Java Programming
Comprehensive Concepts
and Techniques
Third Edition

Gary B. Shelly
Thomas J. Cashman
Joy L. Starks
Michael L. Mick

COURSE TECHNOLOGY
CENGAGE Learning™

Australia • Brazil • Japan • Korea • Mexico • Singapore • Spain • United Kingdom • United States

COURSE TECHNOLOGY
CENGAGE Learning™

Java Programming Comprehensive Concepts and Techniques, Third Edition
Gary B. Shelly, Thomas J. Cashman,
Joy L. Starks, Michael L. Mick

Managing Editor: Alexandra Arnold

Series Consulting Editor: Jim Quasney

Marketing Manager: Dana Merk

Senior Product Manager: Karen Stevens

Product Manager: Reed Cotter

Associate Product Manager: Selena Coppock

Editorial Assistant: Patrick Frank

Print Buyer: Justin Palmeiro

Production Editor: Marissa Falco

Marketing Coordinator: Melissa Marcoux

Quality Assurance: Burt LaFountain Danielle
    Shaw

Copy Editor: Lyn Markowicz

Proofreader: John Bosco

Cover Art: John Still

Compositors: Jeanne Black
            Pre-Press Company, Inc.

For product information and technology assistance, contact us at
Cengage Learning Customer & Sales Support, 1-800-354-9706
For permission to use material from this text or product,
submit all requests online at cengage.com/permissions
Further permissions questions can be emailed to
permissionrequest@cengage.com

ISBN-13: 978-1-4188-5985-5

ISBN-10: 1-4188-5985-0

Course Technology
25 Thomson Place
Boston, Massachusetts 02210
USA

Cengage Learning is a leading provider of customized learning solutions with office locations around the globe, including Singapore, the United Kingdom, Australia, Mexico, Brazil, and Japan. Locate your local office at: **international.cengage.com/region**

Cengage Learning products are represented in Canada by Nelson-Education, Ltd.

For your lifelong learning solutions, visit **course.cengage.com**

Visit our corporate website at **cengage.com**

Printed in the United States of America
5 6 7 11 10 09 08

Java Programming Comprehensive Concepts and Techniques
Third Edition

Contents

CHAPTER 1

An Introduction to Java and Program Design

CHAPTER 4

Decision Making and Repetition with Reusable Objects

CHAPTER 5

Arrays, Loops, and Layout Managers Using External Classes

CHAPTER 6

Creating Menus and Button Arrays Using the Abstract Windows Toolkit

C H A P T E R   7

Swing Interfaces with Sorting and Searching

C H A P T E R   8

Writing Data to a Sequential Data File

CHAPTER 9

Using Collections and Strings in a Reusable Class

CHAPTER 12

Utilizing Servlets for Web Applications

Preface

The Shelly Cashman Series® offers the finest textbooks in computer education. We are proud of the fact that our previous *Java Programming* books have been so well received by instructors and students. This latest edition continues with the innovation, quality, and reliability you have come to expect from this series. In particular, this edition has been updated for Java 2 SDK version 5.0, while continuing to cover the fundamentals of Java programming and design. Valuable Java 2 SDK 5 programming tips are interspersed throughout this latest edition. In addition, the end-of-chapter exercises have been enhanced with critical-thinking problems associated with version 5.0.

Java is one of the more popular programming languages. Java is widely used to implement network interfaces, Web servers, and e-commence solutions, as well as standard business applications. Java provides an object-oriented, portable, and robust framework for application development.

In our *Java Programming* books, you will find an educationally sound and easy-to-follow pedagogy that combines a step-by-step approach with corresponding screens. The Other Ways and Tip features offer in-depth suggestions about alternative ways to complete a task and programming techniques. Every programming chapter builds an application from start to finish following a disciplined development cycle defined in Chapter 1. The Shelly Cashman Series *Java Programming* books will make your programming class exciting and dynamic and one that your students will remember as one of their better educational experiences.

Objectives of This Textbook

Java Programming: Comprehensive Concepts and Techniques, Third Edition is intended for a fifteen-week, three-unit course that teaches Java as the primary component. No experience with a computer is assumed, and no mathematics beyond the high school freshman level is required. The objectives of this book are:

- To teach the fundamentals of the Java programming language
- To teach the basic concepts and methods of object-oriented programming and object-oriented design
- To emphasize the development cycle as a means of creating applications
- To demonstrate how to implement logic involving sequence, selection, and repetition using the Java syntax
- To illustrate well-written and readable programs using a disciplined coding style, including documentation and indentation standards
- To use practical problems to illustrate application-building techniques
- To encourage independent study and help those who are working alone in a distance education environment

The Shelly Cashman Approach

Features of the Shelly Cashman Series *Java Programming* books include:

- **Building Applications**   Each programming chapter builds a complete application using the six phases of the development cycle: (1) analyze requirements; (2) design solution; (3) validate design; (4) implement design; (5) test solution; and (6) document solution.

- **Step-by-Step, Screen-by-Screen Methodology**   Each of the tasks required to build an application within a chapter is identified using a step-by-step, screen-by-screen methodology. Students have the option of learning Java by reading the book without the use of a computer or by following the steps on a computer and building a chapter application from start to finish.

- **More Than Just Step-By-Step**   This book offers extended but clear discussions of programming concepts. Important Java design and programming tips are interspersed throughout the chapters. When a Java statement is introduced, one or more tables follow showing the general form of the statement and the various options available.

- **Other Ways Boxes for Reference**   The Other Ways boxes displayed at the end of many of the step-by-step sequences specify the other ways to do the task completed in the steps. Thus, the steps and the Other Ways box make a comprehensive reference unit.

Organization of This Textbook

Java Programming: Comprehensive Concepts and Techniques, Third Edition provides detailed instruction on how to program using the Java SDK. The material is divided into twelve chapters and five appendices as follows:

Chapter 1 – An Introduction to Java and Program Design   Chapter 1 provides an overview of the capabilities of the Java programming language, application development, program development methodology, program design tools, object-oriented design, and object-oriented programming. The chapter introduces the components of the Java 2 Standard Edition (J2SE) and other development tools.

Chapter 2 – Creating a Java Application and Applet   Chapter 2 introduces students to the process of creating a simple Java program. The chapter begins with a requirements document for the Welcome to My Day application and shows the process of proper design and analysis of the program. Topics include using TextPad to edit, compile, and run Java source code; using comments; creating a class and main() method; and displaying output. Students then learn how to convert the application into an applet that displays both text and a graphic with a color background.

Chapter 3 – Manipulating Data Using Methods   Chapter 3 defines the primitive data types used in storing and manipulating data in Java as students develop the Body Mass Index Calculator. Topics include basic input and output methods, declaring variables, using arithmetic and comparison operators, understanding operator precedence and simple expressions, converting data types, and creating dialog boxes from the Swing class. As students convert the program into an applet, they are introduced to creating and manipulating Labels, TextFields, and Buttons.

Chapter 4 – Decision Making and Repetition with Reusable Objects   Chapter 4 presents students with the fundamental concepts of the selection and repetition structures, as well as an introduction to exception handling. Students create a Commission application that calls user-defined methods. The reusable methods accept and return data to the calling method and use if, switch, and while statements to test input. As an applet, the commission program uses a CheckboxGroup to display option buttons to the user.

Chapter 5 – Arrays, Loops, and Layout Managers Using External Classes   Chapter 5 illustrates how to create and implement an external class complete with constructor and instance methods for use in other programs. Topics include creating and accessing arrays; using a counter-controlled for loop to populate an array; incrementing with unary operators; accumulating with assignment operators; using layout managers to create Frame-based GUI applications; creating TextArea components; and implementing Choice components that display as drop-down lists.

Chapter 6 – Creating Menus and Button Arrays Using the Abstract Windows Toolkit
Chapter 6 creates a Calculator application complete with an array of buttons and a menu system. Topics include implementing private variables; adding components from Java's Menu class including Menu, MenuBar, and MenuItem; using submenus and separator lines in menus; manipulating button arrays and testing for all possible clicks with getActionCommand() and getSource() methods; moving data in and out of the system clipboard employing cut, copy, and paste; using multiple layout managers; programming multiple case solutions; creating an icon on the title bar; and accessing methods from the Toolkit class.

Chapter 7 – Swing Interfaces with Sorting and Searching   Chapter 7 uses the major Swing components to develop a program that searches and sorts data. Topics include the features of the Java Foundation Classes (JFC); comparing and contrasting AWT and Swing components, such as JPanel, JComboBox, JLabel, and JScrollPane; creating a JFrame application; sorting data in parallel arrays; constructing and implementing tool tips; using the super keyword; creating Tabs and Styles in a JTextPane; utilizing Document class methods; and performing linear searches. This chapter also introduces students to Java Look and Feel methods.

Chapter 8 – Writing Data to a Sequential Data File   Chapter 8 presents students with the concept of writing data to a data file. Topics include volatile and nonvolatile data; sequential and random access files; using the UIManager class; creating a stream and writing data to a sequential data file; formatting dates; implementing a showConfirm-Dialog() box; understanding client/server architecture; and identifying the parts of two-tier, three-tier, and multi-tier systems.

Chapter 9 – Using Collections and Strings in a Reusable Class   Chapter 9 presents classes designed for reuse as students develop a generic Password class and use classes such as String, StringBuffer, and the ArrayList class. Topics include instance and class variables, use of the final qualifier, the Collections Framework, overloading constructors, accessor (get) methods, mutator (set) methods, accessing read-only attributes, public versus private methods, and the use of String and StringBuffer methods to encrypt a password. The Password class developed in this chapter is tested, using a JPassword field to mask user input. Thecompleted Password class then is available for reuse in subsequent chapters.

Chapter 10 – Understanding Abstract Classes and Interfaces   Chapter 10 defines a hierarchy of classes used to handle exception conditions with respect to the Password class previously developed. Topics include single versus multiple inheritance, class inheritance versus interface implementation, abstract and concrete classes, relating classes through inheritance, creating and extending an abstract class, using a final method, creating a final class, and concatenation of method calls. As students create a program to test the classes in the PasswordException class hierarchy, they create a user interface that uses multiple windows, establish a callback mechanism, implement a new interface, and use an adapter class.

Chapter 11 – Accessing Databases Using JDBC™   Chapter 11 provides an overview of relational database design as students use Java to create and maintain an Access database that contains Password objects. Topics include persisting objects; implementing the Serializable interface; registering an ODBC data source name; loading a JDBC™ database driver; making a database connection; dropping tables and indexes; creating database tables, indexes, and keys; creating and using a PreparedStatement; performing an SQL query and processing the result set; serializing and deserializing an object; creating a data access class; modifying database records with an SQL update; and committing a database transaction. The data access class developed in this chapter is tested and made available for reuse in the next chapter.

Chapter 12 – Utilizing Servlets for Web Applications   Chapter 12 uses the Model-View-Controller design pattern to redesign the previous application to a Java Web application that uses the same database and also accesses a Web service. Topics include Java Web application components, calling a servlet from an HTML form, using JavaScript in an HTML document, the HTTP GET and POST methods, obtaining form data with input tags, the servlet lifecycle, processing HTTP requests in a servlet, implementing session tracking with HTTP, redirecting or forwarding an HTTP request, outputting HTML code from a servlet, acquiring data from a Web service, synchronizing multithreaded code, and creating a JavaServer Page. To test the Web application using Tomcat, a deployment descriptor file is modified and servlet reloading is enabled.

Appendices   This book concludes with five appendices. Appendix A covers program design tools, including flowcharting and the Unified Modeling Language (UML). Appendix B explains how to install the Java2 SDK, TextPad, and Tomcat, including choosing destination folders, setting environmental variables, and starting and stopping Tomcat. Appendix C demonstrates changing screen resolution and setting TextPad preferences to customize the programming desktop. Appendix D describes how to compile and run Java programs using the Command Prompt window, including instructions on setting window properties and changing the path and classpath of the system. Appendix E presents ways to create HTML documentation using the Javadoc command.

End-of-Chapter Activities

A notable strength of the Shelly Cashman Series *Java Programming* books is the extensive student activities at the end of each chapter. Well-structured student activities can make the difference between students merely participating in a class and students retaining the information they learn. The end-of-chapter activities in the Java books are detailed below.

- **What You Should Know**   A listing of the tasks completed in the chapter in order of presentation together with the pages on which the step-by-step, screen-by-screen explanations appear. This section provides a perfect study review for students.

- **Key Terms**   This list of the key terms found in the chapter together with the pages on which the terms are defined aid students in mastering the chapter material.

- **Homework Assignments**   The homework assignments are divided into three sections: Label the Figure, Short Answer, and Learn It Online. The Label the Figure section, in the chapters where it applies, involves a figure and callouts that students fill in. The Short Answer section includes fill in the blank and short essay questions. The Learn It Online section consists of Web-based exercises that include chapter reinforcement (true/false, multiple choice, and short answer), practice tests, learning games, and Web exercises that require students to extend their learning beyond the material covered in the book.

- **Debugging Assignment**   This exercise requires students to open an application with errors from the Java Data Files that accompanies the book and debug it. Students may obtain a copy of the Java Data Files by following the instructions on the inside back cover of this book.

- **Programming Assignments**   An average of ten programming assignments per chapter require students to apply the knowledge gained in the chapter to build applications on a computer. The initial programming assignments step students through building the application and are accompanied by screens showing the desired interface. Later assignments state only the problem, allowing students to create on their own.

Shelly Cashman Series Instructor Resources

The two categories of ancillary material that accompany this textbook are Instructor Resources (ISBN 1-4188-5965-6) and Online Content. These ancillaries are available to adopters through your Course Technology representative or by calling one of the following telephone numbers: Colleges and Universities, 1-800-648-7450; High Schools, 1-800-824-5179; Private Career Colleges, 1-800-648-7450; Canada, 1-800-268-2222; Corporations with IT Training Centers, 1-800-648-7450; and Government Agencies, Health-Care Organizations, and Correctional Facilities, 1-800-477-3692.

Instructor Resources CD-ROM

The Instructor Resources for this textbook include both teaching and testing aids. The contents of the Instructor Resources CD-ROM are listed below.

- **Instructor's Manual** The Instructor's Manual is made up of Microsoft Word files. The Instructor's Manual includes detailed lesson plans with page number references, lecture notes, teaching tips, classroom activities, discussion topics, projects to assign, and transparency references. The transparencies are available through the Figure Files described below.

- **Syllabus** Any instructor who has been assigned a course at the last minute knows how difficult it is to come up with a course syllabus. For this reason, sample syllabi are included that can be customized easily to a course.

- **Figure Files** Illustrations for every figure in the textbook are available in electronic form. Use this ancillary to present a slide show in lecture or to print transparencies for use in lecture with an overhead projector. If you have a personal computer and LCD device, this ancillary can be an effective tool for presenting lectures.

- **Solutions to Exercises** Solutions and required files for all the chapter projects, Homework Assignments, Debugging Assignments, and Programming Assignments at the end of each chapter are available.

- **Test Bank & Test Engine** The test bank includes 110 questions for every chapter (25 multiple-choice, 50 true/false, and 35 fill-in-the-blank) with page number references, and when appropriate, figure references. A version of the test bank you can print also is included. The test bank comes with a copy of the test engine, ExamView. ExamView is a state-of-the-art test builder that is easy to use. ExamView enables you quickly to create printed tests, Internet tests, and computer (LAN-based) tests. You can enter your own test questions or use the test bank that accompanies ExamView.

- **Data Files for Students** Most of the projects created in this book do not use files supplied by the authors. In the few instances, however, where students are instructed to open a project to complete a task, the files are supplied.

- **PowerPoint Presentation** PowerPoint Presentation is a multimedia lecture presentation system that provides PowerPoint slides for each chapter. Presentations are based on the chapters' objectives. Use this presentation system to present well-organized lectures that are both interesting and knowledge based. PowerPoint Presentation provides consistent coverage at schools that use multiple lecturers in their programming courses.

Online Content

If you use Blackboard or WebCT, the test bank for this book is free in a simple, ready-to-use format. Visit the Instructor Resource Center for this textbook at course.com to download the test bank, or contact your local sales representative for details.

To the Student Getting the Most Out of Your Book

Welcome to *Java Programming: Comprehensive Concepts and Techniques, Third Edition.* You can save yourself a lot of time and gain a better understanding of Java if you spend a few minutes reviewing the figures and callouts in this section.

1 Each Chapter Builds an Application

Each programming chapter builds a complete application, which is carefully described and shown in the first figure of the chapter.

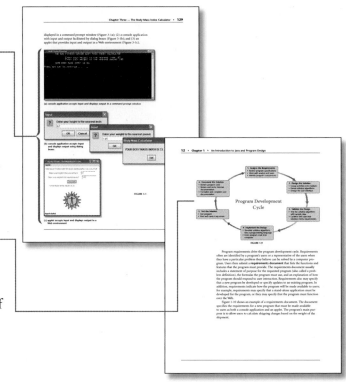

2 Consistent Presentation

The authors use a disciplined approach to building all chapter applications using the six phases of the development cycle. By the end of the course, you will be building applications using this methodology by habit.

3 Pedagogy

Chapter applications are built using a step-by-step, screen-by-screen approach. This pedagogy allows you to build the application on a computer as you read the chapter. Generally, each step is followed by an italic explanation that indicates the result of the step.

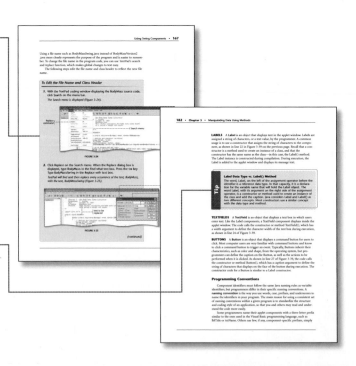

4 More Than Just Step-by-Step

This book offers extended but clear discussions of programming concepts. Important Java design and programming Tips are interspersed throughout the chapters.

5 Review

After successfully stepping through the chapter, a section titled What You Should Know lists the Java tasks with which you should be familiar in the order they are presented in the chapter.

6 Test Preparation

The Key Terms section lists the bold terms in the chapter you should know for test purposes.

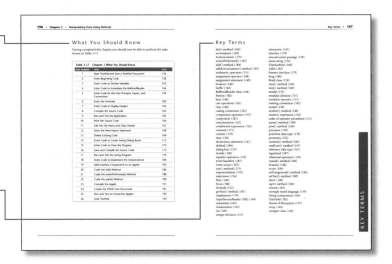

7 Reinforcement and Extension

The Short Answer exercises are the traditional pencil-paper exercises. The Learn It Online exercises are Web-based. Some of these Web-based exercises, such as the Practice Test and Crossword Puzzle, are for reinforcement. Others take you beyond the Java topics covered in the chapter.

8 In the Lab

If you really want to learn how to program in Java, then you must design, program, and debug applications using Java. Every programming chapter includes a Debugging Assignment and several carefully developed Programming Assignments.

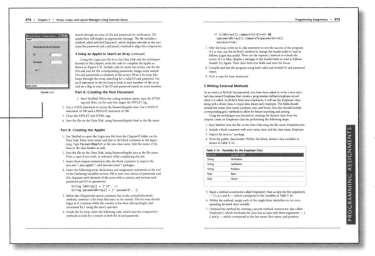

Java Programming, Third Edition CD-ROM

A CD-ROM accompanies this book and can be found on the inside back cover. It includes the following software:

- Sun Java™ SDK, Standard Edition 1.5.0_02
- Sun Java™ SDK, Standard Edition Documentation
- Jakarta Tomcat Server 5.5.7
- Jakarta Tomcat Help
- TextPad 4.7.3 Evaluation
- TextPad Help

Shelly Cashman Series — Traditionally Bound Textbooks

The Shelly Cashman Series presents the following computer subjects in a variety of traditionally bound textbooks. For more information, see your Course Technology representative or call 1-800-648-7450. For Shelly Cashman Series information, visit Shelly Cashman Series at course.com/shellycashman.

COMPUTERS	
Computers	Discovering Computers 2006: A Gateway to Information, Complete
	Discovering Computers 2006: A Gateway to Information, Introductory
	Discovering Computers 2006: A Gateway to Information, Brief
	Discovering Computers: Fundamentals, Second Edition
	Teachers Discovering Computers: Integrating Technology in the Classroom, Third Edition
	Essential Introduction to Computers, Sixth Edition (40-page)

WINDOWS APPLICATIONS	
Microsoft Office	Microsoft Office 2003: Essential Concepts and Techniques (5 projects)
	Microsoft Office 2003: Brief Concepts and Techniques (9 projects)
	Microsoft Office 2003: Introductory Concepts and Techniques, Second Edition (15 projects)
	Microsoft Office 2003: Advanced Concepts and Techniques (12 projects)
	Microsoft Office 2003: Post Advanced Concepts and Techniques (11 projects)
	Microsoft Office XP: Essential Concepts and Techniques (5 projects)
	Microsoft Office XP: Brief Concepts and Techniques (9 projects)
	Microsoft Office XP: Introductory Concepts and Techniques, Windows XP Edition (15 projects)
	Microsoft Office XP: Introductory Concepts and Techniques, Enhanced Edition (15 projects)
	Microsoft Office XP: Advanced Concepts and Techniques (11 projects)
	Microsoft Office XP: Post Advanced Concepts and Techniques (11 projects)
Integration	Teachers Discovering and Integrating Microsoft Office: Essential Concepts and Techniques, Second Edition
	Integrating Microsoft Office XP Applications and the World Wide Web: Essential Concepts and Techniques
PIM	Microsoft Outlook 2002: Essential Concepts and Techniques • Microsoft Office Outlook 2003: Introductory Concepts and Techniques
Microsoft Works	Microsoft Works 6: Complete Concepts and Techniques[1] • Microsoft Works 2000: Complete Concepts and Techniques[1]
Microsoft Windows	Microsoft Windows XP: Comprehensive Concepts and Techniques[2]
	Microsoft Windows XP: Brief Concepts and Techniques
	Microsoft Windows 2000: Comprehensive Concepts and Techniques[2]
	Microsoft Windows 2000: Brief Concepts and Techniques
	Microsoft Windows 98: Comprehensive Concepts and Techniques[2]
	Microsoft Windows 98: Essential Concepts and Techniques
	Introduction to Microsoft Windows NT Workstation 4
Notebook Organizer	Microsoft Office OneNote 2003: Introductory Concepts and Techniques
Word Processing	Microsoft Office Word 2003: Comprehensive Concepts and Techniques[2] • Microsoft Word 2002: Comprehensive Concepts and Techniques2
Spreadsheets	Microsoft Office Excel 2003: Comprehensive Concepts and Techniques[2] • Microsoft Excel 2002: Comprehensive Concepts and Techniques2
Database	Microsoft Office Access 2003: Comprehensive Concepts and Techniques[2] • Microsoft Access 2002: Comprehensive Concepts and Techniques2
Presentation Graphics	Microsoft Office PowerPoint 2003: Comprehensive Concepts and Techniques[2] • Microsoft PowerPoint 2002: Comprehensive Concepts and Techniques[2]
Desktop Publishing	Microsoft Office Publisher 2003: Comprehensive Concepts and Techniques[2] • Microsoft Publisher 2002: Comprehensive Concepts and Techniques[1]

PROGRAMMING	
Programming	Microsoft Visual Basic .NET: Comprehensive Concepts and Techniques[2] • Microsoft Visual Basic 6: Complete Concepts and Techniques[1] • Java Programming: Comprehensive Concepts and Techniques, Second Edition[2] • Structured COBOL Programming, Second Edition • Understanding and Troubleshooting Your PC • Programming Fundamentals Using Microsoft Visual Basic .NET

INTERNET	
Concepts	Discovering the Internet: Brief Concepts and Techniques • Discovering the Internet: Complete Concepts and Techniques
Browser	Microsoft Internet Explorer 6: Introductory Concepts and Techniques, Windows XP Edition • Microsoft Internet Explorer 5: An Introduction • Netscape Navigator 6: An Introduction
Web Page Creation	Web Design: Introductory Concepts and Techniques • HTML: Comprehensive Concepts and Techniques, Third Edition[2] • Microsoft Office FrontPage 2003: Comprehensive Concepts and Techniques[2] • Microsoft FrontPage 2002: Comprehensive Concepts and Techniques[2] • Microsoft FrontPage 2002: Essential Concepts and Techniques • JavaScript: Complete Concepts and Techniques, Second Edition[1] • Macromedia Dreamweaver MX: Comprehensive Concepts and Techniques[2]

SYSTEMS ANALYSIS	
Systems Analysis	Systems Analysis and Design, Sixth Edition

DATA COMMUNICATIONS	
Data Communications	Business Data Communications: Introductory Concepts and Techniques, Fourth Edition

[1]Also available as an Introductory Edition, which is a shortened version of the complete book, [2]Also available as an Introductory Edition and as a Complete Edition, which are shortened versions of the comprehensive book.

1

An Introduction to Java and Program Design

Objectives

You will have
mastered the material in
this chapter when you can:

- Describe characteristics of Java
- Explain the uses of Java and identify types of Java programs
- Identify the phases in the program development life cycle
- Define programs, programming, and applications
- Read, explain, and create a class diagram
- Read, explain, and create an event diagram
- Explain object-oriented programming (OOP) and object-oriented design (OOD)
- Define the terms objects, attributes, methods, and events
- Define and explain encapsulation, inheritance, and polymorphism
- Describe rapid application development (RAD)
- Identify key components of the Java Software Development Kit (SDK)

Introduction

A computer **program** is a step-by-step series of instructions that tells a computer exactly what to do. **Computer programming** is the process of writing that set of instructions for the computer to follow in order to produce a desired result. A **programming language** is a set of words, symbols, and codes that enables a programmer to communicate instructions to a computer. Computer **programmers**, also called **software developers**, design and write programs using a programming language or program development tools. Programming also is referred to as **coding** because the instructions written by a programmer are called computer **code**.

Just as humans understand a variety of languages, such as English, Spanish, and Japanese, a computer programmer can select from a variety of programming languages or program development tools to code a program that solves a particular problem. In fact, more than 2,000 programming languages exist today. This chapter introduces you to basic computer programming concepts to help you learn about fundamental program design and the tools that programmers use to write programs. You will learn these concepts and tools while working with an object-oriented programming language called Java.

Java is a good general-purpose programming language. Schools, businesses, and software development firms are realizing that Java provides the structured basis necessary to write efficient and economical computer programs, which makes Java skills extremely marketable. Most programmers also realize that using an object-oriented approach results in programs that are easier to develop, debug, and maintain than previously accepted approaches. For beginning programmers, who sometimes are overwhelmed by the complexity of programming languages, or those who become carried away with the bells and whistles of graphical user interfaces, Java provides the structure to develop disciplined programming habits.

What Is Java?

Java is a high-level computer programming language. **High-level languages**, like Java, allow programmers to write instructions using English-like commands and words instead of cryptic numeric codes or memory addresses. Each instruction in a high-level language corresponds to many instructions in the computer's machine language. Machine languages consist entirely of numbers and are the only languages understood by computers. The particular set of rules or grammar that specify how the instructions are to be written is called the **syntax** of the language.

Java was designed in the early 1990s by a team from Sun Microsystems led by James Gosling. Java designers began with the basic syntax of languages like C, C++, and Smalltalk. Java initially was designed for use on devices such as cellular phones; however, within a few years, Sun Microsystems was using Java to provide animation and interactivity on the Web. IBM has adopted Java as its major program development language. Many network interfaces, Web servers, and e-commerce solutions now are Java-based — a trend that will continue in the future as businesses learn to take full advantage of the Java language.

Characteristics of Java

Java is the fastest growing programming language in the world, due in part to the design team's successful effort to make the language parsimonious, robust, secure, and portable. Computer professionals use the word **parsimonious** to mean that a language has a compact set of commands without numerous versions or adaptations of the same command. While new commands are periodically added, the original Java commands will not change, meaning that older Java programs still will run on newer versions of the software.

Java is an object-oriented programming language. **Object-oriented programming** (**OOP**) is an approach to programming in which the data and the code that operates on the data are packaged into a single unit called an **object**. A software object represents real objects, such as a person or thing, or abstract objects, such as a transaction or an event — for example, a mouse click. **Object-oriented design** (**OOD**) is an approach to program design that identifies how objects must interact with each other in order to solve a problem. You will learn more about object-oriented programming (OOP) and object-oriented design (OOD) later in this chapter and as you apply the concepts throughout this book.

Being **robust** means that programmers can use Java to develop programs that do not break easily or cause unexpected behaviors; and, if a program fails, it does not corrupt data. Java thus is suitable for developing programs that are distributed over a network. Java is a **strongly typed language**, which means that it checks for potential problems with different types of data — a big plus for beginning programmers. Java is considered **secure** because its programs are easy to protect from viruses and tampering.

A computer program is **portable** if it can be run on a variety of platforms other than the one in which it was created, without requiring major rework. A **platform** is the underlying hardware and software for a system. Java is portable because it is **platform-independent**, which means that you can use Java to write and run a program on many platforms, such as a PC running Windows or Linux, an Apple running Mac OS, or a server running UNIX. Java is based on the idea that the same program should run on many different kinds of computers, PDAs, cellular phones, and other devices. From the time of its initial commercial release in 1995, Java has grown in popularity and usage because of its true portability.

The Java Software Development Kit (SDK)

In addition to being a programming language, Java also is a platform. The Java platform, also known as the **Java Software Development Kit** (**SDK**), is a programming environment that allows you to build a wide range of Java program types. The Java SDK includes programming interfaces, programming tools, and documentation. The Java SDK is described in more detail later in this chapter.

Java Program Types

The Java platform allows you to create programs and program components for a variety of uses. Figure 1-1 on the next page illustrates the types of programs you can create using the Java platform, including console applications, windowed applications with a graphical user interface, applets, servlets, Web services, and JavaBeans. The following sections describe the types of programs you can develop in detail.

Java Program Types

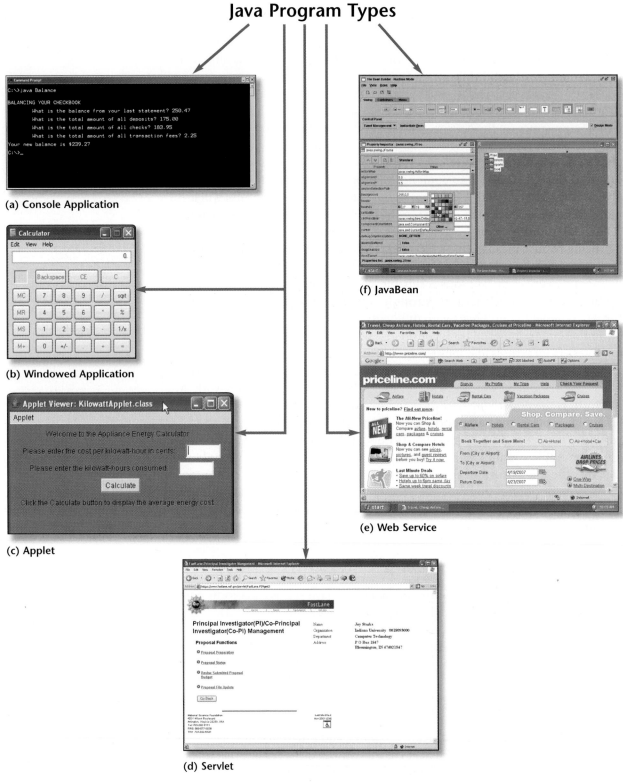

(a) Console Application

(b) Windowed Application

(c) Applet

(d) Servlet

(e) Web Service

(f) JavaBean

FIGURE 1-1

Console and Windowed Applications

An **application** is a program that tells a computer how to accept input from a user and how to produce output in response to those instructions. Typically, applications are designed to complete a specific task, such as word processing or accounting. Java applications are considered to be stand-alone because they can run independent of any other software.

Stand-alone Java applications can be broken down into two types: console applications and windowed applications. A **console application**, also called a console-mode application, uses a command-line interface, such as a command prompt window, to support character output (Figure 1-2). A **windowed application** uses a graphical user interface (GUI) for user input and program output with on-screen elements such as text boxes, buttons, menus, and toolbars to support user interaction (Figure 1-3).

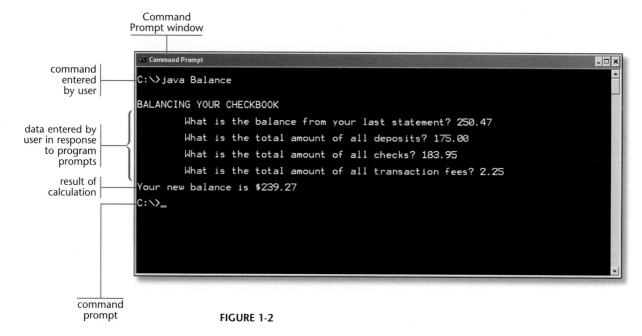

Command Prompt window

command entered by user

data entered by user in response to program prompts

result of calculation

command prompt

FIGURE 1-2

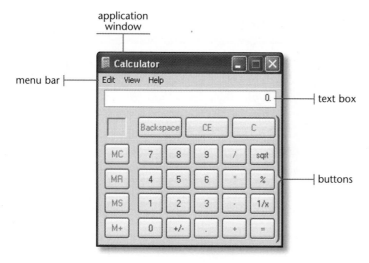

application window

menu bar

text box

buttons

FIGURE 1-3

Applets

An **applet** is a small program that can be downloaded and executed as part of a displayed Web page. Applets, which are intended for general use by people browsing the Web, are considered to be **client-side**, which means the applet executes on the client machine. The client program still may rely on the server or host for some resources, however.

Because applets run within a Web browser, they are subject to security restrictions imposed by the browsers: they cannot read or write files on the client system or connect to any computer other than the applet host. These restrictions made it difficult to use applets for advanced programming applications, such as word processing, until Sun Microsystems introduced a client-side helper application. This helper application, called **Java Web Start**, functions much like Windows Media Player and the RealOne Player, which launch when an audio file is downloaded or opened. The browser launches the Java Web Start helper application when it encounters certain Java commands and statements. For programmers, using the Java Web Start helper application makes deployment of full-featured Java applications as easy as the HTML code used to start applets. For users, Java Web Start means they can download and launch Java applications, such as a complete spreadsheet program, with a single click in a browser.

Some people associate Java's Web capabilities with JavaScript. While JavaScript and Java sometimes are combined in an applet, JavaScript is different from Java. **JavaScript** is a scripting tool, created by Netscape, used to insert code statements directly into the HTML of a Web page, to add functionality and improve the appearance of the Web page. **Hypertext Markup Language** (**HTML**) is a set of special codes called tags that specify how the text and other elements of a Web page display. Unlike a JavaScript statement, which is embedded in the HTML document, a Java applet is sent to the browser as a separate file. A special HTML tag tells the browser where to find and execute the applet file.

Examples of Java applets include a splash screen on the home page of a Web site, an interactive animation or game as part of a Web page, or a program that opens in a new browser window to perform a specific client-side function (Figure 1-4).

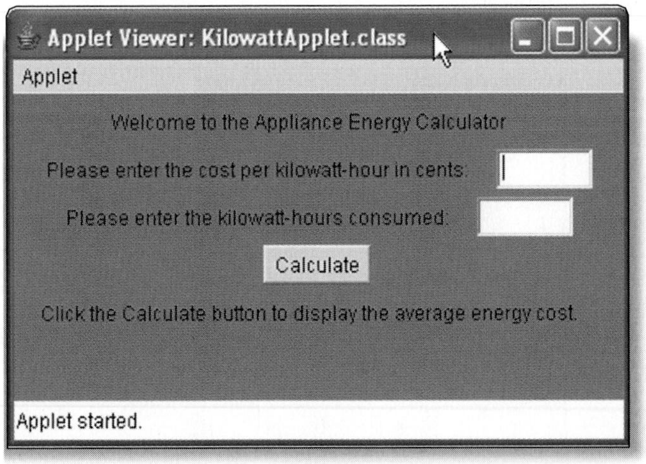

FIGURE 1-4

Servlets

A third use of Java is to create servlets. A **servlet** is a Java program that is hosted and run on a Web server rather than launched from a browser. **Hosting** involves storing Web pages, programs, and other data on a computer that a user connects via a network, intranet, or the Web. A **Web server** is a computer that hosts Web pages, programs, and other files, which it delivers or serves to requesting computers. Web servers use **server software** that responds to incoming requests and serves different forms of data, as well as interfacing with applications and servlets. Thus, servlets are considered to be **server-side**, because the programs are hosted and run on the server and are not executed on the client, as are applets (Figure 1-5).

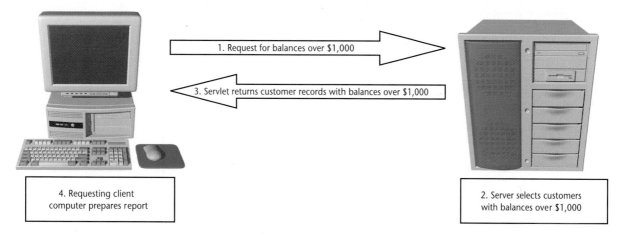

1. Request for balances over $1,000

3. Servlet returns customer records with balances over $1,000

4. Requesting client computer prepares report

2. Server selects customers with balances over $1,000

FIGURE 1-5

Servlets now are widely used to extend Web server and database functionality. Servlets can be used with **Java Server Pages (JSP)**, a server-side technology that extends the Java servlet technology to provide a way to create sophisticated solutions that run on any platform. JSP, when used with servlets, separates the display logic on the client machine (for example, how a Web page or program displays to a user) from the business logic on the server (the rules that define program calculations, responses, and so on). Upon first use, a JSP page is translated into Java source code, which is then compiled into a class file. From then on, it runs similar to any other servlet unless the original JSP file is changed.

Another common use of Java servlets is to connect to databases using **Java Database Connectivity (JDBC)**, a Java interface that enables Java applications to execute queries and interact with most databases.

Programmers use JSP and JDBC to develop data-driven Web applications. Experts estimate that 80 percent of the world's computer applications are database applications; therefore, many programmers use Java servlets to develop database applications for a variety of purposes and deploy them over intranets, extranets, and the Web. Whether a company's human resource department needs to deploy an employee benefits application, or a company needs an enterprise-wide solution for customer service, account management, and inventory control, a programmer can use Java servlets to develop programs to meet those needs. Figure 1-6 displays a Web page that uses a servlet to provide functionality.

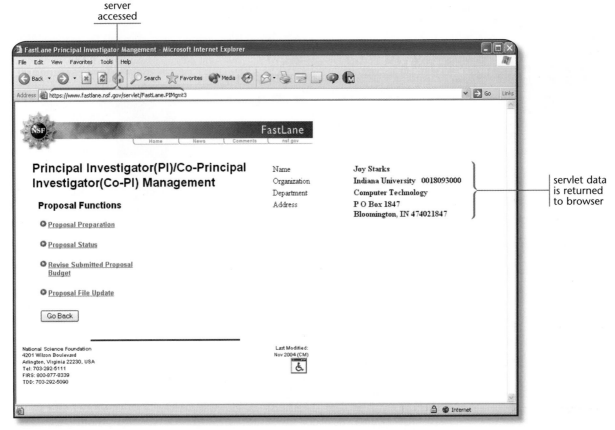

FIGURE 1-6

Web Services

Another use of Java is to create Web services. A **Web service**, sometimes called an application service, is a program that receives a request for information from another program over the Web and then returns data to the requesting program. Web services usually incorporate some combination of programming and data, but may support user input as well. In a typical Web services scenario, a business application sends a request to a service at a given URL using a special Web-based protocol (Figure 1-7). The Web service receives the request, processes it, and returns a response to the application. A typical example of a Web service is that of an automatic stock quote service, in which the request asks for the current price of a specified stock, and the response returns the stock price. Another example might be a service that maps out an efficient route for the delivery of goods. In this case, a business application sends a request containing the delivery destinations, and a Web service processes the request to determine the most cost-effective delivery route.

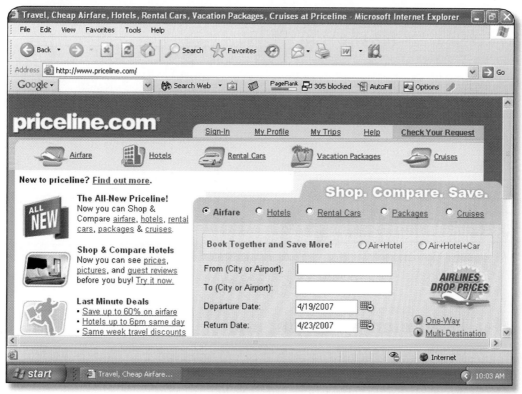

FIGURE 1-7

JavaBeans

Java also can be used to create components for use by other programs. Such a component, called a **JavaBean** or simply a **bean**, is a reusable software component developed in Java, which can be used by any application that understands the JavaBeans format. Beans allow programmers to develop applications visually using standard development tools. Beans provide the benefit of **reusability**, which means they can be used over and over in many programs developed by different programmers. A bean also can store data and retrieve it later. For example, a bank account bean might store an account number and balance. A programmer might write code to display the bean's properties on a secure Web page when the customer requests his or her balance. Figure 1-8 on the next page displays a development tool used to create JavaBeans.

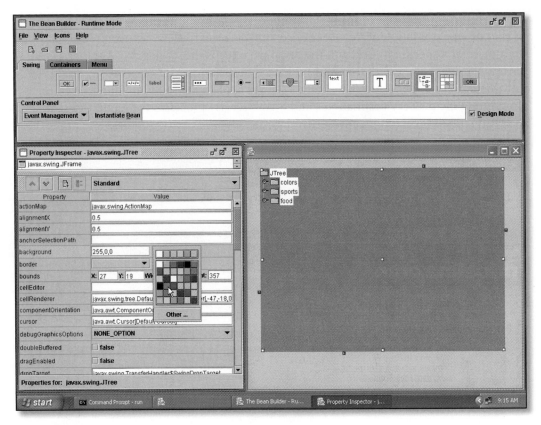

FIGURE 1-8

Programming a Computer

Most computer users do not write their own programs. Programs required for common business and personal applications such as word processing or spreadsheets can be purchased from software vendors or stores that sell computer products. These purchased programs are referred to as **application software packages**.

Even though good application software packages can be purchased inexpensively, software development firms and other companies have a need for developers to build application software packages as well as custom applications. Large companies, for example, need industry-specific software not available in the retail market due to its limited use. Smaller companies want programs that can be adjusted and tailored to fit their needs. Existing programs also need constant maintenance, monitoring, and upgrades. Learning to develop programs, therefore, is an important skill. Learning program development improves logical- and critical-thinking skills for computer-related careers, and it teaches why applications perform as they do. As hardware, networking, and Internet technologies progress and change, developers will be needed to meet the challenge of creating new applications. Programming, a combination of engineering and art, is a very marketable skill.

The Program Development Cycle

Programmers do not sit down and start writing code right away. Instead, they follow an organized plan, or **methodology**, that breaks the process into a series of tasks. Just as there are many programming languages, there are many application development methodologies. These different methodologies, however, tend to be variations of what is called the **program development cycle**. The cycle follows these six phases: (1) analyze the requirements, (2) design the solution, (3) validate the design, (4) implement the design, (5) test the solution, and (6) document the solution. Table 1-1 describes each phase that a programmer goes through to arrive at a computer application. Figure 1-9 on the next page portrays the program development cycle as a continuing, iterative process or loop. When the maintenance phase identifies change, or the program must meet new requirements, a new iteration of the cycle begins again.

Table 1-1   The Program Development Cycle

	PHASE	DESCRIPTION
1	Analyze the requirements	Precisely define the problem to be solved, verify that the requirements are complete, and write program requirements and specifications — descriptions of the program's inputs, processing, outputs, and user interface.
2	Design the solution	Develop a detailed, logical plan using tools such as pseudocode, flowcharts, class diagrams, or event diagrams to group the program's activities into modules; devise a method of solution or algorithm for each module; and test the solution algorithms. Design the user interface for the application, including input areas, output areas, and other necessary elements.
3	Validate the design	Step through the solution design with test data. Receive confirmation from the user that the design solves the problem in a satisfactory manner.
4	Implement the design	Translate the design into an application using a programming language or application development tool by creating the user interface and writing code; include internal documentation (comments and remarks) within the code that explains the purpose of the code statements.
5	Test the solution	Test the program, finding and correcting errors (debugging) until it is error-free and contains enough safeguards to ensure the desired results. Implement the solution at the user level.
6	Document the solution	Review and, if necessary, revise internal documentation; formalize and complete user (external) documentation.

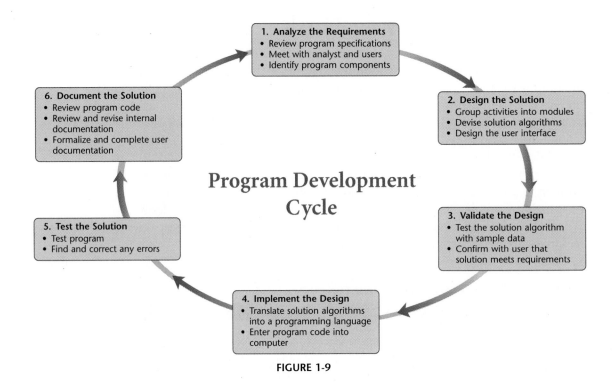

FIGURE 1-9

Program requirements drive the program development cycle. Requirements often are identified by a program's users or a representative of the users when they have a particular problem they believe can be solved by a computer program. Users then submit a **requirements document** that lists the functions and features that the program must provide. The requirements document usually includes a statement of purpose for the requested program (also called a problem definition), the formulas the program must use, and an explanation of how the program should respond to user interaction. Requirements also may specify that a new program be developed or specify updates to an existing program. In addition, requirements indicate how the program will be made available to users; for example, requirements may specify that a stand-alone application must be developed for the program, or they may specify that the program must function over the Web.

Figure 1-10 shows an example of a requirements document. The document specifies the requirements for a new program that must be made available to users as both a console application and an applet. The program's main purpose is to allow users to calculate shipping charges based on the weight of the shipment.

REQUEST FOR NEW APPLICATION

Date submitted:	November 11, 2007
Submitted by:	Vickie Hefner
Purpose:	Legal secretaries and clerks need a quick way to calculate shipping charges as they overnight legal documents to clients and other attorneys.
Application title:	Shipping Charge Calculator

Algorithms:	Shipping charges are based on the weight of the document package in ounces. The secretaries and legal clerks have scales to weigh the package. If the package is 16 ounces or less, the minimum charge is $12.95, then it is 30 cents an ounce for every ounce over 16.
	
	 Calculations can be summarized as follows:
	 Basic Charge = 12.95
	 Extra Charge = (Ounces – 16) * .30
	
	 If ounces are more than 16
	       Total Charge = Basic Charge + Extra Charge
	 Otherwise
	       Total Charge = Basic Charge

Notes:	1) Legal clerks frequently work away from the office. A Web interface would allow them to ship from remote locations. Legal secretaries work mainly from their desks or in the copy room; they have access to a computer, but not always the Web. 2) Employees are accustomed to the terms, shipping charge, and ounces. 3) The application window should allow users to enter the weight and then click a button to see the calculated charge. 4) Packages over 5 lbs (80 ounces) are shipped via a different method. 5) The application should also allow the user to reset the weight, which clears the ounces and charge areas of the screen, so that another calculation can be performed. 6) Use the words, Calculation, Shipping, and Reset, on the buttons.

Approvals

Approval status:	X	Approved
		Rejected
Approved by:	Dennis Louks	
Date:	November 18, 2007	
Assigned to:	J. Starks, Programmer	

FIGURE 1-10

Analyze the Requirements — Phase 1

When a programmer receives a requirements document or similar assignment, the first step is to make sure that the requirements are clear and complete. If equations are included, they need to be correct and precise. If necessary, the programmer must request that the requirements document be revised to address these issues.

Next, the programmer must evaluate the problem to determine that, indeed, it is solvable with a computer program. One way to do this is for the programmer to make a list of the required input and output data. The programmer must also determine whether input data is available for testing purposes. Figure 1-11 shows a sample list of inputs and outputs, along with test data for the Shipping Charge Calculator application.

INPUTS AND OUTPUTS

INPUTS	OUTPUTS
Shipment Weight	Shipping Charge

SAMPLE DATA

INPUTS	OUTPUTS
16 ounces	$12.95
10 ounces	$12.95
26 ounces	$15.95

FIGURE 1-11

The next step is for the programmer to verify that the provided information explains how to convert the input data into output data so that a solution, or **algorithm**, can be developed. The requirements document must clearly state the rules that govern how to convert the input into output. The requirements document in Figure 1-10 on the previous page describes the algorithm in words and in mathematical formulas. When writing an algorithm, consider that the goal of computer programming is to create a correct and efficient algorithm that is a clear and unambiguous specification of the steps needed to solve a problem. **Correct** refers to using logical constructs and valid data in an organized way so that the steps will be carried out correctly and the program will make suitable responses to invalid data, such as displaying a warning message for numbers outside a given range. **Efficient** refers to the program's ability to deliver a result quickly enough to be useful and in a space small enough to fit the environment. For instance, if a program to look up a price on a product takes more than a few seconds, customers may become impatient; or if a computer game takes an enormous amount of memory and hard disk space, it will not be marketable. Computer programs should be as straightforward as possible in the certain event that modifications and revisions will need to be made.

The requirements also must state how the user will interact with the program, such as whether the program must be made available in a windowed application with a graphical user interface, as an applet for Web users, or as a

Web service for use in a larger application. The requirements may include industry-specific terminology with which the user is familiar and which, therefore, must be included in the user interface. These requirements help the programmer determine which technologies to use when designing a solution to the problem. For larger problems, the analysis also should include an initial breakdown of the problem into smaller problems so that programmers can develop solutions gradually and in smaller, more manageable pieces.

The requirements for the Shipping Charge Calculator shown in Figure 1-10 on page 13 specify the input data that should be entered by the user and the algorithm that must be used to calculate the output data. The requirements also explain how users will interact with the program, including the rules that govern valid and invalid input data entered by the user. The end result of the analyze requirements phase is that both the user and the programmer agree in writing that the requirements for the program are clear and complete. At this point, the programmer can begin to design a solution, and the user can begin designing tests to verify that the solution satisfies the program's requirements.

Design the Solution — Phase 2

Designing a program solution usually involves developing a logical model that illustrates the sequence of steps you will take to solve the problem. Programmers use many tools to think algorithmically and to design their programs correctly and efficiently. Programmers use storyboards, class diagrams, flowcharts, and pseudocode to outline the logic of the program.

STORYBOARDS   Because Java often is used to create windowed applications or applets used in Web pages, programmers often create a **storyboard**, or hand-drawn sketch, of how the application window or applet will look and where the user interface elements will be placed in the window. A storyboard also can serve as a reference for the logical names of these elements as you code your program.

The Shipping Charge Calculator may use a similar user interface for both a windowed application and an applet, as shown in the storyboard in Figure 1-12. Although these interfaces may be programmed separately, the user interface is similar, and the same storyboard is useful for both.

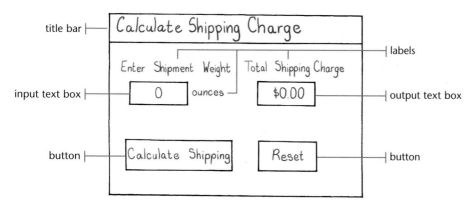

FIGURE 1-12

CLASS DIAGRAMS   As you have learned, programs can be broken into smaller pieces, called objects, which represent a real person, place, event, or transaction. Object-oriented design is an approach to program design that identifies how groups of objects interact with each other in order to solve a problem. A **class** represents the common structure and behavior shared by the same type of objects. A modeling tool that helps developers visualize how a class works within a program is called a class diagram. A **class diagram** illustrates the name, attributes, and methods of a class of objects. The **attributes** of a class are properties used to define characteristics such as appearance. The **methods** of a class are instructions that the class uses to manipulate values, generate outputs, or perform actions. Many times, classes are individual program modules that often can be reused by other programs.

The Shipping Charge Calculator requires that users access the program in one of two ways: a windowed application or an applet. Rather than creating two completely separate applications for these different users, the algorithm used to solve the problem should be programmed only once. By centralizing the program logic for the two application types, maintenance of the program is easier, and the logic needs to be programmed only once, rather than twice. The algorithm can be placed in a class. The Shipment class has an attribute that corresponds to the input, shipment weight. The class requires one method, getShipping(), that tells the class how to manipulate the input value and generate the required output. Method names typically are represented with an active verb phrase followed by parentheses. The getShipping() method performs the calculation after the attribute, weight, is sent to the object by the program. Figure 1-13 shows a class diagram of the Shipment class. Appendix A includes a more detailed discussion of class diagrams.

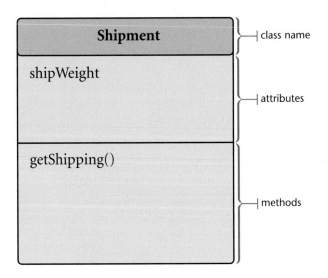

FIGURE 1-13

FLOWCHARTS   Programmers often create a diagram called a **flowchart**, which graphically represents the logic used to develop an algorithm. Table 1-2 shows a standard set of flowchart symbols used to represent various steps, or operations, in a program's logic. When you draw a complete flowchart, you must begin with a terminal symbol connected by a flowline to the first logical step in solving the problem. Most of the time, each step in solving a problem is represented by a separate symbol. Most of the flowcharting symbols, except the decision diamond, have one entering flowline and one exiting flowline. Inside the symbol, you write words describing the logical step. Flowcharts typically do not display programming language commands. Rather, they state the concept in English, pseudocode, or mathematical notation. After the last step, you end a flowchart with a final flowline connected to another terminal symbol. Appendix A includes a more detailed discussion of how to develop flowcharts.

Table 1-2   *Flowcharting Symbols and Their Meanings*

SYMBOL	NAME	MEANING
	Process Symbol	Represents the process of executing a defined operation or group of operations that results in a change in value, form, or location of information; also functions as the default symbol when no other symbol is available
	Input/Output (I/O) Symbol	Represents an I/O function, which makes data available for processing (input) or for displaying processed information (output)
left to right right to left top to bottom bottom to top	Flowline Symbol	Represents the sequence of available information and executable operations; lines connect other symbols; arrowheads are mandatory only for right-to-left and bottom-to-top flow
	Annotation Symbol	Represents the addition of descriptive information, comments, or explanatory notes as clarification; vertical lines and broken lines may be placed on the left, as shown, or on the right
	Decision Symbol	Represents a decision that determines which of a number of alternative paths is to be followed
	Terminal Symbol	Represents the beginning, the end, or a point of interruption or delay in a program
or	Connector Symbol	Represents any entry from, or exit to, another part of the flowchart; also serves as an off-page connector
	Predefined Process Symbol	Represents a named process consisting of one or more operations or program steps that are specified elsewhere

Figure 1-14 shows a flowchart that represents the algorithm used by the getShipping() method to calculate the correct shipping charge. The flowchart includes a **control structure**, which is a portion of a program that allows the programmer to specify that code will be executed only if a condition is met. The control structure in the flowchart, for instance, illustrates how the program decides which shipping rate to use based on the total shipment weight. The breakdown of control structures into sequence, selection, and repetition control structures is explained in detail in Appendix A.

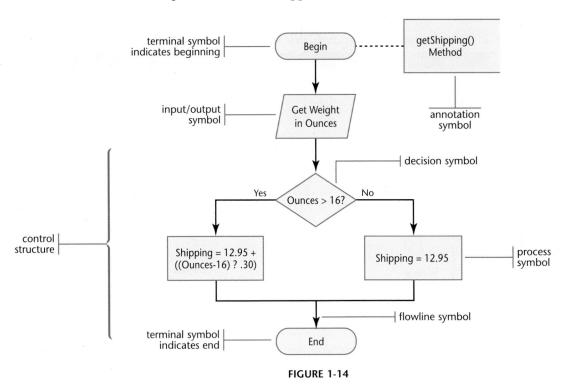

FIGURE 1-14

PSEUDOCODE Some programmers use pseudocode to list the actions a computer should perform and to assist in developing the program logic. **Pseudocode** expresses computer actions using keywords and depicts logical groupings or structures using indentation. Figure 1-15 shows the pseudocode for the getShipping() method of the Shipment object. The pseudocode is not program code but an English representation of how the code should be written. The pseudocode serves as an intermediary between the requirements and the final program code.

```
getShipping() Method

        Accept Weight in Ounces

        ⎧ If Ounces > 16
        ⎪       Shipping = 12.95 + ((Ounces-16) * .30) ─────┤ calculation
decision ├─────⎨ Else
        ⎪       Shipping = 12.95
        ⎩ End If

    End
```

FIGURE 1-15

The end result of designing a program solution is the creation of technical documentation that explains how the program will meet the requirements. Any documents that relate to the design of the user interface should be made available to the user, who must verify that the design is correct and that the program's **usability**, which is a measure of a user's ability to interact with a program in a reasonable and intuitive manner, is acceptable.

Most programmers use combinations and variations of these program design tools. Your instructor or supervisor may prefer one type of design tool to another, and you will probably find one or two more useful than others as you develop your own programming style. In addition, companies often have written standards that specify the tools they use to design programs.

Validate the Design — Phase 3

The third phase in the program development cycle is to **validate** the design, which means that both the programmer and the user must check the program design. The programmer steps through the solution with test data to verify that the solution meets the requirements. The user also must agree that the design solves the problem put forth in the requirements. The validation of the design gives the user one last chance to make certain that all of the necessary requirements were included in the initial requirements document. By comparing the program design with the original requirements, both the programmer and the user can validate that the solution is correct and satisfactory.

The design of the Shipping Charge Calculator can be validated by using a test case for input data and then stepping the test data through both the equation written in the requirements document and the algorithm presented in the program design. The results can be compared to be sure they match.

Implement the Design — Phase 4

The implementation phase of the program development cycle involves writing the code that translates the design into a program and, if needed, creating the user interface. Writing the code, or coding, also includes writing internal documentation, or **comments**, which are notes within the code that explain the purpose of the code. When programmers write the code and create the interface, their job includes testing the code as they write it. Related code that performs a specific task or function should be tested for correctness during the programming process. This type of testing is known as **unit testing**.

Figure 1-16 shows some of the code necessary to implement the getShipping() method for the Shipping Charge Calculator, based on the flowchart in Figure 1-14 on page 18 and the pseudocode in Figure 1-15 on the previous page.

```
1   // this method accepts an integer named ounces
2   // and returns a double named shipping
3   public static double getShipping(int ounces)
4   {
5       double basicCharge;
6       double shipping;
7
8       // set the basic shipping charge to $12.95
9       basicCharge = 12.95;
10
11      // if the ounces are greater than 16 calculate the
12      // extra charge at 30 cents per extra ounce
13      if (ounces > 16)
14          shipping = basicCharge + ((ounces-16) * .3);
15      else
16          shipping = basicCharge;
17
18      return shipping;
19  }
```

FIGURE 1-16

Figure 1-17 shows the user interface developed for the GUI application from the original storyboard design illustrated in Figure 1-12 on page 15.

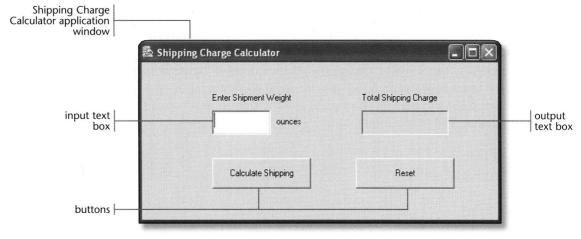

FIGURE 1-17

Test the Solution — Phase 5

Testing the solution is a very important phase in the program development cycle. The purpose of **testing** is to verify that the program meets the requirements from the user's point of view. The program should perform its assigned function correctly under all normal circumstances. If the program includes a user interface, testing should ensure that the user interface also meets requirements. For larger projects, a test plan typically is developed and agreed on during the analyze requirements phase. A **test plan** consists of a collection of test cases. **Test cases** are individual scenarios that include input data and expected output data, and are designed to ensure that the program solves the particular problem indicated in the program requirements.

If a finished application involves several programs or components, **integration testing** must be completed to ensure that all programs and components interact correctly.

The end result of testing the solution includes documentation of any problems with the application. If the user accepts the program as complete and correct, then the user documents this fact, and the program may be put to use. If the testing results are unsatisfactory, then the results are documented and returned to the programmer. The resolution of the problems revealed during testing begins a new iteration of the development cycle, with the outstanding issues serving as requirements.

The Shipping Charge Calculator application requires testing to ensure that all possible cases of valid input data cause the program to calculate the correct result every time. The application must not allow the user to enter values disallowed by the requirements, such as non-numeric data. Test cases also should include input data that would result in the weight being greater than 16 ounces. Based on the requirements, the value of 16 ounces is called a boundary value. **Boundary values** are values that cause a certain rule to become effective. Test cases include the testing of exact boundary values because common logic and programming mistakes occur when boundary values are reached in a problem.

Figure 1-18 shows the Shipping Charge Calculator in the GUI environment being tested with an input value of 24 ounces. Per the requirements, the correct charge should be calculated by adding $12.95 for the first 16 ounces and 30 cents for every ounce thereafter, which results in a total shipping charge of $15.35.

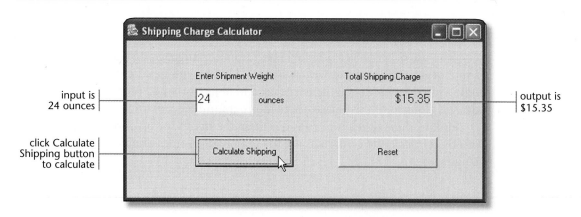

FIGURE 1-18

Document the Solution — Phase 6

The final phase in the development cycle is to document the completed solution. The **documentation** for a completed programming project includes the requirements documents, program design documents, user interface documents, and documentation of the code. The code should be archived electronically so that it can be accessed in the event that a programmer must fix an error in the code or use the code for other purposes.

Final documentation for the Shipping Charge Calculator consists of all documents generated during the development cycle. This also includes electronic archiving and printing the program code and design. The complete set of documents for the project includes the requirements document, approval of requirements by the user and programmer, program design documents, test cases, program code, and printed proof that the test cases were completed successfully.

Object-Oriented Programming and Design

The concepts of object-oriented programming and design represent a relatively recent methodology of application development. As you have learned, Java is an object-oriented programming language, meaning that it packages the data and the code that operates on the data together into a single unit called an object. Object-oriented design is an approach to program design that identifies how objects must interact with each other in order to solve a problem.

Structured programs that are not object-oriented are more linear in nature and must define precisely how the data will be used in each particular program. With such a program, if the structure of the data changes, such as when a new field is added to a table in a database, the program has to be changed. With the dynamic nature of data in this information age, traditionally structured programs have limited use-time and high maintenance costs.

Today, object-oriented programming languages like Java are widely used in many industries. Companies like General Motors, for example, now program their assembly line so that cars (objects) on the assembly line can send messages to paint booths asking for an available slot and color (data). The benefit is that programs developed using an object-oriented approach are easier to develop, debug, and maintain.

Object-Speak

The use of an object-oriented programming language such as Java requires some new terminology, as well as some old terms with new definitions. The following sections define the terms used in object-oriented programming and design, along with the object-oriented programming constructs. A simple way to think of these terms is to consider them the nouns, verbs, and adjectives of object-speak; the constructs are the grammatical rules of object-oriented languages.

NOUNS   Recall that an object is anything real or abstract about which you store both attributes (data) and methods (operations) that manipulate the data. You can think of an object as any noun. Examples of objects are an invoice, a file, a record, a form that allows a user to interact with a program, a sales transaction, or an employee. Parts of a graphical user interface such as menus, buttons, and text boxes are also objects. An object may be composed of other objects, which in turn may contain other objects. **Aggregation** is the term used to describe the concept of an object being composed of other objects. An application window, for example, can aggregate a text box, buttons, and a menu bar.

You can think of an object as a closed or black box; this is because an object is packaged with everything it needs to work in a program. The box receives and sends messages and contains code. A user never should need to see inside the box because the object is self-sufficient. Programmers, however, need to know *how* the object works if they are creating or maintaining code for that object, or *what* the object does if writing code to send messages to the object and use it effectively.

You have learned that a class represents an object or a set of objects that share a common structure and a common behavior. A class also can be thought of as a general category of object types, sometimes called an implementation, which can be used to create multiple objects with the same attributes and behavior.

Each class may have one or more lower levels called a **subclass** or one or more higher levels called a **superclass**. For example, a bank has many types of accounts. A savings account is a subclass, or type, of bank account. A savings account can be broken down further into passbook accounts and certificate accounts. In that relationship, a savings account is a superclass of passbook and certificate accounts. Another example might be when developing a windowed application, programmers can use several types of toolbars. A menu bar is a subclass of a toolbar, but it is also a superclass to a drop-down menu. The relationship among the classes, subclasses, and superclasses forms a hierarchy. A **generalization hierarchy** is an object-oriented design tool used to show the relationships among classes (Figure 1-19).

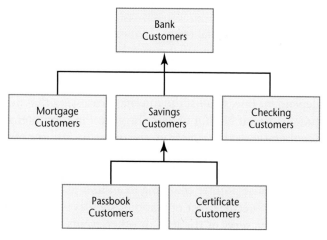

FIGURE 1-19

A unique object — a specific use of a class — is called an **instance**. Think of an instance as a proper noun. For example, option buttons are used in a graphical user interface to allow users to choose one option from a list of options. All option buttons belong to the class of option button objects that have the same attributes and the same method of displaying as selected or not selected. The label that accompanies a specific option button, however, has a unique value and signifies a particular instance of an option button. For example, an option button to select a shipping method is a unique instance of the general class of option button objects. Just as a proper noun represents a unique person or place, each instance has a unique name, such as ShippingOptionButton.

VERBS   An **operation**, or service, is an activity that reads or manipulates the data of an object. You can think of an operation as an active verb. Examples of operations include the standard mathematical, statistical, and logical operations, as well as the input, output, and storage operations associated with computer data. Object-oriented programmers use the term method to refer to code used to perform the operation or service. The Shipment object, for example, performs the operation of calculating shipping charges using the getShipping() method.

For an object to do something, it must receive a message. A **message** activates the code to perform one of the operations. Everything an object can do is represented by the message. The message has two parts — the name of the object to which the message is being sent, and the name of the operation that will be performed. The impetus, or **trigger**, that causes the message to be sent may come from another object or an external user. The entire process of a trigger sending a message that causes an operation to occur is called an **event**. For example, if you click the Calculate Shipping button to determine shipping charges based on weight, clicking the button is the trigger that sends a message to the Shipment object. The Shipment object then uses the getShipping() method to calculate shipping costs, which is the operation. In this example, clicking the Calculate Shipping button is the trigger and the calculation of shipping costs is the operation; together, they make a Calculate Shipping event.

Programmers often draw an **event diagram** to show relationships among events and operations visually and to help plan how they will program events. Event diagrams display the trigger as a shadowed button. When you draw an event diagram, you list the external trigger that causes this event to happen in the shadowed rectangle at the upper-left corner of the diagram (Figure 1-20). Then you begin the next part of the diagram on an independent line, to show that the trigger is external.

On the independent line, you list the internal processing that describes the event. Many students find it helpful to describe what the computer senses at this point or imagine themselves thinking from the processor's point of view.

Operations are shown in rounded rectangles as results of the event. Operation rectangles should be used to describe any visual or procedural inputs and outputs, such as the mouse pointer changing to an hourglass. Some operations cause no other events to occur; other operations, such as the Print request being sent to the printer driver, serve as triggers for other events and send additional messages. When possible, event diagrams are drawn left to right to represent a sequence of events over time.

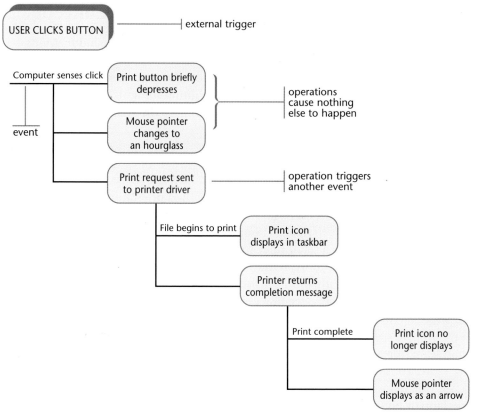

FIGURE 1-20

As shown in Figure 1-20, nothing happens unless the trigger sends a message and causes the event to occur. At the conclusion of the operation, the system again will do nothing until another trigger causes an event to occur. This relationship between events and operations is a key feature of object-oriented programming, and programs that are constructed in this way are said to be **event-driven**.

Event diagrams and class diagrams are part of the **Unified Modeling Language** (**UML**), which provides a standardized model for object-oriented design to depict or describe concepts graphically. The UML is a system of symbols used to describe object behaviors and interaction and to represent how a system should behave. The UML is a relatively new language tool, having been developed in the 1990s from a number of object-oriented design tools. Appendix A includes an introduction to the use of the UML.

ADJECTIVES   In object-oriented terminology, the characteristics of an object are defined by its attributes, or properties. Recall that attributes of an object are values that determine the properties of an individual object, such as its name, size, or background color. Think of attributes as adjectives that describe an object. The attributes of a hyperlink on a Web page might include the font, the color, the font size, and the URL to which it links. Attributes of a bank account object might include a balance and an account number; if the object were an airline flight, the number of passengers would be an attribute. An attribute should not be confused with the data or value assigned to the attribute. Color, for example, is an attribute, while red is the data or value.

Object-Oriented Programming (OOP) Concepts

Object-oriented programming is not just a different set of tools and methods from traditional structured programming. It represents a different philosophy about the nature of computer programs and how those programs are assembled. The following case scenario about two programming students is designed to help illustrate these differences and provide an analogy for discussing object-oriented programming constructs.

Object-Oriented Case Scenario

Paul Randall is a student of traditional structured programming. He wants to create a work/study area in his room where he can write and draw and be able to store his work. He wants to sit at the work area, write, and then store his papers. Paul views the system as a set of three functions: sitting, writing, and storing.

After a great deal of effort in drawing up blueprints, Paul has designed a one-piece integrated study unit, consisting of a writing surface with rolltop cover, a bench, and two drawers. By designing an integrated unit, the functions of sitting, writing, and storing will be compatible with each other, and he will save on material costs and construction time. Paul travels to several lumber and hardware stores and purchases all the materials.

After considerable construction time, Paul is finished and satisfied with the result. He can work comfortably and does not need to reach too far to lift up the desktop or pull open the file drawers. Several weeks pass and Paul begins to think about making enhancements to his system. His bench is not as comfortable as he would like, his writing area feels cramped, and his two drawers are full. Paul decides to live with his system's shortcomings, however, because any change would require substantial effort to dismantle and rebuild the entire system.

Mary Carter is a student of object-oriented programming. She would like to have a study area with the same functionality as Paul's study area. Mary, however, views the system as a set of three objects: a sitting object, a writing surface object, and a storage object. Even though they are separate objects, Mary is confident she can make them interoperate for an effective study area. Mary travels to a furniture factory warehouse and begins evaluating the hundreds of different chairs, desks, and file cabinets for their suitability to her needs and their compatibility with each other.

Mary returns to her room after purchasing a matching chair, two-drawer file cabinet, and rolltop desk. When the desk handle is pulled, it activates a hardware mechanism that raises the rolltop. With little effort, Mary's study area is complete.

Although Mary's furniture cost more than Paul's materials, the savings on her labor costs have more than made up the difference. After several weeks, Mary's file cabinet is full. She returns to the furniture store, buys a three-drawer cabinet of the same style, and replaces the one in her study area.

Encapsulation, Inheritance, and Polymorphism

The conceptual constructs, or building blocks, of object-oriented programming and design include encapsulation, inheritance, and polymorphism. These tools assist programmers with reusing code, and help them create prebuilt objects for rapid application development.

Encapsulation

Encapsulation is the capability of an object to have data (properties) and functionality (methods) available to the user, without the user having to understand the implementation within the object — the closed box concept presented earlier. Traditional structured programming separates data from procedures, which are sections of a program that perform a specific task. In the object-oriented world, an object contains methods as well as its associated data. Encapsulation is the process of hiding the implementation details of an object from its user, making those details transparent. In programming, an action is **transparent** if it takes place without any visible effect other than the desired output. Transparency is a good characteristic of a system because it shields the user from the system's complexity. For example, you do not need to know how the internal parts of a DVD player work in order to view a movie.

This process of making the implementation and programming details transparent to the user sometimes is called **information hiding**. Providing access to an object only through its messages, while keeping the details private, is an example of information hiding. Users know what operations can be requested of an object, but do not know the specifics of how the operations are performed. Encapsulation allows objects to be modified without requiring that the applications that use them also be modified.

In the case scenarios, both Paul and Mary want drawers that cannot be pulled all the way out accidentally. In constructing his system, Paul had to attend to the details of how drawer stops work, which ones to use, and how to build them into the system. For Mary, the safety-stop functionality and behavior is encapsulated within the file cabinet object. As an object-oriented programmer, she does need to understand how her system is constructed. This is not to say that Paul understands his system better than Mary does. From a user's point of view, however, the object-oriented nature of her system means that Mary does not need to concern herself with how the safety stops on her drawers work — only that they *do* work.

Inheritance

Inheritance means that a programmer can use a class, along with its functions and data, to create a subclass, which saves time and coding. A subclass has at least one attribute or method that differs from its superclass, but it inherits functions and data of the superclass. Also known as **subclassing**, this is a very efficient way of reusing code, and provides a way for programmers to define a subclass as an extension of another class without copying the definition. If you let a subclass inherit from a superclass, it automatically will have all the data and methods of the superclass.

In the case scenario, Mary's desk, chair, and cabinet all have similar wood grain, color, and style. If you think of the furniture as a superclass, then Mary's individual pieces are subclasses of that furniture line. Because they are subclasses of the same superclass, they *inherited* the same wood grain, color, and style attributes from the superclass.

Polymorphism

Polymorphism allows an instruction to be given to an object using a generalized rather than a specific, detailed command. The same command will obtain different but somewhat predictable results depending on the object that receives the command. For example, clicking the right mouse button in a windowed environment usually displays a shortcut menu. However, the menu may differ dramatically depending on whether you right-click a folder icon or right-click a toolbar. While the specific actions internal to the object are different, the command, in this case a right-click, would be generally the same.

In the case scenario, when Paul wants to open his desktop, he must perform an open desktop operation. To open his file drawers, he must perform an open drawer operation. Mary's rolltop desk, however, encapsulates the operation of opening within the desk and file cabinet objects. Mary's desk and file cabinet objects are polymorphic with respect to opening, which means Mary can give the same command, opening, to open either object and know that this will result in the same general operation, in which the object opens. As a user, the specific actions internal to the object that cause it to open are not a concern to Mary because the results are generally the same.

Many object-oriented languages, like Java, provide libraries of classes and objects that already have been programmed to work in certain ways. Object-oriented programmers thus can use these classes and objects in programs without knowing the intricacies of the programming behind them. You simply need to know what operations can be requested of a class or object and the results of those operations. Table 1–3 lists 10 object-oriented programming and design concepts in a quick reference format.

Table 1-3 Ten Object-Oriented Programming and Design Concepts

1	An **object** is the basic unit of organization, a combination of a data element and a set of procedures.
2	A **method** is the code to perform a service or operation, including tasks such as performing calculations, storing values, and presenting results.
3	A **class** is an object or a set of objects that shares a common structure and a common behavior. A specific occurrence of an object class is called an **instance**.
4	A **subclass** is a lower-level category of a class with at least one unique **attribute** or method of its own.
5	A subclass **inherits** the attributes, methods, and variables from its superclass. A **superclass** is a higher-level category of class, from which the subclass inherits attributes, methods, and variables.
6	The treelike structure showing the relationship of subclasses and superclasses is called a **generalization hierarchy**.
7	A **message** requests objects to perform a method. A message is composed of the object name and the method.
8	An **event** occurs when a trigger causes an object to send a message.
9	**Encapsulation** is the process of hiding the implementation details of an object from its user by combining attributes and methods.
10	**Polymorphism** allows instructions to be given to objects in a generalized rather than a specific, detailed command.

Rapid Application Development (RAD)

Rapid application development (**RAD**) refers to the use of prebuilt objects to make program development much faster. Using prebuilt objects is faster because you use existing objects rather than creating new ones yourself. The result is shorter development cycles, easier maintenance, and the ability to reuse objects in other projects. One of the major premises on which industry implementation of OOP is built is greater reusability of code.

As shown in Table 1-4, the adoption of an object-oriented approach to programming and program design has many benefits. First, using OOP means that not all members of a development team need to be proficient in an object-oriented programming language such as Java. Second, OOP provides a practical and economical approach to programming because the task of creating objects can be separated from the task of assembling objects into applications. Some programmers, called **class providers**, can focus on creating classes and objects, while other developers, called **class users**, leverage their knowledge of business processes to assemble applications using OOP methods and tools. The end user, or simply user, is the person who interacts with a Java program.

JAVA UPDATE Java 2 v5.0

In 2004, Sun Microsystems came out with a new version of the Java Development Kit (JDK), originally called version 1.5.0. Now commonly called Version 5.0, the new JDK includes a number of new features that can be used to enhance performance and compatibility.

Table 1-4   The Benefits of Object-Oriented Programming

BENEFIT	EXPLANATION
Reusability	The classes are designed so they can be reused in many systems, or so modified classes can be created using inheritance.
Stability	The classes are designed for repeated use and become stable over time.
Easier design	The designer looks at each object as a black box and is not as concerned with the detail inside.
Faster design	The applications can be created from existing components.

What Is the Java SDK?

As previously noted, the Java Software Development Kit (SDK) is a programming package that enables a programmer to develop applications in Java using the included programming interfaces, programming tools, and documentation. As part of the **Java 2 Standard Edition** (**J2SE**) version 5.0, the Java SDK is available for download free from Sun Microsystems on the Web at java.sun.com. It also is included on a CD-ROM in the back of this book. Appendix B discusses how to install J2SE from the CD-ROM.

When you install the J2SE, you can install both the Java Development Kit (JDK) and the Java 2 Runtime Environment (JRE). The tools and components in the Java SDK help you develop Java programs; the tools and components in the **Java 2 Runtime Environment** (**JRE**) help you deploy Java programs. Table 1-5 on the next page outlines some of the components in the Java SDK and the JRE. Several of these components are discussed in detail on the next page.

Table 1-5   Java 2 Standard Edition Components

JAVA 2 STANDARD EDITION (J2SE) COMPONENTS
Java Standard Development Kit (SDK) • Java Compiler • Java Debugger • Other Tools
Java 2 Runtime Environment (JRE) • Java Virtual Machine (JVM) • Java APIs and Class Libraries • Java Applet Viewer • Other Tools

JAVA UPDATE **Java 2** v5.0

There are many reasons to upgrade to Java 5.0. The new version is completely backward compatible, which means your old programs will work in Version 5.0 without any changes. Version 5.0 has improved performance, advanced monitoring and manageability, and runs faster than previous versions. With improved error checking capability and enhanced looping, developers in Version 5.0 will spend less time writing and testing their code.

The Java Compiler

A **compiler** is a program that converts a programmer's code into machine-readable instructions. A compiler is like a person who translates large portions of written text; he or she has the luxury of being able to read the entire text to see how it all fits together during translation. A compiler looks at the entire source code during compilation, searching for errors and inconsistencies with what it knows from other parts of the program. The Java compiler, which is implemented with a program called javac.exe, converts the source code for the entire Java program into object code called **bytecode** (Figure 1-21). The Java compiler is part of the Java SDK.

The Java Virtual Machine

Once the source code is compiled into bytecode, the same bytecode can be run on any computer as long as the computer has an interpreter to execute the Java bytecode. An **interpreter** is a program that executes the machine language instructions to produce results, or answers. An interpreter is like a person who translates orally and dynamically, one sentence at a time, knowing what has been said previously but knowing nothing about future statements.

The language interpreter for Java is included as part of the **Java Virtual Machine** (**JVM**). Execution of Java programs is initiated with the java.exe command; the JVM then interprets or attempts to run commands from the bytecode, one command at a time. For example, once a program is compiled to bytecode, the JVM on any platform — whether Windows, UNIX, or a cell phone — interprets the bytecode (Figure 1-21). The Java Virtual Machine is part of the JRE.

The Java API

The JRE also includes a set of Java application program interfaces, or APIs. An **application program interface** (**API**) is a standard set of interfaces and classes functionally grouped into packages; these APIs are present in any Java implementation. The APIs contain hundreds of pre-written classes that fall into one of more than 50 predefined class packages. **Class packages**, also called **class libraries**, are accessible by every Java program. By using methods and variables

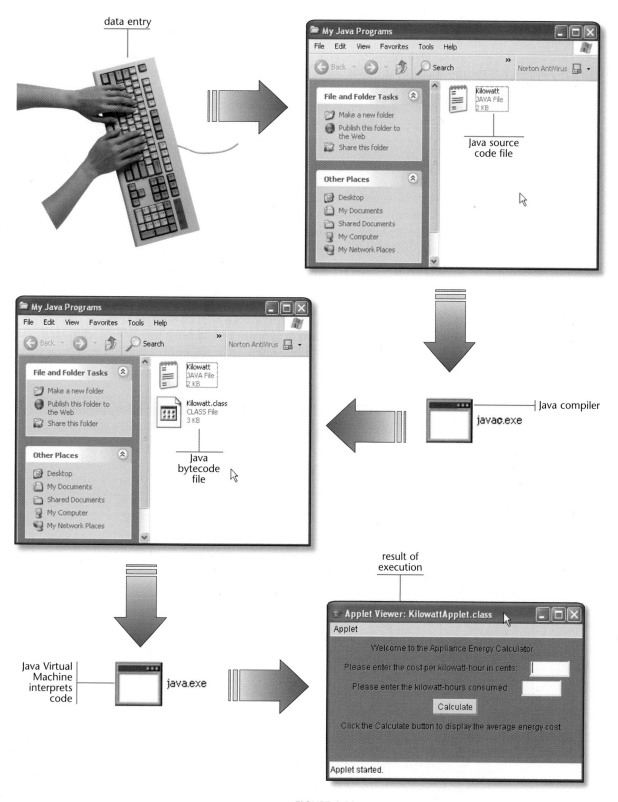

FIGURE 1-21

from these class packages, programmers can reduce the amount of new code
they need to develop and test. Documentation for these APIs is available on the
Sun Microsystems Web site.

The Java Applet Viewer

The **Java Applet Viewer** is a mini-browser designed to display Java applets without any of the version or enabling problems associated with common proprietary browsers such as Microsoft Internet Explorer or Netscape Navigator. For programming development purposes, a program called appletviewer.exe is used to launch the Java Applet Viewer. The Java Applet Viewer is part of the JRE.

Other Java Development Tools

A variety of tools are on the market to help programmers write, compile, and execute Java applications, applets, servlets, and Web services, in conjunction with the Java 2 Standard Edition. While some programmers write code using Microsoft's Notepad program, others use value-added text editors, such as TextPad, JGrasp, or JCreator. A **value-added text editor** (**VATE**) assists programmers by color-coding key elements in the Java code and inserting automatic line numbers. Many VATEs also compile and execute Java programs using buttons and menus. Figure 1-22 shows TextPad, a VATE interface, which you will use in this book to develop Java programs. Instructions for downloading and installing TextPad are included in Appendix B. Appendix C discusses setting the layout to match the screens in this book.

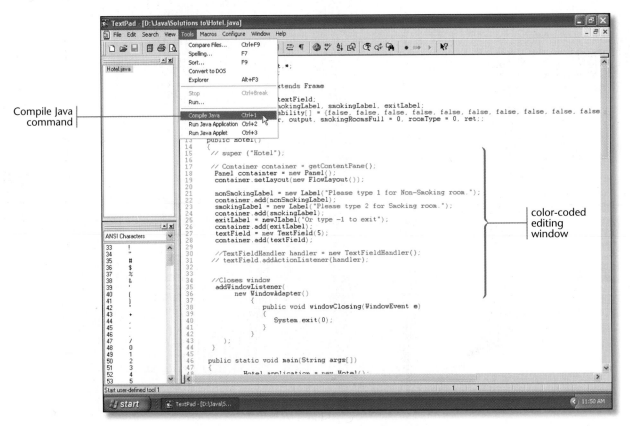

FIGURE 1-22

Another tool developed to assist Java programmers is an **integrated development environment** (**IDE**). An IDE, sometimes also called a **builder tool**, assists programmers by displaying toolbars, menus, windows, and dialog boxes that are designed to facilitate coding and debugging (Figure 1-23). Sun Microsystems' ONE Studio software, for example, is an IDE for Java technology developers. Other IDE examples include JBuilder, Visual Age for Java, and Simplicity. While an IDE does assist programmers with the essential steps in developing programs, IDEs are not well suited for beginning programmers, who must learn to use the IDE while learning Java programming.

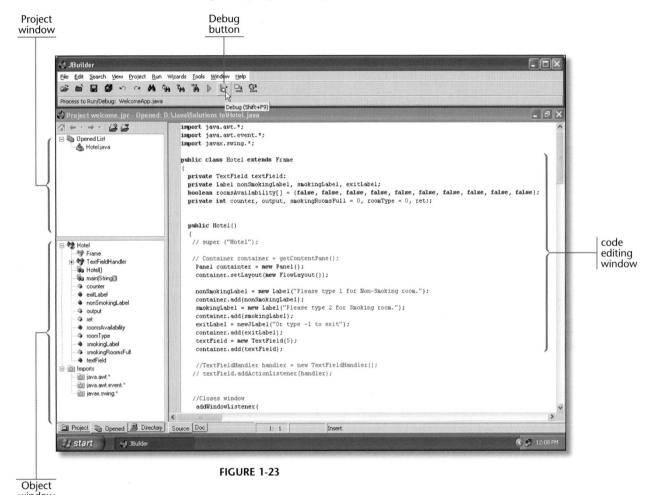

FIGURE 1-23

Once you have developed Java programs, such as servlets, you can deploy them using a Web server, such as Tomcat Web server. Tomcat Web server is a free, open-source implementation for Java servlets and Java Server Pages, which will work on a stand-alone computer system. To run Java programs developed in this book, you can install the Tomcat Web server from the CD-ROM in the back of this book or download and install it from the Web. For more information on downloading the Tomcat Web server, see Appendix B. Your instructor or employer also may direct you to use a different server at your school or business.

Chapter Summary

This chapter provided an overview of computer programming, the Java programming language and its characteristics, and the steps of the program development cycle. The Java platform allows you to build many types of programs, including console applications, windowed applications, applets, servlets, Web services, and beans. The chapter also introduced you to object-oriented programming and design concepts and the use of objects, methods, attributes, and events. You learned how object-oriented programming and design facilitates rapid application development and how the concepts of encapsulation, inheritance, and polymorphism create reusable, stable programs that are easier and faster to design. Finally, the chapter reviewed the components of the Java Software Development Kit (SDK), including the Java compiler, the Java Virtual Machine, APIs, and the Java Applet Viewer, as well as other development tools, such as value-added text editors (VATEs) and integrated development environments (IDEs).

Key Terms

aggregation *(23)*
algorithm *(14)*
applet *(6)*
application *(5)*
application program interface (API)
   (30)
application software packages
   (10)
attributes *(16)*
bean *(9)*
boundary values *(21)*
builder tool *(33)*
bytecode *(30)*
class *(16)*
class diagram *(16)*
class libraries *(30)*
class packages *(30)*
class providers *(29)*
class users *(29)*
client-side *(6)*
code *(2)*
coding *(2)*
comments *(20)*
compiler *(30)*
computer programming *(2)*
console application *(5)*
control structure *(18)*

correct *(14)*
documentation *(22)*
efficient *(14)*
encapsulation *(27)*
event *(24)*
event diagram *(24)*
event-driven *(25)*
flowchart *(16)*
generalization hierarchy *(23)*
high-level languages *(2)*
hosting *(7)*
Hypertext Markup Language (HTML)
   (6)
information hiding *(27)*
inheritance *(27)*
instance *(24)*
integrated development environment
   (IDE) *(33)*
integration testing *(21)*
interpreter *(30)*
Java *(2)*
Java Applet Viewer *(32)*
Java 2 Runtime Environment (JRE)
   (29)
Java 2 Standard Edition (J2SE)
   (29)

Java Database Connectivity (JDBC) *(7)*

Java Server Pages (JSP) *(7)*

Java Software Development Kit (SDK) *(3)*

Java Virtual Machine (JVM) *(30)*

Java Web Start *(6)*

JavaBean *(9)*

JavaScript *(6)*

message *(24)*

methodology *(11)*

methods *(16)*

object *(3)*

object-oriented design (OOD) *(3)*

object-oriented programming (OOP) *(3)*

operation *(24)*

parsimonious *(3)*

platform *(3)*

platform-independent *(3)*

polymorphism *(28)*

portable *(3)*

program *(2)*

program development cycle *(11)*

programmers *(2)*

programming language *(2)*

pseudocode *(18)*

rapid application development (RAD) *(29)*

requirements document *(12)*

reusability *(9)*

robust *(3)*

secure *(3)*

server software *(7)*

server-side *(7)*

servlet *(7)*

software developers *(2)*

storyboard *(15)*

strongly typed language *(3)*

subclass *(23)*

subclassing *(27)*

superclass *(23)*

syntax *(2)*

test cases *(21)*

test plan *(21)*

testing *(21)*

transparent *(27)*

trigger *(24)*

Unified Modeling Language (UML) *(25)*

unit testing *(20)*

usability *(19)*

validate *(19)*

value-added text editor (VATE) *(32)*

Web server *(7)*

Web service *(8)*

windowed application *(5)*

Homework Assignments

Short Answer

1. A(n) _____ is a set of words, symbols, and codes that enables a programmer to communicate instructions to a computer.

2. The particular set of grammar or rules that specify how the instructions are to be written is called the _____ of the language.

3. List some of the characteristics of Java.

4. Define the differences between a Java application, an applet, and a servlet.

5. _____ is a scripting tool created by Netscape in cooperation with Sun Microsystems to insert code statements directly into the HTML of a Web page, in order to add functionality and improve the appearance of the Web page.

(continued)

Short Answer *(continued)*

6. A(n) _____ is a program that receives a request for information from another program over the Web and returns data to the requesting program.

7. Many programmers refer to the entire Java platform as the JDK, which is an acronym for _____.

8. A(n) _____ is a program that converts a programmer's code into machine-readable instructions, whereas a(n) _____ is a program that will execute the bytecode to produce results.

9. The _____ is a standard set of interfaces and classes functionally grouped into packages that are present in any Java implementation.

10. Both _____ and _____ assist programmers by color coding key elements in Java code, as well as inserting line numbers.

11. List the six phases of the program development life cycle in order and briefly describe the purpose of each.

12. List the essential inputs and outputs for a program that calculates and displays sales tax based on a user-supplied dollar amount.

13. List three sets of test data for a program that determines the quotient A/B, where A must be an integer between −1 and 10, and B must be non-zero.

14. Which variable(s) would you test in Figure 1-15 on page 19 to ensure that the entered ounces are a positive integer? Describe the valid range of the variables you select.

15. An employee's weekly gross pay is determined by multiplying the hours worked by the rate of pay. Overtime (hours worked more than 40) is paid at 1.5 times the hourly rate. Answer the following questions:

    a. List the essential inputs and outputs. List sample data that includes boundary values.

    b. Draw a storyboard to label and accept the inputs, and calculate and display the outputs. Identify and label the input and output text boxes, and any buttons on the storyboard.

    c. Draw a class diagram for the Gross Pay object.

    d. Draw a flowchart to calculate the gross pay.

    e. Write the pseudocode that corresponds to the flowchart in Step d above.

    f. Draw an event diagram for the Gross Pay event.

16. Draw a generalization hierarchy chart for a book object. Include a superclass and at least two subclasses. Below the chart, list and label attributes, methods, a trigger, and an instance of a book.

17. Draw a class diagram for a Print button in an application toolbar.

18. Draw an event diagram for an elevator request. Include the user pushing the button as a trigger, the light coming on, and the elevator sensing the request. Follow the event through the elevator arriving at the floor and the doors opening.

19. Write the pseudocode and then draw a flowchart for a program that accepts the age of the user and then tests that value to display one of the following three categories: youth (<18 years), adult (18 to 65 years), or senior (>65 years).

Learn It Online

Start your browser and visit scsite.com/java3e/learn. Follow the instructions in the exercises below.

1. **Chapter Reinforcement TF, MC, and SA**   Click the Chapter Reinforcement link below Chapter 1. Print and then answer the True/False, Multiple Choice, and Short Answer questions.

2. **Practice Test**   Click the Practice Test link below Chapter 1. Answer each question, enter your first and last name at the bottom of the page, and then click the Grade Test button. When the graded practice test displays on your screen, click Print on the File menu to print a hard copy. Continue to take practice tests until you score 80% or better. Hand in a printout of the final practice test.

3. **Crossword Puzzle Challenge**   Click the Crossword Puzzle Challenge link below Chapter 1. Read the instructions, and then enter your first and last name. Click the Play button. Complete the crossword puzzle. When you are finished, click the Submit button. When the crossword puzzle redisplays, click the Print button.

4. **Tips and Tricks**   Click the Tips and Tricks link below Chapter 1. Right-click the information and then click Print on the shortcut menu. Construct a brief example of what the information relates to in Java to confirm that you understand how to use the tip or trick. Hand in the example and printed information.

5. **Newsgroups**   Click the Newsgroups link below Chapter 1. Click a topic that pertains to Chapter 1. Print three comments.

6. **Expanding Your Horizons**   Click the Expanding Your Horizons link below Chapter 1. Click a topic that pertains to Chapter 1. Print the information. Construct a brief example of what the information relates to in Java to confirm that you understand the contents of the article. Hand in the example and printed information.

7. **Search Sleuth**   Select three key terms from the Key Terms section of this chapter and then use the Google search engine at google.com (or any major search engine) to display and print two Web pages for each key term.

Programming Assignments

1 Using Object Terminology

You are a teller at a bank. A customer has come in asking to open a savings account — just one of the many kinds of accounts that you handle. After determining that the customer wants a passbook savings rather than a certificate of deposit, you remind the customer that all accounts are FDIC insured. You assign a unique account number and accept the customer's initial deposit. You explain that while all accounts earn some form of interest, this specific savings account is compounded quarterly. The interest will appear automatically on the monthly statement. The customer now can deposit and withdraw from the account.

(continued)

1 Using Object Terminology *(continued)*

If savings account is the object, give an example of each of the following as it relates to that savings account.

1. superclass _____

2. subclass _____

3. attribute _____

4. method _____

5. instance _____

6. trigger _____

7. event _____

8. inheritance _____

9. encapsulation _____

10. polymorphism _____

2 Writing Pseudocode

Write pseudocode to describe the logic illustrated by the flow-chart shown in Figure 1-24. For additional information about pseudocode, see Appendix A.

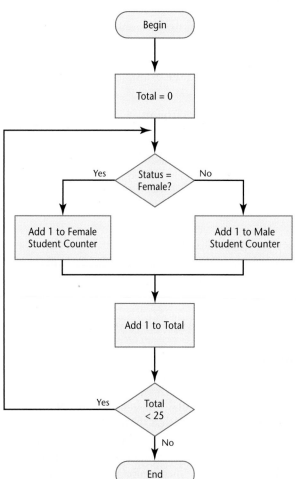

FIGURE 1-24

3 Analyzing Requirements

Review the requirements document in Figure 1-25 and then answer the questions on the next page.

REQUEST FOR NEW APPLICATION

Date submitted:	September 26, 2007
Submitted by:	Ray Lykins
Purpose:	Cattle ranchers rely on feed grains to feed their cattle, along with hay and grazing land. The ranchers use more feed during the winter and less during spring, summer, and fall, unless there is a drought. A field agent helps ranchers calculate the amount of feed they will need. The distribution manager takes the order over the phone and calculates the cost and the shipping.
Application title:	Cattle Feed Calculator (CFC)
Algorithms:	<u>Dietary needs</u>: Each cow consumes 3% of body weight per day in feed (for example, 1,200 lb. cow x 0.03 = 36 lbs. of feed per day). <u>Truck capacity</u>: 2.5 Tons <u>Current market price for dry ration matter</u>: $150 per ton.
Notes:	1) The application should allow users to enter values for the number of cows, the number of days — a calculation based on the commonly used Animal Unit Month (AUM) — and the current market price. 2) The application should also allow the user to reset all values on the screen to zero (0) so that another calculation can be performed. 3) In the near future, we would like to allow the field agents to access the calculator remotely via the Web. 4) The application should include the company logo in the interface. The application window should be sizable so that the user can get a better view of the data. 5) A common dry ration uses a mixture of the following: • grains • grain by-products • protein-rich meals • hays • straws/stubble 6) The user should be able to exit the application at any time.

Approvals

Approval status:	X	Approved
		Rejected
Approved by:	Isaac King	
Date:	October 18, 2007	
Assigned to:	J. Starks, Programmer	

FIGURE 1-25

(continued)

3 Analyzing Requirements *(continued)*

1. List at least three relevant requirements necessary to design a complete program that are missing from the requirements document. Use these new requirements when completing the remaining tasks.

2. List the inputs and outputs necessary to solve the problem.

3. Draw a storyboard for a program that would meet the program requirements.

4. Design three sets of test data and step the test data through the algorithm listed in the requirements in order to test the expected output of the problem.

4 Understanding Flowcharts

Figure 1-26 shows a flowchart that represents part of a cardiovascular disease risk assessment. The higher the point total, the greater the risk of cardiovascular disease. In the spaces provided, write the point total for the following persons using the logic in the flowchart. For additional information about flowcharting, see Appendix A.

1. A 40-year-old smoker with normal blood pressure who eats a low-fat diet.

   _____

2. A 20-year-old nonsmoker with normal blood pressure who eats a high-fat diet.

   _____

3. A 27-year-old smoker with high blood pressure who eats a high-fat diet.

   _____

4. A 16-year-old nonsmoker with normal blood pressure who eats a high-fat diet.

   _____

5. A 63-year-old nonsmoker with high blood pressure who eats a low-fat diet.

   _____

6. A 50-year-old nonsmoker with high blood pressure who eats a high-fat diet.

   _____

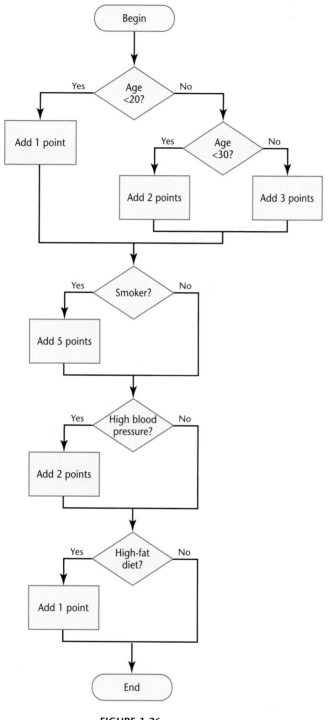

FIGURE 1-26

5 Understanding Event Diagrams

Refer to the event diagram in Figure 1-27 to answer the following questions:

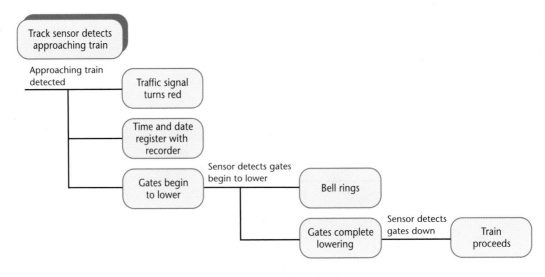

FIGURE 1-27

1. List each message and its corresponding operation.
2. Which of these operations triggers a subsequent message? List any such operation and its subsequent message.
3. Which of these operations changes the value of an attribute of an object? List the operation, the attribute, and the attribute's value before and after the operation.

6 Creating a Generalization Hierarchy

Pick any class of objects that interests you (for example, books, clothes, musical instruments, physical fitness equipment). Create a generalization hierarchy showing at least four levels of subclasses and superclasses. For each subclass, identify several attributes inherited from the superclass.

7 Creating Class Diagrams

Draw a class diagram for each object in Figure 1-27. Include at least two attributes and one method in each diagram.

8 Creating an Event Diagram

Using Figure 1-27 as an example, draw an event diagram to raise the gates when the track sensor has detected the train is clear of the intersection. The trigger is the lack of weight on the tracks. The events that happen include the sensor detecting that loss of weight and the gates rising. Possible operations include traffic signal changing, time and date recording, and gate movement.

9 Thinking Algorithmically

Take one of the following tasks and write a set of instructions that is sufficiently complete so that another person could perform the task without asking questions. Test your solution by giving it to another class member and having him or her perform the steps. If a step in your task is dependent on a condition, use the words if, then, and else to describe the criteria to be met for that condition and the results. If steps in the task repeat, use the phrases do while, do until, or do a certain number of times to describe the repetition. For more information about conditions and repetitions, see Appendix A.

1. light a candle
2. make a cup of tea
3. send an e-mail
4. walk from the classroom to the bookstore
5. log on to your school's network or intranet

10 Identifying Triggers and Events

Figure 1-28 displays a user interface to calculate prices at a movie theater. Notice there is no button labeled Calculate. Using your knowledge of graphical user interfaces, list each object in the window, identify the trigger(s) to select the objects, and then describe the output related to the event and its operations. *Hint*: only one event trigger should cause the price to display.

FIGURE 1-28

11 Understanding Java Components

Create a generalization hierarchy or class diagram of the various JDK components in Java 2 Standard Edition (J2SE), version 5.0. Use information from this chapter and information from the Sun Microsystems Java Web site at java.sun.com. Include such components as the JRE, JVM, and API, among others.

12 Exploring Other Java Technologies

Visit the Sun Microsystems Java Web site at java.sun.com. Choose any one of the listed Java technologies and explore the linked Web pages. Write several paragraphs about your chosen technology. Include a general description of the technology and information on current versions, new enhancements, and compatibility. Describe how the technology interacts with J2SE 5.0.

13 Blog about Java Technology

Visit the Sun Microsystems blog site at java.sun.com/developer/blogs/index.html or an other Java technology blog. Search the site for information related to J2SE 5.0. Print out several references and hand them in to your instructor.

2

Creating a Java Application and Applet

Objectives

You will have
mastered the material in
this chapter when you can:

- Write a simple Java application
- Use TextPad
- Understand the different types and uses of comments
- Use proper naming conventions for classes and files
- Identify the parts of a class header and method header
- Code output
- Use the println() method
- Compile a Java program
- Understand the common types of errors
- Run a Java program
- Edit Java source code to insert escape characters and a system date
- Print source code
- Differentiate between an application and an applet
- Create an applet from Java source code
- Write code to display a graphic, text, color, and the date in an applet
- Create an HTML host document
- Run a Java applet

Introduction

The way in which a user enters data and instructions into a computer and receives feedback from the computer is called a **user interface**. As discussed in Chapter 1, the Java platform allows you to create programs and program components that have many different user interfaces. In a Java console application, for example, the user interface is a command-line interface that displays character input and output on a black screen. A windowed application, by contrast, has a graphical user interface that is displayed in a window. Another type of Java program, an applet, can use a graphical user interface to display output to a user in a browser window.

In this chapter, you will learn how to use TextPad to write, compile, and execute a stand-alone Java program that runs as a console application. Even though communicating with a computer using a command-line interface may seem tedious when compared with today's highly interactive GUI applications, using commands to interact with a computer is a common, easy place to start. Many networking and server applications, for example, use console applications written in Java; console applications also are useful for testing and system configuration. Next you will learn how to create an applet using TextPad. The applets will run and display in the Applet Viewer window, which is the mini-browser supplied with the Java SDK.

In this chapter, you will learn the basic parts of a Java program as well as the use of proper Java syntax, which is the set of grammar or rules that specifies the spelling of its commands and any required symbols. You will learn to analyze a problem and design a solution. You then will learn how to create a console application, compile and test the application, and run the program. Finally you will learn how to create an applet and its HTML hosting file. The applet will display text and a graphic in Java's Applet Viewer window.

Chapter Two — The Welcome to My Day Program

The console application developed in this chapter is the Welcome to My Day program, which displays a welcome message, the user's name, and the system date on a splash screen (Figure 2-1a). A **splash screen** is a screen that is displayed before the main program is displayed. The compiled Java source code will cause text output to display on the screen for the user to read. Creating this console application serves as a first step in creating an electronic calendar application for either a desktop or a handheld computer system.

The same electronic calendar application also will need to be accessible to users via the Web. To create a splash screen for the Web-based version of the calendar application, the console application must be converted to an applet that displays text output and a graphic in the Applet Viewer window (Figure 2-1b). As shown in Figures 2-1a and 2-1b, the console application displays white letters on a black screen, while the applet displays black letters on a light blue (cyan) background, beside the graphic. Both the console application and the applet will become part of the electronic calendar application when it is fully implemented.

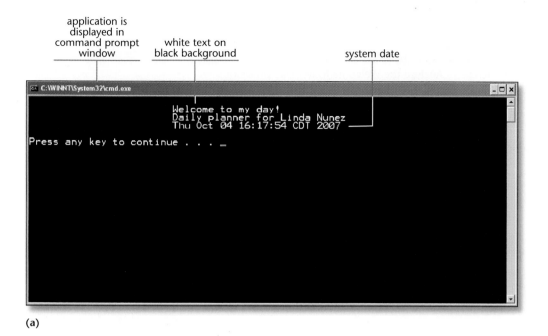

(a)

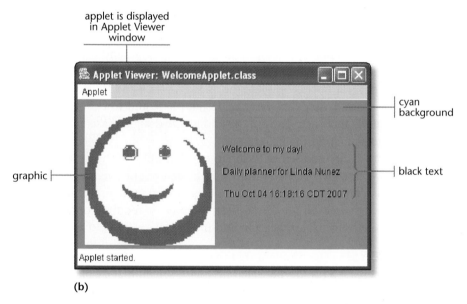

(b)

FIGURE 2-1

Program Development

As you learned in Chapter 1, the tasks involved in developing an application follow the series of six iterative phases outlined in the development cycle. The six phases and corresponding tasks of the development cycle for the Welcome to My Day program are shown in Table 2-1 on the next page.

Table 2-1 Welcome to My Day Program Development Tasks

	DEVELOPMENT PHASE	TASK(S)
1	Analyze the requirements	Analyze the Welcome to My Day problem.
2	Design the solution	Design the user interface for both the application and the applet including output data and placement of the applet graphic. Design the logic to solve the problem.
3	Validate the design	Confirm with the user that the design solves the problem in a satisfactory manner.
4	Implement the design	Translate the design into code for both the application and the applet. Include internal documentation (comments and remarks) within the code that explains the purpose of the code statements. Create the HTML file to host the applet.
5	Test the solution	Test the program. Find and correct any errors (debugging) until it is error-free.
6	Document the solution	Print copies of the application code, applet code, applet interface, and HTML code.

Analysis and Design

The first two phases in the development cycle — analysis and design — involve analyzing the problem to be solved by the program and then designing a solution. Once programmers complete the analysis phase and fully understand the problem to be solved, they can start the design phase and work with users to design a user-friendly interface. Toward the end of the design phase, programmers design the logic behind the program.

Figure 2-2 shows the requirements document that initiates the development cycle for the Welcome to My Day program. The design requirements listed by the user are specific enough to allow for the development cycle to begin. The document specifies the reason for the request, the specific required output, and a description of both the application and the applet.

PROBLEM ANALYSIS The problem that the Welcome to My Day program should solve is to create a prototype welcome splash screen that displays a welcome message, user's name, and the date on the screen. A **prototype** is a functional working model of a proposed system, created to make sure it meets users' needs. The prototype welcome splash screen is the first step in implementing a company-wide electronic calendar application. This prototype later could be modified to interface with the database of the electronic calendar application.

The requirements document has outlined the need for a prototype splash screen. Splash screens generally serve two purposes: (1) to let the user know that the program has started, and (2) to provide information that the user may read while waiting for the entire application to load. As outlined in the requirements document, both the application and the applet versions of the splash screen should display output to the user in the form of text. The text displayed includes a welcome message, the user's name, and the **system date**, which is the current date and time generated by the operating system of a computer. Additionally, the requirements document requests that the applet version of the program includes color and a graphic.

REQUEST FOR NEW APPLICATION .

Date submitted:	August 28, 2007
Submitted by:	Linda Nunez
Purpose:	Our firm has begun the process of implementing an electronic calendar application for each employee. The calendar application needs to run as a stand-alone application on desktop and handheld computers and also be accessible via the Web. The company wants to create a prototype welcome splash screen that displays a welcome message, the user's name, and the system date. This prototype later will be modified to interface with the database of an electronic calendar application purchased from a major software company.
Application title:	Welcome to My Day
Algorithms:	Text and graphics will display on the screen when the program executes.
Notes:	1) As some of our employees have handheld computing devices with small monochrome screens, the stand-alone console application should display text only. 2) If employees choose to view their calendar over the Web, the welcome splash screen should display in an applet. 3) The application and applet should use the system date, so that it is always current. The system date does not have to be formatted in any special way. Our employees are used to reading the system date on printouts and electronic transfer reports. 4) The applet should use color and display a graphic. A sample graphic file is included on the accompanying Data Disk. 5) Employees should be able to close the welcome splash screen at anytime by clicking a standard Close button.

Approvals

Approval status:	X	Approved
		Rejected
Approved by:	David Reneau	
Date:	September 24, 2007	
Assigned to:	J. Starks, Programmer	

FIGURE 2-2

DESIGN THE SOLUTION   Once you have analyzed the problem and understand the needs, the next step is to design the user interface. Figure 2-3a shows an example of a hand-drawn storyboard for the user interface of the Welcome to My Day application; Figure 2-3b on the next page shows a storyboard for the user interface of the Welcome to My Day applet. The displayed output data, as specified in the requirements document, includes a welcome message, the user's name, and the system date.

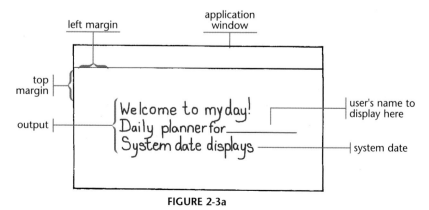

FIGURE 2-3a

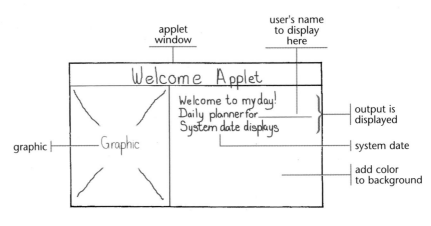

FIGURE 2-3b

When designing a console application, programmers typically use text to display the output. Console applications are used when the program must display information such as prompts, simple menus, and input and output data. In the Welcome to My Day application, the program requires no input from the user, so no prompts for data input display. The program displays three lines of output data as left-justified text. As shown in the storyboard in Figure 2-3a on the previous page, the output text is displayed with a top and left margin to provide space between the window's edge and the output text. Design experts agree that adding top and left margins makes the display look less crowded and creates a more visually appealing display of output.

While the system date display may seem cryptic to those unfamiliar with that sort of notation, the requirements document states that the employees are accustomed to seeing the date display in that manner. When designing an application, it is important to adhere to company standards and practices so as to make users comfortable with the user interface.

The output for the applet will include the same text that the application displays, as well as color and a graphic (Figure 2-3b). The smiley face graphic used in this prototype applet is a placeholder graphic submitted with the requirements document and included on the Data Disk that accompanies this book. When the electronic calendar application is implemented, the graphic would be replaced with a company logo.

The requirements document states that the user will click the Close button to exit the program. Both Java console applications and applets automatically display a standard Close button, which is a **default** or preset feature of the command prompt and Applet Viewer windows. When a user clicks the Close button, the active window closes. The close action is encapsulated into the Click event of the Close button — in other words, the operating system automatically tells the Java program how to close the active window when a user clicks the Close button. In addition to the default Close button, the command prompt and Applet Viewer windows also both include Minimize and Maximize buttons. When developing a program, programmers can assume that those button objects and their corresponding events will work as intended. No further design issues apply to exiting the program.

Exiting a Console Application Using a VATE

Some value-added text editors (VATEs), including TextPad, automatically display a "Press any key to continue" message after displaying all the output in a console application. In most cases, pressing any key exits the program in a manner similar to clicking the Close button.

PROGRAM DESIGN   Once you have designed the interface, the next step is to design the logic to solve the problem and create the desired results. The only programming task is to display three lines of output, one after another, on the screen; therefore, the structure of the program will be sequential in nature. The program code will send a print message to an object — in this case, the default display device of your system (Figure 2-1a on page 47). The program code then will be modified so that the program can run on the Web as an applet. The program code for the applet will display the three lines of output in a window of their own, along with a graphic (Figure 2-1b on page 47). Both the application and the applet versions of the program should contain appropriate documentation and be saved for future use.

Figure 2-4a shows a flowchart that outlines the sequence of steps in the program. Figure 2-4b shows an event diagram that illustrates how the execution of the program triggers the Display event.

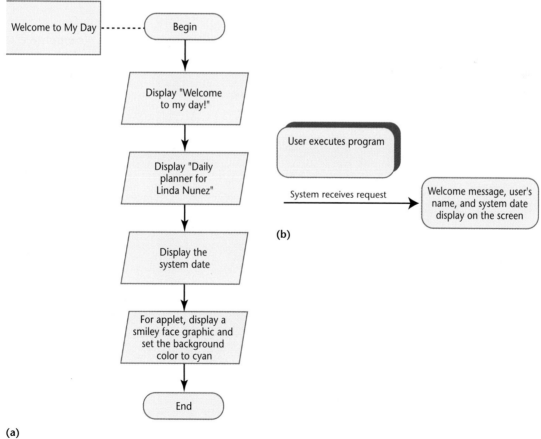

(b)

(a)

FIGURE 2-4

Having analyzed the problem, designed the interface, and designed the program logic, the analysis and design of the application is complete. As shown in Table 2-1 on page 48, the next task in the development cycle is to implement the design using the Java SDK. To complete the steps in this text, you must have downloaded the Java 2 Standard Edition (J2SE) version 5.0 from the Sun Microsystems Web site or installed it from the CD in the back of this book. You also must have downloaded and installed TextPad. This book uses TextPad to edit code, but you can use any text editor available on your system, as indicated by your instructor. For more information on installing the Java SDK and TextPad, see Appendix B.

Using TextPad

This book uses TextPad to enter Java source code—the English-like statements that represent the step-by-step instructions a computer must execute. **TextPad** is a powerful, value-added text editor (VATE) used to create many different kinds of text-based files, one of which is a Java source code file. Any text-editing program capable of creating a text file can be used to write Java programs; however, TextPad displays line numbers and color coding to assist programmers in writing and testing their programs. Additionally, TextPad contains many programmer-friendly tools, including commands to compile and execute both applications and applets.

Starting TextPad

With TextPad installed on your computer, perform the following steps to start TextPad.

To Start TextPad

1. With the Windows desktop displayed, click the Start button on the taskbar and then point to All Programs on the Start menu. Point to TextPad on the All Programs submenu.

The All Programs submenu is displayed (Figure 2-5). Your system may have a different set of menus.

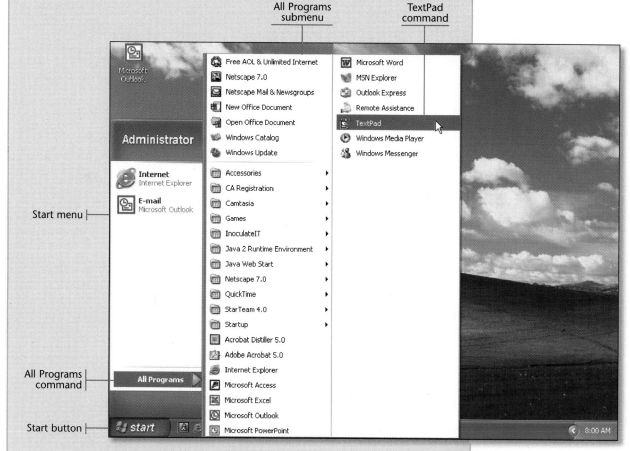

FIGURE 2-5

(continued)

2. Click TextPad. When the TextPad window opens, if necessary, click the Maximize button to maximize the screen. If a Tip of the Day dialog box is displayed, click its Close button.

TextPad starts and displays a blank coding window (Figure 2-6). A Help message box may display briefly. The insertion point and mouse pointer display in the TextPad coding window. Your system may display a shadow or highlight on the line with the mouse pointer. See Appendix C to change your settings to match those in this book.

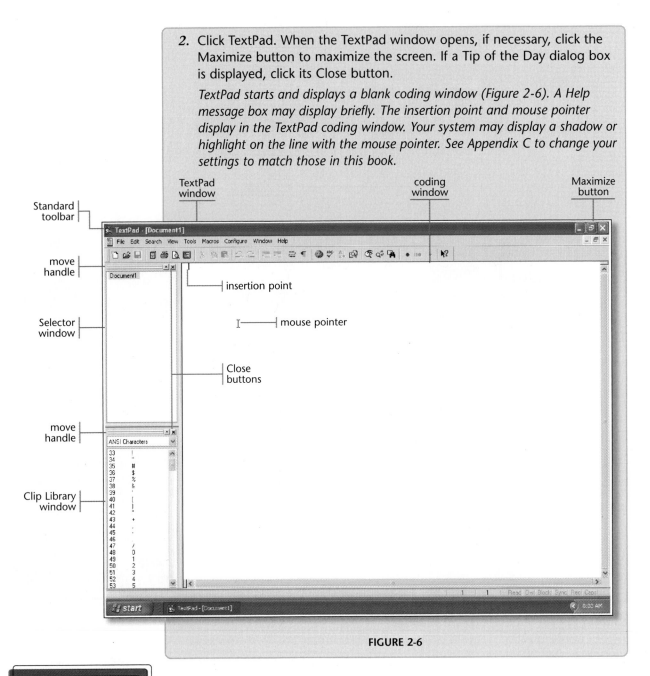

FIGURE 2-6

OTHER WAYS

1. Click TextPad on Start menu
2. Double-click TextPad icon on desktop

The TextPad Window

The TextPad window consists of several window areas and a Standard toolbar to help you create programs. Depending on the task you are performing or the options you choose, other windows and toolbars will display or replace components shown in Figure 2-6.

The TextPad **coding window** is the area where you can enter and edit lines of Java code (Figure 2-6). Also referred to as a list or listing, the code will be entered and edited later in the chapter.

The window in the upper-left corner of the screen shown in Figure 2-6 is the **Selector window**, which displays a list of open TextPad files. Notice that the default file name, Document1, is displayed. The window below the Selector window is the Clip Library window. The **Clip Library window** displays a list of special codes and tags used by some scripting tools and languages such as HTML. You can double-click any code or tag in the list to insert it into the code in the coding window.

Java programmers customize the display of the TextPad window in a variety of ways. For example, a programmer can move both the Selector window and the Clip Library window to any part of the TextPad window by dragging the respective window's move handle, or resize each window by dragging its border. A programmer also can close the windows by clicking their respective Close buttons, in order to maximize the space in the coding window.

Displaying Line Numbers in the TextPad Window

Another way you can customize the TextPad window is to display line numbers in the coding window. TextPad allows you to display **line numbers** that begin with one and progress sequentially down the left side of the coding window. Using line numbers not only allows you to keep track of which line you are on while you enter code but also provides a reference for possible errors when you compile Java source code.

Perform the following steps to display line numbers in the TextPad window.

To Display Line Numbers in the TextPad Window

1. With the TextPad window still open, click View on the menu bar. *The View menu is displayed (Figure 2-7).*

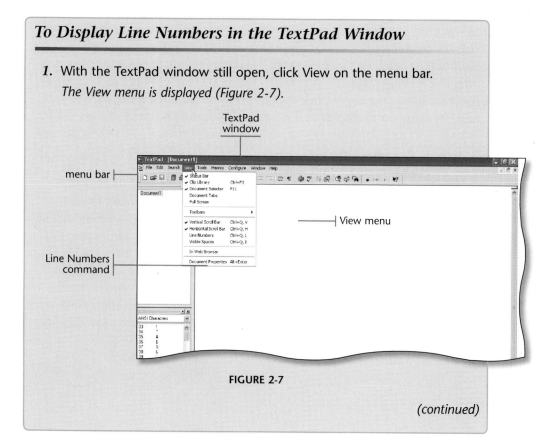

FIGURE 2-7

(continued)

2. Click Line Numbers on the View menu.

Line number 1 is displayed in the coding window (Figure 2-8).

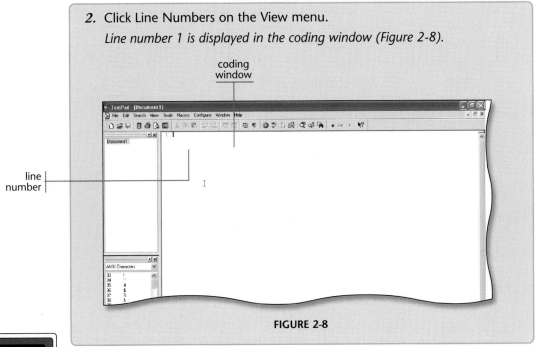

FIGURE 2-8

OTHER WAYS

1. Press CTRL+Q, press L
2. Press ALT+V, press L

By default, TextPad does not display line numbers automatically in the coding window. As shown in the previous steps, you can use the Line Numbers command on the View menu to display line numbers after you start TextPad. If you want line numbers to display each time you start TextPad, you can change TextPad's default setting so that line numbers always display. To change the default setting, click Preferences on the Configure menu. When the Preferences dialog box is displayed, click View in the list on the left and then click Line numbers in the list on the right. Click the OK button to save the changes. This will cause line numbers to display in the coding window each time you start TextPad.

Saving a TextPad Document

Before you type any code, you will save the default TextPad document displayed in the TextPad coding window. Saving the TextPad document before entering any code serves several purposes. First, by saving the document as a Java file type, you notify TextPad that the document includes Java source code, thus enabling TextPad's color-coding capabilities related to Java. Further, after you save the document, the document name is displayed in TextPad's title bar and provides a visual reference as you work. Saving first also allows you to use the Save button on the Standard toolbar for subsequent saves, thus saving time. Finally, having a previously saved document may help you recover lost data in the event of a system crash or power loss.

Perform the following steps to save the TextPad coding window.

To Save a TextPad Document

1. Insert the Data Disk in drive A. See the preface of this book for instructions for downloading the Data Disk or see your instructor for information about accessing the files required in this book.

2. With the TextPad window still open, click File on the menu bar.

The File menu is displayed (Figure 2-9).

FIGURE 2-9

3. Click Save As on the File menu.

The Save As dialog box is displayed (Figure 2-10). Your screen may differ.

FIGURE 2-10

(continued)

4. Type Welcome in the File name text box. Do not press the ENTER key. Click the Save as type box arrow.

   Welcome is displayed in the File name text box as the new file name (Figure 2-11). The Save as type list displays a list of file types supported by TextPad.

FIGURE 2-11

5. Click Java (*.java) in the Save as type list.

   Java (.java) is displayed as the file type (Figure 2-12).*

FIGURE 2-12

6. Click the Save in box arrow.

The Save in list displays the available storage locations (Figure 2-13).

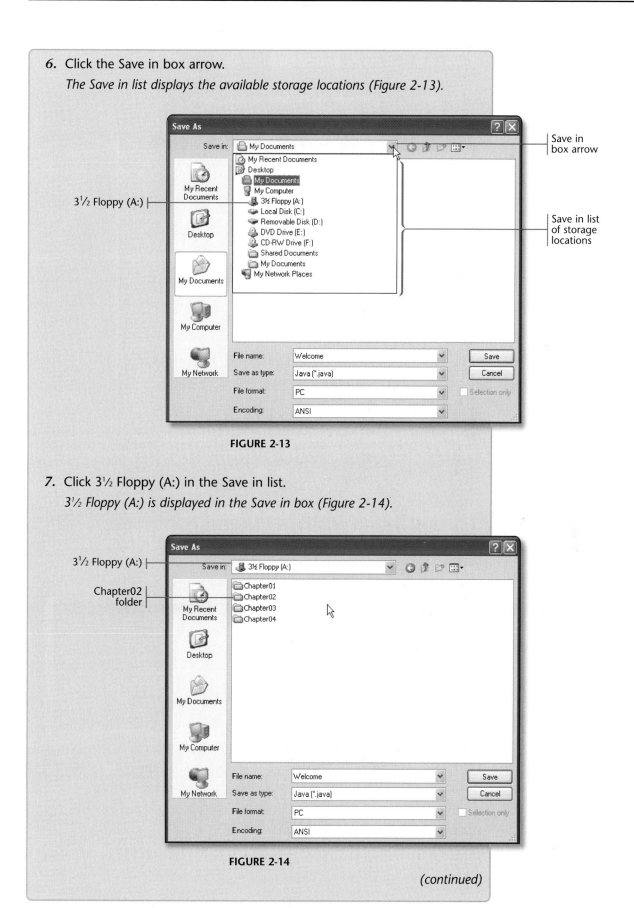

FIGURE 2-13

7. Click 3½ Floppy (A:) in the Save in list.

3½ Floppy (A:) is displayed in the Save in box (Figure 2-14).

FIGURE 2-14

(continued)

8. Double-click the Chapter02 folder or other location as directed by your instructor.

Chapter02 is displayed in the Save in box (Figure 2-15). Your list of files may differ.

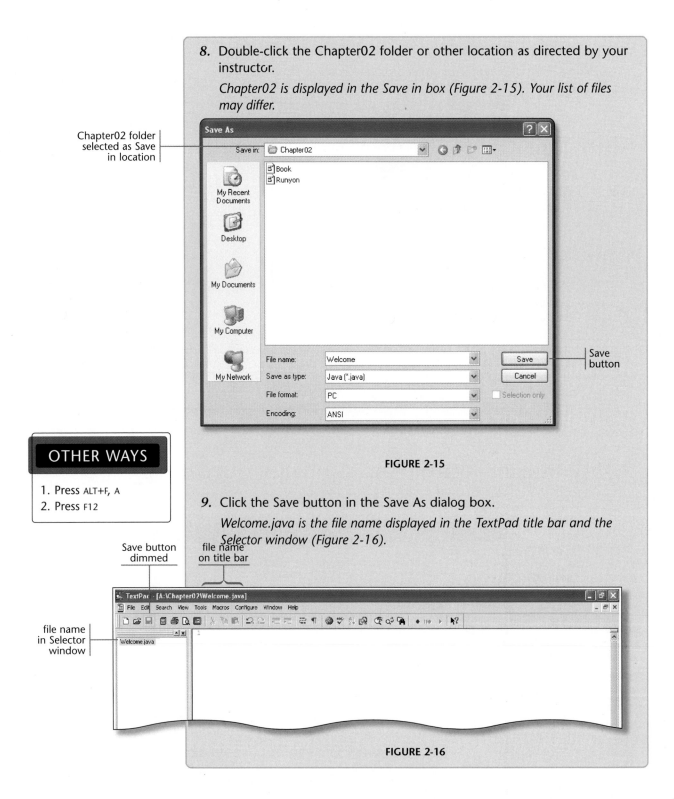

Chapter02 folder selected as Save in location

Save button

FIGURE 2-15

9. Click the Save button in the Save As dialog box.

Welcome.java is the file name displayed in the TextPad title bar and the Selector window (Figure 2-16).

Save button dimmed

file name on title bar

file name in Selector window

FIGURE 2-16

In Figure 2-16, the Save button is dimmed, or disabled. The Save button is enabled only when changes have been made to the document. As you make changes to the document by entering code, it is good practice to save the program periodically. To save the program again in the same folder, you can click the Save button on the Standard toolbar, rather than using the Save As command on the File menu.

Coding the Program

As you have learned, the implementation phase of the program development cycle involves writing the code that translates the design into a program. During program design, a flowchart was used to outline the logic of the program code in the Welcome to My Day application (Figure 2-4a on page 51). As outlined in that flowchart, the task to be performed is to display a welcome message, the user's name, and the system date on the screen. Implementing the code to perform the task, instructing the computer to save that set of instructions, and then learning how to execute those instructions on any computer platform or the Web is a stepping stone to creating larger, more intricate, and more useful programs.

Coding Comments as Documentation

The process of writing code, or coding, includes adding internal documentation in the form of **comments**, which are notes within the code that explain the purpose of the code. These comments describe the purpose of the program, the name of the programmer, the date, and other important information for the programmer and other users.

When writing code, it is a good programming practice to include comments at the beginning of a program and at the start of every major section of a program. When it is necessary for a programmer to review program source code, these comments provide an immediate description of what the program is going to do. Comments also help the programmer think clearly about the purpose of the upcoming code.

Comments are not executed when the program runs. Comment lines display in the coding window and on printouts of the source code, but they do not cause the computer to perform any task.

In Java, comments can take several different forms. A **block comment** begins with a forward slash followed by an asterisk (/*) and ends with the symbols reversed, an asterisk followed by a forward slash (*/). Block comments can span as many lines as necessary within the beginning and ending marks.

Tip

Comment Placement
Comments provide important program information and remind you and other programmers of the purpose of code. Use comments in the following three ways:
1. Place a comment that identifies the file and its purpose at the top of every class or file that contains code. This type of comment typically is called a **comment header**.
2. Place a comment at the beginning of code for each event and method.
3. Place comments near portions of code that need clarification or serve an important purpose.

Typically, each line within a block comment is indented for ease in reading. Block comments can be placed before or after any line of code. All of the lines in the block, however, must stay together in a block; they cannot be interrupted or separated by commands or other lines of code. Programmers may use a block comment at the beginning of a program to describe the entire program, or in the body of a program to describe the function of a specific method.

A second type of block comment, called a **doc comment**, or a documentation comment, begins with a forward slash followed by two asterisks (/**) and ends with an asterisk followed by a forward slash (*/). Doc comments are meant to provide a concise summary of the code, not to comment on specific lines of code. Doc comments can be extracted to HTML files using the javadoc tool. For more information on the javadoc tool, see Appendix E.

A **line comment**, or single line comment, is a comment that spans only a single line or a part of a line. Line comments begin with two forward slashes (//), which cause the rest of the line to be ignored during compilation and execution. Line comments have no ending symbol. A line comment is useful especially when describing the intended meaning of a single line of code, whereas the block comment generally is more useful when describing larger sections of code. Table 2-2 shows the general form of block, doc, and line comment statements.

Table 2-2 *Comment Statements*		

General form:	`/* block comments */`
	`/** doc comments */`
	`// line comments`	

Purpose:	To insert explanatory comments in a program as internal documentation.	

Examples:	1. `/*Chapter 2:    Anita's Antiques Splash Screen`
	`   Programmer:   J. Starks`
	`   Date:         September 3, 2007`
	`   Filename:     Anita.java`
	`   Purpose:      This program displays the name, address,`
	`   and Web site address for a company as a console application.`
	`   */`
	
	2. `/**`
	`   * Returns an Image object that can be painted on the screen.`
	`   * The URL argument must specify an absolute {@link URL}.`
	`   * The name argument is a specifier relative to the URL.`
	`   * <p>`
	`   * @param  url  a URL giving the base location of the image`
	`   *              name and the location, relative to the URL`
	`   * @return       the image at the specified URL`
	`   * @see          Image`
	`   */`
	
	3. `//   The following section sets the object's properties.`	

In the code for the Welcome to My Day application, a comment header identifies the application, programmer, date, and purpose of the Welcome to My Day program. Figure 2-17 shows the comment header in block comment format. Later in the code, a line comment will explain the code used to construct the system date.

```
1   /*
2         Chapter 2:   Welcome to My Day
3         Programmer: J. Starks
4         Date:        October 4, 2007
5         Filename:    Welcome.java
6         Purpose:     This project displays a welcome message, the user's
7                      name, and the system date in a console application.
8   */
9
```

FIGURE 2-17

The code shown in Figure 2-17 includes **tab characters**, which are entered by pressing the TAB key and are used to indent items on each line. For example, in line 2, the tab characters indent the beginning of the line and separate the words, Chapter 2:, from the words, Welcome to My Day. Line 9 is left blank to separate the comments visually from the rest of the program code.

Perform the following step to enter comments in the coding window.

To Code Comments

1. With the insertion point in line 1 in the coding window, type the eight lines of the block comment header as shown in Figure 2-17. Do not type the line numbers. You can insert your own name as the programmer. Press the TAB key at the beginning of lines 2 through 7 and after each colon to indent the text as illustrated in Figure 2-17. You may need to press the TAB key more than once to create the correct indentation, or press the BACKSPACE key if necessary. Press the ENTER key after each line. After typing the comment header, press the ENTER key one more time to create a blank line in line 9.

The code window displays the comment header for the Welcome to My Day application, as shown in Figure 2-18. The insertion point is displayed in line 10.

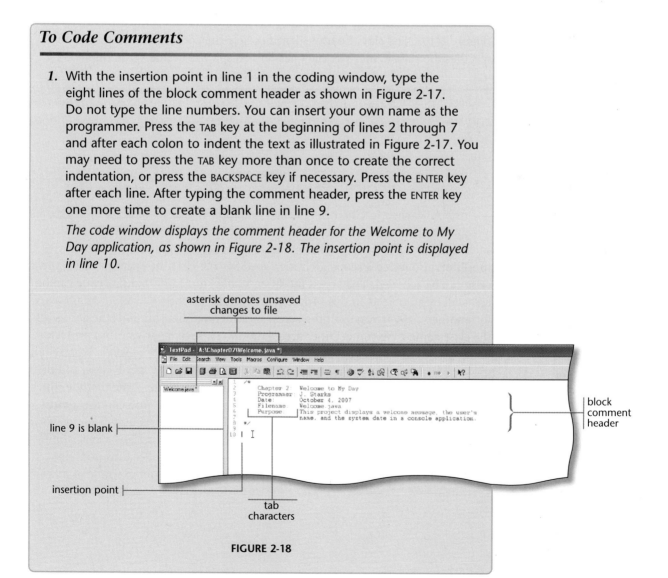

FIGURE 2-18

Notice that TextPad displays comments in the color green (Figure 2-18 on the previous page). Color coding helps you identify which lines of code are included in the comment and which are not. TextPad allows you to customize the colors used for regular code, comments, line numbers, URLs, and other items using the Preferences dialog box.

Tip

Saving Code Files

The Save button on TextPad's Standard toolbar is enabled if the file contains unsaved edits but that is not the only way to determine if the code has been changed. If TextPad displays an asterisk after the file name in its title bar or in the Selector window, the code contains edits that have not been saved (Figure 2-18 on the previous page).

The Class Header

The first line of code entered after the comment lines is the class header (Figure 2-19). The **class header** identifies how the code will be accessed and specifies the class name. The class header is displayed in line 10 in Figure 2-19.

```
10   public   class   Welcome
11   {
12
```

FIGURE 2-19

As you learned in Chapter 1, a class is an object or a set of objects that shares a common structure and a common behavior. In Java, an entire program is considered a class. The word **public** in line 10 is an access modifier. An **access modifier**, also called a scope identifier, specifies the circumstances in which the class can be accessed. The access modifier, public, indicates that this code can be accessed by all objects in this program and can be extended, or used, as a basis for another class. If you omit the access modifier, public, you limit the access to the class named Welcome. Other access modifiers, such as private and protected, are discussed in a later chapter.

In a Java program, an access modifier is followed by the word, class, and then the class name. The class name or class identifier is a unique name that identifies a specific class. In this program, the class name is Welcome. You can use almost any word as a class name, but in general, you should opt for a user-friendly word that is not on the list of keywords shown in Table 2-3. Java assigns a special purpose to these **keywords**, or **reserved words**; the Java compiler thus does not accept them as a class name. The access modifier, public, is an example of a Java keyword.

Table 2-3   Java Keywords

abstract	else	int	super
axiom	enum	interface	switch
boolean	extends	long	synchronized
break	false	native	this
byte	final	new	throw
byvalue	finally	null	throws
case	float	operator	transient
cast	for	outer	true
catch	future	package	try
char	generic	private	var
class	goto	protected	void
const	if	public	volatile
continue	implements	rest	while
default	import	return	
do	inner	short	
double	instanceof	static	

The Java programming language syntax also sets forth certain rules about class names, which specify that a class name cannot contain spaces and must not begin with a number. It also is customary to begin a class name with an upper-case letter; the names of objects and data items customarily begin with lowercase letters. Table 2-4 displays the naming rules and examples of valid or legal class names, as well as invalid or illegal ones.

Table 2-4   Java Class Naming Rules

RULE EXAMPLES	LEGAL EXAMPLES	ILLEGAL
Class names must begin with a letter, an underscore, or a dollar sign. (Letters are preferred to make class names more user-friendly). It is customary to begin class names with an uppercase letter, but not mandatory.	Employee Anita _MyProgram $myFile	123Data 1Calculator3
Class names may contain only letters, digits, underscores, or dollar signs. Class names may not contain spaces.	Record Record123 Record_123	Record#123 Record 123
Class names may not use reserved keywords. (Refer to Table 2-3 for a list of reserved keywords.)	MyClass	class

When you save a Java source code file, the Java compiler will expect the file name to match exactly the class name assigned at the beginning of your program in line 10 of Figure 2-19 on page 64. Java is **case-sensitive**, which means that the Java compiler considers uppercase and lowercase as two different characters. If you use a class name beginning with an uppercase letter, you also must begin the file name with an uppercase letter. Conventionally, Java programmers use uppercase letters, as opposed to underlines, to distinguish words in the class names, such as MyAddressProgram or OctoberPayroll.

All code entered after the class header is considered to be the body of the class and must be enclosed in **braces { }**. The opening brace is displayed in line 11 in Figure 2-19; the closing brace will display later in the code. Perform the following step to enter the class header and its opening brace.

To Code the Class Header

1. With the insertion point in line 10 in the coding window, enter the class header and opening brace in lines 10 and 11, as shown in Figure 2-19 on page 64.

   The class header is displayed (Figure 2-20). The keywords, public and class, are displayed in blue, and the opening brace is displayed in red. When you press the ENTER key after a brace, TextPad automatically indents the next line.

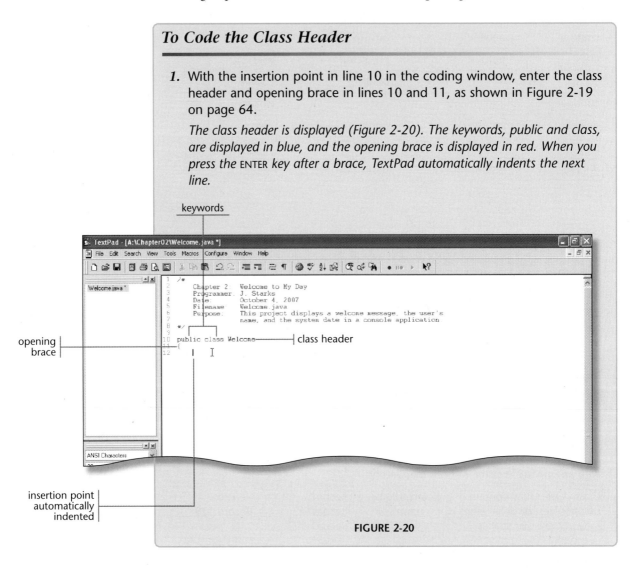

FIGURE 2-20

In Java, using a pair of opening and closing braces to enclose a portion of code indicates that they form a single, logical unit in the program, such as a class. It does not matter if you place the opening brace on the same line as the access modifier and class name or on the next line. When writing code, it is good programming practice to be consistent in the placement of the opening brace.

The Method Header

The first line of code inside the Welcome class is the main() method header. As discussed in Chapter 1, a method is the code to perform a service or operation, including manipulating values, generating outputs, or performing actions. Methods are the basic building blocks in Java code and thus are very important. Where other programming languages have functions, Java has methods.

To code a method in Java, you begin with a method header. The **method header** notifies the Java compiler of the method's attributes, the type of data it will generate (if any), the name of the method, and any other information or parameters the method needs to perform a service or operation. Table 2-5 shows the general form of a method header.

Table 2-5 Method Header	

General form:	modifier returnDataType methodName(DataType parameter)
	{
	        //code to execute when the method is called
	}

Purpose:	To notify the compiler of a method, its attributes, the type of data it will return (if any), and to provide a list of parameters the method may need. A method header can have several access modifiers and several parameters, or it can have none. Any parameters follow the method name in parentheses, with each parameter preceded by its data type. Multiple parameters are separated by commas. A method header can have only one return data type.
Examples:	1. `public static void main(String[] args)` 2. `public void paint(Graphics g)` 3. `public void init( )` 4. `public double getOvertime(double hours, double rate)`

Every stand-alone Java application must contain a **main() method**, which is the starting point during execution. The code in the main() method is performed sequentially during execution; however, the main() method may call other methods in the program. The main() method starts with the main() method header, as shown in line 12 of the Welcome to My Day program (Figure 2-21).

```
12      public   static   void  main( String  []   args )
13          {
14
```

FIGURE 2-21

A method header usually begins with one or more method modifiers. A **method modifier** is used to set properties for the method. In line 12, the access modifier, public, declares the method's visibility just as it did when used as an access modifier for a class. Because the main() method is public, other programs may invoke or use this method. The modifier, **static**, means that this method is unique and can be invoked without creating a subclass or instance. As shown in line 12 in Figure 2-21 on the previous page, the main() method in the Welcome class of the Welcome to My Day program is both public and static.

A typical method header has three parts after the modifiers: a reference to the data type of the return value, the method name, and a list of parameters. A **return value** is the result or answer of a method. A method can return data — similar to the return value of a function in a spreadsheet application — or it can return no data. A method that returns data lists the expected data type. A method that does not return data uses the keyword, **void**, instead of a data type. The main() method in the Welcome class does not create a return value and thus uses the keyword, void.

The method name is next in the method header. As shown in Figure 2-21, the main() method uses the name main. The method name is followed by parentheses. It is easy to recognize a method name in Java because it always is followed by a set of parentheses.

The parentheses enclose a list of parameters used by the method. A **parameter** is a piece of data received by the method to help the method perform its operation. For example, a method to calculate sales tax would need to know the amount of the sale and the tax rate in order to create a return value. The sales amount and the tax rate would be parameters. Later in the chapter, when you learn how to send data to a method, that data will be called an **argument**. Parameters and arguments are closely related concepts.

In the Welcome class, the main() method has one parameter named args. The word, args, is not a keyword; it is an identifier for a piece of data that the main() method may need. An **identifier** is any word you choose to name an item in a Java program. An identifier is used to name a **variable**, which is a location in computer memory that can change values as the code executes. For example, you might use the identifier, sTax, to name a variable that holds the state tax. Java programmers typically use the identifier, args, to name the parameter for the main() method, although you can use other identifiers. Variable names have the same spelling restrictions as class names (see Table 2-4 on page 65).

Each parameter must be preceded by a data type declaration. A **data type** is a word that describes the type or category of data the method uses. The parameter, args, has a String data type, which indicates a series or string of characters. The String data type is indicated by the notation, **String[]**, in line 12 in Figure 2-21. You will learn more about data types in a later chapter.

When documenting information about the main() method, programmers and language documentation would use the following terminology: Java's main() method is public and static, accepts a String parameter named args, and returns void.

The main() method header is placed before the lines of executable code, or **body**, of the main() method. The body is enclosed in pairs of braces, just as the body of the class is enclosed in braces. Line 13 in Figure 2-21 contains the opening brace of the main() method's body. It is common to indent all lines of code entered after the opening brace to facilitate reading.

Perform the following step to enter the method header for the main() method, along with its opening brace.

To Code the Method Header

1. With the insertion point in line 12, type the main() method header and opening brace as shown in Figure 2-21 on page 67.

The main() method header is displayed in line 12 in the coding window (Figure 2-22). The keywords, public, static, and void, display in blue and the opening brace is displayed in red. TextPad automatically indents the line after the opening brace of the method.

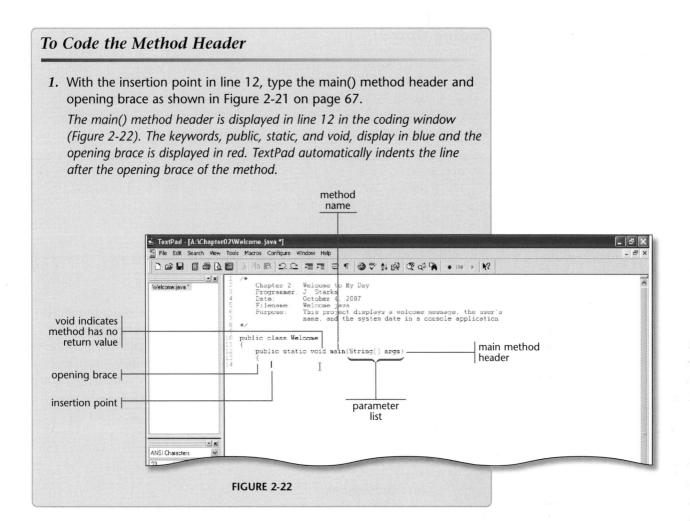

FIGURE 2-22

After the code for the class and the main() method is complete, closing braces indicate the end of each method. To make it easier to see what code is included in the body of the class and main() method, the closing brace for each should be indented so that it aligns underneath the respective opening brace. To facilitate entering methods, TextPad automatically reduces the indent after you type a closing brace.

Tip

Placement of Braces

You can place the opening brace on the same line as the class or method header, or on the line below. Each opening brace must be paired with a closing brace. A simple way to avoid forgetting a closing brace is to immediately place the closing brace on a line below the opening brace before writing the code within the braces. Some Java programmers indent the braces; others do not. When writing code, it is good programming practice to be consistent in the placement of the opening brace. Some programmers place a line comment directly after the closing brace to help remember which class or method the brace closes.

Coding Output

Displaying output in console applications involves sending a message to the standard output device, which in most cases is the monitor of the computer system. In the Welcome to My Day application, the output is displayed as white characters on the black background of the command prompt window. Figure 2-23 shows the code you use to display output.

```
14          System.out.println();
15          System.out.println("Welcome to my day!");
16          System.out.println("Daily planner for Linda Nunez");
17          System.out.println("October 4, 2007");
18          System.out.println();
19
```

FIGURE 2-23

In line 14, the word, System, refers to a specific Java class definition supplied with the SDK. A **class definition** defines the instance and class variables and methods available for use in the class, as well as other information, such as the immediate superclass. The **System class** contains several useful class variables and methods, such as those involving standard input, standard output, and other utility methods. The System class **extends**, or inherits, methods from its superclass, which in this case is Java's Object class. You will learn more about the System and Object classes in later chapters.

> **Tip**
>
> **Class Definitions**
>
> A class definition defines the instance and class variables and methods available for use in the class, as well as other information, such as the immediate superclass. You can use the Java API to view the hierarchy of individual classes and to look up specific methods used by each class.

The word, **out**, refers to the object representing the default display. Perhaps the most often used object from the System class, out represents the device used to display a standard output of text characters. A period (.) separates or delimits the class, System, and the object, out.

Following another period delimiter, the word, println, identifies the **println() method** from the System class. The println() method returns its value to the System.out device. The println() method is *called* from the Java Object package in this case — the programmer is not writing all of the code to make it work. Calling methods such as println() differs from writing methods such as main(). When coding the main() method, which begins with a method header, the programmer must include the code statements for operations that the main() method must perform. Methods such as println() already have been written, so programmers can use the methods without having to write all of the code that each method must perform. Programmers simply call such methods by the method's name and send data along with it, in the form of arguments enclosed in parentheses. You do not need to specify the argument's data type when calling a method.

In the Welcome to My Day program, the argument for the println() method is the data sent to the monitor at run time. In lines 14 and 18, no argument is displayed in the parentheses, so a blank line with no text will be displayed. In line 15, the string of characters enclosed in quotation marks inside the parentheses will be sent to the monitor for display. The string of characters is called a **literal**, which means the data inside the quotes will be displayed exactly as entered in the code. You will learn how to use the println() method to display stored String data, as well as literal and stored numeric data. When using the println() method to output numbers and variables to the display, you do not need to enclose the argument in quotation marks.

Lines 14 through 18 each end with a semicolon (;). Other than headers and braces, all lines of Java code must end with a semicolon. Line 15 uses the object-oriented components of classes, objects, and methods all in one line. System is the name of the class; out is the object that represents the default display; and println() is the name of a method that accepts a String argument.

After entering the code to display output, you will close the class and the main() method by entering the respective closing braces. You then will save the program. Perform the following steps to enter the code to display output, and then save the Java program file on the Data Disk in drive A.

To Enter Code to Display Output and Save the Program File

1. With the insertion point in line 14, enter the code as shown in Figure 2-23, keeping in mind that Java is case-sensitive.

The TextPad window displays the Java source code for the five println() methods (Figure 2-24). Lines 14 and 18 will cause the program to output blank lines.

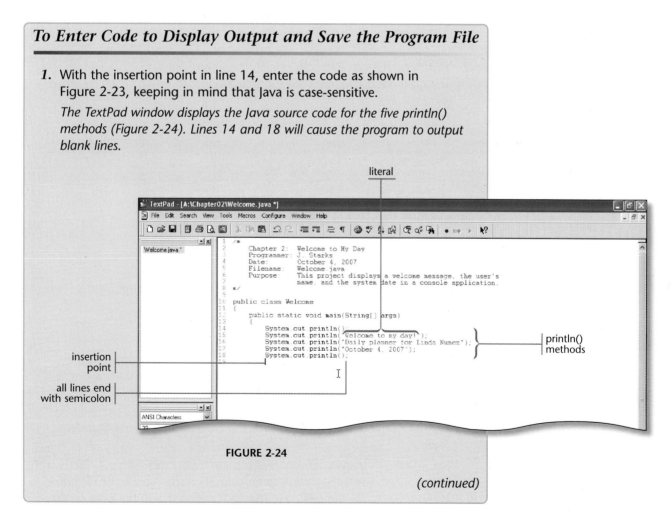

FIGURE 2-24

(continued)

2. With the insertion point in line 19, type a closing brace and then press the ENTER key.

The closing brace for the main() method automatically aligns with the opening brace for the main() method (Figure 2-25).

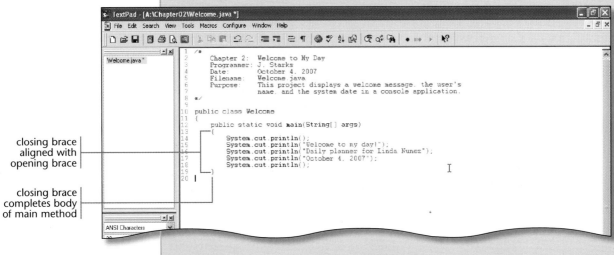

closing brace
aligned with
opening brace

closing brace
completes body
of main method

FIGURE 2-25

3. With the insertion point in line 20, type a closing brace.

The closing brace for the class is displayed aligned with its opening brace (Figure 2-26).

Save button

closing brace
aligned with
opening brace

closing brace
completes
the class

FIGURE 2-26

OTHER WAYS

1. Type code, press
   CTRL+S
2. Type code, press
   ALT+F, S
3. Type code, click
   Save on File menu

4. With the Data Disk in drive A, click the Save button on the Standard toolbar.

Because the file previously was saved to the Data Disk in drive A, TextPad automatically saves the file in the same location using the same file name, Welcome.java. The old version of the file is replaced with the new, edited file.

Unless you use the Save As command and then choose a different Save as type to change the file extension, TextPad automatically saves the file with the same .java extension. If another application, such as Notepad, is used to create the Java program, the file must be saved in plain text format with the extension .java.

Testing the Solution

The fifth phase of the development cycle is to test the solution. After the program solution is designed and then implemented in code, it should be tested to ensure that it runs properly. With Java, testing the solution is a two-step process that involves (1) compiling the source code and then (2) executing the bytecode.

Compiling the Source Code

Java source code must be compiled before it can be executed. TextPad includes a Compile Java command on the Tools menu. The Compile Java command uses the Java compiler command, javac.exe, to translate the Java source code into bytecode that any machine can interpret. The compilation process creates a new file for each class and saves it in the same directory as the source code file.

> **Tip**
>
> **Accessing the Java SDK Compiler**
> The Java compiler needs to access certain files from the Java SDK. If you first installed the Java SDK using its setup program and then installed TextPad, the Java compiler will automatically access the necessary SDK files when you execute the Compile Java command in TextPad. If you are compiling Java source code using the command prompt window, you must use operating system commands to designate the location of the SDK files each time you open the command prompt window. See Appendix D for more information on compiling Java source code at the command prompt.

Perform the following steps to compile the Welcome to My Day program.

To Compile Source Code

1. With the Data Disk in drive A, click Tools on the menu bar.

The Tools menu is displayed (Figure 2-27).

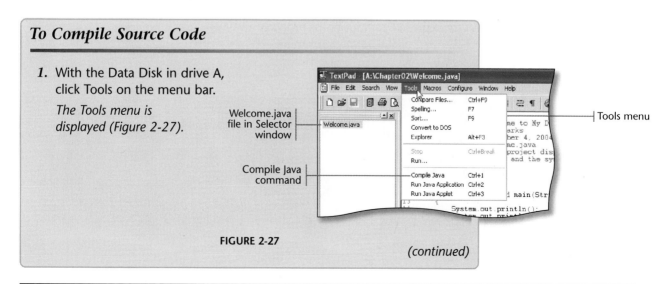

FIGURE 2-27

(continued)

OTHER WAYS

1. Press CTRL+1
2. At command
   prompt, type javac
   Welcome.java

2. Click Compile Java on the Tools menu. If TextPad displays any error messages, click Welcome.java in the Selector window. Fix the errors and repeat Step 1.

If TextPad finds no errors while compiling the source code, TextPad redisplays the source code. The bytecode for the Welcome to My Day application is saved on the Data Disk.

During compilation, the compiler saves the source code again and then adds a file to the disk called Welcome.class, which is the actual bytecode.

If your TextPad installation does not display the Compile Java command on the Tools menu, the SDK may have been moved or installed after TextPad. See Appendix C for more information on configuring TextPad. Recall that compiling Java source code with a VATE program such as TextPad allows you to compile using its menu system. Alternately, you can compile by opening a command prompt window and issuing the compile command, javac. If you are compiling at the command prompt, you may need to change to the directory containing your Data Disk. See Appendix D for more information on compiling in the command prompt window.

Debugging the Solution

If TextPad displays error messages when you compile the source code, you may have a system, syntax, semantic, run-time, or other logic error. The process of fixing errors is called **debugging**. Debugging can be a time-consuming and frustrating process, but it is a skill that will improve as you learn to program.

System Errors

If your system displays an error such as unrecognized command or cannot read file, you may have a system error (Figure 2-28). A **system error** occurs when a system command is not set properly, software is installed incorrectly, or the location of stored files has changed. System errors usually display in the command prompt window. If you get a system error while compiling using TextPad, you may not have first installed the Java SDK (see Appendix B). If you get a system error compiling the program using the javac command, you may not have set the required path locations properly (see Appendix D).

FIGURE 2-28

Syntax Errors

A **syntax error** is an error caused by code statements that violate one or more syntax rules of the Java programming language. Typing mistakes often cause syntax errors. When you compile Java source code, TextPad lists syntax errors in a **Command Results window**, as shown in Figure 2-29.

Command Results listed in Selector window

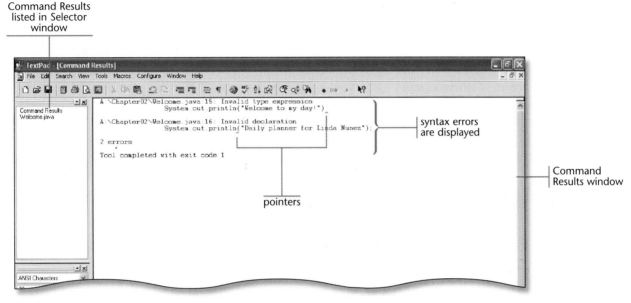

FIGURE 2-29

When it encounters syntax errors, the compiler attempts to isolate the syntax error by displaying a line of code with pointers pointing to the first incorrect character in that line. The error, however, may not be at that exact point. For instance, if you omit a necessary semicolon at the end of a line, TextPad may display error messages, similar to those shown in Figure 2-29. Both errors are due to the same missing semicolon. Without the semicolon in the first line, the compiler cannot find the end of the first line and thus generates an error message with the file name, the line number, and the error message, Invalid type expression. The compiler then tries to compile the two lines together, which results in a second error message, Invalid declaration. Once the semicolon in the code is corrected, neither error message will display.

A rule of thumb to follow when debugging syntax errors is to correct the first mistake in a long list. Doing so may reduce the total number of errors dramatically and allow you to focus on the cause of the remaining errors.

The most common mistakes that cause syntax errors are capitalization, spelling, the use of incorrect special characters, and omission of correct punctuation. Table 2-6 on the next page lists some common syntax errors, the error messages that indicate the specific syntax error, and the method of correction.

Table 2-6   Common Syntax Errors

SYNTAX ERROR	SAMPLE ERROR MESSAGE	METHOD OF CORRECTION
missing semicolon	invalid type expression invalid declaration ';' expected	Add a semicolon at the end of the line.
missing punctuation	')' expected	Insert missing) or }.
incorrect file name	public class must be defined in a file	Make sure class name and file name match exactly, both in spelling and capitalization.
incorrect number of arguments	invalid argument	Add a comma between arguments in an argument list.
incorrect use of mathematical operators	missing term	Correct operand error.

Semantic Errors

While syntax refers to code structure or grammar, a **semantic error** is an error that changes the meaning of the code. To the Java compiler, a semantic error appears as unrecognizable code. For example, if you misspell the println() method in code, the Java compiler will return an error message that it cannot resolve the symbol or that the method was not found (Figure 2-30). If you use a variable name that has not been declared properly, the compiler will return an error message that the variable is undefined. Most semantic errors can be fixed by correcting the spelling of keywords or by properly defining variables and methods.

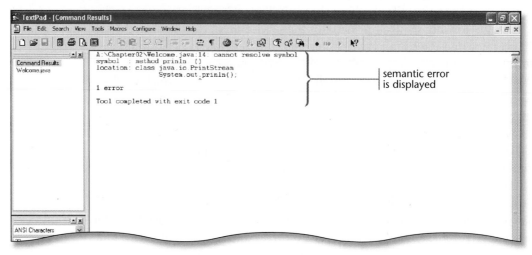

FIGURE 2-30

If TextPad displays error messages when you try to compile a program, click the file name in the Selector window to display the code in the coding window and then correct any syntax or semantic errors. Alternately, you can double-click the first line of the error message itself, and TextPad will open the coding window automatically, placing the insertion point at the beginning of the line in question. Once the errors are fixed, save the file and then compile the program again. If Java still displays error messages after you have corrected all syntax or semantic errors, consult your instructor.

Logic and Run-Time Errors

A **logic error** occurs when a program does not behave as intended due to poor design or incorrect implementation of the design. A **run-time error**, also called an **exception**, is an error that occurs when unexpected conditions arise as you run or execute the program. Even programs that compile successfully may display logic or run-time errors if the programmer has not thought through the logical processes and structures of the program. Your goal should be to have error-free programs, and by implementing the development cycle correctly, you will achieve that goal.

Occasionally, a logic error will surface during execution of the program due to an action the user performs — an action for which the programmer did not plan. For example, if a user inputs numbers outside of valid ranges or enters the wrong types of data, the program may stop executing if the code cannot handle the input. In later chapters, you will learn how to write code to handle data entry errors based on validity, range, and reasonableness. In this chapter, the user inputs no data into the application, so these types of logic errors should not occur.

Other logic or run-time errors may occur as you run a program. For example, if a programmer typed the wrong data or used an incorrect operator in code, the program would compile and run correctly, but the wrong output would display. No run-time error message would occur. These types of errors can be difficult to identify.

A run-time error message also will display if you are executing the program from the command prompt window and misspell the command, misspell the name of the bytecode file, or add an extension by mistake.

Running the Application

After a Java program is compiled into bytecode, and syntax and semantic errors are fixed, the program must be run or executed to test for logic and run-time errors. Programmers run the program to display output, receive input from the user if necessary, and interpret the commands to produce the desired result.

Running the Application

TextPad includes a Run Java Application command on the Tools menu. The Run Java Application command executes the compiled bytecode of the file selected in the Selector window. TextPad automatically looks for the class file with the same name and then executes it. If you are running the application from the command prompt, you type `java` followed by the name of the class file, `Welcome` (no extension). Perform the steps on the next page to run the Welcome to My Day application.

To Run the Application

1. **Click Tools on the menu bar.**

   The Tools menu is displayed (Figure 2-31).

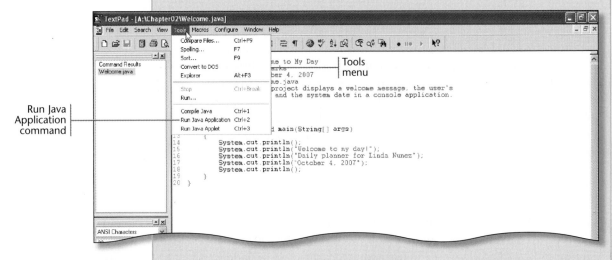

Run Java
Application
command

FIGURE 2-31

2. **Click Run Java Application on the Tools menu.**

   If no error messages display, TextPad executes the application to display three lines of text in the command prompt window (Figure 2-32).

command prompt
window

Close
button

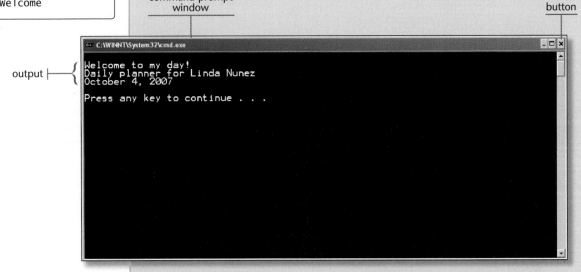

output

FIGURE 2-32

3. **Click the Close button in the command prompt window title bar.**

   The command prompt window closes, and the TextPad coding window is displayed.

The println() method of the System.out object causes each output String to display on a new line in the command prompt window. The System.out object supports other output methods in addition to the println() method. For example, the System.out object supports the print() method, which prints output on a single line, without moving the insertion point down to the next line. The print() method is useful when you want the insertion point to display directly after a prompt to the user. You can use the Java API and language documentation on the Sun Microsystems Web site to research other methods supported by the System.out object.

Editing the Source Code

When you **edit** or modify the source code in any way, you must repeat the steps of saving, compiling, and executing the program. Even if you make a simple change, such as editing the spacing between characters, you should repeat the steps of saving, compiling, and executing the program to ensure that the program runs properly.

The source code of the Welcome to My Day application must be edited so that the application obtains the current date from the operating system, displays the date, and formats the output as requested in the requirements document. Figure 2-33 shows the source code after the edits are complete.

```
1    /*
2          Chapter 2:   Welcome to My Day
3          Programmer:  J. Starks
4          Date:        October 4, 2007
5          Filename:    Welcome.java
6          Purpose:     This project displays a welcome message, the user's
7                       name, and the system date in a console application.
8    */
9
10   import java.util.Date;
11
12   public class Welcome
13   {
14       public static void main(String[] args)
15       {
16           Date currentDate = new Date(); // Date constructor
17           System.out.println();
18           System.out.println("\t\t\tWelcome to my day!");
19           System.out.println("\t\t\tDaily planner for Linda Nunez");
20           System.out.println("\t\t\t" + currentDate);
21           System.out.println();
22       }
23   }
```

FIGURE 2-33

TextPad allows programmers to use standard editing techniques, such as those used in a word processing program, to replace and enter new code in the coding window. The Edit menu in the TextPad menu bar displays commands for many standard editing functions, including cut, copy, paste, insert, and delete. For more information on using shortcuts, selecting text, and moving the insertion point through the coding window, see Appendix C.

Entering Code to Import Packages

The classes and methods needed to display the system date are not immediately available, which means the programmer must tell the compiler to access the storage location in order to use these methods. The SDK includes class packages as part of the standard installation. Recall that class packages, or libraries, contain portable Java bytecode files. Because hundreds of these files are available, Java organizes them, by category, into packages.

Some of the more widely used Java packages and their descriptions are listed in Table 2-7. The Java API contains a complete list of Java packages.

Table 2-7   Java Packages

PACKAGE NAME	DESCRIPTION	EXAMPLES OF CLASSES IN PACKAGE
java.applet	Provides the classes necessary to create an applet and the classes an applet uses to communicate with its applet context.	Class used to create the applet window and methods to initialize, start, and stop the applet.
java.awt	The Abstract Window Toolkit (AWT) provides the classes for creating user interfaces and for painting graphics and images.	Classes to define GUI objects, including Button, Label, TextField, and Checkbox.
java.awt.event	Provides interfaces and classes for dealing with different types of events fired by AWT components, such as button clicks and key press events.	Classes to support events, including ActionEvent, WindowEvent, MouseEvent, and KeyEvent.
java.io	Provides classes that support system input and output through data streams, serialization, and the file system.	Classes to handle I/O methods, including FileReader, InputStreamReader, and BufferedReader.
java.lang	Provides classes that are fundamental to the design of the Java programming language, which facilitate data types, threads, Strings, and others.	Classes such as those related to String, System, Double, Integer, Float, and Thread.
java.net	Provides classes used for networking and client/server applications.	Classes related to networks, such as URL, InetAddress, and NetworkInterface.
java.util	Provides classes for the date and time facilities, internationalization, and miscellaneous utilities.	Classes related to time (such as Date, Calendar, and Timer) and location (such as Locale and TimeZone).
javax.swing	Provides a set of lightweight Java-based components.	Classes to define GUI components such as JApplet, JOptionPane, JLabel, JTextField, and JScrollBar.

The java.lang package is the only package imported automatically without an explicit command; all other packages need an **import statement** to tell the compiler where to access the classes, fields, and methods of an existing class in the package. The import statement is placed at the beginning of the Java source code, most commonly right after the opening documentation. During compilation, the import statement goes to the location where the SDK is stored, and loads the appropriate class or classes. Typing an asterisk (*) after the package name tells the program to load all the classes within a package; typing an individual class name after the package name tells the program to load an individual class.

Tip

Using the import Statement
Using the import statement to import all of the classes in a package does not make the bytecode longer because the compiler uses only the classes it needs. Importing numerous packages does slow the compiler, however, as it checks through each package when it needs a class. To keep compile times reasonable, a programmer should use the import statement to import only packages with the tools the compiler needs.

In the Welcome to My Day application, you will import the Date class from the java.util package, as shown in the following steps.

To Code the Import Statement

1. With the Welcome.java file displayed in the TextPad coding window, click line 9, below the block comment. Press the ENTER key.
   The insertion point displays in line 10 (Figure 2-34).

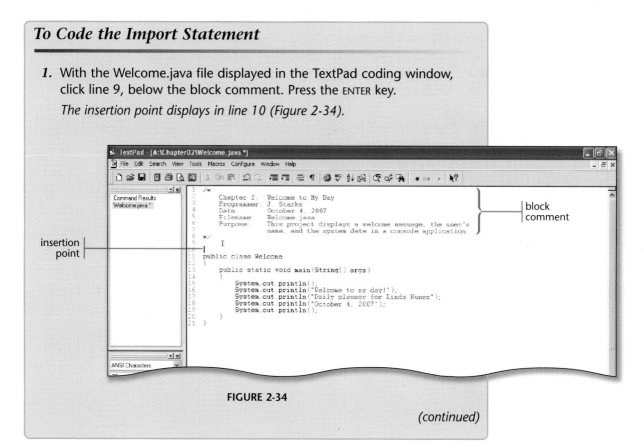

FIGURE 2-34

(continued)

2. Enter line 10 from Figure 2-33 on page 79. Press the ENTER key.

The import statement to import the Date class package from the SDK is displayed in line 10 (Figure 2-35). The Date class from the java.util package will be imported into the Welcome to My Day application. Line 11 is blank.

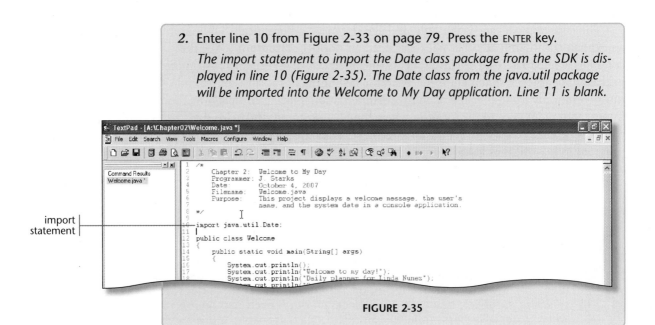

import statement

FIGURE 2-35

Some programmers place import statements before the block comments rather than after them. Either placement is acceptable, provided that the import statements are placed before the class header.

Entering Code to Call a System Date Constructor

The operating system running on your computer keeps track of the current date and time. This system date is kept current by a battery inside the system unit on most computers. The **Date class** in Java represents a specific instant in time, measured to the nearest millisecond. Java creates a Date object and initializes it so that it represents the exact date and time it was allocated.

In order for Java to ask the operating system for that system date, a programmer must create a storage location to hold the system date data. Line 16 in Figure 2-33 on page 79 displays the code to construct the storage location to hold the value for the Date object with the variable name, currentDate. A **constructor**, which is identified by the = new notation, declares the type of data or object to be stored and assigns it a variable name in the computer's memory. Programmers **declare** the type of data or object by entering the name of the Java data type followed by the variable name. In line 16, Date is the data type and currentDate is the variable.

Tip

Use of Date Constructors and Methods

Date constructors in Java are not used to set a particular date or calculate future dates. Recent versions of the Java SDK have **deprecated,** or retired, methods such as setDate() and setTime() in favor of methods related to a newer Calendar object. However, the Date object and its constructor remains an easy way to display the system date on a given computer system.

Perform the following steps to enter code for the Date constructor to construct an instance of the system date.

To Code a Call to a System Date Constructor

1. Click the TextPad coding window, immediately to the right of the main() method's opening brace in line 15.

   The insertion point displays to the right of the brace in line 15 (Figure 2-36).

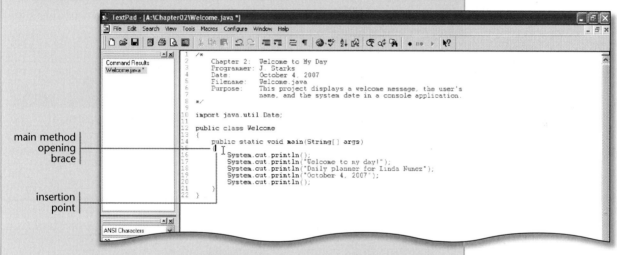

FIGURE 2-36

2. Press the ENTER key and then type line 16 as shown in Figure 2-33 on page 79.

   The Date constructor to construct a system date is displayed (Figure 2-37). A line comment explains the code by noting that this is a Date constructor.

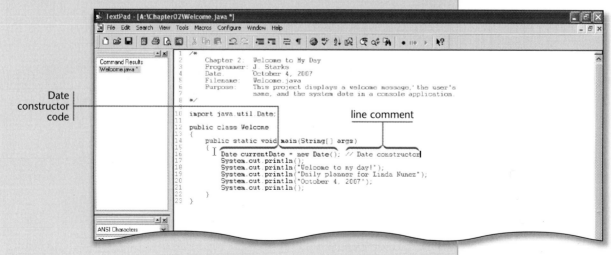

FIGURE 2-37

The Date constructor allows the program to request and store the current system date at the time the program is executed. Once the variable currentDate is constructed, it can be used in other parts of the program.

Formatting Output Using Escape Characters

In the Welcome to My Day program, you will insert special codes to indent and position the output away from the left side of the screen. Java uses **escape characters** inside the String arguments of the println() method to move the insertion point to the right, which thereby moves the text output to the right. Escape characters, also called escape codes or escape sequences, are non-printing control codes. Table 2-8 displays some of the Java escape characters used to move the output of data on a computer screen.

Table 2-8   Java Escape Characters

CODE	CONCEPT	RESULT
\t	horizontal tab	Moves insertion point eight spaces to the right.
\b	backspace	Moves insertion point one space to the left.
\n	new line	Moves insertion point down one line and to the left margin.
\r	carriage return	Moves insertion point to the left margin.

Perform the following steps to edit the code to include escape characters that position the text output.

To Code Escape Characters to Format Output

1. Click immediately to the left of the word, Welcome, in line 18.

The insertion point displays between the quotation mark and the W of Welcome (Figure 2-38).

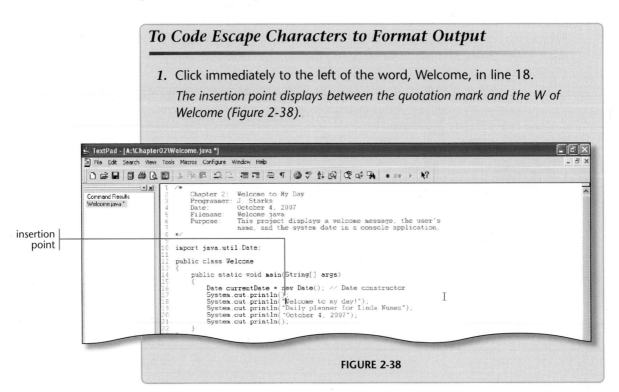

FIGURE 2-38

2. Type \t\t\t after the quotation mark in line 18.

The escape code characters are displayed as part of the String argument (Figure 2-39). The three horizontal tab escape characters will cause the insertion point to move 24 spaces to the right — eight spaces for each escape character — before outputting the words to the screen.

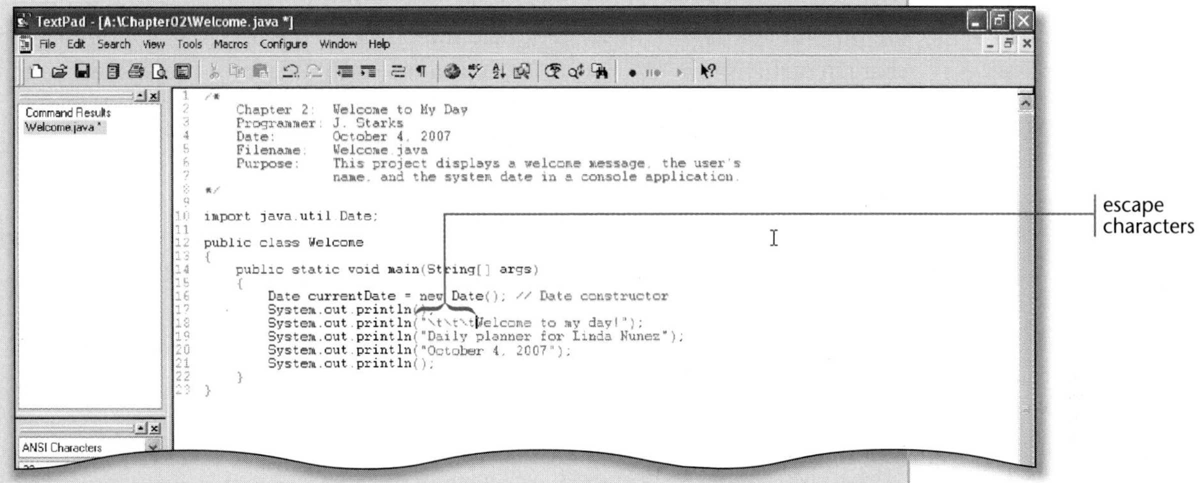

escape characters

FIGURE 2-39

3. Position the insertion point between the quotation mark and the letter D in Daily in line 19. Type \t\t\t after the quotation mark in line 19.

The println() methods in lines 18 and 19 display escape characters in their String arguments (Figure 2-40).

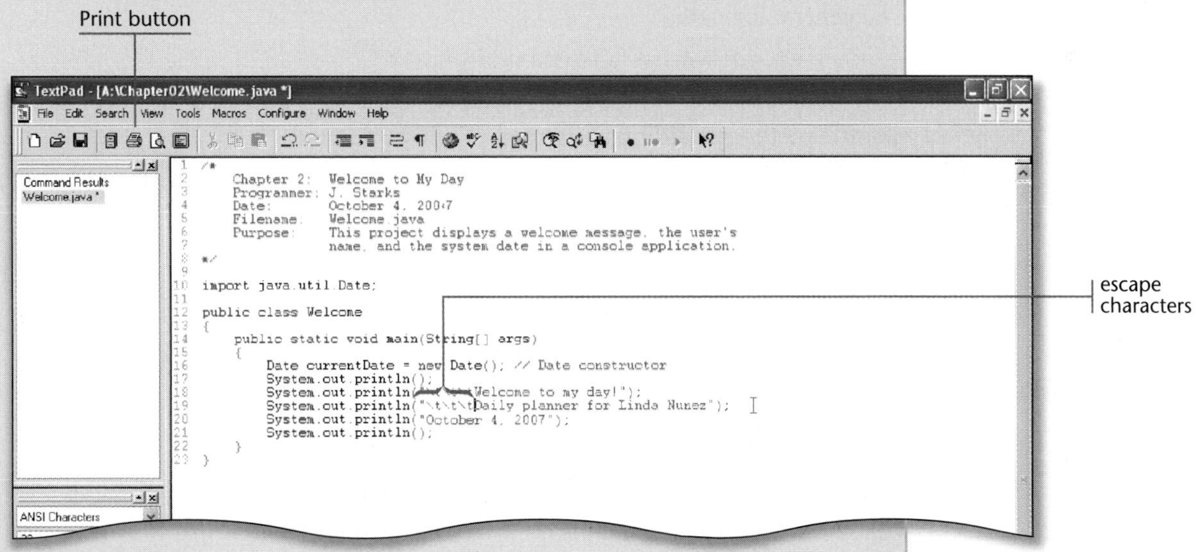

Print button

escape characters

FIGURE 2-40

The final edit is to insert the line of code to display the system date constructed by the Date constructor in line 16. As shown in line 20 of Figure 2-33 on page 79, the code is changed to use the variable currentDate, instead of the previously typed date. Unlike the typed date, the variable currentDate is not enclosed in quotation marks, so it will not literally print the words, currentDate, on the screen. Alternately, it will print whatever value is in the storage location at run time — in this case, the system date.

In the Java programming language, you can use a plus sign (+) to join or **concatenate** two or more Strings: the plus sign (+) typed between the escape characters and the currentDate variable in the println() argument in line 20 tells the program to display the system date directly after the literal String of escape characters that move the insertion point to the right. Perform the following step to enter the code to display the system date.

To Enter Code to Concatenate String Data

1. Select the text "October 4, 2007" in line 20 by dragging through it. Type "\t\t\t" + currentDate as shown in Figure 2-33 on page 79.

The edited code is displayed (Figure 2-33). Line 20 instructs the program to display the system date indented 24 characters to the right.

If you want to embed data within a string of text rather than concatenate it, a new **printf() method** is available in Java 5.0. This functionality, which will help developers who have used the C programming language in the past, uses a percent sign (%) followed by one of several formatting characters to display formatted data. Similar to the escape characters, the percent sign (%) and its formatting character do not print during execution; rather, they are replaced with data indicated by one or more data items or variable names listed in the method. The general format is

```
System.out.printf(format, items);
```

For example, if you wanted to display a stored user's name in a message, the printf() method could be written as

```
System.out.printf("Hello, %s. Welcome to this application.", userName);
```

During execution, the %s is replaced with the data from the variable, userName.

Besides the formatting character s, which is used for String data, Java 5.0 supports other types of data and precision of numbers for formatted output, which you will learn about in Chapter 3.

Recompiling and Running the Application

As you have learned, after compiling, the Java compiler created the file Welcome.class, which contains the bytecode or object code from your program. The bytecode is the code that actually executes when you run the Java application using TextPad or the command prompt window. If you have not recompiled the source code after editing, Java will execute the old bytecode and any updates will not appear. In order to run the most recent version of the application, the source code first must be recompiled into new bytecode.

Follow these steps to recompile and then run the application.

To Recompile and Run the Application

1. Click Tools on the menu bar and then click Compile Java on the Tools menu. If TextPad displays any error messages in the coding window, click Welcome.java in the Selector window. Fix the errors and repeat Step 1.

   The source code is compiled. Clicking the Compile Java command automatically saves the file again.

2. After TextPad successfully compiles the source code, run the program by clicking Tools on the menu bar and then click Run Java Application on the Tools menu.

   The program runs and the println() methods send data to the monitor (Figure 2-41). The output is displayed, with all lines indented from the left side of the command prompt window.

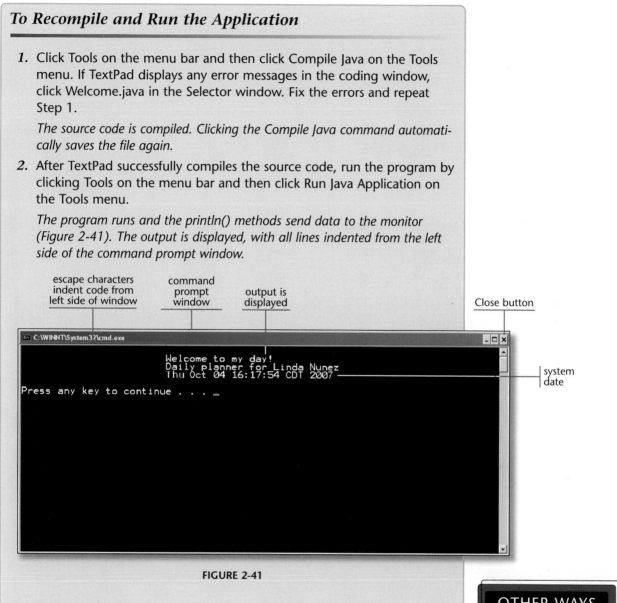

FIGURE 2-41

3. Click the Close button in the command prompt window title bar.

OTHER WAYS

1. Press CTRL+1, CTRL+2
2. At command prompt, type javac Welcome.java, type java Welcome

Printing the Source Code

The final step of the development cycle for this application is to document the program by printing the code. A printed version of the source code is called a **hard copy**, or **printout**. Perform the steps on the next page to print the source code.

To Print the Source Code

1. Ready the printer according to the printer instructions. With the Welcome.java source code displaying in the TextPad window, click the Print button in the Standard toolbar (see Figure 2-40 on page 85).

2. When the printer stops, retrieve the printout.

   TextPad prints a hard copy of the Java source code (Figure 2-42). Your printout may differ.

```
Welcome.java                                              10/4/2007

 1   /*
 2        Chapter 2:   Welcome to My Day
 3        Programmer:  J. Starks
 4        Date:        October 4, 2007
 5        Filename:    Welcome.java
 6        Purpose:     This project displays a welcome message, the user's
 7                     name, and the system date in a console application.
 8   */
 9
10   import java.util.Date;
11
12   public class Welcome
13   {
14       public static void main(String[] args)
15       {
16           Date currentDate = new Date(); // Date constructor
17           System.out.println();
18           System.out.println("\t\t\tWelcome to my day!");
19           System.out.println("\t\t\tDaily planner for Linda Nunez");
20           System.out.println("\t\t\t" + currentDate);
21           System.out.println();
22       }
23   }
```

FIGURE 2-42

OTHER WAYS

1. On File menu, click Print, click OK button
2. Press CTRL+P, click OK button

When you use the Print button to print source code, TextPad prints the entire listing automatically. If your printout does not display line numbers, you may turn the feature on in the Preferences dialog box as discussed in Appendix C. You then can distribute the hard copy or keep it as permanent documentation of the source code for the Welcome to My Day application.

If you want to print multiple copies of the document, click File on the menu bar and then click Print to display the Print dialog box. The Print dialog box has several printing options, including the option to specify the number of copies to print.

Quitting TextPad

After you create, save, compile, execute, test, and print the program, you can quit TextPad. To quit TextPad and return control to Windows, perform the following step.

> ### *To Quit TextPad*
>
> *1.* Click the Close button on the right side of the TextPad title bar.
>
> *If you made changes to the project since the last time it was saved, TextPad displays a TextPad dialog box. If you click the Yes button, you can resave your file and quit. If you click the No button, you will quit without saving changes. Clicking the Cancel button will close the dialog box.*

Moving to the Web

One of the features that makes Java so useful is that programmers can use it to develop programs that are machine-independent and can run on the Web. Much of Java's portability lies in the use of applets. As you learned in Chapter 1, an applet is a small program that can be downloaded and executed as part of a displayed Web page. When run as part of a Web page, applets often are used to perform interactive animations, immediate calculations, or other simple tasks without having to access the computer that is hosting the Web page.

Other major differences between Java applications and Java applets exist. One difference is that applications run as stand-alone programs with full access to system resources, whereas applets can run only within a browser or viewer and are usually delivered to the local computer via the Web. Another difference is in their scope for data handling. An applet cannot be used to modify files stored on a user's system, while an application can. Finally, unlike applets, applications do not need a memory-intensive browser or viewer in order to execute.

The source code for the Welcome to My Day application is complete and can be edited to convert the application into an applet that can run via the Web. The steps to convert the application into an applet include opening the Welcome file in TextPad, editing the code to import two new packages, changing the class name, and specifying that the class is an applet. Then the class code is edited to include a paint method that draws text in the applet window and displays a graphic and color. Once the changes are complete, the file is saved and the applet is compiled.

Opening an Existing File in TextPad

Once you have created and saved a file, you often will have reason to retrieve it from disk. For example, you might want to revise the code or print it again. Earlier you saved the Java source code file created in this chapter on a disk using the file name Welcome. The steps on the next page illustrate how to open the file Welcome.java from the Data Disk in drive A using TextPad.

To Start TextPad and Open an Existing File

1. With the Data Disk in drive A and the Windows desktop displayed, click the Start button on the taskbar and then point to TextPad (Figure 2-43). If TextPad does not display on the Start menu, point to All Programs on the Start menu and then point to TextPad on the All Programs submenu.

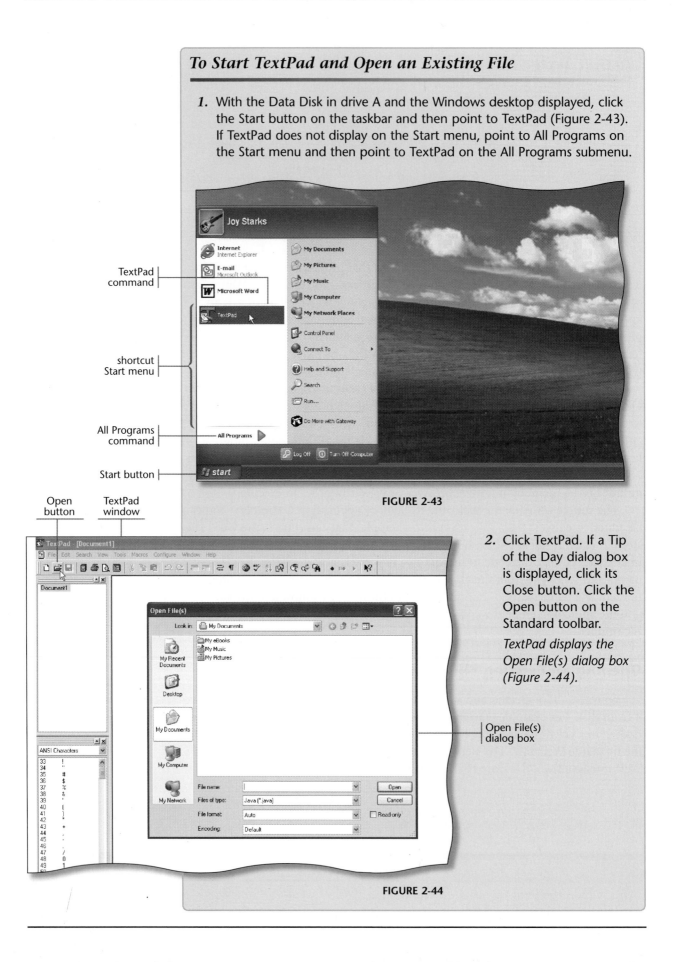

FIGURE 2-43

2. Click TextPad. If a Tip of the Day dialog box is displayed, click its Close button. Click the Open button on the Standard toolbar.

   TextPad displays the Open File(s) dialog box (Figure 2-44).

FIGURE 2-44

3. If necessary, click the Files of type box arrow and then click Java (*.java) in the list. Click the Look in box arrow and then click 3½ Floppy (A:) in the list.

The Look in box displays 3½ Floppy (A:) (Figure 2-45). The names of folders on the Data Disk in drive A display in the Open File(s) dialog box.

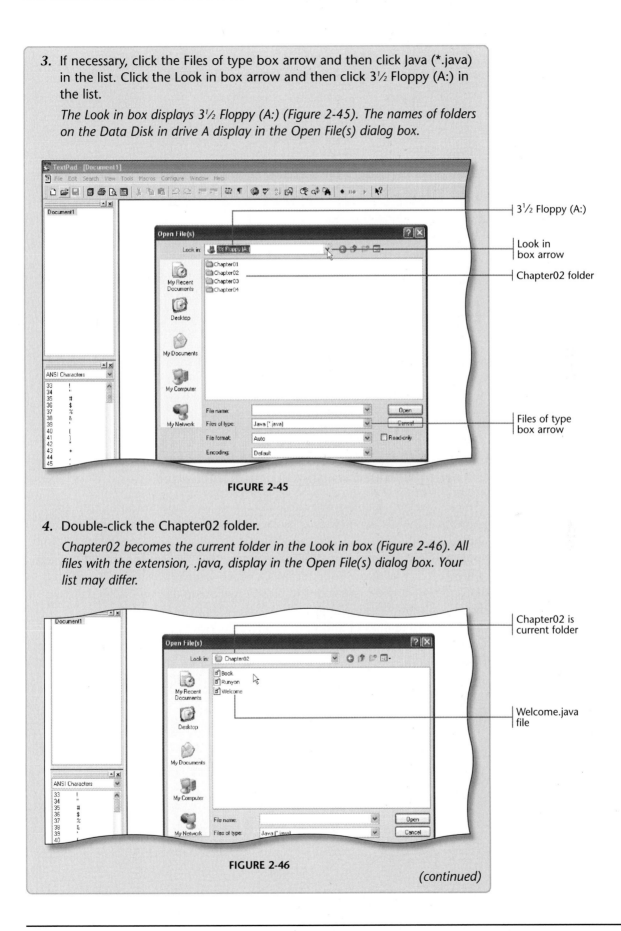

FIGURE 2-45

4. Double-click the Chapter02 folder.

Chapter02 becomes the current folder in the Look in box (Figure 2-46). All files with the extension, .java, display in the Open File(s) dialog box. Your list may differ.

FIGURE 2-46

(continued)

5. Double-click Welcome. If necessary, click View on the menu bar and then click Line Numbers to display line numbers in the coding window.

The Java source code for the Welcome to My Day application is displayed in the coding window (Figure 2-47).

TextPad window

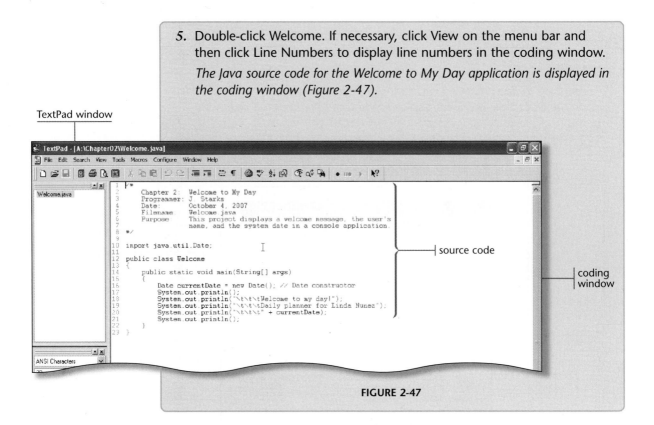

FIGURE 2-47

Entering Code to Import Applet Packages

The first step in converting the Welcome to My Day application into an applet is to import two new class packages that Java will need to support the applet-related methods. The first package is the **applet package**, which allows applets to inherit certain attributes and manipulate classes. The second package is the **Abstract Window Toolkit** (**AWT**), which is a package included with the SDK to provide programs access to color, draw methods, and other GUI elements commonly used in applets.

As shown in lines 11 and 12 in Figure 2-48, two import statements are used to import the applet and AWT packages. Because Java will need to use multiple classes from the two packages, you will insert a period and then an asterisk (*) at the end of the import statement. The asterisk is a wildcard symbol to tell the program to import all necessary classes from the java.awt and java.applet packages.

```
 1   /*
 2       Chapter 2:   Welcome to My Day
 3       Programmer:  J. Starks
 4       Date:        October 4, 2007
 5       Filename:    WelcomeApplet.java
 6       Purpose:     This project displays a welcome message, the user's
 7                    name, the system date, and an image in an applet.
 8   */
 9
10   import java.util.Date;
11   import java.awt.*;
12   import java.applet.*;
13
14   public class WelcomeApplet extends Applet
15   {
16       public void paint(Graphics g)
17       {
18           Date currentDate = new Date(); // Date constructor
19           g.drawString("Welcome to my day!",200,70);
20           g.drawString("Daily planner for Linda Nunez",200,100);
21           g.drawString(currentDate.toString(),200,130);
22           Image smile; // declare an Image object
23           smile = getImage(getDocumentBase(),"Smile.gif");
24           g.drawImage(smile,10,10,this);
25           setBackground(Color.cyan);
26       }
27   }
```

FIGURE 2-48

Perform the following steps to code the import statements to support the applet.

To Code Import Statements

1. With the Welcome.java file displayed in the TextPad coding window, click at the end of line 10 and then press the ENTER key.

2. Type lines 11 and 12, as shown in Figure 2-48.

The applet will import objects and classes from the applet and awt packages, as well as from the Date package.

The remaining edits to the source code will incorporate methods and classes that Java uses from the applet and awt packages.

Changing the Class Name and Extending the Applet Class

Because the purpose of this program now will be to run as an applet on the Web, it is important to change the class name and the file name. The class name is changed to WelcomeApplet in the class header. The file name, which is changed to WelcomeApplet.java, must be updated in the comment header and when the file is saved.

You also will extend the class, which means that this new Java class will be a type or subclass of applet. As shown in line 14 of Figure 2-48 on the previous page, the **extends command** is added to the class header, along with the name of the superclass. Recall that a superclass represents a broader, higher category of a class object, and shares a common structure and behavior with its subclasses. In the Welcome to My Day program, Applet is the superclass you will extend to create the subclass, WelcomeApplet. When a class extends from another class, it inherits attributes and methods from its superclass. The WelcomeApplet subclass will inherit general applet characteristics from the Applet class, such as the ability to run in a browser window.

Perform the following steps to edit the class name and extend the Applet class.

To Edit the Class Name and Extend the Applet Class

1. In the TextPad coding window, click after the word, Welcome, in line 5. Without spacing, type Applet as shown in Figure 2-49.

TextPad displays the comment header with the new file name, WelcomeApplet.java, in line 5 (Figure 2-49).

new file name

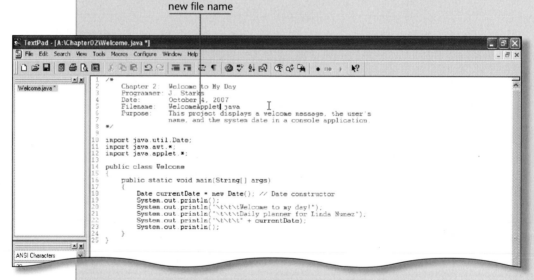

FIGURE 2-49

2. In line 14, click after the word, Welcome, in the class header. Without pressing the SPACEBAR, type Applet extends Applet to complete the line.

The new class header is displayed (Figure 2-50). Adding the extends command instructs the program to consider WelcomeApplet as a subclass of Applet. You also may change the purpose comment to better reflect the applet.

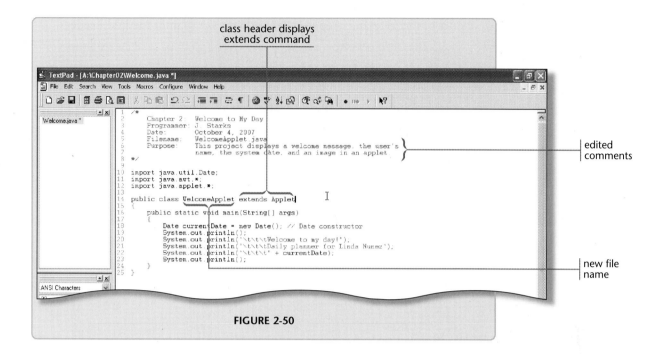

FIGURE 2-50

The relationship of the SDK to its packages, and the packages to their classes, is a perfect example of the superclass, class, and subclass hierarchy discussed in Chapter 1. In a later chapter, you will learn more about creating subclasses and instances of existing classes.

The paint() Method

As you have learned, the main() method is the first method called when any stand-alone Java application is executed. With an applet, Java does not look for a main() method because Java does not execute the applet; the applet is executed from a browser or other calling program. Instead, the **init() method** loads the initial setup of the applet when execution begins. Because the code extends the Applet class, init() and all other applet methods are encapsulated in the Applet class, which means they happen automatically without any additional code being added to the program.

In the Welcome to My Day applet, you also will code a **paint() method** to graphically draw text and an image on the applet screen after the applet is initialized. The source code for the beginning of the paint() method is displayed in lines 16 through 21 in Figure 2-51. As shown in line 16, the paint() method accepts a Graphics parameter. It is common practice to identify the Graphics parameter as g, although any variable name can be used. The paint() method returns no value, so it is void.

```
16      public void paint(Graphics g)
17      {
18          Date currentDate = new Date(); // Date constructor
19          g.drawString("Welcome to my day!",200,70);
20          g.drawString("Daily planner for Linda Nunez",200,100);
21          g.drawString(currentDate.toString(),200,130);
```

FIGURE 2-51

Perform the following step to enter code for the paint() method header.

To Code the paint() Method Header

1. Replace the main() method header in line 16 with the code shown in line 16 of Figure 2-51 on the previous page.

   The paint() method header is displayed in line 16 (Figure 2-52). The Graphics parameter is represented by a g in the parameter list; the keyword, void, indicates that the paint() method returns no return value.

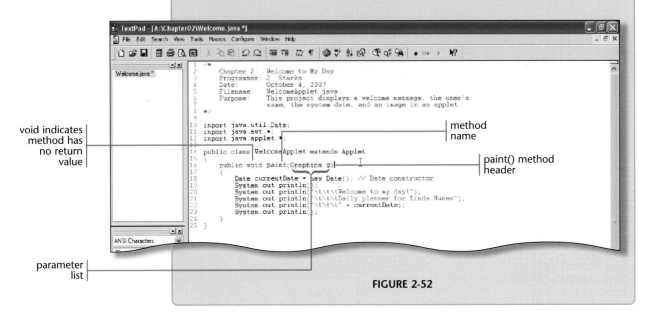

void indicates method has no return value

method name

paint() method header

parameter list

FIGURE 2-52

Some method arguments, like the one used with the println() method, contain data. Other methods, such as the paint() method, refer to a specific instance of an object. When a method refers to an instance of an object, such as Graphics g, the g is called a **reference variable**. Other methods that use a reference variable include those that draw shapes, set colors, and set fonts. You will learn more about reference variables in a later chapter.

The drawString() Method

To instruct the program to display text output, the applet uses the drawString() method instead of println(). The **drawString() method**, which is taken from the awt package, draws text in the applet window. The drawString() method accepts three arguments: the String data to display, the horizontal (X-axis) position or coordinate at which to display the String, and the vertical (Y-axis) coordinate at which to display the String. As shown in lines 19 through 21 in Figure 2-51 on the previous page, the code for the drawString() method uses the identifier g from the method header, followed by a dot, followed by the method name. The three arguments are enclosed in parentheses, with each of the multiple arguments separated by commas.

Tip

Setting Horizontal and Vertical Coordinates

The horizontal and vertical coordinates required by the drawString() method are measured in pixels. A **pixel**, or picture element, is the basic unit of programmable color on a computer display or in a computer image. Think of a pixel as a dot of light; the dots grouped together form characters and images. The physical size of a pixel depends on the resolution of the computer screen. For instance, if your screen resolution is 800 by 600 pixels, a horizontal (X-axis) coordinate of 400 would display approximately halfway across the screen.

The drawString() method must use a String as its first argument. However, the system date object, currentDate, in line 21 is not a String. The **toString() method** can be used to convert currentDate to a String; the code takes the form of the variable currrentDate, followed by a period, followed by toString(). The code is inserted as the first argument of the drawString() method. The toString() method has no arguments in this applet.

Perform the following step to enter three drawString() methods.

To Code the drawString() Methods

1. Replace lines 19, 20, and 21 in the TextPad coding window with the code shown in lines 19, 20, and 21 of Figure 2-51 on page 95. Delete the println() methods in lines 22 and 23. Leave line 22 blank.

   The drawString() methods replace the println() methods in lines 19 through 21 (Figure 2-53). The horizontal and vertical coordinates following each string of characters set the position of the output display and replace the horizontal tab escape characters.

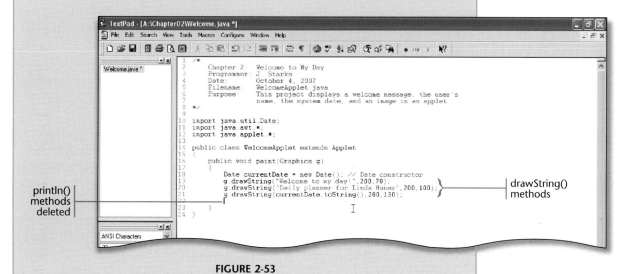

FIGURE 2-53

The drawString() methods instruct the program to display text output in the positions defined by the coordinate parameters. The toString() method in line 21 is an example of polymorphism. As you learned in Chapter 1, polymorphism allows a program to use the same command while obtaining different but somewhat predictable results, depending on the object that receives the command. The toString() method is polymorphic in that the same method name is used to refer to methods that handle many different data types, but the result is always a String conversion. You will learn more about data type conversions in the next chapter.

Entering Code to Draw an Image and Set the Background Color

The final step in editing the source code is to insert the commands necessary to display a graphic in the applet and change the background color of the window. As shown in Figure 2-54, the edited source code will declare an Image object, use a method named getImage() to retrieve a graphic file from the disk, use the drawImage() method to draw the graphic in the applet window, and then use the setBackground() method to change the color of the window.

```
22        Image smile; // declare an Image object
23        smile = getImage(getDocumentBase(),"Smile.gif");
24        g.drawImage(smile,10,10,this);
25        setBackground(Color.cyan);
26    }
27  }
```

FIGURE 2-54

The **Image object** will have a variable name of smile, as declared in line 22. The Image object must be declared before its methods can be used. Java applet images may be one of many different types of graphics including GIF, JPEG, or PNG. In the Welcome to My Day program, the graphic is a GIF file with the file name Smile.gif.

The **getImage() method**, as shown in line 23, is used to load images into an applet. The getImage() method creates and returns an Image object that represents the loaded image. The getImage() method uses a second method called the **getDocumentBase() method**, which allows the applet to pull the image from the current folder in which your applet class is stored. Once the graphic is retrieved, the graphic is assigned to the memory location represented by the smile variable. The logic of assigning a value to a variable in Java works from right to left and uses an equal sign.

Next, the **drawImage() method** in line 24 specifies the location where the program should draw the graphic. Similar to the drawString() method, the drawImage() method accepts horizontal and vertical coordinates as parameters that identify the screen location in pixels. The keyword, this, is required by the drawImage() method to hold the location of the image while it is being loaded from disk.

Notice that the drawString() and drawImage() methods both have a g. in front of the methods. The g refers to the Graphics object that is drawn when the applet initializes. In Java, the period (.) after the g separates an object and its method, or an object and its attribute.

Finally, the **setBackground() method** in line 25 takes a Color object and its attribute, Color.cyan, to change the background color of the applet window. Common color words used by the setBackground() method display are show in Table 2-9.

Table 2-9   Colors Used with the Color Object

black	magenta
blue	orange
cyan	pink
darkGray	red
gray	white
green	yellow
lightGray	

The setBackground() method does not start with the reference variable, g. The object in this case is understood to be the background of the applet window and does not have to be painted or drawn in a certain place, like the graphic. Other related methods, such as setForeground(), setFont(), and setSize(), also can be used to set characteristics of the applet window.

Perform the following step to enter code to declare, retrieve, and draw an image in the applet, as well as to set the background color to cyan.

To Enter Code to Draw an Image and Set the Background Color

1. With the insertion point in line 22, type lines 22 through 25, as shown in Figure 2-54.

   The edited code is displayed (Figure 2-55).

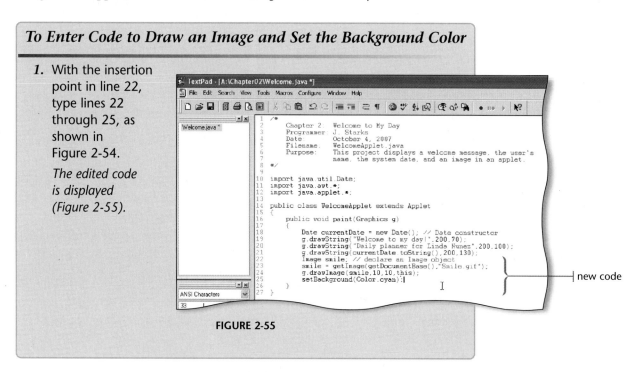

new code

FIGURE 2-55

The source code for the applet now is complete. Lines 22 through 25 of the code declare an Image object and use the getImage() method to retrieve the Smile.gif image file from disk. The drawImage() method then draws the graphic in the applet window. Finally, the setBackground() method changes the background color of the window to cyan.

Saving a Source Code File with a New Name

Once the editing to convert the application to an applet is complete, the file should be saved with a file name that matches the class name, WelcomeApplet, as shown in the following steps.

To Save the Source Code File with a New File Name

1. If necessary, insert the Data Disk in drive A. With the TextPad coding window open, click File on the menu bar and then click Save As on the Tools menu.

2. Type WelcomeApplet in the File name text box. Do not press the ENTER key. If necessary, click the Save as type box arrow and then click Java (*.java) in the list. If necessary, click the Save in box arrow, click 3½ Floppy (A:) in the list, and then double-click the Chapter02 folder.

The file name, WelcomeApplet, is displayed in the File name text box (Figure 2-56). Java (.java) is displayed in the Save as type box. Chapter02 is displayed in the Save in box.*

3. Click the Save button in the Save As dialog box.

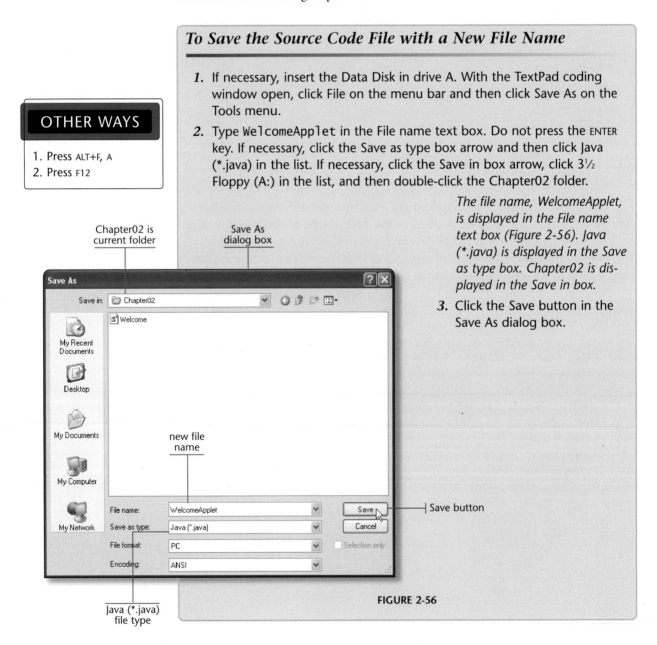

Chapter02 is current folder

Save As dialog box

new file name

Java (*.java) file type

Save button

FIGURE 2-56

Compiling the Applet

When you compile the applet, the compiler looks for the image file in the same directory as the source code file. The image file, Smile.gif, is included in the Chapter02 folder of the Data Disk that accompanies this book. See the preface for instructions on downloading the Data Disk, or see your instructor for a copy of the graphic. The following steps assume that the Smile.gif file is located in the Chapter02 folder on the Data Disk in drive A.

Perform the following steps to compile the applet.

To Compile the Applet

1. With the Data Disk in drive A, click Tools on the menu bar. Click Compile Java on the Tools menu.

2. If any error messages display in the Command Results window, click WelcomeApplet.java in the Selector window, fix the errors, and then repeat Step 1.

TextPad compiles the applet.

OTHER WAYS

1. Press CTRL+1
2. At command prompt, type javac WelcomeApplet.java

As when the Java application was compiled, possible errors that will be generated while compiling the applet include an incorrect location for the Java compiler, typing mistakes, omitting special characters, case-sensitive errors, and file name errors. If you cannot determine and fix a coding error based on the error messages and the information about errors on pages 74 through 77, consult your instructor.

Creating an HTML Host Document

Because an applet is initiated and executed from within another language or run as part of a Web page, you must identify a **host**, or reference program, to execute the applet. The applet for this chapter is run as part of a Web page created in HTML.

As you learned in Chapter 1, Hypertext Markup Language (HTML) is a set of special codes called tags that specify how the text and other elements of a Web page display. Unlike a programming language such as Java, HTML mainly is used to display information; it is not suited to support user interaction to accept input and generate output. A Java applet is thus ideal for adding that interactivity and functionality to a Web page.

An extensive understanding of HTML is not needed to build an HTML host document for an applet. A few simple HTML tags to tell the browser where to find and execute the applet file are all that are necessary to create a host for a Java applet.

Coding an HTML Host Document

In HTML, a **tag**, or markup, is a code specifying how Web page content should display or link to other documents. Each tag actually has two elements: a **start tag**, which is enclosed in angle brackets < >, and an **end tag**, which uses a forward slash and also is enclosed in angle brackets. The tags enclose content or other HTML code to define a section of content or apply a color, style, or other format.

The tag at the beginning and end of the source code for a typical Web page is an example of an HTML tag. At the beginning of the HTML code for a Web page, programmers insert the start tag <HTML>. In order to end the code, programmers need to insert the end tag </HTML>. Figure 2-57 displays the code for the HTML host document for the WelcomeApplet.

```
1  <HTML>
2  <APPLET CODE = "WelcomeApplet.class" WIDTH = "400" HEIGHT = "200">
3  </APPLET>
4  </HTML>
```

FIGURE 2-57

When an HTML host document is loaded in the browser, the Java applet is sent to the browser as a separate file. A special HTML tag, <APPLET>… </APPLET> tells the browser the name of the applet file. In the following series of steps, you will create a simple HTML file to serve as the host document for the applet named WelcomeApplet.

To Code an HTML Host Document

1. With the TextPad coding window open, click File on the menu bar.
The File menu is displayed (Figure 2-58).

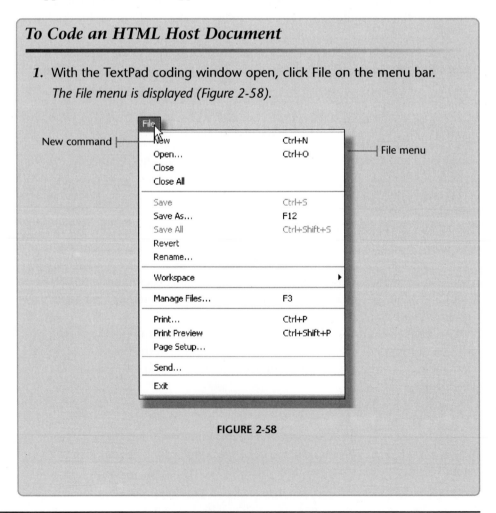

FIGURE 2-58

2. Click New on the File menu. When the new coding window is displayed, if necessary, click View on the menu bar and then click Line Numbers. Click File on the menu bar and then click Save As on the File menu. When the Save As dialog box is displayed, type `WelcomeApplet` in the File name text box. Do not press the ENTER key. Click the Save as type box arrow and then click HTML (*.htm*,*.stm*) in the list. If necessary, click the Save in box arrow, click 3½ Floppy (A:) in the list, and then double-click the Chapter02 folder in the list.

HTML (.htm*,*.stm*) displays as the file type (Figure 2-59). The file, Welcome Applet.html, will be saved in the Chapter02 folder on the Data Disk in drive A. Your file name extension may be .htm.*

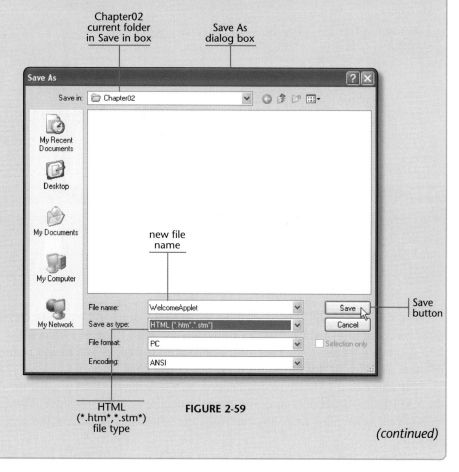

FIGURE 2-59

(continued)

3. Click the Save button in the Save As dialog box.

TextPad saves the file on the Data Disk in drive A. The file name is displayed in the title bar of the TextPad window.

4. In the TextPad coding window, type the HTML code as shown in Figure 2-57 on page 102.

The code for the HTML host document is displayed in the TextPad coding window (Figure 2-60).

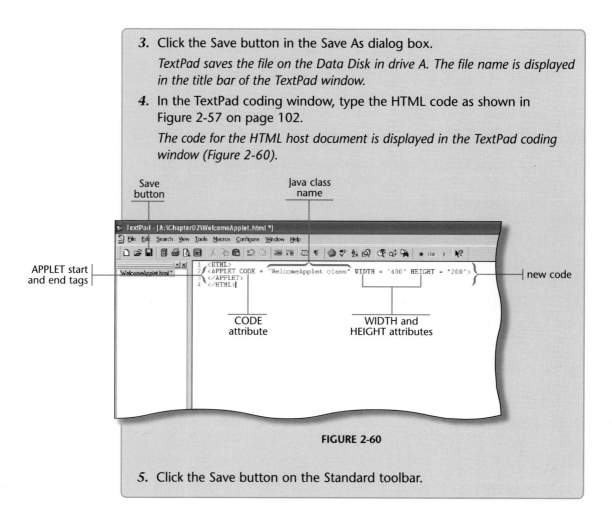

FIGURE 2-60

5. Click the Save button on the Standard toolbar.

The <APPLET> tag, nested within the <HTML> start and end tags, specifies three pieces of information that the Web page will need in order to access the Java applet: the name of the Java bytecode file and the width and height of the window in which to run the applet (Figure 2-57 on page 102).

The name of the Java bytecode file is specified using the CODE attribute of the <APPLET> tag. HTML and its tags generally are not case-sensitive. The name of the referenced class, however, must match exactly because it is a Java class.

The width and height of the window in which to run the applet are specified using the WIDTH and HEIGHT attributes of the <APPLET> tag. The values specified for the width and height are measured in pixels.

Running an Applet

As you have learned, an applet is run by first running the HTML host document. TextPad includes a Run Java Applet command, which opens the HTML host document and executes Java's appletviewer.exe command to display the Applet Viewer window. If you are compiling and running the Java applet from the command prompt, you type appletviewer, followed by the name of the host document.

Applet Viewer provides advantages over a browser for viewing an applet. First, Applet Viewer ignores any HTML that is not immediately relevant to launching an applet. If the HTML host document does not include a correct reference to an applet or similar object, Applet Viewer does nothing. Additionally, Applet Viewer does not have to be Java-enabled, as do some browsers, in order to correctly display the applet. Finally, Applet Viewer uses less memory than does a browser, which makes it a good tool to test that the applet's code works properly before attaching the applet to a Web page.

The following steps show how to run an applet using TextPad.

To Run an Applet

1. Click Tools on the TextPad menu bar.
The Tools menu is displayed (Figure 2-61).

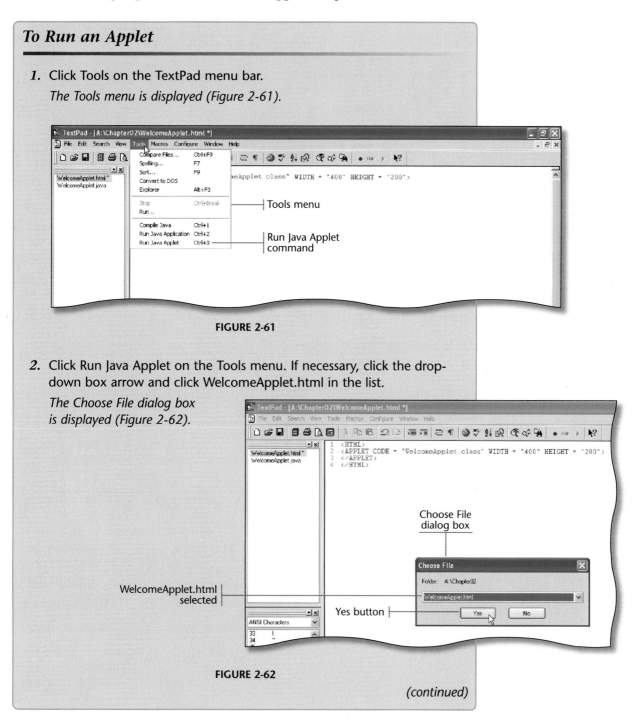

FIGURE 2-61

2. Click Run Java Applet on the Tools menu. If necessary, click the drop-down box arrow and click WelcomeApplet.html in the list.
The Choose File dialog box is displayed (Figure 2-62).

FIGURE 2-62

(continued)

3. Click the Yes button.

After a few seconds, the applet is displayed in the Applet Viewer window, 400 pixels wide and 200 pixels tall, as defined in the HTML code (Figure 2-63).

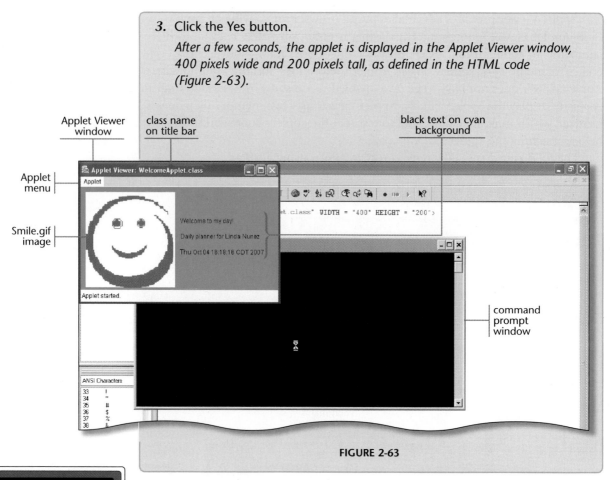

Applet Viewer window

class name on title bar

black text on cyan background

Applet menu

Smile.gif image

command prompt window

FIGURE 2-63

OTHER WAYS

1. Press CTRL+3, click Yes
2. At command prompt, type appletviewer WelcomeApplet .html
3. In browser Address box, type a:\Chapter02\ WelcomeApplet .html

When the applet is displayed in the Applet Viewer window, the Smile.gif image displays to the left, and black text on a cyan background displays to the right. The command prompt window is displayed in the background.

The title bar of the Applet Viewer window displays the name of the class. The Applet Viewer window also displays an Applet menu (Figure 2-63) that allows you to perform such functions as restarting the applet, printing the applet, and closing the applet. For information on running an applet from the command prompt window, see Appendix D.

Documenting the Applet and HTML Host Document

The final step in the program development cycle is to document the applet and HTML host document code. After the applet is documented, the applet can be closed.

Perform the following steps to print a hard copy of the applet display, close the Applet Viewer window, print the HTML code, and then print the applet code.

To Document the Applet and HTML Host Document

1. Ready the printer according to the printer instructions. Click Applet on the Applet Viewer menu bar.

The Applet menu is displayed (Figure 2-64).

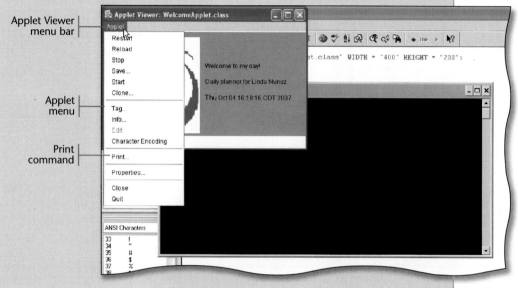

FIGURE 2-64

2. Click Print on the Applet menu.

The Print dialog box is displayed (Figure 2-65). Your display may differ.

FIGURE 2-65

(continued)

3. Click the Print button in the Print dialog box.

   Applet Viewer prints a copy of the applet display on the default printer (Figure 2-66).

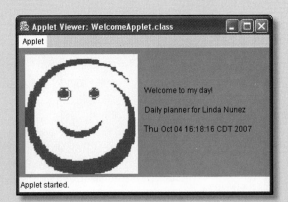

FIGURE 2-66

4. Retrieve the printout from the printer. If necessary, click the Close button in the Applet Viewer window.

   The Applet Viewer window closes, and the TextPad coding window is displayed.

5. If necessary, click WelcomeApplet.html in the Selector window to display the HTML code in the coding window. Click File on the menu bar and then click Print on the File menu. When the Print dialog box displays, click the OK button.

   The HTML code prints on the default printer (Figure 2-67). Your printout may differ.

```
WelcomeApplet.html                                              10/4/2007
1   <HTML>
2   <APPLET CODE = "WelcomeApplet.class" WIDTH = "400" HEIGHT = "200">
3   </APPLET>
4   </HTML>
```

FIGURE 2-67

6. Retrieve the printout from the printer. Click WelcomeApplet.java in the Selector window. Click File on the menu bar and then click Print on the File menu. When the Print dialog box displays, click the Print button.

   The applet code prints on the default printer (Figure 2-68).

```
WelcomeApplet.java                                          10/4/2007

 1   /*
 2        Chapter 2:  Welcome to My Day
 3        Programmer: J. Starks
 4        Date:       October 4, 2007
 5        Filename:   WelcomeApplet.java
 6        Purpose:    This project displays a welcome message, the user's
 7                    name, the system date, and an image in an applet.
 8   */
 9
10   import java.util.Date;
11   import java.awt.*;
12   import java.applet.*;
13
14   public class WelcomeApplet extends Applet
15   {
16       public void paint(Graphics g)
17       {
18           Date currentDate = new Date(); // Date constructor
19           g.drawString("Welcome to my day!",200,70);
20           g.drawString("Daily planner for Linda Nunez",200,100);
21           g.drawString(currentDate.toString(),200,130);
22           Image smile; // declare an Image object
23           smile = getImage(getDocumentBase(),"Smile.gif");
24           g.drawImage(smile,10,10,this);
25           setBackground(Color.cyan);
26       }
27   }
```

FIGURE 2-68

7. Retrieve the printout from the printer.

OTHER WAYS

1. On Standard toolbar, click Print button
2. Press CTRL+P, click OK button

Tip

Text Pad Settings

In TextPad version 4.7 and above, current line highlighting may be enabled to delineate the line of code containing the insertion point. The highlight is not the same as a selection highlight. Rather, it is a slight shadow behind the text to assist programmers in following the line of code across the screen. This new feature may be turned on or off in the Preferences dialog box, as discussed in Appendix C.

Quitting TextPad

After you create, save, compile, execute, test, and document the Welcome to My Day applet, the program is complete and you can quit TextPad. To quit TextPad and return control to Windows, perform the following step.

<table>
<tr><td>

OTHER WAYS

1. Press ALT+F, X
2. On File menu, click Exit

</td><td>

To Quit TextPad

1. Click the Close button on the TextPad title bar.
   The TextPad window closes and the Windows desktop is displayed.

</td></tr>
</table>

Chapter Summary

In this chapter, you learned the basic form of a Java application and an applet. You learned how to use TextPad to enter comments as documentation, enter a class header and a method header, and use the println() method to display output in a console application. The println() method uses character strings, escape characters, and concatenated data to format output. J2SE 5.0 includes the printf() method that can embed data using a percent sign and a formatting character. After learning how to compile the source code and debug any errors, you learned how to run the Java application. Next, you learned how to edit source code in the TextPad window using the import statement to import packages, a Date constructor, and escape characters to format output. You learned how to edit existing source code to convert the application into an applet that can run on the Web. You learned how to import applet packages, change a class name, and extend the Applet class, and how to use the paint, drawString, and getImage methods to complete the applet code. Finally, you created an HTML host document to display the applet and run it using Applet Viewer.

What You Should Know

Having completed this chapter, you should now be able to perform the tasks shown in Table 2-10.

Table 2-10   Chapter 2 What You Should Know

TASK NUMBER	TASK	PAGE
1	Start TextPad	53
2	Display Line Numbers in the TextPad Window	55
3	Save a TextPad Document	57
4	Code Comments	63
5	Code the Class Header	66
6	Code the Method Header	69
7	Enter Code to Display Output and Save the Program File	71
8	Compile Source Code	73
9	Run the Application	78
10	Code the Import Statement	81
11	Code a Call to a System Date Constructor	83
12	Code Escape Characters to Format Output	84
13	Enter Code to Concatenate String Data	86
14	Recompile and Run the Application	87
15	Print the Source Code	88
16	Quit TextPad	89
17	Start TextPad and Open an Existing File	90
18	Code Import Statements	93
19	Edit the Class Name and Extend the Applet Class	94
20	Code the paint() Method Header	96
21	Code the drawString() Methods	97
22	Enter Code to Draw an Image and Set the Background Color	99
23	Save the Source Code File with a New File Name	100
24	Compile the Applet	101
25	Code an HTML Host Document	102
26	Run an Applet	105
27	Document the Applet and HTML Host Document	107
28	Quit TextPad	110

Key Terms

Abstract Window Toolkit (AWT) *(92)*

access modifier *(64)*

applet package *(92)*

argument *(68)*

block comment *(61)*

body *(68)*

braces { } *(66)*

case-sensitive *(66)*

class definition *(70)*

class header *(64)*

Clip Library window *(55)*

coding window *(54)*

Command Results window *(75)*

comment header *(61)*

comments *(61)*

concatenate *(86)*

constructor *(82)*

data type *(68)*

Date class *(82)*

debugging *(74)*

declare *(82)*

default *(50)*

deprecated *(82)*

doc comment *(62)*

drawImage() method *(98)*

drawString() method *(96)*

edit *(79)*

end tag *(101)*

escape characters *(84)*

exception *(77)*

extends *(70)*

extends command *(94)*

getDocumentBase() method *(98)*

getImage() method *(9)*

hard copy *(87)*

host *(101)*

identifier *(68)*

Image object *(98)*

import statement *(81)*

init() method *(95)*

keywords *(64)*

line comment *(62)*

line numbers *(55)*

literal *(71)*

logic error *(77)*

main() method *(67)*

method header *(67)*

method modifier *(67)*

out *(70)*

paint() method *(95)*

parameter *(68)*

pixel *(97)*

printf() method *(86)*

println() method *(70)*

printout *(87)*

prototype *(48)*

public *(64)*

reference variable *(96)*

reserved words *(64)*

return value *(68)*

run-time error *(77)*

Selector window *(55)*

semantic error *(76)*

setBackground() method *(99)*

splash screen *(46)*

start tag *(101)*

static *(68)*

String[] *(68)*

syntax error *(75)*

System class *(70)*

system date *(48)*

system error *(74)*

tab characters *(63)*

tag *(101)*

TextPad *(52)*

toString() method *(97)*

user interface *(46)*

variable *(68)*

void *(68)*

Homework Assignments

Label the Figure

Identify the elements shown in Figure 2-69.

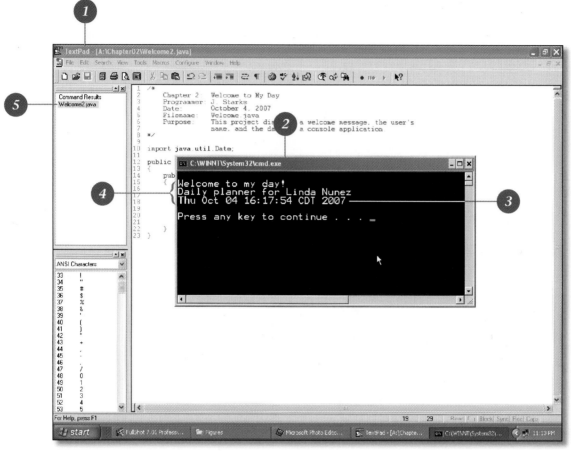

FIGURE 2-69

1. _____
2. _____
3. _____

4. _____
5. _____

Identify Code

Identify the code elements shown in Figure 2-70.

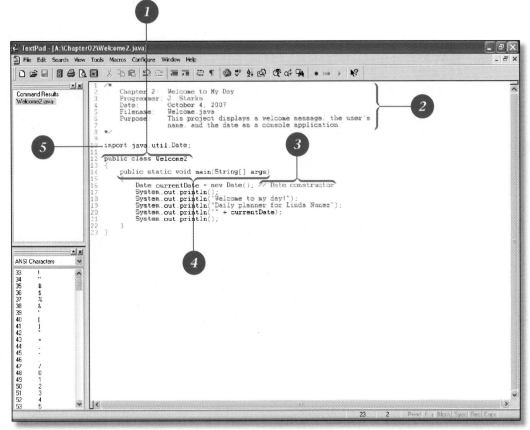

FIGURE 2-70

1. _____   4. _____

2. _____   5. _____

3. _____

Understanding Error Messages

Figure 2-71a displays a Java program that prints a student's name and address on the screen. Figure 2-71b displays the compilation error messages. Use TextPad or a text-editing software to rewrite the code and correct the errors. Print a hard copy of your program.

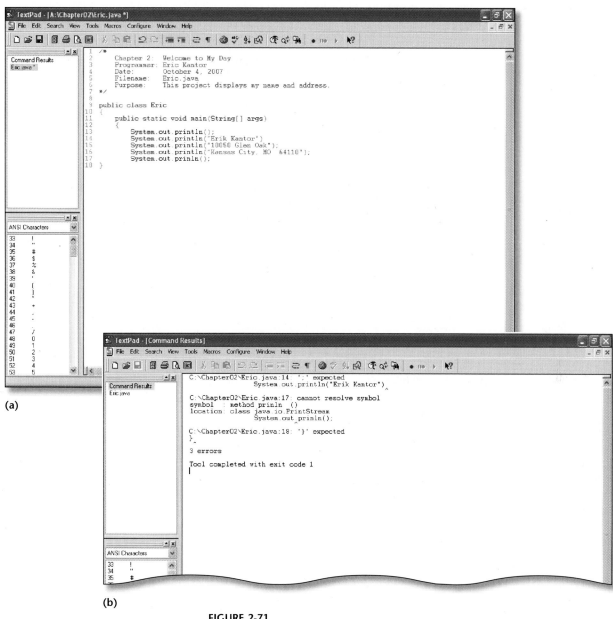

(a)

(b)

FIGURE 2-71

Using the Java API

The Java API is a good tool to look up information about a class with which you may be unfamiliar or to check the syntax of commands and methods you wish to use in your programs. While connected to the Internet, open a browser, type `http://java.sun.com/j2se/1.5.0/docs/api/` in the Address window, and then press the ENTER key to view the Java API Specification on the Sun Web site. The Java API is organized by packages, hierarchically, but many programmers click the Index link located at the top of the page to display the entire list alphabetically.

With the Java API Specification open in the browser window, perform the following steps.

1. Use the scroll down arrow in the top left frame of the Web page to display the java.lang link. Click the java.lang link.

2. When the Package java.lang page is displayed, scroll down to display the Class Summary table. Click the System link in the left column of the table.

3. When the Class System page is displayed, scroll down to display the Field Summary table and click the out link in the right column.

4. When the out definition is displayed (Figure 2-72), select the definition by dragging through it. Click File on the menu bar and then click Print. When the Print dialog box is displayed, click the Selection option button and then click the Print button in the Print dialog box to print the definition.

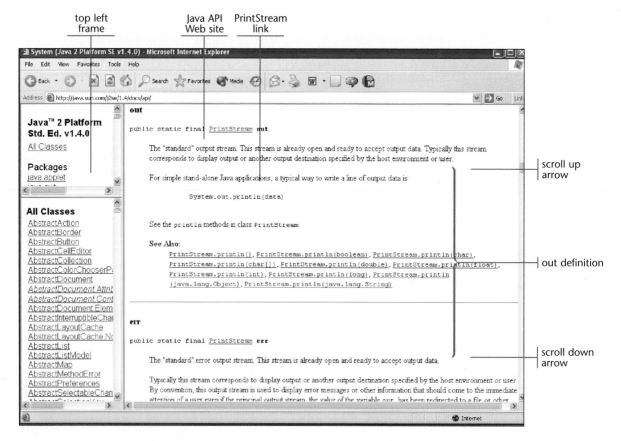

FIGURE 2-72

5. Click the PrintStream link. When the Class PrintStream page is displayed, scroll to the Method Summary table. Choose any five methods and then click the links and read their descriptions. Make a list of the five methods, their return values, and their argument data types.

6. Write a paragraph explaining why you think some of the methods are listed more than once in the Method Summary table.

Short Answer

1. The keyword public is an example of a(n) _____.

2. In Java, every line of code, other than headers and braces, must end with a(n) _____.

3. Line comments begin with _____; block comments begin with _____ and end with _____.

4. _____ is/are collections of classes, sometimes called libraries, which contain portable Java bytecode files.

5. A misspelled method most likely would result in a(n) _____ error.

6. The _____ command is placed at the beginning of Java source code to load the appropriate class package.

7. When you extend the Applet class, you are creating a(n) _____ of the Applet class.

8. The _____ is a current date and time generated by the operating system of a computer.

9. The println() method takes a String _____ in parentheses.

10. The keyword void means the method returns _____.

11. Java looks for the _____ as the usual starting point for all stand-alone applications.

12. A(n) _____, which is easily identified by the = new notation, both declares the type of data or object to be stored and assigns it a variable name in the computer's memory.

13. Describe the difference between the println() and drawString() methods.

14. Describe the code differences between applications and applets.

15. Describe the execution differences between applications and applets.

16. Explain why a Date object cannot be used with the drawString() method.

17. List the three-step process to save, compile, and execute a program.

18. Explain why an HTML host document is needed along with an applet.

19. Write a line of code to declare and construct a Date object named curDate.

20. Write a line of code to assign an image from the current folder to the variable name grandma.

21. Write a line of code that will change an applet's background color to red.

22. Write a line of code to print each of the following in the command prompt window:

    a. your name

    b. a previously declared String named lastName

(continued)

Short Answer *(continued)*

    c. a blank line

    d. the name of your instructor tabbed 24 characters to the right

23. Write a line of code to print each of the following in an applet. The numbers represent pixel locations.

    a. your name (100, 75)

    b. a previously declared and assigned image named grandma (50, 50)

    c. a previously declared Date named myDate (200, 300)

    d. a previously declared String named firstName (150, 250)

24. Give an example of three valid class names and three invalid class names.

25. Write a line of code that uses the printf() method to display a previously declared String named myName.

Learn It Online

Start your browser and visit scsite.com/java3e/learn. Follow the instructions in the exercises below.

1. **Chapter Reinforcement TF, MC, and SA**   Click the Chapter Reinforcement link below Chapter 2. Print and then answer the questions.

2. **Practice Test**   Click the Practice Test link below Chapter 2. Answer each question, enter your first and last name at the bottom of the page, and then click the Grade Test button. When the graded practice test is displayed on your screen, click Print on the File menu to print a hard copy. Continue to take practice tests until you score 80% or better. Hand in a printout of the final practice test.

3. **Crossword Puzzle Challenge**   Click the Crossword Puzzle Challenge link below Chapter 2. Read the instructions, and then enter your first and last name. Click the Play button. Complete the crossword puzzle. When you are finished, click the Submit button. When the crossword puzzle is displayed, click the Print button.

4. **Tips and Tricks**   Click the Tips and Tricks link below Chapter 2. Click a topic that pertains to Chapter 2. Right-click the information and then click Print on the shortcut menu. Construct a brief example of what the information relates to in Java to confirm that you understand how to use the tip or trick. Hand in the example and printed information.

5. **Newsgroups**   Click the Newsgroups link below Chapter 2. Click a topic that pertains to Chapter 2. Print three comments.

6. **Expanding Your Horizons**   Click the Expanding Your Horizons link below Chapter 2. Click a topic that pertains to Chapter 2. Print the information. Construct a brief example of what the information relates to in Java to confirm you that understand the contents of the article. Hand in the example and printed information.

7. **Search Sleuth**   Select three key terms from the Key Terms section of this chapter and then use the Google search engine at google.com (or any major search engine) to display and print two Web pages for each key term.

Debugging Assignment

Start TextPad and open the file Runyon.java from the Chapter02 folder on the Data Disk. See the preface of this book for instructions for downloading the Data Disk or see your instructor for information about accessing the files required in this book.

The Runyon program is a Java application that displays a splash screen for the Runyon Company, listing its name, address, and Web site address. The desired output is shown in Figure 2-73.

FIGURE 2-73

The Runyon program has several syntax, semantic, and logic errors in the program code. Perform the following steps to debug the program.

1. Open the file Runyon.java in TextPad.
2. Read through the code and fix any errors that you see. Insert your name as the programmer in the comment header. Insert the current date.
3. Save the program.
4. Compile the program. As TextPad displays compilation errors, fix the first error, then recompile.
5. When you have fixed all the syntax and semantic errors so that the program will compile without errors, run the program and look for run-time and logic errors. Fix any errors and compile again.
6. When the program compiles and runs to produce the output as shown in Figure 2-73, print a copy of the source code.

DEBUGGING ASSIGNMENT

Programming Assignments

1 Writing Java Code from a Flowchart

Start TextPad. Open the file Book.java from the Data Disk. See the preface of this book for instructions for downloading the Data Disk or see your instructor for information about accessing the files required in this book. Using the techniques you learned in this chapter, write the lines of code inside the main() method to print the bibliographic entry as outlined by the flowchart in Figure 2-74.

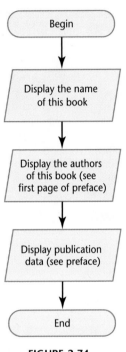

FIGURE 2-74

1. With the Book.java source code displayed in the TextPad coding window, locate the access modifier and class name, Book. Change the class name to Biblio. Change the name to Biblio in the comment header, and enter your name as the programmer.

2. Click inside the main() method braces.

3. After studying the flowchart in Figure 2-74, enter the lines of code necessary to produce the output.

4. Save the file on the Data Disk with the name Biblio. Make sure you choose Java (*.java) in the Save as type box.

5. Compile the program. If errors occur, fix them in the TextPad coding window and compile again.

6. Run the program. If the program runs correctly, return to TextPad and print a copy of the source code. Otherwise, return to Step 3 and correct the errors until the program runs error-free.

2 Analysis and Design

Figure 2-75 shows a requirements document for a new application, as requested by a small business owner. Using the six phases of the development cycle as shown in Table 2-1 on page 48, perform the following steps.

REQUEST FOR NEW APPLICATION

Date submitted:	September 10, 2007
Submitted by:	Donna Van Krimpen
Purpose:	Our small business would like to start thinking about adding e-commerce to our current Web site. As a first step, we need a small window that would open from our current home page. The window would display "coming soon" information as detailed below.
Application title:	Donna's Dutch Doilies
Algorithms:	A three line message will display.
Notes:	1) We would like the following information to display in an applet: Coming soon… Order doilies online at www.DonnasDutchDoilies.com 2) We would like black letters on a yellow background. 3) If possible, have the applet display in a perfect square. 4) The text should be centered as closely as possible. 5) No graphic is necessary.

Approvals

Approval status:	X	Approved
		Rejected
Approved by:		Doug McMann, programmer We Can Do That on the Web A Web Site Consulting Firm
Date:		September 14, 2007
Assigned to:		

FIGURE 2-75

1. Analyze the requirements. Read the requirements document carefully. Think about the requester, the users, the problem, and the purpose of the application.

2. Design the solution. Draw a storyboard for the applet. Pay careful attention to the size and spacing request. Write either pseudocode or draw a flowchart to represent the sequence of events in your program.

(continued)

2 Analysis and Design (continued)

3. Validate the design. Have a classmate or your instructor look over your storyboard and make suggestions before you proceed.

4. Implement the design. Translate the design into code for the applet. Create an HTML document to host the applet.

5. Test the solution. Test the program, finding and correcting errors (debugging) until it is error-free.

6. Document the solution. Print a copy of the source code, the HTML code, and a copy of the applet interface.

7. Hand in all documents to your instructor.

3 Coding Your Own Splash Screen

In order to practice writing, compiling, and running Java, you decide to create a Java application that displays your name and address on the screen. Perform the following steps.

1. Start TextPad. Save the file on the Data Disk with your first name as the file name. Make sure you choose Java (*.java) in the Save as type box. Click the Save in box arrow to save the file on drive A in the folder named Chapter02.

2. Type the block comments to include your name, the date, the program's name, the course number, and the program's purpose. Press the TAB key as needed to align the comments. Remember to use /* to begin the block comment and */ to end it.

3. Type the class header. Use your first name as the name of the class. Do not forget to enter the keywords, public and class, before your name. On the next line, type an opening brace.

4. Type the main() method header, using the keywords public, static, and void. The main() method takes a String[] parameter named args. As you type, remember that Java is case-sensitive. On the next line, type an opening brace.

5. Type three lines that begin System.out.println(" and then include your name, address and city each on a separate line. Do not forget to close the quotation mark and parentheses. Place a semicolon at the end of each line.

6. Type a closing brace for the main() method.

7. Type a closing brace for the class.

8. Compile the program by clicking Compile Java on the TextPad Tools menu. If necessary, fix any errors in the coding window and then compile the program again.

9. Once the program compiles correctly, run the program by clicking Run Java Application on the TextPad Tools menu. After viewing your output, click the Close button in the command prompt window title bar.

10. In the TextPad window, use the Print command on the File menu to print a copy of the source code.

11. Close the TextPad window.

4 Converting an Application to an Applet

After completing the splash screen in Programming Assignment 3, you decide to convert the application into an applet. Perform the following steps.

1. Change the file and class name to SplashApplet every time it displays in the code.

2. Add the words, extends Applet, to the class header.

3. Change the main() method header to a paint() method header.

4. Change each println() method to a drawString() method. Remember to reference the Graphics object (g) as you did on pages 96 and 97.

5. Save the program with the new file name, SplashApplet.

6. Compile the program. If there are errors, fix them in the SplashApplet coding window and then compile again.

7. Create an HTML host document that calls the SplashApplet class. Set the attributes of the applet to have a width of 400 and a height of 300 when it displays in the Applet Viewer window.

8. Run the program.

9. Print a copy of the applet interface by using the Applet menu in the Applet Viewer window. Using TextPad, print a copy of the source code for the Java applet and the HTML code for the host document.

10. For extra credit, edit the program to include a system date.

5 Formatting Output Using Escape Characters

Computer applications typically display a splash screen for users to view while waiting for the entire application to load. The Computer Science department at Middle Illinois College wants to display a splash screen with the school's initials, MIC, as each application loads. The display should use text characters to make large versions of the letters M, I, and C, as shown in Figure 2-76.

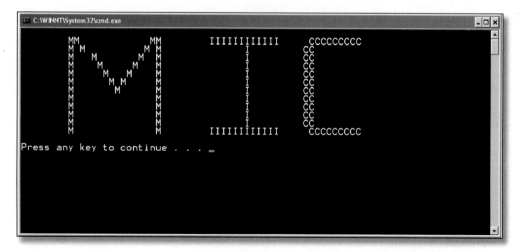

FIGURE 2-76

(continued)

5 Formatting Output Using Escape Characters *(continued)*

1. Start TextPad.

2. Save the program as Java source code with the file name MIC on your Data Disk.

3. Type block comments to include your name, the date, the program's name, the course number, and the program's purpose. Press the TAB key as needed to align the comments. Remember to use /* to begin the block comment and */ to end it.

4. Enter the code from Figure 2-77 in the TextPad window, using the escape code sequence \t as indicated. *Hint:* Eleven spaces separate the Ms in line 5; each successive line has 2 less spaces.

```
 1   public   class   MIC
 2   {
 3       public   static   void   main( String  []   args )
 4       {
 5           System . out . println  ("\tMM              MM\tIIIIIIIIIIIII\t            CCCCCCCC) ;
 6           System . out . println  ("\tM   M            M M\t        I          \tCC" ) ;
 7           System . out . println  ("\tM   M            M M\t        I          \tCC" ) ;
 8       //Add  new  code  here
 9       }
10   }
```

FIGURE 2-77

5. Add three or four more lines of code to complete the school's initials.

6. Compile your program.

7. If no compilation errors occur, run the program.

8. Using TextPad, print a copy of the source code.

6 Creating an Applet with a Background Color

In preparation for creating your own personal Web page, you would like to view some possible background colors that will be easy to read with black text. You decide to write a Java applet that displays black words on a colored background. You will use the setBackground() method, which accepts a color argument in applets.

1. Start TextPad. Save the file as Java source code with the file name MyColorApplet.

2. Type a block header with the information about you and the assignment.

3. Import the java.awt.* and java.applet.* packages.

4. Write the class header for MyColorApplet. Remember to extend the Applet class. Include an opening brace for the class.

5. Write a method header for the paint() method. Include an opening brace for the method.

6. Set the background color to yellow.

7. Use the drawString() method to print the words "This is a color test" at the coordinates 25 and 30.

8. Enter closing braces to close the method and class.

9. Compile the program. Fix errors as necessary.

10. On the TextPad menu bar, click File and then click New. Type the HTML code to reference the MyColor.class with a width of 400 and a height of 200. Be sure to include the start and end <HTML> tags.

11. Save the HTML document with the filename MyColorApplet. Make sure you specify the HTML (*.htm*,*.stm*) file type.

12. Run the program.

13. Edit the program several times and change the color to red, blue, cyan, and orange. Compile and then run the program after each color change.

7 Rick's Riding Rodeo

Rick's Riding Rodeo plans to market its line of saddles on the Web next year. In preparation for Rick to begin e-commerce, write a Java application to display the name of the store on the screen. Use appropriate documentation lines. Compile the program and execute it. Once the program executes with no errors, edit the program to include Rick's e-mail address (RideWithRick@rodeo.com). Save, compile, and execute the program again. Convert the program to display as an applet, and add an appropriate logo (your instructor may supply you with a graphic, or you may download a graphic from the Web). When the applet is complete and generates no compilation errors, write the HTML code to run the applet.

8 Accessing the System Date

Your school would like to print out the programmer's initials and the system date on all printouts from the mainframe computer. As a prototype, write a Java program to print your initials and the system date on a splash screen. Use the escape characters and spacing to print the letters in the correct locations. Compile and execute your program. Print the source code.

9 Looking at Applets

The Web contains many sites that have free Java applets that you may download. Use a search engine to search for Java applets on the Web. When you find a Web page with some applets, use your browser's View Source command to look at the coding. Within that code, look for tags such as <APPLET CODE = >. Print three examples to submit to your instructor.

10 Your School Logo

Companies sometimes use a splash screen on the Web to give the user something to look at while the longer, graphic intensive Web page downloads. Write a splash screen applet that displays the name of your company or school, the address, the Web address, and your school's logo. Ask your instructor for the location of the graphic file. Position the lines using the g.drawString() method with the x and y coordinates. Position the graphic beside the text. Compile and run the applet using TextPad. Then run the applet using a browser such as Internet Explorer or Netscape by typing the path and file name of the HTML file in the browser's Address text box. Compare the two results. Print both the source code for the applet and the HTML file.

11 Creating a Splash Screen

In preparation for future Java programs, create a Java program, called Center, that displays an opening screen with text information about your program centered in the middle of the screen. Include the name of your program, your name, your instructor's name, the date, and any other necessary information. When maximized, the command prompt window displays approximately 25 lines that are 80 characters across. To center vertically, divide the number of lines of text into 25 (dropping any remainder) to determine how many blank lines (\n) to insert before each text line. To center horizontally, count the characters in the line of text, divide that by 2 (dropping any remainder), and then subtract that from 40 to determine how many spaces you should indent from the left margin. Remember that each escape character (\t) moves the text approximately eight characters to the right. Use the SPACEBAR to insert fewer than eight spaces. Compile and execute your program. Save your program on the Data Disk.

12 Creating New Colors

Use the Java API (http://java.sun.com/j2se/1.5.0/docs/api) to research possible colors for use with applets. When the API displays, click the java.awt package. Then click the class, Color. Look at the Field Summary table for possible colors. Then look at the Method Summary table for ways to change those colors. Write an applet that uses some of the methods you found to set both the background and foreground colors in an applet. If necessary, use the Java API Index at the top of the Web page to look up and review the syntax for the setBackground() and setForeground() methods.

3

Manipulating Data
Using Methods

Objectives

You will have
mastered the material in
this chapter when you can:

- Identify, declare, and use primitive
  data types
- Use the System class to create data streams
- Instantiate the BufferedReader class in code
- Use the readLine() method to handle user input
- Convert strings to numbers using the parse() method
- Use assignment statements to store data with proper identifiers
- Use operators and parentheses correctly in numeric and conditional
  expressions
- Round an answer using the round() method of the Math class
- Use Swing components to build the GUI for a Swing program
- Use the exit() method to close a Swing program
- Implement an ActionListener to handle events
- Add interface components to an applet
- Use the init() and paint() methods to load the applet interface
- Use the actionPerformed() method
- Run and test an interactive applet
- Manage Java source code files and Java class files

Introduction

Manipulating data is integral to creating useful computer programs. Programmers must know how to retrieve and store different kinds of data efficiently. **Data** are collections of raw facts or figures, such as words, text, or numbers, which are used in reasoning or calculations (datum is the singular form of the word, data). A computer program performs operations on input data to produce output in the form of information The data used by a program can come from a variety of sources, such as the program itself, from users of the program, or from external files. When developing programs, programmers often embed certain kinds of data, such as constant values that will not change, within the program. Other kinds of data, such as current rates or prices that can change, are input to the program from external files or by users.

In this chapter, you will learn about the numerous ways Java can accept, retrieve, and manipulate data. You will learn how to write code that assigns values to variables, which Java uses to store data temporarily for processing. You also will learn to use classes and methods to set fields to specific values and create instances of classes. As you develop an interactive console application, you will learn to write code to accept a stream of character input from a keyboard, read the line, and then process it. In addition, you will learn how to code formulas with mathematical operators and create a single line of output on the display. In the process of modifying the console application to accept data from a dialog box, you will learn to add Java's Swing components, such as JOptionPane, to an interface to display messages and accept user input via dialog boxes. In converting the application to an interactive applet, you will learn to use an ActionListener to handle events, as well as to call constructors to add Labels, TextFields, and a Button component to the interface, along with an Image. Finally, you will create an HTML host file and then run the applet in the Applet Viewer window.

Chapter Three — The Body Mass Index Calculator

The programs developed in this chapter create a Body Mass Index Calculator for a health club and its staff of trainers to use as they work with health club customers to establish exercise and diet regimens. Body mass index (BMI) is one way to gauge the total body fat in adults by measuring the relationship of weight to height. Studies have shown that adults should strive to maintain a BMI between 20 and 24. The fitness center wants to measure improvement in its customers by taking a before and after measurement of the customer's BMI. The Body Mass Index Calculator will allow the trainers to input data and generate accurate and consistent computerized calculations. To make it easily accessible from any location in the fitness center, the Body Mass Index Calculator will be available on a notebook computer, over the Web, or via a personal digital assistant (PDA).

The compiled Java source code for the Body Mass Index Calculator will cause prompts to display and will accept user input. The program then will calculate the body mass index. Three versions of the Body Mass Index Calculator are developed in this chapter: (1) a console application with input and output displayed in a command prompt window (Figure 3-1a); (2) a console application with input and output facilitated by dialog boxes (Figure 3-1b); and (3) an applet that provides input and output in a Web environment (Figure 3-1c).

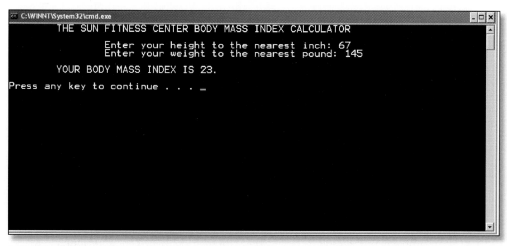

(a) console application accepts input and displays output in a command prompt window

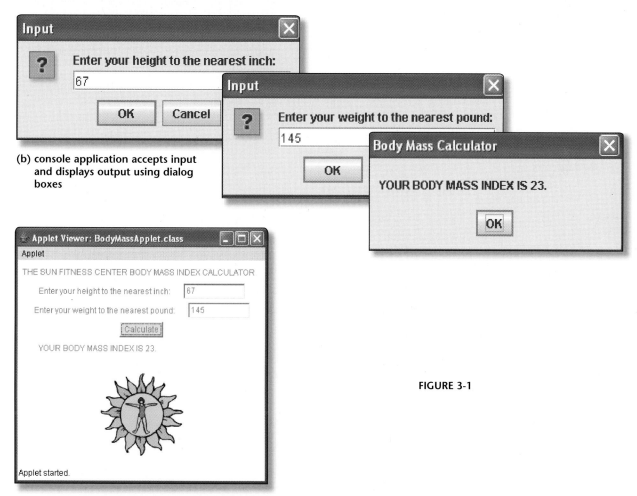

(b) console application accepts input and displays output using dialog boxes

(c) applet accepts input and displays output in a Web environment

FIGURE 3-1

Program Development

The program development cycle for the Body Mass Index Calculator program consists of tasks that correspond to the six development cycle phases, as shown in Table 3-1.

Table 3-1   Body Mass Index Calculator Program Development Tasks

	DEVELOPMENT PHASE	TASK(S)
1	Analyze the requirements	Analyze the Body Mass Index Calculator problem.
2	Design the solution	Design the user interface for both console applications and the applet, including output data and placement of the applet graphic. Design the logic to solve the problem.
3	Validate the design	Confirm with the user that the design solves the problem in a satisfactory manner.
4	Implement the design	Translate the design into code. Include internal documentation (comments and remarks) within the code that explains the purpose of the code statements. Create the HTML file to host the applet.
5	Test the solution	Test the program. Find and correct any errors (debug) until it is error-free.
6	Document the solution	Print copies of the application code, applet code, applet interface, and HTML code.

Analysis and Design

Figure 3-2 shows the requirements document that initiates the development cycle for the Body Mass Index Calculator program. The requirements document specifies the reason for the request, lists the required inputs and outputs, and shows the algorithm used to compute the BMI based on a person's height and weight.

REQUEST FOR NEW APPLICATION

Date submitted:	October 9, 2007
Submitted by:	Sun Fitness Center, Helen Sun - Office Manager
Purpose:	Our staff would like an easy-to-use program that calculates the body mass index of our customers. We measure customers when they first enter our program and then again after several weeks. The body mass index is a metric calculation; thus, our employees have had to convert the height and weight and then calculate the body mass index.
Application title:	Body Mass Index Calculator

Algorithms:	The body mass index is calculated as follows:
	    $kilograms / meters^2$
	
	To convert inches to meters, divide by 39.36
	To convert pounds to kilograms, divide by 2.2
	
	Example: A 5'7" adult that weights 145 pounds has a body mass index of 23 as calculated in the following formulas:
	
	    1.70 meters = 67 inches / 39.36
	    65.91 kilograms = 145 pounds / 2.2
	    23 body mass index = 65.91 kilograms / 1.70 meters^2

Notes:	1. The fitness center staff is accustomed to taking measurements using inches and pounds. 2. The program should allow the user to enter values for the height in inches and the weight in pounds. We do not use decimals or fractions when measuring customers. Please remind program users that they should round the input to the nearest inch or nearest pound. 3. The calculated index can be rounded to the nearest integer. 4. Some of our trainers have PDAs, others have notebook computers. Not all of our locations have Web access in the training room. 5. As we want to distribute this program to all of our locations, please use "THE SUN FITNESS CENTER BODY MASS INDEX CALCULATOR" at the top of the display. 6. In the Web version, please use our Sun Fitness Center logo.

Approvals

Approval status:	X	Approved
		Rejected
Approved by:	Tyler Gilbert	
Date:	October 15, 2007	
Assigned to:	J. Starks, Programmer	

FIGURE 3-2

PROBLEM ANALYSIS   The problem that the Body Mass Index Calculator program should solve is the calculation of a health-related measurement of body fat, called the body mass index (BMI). The BMI is based on the relationship between a person's weight and height. To complete the calculation and generate output for the user, the Body Mass Index Calculator program requires the user to input two values: the height in inches and the weight in pounds.

A **formula** is a mathematical sentence that contains values and operators. As stated in the requirements document in Figure 3-2 on the previous page, the Body Mass Index Calculator program must use the following formulas:

meters = inches / 39.36
kilograms = pounds / 2.2

to convert pounds and inches to the metric measurements of meters and kilograms, respectively. The converted values then are used in the following formula:

index = kilograms / meters^2

to calculate the BMI.

As noted on the previous page, the formulas require two inputs. The first formula divides the first input, inches, by 39.36 to calculate meters. The second formula divides the second input, pounds, by 2.2 to calculate kilograms. The program then uses the converted values in a third formula, which divides kilograms by the square of the meters to produce the output value for body mass index. In the third formula, the word, index, represents the body mass index value. Figure 3-3 displays a list of inputs and outputs, as well as sample data.

INPUTS AND OUTPUTS

INPUTS	OUTPUTS
inches	body mass index
pounds	

SAMPLE DATA

INPUTS	OUTPUTS
67 inches 145 pounds	23
62 inches 110 pounds	20
72 inches 200 pounds	27

FIGURE 3-3

DESIGN THE SOLUTION   Once you have analyzed the problem, the next step is to design the user interface. There are three versions of the Body Mass Index Calculator program with three different kinds of interfaces: (1) a console application with prompts at the command line; (2) a console application with dialog box prompts; and (3) an applet with windowed input and output controls.

Figure 3-4a shows a storyboard for the Body Mass Index Calculator as a console application. As stated in the requirements document, the program will display the title, THE SUN FITNESS CENTER BODY MASS INDEX CALCULATOR, at the top of the window. Two prompts then will be displayed, allowing the user to enter the input values for inches and pounds. The calculated BMI will be displayed below the prompts. An advantage of creating this program as a console application is that a user does not need a GUI-based operating system or a mouse to enter data or view the resulting output. The console application thus is ideal for use on a personal digital assistant (PDA). Another advantage of creating a console application is that a programmer can validate the program logic before designing and creating a GUI version of the program.

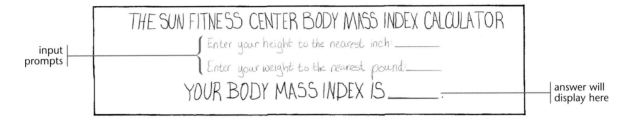

FIGURE 3-4a

Even though a console application will allow you to edit, backspace, and even cut and paste as you enter data, many users feel more comfortable entering data into a text box or text field. Therefore, a second version of the Body Mass Index Calculator is developed as a console application that will accept input via dialog boxes.

A **dialog box** is a small window that displays messages and can accept user input. Figure 3-4b shows a storyboard for a dialog box. To accept user input, a dialog box may include a text box to accept input data, as shown in Figure 3-4b, or it may include option buttons, lists, or other items that allow a user to select from several preset choices. A dialog box has at least one button and may contain an icon. The title bar of a dialog box displays a caption and has a Close button.

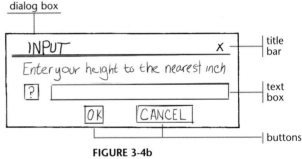

FIGURE 3-4b

A dialog box may be displayed as a result of a user action, such as clicking a button, or it may display as a result of logic in the program. When a dialog box is displayed, it is displayed in front of the application in which it is running. When the user finishes entering information or clicks an appropriate button in the dialog box, the dialog box closes. The program that called the dialog box, however, does not necessarily close when the dialog box closes.

Dialog boxes that require the user to complete a specific action, such as entering data, clicking the Cancel button, or choosing yes or no before returning to the program's interface, are called **modal**. Modal dialog boxes give the programmer control over how the user interacts with the program.

The third version of the Body Mass Index Calculator — an applet with a Web interface — also will accept user input; however, the applet user will type data into text boxes and then click a Calculate button in the applet window. As shown in the storyboard in Figure 3-4c on the next page, the applet window displays the title of the program, two input prompts with associated text boxes for data entry, and a Calculate button that causes the program to calculate body mass index and display the results. The company logo will display as a graphic in the lower portion of the applet window.

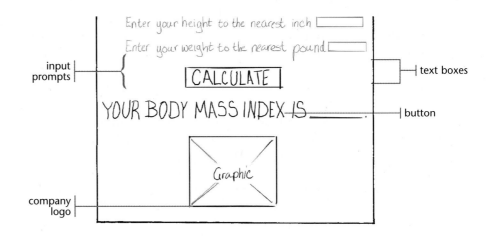

FIGURE 3-4c

Consistent Wording in Applications and Applets

When designing different versions of the same program, as you do when you convert console applications to applets, be sure to code prompts and output messages so that the wording is as similar as possible. Consistent wording will allow users to interpret easily what the program is asking and make it easier if they have to switch between program versions running on a desktop, on a PDA, or via the Web. It also will simplify the programming process, especially if you are editing existing code to create a different version of the program.

PROGRAM DESIGN   Once you have designed the interface, the next step is to design the logic to solve the problem and create the desired results. The only programming task is to calculate the BMI based on input. The user can execute the program code to calculate BMI by answering the prompts in any version of the application program. The applet requires the additional step of clicking the Calculate button.

The program code for the first console application will allow user input, perform calculations, and display an answer, in that order, so the structure of the program will be sequential in nature. Input prompts and output will display using the System.out object, which is the default display device of your system (Figure 3-1a on page 129).

The program code then will be modified to use dialog boxes. This second version of the application will call on a special Java package named **javax.swing**, which provides a set of Java-based GUI components (Figure 3-1b on page 129).

Finally, the program code will be modified to create a third version of the program that can run over the Web as an applet. The program code for the applet will display text, text boxes, a button, and a graphic in an applet window (Figure 3-1c on page 129). Both the application and applet versions of the program should contain appropriate documentation and be saved for future use.

Figure 3-5a shows the pseudocode that represents the logic of the program requirements. The structure of the program will be sequential in nature, meaning that the computer will perform one action after another without skipping any steps or making any decisions that would affect the flow of the logic. Figure 3-5b shows an event diagram that illustrates how the click of the Calculate button in the applet window triggers the calculation and displays the answer in the applet window.

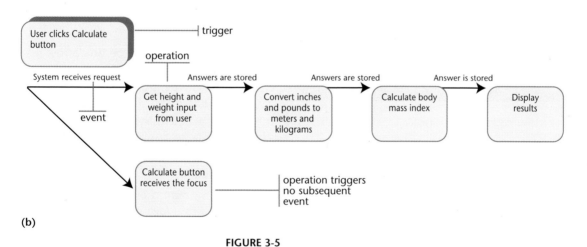

Calculate Body Mass Index

       get height from user

       get weight from user

       convert height and weight to metric

       calculate index

       display index

End

(a)

(b)

FIGURE 3-5

VALIDATE DESIGN   Once you have designed the program, you can validate the design by stepping through the requirements document and making sure that the design addresses each requirement. If possible, you also should step through the solution with test data to verify that the solution meets the requirements. The user also should review the design to confirm that it solves the problem outlined in the requirements. By comparing the program design with the original requirements, both the programmer and the user can validate that the solution is correct and satisfactory.

Having analyzed the problem, designed the interface, and designed and validated the program logic, the analysis and design of the application is complete. As shown in Table 3-1 on page 130, the next task in the development cycle is to implement the design by creating a new Java program using TextPad.

Starting a New Java Program in Textpad

In Chapter 2, you learned how to start TextPad and save a file using a Java file type. The following steps start TextPad and save a TextPad document using a Java file type.

<table>
<tr><td>

OTHER WAYS

1. To start TextPad, click Start button, click TextPad on Start menu
2. To view line numbers, press CTRL+Q, L
3. To save, press F12
4. To save, press ALT+F, A

</td><td>

To Start TextPad and Save a TextPad Document

1. With the Windows desktop displayed, click the Start button on the taskbar and then point to All Programs on the Start menu. Click TextPad on the All Programs submenu.

2. When the TextPad window opens, if necessary, click the Maximize button to maximize the screen. If a Tip of the Day dialog box is displayed, click its Close button. If line numbers do not display in the TextPad coding window, click View on the menu bar and then click Line Numbers on the View menu.

3. Insert the Data Disk in drive A. Click File on the menu bar and then click Save As on the File menu.

4. When the Save As dialog box is displayed, type BodyMass in the File name text box. Do not press the ENTER key.

</td></tr>
</table>

5. Click the Save as type box arrow and then click Java (*.java) in the Save as type list. Click the Save in box arrow and then click 3½ Floppy (A:) in the Save in list.

6. Double-click the Chapter03 folder or a location specified by your instructor.

The file named BodyMass will be saved as a Java source code file in the Chapter03 folder on the Data Disk in drive A (Figure 3-6).

7. Click the Save button in the Save As dialog box.

FIGURE 3-6

Recall that saving the program before entering any code causes TextPad to display Java-related color coding as you begin to enter code. It also causes the file name to display on the title bar, on the Windows taskbar, and in the Selector window, which provides a visual reference as you enter code. Finally, after the file is saved once, you can click the Save button on the Standard toolbar to resave the file to the same folder. TextPad also automatically resaves the file each time the program is compiled.

Coding the Program

As you have learned, the implementation phase of the development cycle involves writing the code that translates the design into a program. During program design, pseudocode was used to outline the logic of the program code in the Body Mass Index Calculator application (Figure 3-5a on page 135). As outlined in that pseudocode, the task to be performed is to accept two inputs of height and weight, convert the input values to metric, calculate body mass index using a given formula, and then display the BMI value as output. The coding process starts with entering the beginning program code.

Entering Beginning Code

Similar to the console application program in Chapter 2, the code for the Body Mass Index Calculator program will include comments, a class header, and a main() method. The code for the Body Mass Index Calculator also will use an import statement to import the java.io package. Recall from Chapter 2 that the java.lang package is the only package imported automatically without an explicit command; all other packages need an import statement to tell the compiler where to access the classes, fields, and methods of an existing class in the package. In this program, the java.io package is imported to provide classes to support system input and output.

When you use certain methods from the java.io package, you must warn the compiler that the possibility of errors exists. For instance, a user might not have authority to open a file, a disk might not be located in the proper disk drive, or the system might be busy with other input. An easy way to keep the program from aborting prematurely due to these kinds of errors is to add the code, throws IOException, to the end of the main() method header. The code, **throws IOException**, gives the program a way to acknowledge and handle potential input or output errors and still compile correctly.

Figure 3-7 on the next page displays the code for the comment header, import statement, class header, and main() method header used in the Body Mass Index Calculator program.

```
1   /*
2        Chapter 3:   The Body Mass Index Calculator
3        Programmer:  J. Starks
4        Date:        October 20, 2007
5        Filename:    BodyMass.java
6        Purpose:     This project calculates the body mass index based
7                     on a person's height and weight.
8   */
9
10  import java.io.*;
11
12  public class BodyMass
13  {
14          public static void main(String[] args) throws IOException
15          {
```

FIGURE 3-7

The following step enters beginning code in the coding window.

To Enter Beginning Code

1. With the insertion point on line 1 in the coding window, type the code as shown in Figure 3-7. In the comment header, insert your own name as the programmer and enter the current date.

TextPad displays the beginning code in the coding window (Figure 3-8). The insertion point displays after the opening brace on line 15.

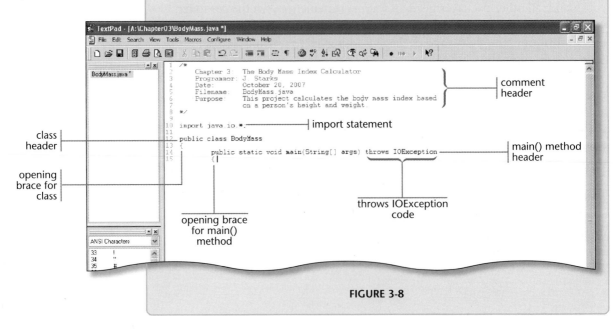

FIGURE 3-8

Comments and commands related to packages, such as the import statement, are the only code allowed outside the class header and its braced block of code. Recall that during compilation, the import statement loads the appropriate class or classes from the location where the SDK is stored. Typing an asterisk (*) after the package name tells the program to load all the classes within a package; typing an individual class name after the package name tells the program to load an individual class.

Storing Data

For a computer program to make use of data, the data must be stored in the memory of the computer. Java makes efficient use of memory by requiring programmers to declare the kind of data they want to store. Java then allocates just enough memory for that data. It is a good programming practice to store data in the smallest location possible while still maintaining the precision and integrity of the data. **Precision** refers to the amount of storage allocated to hold the fractional part of a number. If a greater amount of storage is allocated, a more precise number with additional decimal places can be stored. Thus, the more precision a system uses, the more exactly it can represent fractional quantities.

Before a Java program can manipulate data, the program must identify the types of data to be used, declare a variable identifier, and put actual data into the storage location that the program can access later.

Java Data Types

As you learned in Chapter 2, a data type classifies the data into a particular category of information and tells the computer how to interpret and store the data. Humans easily can distinguish between different types of data. For example, you usually can tell at a glance whether a number is a percentage, a time, or an amount of money by the use of special symbols, such as %, :, or $, which indicate the data type. Similarly, a computer uses special internal codes and words to keep track of and identify the different types of data it processes.

Java is a **strongly typed language**, which means it enforces a set of rules about how you use the objects you create, especially when using different types of data. For instance, every variable must have a data type, which determines the values that the variable can contain and the operations a program can perform on the data. Java programmers thus cannot declare a variable location as an integer and then try to insert a string of characters into that variable location. There would not be enough room because each data type has internal sizes associated with it.

Java supports two categories of data types: primitive and reference. A **primitive data type** is a data type that is structured by Java to hold single data items, such as integer, character, floating point, and true or false values. Java supports eight primitive data types, which help programmers by restricting the kind of data allowed in the declared variable location. If you try to store some other type of value in that variable location, Java displays an error message during compilation. The eight primitive data types, their descriptions, and examples of each are listed in Table 3-2 on the next page.

Table 3-2   Java Primitive Data Types

TYPE	DESCRIPTION	EXAMPLES
boolean	stores data in only one of two states, as a logical value of true or false	true false
byte	stores whole number values in 8-bit signed locations from –128 to +127	75 –14
char	stores any one of the 65,436 single characters of the Unicode set, which includes characters and symbols from many languages	'a' 'M'
double	stores numbers with up to 14 or 15 decimal places as double-precision, floating-point values	87.266975314 100D
float	stores numbers with up to 6 or 7 decimals as single-precision, floating-point values	349.135 954F
int	stores whole number values in 32-bit signed locations from -2^{31} to $+2^{31}-1$	29387 –86421
long	stores whole number values in 64-bit signed locations from approximately $-9*10^{18}$ to $+9*10^{18}-1$	13579286740 7362L
short	stores whole number values in 16-bit signed locations from –32,768 to +32,767	619 –530

As you learned in Chapter 2, when an actual number or character displays as data in code, it is called a literal. Generally speaking, a literal numeric value with no decimal point is treated by the compiler as an int data type. Programmers can specify that the data be treated as a long integer by putting an uppercase L or lowercase l after the number, which overrides the default int storage. An uppercase L is preferred, as it cannot be confused with the digit 1. In the same way, an uppercase D or lowercase d after the literal forces that number to be considered a double. The compiler considers a literal containing digits and a decimal point as a double. Programmers may override that storage to specify a float by putting an F or f after the number.

The two boolean literals are true and false. Programmers use the boolean data type to store a comparative result or one that has only two states — such as true or false, yes or no, 1 or 0 — as a logical value of true or false. A literal char value is any single character between single quote marks.

Tip

Primitive Data Types Are Platform-Independent

In other programming languages, the format and size of primitive data types may depend on the platform on which a program is running. In contrast, the Java programming language specifies the size and format of its primitive data types. Therefore, primitive data types are platform–independent, which means programmers do not have to worry about system dependencies.

Note that the char data type is a primitive and is restricted to storing a single character. When programmers want to store more than one character, they often use the non-primitive String class, which can store more than a single character. Classes such as String, Date (which you accessed in Chapter 2), and arrays (which you will learn about in a later chapter) are considered reference data types or object types. A **reference data type** is a data type whose value is an address. Like a primitive data type, a reference data type is declared with an identifier name, but that identifier references the location of the data rather than the actual data.

Declaring Variables

A **declaration statement** is a line of Java code that identifies, or declares, the data type and names the identifier or variable. Programmers also can use the declaration statement to assign an initial value or call a constructor method to declare an instance of a class as they declare their variables. Table 3-3 shows the general form of declaration statements.

Table 3-3	*Declaration Statements*

General form:	1. dataType identifier; //simple declaration
	2. dataType identifier, identifier, identifier; //multiple declarations
	3. dataType identifier = initialValue; //declaration and initialization
	4. dataType identifier = new constructorMethod(); //declaration and construction

Purpose:	To allocate a storage location and specify the type of data or object it will hold.
Examples:	1. int userAge; 2. boolean flag, done, membership; 3. double taxRate = .05; 4. Date currentDate = new Date();

Figure 3-9 displays the declaration statements that declare the variables used in the Body Mass Index Calculator program. If you want to declare variables with different data types, you must use a separate declaration statement for each data type. If, however, you have several variables of the same data type, you can list the data type once and then include each variable on the same line separated by commas, as shown in lines 18 and 19 in Figure 3-9. You must declare a variable before you can use it in a program; however, you can combine the declaration of a variable with its first value or assignment, as shown in example 3 in Table 3-3.

```
16          // declare and construct variables
17          String height, weight;
18          int inches, pounds;
19          double kilograms, meters, index;
```

FIGURE 3-9

Tip

Using Prefixes in Variable Names

Sun Microsystems has no suggested naming convention for Java variables. It is customary to begin variable names with lowercase letters. Some programmers use single character prefixes in front of their variable names to denote the data type. For example, a double value for sales tax might be named dSalesTax. For non-primitive data types, programmers sometimes use a three-letter prefix, similar to the standard Visual Basic notation for objects. For example, a Label component might be named lblFirstName. Regardless of the convention you follow, it is important to use mnemonic, user-friendly variable names. Naming and coding conventions will be covered in more detail later in the chapter.

The following step enters code to declare variables.

To Enter Code to Declare Variables

1. With the insertion point on line 16 in the coding window, type the line comment and declaration statements, as shown in Figure 3-9 on the previous page.

A line comment in line 16 explains that the following code declares and constructs variables (Figure 3-10). Three declaration statements are displayed in lines 17 through 19. No assignment of values is made.

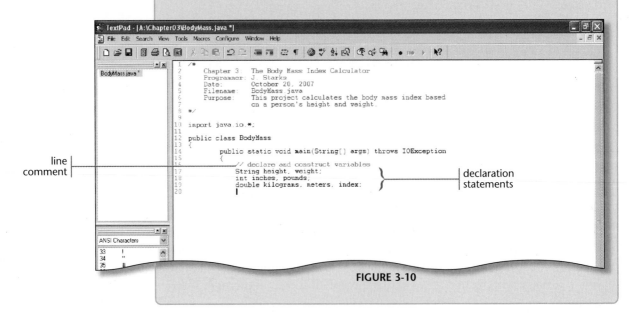

FIGURE 3-10

It may be helpful to remember that the integer data type, as declared in line 18, represents whole numbers, whereas the double data type represents a double-precision, floating-point value. Table 3-2 on page 140 describes a double as a number that is precise up to 14 or 15 decimal places. The word, floating, comes from scientists who refer to large numbers in scientific notation. For instance, 1,200,000 can be notated as 1.2 times 10 to the power of 6. The decimal point *floated* six places to the left.

> **Tip**
>
> **Performing Math with Floats and Doubles**
> Programmers must pay particular attention to data types when multiplying or dividing numbers with decimal places. A rule of arithmetic states that when two numbers are multiplied, the number of decimal places in the answer equals the sum of each number's decimal places. For example, if two numbers with four decimal places each are multiplied together, the answer has eight decimal places. Thus, while you might declare the numbers as floats because they have only four decimal places, you would have to declare the answer as double because it has eight decimal places. Another example is that literal data not specified with an L or F is considered double by the Java compiler. Therefore, you must declare the result of any mathematical operation with a nonspecified literal value as a double. If you try to store the answer in a float location, you will receive an error that states, possible loss of precision found, and the program will not compile.

User Input

Programmers who want to use timely data or data that changes on a regular basis usually do not code literal data into their programs. Instead, programmers code programs to reference an external data source, such as data input by a user. For example, in the banking industry, a programmer must rely on a bank customer to enter data such as a personal identification number (PIN) using the ATM keyboard. In fact, it is more common to rely on data from external sources than it is to include data in the program itself. Using external data allows for flexibility in programming and tailoring of the program to fit the company's or the user's needs.

Interactive is the term used with programs that allow the user to interact with the program by making choices, entering data, and viewing results. Interactive input and output in Java usually involves a user of the program entering data using a mouse and keyboard and viewing results on the screen.

Streams and the System Class

In Java, the act of data flowing in or out of a program is called a **stream**. Examples of streams include data being input from a keyboard or output to a display. Recall that the System class, which was introduced in Chapter 2, contains several useful methods, including those involving standard input and output streams. The System class creates three different streams when a program executes: System.in, System.out, and System.err. Table 3-4 on the next page describes these three System streams or classes. Each has many associated methods; several examples of these methods are listed in the table.

Table 3-4 System Classes

CLASS	FUNCTION	EXAMPLES OF ASSOCIATED METHODS	DEFAULT DEVICE	CODE EXAMPLE
System.in	Accepts input data from the keyboard buffer, wrapped in the InputStreamReader (ISR)	readLine() used with constructed variable	keyboard buffer	String custName = dataIn.readLine();
System.out	Sends output to the display or redirects output to a designated file	print() println() flush()	monitor or other display	System.out.println("Anita's Antiques");
System.err	Sends output to the monitor; used for prompts and error messages	print() println() flush()	monitor or other display	System.err.println("Thread started");

Recall from Chapter 2 that System.out sent a stream to the standard output device, which usually is the monitor. System.out implemented the method, println(), to transfer the stream of characters. When the System.out.println() method executed, the program sent a literal string argument to the display. In the code example in Table 3-4, the text, Anita's Antiques, would appear on the display.

While the Java SDK provides the println() method for output, the SDK contains no simple method for input. System.in actually refers to a buffered input stream. As a user types data into a program interface, the keystrokes are sent to a buffer. A **buffer** is a data area shared by hardware devices or programs, where data are held until they are needed by the processor. Buffering ensures that if a user presses the BACKSPACE key to delete a character, the deleted characters are not sent when the program retrieves the characters from the input buffer.

The java.io package contains several classes used to receive input typed by the user. One of these classes is the InputStreamReader, which is a special reader used to read the input buffer. The **InputStreamReader (ISR)** is a Java class or object that serves as an intermediary between the input buffer and the Java program. Java programmers use the word, **wrap**, to describe how the ISR envelops the stream from the input buffer. The Java code necessary to reference the buffer uses the form

InputStreamReader(System.in)

in which the InputStreamReader() method uses System.in as the argument.

One more step must be completed before a program can use the data from the ISR. The data must be stored and named in an accessible way, as described in the next section.

The BufferedReader Class

The **BufferedReader class** is used to store, or buffer, the input received from another object or class, such as the InputStreamReader class. The BufferedReader class, which is part of the java.io package, is used to increase the efficiency of character input. Input devices, such as a keyboard, typically are much slower than the computer's CPU; buffering the data reduces the number of times the CPU has to interact with the device to obtain the input data.

Recall that an instance is a unique object or a specific occurrence of a class of objects. **Instantiation** is the process of constructing an instance of a data type or object from a previously defined class. As discussed in Chapter 2, you use a special method called a constructor to create an instance of a class of objects. All Java classes have constructors that are used to initialize a new object of that type; the constructor method has the same name as the class.

Line 20 in Figure 3-11 calls a constructor to **instantiate**, or declare an instance of, the BufferedReader class. The resulting line of Java code may seem a bit cryptic; Table 3-5 breaks down and explains the purpose of the constructor code to declare the BufferedReader class.

```
20          BufferedReader dataIn= new BufferedReader(new
            InputStreamReader(System.in));
21
```

FIGURE 3-11

Table 3-5 The BufferedReader Constructor Code

CODE COMPONENTS	TERMINOLOGY	EXPLANATION
BufferedReader	a class from the java.io package	A class that reads text from a character input stream, buffering characters so as to provide for the efficient reading of characters, arrays, and lines.
dataIn	identifier (variable) to hold the inputted data	Variable name assigned by the programmer.
= new	constructor notation	The standard notation to instantiate or construct an instance of a class.
BufferedReader()	method	A constructor or method used to instantiate or construct an instance of the BufferedReader class.
InputStreamReader()	a class from the java.io package	An InputStreamReader is a bridge from byte streams to character streams; it reads bytes and decodes them into characters. It usually is wrapped inside a BufferedReader.
System.in	an object representing input from a buffer	An object representing the standard input device on a computer system, usually the keyboard.

The argument of the BufferedReader() method, on the right side of the constructor notation, instantiates a new InputStreamReader class. The InputStreamReader acts as a bridge to read the stream of bytes from the keyboard buffer and decode the bytes into characters. The BufferedReader() method returns a reference to the input data from the System.in.

Most programmers use a variable identifier such as myIn or dataIn to hold the input data read by the BufferedReader class. As shown in Figure 3-11 on the previous page, line 20 uses the identifier dataIn. When assigned by one of several readLine() methods, dataIn will contain the new data from System.in wrapped in the InputStreamReader. Figure 3-12 shows the flow of the data stream.

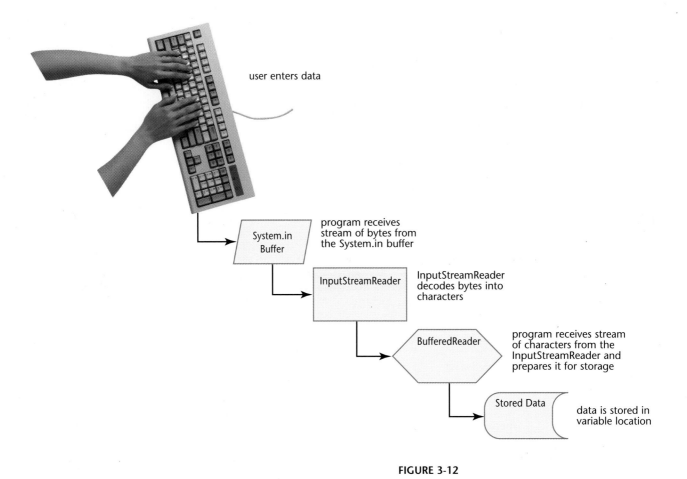

user enters data

System.in Buffer — program receives stream of bytes from the System.in buffer

InputStreamReader — InputStreamReader decodes bytes into characters

BufferedReader — program receives stream of characters from the InputStreamReader and prepares it for storage

Stored Data — data is stored in variable location

FIGURE 3-12

The following step enters code to instantiate the BufferedReader.

To Enter Code to Instantiate the BufferedReader

1. With the insertion point on line 20 in the coding window, enter lines 20 and 21, as shown in Figure 3-11 on the previous page.

The BufferedReader code is displayed in line 20 (Figure 3-13). Line 21 is a blank line.

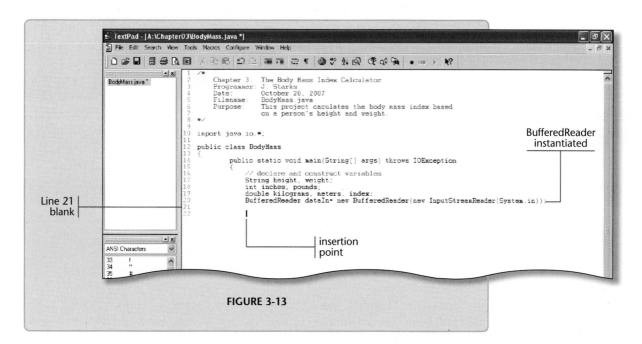

FIGURE 3-13

The BufferedReader could be declared and constructed with two separate lines, but it is more common to perform both actions in one line. Later you will learn that the BufferedReader can be used to efficiently read text and numbers from files as well as from the InputStreamReader (ISR).

Many users and textbooks create their own classes for input and output to simplify the process of reading from the buffer. It is exactly this BufferedReader capability, however, that makes Java easy to adapt to all kinds of input, such as strings, numbers, special characters, and foreign language symbols. It aids in Java's platform independence.

User Prompts, Inputs, and Conversions

As defined during program design, users of this program will respond to prompts on the screen in order to enter the input data for height and weight. The prompts will take the form of questions displayed with the System.out.println() and System.out.print() methods, as shown in lines 23, 24, 25, and 28 of Figure 3-14.

After the user enters text, the **readLine() method** from the BufferedReader class reads the line of inputted text and returns a String containing the contents of the line. Lines 26 and 29 each include a readLine() method that accepts the response from the buffer and stores it in the location named dataIn.

```
22              // print prompts and get input
23              System.out.println("\tTHE SUN FITNESS CENTER BODY MASS INDEX CALCULATOR");
24              System.out.println();
25              System.out.print("\t\tEnter your height to the nearest inch: ");
26                  height = dataIn.readLine();
27                  inches = Integer.parseInt(height);
28              System.out.print("\t\tEnter your weight to the nearest pound: ");
29                  weight = dataIn.readLine();
30                  pounds = Integer.parseInt(weight);
31
```

FIGURE 3-14

The buffer stores input data one character at a time from the keyboard and then delivers a stream of characters to the program wrapped as a String object. Data read from the buffer with the method, readLine(), thus is a string of characters; therefore, it must be declared as a String object. A String is appropriate for data such as a person's name, but Java cannot perform mathematical operations on a String. Consequently, any input data that a programmer plans to use in formulas must be converted from a String to a numeric data type.

In the java.lang package, each primitive data type may use its associated **wrapper class** to provide a way to help primitive data types, such as ints and doubles, conform to their Object class counterparts, such as Strings. Unlike the String class of objects, primitive data types in Java are not objects. Each wrapper class wraps, or packages, the primitive data type value so that it is treated as an object. The Integer class of objects, for example, wraps an int value in an object so that the program can manipulate it as though it were an object. In addition, the Integer class provides several methods for converting a String to an int data type and vice versa.

One of the methods associated with the wrapper classes is the **parse() method**, which allows programmers to convert Strings to a numeric data type. The parse() method is unique to each of its data types. The parseInt() method, as shown in lines 27 and 30 of Figure 3-14 on the previous page, belongs to the Integer class of objects, while the parseDouble() method belongs to the Double class of objects. The basic syntax of any parse() method is to list the object class followed by a period, followed by the specific method name, such as parseInt() or parseDouble(). The String variable to be converted is placed inside the method's parentheses.

For each of the parse() methods, the end result is the same: a String is converted to a number. The difference is the data type of the converted number and the object name listed before the parse method.

Note that lines 27 and 30 are indented below the lines of code that include the println() and print() methods used to display input prompts to the user. Typically, the lines of code that accept and manipulate data in response to user input are indented to show their relationship to the prompt.

Assignment Statements

The parseInt() methods in lines 27 and 30 assign the parsed value on the right of the **assignment operator** (=) to the String variable on the left. An **assignment statement** is a line of code beginning with a location, followed by the assignment operator (=), followed by the new data, method, or formula.

JAVA UPDATE Java 2 v5.0

A new class of Scanner objects used for data entry is available in version 5.0. A Scanner object can accept user input from System.in and then call predefined methods to extract the data. Methods such as **nextInt()**, nextDouble(), and nextBoolean() allow direct assignment to the corresponding variable without parsing.

The **Scanner** class is part of the java.util package that must be imported in programs that use Scanner.

If you want to amend the BodyMass program to incorporate Scanner, replace lines 11, 20, 27, and 30, then comment out lines 26 and 29 as shown in the following code.

```
11   import java.util.*;
      ↓
20   Scanner scannerIn= new Scanner(System.in);
      ↓
26   //height = dataIn.readLine();
27   inches = scannerIn.nextInt();
      ↓
29   //weight = dataIn.readLine();
30   pounds = scannerIn.nextInt();
```

Table 3-6 displays the general form of an assignment statement. Note that the assignment operator, which looks like an equal sign, never is used to represent equality in Java. The equality operator (= =) will be discussed later in the chapter.

Table 3-6   Assignment Statements

General form:	1. identifier = value; //simple assignment
	2. dataType identifier = value; //declaration and assignment
	3. identifier = formula; //assigning the result of a formula
	4. identifier = differentIdentifier; //copying data between identifiers
	5. identifier = object.method(); //assigning the result of a method call
	6. identifier = identifier + value; //accumulator
Purpose:	To assign a value to a storage location
Examples:	1. `userAge = 21;`
	2. `boolean flag = false;`
	3. `totalCharge = sales + tax;`
	4. `newLocation = oldData;`
	5. `inches = Integer.parseInt(height);`
	6. `counter = counter + 1;`

Programmers sometimes declare their data and assign it at the same time, as shown in example 2. When using this type of assignment statement, the literal data must match the data type of the identifier. When a formula is used for assignment, as in example 3, the formula is placed on the right side of the assignment operator and the location to store the result is on the left. In example 4, the assignment is a reference to another storage location; therefore, its data is copied from one location to another. In example 5, the assignment is the result of a method call.

Because Java evaluates the code on the right side of the assignment operator before assigning the result to the left side, a special case may arise in which a value is manipulated and then stored back in the same storage location, as shown in example 6. For instance, if you want to track the number of hits on a Web page, you might write code to add 1 to the current counter value each time the page is downloaded from the Web server. The code then stores the updated counter value back in the original counter storage location. The result is an accumulated total called an **accumulator,** or **counter**. Every time Java executes the line of code, a value of 1 will be added to the current counter total. You will learn more about accumulators and counters in a later chapter.

The step on the next page enters code to prompt the user, accept input, and then parse the String responses. If your code runs over to two lines in the TextPad coding window, let the text wrap to the next line; do not press the ENTER key to split the code into two lines. Even if the code wraps to two or more lines in the coding window, Java looks for the semicolon (;) to indicate the end of the line.

To Enter Code for the User Prompts, Inputs, and Conversions

1. With the insertion point on line 22 in the coding window, enter the code from Figure 3-14 on page 147.

The System.out.println(), print(), readLine(), and parseInt() methods are displayed (Figure 3-15). Line 31 is a blank line.

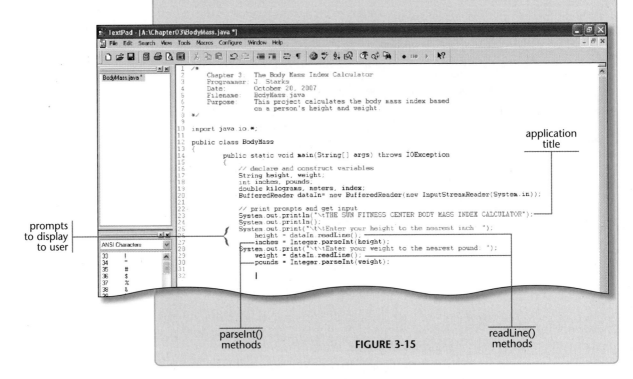

prompts to display to user

application title

parseInt() methods

FIGURE 3-15

readLine() methods

In line 26, the readLine() method takes the value from the dataIn variable location and assigns or copies it to the String location named height. The parseInt() method then converts height to an integer and assigns it to a variable location named inches. Java does not allow two variables with the same name in the same procedure.

Operators

To complete a program task, a Java program may need to manipulate values mathematically, such as adding or subtracting values, or it may need to evaluate values logically, such as testing to see if the hours worked are greater than 40. The Body Mass Index Calculator, for example, must divide the input value for inches by 39.36 to convert it to meters. Performing mathematical or logical operations in Java is similar to other programming languages and uses two basic types of operators: arithmetic and comparison.

Arithmetic Operators

Arithmetic operators manipulate two or more numeric values. Table 3-7 lists seven arithmetic operations, the operator symbols, an example, and example results.

Table 3-7 Arithmetic Operators in Java

OPERATION	OPERATOR SYMBOL	EXAMPLE	RESULT
Cast	(data type) literal or variable	(int) 20.3	20 (conversion to integer results in loss of precision)
Multiplication	*	20 * 3	60
Division	/	20.0/3.0	6.6666667 for float 6.666666666666667 for double
Integer Division	/	20 / 3	6 (the remainder is dropped because the operands both are integers)
Modular Division	%	20 % 3	2 (only the integer remainder is stored)
Addition	+	20 + 3	23
Subtraction	-	20 - 3	17

Table 3-7 lists the arithmetic operators in the order of operator precedence. **Order of operator precedence** is a predetermined order that defines the sequence in which operators are evaluated and resolved when several operations occur in an expression. You may be familiar with most of the arithmetic operators, as operator symbols in Java are similar to regular algebraic symbols. Commonly used arithmetic operators are the plus sign (+), used to add or sum two numbers, and the asterisk (*), used to multiply two numbers.

The less familiar operations, with respect to Java, are integer and modular division. **Integer division** is performed when both the dividend and the divisor are integers. When performing integer division, Java forces the result to be an integer because it is a primitive data type; it then drops any remainder. **Modular division**, or remainder division, is used to store any truncated remainder value from integer division. The **modulus operator** (%), which also is called the remainder operator, is entered between two integers and performs modular division. Modular division is common to many programming languages.

The type of division used in a program can return different results. For example, if you wanted to convert 168 minutes to hours and minutes, regular division using double data types would result in 2.8 hours:

```
decimalAnswer = 168D / 60D;
decimalAnswer = 2.8;
```

On the other hand, using integer or modular division would return a result that separates hours and minutes, rather than the decimal result returned when using regular division. First, integer division would drop the remainder, to result in 2 hours:

integerAnswer = 168 / 60;
integerAnswer = 2;

Modular division, however, would keep only the remainder minutes, to result in 48 minutes:

modulusAnswer = 168 % 60;
modulusAnswer = 48;

The operations of addition, subtraction, multiplication, and division shown in Table 3-7 on the previous page can manipulate any data type. Dividing float or double numbers will yield decimal results. If the operands in a division problem are of different data types, Java **promotes** the integers to floating point values before evaluating the expression.

The integer and modular division operations can manipulate only integers. As previously noted, Java performs integer division only on integer values and drops the remainders in the resulting value. Java performs modular division only on integers and stores the resulting remainder as an integer value. You will learn about other special operators that involve single value arithmetic in a later chapter.

A seventh operation, cast, also is listed in Table 3-7 because it performs a kind of arithmetic on numbers. Sometimes programmers want to force data to convert to a different data type. For example, for calculation or storage purposes, an integer value might be forced to become a double, or the other way around. The **cast operation** converts data from one primitive data type to another by entering the new data type in parentheses before a literal or variable, as shown in Table 3-7.

The ability to cast or convert primitive data types has some advantages. For example, the program in Figure 3-16 calculates the average miles per gallon. The user is asked to input miles and gallons. The input values are parsed in lines 16 and 20 to values that have been declared to be integers in line 9. The average then is calculated by dividing the miles by the gallons (line 23). Normally Java would return an int value because both values in the equation are integers. The average variable, however, has been declared to be a double value. Without the cast, the program would perform the operation on the right side first and would store an integer value in average. With the cast (double) in line 23, the program converts the total to a double before it performs the calculation, which increases the precision of the answer. When Java performs math on mixed data types, the result is always the larger data type. Therefore, when the program divides the casted double named total by the integer named count, the result is a double that subsequently is stored in the variable location named average.

```
1   import java.io.*;
2
3   public class Average
4   {
5        public static void main(String[] args) throws IOException
6        {
7             // declare and construct variables
8             String miles, gallons;
9             int total, count;
10            double average;
11            BufferedReader myIn= new BufferedReader(new InputStreamReader(System.in));
12
13            // print prompts and get input
14            System.out.print("Enter the total number of miles ");
15                miles = myIn.readLine();
16                total = Integer.parseInt(miles);
17
18            System.out.print("Enter the total gallons of gas ");
19                gallons = myIn.readLine();
20                count = Integer.parseInt(gallons);
21
22            // calculations
23            average = (double) total / count;
24
25            // output
26            System.out.println("The average is " + average);
27        }
28  }
```

FIGURE 3-16

Occasionally, programmers use casting in order to truncate decimal places. If, however, a programmer chooses to cast to a smaller data type, he or she then has to assume responsibility for any loss of precision in the operation.

Comparison Operators

Comparison operators involve two values, as do arithmetic operators; however, they compare the numbers rather than perform math on them. As shown in Table 3-8 on the next page, comparison operations include greater than, less than, equal to, or not equal to, or any combination of those operations. While the result in arithmetic formulas evaluates to a numeric value, the result in a comparison operation evaluates to either true or false. Programmers use the boolean data type to store a comparative result of true or false. As an example, the statement

boolean isOvertime = (hours > 40)

would declare a boolean variable, isOvertime, and store a true value if the variable, hours, is greater than 40. The comparison operation is enclosed in parentheses. The identifiers for boolean variables are more easily recognized if a form of the verb, to be, is used as part of the variable name, as in the example above, which uses the variable isOvertime.

Table 3-8 lists the six comparison operations, the operator symbols, and examples of true and false expressions.

Table 3-8   Comparison Operators in Java

OPERATION	OPERATOR SYMBOL	TRUE EXPRESSION	FALSE EXPRESSION
less than	<	(2 < 9)	(9 < 2)
greater than	>	(5 > 1)	(1 > 5)
less than or equal to	<=	(3 <= 4)	(5 <= 4)
greater than or equal to	>=	(8 >= 6)	(3 >= 7)
equal to	==	(9 == 9)	(5 == 9)
not equal to	!=	(4 != 2)	(2 != 2)

The first four comparison operators sometimes are referred to as **relational operators** because they compare the relation of two values; the last two sometimes are called **equality operators**. The double equal sign, ==, is used to differentiate the equal to operation from the assignment operator (=) used in Java. Spaces are not included between comparison operator symbols.

Expressions

When using operators in code, it is important to understand their functions, order of precedence, and purpose in the statement expression. In Java and other programming languages, an **expression** can perform a calculation, manipulate characters, call a method, or test data. Expressions can be divided into two basic categories: numeric and conditional.

Numeric Expressions

A **numeric expression** is any expression that can be evaluated as a number. A numeric expression can include arithmetic operators, values, and variables, as well as methods. The data type of any value in an arithmetic expression must be one of the numeric primitive data types from Table 3-2 on page 140. A numeric expression cannot contain String variables, String literals, or objects.

The values, variables, and methods in a numeric expression often are separated from each other by parentheses and arithmetic operators. A programmer must be concerned with both the form and the evaluation of an expression. It is necessary to consider the purpose of the expression as well as the rules for forming a valid expression before you start to write expressions in Java statements with confidence.

Forming Valid Numeric Expressions

The definition of a numeric expression dictates the manner in which a numeric expression can be validly formed. For example, the following statement formed to assign the identifier, response, twice the value of myAnswer is invalid:

response = 2myAnswer; //Invalid statement

Java will reject the statement because a value (2) and a variable (myAnswer) within the same expression must be separated by an arithmetic operator. The statement can be written validly as:

response = 2 * myAnswer; //Valid statement

It also is invalid to use a String variable or String literal in a numeric expression. The following are invalid numeric expressions:

response = 72 + "BALANCE" / myValue;
response = "45" / myValue + "answer" – 19;

Evaluation of Numeric Expressions

As you form complex numeric expressions involving several arithmetic operations, it is important to consider the order in which Java will evaluate the expression. For example, in evaluating the expression:

answer = 16 / 4 / 2

would the result assign 2 or 8 to the identifer, answer? The answer depends on how you evaluate the expression. If you complete the operation 16 / 4 first, and only then 4 / 2, the expression yields the value 2. If you complete the second operation, 4 / 2, first, and only then 16 / 2, it yields 8.

Java follows the normal algebraic rules to evaluate an expression. The normal algebraic rules that define the order in which the operations are evaluated are as follows: unless parentheses dictate otherwise, reading from left to right in a numeric expression, all multiplications and/or divisions are performed first, then all integer divisions, then all modular divisions, and finally all additions and/or subtractions. Following these algebraic rules, Java would evaluate the expression 16 / 4 / 2 to yield a value of 2.

Tip

Order of Operator Precedence

Unless parentheses dictate otherwise, Java evaluates expressions and performs all operations in the following order:

1. multiplication and/or division
2. integer division
3. modular division
4. addition and/or subtraction

When multiple operations of the same kind exist, Java performs the operations left to right.

This order of operator precedence, which defines the order in which operators are evaluated, sometimes also is called the rules of precedence, or the hierarchy of operations. The meaning of these rules can be made clear with some examples.

For example, the expression 18 / 3 − 2 + 4 * 2 is evaluated as follows:

18 / 3 − 2 + 4 * 2
6 − 2 + 4 * 2
6 − 2 + 8
4 + 8
12

If you have trouble following the logic behind this evaluation, use the following technique. Whenever a numeric expression is to be evaluated, read or scan, the expression from left to right four different times and apply the order of operator precedence rules outlined above each time you read the expression. On the first scan, moving from left to right, every time you encounter the operators, * and /, perform the required operation: multiplication or division. Hence, 18 is divided by 3, yielding 6, and 4 and 2 are multiplied, yielding 8.

On the second scan, from left to right, perform all integer division. On the third scan, from left to right, perform all modular division. This example includes no integer division or modular division, so no operations are performed.

On the fourth scan, moving again from left to right, every time you encounter the operators, + and −, perform addition and subtraction. In this example, 2 is subtracted from 6 resulting in 4. Then it is added to 8 for a total of 12.

The following expression includes five arithmetic operators and yields a value of −3.

5 * 3 % 2 + 7 / 2 − 7
15 % 2 + 7 / 2 − 7   **<-end of first scan – multiplication performed**
15 % 2 + 3 − 7   **<-end of second scan – integer division performed**
1 + 3 − 7   **<-end of third scan – modular division performed**
−3   **<-end of fourth scan – addition and subtraction performed**

In later chapters, you will add to the hierarchy of operations as you learn about operators that manipulate single operands.

Conditional Expressions

A **conditional expression** is any expression that can be evaluated as true or false. A conditional expression can include comparison operators, values, and variables, as well as methods. The resulting data type after a conditional expression is evaluated is boolean. A conditional expression may contain String variables and String literals. Table 3-8 on page 154 displays examples of conditional expressions.

Conditional expressions are governed by validity and operator precedence rules that are similar to those used with numeric expressions. Valid conditional expressions that use two operands must separate the operands with a comparison operator. Unless parentheses dictate otherwise, conditional expressions are evaluated from left to right. When multiple comparison operators exist in the same statement, relational operators take precedence over equality operators. For example, in the following expression, the operations are performed left to right, resulting in a value of false:

10 < 5 = = true
false = = true   <-first scan, less than operator evaluated
false   <-second scan, equality operator evaluated

If you have trouble following the logic behind this evaluation, use the following technique. Whenever a conditional expression is to be evaluated, scan the expression from left to right two different times and apply the order of operator precedence rules outlined above each time you read the expression. On the first scan, moving from left to right, every time you encounter the operators <, >, <=, or >=, perform the required operation: less than, greater than, less than or equal to, greater than or equal to. Hence, 10 < 5 evaluated to false.

On the second scan, moving again from left to right, every time you encounter the operators == and !=, evaluate for equality and nonequality. In the above example, false does not equal true, which results in a false expression. You will learn more about conditional expressions in later chapters.

Using Parentheses in Expressions

Parentheses may be used to change the order of operations. In Java, parentheses normally are used to avoid ambiguity and to group terms in a numeric or conditional expression. The order in which the operations in an expression containing parentheses are evaluated can be stated as follows: when parentheses are inserted into an expression, the part of the expression within the parentheses is evaluated first, then the remaining expression is evaluated according to the normal rules of operator precedence.

Tip

Use of Parentheses in Expressions
When parentheses are inserted into an expression, the part of the expression within the parentheses is evaluated first, then the remaining expression is evaluated according to the normal rules of operator precedence.

If the first numeric expression example were rewritten with parentheses as 18 / (3 − 2) + 4 * 2, then it would be evaluated in the following manner:

18 / (3 − 2) + 4 * 2
18 / 1 + 4 * 2
18 + 4 * 2
18 + 8
26

Evaluating numeric expressions with parentheses should be done as follows: make four scans from left to right within each pair of parentheses, and only after doing this make the standard four passes over the entire numeric expression.

Evaluating conditional expressions with parentheses should be done as follows: make two scans from left to right within each pair of parentheses, and only after doing this make the standard two passes over the entire conditional expression.

When coding a numeric expression, use parentheses freely when in doubt as to the valid form and evaluation of a numeric expression. For example, if you wish to have Java divide 6 * D by 5 * P, the expression may be written correctly as 6 * D / 5 * P, but it also may be written in the following manner:

(6 * D) / (5 * P)

> **Tip**
>
> ### Using Parentheses When Coding Numeric or Conditional Expressions
>
> When coding numeric or conditional expressions, use parentheses freely if you are unsure about operator precedence and the form of a valid expression. Using parentheses helps to provide clarity when the expression is evaluated.

For more complex expressions, Java allows parentheses to be contained within other parentheses. When this occurs, the parentheses are said to be **nested**. In this case, Java evaluates the innermost parenthetical expression first, then goes on to the outermost parenthetical expression. Thus, 18 / 3 * 2 + (3 * (2 + 5)) is broken down in the following manner:

> **18 / 3 * 2 + (3 * (2 + 5))**
> **18 / 3 * 2 + (3 * 7)**
> **18 / 3 * 2 + 21**
> **6 * 2 + 21**
> **12 + 21**
> **33**

When coding expressions, be sure to avoid two common errors. First, check that you have surrounded the correct part of an expression with parentheses. Second, check that you have balanced the parentheses by verifying that the expression has as many close parentheses as open parentheses.

Construction of Error-Free Expressions

If you have written an expression observing the order of precedence rules, Java can translate the expression without generating any error messages. This, however, is no guarantee that Java actually will be able to evaluate it. In other words, although a numeric expression may be formed in a valid fashion, Java may not be able to evaluate it because of the data type of the numbers involved or some other logic error. In situations where error conditions arise during compilation, Java will display an error message.

Applying the following rules when coding expressions should help you avoid such hazards:

1. Do not attempt to divide by zero.
2. Do not attempt to determine the square root of a negative value.
3. Do not attempt to raise a negative value to a non-integer value.

4. Do not attempt to compute a value that is greater than the largest permissible value or less than the smallest permissible nonzero value for the data type.

5. Do not try to compare different data types in a conditional expression.

The Math Class

Numeric expressions in formulas are the most common use of operators in Java, although some math functions cannot be performed with operators alone. Figure 3-17 displays the formulas used in the Body Mass Index Calculator program. While the first two formulas can be written with operators, the third one needs a special method to calculate the answer.

```
32          // calculations
33          meters = inches / 39.36;
34          kilograms = pounds / 2.2;
35          index = kilograms / Math.pow(meters,2);
36
```

FIGURE 3-17

In the first formula, inches are converted to meters by dividing them by 39.36 (line 33). Pounds are converted to kilograms by dividing by 2.2 (line 34). When int variables, such as inches and pounds, are divided by double values such as 39.36 and 2.2, Java stores the answer as the larger data type. Meters and kilograms thus were declared to be double in line 19 (Figure 3-9 on page 141).

The final formula for BMI is calculated by dividing kilograms by the meters squared, which calls for an exponent. The process of raising a number to the power of an exponent is called **exponentiation**. In some math notations, a caret sign ($\wedge$) is used to denote an exponent. For example, $4 \wedge 2$ is the same as 4^2 and is equal to 16, and $3 \wedge 4$ is the same as 3^4 and is equal to 81. Even though Java has no exponentiation operator, it easily is accomplished by using a prewritten method from the Math class. The **Math class**, which is part of the java.lang package, contains methods for a number of useful functions, such as rounding, exponentiation, randomizing, and square roots. Methods from the Math class have the general form shown in Table 3-9 on the next page. The table displays only some of the many methods from the Math class; a complete listing is available in the Java API.

Table 3-9 Methods from the Math Class

General form:	Math.method(arguments)		
Purpose:	The Math class contains methods for performing basic numeric operations such as the elementary exponential, logarithm, square root, and trigonometric functions.		
Examples:			
METHOD	DESCRIPTION	EXAMPLE CODE	RESULT
abs()	Absolute value	Math.abs(-75)	75
max()	Higher of two numbers	Math.max(99,41)	99
min()	Lower of two numbers	Math.min(99,41)	41
pow()	Exponentiation	Math.pow(2,5)	32
random()	Random number generator	Math.random()	0< value >1
round()	Rounding to an integer	Math.round(27.59)	28
sqrt()	Square root	Math.sqrt(144)	12

Recall that the values inside the parentheses are the arguments — the pieces of information the method needs to perform its task. The arguments in most Math methods can be literals (as in the table examples), variables, or calls to other methods. The **pow() method**, used to express exponentiation as in meters squared, requires two arguments: the base number and the exponent. A comma separates the arguments.

Perform the following step to enter the formulas.

To Enter the Formulas

1. With the insertion point on line 32 in the coding window, enter the code from Figure 3-17 on the previous page.

The formulas to convert input values to metric and to calculate the BMI are entered (Figure 3-18). Line 36 is a blank line.

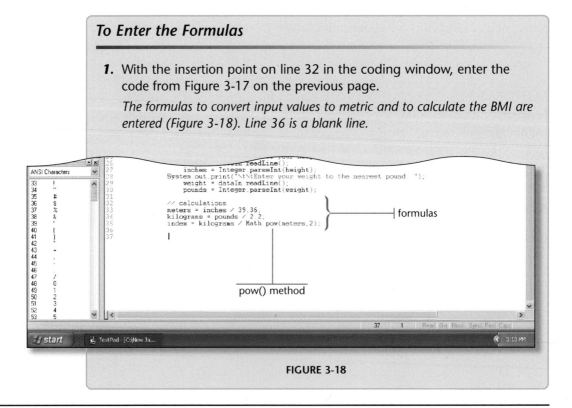

FIGURE 3-18

In general, you invoke Java methods by typing the class name followed by a period followed by the method name. As you have learned, classes must be imported before they can be used. Because the Math class is part of the java.lang default package, it needs no previous import statement.

Program Output

After all calculations are performed, the program should display appropriate output to the user. The output for the Body Mass Index Calculator program is a message indicating the user's calculated BMI.

Using Variables in Output

The println() method commonly displays a string of characters, but it also can display values from variable locations. Table 3-10 displays some forms of the println() method.

Table 3-10 The println() Method	
General form:	1. System.out.println("literal"); 2. System.out.println(String variable); 3. System.out.println(numeric variable); 4. System.out.print("literal"); System.out.println(variable); 5. System.out.println("literal" + variable); 6. System.out.println(Class.method(arguments)); 7. System.out.println("");
Purpose:	To display output on the standard output device

Examples:	```1. System.out.println("Anita's Antiques");```
	```2. System.out.println(firstName);```
	```3. System.out.println(dSalesTax);```
	```4. System.out.print("The answer is ");```
	``` System.out.println(answer);```
	```5. System.out.println("The answer is " + answer);```
	```6. System.out.println(Math.round(answer));```
	```7. System.out.println(""); //prints a blank line```

Remember that System.out refers to the default output device, usually the monitor. The println() method can display a literal string of characters, using code such as that in example 1. For Java to display the values from variable locations to users, the program code must use a variable identifier as the argument of the println() method, as shown in examples 2 and 3.

If you want to combine strings of characters and variables on the same line, the code can take one of two forms. First, you can use the print() method followed by println() method, as in example 4. The print() method does not force a new line after displaying, so any output following a print() method will display in the same line.

A second way, as shown in example 5 on the previous page, combines Strings and variables in the same line using concatenation. Using a plus sign (+), Java allows a **concatenation**, or joining, of these types of data in a single output line of code. In both example 4 and 5, leaving a space after the word, is, keeps the message and the answer from running together.

Additionally, programmers may invoke methods in their output, as shown in example 6. The Math.round() method rounds the answer to the nearest integer; the println() method then prints the answer.

The output code for the Body Mass Index Calculator program is shown in Figure 3-19. Line 39 begins with an escape character tab, followed by text. Then the index value from the previous calculation is rounded to an integer with the Math.round() method and concatenated to the text, YOUR BODY MASS INDEX IS. Finally, a period is concatenated to complete the output sentence. Lines 38 and 40 print blank lines before and after the output message. Lines 41 and 42 are the closing braces for the main() method and class blocks, respectively.

```
37          // output
38          System.out.println();
39          System.out.println("\tYOUR BODY MASS INDEX IS " + Math.round(index) + ".");
40          System.out.println();
41      }
42  }
```

FIGURE 3-19

The following step enters the code that uses variables, concatenation, and the Math.round() method to produce output on the display.

To Enter Code to Display Output

1. With the insertion point on line 37 in the coding window, type the code from Figure 3-19.

   The output code is displayed in the coding window (Figure 3-20). The calculated BMI will display as a rounded integer value in the same line as the output message. Depending on your TextPad settings, the closing brace in line 42 may display in a different column.

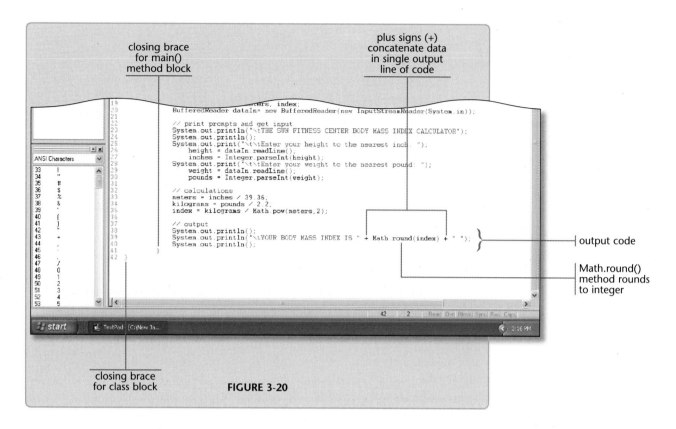

FIGURE 3-20

The program now is complete. You coded the documentation; the opening class and method headers; the declaration of variables; the prompts, inputs, and conversions; the calculations; and the output. Check the code to ensure that the syntax, spelling, capitalization, and indentations are correct. When you are confident everything is correct, you are ready to save and compile your program.

Compiling, Running, and Documenting the Application

The Java source code for the Body Mass Index Calculator program must be compiled before it can be executed and tested. Once the program is running correctly, it is a good idea to print a copy of the source code for documentation.

Compiling the Source Code

Recall that the compiler automatically saves the program and then translates the source code into Java bytecode. To compile the program, you will use the Compile Java command on TextPad's Tools menu, as shown in the step on the next page.

To Compile the Source Code

1. With your Data Disk in drive A, click Tools on the menu bar. Click Compile Java on the Tools menu.

TextPad compiles the program. If TextPad notifies you of compilation errors, fix the errors in the BodyMass coding window and then compile the program again.

Now that the program has been compiled into bytecode, you are ready to execute, or run, the program and test the results of the coded calculations.

Running and Testing the Application

When you run an interactive Java program, such as the console application version of the Body Mass Index Calculator, prompts will be displayed in the command prompt window. The bytecode runs in the command prompt window, pausing every time the readLine() method is executed, to allow the user to enter the data requested in the prompt. To test the program, programmers typically use the sample data that they created during program design and any sample data from the requirements document. During execution and testing, the programmer acts as the user, entering data from a user's perspective as the program runs.

The following steps execute and test the application.

To Run and Test the Application

1. If necessary, click BodyMass.java in the Selector window in TextPad. Click Tools on the menu bar and then click Run Java Application on the Tools menu. Type 67 in response to the first prompt.

The command prompt window displays the first prompt and user response (Figure 3-21).

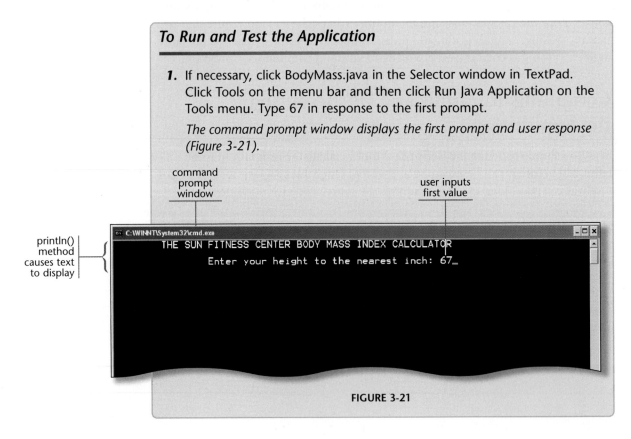

FIGURE 3-21

2. Press the ENTER key. Type 145 in response to the second prompt.

The command prompt window displays the second prompt and user response (Figure 3-22).

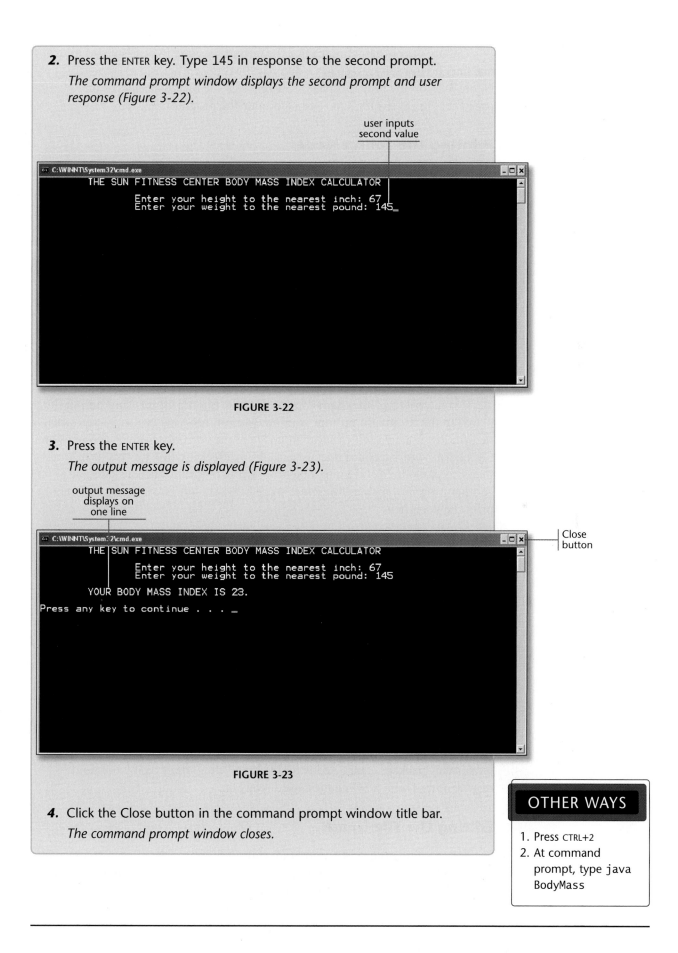

user inputs
second value

```
C:\WINNT\System32\cmd.exe
               THE SUN FITNESS CENTER BODY MASS INDEX CALCULATOR

                    Enter your height to the nearest inch: 67
                    Enter your weight to the nearest pound: 145_
```

FIGURE 3-22

3. Press the ENTER key.

The output message is displayed (Figure 3-23).

output message
displays on
one line

Close
button

```
C:\WINNT\System32\cmd.exe
               THE SUN FITNESS CENTER BODY MASS INDEX CALCULATOR

                    Enter your height to the nearest inch: 67
                    Enter your weight to the nearest pound: 145

          YOUR BODY MASS INDEX IS 23.
Press any key to continue . . . _
```

FIGURE 3-23

4. Click the Close button in the command prompt window title bar.

The command prompt window closes.

OTHER WAYS

1. Press CTRL+2
2. At command prompt, type java BodyMass

The use of concatenation causes the output message to be displayed in one line. If your screen displays a different BMI than what is displayed in Figure 3-23 on the previous page, double check the formulas entered on page 160. Fix any errors, save, and recompile the program.

Printing the Source Code

You may want to print a copy of the BodyMass source code for documentation purposes or for reference, as you modify the program to create different versions of the program. The following steps print a copy of the source code.

To Print the Source Code

1. Click the Print button on the Standard toolbar in the TextPad window. *The source code prints on the printer.*
2. Retrieve the printout from the printer.

If you want to print a hard copy of the title, input prompts, and output displayed in the command prompt window, you can press ALT+PRINT SCREEN when the window is active, which saves an image of the current screen to the Windows Clipboard (your keyboard may use a slightly different name for this key). You then can paste the picture into a picture editing program, such as Paint, or another program, such as Microsoft Word or Microsoft PowerPoint, and then print the document.

Using Swing Components

In 1997, Sun Microsystems introduced a new set of GUI components commonly referred to as **Swing components**. As a part of the newer Java Foundation Classes (JFC) that encompass a group of features to help people build graphical user interfaces, Swing components are implemented with no native code. Because Swing components are not restricted to the least common denominator — that is, the features that are present on every platform — they can have more functionality than Abstract Window Toolkit (AWT) components.

As defined during program design, a second version of the Body Mass Index Calculator must be developed as a console application that will accept input via dialog boxes. As you modify the Body Mass Index Calculator program, you will edit the file name, change the import statement to import classes in the javax.swing package, change code to display a Swing input dialog box, and display output with a Swing message dialog box.

Editing the File Name

Before editing the existing program code, it is appropriate to assign a new file name to the new version of the program code. The new file name not only distinguishes it from the previous version but also better reflects the purpose of the code in the new file. The file thus is given the file name BodyMassSwing.java.

Using a file name such as BodyMassSwing.java instead of BodyMassVersion2 .java more closely represents the purpose of the program and is easier to remember. To change the file name in the program code, you can use TextPad's search and replace function, which makes global changes to text easy.

The following steps edit the file name and class header to reflect the new file name.

To Edit the File Name and Class Header

1. With the TextPad coding window displaying the BodyMass source code, click Search on the menu bar.

The Search menu is displayed (Figure 3-24).

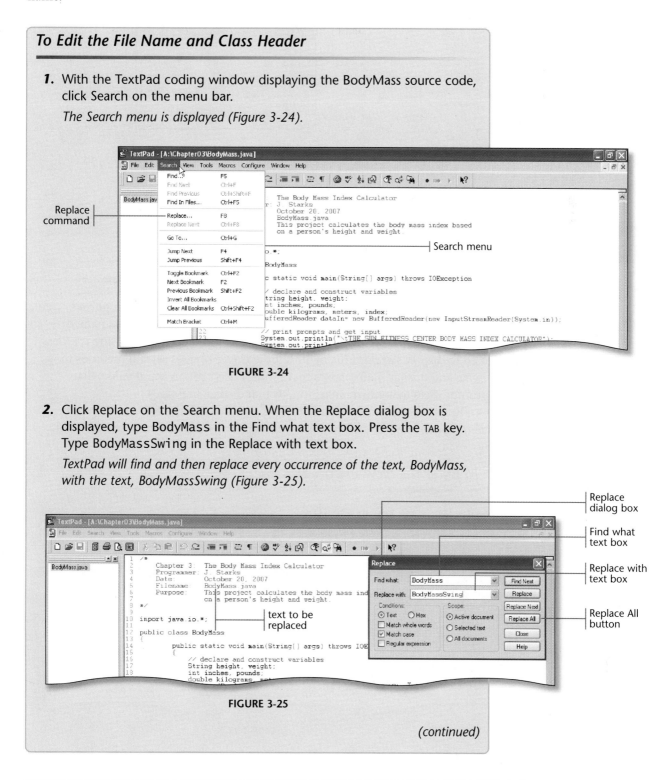

FIGURE 3-24

2. Click Replace on the Search menu. When the Replace dialog box is displayed, type BodyMass in the Find what text box. Press the TAB key. Type BodyMassSwing in the Replace with text box.

TextPad will find and then replace every occurrence of the text, BodyMass, with the text, BodyMassSwing (Figure 3-25).

FIGURE 3-25

(continued)

3. Click the Replace All button.

TextPad replaces the text, BodyMass, with the text, BodyMassSwing, in lines 5 and 12 (Figure 3-26).

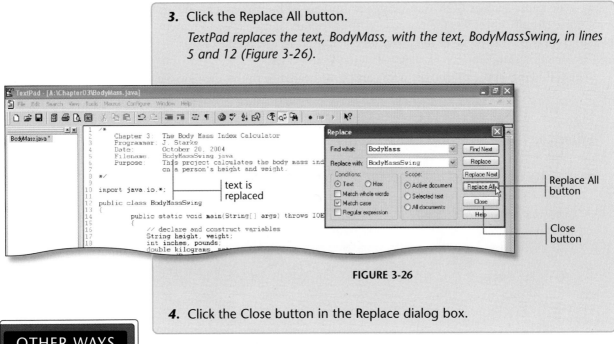

Replace All button

Close button

FIGURE 3-26

4. Click the Close button in the Replace dialog box.

OTHER WAYS

1. On Standard toolbar, click Replace button
2. Press F8

Importing Classes from the javax.swing Package

The import statement in line 10 of the BodyMass.java code imported classes from the java.io package. The new code must import a class named javax.swing.JOptionPane from the javax.swing package. **JOptionPane** is a class used to display standard dialog boxes; the class provides several methods to create and display dialog boxes that prompt users for an input value, that prompt users to confirm an action, or that display messages.

To replace a line of code in TextPad, double-click the line number and then type the new code. The following steps enter the new import statement.

To Enter the New import Statement

1. Select the text in line 10.

The text is selected (Figure 3-27).

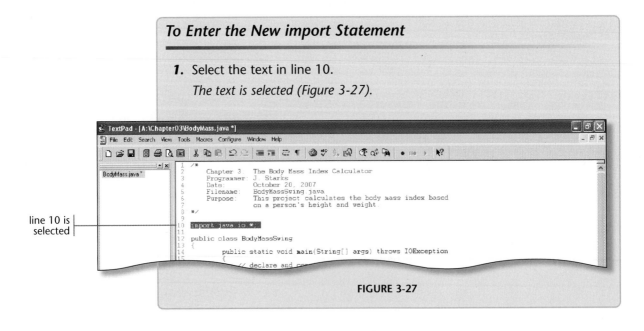

line 10 is selected

FIGURE 3-27

2. Type import javax.swing.JOptionPane; to replace the text. Press the ENTER key if necessary, to maintain a blank line 11.

The JOptionPane class from the javax.swing package will be imported (Figure 3-28).

import statement
to import
JOptionPane class

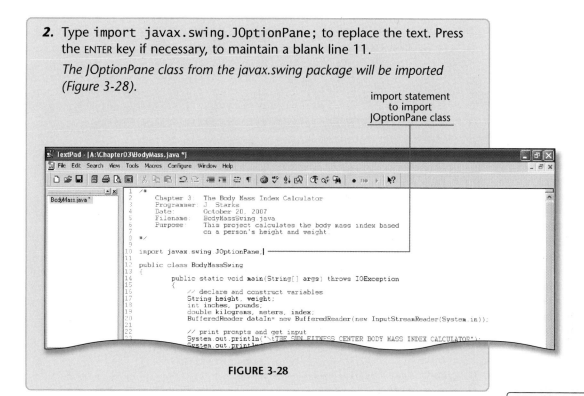

FIGURE 3-28

OTHER WAYS

1. To select line, triple-click line

Deleting Existing Code

In the Swing version of the Body Mass Index Calculator, the Swing dialog boxes will take care of buffering the data from the user and handling IO errors so that classes and methods from the java.io package, such as the BufferedReader class in line 20, are no longer necessary. Additionally, the Swing version of the Body Mass Index Calculator no longer needs blank lines to print in the command prompt window. While these lines do not affect the output or calculations of the program, they are unnecessary.

The following steps remove unnecessary code. To select an entire line, you can double-click the line number or triple-click the line itself.

To Delete Existing Code

1. Drag through the text, throws IOException, in line 14 to select it. Press the DELETE key.

(continued)

2. One at a time, select lines 40, 38, 24, and 20 and then press the DELETE key to delete each line.

The TextPad coding window displays the program code, with the unnecessary code deleted (Figure 3-29).

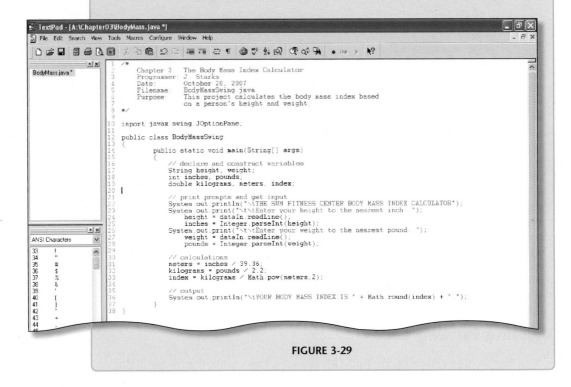

```
1  /*
2     Chapter 3    The Body Mass Index Calculator
3     Programmer:  J  Starks
4     Date:        October 20, 2007
5     Filename.    BodyMassSwing.java
6     Purpose:     This project calculates the body mass index based
7                  on a person's height and weight.
8  */
9
10 import javax.swing.JOptionPane;
11
12 public class BodyMassSwing
13 {
14     public static void main(String[] args)
15     {
16         // declare and construct variables
17         String height, weight;
18         int inches, pounds;
19         double kilograms, meters, index;
20
21         // print prompts and get input
22         System.out.println("\t\tTHE SUN FITNESS CENTER BODY MASS INDEX CALCULATOR");
23         System.out.print("\t\tEnter your height to the nearest inch  ");
24         height = dataIn.readLine();
25         inches = Integer.parseInt(height);
26         System.out.print("\t\tEnter your weight to the nearest pound. ");
27         weight = dataIn.readLine();
28         pounds = Integer.parseInt(weight);
29
30         // calculations
31         meters = inches / 39.36;
32         kilograms = pounds / 2.2;
33         index = kilograms / Math.pow(meters,2);
34
35         // output
36         System.out.println("\tYOUR BODY MASS INDEX IS " + Math.round(index) + ".");
37     }
38 }
```

FIGURE 3-29

Creating Swing Dialog Boxes

The Swing JOptionPane class provides many methods that make it easy for programmers to display standard dialog boxes, including methods to show a confirmation, input, or message dialog box. Table 3-11 shows the basic syntax of any JOptionPane method. Table 3-12 displays some of the show methods associated with the JOptionPane class of dialog boxes.

Table 3-11   JOptionPane Methods

General form:	JOptionPane.method(arguments)
Purpose:	To create a dialog box on the screen
Examples:	1. `String answer = JOptionPane.showInputDialog("What is your name?");` 2. `JOptionPane.showMessageDialog(null, "It's been a pleasure to serve you", "Thank You Box", JOptionPane.PLAIN_MESSAGE);` 3. `JOptionPane.showConfirmDialog(null, "Please choose one", "Confirm Box", JOptionPane.YES_NO_OPTION);`

Table 3-12   JOptionPane show Methods

METHOD	PURPOSE	EXAMPLE
1. showInputDialog()	Prompts for input	JOptionPane.showInputDialog(null, "message");
2. showMessageDialog()	Displays information to the user	JOptionPane.showMessageDialog(null, "message", "title bar caption", messageType);
3. showConfirmDialog()	Asks a confirming question, like yes/no/cancel	JOptionPane.showConfirmDialog(null, "message", "title bar caption", messageType);

In the first example shown in Table 3-11, the showInputDialog() method displays a dialog box with a message and a text box for user input. The showInputDialog() method actually is assigned to a String variable with an assignment statement. Figure 3-30 shows a typical input dialog box that displays when the JOptionPane.showInputDialog() method is used.

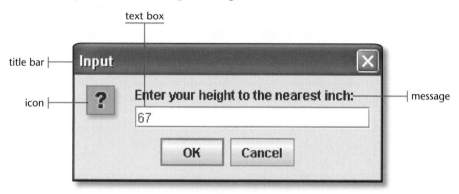

FIGURE 3-30

The second and third examples in Table 3-12 each use four method arguments. The first argument indicates the placement of the dialog box on the screen. The Java keyword, null, instructs the program to display the dialog box centered within the program's active window. The second argument represents the display area inside the dialog box and can be an object, icon, component, or String. The third argument indicates the caption that appears on the title bar. The fourth argument refers to one of various constants defined in the JOptionPane class. A **constant** is a value that Java understands to have a certain, intrinsic meaning. In the case of JOptionPane dialog boxes, the argument refers to one of several styles of dialog boxes with displayed icons, as shown in Table 3-13 on the next page.

Table 3-13   Constant Message Types

MESSAGE TYPE	DISPLAYED ICON
ERROR_MESSAGE	
INFORMATION_MESSAGE	
WARNING_MESSAGE	
QUESTION_MESSAGE	
PLAIN_MESSAGE	no icon display

JOptionPane dialog boxes can return a value. In the case of an input dialog box (example 1 in Table 3-12 on the previous page), the returned value is the data entered into the text box by the user. In example 2, a message box simply displays a message and has no return value. In example 3, the return value is an integer indicating the option selected by the user.

The following steps replace the readLine() methods with JOptionPane showMessageDialog() and showInputDialog() methods, as shown in Table 3-14.

Table 3-14   Replacing Code to Create Swing Dialog Boxes

LINE	DELETE OLD CODE	REPLACE WITH NEW CODE
36	System.out.println("\tYOUR BODY MASS INDEX IS " + Math.round(index) + ".");	JOptionPane.showMessageDialog(null, "YOUR BODY MASS INDEX IS " + Math.round(index) +".", "Body Mass Calculator",JOptionPane.PLAIN_MESSAGE);
26, 27	System.out.print("\t\tEnter your weight to the nearest pound: "); weight = dataIn.readLine();	weight=JOptionPane.showInputDialog(null, "Enter your weight to the nearest pound: ");
23, 24	System.out.print("\t\tEnter your height to the nearest inch: "); height = dataIn.readLine();	height=JOptionPane.showInputDialog(null, "Enter your height to the nearest inch: ");

To Enter Code to Create Swing Dialog Boxes

1. Select line 36. Type the new code from Table 3-14.

2. Select lines 26 and 27. Type the new code from Table 3-14.

3. Select lines 23 and 24. Type the new code from Table 3-14.

The code to create Swing dialog boxes is displayed (Figure 3-31). Your code may wrap differently.

showInputDialog() methods to display input dialog boxes

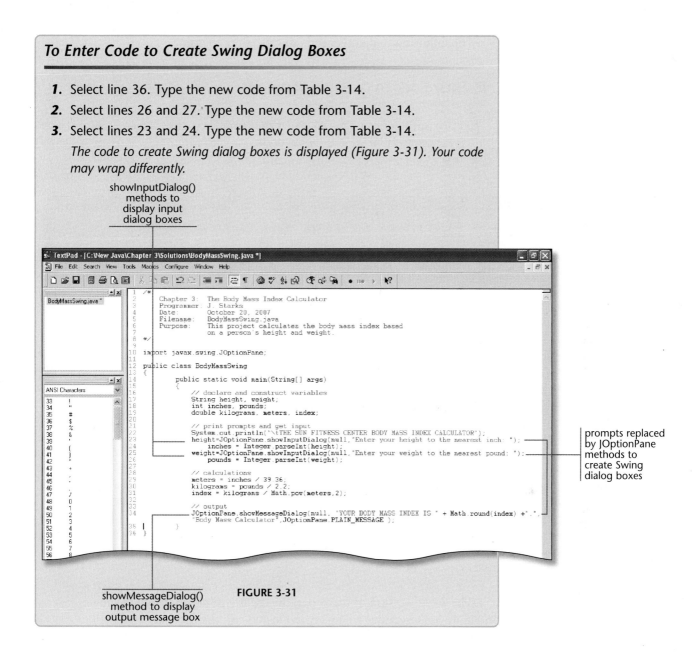

prompts replaced by JOptionPane methods to create Swing dialog boxes

showMessageDialog() method to display output message box

FIGURE 3-31

Closing Programs That Use Swing

One more line of code is necessary in order to close programs that use Swing dialog boxes, after the program ends. The System class provides an **exit() method**, which is used to terminate an application that displays a graphical user interface, such as a dialog box. The method accepts an integer argument that serves as a status code. A 0 (zero) indicates that the application has terminated successfully. A value of 1 typically indicates abnormal termination. If you do not include a System.exit(0); statement at the end of the program code, the command prompt window will not close at the end of the program.

The following step enters code to close the program.

To Enter Code to Close the Program

1. Click at the end of line 34. Press the ENTER key twice. Type
System.exit(0); as the new code.

The code for the System.exit() method is entered (Figure 3-32).

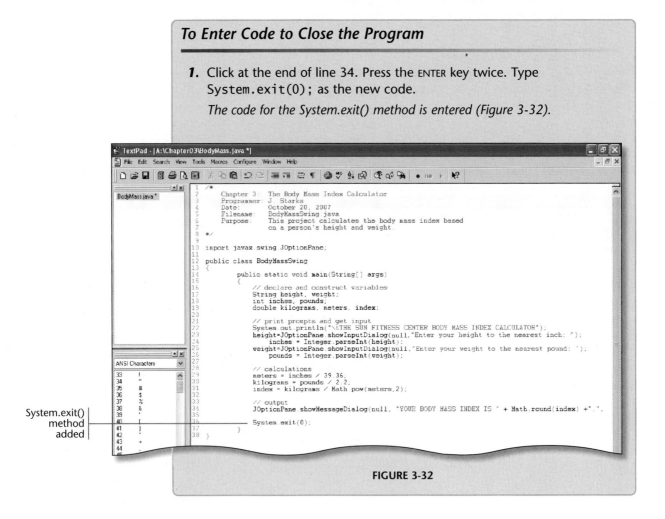

System.exit()
method
added

FIGURE 3-32

The Swing version of the program now is complete. The code shown
in Figure 3-32 includes a new import statement; the new class name,
BodyMassSwing; and has no unnecessary code. It also includes code to
prompt the user and to accept a String answer using dialog boxes. Finally, the
code includes a System.exit() method, so that the program will terminate
properly.

Once the code is complete, check for syntax, proper spelling, capitalization,
and indentations. When you are confident everything is correct, you are ready to
save and compile your program.

Saving, Compiling, and Running the Swing Version

The Java source code for the Swing version of the Body Mass Index Calculator program must be saved with a new file name and then compiled before it can be executed and tested. Once the program is running correctly, a copy of the source code can be printed for documentation.

Saving and Compiling the Swing Version

As you have learned, Java program names must be the same as the class statement at the beginning of the code. The program thus must be saved by using the Save As command and indicating the new file name, BodyMassSwing, before it can be compiled. The following steps save the source code file on the Data Disk with a new file name and then compile the source code.

To Save and Compile the Source Code

1. With the Data Disk in drive A, click File on the menu bar and then click Save As.
2. When the Save As dialog box is displayed, type BodyMassSwing in the File name text box.
3. If necessary, click the Save as type box arrow and then click Java (*.java) in the list.
4. If necessary, click the Save in box arrow and then click 3½ Floppy (A:) in the list. Double-click the Chapter03 folder.
5. Click the Save button in the Save As dialog box.
6. Click Tools on the menu bar and then click Compile Java.

   The program is saved with a new file name on the Data Disk and then compiled. If TextPad notifies you of compilation errors, fix the errors in the BodyMassSwing coding window and then compile the program again.

OTHER WAYS

1. To Save As, press F12
2. To compile, press CTRL+1
3. To compile, at command prompt, type javac BodyMassSwing .java

Running and Testing the Swing Program

When testing different versions of the same program, it is a good idea to use the same sample data for each test. That way you can compare output results to ensure that they are consistent for all versions of the program. The steps on the next page run and test the interactive program BodyMassSwing.

To Run and Test the Swing Program

1. Click Tools on the menu bar and then click Run Java Application on the Tools menu. When the height Input dialog box is displayed, type 67 in the text box.

The command prompt window displays the program name (Figure 3-33). The height Input dialog box, which is displayed in front of the command prompt window, includes a text box for input.

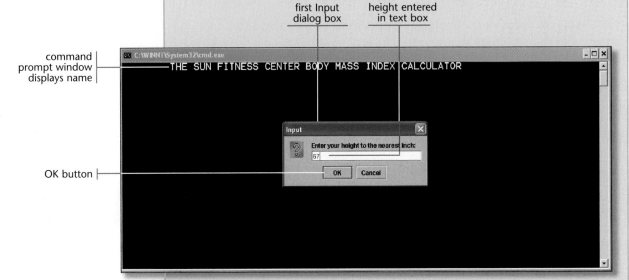

FIGURE 3-33

2. Click the OK button. When the weight Input dialog box is displayed, type 145 in the text box.

The height Input dialog box closes and the weight Input dialog box is displayed (Figure 3-34). The weight value is entered in the text box.

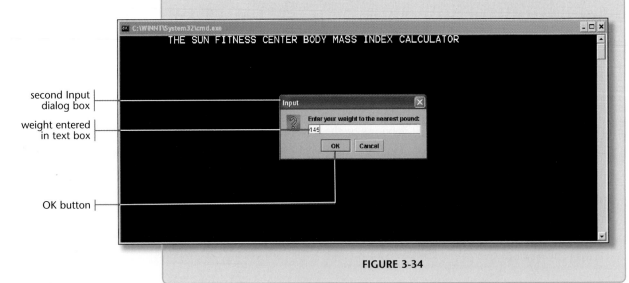

FIGURE 3-34

3. Click the OK button.

The message box showing the user the Body Mass Index is displayed (Figure 3-35). The calculated BMI value displayed should be 23, the same value calculated by the previous version of the program.

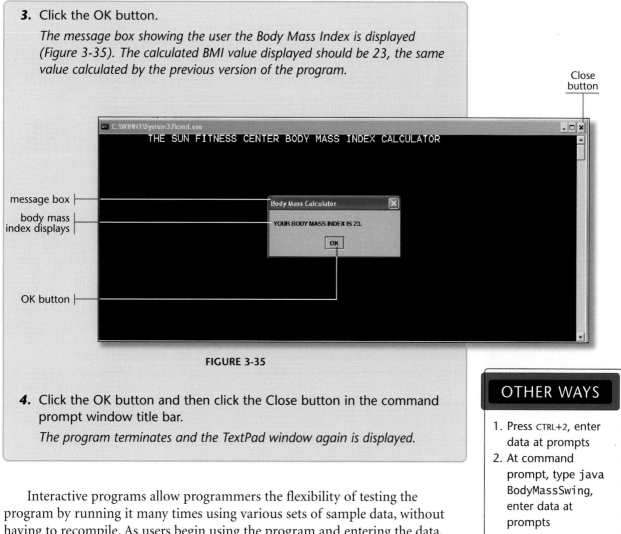

Close button

message box
body mass index displays
OK button

FIGURE 3-35

4. Click the OK button and then click the Close button in the command prompt window title bar.

The program terminates and the TextPad window again is displayed.

Interactive programs allow programmers the flexibility of testing the program by running it many times using various sets of sample data, without having to recompile. As users begin using the program and entering the data, many things could go wrong, such as entering incorrect information or unrealistic data. This chapter does not attempt to account for all of the possible errors that might occur; errors and exception handling are covered in more detail in later chapters. If, however, the program is run with data that makes sense, and the data is entered correctly, the correct answer will display.

Once you have determined that the program runs correctly, you should print a copy of the BodyMassSwing source code for documentation purposes. You can print a copy of the program code from the TextPad coding window by using the Print command on the File menu. A printout of the program code will be sent to the default printer. Figure 3-36 on the next page shows the printout of the program code for the Swing version of the Body Mass Index Calculator. As shown in Figure 3-36, long lines of code sometimes wrap to the next line on hard copies.

Your printout may not display line numbers. To print line numbers, see Appendix C, pages APP 50 through APP 52.

```
     BodyMassSwing.java                                                    10/9/2007
 1   /*
 2         Chapter 3:   The Body Mass Index Calculator
 3         Programmer:  J. Starks
 4         Date:        October 20, 2007
 5         Filename:    BodyMassSwing.java
 6         Purpose:     This project calculates the body mass index based
 7                      on a person's height and weight.
 8   */
 9
10   import javax.swing.JOptionPane;
11
12   public class BodyMassSwing
13   {
14         public static void main(String[] args)
15         {
16              // declare and construct variables
17              String height, weight;
18              int inches, pounds;
19              double kilograms, meters, index;
20
21              // print prompts and get input
22              System.out.println("\tTHE SUN FITNESS CENTER BODY MASS INDEX CALCULATOR");
23              height=JOptionPane.showInputDialog(null,
                     "Enter your height to the nearest inch: ");
24                   inches = Integer.parseInt(height);
25              weight=JOptionPane.showInputDialog(null,
                     "Enter your weight to the nearest pound: ");
26                   pounds = Integer.parseInt(weight);
27
28              // calculations
29              meters = inches / 39.36;
30              kilograms = pounds / 2.2;
31              index = kilograms / Math.pow(meters,2);
32
33              // output
34              JOptionPane.showMessageDialog(null, "YOUR BODY MASS INDEX IS " + Math.round(
                     index) +".", "Body Mass Calculator",JOptionPane.PLAIN_MESSAGE);
35
36              System.exit(0);
37         }
38   }
```

long text lines wrap to next line of printout

FIGURE 3-36

Moving to the Web

The final version of the program for the Body Mass Index Calculator is to create an applet. Recall that an applet is a program called from within another environment, usually a Web page. In order to convert the Body Mass Index Calculator from a console application that runs in the command prompt window to an applet that will display as part of a Web page, you will need to create four kinds of objects: an Image, Labels, TextFields, and Buttons.

In Chapter 2, you learned that an applet uses different Java packages than an application and thus must import the java.awt and java.applet class packages needed to support the applet-related methods. Recall that applets also must extend the Applet class in the class header in order to inherit attributes from the applet package.

Implementing an ActionListener to Handle Events

Because the Body Mass Index Calculator applet will be interactive, the program must have the ability to handle events. Every time the user clicks a button, presses a key on the keyboard, or opens a program window, for example, an event occurs. The event classes are included in the **java.awt.event package**, which provides interfaces and classes for dealing with different types of events triggered by AWT components. (The java.awt.event package is not a subset of java.awt; it is a different package.) Table 3-15 lists several classes in the java.awt.event package, an example of an event represented by the class, and an associated listener interface.

Table 3-15 *java.awt.event Classes*

CLASS	EXAMPLE OF EVENT	ASSOCIATED LISTENER INTERFACE
ActionEvent	User clicks a button, presses the ENTER key, or chooses a menu item	ActionListener
ItemEvent	User selects or deselects an item such as a checkbox or an option button	ItemListener
KeyEvent	User presses a key	KeyListener
MouseEvent	User performs a mouse action, such as select, drag, or enter MouseMotionListener	MouseListener
TextEvent	User changes text in text box	TextListener
WindowEvent	Window changes status by opening, closing, or performing some other action	WindowListener

As shown in Table 3-15, every event class has one or more associated listener interfaces. A **listener interface** — sometimes called simply an **interface** — monitors, or listens, for events during execution of an interactive program. The listener interface used in the applet version of the Body Mass Index Calculator is ActionListener. **ActionListener** is a listener interface that listens for any events that occur during execution of the program, such as when a user clicks a button, double-clicks an item, selects a menu item, or presses the ENTER key. The ActionListener tells the program that some response to the user's action should occur. The keyword, **implements**, is used in the class header to specify which listener interface a programmer wants to use. If more than one listener interface is implemented, those are separated by commas.

Figure 3-37 on the next page shows the comments, import statements, class header, and declarations for the applet. As shown in line 5, the new name of the program will be BodyMassApplet. The applet will import three packages, extend the Applet class, and implement the ActionListener. The BodyMassApplet will declare the same int and double variables that were declared in the BodyMass and BodyMassSwing programs. It also will declare an Image named logo.

```
1   /*
2          Chapter 3:   The Body Mass Index Calculator
3          Programmer:  J. Starks
4          Date:        October 20, 2007
5          Filename:    BodyMassApplet.java
6          Purpose:     This project calculates the body mass index based
7                       on a person's height and weight.
8   */
9
10  import java.applet.*;
11  import java.awt.*;
12  import java.awt.event.*;
13
14  public class BodyMassApplet extends Applet implements ActionListener
15  {
16          //declare variables
17          Image logo; //declare an Image object
18          int inches, pounds;
19          double meters, kilograms, index;
20
```

FIGURE 3-37

As you learned in Chapter 2, programmers sometimes edit existing application code to create applet code. When the required edits are extensive, however, it sometimes is more convenient to start a new document in the coding window. The following steps will start a new document in TextPad in which to code the applet version of the Body Mass Index Calculator. The steps then enter code for comments, import statements, the class header that extends the Applet class and implements the ActionListener, and variable declarations for the applet.

To Enter Code to Implement the ActionListener

1. Click the New Document button on the Standard toolbar in the TextPad coding window. If line numbers do not display, click Line Numbers on the View menu.

2. With the Data Disk in drive A, click File on the menu bar and then click Save As on the File menu.

3. When the Save As dialog box is displayed, type BodyMassApplet in the File name box. If necessary, click Java (*.java) in the Save as type list. If necessary, click the Save in box arrow, click 3½ Floppy (A:) in the list, and then double-click the Chapter03 folder.

4. Click the Save button in the Save As dialog box.

5. Enter the code, as shown in Figure 3-37.

   The new code is entered (Figure 3-38). The class header displays the new class name, extension of Applet class, and implementation of the ActionListener. Lines 17 through 19 declare the variables for the program. Line 20 is blank intentionally, in order to separate sections of code.

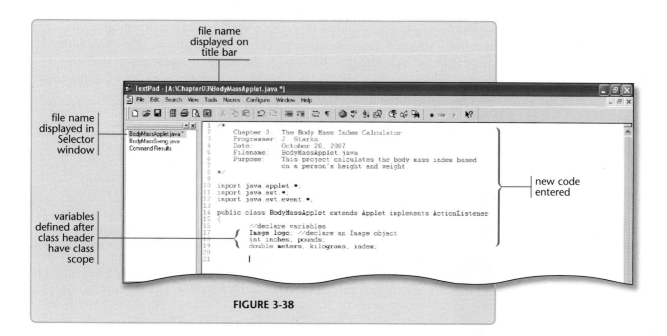

file name displayed on title bar

file name displayed in Selector window

variables defined after class header have class scope

new code entered

FIGURE 3-38

Declaring variables at the beginning of the program, after the class header, creates data that can be accessed by the entire program; that is, the variables are not limited to use by certain methods. The **scope** of an identifier for a variable, reference, or method is the portion of the program that can recognize and use the identifier. The variables in Figure 3-38 have class scope, which means all of the methods defined in this program will be able to utilize these variables.

Adding Interface Components to an Applet

The java.awt package contains components or object data types that you can use to build a user interface for applets. Each **component**, sometimes called a control, is a Java class with methods to construct, add, and manipulate the object. Java AWT components, such as Checkbox, List, or MenuItem, begin with an uppercase letter for each word in the name — referred to as title case. In the applet version of the Body Mass Index Calculator, you will use three components for the java.awt.package: Labels, TextFields, and Buttons. Figure 3-39 shows the code to add the Labels, TextFields, and Button component to the applet window interface.

```
21      //construct components
22      Label companyLabel = new Label("THE SUN FITNESS CENTER BODY MASS INDEX CALCULATOR");
23      Label heightLabel = new Label("Enter your height to the nearest inch: ");
24          TextField heightField = new TextField(10);
25      Label weightLabel = new Label("Enter your weight to the nearest pound: ");
26          TextField weightField = new TextField(10);
27      Button calcButton = new Button("Calculate");
28      Label outputLabel = new Label("Click the Calculate button to see your body mass index.");
29
```

FIGURE 3-39

LABELS A **Label** is an object that displays text in the applet window. Labels are assigned a string of characters, or a text value, by the programmer. A common usage is to use a constructor that assigns the string of characters to the component, as shown in line 22 in Figure 3-39 on the previous page. Recall that a constructor is a method used to create an instance of a class, and that the constructor has the same name as the class — in this case, the Label() method. The Label instance is constructed during compilation. During execution, the Label is added to the applet window and displays its message text.

> **Tip**
>
> **Label Data Type vs. Label() Method**
> The word, Label, on the left of the assignment operator before the identifier is a reference data type. In that capacity, it is a declaration for the variable name that will hold the Label object. The word Label, with its argument on the right side of the assignment operator, is a constructor or method used to create an instance of the class and add the caption. Java considers Label and Label() as two different concepts. Most constructors use a similar concept with the data type and method.

TEXTFIELDS A **TextField** is an object that displays a text box in which users enter text. Like the Label components, a TextField component displays inside the applet window. The code calls the constructor or method TextField(), which has a width argument to define the character width of the text box during execution, as shown in line 24 of Figure 3-39.

BUTTONS A **Button** is an object that displays a command button for users to click. Most computer users are very familiar with command buttons and know to click a command button to trigger an event. Typically, Buttons inherit their characteristics, such as color and shape, from the operating system, but programmers can define the caption on the Button, as well as the actions to be performed when it is clicked. As shown in line 27 of Figure 3-39, the code calls the constructor or method Button(), which has a caption argument to define the string of characters that displays on the face of the button during execution. The constructor code for a Button is similar to a Label constructor.

Programming Conventions

Component identifiers must follow the same Java naming rules as variable identifiers, but programmers differ in their specific naming conventions. A **naming convention** is the way you use words, case, prefixes, and underscores to name the identifiers in your program. The main reason for using a consistent set of naming conventions within a given program is to standardize the structure and coding style of an application, so that you and others may read and understand the code more easily.

Some programmers name their applet components with a three-letter prefix similar to the ones used in the Visual Basic programming language, such as lblTitle or txtName. Others use few, if any, component-specific prefixes, simply calling their components label, title, or name. This convention makes it difficult to remember and identify what kind of component is being used in longer programs.

In this program, the naming convention utilized is to have a word beginning with a lowercase letter to identify the purpose of the component, followed by the component name in title case. A Label, for example, might be named costLabel; a TextField might be named amountField. The naming conventions for a Button use a verb or a response caption, such as OK. The verb or response will be followed by the word Button. For example, a button might be named calcButton or okButton. Whatever naming convention you decide to use in your own programs, it should provide for easy reading and consistency.

Recall in the previous versions of the Body Mass Index Calculator program you indented related lines of code, such as the lines following the user prompt that read and parsed input data. This kind of indentation rule is part of a programmer's **coding convention**. The program code for the Body Mass Index Calculator applet follows the same coding conventions, indenting the component constructors for TextFields associated with prompt Labels. Java currently provides no specific rules about coding conventions; as Java takes a firmer hold in application development, a system of standardized indentations and spacing will follow. For now, as with naming conventions, coding conventions should provide for easy reading, logical grouping, and consistency.

Perform the following step to construct Label, TextField, and Button components in the applet.

To Add Interface Components to an Applet

1. With the insertion point on line 21, enter the code as shown in Figure 3-39 on page 3.55 to construct the components.

The code to construct the components is displayed in the coding window (Figure 3-40).

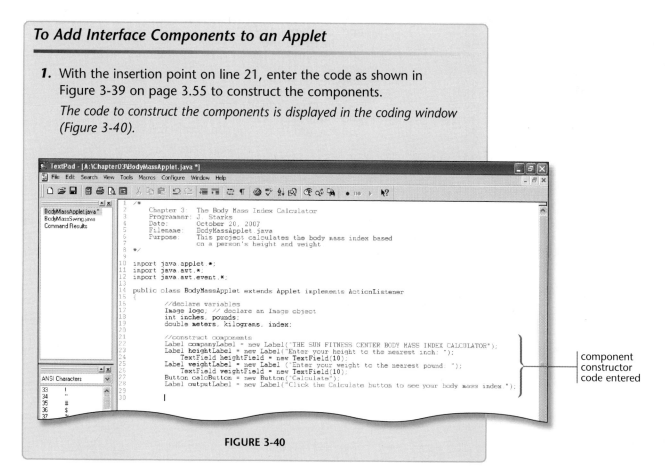

FIGURE 3-40

With the widespread use of graphical user interfaces, users have certain expectations of how they should interact with GUI components. They expect to enter text into text boxes and expect to click buttons to trigger an action or event. Java takes advantage of those expectations and provides the prebuilt classes for typical GUI components. Programmers have these kinds of tools at their fingertips, with many ways to implement them.

The init() Method

The constructors for Labels, TextFields, and Buttons are merely storage locations until the applet actually is displayed on the screen. To display on the screen, the components must be added to the applet interface using the init() method. As you learned in Chapter 2, the init() method loads the initial setup of the applet when execution begins. In the Welcome to My Day applet created in Chapter 2, the init() method automatically was invoked or initialized by the use of the paint() method to graphically draw text and an image on the applet screen.

When the init() method is **defined**, or coded, as it is in line 30 of the Body Mass Index Calculator applet code, the programmer takes control over what attributes and components are added to the applet window when it is initialized (Figure 3-41).

```
30          public void init()
31          {
32               setForeground(Color.red);
33               add(companyLabel);
34               add(heightLabel);
35               add(heightField);
36               add(weightLabel);
37               add(weightField);
38               add(calcButton);
39               calcButton.addActionListener(this);
40               add(outputLabel);
41               logo = getImage(getDocumentBase(), "logo.gif");
42          }
43
```

FIGURE 3-41

Once the applet window is initialized, several methods are used to define the display of the applet window, including how the components display. As shown in Figure 3-41, line 32 changes the foreground or text color of the applet window to red with the **setForeground() method**. The **add() method** in lines 33 through 38 and 40 is used to insert the previously declared objects, such as companyLabel and heightField, in the applet window. Both the setForeground() and add() methods have no object preceding their call, which means the applet itself is the parent object.

Line 39 uses a Button method called the addActionListener() method. Recall that the ActionListener, which was implemented in the class header, is a listener interface that listens for events. If an application is expected to perform some action based on an event from a specific component, such as a Button, the code must (1) implement ActionListener, as it did in line 14 in the class header, and (2) register ActionListener to receive events from the Button, by calling the component's addActionListener() method.

Each component has an **addActionListener() method** that registers, or assigns, an ActionListener to receive action events from that component. In the Body Mass Index Calculator applet, the addActionListener() method for a Button is used to associate the specific Button component, calcButton, with ActionListener. When a user clicks the calcButton, the calcButton sends an action event to ActionListener.

As shown in line 39 of Figure 3-41, the addActionListener() method has only one argument, which is used to assign the specific instance of the Button class that will send action events to the ActionListener. In line 39, the addActionListener() method uses the keyword, this, as the argument for the method. The keyword, this, refers back to the component itself — in this case, the calcButton instance of the Button class. The calcButton thus is the object monitored by the listener interface, ActionListener. In summary, you can think of the ActionListener as telling the applet to listen for the click on the calcButton, and the keyword, this, as identifying which click event code to execute after the user clicks the calcButton.

In line 41, the image for the applet is retrieved from storage and placed in the applet. As in Chapter 2, the getImage() method is used to load an image into an applet. The getImage() method calls a second method called the getDocumentBase() method, which allows the applet to pull the image from the current folder in which your applet class is stored. The getImage() method creates and returns the image object to the variable, logo, which represents the loaded image.

The step on the next page codes the init() method, which adds the components to the applet window, sets the addActionListener() method for the button, and gets the image to display in the applet window.

To Code the init() Method

1. With the insertion point on line 30, enter the code as shown in Figure 3-41 on page 184.

The init() method is entered in the coding window (Figure 3-42).

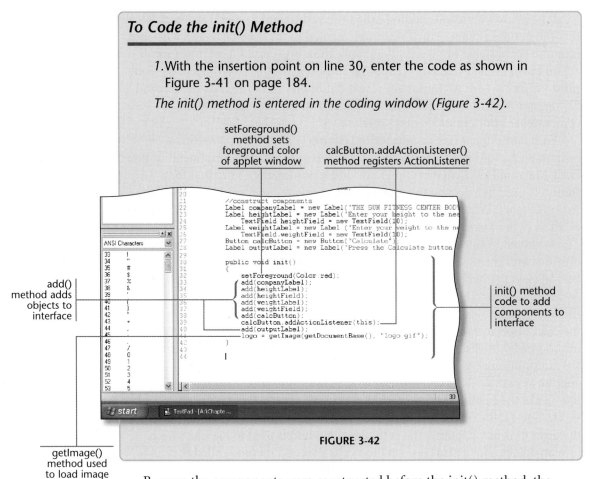

setForeground() method sets foreground color of applet window

calcButton.addActionListener() method registers ActionListener

add() method adds objects to interface

init() method code to add components to interface

getImage() method used to load image

FIGURE 3-42

Because the components were constructed before the init() method, the compiled bytecode contains the implementation of those components even before the applet window is initialized. Constructing the components before coding the init() method will speed processing during execution, as the init() method quickly can access and add the constructed components to the applet on the screen. Also, if you try to add a component at the class level, the compiler sometimes interprets it as a new method without a return data type, and will not compile the code.

As you enter code to add components to a user interface, remember that the components will display in the applet window in the order they are entered in the init() method. To the user, the components thus will display as the applet title (companyLabel), followed by the height label and text box (heightLabel and heightField), the weight label and text box (weightLabel and weightField), the Calculate button (calcButton), and the results message (outputLabel).

Tip

Focus and Applet Text Boxes

When applets use components to display text boxes, the first text box has the **focus**, which means the insertion point displays in that text box. Users may press the TAB key to move to subsequent text boxes. Java programmers should pay close attention to the order in which they add TextFields to applets, as that sets the default tab stop sequence.

The actionPerformed() Method

The final set of code will create the event behind the Calculate button. Once a user clicks the Calculate button and the click is received, a Java applet must perform a task; in this case, it must calculate the Body Mass Index just as it did in the previous two versions of the program.

When an object such as the calcButton causes an event to happen, the object is called an **event source**. Each event source can have one or more listener interfaces, which become **registered**, or paired, with the event source at compile time. In the Body Mass Index Calculator applet, the ActionListener interface is registered with the calcButton using the addActionListener() method.

A listener interface has methods that specify what will happen when an event is sent to the listener interface. These methods are called **event handlers**. ActionListener has one event handler or method, called **actionPerformed()**, which is executed when the click event occurs. The actionPerformed() method takes the general form shown in line 44 of Figure 3-43. It is common practice to identify the ActionEvent parameter as e, although any variable name can be used.

```
44          public void actionPerformed(ActionEvent e)
45          {
46
47              inches = Integer.parseInt(heightField.getText());
48              pounds = Integer.parseInt(weightField.getText());
49              meters = inches / 39.36;
50              kilograms = pounds / 2.2;
51              index = kilograms / Math.pow(meters,2);
52              outputLabel.setText("YOUR BODY MASS INDEX IS " + Math.round(index) + ".");
53          }
54
```

FIGURE 3-43

In lines 47 and 48, the data entered by the user in the text box created by the TextField component are retrieved using the getText() method. The **getText() method** is used to retrieve text from a Label, TextField, or other AWT or Swing component that uses text. Table 3-16 displays the general form of the getText() method.

Table 3-16	getText() Method
General form:	object.getText():
Purpose:	To retrieve text from a Label, TextField, or other AWT or Swing component that uses text. It returns a String composed of the Label's caption or the user-supplied data from a TextField.
Examples:	1. heightField.getText(); 2. myLabel.getText();

In lines 47 and 48 of Figure 3-43 on the previous page, the result of the getText() method is wrapped inside the parseInt() method, which means that after Java gets the text from the TextField, it immediately is converted to an integer. The formulas are calculated in lines 49 through 51, and then the answer is sent back to the applet via the setText() method. The **setText() method** does just the opposite of the getText() method: it assigns the caption or String to an object. In line 52, for example, the setText() method assigns the output message to the outputLabel component. The getText() and setText() methods can be used with both Labels and TextFields, as well as with other text-based objects in the java.awt and javax.swing packages.

The following step enters the code for the actionPerformed() method used to handle the click event.

To Code the actionPerformed() Method

1. With the insertion point on line 44, enter the code as shown in Figure 3-43 on the previous page.

The actionPerformed() method code is entered (Figure 3-44).

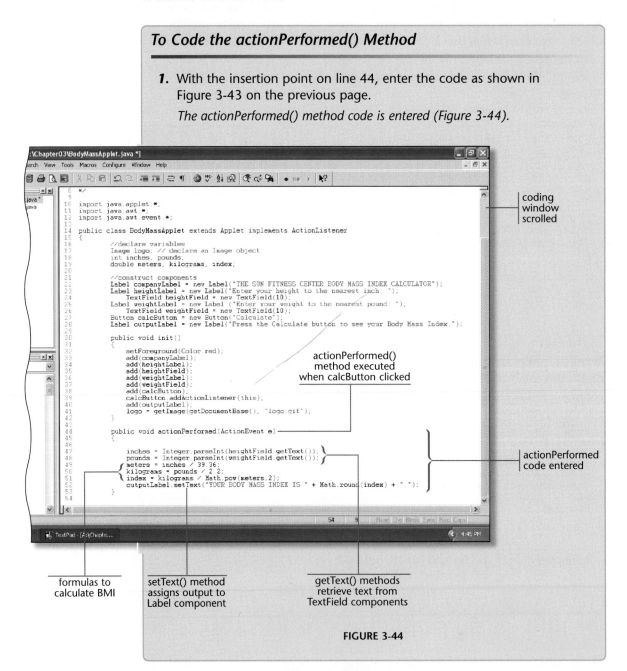

FIGURE 3-44

When the user clicks the calcButton, it triggers the actionPerformed() method. The actionPerformed() method includes the getText() method to retrieve the input values, formulas to calculate BMI, and the setText() method to display output to the user. Anytime you use a TextField component in Java, you can use the getText() and setText() methods to transfer data back and forth easily from the user to the applet, just as you did with the ISR when the program was a console application.

The paint() Method

The final step in coding the Body Mass Index Calculator applet is to enter the code for the paint() method that draws the image in the applet after it is initialized. As shown in Figure 3-45, line 57 will draw the Sun Fitness Center logo image at a location of 125 pixels from the left side of the applet and 160 pixels from the top. The brace in line 58 closes the block of code for the paint() method. Line 59 displays the closing brace for the entire BodyMassApplet class.

```
55          public void paint(Graphics g)
56          {
57              g.drawImage(logo,125,160,this);
58          }
59  }
```

FIGURE 3-45

The following step enters the paint() method.

To Code the paint() Method

1. With the insertion point on line 55, enter the code as shown in Figure 3-45.

The paint() method is entered (Figure 3-46). Line 59 displays the closing brace for the BodyMassApplet class.

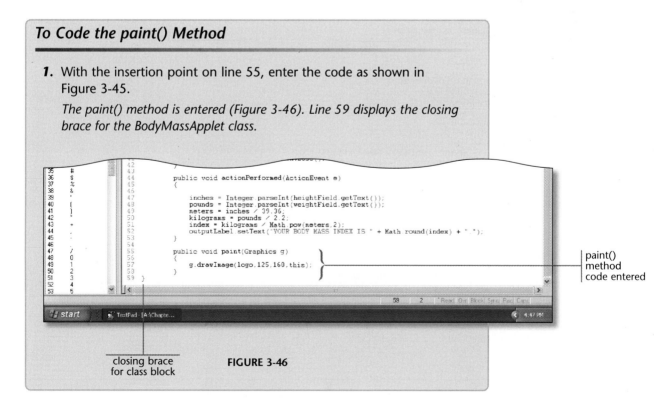

closing brace for class block   **FIGURE 3-46**

paint() method code entered

The applet version of the Body Mass Index Calculator now is complete. You added the import statements, changed the name of the class to BodyMassApplet, and constructed the applet components. You then entered code for the init() method. Next, you included the actionPerformed() method to convert the text to numbers, calculate, and display the answer. Finally, you coded the paint() method to display the company logo in the Applet Viewer window.

Figure 3-47 shows the applet code in its entirety. Check your own code for syntax, proper spelling, capitalization, and indentations. Your lines may wrap differently. When you are confident that everything is correct, you are ready to save and compile your program.

```
1  /*
2      Chapter 3:   The Body Mass Index Calculator
3      Programmer:  J. Starks
4      Date:        October 20, 2007
5      Filename:    BodyMassApplet.java
6      Purpose:     This project calculates the body mass index based
7                   on a person's height and weight.
8  */
9
10 import java.applet.*;
11 import java.awt.*;
12 import java.awt.event.*;
13
14 public class BodyMassApplet extends Applet implements ActionListener
15 {
16         //declare variables
17         Image logo; //declare an Image object
18         int inches, pounds;
19         double meters, kilograms, index;
20
21         //construct components
22         Label companyLabel = new Label("THE SUN FITNESS CENTER BODY MASS INDEX CALCULATOR");
23         Label heightLabel = new Label("Enter your height to the nearest inch: ");
24             TextField heightField = new TextField(10);
25         Label weightLabel = new Label("Enter your weight to the nearest pound: ");
26             TextField weightField = new TextField(10);
27         Button calcButton = new Button("Calculate");
28         Label outputLabel = new Label(
29         "Click the Calculate button to see your body mass index.");
30
31         public void init()
32         {
33             setForeground(Color.red);
34             add(companyLabel);
35             add(heightLabel);
36             add(heightField);
37             add(weightLabel);
38             add(weightField);
39             add(calcButton);
40             calcButton.addActionListener(this);
41             add(outputLabel);
42             logo = getImage(getDocumentBase(), "logo.gif");
43         }
44
45         public void actionPerformed(ActionEvent e)
46         {
47
48             inches = Integer.parseInt(heightField.getText());
49             pounds = Integer.parseInt(weightField.getText());
50             meters = inches / 39.36;
51             kilograms = pounds / 2.2;
52             index = kilograms / Math.pow(meters,2);
53             outputLabel.setText("YOUR BODY MASS INDEX IS " + Math.round(index) + ".");
54         }
55
56         public void paint(Graphics g)
57         {
58             g.drawImage(logo,125,160,this);
59         }
}
```

(Note: line numbers 1–59 appear in the left margin of the code listing.)

FIGURE 3-47

Compiling the Applet

The following step compiles the BodyMassApplet source code.

To Compile the Applet

1. With the Data Disk in drive A, click Tools on the menu bar and then click Compile Java on the Tools menu.

TextPad automatically saves and then compiles the BodyMassApplet source code. If TextPad notifies you of compilation errors, fix the errors in the BodyMassApplet coding window and then compile the program again.

OTHER WAYS

1. Press CTRL+1
2. At command prompt, type javac BodyMassApplet .java

Correcting Errors

In TextPad's Command Results window, you can double-click the first line in an error message to move the insertion point to that error in the coding window, thus eliminating the searching and scrolling necessary to locate the referenced line number.

Creating an HTML Host Document for an Interactive Applet

You may remember that, because an applet is initiated and executed from within another language or run as a part of a Web page, you must identify a host, or reference program, to execute the applet. The interactive Body Mass Index Calculator applet will run as part of an HTML host document that tells the browser, through the use of tags, the name of the applet and the size of the window. HTML hosts may contain other tags as well.

Creating the Host Document

You will use the <HTML> tag and the <APPLET> tag in the host document. The following steps create the HTML host document using TextPad.

To Create the HTML Host Document

1. With the TextPad window open, click the New Document button on the Standard toolbar. If line numbers do not display, click Line Numbers on the View menu.

2. In the TextPad coding window, type the code as shown in Figure 3-48 on the next page.

(continued)

3. Click File on the menu bar and then click Save As on the File menu. When the Save As dialog box is displayed, type `BodyMassApplet` in the File name text box. Do not press the ENTER key. Click the Save as type box arrow and then click HTML (*.htm*,*.stm*) in the list. If necessary, click the Save in box arrow, click 3½ Floppy (A:) in the list, and then double-click the Chapter03 folder in the list.

4. Click the Save button in the Save As dialog box.

TextPad saves the HTML file on the Data Disk in drive A. The file name is displayed on the title bar of the TextPad window and in the Selector window.

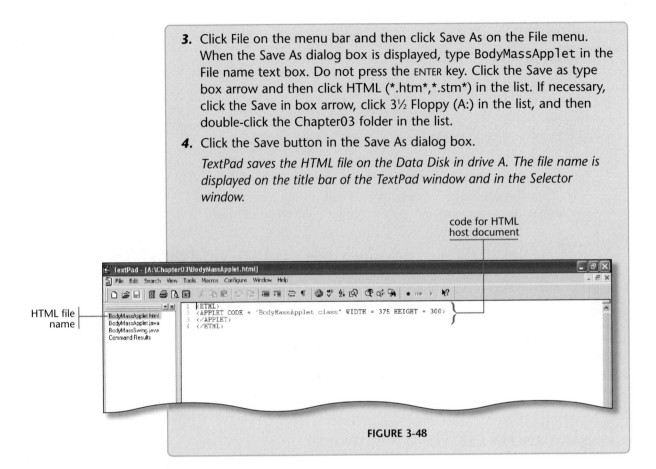

FIGURE 3-48

As you learned in Chapter 2, the <APPLET> tag nested within the <HTML> beginning and ending tags specifies three pieces of information that the Web page needs to access the Java applet: the name of the Java bytecode file, the width of the window, and the height of the window in which to run the applet (Figure 3-48).

Running and Testing an Interactive Applet

You now are ready to run the applet by using TextPad's Run Java Applet command. The Run Java Applet command automatically executes Java's appletviewer.exe command to display the Applet Viewer window.

When testing the applet version of the same program, you again should use the same sample data for testing each version. That way you can compare output results to ensure that they are consistent for all versions of the program.

To Run and Test an Interactive Applet

1. Click Tools on the menu bar and then click Run Java Applet on the Tools menu.

2. If necessary, when the Choose File dialog box is displayed, click the box arrow and choose BodyMassApplet.html in the list. Click the Yes button.

3. When the applet is displayed, type 67 in the inches text box. Press the TAB key.

4. Type 145 in the pounds text box.

5. Click the Calculate button.

The applet is displayed in the Applet Viewer window (Figure 3-49). The calculated body mass index (BMI) is displayed, along with an output message.

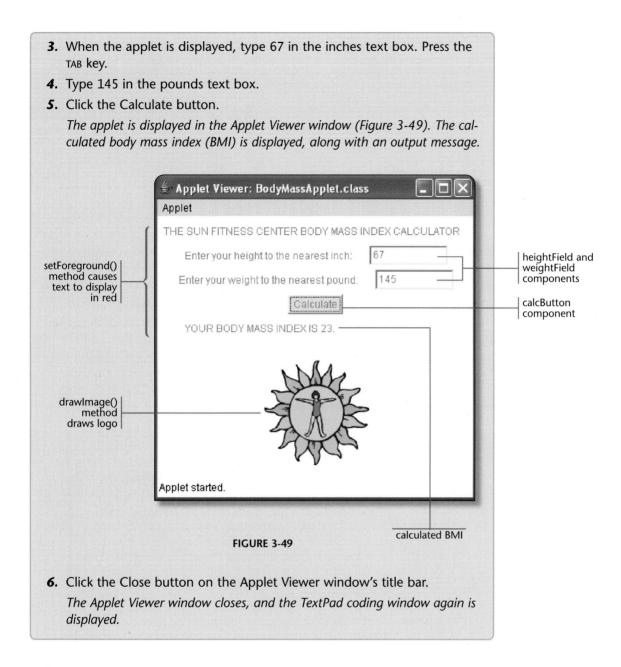

FIGURE 3-49

6. Click the Close button on the Applet Viewer window's title bar.

The Applet Viewer window closes, and the TextPad coding window again is displayed.

To enter different data in the applet, you must close the Applet Viewer window and then execute the program again. In a later chapter, you will learn how to write a clear event that will clear the sample data for the next person, without having to close and execute the program again.

Once you have determined that the program runs correctly, you should print a copy of the BodyMassApplet source code and the HTML host document code for documentation purposes. You can print a copy of the program code from the TextPad coding window by selecting the appropriate document in the Selector window and then using the Print command on the File menu. A printout of the program code will be sent to the default printer. Figure 3-47 on page 190 shows the printout of the program code for the applet version of the Body Mass Index Calculator. As previously noted, the longer lines of code wrap to the next line in the printout.

The final step is to quit TextPad.

To Quit TextPad

1. Click the Close button in the TextPad title bar.

File Management

Performing the steps to code, save, compile, modify, and so on creates several files on your storage device. File naming conventions and the operating system's capability of displaying icons associated with different file types can help you keep everything in logical order. The steps in this chapter created a Java file, BodyMass, which then created a class file on the Data Disk when compiled. The original Java file also was modified twice to create the files BodyMassSwing and BodyMassApplet. These files also were compiled to create two additional class files. An HTML host file, BodyMassApplet, also was created on the Data Disk for a total of seven files. Figure 3-50 displays a list of files created on the Data Disk in this chapter. Finally, the logo file used in the applet version of the program is included on the Data Disk. Your icons may appear differently, based on your installation of the SDK and your default browser.

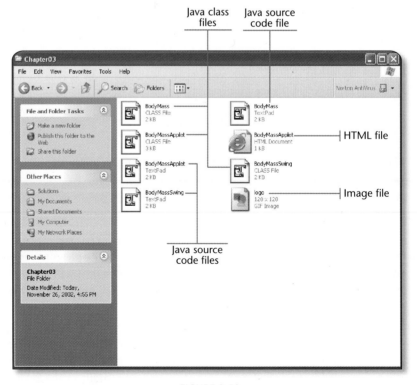

FIGURE 3-50

Chapter Summary

In this chapter, you learned to create a console application to calculate body mass index (BMI). In creating the application, you leaned how to declare variables and write assignment statements to store data with proper identifiers. You also learned to create an instance of a BufferedReader to store, or buffer, the input received from the InputStreamReader (ISR) and to use assignment statements to assign the input data to variables. You learned how to use the readLine() method to make the program pause and wait for user input. In addition, you learned how to code formulas with arithmetic operators, including the use of two methods from the Math class, round() and pow(). You learned to write code that uses variables and concatenation to produce output on the display. You learned to modify the console application to accept data from a dialog box using a Java Swing component called JOptionPane and its associated methods. Finally, you learned how to convert the application to an interactive applet. You learned to use ActionListener to handle events, as well as to use constructors to add Labels, TextFields, and a Button component to the interface. You learned to use the init() method to add components to the applet interface and to use the paint() method to display an image in the Applet Viewer window. After you created an HTML host document to display the applet and run it using the Applet Viewer, you learned about file management and looked at the types of files created by TextPad and the Java SDK.

What You Should Know

Having completed this chapter, you should now be able to perform the tasks shown in Table 3-17.

Table 3-17 **Chapter 3 What You Should Know**

TASK NUMBER	TASK	PAGE
1	Start TextPad and Save a TextPad Document	136
2	Enter Beginning Code	138
3	Enter Code to Declare Variables	142
4	Enter Code to Instantiate the BufferedReader	146
5	Enter Code for the User Prompts, Inputs, and Conversions	150
6	Enter the Formulas	160
7	Enter Code to Display Output	162
8	Compile the Source Code	164
9	Run and Test the Application	164
10	Print the Source Code	166
11	Edit the File Name and Class Header	167
12	Enter the New import Statement	168
13	Delete Existing Code	169
14	Enter Code to Create Swing Dialog Boxes	173
15	Enter Code to Close the Program	174
16	Save and Compile the Source Code	175
17	Run and Test the Swing Program	176
18	Enter Code to Implement the ActionListener	180
19	Add Interface Components to an Applet	183
20	Code the init() Method	186
21	Code the actionPerformed() Method	188
22	Code the paint() Method	189
23	Compile the Applet	191
24	Create the HTML Host Document	191
25	Run and Test an Interactive Applet	192
26	Quit TextPad	194

Key Terms

abs() method *(160)*
accumulator *(149)*
ActionListener *(179)*
actionPerformed() *(187)*
add() method *(184)*
addActionListener() method *(185)*
arithmetic operators *(151)*
assignment operator *(148)*
assignment statement *(148)*
boolean *(140)*
buffer *(144)*
BufferedReader class *(144)*
Button *(182)*
byte *(140)*
cast operation *(142)*
char *(140)*
coding convention *(182)*
comparison operators *(153)*
component *(181)*
concatenation *(162)*
conditional expression *(156)*
constant *(171)*
counter *(123)*
data *(128)*
declaration statement *(141)*
defined *(184)*
dialog box *(133)*
double *(140)*
equality operators *(154)*
event handlers *(187)*
event source *(187)*
exit() method *(173)*
exponentiation *(159)*
expression *(154)*
float *(140)*
focus *(186)*
formula *(132)*
getText() method *(187)*
implements *(179)*
InputStreamReader (ISR) *(144)*
instantiate *(145)*
instantiation *(145)*
int *(140)*
integer division *(151)*

interactive *(143)*
interface *(179)*
java.awt.event package *(178)*
javax.swing *(134)*
JOptionPane *(168)*
Label *(182)*
listener interface *(179)*
long *(140)*
Math class *(159)*
max() method *(160)*
min() method *(160)*
modal *(133)*
modular division *(151)*
modulus operator *(151)*
naming convention *(182)*
nested *(158)*
nextInt() method *(148)*
numeric expression *(154)*
order of operator precedence *(151)*
parse() method *(148)*
pow() method *(160)*
precision *(139)*
primitive data type *(139)*
promotes *(152)*
random() method *(160)*
readLine() method *(147)*
reference data type *(141)*
registered *(187)*
relational operators *(154)*
round() method *(160)*
Scanner *(148)*
scope *(184)*
setForeground() method *(184)*
setText() method *(188)*
short *(140)*
sqrt() method *(160)*
stream *(143)*
strongly typed language *(139)*
Swing components *(166)*
TextField *(182)*
throws IOException *(137)*
wrap *(144)*
wrapper class *(148)*

Homework Assignments

1 Label the Figure

In the spaces provided, identify the various parts of the Java applet shown in Figure 3-51.

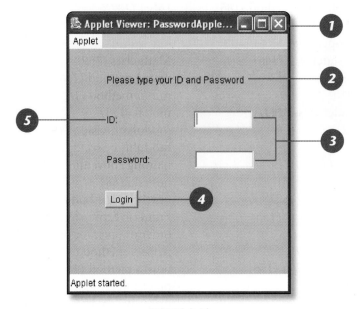

FIGURE 3-51

1. _____   4. _____

2. _____   5. _____

3. _____

2 Identify Code

In Figure 3-52, arrows point to sections of Java code. Identify the code in the spaces provided using the appropriate word from the following list.

comment	constructor
calculation	concatenation
declaration section	conversion
input from buffer	output section
class name	package name

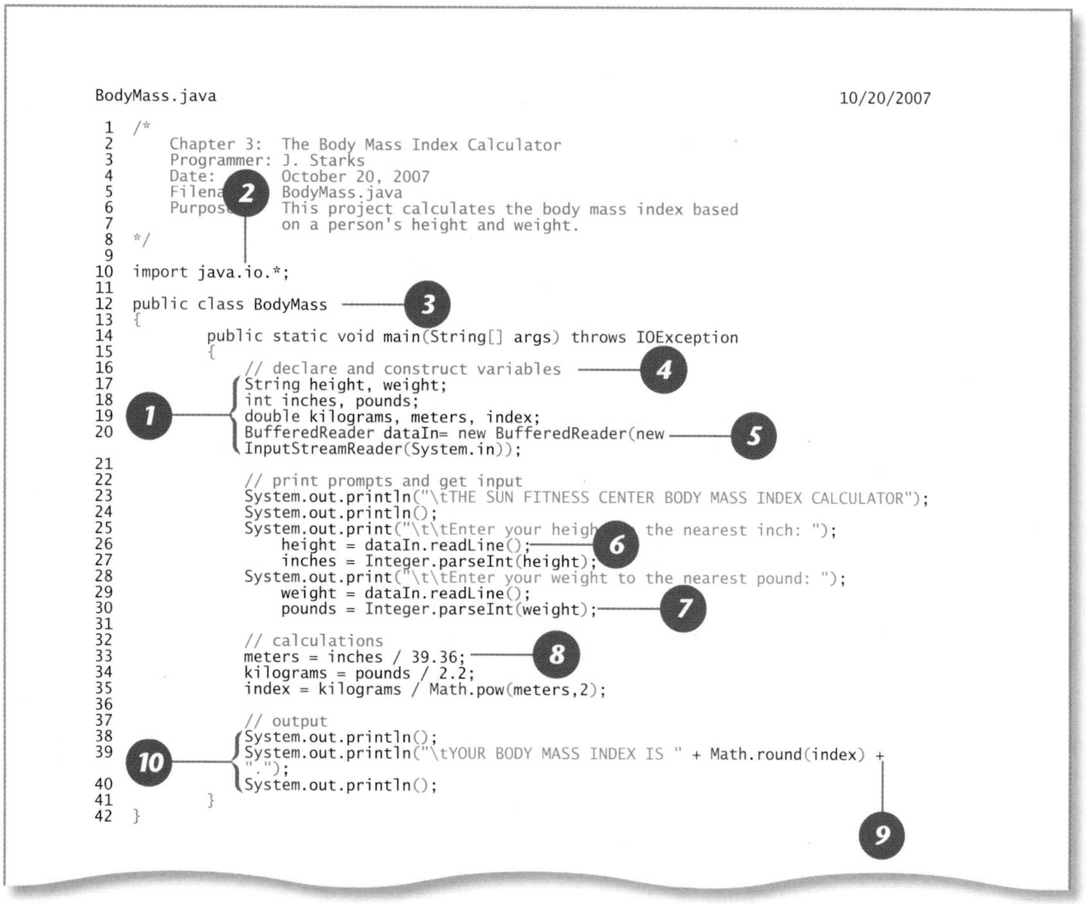

```
BodyMass.java                                                    10/20/2007
 1   /*
 2        Chapter 3:   The Body Mass Index Calculator
 3        Programmer: J. Starks
 4        Date:        October 20, 2007
 5        Filena       BodyMass.java
 6        Purpos       This project calculates the body mass index based
 7                     on a person's height and weight.
 8   */
 9
10   import java.io.*;
11
12   public class BodyMass
13   {
14        public static void main(String[] args) throws IOException
15        {
16             // declare and construct variables
17             String height, weight;
18             int inches, pounds;
19             double kilograms, meters, index;
20             BufferedReader dataIn= new BufferedReader(new
                  InputStreamReader(System.in));
21
22             // print prompts and get input
23             System.out.println("\tTHE SUN FITNESS CENTER BODY MASS INDEX CALCULATOR");
24             System.out.println();
25             System.out.print("\t\tEnter your height   the nearest inch: ");
26                  height = dataIn.readLine();
27                  inches = Integer.parseInt(height);
28             System.out.print("\t\tEnter your weight to the nearest pound: ");
29                  weight = dataIn.readLine();
30                  pounds = Integer.parseInt(weight);
31
32             // calculations
33             meters = inches / 39.36;
34             kilograms = pounds / 2.2;
35             index = kilograms / Math.pow(meters,2);
36
37             // output
38             System.out.println();
39             System.out.println("\tYOUR BODY MASS INDEX IS " + Math.round(index) +
                  ".");
40             System.out.println();
41        }
42   }
```

FIGURE 3-52

1. _____   6. _____

2. _____   7. _____

3. _____   8. _____

4. _____   9. _____

5. _____   10. _____

3 Understanding Error Messages

Figure 3-53 displays a Command Results window with error messages. Using what you know about coding and error messages, list the possible coding errors that might cause TextPad to display the error messages.

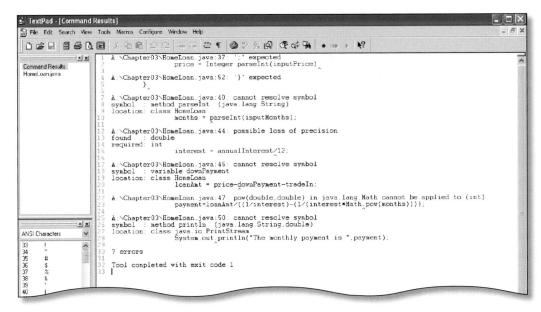

FIGURE 3-53

4 Using the Java API

The Java API is a good tool to look up information about a class with which you may be unfamiliar or to check the syntax of commands and methods you wish to use in your programs. While connected to the Internet, start a browser, type `http://java.sun.com/j2se/5.0/docs/api/` in the Address text box and then press the ENTER key to view the Java API Specification on the Sun Web site. The Java API Specification is organized by the packages, hierarchically, but many programmers click the Index link located at the top of the page to display the entire list alphabetically.

With the Java API Specification open in the browser window, perform the following steps.

1. Use the down scroll arrow in the upper-left frame to display the javax.swing link. Click the javax.swing link.

2. When the javax.swing page is displayed in the lower-left frame, scroll down to display the list of Classes. Click JOptionPane in the list of Classes.

3. When the Class JOptionPane page is displayed in the main frame, read the opening paragraphs that describe the JOptionPane class (Figure 3-54). Read three sections entitled Parameters, Examples, and Direct Use.

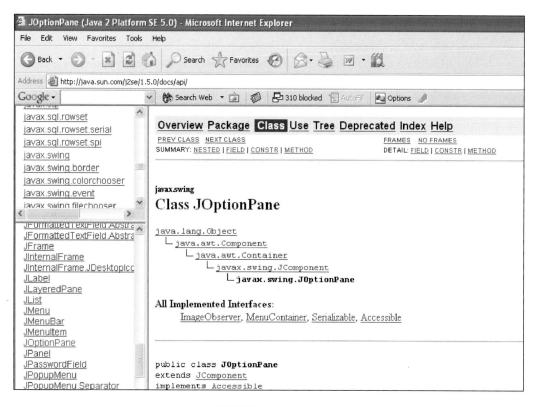

FIGURE 3-54

4. Scroll to display the Field Summary table.

5. Chose any three fields in the Field Summary table. One at a time, click each of the three links. When the field definition is displayed, drag through the definition to select it. Print a copy of the field definition by clicking File on the browser's menu bar and then click Print on the File menu. When the Print dialog box is displayed, click Print selection and then click the Print button in the Print dialog box.

6. Click the Back button on your browser's toolbar to return to the JOptionPane page. Scroll to the Method Summary table. Choose any five methods and then click the links and read their descriptions. Make a list of the five methods, their return values, and their argument data types.

7. Write a paragraph describing a computer application that might make good use of a JOptionPane method.

Short Answer

1. In Java, the process of joining two strings with a plus sign is called

   _____.

2. Data flowing in or out of a program in Java is called _____.

3. ISR stands for _____.

4. _____ is the process of constructing an instance of a data type or object from a previously defined class.

(continued)

Short Answer *(continued)*

5. Adding the Java code, _____, to the end of the main() method header gives a program a way to acknowledge and handle potential input or output errors and still compile correctly.

6. _____ listens for events in an applet.

7. Examples of applet component objects include _____, _____, and _____.

8. The actionPerformed() method is an example of a(n) _____.

9. The main reason for using a consistent set of _____ is to standardize the structure and coding style of an application, so that you and others can read and understand the code easily.

10. Make a list of the primitive data types in Java. Give three different literal examples of each.

11. Evaluate each of the following expressions:
    a. 4 * 3 / 6 − 4 + Math.pow(7,2)
    b. (3 + 4) * 7 − 3
    c. 9 * 2 / 4 + 5 % 3 + 3
    d. 55 = = 55

12. For each of the situations below, explain which type of division (regular, integer, or modular) will result in the more appropriate answer. Your answer may include more than one type of division.
    a. calculating how many busses will be needed for 350 students
    b. figuring an average grade
    c. determining how many quarters are in 685 cents
    d. testing user input for an even number
    e. rounding down

13. Which arithmetic or comparison operation is performed first in the following expressions?
    a. 144 / (6 * 2)
    b. 25<57 != false
    c. answerA + answerB * answerC
    d. 125 / (result * 4)
    e. true = = true != false
    f. 5 * 3 % 2 + 7 / 2 − 7

14. Which of the following expressions are valid and do *not* require the Java compiler to cast?
    a. double answerA = 12.0 / 4.0;
    b. int answerB = 12 / 7;
    c. int answerC = 3 + 4 + "subtotal";
    d. boolean answerD = 9 * 6;
    e. double answerE = 3answerB;
    f. double answerF = 15 % 5;

15. If necessary, insert parentheses so that each numeric expression results in the value indicated on the left side of the assignment operator (=).

    a. 33 = 3 * 6 − 3 + 2 + 6 * 4 − 4 / Math.pow(2,1);

    b. 22 = 7 * 3 + Math.pow(4,2) − 3 / 13;

    c. 1 = 25 % 6 - 18 + 6 * 3;

    d. 5.0 = 3.0/2.0 + 0.5 + Math.pow(3.0,1.0);

16. Assume each of the following values has been entered by the user and stored as a String. Write a line of code to convert each variable to an appropriate primitive data type.

    a. interestRate

    b. age

    c. *pi*

    d. distanceToMoon

    e. numberOfStudents

17. Describe the differences between JOptionPane message boxes and JOptionPane input boxes.

18. Describe the difference between the getText() method and the setText() method. Give examples of each, including components, arguments, and results.

19. Choose any two numbers and write a formula using each of the arithmetic operators with those two numbers. Solve each formula the way Java would solve it.

20. List five boolean expressions using the relational or conditional operators. Use a variable as one part of your expression. Then, list two variable values that would make your expression true and two that would make your expression false.

21. Write a paragraph describing a situation in which casting might be appropriate. Give examples.

22. Define what is meant by a loss of precision.

23. What does it mean to say that Java is a strongly typed language?

24. Describe the difference between primitive data types and reference data types, and give examples of each.

25. List a variable in the Body Mass Index Calculator program that must have class level scope, and explain why.

Learn It Online

Start your browser and visit scsite.com/java3e/learn. Follow the instructions in the exercises below.

1. **Chapter Reinforcement TF, MC, and SA**   Click the True/False, Multiple Choice, and Short Answer link below Chapter 3. Print and then answer the questions.

2. **Practice Test**   Click the Practice Test link below Chapter 3. Answer each question, enter your first and last name at the bottom of the page, and then click the Grade Test button. When the graded practice test is displayed on your screen, click Print on the File menu to print a hard copy. Continue to take practice tests until you score 80% or better. Hand in a printout of the final practice test.

3. **Crossword Puzzle Challenge**   Click the Crossword Puzzle Challenge link below Chapter 3. Read the instructions, and then enter your first and last name. Click the Play button. Complete the crossword puzzle. When you are finished, click the Submit button. When the crossword puzzle is redisplayed, click the Print button.

4. **Tips and Tricks**   Click the Tips and Tricks link below Chapter 3. Click a topic that pertains to Chapter 3. Right-click the information and then click Print on the shortcut menu. Construct a brief example of what the information relates to in Java to confirm that you understand how to use the tip or trick. Hand in the example and printed information.

5. **Newsgroups**   Click the Newsgroups link below Chapter 3. Click a topic that pertains to Chapter 3. Print three comments.

6. **Expanding Your Horizons**   Click the Articles for Java link below Chapter 3. Click a topic that pertains to Chapter 3. Print the information. Construct a brief example of what the information relates to in Java to confirm that you understand the contents of the article. Hand in the example and printed information.

7. **Search Sleuth**   Select three key terms from the Key Terms section of this chapter and then use the Google search engine at google.com (or any major search engine) to display and print two Web pages for each key term.

Debugging Assignment

Start TextPad and open the file, Bert, from the Chapter03 folder on the Data Disk. See the preface of this book for instructions for downloading the Data Disk or see your instructor for information about accessing the files required in this book.

The Bert program is a Java application that calculates the monthly payment on a car by requesting inputs from the user, performing calculations, and displaying output, as shown in Figure 3-55.

```
C:\WINNT\System32\cmd.exe                                                    _□×
What is your name?  Christy Minton
What is the price of the car?  17500
What is the down payment?  500
What is the trade-in value?  1250
For how many months is the loan?  60
What is the decimal interest rate?  .05
The monthly payment for Christy Minton is $297

Press any key to continue . . .
```

FIGURE 3-55

The Bert program has several syntax, semantic, and logic errors in the program code. Perform the following steps to debug the program.

1. Open the file Bert.java in TextPad.
2. Insert your name as the programmer in line 3 of the comment header. Insert the current date in line 4 and write a purpose comment for the program in line 6. Read through the code and fix any errors that you see.
3. Compile the program. As TextPad displays compilation errors, return to the coding window to find the first error, fix it, and then recompile the program.
4. When you have fixed all the syntax and semantic errors so that the program will compile without errors, run the program. Use the following sample data in Table 3-18 to test the program for run-time and logic errors. Fix any errors and compile again.

Table 3-18   Sample Data for Bert Program

Name	Christy Minton
Price	17,500
Down payment	500
Trade-in value	1250
Number of months of loan	60
Decimal interest value	.05

5. When the program compiles and runs to produce the output as shown in Figure 3-55, print a copy of the source code.

DEBUGGING ASSIGNMENT

Programming Assignments

1 Writing Java Code from Pseudocode

Start TextPad. Open the Java source code file SimpleMath.java from the Chapter03 folder on the Data Disk. Using the techniques you learned in this chapter, write the lines of code inside the main() method to perform the simple math operations, as outlined by the pseudocode in Table 3-19.

Table 3-19 Pseudocode for Simple Math Program

Begin SimpleMath
    Get Data
        Get first integer from user
        Get second integer from user
    End Get Data
    Perform Math
        Calculate sum: first + second
        Calculate difference: first - second
        Calculate product: first * second
        Calculate quotient: first / second
    End Perform Math
    Display all answers
End

---

1. With the SimpleMath.java source code displayed in the TextPad coding window, insert your name and date in the comments. Insert an appropriate purpose comment. Change the name of the program to MathProgram in the class header and comments.

2. Click inside the main() method braces.

3. Begin by entering the declaration statements to declare the following variables:
   - declare string variables for user input
   - declare integer variables to store the user input after it has been parsed
   - declare integer variables to store the sum, difference, and product
   - declare a double variable to store the quotient

4. After studying the pseudocode in Table 3-19, enter the lines of code necessary to produce the output.

5. Save the file on the Data Disk with the file name MathProgram.

6. Compile the program. If errors occur, fix them in the TextPad coding window and compile again.

7. Run the program. If the program runs correctly, return to TextPad and print a copy of the source code. Otherwise, return to Step 3, review the code, and correct the errors until the program runs error-free.

2 Analysis and Design

Figure 3-56 shows a requirements document for a new application, as requested by a small business owner. Using the six phases of the development cycle as shown in Table 3-1 on page 130, perform the following steps:

REQUEST FOR NEW APPLICATION

Date submitted:	November 12, 2007
Submitted by:	Patricia Wolinsky
Purpose:	The personnel department often is asked to do a quick computation of an employee's state income tax. Personnel staff would save time and provide more accurate information if members of the staff had a stand-alone application at their disposal to perform the calculation.
Application title:	State Tax Computation
Algorithms:	State tax is computed as follows: State tax = 0.03 x (Income − (600 x Dependents))
Notes:	1) The personnel staff is accustomed to the following terminology: **Taxpayer's income** for Income in the above algorithm, **Number of dependents** for Dependents in the above algorithm, **State tax due** for State tax in the above algorithm. 2) The application should allow the user to enter values for Taxpayer's income and number of dependents, so that state tax due can be computed. 3) The computation should be designated by the term, Compute.

Approvals

Approval status:	X	Approved
		Rejected
Approved by:	Leslie Broda	
Date:	November 19, 2007	
Assigned to:	J. Starks, Programmer	

FIGURE 3-56

1. Analyze the requirements. Read the requirements document carefully. Think about the requester, the users, the problem, and the purpose of the application.
2. Design the solution. Draw a storyboard for the program. Pay careful attention to the inputs and outputs. Write either pseudocode or draw a flowchart to represent the sequence of events in your program.

(continued)

2 Analysis and Design *(continued)*

3. Validate the design. Have a classmate or your instructor look over your storyboard and make suggestions before you proceed.

4. Implement the design. Translate the design into code for the program.

5. Test the solution. Test the program, finding and correcting errors (debugging) until it is error-free.

6. Document the solution. Print a copy of the source code.

7. Hand in all documents to your instructor.

3 Converting from Sample Data to User Input

In order to practice writing interactive programs that require user input, you decide to convert a console application that includes sample data to one that has user prompts and accepts input values. Perform the following steps.

1. Start TextPad. Open the file Money.java from the Chapter03 folder of the Data Disk. The Money.java file contains program code for a program that converts any number of coins into dollars and cents. Change the lines of code that assign sample data into lines of code that prompt the user and store the answers.

2. With the Money.java source code displayed in the TextPad window, insert your name and date in the block comment at the beginning.

3. Use TextPad's Replace dialog box to change each occurrence of the text, Money, to the text, Coins.

4. Save the file on the Data Disk, using Coins as the file name.

5. Add four additional variable declarations for string inputs by typing:

```
String strQuarters;
String strDimes;
String strNickels;
String strPennies;
```

at the appropriate place in the program code.

6. Delete the Assigning Values section of code. Replace it with the following code:

```
System.out.println("Enter the number of quarters.");
    strQuarters = dataIn.readLine();
System.out.println("Enter the number of dimes.");
    strDimes = dataIn.readLine();
System.out.println("Enter the number of nickels.");
    strNickels = dataIn.readLine();
System.out.println("Enter the number of pennies.");
    strPennies = dataIn.readLine();
```

7. Delete the Calculations section of code. Replace the statements that multiply the number of coins by their face value with lines of code that parse the input values and assign the values to variables by typing the following:

quarters = Integer.parseInt(strQuarters) * 25;

dimes = Integer.parseInt(strDimes) * 10;

nickels = Integer.parseInt(strNickels) * 5;

pennies = Integer.parseInt(strPennies) * 1;

8. Compile the program by clicking Tools on the menu bar and then clicking Compile Java. If the compilation results in any errors, correct the errors and recompile the program.

9. Run the program by clicking Tools on the menu bar and then clicking Run Java Application. Enter sample data to test the program. If the program runs correctly, return to TextPad and print a copy of the source code for your instructor. Otherwise, correct any errors and return to step 8.

10. Quit TextPad.

4 Interactive Checkbook Balancing Calculator

The local credit union has asked you to develop a simple program to help customers balance their checkbooks. You decide to write a stand-alone Java application that accepts the beginning balance, the total of the checks written, the total of any deposits, and the fees charged by the bank as inputs. The program then calculates and displays what the ending balance should be. Figure 3-57 displays the results from executing the application. Perform the following steps:

```
C:\WINNT\System32\cmd.exe
BALANCING YOUR CHECKBOOK
        What is the balance from your last statement? 250.47
        What is the total amount of all deposits? 175.00
        What is the total amount of all checks? 183.95
        What is the total amount of all transaction fees? 2.25
Your new balance is $239.27
Press any key to continue . . .
```

FIGURE 3-57

1. Start TextPad. Save the new document as a Java source code file on the Data Disk using the file name Balance.

2. Begin your code by typing a block comment with the Programming Assignment number, your name, the current date, and the program name, Balance.java. Write a description or purpose comment.

3. Type the import statement, class header, and main() method header and their opening braces. Remember to use the phrase, throws IOException, as the program will be interactive.

(continued)

4 Interactive Checkbook Balancing Calculator (continued)

4. Type a constructor for the BufferedReader, as described in this chapter.

5. Declare both String and float variables for beginning balance, total deposits, total checks, and total fees. Declare a float variable for ending balance. Use user-friendly, unique names for each variable.

6. Using System.out.println() methods, enter lines of code to prompt the user for each of the input variables, as shown in Figure 3-57. Include a readLine() method to accept each input and assign it to its corresponding declared String variable.

7. Enter code to convert each input variable to doubles or floats using the appropriate parse() method.

8. Write a formula that takes the beginning balance plus the total deposits minus the checks and fees, and assigns the value to the ending balance.

9. Write an output section that displays an appropriate message and the ending balance on the display.

10. Label each section with an appropriate line comment.

11. Compile your program by pressing CTRL+1.

12. If there are no compilation errors, execute the program by pressing CTRL+2. Enter the sample input data from Figure 3-57; confirm that the program provides correct output data. Run the program again with your own personal data.

13. In the TextPad window, use the Print command on the File menu to print a copy of the code for your instructor.

14. Quit TextPad.

5 Income to Debt Ratio Calculator

Many financial institutions make decisions about extending credit and financing major purchases based on a customer's income to debt ratio. This ratio is the percentage of a customer's income that is spent paying off debts such as mortgages, automobile loans, and other debt, such as credit cards. Typically, all debts are added together and then that total is divided by the customer's monthly income. Customers with a lower income to debt ratio are more likely to qualify for a loan.

As an intern at the Employees' Credit Union, you have been asked to create an interactive income to debt ratio calculation program that can run as a stand-alone application. Input should be via dialog boxes. Table 3-20 on the next page displays the inputs and outputs for the program.

Table 3-20   Inputs and Outputs for Income to Debt Ratio Calculator

INPUTS	OUTPUTS
amount of monthly income	Income to Debt Ratio
amount of mortgage or rent (or zero)	
amount of auto loan (or zero)	
amount of other debt (or zero)	

Perform the following steps.

1. Start TextPad. Save the new document as a Java source code file on the Data Disk. Name the file DebtRatio.

2. Begin your code by typing a block comment with the Programming Assignment number, your name, the current date, and the program name, DebtRatio.java. Write a description or purpose comment.

3. Type a statement to import the javax.swing package.

4. Type the class header and main() method header.

5. Declare the following variables to be Strings: strMonthlyIncome, strMortgage, strAutoLoan, and strOtherDebt.

6. Declare the following variables to be doubles: monthlyIncome, mortgage, autoLoan, otherDebt, and ratio.

7. Create an input section beginning with an appropriate line comment. In order to accept user input, enter showInputDialog() methods to display the prompts and accept user input for monthly income, mortgage, auto loan, and other debt.

8. Create a conversion section, beginning with an appropriate line comment, to parse each of the inputted values.

9. Create a calculation section, beginning with an appropriate line comment, to calculate the income to debt ratio using the following formula: ratio = (mortgage + autoLoan + otherDebt) / monthlyIncome.

10. Create an output section, beginning with an appropriate line comment. Use concatenation to print a message and the variable, ratio, in a JOptionPane dialog or message box.

11. Close both the main() and class methods with closing braces.

12. Compile your program by clicking Tools on the menu bar and then clicking Compile Java.

13. If no compilation errors occur, execute the program by clicking Tools on the menu bar and then clicking Run Java Application. Run the program again with your own personal data.

14. In the TextPad window, use the Print command on the File menu to print a copy of the source code for your instructor.

15. Quit TextPad.

6 Creating an Applet

As Webmaster for a chain of appliance stores, you have been asked to create an applet that will display as part of the store's e-commerce site. The applet will calculate the annual cost of running an appliance. Using text boxes, the applet will ask the user for (1) the cost per kilowatt-hour in cents and (2) the number of kilowatt-hours the appliance uses in a year. Perform the following steps to create the applet. Figure 3-58 displays the applet.

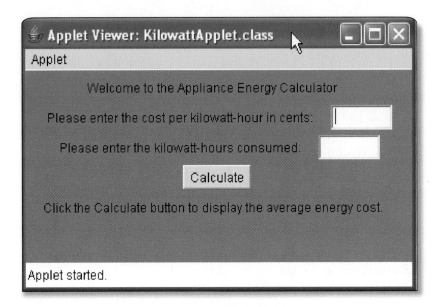

FIGURE 3-58

1. Start TextPad. Save the new document as a Java source code file on the Data Disk using the file name KilowattApplet.

2. Begin your code by typing a block comment with the Programming Assignment number, your name, the current date, and the program name, KilowattApplet.java. Write a description or purpose comment.

3. Type lines of code to import all of the classes from the following packages: java.awt, java.applet, and java.awt.event.

4. Type a class header that extends Applet and implements the ActionListener.

5. Construct the components listed in Table 3-21 on the next page.

Table 3-21 Kilowatt Applet Constructed Components

OBJECT	IDENTIFIER	METHOD PARAMETER (CAPTION OR LENGTH)
Label	welcome	Welcome to the Appliance Energy Calculator
Label	costKwhrLabel	Please enter the cost per kilowatt-hour in cents:
TextField	costKwhrField	5
Label	hoursPerYearLabel	Please enter the kilowatt-hours consumed:
TextField	hoursPerYearField	5
Button	calcButton	Calculate
Label	outputLabel	Click the Calculate button to display the average energy cost.

6. Create an init() method to add all of the above components to the applet interface.

7. Enter the code to add the ActionListener to the calcButton and close the init() method with a brace.

8. Create an actionPerformed() method to convert the input and perform the calculations. Enter the code to get the text from each text box, parse it, and assign it to the appropriate declared variable as shown in Table 3-22.

Table 3-22 KilowattApplet Construction and Conversion Code

```
double costKwhr = Double.parseDouble(costKwhrField.getText());

double kwHours = Double.parseDouble(hoursPerYearField.getText());
```

9. Declare a double variable named average.

10. Write a line of code to perform the calculation that multiplies the cents by the kilowatt-hours in a year and then assigns it to the variable, average.

11. Enter the code from Table 3-23 to round the average with the Math.round() method and assign it to the text of the output label. The Math.round() method includes a casting of the literal 100 to double in order to retain the decimal places.

Table 3-23 KilowattApplet Output Code

```
outputLabel.setText("The average annual cost to operate this appliance is $" +
    Math.round(average* 100)/100D);
```

(continued)

PROGRAMMING ASSIGNMENTS

6 Creating an Applet *(continued)*

12. Close the actionPerformed() method with a closing brace and then close the applet class with a closing brace.

13. Compile your program by clicking Tools on the menu bar and then clicking Compile Java.

14. In the TextPad window, click the New Document button on the Standard toolbar. Type the code from Table 3-24 for the HTML host document.

Table 3-24 HTML Host Document Code

```
<HTML>
<APPLET CODE = "KilowattApplet.class" WIDTH = 430 HEIGHT = 200>
</APPLET>
</HTML>
```

---

15. Save the HTML file on the Data Disk using the file name KilowattApplet.html.

16. Execute the program. Enter the sample data as shown in Table 3-25. Run the program again with your own personal data.

Table 3-25 Sample Data for Appliance Energy Calculator

INPUTS		OUTPUTS
Cost per kilowatt-hour	Number of kilowatt-hours consumed	Annual cost
.086	730	$62.78

---

17. In the TextPad window, use the Print command on the File menu to print a copy of the source code for your instructor; then quit TextPad.

7 Bill's Burgers

Bill's Burgers would like an applet that calculates the sales tax for their front counter help. The applet should let the worker enter the total amount of the customer's order and then calculate a six percent (6%) sales tax. When the worker clicks a Calculate button, the applet should display the amount of the customer's order, the tax, and the total of the customer's order and tax added together. *Hint:* Use a method and formula similar to the one in Table 3-23.

8 Ohm's Law

Ohm's law relates the resistance of an electrical device, such as a portable heater, to the electric current flowing through the device and the voltage applied to it. The law uses the formula

$$I = V/R$$

where V is the voltage, measured in volts; R is the resistance, measured in ohms; and I is the answer, the electrical current, measured in amps. Write an applet that displays a welcome message, two Label prompts, and TextFields. One Label will ask the user to input the voltage; the other Label will ask the user to input the resistance of a device. The applet then will display the current. Remember that because V and R will be entered as integers, the ActionListener will have to parse the numbers into double values in order to perform the division.

9 Calculating the Circumference of a Circle

Your younger brother is studying beginning geometry. He has to calculate the circumference of several different circles and would like to automate the process. Write a stand-alone application for him that calculates the circumference of a circle from the radius. The radius will be an integer value input from the keyboard. Create a method that will accept the integer and perform the calculation using the formula, $2*pi*r$ — that is, 2 times the value of pi times the radius. Use the value 3.14 or the Java variable, Math.PI, in your calculation.

10 Dollars and Cents

Write a program that will spell out the number of dollars and cents based on user numeric input. For instance, if the user inputs 925, the program will print out 9 dollars and 25 cents. For this program, you will use integer arithmetic and will need to avoid floating point arithmetic. Review modular division and the modular operator (%), as discussed in the chapter.

11 Currency Conversion

Because you are an outstanding student, a local civic organization has awarded you a generous sum of money to pursue your education in England. You also plan to do some sightseeing while you are in Europe. The award money is in U.S. dollars, and you want to know how that will convert to the British pound, the euro, and the Russian ruble. Use the concepts and techniques presented in this chapter to create an application that will accept the U.S. dollar amount, convert the U.S. dollar amount, and display the British pound, euro, and Russian ruble equivalents. Use the Web, a newspaper, or a local financial institution to obtain the conversion rates.

12 Using the Sun Microsystems Java Documentation

Use the Java API (http://java.sun.com/j2se/1.5.0/docs/api) to find documentation on Java packages. In particular, search the site for methods in the Math class. Make a list of 8 methods, and describe their arguments and what they return.

13 Moving from the BufferedReader to Scanner

In Programming Assignment 4, you created an interactive checkbook using the BufferedReader to accept input in the console window. Convert the program so that it uses the J2SE version 5.0 Scanner class described on page 148. Import the java.util.* package. You will change the line of code that constructs an instance of the BufferedReader to construct an instance of the Scanner class. Change the lines of code that use the readLine() method to use the nextFloatFloat() method. Insert comment marks in front of lines that previously parsed the data.

14 Moving from Swing to Scanner

In Programming Assignment 5, you created an income to debt ratio calculator with Swing input using dialog boxes. Convert the program so that it uses the J2SE version 5.0 Scanner class described on page 148. Import the java.util.* package. You will construct an instance of the Scanner class. Change the lines of code that use the showInputDialog() method to use the nextDouble() method. Insert comment marks in front of lines that previously parsed the data.

15 Input Usability

Many businesses conduct usability tests evaluating user interfaces. Your job is to provide four versions of user input from which a business may select. Choose any program in this chapter and create the following forms of the same program:

- An application with user input from the BufferedReader at the command prompt, parsing the data from the readLine() method.
- An application with user input from the Scanner class at the command prompt, using the nextInt() or nextDouble() method.
- An application with user input from Swing dialog boxes, parsing the data from the showInputDialog() method.
- An applet with user input from Swing dialog boxes, parsing the data from the showInputDialog() method.

Add comments to each program describing the kind of input and the methods used. Print a copy of each program. Demonstrate the program, in execution, to a classmate. On the back of the printouts, write any feedback about speed, usability, or preferences. Turn the printouts in to your instructor.

16 The Scanner Methods

The Scanner method, new to J2SE version 5.0, uses several different methods to receive user input based on data types. Visit the Sun Microsystems Java API site at http://java.sun.com/j2se/1.5.0/docs/api/. Use the index to find the Scanner class. Scroll to the Method Summary. Choose any four methods that begin with the word, next, and click each one. Read the information provided and write a brief paragraph about each. Turn the paragraphs in to your instructor.

4

Decision Making and Repetition with Reusable Objects

Objectives

You will have
mastered the material in
this chapter when you can:

- Design a program using methods
- Code a selection structure to make decisions in code
- Describe the use of the logical AND, OR, and NOT operators
- Define exceptions and exception handling
- Code a try statement and a catch statement to handle exceptions
- Create a user-defined method
- Code a repetition structure using the while statement
- Write a switch statement to test for multiple values in data
- Format numbers using a pattern and the format() method
- Construct a Color object
- Use a Checkbox and a CheckboxGroup in the user interface

Introduction

Thus far in this book, Java programming examples have included code statements that execute sequentially, from top to bottom, without skipping any code, repeating any code, or branching to another class or method. Realistically, most programs use a **selection structure**, also called an **if...else structure**, to branch to a certain section of code and a **repetition structure** to repeat a certain section of code. Both selection structures and repetition structures are considered to be **control structures,** because the logic of these structures controls the order in which code statements execute. These structures will be covered in detail later in the chapter as you learn how to write code that uses if...else statements, while statements, and switch statements.

You also will learn how to write user-defined methods in Java in order to break tasks into small sections of code that can be reused. You will learn how to write a try statement and a catch statement to handle exceptions, in addition to learning ways to test for validity, reasonableness, and accurate input. Finally, you will learn how to write code to add check boxes and option buttons to an applet.

Chapter Four — Sales Commission

The programs developed in this chapter create a Commission program that GetOuttaTown Travel, a nationwide travel agency, can use to calculate sales commission for their travel agents. The agents at GetOuttaTown Travel can complete three types of sales — telephone, in-store, and outside — each of which earns a different commission percentage. The travel agency requires a computer program that will accept a sales amount and then, based on a choice of commission codes, will calculate a dollar commission amount using the formula, commission = sales amount * commission rate. The commission code identifies the type of sale and commission rate. Telephone sales receive a 10% commission, in-store sales receive a 14% commission, and outside sales receive an 18% commission. Output will include a formatted message displaying the calculated commission.

Two versions of the Commission program are developed in this chapter, as shown in Figure 4-1. First, the Commission program is developed as an application with two dialog boxes that provide text boxes for user input. Next, the Commission program is developed as an applet that uses a text box and option buttons for user input.

(a) User enters sales amount.

(b) User enters commission code.

(c) Application calculates commission.

FIGURE 4-1

(d) Web user enters sales amount and then clicks an option button to display the sales and commission.

Program Development

The program development cycle for the Commission program consists of tasks that correspond to the six development cycle phases, as shown in Table 4-1.

Table 4-1   Commission Program Development Tasks

	DEVELOPMENT PHASE	TASK(S)
1	Analyze the requirements	Analyze the Commission problem.
2	Design the solution	Design the user interface for the console application and the applet, including output data and placement of the applet components and graphic. Design the logic to solve the problem.
3	Validate the design	Confirm with the user that the design solves the problem in a satisfactory manner.
4	Implement the design	Translate the design into code. Include internal documentation (comments and remarks) within the code that explains the purpose of the code statements. Create the HTML file to host the applet.
5	Test the solution	Test the program. Find and correct any errors (debug) until it is error-free.
6	Document the solution	Print copies of the application code, applet code, applet interface, and HTML code.

Analysis and Design

Figure 4-2 shows the requirements document that initiates the development cycle for the Commission program. The requirements document specifies the reason for the request, lists the required inputs and outputs, and shows the algorithm used to compute the commission based on the sales amount and commission rate.

REQUEST FOR NEW APPLICATION

Date submitted:	October 11, 2007
Submitted by:	Patty Witte, GetOuttaTown Travel
Purpose:	Many departments and employees within our travel agency need to calculate sales commission for different types of sales. Our agents receive 10% commission for telephone sales, 14% commission on in-store sales, and 18% commission on outside sales. We need a program that runs both locally and over the Web to give quick feedback on sales commission.
Application title:	Commission
Algorithms:	Users should be able to type in the total sales, select one of the three types of sales mentioned above and then click a button to display the resulting commission. Each type of sales should have a commission code assigned. Sales commission is calculated as follows: • Code 1 = telephone sales amount * .10 • Code 2 = in-store sales amount * .14 • Code 3 = outside sales amount * .18
Notes:	1) You may want to help users enter valid data by reminding them to not enter commas or dollar signs when they enter the sales amount. 2) Please label the commission codes with descriptive words, rather than listing the commission percentages. For example, in the local version running on our desktops, the program should present a simple list with the words, Telephone Sales, In-Store Sales, and Outside Sales, to identify the type of sales. In the Web version, option buttons labeled Telephone Sales, In-Store Sales, and Outside Sales would help users choose the correct commission code. 3) The application should employ dialog boxes to allow users to enter data. Appropriate error messages should display when users enter invalid information. 4) The user should be able to exit the application by clicking a Cancel button or by clicking the Close button in the application window. 5) The attached graphic uses our company colors. Can you try to match the dark red color in the applet?

Approvals

Approval status:	X	Approved
		Rejected
Approved by:	Amir Rubadi	
Date:	October 18, 2007	
Assigned to:	J. Starks, Programmer	

FIGURE 4-2

PROBLEM ANALYSIS   The Commission program should accept and test a numeric value from the user, display a list of codes and test for a valid choice, and then calculate and display results. The program also should include appropriate prompts and messages.

Because this program involves making decisions based on user input, the code that executes each decision can be designed, developed, and tested individually as it is added to the program. Programmers commonly create a small portion of code and then thoroughly test it before moving on to the next section. The object-oriented nature of Java lends itself to this kind of component design, creating reusable portions of code and breaking the programming tasks down into simpler, more manageable steps. Throughout the chapter, the code for each decision is designed and tested as it is added to the program.

DESIGN THE SOLUTION   Once you have analyzed the problem, the next step is to design the user interface and the logic to solve the problem. The Commission program has two versions: a console application and an applet. The console application uses dialog boxes with prompts and text boxes to accept numeric input, and then displays formatted output in a message box, as shown in the storyboard in Figure 4-3a. The applet uses a prompt, a text box, and option buttons to accept input, and then displays formatted output in the applet window, as shown in the storyboard in Figure 4-3b on the next page.

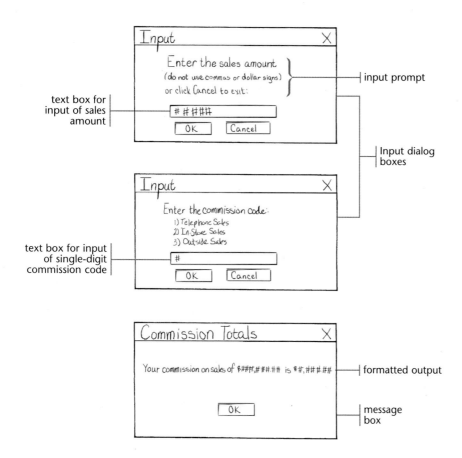

FIGURE 4-3a

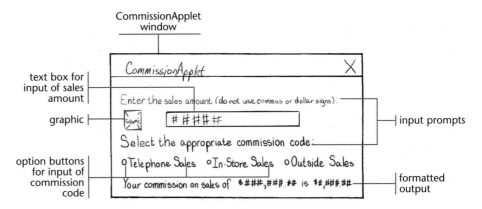

FIGURE 4-3b

PROGRAM DESIGN Once you have designed the interface, the next step is to design the logic to solve the problem and create the desired results. Figure 4-4 shows the flowchart and related pseudocode that represents the logic of the program. Each process symbol references the pseudocode for each of the five methods required in this program. The main() method calls each of these five methods after the program starts.

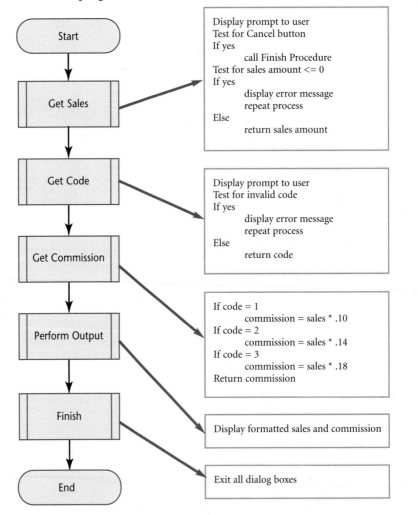

FIGURE 4-4

The getSales() method displays an input dialog box and prompts the user for a sales amount in dollars. If the user clicks the Cancel button or Close button in the user interface, the program will terminate. If not, the getSales() method will make sure the value entered is greater than zero. If the value is not greater than zero, the program will display an error message and allow the user to enter a new value. When a valid value for sales amount is entered, the code returns the value to the main() method for storage.

The getCode() method then displays a list of valid commission codes that the user can enter. The getCode() method also checks for a valid integer between 1 and 3. If an invalid number is entered, the method displays an error message and prompts the user to enter a new value. When a valid value for commission code is entered, the code value is returned to the main() method for storage.

The getComm() method uses the two previous input values to calculate a commission amount using the formula commission = sales amount * commission rate, and then returns it to the main() method for storage.

The output() method displays formatted output with dollar signs, commas, and decimal points. The output message will include the sales amount and the total commission.

The finish() method calls the System.exit() method to close all dialog boxes and then terminate the program.

VALIDATE DESIGN   Once you have designed the program, you can validate the design by stepping through the requirements document and making sure that the design addresses each requirement. If possible, you also should step through the solution with test data to verify that the solution meets the requirements. The user also should review the design to confirm that it solves the problem outlined in the requirements. The user may realize that the instructions the programmer was given do not cover all the company's needs, requiring additional features. By comparing the program design with the original requirements, both the programmer and the user can validate that the solution is correct and satisfactory.

Having analyzed the problem, designed the interface, and designed the program logic, the analysis and design of the application is complete. As shown in Table 4-1 on page 219, the next task in the development cycle is to implement the design by creating a new Java program using TextPad. Implementing the design for this program involves creating Java methods to modularize the task of obtaining a sales amount, using Java's ability to catch errors as they occur, and then creating a module to display an appropriate error message. The program code also involves using code statements that will allow the program to make decisions based on user input.

Starting a New Java Program in TextPad

In Chapter 2, you learned how to start TextPad and save a file using a Java file type. The steps on the next page start TextPad and save the TextPad document using a Java file type.

To Start TextPad and Save a TextPad Document

1. Start TextPad following the steps outlined on page 53. If necessary, click View on the menu bar and then click Line Numbers on the View menu to display line numbers.

2. Insert the Data Disk in drive A. Click File on the menu bar and then click Save As on the File menu.

3. When the Save As dialog box is displayed, type Commission in the File name text box and then click Java (*.java) in the Save as type list. Click the Save in box arrow and then click 3½ Floppy (A:) in the Save in list.

4. Double-click the Chapter04 folder or a location specified by your instructor.

   TextPad will save the file named Commission.java as a Java source code file in the Chapter04 folder on the Data Disk in drive A (Figure 4-5). Your list of files may differ.

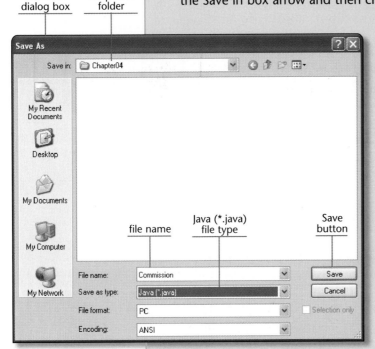

FIGURE 4-5

5. Click the Save button in the Save As dialog box.

OTHER WAYS

1. To start TextPad, click Start button, click TextPad on Start menu
2. To view line numbers, press CTRL+Q, L
3. To save, press F12
4. To save, press ALT+F, A

Coding the Program

As you have learned, the implementation phase of the program development cycle involves writing the code that translates the design into a program. During program design, a flowchart and pseudocode were used to outline the logic of the program code used in the Commission program (Figure 4-4 on page 222). As outlined in that pseudocode, the tasks that the program should perform are to accept two inputs of sales amount and commission code, determine which commission code the user selected, calculate commission using the appropriate formula, and then display the commission as formatted output. The coding process starts with entering the beginning program code.

Entering Beginning Code

Several statements and commands are used as the beginning code in most executable Java programs, including comments, import statements, the class header, and the main method header. In the Commission program, one import statement imports the JOptionPane class from the javax.swing package so that the program can use some of its methods to create and display dialog boxes that display a message or prompt users for an input value. A second import statement imports the DecimalFormat class from the java.text package in order to format the output displayed to the user. The DecimalFormat class will be covered in detail later in the chapter.

The Commission program requires three variables: one to hold the dollar sales amount, one to hold the calculated commission, and one to hold the commission code. Table 4-2 summarizes the data types, variable names, and purposes of the three variables.

Table 4-2   Variables for the Commission Program

DATA TYPE	VARIABLE NAME	PURPOSE
double	dollars	To hold the valid dollar amount of sales
double	answer	To hold the answer returned after commission is calculated
int	empCode	To hold the commission code for the employee's sales

Figure 4-6 displays the comments, import statements, headers, braces, and variable declarations used in the Commission program. Even though this program has no code inside the main() method — other than to declare variables — Java can compile and execute the program successfully.

```
 1  /*
 2        Chapter 4:    Sales Commission
 3        Programmer:  J. Starks
 4        Date:         October 25, 2007
 5        Filename:     Commission.java
 6        Purpose:      This program calculates sales commission using five methods:
 7                      getSales(), getCode(), getComm(), output(), and finish().
 8  */
 9
10  import javax.swing.JOptionPane;
11  import java.text.DecimalFormat;
12
13  public class Commission
14  {
15      public static void main(String[] args)
16      {
17          //declare class variables
18          double dollars, answer;
19          int empCode;
20      }
21  }
```

FIGURE 4-6

This section of code represents a program **stub**, which is an incomplete portion of code entered to allow the developer to compile and test the program. The stub does not actually implement the details of methods, functions, or other elements of the code, but serves as a template or placeholder, in which the developer can later enter code. Using a program stub allows a developer to compile and test a program incrementally while developing the program, to allow for debugging and refinement of code.

The following step enters beginning code.

To Enter Beginning Code

1. Enter the code as shown in Figure 4-6 on the previous page, replacing the programmer name and date shown with your name and the current date.

The TextPad window displays the code for the program stub (Figure 4-7).

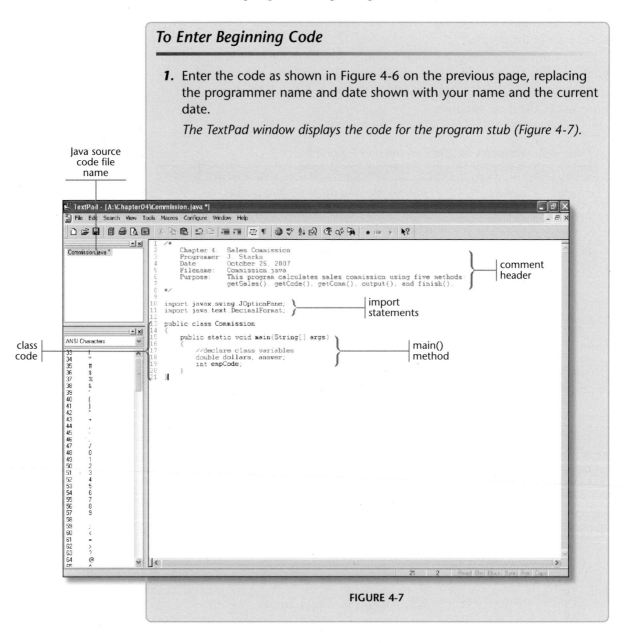

Java source code file name

class code

comment header

import statements

main() method

FIGURE 4-7

Remember that the name of the class must match the name of the Java source code file exactly. In the code entered in the previous step, the Java source code file and the class both use the name Commission. The code created a program stub, which provides the basic template or structure for the code to be entered but does not yet include the detailed code. While the program stub can be compiled and run, it needs additional code to provide the functionality specified in the requirements document.

Compiling and Testing the Program Stub

Recall that the compiler automatically saves the program and then translates the source code into Java bytecode. The following steps show how to test the Commission program stub by compiling the source code and then running the bytecode.

To Compile and Test the Program Stub

1. With the Data Disk in drive A, compile the program by clicking Compile Java on the Tools menu. If TextPad notifies you of errors, click Commission.java in the Selector window, fix the errors, and then compile again.

2. When the program compiles with no errors, if necessary, click Commission.java in the Selector window to display the code in the TextPad window. Click Run Java Application on the Tools menu.

3. When the command prompt window displays, click the Close button in the title bar.

   TextPad compiles and runs the program. No output displays unless the code has errors. If TextPad notifies you of errors, fix the errors and then compile the program again.

OTHER WAYS

1. To compile, press CTRL+1
2. To compile at command prompt, type javac Commission.java
3. To run, press CTRL+2
4. To run at command prompt, type java Commission

Coding, compiling, and then testing a program stub before moving on to the next section of code can provide several benefits. You can check for compilation errors with fewer lines of code, see the results of just one condition or one set of inputs, or debug and look for problems within a narrower framework.

Writing Methods

The object-oriented nature of Java lends itself to modularity in both the program design and implementation processes. **Modularity** is a characteristic of a program in which a larger program's source code is broken down into smaller sections, or modules, of source code. In Java, these modules include methods and classes.

Breaking a large program's source code down into smaller modules applies to both the design process and implementation. As shown in the previous steps, a Java program needs only one public class and one main() method in order to compile the source code. After that, it does not matter how many other methods you add. In a program with many different methods, good program design involves keeping the code for each method in its own separate and reusable section. Thus, instead of writing all code in the main() method, you can write code to transfer execution from the main() method to a user-defined method. The user-defined method (sometimes called a programmer-defined method) is coded in its own separate and reusable section of code, or module.

Recall that a method is a set of instructions used to manipulate values, generate outputs, or perform actions. Methods have a unique name that usually includes an active verb, such as get or write, followed by a descriptive word such as Tax or Output. As with Java-defined methods, any method you write must follow certain syntax rules.

Creating a method is a two-part process that involves writing a call statement and then writing the code for the method itself.

Calling a Method

When you reach the place in the program where the method is to perform its service, you must write code to call the method. The **call** is a line of code stating the name of the method, followed by any data needed by the method in the form of arguments enclosed in parentheses. Once the method performs its service, it may return a value, or an answer, to the program.

Table 4-3 shows the general form of the statements used to call a method.

Table 4-3 *Method Call*	

General form:	1. callMethod(argument); //with one argument
	2. callMethod(argument1, argument2); //arguments separated by commas
	3. callMethod(); //no arguments
	4. firstMethod(secondMethod()); //method used as argument
	5. returnValue = callMethod(argument); //method returns a value

Purpose:	To transfer execution of the program to another method
Examples:	1. `displayOutput(answer);` 2. `getCommission(sales, rate);` 3. `finish();` 4. `System.out.println(output());` 5. `salesTax = getTax(sales);`

In example 1, a method is called and set with one argument, which is enclosed within parentheses. When sending multiple arguments, as in example 2, the arguments are separated by commas. If you have no arguments, as shown in example 3, you still must include the parentheses with nothing inside. As shown in example 4, the method call also can be part of another method or statement. In example 4, the output() method is the argument of the println() method.

In program code, it is quite common to call a method that performs a function designed to return an answer. In that case, the method call becomes part of an assignment statement, as shown in example 5. Example 5 calls a method named getTax(), sends an argument named sales, and receives a return value that the program stores in the variable location named salesTax.

Line 22 in Figure 4-8 shows the line of code that calls the getSales() method in the Commission program. When the method is called, no arguments are sent, but the method returns a value that the program stores in the variable location named dollars.

```
20
21              //call methods
22              dollars = getSales();
23         }
24
25      //The getSales() method asks the user to input a dollar amount and validates it.
26      public static double getSales()
27      {
28              //declare method variables
29              double sales = 0.0;
30
31              String answer = JOptionPane.showInputDialog(null,
                    "Enter the sales amount\n(do not use commas or dollar signs)\n or click Cancel to
                    exit:");
32
33              sales = Double.parseDouble(answer);
34
35              return sales;
36         }
37  }
```

FIGURE 4-8

When a call statement is encountered, the Java compiler looks for a matching method, either a method from an imported package, a method embedded in the application, or a method from an external class. If the call is not accessing a Java-supplied method, the programmer then must write the method header and the section of code statements that define the method.

Coding a Method

When coding a new user-defined method, start the code with the method header. Recall that the method header includes any modifiers, the return value data type or void, the method name, and any parameters in parentheses.

The beginning code for the getSales() method is shown in lines 25 through 36 in Figure 4-8. The purpose of the getSales() method is to receive a valid sales amount and return it to the main() method to be stored in the variable location, dollars. The method header in line 26 contains an access modifier, a method modifier, and the data type of the return value. These three keywords display before the name of the method, getSales(). Recall that an access modifier specifies the circumstances in which the class can be accessed. The access modifier, public, indicates that the method can be accessed by all objects and can be extended, or used, as a basis for another class. The method modifier enables you to set properties for the method, such as where it will be visible and how subclasses of the current class will interact with the method. The method modifier, **static**, indicates that the getSales() method is unique and can be invoked without creating a subclass or instance.

When a method returns a value, the data type of the return value is the third keyword listed before the method name. In this case, the getSales() method returns a double value. Return value identifiers must be declared in the body of the method, as shown in line 29.

After the return data type, the method header then contains the name of the method, getSales. In this program, the method header accepts no passed parameters, so the call statement has no arguments in the parentheses.

When called, the getSales() method will execute the code inside its braces. Line 31 in Figure 4-8 on the previous page uses the showInputDialog() method of the JOptionPane class to instruct the program to display an input dialog box with a message and a text box for user input. The showInputDialog() method has two arguments. The first argument indicates the placement of the dialog box on the screen. The Java keyword, null, instructs the program to display the dialog box centered within the program's active window. The second argument, which is enclosed in quotation marks in line 31, includes the prompt or message to display inside the dialog box. Unless otherwise specified, the showInputDialog() method displays a dialog box with a text box, an OK button, and a Cancel button.

The getSales() method for the Commission program thus causes an input dialog box to display with a message that prompts the user to enter a sales amount. After the user enters the value in the text box and clicks the OK button, line 31 returns and assigns the value to a String variable named answer. In order for math to be performed on the answer, the parseDouble() method in line 33 converts the value to a double data type and assigns it to a variable location named sales.

To return the value to the main() method, the last line inside the getSales() method (line 35) must be a return statement. The **return statement** indicates to the JVM that the method is finished and that execution may return to the main() method. In this program, line 35 returns the value stored in the variable location, sales, back to the main() method. In the main() method, the returned value is assigned to a variable location named dollars. The return value and its resulting storage location, if any, must be of the same data type, but may have different names. For example, the getSales() method declares and uses the variable location, sales, to store the return value, while the main() method declares and uses the variable location, dollars, to store the same return value. When a method is complete, execution always passes back to the next sequential line that follows the call.

This code does not yet validate or test the value entered by the user in any way other than when Java tries to convert it to a double, but it does serve as a stub to allow you to check the method call in line 22.

The following steps enter the code to call the getSales() method and the stub for the getSales() method.

To Enter Code for the getSales() Method

1. Enter lines 20 through 22 as shown in Figure 4-8 on the previous page.

The main() method will call the getSales() method during execution (Figure 4-9). Line 20 is a blank line. As you enter new code, the closing braces for the main() method and class automatically will move down.

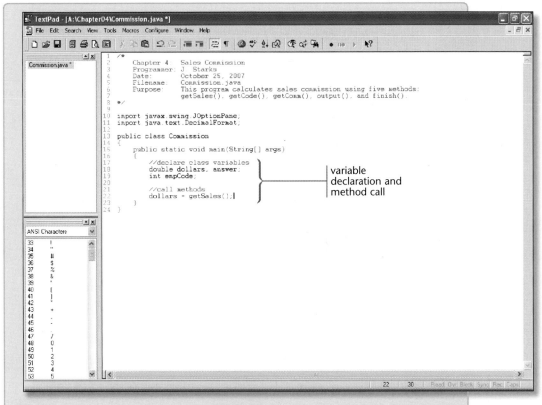

FIGURE 4-9

2. Enter lines 24 through 36 as shown in Figure 4-8 on page 229.

TextPad displays a stub of the getSales() method in the coding window (Figure 4-10). The closing brace for the class moves down to line 37. Depending on your TextPad settings, line 31 may wrap at a different place in your coding window or may not wrap at all.

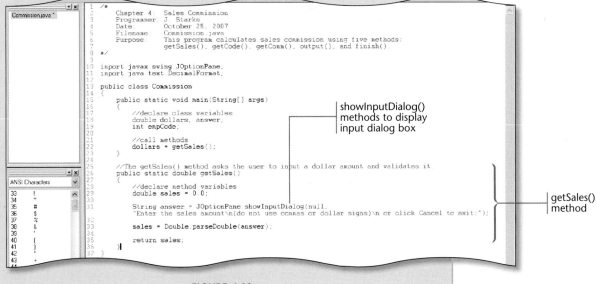

FIGURE 4-10

Tip

Using Word Wrapping in TextPad

In general, you can break a long line of code by pressing the ENTER key after a comma delimiter in the code. Pressing the ENTER key at other places in long lines of code will cause a compile error message to display. Alternatively, you can set TextPad to wrap long lines in the coding window by pressing CTRL+Q and then pressing W. To set TextPad to wrap long lines permanently, click Preferences on the Configure menu. When TextPad displays the Preferences dialog box, click the plus sign next to Document Classes, click Java, and then click the Word wrap long lines check box.

The Commission program now has two internal methods, main() and getSales(). User-defined methods such as getSales() must contain a method header and a set of braces. The only other requirement is that they reside inside a class. Incorrect placement of methods will generate compile errors. In this application, the getSales() method is placed outside of the main() method but within the braces of the Commission class.

Testing the getSales() Method

The following steps test the stub of the getSales() method by compiling and running the source code.

To Compile and Test the getSales() Method

1. With the Data Disk in drive A, compile the program by clicking Compile Java on the Tools menu. If TextPad notifies you of errors, click Commission.java in the Selector window, fix the errors, and then compile again. When the program compiles with no errors, click Run Java Application on the Tools menu.

2. When the Input dialog box displays, type 500 in the text box.

   Entering the test value of 500 confirms that the getSales() method accepts the value input by the user (Figure 4-11).

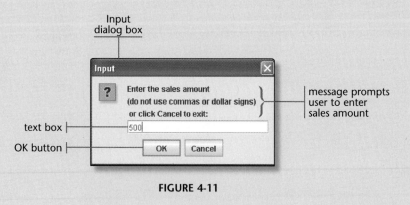

FIGURE 4-11

3. Click the OK button in the Input dialog box.

4. If necessary, click the Close button in the command prompt window title bar.

The Commission program terminates and the command prompt window closes.

OTHER WAYS

1. To compile, press CTRL+1
2. To compile at command prompt, type javac Commission.java
3. To run, press CTRL+2
4. To run at command prompt, type java Commission

When the program runs without any errors, line 33 converts the value entered by the user to a data type of double. No other validation of the data takes place. As you will see in the next section, however, Java provides many tools that programmers can use to test or validate data.

The if...else Statement

The function of the selection structure is to state a condition that allows a program to choose whether to execute one or more lines of code. The selection structure used by Java, also called the **if...else statement**, is used to perform selection or make a decision on whether to execute a particular piece of code based on the evaluation of a condition. The general form of the if...else statement is shown in Table 4-4 on the next page. The if...else logic also is described in detail in Appendix A on page APP 8.

As noted in Table 4-4, the if statement is followed by a condition in parentheses, which is followed by a clause or clauses. A **condition** is a boolean expression that evaluates to true or false. If the condition in an if statement is true, Java acts on the clause or clauses that follow the if statement. A **single-line if statement**, as shown in example 1 in Table 4-4, is used to perform a single task when the condition in the statement is true. A **block if statement**, as shown in example 2, is used to execute more than one command if the condition in the statement is true. Example 3 displays a block if...else specifying that, if the condition in the statement is true, all of the commands in the if clause are executed. If the condition is false, Java acts on the else clause. In either case, after executing the statements in the if clause or else clause, control passes to the statement following the entire if...else statement.

In example 3, if the condition is true, Java takes a path to execute one set of code; if it is false, Java takes a path to execute another set of code. These two paths do not have to have the same number of lines of code; the false condition may result in no action being performed, while the true condition might have many lines of code that execute. The only restriction is that the two paths must come back together after the selection structure, in order to continue processing.

Tip

double vs. Double

Java requires a lowercase d in double when referring to the primitive data type, as programmers do when they declare variables. An uppercase D is required when referring to its wrapper class the – Double class of objects – and its associated methods such as the Double.parseDouble() method. The same is true for other primitive data types and their wrapper classes, such as int and Integer and float and Float.

Table 4-4   The if...else Statement

General form:	1. if (condition) clause; //single result
	2. if (condition)
	    {
	      clause 1;
	      clause 2;
	    } //used for multiple results
	3. if (condition)
	    {
	      clause(s);
	    }
	    else
	    {
	      clause(s);
	    }
	
	where condition is a relation that is evaluated to be boolean (either true or false) and clause is a statement or series of statements; the else keyword and subsequent clause are optional.

Purpose:	To perform selection or make a decision on whether to execute a particular piece of code based on the evaluation of a condition. The words, **if** and **else**, are reserved keywords. The condition must evaluate to a boolean expression. If the condition is true, the clause or clauses following the if statement execute. If the condition is false and an else clause is included, Java executes the else clause. After either clause is executed, control passes to the statement following the if statement in the first form (known as a single-line if statement) and to the statement following the corresponding statement in the second and third forms. Either way, execution passes out of the if statement to the next line of code following the statement.

Examples:	1. `if (age > 65) seniorCount = seniorCount + 1;`
	2. `if (tax >= 0)`
	    `{`
	      `code = "Y";`
	      `text = "Gross Pay";`
	    `}`
	3. `if (marStatus == 1)`
	    `{`
	      `System.out.println("Married");`
	    `}`
	    `else`
	    `{`
	      `System.out.println("Single");`
	    `}`

Each of the single-line if statements, block if statements, or if...else statements may be **nested**, or completely included, within another if statement. For example, in the if...else statement in Figure 4-12, the code in line 15 first tests if the age is greater than 21. If that condition is evaluated as true, a second if statement in line 17 is nested within the first if statement to test if the age is greater than 64. Lines 17 through 26 are said to be nested within the block if statement that begins in line 15.

```
15  if (age > 21)
16  {
17      if (age > 64)
18      {
19          seniorCount = seniorCount + 1;
20          System.out.println("Senior");
21      }
22      else
23      {
24          adultCount = adultCount + 1;
25          System.out.println("Adult");
26      }
27  }
28  else
29  {
30      if (age > 12) System.out.println("Teen");
31      else System.out.println("Youth");
32  }
```

FIGURE 4-12

Lines 30 and 31 are nested within the else clause that begins in line 28; however, because there is only one clause for each of the if and else clauses in lines 30 and 31, no braces are necessary, and the clauses are coded on one line. Programmers normally indent nested structures to facilitate easy reading. TextPad will indent automatically after you type a brace.

When programming selection structures, be careful to use two equal signs (==) in the condition. Beginning programmers sometimes use only one equal sign (=), forgetting that the condition must be boolean, which requires two equal signs (==) for equality. Using only one equal sign (=) results in a compile error. Another common error is forgetting the braces for a block if or else statement. In those cases, Java considers only the first line as part of the condition, incorrectly executing all of the other lines.

Using Operators in an if...else Statement

In many instances, a decision to execute one set of code or another is based on the evaluation of one or more conditions. In Chapter 3, you learned that different types of comparison operators are used in conditional expressions to evaluate the relationship between two expressions or values logically. Relational operators are used to compare the relation of two values; equality operators are used to determine if two values are equal. The values may be variables, constants, numbers, strings, or the result of a function or method.

Another type of operator, the **logical operator**, is used to connect two conditional expressions. As shown in Table 4-5 on the next page, the logical **AND operator** (&&) connects two expressions, x and y, so that both conditions individually must be evaluated as true for the entire expression, x && y, to be evaluated as true. The logical **OR operator** (||) connects two expressions, x and y, so that the whole expression, x || y, evaluates to true if either x or y evaluates to true, or if they both do. The logical **NOT operator** (!) connects two expressions, x and y, so that if x evaluates to true, then the expression !x evaluates to false, and vice versa.

Table 4-5 shows the equality, relational, and logical operators used in Java, including examples of each and the result of evaluating the condition.

Table 4-5 Operator Results in Selection Structures

OPERATOR	MEANING	EXAMPLE	RESULT	TYPE
= =	equal to	2 == 2 1 == 6	true false	equality
!=	not equal to	7 != 4 4 != 4	true false	equality
<	less than	3 < 5 5 < 3	true false	relational
<=	less than or equal to	4 <= 6 7 <= 6	true false	relational
>	greater than	9 > 7 7 > 9	true false	relational
>=	greater than or equal to	8 >= 8 8 >= 10	true false	relational
&&	logical AND (both conditions must be true in order to make the condition true)	(7 > 3) && (0 < 1) (7 > 3) && (1 < 0)	true false	logical
||	logical OR (one of the conditions must be true in order to make the condition true)	(7 > 3) || (1 < 0) (3 > 7) || (1 < 0)	true false	logical
!	logical NOT (condition must evaluate to false in order to make the condition true)	! (5 == 4) ! (a == a)	true false	logical

Coding an if Statement to Test the Cancel Button

As shown in the previous steps, when executed, the getSales() method displays a dialog box prompting the user to enter a dollar amount. The dialog box contains a text box for user input and two buttons: an OK button and a Cancel button. If the user clicks the Cancel button, the program should terminate. If the user clicks the OK button, the method validates the user input.

An if statement, as shown in line 33 of Figure 4-13, is used to test if the user clicked the Cancel button. When clicked, the Cancel button in a JOptionPane dialog box returns a blank value to the variable, answer. Line 33 uses the equal to operator (= =) to compare the variable, answer, against a null. In Java, **null** is a constant that represents the presence of no data. If the return value matches, or is equal to, null, the condition is evaluated to be true and the finish() method is called.

```
31              String answer = JOptionPane.showInputDialog(null,
                "Enter the sales amount\n(do not use commas or dollar signs)\n or click Cancel to
                exit:");
32
33              if (answer == null) finish();
34
35              sales = Double.parseDouble(answer);
36
37              return sales;
38          }
39
40          //The finish() method ends the program.
41          public static void finish()
42          {
43              System.exit(0);
44          }
45      }
```

FIGURE 4-13

The finish() method, displayed in lines 40 through 44, calls the System.exit()
method in line 43 to terminate the program. Note that the if statement in line 33
could call the System.exit() method directly, bypassing the need for the extra
finish() method. While that approach might work within the getSales() method,
coding the System.exit() method in the finish() method allows it to be called
from multiple methods, thus reducing code redundancy and keeping a single
exit for the program no matter which method calls it. Other uses for methods
such as finish() include opportunities to display a closing message, to save data,
or to perform memory clean-up tasks. Later in the chapter, after all data is validated and the commission rate has displayed to the user, an additional call to the
finish() method is added to the program.

The following steps enter an if statement to test the Cancel button.

To Code an if Statement to Test the Cancel Button

1. Enter lines 33 and 34 as shown in Figure 4-13.

*The if statement will compare the variable, answer, to the null constant
(Figure 4-14). Line 34 is a blank line.*

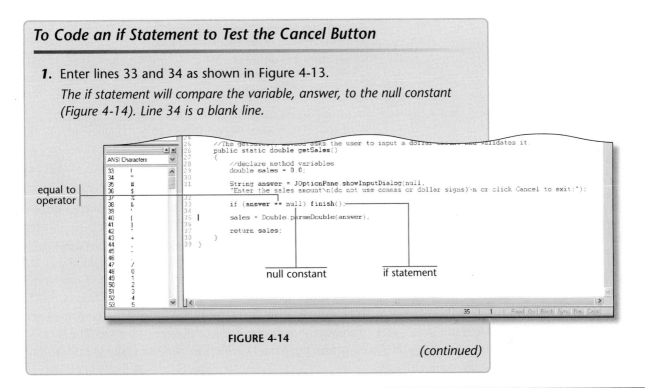

FIGURE 4-14

(continued)

2. Enter lines 39 through 44 as shown from Figure 4-13.

TextPad displays the finish() method in the coding window. The closing brace for the class moves down to line 45. When called, the finish() method will exit the program (Figure 4-15).

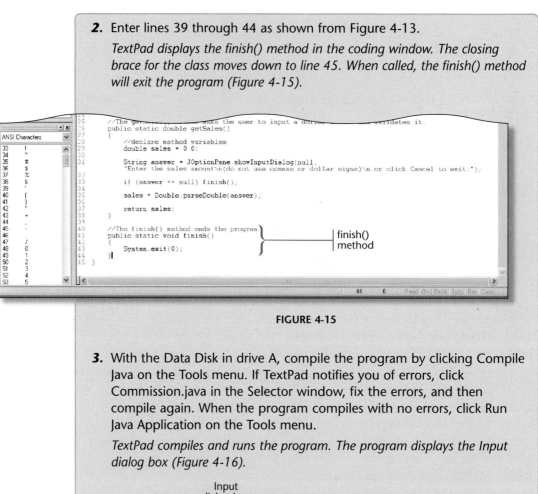

FIGURE 4-15

3. With the Data Disk in drive A, compile the program by clicking Compile Java on the Tools menu. If TextPad notifies you of errors, click Commission.java in the Selector window, fix the errors, and then compile again. When the program compiles with no errors, click Run Java Application on the Tools menu.

TextPad compiles and runs the program. The program displays the Input dialog box (Figure 4-16).

FIGURE 4-16

4. Click the Cancel button. Click the Close button in the command prompt window title bar.

The Commission program terminates and the command prompt window closes.

If the user clicks the Cancel button during program execution, the program does not need to try to convert the input value to a double data type. The if statement thus is placed before the parseDouble() method to make the program code more efficient.

Coding an if Statement to Test Multiple Conditions

The previous steps included code that tested for only one condition at a time. While this is common, an if statement or an if...else statement can test more than one possible condition as well. The logical AND operator (&&) typically would be used for situations in which you might want to test more than one piece of data at the same time. For example, a program that checks for adult male students might compare the gender with a code 1 for male and compare the age with a numeric value. In this case, each condition is enclosed in its own set of parentheses, as shown in the following line of code.

```
if ((gender == 1) && (age >= 18))
```

The logical OR operator (||) typically would be used for testing the same piece of data in two different ways. For example, a program that tests an age for possible child or senior discount might compare the age against two different numeric values, as shown in the following line of code.

```
if ((age < 13) || (age > 65))
```

The logical NOT operator (!) typically would be used for testing a boolean piece of data that evaluates to true or false. For example, a programmer might assign a boolean true value to the variable, done, in response to a user's input to quit the program. If done were not set, then processing would continue. The if statement using the NOT operator might display as shown in the following line of code.

```
if (!done)
```

The logical operators produce boolean results – that is, they evaluate to true or false. The values or operands used in the expressions also must be boolean. An important characteristic of the logical AND and OR is that if the left operand can be sufficient to decide the condition, the right side never is evaluated. For example, if the left side of the logical AND operator (&&) evaluates to false, the condition automatically is false and the right side need not be evaluated. The left operand is sufficient to decide that the condition evaluates to false.

Exception Handling

An **exception** is a Java event resulting from an unusual or erroneous situation which disrupts the normal program flow of instructions. An exception also sometimes is referred to as a **run-time exception** or run-time error, as discussed in Chapter 2. **Exception handling** is the general concept of planning for possible exceptions by directing the program to deal with them gracefully without terminating prematurely. For example, in Chapter 3, possible exceptions were handled by adding the code, throws IOException, to the main() method header. The code gave the program a way to acknowledge and handle potential input or output errors and still compile correctly.

Java has different types of exceptions, including the I/O exceptions covered in Chapter 3, run-time exceptions, and checked exceptions. As you have learned, a run-time exception occurs within the Java run-time system and includes arithmetic exceptions, such as when dividing by zero. Run-time exceptions can occur anywhere in a program and may be quite numerous.

When a run-time exception occurs, the run-time system then looks for a handler, or a way to handle the exception. A **checked exception** is one in which the compiler checks each method during compilation to ensure that each method has a **handler** — the code used to address any possible exceptions.

A method can handle a checked exception in one of two ways: (1) by handling the exception using a catch statement, or (2) by throwing the exception to the code that called the method. By using the keyword, throws, in the method header, the method **claims** the exception; in other words, it lets the compiler know that it may pass along an exception rather than handling it.

Using a checked exception thus allows programmers to catch an exception and handle it in the program. Often programmers write code to catch the exception at the exact point in the program where it might occur, or in other cases, they write code within a calling method, thereby handling it at a higher level.

If the programmer does not code a way to catch the exception, the program may terminate prematurely and display an exception error message. In some cases, Java may throw an exception representing an unrecoverable situation, such as an out of memory error, which is a more serious problem. The object created in response to such an exception can be caught; however, it is not required because it indicates a serious problem that an application should not try to catch.

Handling Exceptions Using try and catch Statements

Java provides several ways to write code that checks for exceptions. One object-oriented way to handle exceptions is to include the lines of code that might cause exceptions inside a try statement. The **try statement** identifies a block of statements that potentially may throw an exception. If an exception occurs, the try statement transfers execution to a handler. Table 4-6 shows an example of the try statement.

Table 4-6   The try Statement

| General form: | ```
try
{
    . . . lines of code that might generate an exception;
    . . .throw new exceptionName;
}
``` |
|---|---|
| Purpose: | To enclose the code statements that might throw an exception. **Try** and **throw new** are reserved words. All statements within the braces in the try statement are monitored for exceptions. Programmers may **explicitly**, or purposefully, cause an exception by typing the words, throw new, followed by the name of a standard Java exception object. A try statement must be followed by a catch statement. |
| Example: | ```
try
{
    answer = 23 / 0; //Java throws exception automatically
    throw new DivideByZeroException(); //programmer explicitly
        throws exception
}
``` |

As noted in Table 4-6, all statements within the braces of the try statement are monitored for exceptions. The try statement notifies the JVM that you plan to deal with them as checked exceptions rather than just allowing them to happen. Any exception occurring as a result of code within the try statement will not terminate the program; rather, you as the programmer will handle the exception through coding.

When an exception occurs, a new exception object is created. The exception object contains information about the exception, such as its location and type. If a run-time exception occurs, the program method that creates the exception object automatically throws it to the run-time system.

You also can cause an exception explicitly, or purposefully, by using a throw statement. The **throw statement** transfers execution from the method that caused the exception to the handler that addresses any possible exceptions. The throw statement is followed by the constructor keyword, new, and a single argument, which is the name of the exception object.

If an exception occurs in the try statement, the throw statement transfers execution from the try statement to the catch statement to handle the exception. The try statement thus must be followed by a catch statement. The **catch statement** consists of the keyword, catch, followed by a parameter declaration that identifies the type of exception being caught and an identifier name in parentheses. The identifier name holds a Java-assigned error value that can access more information about the error through the use of messages. Inside the catch statement braces, you can include statements to either describe the error to the user or fix the error through programming. Table 4-7 shows an example of the catch statement.

Table 4-7   The catch Statement

General form:	catch(ExceptionName identifier)
	{
	   . . . lines of code that handle the exception;
	}

Purpose:	To handle an exception generated in the try statement. **Catch** is a reserved word. ExceptionName is the name of a standard Java exception. Identifier is a variable name to hold a Java-assigned error value. A catch statement optionally may be followed by a finally statement to continue more processing.

Example:	catch(ArithmeticException errNum)
	{
	    System.out.println("An arithmetic error has occurred. " +
	    errNum.getMessage());
	    // message prints with Java-generated data
	}

Used together in a program, the try statement and catch statement are used to handle exceptions. For example, if a user error causes a program to try to divide by zero, the program normally would abort with the following error message:

```
Exception in thread "main" java.lang.ArthmeticException: / by zero
```

If, however, the code is put in a try statement and the same exception occurs, execution is thrown to the corresponding catch statement. The catch statement then can execute code that instructs the program to display a descriptive message to the user and perhaps let the user reenter the data.

As previously discussed, Java may generate the exception, as in the division by zero example above, or you may use the keywords, throw new, to throw the exception explicitly or intentionally. For example, if Java expects an integer input and the user types a decimal point, a NumberFormatException displays and the program terminates. A **NumberFormatException** indicates an operation attempted to use a number in an illegal format. In another example, as shown in Table 4-6 on page 4.24, you could instruct Java to throw a DivideByZeroException if you tried to divide a value by zero by using the following code:

```
throw new DivideByZeroException();
```

Alternately, you might want to create a new exception type. For example, to handle an exception when a user enters the wrong password, you could enter the following line of code:

```
throw new WrongPasswordException();
```

The program then would call the class, WrongPasswordException, if the user entered the wrong password. That new class must be defined by the programmer, however, and be accessible to the class that contains the throw statement.

The throw statement within the try statement causes execution to be transferred to the catch statement. That way, control passes to the same error-handling routine whether the exception is caught by the JVM, as in a data type error, or caught by the programmer testing for an invalid or unreasonable number.

As with the if statement, the try and catch statements can be nested within any other code statements. In addition, you can have more than one catch statement in the same program, or even within the same method, if you are trying to catch multiple types of exceptions.

Catching a NumberFormatException in the getSales() Method

In the Commission program, a valid sales amount must be numeric. The JOptionPane input dialog box, however, does not restrict the type of data entered in the text box. As a result, regardless of what data the user enters, the input is stored in the variable location named answer. If, however, the user has entered alphabetic data and the code tries to parse it, the code will generate a NumberFormatException — an exception that must be caught. To catch the exception, you should include the parse code inside a try statement and write a catch statement to handle the exception.

Figure 4-17 displays the try statement and catch statement used to handle the exception. Lines 35 through 38 show the try statement and the braces enclosing the code that parses the answer value. Lines 39 through 42 catch the NumberFormatException and display a JOptionPane message box. The catch statement will execute only if a NumberFormatException occurs in line 37; when it executes, the catch statement handles the error by displaying a message box rather than allowing Java to terminate the program.

```
34
35          try
36          {
37              sales = Double.parseDouble(answer);
38          }
39          catch(NumberFormatException e)
40          {
41              JOptionPane.showMessageDialog(null,"Your entry was not in the proper format.",
                "Error",JOptionPane.INFORMATION_MESSAGE);
42          }
43          return sales;
```

FIGURE 4-17

The following step enters the try and catch statements.

To Code the try and catch Statements

1. Enter lines 35 through 36 and lines 38 through 42 as shown in Figure 4-18. Use proper spacing and indentation.

The try and catch statements are displayed in the TextPad coding window (Figure 4-18). Line 37 is indented within the braces of the try statement. Line 41 wraps. If your display does not wrap, click Word Wrap on the Configure menu.

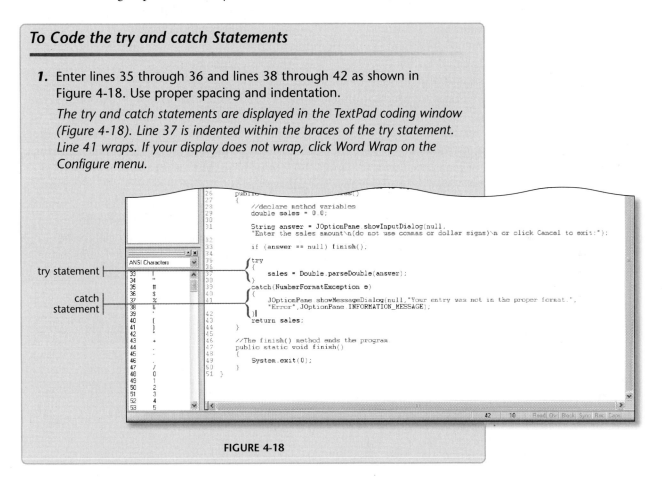

FIGURE 4-18

The try and catch statements may be followed by an optional finally statement, which is placed after the catch statement. The **finally statement** typically contains code to perform any cleanup that might be necessary after executing the try statement and catch statement. The finally statement always is executed, regardless of whether the try statement generates an exception. The most common usage of the finally statement is to release a resource specifically allocated for use by a method, such as an open file.

When execution transfers to the catch statement, the program performs a validity check. Checking **validity** involves testing data to ensure that it uses the correct data type. The code entered in the previous step handles an exception caused by entering values that did not match the type of data the program expected. You did not write the code to test for the condition yourself; you merely caught the JVM interpreter's throw of the NumberFormatException.

Throwing an Exception

Input from the user also should be checked for **reasonableness** — that is, that the values entered are within reason as expected input. For example, in the Commission program, any positive number might be a reasonable answer for the sales amount, as you do not know how many sales a travel agent may have completed to earn commission. Negative amounts and the number zero, while valid integers, would not be reasonable. Additionally, according to the requirements document for the Commission program, a sales amount cannot be negative and cannot be zero. If users input a negative number or zero, a message should display notifying them of their error.

Because you have already coded a catch statement to handle exceptions, you can use a throw statement to create your own NumberFormatException when the user inputs an unreasonable number. The throw statement, followed by the constructor keyword, new, will transfer execution to the catch statement. Using the catch statement to handle this exception, as well as for the previous exception, is an example of how Java allows the reuse of objects.

Line 38 in Figure 4-19 displays an if statement that tests for an unreasonable sales amount that is less than or equal to zero. If the condition is found to be true, the program will generate an exception through an explicit call to the NumberFormatException() method. Because this section of code is within the try statement, execution will transfer to the catch statement.

```
35          try
36          {
37              sales = Double.parseDouble(answer);
38              if (sales <= 0) throw new NumberFormatException();
39          }
```

FIGURE 4-19

The following step enters code to throw an exception explicitly.

To Enter Code to Throw an Exception

1. Enter line 38 as shown in Figure 4-19.

TextPad displays the code to throw an exception in the TextPad coding window (Figure 4-20).

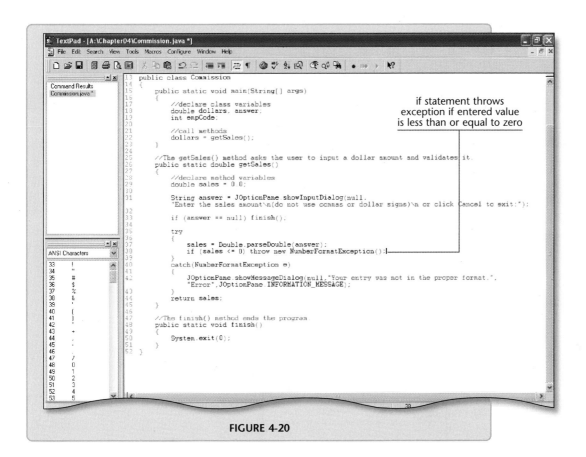

FIGURE 4-20

The try and catch statements are ready to be tested. The code can be tested by entering alphabetic data, a negative sales amount, and a zero sales amount in the Input dialog box. The program will catch the exception and display an Error message box with the message coded in line 42. The following steps compile and test the try and catch statements.

To Compile and Test the try and catch Statements

1. With the Data Disk in drive A, compile the program by clicking Compile Java on the Tools menu. If TextPad notifies you of errors, click Commission.java in the Selector window, fix the errors, and then compile again. When the program compiles with no errors, click Run Java Application on the Tools menu.

2. When the Input dialog box displays, type seventy-nine in the text box. Click the OK button.

3. When the Error dialog box displays, click the OK button. Click the Close button in the command prompt window title bar.

4. Run the program again. When the Input dialog box displays, type –382 in the text box. When the Error dialog box displays, click the OK button. Click the Close button in the command prompt window title bar.

(continued)

5. Run the program again. When the Input dialog box displays, type 0 in the text box. When the Error dialog box displays, click the OK button. Click the Close button in the command prompt window title bar.

With each run, the Error dialog box displays an error message stating that the data entered was not in the proper format (Figure 4-21).

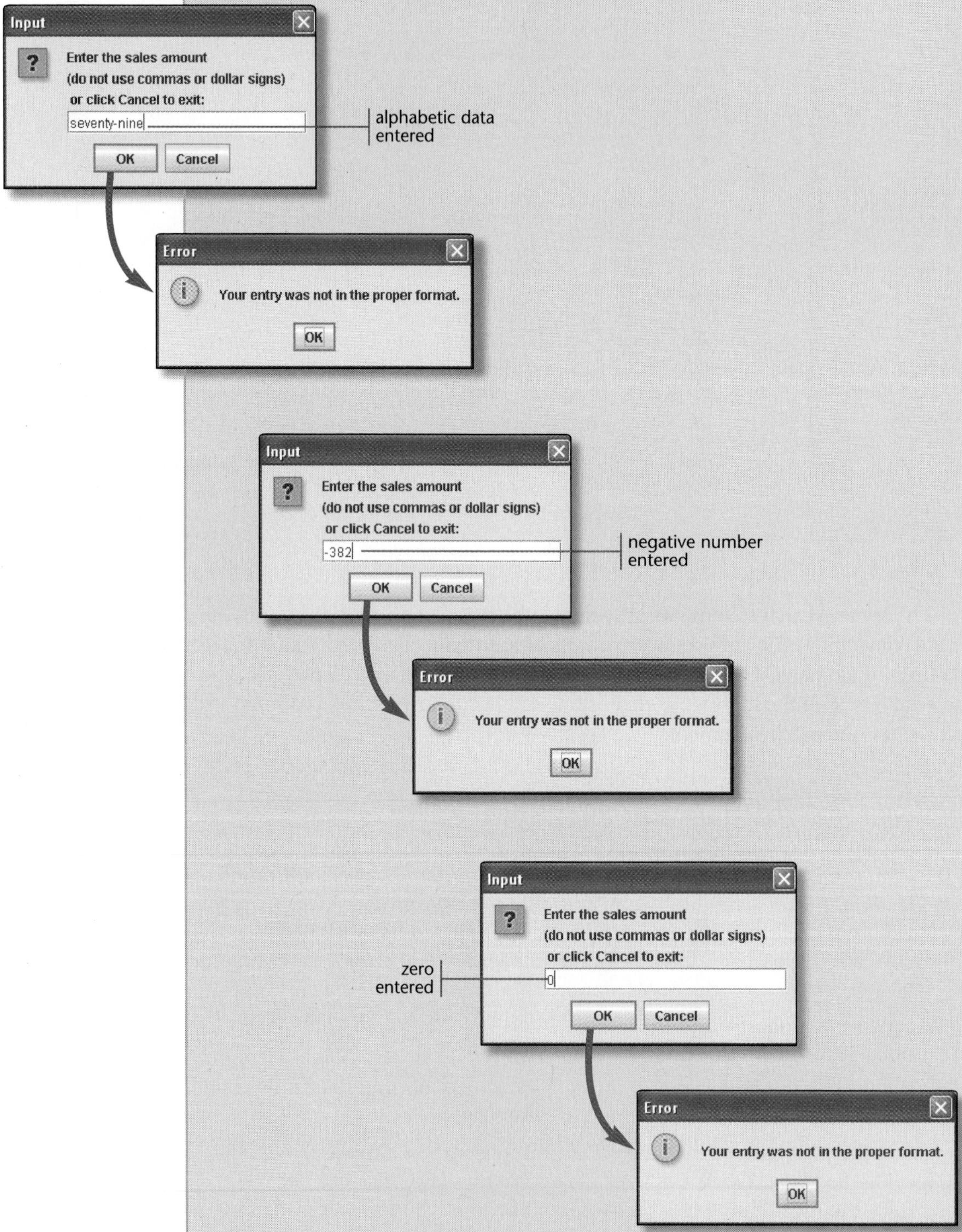

alphabetic data entered

negative number entered

zero entered

FIGURE 4-21

It is important to have a well thought-out and consistent exception-handling strategy for the sake of efficiency and good programming practice. Exception handling should not be considered an afterthought, but an integral part of the development process. Having a consistent exception-handling strategy helps develop applications that are robust and dependable by design rather than by accident. The Java Language Specification states that "an exception will be thrown when semantic constraints are violated," which implies that an exception throws in situations that ordinarily are not possible or in the event of a violation of normal program behavior. Therefore, sometimes it is easier to address data entry errors with simple if statements that display error messages, rather than by throwing exceptions. On the other hand, if the error is related to a type of exception that Java already is handling in the program, it makes sense to reuse that catch code to validate the data entry.

Repetition Structure

Thus far in this program code, if the user enters an invalid or unreasonable number, the program terminates. A message displays notifying the user of the error, but it does not allow the user to reenter the data and try again without rerunning the entire program. As previously noted, Java uses a repetition structure to repeat a certain section of code. This repetitive, or iterative, process is referred to as **looping**. The Commission program will use a repetition structure so that if the user enters an invalid or unreasonable number, it again displays the Input dialog box so that the user can try again to enter valid and reasonable data.

The while Statement

Java uses a special repetition structure, called a **while loop,** for looping when the exact number of repetitions is unknown. To code a while loop, you code a **while statement**, starting with the keyword, while, followed by a condition in parentheses. All of the code that should be repeated, or looped, while the condition evaluates to true is enclosed in braces. Table 4-8 on the next page shows the general form of the while statement. The repetition structure and the while statement also are described in detail in Appendix A on page APP 8.

Table 4-8   The while Statement

General form:	```while(condition)
	{
	. . . lines of code to repeat while above condition is true;
	}```

Purpose:	To create a process that will repeat, or loop through, executing a series of statements while the condition in the while statement is true. The word, **while**, is a reserved keyword. The condition must be a boolean expression that evaluates to true or false. The code repeats as long as the condition is evaluated as true. The condition eventually must evaluate to false in order to exit the loop.

Example:	```while(!done)
	{
	    System.out.println("Are you done (yes or no)");
	    String answer = dataIn.readLine();
	    if (answer == "yes") done;
	}```

The getSales() method requires that its statements continue to be executed while the sales amount data entered by the user is invalid. If the program throws an exception, it should loop back to the JOptionPane input dialog box and allow the user to enter a new sales amount. Figure 4-22 displays the complete getSales() method definition. Lines 30 through 34, line 43, and line 49 are new to the method.

```
25      //The getSales() method asks the user to input a dollar amount and validates it.
26      public static double getSales()
27      {
28          //declare method variables
29          double sales = 0.0;
30          boolean done = false;
31
32          //loop while not done
33          while(!done)
34          {
35              String answer = JOptionPane.showInputDialog(null,
                "Enter the sales amount\n(do not use commas or dollar signs)\n or click Cancel
                to exit:");
36
37              if (answer == null) finish();
38
39              try
40              {
41                  sales = Double.parseDouble(answer);
42                  if (sales <= 0) throw new NumberFormatException();
43                  else done = true;
44              }
45              catch(NumberFormatException e)
46              {
47                  JOptionPane.showMessageDialog(null,
                    "Your entry was not in the proper format.", "Error",
                    JOptionPane.INFORMATION_MESSAGE);
48              }
49          }
50          return sales;
51      }
```

FIGURE 4-22

Line 30 declares a boolean variable, done, and assigns it a value of false, thus allowing the program to enter the loop structure that begins with the while statement in line 33. The exclamation point is the logical NOT operator, thus causing the code in the while statement to loop when the value of done is not true. Recall that boolean variables may be used as conditions. In this example, the variable serves as a flag to notify the loop whether or not to execute. The braces for the while statement in lines 34 and 49 enclose the code that should repeat until the value of done is true.

Within the body of the while loop, some trigger must cause the loop to stop — in other words, something must happen within the code that changes the state of the boolean variable, done. In line 43, an else clause has been added to the selection structure. The else clause is executed if the entered sales amount did not throw an exception automatically when the sales amount was parsed in line 41, and was not greater than zero in line 42. When execution passes back to line 33, the true value will cause the loop created by the while statement to stop executing. Control then will pass to line 50, outside the while statement.

The following step adds the code for the while loop to the getSales() method.

To Enter Code for the while Statement

1. Within the getSales() method in the Commission program, enter new lines 30 through 34, line 43, and line 49 as shown in Figure 4-22. Use appropriate spacing and indentation.

The new code is displayed (Figure 4-23). Your lines may wrap differently.

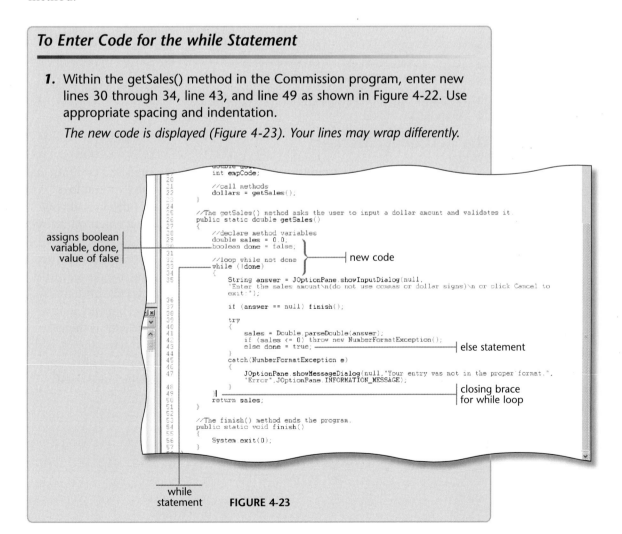

FIGURE 4-23

Testing the while Statement

The following steps compile and test the while statement.

To Compile and Test the while Statement

1. With the Data Disk in drive A, compile the program by clicking Compile Java on the Tools menu. If TextPad notifies you of errors, click Commission.java in the Selector window, fix the errors, and then compile again. When the program compiles with no errors, click Run Java Application on the Tools menu.

2. When the program displays the Input dialog box, type -35000 and then click the OK button.

3. When the program displays the Error dialog box, click the OK button.

4. When the program again displays the Input dialog box, type 35000 and then click the OK button. Click the Close button in the command prompt window title bar.

The program displays an error message when a negative number is entered. The program accepts the positive value as valid input data.

Run the program several more times and test valid and invalid entries for sales amounts, such as zero or alphanumeric data.

The getCode() Method

The next step after obtaining a valid sales amount is to request a commission code. The method to accept a valid commission code from the user employs similar logical constructs as the getSales() method. Figure 4-24 displays the line of code to call the getCode() method (line 23) and the getCode() method definition (lines 53 through 80).

In the getCode() method, line 58 declares the variable, code, and assigns an initial value of 0. Line 59 declares a boolean variable, done, and assigns an initial value of false. Execution then enters the while statement in lines 62 through 78, which repeats until a valid code is entered. The try and catch statements in lines 64 through 77 handle any exceptions by displaying an error message if the user enters an invalid commission code. Note that it is acceptable to reuse the variable name, done, in line 59 because each occurrence is local in scope — that is, the occurrence of the variable, done, is unique to the method in which it is used.

```
23              empCode = getCode();
```

```
53
54          //The getCode() method retrieves a code from the user and validates it.
55          public static int getCode()
56          {
57              //declare method variables
58              int code = 0;
59              boolean done = false;
60
61              //loop while not done
62              while(!done)
63              {
64                  try
65                  {
66                      String message = "Enter the commission code:" +
                        "\n\n1) Telephone Sales\n2) In-Store Sales\n3) Outside Sales\n\n";
67
68                      code = Integer.parseInt(JOptionPane.showInputDialog(null,message))
69
70                      //test for valid codes 1, 2, or 3
71                      if (code<1 || code>3) throw new NumberFormatException();
72                      else done = true;
73                  }
74                  catch(NumberFormatException e)
75                  {
76                      JOptionPane.showMessageDialog(null,"Please enter a 1, 2, or 3.",
                        "Error",JOptionPane.INFORMATION_MESSAGE);
77                  }
78              }
79              return code;
80          }
```

FIGURE 4-24

Line 66 assigns the String data used to define the prompt to a variable named message. The String data includes the user prompt, Enter the commission code:, followed by a numbered list of valid commission codes. Recall that the escape character sequence, \n, will cause the data that follows it to print on a new line. When you convert this program to an applet later in the chapter, you will learn how to create option buttons from which the user can choose a commission code. For this application, however, the numbered list presents an easy to understand set of choices to the user.

In line 68, the variable, message, is included as the second argument of the showInputDialog() method, which will cause the message to display as a prompt in the Input dialog box. The value entered by the user serves as the return value of the method and thus becomes the argument for the parseInt() method. After the input is returned and parsed, it then is assigned to the variable, code. Wrapping a method inside another, as shown in line 68, commonly is used in Java programming because it reduces the number of lines of code.

Line 71 uses the logical OR operator to test for commission codes less than one or greater than three. In either case, a NumberFormatException is explicitly thrown, and execution transfers to the catch statement, which displays a message in an Error dialog box (line 76). The program then loops back to allow the user to reenter a new, valid commission code.

Line 79 returns the valid code to the calling statement in line 23, where it is assigned to the variable, empCode.

The following steps enter code to call and then execute the getCode() method.

To Enter Code for the getCode() Method

1. Enter line 23 as shown in Figure 4-24 on the previous page into the main() method of the Commission program.

The statement calls the getCode() method and assigns its return value to a variable named empCode (Figure 4-25).

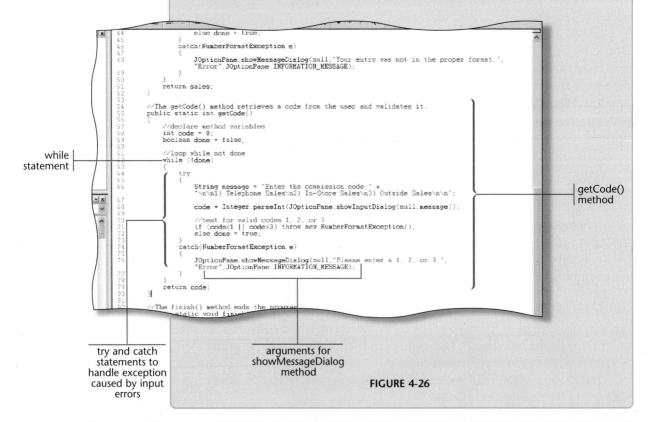

```
13  public class Commission
14  {
15      public static void main(String[] args)
16      {
17          //declare class variables
18          double dollars, answer;
19          int empCode;
20
21          //call methods
22          dollars = getSales();
23          empCode = getCode();            method call
24      }
25
26      //The getSales() method asks the user to input a dollar amount and validates it.
27      public static double getSales()
28      {
29          //declare method variables
30          double sales = 0.0;
31          boolean done = false;
32
33          //loop while not done
34          while (!done)
35          {
36              String answer = JOptionPane.showInputDialog(null,
                  "Enter the sales amount\n(do not use commas or dollar signs)\n or click Cancel to
                  exit:");
```

FIGURE 4-25

2. Enter lines 53 through 80 as shown in Figure 4-24.

TextPad displays the getCode() method in the coding window (Figure 4-26).

```
44              else done = true;
45          }
46          catch(NumberFormatException e)
47          {
48              JOptionPane.showMessageDialog(null,"Your entry was not in the proper format.",
                  "Error",JOptionPane.INFORMATION_MESSAGE);
49          }
50      }
51      return sales;
52  }
53
54      //The getCode() method retrieves a code from the user and validates it.
55      public static int getCode()
56      {
57          //declare method variables
58          int code = 0;
59          boolean done = false;
60
61          //loop while not done
62          while (!done)
63          {
64              try
65              {
66                  String message = "Enter the commission code:" +
                      "\n\n1) Telephone Sales\n2) In-Store Sales\n3) Outside Sales\n\n";
67
68                  code = Integer.parseInt(JOptionPane.showInputDialog(null,message));
69
70                  //test for valid codes 1, 2, or 3
71                  if (code<1 || code>3) throw new NumberFormatException();
72                  else done = true;
73              }
74              catch(NumberFormatException e)
75              {
76                  JOptionPane.showMessageDialog(null,"Please enter a 1, 2, or 3.",
                      "Error",JOptionPane.INFORMATION_MESSAGE);
77              }
78          }
79          return code;
80      }
81
82      //The finish() method ends the program
            static void fini
```

while statement — (points to line 62)

getCode() method — (points to lines 53–80)

try and catch statements to handle exception caused by input errors

arguments for showMessageDialog method

FIGURE 4-26

Testing the getCode() Method

The following steps compile and test the getCode() method.

To Compile and Test the getCode() method

1. With the Data Disk in drive A, compile the program by clicking Compile Java on the Tools menu. If TextPad notifies you of errors, click Commission.java in the Selector window, fix the errors, and then compile again. When the program compiles with no errors, click Run Java Application on the Tools menu.

2. When the program displays the first Input dialog box, type 20000 as the sales amount and then click the OK button. When the program displays the second Input dialog box, type 5 and then click the OK button.

3. When the program displays the Error dialog box, click the OK button.

4. When the program again displays the Input dialog box, type 2 and then click the OK button. Click the Close button in the command prompt window title bar.

   The program displays an error message when a number less than one or greater than three is entered for the commission code. The program accepts any number between one and three as valid input data.

Run the program several more times and test valid and invalid entries for commission code, such as negative numbers, zero, or alphanumeric data.

The Case Structure

Sending a value to a method where it will be tested is a convenient way to make the program easy to read and to test its components. In the case of a menu, for example, there might be many possible, valid choices for the user to input. When there are more than two possible, valid choices, the logical operators become cumbersome and hard to understand, even when the logical AND and OR operators are used.

Most programming languages, including Java, thus contain a variation of the selection structure called a case structure. A **case structure** is a type of selection structure that allows for more than two choices when the condition is evaluated. For example, if a user selects from several choices on a menu, the code evaluates the choice. If a match is found, then the appropriate action is performed. For example, if the user selected Option 1 on the menu, the logic of the code might execute one section of code; if the user selected Option 4 on the menu, an entirely different section of code might execute. Alternatively, if no match is found, the case structure can provide feedback to the user or store the no match result for later use in the program. The case structure is described in detail in Appendix A on page APP 8.

The switch Statement

Java uses a **switch statement** to evaluate an integer expression or value and then conditionally perform statements. The switch statement evaluates its value and then, depending on the value, transfers control to the appropriate **case statement**. Control is transferred to a case statement that has a value following the case keyword that matches the value evaluated by the switch statement. Table 4-9 displays the general form of the switch statement.

Table 4-9   The switch Statement

General form:	switch(value)
	{
	    case value1:
	      . . . statements to execute if value matches value1
	      break;
	
	    case value2:
	      . . . statements to execute if value matches value2
	      break;
	    .
	    .
	    .
	    default:
	      . . . statements to execute if no match is found
	}

Purpose:	To evaluate an integer expression or value and then conditionally perform statements. The words **switch**, **case**, **break**, and **default** are reserved keywords. The switch value is any valid integer data type, variable, or constant. The case value is any valid integer data type, variable or constant. The switch statement compares the value to the case. If they match, the code following that case statement is executed. The default case is optional and executes only if none of the other, previous cases executes.

Example:	switch(flavor)
	{
	    case 1:
	        System.out.println("chocolate");
	        break;
	
	    case 2:
	        System.out.println("vanilla");
	        break;
	
	    case 3:
	        System.out.println("strawberry");
	        break;
	
	    default:
	        System.out.println("Please choose one of our three flavors.");
	}

As shown in Table 4-9, each case statement contains a **break statement** at the end, which forces an exit of the structure when a match is found. After the break, no more statements within the structure are evaluated, thereby reducing processing time.

The getComm() Method

In the Commission program, a method named getComm() will get a commission rate based on the dollar amount of the sales and the employee sales code. Figure 4-27 displays the line of code to call the getComm() method (line 24) and the getComm() method definition (lines 82 through 104).

```
24              answer = getComm(dollars,empCode);
```

```
82
83      //The getComm() method accepts the dollars and code and returns the commission.
84      public static double getComm(double employeeSales, int employeeCode)
85      {
86          double commission = 0.0;
87
88          switch(employeeCode)
89          {
90              case 1:
91                  commission = .10 * employeeSales;
92                  break;
93
94              case 2:
95                  commission = .14 * employeeSales;
96                  break;
97
98              case 3:
99                  commission = .18 * employeeSales;
100                 break;
101         }
102         return commission;
103     }
104
```

FIGURE 4-27

When the getComm() method is called from the main() method in line 24, it sends the arguments, dollars and empCode, to the getComm() method itself. The method returns a double value that is stored in a variable named answer.

The method header for the getComm() method displays in line 84. Its two parameters are declared to accept the values sent from the calling statement. Those values do not have to have different names than the arguments, dollars and empCode, used in line 24; however, because Java considers them different storage locations, visible only in their respective methods, most programmers assign the arguments and parameters different — but user-friendly and related — names. The arguments, dollars and empCode, become the parameters, employeeSales and employeeCode, in the getComm() method.

Tip

Arguments and Parameters

Recall from Chapter 2 that parameters and arguments are closely related concepts: an argument is data to be sent to a method, and a parameter is a piece of data received by a method to help the method perform its operations. When using arguments and parameters in code, you must have the same number of arguments as parameters, they must be in the same order, and they must be of the same data type.

After the return variable, commission, is declared and assigned an initial value of 0.0 (line 86), a switch statement is used to assign a commission rate based on the commission code entered by the user (lines 88 through 101). If the user enters 1, the method call in line 24 sends that value as the argument, emp-Code, to the getComm() method. The getComm() method receives the value and stores it as the parameter, employeeCode, which is local to the getComm() method. The switch statement evaluates the value of employeeCode and, because the value matches the value used in the case statement in line 90, the program assigns the commission variable a commission rate of .10 multiplied by the value for employeeSales. If the user enters a 2, the program assigns a commission rate of .14 multiplied by the value for employeeSales. If a user enters a 3, the program assigns a commission rate of .18 multiplied by the value for employeeSales.

Because the getCode() method already validated the commission code entered by the user to ensure it was in the range of one through three, there is no chance of the switch structure encountering a number outside of the range, which means no default case statement is necessary to handle exceptions.

The following steps enter code to call and execute the getComm() method.

To Enter Code for the getComm() Method

1. Enter line 24 as shown in Figure 4-27 on the previous page.

The main() method of the Commission program includes the statement to call the getComm() method and assign its return value to a variable named empCode (Figure 4-28).

```
15    public static void main(String[] args)
16    {
17        //declare class variables
18        double dollars, answer;
19        int empCode;
20
21        //call methods
22        dollars = getSales();
23        empCode = getCode();
24        answer = getComm(dollars,empCode);          method call
25    }                                               with arguments
26
27    //The getSales() method asks the user to input a dollar amount and validates it
28    public static double getSales()
29    {
30        //declare method variables
31        double sales = 0.0;
32        boolean done = false;
33
34        //loop while not done
35        while (!done)
36        {
37            String answer = JOptionPane.showInputDialog(null,
                 "Enter the sales amount\n(do not use commas or dollar signs)\n or click Cancel to
                 exit:");
```

FIGURE 4-28

> **2.** Enter lines 83 through 104 as shown in Figure 4-27 on page 4.39.
>
> *TextPad displays the getComm() method in the coding window (Figure 4-29).*

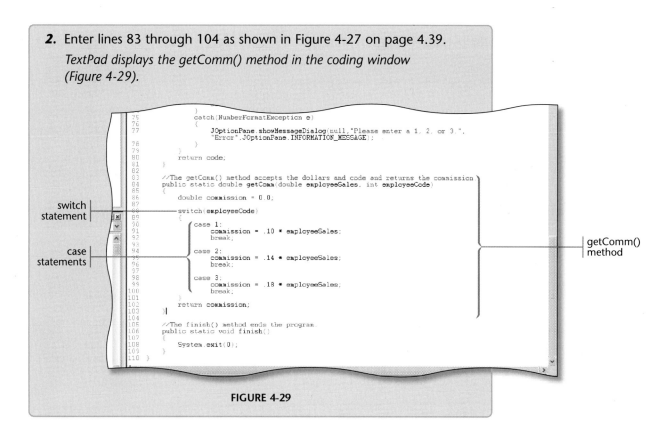

FIGURE 4-29

While the getComm() method is complete, it merely returns a commission rate to the main() method. Additional code must be added to the program to display output showing the calculated commission.

Formatting Numeric Output

As you have learned, both the System.out.println() and the JOptionPane methods can display numeric output, but it is not formatted in any special way. **Formatted numeric output** includes features such as dollar signs, commas, decimal points, leading zeroes, and other formatting symbols, applied automatically to a displayed value.

Java has a special class of methods to handle numeric formatting. For example, the **DecimalFormat class** formats decimal numbers. It has a variety of features designed to make it possible to parse and format numbers in any locale, including support for Western, Arabic, and Indic digits. It also supports different kinds of numbers, including integers (123), fixed-point numbers (123.4), scientific notation (1.23E4), percentages (12%), and currency amounts ($123).

Programmers use the DecimalFormat class to format decimal numbers into Strings for output. This class allows you to control the display of leading and trailing zeroes, prefixes and suffixes, grouping (thousands) separators, and the decimal separator.

A constructor is used to create a named String using the **DecimalFormat() method**. The argument for the DecimalFormat() method is a String called a **pattern**, which determines how the formatted number should be displayed. Table 4-10 on the next page displays some examples of patterns and the resulting output.

Table 4-10   Patterns for the DecimalFormat() Method

UNFORMATTED NUMERIC VALUE	PATTERN	FORMATTED NUMERIC OUTPUT	EXPLANATION
123456.789	###,###.###	123,456.789	The pound sign (#) denotes a digit, the comma is a placeholder for the grouping separator, and the period is a placeholder for the decimal separator.
123456.789	###.##	123456.79	The unformatted numeric value has three digits to the right of the decimal point, but the pattern has only two. The DecimalFormat() method handles this by rounding the number up.
123.78	000000.000	000123.780	The zero (0) character denotes a leading or trailing zero. Because the 0 character is used instead of the pound sign (#), the pattern specifies up to six leading zeroes to the left of the decimal point and three trailing zeroes to the right of the decimal point.
12345.67	$###,###.###	$12,345.67	The first character in the pattern is the dollar sign ($). Note that it immediately precedes the leftmost digit in the formatted output.
12345.67	\u00A5###,###.###	¥12,345.67	The pattern specifies the currency sign for Japanese yen (¥) with the Unicode value 00A5.

Once declared and constructed, the **format() method** can be used to assign the formatting pattern to a specific value. Table 4-11 shows the general form of the DecimalFormat class constructor, the DecimalFormat() method and its argument, and the use of the format() method to assign the formatting specified in a pattern to a value.

Table 4-11   DecimalFormat Class Constructor and DecimalFormat() Method

General form:	DecimalFormat patternName = new DecimalFormat("pattern String"); patternName.format(value);
Purpose:	To provide formatted output of decimal numbers
Examples:	`DecimalFormat twoDigits = new DecimalFormat("$000.00");` `twoDigits.format(123.45);`

Coding the output() Method

The output() method in the Commission program will construct an instance of the DecimalFormat object and assign it a pattern that includes a dollar sign, a comma for a grouping (thousands) separator, a decimal point, and two digits for cents. The DecimalFormat object then is used with the format() method to provide properly formatted numeric output of the sales and commission values in a JOptionPane message dialog box. Figure 4-30 displays the line of code to call the output() method (line 25) and the output() method definition (lines 105 through 113).

```
25            output(answer, dollars);
```

```
105
106        //The output() method displays the commission and sales.
107        public static void output(double commission, double sales)
108        {
109            DecimalFormat twoDigits = new DecimalFormat("$#,000.00");
110
111            JOptionPane.showMessageDialog(null,"Your commission on sales of "+ twoDigits.format
           (sales) + " is " + twoDigits.format(commission),"Commission Totals",JOptionPane.
           INFORMATION_MESSAGE);
112        }
113
```

FIGURE 4-30

When the output() method is called from the main() method in line 25, it sends the arguments, answer and dollars, to the output() method itself. It does not receive a return value.

In line 109 in the output() method, an instance of the DecimalFormat object, named twoDigits, is constructed with a pattern allowing for thousands of dollars, formatted with a dollar sign, a comma thousands separator, and two decimal places.

In line 111, the second argument of the showMessageDialog() method represents the message that will display in the dialog box. The argument is composed of a string of characters concatenated, or joined, with the values for the sales amount and the commission amount. As you learned in Chapter 2, the plus sign (+) is a concatenation symbol used to join String values. In line 111, the twoDigits.format() methods take the numeric arguments, sales and commission, and apply the format pattern defined and assigned in line 109.

The following steps enter code for the output() method.

To Code the output() Method

1. Enter line 25 as shown in Figure 4-30.

TextPad displays the statement to call the output() method and send two arguments (Figure 4-31).

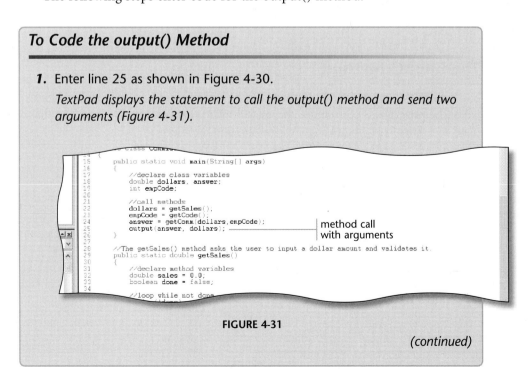

FIGURE 4-31

(continued)

2. Enter lines 106 through 113 as shown in Figure 4-30 on the previous page.

TextPad displays the output() method in the coding window (Figure 4-32).

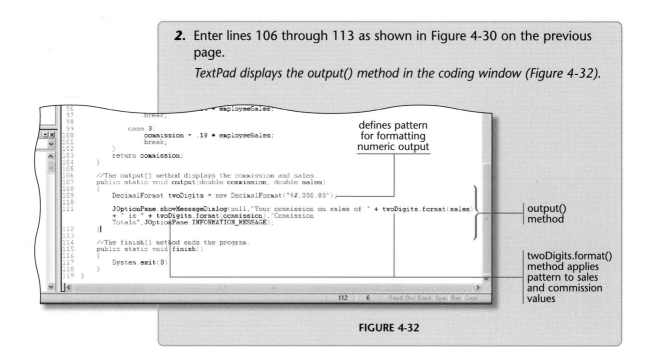

FIGURE 4-32

The DecimalFormat class contains many useful methods to change numeric formatting symbols. For example, instead of formatting a number in the form:

4,200,923.25

Some European countries use different numeric conventions, such as using a comma instead of a period to separate decimal values and a period instead of a comma as the grouping or thousands separator, in the form:

4.200.923,25

The DecimalFormat class offers a great deal of flexibility in the formatting of numbers.

The finish() Method

Finally, the main() method must call the finish() method to exit the system when the program is completed successfully. The complete main() method displays in Figure 4-33, including a call to the finish() method in line 26.

```
15      public static void main(String[] args)
16      {
17          //declare class variables
18          double dollars, answer;
19          int empCode;
20
21          //call methods
22          dollars = getSales();
23          empCode = getCode();
24          answer = getComm(dollars,empCode);
25          output(answer, dollars);
26          finish();
27      }
28
```

FIGURE 4-33

The following step enters code to call the finish() method as shown in Figure 4-33.

To Enter Code for the finish() Method

1. Enter line 26 as shown in Figure 4-33.

The application now is complete. The following steps compile and run the application, testing the application using sample data.

To Compile and Test the Application

1. With the Data Disk in drive A, compile the program by clicking Compile Java on the Tools menu. If TextPad notifies you of errors, click Commission.java in the Selector window, fix the errors, and then compile again. When the program compiles with no errors, click Run Java Application on the Tools menu.

2. When the Input dialog box displays, type 52375 and then click the OK button.

3. When the second Input dialog box displays, type 2 and then click the OK button.

The Commission Totals dialog box displays the formatted sales and the commission (Figure 4-34).

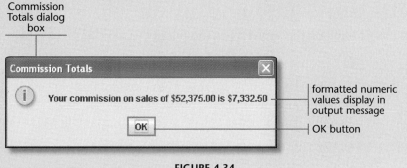

Commission Totals dialog box

formatted numeric values display in output message

OK button

FIGURE 4-34

4. Click the OK button in the Commission Totals dialog box. Click the Close button in the command prompt window title bar.

The Commission program terminates and the command prompt window closes.

The Commission class now contains six working methods: main(), getSales(), getCode(), getComm(), output(), and finish(). You may want to print a copy of the Commission.java source code for reference, as you modify the code to create different versions of the program.

In J2SE version 5.0, the **printf() method** may be used to format numeric output. After importing the java.io.* package, programmers may embed one of several special **conversion characters** that will insert data into a string, as shown in Table 4-12.

Table 4-12   The printf() Method

Conversion Character	sample code
General form:	System.out.printf(String format, Object arguments)
Purpose:	To write a formatted string to an output stream using the specified format string and arguments
Examples:	
%b – Boolean value	System.out.printf("The Boolean value is %b\n", true);
%c – character	System.out.printf("The character %c\n", 'A');
%d – decimal integer	System.out.printf("An integer %d displays from a declared variable, num\n", num);
%f – floating-point number	System.out.printf("%f is a floating-point number representation of 3.1415929\n", 3.1415929);
%e – number in standard scientific notation	System.out.printf("The scientific notation is %e\n", 3.1415929);
%s – String	System.out.printf("The string %s displays\n", "Hi There");

Moving to the Web

Creating the applet version of the Commission program involves using the same techniques of building the applet using modularity, in which a larger program's source code is broken down into smaller sections of source code. First, an HTML host document to call the applet must be created; then the applet stub is created, compiled, and tested. Next, components must be added to the applet and selection structures must be included in the applet code. Finally, the applet should be tested, using sample data to test its error and exception-handling capabilities.

Creating the Host Document

Recall from previous chapters that because an applet is initiated and executed from within another language or run as part of a Web page, you must identify a host, or reference program, to execute the applet. The host document often is a Web page created as an HTML file with an applet tag.

The code to create an HTML file to access the CommissionApplet program is shown in Figure 4-35.

```
1   <HTML>
2   <APPLET CODE = "CommissionApplet.class" WIDTH = "350" HEIGHT = "200">
3   </APPLET>
4   </HTML>
```

FIGURE 4-35

The following steps create the HTML file and save it on the Data Disk in Drive A.

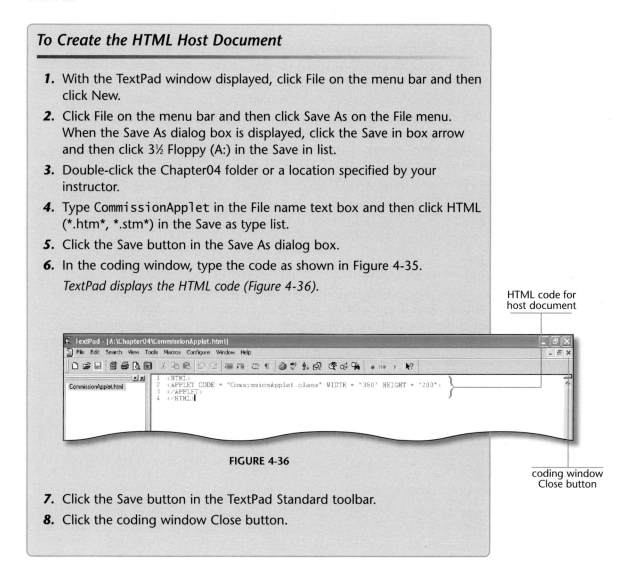

To Create the HTML Host Document

1. With the TextPad window displayed, click File on the menu bar and then click New.

2. Click File on the menu bar and then click Save As on the File menu. When the Save As dialog box is displayed, click the Save in box arrow and then click 3½ Floppy (A:) in the Save in list.

3. Double-click the Chapter04 folder or a location specified by your instructor.

4. Type CommissionApplet in the File name text box and then click HTML (*.htm*, *.stm*) in the Save as type list.

5. Click the Save button in the Save As dialog box.

6. In the coding window, type the code as shown in Figure 4-35.

   TextPad displays the HTML code (Figure 4-36).

HTML code for host document

coding window Close button

FIGURE 4-36

7. Click the Save button in the TextPad Standard toolbar.

8. Click the coding window Close button.

Coding an Applet Stub

As you may recall from previous chapters, creating an applet typically involves importing two class packages that Java will need to support the applet-related methods. First, the java.applet package is imported to lay the foundation for an applet by allowing the applet to inherit certain attributes and manipulate classes.

Programmers commonly enter an import statement to import the Abstract Window Toolkit (AWT), which provides resources that implement rich, attractive, and useful interfaces in Java applets. As you learned in Chapter 2, the java.awt package is included with the SDK and contains all of the classes for creating user interfaces and for painting graphics and images, as well as container classes to add components such as Buttons, TextFields, and Labels. The AWT's Graphics class is quite powerful, allowing you to create shapes and display images.

The other imported package used in many interactive applets is the java.awt.event package. The java.awt.event package provides interfaces and classes for dealing with different types of events triggered by AWT components. The java.awt.event package is not a subset of the java.awt package; rather, it is a separate package enabling you to implement interfaces, such as the ActionListener and the ItemListener.

As you learned in Chapter 3, ActionListener listens for events that occur during execution of the program, such as a user clicking a mouse button or pressing the ENTER key. **ItemListener** can be added to an applet to listen for when the user clicks components such as check boxes. ItemListener has several methods, such as addItemListener() and itemStateChanged(), that enable you to test whether or not items in the user interface are selected. These packages — java.awt, java.applet, and java.awt.event, as well as the java.text.DecimalFormat used in the Commission application — can be imported in any order.

Recall that applets do not have a main() method. Instead, applets use the init() method to initialize the applet from the browser or Applet Viewer. When the applet is loaded, the browser calls the init() method. This method is called only once, no matter how many times you might return to the Web page.

Stubbing in the program will involve typing the general block comments; importing the four classes; and entering the class header, the init() method header, and the itemStateChanged() method header, as shown in Figure 4-37.

```
 1   /*
 2       Chapter 4:   Sales Commission
 3       Programmer:  J. Starks
 4       Date:        October 25, 2007
 5       Filename:    CommissionApplet.java
 6       Purpose:     This applet calculates sales commission using a sales amount
 7                    (input by the user) and a sales code (chosen from among option buttons).
 8   */
 9
10   import java.awt.*;
11   import java.applet.*;
12   import java.awt.event.*;
13   import java.text.DecimalFormat;
14
15   public class CommissionApplet extends Applet implements ItemListener
16   {
17       public void init()
18       {
19       }
20
21       //This method is triggered by the user clicking an option button
22       public void itemStateChanged(ItemEvent choice)
23       {
24       }
25   }
```

FIGURE 4-37

The following steps code the program stub for the Commission applet.

To Code the Applet Stub

1. With the TextPad window displayed, click File on the menu bar and then click New.

2. With the Data Disk in drive A, click File on the menu bar and then click Save As on the File menu. When the Save As dialog box is displayed, type CommissionApplet in the File name text box and then click Java (*.java) in the Save as type list. Click the Save in box arrow and then click 3½ Floppy (A:) in the Save in list. Double-click the Chapter04 folder. Click the Save button.

3. Enter the code as shown in Figure 4-37, using your name and the current date in the block comment.

   TextPad displays the code for the applet stub in the coding window (Figure 4-38).

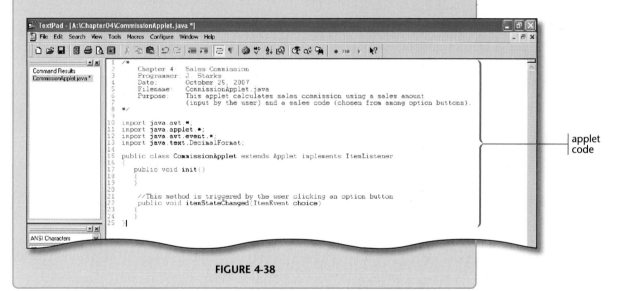

```
/*
    Chapter 4    Sales Commission
    Programmer: J Starks
    Date:       October 25, 2007
    Filename:   CommissionApplet.java
    Purpose:    This applet calculates sales commission using a sales amount
                (input by the user) and a sales code (chosen from among option buttons).
*/

import java.awt.*;
import java.applet.*;
import java.awt.event.*;
import java.text.DecimalFormat;

public class CommissionApplet extends Applet implements ItemListener
{
    public void init()
    {
    }

    //This method is triggered by the user clicking an option button
    public void itemStateChanged(ItemEvent choice)
    {
    }
}
```

applet code

FIGURE 4-38

You can test the applet stub, even without any commands or data components in the applet code. The following steps compile and test the applet stub.

To Compile and Test the Applet Stub

1. With the Data Disk in drive A, compile the program by clicking Compile Java on the Tools menu. If TextPad notifies you of errors, click CommissionApplet.java in the Selector window, fix the errors, and then compile again. When the program compiles with no errors, click Run Java Applet on the Tools menu.

2. When the Choose File dialog box displays, if necessary, click the box arrow and then click CommissionApplet.html in the list.

(continued)

3. Click the Yes button in the Choose File dialog box.

Applet Viewer displays the applet with no components (Figure 4-39). The program stub has no active statements or commands.

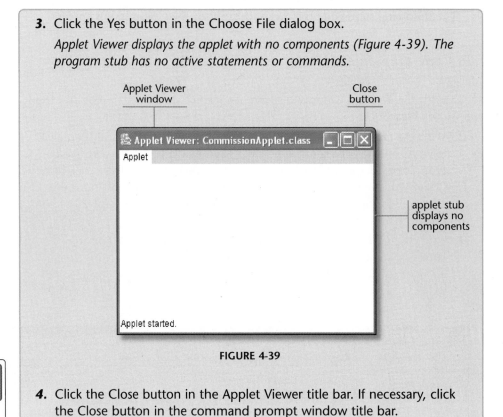

FIGURE 4-39

4. Click the Close button in the Applet Viewer title bar. If necessary, click the Close button in the command prompt window title bar.

Declaring Variables and Constructing Colors

The code for the applet must declare the same variables as those used in the application, along with a new variable to hold an image for the company logo. The code also should construct a dark red color to complement the logo. All of these variables have class scope, which means all of the methods in the applet will have access to their stored values.

Figure 4-40 displays the variable declarations and color constructor. The variables, dollars and answer, will store dollar amounts using the double data type. In line 19, the variable, empCode, will hold the commission code of 1, 2, or 3 using an integer data type. Line 20 declares an Image object named dollarSign. Line 21 constructs a **Color object** named darkRed. As shown in Line 21, the **Color() method** takes three arguments, each of which is a number in the range from 0 to 255 that corresponds to a specified red, green, and blue color. When combined, these three red, green, and blue colors can create a wide range of different colors, including darkRed.

```
17      //declare variables and construct a color
18      double dollars, answer;
19      int empCode;
20      Image dollarSign;
21      Color darkRed = new Color(160, 50, 0);
22
```

FIGURE 4-40

The following step enters code to declare the variables and construct the darkRed color.

To Enter Code to Declare Variables and Construct a Color

1. Enter lines 17 through 22 as shown in Figure 4-40.

TextPad displays the declared variables, including the constructed Color object, in the coding window. All methods in the class will be able to use the declared variables (Figure 4-41).

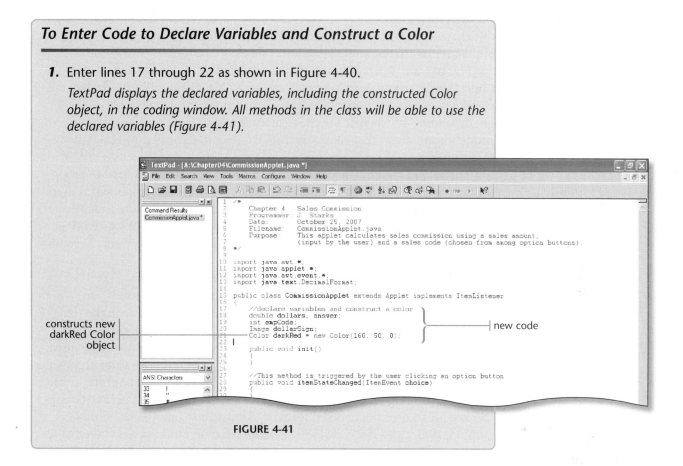

constructs new darkRed Color object

new code

FIGURE 4-41

Making Decisions in Applets

As with the Commission program created in the previous sections, a Java applet also may need to execute a specific section of code based on the actions of the user. For example, if the user enters an invalid number, the applet should display an error message and then give the user a chance to enter another number. Alternatively, if the user makes a choice from a list of options, a Java applet should switch or branch to a certain set of code statements based on that choice.

Through the use of check boxes, Java applets can allow the user to make choices that are evaluated by the applet. For instance, a user can click a check box to select it. The applet uses the ItemListener to listen for that click and then performs a unique set of instructions associated with that component.

Java applets also support the traditional if…else statements as well as the switch statement, to make a decision or determine which code to execute based on a user or program action.

Constructing Checkboxes

In previous chapters, the applets used components from the java.awt package, such as Labels, TextFields, and Buttons, to create the user interface. In this chapter, you will create a constructor for a Checkbox component that is used in the user interface.

Java has two different kinds of Checkboxes. The first is a traditional **Checkbox**, which displays as a small square with a caption. When selected, the Checkbox displays a check mark. The Checkbox has the toggled value of on or off, depending on whether the check mark displays. The Checkbox is an independent component that allows the user to select it, regardless of other choices in the interface.

The second kind of Checkbox, called a **CheckboxGroup,** is used to group together several Checkbox components. When a Checkbox component is used in a CheckboxGroup, it displays as a small circle or option button. Exactly one Checkbox in a CheckboxGroup can be selected, or checked, at any given time. When the user clicks one of the components, the others automatically become deselected.

Table 4-13 displays the general form of the Checkbox() and CheckboxGroup() methods used to add a Checkbox or CheckboxGroup component to the user interface. For a single Checkbox component, the Checkbox() method takes a String argument that represents the **caption**, or label, you want to display beside the Checkbox. When using mutually exclusive Checkboxes in a CheckboxGroup, the Checkbox() method takes three arguments: the caption, the state, and the name of the CheckboxGroup(). The **state** is true or false, depending on whether you want the Checkbox in the CheckboxGroup checked for true, or not checked for false. Because it is a mutually exclusive grouping, only one Checkbox in the CheckboxGroup can have its state value set to true at any given time. The CheckboxGroup name is the identifier previously used when the CheckboxGroup was constructed. The CheckboxGroup name assigns the Checkbox as a member of the particular CheckboxGroup.

Table 4-13   Checkbox() and CheckboxGroup() Methods

General form:	`//Checkbox`
	`Checkbox variableName = new Checkbox("caption");`
	`//grouped Checkbox`
	`CheckboxGroup variableName = new CheckboxGroup();`
	`  Checkbox variableName = new Checkbox("caption", state, GroupName);`

Purpose:	Component allows user to select on or off in a non-grouped Checkbox or to select one from many in a grouped Checkbox. Checkboxes toggle checked and unchecked based on a user's click. Grouped Checkboxes are mutually exclusive. Selecting one from among the group deselects all others.

Examples:	1. `Checkbox mayoBox = new Checkbox("Mayo");`
	`   Checkbox ketchupBox = new Checkbox("Ketchup");`
	`   Checkbox mustardBox = new Checkbox("Mustard");`
	2. `CheckboxGroup sizeGroup = new CheckboxGroup();`
	`   Checkbox smallOpt = new Checkbox("Small", false, sizeGroup);`
	`   Checkbox mediumOpt = new Checkbox("Medium", false, sizeGroup);`
	`   Checkbox largeOpt = new Checkbox("Large", true, sizeGroup);`

Constructing Applet Components

Next, code must be added to the applet to construct Labels for the prompts and output, a TextField in which the user will enter the sales amount, and a CheckboxGroup for the three sales code options. Figure 4-42 displays the code used to construct the applet components.

```
22
23          //Create components for applet
24          Label promptLabel = new Label(
            "Enter the sales amount (do not use commas or dollar signs):");
25              TextField salesField = new TextField(20);
26
27          Label codeLabel = new Label("Select the appropriate commission code:");
28
29          CheckboxGroup codeGroup = new CheckboxGroup ();
30              Checkbox telephoneBox = new Checkbox("Telephone Sales",false,codeGroup)
31              Checkbox inStoreBox = new Checkbox("In-Store Sales",false,codeGroup);
32              Checkbox outsideBox = new Checkbox("Outside Sales",false,codeGroup);
33              Checkbox hiddenBox = new Checkbox("",true,codeGroup);
34
35          Label outputLabel = new Label(
            "Click an option button to calculate the sales commission.");
36
```

FIGURE 4-42

Line 29 in Figure 4-42 constructs an instance of the CheckboxGroup, thus directing the Java compiler that only one Checkbox in the group can be checked at one time. Lines 30 through 33 then construct individual instances of the Checkboxes with unique identifiers. The hidden Checkbox coded in line 33 will not be added to the applet's user interface, as you will see in later steps. Instead, the hidden Checkbox is included so that if you want to clear all the other Checkboxes in the CheckboxGroup, the code can set the hidden Checkbox to true, thus changing the others to false automatically. Because you want none of the visible options to be selected when the applet starts, the hidden Checkbox is set to true, and all other members of the CheckboxGroup are set to false.

The step on the next page enters the code to construct the applet components.

To Construct Applet Components

1. Enter lines 23 through 36 as shown in Figure 4-42 on the previous page.

TextPad displays the code to construct the components (Figure 4-43). The Checkbox constructors use the variable, codeGroup, to include the four Checkboxes as members of the CheckboxGroup named codeGroup.

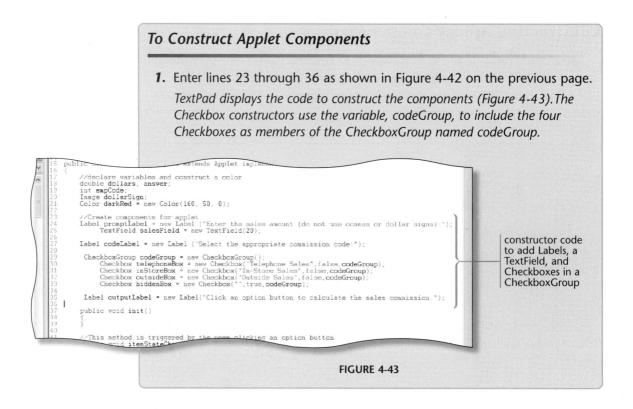

constructor code to add Labels, a TextField, and Checkboxes in a CheckboxGroup

FIGURE 4-43

Table 4-14 displays some of the methods used with a Checkbox. For information on other methods, the Java API contains a table associated with each component.

Table 4-14   Methods Used with the Checkbox Component

METHOD	PURPOSE	EXAMPLE
setState() getState()	To set or determine whether the Checkbox is selected	`boolean answer = myOption.getState();`
setLabel() getLabel()	To set or determine the caption of a Checkbox	`myOption.setLabel("This is the new caption");`
addItemListener()	Allows the Checkbox to become a trigger for an event	`myCheckbox.addItemListener();`

Adding Color, Components, Focus, and Listeners to the Applet

You may recall that the add() method takes an argument of a declared component and adds it to the Applet Viewer window when the applet is initiated. The **addItemListener event** then causes the applet to listen for clicks initiated by the user. When the click occurs, a series of associated objects and methods change, including the getState() method, the itemStateChanged() method, and the ItemEvent() object. Table 4-15 describes the general form of the addItemListener event.

Table 4-15   The addItemListener Event

Syntax:	component.addItemListener(ItemListener object)
Comment:	Causes the applet to listen for clicks initiated by the user. The component must be declared with a constructor before triggering the event. The ItemListener object may be self-referential, using the argument, this, or a constructor of a new ItemListener object.
Example:	`optBlue.addItemListener(this);`

Applets can use graphics and color to keep users interested and provide ease of use. Two methods help you change the color of your applet: the setBackground() method and the setForeground() method. As you learned in Chapter 2, the setBackground() method changes the background color of the applet window or other component. The **setForeground() method** changes the color of the text used in the applet window. You may want to change the foreground (text) color to draw attention to a certain component or use a lighter color to make the text display more clearly on darker backgrounds. Table 4-16 displays the general form of the setBackground() and setForeground() methods.

Table 4-16   The setBackground() and setForeground() methods

METHOD	PURPOSE	EXAMPLE
setBackground()	Set the background color of an applet or other component	1. `setBackground(Color.blue);` 2. `myLabel.setBackground(Color.cyan);`
setForeground()	Set the foreground color of an applet or other component	3. `setForeground(darkRed);` 4. `myTextField.setForeground(Color.cyan);`

Example 1 sets the background of the entire applet window to blue. If you want to set the background color for a specific Label or Checkbox, you must precede the command with the name of the object, as shown in example 2.

The argument of both methods uses a Color object. In example 3, the color darkRed was declared and assigned previously, so the attribute does not need to be preceded by the name of the Color object. In example 4, the Color object is followed by a period delimiter followed by a valid color attribute. The preset color attributes used for most components are medium gray for the background and black for the foreground or text. To review a list of valid attributes for the Color object, see Table 2-9 on page 99.

Another method associated with applets that use TextFields is the requestFocus() method. The **requestFocus() method** moves the insertion point to the component that calls it. In the case of TextFields, when the TextField has the focus, the insertion point displays as a vertical flashing line in the text box. A command button, such as OK or Cancel, may display focus with a dotted rectangle displayed around the button's caption. Displaying the insertion point helps users focus on the appropriate spot to enter the next item of text and commonly is used when clearing an incorrect entry to let the user try another entry.

Coding the init() Method

Figure 4-44 displays the code for the init() method. Lines 39 and 40 set the background and foreground colors of the applet window, and lines 41 and 42 add the promptLabel and salesField to accept user input. Line 43 sets the focus to the salesField and line 44 sets the foreground color of the salesField component to black. Lines 45 through 52 use the add() method to add the components to the applet and to add the ItemListener to each of the Checkbox components.

```
37        public void init()
38        {
39            setBackground(darkRed);
40            setForeground(Color.white);
41            add(promptLabel);
42            add(salesField);
43            salesField.requestFocus();
44            salesField.setForeground(Color.black);
45            add(codeLabel);
46            add(telephoneBox);
47            telephoneBox.addItemListener(this);
48            add(inStoreBox);
49            inStoreBox.addItemListener(this);
50            add(outsideBox);
51            outsideBox.addItemListener(this);
52            add(outputLabel);
53        }
54
```

FIGURE 4-44

It is a common coding practice to set the applet background and foreground colors first and then add additional components and set their background and foreground colors as they are added to the applet interface. The applet components will display in the order they are added. The code to add the ItemListener for each Checkbox component typically is coded directly after the code used to add each Checkbox component.

The following step codes the init() method in the applet.

To Code the init() Method

1. Enter the code from lines 39 thorugh 52 as shown in Figure 4-44.

The init() method code will execute at run time (Figure 4-45). The code completes the init() method by adding the components to the user interface, defining the foreground and background colors for the applet window and components, setting the corresponding ItemListener for each Checkbox, and setting the focus to the salesField TextField component.

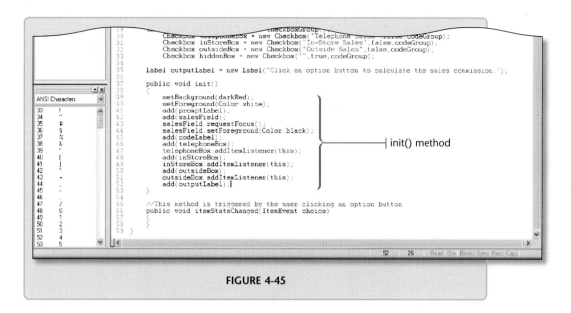

FIGURE 4-45

Compiling and Testing the init() Method

With the init() method complete, the applet will display its Labels, TextField, and Checkboxes, allowing the user to click one Checkbox in the CheckboxGroup. The following steps compile the applet and test the init() method.

To Compile and Test the init() Method

1. With the Data Disk in drive A, compile the program by clicking Compile Java on the Tools menu. If TextPad notifies you of errors, click CommissionApplet.java in the Selector window, fix the errors, and then compile again. When the program compiles with no errors, click Run Java Applet on the Tools menu.

2. When the Choose File dialog box displays, if necessary, click the box arrow and then click CommissionApplet.html in the list.

TextPad displays the Choose File dialog box (Figure 4-46).

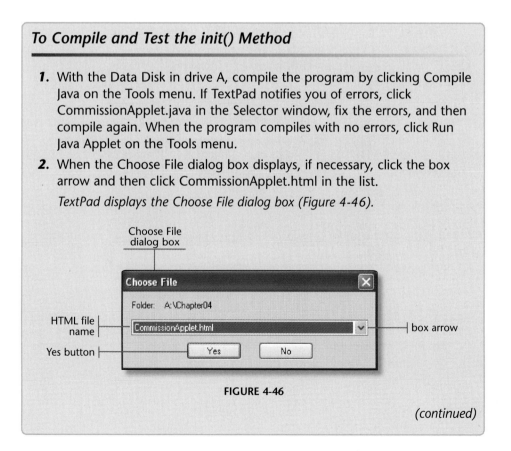

FIGURE 4-46

(continued)

3. Click the Yes button in the Choose File dialog box.

The applet starts and displays the focus in the text box (Figure 4-47). None of the option buttons created by the Checkbox and CheckboxGroup components is selected.

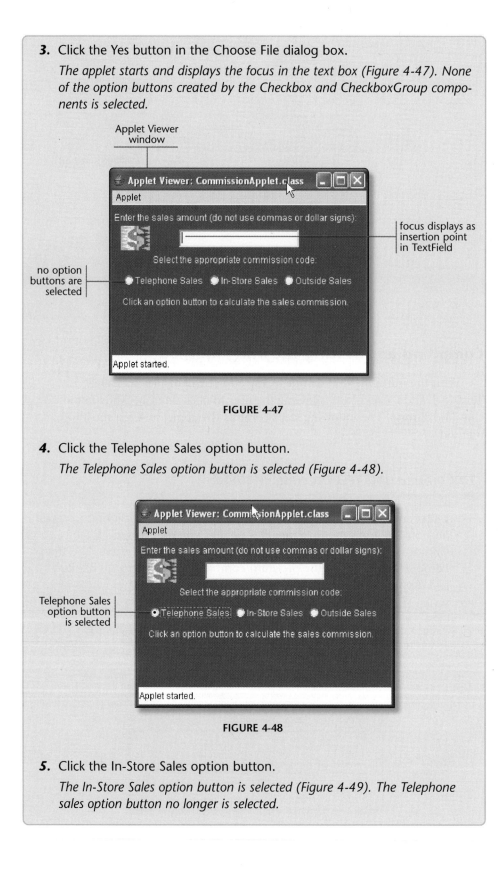

FIGURE 4-47

4. Click the Telephone Sales option button.

The Telephone Sales option button is selected (Figure 4-48).

FIGURE 4-48

5. Click the In-Store Sales option button.

The In-Store Sales option button is selected (Figure 4-49). The Telephone sales option button no longer is selected.

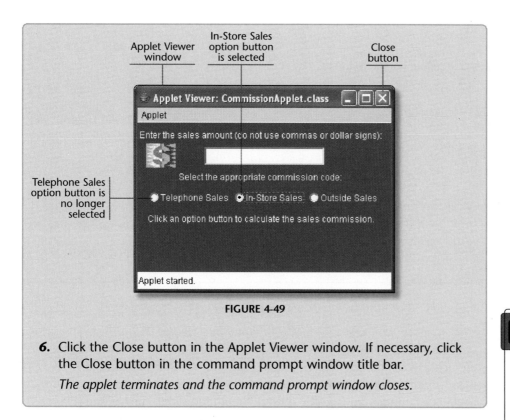

FIGURE 4-49

6. Click the Close button in the Applet Viewer window. If necessary, click the Close button in the command prompt window title bar.

The applet terminates and the command prompt window closes.

OTHER WAYS

1. To compile, press CTRL+1
2. To compile at command prompt, type javac CommissionApplet.java
3. To run, press CTRL+3, choose file, click Yes button
4. To run at command prompt, type appletviewer CommissionApplet.html

Setting the hidden Checkbox to true, as part of the CheckboxGroup, means that when the applet starts, none of the option buttons displayed on the user interface are selected. The hidden Checkbox allows you to control the selection when the applet starts rather than letting a default selection dictate the course of the program.

Handling Exceptions in the Applet Using try and catch Statements

When one of the Checkboxes in the CheckboxGroup is selected by a user during run time, the ItemListener changes the state of the component. That means when a user clicks an option button, the itemStateChanged() method is triggered.

In the applet, the code in the itemStateChanged() method includes a try and catch statement to call the methods used to test for valid data and to handle exceptions. The try and catch statements are shown in Figure 4-50 on the next page.

```
54
55      //This method is triggered by the user clicking an option button
56      public void itemStateChanged(ItemEvent choice)
57      {
58          try
59          {
60              dollars = getSales();
61              empCode = getCode();
62              answer = getComm(dollars,empCode);
63              output(answer, dollars);
64          }
65
66          catch(NumberFormatException e)
67          {
68              outputLabel.setText("You must enter a dollar amount greater than zero.");
69              hiddenBox.setState(true);
70              salesField.setText("");
71              salesField.requestFocus();
72          }
73      }
```

FIGURE 4-50

Lines 58 through 64 show the try statement and the braces enclosing the statements to call the getSales() method that returns a sales amount, the getCode() method that returns a commission code, the getComm() method that calculates a commission, and the output() method used to format and display the output. The try statement is similar to the main() method in the application, except it does not have to call the finish() method to terminate the program. Applets are controlled by their calling programs; therefore, Applet Viewer's Close button will be used to close the applet.

The catch statement, which executes when the try statement encounters an exception, uses the setText() method to display an error message. The message is displayed in line 68 in the outputLabel component on the applet interface. The setState() method in line 69 is used to set the state of the hidden Checkbox to true, thus deselecting the other Checkboxes. The setText() method in line 70 is used to clear the salesField TextField. Finally, in line 71, the requestFocus() method moves the insertion point to the salesField TextField so that the user can reenter a value for the sales amount.

The following step codes the try and catch statements for the applet. As you enter the code for this and the remaining methods in the applet, you may use cutting and pasting techniques to copy appropriate code from the application to the applet.

To Enter Applet Code for the try and catch Statements

1. Enter the code in lines 58 through 72 as shown in Figure 4-50.

TextPad displays the try and catch statements in the coding window
(Figure 4-51).

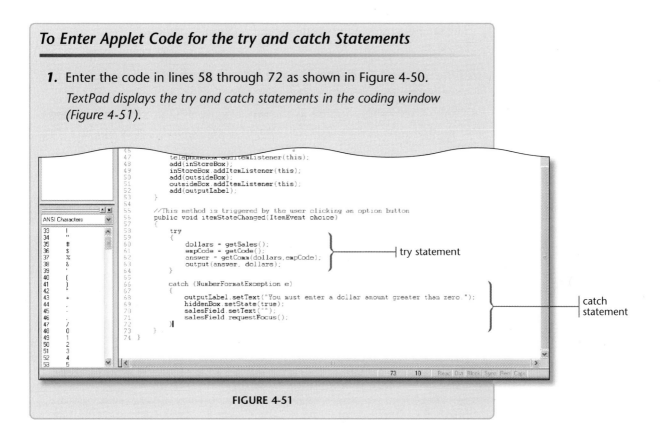

FIGURE 4-51

If the catch statement executes, a message will display in the applet window,
the TextField will be cleared of any invalid input data, focus will be reset to that
TextField, and any option buttons selected via the user interface will be cleared.

Coding the getSales() Method for the Applet

The getSales() method used in the applet, as shown in Figure 4-52, is similar
to that used in the application. The getSales() method parses the data from the
TextField to a double data type and stores it in a declared variable named sales
(line 77). Then, in line 79, it tests to see if sales is less than or equal to zero. If it
is, the getSales() method throws an exception back to the calling init() method.
If the sales amount is valid, line 81 returns the valid sales amount to the init()
method.

```
74
75      public double getSales()
76      {
77          double sales = Double.parseDouble(salesField.getText());
78
79          if (sales <= 0) throw new NumberFormatException();
80
81          return sales;
82      }
```

FIGURE 4-52

The following step enters code for the getSales() method.

To Enter Applet Code for the getSales() Method

1. Enter lines 74 through 82 as shown in Figure 4-52 on the previous page. *TextPad displays the getSales() method in the coding window (Figure 4-53).*

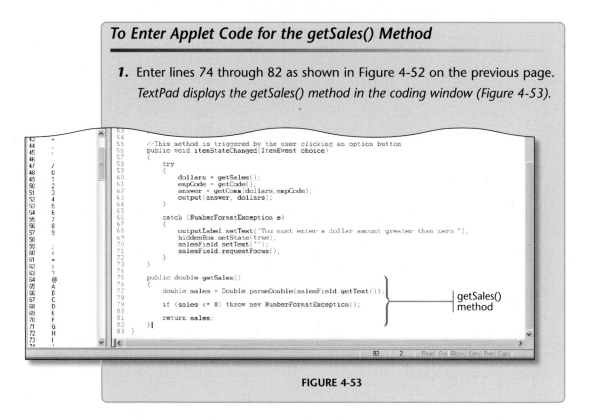

FIGURE 4-53

Coding the getCode() Method for the Applet

The getCode() method, as shown in Figure 4-54, is slightly different than that of the application. Line 86 declares a variable named code and assigns the initial value of 0. The getCode() method uses an if statement with the getState() method to assess the state of each of the Checkboxes in the CheckboxGroup, one after the other. If the getState() method evaluating the first Checkbox returns a true value, the program sets the variable code to 1. Otherwise, the else statement is followed by another if statement, which evaluates the state of the next Checkbox. If the second getState() method returns a true value, the program sets the variable code to 2. The process is repeated for the third Checkbox. The appropriate variable code is returned to the calling init() method in line 92.

```
83
84      public int getCode()
85      {
86          int code = 0;
87          if (telephoneBox.getState()) code = 1;
88          else
89              if (inStoreBox.getState()) code = 2;
90              else
91                  if (outsideBox.getState()) code = 3;
92          return code;
93      }
```

FIGURE 4-54

The following step enters code for the getCode() method.

To Enter Applet Code for the getCode() Method

1. Enter the code in lines 83 through 93 as shown in Figure 4-54.
TextPad displays the getCode() method in the coding window (Figure 4-55).

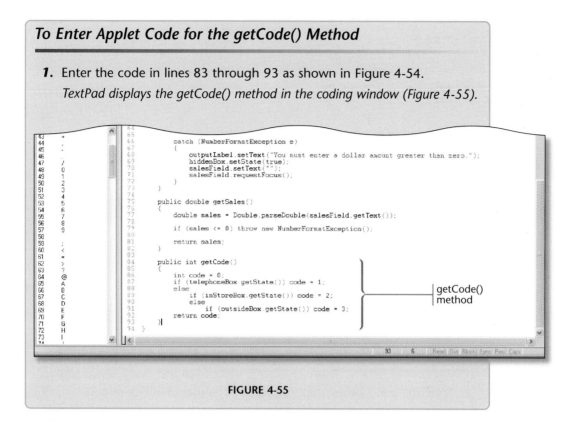

```
        catch (NumberFormatException e)
        {
            outputLabel.setText("You must enter a dollar amount greater than zero.");
            hiddenBox.setState(true);
            salesField.setText("");
            salesField.requestFocus();
        }
    }

    public double getSales()
    {
        double sales = Double.parseDouble(salesField.getText());

        if (sales <= 0) throw new NumberFormatException();

        return sales;
    }

    public int getCode()
    {
        int code = 0;
        if (telephoneBox.getState()) code = 1;
        else
            if (inStoreBox.getState()) code = 2;
            else
                if (outsideBox.getState()) code = 3;
        return code;
    }
}
```

getCode()
method

FIGURE 4-55

In the application, the code uses a switch statement to evaluate the value entered by the user and then transfers control to the appropriate case statement. The switch statement, however, can accept only an integer value as an argument, which means it cannot accept the boolean value of true or false required to test the state of a Checkbox. Because of this, the applet uses nested if statements to determine which Checkbox the user selected. You will learn other ways to check the state of components in a later chapter.

Coding the getComm() Method for the Applet

The getComm() method used in the applet is identical to the getComm() method used in the application. When the getComm() method is called from the init() method, it sends the arguments, dollars and empCode, along to the getComm() method itself. As shown in line 95 in Figure 4-56 on the next page, the arguments, dollars and empCode, become the parameters, sales and code, in the getComm() method. As with the getComm() method in the application, the getComm() method in the applet receives the value of the argument, empCode, and stores it as the parameter, code, which is local to the getComm() method. The switch statement evaluates the value of code, and if the value matches the value used in the case statement in line 100, the program assigns the commission variable a commission rate of .10 multiplied by the value for sales. If the user enters a 2, the program assigns a commission rate of .14 multiplied by the value for sales. If a user enters a 3, the program assigns a commission rate of .18 multiplied by the value for sales.

```
94
95      public double getComm(double sales, int code)
96      {
97          double commission = 0.0;
98          switch(code)
99          {
100             case 1:
101                 commission = .10 * sales;
102                 break;
103
104             case 2:
105                 commission = .14 * sales;
106                 break;
107
108             case 3:
109                 commission = .18 * sales;
110                 break;
111         }
112         return commission;
113     }
```

FIGURE 4-56

The following step enters the code for the getComm() method in the applet.

To Enter Applet Code for the getComm() Method

1. Enter the code for lines 94 through 113 as shown in Figure 4-56.

TextPad displays the getComm() method in the coding window (Figure 4-57).

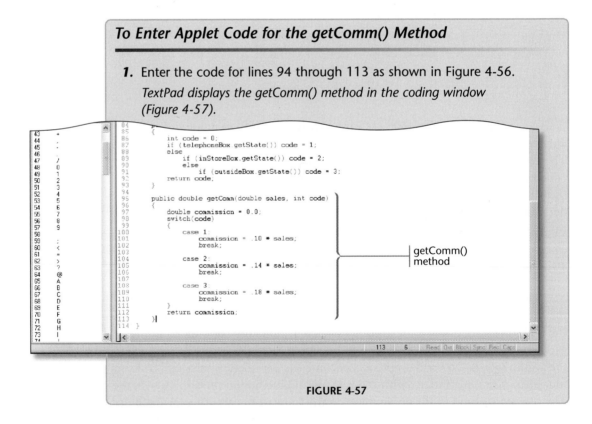

FIGURE 4-57

Coding the output() Method for the Applet

The output() method, shown in Figure 4-58, causes the output to display in the applet. The output() method accepts the commission and sales values (line 115) from the calling method, constructs an instance of the DecimalFormat object with a pattern of dollars and cents (line 117), and then uses the setText() method to send the output to the Label in the applet interface (line 118).

```
114
115        public void output(double commission, double sales)
116        {
117            DecimalFormat twoDigits = new DecimalFormat("$#,000.00");
118            outputLabel.setText("Your commission on sales of " + twoDigits.format(sales) +
                   " is " + twoDigits.format(commission));
119        }
```

FIGURE 4-58

The following step enters code for the output() method in the applet.

To Enter Applet Code for the output() Method

1. Enter the code for lines 114 through 119 as shown in Figure 4-58. *TextPad displays the output() method in the coding window (Figure 4-59).*

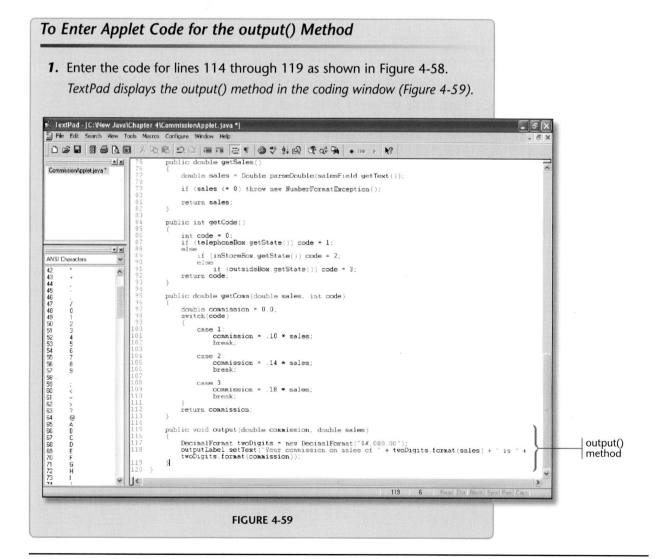

FIGURE 4-59

When used in a pattern for the DecimalFormat method, most characters, both numeric and alphabetic, are taken literally — that is, they are unchanged during formatting. On the other hand, special characters, such as those listed in Table 4-17, stand for other characters, strings, or classes of characters; they are replaced with the appropriate value when the method is called.

Table 4-17   Special Characters Used in Patterns

SYMBOL	PATTERN LOCATION	MEANING
0	Number	Digit; zero shows as leading or trailing zero
#	Number	Digit; zero shows as absent
.	Number	Decimal separator or monetary decimal separator
–	Number	Minus sign
,	Number	Grouping separator
E	Number	Separates mantissa and exponent in scientific notation
;	Subpattern boundary	Separates positive and negative subpatterns
%	Prefix or suffix	Multiply by 100 and show as percentage

Coding the paint() Method

Recall that the paint() method draws text in the applet window and displays graphics and color. Figure 4-60 shows the code for the paint() method used in the CommissionApplet program. Line 123 retrieves the image, dollarSign.gif; line 124 draws the stored image in the applet.

```
120
121     public void paint(Graphics g)
122     {
123         dollarSign = getImage(getDocumentBase(), "dollarSign.gif");
124         g.drawImage(dollarSign,12,28,this);
125     }
```

FIGURE 4-60

The following step enters the paint() method in the applet.

To Enter Applet Code for the paint() Method

1. Enter the code for lines 120 through 125 as shown in Figure 4-60.

TextPad displays the paint() method in the coding window (Figure 4-61).

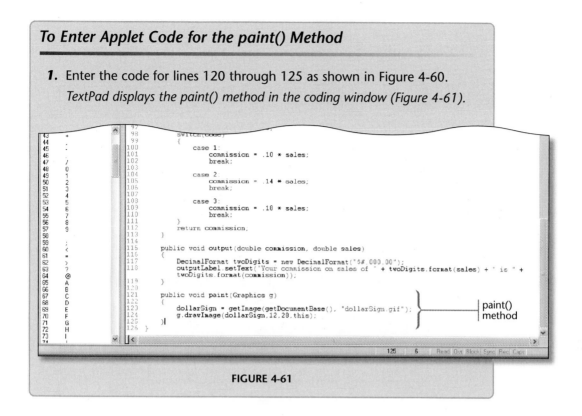

```
switch(code)
{
    case 1:
        commission = .10 * sales;
        break;

    case 2:
        commission = .14 * sales;
        break;

    case 3:
        commission = .18 * sales;
        break;
}
return commission;
}

public void output(double commission, double sales)
{
    DecimalFormat twoDigits = new DecimalFormat("$#,000.00");
    outputLabel.setText("Your commission on sales of " + twoDigits.format(sales) + " is " +
        twoDigits.format(commission));
}

public void paint(Graphics g)                                    ⎤ paint()
{                                                                │ method
    dollarSign = getImage(getDocumentBase(), "dollarSign.gif");  │
    g.drawImage(dollarSign,12,28,this);                          ⎦
}
}
```

FIGURE 4-61

The image file is located in the Chapter04 folder of the Data Disk that accompanies this book; you also can contact your instructor for additional information on how to obtain the image. Remember that the image file and the source code file need to be in the same folder for the applet to compile and run successfully.

Compiling and Testing the Applet

The code for the applet now is complete. You declared variables; constructed components; and wrote code for the init(), itemStateChanged(), and several user-defined methods that were similar to the user-defined methods in the Commission program. Now the applet can be compiled, and then run and tested using test data.

The following steps compile and then test the applet.

To Compile and Test the Applet

1. With the Data Disk in drive A and the image file located in the same folder as the source code, compile the program by clicking Compile Java on the Tools menu. If TextPad notifies you of errors, click CommissionApplet.java in the Selector window, fix the errors, and then compile again. When the program compiles with no errors, click Run Java Applet on the Tools menu.

(continued)

2. When the Choose File dialog box displays, if necessary, click the box arrow and then click CommissionApplet.html in the list. Click the Yes button.

3. When the applet displays, do not enter any data in the text box. Click any one of the option buttons.

The applet clears the option button selection and displays an error message (Figure 4-62).

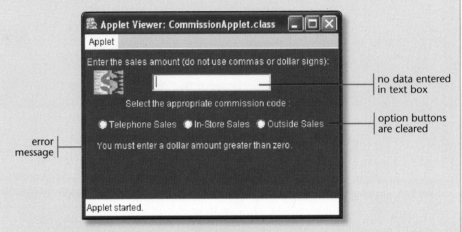

FIGURE 4-62

4. Type two thousand in the text box.

The invalid alphabetic data is displayed in the text box (Figure 4-63).

FIGURE 4-63

5. Click any of the option buttons. When the applet displays an error message and clears the alphabetic data, type 52375 in the text box.

The applet clears the invalid alphabetic data and the option buttons. A valid sales amount is displayed in the text box (Figure 4-64).

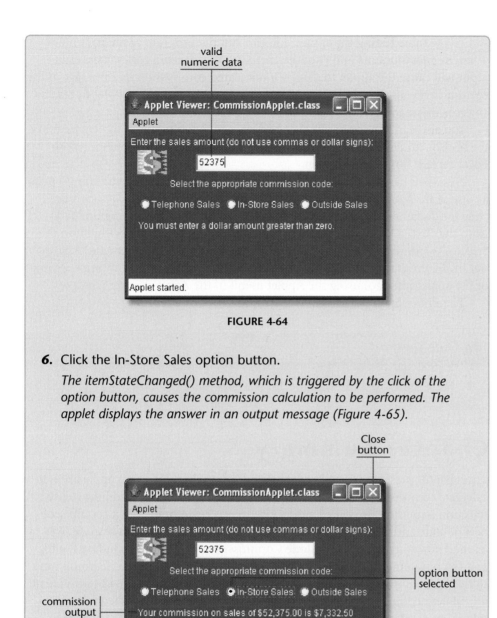

FIGURE 4-64

6. Click the In-Store Sales option button.

The itemStateChanged() method, which is triggered by the click of the option button, causes the commission calculation to be performed. The applet displays the answer in an output message (Figure 4-65).

FIGURE 4-65

7. Click the Close button in the Applet Viewer title bar and, if necessary, click the Close button in the command prompt window title bar.

OTHER WAYS

1. To compile, press CTRL+1
2. To compile at command prompt, type javac Commission.java
3. To run, press CTRL+3, choose file, click Yes button
4. To run at command prompt, type appletviewer CommissionApplet.html

To continue testing the applet, you can run the program again and enter different sales amounts and choose different option button codes. Valid data input will cause the applet to display a calculated commission in a message at the bottom of the applet window; invalid data input will cause the applet to display an error message and then clear the text box and option buttons.

You also can run the applet using a browser by typing the complete path of the host document, a:\Chapter04\CommissionApplet.html, in the Address or Location text box of the browser.

Once you have determined that the program runs correctly, you should print a copy of the CommissionApplet source code and the HTML host document code for documentation purposes. You can print a copy of the program code from the TextPad coding window by selecting the appropriate document in the Selector window and then using the Print command on the File menu. A print-out of the program code will be sent to the default printer. You can print a copy of the applet interface using the Applet menu in the Applet Viewer window.

The final step in the project is to quit TextPad.

To Quit TextPad

1. Click the Close button in the TextPad title bar.

Chapter Summary

This chapter presented a series of steps and a discussion of a Java application to calculate commission based on a dollar sales amount. You learned how to use a selection structure, also called an if...else structure, to branch to a certain section of code and a repetition structure to repeat a certain section of code. You learned how to create a stand-alone Commission application, including the try and catch statements to handle possible exceptions, in addition to learning ways to test for validity, reasonableness, and accurate input. You learned how to create a user-defined method, called the getSales() method, which is called from the main() method and obtains a sales amount after employing an if structure to test for valid entries. You also learned how to code the getCode() method to test for a valid sales code, along with a while statement to allow users to reenter data should they enter inaccurate data. You learned about using a switch statement in the getComm() method to calculate commission based on passed parameters. Finally, you learned to code the output() method to display formatted numeric values and exit a program using the finish() method. At each step of the process, you learned how to code a program stub and then test a small section of code before moving on to the next component.

In the last part of the chapter, you learned to convert the application into an applet with a CheckboxGroup that displays three Checkboxes as option buttons in the user interface. You learned how to use the paint() method to draw a graphic and set foreground and background colors of the applet window and components. You learned how to add components to the applet interface, along with how to code an ItemListener event to listen for the user's click of the option button and to perform the corresponding event code. In both the application and the applet, you learned to use code to perform data validation and display error messages.

What You Should Know

Having completed this chapter, you now should be able to perform the tasks shown in Table 4-18.

Table 4-18 *Chapter 4 What You Should Know*

TASK NUMBER	TASK	PAGE
1	Start TextPad and Save a TextPad Document	224
2	Enter Beginning Code	226
3	Compile and Test the Program Stub	227
4	Enter Code for the getSales() Method	230
5	Compile and Test the getSales() Method	232
6	Code an if Statement to Test the Cancel Button	237
7	Code the try and catch Statements	243
8	Enter Code to Throw an Exception	244
9	Compile and Test the try and catch Statements	245
10	Enter Code for the while Statement	249
11	Compile and Test the while Statement	250
12	Enter Code for the getCode() Method	252
13	Compile and Test the getCode() Method	253
14	Enter Code for the getComm() Method	256
15	Code the output() Method	259
16	Enter Code for the finish() Method	261
17	Compile and Test the Application	261
18	Create the HTML Host Document	263
19	Code the Applet Stub	265
20	Compile and Test the Applet Stub	265
21	Enter Code to Declare Variables and Construct a Color	267
22	Construct Applet Components	270
23	Code the init() Method	272
24	Compile and Test the init() Method	273
25	Enter Applet Code for the try and catch Statements	277
26	Enter Applet Code for the getSales() Method	278
27	Enter Applet Code for the getCode() Method	279
28	Enter Applet Code for the getComm() Method	280
29	Enter Applet Code for the output() Method	281
30	Enter Applet Code for the paint() Method	283
31	Compile and Test the Applet	283
32	Quit TextPad	286

Key Terms

addItemListener event *(270)*

AND operator *(235)*

block if statement *(233)*

break *(254)*

break statement *(254)*

call *(228)*

caption *(268)*

case *(254)*

case statement *(254)*

case structure *(253)*

catch *(241)*

catch statement *(241)*

Checkbox *(268)*

CheckboxGroup *(268)*

checked exception *(240)*

claims *(240)*

Color object *(266)*

Color() method *(266)*

condition *(233)*

control structures *(218)*

conversion characters *(262)*

DecimalFormat class *(257)*

DecimalFormat() method *(257)*

default *(254)*

else *(234)*

exception *(239)*

exception handling *(239)*

explicitly *(240)*

finally statement *(243)*

format() method *(258)*

formatted numeric output *(257)*

handler *(240)*

if *(234)*

if...else statement *(233)*

if...else structure *(218)*

ItemListener *(264)*

logical operator *(235)*

looping *(247)*

modularity *(227)*

nested *(234)*

NOT operator *(235)*

null *(236)*

NumberFormatException *(242)*

OR operator *(235)*

pattern *(257)*

printf() method *(262)*

reasonableness *(244)*

repetition structure *(218)*

requestFocus() method *(271)*

return statement *(230)*

run-time exception *(239)*

selection structure *(218)*

setForeground() method *(271)*

single-line if statement *(233)*

state *(268)*

static *(229)*

stub *(226)*

switch *(254)*

switch statement *(254)*

throw new *(240)*

throw statement *(241)*

try *(240)*

try statement *(240)*

validity *(244)*

while *(248)*

while loop *(247)*

while statement *(247)*

Homework Assignments

Label the Figure

In Figure 4-66, arrows point to components of a Java applet running on the desktop. Identify the various components of the applet in the spaces provided.

1. _____   4. _____

2. _____   5. _____

3. _____

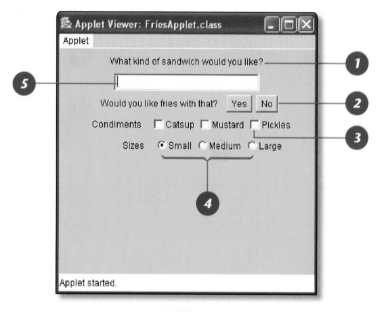

FIGURE 4-66

Identify Code

In Figure 4-67 on the next page, arrows point to sections of Java source code. Identify the code in the spaces provided using the appropriate word from the following list.

arguments	case structure	initialization
concatenation	constructor	exception
data type	selection structure	while loop
header	method	object
pattern	package name	parameters

(continued)

Identify Code (continued)

```
75
76      public double getSales()
77      {                                                                    1
78          double sales = Double.parseDouble(salesField.getText());
79
80          if (sales <= 0) throw new NumberFormatException();
81
82          return sales;
83      }
84
85      public int getCode()                                                 2
86      {
87          int code = 0;
88          if (telephoneBox.getState()) code = 1;
89          else
90              if (inStoreBox.getState()) code = 2;                         3
91              else
92                  if (outsideBox.getState()) code = 3;
93          return code;
94      }                                                                    4
95
96      public double getComm(double sales, int code)
97      {
98          double commission = 0.0;                                         5
99          switch(code)
100         {
101             case 1:
102                 commission = .10 * sales;
103                 break;
104
105             case 2:
106                 commission = .14 * sales;                                6
107                 break;
108
109             case 3:
110                 commission = .18 * sales;
111                 break;
112         }
113         return commission;
114     }                                                                    8                      7
115
116     public void output(double commission, double sales)
117     {
118         DecimalFormat twoDigits = new DecimalFormat("$#,000.00");
119         outputLabel.setText("Your commission on sales of " + twoDigits.format(sales) +
                " is " + twoDigits.format(commission));
120     }
121
122     public void paint(Graphics g)                                        9
123     {
124         dollarSign = getImage(getDocumentBase(), "dollarSign.gif");
125         g.drawImage(dollarSign,12,28,this);
126     }
127 }                                                                        10
```

FIGURE 4-67

1. _____   6. _____

2. _____   7. _____

3. _____   8. _____

4. _____   9. _____

5. _____   10. _____

Understanding Error Messages

Locate the file named Errors in the Chapter04 folder on the Data Disk. Start TextPad and open the file. Compile the program. Using what you know about coding and error messages, list the possible coding errors that might cause TextPad to display the error messages. Or, if your instructor directs you to do so, fix the errors and submit a copy of the program to your instructor.

Short Answer

1. A(n) _____ Checkbox in a CheckboxGroup can be used to clear others in the mutually exclusive set.

2. A statement is referred to as _____ when it is located completely within another statement.

3. Java uses a(n) _____ statement to evaluate a value for the case statement.

4. You can use the _____ method to position the insertion point in a TextField.

5. If the left side of the _____ operator evaluates to false, then the right side is not evaluated. If the left side of the _____ operator evaluates to true, then the right side is not evaluated.

6. The _____ typically contains code to perform any cleanup that might be necessary after executing the try statement and catch statement.

7. A(n) _____ displays as option buttons in the user interface of a Java applet.

8. An operation that attempts to use a float value in a location declared to be an integer is an example of a(n) _____.

9. A(n) _____ check might be used to ensure that data input by the user fits the program's specifications for a correct data type.

10. Conditions in Java are _____ expressions that evaluate to true or false.

11. A control structure that allows for more than two choices when a condition is evaluated is called a(n) _____.

12. When a Checkbox is clicked, the _____ method is called.

13. Study the following conditions and determine whether they evaluate to true or false. In those examples that display more than one condition, tell which condition confirms the true or false state.

    a. 25 == 25
    b. (18 < 19) && (12 > 14)
    c. (18 < 19) || (12 > 14)
    d. 31 <= 31
    e. !(5 == 5)
    f. (a == a) || (b == b) || (c == c)
    g. !((14 > 12) && (27 >= 26))
    h. (45 < 55) && (55 > 45)

(continued)

Short Answer *(continued)*

13. *(continued)*

   i. (100 + 5) != (40 + 65)

   j. (a == a) || !(== a)

14. Given the expression E = 450, S = 670, J = 1, T = 56, I = 34, determine the truth value of the following compound conditions:

   a. ((E < 400) || (J == 1))

   b. ((S == 700) && (T == 400))

   c. ((I == S) || J == 0))

   d. ((S < 300) && ((I < 50) || (J == 1)))

   e. ((S < 300) && (!(I < 50) || (J == 1)))

15. Determine a value of Q that will cause the condition in the if statements below to be true:

   a. if ((Q > 8) || (Q = 3) || (Z / 10))

   b. if ((Q >= 7) && (Q > 0)) strMessage = "Maximum number exceeded."

   c. if (Q / 3 < 9) intCount = intCount + 1

   d. if ((Q > 3) && !(Q == 3)) dblSum = dblSum + dblAmt

16. Given the conditions S == 0, Y == 4, B == 7, T == 8, and X == 3, determine the action taken for each of the following:

   a. if (S > 0) JOptionPane.showMessageDialog(null, "Computation complete.");

   b. if ((B == 4) || (T > 7))

      if (X > 1) JOptionPane.showMessageDialog(null, "Computation complete.");

   c. if ((X == 3) || (T > 2))

      if (Y > 7) JOptionPane.showMessageDialog(null, "Computation complete.");

   d. if ((X + 2) < 5)

     if (B < (Y + X))

     JOptionPane.showMessageDialog(null, "Computation complete.");

17. Given five variables with previously defined values intA, intB, intC, intD, and intE, write an if statement to increment the variable, intTotal, by 1 if all five variables have the exact value of 10.

18. Given the following code, what will display if the variable, answer, is set to 2? What will display if the variable, answer, is set to 4?

```
switch(answer)
{
    case 1:
        System.out.println("true");
        break;
```

```
        case 2:
            System.out.println("false");
            break;
        default:
            System.out.println("unknown");
            break;
    }
```

19. Given the following code, state five appropriate test values for the variable, dollars, that would cause the catch statement to be executed.

```
    try
    {
        double dollars = getSales();
        if (dollars < 0) throw new NumberFormatException;
    }

    catch (NumberFormatException e)
    {
        outputLabel.setText("You must enter a valid dollar amount greater than zero.");
    }
```

20. Assuming correct variable declaration and assignment, write a while statement for each of the following conditions.

    answer is equal to yes

    done is set to false

    moreRecords is set to true

    sex is male and age is greater than or equal to 21

21. Write a try statement and catch statement that will test a value entered by the user into a TextField named myAge. If the value is not a valid age, the catch statement should display a message in a Label named errorLabel. *Hint:* the error message should display for errors in range, validity, and data type.

22. Given two positive integer variables, intA and intB, write a sequence of statements to assign the variable with the larger value to intBig and the variable with the smaller value to intSmall. If intA and intB are equal, assign either to intSame. Be sure to show variable declarations.

23. The values of three variables, intU, intV, and intW, are positive and not equal to each other. Using if and else statements, determine which has the smallest value and assign this value to intLittle. Be sure to show variable declarations.

24. Write a partial program to display a message that reads, "Amanda Hefner, you may be the winner of $10,000.00!" in a JOptionPane dialog box. The message should use the proper concatenation and formatting. The title of the dialog box should be, Amanda Hefner, Lucky Winner. Properly declare any necessary variables. Use the corresponding variables listed below for the first name, last name, and winnings amount, but do not code those values directly into the statements.

```
    String firstName = "Amanda"
    String lastName  = "Hefner"
    double winnings = 10000.00
```

25. Write a partial program that creates a color called purple using RGB values and then displays the color as the background of an applet.

Learn It Online

Start your browser and visit scsite.com/java3e/learn. Follow the instructions in the exercises below.

1. **Chapter Reinforcement TF, MC, and SA** Click the True/False, Multiple Choice, and Short Answer link below Chapter 4. Print and then answer the questions.

2. **Practice Test** Click the Practice Test link below Chapter 4. Answer each question, enter your first and last name at the bottom of the page, and then click the Grade Test button. When the graded practice test is displayed on your screen, click Print on the File menu to print a hard copy. Continue to take practice tests until you score 80% or better. Hand in a printout of the final practice test.

3. **Crossword Puzzle Challenge** Click the Crossword Puzzle Challenge link below Chapter 4. Read the instructions, and then enter your first and last name. Click the Play button. Complete the crossword puzzle. When you are finished, click the Submit button. When the crossword puzzle is redisplayed, click the Print button.

4. **Tips and Tricks** Click the Tips and Tricks link below Chapter 4. Click a topic that pertains to Chapter 4. Right-click the information and then click Print on the shortcut menu. Construct a brief example of what the information relates to in Java to confirm that you understand how to use the tip or trick. Hand in the example and printed information.

5. **Newsgroups** Click the Newsgroups link below Chapter 4. Click a topic that pertains to Chapter 4. Print three comments.

6. **Expanding Your Horizons** Click the Articles for Java link below Chapter 4. Click a topic that pertains to Chapter 4. Print the information. Construct a brief example of what the information relates to in Java to confirm that you understand the contents of the article. Hand in the example and printed information.

7. **Search Sleuth** Select three key terms from the Key Terms section of this chapter and then use the Google search engine at google.com (or any major search engine) to display and print two Web pages for each key term.

Programming Assignments

1 Multiplication Quiz

Start TextPad. Open the file named Multiply from the Chapter04 folder of the Data Disk. Review the program. This Multiplication Quiz application asks students to enter the multiplication table they wish to practice and then prompts them to enter each answer, multiplying their table value by each integer from 0 to 12. Although the program tells students whether they are right or wrong, it does not provide error checking to handle exceptions caused by the input of non-integer values, such as decimal or String values.

Using techniques learned in this chapter, write the try and catch statements to display appropriate messages if students try to enter non-integer numbers. Also write a while statement to create a loop that repeats the input prompt if a student enters invalid data.

1. With the Multiply.java code displayed in the TextPad window, substitute your name and date in the block comment. Type Quiz as the new class name. Edit the name of the class in the class header as well.

2. Save the file on your Data Disk with the file name Quiz.java. If you wish, print a copy of the source code to reference while completing this lab.

3. Compile the program by pressing CTRL+1.

4. Run the program by pressing CTRL+2. When the program executes in the command prompt window, enter an integer value, such as 8, as the value for the multiplication table you wish to practice. Respond to the prompts by entering the correct answers as integers. When you have completed the multiplication table, press any key or click the Close button in the command prompt window to quit the program.

5. Run the program again. Enter 8 as the value for the multiplication table you wish to practice. Respond to the first prompt by entering an incorrect answer, such as 80. Notice that the program tells you the answer is incorrect but does not allow you to try again. Click the Close button on the command prompt window to quit the program.

6. Run the program again. Enter a non-integer value, such as 7.5, as the value for the multiplication table you wish to practice. Java throws an exception, and a NumberFormatException message displays in the command prompt window.

7. Use TextPad to edit the program source code. In the main() method, enclose the section of code starting with the line, //Calling the user-defined methods, in a try statement. Remember to enter the try statement and an opening brace before and a closing brace after that section of code.

8. Below the try statement, enter a catch statement for a NumberFormatException. Write code to print an appropriate error message using the System.out.println() method or a JOptionPane message box.

9. Compile and run the program again, testing with both integer and non-integer values. Notice that an appropriate message now displays, but students must run the program again to answer any additional questions.

(continued)

1 Multiplication Quiz *(continued)*

10. Edit the program to enclose the section of code including the try and catch statements in a while loop. To do this, enter the code:

    ```
    while(!done)
    ```

    and an opening brace before and a closing brace after that section of code.

11. Before the closing brace of the try statement, enter the line of code:

    ```
    done = true;
    ```

    to terminate the loop during execution. Save the file by clicking Save on the File menu.

12. Compile and run the program again, testing with both integer and non-integer values. Notice that users now are directed back to the beginning of the program after the error message displays.

13. Edit the program again. In the takeQuiz() method, find the statement, while (count <= 12). Click below the while statement's opening brace. Enclose all the code within the while statement in a try statement. Include all the code statements in the try statement but not the opening or closing braces of the while statement itself. Move the line

    ```
    count = count + 1;
    ```

    up to position it inside the if statement braces, at approximately line 80.

14. Below the try statement, enter a catch statement for a NumberFormatException. Print an appropriate message using the System.out.println() method or a JOptionPane message box. Compile and run the program again, testing with both integer and non-integer values. Notice that the program now displays an error message if a user enters an incorrect answer and then gives the user a chance to enter a different answer.

15. Print a copy of the revised source code for your instructor.

2 Using switch and try Statements to Validate User Input

You would like to write a program to help beginning Java programmers understand data types. You have noticed that students have trouble differentiating among doubles, ints, Strings, and other data types. You decide to create an application, such as the one in Figure 4-68, that uses input boxes to test their knowledge. Beginning with a try statement, the program should allow users to choose a data type. Then, based on a switch statement and several case statements, the program should prompt the user to enter a value that would fit that specific data type. If the user inputs valid data — that is, data that matches the chosen data type and parses correctly — the program should display positive feedback. If the inputted data does not match the chosen data type, the parse statement will throw a NumberFormatException. The program then should use a catch statement to display an appropriate error message and then allow the user to try again.

FIGURE 4-68

1. Start TextPad. Save the program as a Java source code file with the file name, MyType.

2. Enter general documentation comments, including the name of this lab, your name, the date, and the file name.

3. Import the java.io.* package and the javax.swing.JOptionPane package.

4. Type the class header and an opening brace to begin the class.

5. Type `public static void main(String[] args)` and an opening brace to begin the main() method header.

6. Declare the following variables using the code:

   `String strChoice, strTryString, strTryInt, strTryDouble;`

   `int choice, tryInt;`

   `double tryDouble;`

   `boolean done = false;`

7. Begin a while(!done) loop to repeat as long as the user does not click the Cancel button.

8. Inside a try statement, enter code to display an input box with three choices, as shown in Figure 4-68.

9. Type `choice = Integer.parseInt(strChoice);` on the next line to parse the value for the choice entered by the user.

10. Create a switch statement to test for each of the three choices. Type `switch(choice)` as the header and then press the ENTER key. Type an opening brace.

11. Enter a case statement for each of the three choices, using pages 254 through 257 as a guide for coding the switch, case, and break statements.

    • Case 1: If the user enters a 1, display a message that informs users they are correct, as any input can be saved as a String. Enter the break statement.
    • Case 2: If the user enters a 2, parse the value into tryInt. Display a message that informs users they are correct. Enter the break statement.

(continued)

PROGRAMMING ASSIGNMENTS

2 Using switch and try Statements to Validate User Input
(continued)

- Case 3: If the user enters a 3, parse the value into tryDouble. Display a message that informs users they are correct. Enter the break statement.
- Case 4: Set done equal to true. Enter code to display a closing message. Enter the break statement.
- Case default: throw a new NumberFormatException.

12. Close the switch statement with a closing brace.

13. Create a catch statement by typing `catch(NumberFormatException e)` and then an opening brace.

14. Display an appropriate message directing the user to try again and then close the catch statement with a closing brace.

15. Close the try statement, the while statement, and the main() method with closing braces.

16. Save the file on the Data Disk using the file name MyType.java.

17. Compile the program. If necessary, fix any errors in the TextPad window, save, and then recompile.

18. Run the program. Enter various values for each menu choice. Check your answers.

19. Print a copy of the source code for your instructor.

20. As an extra credit assignment, add choices for long, byte, and boolean data types.

3 Writing User-Defined Methods

A small proprietary school that offers distance-learning courses would like an application that calculates total tuition and fees for their students. Users will input the number of hours; the program then will calculate the total cost. For full-time students taking greater than 15 hours of courses, the cost per credit hour is $44.50. For part-time students taking 15 hours or fewer, the cost per credit hour is $50.00.

1. Start TextPad. Save the file on your Data Disk with the file name Tuition.java.

2. Enter general documentation comments, including the name of this lab, your name, the date, and the file name.

3. Import the java.io.* package and the java.text.DecimalFormat package.

4. Type the class header and opening brace for the public class, Tuition.

5. Enter the main() method header.

6. Declare an integer variable named hours. Declare double variables named fees, rate, and tuition.

7. Enter the following method calls and then close the main() method with a closing brace.

```
displayWelcome();
hours = getHours();
```

```
rate = getRate(hours);
tuition = calcTuition(hours, rate);
fees = calcFees(tuition);
displayTotal(tuition + fees);
```

8. Code the corresponding methods:
   - Type `public static void displayWelcome()` and then, within that method block, code the statements to display a welcome message.
   - Type `public static int getHours()` and then, within that method block, declare strHours as a String and hours as an int, setting hours to an initial value of zero. Display a prompt that allows the user to enter a string value, strHours, for the total number of hours. Parse that value into the integer, hours. The getHours() method also should include a try and catch statement for non-integer input. This method will return the int, hours, to main.
   - Type `public static double getRate(int hours)` and then, within that method block, include an if...else statement for hours greater than 15, which will calculate a rate per credit hour. This method will return the double value, rate, to main() method.
   - Type `public static double calcTuition(int hours, double rate)` and then, within that method block, code the statements to accept two values, multiply them, and return a double value, tuition, to main.
   - Type `public static double calcFees(double tuition)` and then, within that method block, code the statements to accept the double value, tuition, multiply it by .08, and then return a double value, fees, to the main method.
   - Type `public static void displayTotal(double total)` and then, within that method, construct a DecimalFormat pattern for currency. Use the System.out.println method to display the value passed by adding tuition and fees, along with a closing message.

9. Compile the program. If necessary, fix any errors in the TextPad window, save, and then recompile.

10. Run the program. Test the program by entering values both less than and greater than 15. Check your answers.

11. Print a copy of the source code for your instructor.

4 User Decisions

CandleLine is a business that sells designer candles and personal gifts. They cater to customers who want to send gifts for birthdays, holidays, and other special occasions. CandleLine's e-commerce site is an interactive Web site that uses a shopping cart to allow customers to purchase items. As customers choose the candles and gifts they wish to purchase, the items are added to an electronic shopping cart. Approximately 300 people per day are accessing CandleLine's Web site, but many customers have complained that the shipping charges become a hidden cost when they are placing an order. In order to improve customer relations, the company would like to give its customers a choice in shipping methods and would like to create a way for customers to calculate their shipping costs before finalizing their order.

(continued)

4 User Decisions *(continued)*

Create a Java applet similar to the one shown in Figure 4-69 that calculates the shipping cost for customer purchases. Eventually, the program will read the total price of purchases as data from the Web page; for now, the user will be able to enter the total price as an input value and then have the program calculate shipping charges. If a customer wants priority delivery (overnight), then the shipping charge is $16.95. If the customer prefers express delivery (2 business days), then the shipping charge is $13.95. If the customer wants standard delivery (3 to 7 business days) and the total cost of the order is more than $100.00, then CandleLine ships the items to the customer free; if the order is less than $100.00, then CandleLine charges $7.95 for standard delivery.

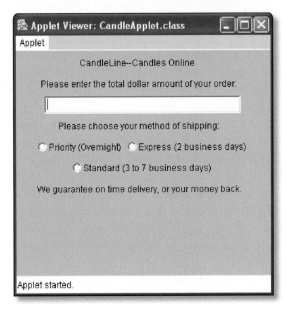

FIGURE 4-69

5 Freddie's Fast Food

Create an applet that displays an interface related to fast-food sandwiches created at Freddie's Fast Food. Using the techniques you learned in Chapter 4, add user interface components, including Checkboxes for the condiments and a CheckboxGroup with Checkboxes for the sizes. Add enough code to the program to make the selection of both the CheckboxGroup and Checkboxes work.

1. Start TextPad. Save the file on the Data Disk using the file name Freddie.java.

2. Enter general documentation comments, including the name of this lab, your name, the date, and the file name.

3. Import the following packages: java.awt.*, java.applet.*, and java.awt.event.*. Remember to use the import statement and conclude each line with a semicolon.

4. Enter a public class header for Freddie that extends Applet and implements ItemListener.

5. Create each of the following components using a constructor: sandwichPromptLabel, sandwichInputField, sizePromptLabel, catsupBox, mustardBox, picklesBox, sizeGroup, smallBox, mediumBox, largeBox. Set all the condiment Checkboxes to false. Set the first size Checkbox in the CheckboxGroup to true and the other sizes to false.

6. Create an init() method by typing `public void init()` as the header and adding an opening brace.

7. Set the background color of the applet window to red.

8. Enter add() methods for each of the components created in Step 5. Use an addItemListener(this) for each of the boxes and buttons. Type the closing braces for the init() method.

9. Type `public void itemStateChanged(ItemEvent choice)` as the header of the itemStateChanged() method. Type an opening brace and closing brace to stub in the event.

10. Compile the program and fix any errors.

11. In TextPad, click New on the File menu and then enter the HTML code to create an HTML host document to display the applet. Be sure to include the beginning and ending HTML and APPLET tags. Use a width of 350 and a height of 300.

12. Save the HTML host document on the Data Disk using the file name Freddie.html.

13. Run the applet. Click each of the buttons and boxes. Notice the Checkboxes toggle on and off, individually, while the grouped Checkboxes are mutually exclusive.

14. Print a copy of the source code for your instructor.

15. As an extra credit assignment, code the itemStateChanged() method to print out a confirmation dialog box of the customer's order.

6 Traffic Violations

You are serving an internship with the traffic court in the city where you live. The clerks in the traffic court office want a simple application that will allow them to enter the actual speed limit, the speed at which the offender was traveling, and the number of previous tickets that person has received. The application should provide interface options to allow users to calculate charges and exit the application. The application should calculate and display how many miles over the speed limit the offender was traveling, the cost of the speeding ticket, and court costs. The program should calculate a charge of $20.00 for each mile per hour over the speed limit. The program should calculate court costs beginning at $74.80 for the first offense and increasing by $25.00 for each subsequent offense up to the third offense (that will represent the maximum court cost).

7 We Love Pets

We Love Pets is a pet clinic with several locations. The office manager has asked you to create an applet that could run from a browser at all the offices. The applet should be designed with individual check boxes for users to select various services such as office visits, vaccinations, hospitalization, heartworm prevention, boarding, dentistry, x-rays, laboratory work, and prescriptions. As each service is selected, the charge for the service should display. After all selections have been made, the charges should be added together to arrive at a total amount due that displays when the user clicks the Calculate button. The office manager also has requested that when the user clicks the Calculate button, the program will clear all the check boxes for the next user.

8 Reasonable Computers Corporation

Reasonable Computers Corporation would like an applet to calculate the cost of adding peripherals to a basic computer system. Use at least six single check boxes for various types of peripheral devices, including printers, monitors, modems, and other devices with which you are familiar. Assume a basic computer system price of $575 and then add appropriate prices based on user checks. Add a button that tells the program to perform the calculation and display the final price. Try various width and height values in your HTML code to help align components.

9 Wright's Garage

Wright's Garage wants an interactive program that requires the mechanic to enter the tire pressure from four tires on any given car that comes into the garage. The program should first display three options to select a driving type: normal, hauling, and rugged terrain. After the mechanic chooses a driving type, the program should prompt the user to enter the tire pressure for each of the four tires. Finally, the program should tell the mechanic what adjustments to make. Assume the following:

- For normal driving, all four tires should be inflated between 33 and 43 pounds per square inch (psi).
- For hauling, rear tire pressure should be approximately 10% greater.
- For rugged terrain, rear tire pressure should be approximately 15% greater.

10 Overdue Books

Your city library has hired you on a consulting basis to provide them with an application to calculate overdue charges. The overdue charges apply to hardcover or paperback books, records, tapes, CDs, and videos. The librarians want an easy way to calculate the overdue charges, keeping in mind that a borrower could be returning multiple overdue items. Some method of looping to enter the next item is necessary. The total number of overdue items and the total amount due should display.

11 Stockbroker's Commission

Draw a flowchart and then develop an application that allows a user to enter a stock purchase transaction and determine the stockbroker's commission. Each transaction includes the following data: the stock name, price per share, number of shares involved, and the stockbroker's name. Assuming price per share = P, the stockbroker's commission is computed in the following manner:

If P (price per share) is less than or equal to $75.00, the commission rate is $0.19 per share; if P is greater than $75.00, the commission rate is $0.26 per share. If the number of shares purchased is less than 150, the commission is 1.5 times the rate per share.

Write code so that the program displays a message box that includes the stock transaction data and the commission paid the stockbroker in a grammatically correct set of sentences. After the message box displays, reset the input values to their original state.

12 Volume Computations

Use good design and programming techniques to develop a program to compute the volume of a box, cylinder, cone, and sphere. The user interface should provide option buttons to allow the users to select a shape. The interface also should include four input fields that allow a user to enter numbers with two decimal places; each input field should indicate that the input value is measured in feet. Label the four input fields as Length, Width, Height, and Radius.

When the user clicks a button to perform the calculation, the button's event procedure first should determine that the user selected a shape type. Next, the event procedure should ensure that only nonzero, positive values have been entered for the measurements required for the particular formula being used. Finally, the program should perform the calculation and display a message box listing the inputs, output, and calculated volume in a suitable format:

For example, the volume of a box with a length of 1.00 feet, a width of 2.00 feet, and a height of 3.00 feet is 6.00 cubic feet.

Use the following formulas to determine the volumes of the various shapes:

1. Volume of a box: V = L x W x H, where L is the length, W is the width, and H is the height of the box

2. Volume of a cylinder: V = pi x R x R x H, where R is the radius and H is the height of the cylinder

3. Volume of a cone: V = (pi x R x R x H)/3, where R is the radius of the base, and H is the height of the cone

4. Volume of a sphere: V = (4/3) x pi x R x R x R, where R is the radius of the sphere

In all of the above formulas, use either 3.14 or the Java constant, Math.PI, for the value of pi. You may use the Math.Pow() method for exponentiation.

13 What's My Color

Write an applet that allows the user to enter three positive integers between 0 and 255, each of which corresponds to a specified red, green, and blue color. Then, when the user clicks a Button object, the background color of the applet changes to match the color created by the red, green, and blue colors. Invalid numbers, less than zero or greater than 255, should display error messages.

14 Formatting Output

Write an application that accepts a double number and then displays it in five different ways, using a combination of dollar signs, thousands separators, decimal places, and other formats. Use the Java API to look up DecimalFormat and discover some formatting patterns that were not covered in this chapter. Use at least two patterns from the API.

15 Using the API

The printf() method, new to J2SE Version 5.0, uses several special characters to provide formatted output based on data types, similar to the C++ programming language. Visit the Sun Microsystems Java API Web site at http://java.sun.com/j2se/1.5.0/docs/api/io/PrintStream.html. Use the index to find the printf() method. Click the link, Format string Syntax. Scroll to display the conversion characters, flags, and their definitions. Using a word processing program, create a table with three columns that lists each character or flag, its definition in your own words, and a sample usage or code. Print the table and turn it in to your instructor.

16 Using the printf() Method

In Programming Assignment 6, you created an application to calculate traffic violation charges. Convert the program to use the J2SE 5.0 printf() method. Use dialog boxes for input, but convert all output to display in the console using forms of the printf() method. Table 4-12 on page 262 displays the various special characters used in the format string to embed data within the output rather than concatenating it to display in a dialog box.

5

Arrays, Loops, and Layout Managers Using External Classes

Objectives

You will have
mastered the material in
this chapter when you can:

- Create and implement an external class
- Write code to create a constructor class method
- Construct an instance method to initialize instance variables
- Declare and construct an array using correct notation
- Use layout managers with container components
- Code a counter-controlled loop using the for statement
- Correctly employ assignment and unary operators
- Use methods with Frame, Panel, TextArea and Choice components

Introduction

This chapter illustrates how to create an object, complete with methods and data, for use in other programs. Recall that Java can store data about objects and that it uses coded methods to trigger operations. An object has three key characteristics: (1) **identity**, which means the object can be called and used as a single unit; (2) **state**, which refers to the various properties of the object, whose values might change; and (3) **behavior**, which means the object can perform actions and can have actions performed on it.

This chapter also shows how to create different kinds of storage locations other than single variables that hold one piece of data. Storing and then manipulating a single value is useful for some applications, but many times a program must deal with larger amounts of data. Manipulating large numbers of variables with individual identifiers is cumbersome and tedious. Thus, Java allows programmers to organize and process data systematically using an **array,** which stores multiple data items of the same data type in a single storage location. Programmers use counter-controlled loops to accomplish many of the array manipulations.

Finally, in the process of creating a windowed application, this chapter introduces four new AWT components: Frame, Panel, TextArea, and Choice components. The AWT components will be placed precisely in the windowed application using a layout manager — one of a set of five classes that help programmers organize components into predefined locations in the window.

Chapter Five — Reservations

The Mahalo Polynesian Restaurant takes reservations during the day for evening use of their eight party rooms. Five of the rooms are for nonsmoking customers, and three of the rooms are for smoking customers. Rooms are reserved for groups of eight or more for the entire evening; there is a maximum of 20 guests per party room. The restaurant only accepts same-day reservations. When a reservation is taken, the customer is asked for a name, a phone number, a smoking preference, and the number of people in the party.

The restaurant wants a stand-alone application that allows the user to book a room and provides the capability to see, at a glance, which rooms are open and which ones are reserved. The Reservations program, as shown in Figure 5-1, is developed in this chapter as a stand-alone windowed application with a graphical user interface that displays a representation of the rooms and provides data input fields allowing the user to reserve a room for a party.

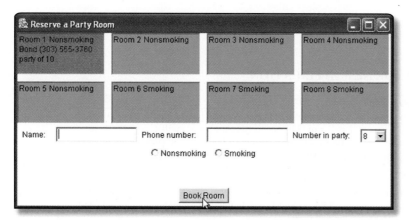

FIGURE 5-1

Program Development

The program development cycle for the Reservations program consists of tasks that correspond to the six development cycle phases, as shown in Table 5-1.

Table 5-1 **Reservations Program Development Tasks**

	DEVELOPMENT PHASE	TASK(S)
1	Analyze the requirements	Analyze the Reservations problem.
2	Design the solution	Design the user interface for the application, including the layout, data, and components. Design the logic to solve the problem.
3	Validate the design	Confirm with the user that the design solves the problem in a satisfactory manner.
4	Implement the design	Translate the design into code. Include internal documentation (comments and remarks) within the code that explains the purpose of the code statements.
5	Test the solution	Test the program. Find and correct any errors (debug) until it is error-free.
6	Document the solution	Print copies of the program code and interface.

Analysis and Design

Figure 5-2 on the next page shows the requirements document that initiates the development cycle for the Reservations program. The requirements document specifies the reason for the request, lists the required inputs and outputs, references the need to set the room status back to available each morning, and notes the need for possible changes to the program to support additional rooms.

REQUEST FOR NEW APPLICATION

Date submitted:	October 15, 2007
Submitted by:	Doreen Anderson, Manager, Mahalo Polynesian Restaurant
Purpose:	Our staff would like an easy-to-use program that would help us reserve party rooms. Customers phone us each day asking for large group reservations (eight or more people, with a maximum of 20). We reserve party rooms on a daily basis (no advanced reservations). We need a quick, easy way to see what rooms are available. After confirming the customer's smoking preference, we then reserve the room for the customer by entering the customer's name, phone number, and number of guests.
Application title:	Reserve a Party Room
Algorithms:	No computations are required; however, all of the rooms should be reset to a status of available when we start the program each morning.
Notes:	1. Reservations are taken during the day for evening use of our party rooms. At this point, we have only eight party rooms (five nonsmoking and three smoking), but we may add a few more in the near future.
	2. We reserve rooms only for the entire evening and do not accept reservations for the next day. The program thus does not need to be concerned with dates and times.
	3. The program should allow the user to select the first available room (either nonsmoking or smoking) and then enter values for the customer's name, the phone numbe r with area code, and the number of guests in the party, from 8 to 20. The program should display that information after the reservation is made to help with seating arrangements.
	4. The program should provide some sort of visual representation of the rooms as well, with different colors for reserved rooms and available rooms.
	5. Our employees will use the program only in-house; it does not need to run or be accessible via the Web.

Approvals

Approval status:	X	Approved
		Rejected
Approved by:	Tyler Gilbert	
Date:	October 28, 2007	
Assigned to:	J. Starks, Programmer	

FIGURE 5-2

PROBLEM ANALYSIS   The problem that the Reservations program should solve is the booking of reservations for party rooms at a local restaurant. Table 5-2 displays the inputs and outputs assembled from the requirements document.

Table 5-2   Inputs and Outputs for the Reservations Program

INPUTS	OUTPUTS
Customer name	Visual indicator of room reservation status (available/reserved)
Phone number with area code	Inputted data for each reserved room
Number in party	
Smoking preference	

When first executed, the program should display eight available rooms. As noted in the requirements document in Figure 5-2, party rooms are reserved during the day for the same evening, which means no permanent data needs to be stored. The rooms are reserved only for parties of eight or more. The maximum number of guests per room is 20.

As customers call to make reservations, the user can enter the customer information into the program and click the Book Room button. The program then should book the room, change some visual element on the user interface to indicate the change in room reservation status (from available to reserved), and display the customer information for the reserved room. The program should be easily changeable as the restaurant adds more party rooms.

DESIGN THE SOLUTION   Once you have analyzed the problem, the next step is to design the user interface. Only one version of the Reservations program is created in this chapter: a stand-alone, windowed application that the restaurant will run on a desktop computer system as it takes reservations. A graphical user interface (GUI) is appropriate for this application, as the user needs a way to input data, book a room reservation, and then view a visual representation of each room and its reservation status, along with the customer information associated with that room.

Figure 5-3 on the next page shows a storyboard for the Reservations program. The interface includes eight different TextArea components, one for each of the eight party rooms at the restaurant. A **TextArea component**, which appears as a rectangular box in the interface, displays larger amounts of data than a TextField. TextArea components have methods to turn on and off the capability to edit the field directly and to display scroll bars. TextArea components also have a setBackground() method, similar to the one used for applets, which can be used to change the TextArea component's background color.

The Reservations program uses eight TextArea components, in two rows of four, to provide a visual representation of the party rooms. When the program runs, the background color of each TextArea component will be set to indicate if the room is available (light green) or reserved (light red). If a room is reserved, the corresponding TextArea component will display the customer information.

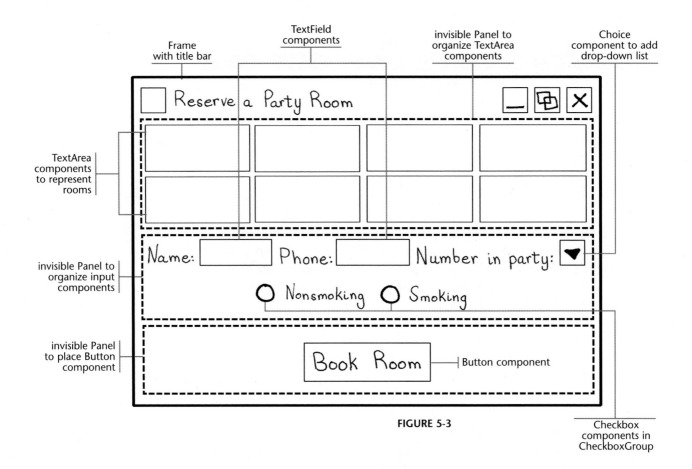

FIGURE 5-3

Two TextField components are appropriate for input of the customer's name and phone number, as they allow users to enter short pieces of data and perform minor editing such as backspacing, cutting, and pasting.

Because the number of guests in a party is a specific number from 8 to 20, the interface should include a drop-down list of valid numbers, rather than asking the user to type in the number. Providing a drop-down list not only will ensure that a user enters a valid number, it also will allow the user to enter the data more quickly. The **Choice component**, which displays as a drop-down list in a graphical user interface, has methods for creating a list of data items and methods to retrieve and reset the user's selection from the list.

Two Checkbox components in a CheckboxGroup are used to create nonsmoking and smoking option buttons in the interface. Recall that Java uses a CheckboxGroup for mutually exclusive selections. A hidden Checkbox component will be used to clear the other option buttons after a room is booked so that the option buttons are clear for entry of the next room reservation.

Finally, a Button component is used to create a button that the user clicks to trigger the booking of each room. After a room is booked, the TextArea component is set to a background color of light red and displays the customer information.

These components will be inserted into a **Frame**, which is an AWT component that serves as a container for a collection of graphical AWT components. A Frame, which is similar to a window with a title bar and border, utilizes methods to set its size, title bar caption, and visibility, among other attributes. In this application, the Frame title bar will display the title, Reserve a Party Room. As the program is created, the chapter steps will discuss organizing the Frame and placement of the components.

Within the Frame, the TextArea, TextField, Choice, Checkbox, and Button components will be placed within one of three Panels. A **Panel** is an AWT component that serves as an invisible container to further refine the arrangement of components within another container, such as a Frame. A Panel is similar to a Frame in that it may contain other components, but it does not have a title bar or any automatic features, such as borders.

PROGRAM DESIGN   Once you have designed the interface, the next step is to design the logic to solve the problem and create the desired results. The programming required in the Reservations program involves the capability to create room objects in memory. Using a graphical user interface, a user should be able to interact with the program to change the state of a room object, store data about the room object, and display that data. Toward that end, the program solution will contain two classes: one class named Reservations, to create the user interface, and another named Rooms, to create and manipulate a room object. The Reservations class is considered a **driver class** — the term used to specify a class that instantiates other classes and calls appropriate methods.

The first task of the Reservations class is to display the Reservations interface that allows for user input. In general, windowed application programs, similar to their applet counterparts, are coded in three basic stages: (1) constructing the components; (2) adding them to the interface; and (3) programming the functionality of the components.

Table 5-3 displays a list of the components and variables used in the Reservations class. Sometimes called a **variable dictionary**, programmers use this kind of tool to ensure consistent use of variables and provide a reference for other programmers. This reference tool is especially useful when multiple programmers are working on developing a complex Java program with many classes, components, and variables.

Table 5-3   Components and Variables Used in the Reservations Class

VARIABLE NAME	DATA TYPE OR COMPONENT	PURPOSE
args	String	References any variable passed to the main() method
available	int	Identifies the value returned by the Rooms object; represents the room number of the first available room (a zero value will indicate no room available)
bookButton	Button	Calls the bookRoom() method from the Rooms class when the Button is clicked
buttonPanel	Panel	Serves as a container to hold and position the Button

(continued)

Table 5-3   Components and Variables Used in the Reservations Class *(continued)*

VARIABLE NAME	DATA TYPE OR COMPONENT	PURPOSE
custNameLabel	Label	Displays a Label prompt for input of customer name
custPhoneLabel	Label	Displays a Label prompt for input of customer phone number
e	ActionEvent	References the object that triggers the actionPerformed() event and windowClosing() event
f	Frame	Holds the instantiation of the Reservations class
hidden	Checkbox	Serves as an option button that will not display, used to reset other option buttons through programming
i	int	Used to increment a loop
inputPanel	Panel	Serves as a container to hold and position input components
lightGreen	Color	Used as a background color for TextArea during certain conditions (room is considered available)
lightRed	Color	Used as a background color for TextArea during certain conditions (room is considered occupied)
nameField	TextField	Serves as a text box to hold user input for customer name
Nonsmoking	Checkbox	Serves as an option button for user to select nonsmoking as smoking preference
numLabel	Label	Displays a Label prompt for input of the number of guests in the party
numberOfGuests	Choice	Adds a drop-down list from 8 to 20 for the number of guests, for user input
options	CheckboxGroup	Adds a logical grouping of option buttons: nonsmoking, smoking, and hidden
phoneField	TextField	Adds a text box to hold user input for customer phone number
room	Variable of type (class) Rooms	Used to store data about the array of Rooms
roomDisplay	Array of type TextArea	Used to display data about the array of Rooms
roomPanel	Panel	Serves as a container to hold and position TextArea components
Smoking	Checkbox	Serves as an option button for user to select smoking as smoking preference

The Reservations class will use four methods to implement the interface. Table 5-4 displays the methods of the Reservations class and their purposes.

Table 5-4   Methods in the Reservations Class

METHOD NAME	PURPOSE
Reservations()	Set layout of the Frame Instantiate TextArea components to display default settings Add components to the user interface Add listeners to all necessary components and to the window
main()	Create an instance of Reservations object Set attributes of the Frame
actionPerformed()	Check to see if the hidden Checkbox still is selected Check to make sure a room is available
clearFields()	Reset all input fields

First, the program will use a constructor method named Reservations() to create a Frame and add various components to it. A **constructor method** is a programmer-defined method that is called when creating an object to ensure that all associated variables are initialized properly. Constructor methods have the same name as the object class they are creating. Constructor methods have no return data type; they have the implicit type of the object that they construct, creating an instance of the object internally. You have called constructors of objects such as Labels and Buttons in previous chapters using the = new notation, which is the standard notation to instantiate or construct an object of a class. In this chapter, however, you will write a new constructor method for the Reservations class to allow other classes to extend the Reservations class. The main() method will instantiate the Frame and set its attributes.

The actionPerformed() method is executed when a user clicks the Book Room button. Figure 5-4 displays a flowchart for the actionPerformed() method, which checks to see if the hidden Checkbox still is selected and then checks to make sure a room that meets the user criteria is available for booking.

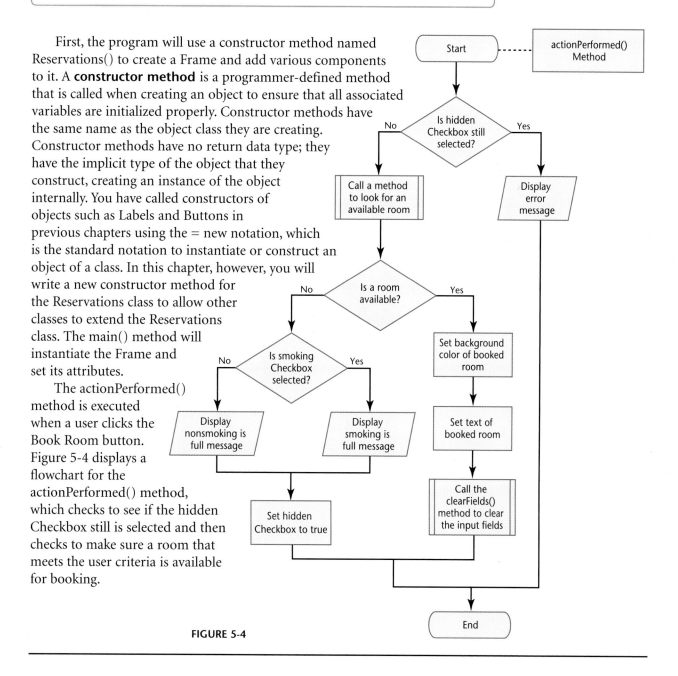

FIGURE 5-4

After the actionPerformed() method is executed, a clearFields() method will reset all of the input values so that the user can enter a reservation for the next customer.

The Rooms class creates a room object. Figure 5-5 displays an object-structure diagram that illustrates the attributes and methods of the Rooms object.

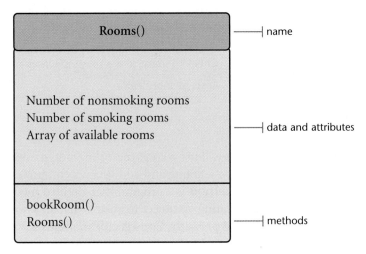

FIGURE 5-5

As shown in Table 5-5, the Rooms class will use two methods, each of which accepts passed parameters and returns a value. The Rooms() constructor method allows driver classes to create instances of the Rooms object. The bookRoom() method allows driver classes to book each room.

Table 5-5 Methods for the Rooms Class

METHOD NAME	PARAMETERS PASSED TO METHOD	RETURN VALUE	PURPOSE
Rooms()	int non int sm	Has no return data type but creates a Rooms object internally	A constructor method called by driver classes to create an instance of an array of rooms, identifying through passed parameters the number of nonsmoking and smoking rooms in the array
bookRoom()	boolean smoking	A method that returns an int	An instance method called by driver classes to obtain a room number (zero for no room available)

Table 5-6 displays the variable dictionary, or list of variables, for the Rooms class.

Table 5-6   Variables for the Rooms Class

VARIABLE NAME	DATA TYPE	PURPOSE
numSmoking	int	An integer variable to hold the number of smoking rooms to be generated
numNonSmoking	int	An integer variable to hold the number of nonsmoking rooms to be generated
occupied[]	array of booleans	An array of boolean values, initially set to false, to indicate the state of each room (occupied or empty)
non	int	An integer variable passed to the Rooms object holding the requested number of nonsmoking rooms
sm	int	An integer variable passed to the Rooms object holding the requested number of smoking rooms
begin	int	An integer variable to hold the first room number to check when attempting a booking
end	int	An integer variable to hold the last room number to check when attempting a booking
roomNumber	int	An integer variable to hold the return value from the bookRoom() method, representing the booked room (zero if none available)
smoking	boolean	A boolean value sent to the bookRoom() method to indicate if the user has chosen a smoking room
i	int	A variable to hold the increment during loop structures

VALIDATE DESIGN   Once you have designed the program, you can validate the design by stepping through the requirements document and making sure that the design addresses each requirement. If possible, you also should step through the solution with test data to verify that the solution meets the requirements. The user also should review the design to confirm that it solves the problem outlined in the requirements. By comparing the program design with the original requirements, both the programmer and the user can validate that the solution is correct and satisfactory.

Having analyzed the problem, designed the interface, and designed and validated the program logic, the analysis and design of the application is complete. As shown in Table 5-1 on page 307, the next task in the development cycle is to implement the design by creating a new Java program using TextPad.

Starting a New Java Program In TextPad

In Chapter 2, you learned how to start TextPad and save a file using a Java file type. The following steps start TextPad and save the TextPad document using a Java file type.

To Start a New Java Program in TextPad

1. Start TextPad. If necessary, click View on the menu bar and then click Line Numbers on the View menu to display line numbers.

2. Insert the Data Disk in drive A. Click File on the menu bar and then click Save As on the File menu.

3. When the Save As dialog box is displayed, type Rooms in the File name text box and then click Java (*.java) in the Save as type list. Click the Save in box arrow and then click 3½ Floppy (A:) in the Save in list.

4. Double-click the Chapter05 folder or a location specified by your instructor.

   The file named Rooms will be saved as a Java source code file in the Chapter05 folder on the Data Disk in drive A (Figure 5-6).

FIGURE 5-6

5. Click the Save button in the Save As dialog box.

Creating an External Class

The Reservations application created in this chapter uses two classes: the Rooms class and the Reservations class. The Rooms class will contain the constructors and methods to define the number of nonsmoking and smoking rooms to be created and to book the reservations for each room. The Reservations class will contain the main() method and the code to implement the user interface. Separating these two processes into two different classes promotes reusability of the Rooms class. For example, the restaurant eventually may want to create an application to reserve party rooms more than one day in advance or to reserve tables for the main dining area. Any new application could call and use the Rooms class without the programmer re-creating the code already packaged into the class.

As you have learned, Java facilitates the reuse of classes, which is good programming practice. In Java, classes can call each other and use each other's public methods. A class or method that is not a driver class is called an **external class**. In this project, the Rooms class is an external class. Once compiled, an external class becomes an object with data and methods that a driver class, such as the Reservations class, can use. An external class must define any method that the driver class may want to use. If a driver class calls a method that does not exist in a class it uses, the code will not compile, as this is a syntax error. An external class usually also contains a constructor method to define itself. As you will see later in the chapter, other methods, known as instance methods, manipulate the data for the external class object.

The following sections examine the Rooms class first, followed by an explanation of the Reservations class.

The Rooms Class

The Rooms class will contain the necessary methods to define the number of nonsmoking and smoking rooms to be created and to book the reservations for each room. Figure 5-7 displays the code for the comments, import statements, and class header.

```
1   /*
2         Chapter 5:    Reserve a Party Room
3         Programmer:   J. Starks
4         Date:         October 28, 2007
5         Filename:     Rooms.java
6         Purpose:      This is an external class called by the Reservations.java program.
7                       Its constructor method receives the number of nonsmoking and smoking rooms
8                       and then creates an array of empty rooms. The bookRoom() method accepts a
9                       boolean value and returns a room number.
10  */
11
12  public class Rooms
13  {
```

FIGURE 5-7

The following step illustrates entering the beginning code for the Rooms class.

To Enter Beginning Code for the Rooms Class

1. Enter the code as shown in Figure 5-7 on the previous page, replacing the programmer name and date shown with your name and the current date.

The TextPad window displays the beginning code for the Rooms class (Figure 5-8).

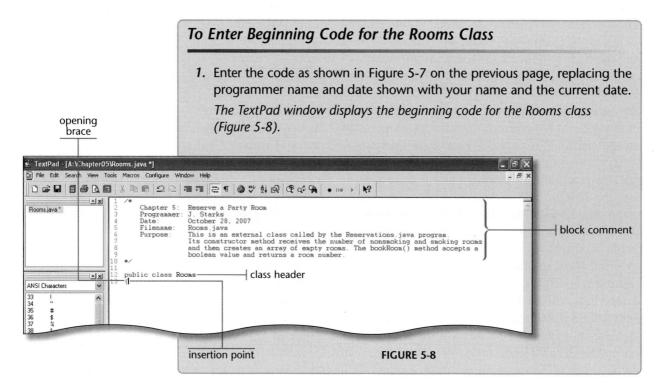

FIGURE 5-8

As shown in line 12, the Rooms class is declared public. As you have learned, public classes are accessible by all objects, which means that public classes can be extended, or used, as a basis for any other class. If you develop a viable Rooms class as a public class, you can use it to create additional, more specific classes, which keeps you from having to start over from scratch. Each new class can become an extension of the original Rooms class, inheriting its data and methods.

The next step in coding the program is to declare variables for the Rooms class. These variables will be used by the Rooms() constructor method to create an array that represents empty rooms.

Arrays

A single piece of data usually is stored as a variable with a unique identifier name and a predetermined data type. When you manipulate that data, you reference its identifier name. Using this approach, a list of related data items, stored in individual locations, each would require a separate line of code to manipulate the values.

Java and other programming languages use a data structure called an array to store lists of related data items and manipulate data more efficiently. As previously noted, Java thus allows programmers to use an array to store multiple data items of the same type in a single storage location. An array stores these multiple data items in a contiguous block of memory, divided into a number of slots. Think of an array as a stretched variable — a location that still has one identifier name, but is larger in that it can hold more than one value. Each item in the array is referred to as a **member**, or **element**, of the array; each element can hold a different value. All of the values, however, must be of the same data type. The data type may be any valid data type including primitive, reference, or a programmer-defined data type.

An **index number**, or **subscript**, is assigned to each element of the array, allowing the program and the programmer to access individual values when necessary. Index numbers are always integers. They begin with zero and progress sequentially by whole numbers to the end of the array. The practice of **zero-indexing** is common to many programming languages. It may help to think of the first array element as being zero elements away from the beginning of the array.

Declaring and Constructing an Array

As with all variables, an array must be declared. The code to declare an array first lists the data type, followed by a set of square brackets, followed by the identifier name. For example, the code

```
int[] ages;
```

declares an array named ages with an integer data type. An alternate declaration, similar to the C and C++ programming languages, places the square brackets after the identifier.

```
int ages[];
```

Java uses brackets instead of parentheses for arrays so that the arrays are not confused with methods.

In the above examples, an array named ages is declared that will hold integer values. The actual array, however, is not constructed by either of these declarations. You must construct the array and specify its **length**, or total number of elements in the array, with an = new constructor statement.

```
ages = new int[100];
```

Often an array is declared and constructed in a single statement.

```
int[] ages = new int[100];
```

This declaration tells the Java compiler that ages will be used as the name of an array containing integers and to construct a new array containing 100 elements. Remember that Java uses zero-indexing, so the 100 constructed elements will be numbered using indices 0 through 99.

An array is an object, and like any other object in Java, it is constructed as the program is running and not at compile time. The array constructor uses different syntax than most object constructors because it must initialize the length of the array, which is established when the array is created at run time. After creation, an array is a fixed-length structure. In other words, once an array has been constructed, the number of elements it contains does not change. If you need to refer to the length of the array in code, you can use the code

```
int size = arrayName.length
```

to refer to the length of the array as a property, and assign it to an integer. Programmers used to other programming languages may be inclined to follow the length property with an empty set of parentheses. In Java, however, length is not a method; it is a property provided by the Java platform for all arrays.

Once an array of primitive data types is declared and constructed, the stored value of each array element will be initialized to zero; however, reference data types such as Strings are not initialized to SPACEBAR blanks or an empty string. You must populate String arrays explicitly.

To reference a single element, the code should include the index number in brackets.

```
System.out.println(answer[5]);
```

In the above example, answer is the name of the array. The sixth element of the array will display during run time because array index numbers begin with zero.

Tip

Using Array Index Numbers

Arrays assign an index number, or subscript, to each element of the array, allowing the program and the programmer to access individual values when necessary. Index numbers are always integers; they begin with zero and progress sequentially by whole numbers to the end of the array. Thus, to reference the sixth array element, you would use the integer, 5, in brackets.

You also can use assignment statements to explicitly place values within arrays, just as you do with single variables.

```
temperature[3] = 78;
```

After it has been executed, the fourth element of the array named temperature will hold the value 78.

Alternately, you can declare, construct, and assign values using one statement, as in the following example.

```
boolean[] results= { true, false, true, true, false };
```

Java provides this shortcut syntax for creating and initializing an array. The length of this boolean array is determined by the number of values provided between the braces, { and }.

Array elements can be used anywhere a variable can be used.

```
overtime = (hours[6] - 40) * rate[6] * 1.5
```

In the above example, overtime is calculated by taking the seventh element of the hours array, subtracting 40, multiplying it by the seventh element of the rate array, and then finally multiplying that product by 1.5 for time-and-a-half pay.

The index number assigned to an element in an array always is an integer data type, but it does not have to be a literal; it can be any expression that evaluates to an integer. For example, if the array has been declared properly, the following code is valid.

```
int index = 8;
myArray[ index ] = 71;
```

In the above example, the ninth element of myArray will be set to the value 71. Using an expression for an array index number is a very powerful tool. As you will see later in this chapter, using expressions within a loop provides an efficient way to manipulate data in an array. Many times a problem is solved by organizing the data into arrays and then processing the data in a logical way using a variable as an index number.

Two-Dimensional Arrays

Sometimes programmers need to create a table of values. In those cases, a two-dimensional array, with two index numbers representing the row and column, is appropriate. For example, the code

```
int[][] myTable = new int[4][3]; \\ constructs the two dimensional array (4 rows, 3 columns)
myTable[1][3] = 487; \\ assigns the value 487 to row 1, column 3
```

creates a two-dimensional array with 4 rows and 3 columns, and then assigns the value 487 to row 1 and column 3 of the array. Theoretically, an array can have many dimensions; however, it is difficult to manipulate an array that is more than two- or three-dimensional.

Declaring Variables in the Rooms Class

Figure 5-9 displays code to declare three variables in the Rooms class: two ints and a boolean array. The two integers will represent the number of smoking and nonsmoking rooms — values kept current for the Rooms object. The boolean array named occupied will hold a list of true and false values to represent the state of each room, using a true value to represent an occupied room and a false value to represent an unoccupied room.

```
14    //declare class variables
15    int numSmoking;
16    int numNonSmoking;
17    boolean occupied[];
18
```

FIGURE 5-9

The following step enters the declaration statements for the class variables.

To Enter Declarations for the Rooms Class

1. Enter the code as shown in Figure 5-9 on the previous page.

   The TextPad window displays the variable declarations for the int variables, numSmoking and numNonSmoking, and the boolean array, occupied (Figure 5-10).

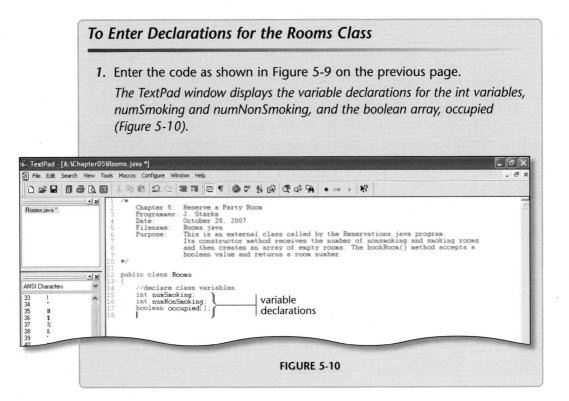

FIGURE 5-10

Constructing an Instance

Declaring variables in the external class, Rooms, is not sufficient to make Rooms a reusable object. A class is just an abstract description of what an object will be like when the object is instantiated, or created. This kind of class definition is like a blueprint for the object. Just as you might understand all the characteristics of an item you intend to manufacture long before the first item rolls off the assembly line, you describe a class before you create a working instance of that class.

Recall that an instance is a unique object or a specific occurrence of a class of objects. You can think of an instance as a proper noun. For example, the word, boy, is a noun; but the word, John, is a proper noun. John defines which boy you are talking about. In Java, declaring the variables for a class indicates that the code will include an object (or, as in the example, a noun, boy). Using a constructor method, you then will define a specific instance of that object (or, as in the example, the proper noun, John).

The Rooms() Constructor Method

In this project, the Rooms() constructor method, which creates a working instance of the Rooms object by defining the components, becomes a constructor for use by driver classes.

Figure 5-11 lists the code for a Rooms() constructor method header within the Rooms class. As shown in line 19, the Rooms() constructor method begins with an access modifier, public, followed by the name of the method. Recall that a constructor method name must match the name of the class object. Just as the Label() method helped construct a Label object in previous programs, the Rooms() method will construct a Rooms object when called by the driver class, Reservations. The constructor method header in line 19 returns an initialized Rooms object. The constructor method header includes two parameters, which are passed to the Rooms() constructor method from the driver class arguments. The parameters represent two integer values: the number of nonsmoking and smoking rooms to be created.

> **Tip**
>
> **Naming Instance Variables**
> Identifier names in driver classes typically use full words to represent variables, such as nonsmoking and smoking. When naming instance variables, however, it is common practice to use shortened names such as non and sm for parameters.

```
19      public Rooms(int non, int sm)
20      {
21          //construct an array of boolean values equal to the total number of rooms
22          occupied = new boolean[sm+non];
```

FIGURE 5-11

Line 22 constructs the array named occupied. The occupied array contains boolean values and has the same number of elements as there are total rooms — the smoking and nonsmoking values from line 19 added together. For example, if the Reservations driver class calls for a set of rooms with nine nonsmoking rooms and five smoking rooms, the Rooms() constructor method will create an array with a length of 14 (that is, 9 + 5).

The following step illustrates how to enter the Rooms() constructor method header and the code to construct an array.

To Enter the Rooms() Constructor Method Header

1. Enter lines 19 through 22 as shown in Figure 5-11 on the previous page. Be sure to use proper indentation.

   The TextPad window displays the code for the Rooms() constructor method header and the code to construct the occupied array (Figure 5-12).

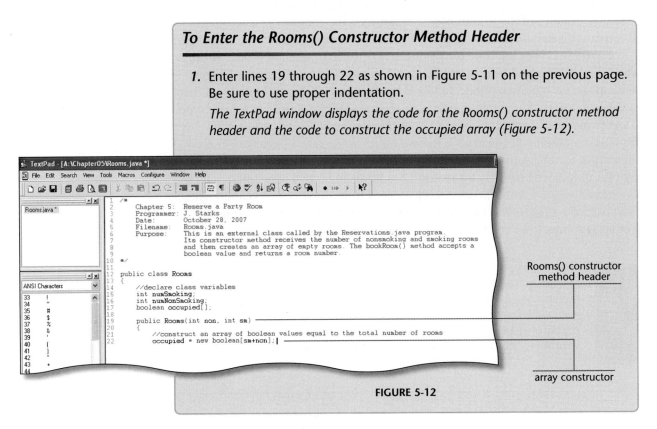

FIGURE 5-12

You can create multiple constructor methods of the same data type if you anticipate a need for multiple instances of an object with different arguments. For example, if you plan to use an instance of the Rooms object in a different application that books reservations only for nonsmoking rooms (passing only a single integer), you can include a second Rooms() constructor method that uses a single parameter. A second constructor method header might be coded as follows:

```
public Rooms(int rms)
```

In that case, whether the driver class passes just one argument or two, the Rooms object would accept the call. This practice of defining more than one method with the same name is called **method overloading**. Later chapters will present additional examples of method overloading.

Counter-Controlled Loops

Recall that when you wanted a program to repeat a set of instructions, you used a repetition structure called a while loop. As you learned in Chapter 4, a while loop works well when you need to perform a task an undetermined number of times. All of the code that should be repeated, or looped, while the condition is evaluated as true is enclosed in braces. The condition must be a boolean expression that evaluates to true or false. The condition repeats as long as the condition is evaluated as true. The condition eventually must evaluate to false in order to exit the loop, based on some condition or user input that changed.

Java provides another type of loop to use if you know exactly how many times you want the program to repeat a set of instructions. A loop that executes a specific number of times is called a **counter-controlled loop**, or **measured loop**.

The for Statement

Java uses a **for statement** to implement a counter-controlled loop, also called a **for loop**. The for statement lists the parameters of a for loop, which include the beginning value, the stop condition that tests whether to continue to loop, and the increment to use for the counter. The three parameters are enclosed in parentheses and separated by semicolons. The for statement is followed by a line of code or a block of statements, enclosed in braces, which execute the number of times defined in the for statement.

Table 5-7 displays the general form of the for statement.

Table 5-7	*The for Statement*

General form:	for (start; stop; counter-control)
	{
	. . . lines of code to repeat;
	}

Comment:	The word, **for**, is a reserved keyword. The start parameter typically is a variable initialized to a beginning value and is done only once per invocation of the loop. The stop parameter is a condition that tests whether to continue the loop. As long as the condition evaluates to true, the loop continues. The **counter-control**, sometimes called the update, typically is an expression indicating how to increment or decrement the counter. Semicolons separate the three parameters enclosed in parentheses.

Examples:	1. `for (int j=1; j<5; j++)`
	//j is initialized to 1; the loop continues while j is less than 5; j is incremented by 1 at each pass of the loop; the loop will execute 4 times.
	2. `for (int counter=6; counter>0; counter--)`
	//counter is initialized to 6; the loop continues while counter is greater than 0; counter is decremented by 1 at each pass of the loop; the loop will execute 6 times.
	3. `for (int evenValues=2; evenValues<=100; evenValues+=2)`
	//evenValues is initialized to 2; the loop continues while evenValues is less than or equal to 100; evenValues is incremented by 2 at each pass of the loop; the loop will execute 50 times.

The first parameter in the for statement is an assignment statement to tell the compiler to store an integer, positive or negative, as the start value. Any valid integer can be used as the start value for the for loop. That value defines where the compiler will start counting as it executes the for loop. For example, if you wanted to manipulate each element of an array in a for loop, you would set your first parameter counter to zero (0), as arrays are numbered beginning with zero. As the start value is incremented or decremented at each pass of the loop, the updated value is stored. The start value typically is declared inside the for statement.

The second parameter determines how many times the loop executes. The parameter must be a condition that results in a boolean value. Typically, the condition tests the value of the counter using a conditional operator. While the value is true, the loop keeps executing; if the condition is false, the loop stops executing. For example, if you were looping to manipulate each element of the array, the loop should continue only while you still have array elements. If the length of the array is 9 (elements numbering 0 through 8), the second parameter in the for statement would compare the counter variable to less than 9 as in the following code:

```
for (int counter=0; counter<9; counter++)
```

The for Statement

Many times students confuse the second parameter of the for statement with a do-until concept. It is better to think of it as a do while. The second parameter notifies the loop to keep performing while a certain condition is true. For example, a loop that prints paychecks for 100 employees might contain a loop condition of number<101 or number<=100. Assuming the loop began with 1 and was incremented by 1 each time, either condition would cause the loop to execute 100 times.

The third parameter manipulates the counter-control value. While a for loop often increments or decrements the counter-control value by one, a for loop can increment or decrement by any integer value other than one, an example of which is shown in example 3 of Table 5-7 on the previous page. For example, if you wanted to increment the start value by five, you might use the add and assign operator to add five to the start value at each pass of the loop, as in the following code:

```
for (int counter=5; counter<=100; counter+=5)
```

An assignment or unary operator typically is used to increment or decrement the counter-control value. The next section discusses both assignment and unary operators in detail.

Assignment and Unary Operators

Recall that to accumulate a running total, you declare a variable, give that variable a beginning value, and then add to it by including the identifier name on both sides of an assignment operator. For example, the following code:

```
variable = variable + newValue;
```

is an assignment statement that is evaluated from right to left. Therefore, in the above example, every time the line is executed, the old value of variable is added to newValue and then reassigned to the original identifier name.

In Java, an **assignment operator**, or **shortcut operator**, is used to perform arithmetic and an assignment operation all with one operator, thus providing a shortened form of that variable accumulation. One of the assignment operators, the **add and assign operator** (+=), performs both addition of a new value and assignment to a storage location, replacing the repetitive portion of the above code with the following code:

```
variable += newValue;
```

For example, if you declare a variable with the identifier name counter and want to add five to it each time the line of code is executed, the code would use the add and assign operator (+=), as follows:

```
counter += 5;
```

Each time the above code is executed, Java adds five to the previous value of counter and writes the new value back into the same storage location, effectively overwriting the earlier value.

An easy way to increment a running count or counter is to use a special operator called a unary operator. A **unary operator** is an operator that needs only one value, or operand, to perform its function. Java supports the use of two unary operators: the **increment operator** (++), which adds one to the operand, and the **decrement operator** (- -), which subtracts one from the operand.

With traditional operators, such as an addition operator, you must supply at least two values to be added. With unary operators, you use a special symbol that performs a mathematical operation on a single value. For example, if you want to increment the variable, i, by one each time the code executes, you could write the following code using an addition operator:

```
i = i + 1;
```

Using an assignment operator, the code becomes a little shorter.

```
i+=1;
```

Using a unary operator, the code becomes even simpler.

```
i++;
```

An interesting feature of unary operators is that they behave differently depending on whether the unary operator is positioned before or after the variable. If the increment operator comes after the variable, as in the above example, the value is incremented after the line of code is executed. If, however, the increment operator precedes the variable, the value is incremented before the line of code is executed. In a single line of code, the placement of the unary operator does not make any difference. If, however, the unary operator is included as part of a formula or in an assignment statement, the placement is crucial. For example, the following code:

```
i = 5;
answer = ++i;
```

results in the value of answer being equal to six, because the variable, i, is incremented before the line of code is executed. Any later references to the value, i, will be evaluated as six, as well.

If the unary operator comes after the variable, as in the following code:

```
i = 5;
answer = i++;
```

the value of answer will be equal to 5, because the variable, i, is incremented after the line of code is executed. Any later references to the value, i, will be evaluated as 6, because i was incremented after the assignment. Like the increment operator, the timing of the decrement is dependent on the placement of the decrement operator.

Table 5-8 lists Java's two unary operators and six assignment operators.

Table 5-8   Unary and Assignment Operators

OPERATOR SYMBOL	OPERATOR NAME	TYPE OF OPERATOR	SAMPLE CODE	VALUE OF ANSWER AFTER EXECUTION
++	increment	unary	answer = 10; answer++;	11
- -	decrement	unary	answer = 10; answer--;	9
=	assign	assignment	answer = 10;	10
+=	add and assign	assignment	answer = 10; answer += 10;	20
-=	subtract and assign	assignment	answer = 10; answer -= 3;	7
*=	multiply and assign	assignment	answer = 10; answer *= 4;	40
/=	divide and assign	assignment	answer = 10; answer /= 5;	2
%=	modulus and assign	assignment	answer = 10; answer %= 3;	1

Table 5-9 displays a series of Java code statements showing how the value of i might change using the increment operator both before and after the operand.

Table 5-9   Changing Values Using the Increment Operator

LINE	CODE	DISPLAYED RESULT	REASON
1	i = 10;		
2	System.out.println(i);	10	i was assigned the value of 10 in line 1
3	i++		
4	System.out.println(i);	11	i was incremented by 1 in line 3
5	System.out.println(i++);	11	i is incremented by 1 after line 5 is executed; value of i thus does not change when printed
6	System.out.println(i);	12	i was incremented by 1 after line 5 executed
7	System.out.println(++i);	13	i is incremented by 1 before line 7 is executed
8	System.out.println(i);	13	i was not changed after line 7

Using Unary Operators in for Loops

To create a simple for loop that is to be repeated 10 times, the following for statement can be used:

```
for (int i = 1; i<11; i++)
```

Many programmers use the identifier, i, instead of spelling out the word increment when creating a for loop. The first parameter declares and sets the i variable to 1. The second parameter tests i to make sure it is less than 11. The third parameter increments the variable by one, using the increment operator, ++.

When a for loop uses a decrement operator in the third parameter, it gives the feeling of counting backward. For example, the following code:

```
for (int counter = 10; counter>0; counter--)
```

creates a for loop that executes 10 times.

When using a decrement operator, the counter in the second parameter must be less than the value in the first parameter. If it is not, as in the following code:

```
for (int counter = 1; counter<10; counter--)
```

the for loop will execute an infinite number of times, because the condition always will be true. If the values in the first and second parameters are the same, as in the following code:

```
for (int counter = 1; counter<1; counter--)
```

the program will compile, but the for loop never will execute.

Figure 5-13 displays the code to assign each element of the occupied array a value of false, using a for loop in the Rooms() constructor method. The for loop beginning in line 23 has only one dependent line of code in line 24 and thus does not include braces. A for loop that has more than one line of code must include braces around that code; if it does not, only the first line of code will repeat. The other lines will execute once after the loop is completed.

When the Rooms object is instantiated in the driver class, lines 26 and 27 assign the passed values to the class level variables for use in all methods of the Rooms class.

```
23          for(int i=0; i<(sm+non); i++)
24             occupied[i] = false; //set each occupied room to false or empty
25          //initialize the number of smoking and nonsmoking rooms
26          numSmoking = sm;
27          numNonSmoking = non;
28       }
29
```

FIGURE 5-13

The following step illustrates how to enter code for the for loop and assignment statements.

To Enter Code for the for Loop and Assignment Statements

1. Enter lines 23 through 29 as shown in Figure 5-13 on the previous page. *The for loop and assignment statements are displayed (Figure 5-14).*

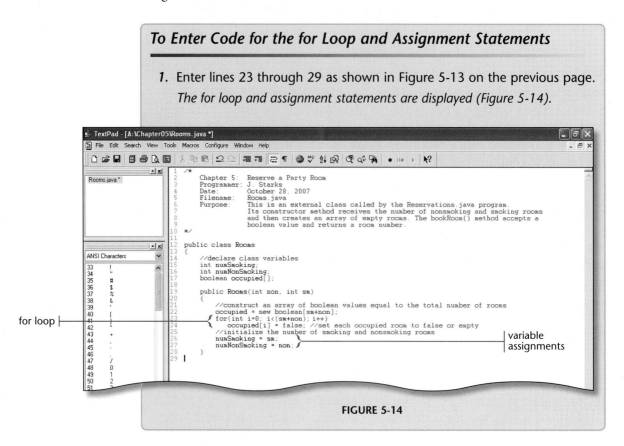

FIGURE 5-14

Line 23 includes a for statement to define the for loop with three parameters. The first parameter declares and sets the i variable to 0. The second parameter tests i to make sure it is less than the sum of the sm and non variables, which represent the number of smoking and nonsmoking rooms respectively. The third parameter increments the variable by one, using the increment operator, ++. Line 24 assigns each element of the occupied array a value of false. The for loop thus will execute until the number of occupied rooms is not less than the total number of rooms.

Lines 26 and 27 assign the passed values, sm and non, to the class variables, numSmoking and numNonSmoking, for use in all methods of the Rooms class. Line 28 is the closing brace for the Rooms() constructor method. This method now can be called from the driver class to create an instance of the Rooms object. When called, it must pass two integer arguments.

Exiting a for Loop Prematurely

Occasionally, you will want to terminate a counter-controlled or for loop based on a different condition. For example, if the purpose of the for loop is to look through a list for a certain item and the program finds the item before the for loop is done, you may not want to continue the for loop. In that case, you can force the counter to equal a number outside the range tested by the condition. For example, if the for loop should loop through items 1 to 10 and the program finds the item at number 3, the following code:

```
for (int counter=1; counter<=10; counter++)
{
        //item found
        counter = 11;
}
```

assigns the counter variable a value of 11, thus causing the condition in the second parameter to evaluate as false and the for loop to exit.

Because the Rooms object will know exactly how many rooms there are, the Rooms() constructor method will use a for loop and increment by 1 as it assigns each element of the array a false state (unoccupied at the beginning).

Nested Loops

The for loop may be nested inside another for loop. Recall that nesting means a code structure is completely enclosed within the braces or constraints of another structure. The following code:

```
for (int i=1; i<=4; i++)
{
        for (int j=1; j<=3; j++)
                System.out.println( i + " - " + j);
}
```

defines a nested for loop that will produce the following 12 lines of output:

```
1 - 1
1 - 2
1 - 3
2 - 1
2 - 2
2 - 3
3 - 1
3 - 2
3 - 3
4 - 1
4 - 2
4 - 3
```

A nested loop is convenient when assigning values to two-dimensional arrays or when keeping track of a table of numbers.

Instance Methods

Just as declaring variables did not fully instantiate the external class, Rooms, constructing an instance by itself does not provide a means to enter data into that instance — for that, you need an instance method. An **instance method** operates or manipulates variables for an external class. While external classes use constructor methods to allow driver classes to instantiate them, external classes use instance methods to allow driver classes to manipulate the object's data. The variables manipulated within an instance method, which are local in scope, are called **instance variables**. When called by the driver class, instance methods must use the class.method() notation, in which class is the name of the external class object.

Java programmers typically use a user-friendly, active verb in the name of the instance methods. For example, an instance method to retrieve data about an invoice might be named getBalance(). An instance method to assign a new balance might be named setBalance(). While other data members are declared private so that the driver class does not change the values, the get() and set() instance methods usually are declared public so that data used in the methods may be validated.

> **Tip**
>
> **Naming Instance Methods**
> When naming an instance method, use a user-friendly, active verb in the name. For example, methods that retrieve and assign data commonly are named with the verbs, get and set. A method to retrieve data about an invoice thus might be named getBalance(). The method to assign a new balance might be named setBalance().

The bookRoom() Method

The Rooms class needs an instance method to book a specific room. Figure 5-15 shows the code for the instance method named bookRoom(), a name that describes the purpose of the instance method. Line 30 sets the bookRoom() method to have public access, thus allowing its use in other programs. The bookRoom() method accepts a passed parameter, which is a boolean value representing whether or not the user has requested a smoking room. The bookRoom() method returns an int value to the driver class, representing the number of the booked room (or the value, zero, if no rooms are available).

```
30      public int bookRoom(boolean smoking)
31      {
32          int begin, end, roomNumber=0;
33
34          if(!smoking)
35          {
36              begin = 0;
37              end = numNonSmoking;
38          }
39          else
40          {
41              begin = numNonSmoking;
42              end = numSmoking+numNonSmoking;
43          }
44
45          for(int i=begin; i<end; ++i)
46          {
47              if(!occupied[i]) //if room is not occupied
48              {
49                  occupied[i] = true;
50                  roomNumber = i+1;
51                  i = end; //to exit loop
52              }
53          }
54          return roomNumber;
55      }
56  }
```

FIGURE 5-15

The bookRoom() method must evaluate each of the desired type of rooms (nonsmoking or smoking), one by one, looking for an unoccupied room (a false element in the array). In the body of the bookRoom() method, three variables are declared: one that will hold the first room to be evaluated, one that will hold the last room to be evaluated, and one that will hold the reserved room number, once it is identified.

An if statement in line 34 determines whether the driver class has asked for a smoking or nonsmoking room. If a nonsmoking room has been requested, the rooms to be evaluated will begin at zero, as stored in a variable named begin in line 36. The evaluation will continue through the total number of nonsmoking rooms (as previously stored by the Rooms() constructor method and assigned to the NonSmoking variable), which is stored in a variable named end (line 37). Otherwise, the bookRoom() method will begin looking at the first smoking room (assigned in line 41) and proceed to the end of the array (calculated and assigned in line 42).

The for loop in lines 45 through 53 goes through the appropriate rooms looking for an unoccupied one. A false value in the boolean array indicates an unoccupied room; if an unoccupied room is found, its value is changed to true in line 49. The room number is assigned and the for loop exits. If the for loop completes without finding an unoccupied room, the initial roomNumber value of zero, previously initialized in line 32, is returned to the calling program indicating that all rooms of that type are full (line 54).

The following step enters code for the bookRoom() method.

To Enter Code for the bookRoom() Method

1. Enter the code as shown in Figure 5-15 on the previous page. *The bookRoom() method is displayed (Figure 5-16).*

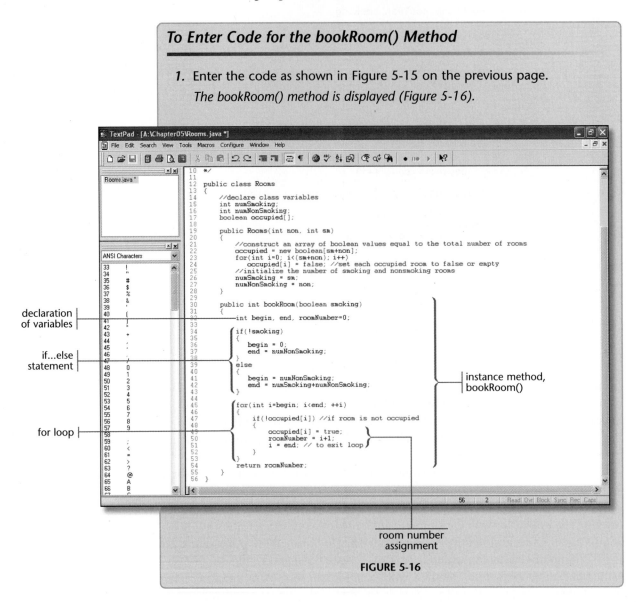

FIGURE 5-16

In line 50, the roomNumber variable is assigned a value of the increment plus one. Remember that arrays are numbered from zero to the end. Therefore, room number 1 actually is the zero member of the array. As most establishments would begin their room numbers with 1, adding one to the array index number gives a more user-friendly numerical representation of the correct room number.

Compiling the Rooms Class Source Code

The Rooms class is complete. The next step is to compile the Rooms class source code to create a reusable class object, as shown in the following steps.

To Compile the Rooms Class Source Code

1. With your Data Disk in drive A, click Compile Java on the Tools menu.
2. If the Rooms class contains errors, fix them in the coding window and then recompile the program.

TextPad compiles the source code for the Rooms class.

OTHER WAYS

1. Press CTRL+1
2. At command prompt, type `javac Rooms.java`

The Rooms class now can be used or called from any Java application that needs this kind of class. If you want to document the source code, you can print a copy of the code for later reference by clicking the Print button on the Standard toolbar in the TextPad window.

Creating Windowed Applications

Recall that the Abstract Window Toolkit is the basic set of Java classes used to build graphical user interfaces for Java applets and applications. Using the AWT, programmers have access to tools for creating common graphical objects such as windows, dialog boxes, buttons, areas in which to manipulate text, and much more. The AWT also specifies an event-handling model that enables a Java program to respond to the keystrokes and mouse-clicks entered by a user.

The AWT is abstract or conceptual, in that it provides only the essential components and functionality that are common to all major operating systems that support windowed applications. For example, Microsoft Windows, Apple Mac OSX, and Unix all allow a user to click a button to execute an action. The physical appearance of the button, precise behavior, and the application program interface (API), however, differ significantly for each of the three environments. (Recall that an application program interface is a standard set of interfaces and classes functionally grouped into packages; these APIs are present in any Java implementation.) Java abstracts the essential behavior of a button and provides an API that is presented to the developer in the AWT. When an instance of the Java Button class is compiled, the actual button presented to the user is obtained from the native, or operating system, environment of the user's computer. The same is true for many of the other AWT components, including the window itself.

Recall that Swing components use lightweight Java implementations of the standard GUI controls. While Swing components increasingly are used to create windowed applications, the Swing classes typically are not used on Java certification exams because they do not create native controls, as do the AWT controls. Additionally, some Swing components do not work with all browsers.

Using Frames in a Windowed Application

A **container** is a special Java object that contains other components, such as user interface controls and other containers. For example, a window is a familiar container for users. It can hold icons, buttons, frames, and other components. Java containers defined in the AWT include Windows, Panels, Frames, Canvases, Dialogs, and ScrollPanes.

The Reservations program will use a Frame container. As previously noted, a Frame is an AWT component that serves as a container for a collection of graphical AWT components. Figure 5-17 displays the hierarchy of AWT components. Notice that the Frame class inherits attributes and methods from the Window class. Similar to a window, a Frame is used in stand-alone applications to create a window with its own title bars, borders, icons, and Minimize, Maximize, and Close buttons. Frames also can include menus and use a number of different insertion point shapes.

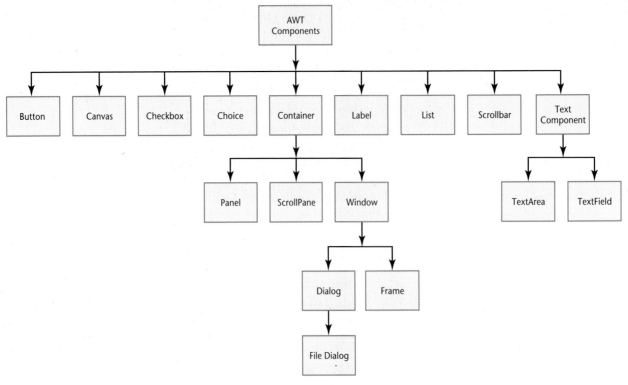

FIGURE 5-17

Frames are a powerful feature of the AWT, because you may use Frames to build stand-alone windowed applications or to create separate windows for applets, as is the case when running an applet outside the main window of a Web browser.

A program that uses a Frame needs to use the word, extends, in the class header. Recall that a program may extend, or build on, a superclass provided by Java, such as a Frame, or it may extend a programmer-defined class.

The Reservations Class

Figure 5-18 displays the beginning code to start the Reservations program by declaring the Reservations class. After the block comment, import statements are used to import three packages. The JOptionPane class of the Swing package will be used to display message dialog boxes when all of the party rooms are occupied. The java.awt and java.awt.event packages will be used for methods related to GUI components and their listeners.

```
1  /*
2        Chapter 5:    Reserve a Party Room
3        Programmer:  J. Starks
4        Date:         October 28, 2007
5        Filename:     Reservations.java
6        Purpose:      This program creates a windowed application to reserve a party room.
7                      It calls an external class named Rooms.
8  */
9
10  import javax.swing.JOptionPane;
11  import java.awt.*;
12  import java.awt.event.*;
13
14  public class Reservations extends Frame implements ActionListener
15  {
```

FIGURE 5-18

As shown in Figure 5-18, line 14 extends the Frame class. The Frame class is the application equivalent of the Applet class, in that it is a logical and visual object in which components are placed. By extending from the Frame class, the Reservations class will be a subclass of the Frame class; this means the Reservations class will behave in a similar manner and will inherit all of the fields and methods declared or inherited in the Frame class. Programs that use a window, or GUI-based interface, typically extend the Frame class and are called windowed applications, or **frame-based applications**. The Reservations class will implement the ActionListener because it will receive input, in the form of a user clicking a button on the program interface.

The following steps enter the beginning code for the Reservations class.

To Enter Beginning Code for the Reservations Class

1. Start TextPad. If TextPad already is running, click the New Document button on the Standard toolbar.

2. Insert the Data Disk in drive A. Click File on the menu bar and then click Save As on the File menu. When the Save As dialog box is displayed, type Reservations in the File name text box and then click Java (*.java) in the Save as type list. Click the Save in box arrow and then click 3½ Floppy (A:) in the Save in list. Double-click the Chapter05 folder or a location specified by your instructor. Click the Save button.

(continued)

3. Enter the code as shown in Figure 5-18 on the previous page, replacing the programmer name and date shown with your name and the current date.

The TextPad window displays the beginning code for the Reservations class (Figure 5-19).

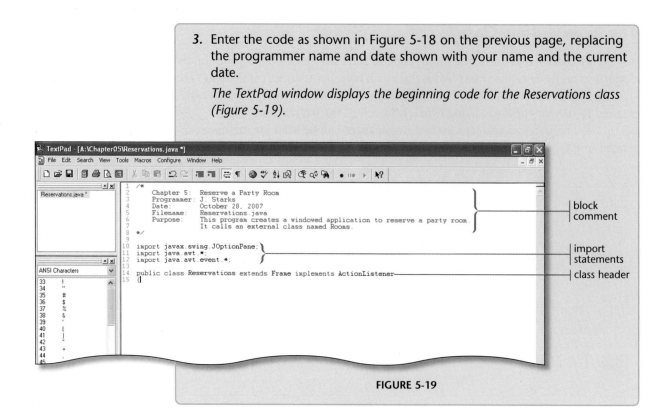

FIGURE 5-19

Using a Choice Component

A Choice component is an AWT component just like Buttons, Labels, and TextFields; however, the Choice component displays as a drop-down list box with a box arrow. Choice components are useful for displaying restricted lists, such as specific states or countries, a list of available colors, or numbers within a range. Java automatically displays the first item in the list and then displays a box arrow that a user can click to view other items in the Choice component list. Users then can select any item in the list.

When a user clicks the box arrow and selects an item from the list, Java associates that click event with a Choice event. The Choice event of clicking the arrow to display the list and then choosing from that list is polymorphic — that is, it happens without any additional components or coding. When you add the Choice component, the functionality comes with it. As you will see later in this chapter, Choice components have some unique features with regard to their creation and population, but they must be constructed with a name and then added to the user interface in a manner similar to other components.

Using an = new constructor, the Choice component must be given a name. The following code:

```
Choice myChoice = new Choice();
```

identifies Choice as the type of component and myChoice as the name of this specific instance of the Choice component. The object type, Choice, must be capitalized. As with the CheckboxGroup component you learned about in an earlier chapter, the Choice component's argument list is null — that is, no arguments are listed inside the parentheses during construction.

The Choice component has several methods used to manipulate items in Choice lists. Table 5-10 lists several of these methods and their purpose.

Table 5-10   Choice Component Methods

METHOD	SAMPLE	PURPOSE
add()	myDropDown.add("First Item");	Populates a drop-down list
Choice()	Choice myDropDown = new Choice();	Serves as constructor method
getIndex()	myDropDown.getIndex();	Returns the index number of the selected item
getItemCount()	myDropDown.getItemCount();	Returns the number of items in this Choice menu
getSelectedItem()	String answer = myDropDown.getSelectedItem();	Returns String of user selection
insert()	myDropDown.insert("new item", 3);	Inserts new item into Choice list at the specified position
remove()	myDropDown.remove("String to remove"): myDropDown.remove(2);	Removes the first occurrence of the String or removes the item at the specified position in Choice list
select()	myDropDown.select("Highlight this one"); myDropDown.select(4);	Sets the selected item in this Choice list to be the specified String or the item at the specified position

Items added to the Choice component are indexed internally by Java, beginning with zero and incremented by 1 for each new item. It sometimes is useful to reference that index number, using the getIndex() method shown in Table 5-10. Programmers also can access the String of characters displayed in an item from the list using the getSelectedItem() method.

In the Reservations program, a Choice component will be constructed, populated with a list of numbers, and then used in the program interface to allow users to select the number of guests in the party.

Coding Constructor Methods for the Reservations Class

Figure 5-20 displays the constructor methods that are called for use in the Reservations class.

```
16        Color lightRed = new Color(255, 90, 90);
17        Color lightGreen = new Color(140, 215, 40);
18
19        Rooms room = new Rooms(5,3);
20
21        Panel roomPanel = new Panel();
22            TextArea roomDisplay[] = new TextArea[9];
23
24        Panel buttonPanel = new Panel();
25            Button bookButton = new Button("Book Room");
26
27        Panel inputPanel = new Panel();
28            Label custNameLabel = new Label("Name:");
29            TextField nameField = new TextField(15);
30            Label custPhoneLabel = new Label("Phone number:");
31            TextField phoneField = new TextField(15);
32            Label numLabel = new Label("Number in party:");
33            Choice numberOfGuests = new Choice();
34            CheckboxGroup options = new CheckboxGroup();
35                Checkbox nonSmoking = new Checkbox("Nonsmoking",false,options);
36                Checkbox smoking = new Checkbox("Smoking",false,options);
37                Checkbox hidden = new Checkbox("",true,options);
38
```

FIGURE 5-20

Lines 16 and 17 construct two new colors, lightRed and lightGreen, with their RGB arguments. Line 19 constructs an instance of the Rooms object, which was coded earlier in this chapter, with the integers 5 and 3 as arguments to represent five nonsmoking rooms and three smoking rooms.

Recall that a Panel is a GUI component that serves as a container for other components. A Panel must be declared and constructed like other components. Lines 21, 24, and 27 declare and construct three Panels named roomPanel, buttonPanel, and inputPanel. The indentation below each Panel constructor serves to visually separate the code and indicate which components will be included in each Panel.

When an array contains values other than primitive data types, such as a reference data type or String, it is considered an **object array,** or **control array**. Line 22 constructs an object array of TextArea components with the name roomDisplay. Creating an array of TextArea components simplifies the code, because you do not have to create separate names and constructors for each of the TextArea components. It also facilitates sending data to the TextArea components, which will be discussed later in the chapter. Even though the restaurant has only eight rooms, the constructor creates nine rooms, numbered 0 through 8. This allows you to relate the TextArea component numbers with the room number without having to add 1 to the index number.

You also can create an object array of programmer-defined data types or classes. For example, you might have an external class named Employee, with constructor and instance methods for one employee. In your driver class, the program might create an array of type Employee as in the following code:

```
Employee empGroup = new Employee[16];
```

An array of 16 employees is constructed and stored in a variable location named empGroup. Again, think of the array as a stretched variable location; in the case of an object array, each member of the array refers to a set of data as opposed to a single data item. An object array of this type still follows the rule about every array member being the same data type; in this example, every member of the array is an Employee object. At compile time, the compiled Employee object must exist for it to be used as a data type in the driver class.

Line 25 constructs a Book Room button that will display in the button panel (line 24). Lines 28 through 32 construct Labels and TextFields for prompts and data input that will display in the input panel (line 27).

Line 33 is the call to the constructor for the Choice component, which is named numberOfGuests. The Choice() method has no arguments. Individual items will be added to the drop-down list later in the program.

Finally, line 34 declares and constructs a CheckboxGroup named options, and lines 35 through 37 construct three Checkbox components to display within the CheckboxGroup. Recall that each Checkbox component in a CheckboxGroup will appear as an option button on the program interface.

The following step enters the declarations for the Reservations class.

To Enter Declarations for the Reservations Class

1. Enter the code as shown in Figure 5-20.

The TextPad window displays the declarations for the Reservations class (Figure 5-21).

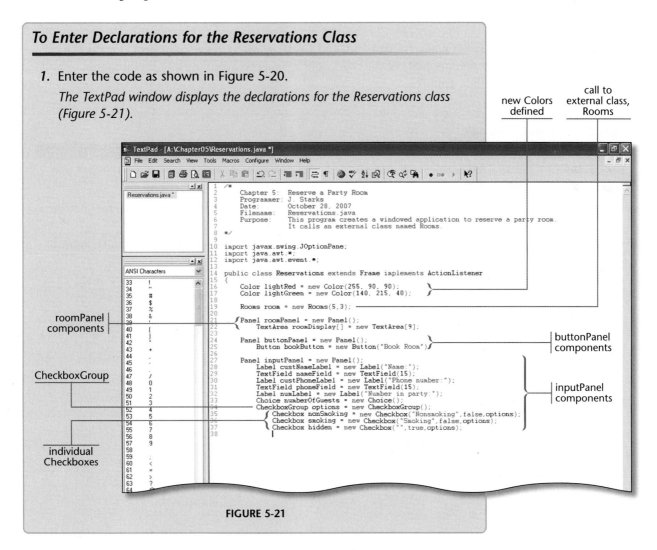

FIGURE 5-21

The code in lines 16 through 37 creates two Colors, a Rooms object, as well as three Panels that include other components, such as a Choice component and a CheckboxGroup. An object array of TextArea components also is created.

Layout Managers

In previous projects, Java or Applet Viewer automatically has determined the placement of components, based on the size of the window listed in the HTML host document, among other considerations. Alternatively, you might have positioned components in a window using coordinates. When you position components using coordinates, however, it can cause problems when someone using a monitor with 640 x 480 resolution tries to run a program designed to fit on a screen with 1280 x 1024 resolution.

To assist in component placement inside containers, Java provides a **layout manager** — one of a set of five classes that help programmers organize components into predefined locations in the window, rather than allowing Java to place them left to right within the space provided. By using layout managers, you can instruct the AWT where to place certain components relative to other components.

The five layout managers provided by Java are FlowLayout, BorderLayout, GridLayout, CardLayout, and GridBagLayout. Table 5-11 provides a quick reference table of the five layout managers, how they handle components, and their features.

Table 5-11   Layout Managers

LAYOUT MANAGER	COMPONENT HANDLING	FEATURES
FlowLayout	Places components in rows from left to right	Three alignment possibilities: LEFT, RIGHT, and CENTER
BorderLayout	Places components at compass points — North, South, East, and West	Placement in five possible areas in the container; specify horizontal and vertical gaps
GridLayout	Places components left to right in a predetermined grid	Specification of number of rows and number of columns
CardLayout	Places components in a stack	Support for methods such as first(), last(), previous(), and next() to display stack components
GridBagLayout	Places components in grids; components may vary in size	Specification of grid and location of components

FlowLayout

FlowLayout is the default, or preset, layout manager for Panels and Applets. If you do not program a layout manager, Java uses FlowLayout, which treats a container as a set of rows. As components are added to the container, FlowLayout places them in rows, from left to right. The height of the item placed in the row determines the height of that entire row. The number of rows is determined by the size of the container. If the component cannot fit on the current row, FlowLayout moves it to the next row. If components do not fill the row, the components are centered in the row.

If you decide to change back to FlowLayout from a different layout manager, the layout manager must be constructed with the **setLayout() method** using the following:

```
setLayout(new FlowLayout());
```

If you want to change FlowLayout's alignment, you can use code such as the following code:

```
setLayout(new FlowLayout(FlowLayout.RIGHT));
```

to specify one of three different alignment constants as an argument or parameter to the constructor for FlowLayout: LEFT, RIGHT, or CENTER. In Java, any **constant**, such as LEFT, RIGHT, or CENTER, is entered in capital letters.

Once FlowLayout has been specified, components can be added to the container with the usual add() method. For example, the following code:

```
add(custNameLabel);
```

adds a Label component with the name custNameLabel. Figure 5-22 displays an application with five Button components added to the container using the default CENTER location of the FlowLayout layout manager.

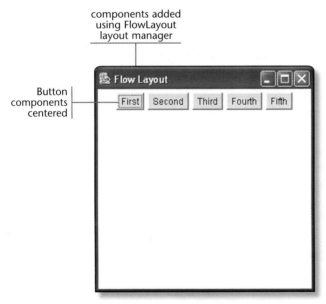

FIGURE 5-22

BorderLayout

The layout manager **BorderLayout** places components into five regions within the container: North, South, East, West, and Center. Figure 5-23 displays an application with five buttons, one in each region, placed using the BorderLayout layout manager.

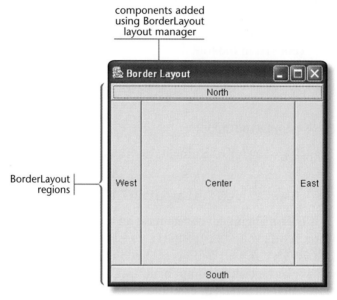

FIGURE 5-23

Components are added to the container by specifying their geographical placement using the add() method, as in the following line of code:

```
add(myButton, BorderLayout.SOUTH);
```

An alternate form adds and constructs a button with a caption, as shown in the following line of code:

```
add("South", new Button("Okay"));
```

Up to five components can be added in any order, but only one component can be added to each region. Additional components added to a region will replace whatever component is in a region. The components placed in the North and South regions extend horizontally to the edge of the container and are as tall as the tallest component. The components in the East and West regions expand vertically between the North and South regions and are as wide as the widest component. The Center component expands to take up all the remaining space. If a North, South, East, or West component is not present, the adjacent components fill the space. If a Center component is not present, the region is left blank.

With BorderLayout, you also can specify the number of pixels between components, using the following line of code:

```
setLayout(new BorderLayout(9,7));
```

This line of code instructs the layout manager to use the BorderLayout with nine pixels horizontally and seven pixels vertically between components.

GridLayout

The **GridLayout** layout manager divides the container into a grid so that components can be placed in rows and columns, from left to right and then top to bottom, within the grid. The following line of code:

```
setLayout(new GridLayout(3,4));
```

instructs the layout manager to use the GridLayout with three rows and four columns. While you can specify the size of the grid to create using the GridLayout layout manager, you cannot specify into which row or column to put a component; GridLayout adds components in order, from left to right, top to bottom, within the grid. Figure 5-24 displays an application with 12 buttons placed in a 3 x 4 grid using the GridLayout layout manager.

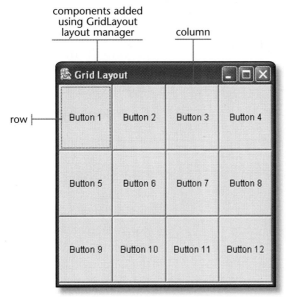

FIGURE 5-24

CardLayout

A more flexible but slightly more complicated layout manager is CardLayout. **CardLayout** is used primarily to house other containers. CardLayout places other containers in a stack similar to a deck of cards. Each container in the stack then can use its own layout manager. The container at the top of the deck is visible when the program is executed.

Often, an instance of CardLayout is constructed for use later in the program, using the code:

```
myCards = new CardLayout();
```

Containers are created and then used to construct the instance, using the code:

```
deck = new Panel();
deck.setLayout(myCards());
```

The add() method then can be used to add the internal containers to the deck, using the code:

```
deck.add(myPanel);
deck.add(myDialog);
```

Only one card is visible at any one time. CardLayout uses four methods — first(), last(), previous(), and next() to display the cards, with the name of the container as an argument, as in the following code:

```
myCards.previous(deck);
```

Figure 5-25 displays an application that is typical of how Java programmers combine some of the different layout managers to achieve certain visual effects. The application combines both the GridLayout and the CardLayout. On the left is a set of Button components positioned using the GridLayout manager. On the right is a Panel component, positioned using the CardLayout manager. The buttons then are programmed to bring a specific panel to the front. The Panel's background color has been set to green to better display its location.

GridBagLayout

Perhaps the most flexible of all the Java layout managers is the GridBagLayout. **GridBagLayout**, which is created in a manner similar to GridLayout, aligns components horizontally and vertically without requiring that the components be the same size. Each GridBagLayout manager uses a rectangular grid of cells, with each component occupying one or more cells. Components may be added in any order. Figure 5-26 displays an application that places components using the GridBagLayout layout manager.

The use of a layout manager offers many benefits, including that of automatically adjusting the size and position of components if the user resizes the Frame.

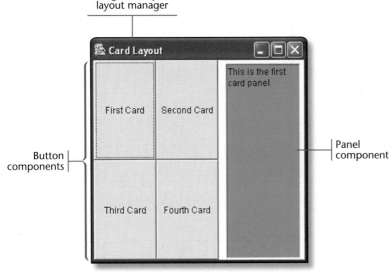

FIGURE 5-25

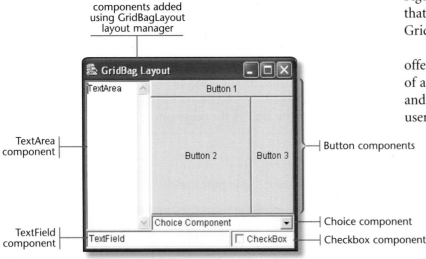

FIGURE 5-26

Using Layout Managers in the Reservations() Constructor Method

Recall that the Reservations class will contain a Reservations() constructor method that defines what the Reservations object will be like when the object is instantiated, or created. Typically, a constructor method of this sort is similar to the init() method in an applet in that it adds components to the interface. In the case of the Reservations() method, the layout manager, BorderLayout, will be defined and the components will be added to Panels, each of which will use its own layout manager. Figure 5-27 displays the code for the Reservations() constructor method.

```
39    public Reservations()
40    {
41        //set Layouts for frame and three panels
42        this.setLayout(new BorderLayout());
43            roomPanel.setLayout(new GridLayout(2,4,10,10));
44            buttonPanel.setLayout(new FlowLayout());
45            inputPanel.setLayout(new FlowLayout());
46
47        //add components to room panel
48        for (int i=1; i<9; i++)
49        {
50            roomDisplay[i] = new TextArea(null,3,5,3);
51            if (i<6)
52                roomDisplay[i].setText("Room " + i + " Nonsmoking");
53            else
54                roomDisplay[i].setText("Room " + i + " Smoking");
55            roomDisplay[i].setEditable(false);
56            roomDisplay[i].setBackground(lightGreen);
57            roomPanel.add(roomDisplay[i]);
58        }
59
60        //add components to button panel
61        buttonPanel.add(bookButton);
62
63        //add components to input panel
64        inputPanel.add(custNameLabel);
65        inputPanel.add(nameField);
66        inputPanel.add(custPhoneLabel);
67        inputPanel.add(phoneField);
68        inputPanel.add(numLabel);
69        inputPanel.add(numberOfGuests);
70            for(int i = 8; i<=20; i++)
71                numberOfGuests.add(String.valueOf(i));
72        inputPanel.add(nonSmoking);
73        inputPanel.add(smoking);
74
75        //add panels to frame
76        add(buttonPanel, BorderLayout.SOUTH);
77        add(inputPanel, BorderLayout.CENTER);
78        add(roomPanel, BorderLayout.NORTH);
79
80        bookButton.addActionListener(this);
81
```

FIGURE 5-27

As shown in line 42 of Figure 5-27, the layout for the entire Frame will be a BorderLayout. The self-referential keyword, this, refers to the entire Reservations() constructor method and thus sets the BorderLayout for the Frame. The Panels, which are described in the storyboard in Figure 5-3 on page 310, use different layout managers: roomPanel will use GridLayout to position the eight TextArea components, and the buttonPanel and inputPanel will use FlowLayout.

JAVA UPDATE Java 2 v5.0

A new feature of J2SE version 5.0 is the inclusion of static imports. A static import is a way for programmers to simplify their code by dropping reference to the BorderLayout manager when specifiying the region.

For example, previously the add() method required programmers to type:

```
add(label,
BorderLayout.SOUTH);
```

In version 5.0, programmers import the static constants with the code:

```
import static
java.awt.
BorderLayout.*;
```

Then when they get ready to add a component to a region, they simply type:

```
add(label, SOUTH);
```

Static imports should be used sparingly and, typically, only for constants.

If you wish to use static imports in the Reservations program, insert new code for line 13, and replace lines 76, 77, and 78.

Lines 48 through 58 add components to the roomPanel. Line 48 starts a for loop that begins at 1 and continues sequentially through 8, while the index number is less than 9. With each pass of the loop, the TextArea() constructor in line 50 takes four arguments: the default String to display (null means no default text), the number of text rows to display (a 3 means three rows of text), approximate average character width that is platform-dependent (in this case 5), and a number representing scroll bar visibility (a 3 means no scroll bars).

An if...else statement in lines 51 through 54 determines whether to add the text, Nonsmoking or Smoking, to the TextArea component. In line 55, the **setEditable() method** locks each TextArea component, which means the user cannot enter text into the TextArea at run time. Line 56 uses the setBackground() method to set the background of each TextArea component to light green.

In line 57, the TextArea component representing a room is added to the roomPanel. As with applets, Java has an add() method for adding each type of component to a container.

In line 61, the bookButton button is added to the buttonPanel. Lines 64 through 73 add the Labels, TextFields, Choice, and Checkbox components to the inputPanel.

In lines 70 and 71, a for loop is used to **populate**, or insert data into, the drop-down list of the Choice component. The population of a drop-down list in a Choice component is similar to adding data to an array. As the data is entered, it is given an index number that begins with zero and increases by one each time new data is entered. The add() method is used to specify the data. Programmers typically place multiple add() methods together in the code, directly after the addition of the object itself. The add() method inserts data into a Choice component, beginning at the top and adding a new line with each pass of the loop. In the case of the Reservations class, the Choice component will display the number of guests in a customer's party reservation, a number between 8 and 20. The for loop's increment value, i, is used to provide the data argument for the add() method. Because this data is an int, it must be converted to a String data type required by the Choice's add() method. The **valueOf() method** returns a String value from its int argument, effectively converting the int to a String. Similar to the toString() method, Java supports a valueOf() method to create a String representation of each primitive data type.

Lines 76 through 80 position each of the three Panels in a BorderLayout region and add the ActionListener to the Button. Notice that you need not include the object name in front of the add() method to add the Panels to the Frame. When no object is specified, the add() method relates to the entire Frame.

```
13    import static java.awt.BorderLayout.*;

76            add(buttonPanel, SOUTH);
77            add(inputPanel, CENTER);
78            add(roomPanel, NORTH);
79
```

The following step enters the code to set the layout managers and add components to the Reservations() constructor method.

> ### To Enter Code for the Reservations() Constructor Method
>
> **1.** Enter the code as shown in Figure 5-27 on page 347.
> *The TextPad window displays the new code (Figure 5-28).*

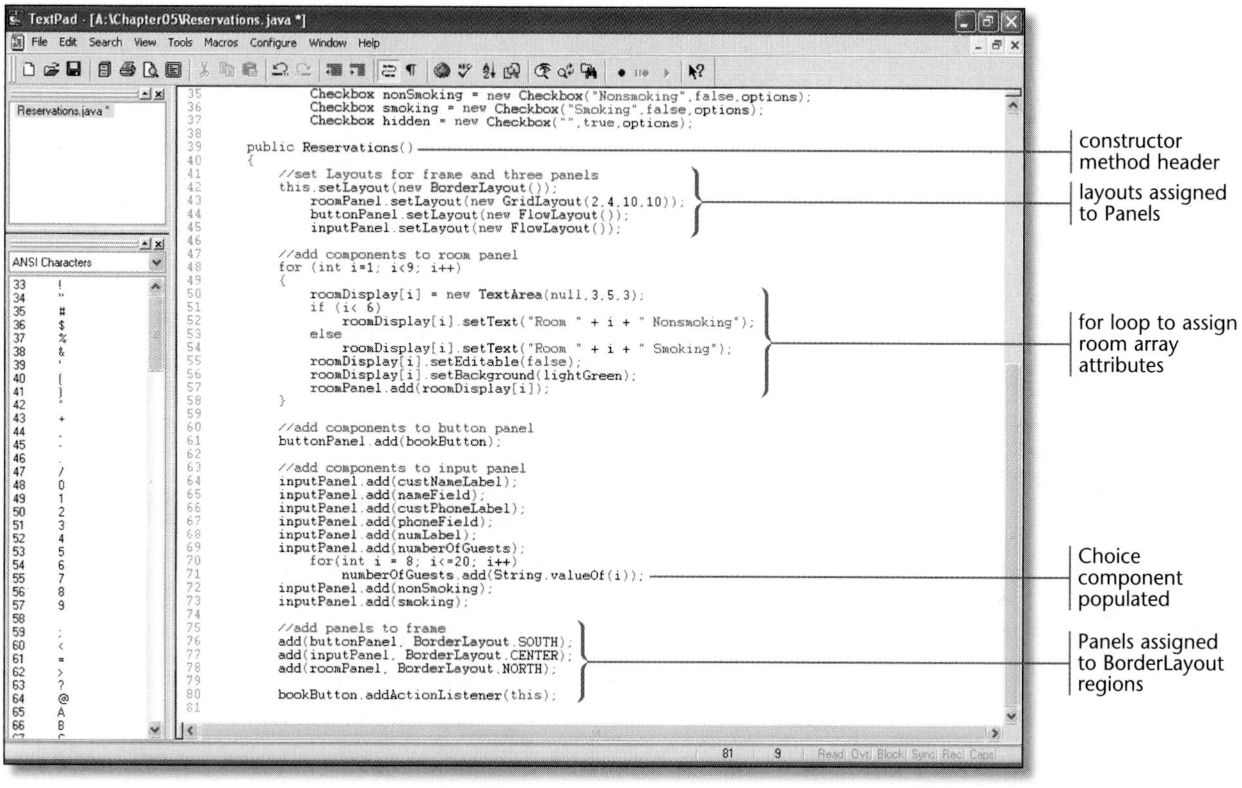

FIGURE 5-28

The Reservations() constructor method shown in Figure 5-28 defines the layout manager, BorderLayout; adds components to three Panels; constructs a list in the Choice component; and positions each Panel in a BorderLayout region.

Window Event-Handling Methods

The JVM, or Java Virtual Machine, is the run-time interpreter portion of the Java SDK. In windowed applications, the JVM handles building the Frame, title bar, and window control buttons in the title bar, based on the native environment of the user's machine. To allow the user to interact with the Frame, or window, the Frame has some inherent events that minimize, maximize, or close the window.

Figure 5-29 on the next page displays the code to add a WindowListener for the Frame. Java's **addWindowListener() method**, which begins in line 83, registers the listener with the Frame. When you **register** a listener with a Frame, you connect two objects so that events from one object, the Frame, are sent to the other object, the listener. The listener tells the Frame object to listen for such events and respond accordingly.

```
82          //overriding the windowClosing() method will allow the user to click the Close
            button
83          addWindowListener(
84              new WindowAdapter()
85              {
86                  public void windowClosing(WindowEvent e)
87                  {
88                      System.exit(0);
89                  }
90              }
91          );
92      } //end of constructor method
93
```

FIGURE 5-29

As shown in Figure 5-29, the addWindowListener() method includes an argument inside the parentheses; the argument extends through line 91 with the closing parenthesis and the semicolon. The argument creates a new occurrence of the WindowAdapter class. **Adapter classes** provide prewritten methods for interfaces. Programmers can override the methods of interest and ignore the others. In this particular case, WindowAdapter is an adapter class with ten window event-handling methods. Table 5-12 displays the ten methods and how they are triggered.

Table 5-12	Window Event-Handling Methods
WINDOW EVENT-HANDLING METHOD	**HOW THE EVENT IS TRIGGERED**
windowActivated()	User starts the application or applet
windowClosed()	Operating system has closed the window
windowClosing()	User clicks the Close button
windowDeactivated()	User clicks in the application to give it the focus
windowDeiconified()	User clicks a minimized button on the taskbar
windowGainedFocus()	User clicks anywhere in the window (or programmed operation selects window)
windowIconified()	User clicks the Minimize button
windowLostFocus()	User clicks away from the window (or programmed operation causes another window to gain focus)
windowOpened()	Operating system has opened the window
windowStateChanged()	Invoked when the window's state changes by virtue of being iconified, maximized, etc.

Each method in the WindowAdapter class is an event listener for a Window or a Frame event. In Java, programmers have the choice of implementing the WindowListener interface and then writing all the methods themselves, or using WindowAdapter and providing only the methods they wish to change or override. It is appropriate to use the WindowAdapter in this case because the program needs to handle only one of the events: closing the window.

In lines 83 through 91 in Figure 5-29, the program overrides the windowClosing() method, telling the program what to do when the user clicks the Close button in the Frame. Normally, the windowClosing() method simply closes the window or Frame, making it invisible, but does not necessarily stop the program. In the Reservations() method, however, it is overridden so that the program terminates and the window closes.

Internally, Java sends this windowClosing() method a WindowEvent object when the title bar Close button is clicked. The method disposes of the current Frame object and then calls System.exit() in line 88 to exit the application.

In previous chapters, you used the System.out() method to direct the operating system to send a stream of characters to the default output device, usually the monitor. When encountered, the System.exit() method causes the operating system to terminate the program. System.exit() has one argument, which is sent to the operating system in which the program is running. Traditionally, System.exit() returns a zero (0) to the operating system when a program ends normally and a one (1) when a program ends due to an error. The System.exit() method is used with applications rather than applets. If necessary, the System.exit() method's argument is used by the JVM when the application terminates.

The following step enters code to add the addWindowListener() method and override the windowClosing() method to close the window.

To Code the Window Event-Handling Method

1. Enter lines 82 through 93, as shown in Figure 5-29.

The TextPad window displays the code for the addWindowListener() method (Figure 5-30). The addWindowListener() method creates an occurrence of the WindowAdapter class. Lines 83 through 91 override the windowClosing() method, so that clicking the title bar Close button terminates the program.

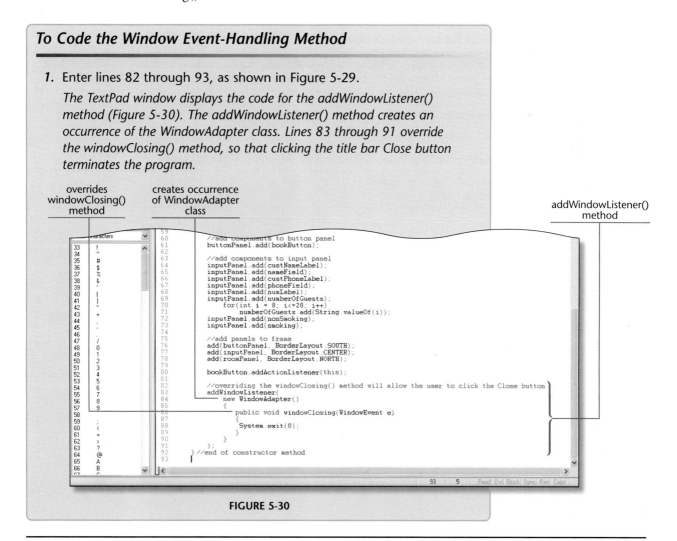

FIGURE 5-30

> ### Tip
>
> **Indenting Code**
>
> Note the indentation used in lines 82 through 93 in Figure 5-30 on the previous page. When using a method as an argument for another method, appropriate indentation can help make the code more readable. It also is important to ensure that beginning and ending parentheses and braces are indented correctly to show where the methods start and end.

Coding the main() Method

Recall that the main() method is where execution begins when running the compiled bytecode in Java. The main() method does not have to be at the beginning of the program; indeed, it can be anywhere within the class braces and still function properly.

In a windowed application, the main() method creates the instance of the Frame using a call to the constructor method. Programmers typically use the letter, f, to name their Frames, but any legal identifier is allowed. They also use the main() method to set beginning attributes of the Frame, using methods such as those listed in Table 5-13.

Table 5-13   Methods Used to Set Frame Attributes

METHOD NAME	PURPOSE	SAMPLE
setBounds()	Sets the screen location of the frame, using the x and y coordinates and the width and height	f.setBounds(200,200,600,300);
setTitle()	Sets the caption in the Frame's title bar	f.setTitle("Reserve a Party Room");
setVisible()	Sets the visibility of the Frame	f.setVisible(true);
isResizable()	Indicates whether this Frame is Resizable by the user	if(f.isResizable());
setIconImage()	Sets the image to be displayed in the Minimize icon for this Frame	f.setIconImage(myPic.gif);

Coding the main() Method in the Reservations Class

In the Reservations class, the Frame will be constructed with the name, f, as shown in line 96 of Figure 5-31. The setBounds() method in line 97 will define the location of the Frame; the setTitle() method in line 98 will assign its title bar caption; and the setVisible() method in line 99 will cause the Frame to display.

```
94      public static void main(String[] args)
95      {
96          Reservations f = new Reservations();
97          f.setBounds(200,200,600,300);
98          f.setTitle("Reserve a Party Room");
99          f.setVisible(true);
100     } //end of main
101
```

FIGURE 5-31

The step below illustrates entering the code for the main() method.

To Enter Code for the main() Method

1. Enter the code as shown in Figure 5-31.

The TextPad window displays the code for the main() method (Figure 5-32).

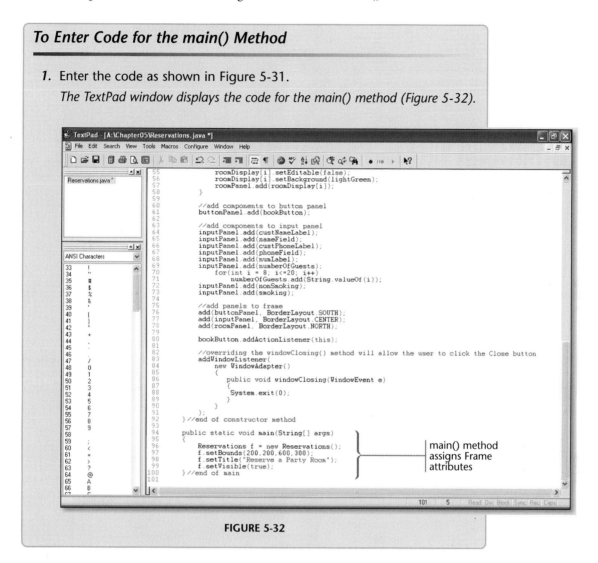

FIGURE 5-32

Coding the actionPerformed() Method

The actionPerformed() method contains the code that will execute when the user clicks the Book Room button. Recall from the flowchart in Figure 5-4 on page 313, that the Book Room button should perform the following tasks:

1. It should make sure the user has selected an option button (nonsmoking or smoking).
2. It should call the bookRoom() method of the Rooms object.
3. If a room is available, the program should change the display; otherwise, a full message should display.

Figure 5-33 on the next page displays the code for the actionPerformed() method. Three different if...else statements are used to test for the required conditions. Line 104 evaluates the state of the hidden Checkbox. If the hidden

Checkbox is selected, then the user has not chosen one of the visible option buttons on the interface, thus causing a message box to display a message prompting the user to select nonsmoking or smoking (line 106).

```
102     public void actionPerformed(ActionEvent e)
103     {
104         if (hidden.getState())
105         {
106             JOptionPane.showMessageDialog(null,"You must select Nonsmoking or Smoking.",
                    "Error",JOptionPane.ERROR_MESSAGE);
107         }
108         else
109         {
110             int available = room.bookRoom(smoking.getState());
111
112             if (available > 0) //room is available
113             {
114                 roomDisplay[available].setBackground(lightRed); //display room as occupied
115                 roomDisplay[available].setText(
116                                         roomDisplay[available].getText() +
117                                         "\n" +
118                                         nameField.getText() +
119                                         " " +
120                                         phoneField.getText() +
121                                         "\nparty of " +
122                                         numberOfGuests.getSelectedItem()
123                                         ); //display info in room
124                 clearFields();
125             }
126             else //room is not available
127             {
128                 if (smoking.getState())
129                     JOptionPane.showMessageDialog(null,"Smoking is full.","Error",
                        JOptionPane.INFORMATION_MESSAGE);
130                 else
131                     JOptionPane.showMessageDialog(null,"Nonsmoking is full.","Error",
                        JOptionPane.INFORMATION_MESSAGE);
132                 hidden.setState(true);
133             } //end of else block that checks the available room number
134         } //end of else block that checks the state of the hidden option button
135     } //end of actionPerformed() method
```

FIGURE 5-33

After the bookRoom() method is called in line 110, the program evaluates the value of available, which represents the returned room number. If the value of available is greater than zero, the program sets the background color of the TextArea component that matches the room number (line 114). Lines 115 through 123 are one long statement that concatenates the user input data of customer's name, phone number, and number of guests in the party, then sets that String to display in the TextArea component.

Tip

Improving Readability in Long Lines of Code

In TextPad, you may press the ENTER key to continue lines at certain locations, such as after operators, commas, or parentheses; Java ignores the extra white space. Breaking long statements into multiple lines improves readability. When you press the ENTER key, TextPad inserts a new line number. If a long line wraps, TextPad does not insert a new line number.

In line 124, a user-defined method named clearFields() is called. You will program the clearFields() method later in this chapter.

Lines 126 through 132 display the code that executes if the return value is zero, indicating that no rooms are available. The program then evaluates the state of the chosen option button and displays one of two error messages using a JOptionPane dialog box. The input data is not cleared, but line 132 again selects the hidden Checkbox so that the user can choose another option button on the interface.

It is sometimes useful in long programs to place line comments at closing braces, such as those in lines 133, 134, and 135, detailing which block of code is being completed.

The step below enters the code for the actionPerformed() method.

To Enter Code for the actionPerformed() Method

1. Enter the code as shown in Figure 5-33. Use the TAB key to indent in lines 116 through 123.

The TextPad window displays the actionPerformed() method (Figure 5-34). Your lines may wrap differently.

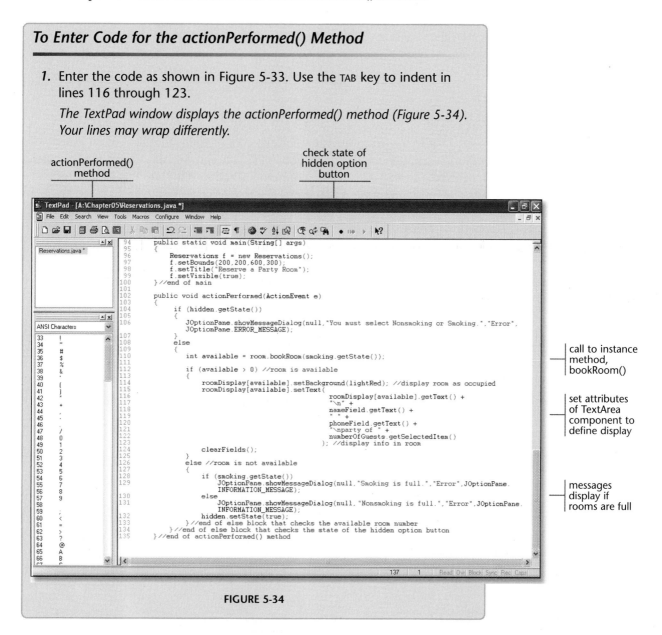

actionPerformed() method

check state of hidden option button

call to instance method, bookRoom()

set attributes of TextArea component to define display

messages display if rooms are full

FIGURE 5-34

Coding the clearFields() Method

The final method in the Reservations class is a user-defined method named clearFields(), which clears the input fields after a successful booking. Figure 5-35 displays the code for the clearFields() method. The method accepts no passed parameters and returns void.

```
136
137        //reset the text fields and choice component
138        void clearFields()
139        {
140            nameField.setText("");
141            phoneField.setText("");
142            numberOfGuests.select(0);
143            nameField.requestFocus();
144            hidden.setState(true);
145        } //end of clearFields() method
146
147    } //end of Reservations class
```

FIGURE 5-35

When called from the actionPerformed() method, the clearFields() method will reset the nameField to a null String (" ") in line 140 and reset the phoneField in line 141. To reset the Choice component in line 142, the **select() method**, with its integer argument that represents the position in the list, is set to zero (the first element in the list). The requestFocus() method in line 143 sets the focus and returns the insertion point to the nameField. The hidden Checkbox again is set to true in line 144 to clear the Nonsmoking and Smoking option buttons on the interface.

The step below enters the code for the clearFields() method.

To Enter Code for the clearFields() Method

1. Enter the code as shown in Figure 5-35.

The TextPad window displays the code for the clearFields() method (Figure 5-36). The closing brace in line 147 ends the Reservations class.

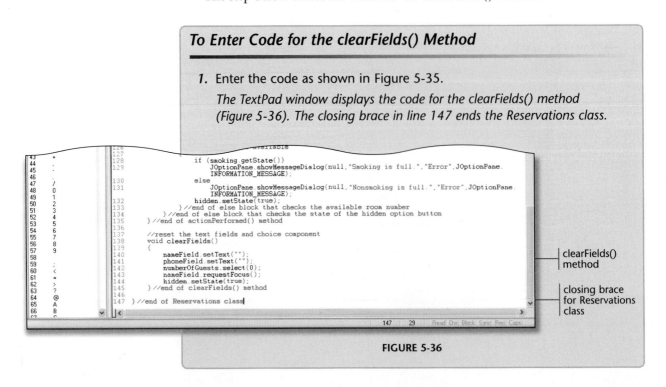

FIGURE 5-36

Testing a Windowed Application

The fifth step in the development cycle is to test the program, find any errors, and correct them until the program is error-free. While compiling the program, the Java compiler checks for some semantic and syntax errors; it is in running the program that programmers may find it hard to detect logic errors. When programs have many variables, inputs, and limit restrictions, such as a maximum number of entries, you must enter data of many different types, including incorrect data, and enter a sufficient number of entries to test any maximum values.

Compiling and Running the Reservations Application

The following steps compile and run the Reservations program. Once the program is running, sample data — such as the data listed in Table 5-14 — should be used to test the application.

Table 5-14   Sample Data for the Reservations Application

NAME	PHONE NUMBER	NUMBER OF GUESTS	SMOKING PREFERENCE
Bond	(303) 555-3760	10	N
Louks	(303) 555-2227	9	N
Thomas	(303) 555-8625	20	S
Gupta	(303) 555-5089	8	N
Amir	(303) 555-1140	14	N
Pipina	(303) 555-8606	12	N
Mitchell	(303) 555-9876	16	N

To Compile and Run the Application

1. In the TextPad window, click Compile Java on the Tools menu.

Java compiles the source code for the Reservations application (Figure 5-37). If you have errors, fix them in the TextPad window, save, and then recompile.

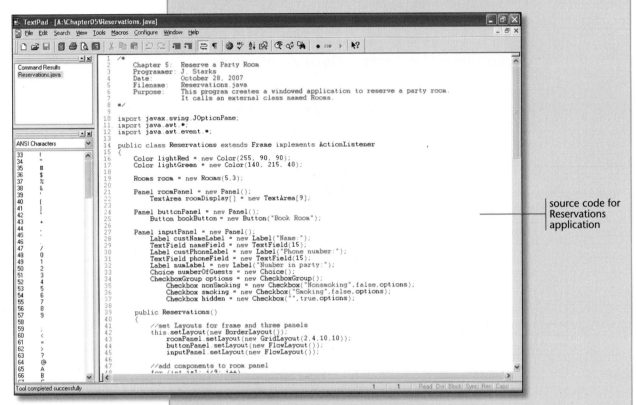

source code for Reservations application

FIGURE 5-37

2. Click Run Java Application on the Tools menu. Click the Name text box.

The Reservations application window is displayed (Figure 5-38). Eight TextArea components display, one for each room.

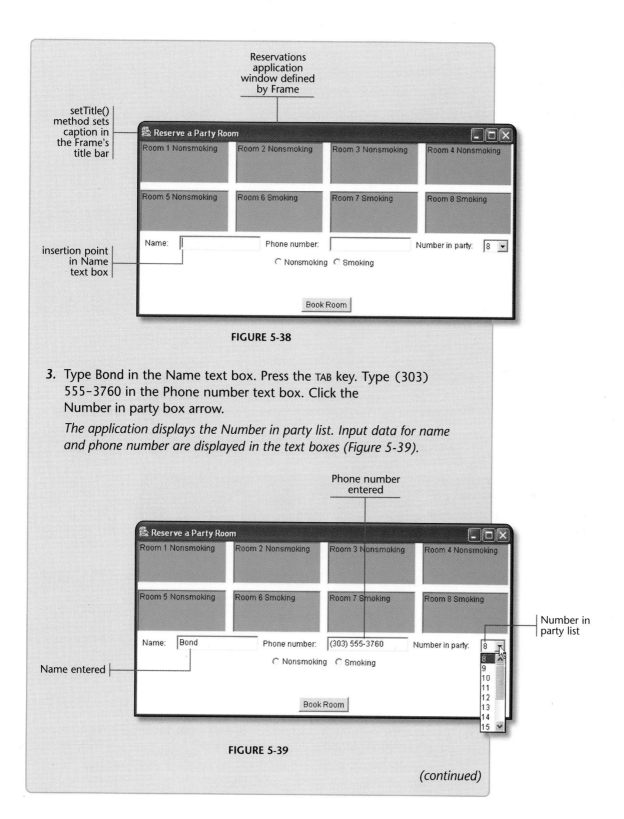

FIGURE 5-38

3. Type Bond in the Name text box. Press the TAB key. Type (303) 555-3760 in the Phone number text box. Click the Number in party box arrow.

The application displays the Number in party list. Input data for name and phone number are displayed in the text boxes (Figure 5-39).

FIGURE 5-39

(continued)

4. Click 10 in the Number in party list. Click the Nonsmoking option button.

The user selections are displayed (Figure 5-40).

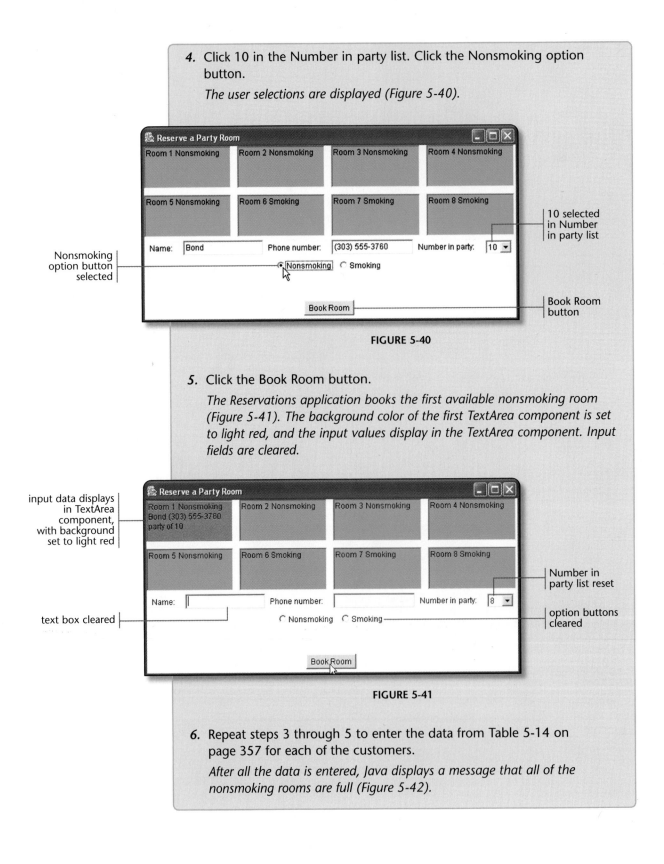

FIGURE 5-40

5. Click the Book Room button.

The Reservations application books the first available nonsmoking room (Figure 5-41). The background color of the first TextArea component is set to light red, and the input values display in the TextArea component. Input fields are cleared.

FIGURE 5-41

6. Repeat steps 3 through 5 to enter the data from Table 5-14 on page 357 for each of the customers.

After all the data is entered, Java displays a message that all of the nonsmoking rooms are full (Figure 5-42).

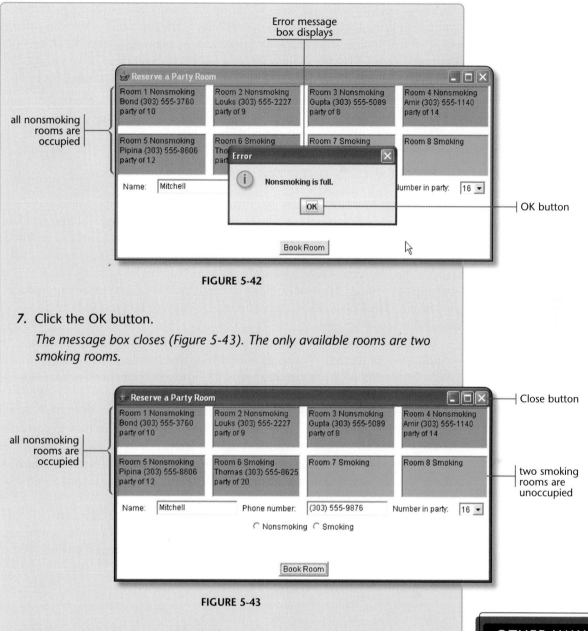

FIGURE 5-42

7. Click the OK button.

The message box closes (Figure 5-43). The only available rooms are two smoking rooms.

FIGURE 5-43

8. Click the Close button in the Reserve a Party Room window. If necessary, click the Close button in the command prompt window.

The window closes and returns to TextPad because you coded an addWindowListener() method. None of the data is saved for the next day of reservations at the restaurant.

OTHER WAYS

1. To compile, press CTRL+1
2. To compile at command prompt, type javac Reservations.java
3. To run, press CTRL+2, enter data
4. To run at command prompt, type java Reservations, enter data

You can print the source code for either the Rooms class or the Reservations application using the Print button in TextPad's Standard toolbar. You can print a copy of the Reservations application interface by pressing ALT+PRINT SCREEN when the window is active, which saves an image of the current screen to the Windows Clipboard (your keyboard may use a slightly different name for this key). You then can paste the picture into a picture-editing program, such as Paint, or into another program, such as Microsoft Word or Microsoft PowerPoint, and then print the document.

Chapter Summary

In this chapter, you learned how to create a windowed application to enter reservations for party rooms at a local restaurant. First, you learned to create and implement an external class named Rooms and to construct an instance method to initialize instance variables. You learned to write code to create a constructor class method, as well as how to declare and construct an array using correct notation to create an array of boolean values, all set to false to represent unoccupied rooms. The Rooms class also included an instance method to book the rooms.

You then learned how to develop a stand-alone Reservations application, including the construction of components such as a Frame, Panels, TextAreas, Labels, TextFields, a CheckboxGroup, and a Choice component. You learned to use a layout manager to place components precisely within the Frame and use the main() method to set attributes of the Frame.

You learned how to use a counter-controlled loop, as well as how to correctly use assignment and unary operators. You then learned how to code a for loop using the increment operator, ++, to loop through the array of boolean values for the state of each room and the array of TextFields that visually represented the rooms on the screen.

You learned how to code the actionPerformed() method and a user-defined method, clearFields(). You also learned how to retrieve data about the rooms and clear fields. Finally, you learned how to save, test, and document the windowed application.

What You Should Know

Having completed this chapter, you now should be able to perform the tasks shown in Table 5-15.

Table 5-15   Chapter 5 What You Should Know

TASK NUMBER	TASK	PAGE
1	Start a New Java Program in TextPad	316
2	Enter Beginning Code for the Rooms Class	318
3	Enter Declarations for the Rooms Class	322
4	Enter the Rooms() Constructor Method Header	324
5	Enter Code for the for Loop and Assignment Statements	330
6	Enter Code for the bookRoom() Method	334
7	Compile the Rooms Class Source Code	335
8	Enter Beginning Code for the Reservations Class	337
9	Enter Declarations for the Reservations Class	341
10	Enter Code for the Reservations() Constructor Method	348
11	Code the Window Event-Handling Method	351
12	Enter Code for the main() Method	353
13	Enter Code for the actionPerformed() Method	355
14	Enter Code for the clearFields() Method	356
15	Compile and Run the Application	358

Key Terms

adapter classes *(350)*
add and assign operator (+=) *(327)*
addWindowListener() method *(349)*
array *(306)*
assignment operator *(327)*
behavior *(306)*
BorderLayout *(344)*
CardLayout *(345)*
Choice component *(310)*
constant *(343)*
constructor method *(313)*
container *(336)*
control array *(340)*
counter-control *(325)*
counter-controlled loop *(325)*
decrement operator (--) *(327)*
driver class *(311)*
element *(318)*
external class *(317)*
FlowLayout *(343)*
for *(325)*
for loop *(325)*

for statement *(325)*
Frame *(311)*
frame-based applications *(337)*
GridBagLayout *(346)*
GridLayout *(345)*
identity *(306)*
increment operator (++) *(327)*
index number *(319)*
instance method *(332)*
instance variables *(332)*
isResizeable() *(352)*
layout manager *(342)*
length *(319)*
measured loop *(325)*
member *(318)*
method overloading *(324)*
object array *(340)*
Panel *(311)*
populate *(348)*
register *(349)*
select() method *(356)*
setBounds() *(352)*
setEditable() method *(348)*
setIconImage() *(352)*

setLayout() method. *(343)*
setTitle() *(352)*
setVisible() *(352)*
shortcut operator *(327)*
state *(306)*
static import *(348)*
subscript *(319)*
TextArea component *(309)*
unary operator *(327)*
valueOf() method *(348)*
variable dictionary *(311)*
windowActivated() *(350)*
windowClosed() *(350)*
windowClosing() *(350)*
windowDeactivated() *(350)*
windowDeiconified() *(350)*
windowGainedFocus() *(350)*
windowIconified() *(350)*
windowLostFocus() *(350)*
windowOpened() *(350)*
windowStateChanged() *(350)*
zero-indexing *(319)*

Homework Assignments

Label the Figure

Identify the elements shown in Figure 5-44.

1. _____
2. _____
3. _____
4. _____
5. _____

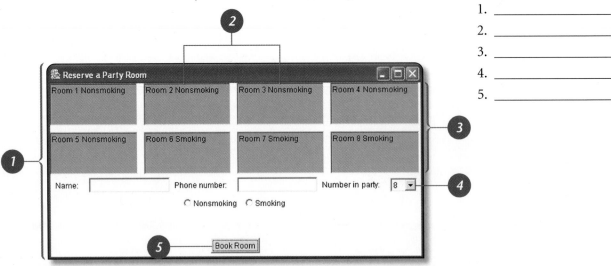

FIGURE 5-44

Identify Code

Identify the code elements shown in Figure 5-45 using the appropriate word from the following list.

add and assign operator   for loop   subscript
array   index number   unary operator
class variables   instance method header
constructor method header   not operator

```
Rooms.java                                                            3/2/2003
 1  /*
 2      Chapter 5:  Reserve a Party Room
 3      Programmer: J. Starks
 4      Date:       October 28, 2007
 5      Filename:   Rooms.java
 6      Purpose:    This is an external class called by the Reservations.java program.
 7                  Its constructor method receives the number of nonsmoking  and smoking rooms
 8                  and then creates an array of empty rooms. The bookRoom() method accepts a
 9                  boolean value and returns a room number.
10  */
11
12  public class Rooms
13  {
14      //declare class variables
15      int numSmoking;
16      int numNonSmoking;
17      boolean occupied[];
18
19      public Rooms(int non, int sm)
20      {
21          //construct an array of boolean values equal to the total number of rooms
22          occupied = new boolean[sm+non];
23          for(int i=0; i<(sm+non);i++)
24              occupied[i] = false; //set each occupied room to false or empty
25          //initialize the number of smoking and nonsmoking rooms
26          numSmoking = sm;
27          numNonSmoking = non;
28      }
29
30      public int bookRoom(boolean smoking)
31      {
32          int begin, end, roomNumber=0;
33
34          if(!smoking)
35          {
36              begin = 0;
37              end = numNonSmoking;
38          }
39          else
40          {
41              begin = numNonSmoking;
42              end = numSmoking+numNonSmoking;
43          }
44
45          for(int i=begin; i<end; ++i)
46          {
47              if(!occupied[i]) //if room is not occupied
48              {
49                  occupied[i] = true;
50                  roomNumber = i+1;
51                  i = end; // to exit loop
52              }
53          }
54          return roomNumber;
55      }
56  }
```

FIGURE 5-45

1. _____

2. _____

3. _____

4. _____

5. _____

6. _____

7. _____

8. _____

9. _____

10. _____

Understanding Error Messages

Figure 5-46 displays a Command Results window with error messages. Using what you know about coding and error messages, list the possible coding errors that might cause TextPad to display the error messages.

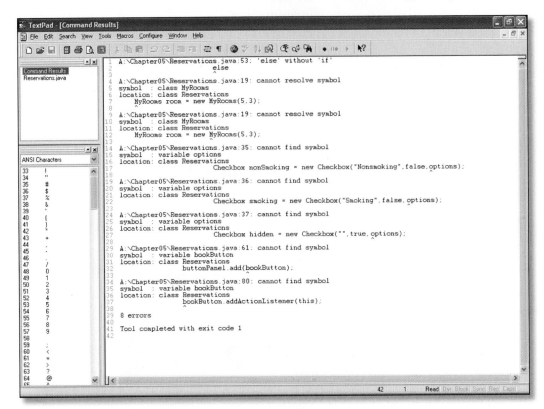

FIGURE 5-46

Using the Java API

The Java API is a good tool for looking up information about a class with which you may be unfamiliar or to check the syntax of commands and methods you wish to use in your programs. While connected to the Internet, start a browser, type `http://java.sun.com/j2se/1.5.0/docs/api/` in the Address text box, and then press the ENTER key to view the Java API Specification on the Sun Web site. (Or, if you downloaded the documentation from the CD that accompanies this book, navigate to the installed version of the Java SDK on your system. Open the index.html file in the docs\api folder.)

With the Java API Specification open in a browser window, perform the following steps.

1. Use the scroll bar in the lower-left frame to scroll to the Frame link. Click the Frame link to display the page shown in Figure 5-47.

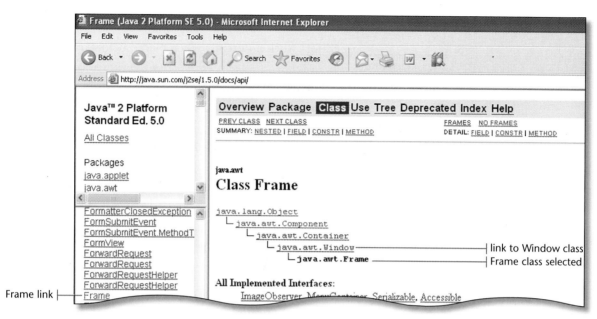

Frame link

FIGURE 5-47

2. Read the description of the Frame class and how its position on the screen can be manipulated relevant to the origin of the physical screen.

3. Scroll to the Method Summary table.

4. Choose any three methods that were not discussed in the chapter. One at a time, click each of the three chosen links. When the field definition is displayed, drag through the definition to select it. Print a copy of the field definition by clicking File on the browser's menu bar and then clicking Print on the File menu. When the Print dialog box is displayed, click Print selection and then click the Print button in the Print dialog box.

5. Click the Back button on your browser's toolbar to return to the Frame page. At the top of the Frame page, click the java.awt.Window link to view information about the superclass, Window (Figure 5-47).

6. Read the definition of a Java Window. Write a paragraph describing the difference between a Window and a Frame. Explain why the Window constructor methods create invisible Windows. Include the reasons that a Frame is a subclass. Describe a situation in which you would use both a Window and a Frame in the same application.

Short Answer

1. A class or method that is not part of the driver class is called a(n) _____.

2. Using the access modifier, _____, in a class header means that the class is accessible by all objects and can be extended, or used, as a basis for any other class.

3. Defining more than one method with the same name is called _____.

4. A(n) _____ is a number referencing a member of an array.

(continued)

Short Answer *(continued)*

5. _____ operators work differently when placed before, rather than after, an operand.

6. The for statement parameters are separated by _____.

7. The _____ component presents a drop-down list of items from which a user can choose.

8. The _____ method adds a new data element to a choice component.

9. Which of the following declares an array of int named scores?

   a. int scores;   b. int[] scores;

   c. new int scores[];   d. int scores = int[];

10. What are the legal index numbers for the array, evenNumbers, given the declaration, int[] evenNumbers = {2, 4, 6, 8}?

    a. 0, 1, 2, 3   b. 1, 2, 3, 4

    c. 2, 4, 6, 8   d. all even numbers

11. For which of the following applications is an array NOT suitable?

    a. storing the scores on 12 midterm exams of a class

    b. storing the name, social security number, age, and income of one individual

    c. storing the temperature readings taken every hour throughout a day

    d. storing a list of animals at the local zoo

12. Which of the following initializes an instance variable?

    a. a constructor method   b. an overload

    c. an initializer   d. a for statement

13. A(n) _____ stores data in a contiguous block of memory, divided into a number of slots.

    a. overload   b. array

    c. element   d. constructor

14. Which of the following is NOT an assignment operator?

    a. +=   b. =\

    c. *=   d. /=

15. In the line of code setLayout(new BorderLayout(10,8); the arguments of the constructor for the BorderLayout() class represent _____.

    a. pixels   b. rows and columns

    c. twips   d. array indices

16. The setEditable() method takes a(n) _____ argument.

    a. String   b. boolean

    c. int   d. read/write

17. The method that governs the action taken when a user clicks the Close button is called the _____ method.

    a. Close()   b. windowMethod()

    c. closeWindow()   d. windowClosing()

18. Which of the following is a layout manager constant?

    a. center

    b. Center

    c. CENTER

    d. c.Center

19. Given the following partial program, what displays when the code is executed?

```java
int first = 0;
for (int i = 0; i<5; i++)
{
        int second = 0;
        first += 1;
        for (int j = 1; j<4; j++)
        {
            second += first;
            System.out.println(first + second);
        }
}
```

20. In the following for statements, determine how many times the counter-controlled loop will be executed. The answer may be zero, any positive integer, or infinite:

    1. `for (int i = 0; i<50; i++)`

    2. `for (int j = 10; j>0; j--)`

    3. `for (int k = 0; k<100; k+=5)`

    4. `for (int m = 7; m<9; m++);`

21. Determine how many lines will print in the following nested loop:

```java
for (int count = 1; count<15; count++)
  for (int nextCount = 1; nextCount<15; nextCount++)
      System.out.println("This line will print");
```

22. List what will display when each line of the following code is executed. In the example, the first line of code declares and constructs an array of ints. Because no values have been assigned, the next line results in the display of a zero, which is the value stored at the zero element of the array. Assume the code progresses sequentially from line 1 through 19.

    1. `int[] myArray = new int[10];`

    2. `System.out.println(myArray[0]);`

    3. `myArray[1] = 28;`

    4. `System.out.println(myArray[1]);`

    5. `myArray[2] = myArray[1];`

    6. `System.out.println(myArray[2]);`

    7. `myArray[3] = ++myArray[2];`

    8. `System.out.println(myArray[3]);`

    9. `myArray[4] = myArray[1]--;`

(continued)

Short Answer *(continued)*

```
10. System.out.println(myArray[4]);
11. myArray[5]+=7;
12. System.out.println(myArray[5]);
13. myArray[6] = myArray[1] /= myArray[5];
14. System.out.println(myArray[1]);
15. for (int i = 0; i<myArray.length; i++)
16. {
17. myArray[i] = i;
18. }
19. System.out.println(myArray[9]);
```

Learn It Online

Start your browser and visit scsite.com/java3e/learn. Follow the instructions in the exercises below.

1. **Chapter Reinforcement TF, MC, and SA**   Click the Chapter Reinforcement link below Chapter 5. Print and then answer the questions.

2. **Practice Test**   Click the Practice Test link below Chapter 5. Answer each question, enter your first and last name at the bottom of the page, and then click the Grade Test button. When the graded practice test is displayed on your screen, click Print on the File menu to print a hard copy. Continue to take practice tests until you score 80% or better. Hand in a printout of the final practice test.

3. **Crossword Puzzle Challenge**   Click the Crossword Puzzle Challenge link below Chapter 5. Read the instructions, and then enter your first and last name. Click the Play button. Complete the crossword puzzle. When you are finished, click the Submit button. When the crossword puzzle is redisplayed, click the Print button.

4. **Tips and Tricks**   Click the Tips and Tricks link below Chapter 5. Click a topic that pertains to Chapter 5. Right-click the information and then click Print on the shortcut menu. Construct a brief example of what the information relates to in Java to confirm that you understand how to use the tip or trick. Hand in the example and printed information.

5. **Newsgroups**   Click the Newsgroups link below Chapter 5. Click a topic that pertains to Chapter 5. Print three comments.

6. **Expanding Your Horizons**   Click the Expanding Your Horizons link below Chapter 5. Click a topic that pertains to Chapter 5. Print the information. Construct a brief example of what the information relates to in Java to confirm that you understand the contents of the article. Hand in the example and printed information.

7. **Search Sleuth**   Select three key terms from the Key Terms section of this chapter and then use the Google search engine at google.com (or any major search engine) to display and print two Web pages for each key term.

Debugging Assignment

Find and fix the error in each line of code. Each line contains only one error. Assume variables have been declared correctly.

1. `public class myFrame extends ActionListener`
2. `for (int i = 0, i<10; i++)`
3. `myPad.setGridLayout(4,4);`
4. `add(myField, BorderLayout.TOP);`
5. `myButton.addActionListener;`
6. `Case 1:`
7. `myArray[i] = new Button(valueOf(i));`
8. `addSystem.exit(0);`
9. `myField.setEditable("");`
10. `add("CENTER", new Button("Center"));`

Programming Assignments

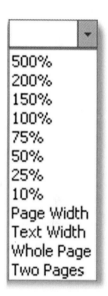

FIGURE 5-48

1 Coding a Choice Component

Figure 5-48 displays a drop-down list created using a Choice component. Write the Java code to declare and construct the Choice component named zoomChoice. Then, write the code to populate the component as shown.

2 What's My Color?

Figure 5-49 displays an interface with five option buttons in a Frame. When clicked, each button changes the background color of the Frame. Perform the following steps to create the application.

FIGURE 5-49

1. Start TextPad. Create a block comment with your name, date, program name, and purpose. Write the code for the class header. Name the file ColorButtons. Save the program on the Data Disk as a Java source code file.

2. Construct an instance of a CheckboxGroup with five Checkboxes.

3. Write the constructor method for ColorButtons(). In that method, assign FlowLayout as the layout manager. Use the add() method to add each of the Checkboxes to the Frame and add the ItemListener to each Checkbox. Write the code for the addWindowListener() method, as was done in the chapter.

(continued)

2 What's My Color? (continued)

4. Write the code for the itemStateChanged() method, which uses the get-State() method to test which Checkbox the user clicked. Use nested if statements.

5. Compile and test the program. Print a copy of the source code for your instructor.

6. For extra credit, convert the five Checkboxes to a control array. Then, instead of multiple ifs, write a for loop that loops through the array using the index number in the getState() method.

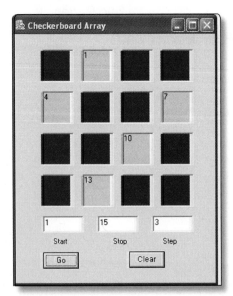

FIGURE 5-50a

FIGURE 5-50b

3 Using a Component Array and Counter-Controlled Loop

You are tutoring programming students and want an application to demonstrate arrays and looping structures. You decide to create a panel containing an array of 16 TextField components that change color to correspond with the start, stop, and step values entered by the user and to create a looping structure that allows the student to specify how many times the loop statements will be executed. Perform the following tasks to create the Checkerboard Array application shown in Figure 5-50a. When the user enters the start, stop, and step fields and then clicks the Go button, the results display as shown in Figure 5-50b.

1. Start TextPad. Create a block comment with your name, date, program name, and purpose.

2. Import the java.awt.* and awt.event.* packages.

3. Create a class named Checkerboard that extends the Frame and implements the ActionListener. Save the program on the Data Disk as a Java source code file with the file name Checkboard.java.

4. Declare variables for the following components included in the Frame:

   a. an array of 16 TextField components

   b. a Panel to hold the array

   c. three individual TextField components

   d. three int variables to receive the start, stop, and step input data

   e. three Labels to display Start, Stop, and Step

   f. a Go button and a Clear button

   g. a Panel to hold the three fields and the Labels

   h. a Panel to hold the two buttons

5. Create a constructor method named Checkerboard(), which includes code that:

   a. constructs each of the components declared above and sets the start, stop, and step variables to zero

b. sets the Frame layout manager to BorderLayout

c. writes a for loop to loop the array and set each of the 16 TextField components in that array so they cannot be edited; within the same loop, set each TextField component's text to match the loop increment *Hint*: Use the setEditable() and setText() methods.

d. sets the upper Panel to GridLayout 4 by 4 and sets the lower Panel to GridLayout 2 by 3

e. adds the components to their respective Panels

f. uses the addActionListener() method to make the button clickable

g. places the panels in the Frame using the appropriate border area

h. enters the addWindowListener() method as described in the chapter

6. To make the buttons work, code an actionPerformed() method as follows:

a. enter the method header, using the identifier, e, as an argument.

b. Write an if statement to test for Go or Clear. If the agument is Go, convert the data from the input fields to ints using the getText() method along with the parseInt() method. Store the result in the variables declared for that purpose in Step 4 above. If the argument is Clear, or integers are not entered properly, set all colors back to white and clear the input fields.

c. Write a loop that goes through the array setting every background color to a darker color, such as magenta.

d. Write a loop based on the user input values. Each time the loop is executed, change the background color to a lighter color, such as yellow.

7. Write a main method that creates an instance of the Checkerboard Frame.

a. Set the bounds of the Frame to 50, 100, 300, and 400.

b. Set the title bar caption as Checkerboard Array.

c. Use the setVisible() method to display the application Frame during execution.

8. Save the file on the Data Disk using the same file name.

9. Compile the source code. Fix any errors and recompile, if necessary.

10. Run the application several times, trying different numbers for the Start, Stop, and Step input values. Remember that the array has a length of 16, so the highest allowable stop value is 15.

11. Print a copy of the source code for your instructor.

12. For extra credit, write code to display a JOptionPane error dialog box if the user enters a value greater than 15.

4 Using an Applet to Search an Array

Many e-commerce Web sites and intranets require that users enter a correct login ID and password in order to access data from the site. You recently have taken a work-study job in the Computer Administration department and have been asked to finish a login applet started by a previous student. The applet will ask the user for an ID and password. Once the user clicks the Login button, the applet will search through an array of IDs and passwords for verification. The applet

(continued)

FIGURE 5-51

then will display an appropriate message. The file includes a method called setEchoCharacter(), which displays asterisks as the user types the password and a setLayout() method to align the components.

4 Using an Applet to Search an Array *(continued)*

Using the Login.java file from the Data Disk and the techniques learned in this chapter, write the code to complete the applet as shown in Figure 5-51. Include code to create two arrays, one for the IDs and one for the corresponding passwords. Assign some sample IDs and passwords to elements of the arrays. Write a for loop that loops through the array, searching for a valid ID and password. Use an if statement in the for loop to look at each member of the array and set a flag to true if the ID and password match an array member.

Part A: Creating the Host Document

1. Start TextPad. When the coding window opens, type the HTML tag and then, on the next line, begin the APPLET tag.

2. Use a CODE statement to access the PasswordApplet.class. Use a WIDTH statement of 300 and a HEIGHT statement of 300.

3. Close the APPLET and HTML tags.

4. Save the file on the Data Disk, using PasswordApplet.html as the file name.

Part B: Creating the Applet

1. Use TextPad to open the Login.java file from the Chapter05 folder on the Data Disk. Enter your name and date in the block comment at the beginning. Type PasswordApplet as the new class name. Edit the name of the class in the class header as well.

2. Save the file on the Data Disk, using PasswordApplet.java as the file name. Print a copy if you wish, to reference while completing this lab.

3. Insert three import statements after the block comment to import the java.awt.*, java.applet.*, and java.awt.event.* packages.

4. Insert the following array declaration and assignment statements at the end of the Declaring variables section. Fill in your own choice of passwords and IDs. Separate each element of the array with a comma, and enclose each password and ID in quotations.
   ```
   String idArray[] = {"id", …};
   String passwordArray[] = {" password", …};
   ```

5. Below the //Sequential search comment line in the actionPerformed() method, construct a for loop that uses i as its counter. The for loop should begin at 0, continue while the counter is less than idArray.length, and increment by 1 using the unary operator.

6. Inside the for loop, enter the following code, which uses the compareTo() methods to look for a match in both the id and password.

```
if ((idArray[i].compareTo(id)==0) &&
   (passwordArray[i].compareTo(password)==0))
   success=true;
```

7. After the loop, write an if...else statement to test the success of the program. If it is true, use the setText() method to change the headerLabel to read as follows: Login Successful. Then use the repaint() method to refresh the screen. If it is false, display a message in the headerLabel to read as follows: Invalid. Try Again. Then clear both text fields and reset the focus.

8. Compile and test the program using both valid and invalid ID and password values.

9. Print a copy for your instructor.

5 Writing External Methods

As an intern at ReTech Incorporated, you have been asked to write a Java external class named Employee that creates a programmer-defined employee record when it is called. As ReTech hires new employees, it will use the Employee class, along with a driver class, to input data about each employee. The fields should include last name, first name, position, rate, and hours. You also should include corresponding get() methods to allow for future searching and sorting.

Using the techniques you learned in creating the Rooms class from the chapter, create an Employee class by performing the following steps:

1. Start TextPad. Save the file on the Data Disk using the file name, Employee.java.

2. Include a block comment with your name, date, and the class name, Employee.

3. Import the java.io.* package.

4. Write the public class header. Within the block, declare class variables as shown in Table 5-16.

Table 5-16   Variables for the Employee Class

DATA TYPE	VARIABLE NAME
String	FirstName
String	LastName
String	Position
float	Rate
float	Hours

5. Begin a method constructor called Employee() that accepts the five arguments — f, l, p, r, and h — which correspond to the variables in Table 5-16.

6. Within the method, assign each of the single letter identifiers to its corresponding declared class variable.

7. Overload the method by creating a second method constructor, also called Employee(), which overloads the class but accepts only three arguments — l, f, and p — which correspond to the last name, first name, and position.

8. Create the following instance methods: getFirstName(), getLastName(), getPosition(), getRate(), and getHours(). The methods need only to return the corresponding class variable.

9. Compile the program. If you have errors, fix them in the TextPad window, save, and then recompile.

10. Print a copy of the source code for your instructor.

6 Creating an Applet with Drop-Down Lists

David Leeson, owner of David's Campground, would like an applet to help his customers reserve camping sites on the Web. His paper reservation system includes fields for the customers' personal information, the date they plan to arrive, and the number of nights they will stay. His paper reservation form also lists the type of hookups, such as water only or water and electricity, the customer wants. David writes down the type of camping vehicles, such as pop-up, travel trailer, and tent.

David would like these fields and lists easily available in the applet window. Additionally, he would like a Submit button and a Clear button, as shown in Figure 5-52.

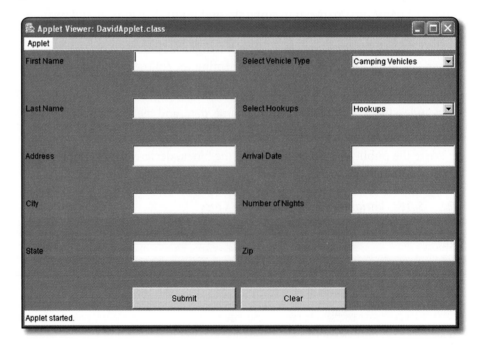

FIGURE 5-52

Part A: Creating the Host Document

1. Start TextPad. When the coding window opens, type the HTML tag and then, on the next line, begin the APPLET tag.

2. Use a CODE statement to access the DavidApplet.class. Use a WIDTH statement of 550 and a HEIGHT statement of 400.

3. Close the APPLET and HTML tags.

4. Save the code as an HTML file on your Data Disk using the file name DavidApplet.html.

Part B: Creating the Applet Source Code

1. Click New on the File menu to open a new document in TextPad.

2. Type a block comment including your name, the current date, the file name DavidApplet.java, and a brief description of the purpose of the program.

3. Import the java.awt.*, java.applet.*, and java.awt.event.* packages.

4. Include a header for the DavidApplet class, which extends Applet and implements the ActionListener.

5. Create components for the applet, including Label, TextField, Button, and Choice components, as shown in Figure 5-52 on the previous page.

6. Create an init() method. Set a background color of your choice. Use the GridLayout method to create six rows and four columns. Add the components you created in Step 5 in order from left to right and then top to bottom as shown in Figure 5-52. Set the focus to the first TextField component. Use add() methods to populate the list of items for the two Choice components as follows:

   Camping Vehicles: tent, pop-up, travel trailer, fifth-wheel, motor home

   Hookups: water only, water and electricity, full hookups, no hookups

7. Use the addActionListener() method to make the buttons clickable.

8. Create an actionPerformed() method that tests for which button was clicked, using the code shown in Figure 5-53.

```
32   public void actionPerformed(ActionEvent e)
33   {
34       String arg = e.getActionCommand();
35       if (arg == "Submit")
36       {
37
38       }
39       if (arg == "Clear")
40       {
41
42       }
43   }
```

FIGURE 5-53

9. Type the closing brace to close the DavidApplet class. The buttons do not have to work.

10. Save the file on the Data Disk, using DavidApplet.java as the file name. Compile and execute the applet.

11. Your component placement may not match the figure exactly. You may experiment with field widths and the Width and Height of the applet itself in the HTML file.

12. As an extra credit assignment, write the code to make the Clear button work. Use the setText() and setSelectedItem() methods to clear each component. Return the focus to the first TextField component.

7 Averaging Grades

Write a Java program that allows you to enter your grades in this course into an array of floats. At the beginning of the program, the application should prompt you for the total number of grades you intend to enter. After entering the grades, the application should call a method to average the grades. Display the grades and the resulting average.

8 Using Layout Managers

Figures 5-22 through 5-26 on pages 343 through 346 display the five different layout managers available with Java's setLayout() method. Choose one of the five, other than BorderLayout, and create the interface using Button components. The components do not need to function, merely display. Print a copy of the source code and hand it in to your instructor. Use static imports as described on page 348.

9 Celebration Movies

Celebration Movies wants an application that allows the user to choose one of six movies and then a number of tickets from drop-down lists. The application should display a check box for users to click so that they can receive a discount if they are purchasing tickets for matinee movies. After selecting the options, the user should be able to click a Calculate Cost button to instruct the application to display the total cost.

10 Using the Web

Using a Web search engine, enter the keywords, Java applets Choice(), to surf the Web looking for examples of Java applets that use drop-down lists. If the source code is not given, use your browser's View menu to look at the source code for the applet. Print the source code and write comments for each line of code describing what the code does, how the drop-down lists are populated, and how the user's choices are evaluated.

11 Preventative Maintenance Schedules

The Pace Trucking Company has hired you to improve its maintenance tracking. After a certain combination of miles and engine hours, truck engines are required to have preventative maintenance. The trucking company would like a program that allows the user to enter the truck's data and then display which maintenance schedule should be performed. After the program asks for the number of trucks to enter, users will enter the cab number, engine hours, and mileage into arrays. Use a loop to go back through the array, checking the hours or miles. If the engine hours are greater than 250 or the miles driven greater than 6,000, then the program should display the cab number and the words, Maintenance Schedule A. If the hours are greater than 500 or the miles greater than 12,000, the program should display the cab number and the words, Maintenance Schedule B. Trucks with more than 1,000 engine hours or 24,000 miles should display the cab number and the words, Maintenance Schedule C.

6

Creating Menus and Button Arrays Using the Abstract Windows Toolkit

Objectives

You will have
mastered the material in
this chapter when you can:

- Create and implement private variables
- Include a menu system in a GUI application
- Manipulate Button arrays
- Move data in and out of the system clipboard
- Differentiate between the getActionCommand() and getSource() methods
- Write code to search for which component was clicked
- Use multiple layout managers
- Program multiple case solutions
- Change the icon in a Java program's title bar
- Access methods from the Toolkit class

Introduction

This chapter illustrates how to design and create a Calculator application that can run as a stand-alone application on any platform, including a desktop or notebook computer, a PDA, a cellular phone, or a kiosk. Even though most operating system software comes with a calculator accessory, other systems—such as a cellular phone, PDA, or kiosk—may not have a calculator immediately available. In addition, not every location that offers an interactive service wants to open up its entire system to the public, as is the case with computers and informational kiosks in libraries, museums, or locations where you pay for usage. Additionally, many companies want to offer software customers a simple calculator that is easily accessible from their desktop to help the user quickly determine costs or savings for their products and services.

In this chapter, as you design and create the calculator application, you will learn how to create a menu system in Java. Using commands on the menu, users of the calculator will be able to clear the display, see information about the program, and exit the application. Additionally, the calculator will work with the system clipboard to allow the user to copy and paste data.

You also will learn how to create a GUI using an array of Button objects and a TextField positioned inside a window to allow a user to perform calculations and display results. You will learn how to write code to ascertain which button the user clicked. Finally, you will learn how to set programmed flags to remember operands and operators needed for compound calculations.

Chapter Six — Calculator Application

A software development firm wants a GUI-based Calculator application written in Java to offer to its clients. The firm programs interactive kiosks on a variety of computer system platforms for museums, libraries, school campuses, and other public places where users have varying levels of access to utility applications, such as a calculator. The calculator needs to be easy-to-use and portable; further, it should allow for copying and pasting of results to other programs. A Java program is ideal for this purpose because of its ability to load quickly and run across platforms.

Figure 6-1 displays the calculator with its numeric and operator buttons. The calculator has a menu with commands such as Clear, Exit, Copy, Paste, and About.

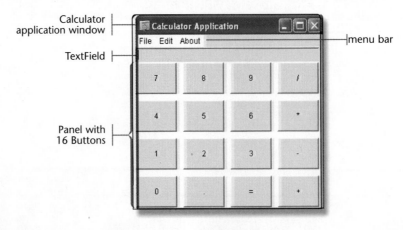

FIGURE 6-1

Program Development

The program development cycle for the Calculator application consists of tasks that correspond to the six development cycle phases, as shown in Table 6-1.

Table 6-1   Calculator Application Development Tasks

	DEVELOPMENT PHASE	TASK(S)
1	Analyze the requirements	Analyze the Calculator problem.
2	Design the solution	Design the user interface for the application and the menu, including placement of the components. Design the logic to make the calculator and its menu work.
3	Validate the design	Confirm with the user that the design solves the problem in a satisfactory manner.
4	Implement the design	Translate the design into code. Include internal documentation (comments and remarks) within the code that explains the purpose of the code statements.
5	Test the solution	Test the program by trying each operator button and each menu option. Find and correct any errors (debug) until it is error-free.
6	Document the solution	Print copies of the application code.

Analysis and Design

Figure 6-2 on the next page shows the requirements document that initiates the development cycle for the Calculator application. The requirements document specifies the reason for the request and describes the features required in the Calculator application.

PROBLEM ANALYSIS A software engineering company wants a Calculator application written in Java with a small set of menu options, including commands to cut and paste. In order to make the calculator as user-friendly as possible, it should display in a standard window with Minimize, Maximize, and Close buttons. In addition, the user should be able to resize the window by dragging its border. As shown in Figure 6-1, the calculator should have ten numeric buttons (numbered 0-9), four operator buttons, a decimal point, and an equal button. When the user clicks a numeric button, the digits should display at the top of the window in a small area similar to an LCD screen on a handheld calculator. When the user clicks an operator button, such as addition (+) or subtraction (−), the program should clear the display and allow for the next operand. The program will need to remember the operands and the operators as the user enters them in order to perform the calculation correctly. When the user clicks the equal button, the calculator should display the answer at the top of the window.

REQUEST FOR NEW APPLICATION

Date submitted:	November 1, 2007
Submitted by:	Fredrick Montgomery – Developer, OpenExhibit Software
Purpose:	Our business customers have requested an easy-to-use desktop calculator that can be used on a variety of platforms. We have customers who program interactive kiosks on a variety of computer system platforms, customers with varying levels of access to utility applications, and others who use dedicated systems without direct access to a calculator or spreadsheet application.
Application title:	Calculator
Algorithms:	Please create an electronic version of a pocket calculator. The calculator application should have a numeric keypad complete with the digits 0 through 9, the decimal point, equal sign, and four arithmetic functions or operators: addition, subtraction, multiplication, and division.
Notes:	The user should not be able to type in the "LCD" area at the top where results display. Instead, they can input data only by using the keypad buttons listed above. Our customers would like a menu system with the following commands: <ul><li>an Exit command (although most users will click the Close button to quit the application)</li><li>a Clear command to clear the display</li><li>Copy and Paste commands, so users can move data in and out of the application</li><li>an About command to display information about our company as follows: Calculator ver. 1.0 OpenExhibit Software Copyright 2007 All rights reserved</li></ul>

Approvals

Approval status:	X	Approved
		Rejected
Approved by:	Violet Cooper	
Date:	November 6, 2007	
Assigned to:	J. Starks, Programmer	

FIGURE 6-2

The requirements document also states that the application should provide the user with commands to exit the application, clear the display, copy and paste data, and view information about the application. The calculator, thus, will include a menu bar at the top of the window; when the user clicks a command on the menu bar, a drop-down menu of commands should display.

DESIGN THE SOLUTION   Once you have analyzed the problem, the next step is to design the user interface and the logic to solve the problem. Utilizing Java's Abstract Windows Toolkit to take advantage of some of the GUI-based objects, a user-friendly window needs to be designed. The Frame should be the size and shape of a simple handheld calculator with appropriately sized buttons, as shown in Figure 6-1 on page 380. The title bar of the application should display an appropriate caption and icon. Below the title bar, a TextField is positioned across the top to display the numbers. Recall from Chapter 5 that the layout manager, BorderLayout, places components into five regions within the container: North, South, East, West, and Center. In the Calculator application, the TextField will be added in the North region of a Frame with BorderLayout. Sixteen buttons will be placed in a Panel using a GridLayout with four rows and four columns; this Panel will be added to the Center of the BorderLayout. No components will be placed in the East, West, or South regions of the BorderLayout.

Each calculator button should have a label with a number or symbol. In order to simplify the declaration, construction, adding, and labeling of the buttons, an array of Button components will be created.

As stated in the requirements document, the Calculator application should provide a menu system with commands including Exit, Clear, Copy, Paste, and About Calculator. Figure 6-3 shows the structure of the menu system to be used in the Calculator application.

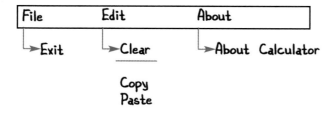

FIGURE 6-3

PROGRAM DESIGN   Once you have designed the interface, the next step is to design the logic to solve the problem and create the desired results. The Calculator application will require each click of a numeric button or the decimal point button to display in the TextField. When the user clicks an operator button (+, −, *, or /), the program should store the number from the TextField and then store the operator for future use in the calculation. If the user clicks the equal sign, the math should be performed and the result should be displayed in the TextField. If the user clicks a menu command on the menu bar, the resulting menu should display available commands.

The program code will include declaration and construction of the various components, including menu commands; however, the majority of the logic will take place in the ActionListener event, which the program uses to listen for and respond to the user clicking a button. Figure 6-4 on the next page displays a flowchart of what will happen when the user clicks each kind of button.

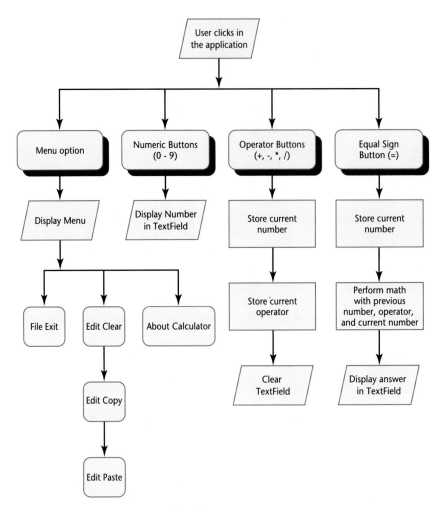

FIGURE 6-4

Each menu option requires its own code, using appropriate if statements to determine which command was clicked. The Exit command will call the System.exit() method. The Clear command will clear the display in the TextField. The Copy and Paste commands will use Java's clipboard access, which is described in detail later in the chapter. Finally, the About Calculator command will display a JOptionPane dialog box with an appropriate message.

The keypad buttons, on the other hand, can share some of the same code because each button is a member of an array referenced by an index number. Recall that a major reason to use arrays in coding is the ease of manipulating data with fewer lines of code. The case structure is ideal for manipulating an array of 16 buttons in the Calculator application. When clicked, numeric buttons, represented in the case structure as cases 0 through 9, will cause the number to display in the TextField, appended to any previous number displayed there. Operator buttons, which are represented in the case structure as cases 10 through 13, store the number and the operator in predetermined variable locations. The Equal button, which is represented in the case structure as case 14, retrieves the data, performs the math, and displays the answer in the TextField. The decimal point is case 15.

VALIDATE DESIGN   Once you have designed the program, you can validate the design by stepping through the requirements document and making sure that the design addresses each requirement. It is appropriate to verify with the user that the menu options display in the correct order and that the placement of the buttons is appropriate. Finally, by comparing the program design with the original requirements, both the programmer and the user can validate that the solution is correct and satisfactory.

Having analyzed the problem, designed the interface, and designed and validated the program logic, the analysis and design of the application is complete. As shown in Table 6-1 on page 381, the next task in the development cycle is to implement the design by creating a new Java program using TextPad.

Starting a New Java Program in TextPad

The following steps start TextPad and save the TextPad document using a Java file type.

OTHER WAYS

1. To start TextPad, click Start button, click TextPad on Start menu
2. To view line numbers, press CTRL+Q, L
3. To Save, press F12
4. To Save As, press ALT+F, A

To Start a New Java Program in TextPad

1. Start TextPad. If necessary, click View on the menu bar and then click Line Numbers to display line numbers.

2. Insert the Data Disk in drive A. Click File on the menu bar and then click Save As on the File menu.

3. When the Save As dialog box is displayed, type Calculator in the File name text box. Click the Save as type box arrow and then click Java (*.java) in the Save as type list. Click the Save in box arrow and then click 3½ Floppy (A:) in the Save in list.

4. Double-click the Chapter06 folder or a location specified by your instructor.

   The file named Calculator will be saved as a Java source code file in the Chapter06 folder on the Data Disk in drive A (Figure 6-5). Your display may differ.

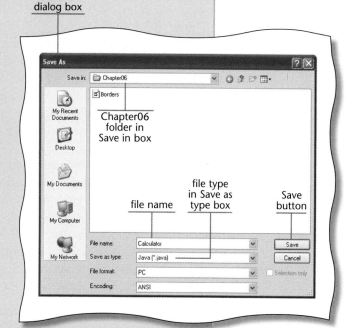

FIGURE 6-5

5. Click the Save button in the Save As dialog box.

Private Variables

All object-oriented languages provide some way to ensure that variables can be shielded from inappropriate outside interference, such as when a class is called from a driver class. In Java, the modifier, **private**, is used to ensure that the driver class cannot change a variable inadvertently. A driver class, thus, cannot access a private variable directly; instead, the driver class must access the private variable through methods designed specifically for that purpose. By contrast, any class in any package can access a public variable.

Declaring private variables creates values that are local in scope and should be used only in the processes and calculations of the class in which they are declared; the outside user has no need to see them or potentially to corrupt them. A key principle of encapsulation is that a class should reveal to the user only what has to be revealed and no more; this concept is referred to as the principle of least privilege and will be discussed in more detail in Chapter 9. In this way, data is protected from misuse, and the class can operate on a more secure basis.

Entering Variables into the Calculator Application

The Calculator application will declare private identifiers for its components and variables. Therefore, a driver class that extends the Calculator class will not be able to change or corrupt any of the components, so it cannot add new buttons, edit the captions, or change the mathematical operations. This does not mean, however, that driver classes cannot use the functions of the buttons and menu. A driver class that calls the Calculator can access the public constructor method to return the value of any of the private values.

The access modifier, private, forces those components and instance variables to have class scope. **Class scope** means that these components and instance variables are not accessible outside the class. Other classes, or clients, that create instances of the Calculator then can use the class without knowing the internal details of how it is implemented or the variables it uses.

The Calculator application will have no get() or set() methods to change any of the values for the variables that will hold the numbers, operators, results, and flags. Recall that a flag is a value that triggers a change in a selection or repetition structure. In Chapter 4, you used a flag variable named done to notify a while loop whether or not to execute. The Calculator application uses private variables named first, foundKey, and clearText as boolean flags to detect a button click and to clear the TextField display.

Table 6-2 briefly explains the purpose of each of the variables used in the Calculator application. Each variable will be explained further as it is used later in the chapter.

> **Tip**
>
> **Declaring Private Variables**
> When you declare private variables, they are local in scope and should be used only in the processes and calculations of the class in which they are declared; this eliminates the potential for them to become corrupted by outside users.

Table 6-2   Private Variables in the Calculator Application

DATA TYPE	VARIABLE NAME	PURPOSE
Button	keys[]	An array of buttons numbered 0 through 15 representing the numeric and operator keys on the calculator.
Panel	keypad	A Panel to display the buttons.
TextField	lcd	A TextField located across the top of the calculator to display numbers as they are clicked and the results of calculations.
double	op1	A double flag that will hold the result of the first operation.
boolean	first	A boolean flag initially set to true for the first operand and then set to false to indicate subsequent operands.
boolean	foundKey	A boolean flag initially set to false. When the user clicks a button, the program will search through the array of buttons looking for a match. When a match is found, the value is set to true to terminate the search.
boolean	clearText	A boolean value initially set to true, but changed when the user begins to click numeric buttons. When the user clicks an operator button, the value is set back to true in order to clear the display.
int	lastOp	An integer to hold the index number of the previous operator.
DecimalFormat	calcPattern	A DecimalFormat variable to hold the pattern for the output display.

Figure 6-6 displays the code to begin the Calculator application. Lines 17 through 25 declare the private variables listed in Table 6-2.

```
1   /*
2         Chapter 6:   Java Calculator
3         Programmer:  J. Starks
4         Date:        November 6, 2007
5         Filename:    Calculator.java
6         Purpose:     This program creates a calculator with a menu.
7   */
8
9   import java.awt.*;
10  import java.awt.event.*;
11  import java.awt.datatransfer.*;
12  import java.text.DecimalFormat;
13  import javax.swing.JOptionPane;
14
15  public class Calculator extends Frame implements ActionListener
16  {
17      private Button keys[];
18      private Panel keypad;
19      private TextField lcd;
20      private double op1;
21      private boolean first;
22      private boolean foundKey;
23      private boolean clearText;
24      private int lastOp;
25      private DecimalFormat calcPattern;
26
```

FIGURE 6-6

The following step enters the beginning code for the comments, import statements, and private variables for the Calculator application.

To Enter Beginning Code

1. Enter lines 1 through 26 as shown in Figure 6-6 on the previous page.
The comments, import statements, class header, and variable declarations display (Figure 6-7).

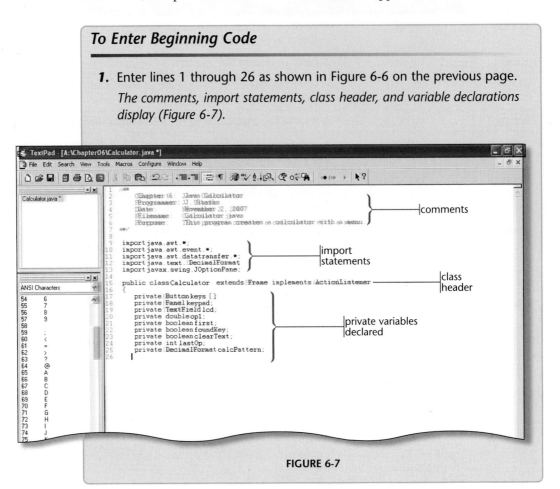

FIGURE 6-7

Line 11 imports the java.awt.datatransfer package. Later in the chapter, classes and methods from the **java.awt.datatransfer package** facilitate moving data in and out of the system clipboard.

By extending from the Frame class, as shown in line 15, the Calculator class will be a subclass or working copy of a Frame. The Calculator class will behave in a similar manner and will inherit all of the fields and methods declared or inherited from the Frame class. The Calculator class also implements the ActionListener because it will receive input, in the form of clicks, from a user.

The next series of steps enter the code to create a constructor method for the Calculator class. This Calculator class will construct its own Frame and embed the following components: a menu system, a TextField, a Panel, and an array of buttons. It will initialize variables, establish a layout manager for itself, and set the TextField display so that the user cannot edit it. Later in this chapter, the main() method will construct an instance of this Calculator() method with a unique name and some specific attributes.

Creating Menus

Most applications contain a menu bar with commands that a user can click to display a menu; each menu, in turn, includes commands that a user can click to perform certain actions. Table 6-3 lists Java's menu components. The **MenuBar** component is used to construct an instance of a menu bar. The **Menu** component with its Menu() constructor method creates a new menu command on the menu bar using the specified label. A second boolean argument indicates whether or not the menu can be implemented as a **tear-off menu**, which remains on the screen after the user releases the mouse button. On platforms that do not support tear-off menus, the tear-off property is ignored. The **MenuItem** component adds a command to a previously declared Menu component, thus resulting in a new command on the drop-down menu. Each of the Java menu components has an associated constructor method, as shown in Table 6-3.

Table 6-3   Java Menu Components

MENU COMPONENT	DESCRIPTION	CONSTRUCTOR METHOD
MenuBar	creates a menu bar	`MenuBar mnuBar = new MenuBar();`
Menu	creates a menu bar command	`Menu mnuEdit = new Menu("Edit", true);`
MenuItem	creates a command on a menu	`MenuItem mnuEditCopy = new MenuItem("Copy");`

After the menu components are constructed, programmers use a variety of methods to assign and populate the menus. Table 6-4 displays some of the more common methods related to menus.

Table 6-4   Menu Methods

METHOD	DESCRIPTION	EXAMPLE
setMenuBar()	automatically displays a previously constructed menu bar at the top of the Frame	`setMenuBar(myMenu);`
add()	adds a command to a menu bar or menu	`myMenu.add(mnuHelp);` `mnuHelp.add(mnuHelpAbout);`
addActionListener()	makes the menu item clickable	`mnuEditCut.addActionListener(this);`
setActionCommand()	sets a String to represent the action of the menu	`mnuEdit.setActionCommand("Edit");`
remove()	removes a menu item from a menu bar or menu	`remove(mnuTools);`
insertSeparator()	inserts a horizontal separator line at the index position	`mnuTable.insertSeparator(1);`

The **setMenuBar() method** assigns the MenuBar to the Frame. The add() method is used in a similar manner to the add() methods used for applets; it adds the object specified in the argument to the container. The addActionListener() method makes the component clickable, as it does with Buttons. Finally, the **setActionCommand() method** takes a String argument that becomes a reference that can be checked with an if statement. The **remove() method** deletes an item from the menu. The **insertSeparator() method** inserts a horizontal separator line at the index position. For example, using the insertSeparator() method with an index of one would draw a horizontal separator line after the first item in the menu.

Using Menus in the Calculator Application

The Calculator application will contain three commands on the menu bar: File, Edit, and About, as shown in Figure 6-1 on page 380. The File menu will contain only the Exit command. The Edit menu will contain three commands: Clear, Copy, and Paste. A horizontal separator line will display between the Clear and Copy commands on the Edit menu. The About menu will contain only the About Calculator command.

When assigning menu variable identifiers, it is common practice to use the prefix, mnu, for each item and then to list the menu bar command before any menu commands in the variable name. For example, the identifier, mnuFile, would be used to name the File command on the menu bar; the identifier, mnuFileExit, would be used to name the Exit command on the File menu; and so forth.

Figure 6-8 displays the beginning of the Calculator() constructor method with its header in line 27. Lines 28 through 54 include the code to set up the menu system for the Calculator application. Line 30 constructs a menu bar named mnuBar, and line 31 sets the menu bar to the Frame by default because no object precedes the method call. Lines 34 through 37 create and populate the File menu. Lines 40 through 48 create and populate the Edit menu, with its three commands and separator line (line 44). Lines 51 through 54 construct and populate the About menu.

FIGURE 6-8

```
27      public Calculator()
28      {
29          // create an instance of the menu
30          MenuBar mnuBar = new MenuBar();
31          setMenuBar(mnuBar);
32
33          // construct and populate the File menu
34          Menu mnuFile = new Menu("File", true);
35          mnuBar.add(mnuFile);
36              MenuItem mnuFileExit = new MenuItem("Exit");
37              mnuFile.add(mnuFileExit);
38
39          // construct and populate the Edit menu
40          Menu mnuEdit = new Menu("Edit", true);
41          mnuBar.add(mnuEdit);
42              MenuItem mnuEditClear = new MenuItem("Clear");
43              mnuEdit.add(mnuEditClear);
44              mnuEdit.insertSeparator(1);
45              MenuItem mnuEditCopy = new MenuItem("Copy");
46              mnuEdit.add(mnuEditCopy);
47              MenuItem mnuEditPaste = new MenuItem("Paste");
48              mnuEdit.add(mnuEditPaste);
49
50          // construct and populate the About menu
51          Menu mnuAbout = new Menu("About", true);
52              mnuBar.add(mnuAbout);
53              MenuItem mnuAboutCalculator = new MenuItem("About Calculator");
54              mnuAbout.add(mnuAboutCalculator);
55
```

Figure 6-9 displays the addActionListener() and setActionCommand() methods for each of the commands on the menus. Because commands on the menu bar itself have no other action except to trigger the display of each menu, they do not need an ActionListener. The capability to display their related menu list is polymorphic.

```
56          // add the ActionListener to each menu item
57          mnuFileExit.addActionListener(this);
58          mnuEditClear.addActionListener(this);
59          mnuEditCopy.addActionListener(this);
60          mnuEditPaste.addActionListener(this);
61          mnuAboutCalculator.addActionListener(this);
62
63          // assign an ActionCommand to each menu item
64          mnuFileExit.setActionCommand("Exit");
65          mnuEditClear.setActionCommand("Clear");
66          mnuEditCopy.setActionCommand("Copy");
67          mnuEditPaste.setActionCommand("Paste");
68          mnuAboutCalculator.setActionCommand("About");
69
```

FIGURE 6-9

The following steps enter code to create and implement the menu system for the Calculator application.

To Enter Code to Create the Menu System

1. Enter lines 27 through 55 as shown in Figure 6-8.

The TextPad window displays the constructor method header, along with the code to construct the menu components (Figure 6-10).

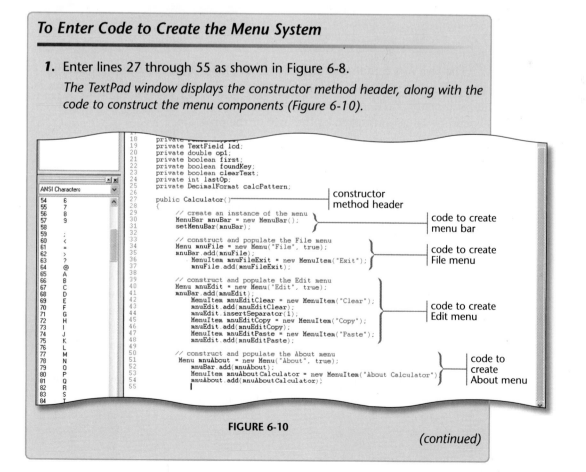

FIGURE 6-10

(continued)

2. Enter lines 56 through 69 as shown in Figure 6-9 on the previous page.

The TextPad window displays the addActionListener() and setActionCommand() methods (Figure 6-11). Both an addActionListener() method and a setActionCommand() method are included for each of the five menu commands.

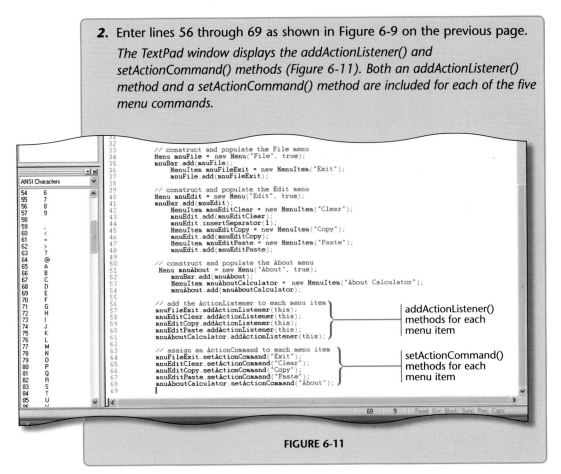

```
31
32
33      // construct and populate the File menu
34      Menu mnuFile = new Menu("File", true);
35      mnuBar.add(mnuFile);
36          MenuItem mnuFileExit = new MenuItem("Exit");
37          mnuFile.add(mnuFileExit);
38
39      // construct and populate the Edit menu
40      Menu mnuEdit = new Menu("Edit", true);
41      mnuBar.add(mnuEdit);
42          MenuItem mnuEditClear = new MenuItem("Clear");
43          mnuEdit.add(mnuEditClear);
44          mnuEdit.insertSeparator(1);
45          MenuItem mnuEditCopy = new MenuItem("Copy");
46          mnuEdit.add(mnuEditCopy);
47          MenuItem mnuEditPaste = new MenuItem("Paste");
48          mnuEdit.add(mnuEditPaste);
49
50      // construct and populate the About menu
51      Menu mnuAbout = new Menu("About", true);
52          mnuBar.add(mnuAbout);
53          MenuItem mnuAboutCalculator = new MenuItem("About Calculator");
54          mnuAbout.add(mnuAboutCalculator);
55
56      // add the ActionListener to each menu item
57      mnuFileExit.addActionListener(this);
58      mnuEditClear.addActionListener(this);
59      mnuEditCopy.addActionListener(this);
60      mnuEditPaste.addActionListener(this);
61      mnuAboutCalculator.addActionListener(this);
62
63      // assign an ActionCommand to each menu item
64      mnuFileExit.setActionCommand("Exit");
65      mnuEditClear.setActionCommand("Clear");
66      mnuEditCopy.setActionCommand("Copy");
67      mnuEditPaste.setActionCommand("Paste");
68      mnuAboutCalculator.setActionCommand("About");
69      |
```

addActionListener() methods for each menu item

setActionCommand() methods for each menu item

69   9   Read Ovr Block Sync Rec Caps

FIGURE 6-11

The Java API contains information about many other methods for adding special features to menus, such as checkmarks, shortcut keys, graphics, arrows, and submenus. Each menu command also can be enabled, disabled, and hidden depending on actions taken by the user or the program.

Initializing the Calculator Variables

Figure 6-12 displays the code to set initial values for the Calculator application. Line 71 is a TextField with a length of 20 that will display in the North region of the interface. As noted in the requirements document in Figure 6-2 on page 382, the user should not be allowed to enter data or change the answers in the calculator by typing into the TextField. Line 72 uses the setEditable() method to limit user input to button clicks. The **setEditable() method**, which takes a boolean argument, is set to false. Users cannot type into a TextField if the setEditable() method is set to false — which means the field will be read only. Using the setEditable() method especially is effective when you want the display to be distinctive, such as black letters on a white background, or when a Label component does not seem appropriate or is not needed. In the Calculator application, the TextField will represent the LCD display on a typical calculator, and users will not be able to type into it.

```
70        // construct components and initialize beginning values
71    lcd = new TextField(20);
72        lcd.setEditable(false);
73    keypad = new Panel();
74    keys = new Button[16];
75    first = true;
76    op1 = 0.0;
77    clearText = true;
78    lastOp = 0;
79    calcPattern = new DecimalFormat("########.########");
80
```

FIGURE 6-12

Line 73 constructs the Panel to hold the array of 16 buttons constructed in line 74; these buttons are used to represent the calculator keypad and will be placed in the Center region of the interface. Lines 75 through 78 set initial values to the variables, first, op1, clearText, and lastOp. Finally, in line 79, the variable, calcPattern, is assigned to hold a DecimalFormat with numbers up to eight digits before and eight digits after the decimal point.

The following step enters code to initialize the calculator variables.

To Enter Code to Initialize Calculator Variables

1. Enter lines 70 through 80 as shown in Figure 6-12.

The TextPad window displays the initialization statements for the calculator variables (Figure 6-13).

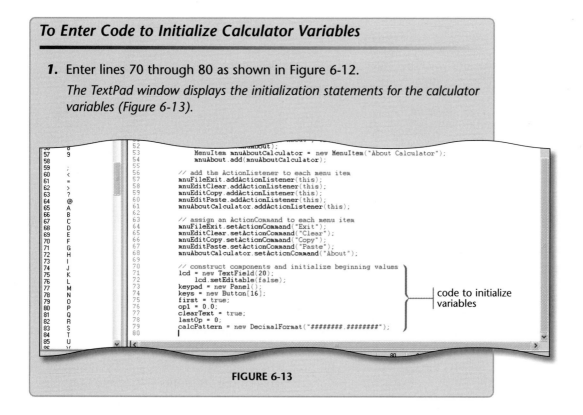

FIGURE 6-13

Recall that the DecimalFormat pattern may contain commas. In this case, however, a comma in the display might not parse correctly if the result were used for subsequent operations. Therefore, the pattern has only placeholders and a decimal point. If the entered number has leading or trailing zeroes, the zeroes will not display in the TextField.

Button Arrays

As specified in the requirements document, the Calculator application must have a keypad complete with buttons for the numbers 0 through 9, a decimal point, an equal sign, and four arithmetic operators (addition, subtraction, multiplication, and division).

Because the Calculator application requires 16 separate buttons to create the keypad, it makes sense to use an array. You may remember that an array is a list that employs a single but inclusive storage location to hold data of the same type with the same identifier name. Using a button array will allow you to use the same code for multiple buttons and will facilitate searching for which button was clicked.

Creating the Keypad

Figure 6-14 displays the code to construct and label the keypad buttons, as well as the method to establish the GridLayout to organize the buttons. As shown in lines 82 and 83, in the case of the Button array named keys, using an array allows the code to construct and label the numeric buttons using a for loop, with only two lines of code instead of ten: one line of code for the for statement (line 82) and another for the construction (line 83).

```
81          // construct and assign captions to the Buttons
82          for (int i=0; i<=9; i++)
83              keys[i] = new Button(String.valueOf(i));
84
85          keys[10] = new Button("/");
86          keys[11] = new Button("*");
87          keys[12] = new Button("-");
88          keys[13] = new Button("+");
89          keys[14] = new Button("=");
90          keys[15] = new Button(".");
91
92          // set Frame and keypad layout to grid layout
93          setLayout(new BorderLayout());
94          keypad.setLayout(new GridLayout(4,4,10,10));
95
```

FIGURE 6-14

The for loop uses an integer, i, to increment through the 10 digits and assign numeric labels to the individual buttons, one at a time. Buttons receive their labels as arguments to the Button method. Recall that Java's valueOf() method converts the numeric value of i to a String. Therefore, in line 83, the argument in the Button constructor becomes the label of the button itself. Because line 83 is the only code in the for loop, block braces are unnecessary; however, indenting line 83 makes the code easier to read and understand.

Lines 85 through 90 explicitly assign the operator, equal sign, and decimal point labels for the other buttons. Line 93 sets the layout of the Frame to BorderLayout, and line 94 sets the layout of the keypad Panel to GridLayout with four rows and four columns.

The following step enters the code that constructs the buttons and sets the layout managers.

To Construct the Buttons and Set the Layout Managers

1. Enter lines 81 through 95 as shown in Figure 6-14.

The TextPad window displays the statements to construct the buttons and set the layouts (Figure 6-15).

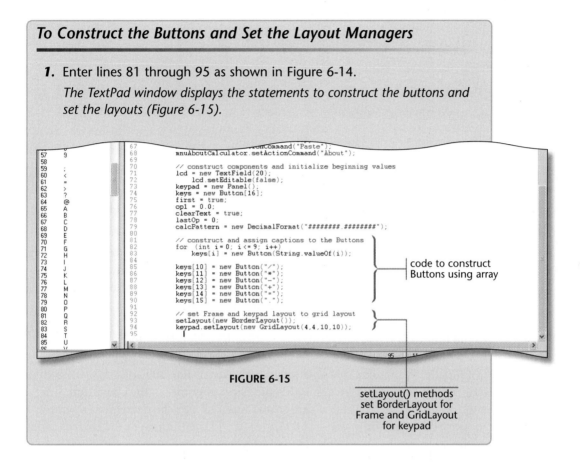

```
67        ...onCommand("Paste");
68    mnuAboutCalculator.setActionCommand("About");
69
70        // construct components and initialize beginning values
71    lcd = new TextField(20);
72        lcd.setEditable(false);
73    keypad = new Panel();
74    keys = new Button[16];
75    first = true;
76    op1 = 0.0;
77    clearText = true;
78    lastOp = 0;
79    calcPattern = new DecimalFormat("########.########");
80
81        // construct and assign captions to the Buttons
82    for  (int i = 0; i <= 9; i++)
83        keys[i] = new Button(String.valueOf(i));
84
85    keys[10] = new Button("/");
86    keys[11] = new Button("*");
87    keys[12] = new Button("-");
88    keys[13] = new Button("+");
89    keys[14] = new Button("=");
90    keys[15] = new Button(".");
91
92        // set Frame and keypad layout to grid layout
93    setLayout(new BorderLayout());
94    keypad.setLayout(new GridLayout(4,4,10,10));
95
```

code to construct Buttons using array

setLayout() methods set BorderLayout for Frame and GridLayout for keypad

FIGURE 6-15

The last two arguments of the GridLayout() method in line 94 specify that 10 pixels will display between each of the four rows and four columns, making the buttons look more like a keypad and adding to the look and feel of the interface.

Adding Components to the Interface

To add components to the interface, the first task is to add the constructed Buttons to the keypad Panel and then add the ActionListener to each Button. The Panel and the TextField then will be added to the Frame.

Because the keypad Panel uses a GridLayout, Java adds buttons beginning in the upper-left corner. Figure 6-16 on the next page displays the code to add the 16 buttons to the panel using the four-row, four-column grid. Line comments within the code will help you understand how each loop and add method takes its turn creating buttons in the keypad.

```
96          for (int i=7; i<=10; i++) // 7, 8, 9, divide
97              keypad.add(keys[i]);
98
99          for (int i=4; i<=6; i++) // 4, 5, 6
100             keypad.add(keys[i]);
101
102         keypad.add(keys[11]); // multiply
103
104         for (int i=1; i<=3; i++) // 1, 2, 3
105             keypad.add(keys[i]);
106
107         keypad.add(keys[12]); // subtract
108
109         keypad.add(keys[0]); // 0 key
110
111         for (int i=15; i>=13; i--)
112             keypad.add(keys[i]); // decimal point, =, add (+) keys
113
```

FIGURE 6-16

The for loop in line 96 adds the row of buttons in the first row of the grid (Buttons 7, 8, 9, and /). The for loop in line 99 adds the numeric buttons in the second row of the grid (Buttons 4, 5, and 6). Line 102 adds the multiplication button (*) to the second row. The for loop in line 104 adds the numeric buttons to the third row of the grid (Buttons 1, 2, and 3). Line 107 adds the subtraction (–) button to the third row.

Finally, the bottom row of the grid is created as line 109 adds the zero button (0), and the for loop in line 111 adds the decimal point (.), the equal sign (=), and the addition (+) buttons. Notice that line 111 uses the decrement operator to move backward from 15 to 13 in order to add the Buttons in the correct order in the last row.

Figure 6-17 displays the code to add the ActionListener to each of the Buttons. The for loop in line 114 goes from 0 to the end of the array, using the length property of the array. It is better to use the length property than to enter the actual numeric length of 16 because if you wish to add more buttons to the calculator, the search will execute accurately without having to change the number in that line of code. Line 115 uses a self-referential, this, to reference the keys array and add the ActionListener to each Button. Recall that the keyword, this, refers back to its own control — in this case, the keys array.

```
114         for (int i=0; i<keys.length; i++)
115             keys[i].addActionListener(this);
116
117         add(lcd, BorderLayout.NORTH);
118         add(keypad, BorderLayout.CENTER);
119
```

FIGURE 6-17

Line 117 adds the lcd TextField to the North region of the BorderLayout, and line 118 adds the keypad Panel to the Center region of the BorderLayout.

The following steps construct the user interface of the Calculator by adding buttons to the Panel, adding the ActionListener to enliven them, and then adding the TextField and Panel to the Frame.

To Create the User Interface

1. Enter lines 96 through 113 as shown in Figure 6-16.

The TextPad window displays the code to add 16 buttons to the Panel (Figure 6-18).

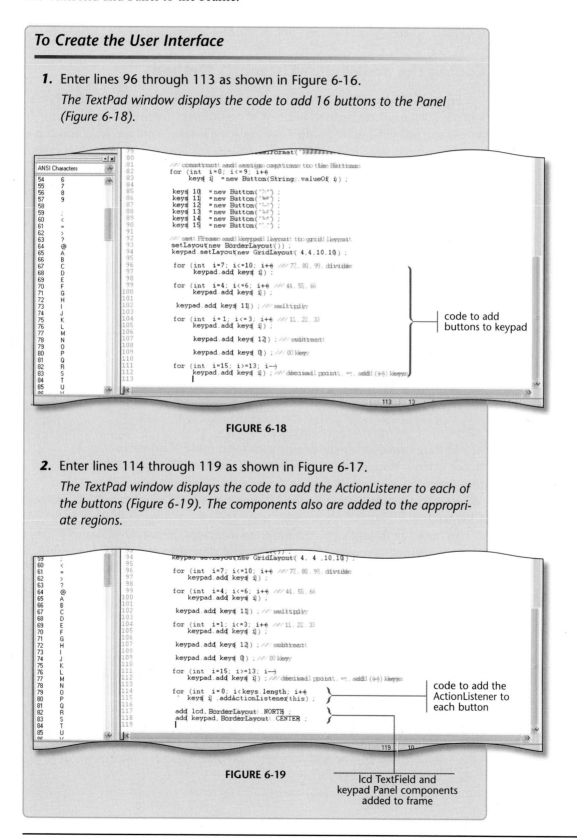

FIGURE 6-18

2. Enter lines 114 through 119 as shown in Figure 6-17.

The TextPad window displays the code to add the ActionListener to each of the buttons (Figure 6-19). The components also are added to the appropriate regions.

FIGURE 6-19

The Panel now is complete, with 16 buttons added to create a keypad. The Panel is a **composite component**, or a container with added components. The act of adding the Panel to the Frame will add all the buttons at once. Later in the program, a call to the actionPerformed() method will determine what action will take place when a user clicks any one of the 16 buttons.

Coding the addWindowListener() Method

Figure 6-20 displays the code to add a WindowListener for the Frame. Java's addWindowListener() method in line 120 registers the listener with the Frame. As you learned in Chapter 5, when you register a listener with a Frame, you connect two objects so that events from one object, the Frame, are sent to the other object, the listener. The listener tells the Frame object to listen for such events and respond accordingly.

```
120          addWindowListener(
121             new WindowAdapter()
122                {
123                public void windowClosing(WindowEvent e)
124                   {
125                      System.exit(0);
126                   }
127                }
128          );
129
130       } // end of constructor method
131
```

FIGURE 6-20

The argument inside the parentheses for the addWindowListener — which extends through line 128, where you see the closing parenthesis and the semicolon — creates a new instance of the WindowAdapter class. The WindowAdapter class provides the window event-handling methods discussed in Chapter 5.

In lines 123 through 126, the program overrides the windowClosing() method, telling the program to terminate and close the window when the user clicks the Close button in the Frame. If the program is not terminated in this manner, it will continue to run.

The following step enters the code for the addWindowListener() method.

To Code the windowClosing() Method

1. Enter lines 120 through 131 as shown in Figure 6-20.

The TextPad window displays the code for the addWindowListener() method (Figure 6-21). The addWindowListener() method creates an occurrence of the WindowAdapter class. Lines 123 through 126 override the windowClosing() method, so that clicking the title bar Close button terminates the program.

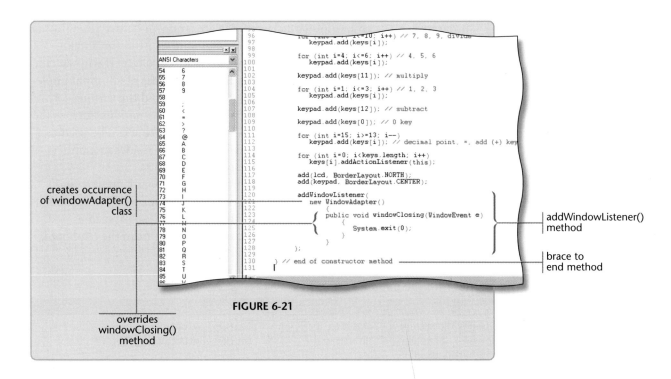

creates occurrence
of windowAdapter()
class

addWindowListener()
method

brace to
end method

overrides
windowClosing()
method

FIGURE 6-21

Although a WindowListener is an interface, the code actually creates an object — a WindowAdapter — which implements the interface.

Saving the Source Code

Because a large amount of code has been added to the Calculator coding window, it is a good idea to save the contents, as shown in the following step.

To Save the Coding Window

1. Click the Save button on the Standard toolbar.

   TextPad saves the source code in the same location on the Data Disk.

Using the System Clipboard

In most modern operating systems, the **clipboard** is a portion of temporary memory reserved for user storage. In Microsoft Windows, that clipboard area originally had the capability to store a single piece of string or numeric data for cut, copy, and paste operations in a single document; today, the clipboard is a storage location that can hold more than 20 pieces of data (including documents, images, and cell ranges in a spreadsheet) to be cut, copied, or pasted across applications. Java's **Clipboard class** implements the system clipboard to transfer data in and out of the clipboard.

Programmers use the Clipboard class to declare a non-primitive variable that will store the clipboard contents. Then, using methods from the Toolkit class and the Transferable interface, programmers write code to perform the cut, copy, and paste operations. The **Toolkit class** is the superclass of all actual implementations of the Abstract Window Toolkit. It is used to bind the various components to particular **native**, or system-dependent, implementations, such as the Clipboard. The **Transferable interface** allows for methods that can be used to provide data for a transfer operation. A Transferable object resides in a buffer between the clipboard and the calling application.

Table 6-5 displays some of the methods from the Clipboard, Toolkit, and Transferable interfaces, along with their purpose and sample code. These methods can be used to obtain information from the operating system, such as desktop properties or print-job information, as well as data from the clipboard.

Table 6-5   Methods Associated with the Clipboard

METHOD	PURPOSE	EXAMPLE
getDefaultToolkit()	Obtains the system toolkit if it exists; however, it usually is combined with another method.	`Toolkit myTools =` `Toolkit.getDefaultToolkit();`
getSystemClipboard()	Gets the most recent value of the system clipboard provided by the native platform.	`Clipboard cb =` `myTools.getSystemClipboard();`
getContents()	Returns a transferable object representing the current contents of the clipboard.	`Transferable fromCb =` `cb.getContents(this);`
setContents()	Sets the current contents of the clipboard to the specified transferable object.	`Transferable toCb =` `cb.setContents();`

getTransferData()	Returns an object, which represents the data to be transferred. The class of the object returned is defined by the representation class of the flavor.	`String s = (String)`
		`content.getTransferData`
		`(DataFlavor.stringFlavor);`

getDesktopProperty()	Obtains a value for the specified desktop property.	`String currentFont =` `getDesktopProperty("win.menu.font");`

getImage()	Obtains an image file from the operating system file structure.	`Image icon =`
		`Toolkit.getDefaultToolkit().getImage`
		`("calcImage.gif");`

The getTransferData() method requires a **DataFlavor** argument that encapsulates information about specific data formats. In the example in the table, the flavor is **stringFlavor**, a static variable in Java representing any generic string of characters. Thus, when the getTransferData(DataFlavor.stringFlavor) statement is executed, any string of characters can be transferred from the buffer. The result usually is cast to be a String so that it can display in TextField or TextArea components.

Selecting Text

A key requirement of copying data to the clipboard is selecting text or numbers. When you **select**, you normally drag the mouse across the data or use the SHIFT+ARROW key (for example, the RIGHT ARROW key) to highlight the text. In the Calculator application, the only piece of data to copy to the clipboard is the data displaying in the lcd TextField. To simplify the copy process, you will program the lcd TextField to be selected automatically when the user clicks the Copy command on the Edit menu. That way, the data in the lcd TextField is transferred to the system clipboard regardless of whether the data in the lcd TextField is selected.

The **StringSelection class** allows programmers to construct an instance of a StringSelection object. When combined with the getText() method, the value in the lcd TextField will automatically become selected.

```
StringSelection contents = new StringSelection(lcd.getText());
```

The **setContents() method** from the Clipboard class then can transfer the data to the clipboard. In the following code, assuming a variable, cb, has been declared properly as a Transferable, the first argument of the setContents() method is the data to be copied, and the second argument is the owner of the clipboard; a null value defaults to the current system and user.

```
cb.setContents(contents, null);
```

Methods from the Clipboard, Toolkit, StringSelection, and Transferable classes will be combined to execute the copy and paste operations needed in the Calculator application.

The actionPerformed() Method

In order to make the Calculator menu system and keypad functional, you must code an actionPerformed() method. Recall that the ActionListener, coded previously, requires an actionPerformed() method. When the user clicks one of the menu options or one of the buttons on the keypad, the ActionListener activates the actionPerformed() method where the action takes place. Also recall that the method takes one argument, usually identified by e, which represents the object passed to it from the ActionListener.

The following paragraphs discuss each portion of the code individually.

Searching for Component Clicks

Recall that in lines 64 through 68 of Figure 6-9 on page 391, you used the setActionCommand() method to establish a keyword command for each of the menu items on the File, Edit, and About menus. When the user clicks the component, the **getActionCommand() method** retrieves that keyword. The keyword can be assigned to a String variable and then used to search through a list of keywords in order to find a match. Alternately, programmers can use the triggered component itself to ascertain what menu item was clicked. The **getSource() method**, a method associated with ActionEvent objects, can be used to compare against a component's variable name. You will use the getActionCommand() method to look at individual keywords associated with the menu items. You will then use the getSource() method to look for which of the individual buttons was clicked.

Searching for the Exit and Clear Commands

Figure 6-22 displays the code used to search the menu items for a click. During program execution, the ActionCommand of any click in the interface, menu, or button will be stored in the variable arg. Line 135 assigns the returned value from the getActionCommand() method to a String variable named arg. Then, if statements compare arg to the assigned keywords. Because there are only five menu options, comparing each sequentially does not require an unreasonable amount of code. Had there been many more options, constructing an array would be a more efficient way to identify which menu item the user clicked.

```
132     public void actionPerformed(ActionEvent e)
133     {
134         // test for menu item clicks
135         String arg = e.getActionCommand();
136         if (arg == "Exit")
137             System.exit(0);
138
139         if (arg == "Clear")
140         {
141             clearText = true;
142             first = true;
143             op1 = 0.0;
144             lcd.setText("");
145             lcd.requestFocus();
146         }
147
```

FIGURE 6-22

As noted above, the ActionCommand of any click in the interface, menu, or button is stored in the variable arg. Line 136 compares the variable, arg, with the keyword, Exit. If a match is found, it means that the user clicked the Exit command on the File menu. The System.exit(0) method is called and the program terminates.

Line 139 compares the variable, arg, with the keyword, Clear. If a match is found, the user has clicked the Clear command on the Exit menu. Lines 141 and 142 then set the boolean flags, clearText and first, back to true, and Line 143 sets the double value, op1, to 0.0 so that the user can begin a new calculation. In line 144, the TextField is set to a null String ("") and the focus is returned to the lcd TextField in line 145.

The following step enters the code to search for clicks of the Exit and Clear commands.

To Enter Code to Search for the Exit and Clear Commands

1. Enter lines 132 through 147 as shown in Figure 6-22.

The TextPad window displays the actionPerformed() method header, followed by an if statement to determine which menu command the user clicked (Figure 6-23). If the user clicked the Exit command, the program will terminate; if the user clicked the Clear command, the program will clear the TextField and reset initial values.

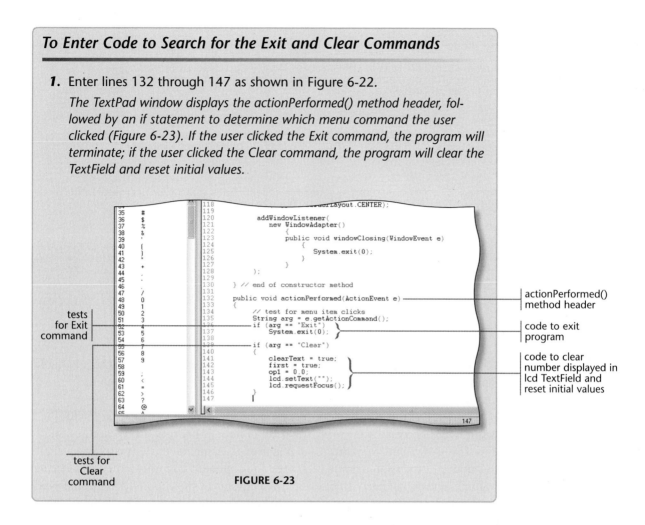

FIGURE 6-23

Even though the user cannot type into the read-only lcd TextField, requesting the focus in line 145 will cause the insertion point to display in the lcd TextField as a visual reminder that the calculator is ready for the next entry.

Searching for the Copy and Paste Commands

Figure 6-24 on the next page displays the code executed if the user clicks Copy or Paste on the Edit menu. Line 148 compares the ActionCommand stored in the variable, arg, with the word, Copy. If a match is found, the code in lines 150 through 152 executes. The getSystemClipboard() method in line 150 is called from within a reference to the operating system toolkit using the getDefaultToolkit() method. The current clipboard then is named cb. It is common to use the period (.) delimiter to link together two methods.

> **Tip**
>
> ### Using the System Clipboard
> By using the clipboard, you can copy and paste data from the calculator into most any other Windows program, or vice versa. Be sure to paste only numeric data into the calculator program, as text will be ignored.

```
148          if (arg == "Copy")
149          {
150              Clipboard cb = Toolkit.getDefaultToolkit().getSystemClipboard();
151              StringSelection contents = new StringSelection(lcd.getText());
152              cb.setContents(contents, null);
153          }
154
155          if (arg == "Paste")
156          {
157              Clipboard cb = Toolkit.getDefaultToolkit().getSystemClipboard();
158              Transferable content = cb.getContents(this);
159              try
160              {
161                  String s = (String)content.getTransferData(DataFlavor.stringFlavor);
162                  lcd.setText(calcPattern.format(Double.parseDouble(s)));
163              }
164              catch (Throwable exc)
165              {
166                  lcd.setText("");
167              }
168          }
169
```

FIGURE 6-24

In line 151, the text from the lcd TextField is selected and stored in a variable named contents. Line 152 then sends contents to cb with the setContents() method.

Line 155 compares the ActionCommand stored in the variable, arg, with the word, Paste. If a match is found, the code in lines 157 through 167 executes. In line 157, getSystemClipboard() again is used to name the current clipboard, cb. It is important to assign a name each time the clipboard is implemented because its value may have changed. In line 158, the contents of the clipboard are transferred to the buffer. This two-step approach of transferring data to the buffer and then to the String variable is necessary because the data may or may not contain values capable of being pasted. Within the try block that begins in line 159, the data is transferred from the buffer to a String variable; then, in line 162, it is parsed, formatted, and sent to the lcd TextField. By including those lines in a try statement, the program will continue rather than abort prematurely if the data is a stream of characters and not numeric. Indeed, in line 166, if an error has been thrown, the lcd TextField is set to a null string, so no data is pasted.

The following step enters the code to determine if the user clicked the Copy or Paste commands on the Edit menu.

To Enter Code to Search for the Copy and Paste Commands

1. Enter lines 148 through 169 as shown in Figure 6-24.

The TextPad window displays the if statements to determine which menu command the user clicked (Figure 6-25). If the user clicked the Copy command, the program will transfer the selected data to the system clipboard; if the user clicked the Paste command, the program will transfer the data from the system clipboard to the TextField.

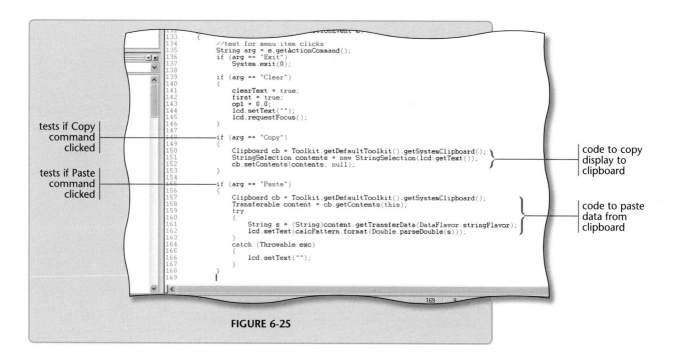

tests if Copy command clicked

tests if Paste command clicked

code to copy display to clipboard

code to paste data from clipboard

FIGURE 6-25

The class, **Throwable**, in line 164 is the superclass of all errors and exceptions in the Java language, used in this case to generically catch any exception that might occur. Only objects that are instances of this class (or one of its subclasses) are thrown by the Java Virtual Machine or can be thrown by the Java throw statement. Similarly, only this class or one of its subclasses can be the argument type in a catch clause. For example, NumberFormatException is a subclass of Throwable.

Searching for the About Calculator Command

According to the requirements document in Figure 6-2 on page 382, if the user clicks the About Calculator command on the About menu, the program should display a message box with information about the program.

Figure 6-26 displays the code to search for the About Calculator command. In line 172, a message is created and stored. Line 173 displays the message in a message box using the showMessageDialog() method.

```
170            if (arg == "About")
171            {
172                String message =
                   "Calculator ver. 1.0\nOpenExhibit Software\nCopyright 2007\nAll rights reserved";
173                JOptionPane.showMessageDialog(null,message,"About Calculator", JOptionPane.
                   INFORMATION_MESSAGE);
174            }
175
```

FIGURE 6-26

The step on the next page enters the code to determine if the user clicked the About Calculator command on the About menu.

To Enter Code to Search for the About Command

1. Enter lines 170 through 175 as shown in Figure 6-26.

The TextPad window displays the remainder of the if statement to determine which menu command the user clicked (Figure 6-27). If the user clicked the About Calculator command, the program will display information about the program in a message box (Figure 6-27).

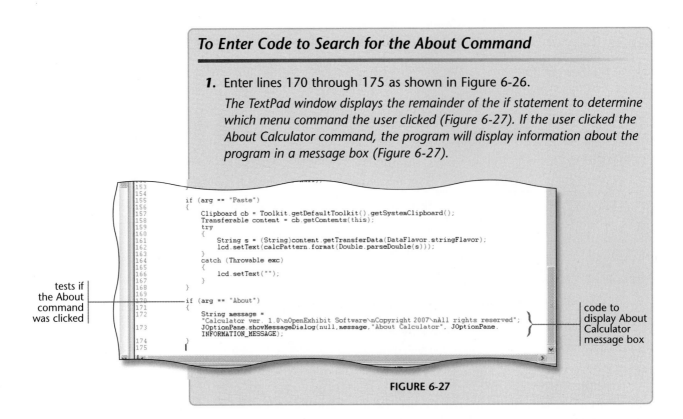

tests if the About command was clicked

code to display About Calculator message box

```
153
154
155    if (arg == "Paste")
156    {
157        Clipboard cb = Toolkit.getDefaultToolkit().getSystemClipboard();
158        Transferable content = cb.getContents(this);
159        try
160        {
161            String s = (String)content.getTransferData(DataFlavor.stringFlavor);
162            lcd.setText(calcPattern.format(Double.parseDouble(s)));
163        }
164        catch (Throwable exc)
165        {
166            lcd.setText("");
167        }
168    }
169
170    if (arg == "About")
171    {
172        String message =
           "Calculator ver. 1.0\nOpenExhibit Software\nCopyright 2007\nAll rights reserved";
173        JOptionPane.showMessageDialog(null,message,"About Calculator", JOptionPane.
           INFORMATION_MESSAGE);
174    }
175    {
```

FIGURE 6-27

Recall that the arguments for the showMessageDialog() include placement of the message box (null defaults to centered), a message, a title bar caption, and an intrinsic constant representing one of the message icons.

Searching the Numeric Buttons

Figure 6-28 displays the code to search the array of buttons to determine which button the user clicked and to add functionality to the numeric buttons and the decimal point in the actionPerformed() method.

```
176    // test for button clicks
177    foundKey = false;
178
179    // search for the clicked key
180    for (int i=0; i<keys.length && !foundKey; i++)
181    {
182        if(e.getSource() == keys[i])
183        {
184            foundKey = true;
185            switch(i)
186            {
187                // number and decimal point buttons
188                case 0: case 1: case 2: case 3: case 4: case 5: case 6: case 7: case 8:
                   case 9: case 15:
189                    if(clearText)
190                    {
191                        lcd.setText("");
192                        clearText = false;
193                    }
194                    lcd.setText(lcd.getText() + keys[i].getLabel());
195                    break;
196
```

FIGURE 6-28

In line 177, a flag variable named foundKey is set to false. Setting a flag variable such as this one to false later will allow testing to prevent actions from being performed unless a button is clicked directly (for example, a user might accidentally click the display field, the title bar, or a border of the Frame). If a button click is detected, the foundKey flag variable will be set to true.

Next, the actionPerformed() method performs a sequential search, checking each button to determine if it was clicked by the user. Starting in line 180, the code first looks for which key was pressed by traversing, or going through, the array one item at a time.

Notice that the termination of the for loop occurs when the increment goes beyond the length of the array and the foundKey is false (line 180). Line 180 uses the length property rather than the actual number of items in the array (in this case, 16 for the 16 buttons). This ensures that if you wish to add more buttons to the calculator, the search will execute accurately without requiring a change to the number in that line of code.

If the source of the click, stored in the object e, matches one of the buttons in the keys (line 182), the code inside the if block begins. Line 184 toggles the foundKey variable to true when a match is found. The location of the match, at the i position in the array, becomes the variable used in the subsequent switch statement in line 185.

The different case statements in line 188 of the switch structure deserve special consideration. As you have learned, Java uses a switch structure to test a variable against multiple possibilities. Typically, each case ends with a break statement; however, you can use one break statement for multiple cases if that one action can serve for multiple cases. For example, in the Calculator application, the first possibility is that the user may click one of the numeric buttons or the decimal point. Line 188 combines all of these cases, delimited with colons (:), into one line of code. Java allows each case to perform the same action as long as break statements do not separate the cases.

Lines 189 though 195 define the action that results when a user clicks a number key or the decimal point key. First, an if statement in line 189 tests clearText. Recall that the variable, clearText, was initialized to true at the beginning of the program. Therefore, the first button click will execute the code inside the if statement automatically. The code in line 191 then clears the lcd TextField by setting the text to a null String. Line 192 sets the clearText flag to false. When the actionPerformed() method is called with each button click, line 194 causes the program to display the label from the clicked button in the lcd TextField, regardless of whether it is the first click or a subsequent click. To display a number with multiple digits, such as 12345, the result of the **getLabel() method** is concatenated with previous text to display in the lcd TextField, thereby displaying the entire number in correct order.

For example, assume that the user begins the program and enters the number 27. When the user clicks the 2 button, the actionPerformed event picks up the click and then clears the lcd TextField. The label from keys[2] then is displayed in the lcd TextField. When the user then clicks a 7, the label from keys[7] is concatenated (+) with the previous text in the field, and 27 displays in the lcd TextField. The integers 0 through 9 and the decimal points are entered this way.

The step on the next page enters the code that executes when a user clicks a numeric button or the decimal point button.

To Enter Code for the Numeric and Decimal Point Button Clicks

1. Enter lines 176 through 196 as shown in Figure 6-28 on page 406.

The TextPad window displays the code to test for button clicks of the numeric buttons or the decimal point button (Figure 6-29). When executed, the array will be searched, and the switch structure will look for numeric buttons and the decimal point. When found, the labels from the buttons will display in the lcd TextField, concatenated with previously displayed labels as needed.

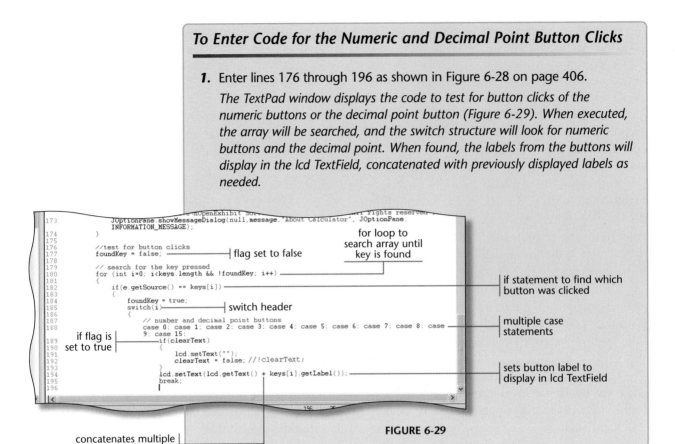

FIGURE 6-29

The boolean flag, foundKey, allows the program to exit the loop if a match is found in line 184, thereby saving time and making the program more efficient.

Searching for the First Operator Button Click

Figure 6-30 displays the code to search the array and add functionality to the operator buttons within the actionPerformed() method. Line 198 displays the case statements that correspond to the operator buttons in the keys. If any of the cases occur, meaning that the user clicked one of the buttons between 10 through 14, execution of the code passes to the first non-case statement, which is seen in line 199.

```
197                    // operator buttons
198                    case 10: case 11: case 12: case 13: case 14:
199                        clearText = true;
200
201                        if (first) // first operand
202                        {
203                            if(lcd.getText().length()==0) op1 = 0.0;
204                            else op1 = Double.parseDouble(lcd.getText());
205
206                            first = false;
207                            clearText = true;
208                            lastOp = i; // save last operator
209                        }
```

FIGURE 6-30

Line 199 sets the clearText field to true. Recall that the identifier clearText was set to false in line 192 after the first operand was entered. Now that an operator is entered, setting clearText back to true will clear the display when the user clicks the next numeric button.

The if statement in lines 201 through 209 executes only when the first operand is clicked. If no values are in the lcd TextField, clicking an operator will store 0.0 in the variable named op1 (line 203). Otherwise, if a number is stored in the lcd TextField, that value is stored in op1 (line 204). The first flag will be set to false (line 206), and the location index of the operator will be stored for later use in the lastOp variable (line 208).

The following step enters the code that executes when a user clicks the first operator button in any calculation.

To Enter Code for the First Operator Button Click

1. Enter lines 197 through 209 as shown in Figure 6-30.

The TextPad window displays the code to handle the first operator button click in a calculation (Figure 6-31). When executed, the array will be searched, and the switch structure will look for an operator button.

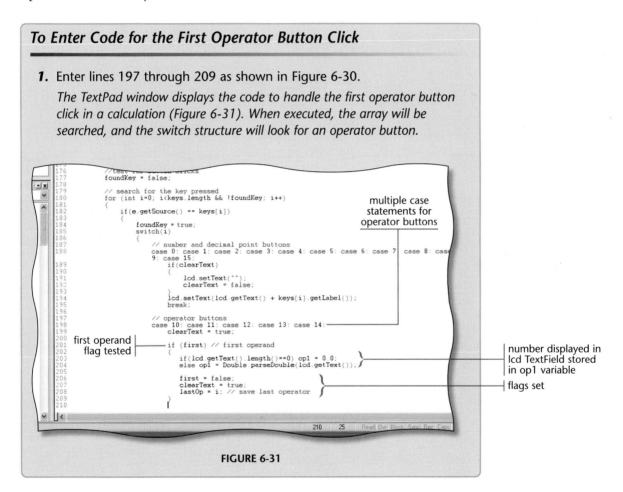

FIGURE 6-31

Period (.) delimiters link, or concatenate, method calls, such as the getText() method and the length() method in line 203. The name of the TextField, lcd, is followed by the getText() method and then by the length() method. Once Java determines the text stored in the lcd TextField using the getText() method, it then can count the characters to return the length.

Searching for Subsequent Operator Clicks

Figure 6-32 displays the code that executes on subsequent operator clicks. Beginning with the else statement that executes if the variable first is false (line 210), the code continues with a switch structure to determine which of the operators was clicked, using the variable lastOp (line 212). The program tests that variable in line 212 to determine which calculation to perform. The four possible cases each use an assignment operator to accumulate the result and assign it to op1, as shown in lines 215, 218, 221, and 224. Recall that the valueOf() method converts text from the lcd TextField to doubles in order to perform the operation; each assignment statement, thus, uses a double data type with a parseDouble() method.

```
210                          else  // second operand
211                          {
212                              switch(lastOp)
213                              {
214                                  case 10: // divide button
215                                      op1 /= Double.parseDouble(lcd.getText());
216                                      break;
217                                  case 11: // multiply button
218                                      op1 *= Double.parseDouble(lcd.getText());
219                                      break;
220                                  case 12: // minus button
221                                      op1 -= Double.parseDouble(lcd.getText());
222                                      break;
223                                  case 13: // plus button
224                                      op1 += Double.parseDouble(lcd.getText());
225                                      break;
226                              }  // end of switch(lastOp)
227                              lcd.setText(calcPattern.format(op1));
228                              clearText = true;
229
```

FIGURE 6-32

Finally, in line 227, the result is formatted and then assigned to the lcd TextField. Line 228 sets the flag, clearText, to true so that subsequent numeric button clicks will begin a new calculation.

The following step enters the code that executes when a user clicks a subsequent operator button — after clicking the first operator button — in any calculation.

To Enter Code for Subsequent Operator Button Clicks

1. Enter lines 210 through 229 as shown in Figure 6-32.

The TextPad window displays the code to handle subsequent operator button clicks in a calculation (Figure 6-33). When executed, the else statement and switch structure will look for subsequent operator button clicks.

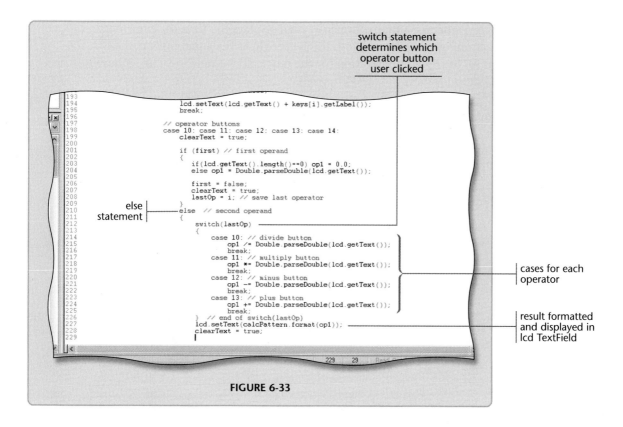

FIGURE 6-33

No matter what the operand, in line 227, the format() method from the DecimalFormat class automatically converts the value op1 to a String. If you had not used the format() method, you would have had to convert the value using a method such as toString() in order for it to be placed in the TextField because TextFields can accept only String data.

Searching for the Equal Button

Notice that the previous switch structure does not contain a case for the equal button, although lines 227 and 228 execute for all operands after the first one. When the user specifically clicks the equal button, the lastOp variable is assigned a value of 14, which is the index number of the equal button. Because a value of 14 does not match any of the cases, execution will pass directly to line 230, as shown in Figure 6-34.

```
230                          if(i==14) first = true;// equal button
231                          else lastOp = i; // save last operator
232                      } // end else
233                      break;
234                  } // end of switch(i)
235              } // end of if
236          } // end of for
237      } // end of actionPerformed
238
```

FIGURE 6-34

Figure 6-34 on the previous page displays the final code for the actionPerformed() method. If the user clicks the equal button, the first flag is set to true in preparation for the next calculation (line 230); otherwise, the lastOp location (line 231) is saved.

Line 232 closes the else structure begun in line 211. Line 233 is the final break for the case structure begun in line 198. Line 234 closes the switch structure begun in line 185. Line 235 closes the if structure begun in line 182. Line 236 ends the for structure begun in line 180, and line 237 closes the actionPerformed() method entirely. The following step enters the code that executes when a user clicks the equal button.

To Enter Code for the Equal Button Click

1. Enter lines 230 through 238 as shown in Figure 6-34.

The TextPad window displays the code to handle a click of the equal button, represented by the subscript 14 in the array (Figure 6-35). Line comments help you know to which structure each closing brace applies.

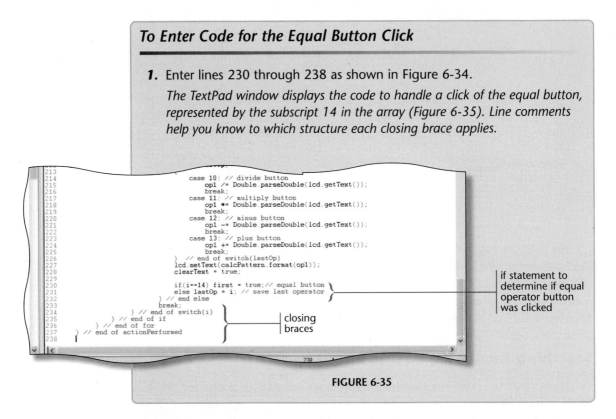

FIGURE 6-35

Tip

Matching Braces

One of the most common errors made by beginning Java programmers is the mismatching of opening and closing braces in control structures and class blocks. Some programmers insert a short line comment for each ending brace specifying what structure is closing. Your instructor may advise you to add other line comments.

Coding the main() Method for the Calculator Class

The main() method for the Calculator application constructs an instance of the Calculator class and then sets three attributes, as shown in Figure 6-36.

```
239     public static void main(String args[])
240     {
241         // set frame properties
242         Calculator f = new Calculator();
243         f.setTitle("Calculator Application");
244         f.setBounds(200,200,300,300);
245         f.setVisible(true);
246
247         // set image properties and add to frame
248         Image icon = Toolkit.getDefaultToolkit().getImage("calcImage.gif");
249         f.setIconImage(icon);
250
251     } // end of main
252 } // end of class
```

FIGURE 6-36

In line 242, an instance of the Calculator Frame, named f, is constructed. Recall that the setTitle() method, shown in line 243, takes a String argument, literal or variable. The argument displays as the title bar caption of the running application. The setBounds() method in line 244 will cause the Frame to display 300 pixels from the top and 300 pixels from the left of the user's screen, 200 pixels wide and 200 pixels tall. The setVisible() method in line 245 will cause the Frame to display at the beginning of the application. The setVisible() method is useful especially when several Frames are used in an application. By using the setVisible() method, you can decide exactly when or what event will make any given Frame visible.

In line 248, the image file, calcImage.gif, is extracted from the file system using the getImage() method of the default toolkit. The **setIconImage() method** in line 249 then assigns the image to the Frame's title bar icon. The following step enters code for the main() method for the Calculator application.

To Code the main() Method

1. Enter lines 239 through 252 as shown in Figure 6-36.
The main() method displays (Figure 6-37).

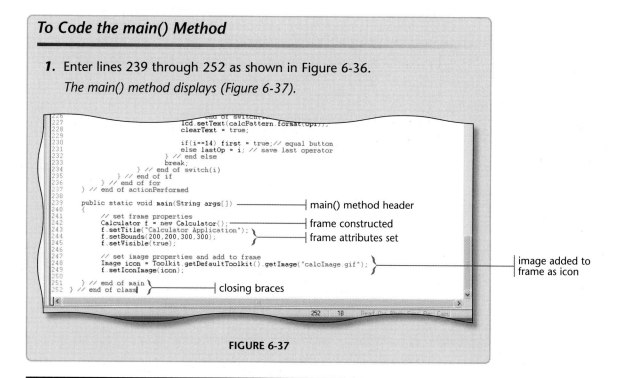

FIGURE 6-37

The size of the Frame, as specified in line 244, does not limit the user to that size in the running application. The border of the Java frame can be resized by dragging; using the setBounds() method merely sets the size when the application first displays.

The Calculator application now is complete. In the next steps, you will compile and execute the Calculator application and then test the Frame's attributes and the functionality of the buttons and menus.

Compiling, Running, and Testing the Application

As you have learned, thoroughly testing an application involves trying out all possible inputs and entering sample data both correctly and incorrectly. In the next series of steps, you will compile and execute the Calculator application. You then will enter data and try different kinds of calculations in order to test the application fully.

Compiling and Running the Application

The image file calcImage.gif is located on the Data Disk that accompanies this book in the folder named Chapter06. The following steps compile and run the Calculator application.

To Compile and Run the Application

1. With the Data Disk in drive A, compile the program by clicking Compile Java on the Tools menu. If TextPad notifies you of errors, click Calculator.java in the Selector window, fix the errors, and then compile again.

2. When the program compiles with no errors, if necessary, click Calculator.java in the Selector window to display the code in the TextPad window. Click Run Java Application on the Tools menu.

TextPad compiles and runs the program. The Calculator application is displayed (Figure 6-38). Your display may differ.

Calculator
Application
window is
displayed

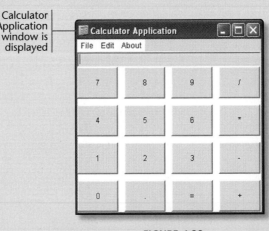

FIGURE 6-38

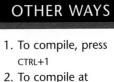

OTHER WAYS

1. To compile, press CTRL+1
2. To compile at command prompt, type javac Calculator.java
3. To run, press CTRL+2
4. To run at command prompt, type java Calculator

Testing the Calculator Application

Testing the Calculator application will involve performing operations and displaying results. The following steps test the calculations performed by the Calculator application.

To Test the Application

1. With the Calculator Application window still open, click the 2 button and then click the 7 button on the keypad.

The digits display in the lcd TextField at the top of the window (Figure 6-39). As the user clicks each button, the actionPerformed() method is executed, and the label from the button is concatenated to the lcd TextField.

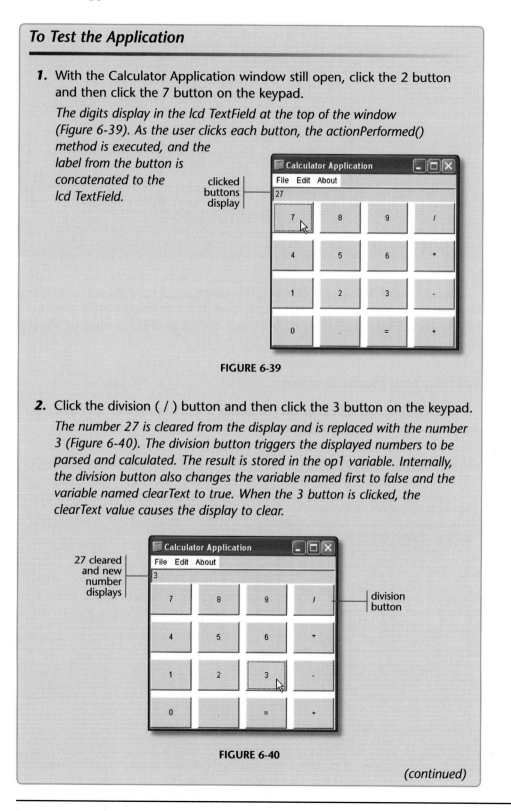

FIGURE 6-39

2. Click the division (/) button and then click the 3 button on the keypad.

The number 27 is cleared from the display and is replaced with the number 3 (Figure 6-40). The division button triggers the displayed numbers to be parsed and calculated. The result is stored in the op1 variable. Internally, the division button also changes the variable named first to false and the variable named clearText to true. When the 3 button is clicked, the clearText value causes the display to clear.

FIGURE 6-40

(continued)

3. Click the equal button.

The answer, 9, displays (Figure 6-41). Because the variable named first was changed to false, the equal button displays the result and then resets the flag variables, so that the calculator is ready for the next calculation.

answer
displays

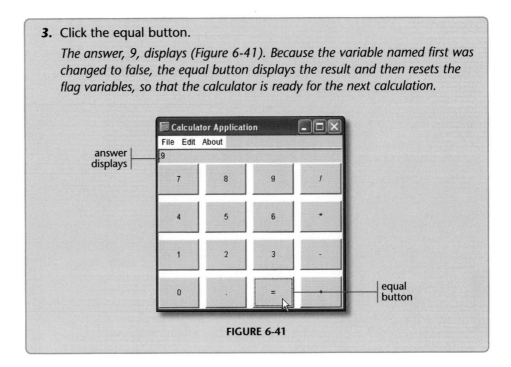

equal
button

FIGURE 6-41

You may continue to test other possible scenarios by entering other calculations using different operators and multiple operands to test the application further. Each time you click the equal button, the result of the calculation should display.

Testing the Menu System

Testing the menu system of the Calculator application will involve clicking the Clear, Cut, and Paste commands on the Edit menu, as well as the About Calculator command on the About menu and the Exit command on the File menu. The following steps test the menu system of the Calculator application.

To Test the Menu System

clicked
buttons
display

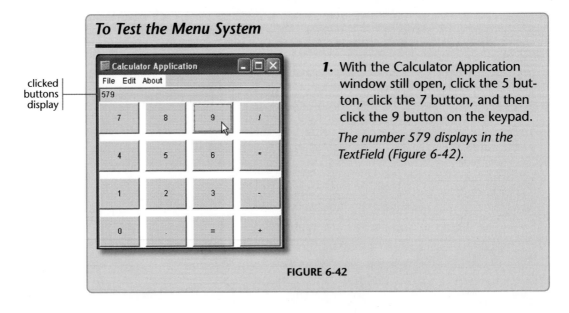

1. With the Calculator Application window still open, click the 5 button, click the 7 button, and then click the 9 button on the keypad.

The number 579 displays in the TextField (Figure 6-42).

FIGURE 6-42

2. Click Edit on the menu bar.

The Edit menu is displayed (Figure 6-43). A separator bar separates the Clear command from the other commands.

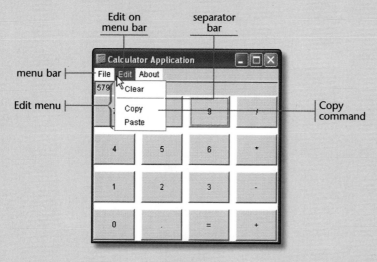

FIGURE 6-43

3. Click Copy. Click Edit on the menu bar. Click Clear.

The Copy command instructs the application to store the number 579 on the system clipboard. The Clear command instructs the application to clear the lcd TextField, so that the number no longer is displayed (Figure 6-44).

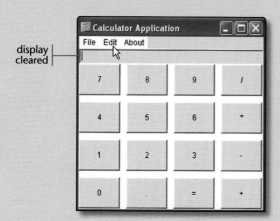

FIGURE 6-44

(continued)

4. Click About on the menu bar and then click About Calculator.

The About Calculator message box is displayed (Figure 6-45).

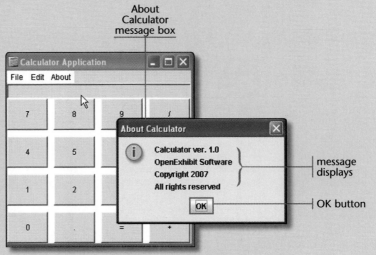

FIGURE 6-45

5. Click the OK button in the About Calculator message box. Click Edit on the menu bar and then click Paste.

The previously copied number, 579, is pasted from the system clipboard to the lcd TextField. The TextField displays the number (Figure 6-46).

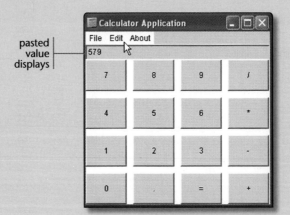

FIGURE 6-46

6. Click File on the menu bar and then click Exit. If necessary, click the Close button on the Command Prompt window title bar.

The Calculator application closes as the exit() method executes.

When you compiled the Calculator application, Java created a file in addition to the Java bytecode file. When a program contains an internal class with the same name as the host file, Java compiles them separately. If you examine the Chapter06 folder on your floppy disk, you will see the usual Java bytecode file named Calculator and another file named Calculator$1. The Calculator$1 file is the compiled Frame object you created and named Calculator.

Chapter Summary

In this chapter, you learned about using Java's Abstract Window Toolkit to create a Calculator application with a menu system. You also learned how to set flags and create an array of Buttons to place in a keypad Panel.

As you designed the menu system for the application, you learned about the MenuBar, the Menu commands, and the MenuItem commands. You added each menu component to its respective container and then added the ActionListener to each of the MenuItems used to create the commands. You also set the action of each command that the user clicks.

You learned that registering a WindowListener event and overriding the windowClosing allows you to customize exactly what will happen when the user clicks the Close button on a frame-based application. You also learned how to write code to set a window's other attributes using Java's setBounds(), setTitle(), and setVisible() methods, among others.

As you learned how to code the ActionPerformed() method, you learned about special classes and methods used to manipulate the system clipboard. You used the getDefaultToolkit() method from the Toolkit class to access the operating system tools, and with the getSystemClipboard() method, you learned how to copy data to the clipboard. The Transferable interface was used to create a buffer to store the contents from the clipboard and evaluate it before using it in a paste operation to paste data from the clipboard.

You learned how to use both if statements and switch statements to determine which button a user clicked on the Calculator application interface. You also learned how to code the getActionCommand() method to retrieve the action event from menu clicks and the getSource() method to retrieve the event object from the numeric and operator button clicks. Finally, you coded the buttons to display and perform mathematic calculations correctly.

Tip

Testing with the System Clipboard

You can use the calculator program to compute a result and then select and copy the answer into another Windows program, such as Notepad, Word, or Excel. Try the reverse action of typing a number in the second application, selecting and copying it, and then pasting the number into the calculator program. Perform a mathematical operation, such as adding 10 to the pasted number, to verify that a valid number was pasted into the calculator.

What You Should Know

Having completed this chapter, you now should be able to perform the tasks shown in Table 6-6.

Table 6-6   Chapter 6 What You Should Know

STEP	TASK	PAGE
1	Start a New Java Program in TextPad	385
2	Enter Beginning Code	388
3	Enter Code to Create the Menu System	391
4	Enter Code to Initialize Calculator Variables	393
5	Construct the Buttons and Set the Layout Managers	395
6	Create the User Interface	397
7	Code the windowClosing() Method	398
8	Save the Coding Window	399
9	Enter Code to Search for the Exit and Clear Commands	403
10	Enter Code to Search for the Copy and Paste Commands	404
11	Enter Code to Search for the About Command	406
12	Enter Code for the Numeric and Decimal Point Button Clicks	408
13	Enter Code for the First Operator Button Click	409
14	Enter Code for Subsequent Operator Button Clicks	410
15	Enter Code for the Equal Button Click	412
16	Code the main() Method	413
17	Compile and Run the Application	414
18	Test the Application	415
19	Test the Menu System	416

Key Terms

class scope *(386)*
clipboard *(399)*
Clipboard class *(399)*
composite component *(398)*
DataFlavor *(400)*
getActionCommand() method *(401)*
getLabel() method *(407)*
getSource() method *(401)*
insertSeparator() method *(390)*
java.awt.datatransfer package *(388)*
Menu *(389)*
MenuBar *(389)*
MenuItem *(389)*
native *(400)*

private *(386)*
remove() method *(390)*
select *(401)*
setActionCommand() method *(390)*
setContents() method *(401)*
setEditable() method *(392)*
setIconImage() method *(413)*
setMenuBar() method *(390)*
stringFlavor *(400)*
StringSelection class *(401)*
tear-off menu *(389)*
Throwable *(405)*
Toolkit class *(400)*
Transferable interface *(400)*

Homework Assignments

Label the Figure

Identify the elements shown in Figure 6-47.

1. _____
2. _____
3. _____
4. _____
5. _____

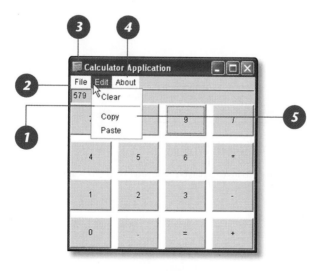

FIGURE 6-47

Identify Code

Identify the code elements shown in Figure 6-48 using the appropriate phrase from the following list.

> literal assigned to action command
> variable containing action command
> variable containing selected text
> WindowListener event
> variable containing clipboard contents
> constructed menu bar
> menu bar command variable
> Edit menu command variable

```
18    public Calculator()
19    {
20        // create an instance of the menu
21        MenuBar mnuBar = new MenuBar();
22        setMenuBar(mnuBar);
23
24        Menu mnuEdit = new Menu("Edit", true);
25        mnuBar.add(mnuEdit);
26            MenuItem mnuEditClear = new MenuItem("Clear");
27            mnuEdit.add(mnuEditClear);
28            mnuEdit.insertSeparator(1);
29            MenuItem mnuEditCopy = new MenuItem("Copy");
30            mnuEdit.add(mnuEditCopy);
31            MenuItem mnuEditPaste = new MenuItem("Paste");
32            mnuEdit.add(mnuEditPaste);
33
34
35        mnuEditCopy.addActionListener(this);
36        mnuEditPaste.addActionListener(this);
37
38        mnuEditCopy.setActionCommand("Copy");
39        mnuEditPaste.setActionCommand("Paste");
40
41        addWindowListener(
42            new WindowAdapter()
43                {
44                    public void windowClosing(WindowEvent e)
45                    {
46                        System.exit(0);
47                    }
48                }
49        );
50
51    } // end of constructor method
52
53    public void actionPerformed(ActionEvent e)
54    {
55        //test for menu item clicks
56        String arg = e.getActionCommand();
57
58        if (arg == "Copy")
59        {
60            Clipboard cb = Toolkit.getDefaultToolkit().getSystemClipboard();
61            StringSelection contents = new StringSelection(lcd.getText());
62            cb.setContents(contents, null);
63        }
64
65        if (arg == "Paste")
66        {
67            Clipboard cb = Toolkit.getDefaultToolkit().getSystemClipboard();
68            Transferable content = cb.getContents(this);
69            try
70            {
71                String s = (String)content.getTransferData(DataFlavor.stringFlavor);
72                lcd.setText(calcPattern.format(Double.parseDouble(s)));
73            }
74            catch (Throwable exc)
75            {
76                lcd.setText("");
77            }
78        }
```

FIGURE 6-48

1. _____
2. _____
3. _____
4. _____
5. _____
6. _____
7. _____
8. _____

Creating a Menu System

Figure 6-49 displays a sketch of a menu system. On paper, write the lines of code necessary to create the menu system using MenuBar, Menu, and MenuItem components. Use appropriate, user-friendly variable names.

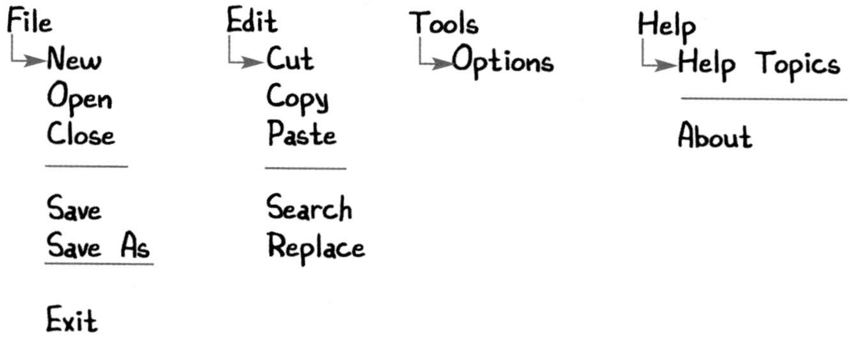

```
File          Edit          Tools         Help
 └►New         └►Cut          └►Options      └►Help Topics
   Open          Copy                          _____
   Close         Paste                         About
   _____       _____
   Save          Search
   Save As       Replace

   Exit
```

FIGURE 6-49

Using the Java API

The Java API is a good tool to look up information about a class with which you may be unfamiliar or to check the syntax of commands and methods you wish to use in your programs. While connected to the Internet, start a browser and then enter `http://java.sun.com` in the Address text box. When the home page displays, enter the phrase `"Windows Desktop Property Support"` in the Search text box and then click the Search button (be sure to include the quotation marks). When the Results page displays, click the page labeled Windows Desktop Property Support in the results list. When the Windows Desktop Property Support page displays, read the information.

Create a short application named Properties that executes the first set of code statements listed on the page. **Hint:** You must import the classes from the java.awt package. Compile and run the program. View the results.

Then, using the Geometry Properties table along with what you learned in this chapter about the getDefaultToolkit() method, write a statement to retrieve the operating system Menu font. Assign it to an object variable. Then use the System.out.println() method to print the value.

Short Answer

1. The modifier, _____, is used to ensure that a driver class cannot change a variable inadvertently.

2. _____ means that components and instance variables are not accessible outside the class.

3. Classes and methods from the _____ package facilitate moving data in and out of the system clipboard.

4. The _____ component is used to construct an instance of a menu bar.

5. The _____ method assigns the MenuBar to the frame.

6. The _____ method deletes an item from the menu.

7. The _____ is a portion of temporary memory reserved for user storage.

8. Java's _____ class implements the system clipboard to transfer data in and out of the clipboard.

9. The Toolkit class is the _____ of all actual implementations of the Abstract Window Toolkit.

10. The _____ interface allows for methods that can be used to provide data for a transfer operation.

11. The getTransferData() method requires a(n) _____ argument, which encapsulates information about specific data formats.

12. The variable, stringFlavor, is a(n) _____ variable, representing any generic string of characters.

13. The _____ method, a method associated with ActionEvent objects, can be used to compare against a component's variable name.

14. The class, _____, is the superclass of all errors and exceptions in the Java language.

15. The ActionListener interface requires a(n) _____ method.

16. Explain the logic presented in Figure 6-4 on page 384.

17. List and explain the function of each line of code in the program presented in this chapter containing one or more of the variables listed in Table 6-2 on page 387.

18. List and describe three constructor methods for Menu components.

19. Explain the purpose of four of the methods commonly related to menus.

20. Explain the purpose of five of the methods related to the Clipboard.

Learn It Online

Start your browser and visit scsite.com/java3e/learn. Follow the instructions in the exercises below.

1. **Chapter Reinforcement TF, MC, and SA** Click the Chapter Reinforcement link below Chapter 6. Print and then answer the questions.

2. **Practice Test** Click the Practice Test link below Chapter 6. Answer each question, enter your first and last name at the bottom of the page, and then click the Grade Test button. When the graded practice test is displayed on your screen, click Print on the File menu to print a hard copy. Continue to take practice tests until you score 80% or better. Hand in a printout of the final practice test.

3. **Crossword Puzzle Challenge** Click the Crossword Puzzle Challenge link below Chapter 6. Read the instructions, and then enter your first and last name. Click the Play button. Complete the crossword puzzle. When you are finished, click the Submit button. When the crossword puzzle is redisplayed, click the Print button.

4. **Tips and Tricks** Click the Tips and Tricks link below Chapter 6. Click a topic that pertains to Chapter 6. Right-click the information and then click Print on the shortcut menu. Construct a brief example of what the information relates to in Java to confirm that you understand how to use the tip or trick. Hand in the example and printed information.

5. **Newsgroups** Click the Newsgroups link below Chapter 6. Click a topic that pertains to Chapter 6. Print three comments.

6. **Expanding Your Horizons** Click the Expanding Your Horizons link below Chapter 6. Click a topic that pertains to Chapter 6. Print the information. Construct a brief example of what the information relates to in Java to confirm that you understand the contents of the article. Hand in the example and printed information.

7. **Search Sleuth** Select three key terms from the Key Terms section of this chapter and then use the Google search engine at google.com (or any major search engine) to display and print two Web pages for each key term.

Programming Assignments

1 Enhancing a Frame

Start TextPad. Open the file named Borders.java from the Data Disk (see inside back cover for instructions on how to obtain a copy of the Data Disk).

1. Change the name of the program to Buttons.java. Use TextPad's Replace command to change each occurrence of the word, Borders, to the word, Buttons. Insert your name and the current date in the comments.

2. Save the file as Buttons.java on the Data Disk. Print a copy of the source code.

3. Compile and run the program. While running, the program displays as shown in Figure 6-50.

FIGURE 6-50

(continued)

1 Enhancing a Frame (continued)

4. Make the following changes to the program:

   a. In the main() method, set the background color to red.

   b. Enter two arguments for the BorderLayout to set the spacing between components as 20 pixels horizontally and 5 pixels vertically.

5. Save the source code in TextPad using the same file name. Compile the program and fix any errors, if necessary. Run the program.

6. Make the following changes to the program.

   a. Implement the ActionListener in the class header.

   b. Change the names of the Buttons to Red, Yellow, Cyan, Magenta, and White. Add the ActionListener to each Button.

   c. Below the main() method but still within the class block, enter an actionPerformed() method using the header, `public void actionPerformed(ActionEvent e)` and an opening brace.

   d. Declare and assign a variable, arg, by typing, `String arg = e.getActionCommand();` within the block.

   e. Test for the click of each button by writing an if statement similar to the following: `if (arg == "Yellow")`. The result of a button click should be a change in the background color of the application.

7. Save the source code. Compile, correct any errors, and then run the applet. Print a copy of the source code.

8. Finally, make the following changes to the program:

   a. Delete the button in the center area. Replace it with a Choice component named colors.

   b. Use the add() method to populate the Choice component with the colors from step 6b above.

   c. At the end of the Buttons class header, insert a comma, and then type `ItemListener` to implement the ItemListener.

   d. Add an itemListener to the Choice component and then add the Choice component to the center area of the BorderLayout.

   e. Write an itemStateChanged() method to test for each item in the Choice component using the header, `public void itemStateChanged (ItemEvent ie)`, and an opening brace. Use the same code as you did in the actionPerformed() method to test for the click of each choice (step 6e above).

9. Save the source code. Compile, correct any errors, and then run the program. Print a copy of the source code.

2 Creating a Telephone Keypad Application

Many computer systems are connected to modems, telephones, and fax systems. As part of the programming team at WebPhone, you have been asked to design the user interface for a telephone keypad that displays on the screen. Figure 6-51 displays a sample of how the user interface of the application should look after programming is complete.

Using the techniques you have learned, including the steps you performed in this chapter, write a Java application that displays a telephone keypad. Add functionality so that when a button is clicked, the number or symbol label for each button displays in the TextField. Perform the following steps to create the Telephone program.

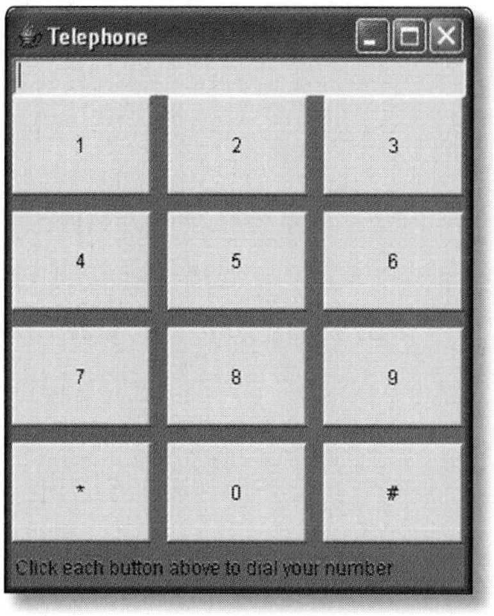

FIGURE 6-51

1. Start TextPad. Create a block comment with your name, date, program name, and purpose.

2. Import Java's awt and awt.event packages.

3. Create a class named Telephone that extends the Frame and implements the ActionListener.

4. Declare public variables as follows:

   an array of buttons

   a keypad

   a TextField

   a Label

   a variable named foundKey

5. Create a Telephone() constructor method and include the following:

   a. Write a constructor for the TextField with a length of 20.

   b. Write a constructor to create the keypad Panel.

   c. Write a constructor to set the array to be of length 12.

   d. Set the Buttons' labels to match the nine buttons shown in Figure 6-51.

   e. Set the TextField to be not editable.

   f. Type `setBackground(Color.magenta);` to change the color of the Frame's background.

   g. Type `setLayout(new BorderLayout());` to declare the layout manager for the Frame.

   h. Type `keyPad.setLayout(new GridLayout(4,3,10,10));` to declare the layout manager for the Panel.

   i. Add the buttons to the keypad in order from upper-left to lower-right.

   j. Add the TextField to the North area of the Frame.

   k. Add the Panel to the Center area of the Frame.

   l. Add the Label to the South area of the Frame.

6. Register a WindowListener by typing the code as shown in Figure 6-20 on page 398.

7. Create an actionPerformed event to include the following:

   a. Write a loop to traverse the array. Test the member of the array at the index number to see if it matches the argument passed to the actionPerformed event. Your code will look similar to `if(e.getSource() == keys[i])` although your variable names may differ.

(continued)

2 Creating a Telephone Keypad Application *(continued)*

    b. When a match is found, transfer the label from the button to TextField, concatenating any previous entries. Your code will look similar to `lcdTextField.setText(lcd TextField.getText() + keys[i].getLabel( ));` although your variable names may differ.

8. Create a main() method with the following code:

    a. Construct an instance of the Telephone.

    b. Set the bounds of the Frame to 50, 130, 250, and 300.

    c. Set the title of the Frame to Telephone.

    d. Set the visibility of the Frame to true.

9. Enter the closing brace for the class. Print a copy to double-check the matching of braces and parentheses before compiling.

10. Save the file as Telephone.java on the Data Disk.

11. Compile the source code. Fix any errors and recompile, if necessary.

12. Run and then test the application by clicking each number and symbol.

13. Print a copy of the source code for your instructor.

14. Several WebPhone customers have asked if the telephone keypad could include a CLR button to clear the display. If directed by your instructor as an extra credit assignment, convert the application to an applet and then add a CLR button to clear a previous number or erase numbers entered in error.

3 Creating a Clickable Applet

Figure 6-52 displays an applet with a graphic. The buttons in the Panel at the bottom of the applet direct the movement of the graphic. The Java cup graphic, cup.gif, is on the Data Disk that is provided with this book. If you wish, you may substitute your own graphic. Be sure to place the graphic in the same directory as your program.

In this applet, you will use the getDocumentBase() method to import a graphic and the repaint() method along with drawImage. The four arguments needed by the drawImage() method are the name of the image, the top pixel, the left pixel, and the self-referential, this. Perform the following steps to create the host document and source code file.

FIGURE 6-52

1. In the TextPad window, create an HTML host document that calls the file MoveIt.class, using a width of 325 and a height of 250.

2. Save the file as MoveIt.html on your Data Disk.

3. Open a new TextPad file and save it as a Java source code file on the Data Disk with the file name MoveIt.java.

4. Create a block comment with your name, date, program name, and purpose.

5. Import the java.awt.*, java.awt.event.*, and java.applet.* packages.

6. Create a public class header with the name MoveIt that extends Applet and implements the ActionListener.

7. Declare the following variables:

```
private Image cup;
private Panel keyPad;
public int top = 15;
public int left = 15;
private Button keysArray[];
```

8. Begin an init method with the following code:

```
public void init()
{
    cup = getImage(getDocumentBase(), "cup.gif");
    Canvas myCanvas = new Canvas();
```

9. Construct the keypad Panel and the five buttons, labeled: Up, Left, Right, Down, and Center.

10. Set the background color to blue.

11. Set the layout manager of the Frame to be BorderLayout and then set the keypad layout manager to be BorderLayout.

12. Add the buttons to the keypad Panel in the appropriate areas.

13. Add myCanvas to the North and keypad to the South of the Frame.

14. Enter five addActionListener statements with the self-referential, this — one for each of the buttons.

15. Enter the following code to drag the image using the paint method:

```
public void paint( Graphics g )
{
    g.drawImage( cup, left, top, this );
}
```

16. Create an actionPerformed() method. **Hint:** Remember to use the getActionCommand method and assign it to a variable, as you did in the chapter.

17. Within the actionPerformed() method, write an if statement to test each of the buttons as follows:

    a. If the user clicks the Up button, subtract 15 from the top variable.

    b. If the user clicks the Down button, add 15 to the top variable.

    c. If the user clicks the Left button, subtract 15 from the left variable.

    d. If the user clicks the Right button, add 15 to the left variable.

    e. If the user clicks the Center button, set the top variable to 60 and the left variable to 125.

18. Enter the code `repaint();` to instruct the program to repaint the screen.

19. Compile the source code. Fix any errors and recompile, if necessary.

20. Run and then test the application by clicking each number and symbol.

21. Print a copy of the source code for your instructor.

4 Creating a Cellular Phone Keypad Applet

The WebPhone company now would like an applet that represents a cellular phone keypad. As you did in Programming Assignment 2 on page 426, create an applet that displays a text area across the top of the window, similar to the LCD panel of most cellular phones. Include buttons for the 10 digits, a star key (*), and a pound key (#). When clicked, the appropriate digit or symbol should display in the text area. No additional functionality is required until WebPhone approves your prototype.

5 Creating a Menu System

Using the menu system displayed in Figure 6-49 on page 423, create a Frame-based application that has one large TextArea placed in the Center region. Create the menu system and code the ActionPerformed() event to make at least five of the menu items work properly.

6 My Classes

Create a Frame-based application that displays an array of nine buttons on a Panel. Assign the Panel to the Center of your frame. Each button should display the name of a course in your department. Include a TextField in the South. When the user clicks a button, the course name should display in the TextField.

7 Adding Extra Buttons to the Calculator

Open the Calculator.java file created for the Calculator application in this chapter. Modify the application to include buttons for Add to Memory (addM), Paste from Memory (pasteM), Backspace (Bksp), and Clear (CLR). Create a fifth row for the new buttons. Increase the length of the keys array. Construct each button and add the ActionListener to each of the new buttons. Then, in the actionPerformed() method, write a switch structure to search for each of the buttons. Write the code for each case. *Hint:* For the Backspace key, use the following code:

```
lcd.setText(lcd.getText().substring(0,lcd.getText().length()-1));
```

8 Researching the setBounds() Method

Chapter 6 uses a method called setBounds() to set certain attributes of a Frame; the setBounds() method is one of the methods inherited from Component class. Use the online Java documentation for Java 2 ver. 5.0 to look up the setBounds() method. You will find several setBounds() with different arguments. Write a paragraph describing each and explain the difference. Draw a picture of the object hierarchy of the setBounds() method.

9 Researching the Frame Class

Use the online Java documentation for Java 2 ver. 5.0 to create a tree or hierarchy chart of the Frame class, similar to the hierarchy chart of AWT components in Figure 5-17 on page 336. Include both superclasses and subclasses. Explain how the AWT interacts with the applet class to use Panels in both applications and applets.

Swing Interfaces with Sorting and Searching

Objectives

You will have
mastered the material in
this chapter when you can:

- List features of the Java Foundation
  Classes (JFC)
- Differentiate between AWT and Swing components
- Create a JFrame application
- Sort data in parallel arrays
- Use the keyword, super, in a constructor method
- Create a tool tip
- Use methods associated with JPanels, JComboBoxes, JLabels, JTextPanes,
  and JScrollPanes
- Use Tabs and Styles in a JTextPane
- Use methods associated with the Document class
- Perform linear searches
- Incorporate look and feel methods in an interface

Introduction

In previous chapters, you learned that the Java GUI components—called Swing components—provide a wide range of objects and methods to help programmers build user interfaces. Swing components include lightweight objects with hundreds of methods that allow programmers to tailor windows using Java-based components, such as option buttons, check boxes, lists, combo boxes, and scroll bars.

In this chapter, you will learn how to design and create a program for a DVD collection of classic movies, which will store the movie title, studio, and year the movie was released. You also will learn how to use Swing components to create the program's graphical user interface; use JMenu objects and methods to create a user-friendly menu system that will allow users to add movies to the list; and display the movies sorted in various ways.

In this chapter, you will also, learn how to use JComboBoxes that display as drop-down lists in the interface and how to create an array of String variables to populate the list displayed in each JComboBox. You will learn how to program an efficient sort routine that quickly will alphabetize the elements in the array for display.

As you learn how to use methods to check the state of various Swing components, the program will display a formatted list with scrolling capabilities in the interface. You will learn how to retrieve the selected item from the JComboBox and have it display in a JScrollPane. You also will learn how to set tabs, fonts, and styles of text. Finally, you will learn how to add a special Java "look and feel" to the interface window.

Chapter Seven — Classics on DVD

An Internet-based collectors club wants to see a prototype of a program with a graphical user interface that allows members to organize their classic movies on DVD. Using the program, club members will be able to search and sort their movies by title, studio, or year. They also will be able to add new movies to the list.

The program will display a formatted list of the movies. Club members will use the display to verify their collections. As users add new movies to the list, the list must be sorted again to display alphabetically.

The Classics on DVD program interface (Figure 7-1) includes both a drop-down list and a scrollable display. The commands available on the Edit menu will allow users to add new movies to the list and search for specific movies. The File menu includes a command that will allow users to exit the program.

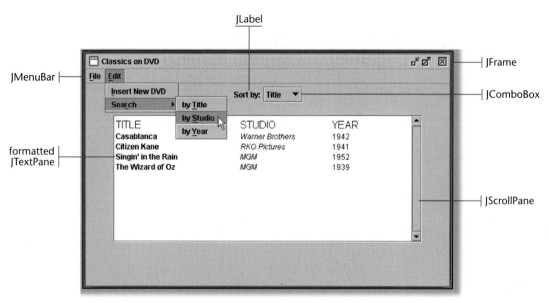

FIGURE 7-1

Program Development

The program development cycle for the Classics on DVD program consists of tasks that correspond to the six development cycle phases, as shown in Table 7-1.

Table 7-1   Classics on DVD Program Development Tasks

	DEVELOPMENT PHASE	TASK(S)
1	Analyze the requirements	Analyze the Classics on DVD problem.
2	Design the solution	Design the user interface. Design the logic to solve the problem.
3	Validate the design	Confirm with the user that the design solves the problem in a satisfactory manner.
4	Implement the design	Translate the design into code. Include internal documentation (comments and remarks) within the code that explains the purpose of the code statements.
5	Test the solution	Test the program. Find and correct any errors (debug) until it is error-free.
6	Document the solution	Print copies of the application code.

Analysis and Design

Figure 7-2 on the next page shows the requirements document that initiates the development cycle for the Classics on DVD program. The requirements document specifies the reason for the request and lists the required components.

REQUEST FOR NEW APPLICATION

Date submitted:	November 3, 2007
Submitted by:	Classics on DVD Collectors Club
Purpose:	Our users have requested an easy-to-use desktop interface to organize their classic DVD collections. The program should work on a variety of platforms. At this time we would like a prototype.
Application title:	Classics on DVD

Algorithms:	Please create a user-friendly interface with the following:
	
	Display:
	     Drop-down list with Title, Studio, and Year choices
	     Formatted output area
	Menu
	     File menu with Exit command
	     Edit menu with Insert and Search commands
	     Search command should display submenu listings for Title, Studio, and Year

Notes:	We have seen some programs with Java's Decorated Look and Feel. It has a kind of multimedia "look" to it. Can you use that in the prototype? Also, many of our users like the shortcut keys on menus. The Insert menu command should immediately sort the list after adding the new DVD, to always present the DVDs in order. Some of our members have many classic movies on DVD, so the display area should scroll to display as many titles as necessary. The display area should use all caps for column headings and bold for the movie names.

Approvals

Approval status:	X	Approved
		Rejected
Approved by:	Ruby Wrinkle	
Date:	November 4, 2007	
Assigned to:	J. Starks, Programmer	

FIGURE 7-2

PROBLEM ANALYSIS An Internet-based collectors group has requested a prototype program to organize their classic movies. The problem that the program should solve is the organization of classic movies on DVD by title, corresponding studio, and year released. The program should allow the user to insert new titles, search, sort, and display.

A **search** is a generic term for the process a computer performs to ascertain the presence of a specific piece of data in a list or storage location. The data entered by the user is called the search argument. A user enters a search argument, and the computer looks it up. For example, a user of the Classics on DVD program may know the title of a movie but not know if the movie is located in the collection. In another example, users may need to find more information about the movie, such as the studio or year it was released. In a search, the user enters the title of the movie, and the application program compares the title with the titles in the program's list and then displays the results.

A **sort** is a generic term that refers to the ways to organize data alphanumerically based on specific criteria. Typically, users request a sort based on a certain field of data, such as sort by title, sort by studio, or sort by year. Once the sort field is determined, the application program reorders or alphabetizes all accompanying data based on that specific field.

DESIGN THE SOLUTION   Once you have analyzed the problem, the next step is to design the user interface. The requirements document for the Classics on DVD program requests a Swing interface with a scrollable text area to display a formatted, detailed listing of the movies (Figure 7-3a). A drop-down list component is required to choose how to sort. Because the request is specific about desired menu options, a **menu storyboard** (Figure 7-3b on the next page) is a good way to verify with the customer that the menu titles and shortcut keys satisfy their needs. A **shortcut key**, or **access key**, is a special key combination used to invoke commands on a menu. A shortcut key usually is an alternative to using the mouse. For example, when you use CTRL+C to copy selected text, you are using a shortcut key. In Figure 7-3b, the underlined letters in the menu system are shortcut keys.

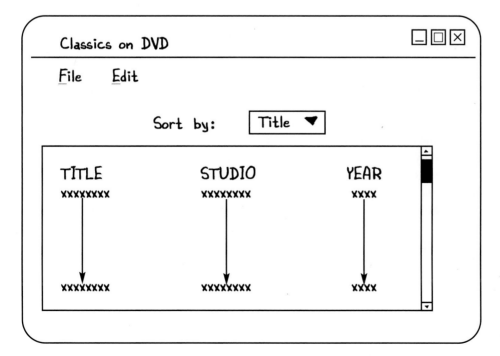

FIGURE 7-3a

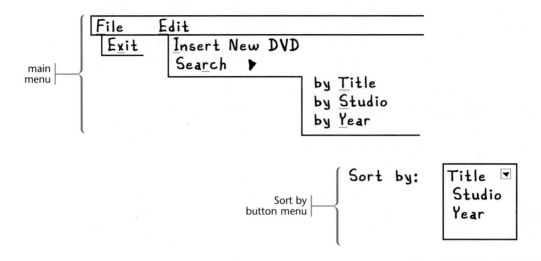

FIGURE 7-3b

The display should be formatted for easy viewing. Because so many different fonts are available, it is good practice to provide users with samples of formatted text from which they may choose. The display area in Figure 7-1 on page 433 uses a Sans Serif (without flourish) family of fonts, including italic, bold, and large font attributes.

PROGRAM DESIGN   Once you have designed the interface, the next step is to design the logic to solve the problem and create the desired results. The Classics on DVD program will involve three logic tasks: data storage, searching, and sorting.

First, because this is only a prototype while the program is running, the data can be stored in arrays rather than in a database. While final versions of the application would probably store the data on external storage devices, this program will use three arrays to store data: one for the movie title, one for the name of the studio, and one for the year the movie was released. These arrays will have to be kept **parallel**, or in sync, with one another as they are sorted to keep the correct movie with the correct studio with the correct year. The subscript number of a movie title must be the same as the subscript number of the matching studio and year in the respective arrays for purposes of displaying the information correctly as well as for sorting. The subscript is the same for each piece of movie data, forming a complete record stored at the same number across these parallel arrays (Figure 7-4). Java handles parallel arrays efficiently, but programmers must be careful with their logic when using them. You will learn more about storing data permanently in a later chapter.

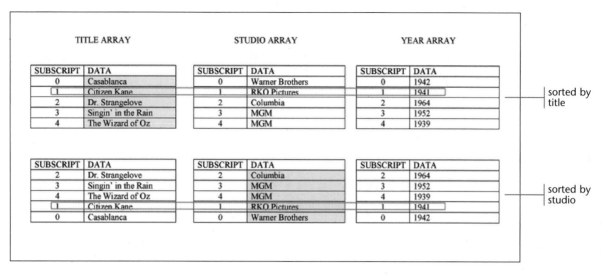

FIGURE 7-4

The second logic task is to search for a user-requested movie. As the list of movies in the prototype is relatively short, a linear search might be appropriate. Performing a **linear search** — also known as a **sequential search** — means searching the list one by one from top to bottom. Search data will be entered by the user via a JOptionPane input dialog box. The data then will be compared with each member of the array, looking for a match. If found, the corresponding data is displayed; otherwise, a message box displays, notifying the user that no results were found. Figure 7-5 displays the message box.

FIGURE 7-5

The third logic task will be to sort the data by a given field. With each array representing a field of data, input from the user will specify which array to sort. Because the arrays are parallel, the other two arrays must be sorted in a manner consistent with the first. As the sort moves an item in the first array, the same move will be made in the other two, keeping the record together across the arrays (Figure 7-4).

VALIDATE DESIGN Once you have designed the program, you can validate the design by stepping through the requirements document and making sure that the design addresses each requirement. The validation process becomes extremely important with a prototype. Together, you and the user should step through the solution with test data to verify that the solution meets the requirements, confirming that the design adequately solves the problem outlined in the requirements. By comparing the program design with the original requirements, both the programmer and the user can validate that the solution is correct and satisfactory.

Having analyzed the problem, designed the interface, and planned and validated the program logic, the analysis and design of the application is complete. As shown in Table 7-1 on page 433, the next task in the development cycle is to implement the design.

Starting a New Java Program in TextPad

The following steps start TextPad and save a TextPad document using a Java file type.

OTHER WAYS

1. To start TextPad, click Start button, click TextPad on Start menu
2. To view line numbers, press CTRL+Q, L
3. To Save As, press F12
4. To Save As, press ALT+F, A

To Start TextPad and Save a TextPad Document

1. With the Windows desktop displayed, click the Start button on the taskbar and then point to All Programs on the Start menu. Point to TextPad on the All Programs submenu.

2. Click TextPad. When the TextPad window opens, if necessary, click the Maximize button to maximize the screen. If a Tip of the Day dialog box is displayed, click its Close button. If line numbers do not display in the TextPad coding window, click View on the menu bar and then click Line Numbers on the View menu.

3. Insert the Data Disk in drive A. Click File on the menu bar and then click Save As on the File menu.

4. When the Save As dialog box is displayed, type DVD in the File name text box. Do not press the ENTER key.

5. Click the Save as type box arrow and then click Java (*.java) in the Save as type list. Click the Save in box arrow and then click 3½ Floppy (A:) in the Save in list.

6. Double-click the Chapter07 folder or a location specified by your instructor.

   The file named DVD will be saved as a Java source code file in the Chapter07 folder on the Data Disk in drive A (Figure 7-6). Your list of files may differ.

7. Click the Save button in the Save As dialog box.

folder name

file name   file type

Save button

FIGURE 7-6

Swing Components and Java Foundation Classes

Recall that Swing is a lightweight set of components that are a part of the Java Foundation Classes (JFC). The **JFC** is defined as containing the features summarized in Table 7-2.

Table 7-2 Features of the Java Foundation Classes (JFC)

FEATURE	DESCRIPTION
Swing Components	Swing components are implemented with no native code. **Native** refers to code and components that are embedded in the operating system. Swing components, therefore, may not appear identical to the components users are used to seeing in their operating system. For example, a Windows message box looks different from a JOptionPane message box because the Windows version uses the native common dialog window. Swing components include everything from panels to buttons to split panes to tables. Swing components begin with an uppercase J. You have used JOptionPane Swing components in previous chapters.
Pluggable Look and Feel Support	The **look and feel methods** offer any program using Swing a choice of how windows, title bars, and other components will display. For example, the same program can use either the Java look and feel or the Windows look and feel.
Accessibility API	This JFC API enables assistive technologies, such as screen readers and Braille displays, to obtain information from the user interface.
Java 2D API	The 2D API enables programmers to incorporate high-quality 2D graphics, text, and images in applications and applets.
Drag and Drop Support	First popularized by Microsoft Window applications, Java contains JFC methods to provide drag and drop capabilities between a Java application and a native application.

Swing Components versus AWT Components

Although the Java 2 Platform still supports the AWT components, it is recommended that you use Swing components instead because they contain more methods to manipulate and implement basic GUI-related features. Swing components are not restricted to the least common denominator, or the features present on every platform; therefore, they have more functionality than AWT components. Even the simplest Swing components have capabilities beyond what the AWT components offer.

The major difference between AWT components and Swing components is that the latter are implemented with no native code. Therefore, Swing components are backward compatible, which means they can be added on to older versions of the JDK. Swing components are considered **lightweight,** which means they borrow screen resources from the operating system and therefore do not have to support their own. **Heavyweight** components, such as those used with the AWT, are associated with their own native resource, or peer. Lightweight components make more efficient use of their resources, provide consistency across platforms, and have a cleaner look and feel integration. Recall that AWT components are in the java.awt package, while Swing components are in the javax.swing package.

Swing Components
Although the Java 2 platform still supports the AWT components, it is recommended that you use Swing components instead because they contain more methods to manipulate and implement basic GUI-related features.

Table 7-3 lists some of the advantages of using Swing components.

Table 7-3   Swing Component Advantages

ADVANTAGES OF USING SWING COMPONENTS
1. Swing Buttons and Labels can display images instead of, or in addition to, text.
2. Borders may be drawn around most Swing components.
3. Swing components do not have to be rectangular. JButtons, for example, can be round.
4. Assistive technologies can obtain information from Swing components. For example, a screen reader easily can read the text that is displayed on a JButton or JLabel.
5. Swing components allow programmers and developers to specify the look and feel of the GUI. By contrast, AWT components always have the look and feel of the native platform.
6. Some Swing components use external objects to hold information about the state of the component. The Swing slider bar, JSlider, for example, automatically is associated with a BoundedRangeModel object to hold its current value and range of legal values.

Most of the AWT components have a counterpart in the Swing package. The AWT button class, for example, is named Button, while the Swing button class is named JButton. The AWT container, Frame, has a JFrame version that provides the same functionality but with more features. Table 7-4 displays a comparison list of AWT and Swing components.

Table 7-4   Swing Components versus AWT Components

SWING COMPONENTS	AWT COMPONENTS	ADVANTAGES OF USING SWING COMPONENTS
JLabel	Label	May use text or image or both
JTextField	TextField	More methods to manipulate text; can be overlaid with a viewport for additional layering of components
JCheckBox JOptionButton	Checkbox	Uses two different controls with more methods, whereas AWT groups a single control
JButton	Button	May have images on the button; button may take different shapes
JComboBox	ComboBox	May take two different forms: editable and uneditable
JTextArea	TextArea	Separates the scrolling capability, size, word wrap, and other properties to a viewport or JScrollPane for more flexibility
JPanel	Panel	Supports all the Swing methods inherited from containers
JFrame	Frame	Uses a content pane container to provide more flexibility
JApplet	Applet	Supports the JFC/Swing component architecture
JMenuBar	MenuBar	Creates menus as buttons for greater flexibility in creating shortcut menus and pop-up menus

Swing Container Hierarchy

The container hierarchy for any window or applet that includes Swing components must have a Swing top-level container rather than an AWT container. A **top-level container**, also called a **root container** is an object at the top of the container hierarchy that displays a border and title bar. For example, a main window should be implemented as a JFrame instance rather than as a Frame instance if the main window will contain Swing components. Table 7-5 displays the container hierarchy. Containers exist in both AWT and Swing packages, but they play a more important role in Swing applications.

Table 7-5   The Swing Container Hierarchy

TYPE OF CONTAINER	PURPOSE	SWING EXAMPLE
Top-Level Containers	The components at the top of any Swing containment hierarchy	JApplet JDialog JFrame
General-Purpose Containers	Intermediate containers that can be used to display components	JPanel JScrollPane JSplitPane JToolbar JTabbedPane
Special-Purpose Containers	Intermediate containers that play specific roles in the user interface, such as layered panes or internal panes	content pane JLayeredPane JInternalPane JDesktopPane
Basic Controls	Low-level components that exist primarily to get input from the user	JButton JComboBox JList JMenu JSlider JSpinner JTextField
Uneditable Information Displays	Low-level components that exist solely to give the user information	JLabel JProgressBar JToolTip
Interactive Displays of Highly Formatted Information	Low-level components that display highly formatted information that may be modified by the user	JColorChooser JFileChooser JTable JText JTree

Low-level components, also called **atomic components**, can stand alone in the interface or be added to a higher level component in the hierarchy; however, programmers should not add components directly to a top-level container, such as a JFrame. The preferred method is to use a special-purpose container to hold components, called a **content pane**. The **getContentPane() method** is used to create an instance of the Container class, similar to a Panel, which does not display a border. Content panes hold individual components and are added to, and therefore contained by, the JFrame. Programs that use a content pane extend JFrame and use add() methods to add components to the instance of the content pane.

In general, do not combine complex AWT components, such as Menus and Panels, in the same container control as Swing components. The reason for this is because when lightweight components, such as Swing, overlap with heavyweight components, such as AWT, the heavyweight component is painted on top.

Entering Code to Extend JFrame

Figure 7-7 displays the comments, the import statements, and the class header for the Classics on DVD program. Line 14 extends the top-level container JFrame and implements the ActionListener.

```
1   /*
2       Chapter 7:   Classics on DVD
3       Programmer:  J. Starks
4       Date:        November 12, 2007
5       Filename:    DVD.java
6       Purpose:     This program creates a Swing interface for sorting a DVD collection.
7   */
8
9   import java.awt.*;
10  import java.awt.event.*;
11  import javax.swing.*;
12  import javax.swing.text.*;
13
14  public class DVD extends JFrame implements ActionListener
15  {
```

FIGURE 7-7

The following step enters the code to extend JFrame in the class header, as you begin coding the Classics on DVD program.

To Extend JFrame in the Class Header

1. Enter the code as shown in Figure 7-7, replacing the programmer name and date shown with your name and the current date.

TextPad displays the beginning code for the DVD class (Figure 7-8). The comments, import statements, and class header are displayed.

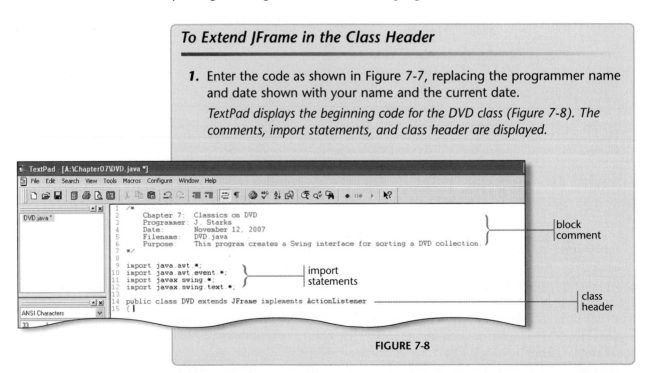

FIGURE 7-8

> **Combining AWT and Swing Components**
> Do not combine complex AWT components—such as Menus and Panels—with Swing components in the same container. Heavy-weight AWT components paint on top of lightweight Swing components.

You learned already that implementing ActionListener allows the program to listen for a click event. You cannot compile the program yet because programs implementing the ActionListener must include an actionPerformed() event before they will compile successfully. JMenu and JComboBox components, coded later in the program, will require clicks by the user, thereby making the ActionListener necessary.

Constructing Class-Level Components

Components that are declared and constructed at the beginning of the class and that are external to any other method are class-level components, which become visible to all other methods within the class. The Classics on DVD program will contain three Swing components and three String arrays that will have class-level scope.

Constructing Swing Components

The three Swing components that will be constructed as class-level components are JLabel, JComboBox, and JTextPane. A JLabel will be used to display the words, Sort by:, at the top of the interface. A **JLabel** is similar to an AWT Label in that it displays information in a GUI application. JLabels, however, also can display borders and images.

A **JComboBox**, Java's Swing version of a drop-down list, will display the sort fields from which users may choose. A **combo box** is a drop-down list that displays when users click a box arrow in the interface. A JComboBox can have two different forms. The first form is the **uneditable combo box**, which features a button and a drop-down list of values. The button displays a word and an arrow; when a user clicks the button, its drop-down list displays. The second form, the **editable combo box**, features a text box with a box arrow. This type of combo box allows the user to type a value in the text box or click the box arrow to display a drop-down list. The setEditable() method is used to set the JComboBox to one of the two forms. The uneditable combo box is the default. Figure 7-9 displays the two forms of the JComboBox.

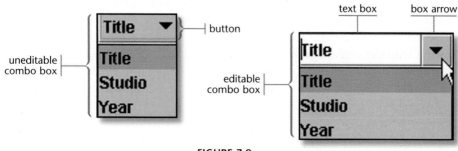

FIGURE 7-9

A JComboBox requires little screen space, and the editable form is useful for allowing the user to choose a value quickly without being limited to the displayed values. Typically, the drop-down list would include the choices selected most often, while the program would allow for other choices as well.

Table 7-6 displays some of the JComboBox methods.

Table 7-6   JComboBox Methods

METHOD	PURPOSE	EXAMPLE
JComboBox()	Constructor method to display drop-down list choices that users may click; may accept a String array of choices to display	`myCombo = new JComboBox(stringArray);`
setSelectedIndex()	Sets which item is selected in the displayed list of choices; useful for resetting the JComboBox back to its default value	`printerListCombo.setSelectedIndex(0);`
addItem()	Adds new items to the drop-down list	`colorCombo.addItem("Blue");`
getItemCount()	Returns the number of items in the drop-down list	`int howMany = myCombo.getItemCount();`
setEditable()	Determines whether the JComboBox is editable (true) or uneditable (false)	`editableCombo.setEditable(true);`
removeItem()	Removes an item from the drop-down list	`coursesCombo.removeItem(4);`

Programmers can add commands to, or populate, JComboBoxes with the addItem() method, as shown in Table 7-6; however, the ability to declare, construct, and populate a JComboBox in a single line of code makes it easier to create long lists of options from which users may choose. For example, a typical interface requesting address information from a user may include a drop-down list of the 50 states. The String array of two-letter postal codes is available from many Web sources; therefore, Java programmers easily can create what otherwise would be a complicated, long segment of code with just a single line.

```
JComboBox statesCombo = new JComboBox(stateArray);
```

The Classics on DVD program will employ a JComboBox that will be populated later in the program.

The third Swing component, a **JTextPane**, is a text component that displays with graphic attributes. This component models paragraphs composed of a series of characters with character attributes. Each paragraph has a logical style attached to it with default attributes, which can be changed by overriding the default with the **setParagraphAttributes() method.** In addition to paragraph attributes, components and images may be embedded in JTextPanes.

Figure 7-10 displays the code to declare and construct the three Swing components.

```
16        //construct components
17        JLabel sortPrompt = new JLabel("Sort by:");
18        JComboBox fieldCombo = new JComboBox();
19        JTextPane textPane = new JTextPane();
20
```

FIGURE 7-10

The following step enters the code to construct the Swing components.

To Construct the Swing Components

1. Enter the code as shown in Figure 7-10.

TextPad displays the declaration and construction code of the Swing components (Figure 7-11).

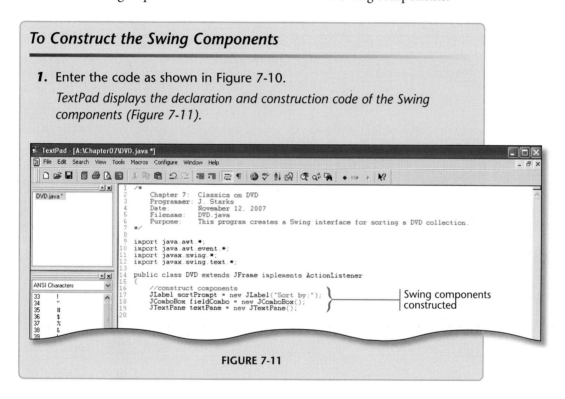

FIGURE 7-11

As class-level components, the JLabel, JComboBox, and JTextPane components all will be visible to other methods in the DVD class.

Populating a JComboBox

The ability to declare, construct, and populate a JComboBox in a single line of code makes it easier to create long lists of options from which users may choose. For shorter lists, populate a JComboBox using the addItem() method.

Constructing Parallel Arrays

Part of the logic necessary for the Classics on DVD prototype program requires that the data can be searched and sorted. Without permanent storage of the data, the most efficient way to manipulate data is in arrays. The Classics on DVD program will use three arrays, one for each of the fields of information: title, studio, and year.

Figure 7-12 displays the code to declare, construct, and populate the String arrays. Recall from Chapter 5 that arrays may be populated as they are constructed, which additionally assigns the length of the array to the number of elements within the braces, as shown in lines 22, 23, and 24.

```
21      //initialize data in arrays
22      String title[] = {"Casablanca", "Citizen Kane", "Singin' in the Rain",
        "The Wizard of Oz"};
23      String studio[] = {"Warner Brothers", "RKO Pictures", "MGM", "MGM"};
24      String year[] = {"1942", "1941", "1952", "1939"};
25
```

FIGURE 7-12

The following step declares and assigns data to the arrays.

To Declare and Assign Arrays

1. Enter the code as shown in Figure 7-12.

TextPad displays the declarations and assignments of the three arrays (Figure 7-13). Your lines may wrap differently.

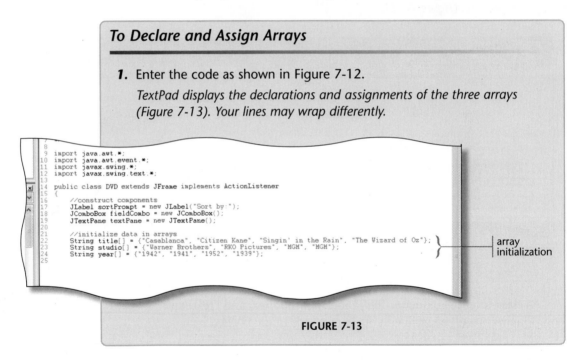

FIGURE 7-13

In this solution, the arrays are populated in the same line of code as the construction. The arrays then have their length automatically set equal to the number of items in the constructor method. For instance, in lines 22, 23, and 24, the arrays are set to have a length of 4, with index numbers 0, 1, 2, and 3. The alternative to populating the arrays in the same line of code is to fill the arrays during initial execution by reading the values from a database.

Using the super Keyword

Recall that a constructor method, which is named the same as the class itself, is called implicitly when another program defines an instance of the class. Therefore, a constructor must exist to create an object of the class. If a class has no constructors, the compiler will create a default constructor.

When inheriting from another class, a constructor, as its first statement, must call a constructor of its immediate parent, or superclass, without creating another instance of the superclass. A superclass default constructor can be called implicitly and so does not require an explicit call. An explicit call, if needed, is done by using the keyword, **super**. Although the JFrame class has a default constructor, classes extending JFrame can explicitly call a JFrame constructor and pass a string to be set as the title bar caption. Because a class can have only one parent, the keyword, super, always refers to the immediate superclass.

The super Keyword

Programmers use the super keyword to substitute for a class name and to invoke an overridden base class method in a derived class.

The DVD() Constructor Method

Figure 7-14 displays the code for the DVD() constructor method. Line 29 uses the keyword, super, to create an instance of the DVD frame and assign it the title, Classics on DVD.

```
26      //construct instance of DVD
27      public DVD()
28      {
29          super("Classics on DVD");
30      }
31
```

FIGURE 7-14

The following step inserts the constructor method code into the Classics on DVD program.

To Code the DVD() Constructor Method

1. Enter the code from Figure 7-14.

TextPad displays the constructor method code (Figure 7-15).

```
11  import ja
12  import javax.swing.text.*;
13
14  public class DVD extends JFrame implements ActionListener
15  {
16      //construct components
17      JLabel sortPrompt = new JLabel("Sort by:");
18      JComboBox fieldCombo = new JComboBox();
19      JTextPane textPane = new JTextPane();
20
21      //initialize data in arrays
22      String title[] = {"Casablanca", "Citizen Kane", "Singin' in the Rain", "The Wizard of Oz"};
23      String studio[] = {"Warner Brothers", "RKO Pictures", "MGM", "MGM"};
24      String year[] = {"1942", "1941", "1952", "1939"};
25
26      //construct instance of DVD
27      public DVD()
28      {
29          super("Classics on DVD");
30      }
31
```

constructor method

superclass reference

FIGURE 7-15

A subclass like JFrame inherits state and behavior from all of its ancestors. For example, the DVD class can refer to any method or variable belonging to JFrame, JFrame's superclass of Frame, or Frame's superclass of Container.

Creating a JMenuBar

A JMenuBar is the Swing version of the AWT MenuBar. The constructor method of the JMenuBar creates an object that can be set at the top of a JFrame through the use of the **setJMenuBar() method**. Each command on a JMenuBar is constructed as a JMenu. The commands that display on the drop-down list for each JMenu are constructed as JMenuItems. Figure 7-16 displays the three components (JMenuBar, JMenu, and JMenuItem) used in common Swing menus.

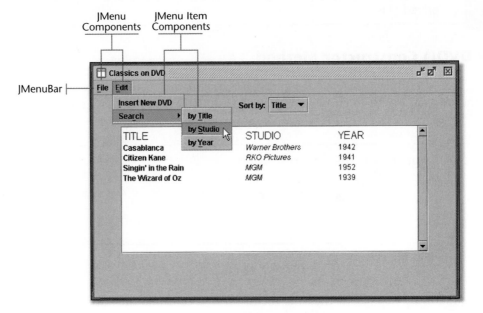

FIGURE 7-16

More methods are available with Swing menus than with AWT menus. Table 7-7 displays some of the common methods and examples.

Table 7-7 Swing Menu Methods

METHOD	PURPOSE	EXAMPLE
setDisplayedMnemonicIndex()	Specifies which letter in the keyword command will act as a shortcut key.	`mnuFormat.setDisplayedMnemonicIndex(1);`
setActionCommand()	Specifies a String that can be used in the actionPerformed() method to test which command was clicked.	`mnuTools.setActionCommand("Tools");`
add()	Adds commands to the JMenuBar or to a JMenu menu.	`mnuBar.add(mnuFile);`
JMenuBar()	Constructs an instance of the JMenuBar object to display as a primary menu bar in an application.	`appMenu = new JMenuBar();`

JMenu()	Constructs an instance of the JMenu object to display as a menu bar command. The first argument is the displayed command keyword. A second, optional boolean argument specifies if the JMenu can act as a tear-off.	`JMenu = mnuFile new JMenu("File");`
		`JMenu = mnuFile new JMenu("Edit",`
		`true);`

addSeparator()	Appends a new separator to the end of the menu.	`mnuHelp.addSeparator();`
JMenuItem()	Constructs an instance of the JMenuItem object to display as a command in a drop-down list. The argument is the displayed command keyword.	`JMenuItem mnuEditCopy = new` `JMenuItem("Copy");`
addActionListener()	Enables the command to hear clicks from the user, activating the action event.	`mnuView.addActionListener(this);`
setJMenuBar()	Assigns the menu bar argument to the application's interface.	`setJMenuBar(appBar);`

Creating a Menu System for the Classics on DVD Program

Recall how the menu system specified in the requirements document included a menu bar with two commands and drop-down lists. Later in the program, the main() method will call a method named createMenuBar(). The createMenuBar() method, as shown in Figure 7-17, will declare and construct instances of the JMenuBar, two JMenu commands, and several JMenuItems. The createMenuBar() method takes no arguments but returns a completed JMenuBar item.

```
32      //create the menu system
33      public JMenuBar createMenuBar()
34      {
35          //create an instance of the menu
36          JMenuBar mnuBar = new JMenuBar();
37          setJMenuBar(mnuBar);
38
39          //construct and populate the File menu
40          JMenu mnuFile = new JMenu("File", true);
41              mnuFile.setMnemonic(KeyEvent.VK_F);
42              mnuFile.setDisplayedMnemonicIndex(0);
43              mnuBar.add(mnuFile);
44
45          JMenuItem mnuFileExit = new JMenuItem("Exit");
46              mnuFileExit.setMnemonic(KeyEvent.VK_X);
47              mnuFileExit.setDisplayedMnemonicIndex(1);
48              mnuFile.add(mnuFileExit);
49              mnuFileExit.setActionCommand("Exit");
50              mnuFileExit.addActionListener(this);
51
52          //construct and populate the Edit menu
53          JMenu mnuEdit = new JMenu("Edit", true);
54              mnuEdit.setMnemonic(KeyEvent.VK_E);
55              mnuEdit.setDisplayedMnemonicIndex(0);
56              mnuBar.add(mnuEdit);
57
58          JMenuItem mnuEditInsert = new JMenuItem("Insert New DVD");
59              mnuEditInsert.setMnemonic(KeyEvent.VK_I);
60              mnuEditInsert.setDisplayedMnemonicIndex(0);
61              mnuEdit.add(mnuEditInsert);
62              mnuEditInsert.setActionCommand("Insert");
63              mnuEditInsert.addActionListener(this);
64
65          JMenu mnuEditSearch = new JMenu("Search");
66              mnuEditSearch.setMnemonic(KeyEvent.VK_R);
67              mnuEditSearch.setDisplayedMnemonicIndex(3);
68              mnuEdit.add(mnuEditSearch);
69
70          JMenuItem mnuEditSearchByTitle = new JMenuItem("by Title");
71              mnuEditSearchByTitle.setMnemonic(KeyEvent.VK_T);
72              mnuEditSearchByTitle.setDisplayedMnemonicIndex(3);
73              mnuEditSearch.add(mnuEditSearchByTitle);
74              mnuEditSearchByTitle.setActionCommand("title");
75              mnuEditSearchByTitle.addActionListener(this);
76
77          JMenuItem mnuEditSearchByStudio = new JMenuItem("by Studio");
78              mnuEditSearchByStudio.setMnemonic(KeyEvent.VK_S);
79              mnuEditSearchByStudio.setDisplayedMnemonicIndex(3);
80              mnuEditSearch.add(mnuEditSearchByStudio);
81              mnuEditSearchByStudio.setActionCommand("studio");
82              mnuEditSearchByStudio.addActionListener(this);
83
84          JMenuItem mnuEditSearchByYear = new JMenuItem("by Year");
85              mnuEditSearchByYear.setMnemonic(KeyEvent.VK_Y);
86              mnuEditSearchByYear.setDisplayedMnemonicIndex(3);
87              mnuEditSearch.add(mnuEditSearchByYear);
88              mnuEditSearchByYear.setActionCommand("year");
89              mnuEditSearchByYear.addActionListener(this);
90
91          return mnuBar;
92      }
93
```

FIGURE 7-17

The **setMnemonic() method** in lines 41, 46, 54, 59, 66, 71, 78, and 85 sets the keyboard mnemonic for a Menu object or a MenuItem object. A **mnemonic** is a device used as an aid in remembering. The mnemonic key is the keyboard letter that — when combined with another key, such as ALT — will activate the object if the window has the focus. A mnemonic must correspond to a single key on the keyboard and should be specified using one of the VK keycodes. Java uses a **VK keycode**, or virtual key keycode, to determine which keyboard key has been pressed. VK keycodes belong to the **KeyEvent class**, a class of methods associated with keyboard events such as pressing a key, releasing a key, or typing into a text box. The general format of the setMnemonic() method is as follows.

```
object.setMnemonic(KeyEvent.keycode);
```

Java supports a VK keycode for each of the letter numbers, and function keys on a standard keyboard by using the syntax, VK_, followed by the appropriate key. For example, to set the mnemonic to the letter F in a File menu, the object would be the name of the menu and the keycode would be VK_F.

```
mnuFile.setMnemonic(KeyEvent.VK_F);
```

Mnemonics are not case sensitive; therefore, a KeyEvent with the corresponding keycode would cause the button to be activated whether or not the SHIFT key was pressed.

Java uses a second method involving mnemonics to specifically assign a visual underline to a certain letter in a menu or label for use as a shortcut key. The **setDisplayedMnemonicIndex() method** in lines 42, 47, 55, 60, 67, 72, 79, and 86 assigns the shortcut key to a letter in the command's keyword, underlining the letter in the menu or label. Java indexes the keyword characters beginning with zero and progressing sequentially. Therefore, in line 86, setting the mnemonic index to 3 will assign the fourth element of the Menu's caption string — in this case, the letter Y — as the shortcut. Thus, the second occurrence of the letter Y in the caption, by Year, will display underlined. Pressing ALT+Y will trigger the command in the same way as clicking the menu command. Mnemonics are assigned to each of the menu system commands to use as shortcuts in the same way.

Setting a Shortcut Key
Use the setDisplayedMnemonicIndex() method to assign a visual underline to a specific letter in a menu or label for use as a shortcut key.

The setActionCommand() method in lines 49, 62, 74, 81, and 88 assigns a String that can be evaluated in the actionPerformed() method. An if statement will match the assigned action with the action of the clicked object; in this way, it is able to determine which command was clicked. For example, in line 62, the setActionCommand() method sets a String to the word, Insert, which then will be evaluated later in the actionPerformed() method.

The addActionListener() method in lines 50, 63, 75, 82, and 89 causes the click of the menu command to trigger the corresponding action event. Recall that the self-referential keyword, this, connects the ActionListener to the object itself rather than activating some other object's click event.

In line 91, the return statement is used to return the constructed JMenuBar item to the calling method.

The following step enters code for the createMenuBar() method.

To Code the createMenuBar() Method

1. Enter the code from Figure 7-17 on page 450.

TextPad displays the code for the createMenuBar() method (Figure 7-18).

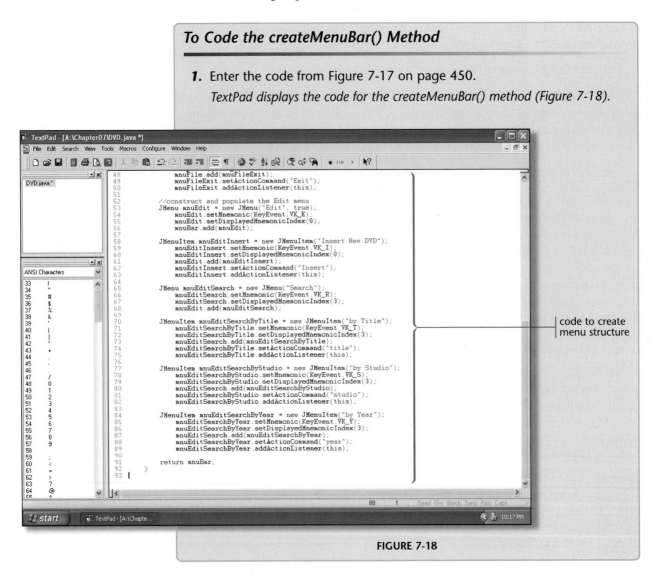

code to create menu structure

FIGURE 7-18

The add() method in lines 43, 48, 56, 61, 68, 73, 80, and 87 takes the object listed in the method argument and adds it to the menu system, just as it did in its AWT counterpart. For example, in line 48, the Exit command is added to the File menu when the mnuFileExit object is added to mnuFile. It is common practice to name JMenu and JMenuItem objects with the prefix, mnu, followed by the command's location and keyword.

Naming Menu Components

Use the prefix, mnu, in the variable name for menu components. Follow the prefix with the Menu's location and a keyword. For example, the Copy command on the Edit menu might be named mnuEditCopy.

Creating the Content Pane

You learned earlier that a content pane is a special-purpose container similar to a Panel. Content panes hold individual components and are added to and, therefore, contained by the JFrame. Many programmers and developers write a method to create the content pane to prevent its components from being confused with another part of the program.

Coding the createContentPane() Method

The createContentPane() method accepts no arguments, but it returns a Container object. **Container** is the superclass for all containers in the API. Inside the Classics on DVD program content pane, there will be a JPanel in the north with a JComboBox and JLabel, and a JPanel in the center with a JTextPane and JScrollPane.

Figure 7-19 displays the code for the createContentPane() method.

```
94      //create the content pane
95      public Container createContentPane()
96      {
97          //populate the JComboBox
98          fieldCombo.addItem("Title");
99          fieldCombo.addItem("Studio");
100         fieldCombo.addItem("Year");
101         fieldCombo.addActionListener(this);
102         fieldCombo.setToolTipText("Click the drop-down arrow to display sort fields.");
103
104         //construct and populate the north panel
105         JPanel northPanel = new JPanel();
106             northPanel.setLayout(new FlowLayout());
107             northPanel.add(sortPrompt);
108             northPanel.add(fieldCombo);
109
110         //create the JTextPane and center panel
111         JPanel centerPanel = new JPanel();
112             setTabsAndStyles(textPane);
113             textPane = addTextToTextPane();
114             JScrollPane scrollPane = new JScrollPane(textPane);
115                 scrollPane.setVerticalScrollBarPolicy(JScrollPane.VERTICAL_SCROLLBAR_ALWAYS);
116                 scrollPane.setPreferredSize(new Dimension(500, 200));
117             centerPanel.add(scrollPane);
118
119         //create Container and set attributes
120         Container c = getContentPane();
121             c.setLayout(new BorderLayout(10,10));
122             c.add(northPanel,BorderLayout.NORTH);
123             c.add(centerPanel,BorderLayout.CENTER);
124
125         return c;
126     }
127
```

FIGURE 7-19

Lines 98 through 100 add the three choices to the JComboBox. Line 101 adds the Action Listener.

Line 102 sets a tool tip for the JComboBox. The **setToolTipText() method** creates a **tool tip**, which is a short descriptive message indicating the name of a specific component or tool, or instructions on how to use it. Tool tips display when the user moves the mouse over an object enabled with the setToolTipText() method. Tool tip messages usually display in a highlighted box. When users move the mouse over the JComboBox, the tool tip displays the words, Click the drop-down arrow to display sort fields. Figure 7-20 shows the tool tip.

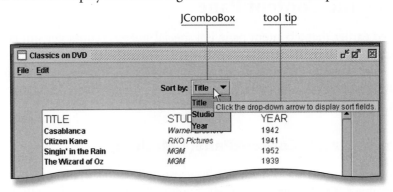

FIGURE 7-20

JAVA UPDATE **Java 2** v5.0

A tool tip is different from a pop-up display or menu. In J2SE version 5.0, programmers may use pop-ups more freely because the coding has been simplified. The listener interface that listens for a right-click of the user's mouse no longer has to be installed, and programmers do not have to register the appropriate key bindings. A JPopupMenu() method may be used anywhere you want a menu to display.

Two JPanels also are created in this method: the northPanel and the centerPanel. The northPanel, created in lines 105 through 108, will hold a JLabel prompt and the JComboBox containing the sort fields. The northPanel uses a FlowLayout. The centerPanel, created in lines 111 through 117, will display information about the movies in a JTextPane declared previously. Line 112 calls a user-defined method named setTabsAndStyles() to provide formatting for the text pane. Line 113 calls another user-defined method named addTextToTextPane() to add text. You will write the methods themselves later in the chapter.

The centerPanel also contains a JScrollPane, constructed in line 114. A **JScrollPane** facilitates a scrollable view of another Swing component, such as a JTextPane. Java uses the term, **viewport,** to identify the portion of the text component displayed within the JScrollPane at any given time. When screen space is limited, programmers employ a JScrollPane to display a component that is large or one whose size can change dynamically.

Table 7-8 displays some of the methods associated with JScrollPanes.

Line 115 uses the attribute, VERTICAL_SCROLLBAR_ALWAYS, as the argument for the setVerticalScrollBarPolicy() method, so that vertical scroll bars will display on the right of the JTextPane.

Line 116 sets the preferred size of the JScrollPane to 500 by 200 pixels as a Dimension object is constructed. A **Dimension** is a logical size object, conceptually similar to a rectangle. The Dimension class encapsulates in a single object the width and height of a component.

Finally, the getContentPane() method in line 120 constructs an instance of the content pane. Its overall layout manager is BorderLayout, as specified in line 121. The JPanels are added to their respective regions, and the content pane is returned to the calling method.

Table 7-8   JScrollPane Methods

METHOD	PURPOSE	EXAMPLE
JScrollPane()	Accepts a Swing component as an argument	myScrollPane = new JScrollPane(myTextPane);
setVerticalScrollBarPolicy()	Determines when the vertical scrollbar appears in the JScrollPane	myScroll.setVerticalScrollBarPolicy (JScrollPane. VERTICAL_SCROLLBAR_ALWAYS);
setPreferredSize()	Sets the size of the JScrollPane	paneScrollPane.setPreferredSize(new Dimension(500,200));
setWheelScrollingEnabled()	Enables/disables scrolling in response to movement of the mouse wheel	aScroll.setWheelScrollingEnabled(true);
setViewportBorder()	Adds a border around the viewport	dataScroll.setViewport(borderStyle);

The following step enters code for the createContentPane() method.

To Code the createContentPane() Method

1. Enter the code from Figure 7-19 on page 453.

TextPad displays the code for the createContentPane() method (Figure 7-21).

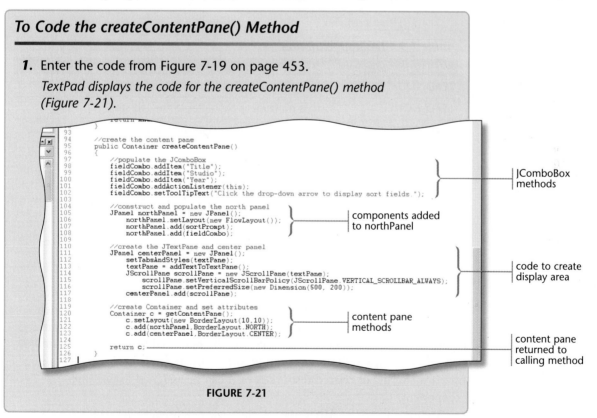

FIGURE 7-21

The getContentPane() method from the Container class can be used with JApplets or JFrames. When used with JApplets, the creation of the content pane must take place in the init() method because the content pane connects its components with the applet itself upon execution. With JFrames, the creation of the content pane takes place in main() or in the constructor method.

JAVA UPDATE Java 2 v5.0

In J2SE version 5.0, programmers may simplify their programs by omitting the getContentPane() method reference when adding components. For example, myJFrame.add() is equivalent to myJFrame.getContent-Pane.add(). Similarly, the setContentPane() method may be omitted.

If you want to amend the DVD program to use the add() methods without the direct reference to the get() and set() methods associated with the content pane, you must replace lines 87, 113, 114, 115, and 321 (created later in the chapter) and comment out lines 112 and 117 as shown in the following code. The createContent-Pane() method no longer will return a Container data type but simply will be called from the main() method.

```
 87   public void createContentPane()
       ↓
112   //Container c = getContentPane();
113     setLayout(new BorderLayout(10,10));
114     add(northPanel,BorderLayout.NORTH);
115     add(centerPanel,BorderLayout.CENTER);
116
117   //return c;
       ↓
321   f.createContentPane();
```

Tabs and Styles

Tabs and styles apply to various text components, such as JTextAreas and JTextPanes. The **TabStop class** allows programmers to create predetermined tab positions at specified distances from the left margin—aligned in a specified way and with an optional specified leader. TabStops usually are contained in TabSets. The **TabSet class** is composed of multiple TabStops and offers methods for locating the closest TabStop to a given position and finding all the potential TabStops. Table 7-9 displays some of the available TabStop attributes.

Table 7-9   TabStop Attributes

ATTRIBUTE	FUNCTION
LEAD_EQUALS	Assigns a leading character to the tab stop
LEAD_NONE	Assigns no leading character to the tab stop
LEAD_DOTS	Assigns periods (or dots) as the leading character to the tab stop
ALIGN_RIGHT	Sets a right-aligned tab stop
ALIGN_CENTER	Sets a centered tab stop
ALIGN_JUSTIFED	Sets a justified tab stop
ALIGN_LEFT	Sets a left-aligned tab stop

Formatting styles associated with JTextPanes can be more complicated. First-time programmers typically create a style context for elements in their JTextPanes. The **StyleContext** class contains a pool of styles—such as font and color—and their associated resources, which are reused by various style definitions. If desired, a StyleContext can be shared by multiple components to maximize the sharing of related resources, or it can be assigned to just one component.

Methods from the **AttributeSet class** use a defined StyleContext to set attributes for the current object. Attributes are used to describe features that will contribute to a graphical representation, such as tabs or paragraph formatting.

A Style is a related concept, but larger and more inclusive. The **Style** class allows programmers to store a collection of attributes associated with an element in a document. Styles must be declared and assigned and typically are used to associate character and paragraph styles with the element. The following code obtains the default style:

```
Style myStyle =
StyleContext.getDefaultStyleContext().getStyle(StyleContext.
DEFAULT_STYLE);
```

Once a style is defined, several methods from the StyleConstants class can be used to set various characteristics. **StyleConstants** are a collection of common text attributes and methods, such as setBold(), setItalic(), and setUnderline().

The following code uses the **setFontFamily() method** to assign the Arial font to a previously declared Style and the **setFontSize() method** to assign a font size of 16.

```
StyleConstants.setFontFamily(myStyle, "Arial");
StyleConstants.setFontSize(myStyle, 16);
```

A defined Style may be used as a starting point to create additional Styles. The **addStyle() method** uses a previously defined Style as well as a String keyword to identify a specific attribute for use in other parts of the program. For example, the following code assigns the word, italic, to a style named newStyle.

```
Style newStyle = textPane.addStyle("italic", myStyle);
```

Coding the setTabsAndStyles() Method

Figure 7-22 displays the code for the setTabsAndStyles() method. The setTabsAndStyles() method accepts a JTextPane argument and returns nothing. Therefore, a JTextPane is passed to this method, which then formats it.

```
128    //method to create tab stops and set font styles
129    protected void setTabsAndStyles(JTextPane textPane)
130    {
131        //create Tab Stops
132        TabStop[] tabs = new TabStop[2];
133            tabs[0] = new TabStop(200, TabStop.ALIGN_LEFT, TabStop.LEAD_NONE);
134            tabs[1] = new TabStop(350, TabStop.ALIGN_LEFT, TabStop.LEAD_NONE);
135        TabSet tabset = new TabSet(tabs);
136
137        //set Tab Style
138        StyleContext tabStyle = StyleContext.getDefaultStyleContext();
139        AttributeSet aset =
140            tabStyle.addAttribute(SimpleAttributeSet.EMPTY, StyleConstants.TabSet, tabset);
141        textPane.setParagraphAttributes(aset, false);
142
143        //set Font Style
144        Style fontStyle =
145            StyleContext.getDefaultStyleContext().getStyle(StyleContext.DEFAULT_STYLE);
146
147        Style regular = textPane.addStyle("regular", fontStyle);
148        StyleConstants.setFontFamily(fontStyle, "SansSerif");
149
150        Style s = textPane.addStyle("italic", regular);
151        StyleConstants.setItalic(s, true);
152
153        s = textPane.addStyle("bold", regular);
154        StyleConstants.setBold(s, true);
155
156        s = textPane.addStyle("large", regular);
157        StyleConstants.setFontSize(s, 16);
158    }
159
```

FIGURE 7-22

In lines 133 and 134, two TabStops are created at 200 and 350 pixels; they become part of the TabSet for the JTextPane. Lines 138 through 141 set the style and attributes for the tabs.

Lines 144 through 157 create the font style. First, a default style is assigned in line 145. Next, that style is used to create a keyword, regular, in line 147. Then, the font is set to SansSerif in line 148. Italic, bold, and large attributes are set in lines 150, 153, and 156, respectively.

The following step enters code for the setTabsAndStyles() method.

To Code the setTabsAndStyles() Method

1. Enter the code shown in Figure 7-22 on the previous page.

TextPad displays the code for the setTabsAndStyles() method (Figure 7-23).

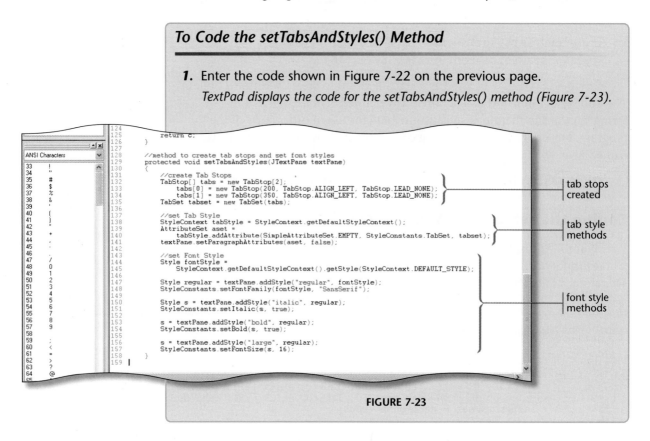

FIGURE 7-23

When another part of the program calls it, the setTabsAndStyles() method will format the text pane with the appropriate tabs and styles.

The Document Class

The **Document class** creates a container for text serving as the model for Swing text components. Rather than inserting text directly into a JTextPane, for example, programmers sometimes will use a Document class to hold the text; this is useful for appending and refreshing text-based Swing components. Table 7-10 displays some useful methods in the Document class.

Table 7-10   Document Class Methods

METHOD	PURPOSE	EXAMPLE
getText()	Gets the text contained within the given portion of the document.	`String myLine = myPane.getText(0, 80);`
remove()	Removes text in a certain area of the component. The method takes two integer arguments that relate to the beginning and end of the area to remove.	`doc.remove(0, 255));`
getLength()	Returns the length of the text in the component.	`int len = myDocument.getLength();`
insertString()	Appends text to an integer location in the text component.	`insertString(doc.getLength(), title[j] + "\t", textPane.getStyle("bold"));`

Coding the addTextToTextPane() Method

Figure 7-24 displays the code for the addTextToTextPane() method. First, line 163 creates a Document, named doc, which uses the previously declared class level JTextPane. Then, the previous text is removed in line 167. The **insertString() method** in line 170 appends the headings, TITLE, STUDIO, and YEAR, using the large style created earlier.

```
160        //method to add new text to the JTextPane
161        public JTextPane addTextToTextPane()
162        {
163            Document doc = textPane.getDocument();
164            try
165            {
166                //clear previous text
167                doc.remove(0, doc.getLength());
168
169                //insert title
170                doc.insertString(0,"TITLE\tSTUDIO\tYEAR\n",textPane.getStyle("large"));
171
172                //insert detail
173                for (int j = 0; j<title.length; j++)
174                {
175                    doc.insertString(doc.getLength(), title[j] + "\t",
                            textPane.getStyle("bold"));
176                    doc.insertString(doc.getLength(), studio[j] + "\t", textPane.getStyle(
                            "italic"));
177                    doc.insertString(doc.getLength(), year[j] + "\n",
                            textPane.getStyle("regular"));
178                }
179            }
180            catch(BadLocationException ble)
181            {
182                System.err.println("Couldn't insert text.");
183            }
184
185            return textPane;
186        }
187
```

FIGURE 7-24

Finally, a loop (lines 173 through 178) goes through the arrays and inserts each member. The **getLength() method** notifies the Document class where to append. The getStyle() method specifies the font style.

Because errors might occur when removing and inserting new text in the JTextPane, the code is included in a try block. If the remove(), insertString(), or getLength() methods generate an error, it is caught, and a System error message is generated by line 182.

The following step enters code for the addTextToTextPane() method.

To Code the addTextToTextPane() Method

1. Enter the code shown in Figure 7-24 on the previous page.

TextPad displays the code for the addTextToTextPane() method (Figure 7-25).

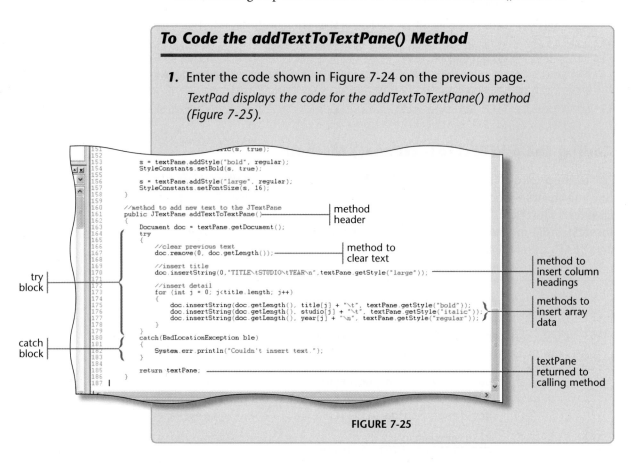

FIGURE 7-25

The addTextToTextPane() returns a new, refurbished JTextPane in line 185. The returned object is used locally in the createContentPane() method (line 113 in Figure 7-19 on page 453).

The actionPerformed() Event

Recall that the actionPerformed() event specifies what will happen when users click various components in the interface. Two methods typically are used to determine what object was clicked. The getActionCommand() returns the String previously assigned to a component, and the **getSource() method** returns the clicked object itself.

getActionCommand() versus getSource()
The getActionCommand() method is preferred over the getSource() method for objects that can have multiple states, such as menus and buttons.

Coding the actionPerformed() Method

In the Classics on DVD program, several objects may be clicked. Previously, action Strings were assigned to each of the menu commands. Besides the menu commands, a user also can click the JComboBox. On any of those occasions, the program should perform the correct operation.

Figure 7-26 displays the code for the actionPerformed() event.

```
188    //event to process user clicks
189    public void actionPerformed(ActionEvent e)
190    {
191        String arg = e.getActionCommand();
192
193        //user clicks the sort by combo box
194        if (e.getSource() == fieldCombo)
195        {
196            switch(fieldCombo.getSelectedIndex())
197            {
198                case 0:
199                    sort(title);
200                    break;
201                case 1:
202                    sort(studio);
203                    break;
204                case 2:
205                    sort(year);
206                    break;
207            }
208        }
209
210        //user clicks Exit on the File menu
211        if (arg == "Exit")
212            System.exit(0);
213
214        //user clicks Insert New DVD on the Edit menu
215        if (arg == "Insert")
216        {
217            //accept new data
218            String newTitle = JOptionPane.showInputDialog(null,
                   "Please enter the new movie's title");
219            String newStudio = JOptionPane.showInputDialog(null,
                   "Please enter the studio for " + newTitle);
220            String newYear = JOptionPane.showInputDialog(null,
                   "Please enter the year for " + newTitle);
221
222            //enlarge arrays
223            title = enlargeArray(title);
224            studio = enlargeArray(studio);
225            year = enlargeArray(year);
226
227            //add new data to arrays
228            title[title.length-1] = newTitle;
229            studio[studio.length-1] = newStudio;
230            year[year.length-1] = newYear;
231
```

FIGURE 7-26

(continued)

```
              //call sort method
232           sort(title);
233           fieldCombo.setSelectedIndex(0);
234        }
235
236     //user clicks Title on the Search submenu
237     if (arg == "title")
238         search(arg, title);
239
240     //user clicks Studio on the Search submenu
241     if (arg == "studio")
242         search(arg, studio);
243
244     //user clicks Year on the Search submenu
245     if (arg == "year")
246         search(arg, year);
247   }
248
249
```

FIGURE 7-26 (*continued*)

In line 191, the Action Event is returned to a String variable named arg, as in previous chapters. The variable, arg, then can reference any of the menu commands.

In line 194, the source of the click first is compared with the JComboBox named fieldCombo. If fieldCombo is the object that the user clicked, the index number of the clicked item in the list becomes the integer for the switch statement. If the index is 0, the user clicked Title. If it is 1, the user clicked Studio, and so on. With each click in the JComboBox, a sort() method is called, which will be coded later in the chapter.

Then, one at a time, the actionPerformed() method evaluates each of the menu options for possible clicks. For example, if the user clicks the Exit command, then the program exits in line 212. If the user clicks Insert, the JOptionPane dialog boxes are displayed to collect the new information in lines 218, 219, and 220.

Arrays are not dynamically enlarged in Java; therefore, an enlargeArray() method will be coded later in the chapter to accept the old data and create a new array with additional elements. The new array is rewritten over the top of the old array in lines 223, 224, and 225. Next, the new data is added to each array (lines 228, 229, and 230); the new array is sent to the sort() method in line 233, and the JComboBox is reset in line 234.

If the user clicks any of the three commands on the Search submenu, the field name and array are sent to a method called search(), coded later in the chapter (lines 238 through 247).

The following step enters code for the actionPerformed() method.

To Code the actionPerformed() Method

1. Enter the code as shown in Figure 7-26 on pages 461 and 462.

TextPad displays the code for the actionPerformed() method (Figure 7-27).

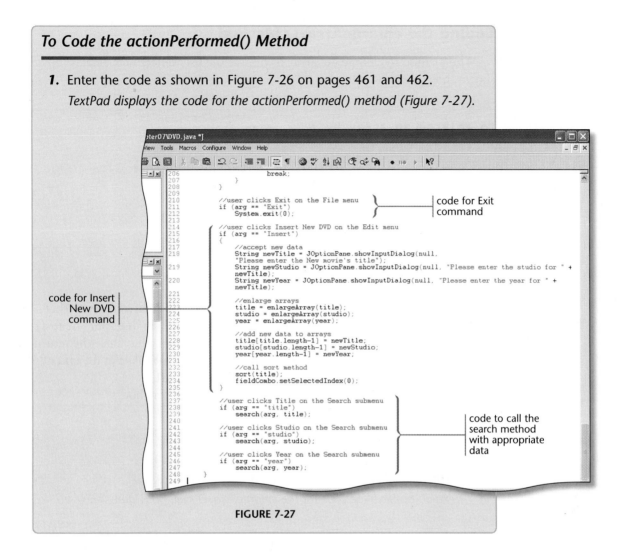

FIGURE 7-27

It can be difficult to know whether to use the getActionCommand() method or the getSource() method to ascertain what item was clicked. The getActionCommand() method is preferred for objects that may have multiple states, such as menus and buttons. For example, a Show/Hide button sometimes might display the word, Show, and other times it might display the word, Hide. The getSource() method would indicate that the button was clicked, but would not indicate the caption of the button at the time of the click. The getActionCommand() method, however, would return a String allowing a modal component like the Show/Hide button to specify its current state. The getSource() method would return the same source object in each case, but the getActionCommand() method would identify the intended action.

Tip

Coding All Possible Clicks

It is important to provide code for all possible user clicks in the interface. Use a storyboard when possible to account for each menu item and each button, making sure you have written an if statement for each in the actionPerformed() method.

Coding the enlargeArray() Method

The method to enlarge the array by one, as the user enters new data, is shown in Figure 7-28.

```
250     //method to enlarge an array by 1
251     public String[] enlargeArray(String[] currentArray)
252     {
253         String[] newArray = new String[currentArray.length + 1];
254         for (int i = 0; i<currentArray.length; i++)
255             newArray[i] = currentArray[i];
256         return newArray;
257     }
258
```

FIGURE 7-28

The method accepts the currentArray passed to it and returns a new String array. The new array is constructed to be one record longer in line 253. The for() loop beginning in line 254 populates the array with the old data. Once the return is executed, the actionPerformed() method inserts the newest data at the end of the array (lines 228 through 230 in Figure 7-26 on page 461).

The following step enters code for the enlargeArray() method.

To Code the enlargeArray() Method

1. Enter the code shown in Figure 7-28.

TextPad displays the code for the enlargeArray() method (Figure 7-29).

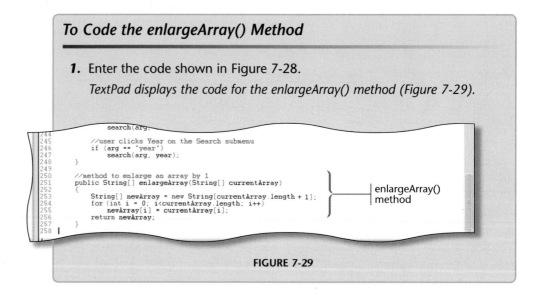

FIGURE 7-29

The methods needed to create the menu system — add components to the content pane, insert new data into arrays, and respond to clicks in the interface — now are complete. The next two sections in the chapter present the sort and search algorithms.

Sorting an Array

Sorting an array is the process of arranging the array's elements in ascending or descending order. Any time large amounts of data are maintained, the data needs to be arranged in a particular order for simplified searching or for logical retrieval. For example, banks sort transactions by check number or date, and telephone directories sort telephone numbers by last name and first name. Teachers sort exam grades from highest to lowest to look for patterns in learning.

Many different computer algorithms for sorting have been implemented over the years, and some have proven more efficient than others. A sorting algorithm looks at pairs of elements to determine if they are in order. If they are not in order, the pair must be interchanged. The algorithm traverses the array, checking pairs, until a complete pass yields no interchange. This is a tedious task by hand but one well-suited for Java. A popular method of sorting is the **bubble sort**, so named because when a pair of elements is examined, the interchanged value moves, or bubbles up, to the top of the array.

Another method of sorting is the **selection sort**, in which the entire array is searched for its lowest-value element. That element then is positioned at the beginning of the array. The process is repeated for the remaining elements; the lowest of that group then is placed in the second position. Each search examines one fewer element than the previous and continues to place elements in order until no elements remain.

An **insertion sort**, well-suited for small arrays, creates a new array and inserts the values in order. A **merge sort** takes two previously sorted arrays of the same data type and sorts them into one list.

Sorting the Classics on DVD Collection

Figure 7-30 displays the sort algorithm that will be used in the Classics on DVD program. The array to be sorted is passed as a temporary array to the sort() method in line 260. A loop then passes through the array, beginning in line 263, for the same number of times as there are elements in the array (length − 1).

```
259        //method to sort arrays
260        public void sort(String tempArray[])
261        {
262            // loop to control number of passes
263            for (int pass = 1; pass < tempArray.length; pass++)
264            {
265                for (int element = 0; element < tempArray.length - 1; element++)
266                    if (tempArray[element].compareTo(tempArray[element + 1])>0)
267                    {
268                        swap(title, element, element + 1);
269                        swap(studio, element, element + 1);
270                        swap(year, element, element + 1);
271                    }
272            }
273            addTextToTextPane();
274        }
275
276        //method to swap two elements of an array
277        public void swap(String swapArray[], int first, int second)
278        {
279            String hold;   //temporary holding area for swap
280            hold = swapArray[first];
281            swapArray[first] = swapArray[second];
282            swapArray[second] = hold;
283        }
284
```

FIGURE 7-30

The first element of the temporary array is compared with the second element in line 266. If an interchange or swap is necessary, the sort() method calls the swap() method with three arguments: the array, the first element, and the second element. The swap() method uses the variable, hold, to temporarily house the first element while the second element is assigned to the first element's location. The hold variable then is transferred into the second element's position (line 282), completing the swap.

As part of the sort routine, Java compares the current array member with the previous array member. Line 266 uses a method named compareTo(), which Java utilizes as a comparison operator. The **compareTo() method** returns a value less than zero when the String object inside its parenthetical argument is less than the given string; a value of zero when the strings are equal; and a value greater than zero when the String object is greater than the given string. It is the comparison operator's return value that indicates whether the two names, and their corresponding fields, should be swapped. Line 266 compares two elements of the array. If compareTo() returns a value greater than zero, then a swap should be made.

The following step enters code for the sort() and swap() methods.

> ### To Code the sort() and swap() Methods
>
> **1.** Enter the code shown in Figure 7-30 on the previous page.
>
> TextPad displays the code for the sort() and swap() methods (Figure 7-31).

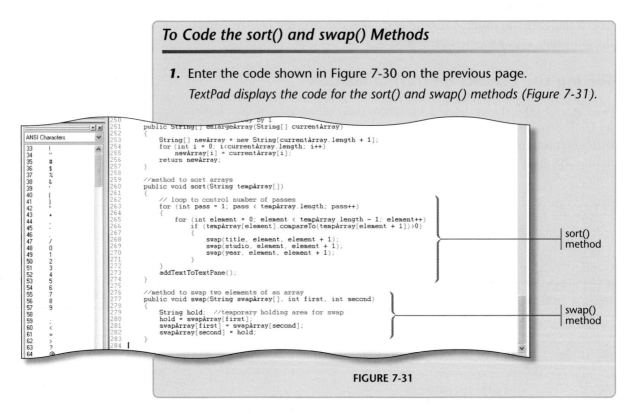

```
250
251    public String[] enlargeArray(String[] currentArray)
252    {
253        String[] newArray = new String[currentArray.length + 1];
254        for (int i = 0; i<currentArray.length; i++)
255            newArray[i] = currentArray[i];
256        return newArray;
257    }
258
259    //method to sort arrays
260    public void sort(String tempArray[])
261    {
262        // loop to control number of passes
263        for (int pass = 1; pass < tempArray.length; pass++)
264        {
265            for (int element = 0; element < tempArray.length - 1; element++)
266                if (tempArray[element].compareTo(tempArray[element + 1])>0)
267                {
268                    swap(title, element, element + 1);
269                    swap(studio, element, element + 1);
270                    swap(year, element, element + 1);
271                }
272        }
273        addTextToTextPane();
274    }
275
276    //method to swap two elements of an array
277    public void swap(String swapArray[], int first, int second)
278    {
279        String hold;   //temporary holding area for swap
280        hold = swapArray[first];
281        swapArray[first] = swapArray[second];
282        swapArray[second] = hold;
283    }
284
```

sort() method

swap() method

FIGURE 7-31

Searching an Array

Searching an array involves accepting a search argument from the user and then comparing it with elements in the array. You learned that if an array is short, performing a linear search — or looking through the list one by one — might be appropriate. A linear search is necessary when the data is not in order. Figure 7-32 displays a flowchart for a linear search.

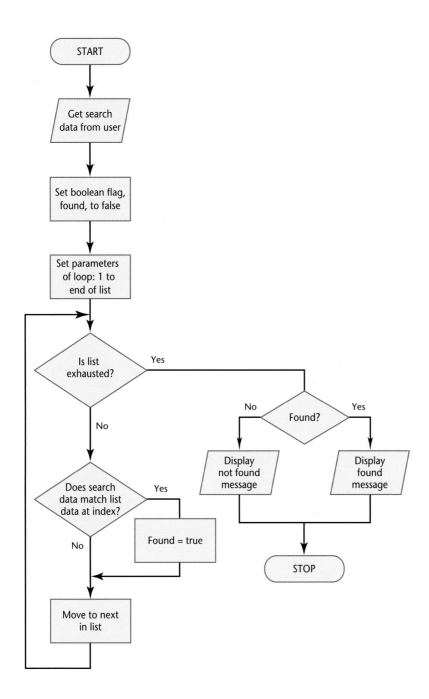

FIGURE 7-32

A linear search may be inefficient, however, for large amounts of data. For example, if the array had 10,000 unordered members, the linear search may have to look at 9,999 items before finding the desired element. A **binary search**, suited for large arrays of sorted data, is more efficient because it reduces the number of times the program must compare search data with stored data. A binary search is similar to the children's game of High-Low. A player might be asked to think of a number between 1 and 100. Most players would respond with the answer, 50, at which time they would be told to guess higher or lower. The process repeats as the player tries to narrow the guesses down to the right number.

In the case of an array, the range is equal to the highest and lowest number possible: the length of the array and zero. Then, the "guess," or search data, is compared with the middle of that range. If the search data is lower than the middle element in the array, the middle element becomes the new high for future guesses. Alternately, if the search data is higher than the middle element in the array, the middle element becomes the new low. Guesses continue to reduce the array to be searched by one-half until the number is found. Figure 7-33 displays a flowchart for a binary search.

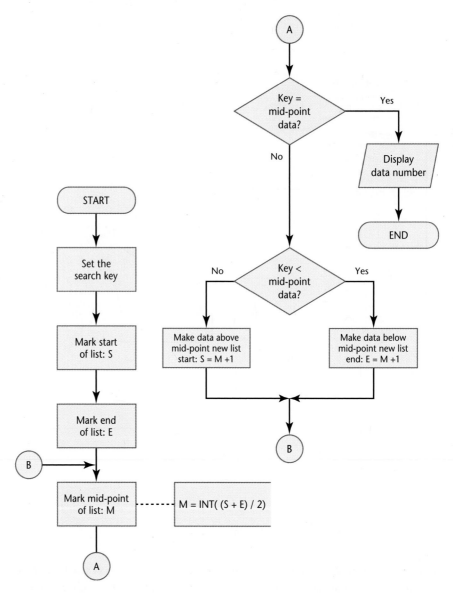

FIGURE 7-33

Searching for a DVD

The search() method is shown in Figure 7-34. For this particular prototype, it is a linear search. Recall that the actionPerformed() method sent the search() method two pieces of information: the search field and the array to search. The first task of the search() method, in lines 289 through 293, is to clear the JTextPane and display the headings as it did in the addTextToTextPane() method.

```
285     public void search(String searchField, String searchArray[])
286     {
287         try
288         {
289             Document doc = textPane.getDocument(); //assign text to document object
290             doc.remove(0,doc.getLength()); //clear previous text
291
292             //display column titles
293             doc.insertString(0,"TITLE\tSTUDIO\tYEAR\n",textPane.getStyle("large"));
294
295             //prompt user for search data
296             String search = JOptionPane.showInputDialog(null, "Please enter the "+
                searchField);
297             boolean found = false;
298
299             //search arrays
300             for (int i = 0; i<title.length; i++)
301             {
302                 if (search.compareTo(searchArray[i])==0)
303                 {
304                     doc.insertString(doc.getLength(), title[i] + "\t",
                        textPane.getStyle("bold"));
305                     doc.insertString(doc.getLength(), studio[i]
                        +"\t", textPane.getStyle("italic"));
306                     doc.insertString(doc.getLength(), year[i] + "\n",
                        textPane.getStyle("regular"));
307                     found = true;
308                 }
309             }
310             if (found == false)
311             {
312                 JOptionPane.showMessageDialog(null, "Your search produced no results.",
                    "No results found",JOptionPane.INFORMATION_MESSAGE);
313                 sort(title);
314             }
315         }
316         catch(BadLocationException ble)
317         {
318             System.err.println("Couldn't insert text.");
319         }
320     }
321
```

FIGURE 7-34

Line 296 displays a JOptionPane input dialog box, which asks the user to enter the search argument for the passed search field. A boolean flag named found is set to false. The for() loop that begins in line 300 continues through the entire array. Line 302 uses the compareTo() method to compare the search data with the array member. If the method returns a 0, a match is found and inserted in the Document, the flag is set to true (line 307), and the for() loop continues evaluating the remaining elements in the array.

If the flag is not set to true, then a match was not found. Line 312 then displays a message dialog box, and the data displays sorted again, by title, in line 313. The code involved in inserting new information in the JTextPane Document is placed inside a try block, as it was in the addTextToTextPane() method.

The following step enters code for the search() method.

To Code the search() Method

1. Enter the code from Figure 7-34 on the previous page.

TextPad displays the code for the search() method (Figure 7-35). Your lines may wrap differently.

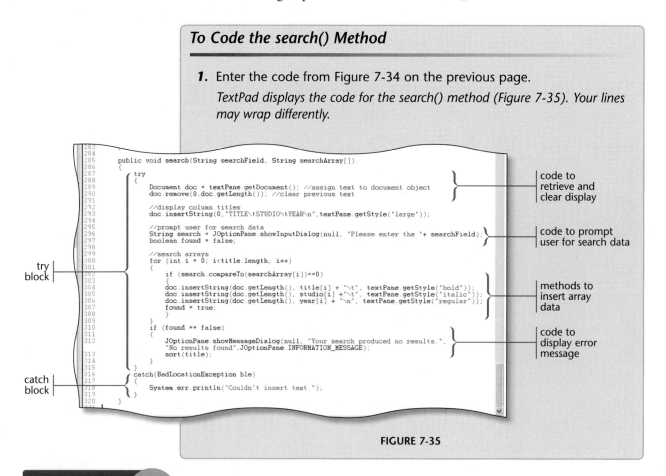

```
283
284
285    public void search(String searchField, String searchArray[])
286    {
287        try
288        {
289            Document doc = textPane.getDocument(); //assign text to document object          code to
290            doc.remove(0,doc.getLength()); //clear previous text                              retrieve and
291                                                                                              clear display
292            //display column titles
293            doc.insertString(0, "TITLE\tSTUDIO\tYEAR\n",textPane.getStyle("large"));
294
295            //prompt user for search data
296            String search = JOptionPane.showInputDialog(null, "Please enter the "+ searchField);   code to prompt
297            boolean found = false;                                                                  user for search data
298
299            //search arrays
300            for (int i = 0; i<title.length; i++)
301            {
302                if (search.compareTo(searchArray[i])==0)
303                {
304                    doc.insertString(doc.getLength(), title[i] + "\t", textPane.getStyle("bold"));      methods to
305                    doc.insertString(doc.getLength(), studio[i] +"\t", textPane.getStyle("italic"));    insert array
306                    doc.insertString(doc.getLength(), year[i] + "\n", textPane.getStyle("regular"));    data
307                    found = true;
308                }
309            }
310            if (found == false)
311            {
312                JOptionPane.showMessageDialog(null, "Your search produced no results.",                 code to
                   "No results found",JOptionPane.INFORMATION_MESSAGE);                                  display error
313                sort(title);                                                                             message
314            }
315        }
316    }
317    catch(BadLocationException ble)
318    {
319        System.err.println("Couldn't insert text.");
320    }
     }
```

try block
catch block

FIGURE 7-35

JAVA UPDATE **Java 2 v5.0**

If no look and feel is specified in a Java 5.0 program, the compiler will assign the Ocean look and feel. New to J2SE 5.0, the Ocean look and feel incorporates a more modern looking icon within dialog boxes, a more colorful Java icon in applet title bars, and dialog box buttons that display a light colored bar or wave pattern behind their text.

Look and Feel

Earlier you learned that the look and feel methods give any program using Swing components a choice of how the windows, title bars, and components will appear. For example, the same program can use either the Java look and feel or the Windows look and feel. The LookandFeelDecorated() method displays a different, more modern window than those generated by Windows or UNIX. Figure 7-36 displays a LookandFeelDecorated window. Notice that the title bar now has a pattern to it. The clip controls — minimize, maximize, and close — display with different buttons and without tool tips. You can see that the default background color is gray rather than white, and the Menu options are displayed more like buttons than typical menu commands. Java refers to these changes as **window decorations**. Developers can design their own window decorations and save them as a look and feel object.

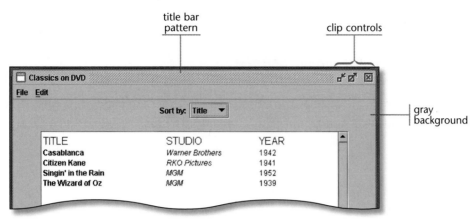

FIGURE 7-36

The main() Method

The look and feel will be set in the main() method, as shown in Figure 7-37. In line 325, the **setDefaultLookAndFeelDecorated() method** specifies that newly created JFrames should have their window decorations (such as borders, clip controls, and title bars) provided by the current look and feel of the user's system. The code in Figure 7-37 constructs an instance of the DVD object and sets its attributes. Instead of overriding the windowClosing() method as in previous chapters, the setDefaultCloseOperation() method will be used. The **setDefaultCloseOperation() method**, which is a Swing method that applies to JFrame components, sets the operation that executes by default when the user initiates a close on the JFrame. Line 328 calls the createMenuBar() method, which is wrapped inside Java's setJMenuBar() method. In a similar fashion, line 329 creates the content pane by calling the createContentPane() method wrapped inside Java's **setContentPane() method**.

```
322     //main method executes at run time
323     public static void main(String args[])
324     {
325         JFrame.setDefaultLookAndFeelDecorated(true);
326         DVD f = new DVD();
327         f.setDefaultCloseOperation(JFrame.EXIT_ON_CLOSE);
328         f.setJMenuBar(f.createMenuBar());
329         f.setContentPane(f.createContentPane());
330         f.setSize(600,375);
331         f.setVisible(true);
332     }
333 }
```

FIGURE 7-37

Tip

Freeing System Resources
When using multiple windows in an application, dispose of windows you no longer need to free system resources without exiting the program. Hidden windows are appropriate for totals or summaries that may display repeatedly. Disable Close buttons sparingly and only as a temporary measure while the program demands further user input.

The following step enters code for the main() method.

To Code the main() Method

1. Enter the code as shown in Figure 7-37 on the previous page.
TextPad displays the code for the main() method (Figure 7-38).

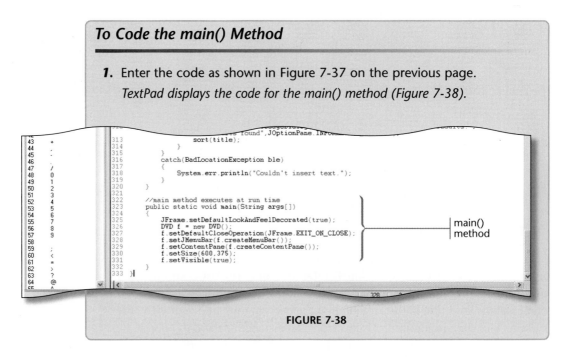

```
313        sort(title);
314        }
315    }
316    catch(BadLocationException ble)
317    {
318        System.err.println("Couldn't insert text.");
319    }
320 }
321
322 //main method executes at run time
323 public static void main(String args[])
324 {
325     JFrame.setDefaultLookAndFeelDecorated(true);
326     DVD f = new DVD();
327     f.setDefaultCloseOperation(JFrame.EXIT_ON_CLOSE);
328     f.setJMenuBar(f.createMenuBar());
329     f.setContentPane(f.createContentPane());
330     f.setSize(600,375);
331     f.setVisible(true);
332 }
333 }
```

main()
method

FIGURE 7-38

Other constants available with the setDefaultCloseOperation()
method besides EXIT_ON_CLOSE include DO_NOTHING_ON_CLOSE,
DISPOSE_ON_CLOSE, and HIDE_ON_CLOSE. When using multiple windows
in an application, those no longer needed should be disposed of so that they free
system resources without exiting the program. Hidden windows are appropriate
for totals or summaries that display repeatedly, interspersed with other windows.
The DO_NOTHING_ON_CLOSE should be used sparingly and only as a temporary state when the program demands further interaction by the user before
closing the window.

Compiling the Prototype

Compiling the program will test for specific Java errors associated with syntax
and construction. Once the program is error free, it can be tested. Each menu
option and each item in the drop-down list should be tested.
The following step shows how to compile the Classics on DVD prototype.

OTHER WAYS

1. Press CTRL+1
2. To compile at
   command prompt,
   type `javac DVD.java`

To Compile the Classics on DVD Prototype

1. Click Tools on the menu bar, and then click Compile Java.
The program compiles.

If you have compilation errors, refer to the various figures in this chapter to double-check your code. Fix the errors and then recompile.

Testing the Prototype

It now is time to test the program. The first test looks at the sort capabilities of the Classics on DVD program by clicking the JComboBox and choosing both studio and year. The next test adds a new DVD movie title. The last test searches for a specific title, studio, or year.

Testing the Sort Capabilities

The following steps test the sort() method.

To Test the sort() Method

1. Click Tools on the menu bar and then click Run Java Application.

The program starts, and the Classics on DVD window opens (Figure 7-39).

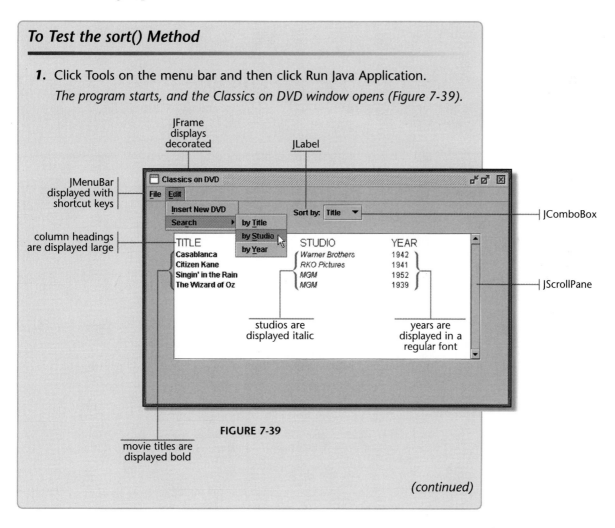

FIGURE 7-39

(continued)

2. In the Classics on DVD window, click the JComboBox.

Java displays the JComboBox choices (Figure 7-40). The JComboBox displays the tool tip.

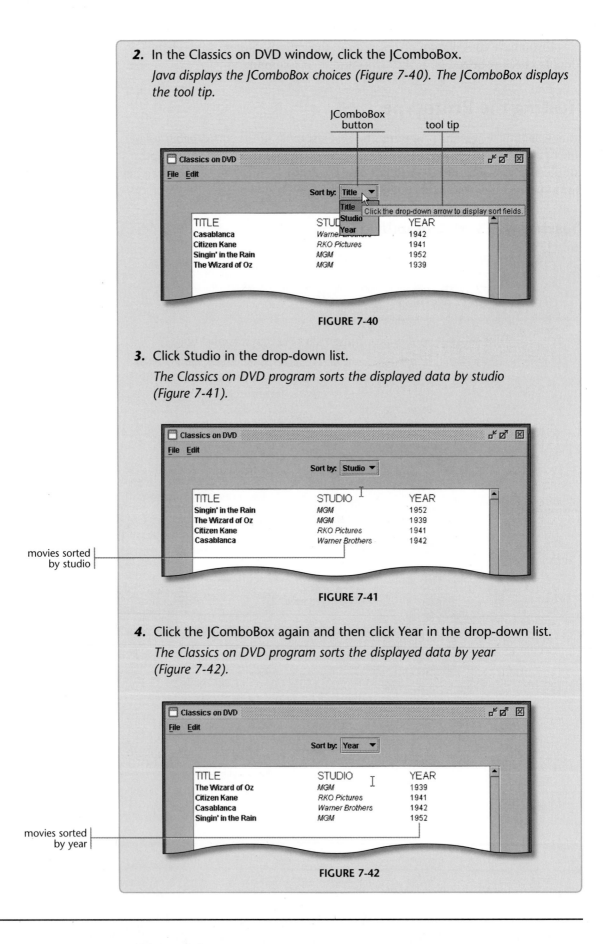

FIGURE 7-40

3. Click Studio in the drop-down list.

The Classics on DVD program sorts the displayed data by studio (Figure 7-41).

FIGURE 7-41

4. Click the JComboBox again and then click Year in the drop-down list.

The Classics on DVD program sorts the displayed data by year (Figure 7-42).

FIGURE 7-42

The sort() method will be tested again when new information is inserted.

Testing the Addition of a DVD Title

The following steps test the Insert New DVD command by inserting a new DVD title, studio, and year.

To Test the Insert New DVD Command

1. If necessary, run the program again by clicking Run Java Application on the Tools menu. Click Edit on the menu bar and then click Insert New DVD.

The program displays the first of three input dialog boxes (Figure 7-43).

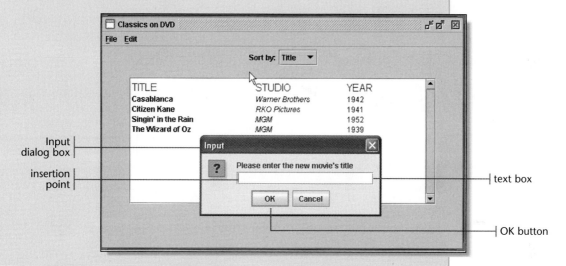

FIGURE 7-43

2. Type Dr. Strangelove in the text box and then click the OK button. When the input dialog box asking for the studio is displayed, type Columbia and then click the OK button. When the input dialog box asking for the year is displayed, type 1964 and then click the OK button.

The program automatically displays the new data sorted by title in the list (Figure 7-44).

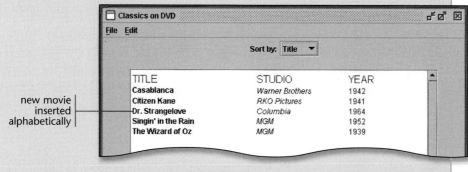

FIGURE 7-44

Testing the Search Capabilities

The following steps show how to test the search() method by searching the arrays for a specific title, studio, and year in order to verify that all three searches work properly.

To Test the search() Method

1. Click Edit on the menu bar and then point to Search.

The program displays three Search options on the Search submenu (Figure 7-45).

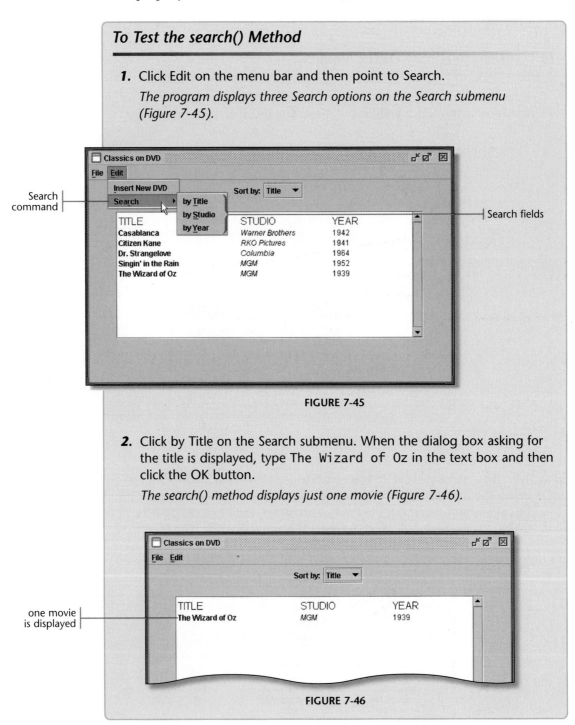

FIGURE 7-45

2. Click by Title on the Search submenu. When the dialog box asking for the title is displayed, type The Wizard of Oz in the text box and then click the OK button.

The search() method displays just one movie (Figure 7-46).

FIGURE 7-46

3. Click Edit on the menu bar, point to Search, and then click by Studio on the Search submenu. When the dialog box is displayed, type MGM in the text box and then click the OK button.

The search() method returns two movies (Figure 7-47).

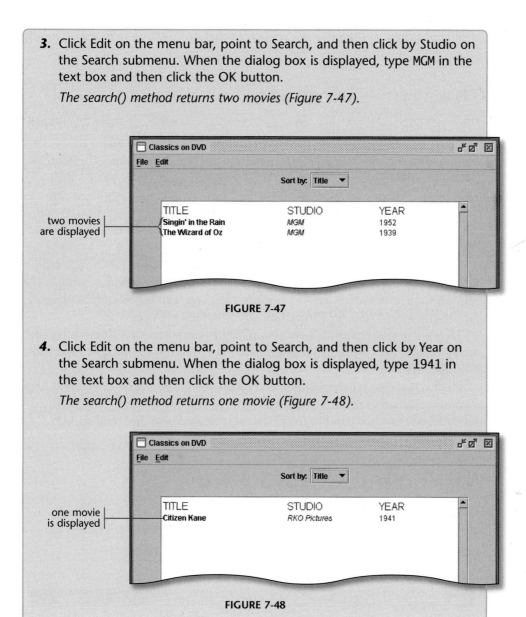

two movies are displayed

FIGURE 7-47

4. Click Edit on the menu bar, point to Search, and then click by Year on the Search submenu. When the dialog box is displayed, type 1941 in the text box and then click the OK button.

The search() method returns one movie (Figure 7-48).

one movie is displayed

FIGURE 7-48

The final step is to exit the program by accessing the File menu with the shortcut key.

To Exit the Program Using a Shortcut Key

1. Press ALT+F.

The File menu is displayed. The shortcut key for the Exit command is the letter, x, which is displayed underlined on the File menu.

2. Press ALT+X.

The program closes.

The prototype for the Classics on DVD program has been fully tested. It now is ready to send to the Internet-based collectors club.

Chapter Summary

In this chapter, you learned to use Swing components. You began with a top-level container, named JFrame, and used a content pane to place the Swing components in the interface. You learned how methods associated with JPanels, JLabels, JTextPanes, JScrollPanes, and JComboBoxes are used to create a drop-down list as well as formatted, scrollable text components in the content pane.

To assist the user, this program created a JMenu system, complete with sub-menus and shortcut keys. It used the keyword, super, to place a title in the title bar of the GUI interface.

You learned how Java supports its Java Foundation Classes (JFC) with look and feel functionality, as well as how to use window decorations and Swing methods to give a modern feel to your interface. You learned about tabs, styles, and the Document class for formatting a JTextPane.

To assist the user of the Classics on DVD program, you added searching and sorting capabilities. You discovered when a linear search is required and learned about the different sorting algorithms.

Finally, this chapter showed how to test the JComboBox and each menu item by running the program and inserting a new movie. The program implemented and enlarged the three parallel arrays that you created, searched, and sorted based on given fields and array index numbers.

What You Should Know

Having completed this chapter, you should now be able to perform the tasks shown in Table 7-11.

Table 7-11   What You Should Know

TASK NUMBER	TASK	PAGE
1	Start TextPad and Save a TextPad Document	438
2	Extend JFrame in the Class Header	442
3	Construct the Swing Components	442
4	Declare and Assign Arrays	446
5	Code the DVD() Constructor Method	447
6	Code the createMenuBar() Method	452
7	Code the createContentPane() Method	455
8	Code the setTabsAndStyles() Method	458
9	Code the addTextToTextPane() Method	460
10	Code the actionPerformed() Method	463
11	Code the enlargeArray() Method	464

Table 7-11 *What You Should Know (continued)*

TASK NUMBER	TASK	PAGE
12	Code the sort() and swap() Methods	466
13	Code the search() Method	470
14	Code the main() Method	472
15	Compile the Classics on DVD Prototype	472
16	Test the sort() Method	473
17	Test the Insert New DVD Command	475
18	Test the search() Method	476
19	Exit the Program Using a Shortcut Key	477

Key Terms

access key *(435)*

addStyle() method *(457)*

atomic components *(441)*

AttributeSet class *(456)*

binary search *(467)*

bubble sort *(465)*

combo box *(443)*

compareTo() method *(466)*

Container *(453)*

content pane *(441)*

Dimension *(454)*

Document class *(458)*

editable combo box *(443)*

getContentPane() method *(441)*

getLength() method *(460)*

getSource() method *(460)*

heavyweight *(439)*

insertion sort *(465)*

insertString() method *(459)*

JComboBox *(443)*

JFC *(439)*

JLabel *(443)*

JScrollPane *(454)*

JTextPane *(444)*

KeyEvent class *(451)*

lightweight *(439)*

linear search *(437)*

look and feel methods *(439)*

menu storyboard *(435)*

merge sort *(465)*

mnemonic *(451)*

native *(439)*

parallel *(436)*

root container *(441)*

search *(435)*

selection sort *(465)*

sequential search *(437)*

setContentPane() method *(471)*

setDefaultCloseOperation() method *(471)*

setDefaultLookAndFeelDecorated() method *(471)*

setDisplayedMnemonicIndex() method *(451)*

setFontFamily() method *(457)*

setFontSize() method *(457)*

setJMenuBar() method *(448)*

setMnemonic() method *(451)*

setParagraphAttributes() method *(444)*

setToolTipText() method *(454)*

shortcut key *(435)*

sort *(435)*

sorting *(464)*

Style *(456)*

StyleConstants *(457)*

StyleContext *(456)*

super *(447)*

TabStop class *(456)*

TabSet class *(456)*

tool tip *(454)*

top-level container *(441)*

uneditable combo box *(443)*

viewport *(454)*

VK keycode *(451)*

window decorations *(470)*

Homework Assignments

1 Label the Figure

Identify the elements shown in Figure 7-49.

1. _____
2. _____
3. _____
4. _____
5. _____

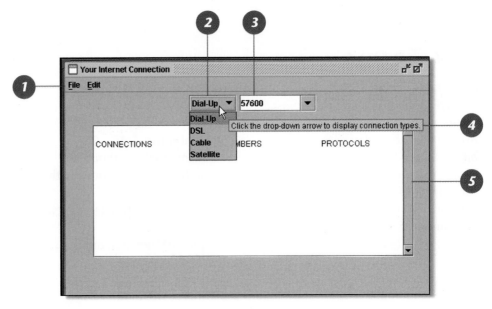

FIGURE 7-49

2 Identify Code

On the lines below, write the line number from a *single line* of code in Figure 7-50 illustrating each of the following:

1. Swing component constructor _____
2. use of a constant _____
3. tab column assignment _____
4. shortcut key assignment _____
5. font family specification _____
6. array declaration _____
7. method header _____
8. creation of a tool tip _____
9. deleting text in a Document object _____
10. accessing a superclass _____

```
1    JComboBox fieldCombo = new JComboBox();
2    JScrollPane scrollPane = new JScrollPane();
3    JTextPane textPane = new JTextPane();
4    String title[] = {"Casablanca", "Citizen Kane", "Singin' in the Rain", "The Wizard of
     Oz"};
5
6    public DVD()
7    {
8        super("Classics on DVD");
9    }
10
11   public JMenuBar createMenuBar()
12   {
13       JMenuBar mnuBar = new JMenuBar();
14       setJMenuBar(mnuBar);
15       JMenu mnuFile =new JMenu("File", true);
16           mnuFile.setDisplayedMnemonicIndex(0);
17           mnuBar.add(mnuFile);
18       return mnuBar;
19   }
20
21   public Container createContentPane()
22   {
23       fieldCombo.addItem("Title");
24       fieldCombo.addItem("Studio");
25       fieldCombo.setToolTipText("Click the drop-down arrow to display sort fields.");
26       JPanel centerPanel = new JPanel();
27           setTabsAndStyles(textPane);
28           JTextPane internalTextPane = addTextToTextPane();
29           JScrollPane paneScrollPane = new JScrollPane(internalTextPane);
30           centerPanel.add(paneScrollPane);
31       Container c = getContentPane();
32           c.setLayout(new BorderLayout(10,10));
33           c.add(centerPanel,BorderLayout.CENTER);
34       return c;
35   }
36
37   protected void setTabsAndStyles(JTextPane textPane)
38   {
39       TabStop tab = new TabStop(200, TabStop.ALIGN_LEFT, TabStop.LEAD_NONE);
40       TabSet tabset = new TabSet(tab);
41       Style fontStyle =
42           StyleContext.getDefaultStyleContext().getStyle(StyleContext.DEFAULT_STYLE);
43       StyleConstants.setFontFamily(fontStyle, "SansSerif");
44
45   }
46
47   public JTextPane addTextToTextPane()
48   {
49       Document doc = textPane.getDocument();
50       try
51       {
52           doc.remove(0,doc.getLength());
53           doc.insertString(0,"TITLE\tSTUDIO\tYEAR\n",textPane.getStyle("large"));
54       }
55       catch(BadLocationException ble)
56       {
57       }
58       return textPane;
59   }
60
61   public static void main(String args[])
62   {
63       DVD f = new DVD();
64       f.setDefaultCloseOperation(JFrame.EXIT_ON_CLOSE);
65       f.setJMenuBar(f.createMenuBar());
66       f.setContentPane f.createContentPane());
67       f.setSize(600,375);
68       f.setVisible(true);
69   }
```

FIGURE 7-50

3 Understanding Error Messages

Using TextPad, open the file named Connections from the Chapter07 folder of the Data Disk that accompanies this book. Use the Replace command on the Search menu to replace all occurrences of the word, Connections, with the word, Modems. Save the file as a Java source code file with the file name Modems. Then, compile the program. When TextPad displays errors in the Command Results window, double-click the first line of the first error message to return to that line in the TextPad coding window. Fix the error. If directed by your instructor, insert a comment line in your code identifying what caused the error. Compile again and repeat the process until the program is error free. Submit your source code to your instructor electronically or on paper as directed.

4 Using the Java API and Java Tutorials

The Java API is a good tool to look up information about a class with which you may be unfamiliar or to check the syntax of commands and methods you wish to use in your programs. While connected to the Internet, start a browser, type `http://java.sun.com/j2se/1.5.0/docs/api/` in the Address text box, and then press the ENTER key to view the Java API Specification on the Sun Web site. (Or, if you downloaded the documentation from the CD-ROM that accompanies this book, navigate to the installed version of the Java SDK on your system. Open the index.html file in the docs/api folder.)

With the Java API Specification open in a browser window, perform the following steps.

1. Click the NO FRAMES link and then click the Index link at the top of the page. When the Index is displayed, click the J link. Scroll downward and then click the JTextPane link to display the Web page shown in Figure 7-51.

2. Review the hierarchy of the JTextPane and then scroll down and read the description of the JTextPane.

3. If your system is connected to the Web, click the Using Text Components link to the tutorial.

4. When the tutorial is displayed, read the information. Scroll down and click the link, example index.

5. Download the example, TextSamplerDemo.java, and open it in TextPad. Insert comments for the lines that contain Swing component references. Print a copy for your instructor.

6. Return to the API and use the Index to research the class definition for each Text component. Click the class or method definitions and report on what you have read, as directed by your instructor.

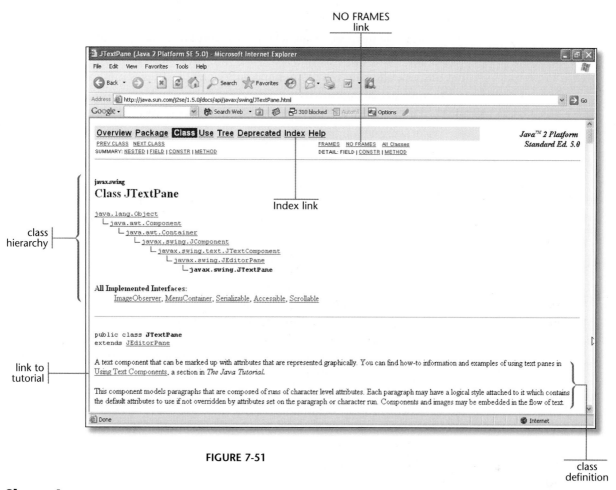

FIGURE 7-51

Short Answer

1. A(n) _____ is a generic term for the process that the computer goes through to ascertain the presence of a specific piece of data in a list or storage location.

2. A(n) _____ is a generic term that refers to ways to organize data alphanumerically based on some criteria.

3. As the list of movies in the prototype is relatively short, performing a(n) _____ search, or _____ search–which means looking through the list one by one–might be appropriate.

4. List four features of the JFC.

5. List the hierarchy of Java Swing Containers from the top down. Give an example of each.

6. Describe the purpose of the content pane. Use examples to explain why the content pane is not constructed like other components. List reasons why you think J2SE version 5.0 allows programmers to omit direct references to the getContentPane() method.

7. What are the main differences between Swing JButtons and AWT Buttons?

8. Write the code to convert a JComboBox named myCombo into one that will accept user input as well as display a drop-down list.

(continued)

Short Answer *(continued)*

9. What is the purpose of the keyword, super? Give examples of how programmers use it.

10. Describe the hierarchy of menu components. List three methods related to menus that change attributes, and give an example of each.

11. Research other sort and search algorithms on the Web and in other books. Write several paragraphs describing the algorithm. If you find a sample program, print a copy of the source code.

Learn It Online

Start your browser and visit scsite.com/java3e/learn. Follow the instructions in the exercises below.

1. **Chapter Reinforcement TF, MC, and SA** Click the Chapter Reinforcement link below Chapter 7. Print and then answer the questions.

2. **Practice Test** Click the Practice Test link below Chapter 7. Answer each question, enter your first and last name at the bottom of the page, and then click the Grade Test button. When the graded practice test is displayed on your screen, click Print on the File menu to print a hard copy. Continue to take practice tests until you score 80% or better. Hand in a printout of the final practice test.

3. **Crossword Puzzle Challenge** Click the Crossword Puzzle Challenge link below Chapter 7. Read the instructions, and then enter your first and last name. Click the Play button. Complete the crossword puzzle. When you are finished, click the Submit button. When the crossword puzzle is redisplayed, click the Print button.

4. **Tips and Tricks** Click the Tips and Tricks link below Chapter 7. Click a topic that pertains to Chapter 7. Right-click the information and then click Print on the shortcut menu. Construct a brief example of what the information relates to in Java to confirm that you understand how to use the tip or trick. Hand in the example and printed information.

5. **Newsgroups** Click the Newsgroups link below Chapter 7. Click a topic that pertains to Chapter 7. Print three comments.

6. **Expanding Your Horizons** Click the Expanding Your Horizons link below Chapter 7. Click a topic that pertains to Chapter 7. Print the information. Construct a brief example of what the information relates to in Java to confirm that you understand the contents of the article. Hand in the example and printed information.

7. **Search Sleuth** Select three key terms from the Key Terms section of this chapter and then use the Google search engine at google.com (or any major search engine) to display and print two Web pages for each key term.

Editing Code

The code in Figure 7-52 sorts a temporary array in ascending order. Make the necessary changes so that the array can be sorted in descending order.

```
 1  for (int pass = 1; pass < tempArray.length; pass++)
 2  {
 3      for (int element = 0; element < tempArray.length - 1; element++)
 4          if (tempArray[element].compareTo(tempArray[element + 1])>0)
 5          {
 6              swap(title, element, element + 1);
 7              swap(studio, element, element + 1);
 8              swap(year, element, element + 1);
 9          }
10  }
```

FIGURE 7-52

Programming Assignments

1 Create a Bibliography

Write a program that accepts the following input data from a user: author, title of book, publisher, year, and number of pages. Display the data in a formatted text pane using a standard MLA- or AP-style bibliography entry. Include a font family, a style, and tabs in your solution.

2 Your Music

Create a Swing program with a Windows look and feel to display data about your favorite musical artists. Construct parallel arrays with data such as artist name, genre, greatest hit, and record label. Create an interface to display the data in a formatted JTextPane with scrolling capabilities. Create a menu structure that allows you to add new data to your arrays. Rather than using the JComboBox, create a Sort command on the menu with a submenu that displays the field names. Change the scrolling capabilities to include both horizontal and vertical scroll bars.

3 Creating JComboBoxes

Write a Swing program that uses a content pane to display components. Include JLabels and JTextFields for typical personal data entered by users in your city, such as first name, last name, city, state, and zip code. Use an uneditable JComboBox for the states, using an array of state names. *Hint:* Many Web sites offer state data. Use an editable JComboBox for zip codes. Include at least five local zip codes in the list.

4 Averaging Grades

Write a Swing program that declares an empty array of grades with a maximum length of 50. Implement a JOptionPane input box within a while loop to allow the user to enter the grades using a -1 as a sentinel value. After the grades are entered, a content pane should display the grades sorted from lowest to highest. Write a loop that goes through the array looking for elements that are greater than 0. Keep a running count of those elements and accumulate them into a grand total. Divide the grand total by the total number of grades entered to find an average. Display the average in the JTextPane, and use the DecimalFormat method to round the average.

5 Usability in the DVD Program

Add the following functionality to the DVD program created in this chapter. Make sure that each function works before proceeding to the next. Include as many functions as directed by your instructor.

a. When a user attempts to insert a new DVD, make the Cancel button that displays in the JOptionPane input box work properly. *Hint:* Chapter 4 describes the use of the null constant.

b. Test input data for a valid Year before adding it to the String array.

c. Give users a choice of fonts by inserting two more menu options on the Edit menu: one that says SansSerif and one that says Arial. Add functionality to the two items by using the setFontFamily() method.

d. Add a fourth array to the program with data about the director of the movie. You may need to increase the size of the content pane. Remember to add a new question to the Insert portion of the actionPerformed() method.

e. *Reminder:* The array must be sorted with each new entry.

6 Using Fonts

Write a Swing program to display the name of your school in a variety of fonts and sizes. The interface should include a JTextPane, a Font combo box, and a Font Size combo box. Use the insertString() method to display the name in the JTextPane. Use at least two different fonts and three different sizes in the respective combo boxes. When the program runs, choosing different items from the combo boxes should change the display.

7 Converting Code from AWT to Swing

Choose any Frame-based application that you have programmed before or one suggested by your instructor and convert all the components to Swing components. Remember to change the constructors, methods, and attributes. Create a content pane to hold your Swing atomic components and extend JFrame.

8 Using Tutorials

Go to the following Web site: http://java.sun.com/docs/books/tutorial/uiswing/components/components.html and work through the tutorial on Swing components. Download at least one example of code explained in the tutorial. Compile and run the code. Add comments to the code, and print a copy as directed by your instructor.

9 Using Ocean Look and Feel Java 2 .5.0

Open the DVD program you created in Chapter 7. Compile the program and run it. Look at the various components in the interface, such as the title bar, menus, drop-down boxes, and dialog boxes. Close the program and look at the code in TextPad. Line 325 sets the look and feel to the user's operating system. Comment out line 325 to cause the program to use the Ocean look and feel, which is the default for J2SE version 5.0. Recompile and run the program again. Make a table of all the components in the interface and describe the changes. Turn the table in to your instructor.

8

Writing Data to a Sequential Data File

Objectives

You will have
mastered the material in
this chapter when you can:

- Explain the use of volatile and nonvolatile
  data
- Set the Look and Feel using the UIManager class
- Customize a JFrame using the setResizable() and setLocation() methods
- Format dates using letter descriptors and the SimpleDataFormat class
- Concatenate a formatted date String onto a file name
- Understand the data hierarchy
- Differentiate between sequential and random access files
- Create a sequential file using Java's DataOutputStream
- Construct an instance of the DataOutputStream
- Describe user events and listener types
- Implement the showConfirmDialog() method
- Use write() methods to send data to a secondary storage device
- Verify the existence of a data file

Introduction

This chapter illustrates how a Java program accepts and writes data to a file on a secondary storage device, such as a disk. A **data file** is a collection of related facts organized in a systematic manner. Data files do not have to be electronic. A telephone book is an example of a data file that contains the names, addresses, and telephone numbers of individuals and businesses in a community. In this chapter, you will learn how to use Java to write data to a sequential data file. A **sequential data file**, or **sequential file**, is a file composed of fields of data stored one after another on a storage device. Each primitive data type has an associated **write()** **method** from the DataOutputStream class that programmers use to transfer data to a storage device.

Thus far, the programs discussed in this book have manipulated only volatile data. **Volatile data**, or electricity-dependent data, is stored in the computer's memory only while electricity is being supplied to the computer and the program is running. Once the computer is powered off, the data is erased. **Nonvolatile data** is stored and can be retrieved later.

Chapter Eight — Crandall Power and Light

This chapter provides an introduction to working with sequential data files by building a BillPayer program for the company Crandall Power and Light. The company wants to automate its payment-collection service by standardizing its user interface at all remote locations. The BillPayer program needs to accept payment information from users who pay their bills at remote locations, such as grocery stores and banks.

The BillPayer program should accept the following information from the user: account number, payment amount, first name, last name, address, city, state, and zip code. When the user clicks the Submit button, the program should verify that all fields are complete (non-blank) and, if the data is valid, write the fields to the sequential file. If a field is blank, a message box should display alerting the user of the incomplete field.

Figure 8-1 displays the data entry screen.

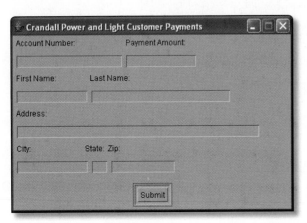

FIGURE 8-1

Program Development

The program development cycle for the Crandall Power and Light BillPayer program consists of tasks that correspond to the six development cycle phases, as shown in Table 8-1.

Analysis and Design

Figure 8-2 shows the requirements document that initiates the development cycle for the Crandall Power and Light BillPayer program. The requirements document specifies the reason for the request, lists the required inputs and outputs, and describes the sequence of data entry.

Table 8-1   BillPayer Program Development Tasks

	DEVELOPMENT PHASE	TASK(S)
1	Analyze the requirements	Analyze the Crandall Power and Light problem.
2	Design the solution	Design the user interface for the program, and organize how the data will be output to the storage device. Include an automatic date feature. Design the logic to solve the problem.
3	Validate the design	Confirm with the user that the design solves the problem in a satisfactory manner.
4	Implement the design	Translate the design into code. Include internal documentation (comments and remarks) within the code that explains the purpose of the code-statements.
5	Test the solution	Test the program. Find and correct any errors (debug) until it is error free. Use sample data to test both valid and invalid entries.
6	Document the solution	Print copies of the program code, and verify data output with a sample file.

REQUEST FOR NEW APPLICATION

Date submitted:	November 15, 2007
Submitted by:	Natani Rebeau Manager of Payment Services Crandall Power and Light
Purpose:	We want to standardize the interface that remote locations use to accept payments from our customers. All data is to be stored in a file for nightly uploading to the central server.
Application title:	BillPayer
Algorithms:	The interface should accept data for the following eight fields. • Account Number • Address • Payment Amount • City • First Name • State • Last Name • Zip The data needs to be verified for completeness before it is written. Clicking the Close button should generate an "Are you sure?" type of dialog box to guard against inadvertent closing before the end of the day. The name of the data file should include the system date to make the name unique.
Notes:	Use the Swing Motif Look and Feel. Make the interface appear the same size and in the same place each time the program is run. The user should not be able to resize the window.

Approvals

Approval status:	X	Approved
		Rejected
Approved by:	Gregg Saffell, IT manager	
Date:	November 19, 2007	
Assigned to:	J. Starks, Programmer	

FIGURE 8-2

PROBLEM ANALYSIS   A clear and easy interface needs to be designed to maximize user efficiency for the BillPayer program. The program should accept eight fields of information from the user and then write the data to a sequential data file. The program should test that all eight fields have been completed.

    The user must be notified by the program when the data has been submitted successfully, and the program should clear all eight fields for the next entry. Additionally, to prevent users from inadvertently closing the file without saving before the end of the day, the user must be notified when the entire file is ready to be saved permanently. Each day creates a new and different data file that will be uploaded external to the program; therefore, it is important that the file name include the date. The date will ensure that each file name is unique and cannot be overwritten. The program also should include appropriate prompts and messages, such as a confirmation dialog box that displays when the user attempts to exit the program.

DESIGN THE SOLUTION   Once the problem has been analyzed, the next step is to design the user interface and the logic to solve the problem. The program is designed in three stages. First, the window is created. Second, the components are added to the interface with appropriate labels, text boxes, and a button. Finally, functionality is added to the components so that users can enter data and store it in a sequential file. The BillPayer program has a single interface that can generate various dialog message boxes. Crandall Power and Light has chosen the Swing Motif Look and Feel for the interface. Because the rows vary in the number of elements they can hold and they each have different widths, each row of components will be stored in its own panel. A storyboard labeling the panels and layouts is shown in Figure 8-3. Using Java's BorderLayout manager, the JPanels, which contain JLabels and JTextFields, are placed in the Center area; the JPanel containing the Submit button is placed in the South area.

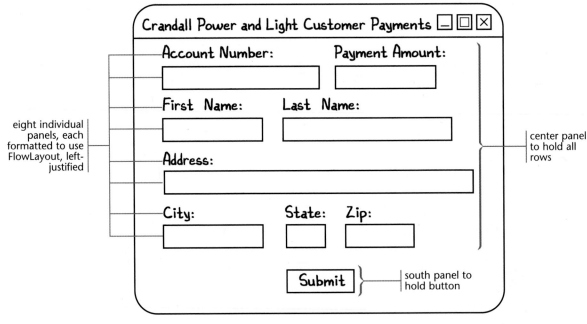

FIGURE 8-3

Five message and dialog boxes summarized in Table 8-2 will be needed. The solution should use one of the JOptionPane show() methods to specify the type of box that displays with the appropriate title, prompt, icon, and buttons.

Table 8-2   BillPayer Message and Dialog Boxes

	TYPE OF BOX	TITLE	PROMPT	ICON	BUTTONS
1	MessageDialog	Error	The UIManager could not set the Look and Feel for this application.	Information	OK
2	MessageDialog	Error	The program could not create a storage location. Please check the disk drive and then run the program again.	Information	OK
3	ConfirmDialog	File Submission	Are you sure you want to exit and submit the file?	Question	YES/NO
4	MessageDialog	Submission Successful	The payment information has been saved.	Information	OK
5	MessageDialog	Data Entry Error	You must complete all fields.	Warning	OK

Box 1 displays if the program generates an exception because it is unable to access the chosen Look and Feel. Box 2 displays if the program generates an exception because the disk is full or the program cannot access the secondary storage device. Box 3 displays when the user clicks the Close button on the title bar. Box 4 displays when the user clicks the Submit button. Finally, Box 5 displays if the user clicks the Submit button and one or more of the text boxes are empty.

PROGRAM DESIGN   Once the interface is designed, the next step is to design the logic to solve the problem and create the desired results. Figure 8-4 shows the pseudocode that represents the logic of the program.

After the interface components are constructed and added to the appropriate containers, the program should open the sequential file and display the interface. The user then has three possible choices: enter data into the text fields, click the Submit button, or click the Close button on the title bar. If the user clicks the Submit button with a field blank, the program should display an error message; otherwise, the data should be written to the sequential file, and a submission message should display. In order to maximize the speed of data entry, users will not be required to enter the payment amount using a certain format.

```
Create BillPayer application

        Construct components

        Construct window and set attributes

        Add components to window

        Try to open output file
        If storage is inaccessible
                Notify user
                Exit program

        Display interface

        When Close button is clicked
                Display confirmation display box
                If yes
                        Close program
                Else
                        Return to interface

        When Submit button is clicked
                If any field is empty
                        Display error message
                        Return to interface
                Else
                        Write data to disk
                        Display submission message
                        Clear fields
                        Return to interface

End BillPayer application
```

FIGURE 8-4

The payment data should be written in a generic format. Once the data is written, the program should clear the fields and display the BillPayer interface again. If the user clicks the Close button, a confirmation dialog box should display asking the user if he/she wants to exit the program.

Starting a New Java Program in TextPad

The following steps start TextPad and save the TextPad document using a Java file type.

To Start a New Java Program in TextPad

1. Start TextPad. If necessary, click View on the menu bar and then click Line Numbers to display line numbers.
2. Insert the Data Disk in drive A. Click File on the menu bar and then click Save As on the File menu.
3. When the Save As dialog box is displayed, type `BillPayer` in the File name text box. Click the Save as type box arrow and then click Java (*.java) in the Save as type list. Click the Save in box arrow and then click 3½ Floppy (A:) in the Save in list.
4. Double-click the Chapter08 folder or a location specified by your instructor.

   The file named BillPayer is saved as a Java source code file in the Chapter08 folder on the Data Disk in drive A (Figure 8-5). Your display may differ.

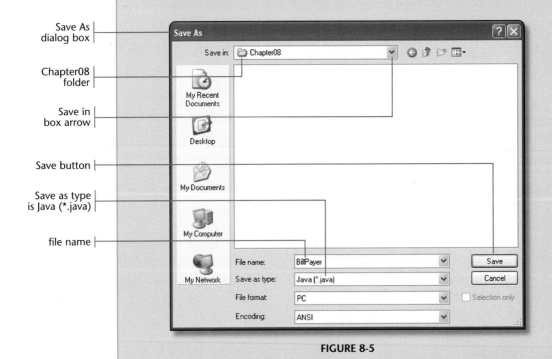

FIGURE 8-5

5. Click the Save button in the Save As dialog box.

Creating the Interface

The first step in creating a GUI-based program, such as the one for Crandall Power and Light, is to create the window. This step involves creating a class named BillPayer that constructs an instance of a JFrame and then sets properties for the Look and Feel in its main() method, along with other attributes. Because the program requires user input, the BillPayer class uses an ActionListener.

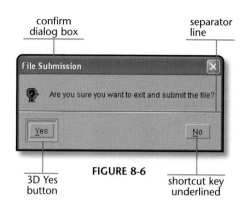

FIGURE 8-6

The Swing Motif Look and Feel

The requirements document specifies the Swing Motif Look and Feel for the BillPayer program. Recall that the LookAndFeel() methods offer any program that uses Swing a choice of how windows, title bars, and other components are displayed. The **Motif Look and Feel** displays a modern looking window, different from those normally generated by Windows or UNIX. Motif interfaces display a dark gray background color, and text boxes display as 3D, in the same dark gray color. When the component with focus is displayed, a thin, pink border is added around it. The text in the window is displayed in black. Window decorations in the title bar are displayed using the system default. Dialog boxes in the Motif Look and Feel display buttons below a separator line; the buttons are displayed using a special 3D look and automatically display shortcut key designations. Figure 8-6 displays a Motif confirm dialog box.

Motif is just one of several Look and Feel interfaces. Table 8-3 displays some of the available Look and Feel formats that accompany the Java SDK.

Table 8-3 **Examples of Look and Feel Formats**

NAME	SETTING	SAMPLE
Ocean version 1.5	javax.swing.plaf.metal.MetalLookAndFeel	*Ocean Look and Feel*
Metal version 1.4	javax.swing.plaf.metal.MetalLookAndFeel	*Metal Look and Feel*
Motif	com.sun.java.swing.plaf.motif .MotifLookAndFeel	*Motif Look and Feel*
Windows	com.sun.java.swing.plaf.windows .WindowsLookAndFeel	*Windows Look and Feel*
GTK	com.sun.java.swing.plaf.gtk.GTKLookAndFeel	Unix-based Look and Feel
Cross Platform	UIManager.getCrossPlatformLookAndFeel ClassName();	Same as Metal

Ocean Look and Feel is the default value for Java applications and applets. Motif is an alternate Look and Feel supplied with the Java SDK. Windows Look and Feel uses Windows operating system properties and appearance settings to design its interface. **GTK** stands for GIMP Tool Kit, which is a set of graphics and images used to create application programs in UNIX-based systems. GIMP is an acronym for the GNU Image Manipulation Program — a graphics editing program originally designed for Linux.

Programmers are not limited to the Look and Feels supplied with the Java platform, however. You can use any Look and Feel located in your program's class path. External Look and Feels usually are provided in one or more JAR files that you add to your program's class path at run time. **JAR files** are archive files created with the Java Archive tool that comes with Java SDK. **Archive files** are compressed files similar to zipped files. Typically, a JAR file contains the class files and auxiliary resources associated with applets and applications. Many free Look and Feel downloads are available via the Web. Once an external Look and Feel is in the program's class path, the program can use it in the same way it would use any of the Look and Feels shipped with the Java platform.

> **Tip**
>
> **Using External Look and Feels**
> External Look and Feels usually are provided in one or more JAR files that you add to your program's class path at run time. Look and Feels may be created by other programmers or downloaded from the Web.

The UIManager Class

Setting the Look and Feel should be the very first step for programs that use it. Otherwise, Java will initialize the Look and Feel regardless of the code. The reason for this is because when a static field references a Swing class, it causes the Look and Feel to be loaded. When a program does not set its Look and Feel, the Swing UIManager is required to determine which Look and Feel to use. The **UIManager** class keeps track of the current Look and Feel and its defaults. Java manages three levels of defaults: user defaults, Look and Feel defaults, and system defaults. A call to UIManager.get(), however, checks all three levels in sequence and returns the first non-null value. A call to UIManager.put() affects only the user defaults. A call to the setLookAndFeel() method does not affect the user defaults but merely replaces the middle defaults level. Table 8-4 displays some of the available methods from the UIManager class.

First, the UIManager checks whether the programmer has specified a preferred Look and Feel through the operating system. If the user has specified a Look and Feel, the UIManager attempts to use it. If the user has not, or if the user's choice is not valid, the UIManager chooses the Java Look and Feel.

JAVA UPDATE **Java 2 v5.0**

One of the most noticeable changes implemented in J2SE version 5.0 is in the look and feel of applications. If you use the Java look and feel, your application will automatically get the new default setting, called Ocean. Ocean was designed with compatibility in mind so the size of GUI components did not change. Ocean is a derivative of the Metal theme; therefore, the code in Table 8-4 that references the Metal look and feel will generate the new Ocean settings. If you have created a custom look and feel, your application will look the same as it did in previous versions of Java.

If you are using Java 5.0 and wish to view the BillPayer program with the new Ocean Look and Feel rather than the Motif Look and Feel, replace line 22 on page 496 with the following code:

```
22  UIManager.setLookAndFeel("javax.swing.plaf.metal.MetalLookAndFeel");
```

Table 8-4   UIManager Methods

METHOD NAME	PURPOSE	EXAMPLE
get()	Returns an object from the defaults table	`Object fileIcon =` `UIManager.get("DirectoryPane.fileIcon");`
getLookAndFeel()	Returns the current default Look and Feel or null	`UIManager.getLookAndFeel().getClass().getName();`
put()	Stores an object in the defaults table	`UIManager.put("Label.font",new` `Font("SansSerif",Font.ITALIC,10));`
setLookAndFeel()	Sets the current default Look and Feel using a LookAndFeel object	`UIManager.setLookAndFeel` `("javax.swing.plaf.metal.MetalLookAndFeel");`

Creating a Window

Figure 8-7 displays the initial stub of code in the BillPayer program. Recall that stubbing is the process of creating just enough code to compile and run the program, but not enough code to make the program fully functional. In line 15, the BillPayer class extends JFrame. Recall that a Java program may extend, or build on, a superclass provided either by Java or by classes you create. By extending JFrame, BillPayer will be a subclass, or working copy, of the JFrame class. The BillPayer class will behave identically to the original class and have all the fields and methods declared in or inherited from the JFrame class. Also, the BillPayer class implements ActionListener; as you learned earlier, this enables the program to listen for mouse clicks from the user.

```
1  /*
2     Chapter 8        BillPayer Power & Light
3     Programmer:      Joy Starks
4     Date:            November 19, 2007
5     Program Name:    BillPayer
6  */
7
8  import java.io.*;
9  import java.awt.*;
10 import java.awt.event.*;
11 import javax.swing.*;
12 import java.text.*;
13 import java.util.*;
14
15 public class BillPayer extends JFrame implements ActionListener
16 {
```

FIGURE 8-7

In Figure 8-8, the main() method in lines 17 through 37 is required in order to run the program stub. Line 22 sets the Motif Look and Feel inside a try block so that the UIManager does not generate an exception. Line 27 displays an appropriate error message box if the UIManager cannot set the Look and Feel (Box 1 from Table 8-2 on page 491).

```
17    public static void main(String[] args)
18    {
19        //set the look and feel of the interface
20        try
21        {
22            UIManager.setLookAndFeel("com.sun.java.swing.plaf.motif.MotifLookAndFeel");
23
24        }
25        catch(Exception e)
26        {
27            JOptionPane.showMessageDialog(null,
                  "The UIManager could not set the Look and Feel for this application.","Error",
                  JOptionPane.INFORMATION_MESSAGE);
28        }
29
30        BillPayer f = new BillPayer();
31        f.setDefaultCloseOperation(JFrame.DO_NOTHING_ON_CLOSE);
32        f.setSize(450,300);
33        f.setTitle("Crandall Power and Light Customer Payments");
34        f.setResizable(false);
35        f.setLocation(200,200);
36        f.setVisible(true);
37    }
38
39    public BillPayer()
40    {
41    }
42
43    public void actionPerformed(ActionEvent e)
44    {
45    }
46 }
```

FIGURE 8-8

Line 30 constructs an instance of the JFrame, and the lines following set the attributes. The **setResizable() method** in line 34 prohibits the user from resizing the window and disables the Maximize button. The **setLocation() method** in line 35 sets the location of the object relative to the parent object, which in this case is the user's screen.

Recall from Chapter 7 that you used the setDefaultCloseOperation() method (line 31 in Figure 8-8) to automatically close a Swing application when the user clicked the Close button. Because the BillPayer program specifies that the Close button should display a dialog box asking if the user really wants to exit the program and submit the file, the constant, **DO_NOTHING_ON_CLOSE**, is used as the method's argument. Therefore, the programmer can override the windowClosing event.

Finally, you must stub in the constructor and an actionPerformed() method because the BillPayer class uses a BillPayer() constructor method and implements the ActionListener.

The following steps create a stub that will display the BillPayer window at run time.

To Create the BillPayer Window

1. Enter the code from Figure 8-7 on page 495.

   The TextPad window displays the comments, import statements, and class header (Figure 8-9).

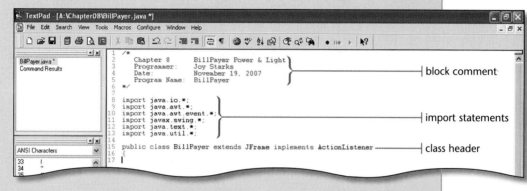

FIGURE 8-9

2. Enter the code from Figure 8-8.

   The TextPad window displays the main() method and the stub for both the BillPayer() and actionPerformed() methods (Figure 8-10).

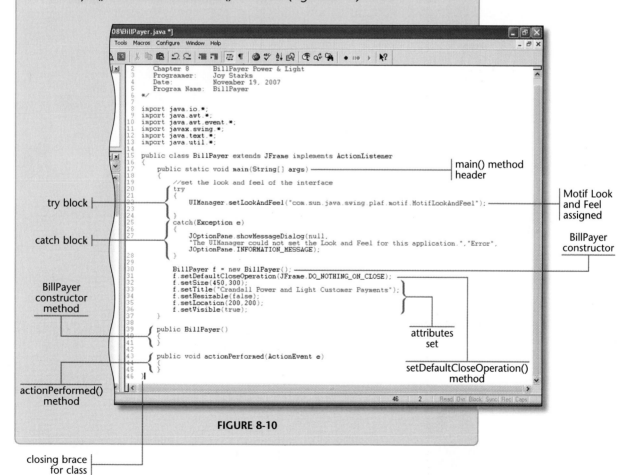

FIGURE 8-10

To test the functionality of the window created by the BillPayer class, you must first compile and then execute the program, as shown in the following steps.

To Test the Functionality of the Window

1. With the Data Disk in drive A, compile the program by clicking Tools on the menu bar and then clicking Compile Java. If TextPad notifies you of errors, click BillPayer.java in the Selector window, fix the errors, and then compile again.

2. When the program compiles with no errors, if necessary, click BillPayer.java in the Selector window to display the code in the TextPad window. Click Tools on the menu bar and then click Run Java Application.

   The program displays the empty Crandall Power and Light Customer Payments window (Figure 8-11).

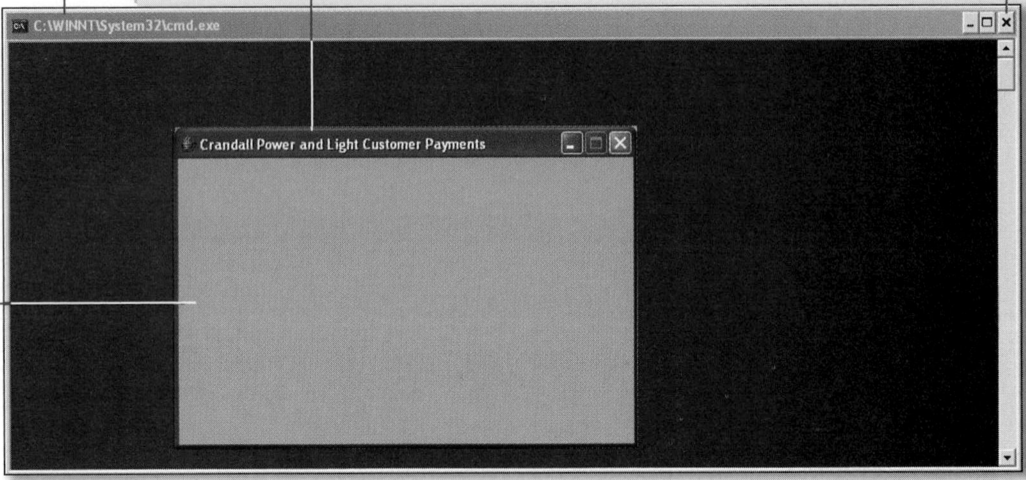

command prompt window

application window

Close button

Motif background

FIGURE 8-11

3. To quit the program, click the Close button on the command prompt window title bar.

OTHER WAYS

1. To compile, press CTRL+1
2. To compile at command prompt, type javac BillPayer.java
3. To run, press CTRL+2, enter data
4. To run at command prompt, type java BillPayer and then enter data

Because line 31 in Figure 8-10 on the previous page overrides the Close button, you must quit the running program by clicking the Close button in the command prompt window. Testing your program interface for the ability to display the basic window is one way to build a program in stages; it allows you to test individual attributes, such as the location and title of the window, before entering additional code.

Tip

Testing the Interface
When creating a program in stages, test the interface for its ability to display the basic window before adding components.

Adding Components to the Interface

Adding components to the BillPayer interface involves the following:
(1) constructing the components, (2) implementing layout managers for placement, and (3) using the add() methods to insert the components into the JFrame. The components in the BillPayer interface include the JFrame, which already was created; the content pane to hold all of the components; JLabels to hold words, instructions, or prompts; JTextFields to allow for user data entry; JButtons to add functionality to the interface; and JPanels to assist with component placement. You may remember that JPanels and JFrames are special containers that house other components, such as user-interface controls and other containers.

Constructing the Components

Figure 8-12 displays the constructors for the BillPayer interface and the declaration of the variable to hold the DataOutputStream. Eight JPanel containers are created in lines 21 through 28. Recall from the storyboard in Figure 8-3 on page 490 that each row of JLabels and JTextFields will be placed in its own panel. Then, in line 31, a larger panel, named fieldPanel, will contain all of the rows. Finally, line 32 constructs the buttonPanel.

```
15   public class BillPayer extends JFrame implements ActionListener
16   {
17       //Declare output stream
18       DataOutputStream output;
19
20       //Construct a panel for each row
21       JPanel firstRow = new JPanel();
22       JPanel secondRow = new JPanel();
23       JPanel thirdRow = new JPanel();
24       JPanel fourthRow = new JPanel();
25       JPanel fifthRow = new JPanel();
26       JPanel sixthRow = new JPanel();
27       JPanel seventhRow = new JPanel();
28       JPanel eighthRow = new JPanel();
29
30       //Construct a panel for the fields and buttons
31       JPanel fieldPanel = new JPanel();
32       JPanel buttonPanel = new JPanel();
33
34       //Construct labels and text boxes
35       JLabel acctNumLabel = new JLabel("Account Number:          ");
36           JTextField acctNum = new JTextField(15);
37       JLabel pmtLabel = new JLabel("Payment Amount:");
38           JTextField pmt = new JTextField(10);
39       JLabel firstNameLabel = new JLabel("First Name:      ");
40           JTextField firstName = new JTextField(10);
41       JLabel lastNameLabel = new JLabel("Last Name:");
42           JTextField lastName = new JTextField(20);
43       JLabel addressLabel = new JLabel("Address:");
44           JTextField address = new JTextField(35);
45       JLabel cityLabel = new JLabel("City:          ");
46           JTextField city = new JTextField(10);
47       JLabel stateLabel = new JLabel("State:");
48           JTextField state = new JTextField(2);
49       JLabel zipLabel = new JLabel("Zip:");
50           JTextField zip = new JTextField(9);
51
52       //Construct button
53       JButton submitButton = new JButton("Submit");
54
55       public static void main(String[] args)
```

FIGURE 8-12

Figure 8-12 on the previous page also displays the constructors to create the JLabel, JTextField, and JButton components. In lines 35, 39, and 45, extra spaces are included in the JLabel() method arguments to cause the length of the label prompt to align with the displayed JTextField that is constructed in the next line. Manipulating components in this manner prevents programmers from coding absolute placement or further complicating the coding with multiple varieties of subsetted layout managers.

The following step enters the constructor method code.

To Construct the Components

1. Enter the code from Figure 8-12 on the previous page, lines 17 through 54.

The TextPad window displays the constructor code (Figure 8-13).

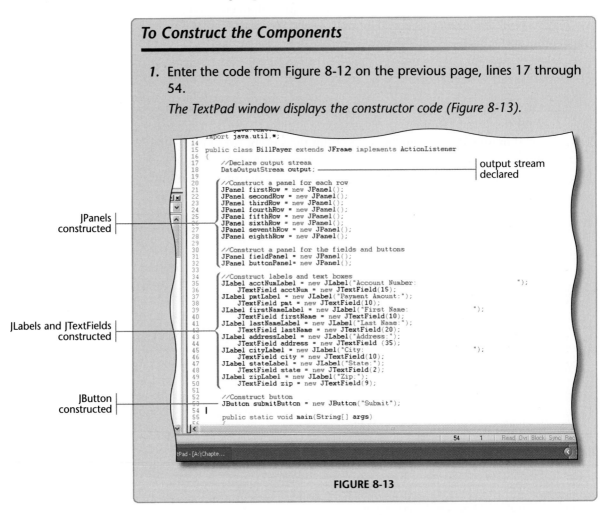

FIGURE 8-13

Although the application contains only one button, placing it in a panel allows it to retain its normal size rather than stretching it across the interface.

Setting the Layout Managers

The next step is to establish the placement of the components in the interface. Because you are using a Swing application, a content pane is necessary. The code in Chapter 7 created a separate createContentPane() method. It is permissible, however, to assign the container in the constructor method for the entire class, especially if no extenuating tabs, styles, or scroll bars exist. The content pane contains two panels. The fieldPanel and buttonPanel are placed using the BorderLayout manager, and the subsetted row panels use the FlowLayout manager.

Figure 8-14 displays the getContentPane() and the setLayout() methods for the BillPayer interface. Line 79 creates a content pane, and line 80 sets BorderLayout as the layout manager. In line 81, the panel to hold all the rows, named fieldPanel, uses the GridLayout manager and is set to contain eight rows and one column. In line 82, an instance of the FlowLayout manager is created with left justification and with pixel settings for the horizontal and vertical placement of the components. The instance, named rowSetup, then is used in lines 83 through 90 as the layout manager for each row. Line 91 sets the buttonPanel to a centered FlowLayout.

```
77        public BillPayer()
78        {
79            Container c = getContentPane();
80            c.setLayout((new BorderLayout()));
81            fieldPanel.setLayout(new GridLayout(8,1));
82            FlowLayout rowSetup = new FlowLayout(FlowLayout.LEFT,5,3);
83                firstRow.setLayout(rowSetup);
84                secondRow.setLayout(rowSetup);
85                thirdRow.setLayout(rowSetup);
86                fourthRow.setLayout(rowSetup);
87                fifthRow.setLayout(rowSetup);
88                sixthRow.setLayout(rowSetup);
89                seventhRow.setLayout(rowSetup);
90                eighthRow.setLayout(rowSetup);
91            buttonPanel.setLayout(new FlowLayout(FlowLayout.CENTER));
92        }
```

FIGURE 8-14

The following step enters the code to set the layout managers.

To Set the Layout Managers

1. Enter the code from Figure 8-14, lines 79 through 91.

TextPad displays the setLayout() methods (Figure 8-15). The LEFT and CENTER attributes specify alignment for FlowLayout.

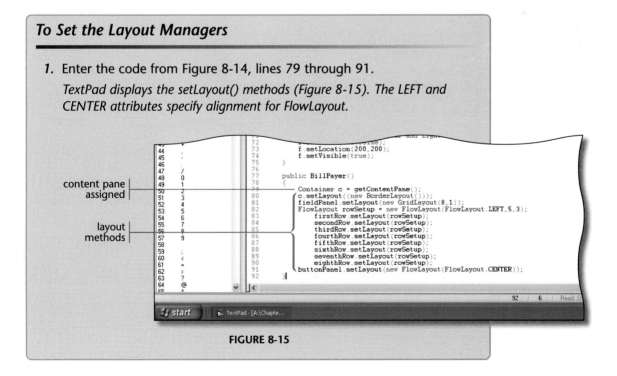

FIGURE 8-15

Adding Components to the JFrame

The last step in creating the BillPayer() constructor method is to add the previously constructed components to the JFrame. Figure 8-16 displays the add() methods and explanatory comments. The components are added to their respective new panels (lines 94 through 117) in order, from left to right and top to bottom. The new panels then are added to the fieldPanel (lines 120 through 127 and 131), and in turn, the fieldPanel and buttonPanel are added to the interface (lines 134 and 135).

```
92
93          //Add fields to rows
94          firstRow.add(acctNumLabel);
95          firstRow.add(pmtLabel);
96
97          secondRow.add(acctNum);
98          secondRow.add(pmt);
99
100         thirdRow.add(firstNameLabel);
101         thirdRow.add(lastNameLabel);
102
103
104         fourthRow.add(firstName);
105         fourthRow.add(lastName);
106
107         fifthRow.add(addressLabel);
108
109         sixthRow.add(address);
110
111         seventhRow.add(cityLabel);
112         seventhRow.add(stateLabel);
113         seventhRow.add(zipLabel);
114
115         eighthRow.add(city);
116         eighthRow.add(state);
117         eighthRow.add(zip);
118
119         //Add rows to panel
120         fieldPanel.add(firstRow);
121         fieldPanel.add(secondRow);
122         fieldPanel.add(thirdRow);
123         fieldPanel.add(fourthRow);
124         fieldPanel.add(fifthRow);
125         fieldPanel.add(sixthRow);
126         fieldPanel.add(seventhRow);
127         fieldPanel.add(eighthRow);
128
129
130         //Add button to panel
131         buttonPanel.add(submitButton);
132
133         //Add panels to frame
134         c.add(fieldPanel, BorderLayout.CENTER);
135         c.add(buttonPanel, BorderLayout.SOUTH);
136
137         //Add functionality to buttons
138         submitButton.addActionListener(this);
```

FIGURE 8-16

Line 138 adds the Action Listener to the Submit button. Recall that the addActionListener() method is necessary for the program to listen for the user's mouse click and to trigger the appropriate event. The following step adds the components to the JFrame.

To Add the Components to the JFrame

1. Enter the code from Figure 8-16, lines 92 through 138.

TextPad displays the add() methods (Figure 8-17). The fieldPanel is added to the Center region, and the buttonPanel is added to the South region.

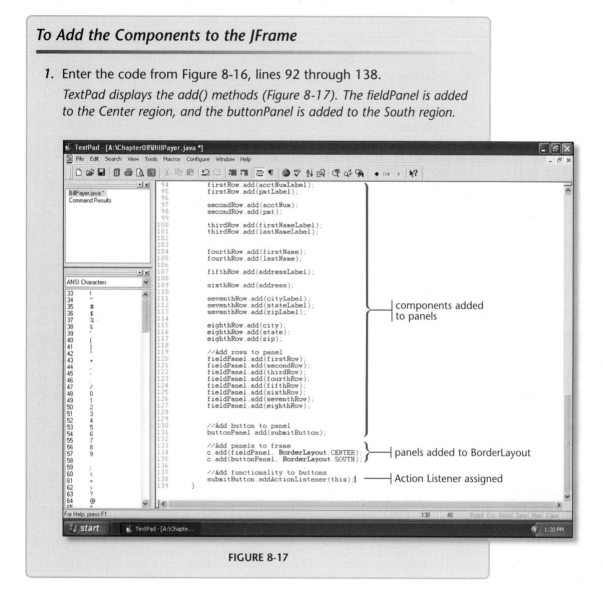

FIGURE 8-17

The following steps test the BillPayer window layout managers.

To Test the Layout Managers

1. Compile the program by clicking Tools on the menu bar and then clicking Compile Java. If TextPad notifies you of errors, click BillPayer.java in the Selector window, fix the errors, and then compile again.

2. When the program compiles with no errors, if necessary, click BillPayer.java in the Selector window to display the code in the TextPad window. Click Tools on the menu bar and then click Run Java Application.

   The program displays the BillPayer window with its components (Figure 8-18).

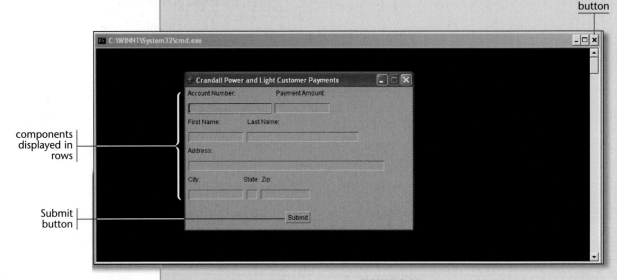

Close button

components displayed in rows

Submit button

FIGURE 8-18

3. Click the Close button in the Command Prompt window.

Recall how Java's BorderLayout manager stretches components to fill empty areas. The fieldPanel component fills the North, East, West, and Center areas.

Creating a File Name with a System Date

Crandall Power and Light wants to ensure that no data is lost; therefore, it is important to keep the data for each day separate for the evening upload to the central server. If the BillPayer program used the same file name for each data file, the previous day's data would be overwritten each time the file is constructed. Appending the system date to the end of the file name creates a unique file, as shown in Figure 8-19.

```
139
140          //Get the current date and open the file
141          Date today = new Date();
142          SimpleDateFormat myFormat = new SimpleDateFormat("MMddyyyy");
143          String filename = "payments" + myFormat.format(today);
144
```

FIGURE 8-19

Line 141 constructs an instance of the date by using the Date() method. Recall that the Date() method constructs a Date object by utilizing the user's system date, which may include the month, day, year, and time. The **SimpleDateFormat** class and constructor method allows programmers to specify how the date should display. Letter **descriptors**, displayed in the SimpleDateFormat() method's argument, describe the pattern in which the date should display. Table 8-5 summarizes some of the available formats.

Table 8-5   Some SimpleDateFormat Strings

LETTER	DATE OR TIME COMPONENT	DESCRIPTOR	EXAMPLES
G	Era designator	GG	AD
y	Year	yyyy yy	2007 07
M	Month in year	MM MMM	07 Jul
w	Week in year	ww	27
D	Day in year	DDD	189
d	Day in month	dd	10
E	Day in week	EEE EEEEEEE	Tue Tuesday
a	am/pm marker	aa	PM
H	Hour in day (0-23)	HH	0
k	Hour in day (1-24)	kk	24
K	Hour in am/pm (0-11)	KK	0
h	Hour in am/pm (1-12)	hh	12
m	Minute in hour	mm	30
s	Second in minute	ss	55

Line 142 assigns a pattern to the variable myFormat. If today's date were November 19, 2007, then the format "MMddyyyy" in line 142 would produce 11192007. Line 143 concatenates the named format to the word, payments, to create the file name payments11192007.

Data File Concepts

Programs often need to read data from a data file or write data to a data file on a secondary storage device, such as a disk. Storing data in locations within the computer's memory is temporary; data easily can be overwritten or lost when the computer is turned off. Therefore, any permanent storage of data should be on a secondary storage device. Data typically is stored in data files, which are collections of fields within records.

To read data, a Java program must open a stream to the data file. Once the data source is streamed, Java reads the information serially. Similarly, a Java program can write data to a secondary storage device by opening a stream to the data and writing the data serially.

Data Hierarchy

Data is organized in a hierarchy, in which each level contains one or more elements from the level beneath it. The levels in the hierarchy of data, from lowest to highest, are bit, byte, field, record, and file (Table 8-6).

Table 8-6   Hierarchy of Data

DATA ELEMENT	CONTAINS	DESCRIPTION	EXAMPLE
bit	lowest level	binary digit 0 or 1	Bits can represent any two-state condition, such as on or off, but usually are combined with bytes to represent data
byte	group of related bits	one character or other unit of information consisting of eight bits	01000001 (letter A)
field	group of related bytes	individual elements of data, such as a person's first name	Ethel
record	group of related fields	related groups of fields, such as a person's name, address, and telephone number	Ethel Malson 202 N. Van Buren Albany, MO 64402 (816) 555-5519
file	group of related records	Many related records	Ethel Malson, 202 N. Van Buren… Idris Evans, R.R. 1 Box 199… Elsie Amos, 1306 Minuteman Dr.…

All data in memory appears as combinations of zeroes and ones, because electronic devices can assume one of two stable states: off and on. This **binary digit**, or **bit**, is the smallest piece of data a computer can understand. Usually a bit is combined with other bits to represent data. The combination of bits within a coding scheme is called a **byte**. A byte can represent a character, such as a letter (A), a number (7), or a symbol (&). A logical grouping of bytes that form a piece of meaningful data (such as a last name or an ID number) is called a **field**. A **record** is a group of related fields. For example, an employee record would contain all the fields about an employee, such as name, date of birth, address, and social security number. A **file** is a collection of related records stored under a single name. A school's student file, for example, would consist of thousands of individual student records. Each student record would contain the same fields as the other records.

The java.io package contains a collection of file and stream classes that support reading and writing data. Java is not concerned about the concept of a record; therefore, it is the programmer's responsibility to organize and structure the data to meet the requirements of the program.

Sequential versus Random Access Files

Java views each file as a sequential stream of bytes. **Sequential** means that items are placed in a specific sequence — or in order — one after another. Java reads and writes sequential files as streams of bytes from beginning to end. Sequential files are used when data elements are manipulated in the order they are stored. For example, a Java programmer might create a sequential file to receive input data from a user or to back up a set of transactions in a batch. The advantages of using sequential files include an increase in the speed at which the program reads and writes data as well as contiguous storage of that data. Storing data sequentially, however, can be tedious when frequent updates are required or when specific records, often out of order, need retrieval. Think of a sequential file as being like a cassette tape of recorded music: it plays from beginning to end. Adding a new song in the middle involves recording the first half of the original cassette tape on another cassette tape, then adding the song to the new cassette tape. Finally, you would record the rest of the cassette tape to finish the project.

If constant updating like inserting, deleting, and changing is involved, or if direct access is needed, Java provides another file mechanism that does not involve traversing the entire file. **Random access** files store data in noncontiguous locations; their records can be retrieved in any order. Because they can locate a particular record directly without reading all of the preceding records, random access files also are called **direct access** files.

The java.io package, imported at the beginning of the BillPayer program, provides classes that handle input and output for both sequential and random access files. The requirement for the BillPayer program is to write data to a sequential data file.

Opening a Connection to an External File

Reading data from or writing data to a data file is a three-step process: (1) declare a variable to hold the stream of data; (2) construct an instance of the stream and assign it to a file; and (3) read or write the data.

Table 8-7 displays the typical code for the declaration, construction, and movement of data between the storage device and the program.

Table 8-7   Code to Create External Data Files

PROCESS	INPUT	OUTPUT
Declaration	`DataInputStream input`	`DataOutputStream output`
Construction	`input = new DataInputStream(new FileInputStream(existingFilename));`	`output = new DataOutputStream(new FileOutputStream(newFilename));`
Moving data	`read()` methods	`write()` methods

The stream of data is declared as either DataInputStream or DataOutputStream; however, it is at the time of construction that the program actually accesses the storage device. The file is opened if it is a read process; the file is created if it is a write process. The **DataOutputStream() method** lets a program write primitive Java data types to an output stream in a portable way. A program then can use a **DataInputStream() method** to read the data from the data file.

The DataOutputStream and DataInputStream classes are wrapper classes, which can be chained or connected to the corresponding File stream classes to implement the reading or writing of formatted data. Wrapper classes were used in earlier chapters to wrap the InputStreamReader to accept the keyboard buffer.

```
BufferedReader dataIn = new BufferedReader(new
InputStreamReader(System.in));
```

In the same way, you can wrap the FileInputStream inside the DataInputStream for formatted data.

```
DataOutputStream output = new DataOutputStream(new
FileOutputStream(filename));
```

FileInputStream and **FileOutputStream** are used, respectively, to read and write data to a given file. The file name is specified in the argument of the FileInputStream() or FileOutputStream() method.

As indicated earlier, the BillPayer program creates a sequential file. If all fields are complete, each time a user clicks the Submit button, formatted output is sent to the data file. As with the BufferedReader, when Java attempts input or output, the program must provide a way to catch possible errors. The try and catch structure will be used to catch possible errors.

Opening the Data File

Earlier, line 18 (Figure 8-12 on page 499) was entered to declare a variable named output as a data type of DataOutputStream. The code shown in Figure 8-20 constructs the instance of this variable.

```
145            try
146            {
147                output = new DataOutputStream(new FileOutputStream(filename));
148            }
149            catch(IOException io)
150            {
151                JOptionPane.showMessageDialog(null,
                   "The program could not create a storage location. Please check the disk drive and
                   then run the program again.","Error",JOptionPane.INFORMATION_MESSAGE);
152
153                System.exit(1);
154            }
155
```

FIGURE 8-20

Line 147 opens a new data file on disk. Because Java requires that the program handle all possible errors, the try structure is employed in lines 145 through 148. A corresponding catch structure, lines 149 through 154, contains the code to execute if an error occurs. The message dialog box that displays is Box 2 from the list in Table 8-2 on page 491. If the file cannot be opened in line 147, the catch will execute and the program will close with the System.exit() method in line 153.

Closing the Data File

Recall that the main() method required the program not to close automatically when the user clicked the Close button. Therefore, you must write code to override the windowClosing event. Figure 8-21 displays the code for the addWindowListener() method, similar to that coded in Chapter 5.

```
156            addWindowListener(
157                new WindowAdapter()
158                {
159                    public void windowClosing(WindowEvent e)
160                    {
161                        int answer = JOptionPane.showConfirmDialog(null,
                           "Are you sure you want to exit and submit the file?", "File Submission",
                           JOptionPane.YES_NO_OPTION);
162                        if (answer == JOptionPane.YES_OPTION)
163                            System.exit(0);
164                    }
165                }
166            );
```

FIGURE 8-21

Java uses many different listeners, depending on how the user triggers the event. Table 8-8 displays some of the user events and listener types.

Table 8-8   User Events and Listener Types

EVENT	LISTENER TYPE
User clicks a button, presses the ENTER key while typing in a text field, or chooses a menu item.	ActionListener
User closes a frame (main window).	WindowListener
User presses a mouse button while the mouse pointer is positioned on a component.	MouseListener
User moves the mouse over a component.	MouseMotionListener
Component becomes visible.	ComponentListener
Component gets the keyboard focus.	FocusListener
Table or list selection changes.	ListSelectionListener

When the user clicks the Close button, line 161 causes a showConfirmDialog box to display with the buttons Yes and No. The **showConfirmDialog() method** can display one of several common dialog boxes with the chosen Look and Feel. The showConfirmDialog() method may display different arrangements of buttons, as listed in Table 8-9. The return values, represented internally as integers, indicate how the user has interacted with the dialog box, or which button he/she has clicked.

Table 8-9   Options of the showConfirmDialog Box

BUTTON OPTIONS	RETURN OPTIONS
DEFAULT_OPTION	YES_OPTION
YES_NO_OPTION	NO_OPTION
YES_NO_CANCEL_OPTION	CANCEL_OPTION
OK_CANCEL_OPTION	OK_OPTION
	CLOSED_OPTION

Line 161 (Figure 8-21 on the previous page) specifies the YES_NO_OPTION, which causes the confirm dialog box to display the Yes and No buttons. Line 162 tests against the YES_OPTION to verify that the user clicked the Yes button. Option buttons are not limited to the displayed set of option buttons. Any button can be selected by using the options parameter.

In line 161, the return value of the user's choice is stored in a variable named answer. Then, line 162 compares the variable, answer, to the JOptionPane, **YES_OPTION**. If the user actually clicked the Yes button, the program exits with no error, resulting in the file being closed. The confirm dialog box is Box 3 from Table 8-2 on page 510.

The following steps illustrate how to write code to create a file name, open the data file, and apply the window listener.

To Open the Data File with a Unique Name

1. Enter the code from Figure 8-19 on page 505.

   The TextPad window displays the code to create a file name with the formatted date appended at the end (Figure 8-22).

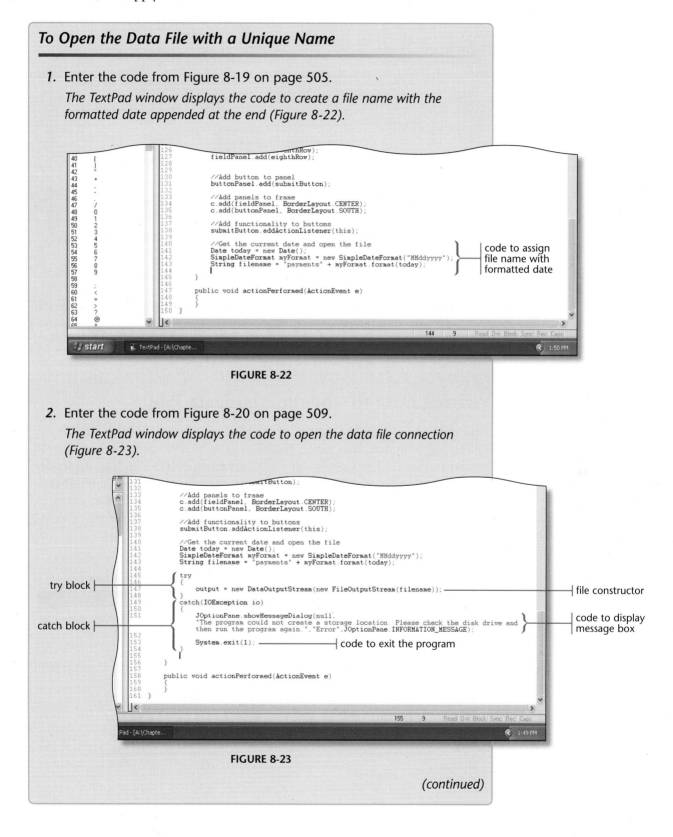

FIGURE 8-22

2. Enter the code from Figure 8-20 on page 509.

   The TextPad window displays the code to open the data file connection (Figure 8-23).

FIGURE 8-23

(continued)

3. Enter the code from Figure 8-21 on page 509.

The TextPad window displays the code for the window listener, which completes the BillPayer() constructor method (Figure 8-24).

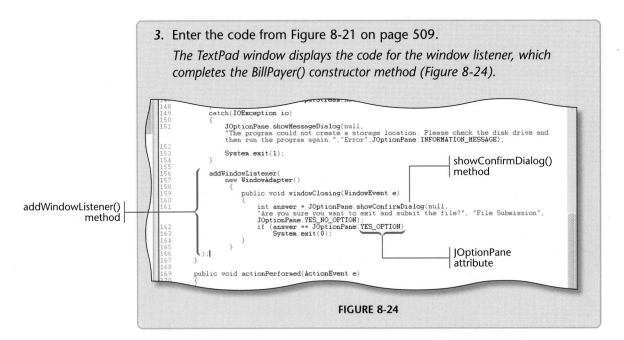

FIGURE 8-24

The System.exit argument usually is one (1) if the program terminates for an error and zero (0) if the program proceeds to its natural conclusion (i.e., the user clicks the Close button). If the window is closed successfully, the open data file also will close.

Writing Data to a Sequential Data File

Table 8-10 summarizes the methods from the Data Stream class that transfer data to and from data files. Notice that there is no writeString() method. Instead, Java Strings are read or written using a UTF() method. **UTF** stands for **Unicode Transformation Format**, which is an encoding scheme that assigns a number to each symbol. The UTF() methods provide a way to read and write formatted data without concern for the specific data type, although the underlying mechanism still is reading one byte at a time.

Table 8-10   Methods to Read and Write from the Data Stream Class

TYPE OF DATA	INPUT METHOD	OUTPUT METHOD	EXAMPLE
boolean data	readBoolean()	writeBoolean()	true or false, stored as a 1 or 0
single character data	readChar()	writeChar()	a
integer	readInt()	writeInt()	7
double	readDouble()	writeDouble()	3.12E+10
float	readFloat()	writeFloat()	5.21
long	readLong()	writeLong()	$9 * 10^{18}$
Strings	readUTF()	writeUTF()	Cashman's

Viewing the Contents of a Data File

To view the contents of the payment data file, programmers construct a program that creates an instance of the DataInputStream and then uses the readUTF() methods, in the same way as the BillPayer program used the DataOutputStream() and writeUTF() methods. For example, to create a program to read the payment data, declare a variable with the data type DataInputStream.

```
DataInputStream input;
```

Then, wrap it in the FileInputStream buffer.

```
input = new DataInputStream(new
FileInputStream("payment11192007"));
```

Finally, code a readUTF() method for each field to read the data from the file.

```
name.setText(readUTF());
```

It also is possible to view the contents by opening the file in a text editor, such as TextPad or Notepad. Be careful not to use a text editor to resave a data file created in Java because text editors will corrupt the binary nature of the file. For example, a text editor might display commas or special characters in place of field separators in a text editor window. If the data file is saved back to disk, the text editor will save the contents of the data file incorrectly.

Moving to the Web

Many companies are moving their payment services to the Web. As individuals and companies continue to expand their e-commerce, utility companies, as well as government agencies, are eager to jump on the Web bandwagon. Most financial-based institutions such as banks, credit card companies, and stock brokerage firms offer services 24 hours a day over the Web. The anytime, anywhere capability of the Internet allows information and services to be more available to more people, with greater convenience and lower cost to customers. Not only do businesses see the Web as a way to save time and money while serving customers around the clock, but the Web also prevents them from becoming outdated or left behind. Analysts predict that by the year 2007, the number of U.S. households with Internet access will rise to 180 million, doubling from the year 2004.

It is easy to think of the Web exclusively as new technology; it is far more useful to think of it as a new way to deliver services. Web services combine traditional functions — such as publishing, business transactions, information gathering, and data search and retrieval — into a single form of presentation. Web services also have unique characteristics that require special policy, management, and technical attention. The most obvious of these is the speed of technological change and the rapidly expanding variety of tools and technologies. A less obvious but perhaps more important characteristic is the completely public nature of the interaction between an agency and a Web user. In theory, anyone, anywhere, at any time can have access to an agency on the Web. Customer service on a Web site can be linked to other sites without the user's permission or knowledge. Material can be copied, distributed, and used in ways neither planned for nor expected. This characteristic gives the Web its excitement and vitality, but it means a new way of thinking for most government organizations.

Because it would not represent the way programmers and database administrators use Java, you will not convert the BillPayer program in this chapter to an applet. Due to security issues relating to applet constraints and data integrity, most Web interfaces use a layer of security between the applet and the data. As you read the next section, you will learn about the layers of security and the client-server concepts typically employed by computer installations and database administrators.

Client-Server Concepts

In the past, the Internet interface for businesses has been written in C++, Visual Basic, or PowerBuilder. The database behind the interface has typically been Microsoft Access or Oracle. The **client** is the computer providing the user interface; the **server**, which is a computer that hosts a network or database, handles data manipulation and connectivity issues. **Client-server architecture** is a general description of a networked system in which a client program initiates contact with a separate server program for a specific purpose. The client requests a service provided by the server. This separation of the client and the server is called a **two-tier system**. The two-tier system, also called a first-generation system architecture, contains application logic typically tied to the client, with heavy network utilization required to mediate the client-server interaction.

A second generation client-server system takes this a step further by adding a middle tier to achieve a three-tier system architecture. In a **three-tier system**, the application is split into three parts: the user interface, the application server, and the database server. This leads to faster network communications, greater reliability, and improved overall performance.

With the advent of Java and the Internet, many businesses have taken a **multitier approach**, in which data moving from a client to a server goes through several stages. The middle tier is expanded to provide connections to various types of services, integrating and coupling them to the client and to each other. Partitioning the application logic among various hosts also can create a multitier approach. This encapsulation of distributed functionality provides significant advantages, such as reusability and, therefore, reliability.

In a client-server system, Java applets with their own objects and methods create the interface. A Java applet has a distinct set of capabilities and restrictions within the language framework, especially from a security standpoint. Java applets can neither read nor write files on a local system unless special permissions are assigned and accepted. Applets cannot create, rename, or copy files or directories on a local system. They also cannot make outside network connections except to the host machine from which they originated.

Most businesses, therefore, create a client interface with HTML or a scripting tool to allow users to enter data. The database itself is separated from the interface by a Web server, usually complete with a firewall to protect the database from the Internet. The program on the Web server that provides the connectivity is in control. Sun Microsystems provides an application programing interface (API) called the **Java Database Connectivity** (**JDBC**) that has its own set of objects and methods to interact with underlying databases.

Another solution is to use a Java servlet. Recall that servlets are modules that run inside request/response-oriented servers — such as Java-enabled Web servers — and extend them. For example, a servlet might be responsible for taking data in an HTML order-entry form and then applying the logic necessary to update a company's order database.

Servlets replace cumbersome and less robust Common Gateway Interface (CGI) programs, which are platform dependent. Because they are written in Java, servlets can be used on many different platforms hosting Web servers. Servlets also offer substantial performance advantages for developers and Webmasters because — unlike CGI code — servlets do not create additional processes each time a request is made from a browser. Servlets are developed with the Java Servlet API, a standard Java extension. Many popular Web servers already support servlets.

Quitting TextPad

The following step quits TextPad and returns control to Windows.

To Quit TextPad

1. Click the TextPad program button on the taskbar to redisplay the TextPad window.
2. Click the Close button on TextPad's title bar.
   The TextPad window closes and the Windows desktop is displayed.

OTHER WAYS

1. Press ALT+F, X

Chapter Summary

In this chapter, you were introduced to writing data to a data file on disk. You learned how to construct an interface window and set attributes for the size, location, and Look and Feel. You then learned how to add JLabels, JTextFields, a JButton, and JPanels to the interface. Next, you learned how to use multiple subsetted layout managers to place components in the window and wrapped the data from the FileOutputStream inside the DataOutputStream to construct a new file. To incorporate additional functionality and user-friendly features, the chapter showed you how to create several JOptionPane boxes to inform users when data was submitted successfully, as well as to warn them when a field was left empty. The file name had the system date appended to it. Then, using the writeUTF() method, the chapter introduced you to transferring data from the interface to the data file.

You also were introduced to methods for verifying the existence of the data file, as well as procedures to view the data file. Finally, you learned about client-server architectures, the core of information technology from databases to the Web. You also learned that two-tier, three-tier, and multitier systems allow for protection of databases and world access.

What You Should Know

Having completed this chapter, you now should be able to perform the tasks shown in Table 8-13.

Table 8-13   *Chapter 8 What You Should Know*

TASK NUMBER	TASK	PAGE
1	Start a New Java Program in TextPad	492
2	Create the BillPayer Window	497
3	Test the Functionality of the Window	498
4	Construct the Components	500
5	Set the Layout Managers	501
6	Add the Components to the JFrame	503
7	Test the Layout Managers	504
8	Open the Data File with a Unique Name	511
9	Code the actionPerformed() Method	513
10	Code the checkFields() Method	515
11	Code the clearFields() Method	516
12	Test the Program	517
13	Verify the Existence of the Data File	520
14	Quit TextPad	523

Key Terms

archive files *(494)*
binary digit *(506)*
bit *(506)*
byte *(506)*
client *(522)*
client-server architecture *(522)*
data file *(488)*
DataInputStream() method *(508)*
DataOutputStream() method
   (508)
descriptors *(505)*
direct access *(507)*
DO_NOTHING_ON_CLOSE *(496)*
field *(507)*
file *(507)*
FileInputStream *(508)*
FileOutputStream *(508)*
GTK *(494)*
JAR files *(494)*
Java Database Connectivity (JDBC)
   (522)
Motif Look and Feel *(493)*

multitier approach *(522)*
nonvolatile data *(488)*
random access *(507)*
record *(507)*
seek() method *(514)*
sequential *(507)*
sequential data file *(488)*
sequential file *(488)*
server *(522)*
setLocation() method *(496)*
setResizable() method *(496)*
showConfirmDialog() method *(510)*
SimpleDateFormat *(505)*
three-tier system *(522)*
two-tier system *(522)*
UIManager *(494)*
Unicode Transformation Format *(512)*
UTF *(512)*
volatile data *(488)*
write() method *(488)*
YES_OPTION *(510)*

Homework Assignments

Short Answer

1. _____ data is stored in the computer's memory while the electricity is supplied to the computer and while the program is running.
2. A(n) _____ is the computer that provides the interface, whereas a(n) _____ is the computer that houses the network or a database.
3. The _____ method is used to write numeric data to a storage device.
4. _____ and _____ classes are wrapper classes.
5. _____ files use the seek() method to look for data.
6. The _____ Look and Feel is the default for Swing applications.
7. Programs that use a window or a GUI-based interface typically extend JFrame and are called _____.
   a. frame implementations
   b. applets
   c. ActionListener events
   d. frame-based applications

(continued)

Short Answer *(continued)*

8. The binary state representing the smallest piece of data a computer can understand is called a _____.

   a. bit

   b. byte

   c. field

   d. record

9. A message box usually contains all of the following except a(n) _____.

   a. title bar

   b. menu

   c. message

   d. OK button

10. The DataOutputStream is a member of the _____ package.

    a. java.awt

    b. java.awt.event

    c. java.io

    d. java.applet

11. Files that must be read from beginning to end when looking for a piece of data are called _____ access files.

    a. sequential

    b. random

    c. stream

    d. ordered

12. A _____ is a collection of related records.

    a. record

    b. field

    c. file

    d. database

13. In a _____ system, the program uses a Web browser, an application server, and a database server; this leads to faster network communications, greater reliability, and improved overall performance.

    a. two-tier

    b. three-tier

    c. multitier

    d. firewall

14. JDBC stands for _____.

    a. Java Data Building Computer

    b. Java Direct Business Connection

    c. Java's DataBase Creation program

    d. Java Database Connectivity

15. Describe the differences between Metal, Motif, and Windows Look and Feel formats.

16. Write the descriptor patterns to display the system date for each of the following formats:

    a. Nov. 19, 2007

    b. 19 NOV 2007

    c. November 2007

    d. 11/19/07

17. Draw a hierarchy pyramid representing all of the parts of a database.

18. List the methods you learned about that set attributes for Frames and JFrames.

19. Use the Java API to discover five different methods used to set or retrieve Look and Feel attributes.

Learn It Online

Start your browser and visit scsite.com/java3e/learn. Follow the instructions in the exercises below.

1. **Chapter Reinforcement TF, MC, and SA** Click the Chapter Reinforcement link below Chapter 8. Print and then answer the questions.

2. **Practice Test** Click the Practice Test link below Chapter 8. Answer each question, enter your first and last name at the bottom of the page, and then click the Grade Test button. When the graded practice test is displayed on your screen, click Print on the File menu to print a hard copy. Continue to take practice tests until you score 80% or better. Hand in a printout of the final practice test.

3. **Crossword Puzzle Challenge** Click the Crossword Puzzle Challenge link below Chapter 8. Read the instructions, and then enter your first and last name. Click the Play button. Complete the crossword puzzle. When you are finished, click the Submit button. When the crossword puzzle is redisplayed, click the Print button.

4. **Tips and Tricks** Click the Tips and Tricks link below Chapter 8. Click a topic that pertains to Chapter 8. Right-click the information and then click Print on the shortcut menu. Construct a brief example of what the information relates to in Java to confirm that you understand how to use the tip or trick. Hand in the example and printed information.

5. **Newsgroups** Click the Newsgroups link below Chapter 8. Click a topic that pertains to Chapter 8. Print three comments.

6. **Expanding Your Horizons** Click the Expanding Your Horizons link below Chapter 8. Click a topic that pertains to Chapter 8. Print the information. Construct a brief example of what the information relates to in Java to confirm that you understand the contents of the article. Hand in the example and printed information.

7. **Search Sleuth** Select three key terms from the Key Terms section of this chapter and then use the Google search engine at google.com (or any major search engine) to display and print two Web pages for each key term.

Programming Assignments

1 Understanding Import Statements

The BillPayer program created in this chapter used six import statements. Make a list of the import statements and, under each one, list all of the classes and methods used in the program that come from that imported package. If necessary, use the Java API to help you discover which methods belong to which classes. Another way you can discover to which package a class or method belongs is to insert a comment mark (//) before the import statements, one at a time, and try to compile the program. TextPad will tell you it cannot resolve the symbol for the class that has no associated import statement.

2 Creating JOptionPane boxes

Figure 8-36 displays a program that accepts data for city sticker applications in the town of Flora. The Flora program is located in the Chapter08 folder of the Data Disk that accompanies this book. A Java source code file named MessageBox also is on the Data Disk. The Flora program needs to generate several message boxes for the user, but calls a programmer-supplied MessageBox class rather than using JOptionPane. You have been asked to update the Flora program to use appropriate JOptionPane boxes.

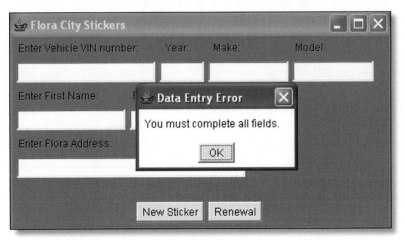

FIGURE 8-36

Perform the following steps.

1. Start TextPad and open the file named MessageBox. Print a copy for your reference.
2. Compile the MessageBox file.
3. Open the file named Flora. Print a copy for your reference.
4. Compile and run the Flora program.
5. Try entering data appropriately, then try omitting data fields. Notice when the message boxes are displayed. Close the program.

6. Look through the source code for the Flora.java file. Insert comment marks (//) at the beginning of all lines involving any of the message boxes, except for the MessageBox declaration statements. Directly underneath the lines that are commented out, insert new code to generate JOptionPane dialog boxes that replace the message boxes. Use the same titles, prompts, and buttons. Do not forget to import the necessary Swing packages.

7. Compile the Flora program again and fix errors if necessary.

8. Run the program and enter both appropriate and incorrect data. Try leaving some fields blank.

9. If necessary, fix any logic errors and then repeat steps 7 and 8 until the program runs correctly.

10. Print a copy of the updated Flora.java file for your instructor.

3 Converting Programs to Swing

Using the Flora program you updated in Programming Assignment 2, convert the interface to a Swing interface with the Motif Look and Feel. Convert all of the AWT components to Swing. Compile, debug, and run the program. Specifically, look at the changes in the dialog box. Print a copy of the updated Flora program for your instructor.

4 Creating a Requirements Document

Using the Flora program updated in Programming Assignment 2 or 3, create the requirements document that generated the production of the Flora program. Use your name as the programmer and the current date as the date. A blank requirements document, in Microsoft Word format, is located in the Chapter01 folder on your Data Files for Students disk. Include the purpose, necessary algorithms, and any notes the programmer might need. Use Figure 8-2 on page 489 as a model.

5 Understanding Layout Managers

Figure 8-37 displays a Java program that creates a window interface used by Ye Olde Ice Cream Shoppe in order to fill ice cream orders. Draw two different storyboards to explain how the layout managers might have been subsetted in order to achieve the components' placement.

FIGURE 8-37

6 Validity Checks

Update the BillPayer program created in this chapter to include validity checks on several fields before writing them to the external file. Check the account number field for a length of 10. Check the payment amount field to verify that it will parse to a double, thereby confirming it is numeric. Check the state field for a length of 2, and parse the zip code to an integer. Provide appropriate error message boxes and return the user to the field in question if the data is not valid. You may continue to use the writeUTF() methods, even though some of the data will be numeric.

7 Reading Data from the Payment File

The program developed in Chapter 8 sent data to an external, sequential data file named payment11192007 (or payment plus the system date for your computer). It opened a connection to the DataOutputStream and used the writeUTF() methods to transfer data to the disk. Write a new program named PaymentReader to read the data into a Swing interface that displays each record. Include a Next button.

8 Entering Course Substitutions

The registrar at your school would like an interface to enter course information for transfer students. The created data file should be sequential in nature, with the student's name, his/her ID number, the course number from the previous college, and the accepted course number at your school. The registrar then will give the data file to the transcript officer who will update the student's permanent files.

Figure 8-38 displays the interface.

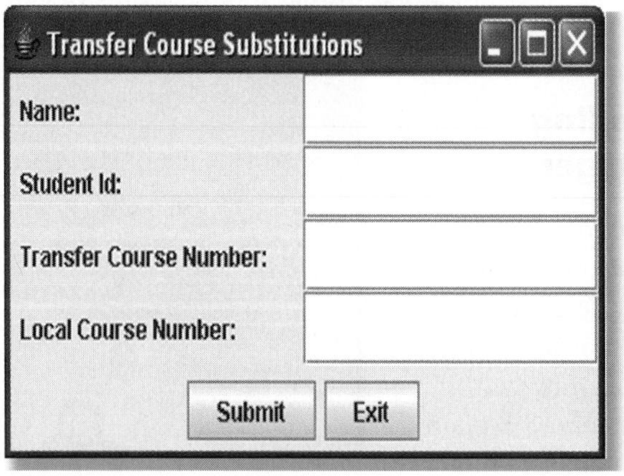

FIGURE 8-38

Using the concepts you learned in Chapter 8, perform the following steps:

1. Start TextPad. Enter the program comments, then import the java.io.*, java.awt.*, java.awt.event.*, javax.swing.*, java.text.*, and java.util.* packages.

2. Create a class header named Transfer, which extends JFrame and implements ActionListener.

3. Save the file on your Data Disk using the file name Transfer.java.

4. Type `DataOutputStream output;` to declare an output stream connection to the data file.

5. Construct two JPanels, four JLabels, four JTextFields, and two JButtons. Give them user-friendly names.

6. Create a main method that instantiates a Transfer window and then sets its title, size, and visibility.

7. Create a constructor method named Transfer, which sets a content pane to a BorderLayout, sets the first panel to a 4 × 2 GridLayout, and sets the second panel to a FlowLayout.

8. Within the Transfer() method, add the labels to the first panel and the buttons to the second panel. Add the panels to the BorderLayout and add the ActionListener to each button.

9. Type the code, `output = new DataOutputStream(new FileOutputStream("Transfer.dat"));` inside a try block.

10. Type the code, `System.exit(1);` inside the catch(IOException ex) block.

11. Lines 156 through 166 in Figure 8-21 on page 509 display the addWindowListener() method. Enter those lines to construct the window listener at the end of the Transfer() constructor method.

12. Create an actionPerformed() method. Within the block, type `String arg = e.getActionCommand();` to declare the button's argument, which is passed to the actionPerformed event when the user clicks a button.

13. Type `if (arg == "Submit")` and then press the ENTER key. Type an opening brace to begin the if block.

14. Create a second try block that contains output.writeUTF() methods to send each of the four JTextFields to the data file. For example, if your JTextField is called student, the code `output.writeUTF(student.getText());` would send that data to the data file. After the four statements, close the try block.

15. Create a catch(IOException ex) block that calls the System.exit() method.

16. Call a method named clearFields() and then close the if block.

17. Create an else block by typing the code from Table 8-14 on the next page.

(continued)

PROGRAMMING ASSIGNMENTS

8 Entering Course Substitutions *(continued)*

Table 8-14

CODE

```
else  //code to execute if the user clicks Exit
{
    try
    {
        output.close();
    }
    catch(IOException c)
    {
        System.exit(1);
    }
    System.exit(0);
}
```

---

18. Close the actionPerformed() method. Define the clearFields() method that is called in Step 16 on the previous page.

19. Compile the program. If errors occur, fix them in the TextPad source code window and then compile the program again.

20. Run the program and enter sample data for five students with fictitious ID numbers and transfer courses.

21. Print the source code for your instructor.

9 Displaying Stock Information

Open the file hotStocks.java from the Data Disk (see the inside back cover of this book for instructions on how to obtain a copy of the Data Disk).

You have accepted a job as an intern at a stock brokerage firm. Your first task is to create an interface to read in the previous day's "hottest" stocks, which are stored sequentially in a binary file named hotStocks.dat (also on the Data Disk).

Create a storyboard similar to the program interface displayed in Figure 8-39. Decide on your colors, your layout manager(s), and the names of your components.

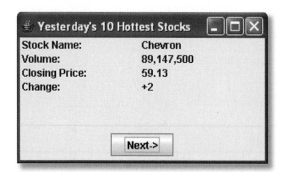

FIGURE 8-39

The data file contains the following fields: Stock Name, Volume, Closing Price, and Change, as displayed in Table 8-15. The Next button should progress through the data, one record at a time.

Table 8-15   Stock Data

STOCK NAME	VOLUME	CLOSING PRICE	CHANGE
Chevron	89,147,500	59.13	+2
Promina	65,323,400	44.44	+.56
Yahoo	60,709,500	29	+2.94
DellCptr	40,835,400	33.44	+1
Westpac	26,358,300	31.88	+2
Microsft	25,092,700	61.31	+.69
ExodusC	24,999,200	49.13	-4.13
EricTel	23,418,800	15.94	-.13
Alumina	22,579,400	63.88	...

The hotStocks.java file contains comments to assist you in entering Java statements in the correct places within the program. Perform the following steps:

1. Change the name of the class in the comments and class header in the hotStocks.java file to Stock. Save the file on the Data Disk or another location specified by your instructor using the file name Stock.java.

2. Type `DataInputStream input;` to declare an input stream connection to the data file.

3. Construct two panels, eight labels, and a button by entering the code from Table 8-16 in the class block.

Table 8-16

```
CODE
JPanel fieldPanel = new JPanel();
JPanel buttonPanel = new JPanel();
JLabel stockLabel = new JLabel("Stock Name:");
JLabel stock = new JLabel("                    ");
JLabel volumeLabel = new JLabel("Volume:");
JLabel volume = new JLabel("                ");
JLabel priceLabel = new JLabel("Closing Price:");
JLabel price = new JLabel("                ");
JLabel changeLabel = new JLabel("Change:");
JLabel change = new JLabel("                ");
JButton next = new JButton("Next->");
```

(continued)

9 Displaying Stock Information *(continued)*

4. In the constructor method Stock, set the background color to blue and the foreground color to white so that the interface has white letters on a blue background. Set the Next button's foreground color to black by typing `next.setForeground(Color.black);` so that the button has black letters.

5. Type `setLayout(new BorderLayout());` to set the frame's layout.

6. Type `fieldPanel.setLayout(new GridLayout(4,2));` to set the data panel layout.

7. Type `buttonPanel.setLayout(new FlowLayout());` to set the button area's layout.

8. Add the components and the ActionListener to the interface by entering the methods from Table 8-17.

Table 8-17

CODE

```
        fieldPanel.add(stockLabel);
        fieldPanel.add(stock);
        fieldPanel.add(volumeLabel);
        fieldPanel.add(volume);
        fieldPanel.add(priceLabel);
        fieldPanel.add(price);
        fieldPanel.add(changeLabel);
        fieldPanel.add(change);
        buttonPanel.add(next);
        add(fieldPanel, BorderLayout.NORTH);
        add(buttonPanel, BorderLayout.SOUTH);
        next.addActionListener(this);
```

9. In the try block of the actionPerformed() method, enter the code from Table 8-18 to read the String data into the appropriate labels.

Table 8-18

CODE

```
stock.setText(input.readUTF());
volume.setText(input.readUTF());
price.setText(input.readUTF());
change.setText(input.readUTF());
```

10. When the end of the file is reached, a message should display and the fields should be cleared. Enter the code from Table 8-19 in the catch block of the actionPerformed() method.

Table 8-19

CODE
| ```
stock.setText("End of File");
volume.setText("");
price.setText("");
change.setText("");
``` |

11. Save the file. Compile the program. If errors occur, correct them in the source code window, save the file, and then compile the program again.

12. Run the program. Click the Next button to look at all nine stocks. When you are finished, click the Close button in the program's title bar.

13. Print a copy of the source code for your instructor.

14. For extra credit, redo the data file with current stock information from the Web or newspaper.

10 Creating a Meteorology Data File

Your friend is majoring in meteorology. As a class project, she has been manually recording the daily rainfall amounts from the last 30 days. She now would like to generate an electronic data file to store the information. Create a Java application with a for loop that runs from 1 to 30. Components should include an input JTextField, a submit button, and appropriate prompts. Store the data file with the name RainfallReadings.dat on the Data Disk or in another location specified by your instructor.

11 On-Time Plumbers

On-Time Plumbers wants an interface with the Motif Look and Feel that allows its dispatcher to enter and record service calls each day and store them in a data file on a floppy disk. The fields should include time of the call, customer name, address, telephone number, and a description of the problem. The program should store the generated data file with the name Dispatch.dat on your Data Disk. Enter seven sample customers and then open the data file with TextPad. Print its contents, but do not resave the file.

12 Creating Message Boxes

Add a message box to any frame-based program that you created in this chapter or the previous chapter. The message box should display when the user clicks the Close button on the title bar. The message box should display the words, Are you sure you want to quit?, in its message. Place the statement before the System.exit command. Add functionality to both buttons. Save, compile, and execute your program. Print a copy of the source code.

PROGRAMMING ASSIGNMENTS
```

13 Creating an Assignment Data File

Create an interface that lets you enter a description of your Java lab assignments and the grades you receive, storing them in a file on your floppy disk. Create a Submit button for the submission of each grade and a Done button to close the file. When you click the Done button, the Submit button should disappear and a Retrieve button should take its place. Use the new Ocean Look and Feel. Add functionality to each button. Print a copy of the source code.

14 The W-2 Form

Assume that employee W-2 information has been stored in a sequential access file. Obtain a copy of a sample W-2 form from your local post office or the IRS Web site (www.irs.gov) and then create a storyboard, identifying the components and containers. Write the code to make the interface look like the form. Name each field appropriately. Finally, write the code to retrieve the information and fill in the form. Print a copy of the source code.

15 Using Version 5.0 Features

The BillPayer program created in this chapter uses a content pane, adding components by directly referring to the content pane. Read the Java 5.0 update on page 454. J2SE version 5.0 allows programmers to add components to the interface without explicitly referring to the content pane. Remove all references to the content pane and compile the program. Fix any errors and submit a printout of the code to your instructor.

9

Using Collections and Strings in a Reusable Class

Objectives

You will have
mastered the material in
this chapter when you can:

- Develop a class for reuse
- Understand class and instance variables
- Use the final qualifier
- Understand the Collections Framework
- Create an ArrayList object
- Create overloaded constructors
- Code accessor (get) methods
- Code mutator (set) methods
- Code accessor methods for read-only attributes
- Understand when to use public and private methods
- Code public instance methods
- Use an ArrayList method
- Understand and use the String and StringBuffer classes
- Code private helper methods
- Test a reusable class
- Use a JPassword field

Introduction

As you learned in Chapter 1, one of the key design principles in object-oriented programming is reusability, which provides programmers the ability to use existing code to develop a new application. We are accustomed to reuse in our physical environment: automobiles are assembled using previously manufactured components, such as transmissions, engines, and seats; and even custom-built houses are constructed using components, such as trusses, prehung windows and doors, and plumbing fixtures. Although automobiles or houses can be built with only raw materials, it is much more efficient to assemble the final product from preassembled components, each of which has a specific use. Additionally, those same components may be used for different end products, built at different times by different people.

The same concept applies to software. It may seem obvious that it is more efficient to write software components once and then reuse them, as opposed to developing everything from scratch each time. In practice, it is all too easy to write code that directly addresses the problem at hand, rather than designing the code with reuse in mind. To design for reuse, you must **abstract**, or separate out, the specific functionality of a given class and design it to provide that functionality regardless of the particular application where it is used.

In this chapter, you will learn how to incorporate some classes that already are developed for general use into your code, thus reusing this code. Using Java, you already have done this to some extent when you used classes such as Applet or Date, even if you did not realize it. You also will learn how to develop a class that can be reused in other programs to provide specific functionality.

Chapter Nine — Developing a Reusable Password Class

The class developed in this chapter encapsulates the concept of a password. When gaining access to a computer system or a software application, users often are required to enter a valid user name and a password associated with that user name. Because a password may be used in many different contexts, it seems a likely candidate to encapsulate this functionality in a reusable class. AccessFour Software is a company that has a number of applications where users are required to enter a valid user name and a password associated with that user name to gain access; however, the current password functionality varies from application to application. The information technology department at AccessFour Software thus would like to develop a reusable Password class, which will ensure that the same password functionality is used across multiple applications.

A password can have numerous characteristics or functionality. The password itself may have certain rules and restrictions placed upon it, such as a minimum length or a requirement for numeric characters. For increased security purposes, passwords also can expire after some period of use, requiring the user to change his or her password to a new value. Further, a history of previously used passwords can be maintained, so that the user cannot immediately reuse the same password when the current password expires. Additionally, passwords often are **encrypted**, meaning that they are encoded so as to be unintelligible to unauthorized parties. It becomes obvious that a password may have considerable functionality, all of which is inherent within the password itself. That is, the function of a password does not depend necessarily on the particular application, but instead depends on the definition of what a password is.

It is worth noting that such a definition of a password does not depend on or impact the user interface or how it is presented to the user. It is the functionality, not the presentation, which is encapsulated in the class. Consequently, the Password class can be used in a variety of applications.

In addition to the Password class developed in this chapter, a small Java program is provided to test the Password class once it is developed. This test program, called the PasswordDemo program, will provide a user interface for testing the Password class, to verify that the class works as required (Figure 9-1).

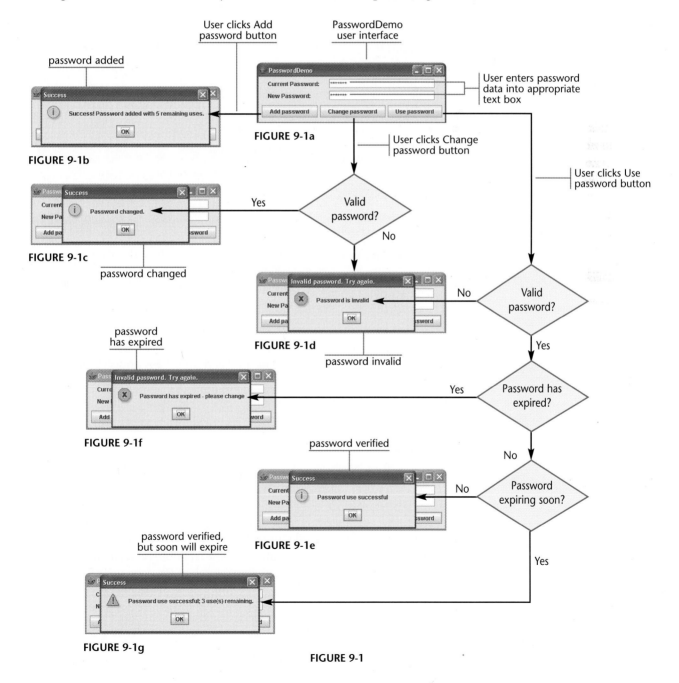

FIGURE 9-1

The main screen, as shown in Figure 9-1a on the previous page, allows a user to enter a password and then choose one of three options: (1) add a new password, (2) change an existing password, or (3) use a current password. A series of dialog boxes display results of successful or unsuccessful actions, such as adding a new password (Figure 9-1b), changing a password (Figure 9-1c), entering an invalid password (Figure 9-1d), using an existing password successfully (Figure 9-1e), trying to use a password that has already expired (Figure 9-1f), or using a password that soon will expire (Figure 9-1g). Each of these dialog boxes is displayed as the result of testing a different logical path in the Password class.

Program Development

The six development cycle phases and corresponding tasks for the Password class are shown in Table 9-1. You should note that, in object-oriented development, these tasks are often **iterative**, or repeating — particularly with regard to the design, implementation, and testing tasks.

Table 9-1   Password Class Development Tasks

	DEVELOPMENT PHASE	TASK(S)
1	Analyze the requirements	Analyze the Password class problem.
2	Design the solution	Design the logic to solve the problem.
3	Validate the design	Confirm with the user that the design solves the problem in a satisfactory manner.
4	Implement the design	Translate the design into code. Include internal documentation (comments and remarks) within the code that explains the purpose of the code statements. Design and code the user interface program used for testing the Password class.
5	Test the solution	Using the test program, test the Password class. Find and correct any errors (debug) until it is error-free.
6	Document the solution	Print copies of the Password class code and the test program code.

Analysis and Design

Figure 9-2 shows the requirements document that initiates the development cycle for the Password class. This document illustrates that a request can come from within the computer systems or information technology department, as well as from end users. Typically, this will happen when the request is for software to support the development of other applications, as is the case with the Password class.

REQUEST FOR NEW APPLICATION

Date submitted:	November 26, 2007
Submitted by:	Mark Allen, Staff Senior Systems Analyst, AccessFour Software
Purpose:	We have a number of applications where a user must enter a password to gain access; however, the current password functionality varies from application to application. There is a need for a reusable Password class, which will present the same functionality to be used across multiple applications so that users have consistent experience when entering a user name and password in any of the applications.
Application title:	Password class
Algorithms:	Encrypt passwords by (a) swapping the first and last halves of the original password string, (b) reversing the order of all resulting characters, (c) performing a bitwise AND operation on the bits of each character of the encrypted password with those of the corresponding character in the original password, and then (d) appending a hash code of the original password to the end of the encrypted password.
Notes:	1. All instances should have a minimum size of 6 characters and a maximum size of 15 characters, including at least one numeric.
	2. All instances should maintain a collection of the most recent encrypted password values used in an appropriate data structure. The number of passwords to keep in the history should be modifiable within a range of 1 to 10. Keep, by default, an active history of up to four passwords, including the current password value. New passwords cannot match any contained in the active history.
	3. If the password is set to expire, all instances should notify users of an expiring password when remaining uses value is 3 or less. This value should be modifiable within a range of 2 to 20.
	4. Each instance should have a maximum number of uses before expiration. This should be 120 by default.
	5. Each instance should track the number of remaining uses of the current password. Initially, this is the same as the maximum by default.
	6. Each instance should track whether or not it should expire automatically. The default value is true.
	7. The class should support only constructors that establish a new password value, and, optionally, set the maximum uses and/or the automatic expiration flag. When a new password is created, or when replacing an older password, the class should set a verified and encrypted password as the new current password.
	8. The class should validate against the current password any password given for use by the user, indicate if it is invalid or expired, and then if both valid and set to expire automatically, decrement the number of remaining uses.
	9. The class should verify the format of a given password.
	10. Users should be able to determine the number of remaining uses of a password.
	11. Users should be able to determine and to reset automatic password expiration.

Approval Status:	X	Approved
		Rejected
Approved by:	Wilson Davis, Director of IT, AccessFour Software	
Date:	November 28, 2007	
Assigned to:	M. Mick, Programmer	

FIGURE 9-2

PROBLEM ANALYSIS The problem that the Password class should solve is to encapsulate consistent password functionality that will be used by other programs, rather than to be an independent program. The requirements document shown in Figure 9-2 outlines several attributes and behaviors for the Password class. The Password class is to encrypt all passwords according to the algorithm presented in the requirements document.

The Password class also will contain several values that apply to all passwords, such as a minimum password size (6 characters), a maximum password size (15 characters), the maximum number of entries in the password history (4), and a usage expiration notification limit (3) that, when reached, triggers a notification to the user that the current password is expiring. The values of these items are the same for all Password objects. The Password class also contains some values that vary for each Password object, such as the maximum number of uses, the remaining number of uses, whether the password is set to expire automatically, if it has expired, and the history of passwords used.

The Password class will accumulate a history, or collection, of recently used passwords, including the current password; verify the format of all passwords to ensure that they are between the minimum and maximum length and that they contain at least one numeric character; validate a given password against the current password value; determine if the current password is approaching expiration; provide the number of remaining uses to a user; provide whether the password is set to expire automatically for a user; and allow the automatic expiration to be activated or inactivated.

DESIGN THE SOLUTION Once you have analyzed the problem and understand the needs, the next step is to design the class. Figure 9-3 shows an example of a class diagram for the Password class, with the attributes and methods determined from the analysis of the requirements document. The top four attributes apply equally to all instances of the class, while the next five may have unique values for each object. Of the 15 methods listed, the last two are needed only within the class, while the remaining 13 methods are available to all users. Constructor methods are not listed, as a general need for constructors is assumed, and because constructors differ only in their parameter lists, which are not shown here for any of the methods. Table 9-2 summarizes the methods in the Password class.

Password
MIN_SIZE MAX_SIZE maxHistory expiresNotifyLimit maxUses remainingUses autoExpires expired pswdHistory
getAutoExpires() setAutoExpires() isExpired() setExpired() getExpiresNotifyLimit() setExpiresNotifyLimit() getMaxHistory() setMaxHistory() getHistorySize getRemaining Uses() isExpiring set() validate() verifyFormat() encrypt()

FIGURE 9-3

Table 9-2   Methods of the Password Class

ACCESS	RETURN DATA TYPE	METHOD	PARAMETERS	PURPOSE
public	boolean	getAutoExpires()	none	Returns value of autoExpires attribute
public	void	setAutoExpires()	boolean	Sets value of autoExpires attribute
public	void	setExpired()	none	Sets value of expired attribute to true
public	boolean	isExpired()	none	Returns value of expired attribute
public	int	getExpiresNotifyLimit()	none	Returns value of expiresNotifyLimit attribute
public	void	setExpiresNotifyLimit()	int	Sets value of expiresNotifyLimit attribute
public	int	getMaxHistory()	none	Returns value of maxHistory attribute
public	void	setMaxHistory()	int	Sets value of maxHistory attribute; reduces the size of the password history list, if necessary
public	int	getHistorySize()	none	Returns the size of the ArrayList containing the password history
public	int	getRemainingUses()	none	Returns value of the remainingUses attribute
public	boolean	isExpiring()	none	Returns true if the password auto-expires and the number of remaining uses has reached the limit at which the user should be notified; otherwise, returns false
public	void	set()	String; unencrypted new password value	Sets the new password value if not in the recently used history; deletes oldest password from history, if necessary; resets expired and remaining uses, if necessary
public	void	validate()	String; unencrypted password value	Checks if password matches current password; if password has expired; if auto-expiring, reduces remaining uses, and sets expired flag, if necessary
private	void	verifyFormat()	String; unencrypted password value	Verifies password length and format meet requirements
private	String	encrypt()	String; unencrypted password value	Encrypts password string

When designing an object, keep in mind that the object may be used for other, future applications, so you want it to be as flexible as possible. The methods available for use by other programs generally need public accessibility. These methods are referred to as the **public interface** of the object. Be extremely careful defining the public interface. Once an object is put into use, changing its public interface might affect existing programs. It is good programming practice to publish the headers of any methods used as the public interface as part of the program documentation. You can change the **implementation** of a public method, that is, how the method works, without changing the public interface. For example, you may change how a password is validated without changing the header of the method called to validate a password. In such a case, programs that use the Password object might not need to be modified or even recompiled.

> **Documenting Methods Used in the Public Interface**
> It is good programming practice to publish as part of the program documentation the headers of any methods used as the public interface.

A method that is used to help an object accomplish its tasks and is not intended to be called by other programs commonly is referred to as a **helper method** and is made private.

When deciding whether methods should be public or private, remember that not everything an object does needs to be publicly available. If an action is self-contained — that is, it does not need to exchange data with other programs — consider making it private. For public methods, remember that only *what* is done is public, not *how* it is done. Design your classes to keep data and methods as private as possible, thus adhering to the principle of **least privilege** — restricting access from outside of the class to the minimum level necessary to perform the task.

> **Deciding between Public and Private Methods**
> Make methods public only if they must be accessible outside of the class. Try to keep methods private, if possible. It is more difficult to remove or modify a public method than a private method, because you may not know all of the classes that are using the public method.

PROGRAM IMPLEMENTATION   Once you have designed the class and validated the design, the next step in the development cycle is to implement the design, as shown in Table 9-1 on page 540. Implementing the design of the Password class involves writing code for attributes (data or variables) and methods, so as to provide the desired behavior. The analysis and design of the class indicate the data and methods expected for use. You may discover a need for additional changes to the design as you proceed through implementation. This is characteristic of the iterative nature of object-oriented programming: the ability to go back and make continual refinements. Be careful, however, to stay within the scope of the original project and make such refinements only when clearly warranted.

Starting a New Java Program in TextPad

The following steps start TextPad and save the TextPad document using a Java file type.

To Start a New Java Program in TextPad

1. Insert the Data Disk in drive A.

2. Start TextPad. If necessary, click View on the menu bar and then click Line Numbers on the View menu to display line numbers.

3. Click File on the menu bar and then click Save As on the File menu. When the Save As dialog box is displayed, click the Save in box arrow and then click 3½ Floppy (A:) in the Save in list.

4. Double-click the Chapter09 folder or a location specified by your instructor.

5. Type Password in the File name text box and then click Java (*.java) in the Save as type list. Click the Save button.

The file named, Password, is saved as a Java source code file in the Chapter09 folder on the Data Disk in drive A (Figure 9-4).

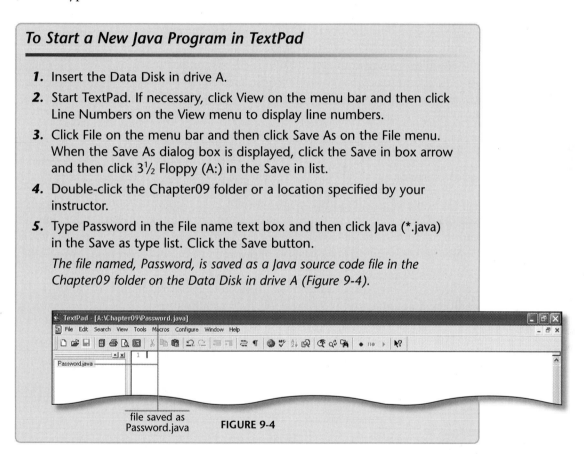

file saved as
Password.java   **FIGURE 9-4**

Class, Instance, and Final Variables

The requirements document in Figure 9-2 on page 541 indicates that some attributes of the Password class apply equally to all instances of the class, effectively sharing the variables among objects, while other attributes have unique values for each instance. This indicates a need for both class and instance variables.

Understanding Class and Instance Variables

A **class variable** is a variable shared by all objects of a class — that is, all instances. A class variable has only one value regardless of the particular object using it. If its value is changed for one object, then it is changed for all objects.

Additionally, class variables may exist and be accessible even when no object of the class exists. The access qualifier, **static**, is used to indicate variables or methods associated with the class rather than an instance. In contrast, an **instance variable** exists only when an object — that is, an instance of the class — exists and its value is not shared among objects. Each object has its own set of values for instance variables. Changing the value of an instance variable in one object does not necessarily affect the value of the same variable in another object. Furthermore, instance variables are often defined as **private**, limiting their access to within the class.

Both class and instance variables are defined outside of the method definitions in a class and are in scope, which means that they are accessible from any method within the class. A **local variable**, however, is a variable defined within a method or in the parameter list of a method, and is in scope only within that method. Local variables should be considered as temporary storage because once the method exits, they no longer are usable. If the method is executed again, new local variables are created.

Using the Final Qualifier

Variables, by definition, contain values that can change. In some cases, however, a programmer needs to ensure that the value of a class or instance variable is not changed, even inadvertently; the variable should contain a constant value. Such a variable is sometimes called a **named constant**, a **constant variable**, or in Java, a **final variable**. Using a final variable allows a constant to have a name, which the Java program can use in multiple places. Giving a constant a name avoids having duplicates of a literal, such as 25 or 'a', throughout the program and improves readability and maintainability of the code. In Java, a final variable is declared with the **final** qualifier and, by convention, is written using all capital letters.

Final instance variables can be left uninitialized when defined. Such a variable is called a **blank final**. The compiler will require the constructor(s) to initialize such a variable, but each constructor need not supply the same value. Consequently, the same value may not be used for all instances.

Blank Finals

Blank finals allow objects of the same class to have the same named constant, but with potentially different values. These values may be obtained from an external file used to configure the application. Although very flexible, this is potentially confusing and, as a consequence, blank finals often are not used.

Figure 9-5 displays the code for the initial comments, the import statement, and the declaration of class and instance variables, including two final variables. Lines 1 through 7 add the block comment, line 9 imports the java.util.* package, and line 11 includes the Password class header. Lines 13 through 16 declare four class variables, including two final variables, MIN_SIZE and MAX_SIZE, which set the minimum length of a password to 6 characters and the maximum length of a password to 15 characters. Lines 18 through 23 declare five instance variables. Table 9-3 lists the class and instance variables of the Password class.

Table 9-3   Class and Instance Variables of the Password Class

VARIABLE SCOPE	DATA TYPE	VARIABLE NAME	PURPOSE
Class	int (final)	MIN_SIZE	Indicates the minimum size (length) of a password
Class	int (final)	MAX_SIZE	Indicates the maximum size (length) of a password
Class	int	maxHistory	Indicates the maximum number of entries in password history list
Class	int	expiresNotifyLimit	Indicates the number of remaining uses when password nears expiration
Instance	int	maxUses	Indicates the maximum number of uses for an auto-expiring password
Instance	int	remainingUses	Indicates the number of remaining uses for an auto-expiring password
Instance	boolean	autoExpires	Indicates whether password should automatically expire
Instance	boolean	expired	Indicates whether password has expired
Instance	ArrayList	pswdHistory	Contains a list of current and recently used passwords

The following steps enter the code to declare class and instance variables, including the final variables, for the Password class.

```
1  /*
2       Chapter 9:   The Password Class
3       Programmer:  Michael Mick
4       Date:        November 28, 2007
5       Filename:    Password.java
6       Purpose:     To provide a reusable Password class
7  */
8
9  import java.util.*;
10
11 public class Password
12 {
13     final static int MIN_SIZE = 6;
14     final static int MAX_SIZE = 15;
15          static int maxHistory = 4;
16          static int expiresNotifyLimit = 3;
17
18     private int maxUses = 120;
19     private int remainingUses = maxUses;
20     private boolean autoExpires = true;
21     private boolean expired = false;
22
23     private ArrayList pswdHistory;
24
```

FIGURE 9-5

To Create Class and Instance Variables

1. Enter lines 1 through 16 as shown in Figure 9-5 on the previous page. In the comments, insert your own name as programmer and enter the current date.

TextPad displays code for the initial comments, import statement, class header, and class variables in the coding window (Figure 9-6). The first two variables are constants because of the keyword, final, while the next two are not. The indentation used helps to make the distinction more noticeable.

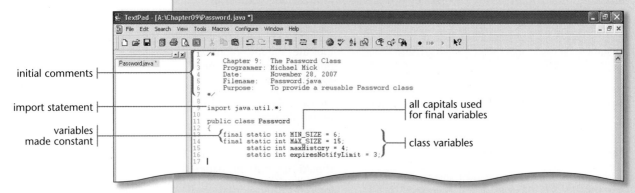

FIGURE 9-6

2. Enter lines 17 through 24 as shown in Figure 9-5.

TextPad displays the code for the instance variables in the coding window (Figure 9-7). The instance variable of type ArrayList required the import of java.util. to make the ArrayList class from this package available for use in the class.*

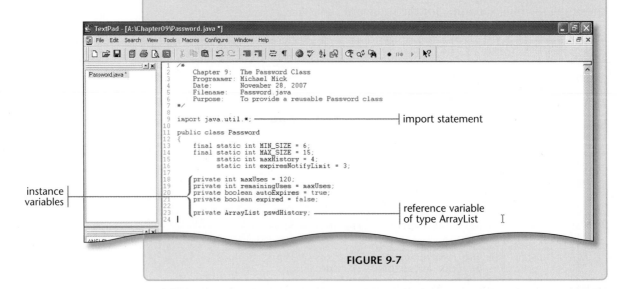

FIGURE 9-7

The code entered in the previous steps sets the initial values of the class and instance variables to match the requirements defined in the requirements document in Figure 9-2 on page 541. For example, the maxHistory variable is set to 4, so that the password class keeps an active history of four passwords by default, while the expiresNotifyLimit variable is set to 3 so that users are notified of an expiring password when the number of remaining uses is 3 or less. As shown in lines 13 and 14, you should make final variables static whenever possible. This reduces the required memory, as static variables are shared across all instances.

Making Final Variables Static
Making final variables static ensures that the same value is used for all instances. Also, if you forget to initialize such a variable, the compiler will generate an error message to remind you.

Understanding the Collections Framework

A **data structure** is simply a format for storing a group, or **collection**, of data. The format may indicate, whether implicitly or explicitly, how the data is to be accessed or otherwise manipulated. For example, as you learned in Chapter 5, an array is a type of general data structure that utilizes an index to access data stored in the array.

Java provides an application program interface (API) for dealing with a number of common data structures, or collections, called the **Collections Framework**. The Collections Framework provides interfaces, implementations, and algorithms for representing and manipulating collections. Among other uses, interfaces are used to provide a general means for manipulating collections independent of how the collections are represented (for example, as lists, maps, or sets); interfaces will be discussed in detail in a later chapter. The implementations provide essentially reusable data structures from the collections interfaces, such as **ArrayList**, which is a list implemented as an array. A **list** is simply an ordered collection, such as a list of names. The algorithms provide a means of performing operations — such as adding to or retrieving from the list, searching, and sorting — on objects that implement the Collections Framework interfaces. Figure 9-8 represents the hierarchy of interfaces in the Collections Framework. The Collections Framework is based on the collections listed in Table 9-4 on the next page.

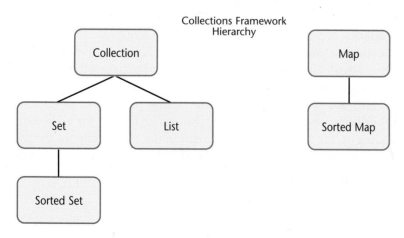

FIGURE 9-8

Table 9-4 *The Collections Framework*

CORE COLLECTION INTERFACES	DESCRIPTION	GENERAL-PURPOSE IMPLEMENTATIONS PROVIDED
Collection	The root of the collection hierarchy.	No implementation
Set	A collection that cannot contain duplicates. Models the mathematical abstraction of a set. Inherits from Collection.	HashSet, TreeSet
SortedSet	A Set in ascending element order. Inherits from Set.	No implementation
List	An ordered collection which can contain duplicates. Inherits from Collection.	ArrayList, LinkedList
Map	Maps keys (unique identifier values) to at most one other value each; cannot contain duplicate keys. Not a true collection, so it does not inherit from Collection. Included in the Collections Framework because it contains operations which allow manipulation as a collection.	HashMap, TreeMap
SortedMap	A Map in ascending key order. Inherits from Map.	No implementation

The requirements for the Password class indicate that a collection of previously encrypted password values be kept in a password history list. The Collections Framework provides an appropriate means of storing and manipulating such a collection with relative ease. The specific implementation for the collection used within the Password class is independent of users of the class, which means it can be changed later, if necessary, without affecting programs dependent on the functionality of the Password class.

Creating an ArrayList

The requirement for the Password class to maintain a collection of password values can be implemented in a variety of ways. It seems intuitive, however, that because a list of passwords is needed, an implementation using the List collection would be most appropriate. The framework provides two general-purpose implementations of List: LinkedList and ArrayList. ArrayList allows programmers to resize the length of the list, inserting and deleting list members. The ability to resize the list of passwords is specified in the requirements document. The **capacity** of the ArrayList is the size of the array used to store the array elements, which is always at least as large as the list **size** — that is, the number of elements actually in the list. As elements are added, when the list size reaches the capacity, the capacity is increased automatically. Additionally, ArrayList typically yields faster access than LinkedList. The time to position to an element in an ArrayList is the same for any element, but varies linearly for a LinkedList, depending on the location of the element in the list. Because of the way the password list will need to be manipulated, ArrayList is the most appropriate implementation to use.

ArrayList vs. LinkedList
ArrayList typically yields faster access than LinkedList. With an ArrayList, accessing any element requires the same time regardless of the size of the array.

In Figure 9-5 on page 547, line 23 declared an instance variable with a type of ArrayList. To create an ArrayList object, you need to call the appropriate constructor using the new keyword, as you would with any other object, and assign it to the instance variable. This constructor is listed in the SDK documentation as

```
ArrayList(int initialCapacity)
```

When constructed, the ArrayList() method has one parameter: an int value that represents the initial capacity of the list. As you will see, this ArrayList constructor will be called in each of the constructors of the Password class.

Creating Overloaded Constructors

You may remember that a constructor is called automatically when you create a new instance of a class (that is, an object). Recall that a constructor is a special kind of instance method that has the same name as the class and has no return data type, not even void; further, a constructor may or may not have a parameter list. A Java constructor that has no parameters (and therefore requires no arguments to be passed when called) is termed a **default constructor**. If a class has no constructors coded, then the compiler creates a default constructor that serves only as a target for the operator, new, which causes a constructor to be called. If even a single constructor is coded, then the compiler will not create a default constructor; in such cases, if the class is to have a default constructor, the programmer then must code it.

The major function of a constructor is to ensure that all instance variables of the class are initialized appropriately. The variables can be initialized by directly assigning a value, by allocating resources such as new instances of other objects, or by calling other methods within the class to establish a valid value. When a constructor is called with an empty argument list it uses default values for all instance variables. A **default value** is the value used when no other value is supplied. The values assigned to each of the instance variables coded in lines 18 through 21 are the initial, or default, values that are used unless replaced with a new value in a constructor.

If no constructors were coded, the default values always would be the initial values for these variables each time an object was created. Depending on the circumstances, you may want different initial values for different objects. Furthermore, when an instance variable is a reference to another object, as is the pswdHistory variable in line 23, that other object must be constructed for the reference variable to have an initial value other than null — a process typically performed by the constructor.

The requirements document states that the Password class should support only constructors which are supplied, at a minimum, with a password value. Therefore, this class will not support a default constructor. Additionally, the requirements document states that users should have the option to supply values for the maximum number of uses, for automatic expiration, or both. This indicates that at least four different constructors with a parameter for a new password value are needed. Each constructor will have a String parameter for a new password value. The first constructor will use default values for all other instance variables, so only one parameter is passed. The second constructor will have an additional int parameter for the maximum number of uses. The third constructor will have a boolean parameter for automatic expiration. The fourth constructor will have both the int parameter for the maximum number of uses and the boolean parameter for automatic expiration. This is possible because a Java class can have multiple constructors, each having the same name as the class.

As you learned in Chapter 5, the practice of defining more than one method with the same name is called method overloading. When a program contains multiple methods (whether they are constructors or not) all having the same name, the methods are said to be **overloaded**.

When creating an object, only one constructor is called, so a means is required by which the compiler can uniquely identify the indicated method. This is done through the **method signature**, which is obtained from a combination of the method name and the formal parameter list in the method header. Because overloaded methods have the same name, they must have unique parameter lists, either in the number of parameters used or in the order of the data types. For example, the following two method headers are valid overloaded methods.

```
public float calcCommission(String name, float commission)

public float calcCommission(float commission, String name)
```

Although the methods have the same names and number of parameters, each parameter list has a different order of data types: the first has a String followed by a float, while the second has a float followed by a String. The return data type is not used in determining the method signature; therefore, changing only the return data type would not result in overloaded methods with unique method signatures. Because constructors do not have return data types and they all have the same name, it is even more obvious that only unique parameter lists provide unique signatures in overloaded methods.

Use Unique Parameter Lists for Overloaded Methods
Multiple methods may be defined with the same name, but they must not have identical parameter lists. The method name plus the parameter list form the method signature, which must be unique.

Figure 9-9 displays the code for the four overloaded constructors for the Password class. Within each constructor, a new ArrayList object named pswdHistory is created. This object has a capacity indicated by the class variable, maxHistory. Within each constructor, instance variables are assigned new values as appropriate. The constructor in lines 27 through 31 will use default values for all instance variables. The second constructor in lines 33 through 39 has an additional parameter for the maximum number of uses; the int value, numMaxUses, is passed to the constructor and assigned to both the class variables, maxUses and remainingUses (lines 36 and 37). Lines 41 through 46 include a third constructor with parameters for automatic expiration; the boolean parameter pswdAutoExpires is assigned to the instance variable autoExpires. Lines 48 through 55 include a fourth constructor that has parameters for the maximum number of uses and for automatic expiration.

Any instance variables not assigned new values retain their initial, or default, values assigned at declaration. Because each constructor receives a password value, each calls the set() method to set the current password to the new value. The set() method, to be coded later, will verify that the new password value uses the proper format and has not been used recently, and then it will call the appropriate method to encrypt the new value. Because the set() method, as well as other methods it calls, may throw an exception to indicate a problem with the new password, the constructors must claim the exception, as they will not handle them. Because no specific type of exception yet exists for an invalid password, each constructor simply claims a general Exception by using the keyword, throws, followed by the word, Exception, in the method header (lines 27, 33, 41, and 48 of Figure 9-9).

```
25
26      // Constructors for objects of class Password
27      public Password(String newPassword) throws Exception
28      {
29          pswdHistory = new ArrayList(maxHistory);
30          set(newPassword);
31      }
32
33      public Password(String newPassword, int numMaxUses) throws Exception
34      {
35          pswdHistory = new ArrayList(maxHistory);
36          maxUses = numMaxUses;
37          remainingUses = numMaxUses;
38          set(newPassword);
39      }
40
41      public Password(String newPassword, boolean pswdAutoExpires) throws Exception
42      {
43          pswdHistory = new ArrayList(maxHistory);
44          autoExpires = pswdAutoExpires;
45          set(newPassword);
46      }
47
48      public Password(String newPassword, int numMaxUses, boolean pswdAutoExpires) throws
        Exception
49      {
50          pswdHistory = new ArrayList(maxHistory);
51          maxUses = numMaxUses;
52          remainingUses = numMaxUses;
53          autoExpires = pswdAutoExpires;
54          set(newPassword);
55      }
56
```

FIGURE 9-9

The following step enters code to create the overloaded constructors.

To Create Overloaded Constructors

1. Enter lines 25 through 55 as shown in Figure 9-9 on the previous page.
TextPad displays the code for the constructors in the coding window (Figure 9-10). Each constructor creates a new ArrayList object to assign to the instance variable of type ArrayList. The set() method called in each constructor will be coded later.

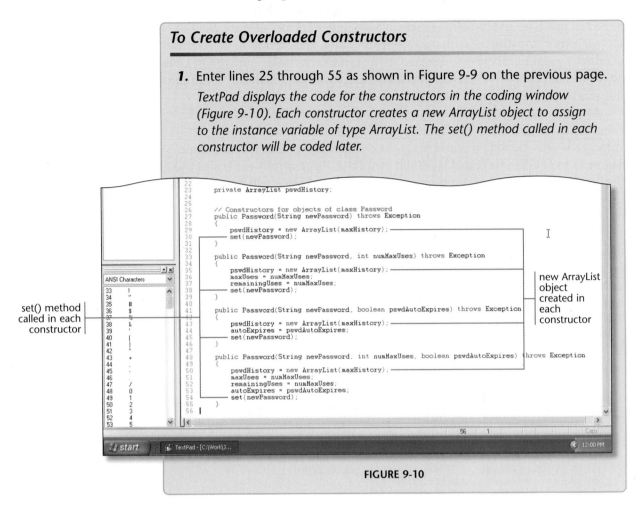

FIGURE 9-10

The overloaded constructors now are completed. To complete the Password class, however, additional instance methods are needed.

Understanding Accessor (Get) and Mutator (Set) Methods

Recall that instance variables (attributes) typically are kept private in order to support the concept of information hiding. Applications that will use the Password class, also called **user programs**, do not need to know the specifics of the instance attributes. Only methods within the class have access to private variables, so user programs — that is, any object outside of the class — must call instance methods of the class in order to gain access to the variables, either to obtain or change their value. Typically, a class will provide methods strictly for the purpose of obtaining or changing the value of instance variables.

Coding Accessor Methods

An **accessor method** provides the value of a private variable within the class to a user program. These methods sometimes are called get or getter methods because of a common naming convention, in which the methods often are named using the verb, get, followed by the name of the returned instance variable. For example, the accessor method, getMaxHistory(), returns the value of the maxHistory instance variable. For boolean variables, accessor methods sometimes are coded with the word, is, followed by the variable name, rather than the word, get. For example, the boolean instance variable, expired, could have an accessor method named either getExpired() or isExpired().

An accessor method is coded with no parameters; however, its return data type must match the variable whose value it returns. For example, the maxHistory variable is of type int; therefore, the header for its accessor method would be

```
public int getMaxHistory()
```

In the body of such an accessor method, the code typically may do no more than simply return the corresponding variable value, and as such is quite simple. An accessor method is necessary in order for a user program to obtain the value of a private instance variable.

Coding Mutator Methods

A **mutator method** accepts a proposed new value for the variable and sometimes is called a set or setter method, again because of a common naming convention. In this case, set is added in front of the variable name to form the method name, as in setMaxHistory(). With mutator methods, the return type typically is void, although sometimes it is boolean so the method can indicate whether the proposed change was accepted. The single parameter represents the proposed new value for the given variable. For the maxHistory variable, the mutator method header would be written as

```
public void setMaxHistory(int newMaxHistory)
```

The mutator method then is responsible for determining if the new value is valid — in this case, within an acceptable range. A user program would call the setMaxHistory() method, sending a proposed new value for the instance variable. If the proposed value is accepted, the mutator method would change the value of the corresponding instance variable.

The new value is only a proposed value, because the mutator method may determine that it is not valid and reject it without making the modification. This action illustrates another aspect of encapsulation: that objects are responsible for their own data. Encapsulating the data and the methods that access and change the data within the object allows the object to determine if a new value is valid before the attribute is changed. For example, the requirements document states that the number of passwords to keep in the history can be changed, but only within a range of one to ten. Therefore, the mutator method for this attribute must verify that any new value is within this range before allowing the current value to be changed. In many non-object-oriented languages, variables may be assigned new values from many different places in the program code and possibly without performing appropriate validation beforehand. By having the object take responsibility for validating any potential change, value assignment for attributes have a single point of control — within the object itself.

The autoExpires Accessor and Mutator Methods

Figure 9-11 displays the accessor method and mutator method for the autoExpires instance variable of the Password class.

```
57      public boolean getAutoExpires()
58      {
59          return autoExpires;
60      }
61
62      public void setAutoExpires(boolean autoExpires)
63      {
64          this.autoExpires = autoExpires;
65          if(autoExpires)
66              remainingUses = maxUses;
67
```

FIGURE 9-11

Both methods are quite short. The accessor method, getAutoExpires(), in lines 57 through 60 returns the value of the instance variable, autoExpires. The mutator method, setAutoExpires(), in lines 62 through 67, sets the value of the instance variable to the value retrieved from the parameter. Because the variables are of the boolean data type, the parameter does not need to be validated; it can have only the value of either true or false, both of which are valid.

The code may be somewhat confusing, however, in that the parameter in line 62 and the corresponding instance variable have the same name, autoExpires. This is a legal and an acceptable way to code the mutator method, setAutoExpires(). Because of the scope of local variables, as discussed earlier, the passed parameter or local variable — defined in the parameter list in line 62 — takes precedence over the instance variable with the same name. Consequently, any use of the variable name, autoExpires, using just the name of the variable refers to the local variable — that is, the parameter, and not the instance variable. To differentiate and refer to the instance variable, programmers must specify a reference to the current object along with the variable name. The keyword, **this**, in line 64 provides an explicit reference to the current object within the class. To illustrate, if the assignment statement were coded

```
autoExpires = autoExpires;
```

it simply would assign the value of the parameter back to itself. No error would occur, but the instance variable would not be changed. This is a common logic error with beginning Java programmers. The statement can be corrected in one of two ways. The first is to use the reference, this, with the instance variable, as in

```
this.autoExpires = autoExpires;
```

This statement, shown in line 64 of Figure 9-11, assigns the value of the parameter, autoExpires, to the instance variable associated with the current object, this.autoExpires, as desired. The second way to correct the assignment statement is to use distinct names for parameters which do not conflict with instance variable names, as in

`autoExpires = pswdAutoExpires;`

where pswdAutoExpires is the name of the parameter. This second technique is the safest for programmers new to Java.

Using Variable Names in Assignment Statements

Beginning Java programmers writing assignment statements should use for parameters distinct names that do not conflict with instance variable names.

Finally, lines 65 and 66 of the mutator method, setAutoExpires(), check to see if the password has been changed to expire automatically and, if so, the method resets the remainingUses value. In line 65, an if statement tests the value of the autoExpires variable. If the user program has sent a true value to the method in order to say that the password should be changed to expire automatically, the method then sets the remaining uses of the password back to the maximum.

The following steps enter code for the accessor and mutator methods for the autoExpires instance variable of the Password class.

To Code Accessor and Mutator Methods for the autoExpires Instance Variable

1. Enter lines 57 through 60 as shown in Figure 9-11.

TextPad displays the accessor method, getAutoExpires(), for the autoExpires instance variable in the Password class (Figure 9-12). The return data type is boolean because the method is returning the value of the instance variable, autoExpires, which is of type boolean.

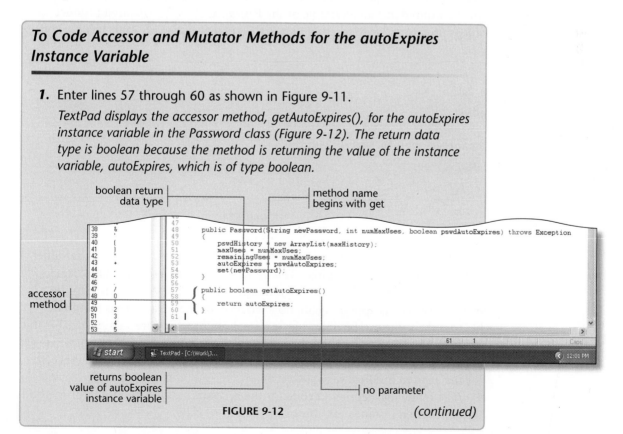

FIGURE 9-12   *(continued)*

2. Enter lines 62 through 67 as shown in Figure 9-11 on page 556.

TextPad displays the mutator method, setAutoExpires(), for the autoExpires variable (Figure 9-13). The use of the keyword, this, in line 64 distinguishes the instance variable from the parameter.

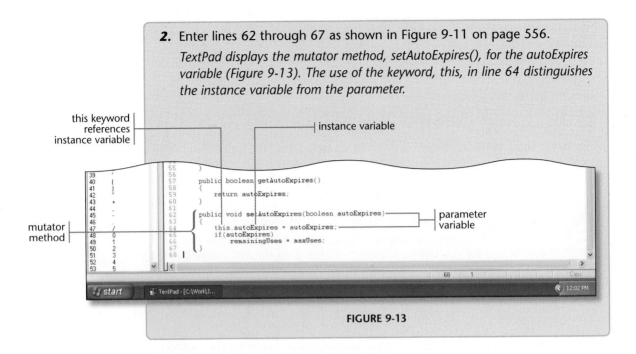

FIGURE 9-13

expired ACCESSOR AND MUTATOR METHODS   As illustrated in the previous steps, accessor and mutator methods typically are grouped in matching pairs of get and set methods for ease of maintenance. As discussed earlier, a boolean variable may have an accessor method with a name that begins with is rather than get. Figure 9-14 displays the accessor method and mutator method for the expired instance variable of the Password class. The expired instance variable is used to indicate whether or not the current password value has expired.

```
69      public boolean isExpired()
70      {
71          return expired;
72      }
73
74      public void setExpired(boolean newExpired)
75      {
76          expired = newExpired;
77      }
```

FIGURE 9-14

The accessor method, isExpired(), in lines 69 through 72 returns the value of the instance variable, expired. The mutator method, setExpired(), accepts a boolean value from the user program and then, in line 76, assigns it to the instance variable, expired. Again, no validation of the parameter is required because the value can be only true or false, both of which are valid values for this method. Note that using a unique name for the parameter — that is, newExpired instead of expired — eliminates the need to use the explicit object reference, this, for the expired instance variable.

The following steps enter code for the accessor method and mutator method for the expired instance variable of the Password class.

To Code Accessor and Mutator Methods for the expired Instance Variable

1. Enter lines 69 through 72 as shown in Figure 9-14.

TextPad displays the accessor method for the expired variable (Figure 9-15). The method name begins with is, rather than get.

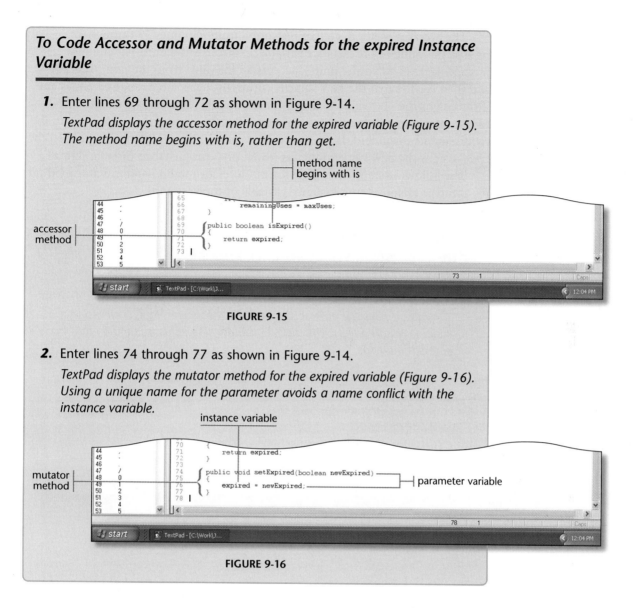

FIGURE 9-15

2. Enter lines 74 through 77 as shown in Figure 9-14.

TextPad displays the mutator method for the expired variable (Figure 9-16). Using a unique name for the parameter avoids a name conflict with the instance variable.

FIGURE 9-16

expiresNotifyLimit ACCESSOR AND MUTATOR METHODS

Figure 9-17 displays the accessor method and mutator method for the expiresNotifyLimit instance variable of the Password class. Recall that the number contained in this variable is used to determine if the password will expire soon.

```
79    public int getExpiresNotifyLimit()
80    {
81        return expiresNotifyLimit;
82    }
83
84    public void setExpiresNotifyLimit(int newNotifyLimit)
85    {
86        if(newNotifyLimit >= 2 && newNotifyLimit <= 20)
87            expiresNotifyLimit = newNotifyLimit;
88    }
```

FIGURE 9-17

The accessor method, getExpiresNotifyLimit(), in lines 79 through 82 returns the value of the instance variable, expiresNotifyLimit. The mutator method, setExpiresNotifyLimit(), accepts an int value from the user program and then verifies that the new value is within the acceptable range of values and, if so, assigns the new value to the instance variable. Line 86 uses a logical AND to test the parameter for a value between 2 and 20, inclusively, as specified in the requirements document. If the new value is within the acceptable range, then the code assigns the new value to the expiresNotifyLimit instance variable (line 87).

The following steps enter code for the accessor method and mutator method for the expiresNotifyLimit instance variable of the Password class.

To Code Accessor and Mutator Methods for the expiresNotifyLimit Instance Variable

1. Enter lines 79 through 82 as shown in Figure 9-17 on the previous page.

   TextPad displays the accessor method for the expiresNotifyLimit instance variable (Figure 9-18). The method is quite simple, as is common for accessor methods.

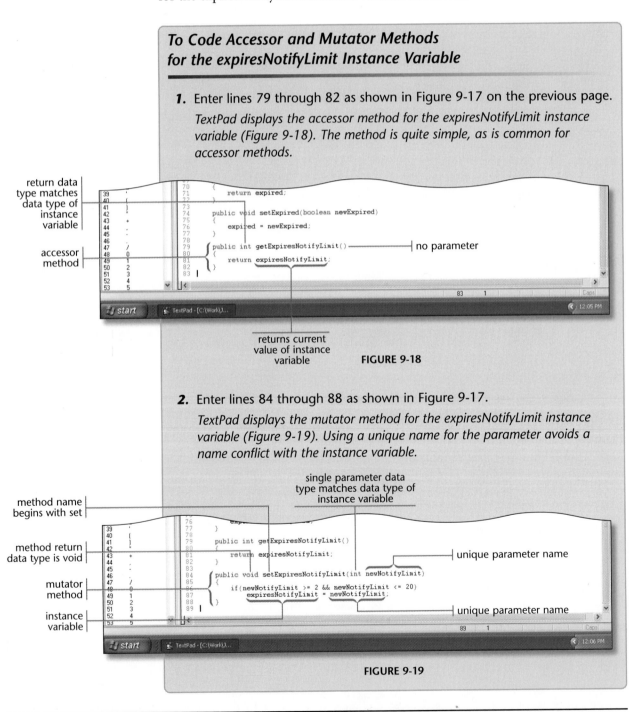

FIGURE 9-18

2. Enter lines 84 through 88 as shown in Figure 9-17.

   TextPad displays the mutator method for the expiresNotifyLimit instance variable (Figure 9-19). Using a unique name for the parameter avoids a name conflict with the instance variable.

FIGURE 9-19

maxHistory ACCESSOR AND MUTATOR METHODS Figure 9-20 displays the pseudocode that outlines the logic for the setMaxHistory() method. Figure 9-21 displays the code for the accessor method and mutator method for the maxHistory instance variable of the Password class.

setMaxHistory() method   (no return data; parameter is integer: new max history limit)

Begin
    If new max history limit between 1 and 10, inclusive
        max history limit = new max history limit
        overage = size of password history list – max history limit
        If overage > 0   (if positive, number of elements exceeds limit)
            Do
                remove oldest element in password history list
                decrease overage by 1
            While overage > 0

only done if size of password history list > max history limit

            trim capacity of password history list to current size (max history limit)
        End If
    End If
End

FIGURE 9-20

```
90          public int getMaxHistory()
91          {
92              return maxHistory;
93          }
94
95          public void setMaxHistory(int newMaxHistory)
96          {
97              int overage = 0;
98              if(newMaxHistory >= 1 && newMaxHistory <= 10)
99              {
100                 maxHistory = newMaxHistory;
101                 overage = getHistorySize() - maxHistory;
102                 if(overage > 0)                          // if size > max allowed
103                 {
104                     do {
105                         pswdHistory.remove(0);           // then remove overage number
106                         overage--;                       // of oldest pswds from list
107                     } while(overage > 0);
108
109                     pswdHistory.trimToSize();            // resize capacity to max allowed
110                 }
111             }
112         }
```

FIGURE 9-21

This pair of accessor and mutator methods is similar to the pairs coded in the previous steps. The accessor method, getMaxHistory(), in lines 90 through 93 simply returns the value of the instance variable, maxHistory. The mutator method, setMaxHistory(), is somewhat more complex. First, the setMaxHistory() method verifies that the new value is within the acceptable range of values for passwords stored in the password history list — that is, between 1 and 10, inclusively, as specified in the requirements document (line 98). If the new value is not valid, it is ignored. If the new value is valid, the setMaxHistory() method assigns the new value to the instance variable, maxHistory (line 100). Line 101 then subtracts maxHistory from the current history size (ascertained by a method call to the accessor method). The result of the subtraction is assigned to a variable named overage. If the new value assigned to overage is greater than zero (line 102), the oldest passwords in the history must be removed until the history is not larger than the new value represented by maxHistory. The ArrayList class does have a method to remove a range of values; however, that method is protected and not available for use by methods in the Password class.

The only accessible method, the **remove() method**, removes elements from the ArrayList one at a time. Lines 104 through 107 thus include a do…while loop that removes the older passwords from the list until the overage number is equal to zero. Line 109 uses the **trimToSize() method** to reset the capacity of the ArrayList, pswdHistory, to the new maximum size, which is also the number of current elements. The remove() and trimToSize() methods are discussed in more detail later in the chapter, along with additional ArrayList methods.

The following steps enter the code for the accessor method and mutator method for the maxHistory instance variable of the Password class.

To Code Accessor and Mutator Methods for the maxHistory Instance Variable

1. Enter lines 90 through 93 as shown in Figure 9-21 on the previous page.

TextPad displays the accessor method for the maxHistory variable in the coding window (Figure 9-22).

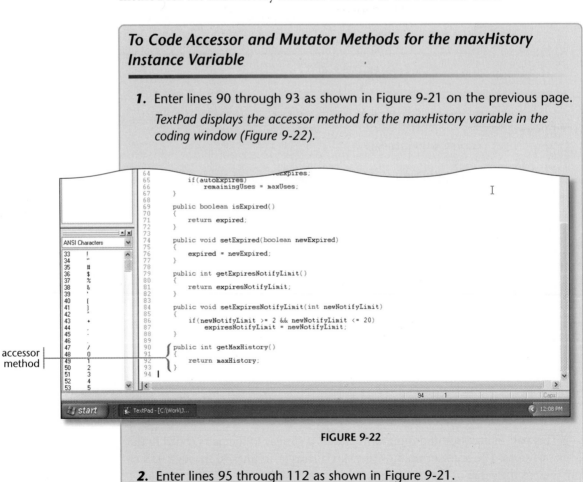

FIGURE 9-22

2. Enter lines 95 through 112 as shown in Figure 9-21.

TextPad displays the mutator method for the maxHistory variable in the coding window (Figure 9-23). If the new history size is greater than or equal to the current size, no old password elements are removed from the password history list.

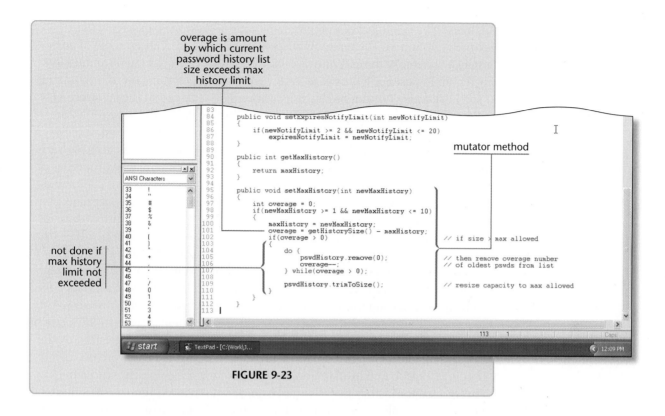

FIGURE 9-23

Setting the maximum size of the password history less than the current size might be done rarely, if at all. The mutator method, setMaxHistory(), must ensure that the number of passwords stored in the history never is more than the maximum size. To do so, any excess entries in the history must be removed, beginning with the oldest entry.

Coding Accessor Methods for Read-Only Attributes

As shown in the previous section, accessor and mutator methods often are coded successively, so it is obvious to the programmer when they exist in pairs. Some attributes, however, have an accessor method, but no mutator method. These attributes sometimes are called **read-only** attributes, because the user can obtain their value but cannot change it, effectively providing read-only access to the attributes.

Figure 9-24 displays the code for the accessor methods to read-only values for the Password class.

```
114     public int getRemainingUses()
115     {
116         return remainingUses;
117     }
118
119     public int getHistorySize()
120     {
121         return pswdHistory.size();
122     }
```

FIGURE 9-24

Lines 114 through 117 in Figure 9-24 on the previous page create the accessor method for the remainingUses attribute, which is an example of an instance variable with read-only access. With the current design, once the value for remaining uses of a password is set by the constructor, it cannot be changed. If such a feature were desired later, it easily could be added to the Password class without affecting current users of the class. This illustrates the iterative nature of object-oriented programming described earlier in this chapter.

Some attributes, or properties, of an object may not appear as instance variables in the class definition. These attributes, or properties, may be properties of a parent class which the object has inherited; in this case, the parent class should provide accessor and/or mutator methods to provide access, as appropriate. For example, a user program may need to know the size of the pswdHistory list, but that attribute is not specifically declared in the Password class. The pswdHistory object inherits certain attributes from ArrayList, such as size. Access is needed, therefore, to the properties of another object, which is itself an instance variable of the class. Such is the case with the ArrayList object in the Password class. Lines 119 through 122 code the accessor method, getHistorysize(), which needs to get the password history size to return the number of elements stored in the history. The password history size is a property of the ArrayList object referenced by the instance variable, pswdHistory, and is not a property of the Password class. Objects of type ArrayList have an accessor method, size(), which returns the desired value for history size. The getHistorySize() method returns the value obtained from calling the size() method of the ArrayList, pswdHistory. In doing so, the getHistorySize() method provides a type of read-only value, even though it does not return the value of an instance variable of Password.

Occasionally, users will need to know some aspect of an object which is not modeled by a single attribute, but by some condition, calculation, or combination of attribute values. Such is the case with the requirement to notify users if a password is expiring. This condition does not have a direct attribute to indicate the password is expiring. Note that this condition is different from a password that has expired, for which there is an attribute. Rather, it is a combination of two conditions: (1) if the password is set to expire automatically, and (2) if the number of remaining uses is at or below the threshold, or limit, for notifying users. Figure 9-25 displays the code for the isExpiring() read-only accessor method for the Password class. Line 126 sets the value of the boolean variable, expiring, to false. Line 128 then checks to see if the password is set to expire automatically and if the number of remaining uses is at or below the threshold, or limit, for notifying users. If both conditions are true, line 129 changes the value of expiring to true and line 131 returns the value.

Even though the isExpiring() method does not return the value of a given instance variable, you can write a method that provides information on a combination of attributes — such as, if the current password is at the point where it will soon expire. In the Password class, the isExpiring() method will return a boolean value named, expiring. As such, it can be viewed as a type of pseudo-accessor method that provides a read-only value.

```
124        public boolean isExpiring()
125        {
126            boolean expiring = false;
127
128            if(autoExpires && remainingUses <= expiresNotifyLimit)
129                expiring = true;
130
131            return expiring;
132        }
```

FIGURE 9-25

The following steps enter code for the read-only accessor methods for the Password class.

To Code Read-Only Accessor Methods

1. Enter lines 114 through 117 as shown in Figure 9-24 on page 563.

TextPad displays the getRemainingUses() accessor method that provides read-only access to an instance variable, remainingUses (Figure 9-26). Because remainingUses is a read-only attribute, no corresponding mutator methods exist.

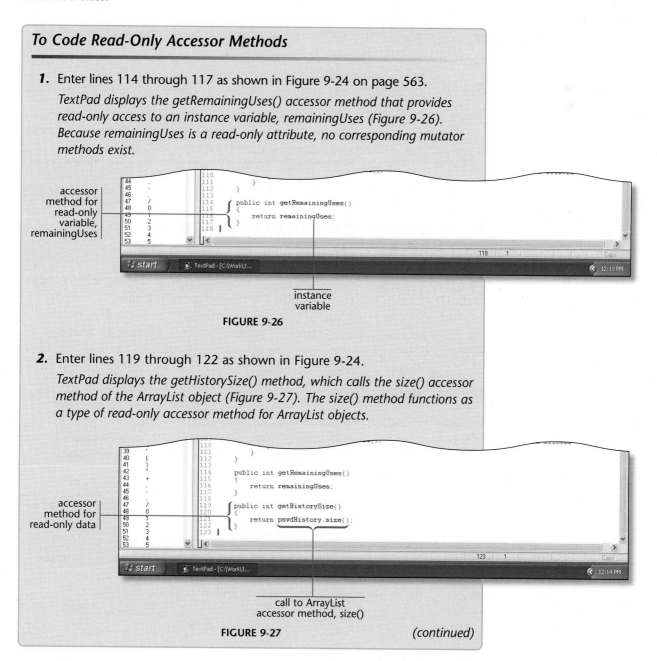

FIGURE 9-26

2. Enter lines 119 through 122 as shown in Figure 9-24.

TextPad displays the getHistorySize() method, which calls the size() accessor method of the ArrayList object (Figure 9-27). The size() method functions as a type of read-only accessor method for ArrayList objects.

FIGURE 9-27   *(continued)*

3. Enter lines 124 through 132 as shown in Figure 9-25 on the previous page.

TextPad displays the isExpiring() method, the pseudo-accessor method for the Password class (Figure 9-28). This method evaluates two conditions and then returns a boolean value based on the result of the evaluation.

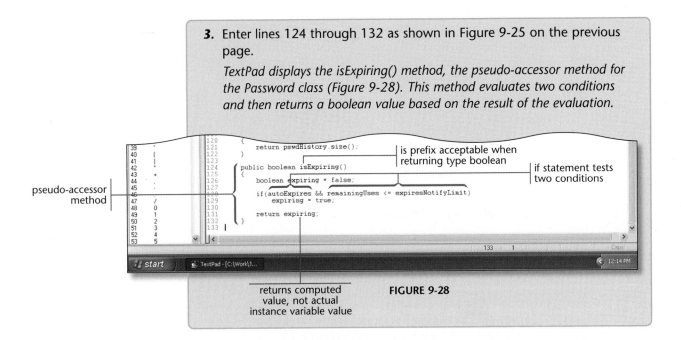

pseudo-accessor method

is prefix acceptable when returning type boolean

if statement tests two conditions

returns computed value, not actual instance variable value

FIGURE 9-28

The requirements document in Figure 9-2 on page 541 requires several additional methods to be coded, including the set() method called earlier. Before coding these methods, it is important to understand why some methods have public access and others have private access and when to use them.

Understanding When to Use public and private Methods

Eleven methods have been coded for the Password class, including seven accessor methods and four mutator methods. The class diagram in Figure 9-3 on page 542 indicates that an additional four instance methods are needed to complete the Password class, including the set() method, which is called in each of the overloaded constructors to create new ArrayList objects.

As previously discussed, methods that users can access directly are, therefore, part of the public interface and must be public. Those methods which are designed for use only within the class should be private. In the Password class, the set() method should be public, as it is called when a user wants to set a new password value, whether by adding a new password or changing an existing password. The validate() method also must be public to allow user programs to access its functionality.

The principal use of a password is to limit access to valid users only. Programs using a Password object have the responsibility for validating users and granting access, as certain users may be granted access to other user accounts without providing the current user password. An example of this would be a superuser, who requires access to various accounts for administrative purposes. When a user program needs to validate whether a password matches the current password, the Password object itself is responsible for doing the validation.

Generally, methods should be kept reasonably short and focused on one task. If other tasks need to be done, it is possible that additional methods might be needed, rather than cluttering a single method with too much code. It is important to understand exactly what a given method needs to do in order to keep the focus on this single task and to delegate ancillary tasks to other methods.

Keep Methods Short and Focused

Keep methods short and focused on a single task. In general, keep the code to one or two printed pages, at a maximum. If you can see all of the code in a method at once, it is easier to grasp what it is doing.

Coding public Instance Methods

The two primary actions of the Password class are setting a new password value as the current password and validating a password entered by a user as current and not expired. These actions are implemented in the set() and validate() methods, respectively. As previously discussed, both the set() method and validate() method must be public to allow programs to access their functionality.

The set() method sets a new password value as the current value of the Password object. Setting a new password value is the essential action when an existing password value is changed or when a password initially is created. This is why the set() method is called in the constructors of the Password class. Figure 9-29 displays the pseudocode that outlines the logic for the set() method.

As illustrated by the pseudocode in Figure 9-29, before the set() method establishes a new string value as the new password, several other actions are taken on the string value entered by the user. First, the **trim() method** of the String class is called to remove any leading or trailing white space, as the user may have entered these spaces accidentally.

```
set() method   (no return data; parameter is String: new password)

Begin
    remove leading and trailing white space from new password
    verify format of new password
    encrypt new password

    If new encrypted password not in list
        If list is at max size
            Remove oldest element in list
        End If

        Add new encrypted password to end of list

        If password not added
            throw Exception: internal list error
        End If

        If password has expired
            Reset password to not expired
        End If

        If password autoexpires
            remaining uses = maximum uses
        End If
    Else
        throw Exception: password recently used
    End If
End
```

FIGURE 9-29

Next, the new password is verified as having an acceptable format that is within the minimum and maximum size limits and contains at least one numeric value. The verifyFormat() method of the Password class, which is discussed later in the chapter, completes this verification. Because only encrypted password values are stored in the password history, the encrypt() method of the Password class then encrypts the new password. The encrypt() method is discussed later in this chapter.

As noted in the requirements document, new passwords cannot match any contained in the active history. The set() method thus calls the **contains() method** of the ArrayList object to determine whether the encrypted password value is in the password history list. If the encrypted password value is in the password history list, an exception is thrown.

If a new password passes all of these conditions, it is ready to be added to the password history list. If the list already is at its maximum size, the oldest password is removed. The new password now is added to the list by calling the ArrayList **add() method**, which returns a boolean value indicating that the item was added. A collection that supports an add() method must return false only if the collection does not allow duplicate items and the item is already in the collection. Because an ArrayList does allow duplicates, this method always should return true. If it does not, this indicates an internal error in the implementation of the ArrayList collection, which is unlikely. The set() method then must determine if the password should expire automatically. If so, the set() method must set the remaining uses to the maximum uses for a new password.

When a user enters a password, the validate() method of the Password class validates the password by comparing it to the current password and, if it matches, by determining that the password has not expired. Additionally, if the password is set to expire automatically upon each successful use, the validate() method decrements the remaining uses. Figure 9-30 displays the pseudocode that outlines the logic for the validate() method.

The validate() method is similar to the set() method, in that it must verify and encrypt the password value provided as a parameter. The validate() method, however, does not trim the entered password to eliminate leading and trailing white space, because a user always is required to supply exactly the correct password.

The remainder of the logic for these two methods is rather different. The set() method must determine that the supplied password value is not in the password history list and then, if it is not, add it to the password history list as the current password. The validate() method, however, not only must determine that the supplied password value *is* in the password history list, but also that it is the latest, or current, entry. This validation can be completed only if the history

JAVA UPDATE Java 2 v5.0

Autoboxing/unboxing

To use a primitive data type where you need an object requires converting the primitive by boxing it with its corresponding wrapper class, as in converting from an int to an Integer to add it to an ArrayList. To obtain the int value from the Integer object, you would unbox it by using the intValue() method. Autoboxing and unboxing automate this process. Although primitives appear as interchangeable with objects, the conversions are still taking place. When used with generics (see page 574), the coding is greatly simplified.

The following code compares adding and then getting an item from an ArrayList of Integers with and without autoboxing/unboxing.

```
//Without Autoboxing/auto-unboxing:
list.add(0, new Integer(5));          // boxing an int with Integer
int number = (list.get(0)).intValue();  // unboxing int value from Integer

//With Autoboxing/auto-unboxing:
list.add(0, 10);                      // autoboxing int to Integer
int number2 = list.get(0);            //auto-unboxing int from Integer
```

```
validate() method (no return data; parameter is String: entered password)

Begin
    verify format of new password
    encrypt entered password

    If the history is not empty
        Obtain the current password from history
        If entered password <> current password
            throw Exception: invalid password
        End If

        If password has expired
            throw Exception: password has expired
        End If

        If password autoexpires
            decrement remaining uses by 1
            If no remaining uses
                Set password to expired
            End If
        End If
    Else
        throw Exception: no password in history
    End If
End
```

FIGURE 9-30

is not empty. Thus, the password history list, thus, always should contain at least one value for a given Password object, unless the history list somehow was corrupted. Although it never should happen, it is safest to check for an empty list.

Because items in an ArrayList can be accessed much like items in any ordinary array, any password value in the history list can be accessed directly by using the proper index value. The current password is the latest one in the list, which has an index equal to the size of the list minus one. Line 176, as shown in Figure 9-32 on the next page, calculates the current password index and then line 177 obtains the item in the ArrayList with this index.

Next, the validate() method verifies that the entered password matches the latest entry in the password history list. If it does not match, an exception is thrown. If it does match, the validate() method then determines if the password is set to expire automatically, which is true by default. If the password is set to expire automatically and the number of remaining uses is zero, then the validate() method must throw an exception; otherwise, the method simply decrements the remaining uses.

Figures 9-31 and 9-32 on the next page display the code for the set() and validate() methods, respectively.

```
134        // Sets password to a new value; keeps current & previous values in history up to max
           number
135        public void set(String pswd) throws Exception
136        {
137            String encryptPswd;
138            boolean pswdAdded = true;
139
140            pswd = pswd.trim();                        // remove any leading, trailing white space
141            verifyFormat(pswd);                       // verify password was entered properly
142            encryptPswd = encrypt(pswd);              // convert to encrypted form
143
144            if(!pswdHistory.contains(encryptPswd))          // if pswd not in recently used list
145            {
146                if(pswdHistory.size() == maxHistory)        // if list is at max size
147                    pswdHistory.remove(0);                  // remove 1st, oldest, pswd from list
148
149                pswdAdded = pswdHistory.add(encryptPswd); // add new pswd to end of ArrayList
150
151                if(!pswdAdded)                            // should never happen
152                    throw new Exception("Internal list error - Password not accepted");
153
154                if(expired)                               // if pswd has expired,
155                    expired = false;                      // reset to not expired
156
157                if(autoExpires)                           // if pswd auto expires,
158                    remainingUses = maxUses;              // reset uses to max
159            }
160            else
161                throw new Exception("Password recently used");
162        }
```

FIGURE 9-31

```
164        // Validates entered password against most recently saved value
165        public void validate(String pswd) throws Exception
166        {
167            String encryptPswd;
168            String currentPswd;
169            int currentPswdIndex;
170
171            verifyFormat(pswd);               // verify password was entered properly
172            encryptPswd = encrypt(pswd);      // convert to encrypted form
173
174            if(!pswdHistory.isEmpty())        // at least one password entry is in history
175            {
176                currentPswdIndex = pswdHistory.size()-1;
177                currentPswd = (String)pswdHistory.get(currentPswdIndex);
178
179                if(!encryptPswd.equals(currentPswd)) // if not most recent pswd
180                    throw new Exception("Password is invalid");
181
182                if(expired)
183                    throw new Exception("Password has expired - please change");
184
185                if(autoExpires)
186                {
187                    --remainingUses;
188                    if(remainingUses <= 0)
189                        expired = true;
190                }
191            }
192            else
193                throw new Exception("No password on file - list corrupted!"); // should never
                   happen
194
195
196        }
```

FIGURE 9-32

The following steps enter the code for the public instance methods, set() and validate(), for the Password class.

To Code public Instance Methods

1. Enter lines 134 through 162 as shown in Figure 9-31.

TextPad displays the code for the set() method in the coding window (Figure 9-33).

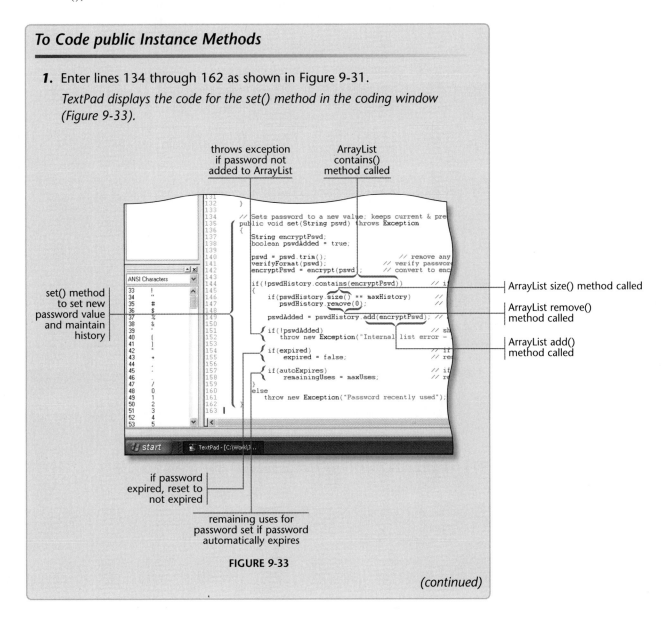

FIGURE 9-33

(continued)

2. Enter lines 164 through 196 as shown in Figure 9-32 on page 570.

TextPad displays the code for the validate() method in the coding window (Figure 9-34). Comments again are used to document the code.

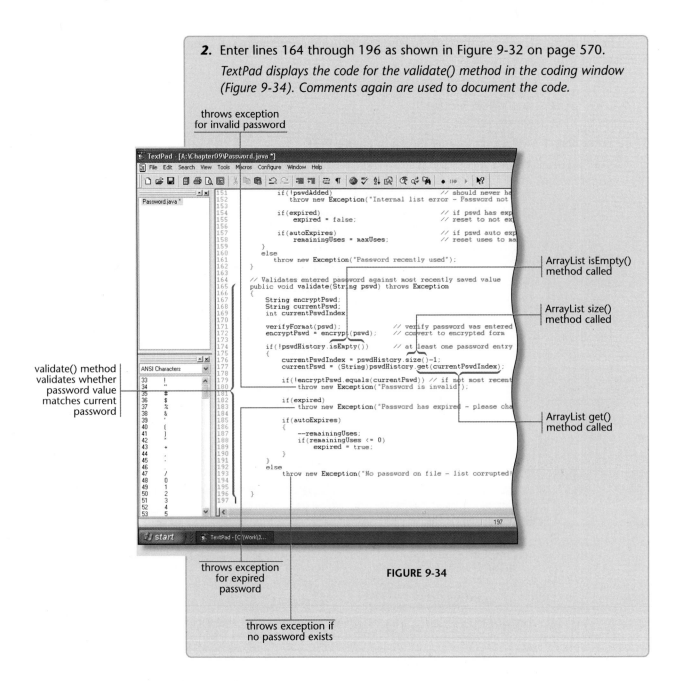

FIGURE 9-34

Notice that both the set() and validate() methods are relatively short. It is not uncommon in object-oriented code to have many smaller methods rather than fewer, larger ones. This contributes to making the code more understandable and easier to maintain.

Using ArrayList Methods

Both of the set() and validate() instance methods call methods of the ArrayList object created in the constructors. Earlier in the chapter, a brief rationale was presented as to why an ArrayList was an appropriate collection to use for the password history list. Although a LinkedList could be used to implement the required functionality for this Password class, an ArrayList provides more efficient access, because many of its operations take a constant time regardless of the size of the list; this access time is low compared to that for a LinkedList. Because the list will have a known size, but a size that might be changed, the resizeable array provided by the ArrayList class is an appropriate solution. As discussed earlier, the ArrayList class has a known size or capacity, which expands automatically as items are added beyond the initial capacity. It does not reduce automatically, however, even if members are removed. The capacity can be explicitly reduced, as was done earlier by calling the trimToSize() method; however, it never should be reduced to less than the current number of elements.

Another important issue when considering the appropriate collection to use for the password history list is if the collection supports all required functionality with relative ease of use for the programmer. The ArrayList object provides several methods — including those called by the set() and validate() methods coded in the previous steps — that provide the required functionality for the password history list. Table 9-5 lists the ArrayList methods used in the Password class created in this chapter.

Table 9-5   ArrayList Methods Used in the Password Class

METHOD	DESCRIPTION
boolean add(Object o)	Appends the element, which can be any object type, to the end of the list. The method returns true because a List collection typically allows duplicate elements.
boolean contains(Object o)	Returns true if the list contains the specified object as an element.
Object get(int index)	Returns the element in the list at the position specified by index.
boolean isEmpty()	Returns true if the list has no elements; otherwise, returns false.
Object remove(int index)	Removes the element at the specified index.
int size()	Returns the number of elements in the list.
trimToSize()	Trims the capacity of the list to the list's current size.

As defined in the requirements document, the Password class is required to keep a password history list of up to 10 old password values. The reason for maintaining a password history list is to prevent reuse of a recent password value when the user changes the current password value. The password history list should, therefore, provide a means to determine whether the new password value entered by the user already exists in the list. The contains() method in line 144 in Figure 9-31 on page 570 provides this capability, returning true if the password history list already contains the new password value.

JAVA UPDATE

Generics

The Java Collections Framework now uses generics, also known as parameterized data types, so the program may specify the exact type of object a given collection can store, rather than treating all elements as Objects. This removes the requirement to cast down a retrieved object to a valid type. It also prevents throwing an exception due to miscasting a retrieved object. Because the data type of objects stored in the collection is specified, an attempt to store a different type of object will generate a compile-time error. Validating the data type at compile time is said to make the collection **typesafe**.

To specify a data type for use with a collection, place the data type within angle brackets, < >, after the collection name. Only reference types, not primitives, can be used with generics, although autoboxing may make it appear otherwise.

If you want to modify the Password class to make its use of the ArrayList collection typesafe, replace lines 23, 29, 43, 50, and 177, as shown in the following code.

The **size() method** (line 146 of Figure 9-31 on page 570) returns the current number of elements in the ArrayList and, therefore, can be used to determine if the maximum password history list size has been reached. As with most kinds of arrays and lists in Java, the numbering of elements begins with zero. Once the password history list has reached its maximum size, an additional password value is added only after the oldest value is removed by using the remove() method in line 147 to remove the element at index zero. In this way, the password history list is maintained within the maximum size limit.

As indicated in the requirements document, new passwords cannot match any contained in the active password history list. Previously used passwords are allowed for reuse, but only when they no longer are in the password history list. The password history list thus should store passwords in the order added; this ensures that the older a password value is, the sooner it will be available for reuse. The ArrayList add() method in line 149 adds a new object to the end of the list. Adding the object to the end of the list maintains items in the order they were added, with the oldest having an index value of zero and the newest having an index value of one less than the size of the list. The Collection interface specifies that the add() method returns true if the element is added and false if it is rejected as a duplicate. As discussed earlier, the ArrayList implementation of the add() method returns true. If the element is not added for any other reason, an exception is thrown.

As shown in line 174 of Figure 9-32 on page 570, the validate() method calls the ArrayList **isEmpty() method**, allowing for a quick determination of whether any items exist in the password history list or not. If the list is not empty, the size() method is called in line 176 to obtain the current size of the password history list. The result of this call can be used to obtain the index of the latest item added, which is one less than the current size of the password history list. This index then is used with the **get() method** to access the indexed ArrayList item directly (the current password value, in this case), regardless of the size of the list.

The get() method in line 177 of Figure 9-32 returns a reference to an element of type Object, even though the passwords in the list are String objects. All objects in Java inherit Object as the root parent class, so any object may be referenced most generally as an instance of Object, regardless of its data type. This is how an ArrayList can maintain a list of any type of object. Recall from Chapter 3 that the cast operation converts from one data type to another, by entering the new data type in parentheses before a literal or variable. Referencing an object as an instance of a more general parent class is called **upcasting** and can be done implicitly, that is, without using the cast operator. When a programmer is ready to retrieve data from an ArrayList, the cast operator must be used to reference an object as an instance of a more specific class. Casting from a more general type

```
23        private ArrayList<String> pswdHistory;

29            pswdHistory = new ArrayList<String>(maxHistory);

43            pswdHistory = new ArrayList<String>(maxHistory);

50            pswdHistory = new ArrayList<String>(maxHistory);

177            currentPswd = pswdHistory.get(currentPswdIndex);
```

to a more specific type is called **downcasting**. Only objects that actually are instances of a more specific class should be downcast. For example, any String also is an Object, but the reverse is not true. In this case, the Object returned from the get() method can be downcast safely to a String, because String objects originally were stored in the ArrayList. If you do not know that an object, referenced as a more general parent class, also is a member of a child class, use the **instanceof operator** before trying to downcast the object, as in the code

```
if(pswd instanceof String) ...
```

The resulting String, which is the current password, can be compared to the password value provided by the user program by using the equals() method, as shown in line 179 of Figure 9-32 on page 570. The **equals() method** compares two Strings and returns a boolean value — true or false. If the value is false, then an exception is thrown with the message, Password is invalid (line 180). Note that the String equals() method requires only an Object as an argument, so a downcast would not be required to use it. The method returns true, however, only if the Object actually is a String with a matching character sequence. Other String comparison methods are available that take an Object, a String, or a StringBuffer as an argument.

The remaining methods for the Password class are not part of the public interface; that is, they are used only for internal purposes and are not made available for public use. Before coding these methods, it is important to understand the String and StringBuffer classes because they are used in these methods.

Understanding the String and StringBuffer Classes

Most applications have a need to deal with characters grouped together, such as a name or some other textual value, rather than as individual, separate characters. Many programming languages have features for dealing with such groupings of characters, or strings, inherent in the language itself. Java, however, does not have a primitive data type for strings. Rather, some central classes, or **core classes**, are provided with the language that offer functionality for dealing with this type of data. The String and StringBuffer classes are the primary core classes in Java for manipulating string values.

Using the String Class

The String class is the Java class that supports **immutable** string values — that is, their values cannot be changed because String objects are constants. Recall that String literals, which are designated by characters within double quotes such as "abc123", are implemented as instances of the String class. When it encounters that String literal, Java creates a String object whose value is abc123.

You also can create String objects using the new keyword and a constructor, as in `String phrase = new String("Java is fun");` which assigns the initial value, Java is fun, to the string. If you assign a new value to a String, it does not replace the old value; the String reference simply refers to the new String, and the old String is abandoned to be removed later by the garbage collector of the Java Virtual Machine (JVM). The **garbage collector** is a routine provided by the JVM that frees previously allocated memory for objects which are no longer in use. Strings have a number of useful methods, including methods for examining individual characters in a string, for comparing strings, for searching strings, and for creating a copy of a string with all characters changed to uppercase or to lowercase. Table 9-6 lists the String methods used in the Password class.

Table 9-6   String Methods Used in the Password Class

METHOD	DESCRIPTION
char charAt(int index)	Returns the character at the index specified
boolean equals(Object obj)	Returns true when obj is a String with a matching character sequence
int hashCode()	Returns a hash code (calculated numeric value) for the string
int length()	Returns the length of the string
String substring(int beginIndex)	Returns as a new String a subset of this string from the beginning index through the end of the string
String substring(int beginIndex, int endIndex)	Returns as a new String a subset of this string from the beginning index through the ending index-1
String trim()	Returns as new String a copy of the current string with leading and trailing white space omitted

As you have learned, the toString() method of the Object class provides conversion support by returning a string value that represents an object. Because String objects are immutable, it might appear that trying to concatenate strings, with or without other non-strings (for example, strX = "abc"+12+"def"), would create a series of new String objects, which would not be used again after the concatenation. This would be true if the concatenation were implemented using only String objects. String concatenation, however, is implemented with the StringBuffer class and its append() method, resulting in a more efficient implementation.

Using the StringBuffer Class

The **StringBuffer class** implements a **mutable** sequence of characters — that is, a string that can be modified. The length and content of the StringBuffer can be changed at any point in time. Each StringBuffer has an internal buffer with a particular capacity. As long as the content does not exceed the capacity, no internal reallocation of the array is necessary. If the capacity of the internal buffer is exceeded, it is expanded automatically.

A new StringBuffer object may be created with no content, in which case the capacity is set to 16 by default. A new StringBuffer object also may be created by using a String (either a reference variable or a string literal) as an argument to the constructor. In this case, the new StringBuffer will represent the same sequence of characters as the original String — that is, a copy of the String. The same constructor can take a concatenation of multiple strings as an argument, because the result of the concatenation is itself a string.

The two principal operations of a StringBuffer are implemented using the insert() and append() methods. The **insert() method** allows any string to be inserted at any given point within the StringBuffer, moving remaining characters to the right. For example, given a StringBuffer object, buf, with the current string contents of book text, the code

```
buf.insert(4, "mark");
```

would alter the string buffer contents to be bookmark text. Using the **append() method** adds new characters to the end of the buffer. If the capacity of the buffer is reached, it is expanded automatically, as indicated earlier. The append() method also is used in the implementation of String concatenation. For example, the previously discussed example

```
strX = "abc"+12+"def";
```

is implemented in the String class by creating a new StringBuffer and then successively appending "abc", 12, and "def" to the buffer and then invoking its toString() method to return a new String with the appended values. Non-string values, such as 12, are converted to Strings by the corresponding String.valueOf() method before appending. The String **valueOf() method** returns a String representing the value of the argument passed to it. This method is overloaded to provide a conversion for many different data types.

Although the insert() and append() methods perform the principal operations, StringBuffer objects also have a number of other useful methods. Table 9-7 lists the StringBuffer methods used in the Password class.

Table 9-7   StringBuffer Methods Used in the Password Class

METHOD	DESCRIPTION
StringBuffer append(int i) StringBuffer append(String str)	Appends the string or a string representation of the argument to the string buffer. This method is overloaded to accept a variety of different argument types.
char charAt(int index)	Returns the character at the specified index in the string buffer.
int length()	Returns the length of the string, in terms of the character count, not the capacity.
StringBuffer reverse()	Replaces the character sequence contained in the string buffer with the reverse sequence.
void setCharAt(int index, char ch)	The character in the sequence at the index specified is replaced by the character ch.
String toString()	Returns a new String object containing the character sequence represented by the string buffer.

Coding private Helper Methods

When two or more methods must perform the same task, it is likely that the task should be implemented in another method. The likelihood grows stronger as the complexity of the task increases. Placing such a task into a separate method provides two advantages: it lessens the complexity of the current method, and it minimizes the duplication of code. The second point becomes increasingly important when making changes to the code, either for future enhancements or for elimination of errors, or bugs.

As previously discussed, methods that are used to help an object accomplish its tasks and are not intended to be called by other programs commonly are referred to as helper methods and are made private. Using the private access specifier makes the method available only to methods within the class. Two such helper methods are in the Password class: the verifyFormat() method and the encrypt() method.

The verifyFormat() method has the task of verifying that the password value provided is within the established rules as acceptable for passwords in the Password class. Figure 9-35 displays the pseudocode that outlines the logic for the verifyFormat() method. Figure 9-36 displays the code for the verifyFormat() method of the Password class.

```
verifyFormat() method        (no return data; parameter is String: entered password)

Begin
    Set number found to false

    If password is empty string
        Throw Exception: no password provided
    End If

    If password length < minimum size
        Throw Exception: password < minimum size
    End If

    If password length > maximum size
        Throw Exception: password > maximum size
    End If

    Loop through all characters in password or until numeric is found
        If character at current index of password is a digit
            Set number found to true
        End If
    End Loop

    If number found is false
        throw Exception: password invalid – no numeric digit
    End If
End
```

FIGURE 9-35

The verifyFormat() method receives a password from its caller as a String parameter named pswd (line 199). Using the **length() method** of the String provides the ability to verify that a password value was submitted and that it is within the acceptable range for number of characters, with at least 6 characters and no more than 15 characters. As shown in lines 203 and 204 of Figure 9-36, if no password is supplied at all (a null, or zero-length, string), there is nothing to

```
198        // Verifies password has proper format
199        private void verifyFormat(String pswd) throws Exception
200        {
201            boolean numFound = false;
202
203            if(pswd.length() == 0)
204                throw new Exception("No password provided!");
205
206            if(pswd.length() < MIN_SIZE)
207                throw new Exception("Password must be at least "+MIN_SIZE+
                    " characters in length");
208
209            if(pswd.length() > MAX_SIZE)
210                throw new Exception("Password cannot be greater than "+MAX_SIZE+
                    " characters in length");
211
212            // scan through password to find if at least 1 number is used
213            for(int i=0; i < pswd.length() && !numFound; ++i)
214                if(Character.isDigit(pswd.charAt(i)))
215                    numFound = true;
216
217            if(!numFound)
218                throw new Exception("Password is invalid - must have at least one numeric
                    digit");
219        }
```

FIGURE 9-36

verify, and an exception is generated with the message, No password provided! It may be that no password value is supplied, even though this method is used only within the class. If the validate() or set() methods receive a null string, or one with only white space characters which subsequently are trimmed, then no password value is available to verify. If, at some later time, the verifyFormat() method were made public, so as to provide users with the ability to verify the format of potential passwords before submitting them, then the possibility of a null string would only increase. In either case, it is better to check for and handle this potential exception condition.

Lines 206 through 210 of Figure 9-36 verify that the password value is between the minimum and maximum lengths. If the password has fewer characters than the value specified as the value for MIN_SIZE (in this case, 6 characters), then the exception is thrown with the error message, Password must be at least 6 characters in length. If the password is longer than the value specified as the value for MAX_SIZE (in this case, 15 characters), then the exception is thrown with the error message, Password cannot be greater than 15 characters in length.

The final requirement for a valid password format is that it contains at least one numeric character, and this is implemented by the code in lines 213 through 215. The **charAt() method** of the String class (line 214) provides the character at a given index within the character sequence of the string. By iterating through the characters in the string, each character can be examined one at a time to see if it is numeric. The loop needs to continue only until all characters have been examined or a numeric character is found. The charAt() method, as it returns the character value at the given index, becomes the argument of the isDigit() method to determine if a numeric character exists. The **isDigit() method,** a static method of the Character class, passes the character being examined and returns true if the character is a digit, or number (line 214). If none of the characters in the password is numeric, an exception is thrown with the error message, Password is invalid — must have at least one numeric digit (lines 217 and 218).

The following step enters the code for the verifyFormat() method of the Password class.

To Code the verifyFormat() Private Helper Method

1. Enter the code in lines 198 through 219 as shown in Figure 9-36 on the previous page.

TextPad displays the helper method, verifyFormat(), for the Password class (Figure 9-37). This method has private access, limiting its use to methods within the Password class.

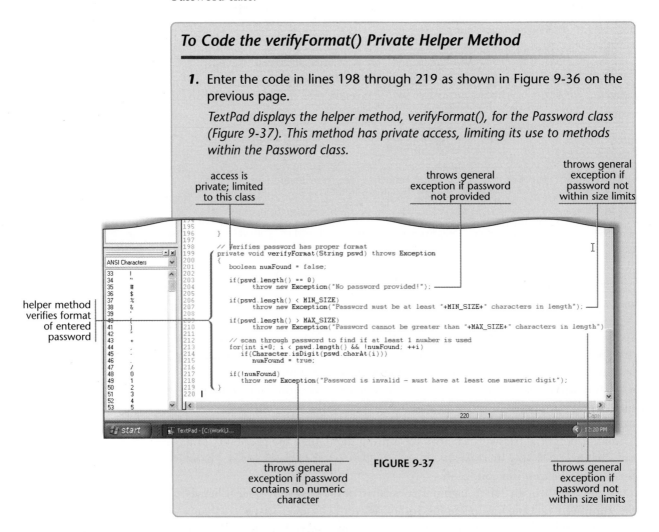

FIGURE 9-37

The encrypt() Method

The encrypt() method is responsible for encrypting the given password value according to the algorithm provided in the requirements document. Many techniques exist to perform the process of **encryption,** which is the conversion of data into a form not understood easily by unauthorized users. Some of these encryption techniques include substitution of letters and numbers or the rotation of letters in the alphabet. Encrypted data is called **ciphertext**, as opposed to unencrypted data, which is called **plaintext**. The process of converting ciphertext into plaintext is called **decryption**.

The algorithm used in the Password class is used primarily to illustrate certain String and StringBuffer methods. Additionally, the hash code used to make the encrypted value unique may not always provide a consistent result, depending on the implementation. Consequently, this code should not be used as a basis for providing secure and reliable encryption.

Figure 9-38 displays the pseudocode that outlines the logic for the encrypt() method. The encryption method specified in the requirements document requires the password to be cut in half and the two halves inverted. Then the order of the characters in the resulting string is reversed (spelled backward). Each character is compared with the character in the original string and manipulated bitwise. Finally, a hash code is computed for the original password and appended to the encrypted one.

encrypt() method (returns String: encrypted password; parameter String: password)

Begin
    Obtain password length
    Calculate midpoint of password
    Encrypted password = last half of password (from midpoint to end)
                    + first half of password (from beginning to midpoint, exclusive)

    Reverse order of characters in encrypted password

    Loop through all characters in the encrypted password
        Set current character to a bitwise AND with corresponding original character
    End loop

    Compute hash code for original password
    Append hash code to encrypted password

    Return string value of encrypted password
End

FIGURE 9-38

Figure 9-39 displays the code for the encrypt() method of the Password class.

```
221        // Encrypts original password returning new encrypted String
222        private String encrypt(String pswd)
223        {
224            StringBuffer encryptPswd;
225            int pswdSize = 0;
226            int midpoint = 0;
227            int hashCode = 0;
228
229            // swap first and last half of password
230            pswdSize = pswd.length();
231            midpoint = pswdSize/2;
232            encryptPswd = new StringBuffer(pswd.substring(midpoint)    // get last half of pswd
233                + pswd.substring(0,midpoint));                        // and concatenate first
                                                                          half
234
235            encryptPswd.reverse();   // reverses order of characters in password
236
237            for(int i=0; i < pswdSize; ++i)                           // encrypt each character
238                encryptPswd.setCharAt(i, (char)(encryptPswd.charAt(i) & pswd.charAt(i)) );
239
240            hashCode = pswd.hashCode();  // hash code for original password
241            encryptPswd.append(hashCode);
242
243            return encryptPswd.toString();
244        }
245    }
```

FIGURE 9-39

The first step in the encryption algorithm implemented by the encrypt() method is to exchange the first half of the password with the last half. As shown in Figure 9-39, this is accomplished in code by obtaining the length of the string, using the String length() method (line 230 of Figure 9-39) and then using integer division to divide the length value in half (line 231). The result is used as the midpoint of the original string, obtaining two equal length substrings for a password with an even number of characters. For a password with an odd number of characters, the substring obtained from the last half is longer by one character.

Because the password value will have its characters modified in the process of encryption, and because String objects are immutable while StringBuffer objects are mutable, lines 232 and 233 place the swapped halves of the original password in a new StringBuffer object for further manipulation, leaving the original password String unchanged. This is accomplished by using two forms of the String method, substring(). The **substring() method** returns a portion, or substring, of a String object. The form with a single argument, as in

`pswd.substring(midpoint)`

returns a new String with the same character sequence as the String pswd, beginning at the midpoint index and continuing through the end of the string, which, in this program, represents the last half of pswd. The form with two int arguments specifies a substring with a beginning and ending location in the String. For example, the code

`pswd.substring(0, midpoint)`

returns a new String with the same character sequence as pswd, beginning at offset zero (the beginning of the string) and extending to the character at midpoint — 1; this string represents the first half of pswd. Concatenating the two resulting strings, the right half and then the left half of the password, provides the argument for the StringBuffer constructor to create a string value for further manipulation.

The next step in the algorithm is to reverse the order of the characters in the encryption string. The StringBuffer method, reverse(), in line 235 accomplishes this with a single method call that replaces the character sequence contained in the string buffer with the reverse of the sequence.

The next step is to loop through all of the characters (line 237) and encrypt them by performing a bitwise AND operation (line 238), which uses the operator, &, as contrasted with the logical AND operator, &&. Individual bits (binary digits) can have a value of zero (off) or one (on). A **bitwise AND** examines the bits of each character and, where two corresponding bits are both set on (have a value of one), the corresponding bit in the result is set to one. In all other cases, the resulting bit is set to off, or zero. The bitwise AND operator works only on integer types, such as char; however, the result of a bitwise AND operation on two char values will be placed in an int by the compiler, if not otherwise specified, to avoid a possible loss of precision. Line 238 casts the result back to a char by placing the char keyword in parentheses before the resulting expression. The result is used as an argument to the StringBuffer method, setCharAt(), to change the value of each character in the encrypted password.

Line 240 obtains a hash code of the original password value from the String method, hashCode(). A **hash code** is a transformation of a string of characters into a shorter, fixed-length value (typically an integer) that represents the original string. Hash codes are not necessarily unique, in that more than one string can produce the same hash code; however, to produce the same hash code, the strings generally have to be similar. The **hashCode() method** returns a hash code for the pswd string. In the encrypt() method, the obtained hash code then is appended to the string using the StringBuffer append() method in line 241, and the resulting string is returned from the method. Finally, the returned string is obtained from the StringBuffer toString() method in line 243, which returns a new String object — the return data type required by the encrypt() method.

The following step enters code for the encrypt() method of the Password class.

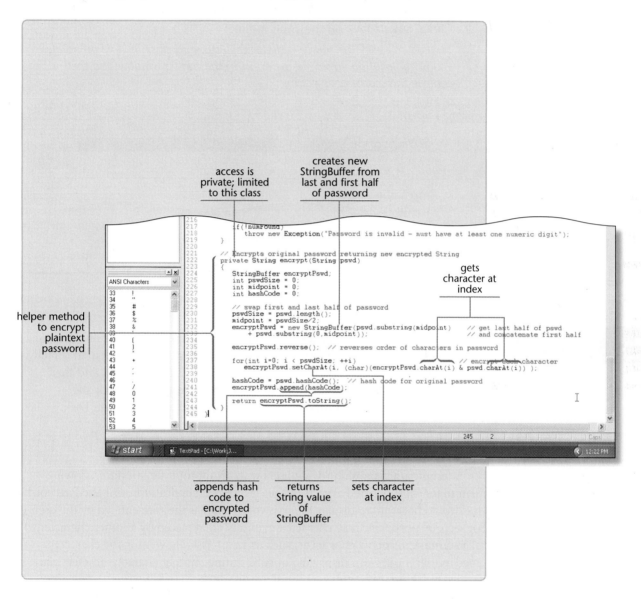

The code for the Password class now is complete. This class does not support a user interface, nor is it an application or applet that can be run. It is simply a definition of a class that is usable by other programs for creating Password objects. To build the class file for use with other programs, the changes must be saved and the source file must be compiled. The steps on the next page save and compile the Password class source file.

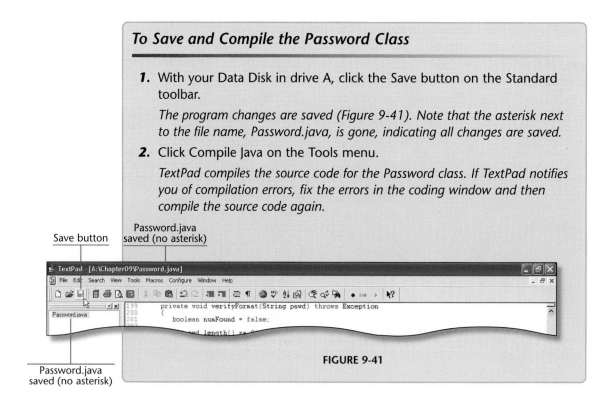

To Save and Compile the Password Class

1. With your Data Disk in drive A, click the Save button on the Standard toolbar.

The program changes are saved (Figure 9-41). Note that the asterisk next to the file name, Password.java, is gone, indicating all changes are saved.

2. Click Compile Java on the Tools menu.

TextPad compiles the source code for the Password class. If TextPad notifies you of compilation errors, fix the errors in the coding window and then compile the source code again.

Save button

Password.java saved (no asterisk)

Password.java saved (no asterisk)

FIGURE 9-41

Testing a Reusable Class

OTHER WAYS

1. Press CTRL+1

The Password class should be tested to verify that all methods work as expected. Because it has no main( ) method, the Password class cannot be executed directly. A test program must be coded that creates objects of type Password and then calls the appropriate public methods to test them. A test program for the Password class, the PasswordDemo program, is provided on the Data Disk.

Using a JPassword Field

A test program should provide users with an appropriate interface, allowing them to test all supported aspects of the class. A real application using the Password class would not want to display the password values as they are entered by the user. For security purposes, these characters typically are replaced by another character, called a **mask**, or **echo character**, such as an asterisk. Preventing the characters typed as user input from displaying or substituting another character in their place is called **masking**. Although a command-line interface could be used, a test program using a graphical user interface (GUI) gives the feel of a typical application using a password. It also allows for use of a **JPassword field**, which provides masking of the entered password with alternate characters. The echo character is an asterisk, by default, but can be changed to any character of your choice. The PasswordDemo program supplied on the Data Disk provides a graphical user interface (GUI) using two JPassword fields for testing the Password class (Figure 9-42). Figure 9-43 displays the PasswordDemo source code.

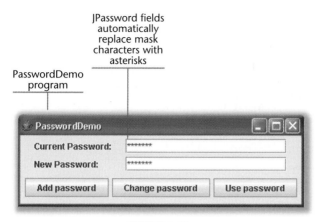

FIGURE 9-42

```
1   /**
2    * Class PasswordDemo used to test class Password
3    *
4    * @author Michael Mick
5    * @version 1.0
6    */
7   import javax.swing.*;
8   import java.awt.*;
9   import java.awt.event.*;
10
11  public class PasswordDemo
12  {
13      public static void main(String[] argv)
14      {
15          int width = 400;
16          int height = 130;
17          final demoFrame f = new demoFrame("PasswordDemo");
18
19          f.pack();
20          f.setDefaultCloseOperation(JFrame.EXIT_ON_CLOSE);
21          f.setSize(width, height);
22          f.centerOnScreen(width, height);
23          f.setVisible(true);
24      }
25  }
26
27  class demoFrame extends JFrame implements ActionListener
28  {
29      Password password = null;
30      String pswd, newPswd;
31
32      JPasswordField pswdField;
33      JPasswordField newPswdField;
34      JButton jbtAddPswd, jbtChangePswd, jbtUsePswd;
35
36      public demoFrame(String title)
37      {
38          super(title); // call super (JFrame) constructor
39
40          JLabel label1 = new JLabel("Current Password:");
41          pswdField = new JPasswordField(20);
42          pswdField.setEchoChar('*');
43
44          JLabel label2 = new JLabel("New Password:", JLabel.RIGHT);
45          newPswdField = new JPasswordField(20);
46          newPswdField.setEchoChar('*');
47
48          jbtAddPswd = new JButton("Add password");
49          jbtChangePswd = new JButton("Change password");
50          jbtUsePswd = new JButton("Use password");
51
```

FIGURE 9-43

(continued)

```
52              jbtAddPswd.addActionListener(this);
53              jbtChangePswd.addActionListener(this);
54              jbtUsePswd.addActionListener(this);
55
56              JPanel pswdPanel= new JPanel(new BorderLayout(10,10));
57              pswdPanel.add(label1,BorderLayout.WEST);
58              pswdPanel.add(pswdField,BorderLayout.EAST);
59
60              JPanel newPswdPanel= new JPanel(new BorderLayout(19,19));
61              newPswdPanel.add(label2,BorderLayout.WEST);
62              newPswdPanel.add(newPswdField,BorderLayout.EAST);
63
64              JPanel buttonPanel= new JPanel(new FlowLayout());
65              buttonPanel.add(jbtAddPswd);
66              buttonPanel.add(jbtChangePswd);
67              buttonPanel.add(jbtUsePswd);
68
69              JPanel contentPanel= new JPanel(new FlowLayout());
70              contentPanel.add(pswdPanel);
71              contentPanel.add(newPswdPanel);
72              contentPanel.add(buttonPanel);
73              setContentPane(contentPanel);
74
75              // Enable Enter key for each JButton so user can tab to button
76              // and press the Enter key, rather than click button with mouse
77              InputMap map;
78              map = jbtAddPswd.getInputMap();
79              if (map != null){
80                  map.put(KeyStroke.getKeyStroke(KeyEvent.VK_ENTER,0,false), "pressed");
81                  map.put(KeyStroke.getKeyStroke(KeyEvent.VK_ENTER,0,true), "released");
82              }
83              map = jbtChangePswd.getInputMap();
84              if (map != null){
85                  map.put(KeyStroke.getKeyStroke(KeyEvent.VK_ENTER,0,false), "pressed");
86                  map.put(KeyStroke.getKeyStroke(KeyEvent.VK_ENTER,0,true), "released");
87              }
88              map = jbtUsePswd.getInputMap();
89              if (map != null){
90                  map.put(KeyStroke.getKeyStroke(KeyEvent.VK_ENTER,0,false), "pressed");
91                  map.put(KeyStroke.getKeyStroke(KeyEvent.VK_ENTER,0,true), "released");
92              }
93          }
94
95      public void centerOnScreen(int width, int height)
96      {
97          int top, left, x, y;
98
99          // Get the screen dimension
100         Dimension screenSize = Toolkit.getDefaultToolkit().getScreenSize();
101
102         // Determine the location for the top left corner of the frame
103         x = (screenSize.width - width)/2;
104         y = (screenSize.height - height)/2;
105         top = (x < 0) ? 0 : x;
106         left = (y < 0) ? 0 : y;
107
108         // Set the frame to the specified location
109         this.setLocation(top, left);
110     }
111
112     public void actionPerformed(ActionEvent e)
113     {
114         String msg;
115         String title;
116         int optionType;
117         try
118         {
119             if(e.getSource() == jbtUsePswd)      // user clicked Use password
120             {
121                 pswd = new String(pswdField.getPassword());   // get current pswd entered
122                 password.validate(pswd);
123
```

FIGURE 9-43

(continued)

```
124                        if(password.isExpiring())
125                        {
126                            msg = "Password use successful; " + password.getRemainingUses()+
                                  " use(s) remaining.";
127                            title = "Success";
128                            optionType = JOptionPane.WARNING_MESSAGE;
129                        }
130                        else
131                        {
132                            msg = "Password use successful";
133                            title = "Success";
134                            optionType = JOptionPane.INFORMATION_MESSAGE;
135                        }
136                    }
137                    else if(e.getSource() == jbtChangePswd)      // user clicked Change password
138                    {
139                        newPswd = new String(newPswdField.getPassword());
140                        password.set(newPswd);
141
142                        msg = "Password changed.";
143                        title = "Success";
144                        optionType = JOptionPane.INFORMATION_MESSAGE;
145                    }
146                    else if(e.getSource() == jbtAddPswd)         // user clicked Add password
147                    {
148                        newPswd = new String(newPswdField.getPassword());
149                        password = new Password(newPswd,5); // auto expires after 5 additional uses
150
151                        if(password.getAutoExpires())
152                            msg = "Success! Password added with "+password.getRemainingUses()+
                                  " remaining uses.";
153                        else
154                            msg = "Success! Password added - not set to expire.";
155
156                        title = "Success";
157                        optionType = JOptionPane.INFORMATION_MESSAGE;
158                    }
159                    else     // can never happen
160                    {
161                        msg = "Please choose a valid action.";
162                        title = "Invalid Action";
163                        optionType = JOptionPane.WARNING_MESSAGE;
164                    }
165
166                    JOptionPane.showMessageDialog(this, msg, title, optionType);
167                    pswdField.setText("");
168                    newPswdField.setText("");
169                    pswdField.requestFocus();
170
171            }// end of try
172            catch (NullPointerException ex)
173            {
174                JOptionPane.showMessageDialog(this,"No Password yet created",
175                                              "Invalid password. Try again.",
176                                              JOptionPane.ERROR_MESSAGE);
177            }
178            catch (Exception ex)
179            {
180                JOptionPane.showMessageDialog(this, ex.getMessage(),
181                                              "Invalid password. Try again.",
182                                              JOptionPane.ERROR_MESSAGE);
183            }
184        }
185  }
```

FIGURE 9-43

The following steps open the PasswordDemo program from the Data Disk and then compile and execute the program.

To Open, Compile, and Execute the PasswordDemo Program

1. With your Data Disk in drive A, click the Open button on the Standard toolbar. If necessary, click the Look in box arrow and then select the Chapter09 folder on the Data Disk in drive A.

   The Open File(s) dialog box displays the files in the Chapter09 folder. If you do not see any files, or you do not see any Java source files, verify that the Files of type list box displays All Files (*.*).

2. Click the file, PasswordDemo.java, and then click the Open button.
3. Click Compile Java on the Tools menu.
4. Click Run Java Application on the Tools menu.

New passwords are created by typing an appropriate value in the New Password text box and then clicking the Add password button. To enter a current password and validate it against the current Password object (for example, to log into an application), type the password in the Current Password text box and then click the Use password button. To change the value of the current password, type a new password in the New Password text box and then click the Change password button. To test the Password class sufficiently, both valid and invalid actions should be tested, such as adding passwords without a numeric character, shorter than six characters, or longer than fifteen characters. After adding a password successfully, you should try to use the password, change the password, and use a different password.

Print the Source Code

After testing the Password class, both the Password class source code and the test program, PasswordDemo, source code should be printed. The following steps print the source code for both programs.

To Print the Source Code

1. Click the Print button on the TextPad Standard toolbar.

   The PasswordDemo source code is printed.

2. Click Password.java in the Selector Window to display the Password class source code.

   The Password class source code is displayed in the coding window.

3. Click the Print button on the TextPad Standard toolbar.

   The Password source code is printed.

Quitting TextPad

After you create, save, compile, execute, test, and print the Password class, the program is complete and you can quit TextPad. The following step quits TextPad and returns control to Windows.

OTHER WAYS

1. Press ALT+F, X

To Quit TextPad

1. Click the Close button on the TextPad title bar.
The TextPad window closes and the Windows desktop is displayed.

Chapter Summary

In this chapter, you learned how to create a reusable Java class that can be used to create objects for other programs. You learned how to create class and instance variables and to use the final qualifier. After learning about the Collections Framework, you learned how to code overloaded constructors for the Password class and created an ArrayList object. Next, you learned about accessor methods and mutator methods and created methods to maintain several instance variables. You also learned about accessor methods for read-only attributes, and you coded methods to provide attributes from a combination of variables. You learned about public and private methods and used ArrayList, String, and StringBuffer objects and their methods. Finally, you learned about testing a reusable class with a program that uses a JPassword field for password security.

What You Should Know

Having completed this chapter, you now should be able to perform the tasks shown in Table 9-8.

Table 9-8   Chapter 9 What You Should Know

TASK NUMBER	TASK	PAGE
1	Start a New Java Program in TextPad	545
2	Create Class and Instance Variables	548
3	Create Overloaded Constructors	554
4	Code Accessor and Mutator Methods for the autoExpires Instance Variable	557
5	Code Accessor and Mutator Methods for the Expired Instance Variable	559
6	Code Accessor and Mutator Methods for the expiresNotifyLimit Instance Variable	560
7	Code Accessor and Mutator Methods for the maxHistory Instance Variable	562
8	Code Read-Only Accessor Methods	565
9	Code Public Instance Methods	571
10	Code the verifyFormat() Private Helper Method	580
11	Code the encrypt() Private Helper Method	583
12	Save and Compile the Password Class	584
13	Open, Compile, and Execute the PasswordDemo Program	588
14	Print the Source Code	588
15	Quit TextPad	589

Key Terms

abstract *(538)*
accessor method *(555)*
add() method *(568)*
append() method *(577)*
ArrayList *(549)*
bitwise AND *(582)*
blank final *(546)*
capacity *(550)*
charAt() method *(579)*
ciphertext *(580)*
class variable *(545)*
collection *(549)*
Collections Framework *(549)*
constant variable *(546)*
contains() method *(568)*
core classes *(575)*
data structure *(549)*
decryption *(580)*
default constructor *(551)*
default value *(551)*
downcasting *(575)*
echo character *(584)*
encrypted *(538)*
encryption *(580)*
equals() method *(575)*
final *(546)*
final variable *(546)*
garbage collector *(576)*
get() method *(574)*
hash code *(582)*
hashCode() method *(583)*
helper method *(544)*
immutable *(575)*
implementation *(544)*

insert() method *(577)*
instance variable *(546)*
instanceof operator *(575)*
isDigit() method *(580)*
isEmpty() method *(574)*
iterative *(540)*
JPassword field *(584)*
least privilege *(544)*
length() method *(579)*
list *(549)*
local variable *(546)*
mask *(584)*
masking *(584)*
method signature *(552)*
mutable *(576)*
mutator method *(555)*
named constant *(546)*
overloaded *(552)*
plaintext *(580)*
private *(546)*
public interface *(544)*
read-only *(563)*
remove() method *(562)*
size *(550)*
size() method *(574)*
static *(546)*
StringBuffer class *(576)*
substring() method *(582)*
this *(556)*
trim() method *(567)*
trimToSize() method *(562)*
upcasting *(574)*
user programs *(554)*
valueOf() method *(577)*

Homework Assignments

Identify Code

Identify the code elements shown in Figure 9-44.

```
 ②  { final static int MIN_SIZE = 6;
    { final static int MAX_SIZE = 15;          }
          static int maxHistory = 4;         ① 
          static int expiresNotifyLimit = 3; }

 ③  { private int maxUses = 120;
    { private int remainingUses = maxUses;
    { private boolean autoExpires = true;
    { private boolean expired = false;

    { private ArrayList pswdHistory;


     // Constructors for objects of class Password
    { public Password(String newPassword) throws Exception
    {
          pswdHistory = new ArrayList(maxHistory);
          set(newPassword);
    }

    { public Password(String newPassword, int numMaxUses) throws Exception
    {
          pswdHistory = new ArrayList(maxHistory);
          maxUses = numMaxUses;
          remainingUses = numMaxUses;
          set(newPassword);
    }

 ④  { public Password(String newPassword, boolean pswdAutoExpires) throws Exception
    {
          pswdHistory = new ArrayList(maxHistory);
          autoExpires = pswdAutoExpires;
          set(newPassword);
    }

    { public Password(String newPassword, int numMaxUses, boolean pswdAutoExpires) throws Exception
    {
          pswdHistory = new ArrayList(maxHistory);
          maxUses = numMaxUses;
          remainingUses = numMaxUses;
          autoExpires = pswdAutoExpires;
          set(newPassword);
    }

    { public boolean getAutoExpires()
 ⑤  {
          return autoExpires;
    }
```

FIGURE 9-44

1. _____

2. _____

3. _____

4. _____

5. _____

Understanding Error Messages

Figure 9-45a displays a portion of a Java program. Figure 9-45b displays the compilation error messages. Using what you know about error messages, list the coding error that caused TextPad to display these errors.

```
1
2    public class ErrorMsg
3    {
4
5        private final int minSize;
6        private boolean found = true;
7
8        private ArrayList objList;
9
10
11       public ErrorMsg()
12       {
13           minSize = 12;
14           objList = new ArrayList(minSize);
15       }
16
17       public ErrorMsg(int newMinSize) throws Exception
18       {
19           minSize = newMinSize;
20           objList = new ArrayList(minSize);
21       }
22
23
24
25   }
```

FIGURE 9-45a

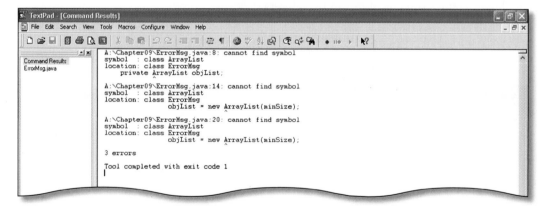

FIGURE 9-45b

Using the Java API

The Java API is a good tool to look up information about a class with which you may be unfamiliar or to check the syntax of commands and methods you wish to use in your programs. While connected to the Internet, start a browser, type http://java.sun.com/j2se/1.5/docs/api/ in the Address text box, and then press the ENTER key to view the Java API Specification on the Sun Web

Using the Java API *(continued)*

site. (Or, if you downloaded the documentation from the CD that accompanies this book, navigate to the installed version of the Java SDK on your system. Open the index.html file in the docs\api folder.)

The Java API is organized by the packages, hierarchically, but many programmers click the Index link located at the top of the page to display the entire list alphabetically. With the Java API Specification open in the browser window, perform the following steps:

1. Use the scroll down arrow in the top left frame of the main frame to display the java.util link. Click the java.util link.

2. When the Package java.util page is displayed in the lower-left frame, if necessary, scroll down to display the list of Classes. Click ArrayList in the list of Classes.

3. When the Class ArrayList page is displayed, read the first four paragraphs, including those that describe the capacity of an ArrayList.

4. Scroll down to display the ensureCapacity() method in the Method Summary. Click ensureCapacity.

5. When the description of the ensureCapacity() method is displayed (Figure 9-46), select the text by dragging through it. Click Print on the File menu. When the Print dialog box is displayed, click the Selection option button and then click the Print button in the Print dialog box to print the definition.

6. Based on your reading, write a paragraph explaining why you think the ensureCapacity() method was not used to set or increase the capacity of the ArrayList object in this chapter.

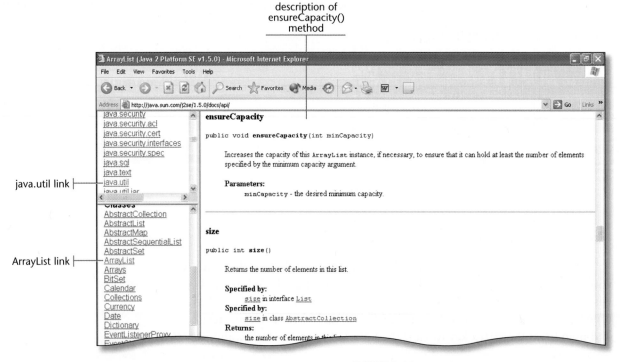

FIGURE 9-46

Short Answer

1. The keyword _____ is used to indicate a helper method available only to the class in which it is defined.

2. Collectively, the public methods of a class are known as the _____.

3. A(n) _____ variable represents a shared value among objects of the same class and is indicated by the keyword _____.

4. A format for storing a group of data is known as a(n) _____.

5. String values that are constant are described as being _____.

6. For modifiable string values, you should use objects of type _____.

7. Encoding text to make it unintelligible to unauthorized users is called _____.

8. The design principle of _____ means being able to use existing software to develop a new application.

9. The principle of _____ means allowing only the minimum access necessary to do the job.

10. Every object has its own set of values for its _____ variables.

11. The _____ of a variable refers to where in the program the variable is accessible.

12. A(n) _____ represents temporary storage available only within a given method.

13. A variable whose value cannot be changed is declared as _____.

14. An uninitialized named constant is called a(n) _____.

15. An API in Java for dealing with a number of common data structures, or collections, is the _____.

16. A(n) _____ is a reusable class representing a list implemented as an array.

17. A(n) _____ is a reusable class that relates keys to, at most, one value each.

18. A method that has the same name as the class and no return data type is called a(n) _____.

19. A method that has the same name as the class, no return data type, and no parameters is called a(n) _____.

20. When no other value is supplied, the initial value used for a variable is called the _____.

21. Any two or more methods having the same names and defined in the same class are considered to be _____.

22. The method name and parameter list, but not the return data type, comprise the _____.

23. A(n) _____ method, sometimes called a set or setter method, is used to change the value of a private variable.

24. The keyword _____ provides an explicit reference to the current object within the class.

(continued)

Short Answer *(continued)*

25. Encrypted data is called _____ as opposed to plaintext.

26. A(n) _____ is a transformation of a string value into an integer number that represents the original string.

27. Use a(n) _____, or echo character, to prevent typed characters from being displayed.

28. Use _____ to convert a more general object reference to a more specific reference.

29. _____ is done automatically when using a more general object reference for a more specific object.

30. To determine if an object of a given class also is an object of another class, particularly of a child class, use the _____ operator.

Learn It Online

Start your browser and visit scsite.com/java3e/exs. Follow the instructions in the exercises below.

1. **Chapter Reinforcement TF, MC, and SA**   Click the Chapter Reinforcement link below Chapter 9. Print and then answer the questions.

2. **Practice Test**   Click the Practice Test link below Chapter 9. Answer each question, enter your first and last name at the bottom of the page, and then click the Grade Test button. When the graded practice test is displayed on your screen, click Print on the File menu to print a hard copy. Continue to take practice tests until you score 80% or better. Hand in a printout of the final practice test.

3. **Crossword Puzzle Challenge**   Click the Crossword Puzzle Challenge link below Chapter 9. Read the instructions, and then enter your first and last name. Click the Play button. Complete the crossword puzzle. When you are finished, click the Submit button. When the crossword puzzle is displayed, click the Print button.

4. **Tips and Tricks**   Click the Tips and Tricks link below Chapter 9. Click a topic that pertains to Chapter 9. Right-click the information and then click Print on the shortcut menu. Construct a brief example of what the information relates to in Java to confirm you understand how to use the tip or trick. Hand in the example and printed information.

5. **Newsgroups**   Click the Newsgroups link below Chapter 9. Click a topic that pertains to Chapter 9. Print three comments.

6. **Expanding Your Horizons**   Click the Expanding your Horizons link below Chapter 9. Click a topic that pertains to Chapter 9. Print the information. Construct a brief example of what the information relates to in Java to confirm you understand the contents of the article. Hand in the example and printed information.

7. **Search Sleuth**   Select three key terms from the Key Terms section of this chapter and then use the Google search engine at google.com (or any major search engine) to display and print two Web pages for each key term.

Debugging Assignment

The UserList program is a Java application that accepts a user name and adds it to a list, if it does not already exist. It accepts a maximum number of user names and when full, responds with a message displaying the last name entered. The program will not accept the user name, username, as a valid entry.

The UserList program has several syntax, semantic, and logic errors in the program code. Perform the following steps to debug the program.

1. Start TextPad and open the file, UserList.java, from the Chapter09 folder on the Data Disk. See the preface of this book for instructions for downloading the Data Disk or see your instructor for information about accessing the files required in this book.

2. Read through the code and fix any errors that you see. Insert today's date and your name as the programmer in the comment header.

3. Save the program.

4. Compile the program. As TextPad displays compilation errors, fix the first error, then recompile.

5. When you have fixed all the syntax and semantic errors so that the program will compile without errors, run the program and look for run-time and logic errors. Fix any errors and compile again.

6. When the program compiles and runs to produce the output as shown in Figure 9-47, print a copy of the source code.

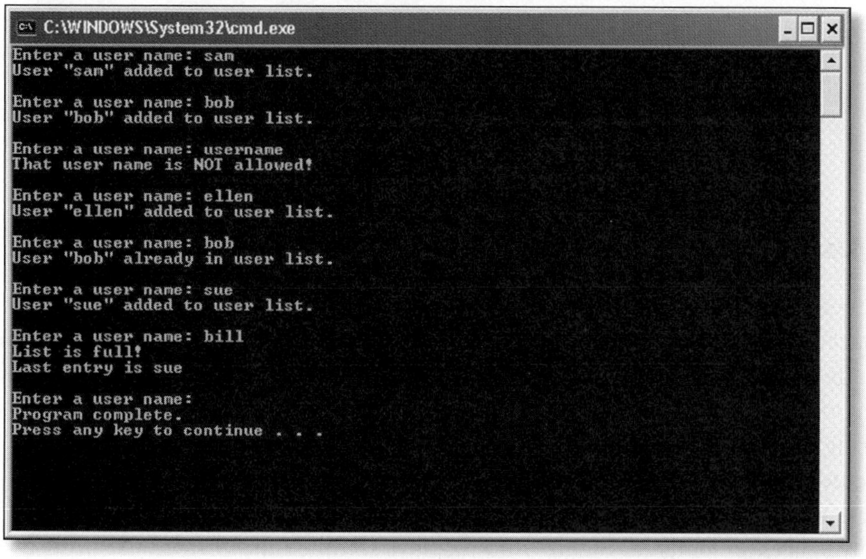

FIGURE 9-47

Programming Assignments

1 Processing Palindromes with StringBuffers

Palindromes are words spelled the same way backwards as they are forwards, such as dad or mom. Using methods from the String and StringBuffer classes, write a program that will accept input from the keyboard and then determine if the entered word is a palindrome. The program should continue as long as the user enters any values. For an extra challenge, modify the program to determine if a phrase is a palindrome. For simplicity, do not use punctuation and remove embedded spaces. *Hint:* You can use a StringBuffer method to delete an individual character at a specified index. Figure 9-48 displays sample output from the program.

FIGURE 9-48

2 Using String Methods to Count Characters

Generally, word processing programs can count and then display the number of characters in a document, either including or excluding blank characters. Using methods from the String class, write a program that will accept input from the keyboard and then display three values: (1) the count of all characters in the string, including leading and trailing blanks; (2) the count of characters not including leading and trailing blanks; and (3) the count of all non-blank characters. The program should continue as long as the user enters any values, even if only spaces are entered. Figure 9-49 displays sample output from the program.

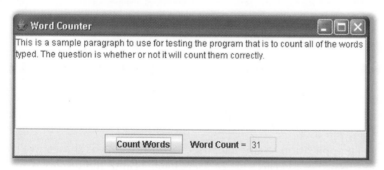

FIGURE 9-49

3 Using String Methods to Count Words

Word processing programs also can count and then display the number of words in a document, in addition to the number of characters. Using methods from the String class, write a program that will count the number of words which are separated by blanks in a String. For simplicity, use strings without punctuation or other white space characters (tabs, newlines, etc.). Use a JTextArea to allow a user to enter the text and allow the text area to scroll, if necessary. When the user clicks a button to count the words, the total number of words counted is displayed in a text box that cannot be modified by the user. For Java 5.0, use static imports where appropriate. For an additional challenge, allow words to be separated by multiple blanks and by one or more newline characters. Figure 9-50 displays sample output.

FIGURE 9-50

4 Using StringBuffers to Modify Strings

Data communication protocols often must wrap data with other characters, surrounding the data with an envelope of characters, much as a letter is within an envelope when mailed. As the data passes through different layers of the communication system, additional layers are wrapped and later unwrapped to guide the data to its intended destination.

Programming Assignments *(continued)*

To simulate this action, write a method to wrap a given number of occurrences of a character at the beginning and the end of a string. For example,

```
wrap(message, 4, '!')
```

should add 4 exclamation marks to the beginning and the end of the string, message. The program should continue to wrap as long as the user enters a wrap character. So, a subsequent call to wrap(message, 2, '?') should result in the message being wrapped by ??!!!! at the beginning and !!!!?? at the end. When the user no longer enters a wrap character, the program should prompt for another string and continue as long as the user enters a string to wrap. Figure 9-51 displays sample output.

ENTER key pressed
with no wrap
character entered

new string
entered

```
C:\WINDOWS\System32\cmd.exe

Enter a string: some text to wrap

Enter a wrap character: ?

Number of characters to wrap: 2
Wrapped string = ??some text to wrap??

Enter a wrap character: !

Number of characters to wrap: 3
Wrapped string = !!!??some text to wrap??!!!

Enter a wrap character:

Enter a string: more text

Enter a wrap character: "

Number of characters to wrap: 2
Wrapped string = ""more text""

Enter a wrap character:

Enter a string:
Program complete.
Press any key to continue . . .
```

FIGURE 9-51

5 Simulating User Logon Tracking with an ArrayList

Computer systems typically track the number of users logged on to the system at any point in time. Some systems do not allow more than one simultaneous logon by a given user.

Write an application to simulate user logon tracking as shown in Figure 9-52. The application should keep a list of users logged on to the system. A user name always must be entered in the User text box to log on or log off. The program also should ensure that only users not already logged on to the system can log on, and only those already logged on can log off. Keep track of the number of users logged on at any point in time, and display this number in a text box that the user cannot modify. Display appropriate messages when a user successfully logs on or off and appropriate error messages when an action fails. For Java 5.0, use a typesafe ArrayList and any other features, such as static imports, as appropriate.

FIGURE 9-52

6 Maintaining a Phone Book with ArrayLists

Computers and personal digital assistant (PDA) devices help to organize many aspects of one's life. A common application is a contact list, or phone book, where names, phone numbers, and often much more information about friends and business contacts is maintained.

Write a Java application to create and maintain a phone book as shown in Figure 9-53. Users should be able to add a new contact, delete an existing contact, update the phone number of an existing contact, or enter a name to find the phone number of an existing contact. Once a contact is entered, the name cannot be changed. Display appropriate messages when a user successfully adds, updates, or deletes a contact. If a requested contact successfully is found in the phone book list, display the name and phone number in the Name and Phone number text boxes, respectively. Display appropriate error messages when any action fails. For Java 5.0, use typesafe ArrayLists and static imports, where appropriate. *Hint:* Use two ArrayLists, one for names and one for phone numbers. For an additional challenge, add the capability to update the name of an entry without deleting the entry first.

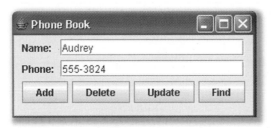

FIGURE 9-53

7 Analysis and Design of a Reusable Tally Class

A tally is a list of different items, with a count for the number of each item. For example, a tally of computer parts might show 12 monitors, 3 CD-ROM drives, 4 floppies, and so forth. Figure 9-54 on the next page shows a requirements document for a reusable Tally class. Using the six phases of the development cycle as shown in Table 9-1 on page 539, perform the steps on the next page:

REQUEST FOR NEW APPLICATION

Date submitted:	December 3, 2007
Submitted by:	Ellen Venloft, Staff Principal Systems Analyst
Purpose:	We have several applications which will need to maintain a tally of various items, such as a tally of computer parts. A tally is a simple list of items along with a count for the quantity of each item. Rather than duplicate code to handle common functionality, we need a common class these applications can use.
Application title:	Tally class
Algorithms:	None. Items and their respective counts must be maintained in pairs.
Notes:	1. User programs should be able to create a tally with or without a title (a name for the tally). Use "Unnamed tally" as the default title. 2. Provide the current title of the tally as a string. 3. Provide the count of a particular item in a tally. 4. Provide the total count of distinct tally items. 5. Add an item to the tally without specifying a quantity. A quantity of 1 is assumed. 6. Add a specified quantity of an item to the tally. 7. When adding an item to the tally, if the item already is in the tally, add the quantity to the current count for the item. If the item is not already in the tally, add the item to the tally with this quantity and increment the count of tally items. 8. Remove an item from the tally without specifying a quantity. A quantity of 1 is assumed. 9. Remove a specified quantity of an item from the tally. 10. Remove all quantities of an item from the tally without requiring that a quantity be specified. 11. When removing any quantity of an item from the tally, if the count for this item reaches zero, then purge the item from the tally and decrement the count of tally items. 12. Remove all items from the tally and set the count of tally items to zero.

Approval Status:	X	Approved
		Rejected
Approved by:	Wilson Davis	
Date:	December 5, 2007	
Assigned to:	M. Mick, Programmer	

FIGURE 9-54

1. Analyze the requirements document carefully. Think about the requester, the users, the problem, and the purpose of the class.

2. Design the solution. Draw a class diagram for the program. Pay careful attention to the methods needed. Write either pseudocode or draw a flowchart to represent the logic in your methods, as appropriate.

3. Validate the design. Have a classmate or your instructor look over your class diagram and logic, making suggestions before you proceed.

4. Implement the design. Translate the design into code for the program. For Java 5.0, use typesafe ArrayLists and autoboxing/unboxing.

5. Test the solution. Create a test program to test the Tally class, finding and correcting errors (debugging) until it is error-free.

6. Print a copy of the source code, and then submit all documents to your instructor.

10

Understanding Abstract Classes and Interfaces

Objectives

You will have
mastered the material in
this chapter when you can:

- Describe an inheritance hierarchy
- Discuss single versus multiple inheritance
- Identify class inheritance versus interface implementation
- Distinguish between abstract and concrete classes
- Create related classes using inheritance
- Create an abstract class
- Extend an abstract class
- Use a final method
- Create a final class
- Explain how to concatenate method calls
- Create a multiple Window user interface
- Use a callback mechanism
- Implement an interface
- Use adapter classes

Introduction

Previously, you learned about developing a class so it can be reused by other user programs. Developing a reusable class is useful when multiple applications, particularly unrelated applications, share a need for some common functionality. Reusing a previously developed and thoroughly tested class to provide specific functionality allows a programmer to be more productive by concentrating on new aspects of the application at hand, instead of the functionality provided by the reusable class. Using a reusable class also reduces the opportunity for errors in the application code, because the functionality provided by the class already is tested.

Whenever you create an instance of any previously defined class in a new application — whether from a class library or your own code — you are reusing a class. As long as the reusable class provides exactly the functionality required, you need only use it in your application. If you must have additional capabilities, you still may be able to use the original class as the basis for a new subclass that inherits the functionality of the original class and then adds to, or extends, it. As you learned in previous chapters, this process of **extending a class**, which is indicated by the keyword, extends, is the means of implementing inheritance in Java. As discussed in Chapter 1, inheritance is the ability of one class (and, of course, the objects instantiated from the class) to inherit attributes and behaviors from another class. Aggregation, by contrast, is the term used to describe the concept of an object being composed of other objects, that is, an object having another object as an instance variable.

In this chapter, you will learn how to use inheritance to build classes that have common functionality; how and when to use aggregation, rather than inheritance; and how to enforce additional common functionality with interfaces and abstract classes. You also will learn how a class can limit the overriding of inherited methods or even prevent inheritance from taking place.

Chapter Ten — Developing a PasswordException Class and Subclasses

In Chapter 9, a reusable Password class was developed so that AccessFour Software could use the class to provide the same password functionality across multiple applications. An application using that Password class, however, currently cannot determine if a generated exception is due to expiration or to an invalid password value. AccessFour Software now has a need for applications to be able to differentiate between the various exception conditions generated by the Password class.

In this chapter, a new PasswordException class and six subclasses are created, and the Password class developed in Chapter 9 is modified to allow for better exception handling. The new and modified classes add functionality so that, if the exception is due to expiration, the user is allowed to log on and change his or her password. If the exception is due to an invalid value, the user is denied access.

The chapter also focuses on developing a stock list application to test the PasswordException class, its subclasses, and the Password class. This test application, the StockListDemo application, allows users to log on and build a list of stock symbols. The stock list application uses multiple windows. Using multiple windows in an application is appropriate if the application must present to a user more information than will fit in a single window or if the application must present information or obtain input before the user can continue working with the application. In either case, the programmer needs the ability to use multiple windows in the application.

In the stock list application developed in this chapter, the process of identifying whether a user's logon information is valid is distinct from the action of tracking specific stocks; the stock list application, thus, presents these actions to the user in two separate windows. As shown in Figure 10-1, after the user logs on to the application (Figure 10-1a), the logon window will close, and a window for building a list of stocks opens (Figure 10-1b). When this stock window closes after the user closes it or logs out, the application reopens the original logon window. Because this test application does not retain user information between executions, the logon window also is used to add new users (Figure 10-1c) or to allow a user to change his or her password to a new password (Figures 10-1d and 10-1e). If a PasswordException is thrown, indicating that the current password is expiring, an informational message displays prior to displaying the stock list window (Figure 10-1f). If a PasswordException is thrown, indicating that the current password has expired or that an invalid password was entered, an appropriate error message displays to the user (Figures 10-1g through 10-1k on the next page).

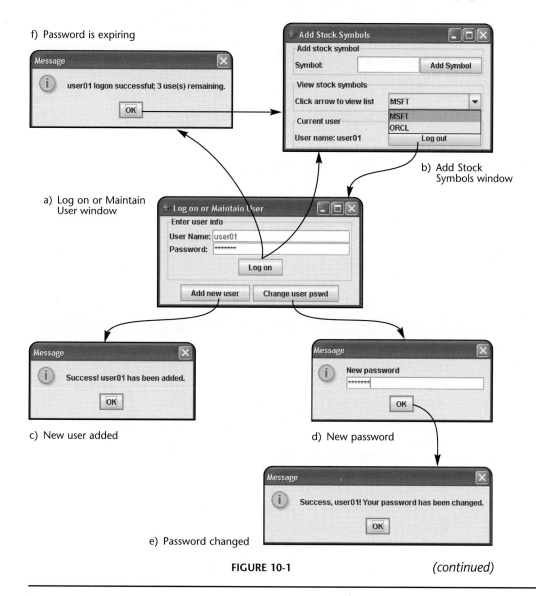

f) Password is expiring

b) Add Stock Symbols window

a) Log on or Maintain User window

c) New user added

d) New password

e) Password changed

FIGURE 10-1   (continued)

g) Password has expired

h) Invalid password — not in list

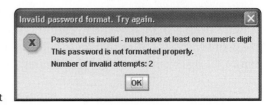

i) Invalid password; no numeric digit

j) Invalid password; less than minimum size

k) Invalid password; greater than maximum size

FIGURE 10-1

Program Development

The program development cycle and corresponding tasks for this project are shown in Table 10-1.

Table 10-1 PasswordException Class Development Tasks

	DEVELOPMENT PHASE	TASK(S)
1	Analyze the requirements	Analyze the PasswordException class problem.
2	Design the solution	Design the logic to solve the problem.
3	Validate the design	Confirm with the user that the design solves the problem in a satisfactory manner.
4	Implement the design	Translate the design into code. Include internal documentation (comments and remarks) within the code that explains the purpose of the code statements. Design and code the StockListDemo application used for testing the PasswordException class and subclasses.
5	Test the solution	Using the StockListDemo test application, test the PasswordException classes. Find and correct any errors (debug) until they are error-free.
6	Document the solution	Print copies of all source code, including the test program code.

Analysis and Design

Figure 10-2 shows the requirements document that initiates the development cycle for the PasswordException class and subclasses, along with the StockList demo program. This document illustrates that a development request may require enhancements to existing programs, rather than building an entirely new program. For object-oriented software, adding enhancements to existing programs often involves creating new classes, which also may require extending either new or existing classes.

REQUEST FOR NEW APPLICATION

occurs. The class should provide a means for user programs to obtain this count. The count should be reset to zero when a valid password is used successfully.

5. All password exceptions must have a default constructor and a constructor that requires only a String message, except for size exception and internal exception.

6. The password size exception constructor must require a String message, the current password size, the maximum password size, and the minimum password size as parameters. It must have no default constructor.

7. The password internal exception constructor must require a String message only and have no default constructor.

8. The test application used to test the classes outlined above should be a multiple window stock list application that allows a user to log on to the application using one window and then enter stocks into a list using a stock window. Only one window at a time should display to the user. When the user logs out of the stock window, the logon window should be redisplayed.

9. When a class generates a password exception, the test application should display appropriate error messages to users, indicating the type of password exception generated.

Approval Status:	X	Approved
		Rejected
Approved by:		Wilson Davis, Director of IT, AccessFour Software
Date:		December 5, 2007
Assigned to :		M. Mick, Programmer

REQUEST FOR NEW APPLICATION

Date submitted:	December 3, 2007
Submitted by:	Mark Allen, Staff Senior Systems Analyst, AccessFour Software
Purpose:	We have a need for applications to be able to differentiate between the various exception conditions generated by the Password class. Presently, when a password expires or an invalid password is used, an exception is generated. An application using the Password class, however, currently cannot determine if the generated exception is due to expiration or to an invalid password value. We also have a need for an application to test the new classes required to support the functionality described above. The test application should be a multiple window stock list application, similar to a stock application that later will incorporate these classes.
Application title:	PasswordException classes
Algorithms:	None specified.

Notes:	1. An application using the Password class currently cannot determine if the generated exception is due to expiration or to an invalid password value. Any new classes should provide functionality so that when a password expires or an invalid password is used, an exception is generated. If the exception is due to expiration, the user should be allowed to log on and change his or her password. If due to an invalid value, the user should be denied access.
	
	2. All password exception objects must be specific to the type of exception generated. All password exceptions should implement a method describing their usage. This method should return a String that could be used as an informational message by a user program. There should be a common, generic reference for all password exceptions; however, no generic password exception objects are to be used in the programs.
	
	3. Programs must be notified of the following password exceptions generated by the Password class when:
	  a. the Password class generates an exception due to an expired password.
	  b. the Password class generates an exception due to an invalid password. This is an entered password that does not match the value of the current password.
	  c. the Password class generates an exception due to an invalid password format. This is considered a type of invalid password.
	  d. the Password class generates an exception due to an invalid password size. The current password size, as well as the maximum and minimum sizes allowed should be available to the exception handler. This is considered a type of invalid password.
	  e. the Password class generates an exception due to the password being in the list of recently used values.
	  f. the Password class generates an exception due to an internal problem with storing the password list. This type of exception is not extensible.
	
	4. A count of invalid password attempts must be provided. This count is incremented automatically each time an invalid password exception

FIGURE 10-2

PROBLEM ANALYSIS The problem that the PasswordException class should solve is to allow other programs to differentiate between the exceptions generated by the Password class for expired or invalid passwords. It also must allow a common, generic reference to all password exceptions from the Password class.

The requirements document outlines several attributes and behaviors for the PasswordException class and subclasses. The PasswordException class and subclasses must generate specific exceptions for expired passwords; invalid passwords (passwords that meet format requirements, but do not match the current password value for the user); passwords with an invalid format (for example, a password without a numeric character); passwords with an invalid size; passwords recently used; and passwords that encountered an internal error when being stored in the password history. Additionally, all subclasses of PasswordException must have a method that returns a short message indicating the condition under which the exception is used.

The requirements document also specifies that any attempt to use an invalid password should increment an internal count when an invalid password exception is generated. User programs must be able to obtain the value of this count, as they will determine the number of invalid attempts allowed. Using a valid password will reset the count to zero. Because the Password class determines when a password is valid, a Password object is responsible for triggering the resetting of the invalid password count back to zero.

The requirements document further specifies that when a password size exception is generated, the exception object must provide the user program with the following information: an error message, the current password size, maximum password size, and minimum password size at the time of the exception. This information allows the user program to take the appropriate action.

Finally, the requirements document requires a multiple window application to test the PasswordException classes. This application displays a single window to the user at one time, hiding the window not in use.

DESIGN THE SOLUTION Once you have analyzed the problem and understand the needs, the next step is to design the PasswordException class. The purpose of creating the PasswordException class and its subclasses is to allow a more specific identification of the kind of exception thrown so the user program can take more appropriate action. Figure 10-3 shows an example of a generalization hierarchy for the PasswordException class and subclasses. As you learned in Chapter 1, a generalization hierarchy, or **inheritance hierarchy**, is an object-oriented design tool used to show the relationships among classes and to describe the inheritance relationships between classes. By convention, abstract classes, interfaces, and abstract methods are shown in italics in a class diagram.

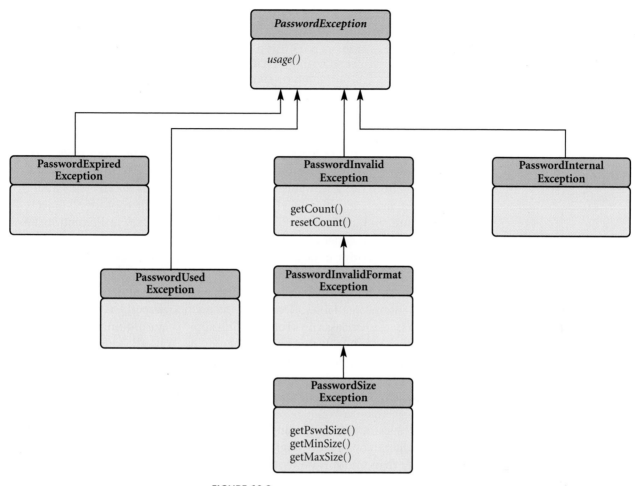

FIGURE 10-3

Examining an Inheritance Hierarchy

In this case, the PasswordException class is at the top, or **root**, of this inheritance hierarchy, making it the **base class** for this inheritance hierarchy. Being a base class means that all classes listed below it are subclasses of the PasswordException class and may inherit from the PasswordException class. As you learned in Chapter 1, the class providing the inherited features is the superclass, or **parent class**, and the class inheriting attributes and behaviors is called the subclass, or **child class**.

A subclass always is below a superclass in an inheritance hierarchy; however, inheritance is not limited to only one level of parent and child classes, or superclass and subclasses. Just as a human parent is a child of his or her own parent, so a parent class can be a child of another class, thereby inheriting features from its parent class. Therefore, as illustrated by the inheritance hierarchy in Figure 10-3, the PasswordSizeException class not only inherits from the PasswordInvalidFormatException class, but also from the PasswordInvalidException class and the PasswordException class. PasswordSizeException, therefore, is said to be a type of PasswordException, and in this case, a type of the other exception classes between them in the hierarchy (PasswordInvalidException and PasswordInvalidFormatException).

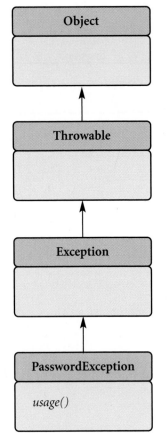

FIGURE 10-4

Furthermore, although PasswordException is shown as the root in the example of the inheritance hierarchy in Figure 10-3 on the previous page, it is also a subclass, as it inherits from the Exception class. The Exception class, in turn, inherits from the Throwable class, the superclass class for all errors and exceptions in Java, and ultimately from the Object class, the root for all objects in Java (Figure 10-4). A PasswordSizeException also is a PasswordException, an Exception, and most generically, an Object.

Although methods can be inherited by a subclass, a subclass does not inherit the constructor methods of its superclass. When a subclass constructor is called, it must call a superclass constructor as its first action, so that the superclass may initialize its instance variables. Recall that the method, super(), is how a subclass explicitly calls a superclass constructor, using appropriate arguments, if any. If the superclass has a default constructor, then no explicit call is needed, as the compiler inserts an implicit call to the superclass default constructor.

Single versus Multiple Inheritance

Java has specific rules regarding inheritance. You may have noticed that the inheritance hierarchy is like a single-sided (one parent) family tree. Java supports single, rather than multiple, inheritance. **Single inheritance** means that an object can inherit from only a single parent. Some object-oriented languages, such as C++, support **multiple inheritance**, where an object can inherit from more than one parent. Using multiple inheritance introduces some problems, such as how to handle instance variables with the same name that were inherited from multiple parents. Even more complex is how to handle inheritance from multiple parents when the parents ultimately have a common parent! Java avoids these problems by supporting only single inheritance.

Class Inheritance versus Implementing Interfaces

As you have learned, when a subclass inherits from a superclass, it may inherit both variables and methods. For example, if your program extends the Applet class, then your program is an Applet and has all of the expected capabilities of an Applet. That program also may need to listen for, or receive notice about, certain actions, such as when a user clicks a button. If Java allowed multiple inheritance, you might expect to inherit this capability from another parent class. Because this is not possible, another means must be used to ensure that your Applet program also will implement the expected behavior appropriate to a program listening for a button click.

As you learned in Chapter 3, a class that implements a listener interface monitors, or listens, for events during execution of an interactive program. For example, by implementing the listener interface, ActionListener, a class provides the capability to listen for mouse clicks on a button, once the class is registered as a listener for the button.

Sometimes an application may need to implement behaviors designated by multiple interfaces. Java allows multiple implementation of interfaces rather than multiple inheritance of classes. This is understandable when you realize that an interface contains only method declarations and/or constants and does not provide implementations for the methods declared within it. Implementing an interface provides a means of ensuring that a class will support a certain behavior without the potential of inheriting two or more means of implementing that behavior. Java classes inherit interface files by use of the keyword, implements; because they must provide the code to implement all methods from the interface, they are said to implement the interface. Because interfaces do not implement the methods that they declare, they cannot be used by themselves to create an object. For this reason, an interface may use the keyword, extends, to inherit from multiple interfaces, although a class may not inherit from multiple classes. In this chapter, two classes, LogonFrame and StockFrame, will implement multiple interfaces. They both will implement the ActionListener interface to listen for mouse clicks on buttons. The StockFrame class also will implement the WindowListener interface in order to take certain actions when its window is opened or closed. The LogonFrame class also will implement a new interface that you will create for activating the display of the windows.

In addition to defining a class to create objects using inheritance, an object also may be composed of other objects. As you learned in Chapter 1, this is called aggregation. Aggregation and inheritance both provide models for object relationships. When designing an object, decide the appropriate model to use by asking if there is an **is-a relationship** (inheritance) or a **has-a relationship** (aggregation). If a Dog is-a Animal, then Dog inherits from Animal. If a Dog has-a Owner, then the Dog class may need an Owner object as a component (attribute). As each user of this application has a password associated with the user, the User class in this chapter uses aggregation to incorporate a Password for each User object.

Tip

Inheritance versus Aggregation

Inheritance and aggregation are not mutually exclusive. A class both can inherit from a parent and contain an object reference. For example, a woman both can be a daughter (is-a) and have a daughter (has-a), and an employee both can be a supervisor (is-a) and have a supervisor (has-a). It all depends on how your classes are designed.

Abstract and Concrete Classes

Like interfaces, classes also may have method headers without implementations. A method that includes only a method header without the implementation is called an **abstract method**. Because a class typically provides the implementation for most methods, simply omitting the implementation would cause a compiler error. To distinguish methods that intentionally do not have an implementation, Java uses the keyword, **abstract**, with the method header. In an interface, all methods are required to be abstract. Therefore, the use of the keyword, abstract, is not required for method headers in an interface.

Whenever a class contains an abstract method, it cannot be used to instantiate an object and must be declared as an abstract class. An **abstract class** is a class that cannot be used to create an object and is used only for purposes of inheritance, that is, to establish a base, or parent, class for future subclasses. An abstract class is designated by use of the keyword, abstract, in the class header. In this chapter, the PasswordException class is defined as an abstract class used to provide a parent class for the six child classes shown in Figure 10-3 on page 609.

> **Tip**
>
> **Deciding between Abstract Classes and Interfaces**
> If you want to prevent instantiation of an object, but need to define instance variables, implemented instance methods, or static methods, then you need to use an abstract class. If you need to enforce behavior through multiple inheritance, then you need to use an interface.

By contrast, a **concrete class** is a class from which an object may be created and may or may not be a parent class. A concrete class cannot contain any abstract methods. If a class, which otherwise would be considered as concrete, inherits an abstract method, it must provide an implementation for that method. If it does not, then the class must be declared as an abstract class. When declaring a method or a class as abstract, the method or class also must be declared as public.

PROGRAM IMPLEMENTATION Once you have designed the class and validated the design, the next step in the development cycle is to implement the design, as shown in Table 10-1 on page 606. In this project, several subclasses of the PasswordException class are needed, rather than a single, comprehensive PasswordException class. In Java, it is not uncommon to create a number of smaller classes, especially when using inheritance. Although not strictly necessary, the new PasswordException class and subclasses should be created in the same location as the Password class. Doing so ensures that the compiler can locate the new classes when compiling the Password class, which also will require changes.

Further, because each subclass or child class depends on the existence of the parent class from which it inherits, the parent and child classes must be coded in the proper order before they can be compiled. For example, the base class, PasswordException, must be coded first, before any of the child classes can be coded.

Starting a New Java Program in TextPad

The following steps start TextPad and save the TextPad document using a Java file type.

To Start a New Java Program in TextPad

1. Insert the Data Disk in drive A.

2. Copy the Password.java file from the location where you saved it in the previous chapter (the Chapter09 folder or the location specified by your instructor) and paste the file in the Chapter10 folder or a location specified by your instructor.

3. Start TextPad. If necessary, click Line Numbers on the View menu to display line numbers.

4. Click File on the menu bar and then click Save As on the File menu. When the Save As dialog box is displayed, click the Save in box arrow and then click 3½ Floppy (A:) in the Save in list.

5. Double-click the Chapter10 folder or a location specified by your instructor.

6. Type PasswordException in the File name text box and then click Java (*.java) in the Save as type list. Click the Save button in the Save As dialog box.

   The file named, PasswordException, is saved as a Java source code file in the Chapter10 folder on the Data Disk in drive A (Figure 10-5).

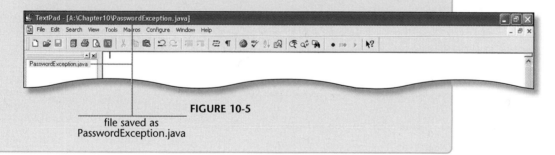

FIGURE 10-5

file saved as
PasswordException.java

Creating Related Classes Using Inheritance

The requirements document in Figure 10-2 on page 607 and the inheritance hierarchy in Figure 10-3 on page 609 describe the relative relationships between the parent class, PasswordException, and the child classes. For the program to be able to distinguish between the various child classes, each must have its own type; however, for the program to refer to an object of any of the child classes using a common type, each must have a common parent, which means they all must inherit from the PasswordException class.

Creating an Abstract Class

As indicated in the requirements document, an object of type PasswordException never should be created; only objects of the subclasses should be created. To ensure this, the PasswordException class should be defined as an abstract class, because an abstract class cannot be used to instantiate an object, and abstract classes are used only as a basis for inheritance.

Figure 10-6 displays the code for the abstract class, PasswordException. Lines 1 through 7 add the block comment. Line 9 declares the PasswordException class as an abstract class using the keyword, abstract. As indicated by the keyword, extends, the PasswordException class extends the Exception class and thus, inherits its attributes and behaviors.

The PasswordException class has two constructors. The first constructor in lines 11 through 14 has no parameters and, therefore, is the default constructor. The second constructor in lines 16 through 19 has a single parameter consisting of a String passed by the calling program. Programs that create Exception objects typically create Exception objects with or without a corresponding informational message; these two types of constructors, thus, are common among Exception classes. Both constructors also call the superclass constructor (lines 13 and 18) and pass a String argument, which is used to initialize a detail message in the superclass, Exception. This detail message later can be accessed by a user program. Line 21 includes the abstract method, usage(), which includes a header but no implementation. The usage() method is used to provide common behavior for all of the PasswordException subclasses, so that when an exception is generated, each PasswordException subclass contains an additional informational message, which also can be accessed by a user program.

```
1   /*
2        Chapter 10: The PasswordException Class
3        Programmer: Michael Mick
4        Date:       December 5, 2007
5        Filename:   PasswordException.java
6        Purpose:    To provide an abstract base class for password exceptions
7   */
8
9   public abstract class PasswordException extends Exception
10  {
11      public PasswordException()
12      {
13          super("Password exception");
14  }
15
16      public PasswordException(String msg)
17      {
18          super(msg);
19      }
20
21      public abstract String usage();
22  }
```

FIGURE 10-6

The following step enters code to create the abstract class, PasswordException.

To Create an Abstract Class

1. Enter lines 1 through 22 as shown in Figure 10-6. In the comments, insert your own name as programmer and enter the current date.

TextPad displays code for the initial comments, the abstract class header, constructors, and the abstract usage() method in the coding window (Figure 10-7). The keyword, abstract, indicates that the PasswordException class is an abstract class and that the usage() method is an abstract method.

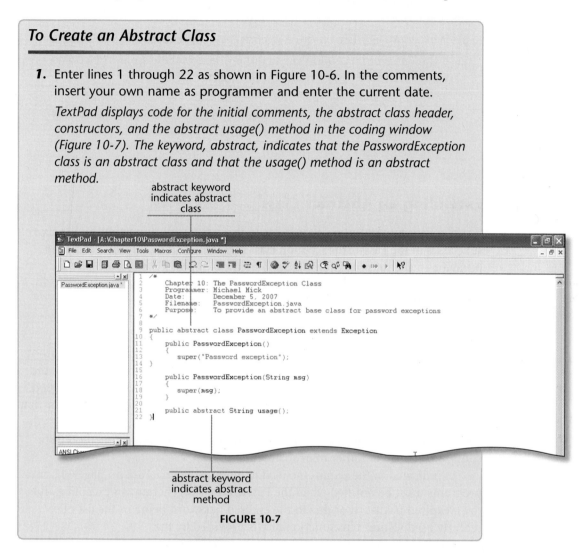

abstract keyword
indicates abstract
class

abstract keyword
indicates abstract
method

FIGURE 10-7

As previously discussed, the PasswordException class must be declared as abstract because it contains an abstract method. Abstract classes are not required to contain an abstract method; however, if a class does include an abstract method, the keyword, abstract, must be used to declare the class as abstract and, thus, prevent instantiation.

The PasswordException class now is completely coded. Remember, this abstract class does not support a user interface, is not an executable application or applet, and cannot be used to create objects. Instead, the PasswordException class is used only for purposes of inheritance — that is, to establish a parent class for child classes of the PasswordException type.

To build the class file for use with child classes, the code must be saved and this source file compiled. The steps on the next page save and compile the PasswordException class source file.

To Save and Compile the PasswordException Class

1. With your Data Disk in drive A, click Compile Java on the Tools menu.

2. If the PasswordException class contains errors, fix them in the coding window and then recompile the program.

TextPad automatically saves and then compiles the source code for the PasswordException class. If TextPad notifies you of compilation errors, fix them in the PasswordException coding window and then compile again.

OTHER WAYS

1. Press CTRL+1

Extending an Abstract Class

The PasswordException class exists to provide a common parent to the six subclasses in the PasswordException class hierarchy and to enforce a common behavior — that of providing a usage() method to provide an informational message to a user program. As indicated by the inheritance hierarchy in Figure 10-3 on page 609, four classes inherit directly from PasswordException. Of these, three classes — PasswordExpiredException, PasswordUsedException, and PasswordInvalidException — can themselves be extended. The class, PasswordinternalException, is designated as a **leaf node**, which means it cannot have any child classes. Each child class extends the PasswordException class and is a concrete class from which an object can be created. As previously discussed, if a class inherits an abstract method, it must provide an implementation for that method to be considered concrete. Each PasswordException subclass inherits the abstract method, usage(), and thus, must implement the usage() method to be considered concrete rather than abstract.

As indicated in the requirements document in Figure 10-2 on page 607, user programs must be notified when the Password class generates an exception due to an expired password or due to the entered password being in the list of recently used values. This functionality is provided by the PasswordExpiredException and PasswordUsedException classes, respectively.

Figures 10-8 and 10-9 display the code for the PasswordExpiredException and PasswordUsedException classes. In the code for the PasswordExpiredException class in Figure 10-8, lines 1 through 7 add the block comment. Line 9 declares the PasswordExpiredException class. As indicated by the keyword, extends, the PasswordExpiredException class extends the PasswordException class and thus, inherits its attributes and behaviors. Lines 11 through 19 add two constructors: the first as a default constructor (lines 11 through 14) and the second constructor with a single parameter consisting of a String passed by the calling program (lines 16 through 19). Lines 21 through 26 implement the abstract method, usage(), which was inherited from the parent class. When a PasswordExpiredException exception is generated, the usage() method is available to return the concatenated string message in lines 23 and 24.

```
 1   /*
 2        Chapter 10: The PasswordExpiredException Class
 3        Programmer: Michael Mick
 4        Date:        December 5, 2007
 5        Filename:    PasswordExpiredException.java
 6        Purpose:     To provide an exception for expired passwords
 7   */
 8
 9   public class PasswordExpiredException extends PasswordException
10   {
11        public PasswordExpiredException()
12        {
13            super("Password has expired.");
14        }
15
16        public PasswordExpiredException(String msg)
17        {
18            super(msg);
19        }
20
21        public String usage()
22        {
23            return new String("This password is set to expire automatically,\n"+
24                              "and its number of remaining uses has reached zero");
25        }
26   }
```

FIGURE 10-8

```
 1.  /*
 2        Chapter 10: The PasswordUsedException Class
 3        Programmer: Michael Mick
 4        Date:        December 5, 2007
 5        Filename:    PasswordUsedException.java
 6        Purpose:     To provide an exception for passwords recently used
 7   */
 8
 9   public class PasswordUsedException extends PasswordException
10   {
11        public PasswordUsedException()
12        {
13            super("Password recently used.");
14        }
15
16        public PasswordUsedException(String msg)
17        {
18            super(msg);
19        }
20
21        public String usage()
22        {
23            return new String("This password cannot be reused at this time.");
24        }
25   }
```

FIGURE 10-9

The code for the PasswordUsedException class is very similar to the code for the PasswordExpiredException class. In Figure 10-9, line 9 declares the PasswordUsedException class; the keyword, extends, indicates that it extends the PasswordException class. Lines 21 through 25 implement the abstract method, usage(), and define a concatenated string message that is returned when the usage() method of the PasswordUsedException exception is called.

The steps on the next page enter code for the PasswordExpiredException and PasswordUsedException classes to extend the abstract class, PasswordException.

To Extend an Abstract Class

1. In the TextPad window, click the New Document button on the Standard toolbar.

2. Click File on the menu bar and then click Save As on the File menu. When the Save As dialog box is displayed, click the Save in box arrow and then click 3½ Floppy (A:) in the Save in list.

3. Double-click the Chapter10 folder or a location specified by your instructor.

4. Type PasswordExpiredException in the File name text box and then click Java (*.java) in the Save as type list. Click the Save button in the Save As dialog box.

5. Enter lines 1 through 26 as shown in Figure 10-8 on the previous page. In the comments, insert your own name as programmer and enter the current date.

TextPad displays code for the initial comments, PasswordExpiredException class header, constructors, and usage() method in the coding window (Figure 10-10). The PasswordExpiredException class inherits from PasswordException by using the keyword, extends, and implements the abstract method, usage(), inherited from PasswordException.

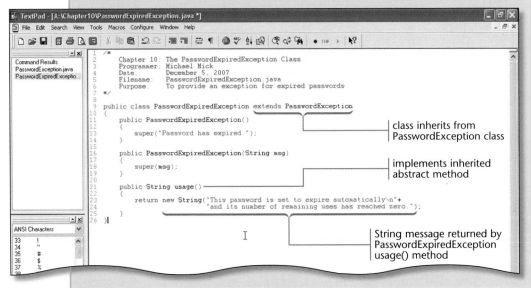

FIGURE 10-10

6. Save and compile the PasswordExpiredException class.

7. Repeat steps 1 through 6 for the class, PasswordUsedException. In step 5, enter lines 1 through 25 as shown in Figure 10-9 on the previous page.

TextPad displays code for the initial comments, PasswordUsedException class header, constructors, and usage() method in the coding window (Figure 10-11). The PasswordUsedException class inherits from PasswordException by using the keyword, extends, and implements the abstract method, usage(), inherited from PasswordException. TextPad displays the new Java source files in the document selector window.

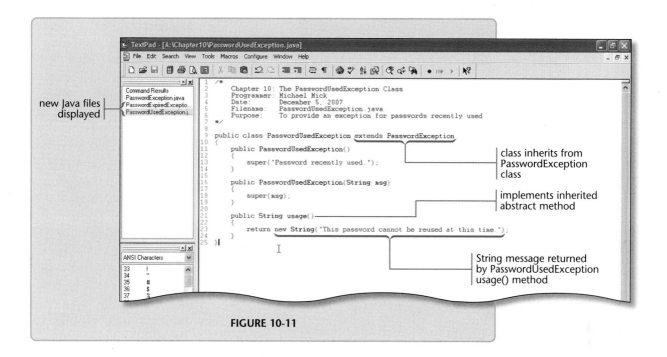

new Java files displayed

class inherits from PasswordException class

implements inherited abstract method

String message returned by PasswordUsedException usage() method

FIGURE 10-11

As shown in the previous steps, extending an abstract class is no different than extending any other class, such as Applet, except that you must implement any abstract methods the abstract class may declare. Both the PasswordInvalidException class and the PasswordUsedException class, thus, implement the abstract method, usage(), which is inherited from the abstract class, PasswordException.

Using a Final Method in a Class

As indicated in the requirements document in Figure 10-2 on page 607, programs must be notified when the Password class generates an exception due to an invalid password — that is, when an entered password does not match the value of the current password. As shown in Figure 10-3 on page 609, the PasswordInvalidException class also inherits from the parent class, PasswordException. The PasswordInvalidException class, however, has some additional components that the previous two classes — PasswordExpiredException and PasswordUsedException — did not have. Figure 10-12 on the next page displays the code for the PasswordInvalidException class. Line 9 declares the PasswordInvalidException class; the keyword, extends, indicates that it extends the PasswordException class.

Line 11 declares the class variable, count, with an int data type. According to the requirements document in Figure 10-2, a count of the number of invalid passwords used should be kept. Because an invalid password triggers a PasswordInvalidException, a variable in the PasswordInvalidException class is an appropriate place to increment such a count. That is, when a user enters an invalid password, this exception is generated, and the called constructor, of the two constructors in lines 13 through 23, increments the count by one. The user program then can continue and give the user another opportunity to enter the correct password. If the user enters another invalid password, a new PasswordInvalidException object is generated. The previous PasswordInvalidException object no longer is in

```
 1  /*
 2       Chapter 10: The PasswordInvalidException Class
 3       Programmer: Michael Mick
 4       Date:       December 5, 2007
 5       Filename:   PasswordInvalidException.java
 6       Purpose:    To provide an exception for invalid passwords
 7  */
 8
 9  public class PasswordInvalidException extends PasswordException
10  {
11      private static int count;
12
13      public PasswordInvalidException()
14      {
15          super("Invalid password.");
16          ++count;
17      }
18
19      public PasswordInvalidException(String pswd)
20      {
21          super(pswd);
22          ++count;
23      }
24
25      public String usage()
26      {
27          return new String("This password does not match any\n"+
28                            "value in the password history.");
29      }
30
31      public final void resetCount()
32      {
33          count = 0;
34      }
35
36      public final int getCount()
37      {
38          return count;
39      }
40  }
```

FIGURE 10-12

use and may be a candidate for the garbage collector. You learned in Chapter 9 that the garbage collector is the Java Virtual Machine (JVM) process that releases memory for objects no longer in use. The constructor of a new PasswordInvalidException object increments again the count of invalid passwords used. Adding one to the number of previous invalid uses requires that the value stored in the count variable be maintained across multiple instances of the PasswordInvalidException class.

Recall that to share a variable across multiple instances of a class means the variable must be declared as static, as is the count variable in line 11. Any instance of the PasswordInvalidException class, therefore, can have access to this variable. Additionally, any instance of the PasswordInvalidException class can be used to get or reset the value of this variable, via the accessor method, getCount(), in lines 36 through 39 and the mutator method, resetCount(), in lines 31 through 34.

Because the count variable is declared as private in line 11, a subclass, such as PasswordInvalidFormat or PasswordSizeException, would not have direct access to the count variable. By overriding the resetCount() method, a subclass could prevent the count from being reset, because the original method might not ever be called. Likewise, overriding the getCount() method might result in an incorrect value being returned to the user program. Therefore, any subclass should not be allowed to override either of these two methods. This is accomplished by declaring the methods as final. A **final method** is a method that can be inherited, but cannot be overridden by a subclass. When coding, use final methods carefully, because they can inhibit extensibility of your classes. Often, a method is declared as final if it has an implementation that should not be changed, because it is critical to the behavior or state of the object.

Tip

Using Final Methods

Use final methods carefully, because they can inhibit extensibility of your classes. If the method should not be used by a subclass, consider making it private. Make it final only if the method must be accessible by the subclass, but not overridden.

The following steps enter code to create the PasswordInvalidException class and declare two final methods.

To Create Final Methods

1. Create and then save a new document in the Chapter10 folder, or a location specified by your instructor, typing PasswordInvalidException as the file name and selecting Java (*.java) as the file type. Enter lines 1 through 30 as shown in Figure 10-12. In the comments, insert your own name as programmer and enter the current date.

TextPad displays code for the initial comments, PasswordInvalidException class header, constructors, and the usage() method in the coding window (Figure 10-13). The PasswordInvalidException class inherits from PasswordException by using the keyword, extends. The method, usage(), overrides the abstract method declared in the parent class. The class variable, count, is incremented in the constructors.

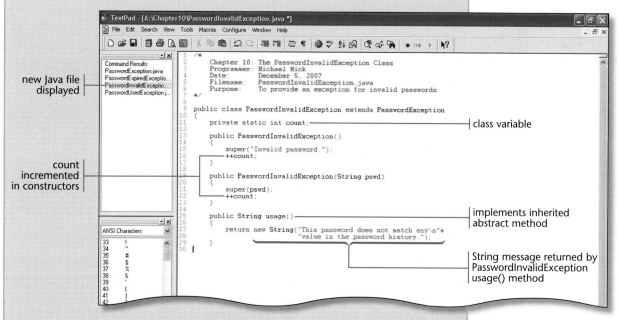

FIGURE 10-13

2. Enter lines 31 through 40 as shown in Figure 10-12.

(continued)

3. Save and compile the PasswordInvalidException class.

TextPad displays code for the accessor method, getCount(), and the mutator method, resetCount(), for the class variable, count (Figure 10-14). The use of the keyword, final, indicates that these methods cannot be overridden by a subclass.

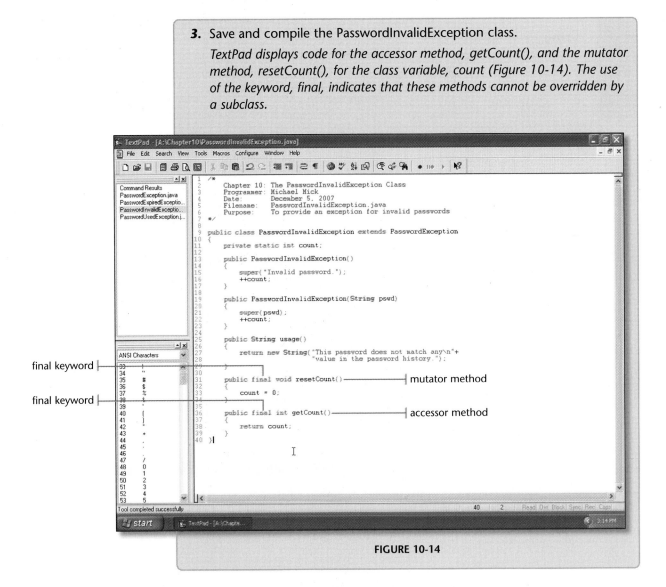

FIGURE 10-14

Extending a Child Class

As indicated in the requirements document in Figure 10-2 on page 607, programs must be notified when the Password class generates an exception due to an invalid password format. The inheritance hierarchy in Figure 10-3 on page 609 shows the PasswordInvalidFormatException class as a child of the PasswordInvalidException class. As such, the only required elements of the PasswordInvalidFormatException class are its constructors.

Figure 10-15 displays the code for the PasswordInvalidFormatException class. Line 9 declares the class and uses the keyword, extends, to indicate that the PasswordInvalidFormatException class inherits from the PasswordInvalidException class. Lines 11 through 19 include two constructors, and lines 21 through 24 include the usage() method. Because the usage() method was implemented in the parent class, the child class is not required to implement the usage() method. Line 21, however, overrides the usage() method so that the program can return a different String message than the one used in the parent class.

```
 1    /*
 2          Chapter 10: The PasswordInvalidFormatException Class
 3          Programmer: Michael Mick
 4          Date:       December 5, 2007
 5          Filename:   PasswordInvalidFormatException.java
 6          Purpose:    To provide an exception for improperly formatted passwords
 7    */
 8
 9    public class PasswordInvalidFormatException extends PasswordInvalidException
10    {
11          public PasswordInvalidFormatException()
12          {
13              super("Invalid password format.");
14          }
15
16          public PasswordInvalidFormatException(String msg)
17          {
18              super(msg);
19          }
20
21          public String usage()
22          {
23              return new String("This password is not formatted properly.");
24          }
25    }
```

FIGURE 10-15

As indicated in the requirements document in Figure 10-2 on page 607, programs must be notified when the Password class generates an exception due to an invalid password size. The current password size, as well as the maximum and minimum sizes allowed, should be available to the exception handler. The inheritance hierarchy in Figure 10-3 on page 609 also shows the PasswordSizeException class as a child of the PasswordInvalidException class. As such, it inherits attributes and behaviors from its parent classes. The reason for extending classes typically is to incorporate additional functionality, beyond what any of the parent classes provide. The PasswordSizeException class, for example, needs to retain information about the size of the password entered by the user, as well as the maximum and minimum sizes allowed, so that this information can be passed to the user program, if desired.

Figure 10-16 on the next page displays the code for the PasswordSizeException classes. Lines 12 through 14 declare three private instance variables to hold the values for the size of the password entered by the user, as well as the maximum and minimum sizes allowed. In lines 22 through 24, the keyword, this, is used to distinguish between the three instance variables and constructor parameters of the same name in line 19. Lines 27 through 40 include three accessor methods to allow access to these values. There are no mutator methods, as these values are set at the time the object is constructed. Further, because it has no default constructor, PasswordSizeException objects must be created passing the required size information, in addition to a String message. Finally, because the method, usage(), is not overloaded, the method supplied by the immediate parent class (PasswordInvalidFormatException) will be used when called for objects of this class.

```
 1   /*
 2        Chapter 10: The PasswordSizeException Class
 3        Programmer: Michael Mick
 4        Date:       December 5, 2007
 5        Filename:   PasswordSizeException.java
 6        Purpose:    To provide an exception for passwords not meeting size requirements
 7   */
 8
 9   public class PasswordSizeException extends PasswordInvalidFormatException
10   {
11        // instance variables
12        private int pswdSize;
13        private int minSize;
14        private int maxSize;
15        /**
16         * Constructor for objects of class PasswordSizeException
17         */
18
19        public PasswordSizeException(String msg, int pswdSize, int minSize, int maxSize)
20        {
21             super(msg);
22             this.pswdSize = pswdSize;
23             this.minSize = minSize;
24             this.maxSize = maxSize;
25        }
26
27        public int getPswdSize()
28        {
29             return pswdSize;
30        }
31
32        public int getMinSize()
33        {
34             return minSize;
35        }
36
37        public int getMaxSize()
38        {
39             return maxSize;
40        }
41   }
```

FIGURE 10-16

The following steps enter code to extend the child class, PasswordInvalidException, to create two additional child classes, PasswordInvalidFormatException and PasswordSizeException.

To Extend a Child Class

1. Create and then save a new document in the Chapter10 folder, or a location specified by your instructor, typing PasswordInvalidFormatException as the file name and selecting Java (*.java) as the file type. Enter lines 1 through 25 as shown in Figure 10-15 on the previous page. In the comments, insert your own name as programmer and enter the current date. Save and compile the PasswordInvalidFormatException class.

TextPad displays code for the initial comments, class header, constructors, and the method, usage(), in the coding window (Figure 10-17). Note that this class extends the concrete class, PasswordInvalidException, not the abstract class, PasswordException. The method, usage(), although not required, overrides the method defined in the parent class.

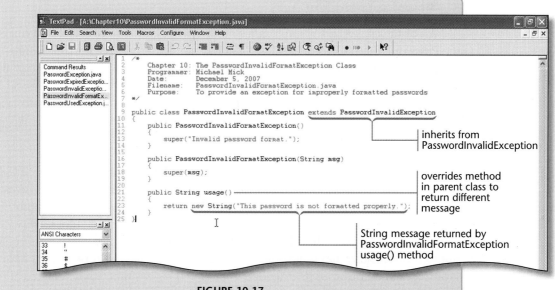

FIGURE 10-17

2. Create and then save a new document in the Chapter10 folder, or a location specified by your instructor, typing PasswordSizeException as the file name and selecting Java (*.java) as the file type. Enter lines 1 through 41 as shown in Figure 10-16. In the comments, insert your own name as programmer and enter the current date. Save and compile the PasswordSizeException class.

TextPad displays code for the initial comments, instance variables, class header, constructor, and the accessor methods (Figure 10-18). This class extends the concrete class, PasswordInvalidFormatException. The keyword, this, is used to distinguish between instance variables and constructor parameters of the same name.

FIGURE 10-18

Creating a Final Class

All of the classes in the inheritance hierarchy diagram are coded except one: the PasswordInternalException class. The PasswordInternalException class notifies programs when the Password class generates an exception due to an internal problem with storing the password list.

The PasswordInternalException class also inherits from the abstract base class, PasswordException. As shown in Figure 10-3 on page 609, however, it is designated as a leaf node, which means it cannot have any child classes; therefore, it is not extensible.

Generally, class designers expect their classes to be extended. Often, they build classes, as in this chapter, specifically for the purpose of extending them. On occasion, the designer will build a class that should not be extended. To do so might open an opportunity for some misuse of the system, expose some vulnerability, or simply not be necessary. In this chapter, the PasswordInternalException class is not to be extensible; that is, it should be defined as a final class. A **final class** in Java is a class that cannot be extended; that is, it is a class that can be only a child class and not a parent class. In Java, the means for inhibiting extensibility of a class is to declare the class with the final qualifier.

Because final classes cannot be extended, think of them as dead ends in your inheritance hierarchy. Use care when making a class final, as it is difficult to foresee future uses of your class.

```
1   /*
2        Chapter 10: The PasswordInternalException Class
3        Programmer: Michael Mick
4        Date:       December 5, 2007
5        Filename:   PasswordInternalException.java
6        Purpose:    To provide an exception when an error occurs in the
7                    collection used for maintaining the password history.
8                    Such an error never should occur.
9   */
10
11  public final class PasswordInternalException extends PasswordException
12  {
13      public PasswordInternalException(String msg)
14      {
15          super(msg);
16      }
17
18      public String usage()
19      {
20          return new String("Internal error in the collection "+
21                            "containing the password history. This never should occur.");
22      }
23  }
```

FIGURE 10-19

> **Tip**
>
> **Final Classes**
> By making a class final, you are not allowing any new classes to enhance its functionality. Before making a class final, be certain this truly is necessary, as it is difficult to foresee future uses of your class.

Figure 10-19 displays the code for the PasswordInternalException class. The final keyword in line 11 declares the class as a final class. Lines 18 through 23 include a usage() method. Because this class extends the abstract class, PasswordException, it is required to override the method, usage(). The following step enters code to create a final class.

To Create a Final Class

1. Create and then save a new document in the Chapter10 folder, or a location specified by your instructor, typing `PasswordInternalException` as the file name and selecting Java (*.java) as the file type. Enter lines 1 through 23 as shown in Figure 10-19. In the comments, insert your own name as programmer and enter the current date. Save and compile the PasswordInternalException class.

TextPad displays code for the initial comments, class header, constructor, and the method, usage(), in the coding window (Figure 10-20).

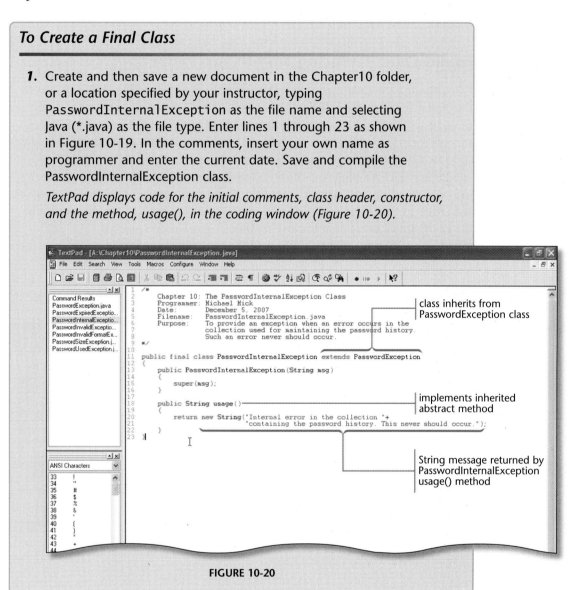

FIGURE 10-20

All of the classes in the PasswordException hierarchy are complete and ready for use. These classes were designed for use by the Password class, which now must be modified accordingly.

Using the PasswordException Classes and Subclasses

The purpose of creating the PasswordException class and its subclasses was to allow a more specific identification of the kind of exception thrown so the user program could take more appropriate action. Consequently, all methods in the Password class that throw an Exception now should be modified to throw a PasswordException.

Finding and Replacing Text in TextPad

Although the Password class is fairly small, as is typical for object-oriented programs, it still may be difficult or tedious to find every place where a change must be made simply by scrolling through the code. TextPad provides features that can help in finding code to change and then replacing the code with new code to make those changes quickly and accurately.

Figure 10-21 displays the modified code for the Password class. The following steps that begin on page 632 find the code, throws Exception, and replace it with the code, throws PasswordException, so that all throws of an Exception in the Password class are changed to throws of a PasswordException.

```
1   /*
2       Chapter 10: The Password Class
3       Programmer: Michael Mick
4       Date:       December 5, 2007
5       Filename:   Password.java
6       Purpose:    To provide a reusable Password class which uses PasswordException
7   */
8
9   import java.util.*;
10
11  public class Password
12  {
13      final static int MIN_SIZE = 6;
14      final static int MAX_SIZE = 15;
15          static int maxHistory = 4;
16          static int expiresNotifyLimit = 3;
17
18      private int maxUses = 120;
19      private int remainingUses = maxUses;
20      private boolean autoExpires = true;
21      private boolean expired = false;
22
23      private ArrayList pswdHistory;
24
25
26      // Constructors for objects of class Password
27      public Password(String newPassword) throws PasswordException
28      {
29          pswdHistory = new ArrayList(maxHistory);
30          set(newPassword);
31      }
32
33      public Password(String newPassword, int numMaxUses) throws PasswordException
34      {
35          pswdHistory = new ArrayList(maxHistory);
36          maxUses = numMaxUses;
37          remainingUses = numMaxUses;
38          set(newPassword);
39      }
40
```

FIGURE 10-21

```
41      public Password(String newPassword, boolean pswdAutoExpires) throws PasswordException
42      {
43          pswdHistory = new ArrayList(maxHistory);
44          autoExpires = pswdAutoExpires;
45          set(newPassword);
46      }
47
48      public Password(String newPassword, int numMaxUses, boolean pswdAutoExpires) throws
        PasswordException
49      {
50          pswdHistory = new ArrayList(maxHistory);
51          maxUses = numMaxUses;
52          remainingUses = numMaxUses;
53          autoExpires = pswdAutoExpires;
54          set(newPassword);
55      }
56
57      public boolean getAutoExpires()
58      {
59          return autoExpires;
60      }
61
62      public void setAutoExpires(boolean autoExpires)
63      {
64          this.autoExpires = autoExpires;
65          if(autoExpires)
66              remainingUses = maxUses;
67      }
68
69      public boolean isExpired()
70      {
71          return expired;
72      }
73
74      public void setExpired(boolean newExpired)
75      {
76          expired = newExpired;
77      }
78
79      public int getExpiresNotifyLimit()
80      {
81          return expiresNotifyLimit;
82      }
83
84      public void setExpiresNotifyLimit(int newNotifyLimit)
85      {
86          if(newNotifyLimit >= 2 && newNotifyLimit <= 20)
87              expiresNotifyLimit = newNotifyLimit;
88      }
89
90      public int getMaxHistory()
91      {
92          return maxHistory;
93      }
94
95      public void setMaxHistory(int newMaxHistory)
96      {
97          int overage = 0;
98          if(newMaxHistory >= 1 && newMaxHistory <= 10)
99          {
100             maxHistory = newMaxHistory;
101             overage = getHistorySize() - maxHistory;
102             if(overage > 0)                              // if size > max allowed
103             {
104                 do {
105                     pswdHistory.remove(0);               // then remove overage number
106                     overage--;                           // of oldest pswds from list
107                 } while(overage > 0);
108
109                 pswdHistory.trimToSize();                // resize capacity to max allowed
110             }
111         }
112     }
113
```

FIGURE 10-21

(continued)

```
114        public int getRemainingUses()
115        {
116            return remainingUses;
117        }
118
119        public int getHistorySize()
120        {
121            return pswdHistory.size();
122        }
123
124        public boolean isExpiring()
125        {
126            boolean expiring = false;
127
128            if(autoExpires && remainingUses <= expiresNotifyLimit)
129                expiring = true;
130
131            return expiring;
132        }
133
134        // Sets password to a new value; keeps current & previous values in history up to max
           number
135        public void set(String pswd) throws PasswordException
136        {
137            String encryptPswd;
138            boolean pswdAdded = true;
139
140            pswd = pswd.trim();                    // remove any leading, trailing white space
141            verifyFormat(pswd);                    // verify password was entered properly
142            encryptPswd = encrypt(pswd);           // convert to encrypted form
143
144            if(!pswdHistory.contains(encryptPswd))        // if pswd not in recently used list,
145            {
146                if(pswdHistory.size() == maxHistory)      // if list is at max size
147                    pswdHistory.remove(0);                // remove 1st, oldest, pswd from list
148
149                pswdAdded = pswdHistory.add(encryptPswd); // add new pswd to end of ArrayList
150
151                if(!pswdAdded)                            // never should happen
152                    throw new PasswordInternalException(
                        "Internal list error - Password not accepted");
153
154                if(expired)                               // if pswd has expired,
155                    expired = false;                      // reset to not expired
156
157                if(autoExpires)                           // if pswd auto expires,
158                    remainingUses = maxUses;              // reset uses to max
159            }
160            else
161                throw new PasswordUsedException("Password recently used");
162        }
163
164        // Validates entered password against most recently saved value
165        public void validate(String pswd) throws PasswordException
166        {
167            String encryptPswd;
168            String currentPswd;
169            int currentPswdIndex;
170
171            verifyFormat(pswd);                // verify password was entered properly
172            encryptPswd = encrypt(pswd);       // convert to encrypted form
173
174            if(!pswdHistory.isEmpty())         // at least one password entry is in history
175            {
176                currentPswdIndex = pswdHistory.size()-1;
177                currentPswd = (String)pswdHistory.get(currentPswdIndex);
178
179                if(!encryptPswd.equals(currentPswd)) // if not most recent pswd
180                    throw new PasswordInvalidException("Password is invalid");
181
```

FIGURE 10-21

```
182                    if(expired)
183                        throw new PasswordExpiredException("Password has expired - please change.");
184
185                    if(autoExpires)
186                    {
187                        --remainingUses;
188                        if(remainingUses <= 0)
189                            expired=true;
190                    }
191            }
192            else
193                throw new PasswordInvalidException("No password on file!");
194
195            new PasswordInvalidException().resetCount(); // resets count of invalid exceptions
196        }
197
198        // Verifies password has proper format
199        private void verifyFormat(String pswd) throws PasswordException
200        {
201            boolean numFound = false;
202
203            if(pswd.length() == 0)
204                throw new PasswordInvalidFormatException("Required password missing!");
205
206            if(pswd.length() < MIN_SIZE)
207                throw new PasswordSizeException("Password < minimum size",pswd.length(),
                       MIN_SIZE,MAX_SIZE);
208
209            if(pswd.length() > MAX_SIZE)
210                throw new PasswordSizeException("Password > maximum size",pswd.length(),
                       MIN_SIZE,MAX_SIZE);
211
212            // scan through password to find if at least 1 number is used
213            for(int i=0; i < pswd.length() && !numFound; ++i)
214                if(Character.isDigit(pswd.charAt(i)))
215                    numFound = true;
216
217            if(!numFound)
218                throw new PasswordInvalidFormatException(
                       "Password is invalid - must have at least one numeric digit');
219        }
220
221        // Encrypts original password returning new encrypted String
222        private String encrypt(String pswd)
223        {
224            StringBuffer encryptPswd;
225            int pswdSize = 0;
226            int midpoint = 0;
227            int hashCode = 0;
228
229            // swap first and last half of password
230            pswdSize = pswd.length();
231            midpoint = pswdSize/2;
232            encryptPswd = new StringBuffer(pswd.substring(midpoint)      // get last half of pswd
233                          + pswd.substring(0,midpoint));                  // and concatenate first
                          half
234
235            encryptPswd.reverse();   // reverses order of characters in password
236
237            for(int i=0; i < pswdSize; ++i)                             // encrypt each character
238                encryptPswd.setCharAt(i, (char)(encryptPswd.charAt(i) & pswd.charAt(i)) );
239
240            hashCode = pswd.hashCode();  // hash code for original password
241            encryptPswd.append(hashCode);
242
243            return encryptPswd.toString();
244        }
245 }
```

FIGURE 10-21

To Find and Replace All Occurrences of Text in TextPad

1. Open the Password.java file that you previously copied from the preceding chapter and placed in the Chapter10 folder, or in a location specified by your instructor. If necessary, click Line Numbers on the View menu to display line numbers. Update the comments to reflect Chapter 10, your name, the current date, and the purpose. With the insertion point on line 1, click Search on the menu bar.

The Search menu provides many choices for finding and optionally replacing text (Figure 10-22).

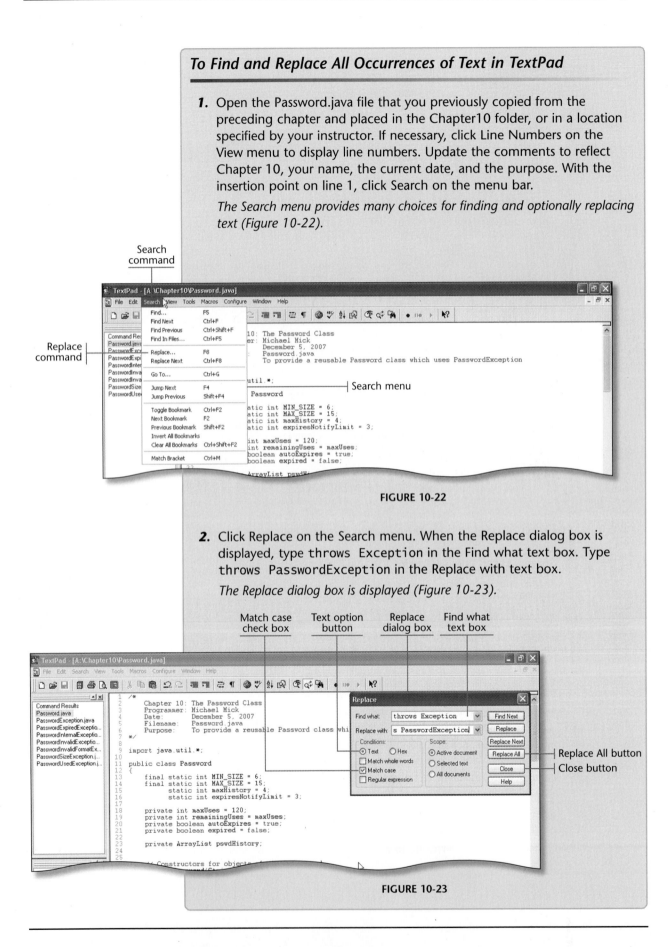

FIGURE 10-22

2. Click Replace on the Search menu. When the Replace dialog box is displayed, type throws Exception in the Find what text box. Type throws PasswordException in the Replace with text box.

The Replace dialog box is displayed (Figure 10-23).

FIGURE 10-23

3. Verify that the Text option button and the Match case checkbox are selected in the Conditions area. Verify that the Active document option button is selected in the Scope area. Click the Replace All button. Click the Close button.

All occurrences of the phrase, throws Exception, now are changed to, throws PasswordException, throughout the entire Password class (Figure 10-24).

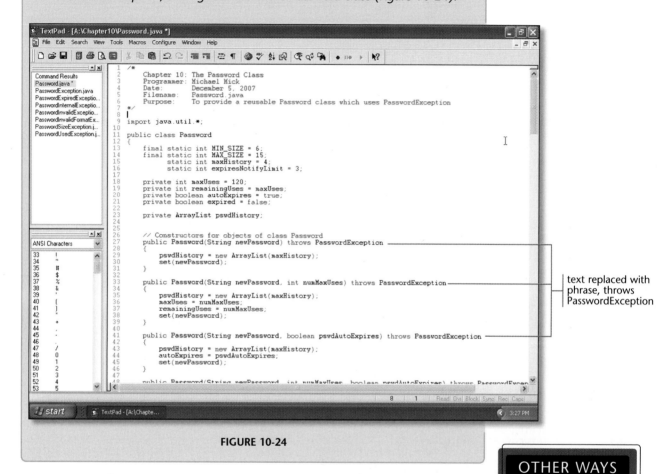

text replaced with phrase, throws PasswordException

FIGURE 10-24

OTHER WAYS

1. Press ALT+S, R
2. Press F8

Each of the four constructors in the Password class claims a PasswordException because they each call the set() method, which can create more than one type of password exception. Similarly, the validate() and verifyFormat() methods can create more than one type of password exception, whether due to password expiration or to an invalid password value. When generating an exception, these methods do not create a PasswordException object, as that class is abstract and cannot be used for creating objects. Instead, one of the subclasses of the PasswordException class — which are specific, concrete classes — must be used.

Any subclass of PasswordException may be referenced more generally as a PasswordException. Therefore, a method that claims (throws) a PasswordException actually may be throwing any of the concrete subclass objects of PasswordException. In this way, only one exception must be listed in the throws clause for each method, rather than listing all specific types of exceptions that the method may throw. The exception still may be caught by its more specific reference, for example, as a PasswordInvalidException or a

PasswordUsedException, or may be caught by the more general reference of a PasswordException.

Figure 10-25 displays the modified code for the set(), validate(), and verifyFormat() methods of the Password class. TextPad can help to locate occurrences of text by marking each occurrence with a **bookmark**, which is a triangle shape located at the beginning of a line containing the desired text.

```
134   // Sets password to a new value; keeps current & previous values in history up to max
      number
135   public void set(String pswd) throws PasswordException
136   {
137       String encryptPswd;
138       boolean pswdAdded = true;
139
140       pswd = pswd.trim();                 // remove any leading, trailing white space
141       verifyFormat(pswd);                 // verify password was entered properly
142       encryptPswd = encrypt(pswd);        // convert to encrypted form
143
144       if(!pswdHistory.contains(encryptPswd))       // if pswd not in recently used list,
145       {
146           if(pswdHistory.size() == maxHistory)     // if list is at max size
147               pswdHistory.remove(0);               // remove 1st, oldest, pswd from list
148
149           pswdAdded = pswdHistory.add(encryptPswd); // add new pswd to end of ArrayList
150
151           if(!pswdAdded)                           // never should happen
152               throw new PasswordInternalException(
                  "Internal list error - Password not accepted");
153
154           if(expired)                              // if pswd has expired,
155               expired = false;                     // reset to not expired
156
157           if(autoExpires)                          // if pswd auto expires,
158               remainingUses = maxUses;             // reset uses to max
159       }
160       else
161           throw new PasswordUsedException("Password recently used");
162   }
163
164   // Validates entered password against most recently saved value
165   public void validate(String pswd) throws PasswordException
166   {
167       String encryptPswd;
168       String currentPswd;
169       int currentPswdIndex;
170
171       verifyFormat(pswd);                 // verify password was entered properly
172       encryptPswd = encrypt(pswd);        // convert to encrypted form
173
174       if(!pswdHistory.isEmpty())          // at least one password entry is in history
175       {
176           currentPswdIndex = pswdHistory.size()-1;
177           currentPswd = (String)pswdHistory.get(currentPswdIndex);
178
179           if(!encryptPswd.equals(currentPswd)) // if not most recent pswd
180               throw new PasswordInvalidException("Password is invalid");
181
182           if(expired)
183               throw new PasswordExpiredException("Password has expired - please change.");
184
185           if(autoExpires)
186           {
187               --remainingUses;
188               if(remainingUses <= 0)
189                   expired=true;
190           }
191       }
```

FIGURE 10-25

```
192            else
193                throw new PasswordInvalidException("No password on file!");
194
195            new PasswordInvalidException().resetCount(); // resets count of invalid exceptions
196        }
197
198        // Verifies password has proper format
199        private void verifyFormat(String pswd) throws PasswordException
200        {
201            boolean numFound = false;
202
203            if(pswd.length() == 0)
204                throw new PasswordInvalidFormatException("Required password missing!");
205
206            if(pswd.length() < MIN_SIZE)
207                throw new PasswordSizeException("Password < minimum size",pswd.length(),
                        MIN_SIZE,MAX_SIZE);
208
209            if(pswd.length() > MAX_SIZE)
210                throw new PasswordSizeException("Password > maximum size",pswd.length(),
                        MIN_SIZE,MAX_SIZE);
211
212            // scan through password to find if at least 1 number is used
213            for(int i=0; i < pswd.length() && !numFound; ++i)
214                if(Character.isDigit(pswd.charAt(i)))
215                    numFound = true;
216
217            if(!numFound)
218                throw new PasswordInvalidFormatException(
                        "Password is invalid - must have at least one numeric digit');
219        }
```

FIGURE 10-25

The following steps illustrate how to locate and subsequently replace each occurrence of a new Exception with a more specific password exception.

To Bookmark All Occurrences of Text in TextPad

1. With the insertion point on line 1 in the coding window, click Search on the menu bar and then click Find on the Search menu.

The Find dialog box is displayed (Figure 10-26). The text from the previous Find operation is displayed in the Find what text box.

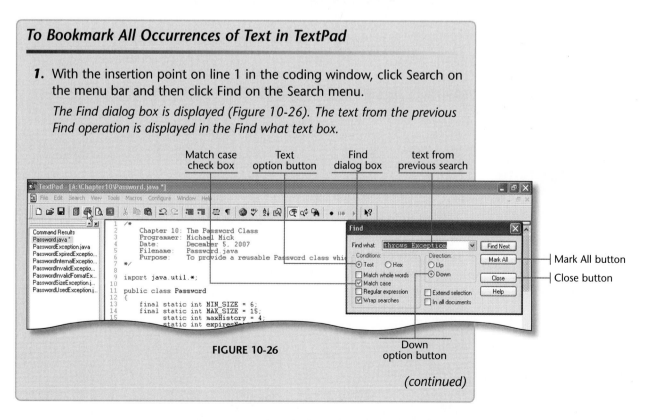

FIGURE 10-26

(continued)

2. When the Find dialog box is displayed, type `throw new Exception` in the Find what text box. Verify that the Text option button and Match case checkbox in the Conditions area and the Down option button in the Direction area are selected. Click the Mark All button. Click the Close button.

All lines with occurrences of the text, throw new Exception, are bookmarked with a triangle next to the line number (Figure 10-27). TextPad automatically moves the insertion point to the first bookmarked line.

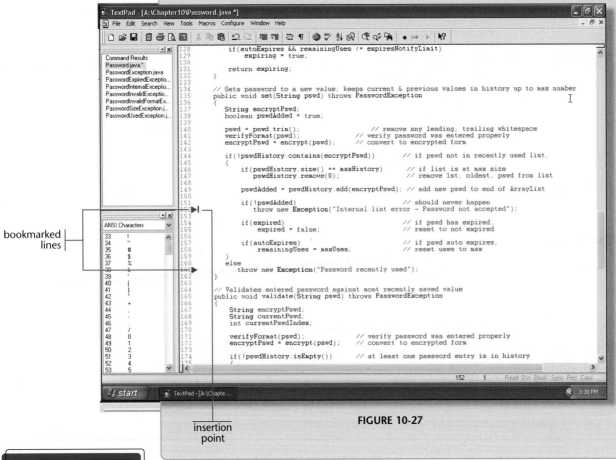

FIGURE 10-27

OTHER WAYS

1. Press ALT+S, F
2. Press F5

Each occurrence of the text, throw new Exception, is located and bookmarked in the source code. The code in each bookmarked line must be modified so that an exception generates an exception of the proper type. After the code is modified, the bookmark indicating the line where the original text was found should be cleared. The following steps change the code and toggle the bookmark off so it no longer displays.

To Modify the Exception Code for Methods

1. Double-click the word Exception in line 152 to select it and then type PasswordInternalException as the new code. Click Search on the menu bar.

The code is changed to create a new PasswordInternalException, rather than a new Exception (Figure 10-28).

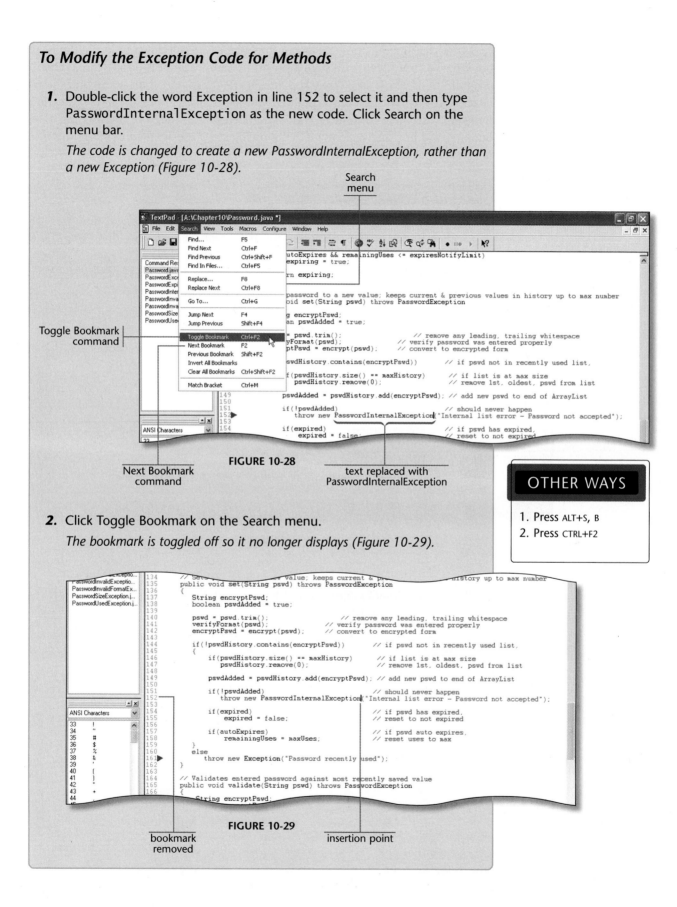

FIGURE 10-28

Next Bookmark command

text replaced with PasswordInternalException

2. Click Toggle Bookmark on the Search menu.

The bookmark is toggled off so it no longer displays (Figure 10-29).

FIGURE 10-29

bookmark removed

insertion point

OTHER WAYS

1. Press ALT+S, B
2. Press CTRL+F2

After clearing the bookmark on a line, you can scroll down to locate the next bookmarked line. Even with such a prominent indicator, it is possible in a large program to overlook a bookmarked line. TextPad provides a means to find the next bookmark, without requiring that you manually scan for the next indicator. By using TextPad to find the next bookmark, you are assured of not missing a bookmarked line inadvertently. The following steps use TextPad to locate the next bookmarked line automatically.

To Find the Next Bookmarked Line

1. Click Search on the menu bar and then click Next Bookmark on the Search menu.

The bookmarked line briefly is selected, and the insertion point is positioned next to the bookmark at the beginning of line 161 (Figure 10-30).

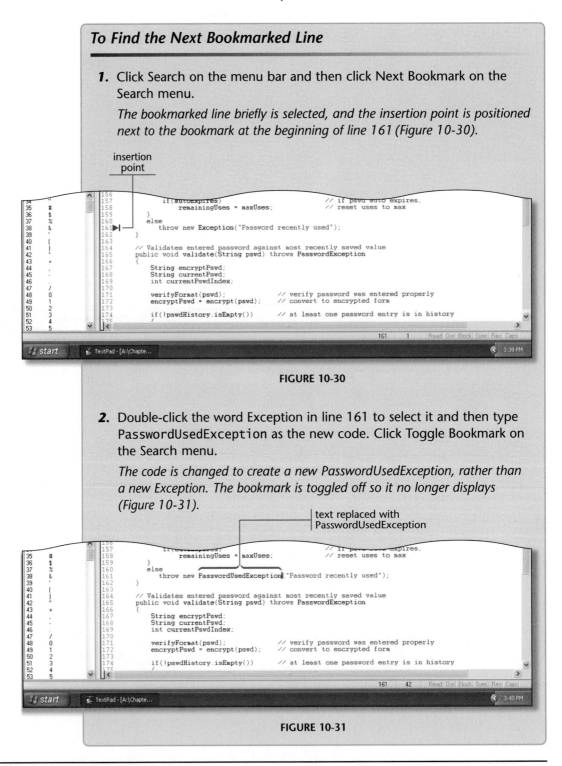

FIGURE 10-30

2. Double-click the word Exception in line 161 to select it and then type PasswordUsedException as the new code. Click Toggle Bookmark on the Search menu.

The code is changed to create a new PasswordUsedException, rather than a new Exception. The bookmark is toggled off so it no longer displays (Figure 10-31).

FIGURE 10-31

3. Repeat steps 1 and 2 to find the remaining bookmarked lines and replace the text, Exception, with the exceptions and parameters listed in Table 10-2. When you have finished, click Toggle Bookmark on the Search menu.

All exceptions are changed appropriately, and all bookmarks are cleared from the code (Figure 10-32).

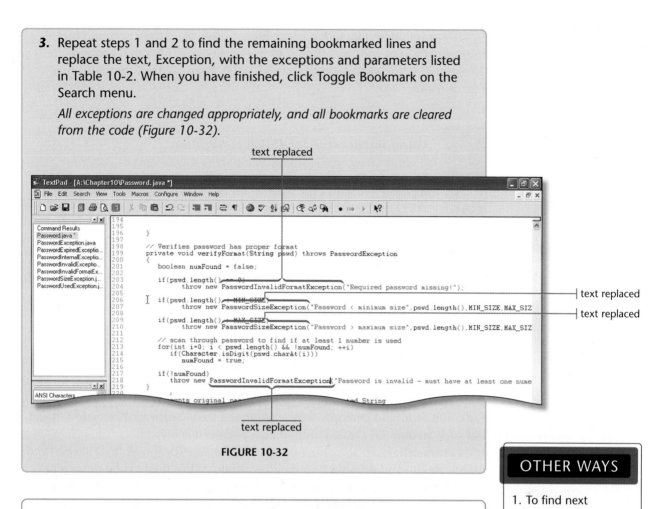

FIGURE 10-32

OTHER WAYS

1. To find next bookmark, press ALT+S, E
2. To find next bookmark, press F2
3. To clear all bookmarks, press CTRL+SHIFT+F2

Table 10-2   Replacement Exception Code on Bookmarked Lines

LINE	REPLACEMENT EXCEPTION	REPLACEMENT ARGUMENTS
180	PasswordInvalidException	
183	PasswordExpiredException	
193	PasswordInvalidException	
204	PasswordInvalidFormatException	
207	PasswordSizeException	"Password < minimum size", pswd.length(), MIN_SIZE, MAX_SIZE
210	PasswordSizeException	"Password > maximum size", pswd.length(), MIN_SIZE, MAX_SIZE
218	PasswordInvalidFormatException	

As shown in Table 10-2 and Figure 10-32, the arguments for creating the new PasswordSizeException object are modified in lines 207 and 210 so that the object retains information about the size of the password entered by the user, as well as the maximum and minimum sizes allowed.

If you want to bookmark a single line of code, place the insertion point in the desired line of code and then click Toggle Bookmark on the Search menu. To clear all of the bookmarks in the code, click Clear All Bookmarks on the Search menu.

Using Bookmarks for Quick Navigation

If you need to navigate quickly between two lines of code, set a bookmark at each line and then use the F2 key (Next Bookmark) to navigate back and forth between the two lines.

Concatenating Method Calls

Finally, one additional line of code is needed in the validate() method. Recall that each PasswordInvalidException increments a count of the times this exception was generated. This count is stored in the class variable, count. Once a correct password is entered, this count should be reset to zero by calling the resetCount() method of a PasswordInvalidException object; however, when a given password is verified successfully, no PasswordInvalidException object, or even any Exception object, exists. By definition, a valid password should not generate an exception. This problem seems difficult to resolve: the code must clear the count of invalid attempts, which requires a PasswordInvalidException object, but such an object is created only when a password is invalid.

Fortunately, exception objects, including the PasswordInvalidException object, are full-fledged objects in their own right. While they can be thrown to indicate an error condition, they do not have to be thrown to be created, then used, and eventually garbage-collected when no longer needed. A PasswordInvalidException object can be created simply to provide access to the resetCount() method, and not to throw as an exception. Furthermore, because this object is used only once to perform a method call and is no longer needed, no reference to the new object is required. The object can be created, and the call to the resetCount() method can be concatenated, or chained, to the call to the constructor.

Method call concatenation, or **method call chaining**, is a means of performing multiple method calls by concatenating calls with period separators. Each call in the concatenated method call, except for the last, must return a reference to an object. Each method must be a valid method for the object referenced.

As an example of method call concatenation, a DogOwner object might have a method, getDog(). This method returns a reference to a Dog object, which has a method, bark(). To invoke the bark() method, you need a Dog object, not a DogOwner object. Using method call concatenation, you could use a DogOwner object; call its getDog() method to get a reference to a Dog assign the reference to a Dog reference variable, myDog; and then use this variable to call the bark() method, as in

```
DogOwner Bob = new DogOwner();

Dog myDog;

myDog = Bob.getDog();

myDog.bark();
```

If you needed to reference myDog for only this one method call, then you could avoid creating the new reference variable, myDog, by concatenating the method calls, using the following code

```
Bob.getDog().bark();
```

To understand what happens in a concatenated method call, read the code from left to right, starting with the object reference and first method. Determine the type of data returned, which must be a reference to an object. Using that object type reference, read the next method call, which is a method of the referenced object.

Thus, in the above code example, the line of code first would use Bob, a DogOwner object, to call getDog(), which returns a reference to a Dog object. This reference is used implicitly to call its bark() method. Although Bob (the DogOwner object) does not have a bark() method, the returned reference to a Dog object does.

Tip

Understanding Concatenated Method Calls

You can understand what happens in a concatenated method call by first reading from the left only the object reference and first method. Determine the type of data returned. It must be a reference to an object. Using that object type, read the next method call, and so forth, until the last method is called.

In this chapter, the same technique is used to invoke the resetCount() method from a newly created PasswordInvalidException object in the validate() method of the Password class. Figure 10-33 displays the code for the chained method call in the validate() method of the Password class. The line of code first includes a constructor to create a PasswordInvalidException object. Once the object is created, the reference is used to call the resetCount() method of the PasswordInvalidException object.

```
195        new PasswordInvalidException().resetCount(); // resets count of invalid exceptions
```

FIGURE 10-33

The following step enters code for a concatenated method call to the resetCount() method of the PasswordInvalidException object.

> ### To Create a Concatenated Method Call
>
> **1.** Enter line 195 as shown in Figure 10-33 on the previous page. Save and compile the changes to the Password class.
>
> *The newly entered code displays (Figure 10-34). This line of code concatenates method calls to create a new PasswordInvalidException object and call its resetCount() method, after which the object will be available for garbage collection.*

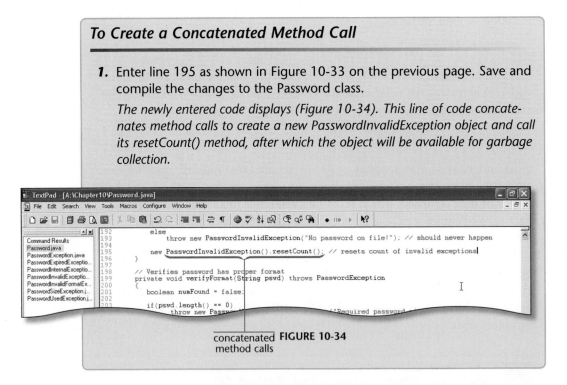

concatenated method calls **FIGURE 10-34**

The changes to the Password class now are complete. This class now uses the PasswordException class and subclasses to handle exceptions, rather than the more general Exception class.

Creating a Program to Test the PasswordException Classes and Subclasses

To effectively test the Password class with the new PasswordException classes requires a test program that uses the classes to verify the password of an existing user. As shown in Figure 10-1 on page 605, this test application, the StockListDemo application, allows users to log on and build a list of stock symbols. In the previous chapter, the Password class was tested without respect to a user. It is more realistic, however, to have a user associated with the password.

Creating a Class Using Aggregation

Because the test program does not use a database, a list of users will be maintained in memory, much like the list of passwords in the previous chapter. Each user in the list will have a name and an associated Password object. To maintain this list of users, a simple User class is created with two attributes: a String for name and a Password object. By incorporating the Password object, the User class illustrates the use of aggregation. As you have learned, aggregation is used to describe the concept of an object being composed of other objects, that is, an object having another object as an instance variable.

In this example, User and Password have a has-a relationship; that is, a User has-a Password. Because the Password object is private to the User, the User class handles all interaction with the Password object and must provide public methods for an application to validate or change a password.

Figure 10-35 displays the code for the User class. Line 9 includes the User class header. Lines 11 and 12 declare two variables, name and pswd, to store the user logon information. By incorporating a reference to a Password object as an instance variable, line 12 illustrates the use of aggregation. Lines 14 through 30 include constructors for the User class.

```
1   /*
2       Chapter 10: The User Class
3       Programmer: Michael Mick
4       Date:       December 5, 2007
5       Filename:   User.java
6       Purpose:    To provide a User class to test the Password class
7   */
8
9   public class User
10  {
11      private String name;
12      private Password pswd;
13
14      public User(String aName, String password) throws PasswordException
15      {
16          name = new String(aName);
17          pswd = new Password(password);
18      }
19
20      public User(String aName, String password, int pswdUses) throws PasswordException
21      {
22          name = new String(aName);
23          pswd = new Password(password,pswdUses);
24      }
25
26      public User(String aName, String password, boolean autoExpirePswd) throws
        PasswordException
27      {
28          name = new String(aName);
29          pswd = new Password(password,autoExpirePswd);
30      }
31
32      public String getName()
33      {
34          return new String(name);
35      }
36
37      public boolean pswdAutoExpires()
38      {
39          return pswd.getAutoExpires();
40      }
41
42      public boolean pswdIsExpiring()
43      {
44          return pswd.isExpiring();
45      }
46
47      public int getPswdUses()
48      {
49          return pswd.getRemainingUses();
50      }
51
52      public void validate(String password) throws PasswordException
53      {
54          pswd.validate(password);
55      }
56
```

FIGURE 10-35

(continued)

```
57        public void changePassword(String oldPassword,String newPassword) throws PasswordException
58        {
59            try
60            {
61                pswd.validate(oldPassword);
62            }
63            catch(PasswordExpiredException ex)
64            {}
65
66            pswd.set(newPassword);
67        }
68    }
```

FIGURE 10-35

Lines 32 through 50 include code for the accessor methods of the User class. Note that most methods simply call a corresponding method in the Password class; access to attributes of the Password class, thus, is provided through accessor methods in the Password class.

In the previous chapter, because the application could not distinguish an exception due to an expired password, invalid password, or any other exception, the current password was not validated before allowing it to be changed. The changePassword() method in lines 57 through 67, however, has the ability to distinguish between an exception due to an expired password versus other types of exceptions. This allows the program to validate the current password (line 61) and, if the only exception generated is due to an expired password, ignore that exception (lines 63 and 64) and set the new password (line 66). Any other exception prevents the change from occurring.

The following steps enter code to create the User class using aggregation.

To Create a Class Using Aggregation

1. Create a new TextPad document and save it in the Chapter10 folder, or a location specified by your instructor, typing User in the File name text box and selecting Java (*.java) as the file type. Enter lines 1 through 31 as shown in Figure 10-35. In the comments, insert your own name as programmer and enter the current date.

TextPad displays code for the initial comments, class header, and constructors in the coding window (Figure 10-36). Note the use of aggregation by the incorporation of references to other objects as instance variables.

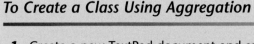

name variable is
String object reference

pswd variable is
Password object reference

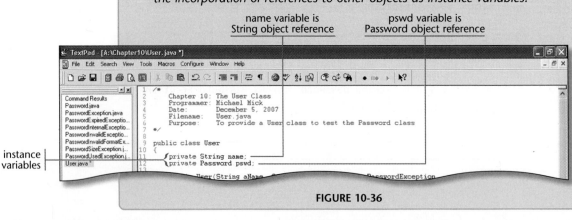

instance variables

FIGURE 10-36

2. Enter lines 32 through 51 as shown in Figure 10-35.

TextPad displays code for the accessor methods in the coding window (Figure 10-37). Note that access to attributes of the Password class is provided through accessor methods in the Password class.

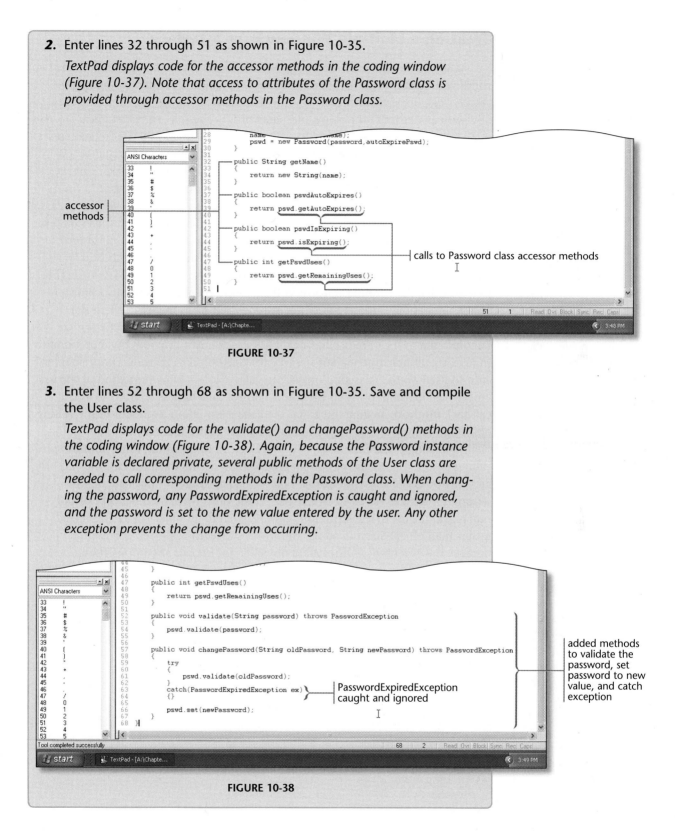

FIGURE 10-37

3. Enter lines 52 through 68 as shown in Figure 10-35. Save and compile the User class.

TextPad displays code for the validate() and changePassword() methods in the coding window (Figure 10-38). Again, because the Password instance variable is declared private, several public methods of the User class are needed to call corresponding methods in the Password class. When changing the password, any PasswordExpiredException is caught and ignored, and the password is set to the new value entered by the user. Any other exception prevents the change from occurring.

FIGURE 10-38

The User class now is complete and available for use with the application.

Creating a Multiple Window User Interface

JAVA UPDATE Java 2 v5.0

Emumerated Types (Enums)

Instead of using of a series of unrelated named int constants to represent a set of values (e.g., Quarters of FALL = 0, WINTER = 1, SPRING = 2, SUMMER = 3), Java now supports true, more flexible, enumerated types with the reserved word, **enum**. Enums are implicitly public static final (may declare explicitly as private) and provide constants in a typesafe manner, so usage can be limited to valid values and actions. (For example, Quarter = SPRING + WINTER does not make sense, nor does Quarter = 7, but this is valid when using int constants.) Enums created in your code are a subclass of java.lang.Enum and so have the ability to inherit (as with the toString(), valueOf(), and values() methods) and to contain additional data and methods. Enums can be used in switch() statements, compared with equals or ==, and sorted. They cannot be defined locally.

The code to the right shows an enum in the simplest form as a list of constants, and as a more complex class, with added data and methods.

As shown in Figure 10-1 on page 605, the StockListDemo application has two windows that comprise the user interface. One window, created by the LogonFrame class, displays the logon window that allows a user to log on to the application with an existing user name and password. Because it is a test application, this same logon window also is used to add new users or to allow a user to change his or her password. In a completed or production application, rather than a test application, the functions of adding a new user or changing a password likely would be completed in a different window, with access limited to valid users or administrators of the system. A second window, created by the StockFrame class, is used to simulate a working stock list application. This window displays data for the current user and provides a means for the user to log off.

Because these two windows are not displayed simultaneously, the current window must close when control transfers to the other window. To provide this functionality, the LogonFrame object creates and then displays a StockFrame object, and, at that time, it can close, or hide itself from the user. When the StockFrame object closes, however, the program needs a way to notify the LogonFrame so it can redisplay. A callback mechanism provides this functionality. In Java, a **callback mechanism** is a way for one object to provide a generic reference to itself, so that a second object can call back to a known method of the first object. The method to which the second object calls back is referred to as the **callback method**. To guarantee that the callback method is present in the calling object, the calling object must implement an interface that requires that method.

Interestingly, the called object does not need to know anything about the calling object, as long as the calling object implements the required interface. In fact, any object of any type can be called back, as long as it implements the required interface. Recall from Chapter 1, the object-oriented concept of polymorphism means that instructions can be given to an object in a generalized rather than object-specific command. In this case, the callback is polymorphic, because the exact type of the called object is not known at compile time.

```
// simple enum
private enum Quarter {FALL, WINTER, SPRING, SUMMER} // values of 0, 1, 2, and 3, respectively

Quarter session = Quarter.WINTER;            //assigns to variable, session
System.out.println("Session = "+session);    //prints WINTER using toString()
session = Quarter.valueOf("SPRING");          //sets session to Quarter.SPRING
System.out.println("Session = "+session);    //prints SPRING

public enum Grade // enum class definition
{
  A("Superior"), B("Good"), C("Average"), D("Poor"), P("Passing"), F("Failed"), I("Incomplete"

  private final String desc;

  Grade(String desc)
  {
    this.desc = desc;
  }

  public String desc()
  {
    return desc.toString();
  }
}

//values() returns an array of Grade, each element has one of the enumerated type's -lues
for (Grade g : Grade.values())
    System.out.print(g + ": \t" + g.desc());
```

In this case, the **activate() method** is the callback method that reactivates the original LogonFrame window. The activate() method activates the object associated with the Activator interface. LogonFrame, thus, implements the **Activator interface**, which includes the activate() method and facilitates the activation of an object from another object.

Figure 10-39 displays the code for the Activator interface containing the abstract method, activate(). Later in the chapter, code for the LogonFrame class will be developed to implement the Activator interface so that the LogonFrame class can pass a reference of itself to the new StockFrame.

```
1   /*
2        Chapter 10:  The Activator Interface
3        Programmer:  Michael Mick
4        Date:        December 5, 2007
5        Filename:    Activator.java
6        Purpose:     Provides an interface for demonstrating a callback method
7   */
8
9   public interface Activator
10  {
11       public void activate();
12  }
```

FIGURE 10-39

The following step enters code for the Activator interface.

To Create an Activator Interface

1. Create a new TextPad document and save it in the Chapter10 folder, or a location specified by your instructor, typing Activator as the file name and selecting Java (*.java) as the file type. Enter lines 1 through 12 as shown in Figure 10-39. In the comments, insert your own name as programmer and enter the current date. Save and compile the Activator interface.

TextPad displays code for the Activator interface (Figure 10-40). The interface contains a single abstract method, activate(). The keyword, abstract, is not required because all methods in an interface definition are abstract.

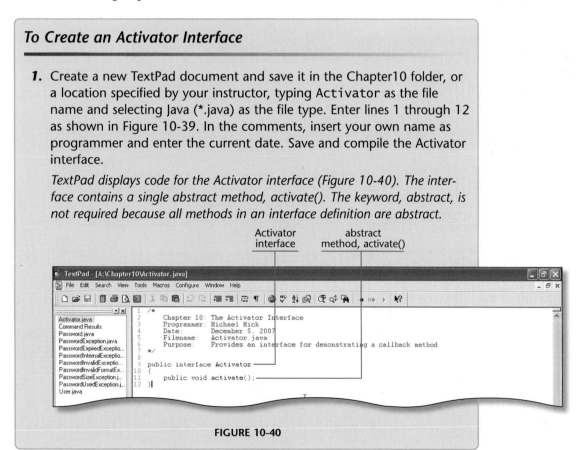

FIGURE 10-40

Using a Callback Mechanism in a Class

Because the StockFrame object is created by the LogonFrame, the StockFrame must be coded first. Figure 10-41 displays the code for the StockFrame class. Lines 9 through 14 import packages used by the class, including those used to create the user interface.

```
1   /*
2       Chapter 10:  The StockFrame Class
3       Programmer:  Michael Mick
4       Date:        December 5, 2007
5       Filename:    StockFrame.java
6       Purpose:     Provides a user interface for a stock list to test the Password class
7   */
8
9   import javax.swing.*;
10  import java.awt.*;
11  import java.awt.event.*;
12  import java.util.*;
13  import java.io.*;
14  import javax.swing.border.TitledBorder;
15
16  class StockFrame extends JFrame implements ActionListener, WindowListener
17  {
18
19      //define instance variables
20      String stockSymbol;
21
22      JTextField jtfStockSymbol;
23      JButton jbtAddStock, jbtLogout;
24      JComboBox jcbStockList;
25      Activator caller;
26
27      public StockFrame(User user, Activator callerObj)
28      {
29          super("Add Stock Symbols"); // call super (JFrame) constructor
30
31          int width = 330;
32          int height = 170;
33          caller = callerObj;      // save reference to caller object
34
35          // Define components for panel 1
36          JLabel label1 = new JLabel("Symbol:");
37          jtfStockSymbol = new JTextField(4);
38          jbtAddStock = new JButton("Add Symbol");
39
40          JPanel p1= new JPanel();
41          p1.setLayout(new GridLayout(1,3));
42          p1.add(label1);
43          p1.add(jtfStockSymbol);
44          p1.add(jbtAddStock);
45          p1.setBorder(new TitledBorder("Add stock symbol"));
46
47          // Define components for panel 2
48          JLabel label2 = new JLabel("Click arrow to view list");
49          jcbStockList = new JComboBox();
50
51          JPanel p2= new JPanel();
52          p2.setLayout(new GridLayout(1,2));
53          p2.add(label2);
54          p2.add(jcbStockList);
55          p2.setBorder(new TitledBorder("View stock symbols"));
56
```

FIGURE 10-41

```
57                  // Define components for panel 3
58                  JLabel label3 = new JLabel("User name: "+user.getName());
59                  jbtLogout = new JButton("Log out");
60
61                  JPanel p3= new JPanel();
62                  p3.setLayout(new GridLayout(1,2));
63                  p3.add(label3);
64                  p3.add(jbtLogout);
65                  p3.setBorder(new TitledBorder("Current user"));
66
67                  // Use nested panels for positioning
68                  JPanel p4= new JPanel();
69                  p4.setLayout(new GridLayout(3,1,10,5)); // rows, cols, hgap, vgap
70                  p4.add(p1);
71                  p4.add(p2);
72                  p4.add(p3);
73
74                  JPanel p5 = new JPanel(new BorderLayout(10,10));
75                  p5.add(p4, BorderLayout.WEST);
76                  JPanel p6 = new JPanel(new BorderLayout(10,10));
77                  p6.add(p5, BorderLayout.EAST);
78
79                  setContentPane(p6);
80
81                  // Register listeners
82                  addWindowListener(this);
83                  jbtAddStock.addActionListener(this);
84                  jbtLogout.addActionListener(this);
85                  jcbStockList.addActionListener(this);
86
87                  // Prepare for display
88                  pack();
89                  if( width < getWidth())          // prevent setting width too small
90                      width = getWidth();
91                  if(height < getHeight())         // prevent setting height too small
92                      height = getHeight();
93                  centerOnScreen(width, height);
94                  jtfStockSymbol.setText("");
95                  jtfStockSymbol.requestFocus();
96          }
97
98      public void centerOnScreen(int width, int height)
99      {
100         int top, left, x, y;
101
102         // Get the screen dimension
103         Dimension screenSize = Toolkit.getDefaultToolkit().getScreenSize();
104
105         // Determine the location for the top left corner of the frame
106         x = (screenSize.width - width)/2;
107         y = (screenSize.height - height)/2;
108         left = (x < 0) ? 0 : x;
109         top = (y < 0) ? 0 : y;
110
111         this.setBounds(left, top, width, height);
112     }
113
114     public boolean stockInList(String stock)
115     {
116         boolean inList = false;
117         int numItems;
118
119         numItems = jcbStockList.getItemCount();
120
121         stock.trim(); // remove any leading, trailing white space
122
```

FIGURE 10-41

(continued)

```
123            if(numItems > 0) // at least one entry is in list
124            {
125                for(int i=0; i < numItems && !inList; ++i)
126                {
127                    if(stock.equals((String)jcbStockList.getItemAt(i)))
128                        inList = true;
129                }
130            }
131
132            return inList;
133        }
134
135    public void actionPerformed(ActionEvent e)
136    {
137            if(e.getSource() == jbtLogout)
138            {
139                logoutUser();
140            }
141            else
142            if(e.getSource() == jbtAddStock)
143            {
144                stockSymbol = jtfStockSymbol.getText();
145                if(stockSymbol.equals(""))
146                    JOptionPane.showMessageDialog(this, "Please enter a stock symbol to
                        add.");
147                else
148                {
149                    if(!stockInList(stockSymbol))
150                        jcbStockList.addItem(stockSymbol);
151                }
152                jtfStockSymbol.setText("");
153                jtfStockSymbol.requestFocus();
154            }
155            else
156            if(e.getSource() == jcbStockList)
157            {
158                stockSymbol = (String)jcbStockList.getSelectedItem();
159                if(stockSymbol == null)
160                    JOptionPane.showMessageDialog(this, "Please add a stock to the list.")
161                else
162                    jtfStockSymbol.setText(stockSymbol);
163            }
164            else
165            {
166                JOptionPane.showMessageDialog(this, "Please choose a valid action.");
167            }
168    }
169
170    private void logoutUser()
171    {
172      this.setVisible(false);
173      dispose();
174      caller.activate();    // call activate method of caller object
175    }
176
177    // Handler for window opened event
178    public void windowOpened(WindowEvent event)
179    {
180        jtfStockSymbol.setText("");
181        jtfStockSymbol.requestFocus();
182    }
183    // Handler for window closing event
184    public void windowClosing(WindowEvent event)
185    {
186      logoutUser();
187    }
188    // Handler for window closed event
189    public void windowClosed(WindowEvent event)
190    {
191    }
192    // Handler for window iconified event
193    public void windowIconified(WindowEvent event)
194    {
195    }
```

FIGURE 10-41

```
196        // Handler for window deiconified event
197        public void windowDeiconified(WindowEvent event)
198        {
199        }
200        // Handler for window activated event
201        public void windowActivated(WindowEvent event)
202        {
203        }
204        // Handler for window deactivated event
205        public void windowDeactivated(WindowEvent event)
206        {
207        }
208  }
```

FIGURE 10-41

Line 16 in Figure 10-41 indicates that the StockFrame class implements the ActionListener interface and the WindowListener interface. The ActionListener interface provides the ability to listen for mouse clicks on a button, once the listener interface is registered with the button; the WindowListener interface listens for the user opening or closing the window. In the StockDemo application, once a user has finished entering stocks in the StockListDemo application, the user closes the StockFrame window by clicking the Log out button or the Close button on the StockFrame user interface. When the StockFrame window closes, the LogonFrame window must be redisplayed. The StockFrame window, thus, must hide itself, dispose of its resources, and call the callback method of the Activator — LogonFrame, in this case — that originally created the StockFrame object. The StockFrame object, therefore, must listen for these actions by the user, using the ActionListener and the WindowListener interfaces coded in line 16. Additionally, the StockFrame object must listen for when its window is opened in order to position the insertion point in the text field for entering a stock symbol.

The StockFrame will use the callback mechanism to take a reference to the caller object — in this case, the LogonFrame object — and call its activate() method. As previously noted, however, the call to the caller object is polymorphic, which means that StockFrame never needs to refer to an object of type LogonFrame, but only to an object of type Activator, as in line 25 in Figure 10-41. This has two implications. First, any object can be called back by StockFrame as long as that object implements the Activator interface and passes a reference to itself when creating a StockFrame object. Second, such objects can be referenced generically by StockFrame as objects of type Activator, regardless of whatever type these objects are. StockFrame, therefore, is reusable by any object implementing the Activator interface.

Line 27 begins a StockFrame constructor, which contains references to a User object and to an Activator object. Lines 29 through 133 create the user interface and functionality for the StockFrame window, including displaying the window centered and preventing the user from adding duplicate stock symbols to the list.

Lines 135 through 168 add the actionPerformed() method required by the ActionListener interface. Lines 170 through 175 include code for the logoutUser() method, which hides the current window, disposes of its resources, and invokes the callback method, activate(), in the calling object, LogonFrame.

As you learned in Chapter 5, the WindowListener interface requires that seven methods be implemented. Only two of the methods — the windowOpened() method in lines 177 through 182 and the windowClosing() method in lines 183 through 187 — are used by the StockFrame object. The remaining methods must be implemented in lines 188 through 207, but are empty and, therefore, take no action if invoked.

The following steps enter code to create the StockFrame class, which uses a callback mechanism to call the LogonFrame class.

To Create a Callback Mechanism in a Class

1. Create a new TextPad document and save it in the Chapter10 folder, or a location specified by your instructor, typing StockFrame as the file name and selecting Java (*.java) as the file type. Enter lines 1 through 26 as shown in Figure 10-41 on page 648. In the comments, insert your own name as programmer and enter the current date.

TextPad displays code for the initial comments, class header, and instance variables in the coding window (Figure 10-42). The class implements both the ActionListener and the WindowListener interfaces. A reference to an Activator object is declared in line 25.

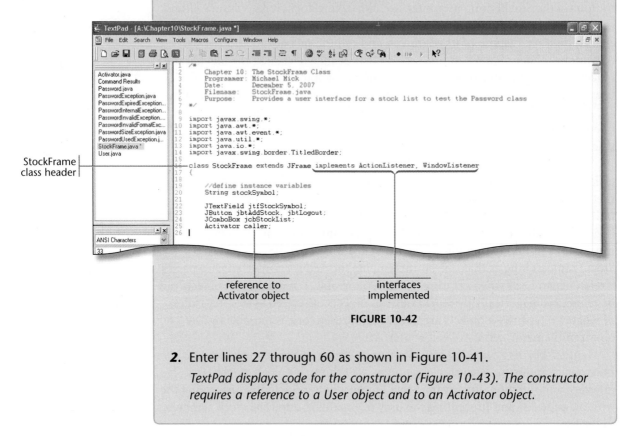

StockFrame class header

reference to Activator object

interfaces implemented

FIGURE 10-42

2. Enter lines 27 through 60 as shown in Figure 10-41.

TextPad displays code for the constructor (Figure 10-43). The constructor requires a reference to a User object and to an Activator object.

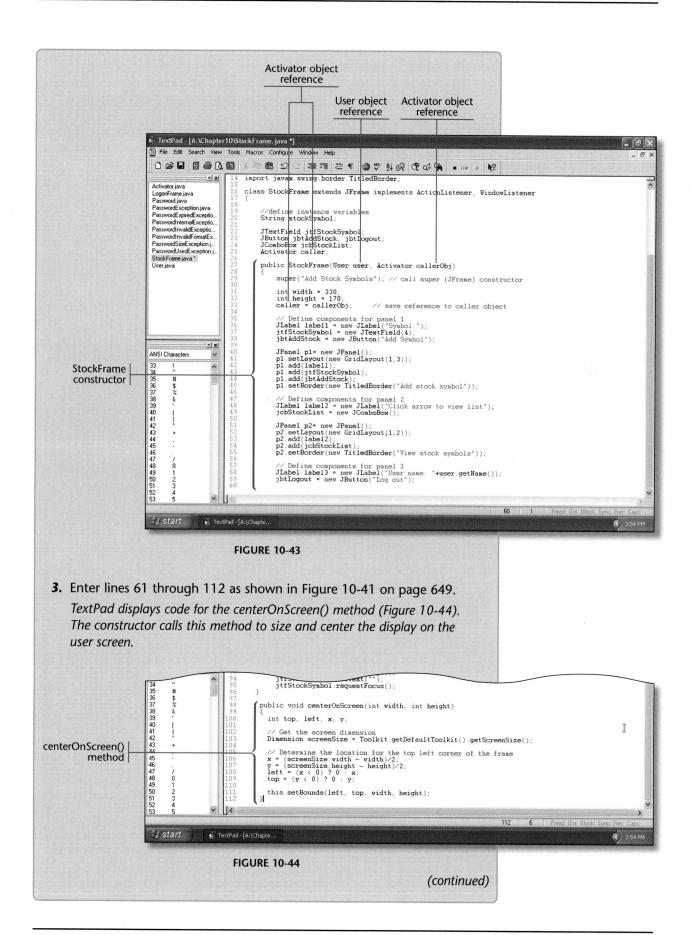

FIGURE 10-43

3. Enter lines 61 through 112 as shown in Figure 10-41 on page 649.

TextPad displays code for the centerOnScreen() method (Figure 10-44). The constructor calls this method to size and center the display on the user screen.

FIGURE 10-44

(continued)

4. Enter lines 113 through 133 as shown in Figure 10-41 on page 649.

TextPad displays code for the stockInList() method (Figure 10-45). The actionPerformed() method calls this method to prevent adding a duplicate stock symbol to the list.

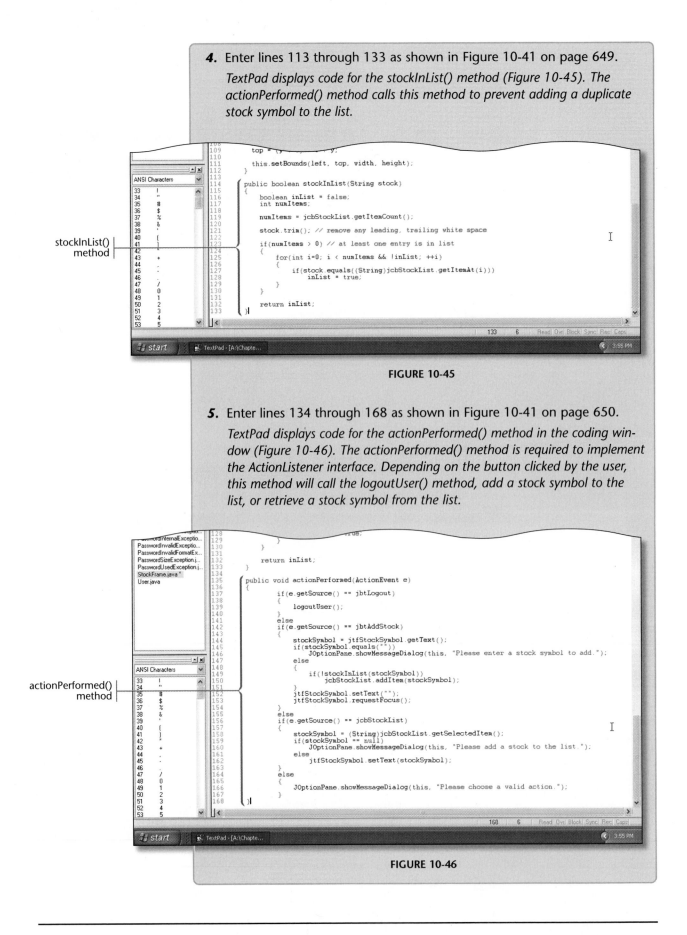

```
109    top = (y   e   y;
110
111        this.setBounds(left, top, width, height);
112    }
113
114    public boolean stockInList(String stock)
115    {
116        boolean inList = false;
117        int numItems;
118
119        numItems = jcbStockList.getItemCount();
120
121        stock.trim(); // remove any leading, trailing white space
122
123        if(numItems > 0) // at least one entry is in list
124        {
125            for(int i=0; i < numItems && !inList; ++i)
126            {
127                if(stock.equals((String)jcbStockList.getItemAt(i)))
128                    inList = true;
129            }
130        }
131
132        return inList;
133    }
```

stockInList() method

FIGURE 10-45

5. Enter lines 134 through 168 as shown in Figure 10-41 on page 650.

TextPad displays code for the actionPerformed() method in the coding window (Figure 10-46). The actionPerformed() method is required to implement the ActionListener interface. Depending on the button clicked by the user, this method will call the logoutUser() method, add a stock symbol to the list, or retrieve a stock symbol from the list.

```
128                }
129            }
130        }
131
132        return inList;
133    }
134
135    public void actionPerformed(ActionEvent e)
136    {
137        if(e.getSource() == jbtLogout)
138        {
139            logoutUser();
140        }
141        else
142        if(e.getSource() == jbtAddStock)
143        {
144            stockSymbol = jtfStockSymbol.getText();
145            if(stockSymbol.equals(""))
146                JOptionPane.showMessageDialog(this, "Please enter a stock symbol to add.");
147            else
148            {
149                if(!stockInList(stockSymbol))
150                    jcbStockList.addItem(stockSymbol);
151            }
152            jtfStockSymbol.setText("");
153            jtfStockSymbol.requestFocus();
154        }
155        else
156        if(e.getSource() == jcbStockList)
157        {
158            stockSymbol = (String)jcbStockList.getSelectedItem();
159            if(stockSymbol == null)
160                JOptionPane.showMessageDialog(this, "Please add a stock to the list.");
161            else
162                jtfStockSymbol.setText(stockSymbol);
163        }
164        else
165        {
166            JOptionPane.showMessageDialog(this, "Please choose a valid action.");
167        }
168    }
```

actionPerformed() method

FIGURE 10-46

6. Enter lines 169 through 175 as shown in Figure 10-41 on page 650.

TextPad displays code for the logoutUser() method in the coding window (Figure 10-47). This logoutUser() method hides the current window, disposes of its resources, and invokes the callback method, activate(), in the calling object.

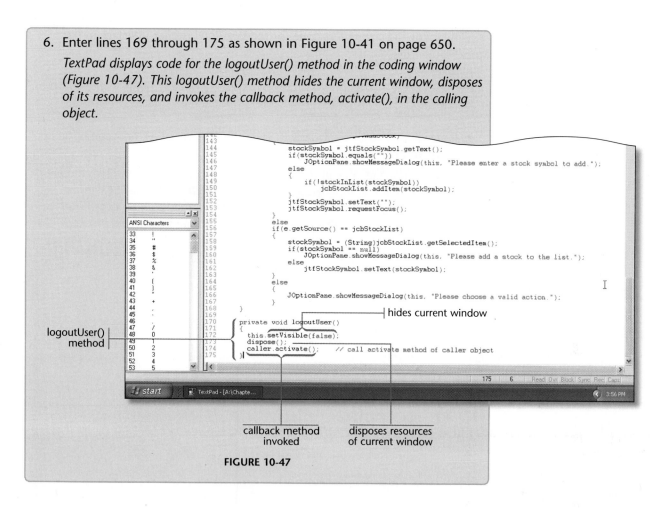

FIGURE 10-47

Calling the setVisible() method with a parameter of false hides the current window. Calling the dispose() method in the logoutUser() method before invoking the callback method, activate(), releases all of the resources used by this window and makes any memory used by the window available to the operating system. Line 174 includes the callback mechanism that calls back to the activate() method of the caller object, LogonFrame.

Implementing the WindowListener Interface

Because the StockFrame class indicates that it will implement the WindowListener interface (line 16 of Figure 10-41 on page 648), it must define the required methods of the interface to be a concrete class. As previously noted, the WindowListener interface requires seven methods be implemented to handle each of seven possible Window events. Only two of the methods — the windowOpened() method and the windowClosing() method — are used by the StockFrame object. The **windowOpened()** method in lines 178 through 182 prepares the StockSymbol JTextField for user data entry when the window first is opened. When the user closes the window, the **windowClosing()** method in lines 184 through 187 calls the logoutUser() method, as both methods take the same action. The remaining methods must be implemented, but are empty and, therefore, take no action if invoked.

The following step enters code for the WindowListener interface in the StockFrame class.

To Implement the WindowListener Interface

1. Enter lines 176 through 208 as shown in Figure 10-41 on page 650. Save and compile the StockFrame class.

TextPad displays code in the coding window for the seven methods required to implement the WindowListener interface (Figure 10-48). The windowOpened() method and windowClosing() method contain code. The remaining methods are empty and, therefore, take no action if invoked.

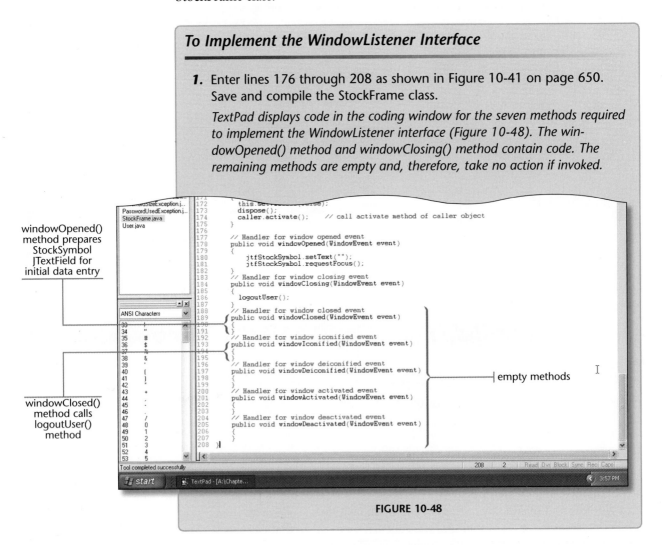

windowOpened() method prepares StockSymbol JTextField for initial data entry

windowClosed() method calls logoutUser() method

empty methods

FIGURE 10-48

Now that the StockFrame class is complete, the LogonFrame class that uses it can be created. Figure 10-49 displays the code for the LogonFrame class. As shown in line 16, the LogonFrame class implements the Activator interface created earlier. Doing so allows the LogonFrame to pass a reference to itself to the StockFrame constructor and allows the StockFrame object to call back to the activate() method in the LogonFrame object. Line 16 also implements the ActionListener interface to listen for mouse clicks on a button, once the listener interface is registered with a button. Lines 16 through 158 create the user interface and functionality for the LogonFrame window, including displaying the window centered, determining if a user already is in the collection, and adding a user to the collection of users. As this is very similar to earlier tasks, this code is provided on the Student Data Disk. Note that line 18 defines the variable, maxUsers, which is the maximum number of users that can be added simultaneously to the test application. Note also that line 10 imports a specific class to support the creation of a TitledBorder object. A **Border** is an object used to draw titles, empty spaces, lines, or fancy edges in the area around a component. A

TitledBorder object is a Border object with text that, by default, displays in a line surrounding the component for which it is used. In line 67, a TitledBorder object using the string, "Enter user info," for the title text, is created and then passed to the **setBorder()** method, which sets a Border object for the JPanel.

In line 120, the method **getDefaultToolkit()** gets the default implementation of the AWT(Toolkit) for the current platform. The **getScreenSize()** method of the Toolkit object gets the size of the screen in pixels and returns a Dimension object, which encapsulates the width and height of the screen. This allows the width and height of the screen to be used to center the current component. Lines 160 through 166 create a doStockActivity() method that creates a new StockFrame object and makes it visible after hiding the LogonFrame. Lines 168 through 173 include code for the callback method, activate().

Lines 175 through 306 include code for the actionPerformed() method, which is required to implement the ActionListener interface. The actionPerformed() method catches the various password exceptions to allow for better error handling than catching only general exceptions. Line 201 checks if the Add new user button was clicked; if so, line 205 creates the new user object with the given user name and password that automatically expires after four uses. Line 214 tests if the Log on button was clicked. If so, line 216 verifies that the user is in the user list. For an existing user, line 218 validates the password entered for the user. For a valid password, line 220 checks if the password is expiring, and if so, displays a message indicating the number of remaining uses. For a valid user with a valid password, line 223 calls the doStockActivity() method which was created earlier. Line 229 tests if the Change user pswd button was clicked. If so, line 231 verifies that the user is in the user list. For an existing user, line 233 validates the password entered for the user. For a user with a valid password, the user is presented with a screen to enter a new password. Line 240 changes the password for the current user and then line 243 calls the doStockActivity() method. Note that beginning in line 256, the exceptions caught are in order from more specific to more general, up to and including a general Exception.

JAVA UPDATE Java 2 v5.0

Enhanced for() Loop

When looping through all items in an array or a Collection, such as an ArrayList, instead of incrementing an index and comparing it to the size of the array or Collection to avoid exceeding the bounds, Java 5.0 provides for an enhanced for() loop. Using the enhanced for() loop simplifies code, especially as compared to iterating through a Collection with an Iterator object. Because you do not use an index value and the only test for continuing the loop is whether you have accessed all elements, the only way to prematurely exit the loop is by using the break statement, which is unstructured. In the right circumstances, the enhanced for() loop can be very useful, but use it with care and do not expect to use it in all loop situations. To help understand the new syntax, read it as "for each Type variableName in array/Collection", as in "for each int num in numArray" or "for each User user in userList".

The following code shows use of the enhanced for() loop with an array of int (intArray) and with an ArrayList of Integers (list), summing the contents of each into an int variable.

```
for(int num : intArray)      // for each int "num" in array of int "intArray"
   total += num;             // auto-unboxing Integer j to int, add to total

for(Integer j : list)        // for each Integer "j" in ArrayList "list"
   sum += j;                 // auto-unboxing Integer j to int, add to sum
```

```
1   /*
2        Chapter 10:   The LogonFrame Class
3        Programmer:   Michael Mick
4        Date:         December 5, 2007
5        Filename:     LogonFrame.java
6        Purpose:      Provides a user interface for a log on to test the Password class
7   */
8
9   import javax.swing.*;
10  import javax.swing.border.TitledBorder;
11  import java.awt.*;
12  import java.awt.event.*;
13  import java.util.*;
14  import java.io.*;
15
16  public class LogonFrame extends JFrame implements ActionListener, Activator
17  {
18      int maxUsers = 3;
19      ArrayList userList = new ArrayList();
20      User user = null;
21      String userName;
22      String password;
23
```

FIGURE 10-49

```
24          JTextField userNameField;
25          JPasswordField passwordField;
26          JButton jbtAddUser, jbtChgPswd, jbtLogon;
27
28          public LogonFrame()
29          {
30              super("Log on or Maintain User"); // call super (JFrame) constructor
31
32              int width = 330;
33              int height = 170;
34
35              // define GUI components
36              JLabel label1 = new JLabel("User Name: ");
37              userNameField = new JTextField(20);
38
39              JLabel label2 = new JLabel("Password:    ");
40              passwordField = new JPasswordField(20);
41              passwordField.setEchoChar('*');
42
43              jbtAddUser = new JButton("Add new user");
44              jbtChgPswd = new JButton("Change user pswd");
45              jbtLogon = new JButton("Log on");
46
47              // set up GUI
48              JPanel userPanel= new JPanel(new BorderLayout());
49              userPanel.add(label1,BorderLayout.WEST);
50              userPanel.add(userNameField,BorderLayout.CENTER);
51
52              JPanel pswdPanel= new JPanel(new BorderLayout());
53              pswdPanel.add(label2,BorderLayout.WEST);
54              pswdPanel.add(passwordField,BorderLayout.CENTER);
55
56              JPanel logonButtonPanel= new JPanel(new FlowLayout());
57              logonButtonPanel.add(jbtLogon);
58
59              JPanel maintButtonPanel= new JPanel(new FlowLayout());
60              maintButtonPanel.add(jbtAddUser);
61              maintButtonPanel.add(jbtChgPswd);
62
63              JPanel contentPanel= new JPanel(new BorderLayout());
64              contentPanel.add(userPanel, BorderLayout.NORTH);
65              contentPanel.add(pswdPanel, BorderLayout.CENTER);
66              contentPanel.add(logonButtonPanel, BorderLayout.SOUTH);
67              contentPanel.setBorder(new TitledBorder("Enter user info"));
68
69              JPanel p2 = new JPanel(new BorderLayout());
70              p2.add(contentPanel, BorderLayout.NORTH);
71              p2.add(maintButtonPanel, BorderLayout.SOUTH);
72
73              JPanel p3 = new JPanel(new BorderLayout(10,10));
74              p3.add(p2, BorderLayout.WEST);
75              JPanel p4 = new JPanel(new BorderLayout(10,10));
76              p4.add(p3, BorderLayout.EAST);
77
78              setContentPane(p4);
79
80              // add listeners
81              jbtAddUser.addActionListener(this);
82              jbtChgPswd.addActionListener(this);
83              jbtLogon.addActionListener(this);
84
85              addWindowListener(new WindowAdapter() {
86                  public void windowClosing(WindowEvent e) { System.exit(0); }
87                  });
88
89              // Enable Enter key for each JButton
90              InputMap map;
91              map = jbtAddUser.getInputMap();
92              if (map != null){
93                  map.put(KeyStroke.getKeyStroke(KeyEvent.VK_ENTER,0,false), "pressed");
94                  map.put(KeyStroke.getKeyStroke(KeyEvent.VK_ENTER,0,true), "released");
95              }
96              map = jbtChgPswd.getInputMap();
```

FIGURE 10-49

(continued)

```
 97              if (map != null){
 98                  map.put(KeyStroke.getKeyStroke(KeyEvent.VK_ENTER,0,false), "pressed");
 99                  map.put(KeyStroke.getKeyStroke(KeyEvent.VK_ENTER,0,true), "released");
100              }
101              map = jbtLogon.getInputMap();
102              if (map != null){
103                  map.put(KeyStroke.getKeyStroke(KeyEvent.VK_ENTER,0,false), "pressed");
104                  map.put(KeyStroke.getKeyStroke(KeyEvent.VK_ENTER,0,true), "released");
105              }
106
107              pack();
108              if( width < getWidth())                 // prevent setting width too small
109                  width = getWidth();
110              if(height < getHeight())                // prevent setting height too small
111                  height = getHeight();
112              centerOnScreen(width, height);
113          }
114
115          public void centerOnScreen(int width, int height)
116          {
117              int top, left, x, y;
118
119              // Get the screen dimension
120              Dimension screenSize = Toolkit.getDefaultToolkit().getScreenSize();
121
122              // Determine the location for the top left corner of the frame
123              x = (screenSize.width - width)/2;
124              y = (screenSize.height - height)/2;
125              left = (x < 0) ? 0 : x;
126              top = (y < 0) ? 0 : y;
127
128              // Set the frame to the specified location & size
129              this.setBounds(left, top, width, height);
130          }
131
132          private boolean userExists(String userName)
133          {
134              boolean userInList = false;
135
136              userName.trim(); // remove any leading, trailing whitespace
137
138              if(userList.size()>0) // at least one entry is in list
139              {
140                  for(int i=0; i < userList.size() && !userInList; ++i)
141                  {
142                      user = (User)userList.get(i);
143                      if(userName.equals(user.getName()))
144                          userInList = true;
145                  }
146              }
147
148              return userInList;
149          }
150
151          private boolean addToList(User user)
152          {
153              boolean success = false;
154              if(userList.size() < maxUsers)
155                  success = userList.add(user);
156
157              return success;
158          }
159
160          private void doStockActivity()
161          {
162              StockFrame frame = new StockFrame(user,this);
163              frame.pack();
164              setVisible(false);
165              frame.setVisible(true);
166          }
167
```

FIGURE 10-49

(continued)

```
168      public void activate()
169      {
170          setVisible(true);
171          userNameField.setText("");
172          userNameField.requestFocus();
173      }
174
175      public void actionPerformed(ActionEvent e)
176      {
177          try
178          {
179              userName = userNameField.getText();
180              if(userName.equals(""))
181              {
182                  JOptionPane.showMessageDialog(this,
183                      "Please enter a valid user name.",
184                      "Missing User Name.",
185                      JOptionPane.ERROR_MESSAGE);
186                  userNameField.requestFocus();
187              }
188              else
189              {
190                  password = new String(passwordField.getPassword());
191                  if(password.equals(""))
192                  {
193                      JOptionPane.showMessageDialog(this,
194                          "Please enter a valid password.",
195                          "Missing Password.",
196                          JOptionPane.ERROR_MESSAGE);
197                      passwordField.requestFocus();
198                  }
199                  else
200                  {
201                      if(e.getSource() == jbtAddUser)
202                      {
203                          if(!userExists(userName))
204                          {
205                              user = new User(userName,password,4);  // auto expires after 4
                                                                       uses
206                              if(addToList(user))
207                                  JOptionPane.showMessageDialog(this, "Success! " +
                                      user.getName()+" has been added.");
208                              else
209                                  JOptionPane.showMessageDialog(this,
                                      "Could not add new user " +user.getName());
210                          }
211                          else
212                              JOptionPane.showMessageDialog(this, "User "+user.getName() +
                                  " already exists!");
213                      }
214                      else if(e.getSource() == jbtLogon)
215                      {
216                          if(userExists(userName))
217                          {
218                              user.validate(password);
219
220                              if(user.pswdIsExpiring())
221                                  JOptionPane.showMessageDialog(this, user.getName() +
                                      " logon successful; "
222                                  +user.getPswdUses()+" use(s) remaining.");
223                              doStockActivity();
224
225                          }
226                          else
227                              JOptionPane.showMessageDialog(this, "Invalid user.");
228                      }
229                      else if(e.getSource() == jbtChgPswd)
230                      {
231                          if(userExists(userName))
232                          {
233                              user.validate(password);
234                              JLabel passwd=new JLabel("New password");
235                              JPasswordField pword=new JPasswordField(20);
236                              Object[] ob={passwd,pword};
237                              JOptionPane.showMessageDialog(this, ob);
238                              String newPassword = new String(pword.getPassword());
239
```

FIGURE 10-49   *(continued)*

```
240                                 user.changePassword(password,newPassword);
241                                 JOptionPane.showMessageDialog(this, "Success, "+user.getName()
242                                             +"! Your password has been changed.");
243                                 doStockActivity();
244                             }
245                             else
246                                 JOptionPane.showMessageDialog(this, "Invalid user.");
247                         }
248                         else
249                             JOptionPane.showMessageDialog(this, "Please choose a valid
                                action.");
250                     }
251                 }
252             userNameField.setText("");
253             passwordField.setText("");
254             userNameField.requestFocus();
255         }// end of try
256         catch (PasswordUsedException ex)
257         {
258             JOptionPane.showMessageDialog(this,
259                 ex.getMessage()+'\n'+ex.usage(),
260                 "Invalid password. Try again.",
261                 JOptionPane.ERROR_MESSAGE);
262         }
263         catch (PasswordSizeException ex)
264         {
265             JOptionPane.showMessageDialog(this,
266                 ex.getMessage()+'\n'+ex.usage(),
267                 "Invalid password. Try again.",
268                 JOptionPane.ERROR_MESSAGE);
269         }
270         catch (PasswordInvalidFormatException ex)
271         {
272             if(ex.getCount() > 2) // allows only 3 tries, then exits program
273                 System.exit(0);
274             else
275                 JOptionPane.showMessageDialog(this,ex.getMessage()
276                                 +"\n"+ex.usage()
277                                 +"\nNumber of invalid attempts: " +ex.getCount(),
278                                 "Invalid password format. Try again.",
279                                 JOptionPane.ERROR_MESSAGE);
280         }
281         catch (PasswordInvalidException ex)
282         {
283             if(ex.getCount() > 2) // allows only 3 tries, then exits program
284                 System.exit(0);
285             else
286                 JOptionPane.showMessageDialog(this,ex.getMessage()
287                                 +"\n"+ex.usage()
288                                 +"\nNumber of invalid attempts: " +ex.getCount(),
289                                 "Invalid password. Try again.",
290                                 JOptionPane.ERROR_MESSAGE);
291         }
292         catch (PasswordException ex)
293         {
294             JOptionPane.showMessageDialog(this,
295                 ex.getMessage()+'\n'+ex.usage(),
296                 "Invalid password. Try again.",
297                 JOptionPane.ERROR_MESSAGE);
298         }
299         catch (Exception ex)
300         {
301             JOptionPane.showMessageDialog(this,
302                 ex.getMessage(),
303                 "Unspecified exception.",
304                 JOptionPane.ERROR_MESSAGE);
305         }
306     }
307 }
```

FIGURE 10-49

The steps on the next page create the LogonFrame class and implement the Activator interface.

To Implement the Activator Interface

1. Start TextPad and open the file, LogonFrame.java, from the Chapter10 folder on the Data Disk. Replace lines 1 through 16 as shown in Figure 10-49 on page 657. In the comments, insert your own name as programmer and enter the current date.

   TextPad displays code for the initial comments, class header, instance variables, and constructor header for the LogonFrame class (Figure 10-50). The LogonFrame class implements both the ActionListener and the Activator interfaces.

LogonFrame.java

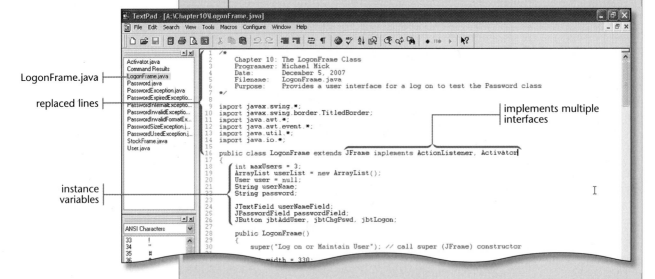

FIGURE 10-50

2. Replace lines 160 through 174 as shown in Figure 10-49.

   TextPad displays code for the method, doStockActivity(), and the callback method, activate() (Figure 10-51). The keyword, this, is used to indicate that a reference to the current object is passed to a new StockFrame object.

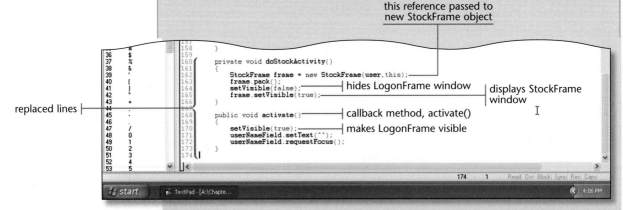

FIGURE 10-51

3. Enter lines 175 through 307 as shown in Figure 10-49 on page 660. Save and compile the LogonFrame class.

TextPad displays code for the actionPerformed() method in the coding window (Figure 10-52). The actionPerformed() method is required to implement the ActionListener interface; it also catches the various password exceptions, allowing for better error handling. Lines 272 and 283 will exit the program if more than two invalid password entries are attempted in sequence.

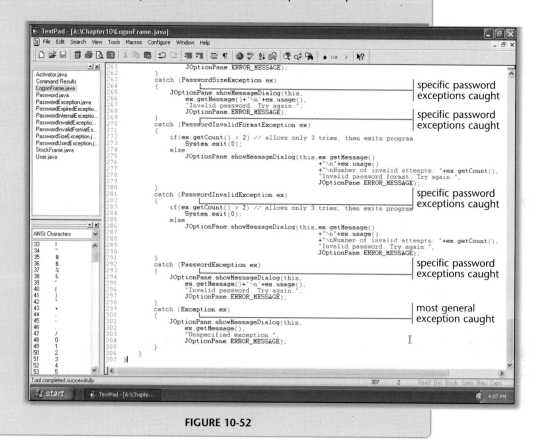

FIGURE 10-52

Using Adapter Classes

Implementing interfaces is fairly simple, but can become tedious if the interface declares many methods and you wish to implement only one or two. To implement the interface in a concrete class, you must define each of the abstract methods, even if they do not do anything, as shown in the StockFrame class. An alternative to implementing a number of empty methods of an interface is to use an adapter class. As you learned in Chapter 5, adapter classes implement an abstract class, providing prewritten methods for all of the methods of the abstract class. An adapter class is a concrete class that implements an interface by providing an empty method for each abstract method declared in the interface. By creating an object from, or inheriting from, the adapter class, the empty implementations are inherited. Overriding any method of interest provides the desired behavior without having to implement each method in your code.

Notice that the LogonFrame class also needs to have a WindowListener to listen for the user closing the window, much as the StockFrame class did for itself. When the user closes the LogonFrame window, the application terminates by exiting, or returning control, to the operating system. The LogonFrame class, however, does not implement the WindowListener interface. Instead, it uses an adapter class, **WindowAdapter**, to be the listener. It then uses the WindowAdapter object to override the windowClosing() method, as this is the only method that is needed by the LogonFrame class. Lines 85 through 87 in Figure 10-49 on page 658 in the LogonFrame class create a new WindowAdapter object and override the windowClosing() method.

Because the WindowAdapter is referenced only when adding it as the listener, no reference variable is needed when the WindowAdapter object is created. An object created without a reference variable is called an **anonymous object**. It is common to see such objects used in Java programs, particularly with respect to larger interfaces where only a single method is needed, such as with establishing a WindowListener object to listen for the closing of a window.

All of the necessary classes now are defined and compiled. To run the test application, a class with a main() method is required. Figure 10-53 displays the code for the StockListDemo class. The only purpose of this StockListDemo class is to provide an entry point for executing the application, which consists of a LogonFrame class and a StockFrame class. As shown in Figure 10-53, the StockListDemo class contains only a main() method, which creates and activates a LogonFrame object. The following step creates the StockListDemo class.

```
1   /*
2        Chapter 10: The StockListDemo Class
3        Programmer: Michael Mick
4        Date:       December 5, 2007
5        Filename:   StockListDemo.java
6        Purpose:    Provides a main() for testing the Password class using a LogonFrame
7   */
8
9   public class StockListDemo
10  {
11      public static void main(String[] argv)
12      {
13          final LogonFrame f = new LogonFrame();
14          f.setVisible(true);
15      }
16  }
```

FIGURE 10-53

To Create the StockListDemo Class

1. Create a new TextPad document and save it in the Chapter10 folder, or a location specified by your instructor, typing `StockListDemo` as the file name and selecting Java (*.java) as the file type. Enter lines 1 through 16 as shown in Figure 10-53. In the comments, insert your own name as programmer and enter the current date.

TextPad displays code for the StockListDemo class in the coding window (Figure 10-54). The class contains only a main() method, which creates and activates a LogonFrame object.

StockListDemo.java

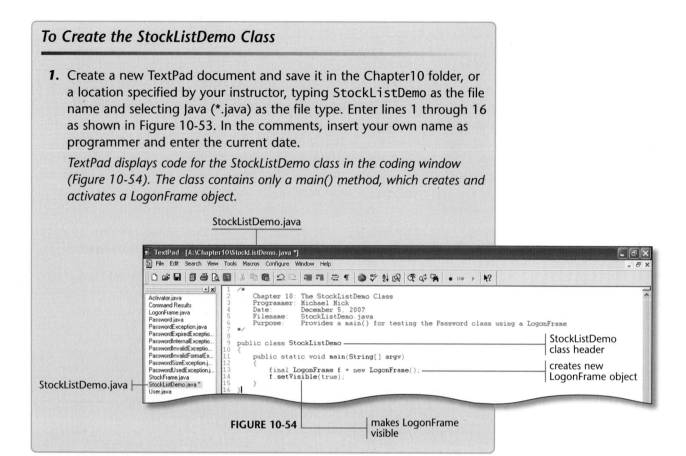

StockListDemo.java

StockListDemo class header

creates new LogonFrame object

FIGURE 10-54

makes LogonFrame visible

While the main() method could be included in the LogonFrame class (or in any class for that matter), it can be in a separate class, as in this case, where the main() method is included in the StockListDemo class. As long as an object of the LogonFrame class is created and made visible, where the main() method for this application resides is not an issue.

The following steps save and compile the StockListDemo Class.

To Save and Compile the StockListDemo Class

1. With your Data Disk in drive A, click the Save button on the Standard toolbar.

The program changes are saved. Note that the asterisk next to the file name, StockListDemo.java, is gone, indicating all changes are saved.

2. Click Compile Java on the Tools menu.

TextPad compiles the source code for the Password class. If TextPad notifies you of compilation errors, fix the errors in the coding window and then compile the source code again.

OTHER WAYS

1. Press CTRL+1

Testing the PasswordException Classes and Subclasses

A user must be added before attempting to log on to use the stock list application to test the PasswordException classes and subclasses. New users are added by typing appropriate values in the User Name text box and the Password text box, and then clicking the Add new user button. To change the password for an existing user, type the user name in the User Name text box and the current password in the Password text box and then click the Change user pswd button. To log on as an existing user, type the user name in the User Name text box and the current password in the Password text box and then click the Log on button.

Testing the PasswordException Classes and Subclasses

To test the application sufficiently, both valid and invalid inputs should be tested. The following steps use the StockListDemo test application to test the PasswordException classes and subclasses and view the various exceptions generated by valid and invalid inputs.

To Test the PasswordException Classes and Subclasses

1. Click Run Java Application on the Tools menu.

   The Log on or Maintain User window displays (Figure 10-1a on page 605).

2. Add a new user by typing user01, or a name of your choice, in the User Name text box and admin01 in the Password text box. Click the Add new user button.

   The new user is added to the list of users and the New user added dialog box displays (Figure 10-1c on page 605).

3. Click the OK button.

   The New user added dialog box closes. You may add as many users as allowed by the variable, maxUsers, in the LogonFrame class, which currently is set to 3.

4. In the Log on or Maintain User window, type user01 (or the user name entered in the previous step) in the User Name text box and the corresponding password, admin01, in the Password text box. Click the Log on button. When the Log on Successful dialog box displays, click the OK button.

   The Add Stock Symbols window displays with the current user name (Figure 10-1b on page 605).

5. Type MSFT, or a stock symbol of your choice, in the Symbol text box and then click the Add Symbol button. Repeat this step, typing ORCL as the stock symbol. Click the Click arrow to view list box arrow in the View stock symbols area.

   The added stock symbols are displayed in the drop-down list (Figure 10-1b).

6. Click the Log out button. When the Log on or Maintain User window displays, repeat Step 2 through Step 4, as appropriate, for the remaining user names, passwords, and actions listed in Table 10-3.

The result for each action and the dialog box displayed are listed in Table 10-3 and shown in Figure 10-1 on pages 605 and 606.

Table 10-3 Data Entry, Actions, and Results for Testing PasswordException Class

USER	PASSWORD	ACTION	RESULT	DISPLAYS	RESPONSE
user01	admin01	Click Add new user button	User added successfully	Success! user01 has been added. (Figure 10-1c)	Click OK button
user02	admin02	Click Add new user button	User added successfully	Success! user02 has been added.	Click OK button
user03	admin03	Click Add new user button	User added successfully	Success! user03 has been added!	Click OK button
user03	admin03	Click Change user pswd	New password dialog box displays (Figure 10-1d); Click New Password text box; Enter new password; click OK button	Success, user03! Your password has been changed. (Figure 10-1e)	Click OK button; click Log out button
user01	admin01	Click Log on button	Password is expiring	User01 logon successful; 3 use(s) remaining. (Figure 10-1f)	Click OK button; Click Log out button
user01	admin01	Click Log on button	Password is expiring	User01 logon successful; 2 use(s) remaining.	Click OK button; Click Log out button
user01	admin01	Click Log on button	Password is expiring	user01 log on successful; 1 use(s) remaining.	Click OK button; Click Log out button
user01	admin01	Click Log on button	Password is expiring	user 01 logon successful; 0 use(s) remaining.	Click OK button; Click Log out button
user01	admin01	Click Log on button	Password has expired	Password has expired — please change. This password is set to automatically expire and its number of remaining uses has reached zero. (Figure 10-1g)	Click OK button

(continued)

Table 10-3   Data Entry, Actions, and Results for Testing PasswordException Class, continued

USER	PASSWORD	ACTION	RESULT	DISPLAYS	RESPONSE
user02	user02	Click Log on button	Invalid password; not in list	Password is invalid This password does not match a value in the password history. Number of invalid attempts: 1 (Figure 10-1h)	Click OK button
user02	administrator	Click Log on button	Invalid password; no numeric digit	Password is invalid — must have at least one numeric digit This password is not formatted properly. Number of invalid attempts: 2 (Figure 10-1i)	Click OK button
user03	user	Click Log on button	Invalid password; less than minimum size	Password < minimum size This password is not formatted properly. (Figure 10-1j)	Click OK button
user03	user123456789012	Click Log on button	Invalid password; greater than maximum size	Password > maximum size This password is not formatted properly. (Figure 10-1k)	Click OK button

Print the Source Code

After testing the application to verify the Password class uses the PasswordException class and subclasses appropriately, all source code for the modified Password class and the PasswordException class and subclasses — as well as the Activator interface, LogonFrame, StockFrame, and StockListDemo classes — should be printed. The following steps print the source code for all programs.

To Print Source Code

1. In the TextPad window, click the Print button on the Standard toolbar.
The StockListDemo source code is printed.

2. Click Activator.java in the Selector Window to display the Activator interface source code.
The Activator source code is displayed in the coding window.

3. Click the Print button on the Standard toolbar.
The Activator source code is printed.

4. Repeat steps 2 and 3 for each Java source code file in the Selector Window.

OTHER WAYS

1. Press CTRL+P
2. Press ALT+F, P

Quitting TextPad

After you create, save, compile, test, and print the source code for the PasswordException classes and subclasses, as well as the classes for the StockListDemo application, the program is complete and you can quit TextPad. The following step quits TextPad and returns control to Windows.

To Quit TextPad

1. Click the Close button on the TextPad title bar.

The TextPad window closes and the Windows desktop is displayed.

OTHER WAYS

1. Press ALT+F, X

Chapter Summary

In this chapter, you learned about inheritance and the difference between single and multiple inheritance. You learned how to use inheritance to construct objects, modeling an is-a relationship between objects, and how that differs from using aggregation to model a has-a relationship. You explored abstract classes and how they differ from concrete classes. You learned how to create and use abstract classes and methods in Java. You also learned about using final methods to prevent method overriding in subclasses, and about final classes and how they can be used to prevent inheritance. You learned about extending child classes to create an inheritance hierarchy. You learned about finding and replacing text and setting, clearing, and finding bookmarks in TextPad. You learned about interfaces and how to create an interface and implement the interface in Java. You learned how to chain, or concatenate, method calls and how to code a callback mechanism using a callback method. Finally, you learned about adapter classes and anonymous objects.

What You Should Know

Having completed this chapter, you now should be able to perform the tasks shown in Table 10-4.

Table 10-4   Chapter 10 What You Should Know

TASK NUMBER	TASK	PAGE
1	Start a New Java Program in TextPad	613
2	Create an Abstract Class	615
3	Save and Compile the PasswordException Class	616
4	Extend an Abstract Class	618
5	Create Final Methods	621
6	Extend a Child Class	624
7	Create a Final Class	627
8	Find and Replace All Occurrences of Text in TextPad	632
9	Bookmark All Occurrences of Text in TextPad	635
10	Modify the Exception Code for Methods	637
11	Find the Next Bookmarked Line	638
12	To Create a Concatenated Method Call	642
13	Create a Class Using Aggregation	644
14	Create an Activator Interface	647
15	Create a Callback Mechanism in a Class	652
16	Implement the WindowListener Interface	656
17	Implement the Activator Interface	662
18	Create the StockListDemo Class	664
19	Save and Compile the StockListDemo Class	665
20	Test the PasswordException Classes and Subclasses	666
21	Print Source Code	668
22	Quit TextPad	669

Key Terms

abstract *(612)*

abstract class *(612)*

abstract method *(611)*

activate() method *(647)*

Activator interface *(647)*

anonymous object *(664)*

base class *(609)*

bookmark *(634)*

Border *(656)*

callback mechanism *(646)*

callback method *(646)*

child class *(609)*

concrete class *(612)*

extending a class *(604)*

enum *(646)*

final class *(626)*

final method *(620)*

getDefaultToolkit() *(657)*

getScreenSize() *(657)*

has-a relationship *(611)*

inheritance hierarchy *(608)*

is-a relationship *(611)*

leaf node *(616)*

method call chaining *(640)*

method call concatenation *(640)*

multiple inheritance *(610)*

parent class *(609)*

root *(609)*

setBorder() *(656)*

single inheritance *(610)*

TitledBorderObject *(656)*

WindowAdapter *(610)*

WindowClosing() *(655)*

WindowOpened() *(655)*

Homework Assignments

Identify Code

Identify the code elements shown in Figure 10-55.

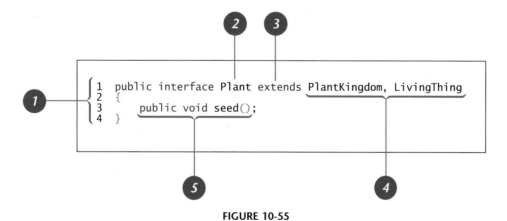

FIGURE 10-55

1. _____

2. _____

3. _____

4. _____

5. _____

Understanding Error Messages

Figure 10-56a displays a portion of a Java program. Figure 10-56b displays the compilation error messages. Using what you know about error messages, list the coding error that caused TextPad to display these errors.

```
1   public class Oak extends BigTree, Plant
2   {
3       public Oak()
4       {
5           super();
6           System.out.println("Created an Oak!");
7       }
8
9       public void grow()
10      {
11          System.out.println("From little acorns grow mighty oaks!");
12      }
13
14      public void seed()
15      {
16          System.out.println("Acorns are seeds for oaks.");
17      }
18
19      public void hasLife()
20      {
21          System.out.println("I'm a Living Thing and I have LIFE!");
22      }
23
24  }
```

FIGURE 10-56a

```
A:\Chapter10\Oak.java:1: '{' expected
public class Oak extends BigTree, Plant
                                ^
A:\Chapter10\Oak.java:24: '}' expected
}
 ^
A:\Chapter10\Oak.java:1: Oak should be declared abstract; it does not define
grow() in BigTree
public class Oak extends BigTree, Plant
                 ^
3 errors

Tool completed with exit code 1
```

FIGURE 10-56b

Using the Java API

The Java API is a good tool to look up information about a class with which you may be unfamiliar or to check the syntax of commands and methods you wish to use in your programs. While connected to the Internet, start a browser, type http://java.sun.com/j2se/1.5.0/docs/api/ in the Address text box and then press the ENTER key to view the Java API Specification on the Sun Web site. The Java API is organized by the packages, hierarchically, but many programmers click the Index link located at the top of the page to display the entire list alphabetically. With the Java API Specification open in the browser window, perform the following steps.

1. Use the scroll down arrow in the top left frame of the main frame to display the java.awt.event link. Click the java.awt.event link.

2. When the Package java.awt.event page is displayed in the lower-left frame, if necessary, scroll down to display the Interfaces. Click the WindowListener link in the list of Interfaces.

3. When the Interface WindowListener page is displayed (Figure 10-57a), read the paragraph that describes the WindowListener interface. Select the header and the first paragraph of text by dragging through them. Click Print on the File menu. When the Print dialog box is displayed, click the Selection option button and then click the Print button in the Print dialog box to print the selection.

4. Under the line, All Known Implementing Classes, click the WindowAdapter link.

5. When the Class WindowAdapter page is displayed (Figure 10-57b on the next page), scroll down, if necessary, and read the three paragraphs that describe the WindowAdapter class. Select the header and the first three paragraphs by dragging through them. Click File on the menu bar and then click Print. When the Print dialog box is displayed, click the Selection option button and then click the Print button in the Print dialog box to print the selection.

6. Based on this reading, write a paragraph explaining the necessary conditions for using the WindowAdapter class versus implementing the WindowListener interface.

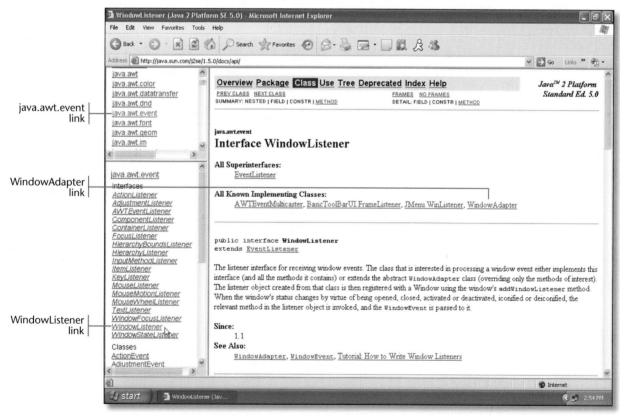

FIGURE 10-57a

(continued)

Using the Java API *(continued)*

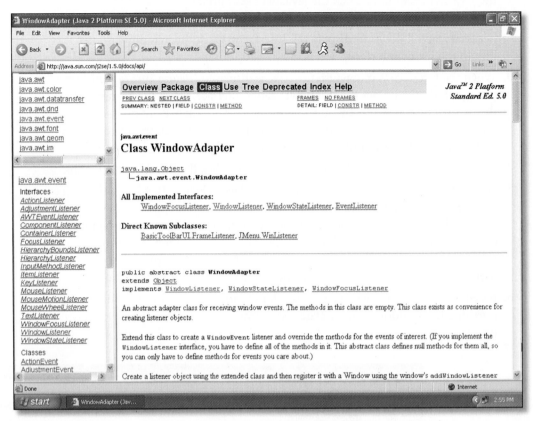

FIGURE 10-57b

Short Answer

1. Java supports _____ inheritance of interfaces, but only _____ inheritance of classes.

2. A class that cannot be used to create an object is known as a(n) _____ class.

3. A class that can be used to create an object is known as a(n) _____ class.

4. A(n) _____ is an object-oriented design tool used to show the relationships among parent-child classes and to describe the inheritance relationships between classes.

5. A method that includes only a method header without the implementation is called a(n) _____ method.

6. A class that contains an abstract method is a(n) _____ class.

7. _____ and _____ model object relationships in Java.

8. Inheritance is used to model a(n) _____ relationship in Java.

9. Aggregation is used to model a(n) _____ relationship in Java, in which an object is composed of other objects.

10. The process of _____ a class is the means of implementing inheritance in Java.

11. A(n) _____ class provides an empty method for each abstract method declared in an interface.

12. An object created without a reference variable is called a(n) _____ object.

13. Declaring a class as _____ prevents it from being inherited.

14. A class depicted as a(n) _____ in an inheritance hierarchy has no subclasses.

15. A(n) _____ class is any class that provides inherited features to a subclass or child class.

16. A(n) _____ class is any class that inherits attributes and behaviors from the superclass or parent class.

17. The _____ class in an inheritance hierarchy is the topmost superclass.

18. Declaring a method as _____ prevents it from being overridden in a subclass.

19. Java provides a(n) _____ to remove unused objects and return their memory to the operating system.

20. The Java keyword, _____, indicates an interface rather than a class will be used.

21. Method call _____, or _____, is a means of coding multiple method calls separated by period separators.

22. To return quickly to a line, or multiple lines, of code in TextPad, you can _____ each line.

23. A(n) _____ is a way for one object to provide a generic reference to itself, so that a second object can call back to a known method of the first object.

24. A(n) _____ method is a method of an object called from a second object using a callback mechanism.

25. A(n) _____ is a Java file that contains only method declarations and/or constants.

Learn It Online

Start your browser and visit scsite.com/java3e/exs. Follow the instructions in the exercises below.

1. **Chapter Reinforcement TF, MC, and SA**   Click the Chapter Renforcement link below Chapter 10. Print and then answer the questions.

2. **Practice Test**   Click the Practice Test link below Chapter 10. Answer each question, enter your first and last name at the bottom of the page, and then click the Grade Test button. When the graded practice test is displayed on your screen, click Print on the File menu to print a hard copy. Continue to take practice tests until you score 80% or better. Hand in a printout of the final practice test.

(continued)

HOMEWORK ASSIGNMENTS

Learn It Online *(continued)*

3. **Crossword Puzzle Challenge**   Click the Crossword Puzzle Challenge link below Chapter 10. Read the instructions, and then enter your first and last name. Click the Play button. Complete the crossword puzzle. When you are finished, click the Submit button. When the crossword puzzle is displayed, click the Print button.

4. **Tips and Tricks**   Click the Tips and Tricks link below Chapter 10. Click a topic that pertains to Chapter 10. Right-click the information and then click Print on the shortcut menu. Construct a brief example of what the information relates to in Java to confirm you understand how to use the tip or trick. Hand in the example and printed information.

5. **Newsgroups**   Click the Newsgroups link below Chapter 10. Click a topic that pertains to Chapter 10. Print three comments.

6. **Expanding Your Horizons**   Click the Expanding Your Horizons link below Chapter 10. Click a topic that pertains to Chapter 10. Print the information. Construct a brief example of what the information relates to in Java to confirm you understand the contents of the article. Hand in the example and printed information.

7. **Search Sleuth**   Select three key terms from the Key Terms section of this chapter and then use the Google search engine at google.com (or any major search engine) to display and print two Web pages for each key term.

Debugging Assignment

The TestCircle class is a Java application that creates a Circle object using the class, Circle, which incorporates the class, Shape. The TestCircle class displays the name of the shape; the radius as an X, Y coordinate location; and the area. It also changes the radius to a new value and then displays the same information in a different format. The class should not be able to create an object of type Shape.

The source code for the TestCircle, Circle, and Shape classes have several syntax, semantic, and logic errors. Perform the following steps to debug the classes.

1. Start TextPad and open the files, TestCircle.java, Circle.java, and Shape.java, from the Chapter10 folder on the Data Disk.

2. Read through the code and fix any errors that you see. Create comment headers and insert your name as the programmer along with today's date in each program.

3. Save the files.

4. Compile the classes. If TextPad displays any compilation errors, fix the errors and then recompile.

5. When you have fixed all the syntax and semantic errors so that the classes will compile without errors, run the TestCircle program and look for run-time and logic errors. Fix any errors and compile again.

6. When the program compiles and runs to produce the output as shown in Figure 10-58, print a copy of the source code of each of the classes.

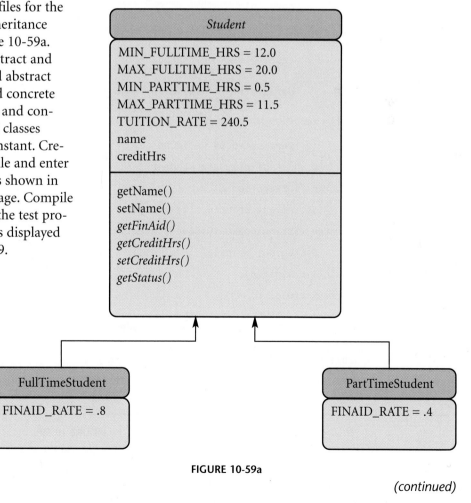

FIGURE 10-58

Programming Assignments

1 Extending Classes in an Inheritance Hierarchy

Create the Java source code files for the three classes listed in the inheritance hierarchy displayed in Figure 10-59a. The base class should be abstract and should contain the indicated abstract methods, as well as the listed concrete methods, instance variables, and constants. Each of the two child classes should contain the listed constant. Create a new Java source code file and enter code for the test program, as shown in Figure 10-59b on the next page. Compile all source code and execute the test program to obtain the output as displayed in Figure 10-59c on page 679.

Student

MIN_FULLTIME_HRS = 12.0
MAX_FULLTIME_HRS = 20.0
MIN_PARTTIME_HRS = 0.5
MAX_PARTTIME_HRS = 11.5
TUITION_RATE = 240.5
name
creditHrs

getName()
setName()
getFinAid()
getCreditHrs()
setCreditHrs()
getStatus()

FullTimeStudent

FINAID_RATE = .8

PartTimeStudent

FINAID_RATE = .4

FIGURE 10-59a

(continued)

1 Extending Classes in an Inheritance Hierarchy *(continued)*

```
1    import javax.swing.JOptionPane;
2    import java.text.DecimalFormat;
3    import java.io.*;
4
5    public class Test
6    {
7        public static void main(String[] args)
8        {
9            BufferedReader dataIn = new BufferedReader(new InputStreamReader(System.in));
10
11           boolean terminated = false;
12           boolean validChoice = true;
13           Student student = null;
14
15           String fullOrPartTime;
16
17           do {
18               validChoice = true;
19               System.out.print("Please enter full-time (F), part-time (P), "
20                               +"or 'Q' to quit: ");
21               try
22               {
23                   fullOrPartTime = dataIn.readLine();
24
25                   switch(fullOrPartTime.charAt(0))  // look at first character entered
26                   {
27                       case 'f':
28                       case 'F': // full-time student
29                               student = new FullTimeStudent();
30                               break;
31                       case 'p':
32                       case 'P': // part-time student
33                               student = new PartTimeStudent();
34                               break;
35                       case 'q':
36                       case 'Q': // quit program
37                               terminated = true;
38                               break;
39                       default : // invalid response
40                               validChoice = false;
41                               System.out.print("Please enter only an F, P, or Q.");
42                   }
43
44                   if(!terminated && validChoice)
45                       if(getData(student))     // data input with no errors
46                           displayData(student);
47               }
48               catch (IOException e)
49               {
50                   System.out.println("Invalid entry.");
51               }
52               catch (StringIndexOutOfBoundsException e)
53               {
54                   System.out.println("Invalid entry. Enter 'Q' to quit.");
55               }
56           } while(!terminated);
57
58           System.exit(0);
59       }
60
61       private static boolean getData(Student student)
62       {
63           boolean success = true;
64           double hrs = 0.0;
65           String name, hours;
66           BufferedReader dataIn = new BufferedReader(new InputStreamReader(System.in));
67
```

FIGURE 10-59b

(continued)

```
68              System.out.print("Please enter student name: ");
69              try
70              {
71                  name = dataIn.readLine();
72                  if(student.setName(name))
73                  {
74                      System.out.print("Please enter credit hours for "+name+": ");
75                      hours = dataIn.readLine();
76                      hrs = Double.parseDouble(hours);
77                      if(!student.setCreditHrs(hrs))
78                      {
79                          System.out.println("Hours invalid for "+student.getStatus()
80                                             +" student.\n");
81                          success = false;
82                      }
83                  }
84                  else
85                  {
86                      System.out.println("Name entered is not valid.\n");
87                      success = false;
88                  }
89              }
90              catch (IOException e)
91              {
92                  System.out.println("Invalid entry.\n");
93                  success = false;
94              }
95              catch (NumberFormatException e)
96              {
97                  System.out.println("Invalid hours entered.\n");
98                  success = false;
99              }
100
101             return success;
102         }
103
104         private static void displayData(Student student)
105         {
106             DecimalFormat twoDigits = new DecimalFormat("$##,##0.00");
107
108             System.out.println("\nStudent : "+student.getName() + " is taking "
109                                +student.getCreditHrs() + " credit hours,");
110             System.out.println("and is receiving "+ twoDigits.format(student.getFinAid()) +
111                                " in financial aid.\n\n");
112         }
113 }
```

FIGURE 10-59b

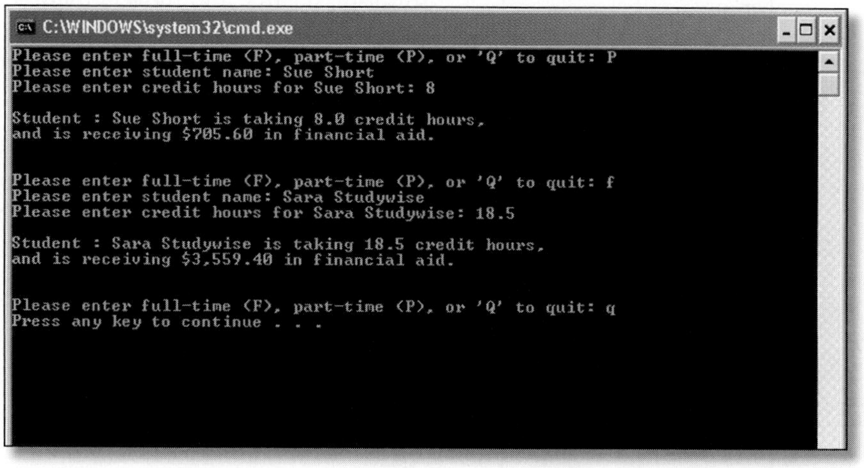

FIGURE 10-59c

2 Using Abstract Classes and Methods

Create the Java source code files for the classes listed in the inheritance hierarchy displayed in Figure 10-60a. Create a new Java source code file and enter code for the AbstractTest.java test program, as shown in Figure 10-60b. Compile all source code and execute the test program to obtain the output as displayed in Figure 10-60c. Perform the following steps to complete these tasks:

1. Create an abstract base class, Animal. The single constructor requires a String to indicate the type of animal, which then is stored in an instance variable.

2. Create a concrete class, Cat, which inherits from Animal. Cat has two instance variables, both Strings: name, which has private access and breed, which has protected access.

3. Create an abstract class, Bird, which inherits from Animal. Bird has a single instance variable, breed, of type String with protected access. Bird implements only the required move() method.

4. Create a concrete class, Robin, which inherits from Bird. Robin has a single instance variable, name, of type String with private access. Robin implements the remaining required methods.

5. Compile all source code and execute the test program to obtain the output as displayed in Figure 10-60c.

6. Create a Dog class and a Fish class, both inheriting from Animal.

7. Re-write AbstractTest (Figure 10-60b) as LoopTest.java. Create an arrray of Animal and then loop through the array using an enhanced for(), calling the describe(), sound(), sleep(), and move() methods, successively. Save and then print your source code.

8   Change LoopTest.java to use an ArrayList instead of an array. Print your source code and indicate whether or not your for() loop had to be modified when changing from an array to an ArrayList.

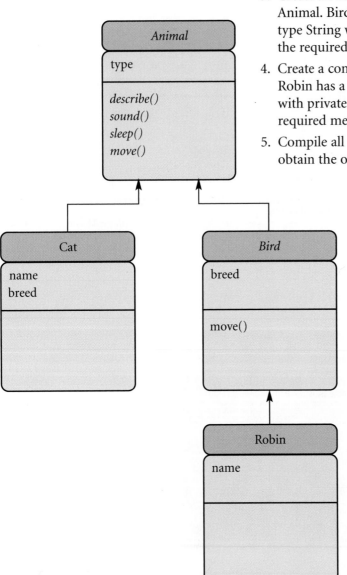

FIGURE 10-60a

```
 1  public class AbstractTest
 2  {
 3      public static void main(String[] args)
 4      {
 5          Cat cat = new Cat("Kitty", "Angora");
 6          Robin bird = new Robin("Rockin");
 7
 8          System.out.println("For the cat:  ");
 9          System.out.print("This is:  ");  cat.describe();
10          System.out.print("Sound:    ");  cat.sound();
11          System.out.print("Sleeping: ");  cat.sleep();
12          System.out.print("Moving:   ");  cat.move();
13          System.out.println("\n");
14
15          System.out.println("For the robin:  ");
16          System.out.print("This is:  ");  bird.describe();
17          System.out.print("Sound:    ");  bird.sound();
18          System.out.print("Sleeping: ");  bird.sleep();
19          System.out.print("Moving:   ");  bird.move();
20          System.out.println("\n");
21
22          System.out.println("\nEnd of program.");
23      }
24  }
```

FIGURE 10-60b

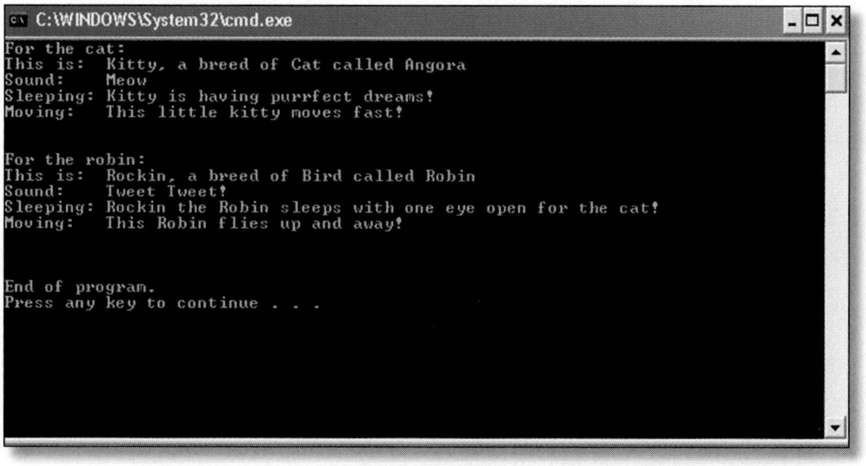

FIGURE 10-60c

3 Polymorphic Behavior Provided by Inheritance

Create the Java source code files for the classes listed in the inheritance hierarchy displayed in Figure 10-61a on the next page. Create a new Java source code file and enter code for the PolyTest.java test program, as shown in Figure 10-61b on page 683. Compile all source code and execute the test program to obtain the output as displayed in Figure 10-61c on page 683. Perform the following steps to complete these tasks:

1. Create an abstract base class, Ball. The single constructor requires a String to indicate the type of ball, which then is stored in an instance variable. The instance method, getType(), returns a new String containing the type of ball. The class declares an abstract method, play(), which returns void.

3 Polymorphic Behavior Provided by Inheritance *(continued)*

2. Create an abstract class, Bounceable, which inherits from Ball. Bounceable has a single abstract method, bounce(), which returns a String. There are no instance variables.

3. Create two concrete classes, Baseball and Bowlingball, which inherit from Ball. No instance variables or additional methods are required, only implementation of any inherited abstract methods.

4. Create two concrete classes, Tennisball and Basketball, which inherit from Bounceable. No instance variables or additional methods are required, only implementation of any inherited abstract methods.

5. Compile all source code and execute the test program to obtain the output as displayed in Figure 10-61c. The program, PolyTest.java, creates an array of Ball and references the various objects polymorphically through the parent class, using downcasting to access the bounce() method when appropriate.

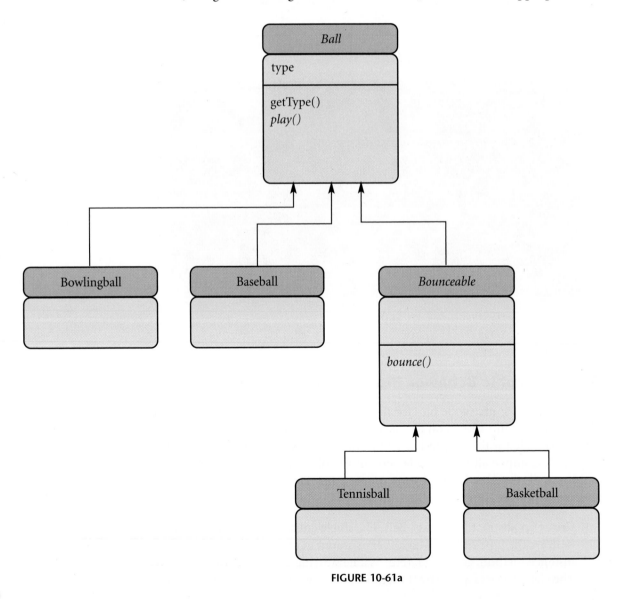

FIGURE 10-61a

```
1   public class PolyTest
2   {
3       public static void main(String[] args)
4       {
5           Ball[] ball = {new Baseball(),new Basketball(),new Bowlingball(),new Tennisball()};
6
7
8           System.out.println("For each type of ball...\n");
9
10          for(int i=0; i<ball.length;++i)
11          {
12              System.out.println("Ball #"+(i+1)+" is a "+ball[i].getType());
13
14              System.out.print("Playing: ");
15              ball[i].play();
16              // checks to see if it is an object of type Bounceable
17              if( ball[i] instanceof Bounceable)
18                  // if so, call bounce method of Bounceable object
19                  System.out.println("Bouncing "+((Bounceable)ball[i]).bounce());
20              else
21                  System.out.println("You can't bounce this ball!");
22
23              System.out.println("\n");
24          }
25
26          System.out.println("\nEnd of program.");
27      }
28  }
```

FIGURE 10-61b

FIGURE 10-61c

4 Polymorphic Behavior Provided by an Interface

When specific behavior is inherited, yet implemented uniquely within child classes, an abstract class may be used. Often, this same behavior can be required through the use of an interface, rather than through inheritance. This allows a change in the inheritance hierarchy, removing a layer of direct inheritance and using Java's implementation of multiple inheritance through interfaces.

(continued)

4 Polymorphic Behavior Provided by an Interface *(continued)*

Use the same test program, PolyTest.java, from Programming Assignment 3 to produce the same output as from Programming Assignment 3, by modifying the classes according to the inheritance hierarchy displayed in Figure 10-62. Change the abstract class, Bounceable, to an interface and modify the appropriate concrete classes from the previous exercise to implement the new interface.

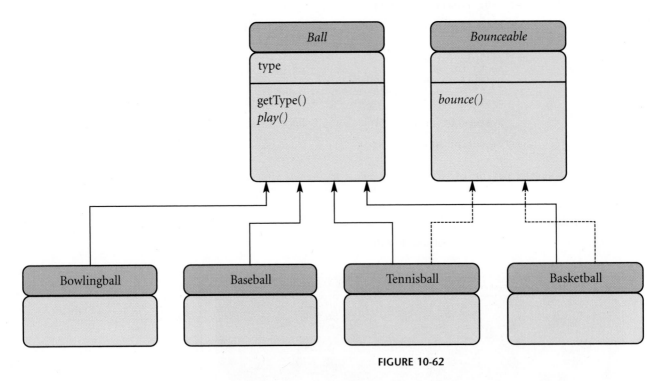

FIGURE 10-62

5 Using Final Classes and Methods

Create the Java source code files for the classes listed in the inheritance hierarchy displayed in Figure 10-63a. Create a new Java source code file and enter code for the FinalTest.java test program, as shown in Figure 10-63b on page 686. Compile all source code and execute the test program to obtain the output as displayed in Figure 10-63c on page 686. Perform the following steps to complete these tasks:

1. The abstract base class, SecurityAlarm, has three constant values used for the state of the alarm: no alarm, sensor failure, and activated alarm. One method, alarmFailure(), cannot be overridden by any subclass. The other two methods, alarm() and sensorSample(), are abstract.

2. The class, EntryAlarm, inherits from SecurityAlarm and has a single constant value as a threshold. If the simulation of the alarm sensor exceeds the threshold, the entry alarm is triggered. An EntryAlarm does not fail; it either signals no alarm or it activates an alarm.

3. The class, FireAlarm, inherits from SecurityAlarm and has two constant values. One indicates a maximum temperature threshold. If the simulation of the alarm sensor exceeds the threshold, the fire alarm is activated. The other constant indicates a temperature failure threshold, to prevent false alarms. If the simulation of the alarm sensor yields a temperature below this value, the fire alarm has malfunctioned. The source code for this class, FireAlarm.java, is located in the Chapter10 folder on the Student Data Disk.

4. The class, COAlarm, inherits from SecurityAlarm and has two constant values. One indicates a maximum carbon monoxide threshold. If the simulation of the alarm sensor exceeds the threshold, the carbon monoxide alarm is activated. The other constant indicates a carbon monoxide failure threshold, to prevent false alarms. If the simulation of the alarm sensor yields a carbon monoxide level below this threshold, the carbon monoxide alarm has malfunctioned.

5. The sensorSample() method is used to simulate alarm conditions by generating a random number value simulating a sensor reading. If the alarm is activated, this method calls the alarm() method. If the alarm fails, this method calls the alarmFailure() method. Compile all source code and execute the test program to obtain the output as displayed in Figure 10-63c on the next page.

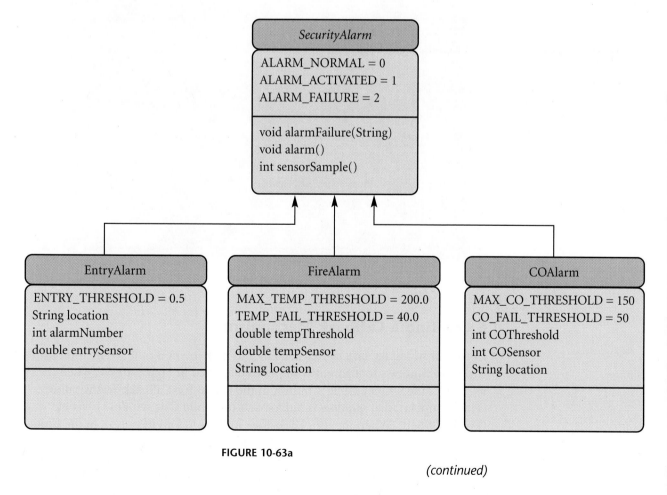

FIGURE 10-63a

(continued)

5 Using Final Classes and Methods (continued)

```
1  public class FinalTest
2  {
3      public static void main(String[] args)
4      {
5          SecurityAlarm[] alarm = {new FireAlarm("kitchen", 120.0),
6                                   new EntryAlarm("rear entrance", 10),
7                                   new COAlarm("furnace room", 130) };
8
9          int status = 0;
10
11         System.out.println("Simulation of Alarm Testing.\n");
12
13         // test alarm simulations
14         for(int i=0; i < 3;++i)
15             for(int j=0; j < alarm.length;++j)
16                 status = alarm[j].sensorSample();
17
18         System.out.println("\nEnd of program.");
19     }
20 }
```

FIGURE 10-63b

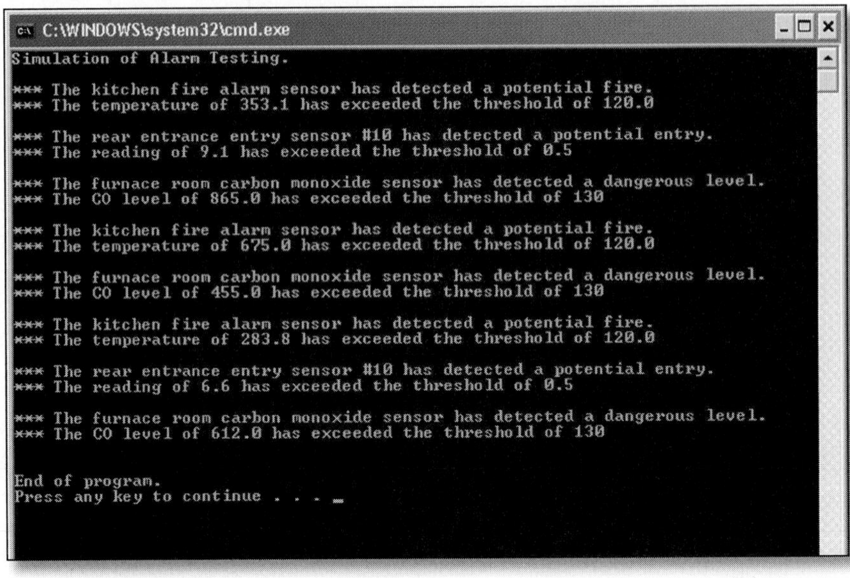

FIGURE 10-63C

6 Creating a Callback Mechanism

Create the necessary Java source code files to implement a callback method from two child windows to a parent window, as displayed in Figure 10-64. When the user clicks the Display Child 1 button in the Parent for Callback Test window (Figure 10-64a), that window is hidden and the Child One window is visible (Figure 10-64b). When the user clicks the Go Back to Parent button in the Child One window, the Child One window is hidden, and the Parent for Callback Test window is visible (Figure 10-64a). The same action occurs for the Display Child 2 button and the Child Two window (Figure 10-64c). The Parent for Callback Test window must implement an interface that provides a callback method.

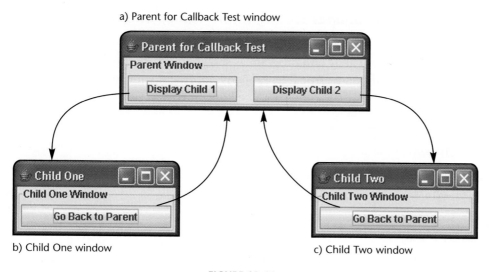

a) Parent for Callback Test window

b) Child One window

c) Child Two window

FIGURE 10-64

7 Constructing Shapes through Inheritance and Aggregation

Using the files, TestCircle.java, Circle.java, and Shape.java, from the Chapter 10 folder on the Data Disk, modify the code from the completed Debugging Assignment to use inheritance, an interface, and aggregation by completing the following steps:

1. In the Shape class, eliminate the concrete methods, area() and perimeter(); create an instance variable of type String called name; and make a constructor that requires a String, shapeName, as the name of the new Shape object. Keep the method getLocation(), and keep the Shape class abstract.

2. Create an interface, Shape2D, which requires the methods, area() and perimeter(), which were eliminated from Shape.

3. Create a new class, Point, which inherits from Shape and contains two private instance variables of type int, x and y, which store the coordinates for the Point. Point should have both a default constructor and a constructor that takes two int values for the coordinates x and y. For the default constructor, set both x and y to zero.

4. Modify the class, Circle, to inherit from Shape as well as use the interface, Shape2D. Circle should have only two private instance variables: a double named, radius, and a Point object reference named, center. Circle should have two constructors, a default constructor and a constructor that takes a double as a new radius value and two ints as the x and y coordinates of the center. Circle does not store the x and y values as ints, but instead creates a Point object with these coordinates. The location of a Circle is the location of its center, Point.

7 Constructing Shapes through Inheritance and Aggregation
(continued)

5. Modify the TestCircle.java program as shown in Figure 10-65 to test your classes until they are error-free. Properly document your solution. Print a copy of the source code and submit all documents to your instructor.

```
1   import java.text.DecimalFormat;
2
3   public class TestCircle
4   {
5       public static void main(String[] args)
6       {
7           DecimalFormat showTwoDecimals = new DecimalFormat( "0.00" );
8           Circle c1 = new Circle(2.5, 22, 44);
9           double newRadius = 6.0;
10
11          System.out.println("This shape is a " + c1.getName() +
12                      "\nlocated at " + c1.getLocation() +
13                      "\nRadius is " + c1.getRadius());
14
15          System.out.println("The shape area is: "
16                      + showTwoDecimals.format(c1.area())+"\n");
17
18          System.out.println("The shape perimeter (circumference) is: " +
19                      showTwoDecimals.format(c1.perimeter())+"\n");
20
21          System.out.println("After changing the radius to "+newRadius);
22          c1.setRadius(newRadius);
23          System.out.println(", it is a"+ c1 + "\nArea is "
24                      + showTwoDecimals.format(c1.area())+"\n");
25          System.out.println("The shape perimeter (circumference) is: " +
26                      showTwoDecimals.format(c1.perimeter())+"\n");
27      }
28  }
```

FIGURE 10-65

8 Using the Enhanced for() with an Array

Rewrite PolyTest from Programming Assignment 3 (see Figure 10-61b) to incorporate use of the enhanced for() loop to iterate through an array. The same code also should work with Programming Assignment 4.

9 Creating and Using an Enum class

Rewrite Programming Exercise 5 such that it uses a new enum class, AlarmStatus, which defines serial values of NORMAL, ACTIVATED, and FAILURE. Use these values instead of the constants defined in the SecurityAlarm class as shown in Figure 10-63a. Modify other classes, including FinalTest, as necessary. Use the AlarmStatus returned from the method sensorSample() in a switch statement to display when the system is normal, is activated, has failed, or has an unknown status.

11

Accessing Databases Using JDBC™

Objectives

You will have
mastered the material in
this chapter when you can:

- Design a relational database
- Describe a persistent object
- Implement the Serializable interface
- Register an ODBC data source name
- Load a JDBC™ database driver and make a connection
- Drop tables and indexes in a database
- Create tables, indexes, and keys
- Create and execute a PreparedStatement object
- Perform an SQL database query and process the result set
- Serialize and deserialize an object
- Create a data access (DA) class
- Modify records with an SQL update
- Use a committed transaction to delete related records
- Test the StockTrackerDB data access class

Introduction

Previously, you were introduced to applications that were used simply to test the functionality of a reusable Password class, as well as a hierarchy of PasswordException classes. Application data, such as users, passwords, and their respective lists of stocks, were stored in memory and had to be entered each time the test programs were run. In a more realistic application, such data would be entered once and stored in a database for later retrieval and manipulation.

In this chapter, you will learn how to store and access data in a relational database. A **relational database** maintains data in tables, allowing relationships between the tables to be specified, and typically is controlled by a vendor-specific software called a database management system (DBMS), as you previously learned. A **database table** provides a grouping of related data in terms of rows and columns, much as with any table of data, even on a printed page. Fortunately, Java makes using databases fairly simple through JDBC™. **JDBC** provides an API for database-independent connectivity between the Java programming language and a wide range of tabular data sources, including relational databases. Although often perceived as an acronym for Java Database Connectivity, officially, JDBC is a trademarked name, not an acronym; it simply is JDBC. Through JDBC, Java programs can issue **Structured Query Language** (**SQL**) statements to manipulate the database. SQL provides a fairly standard set of commands to create, update, delete, and query relational databases with relative simplicity. In this chapter, you will learn how to set up a Microsoft Access database as a data source and how to use JDBC in Java to create and delete the table structures within the database. Finally, you will learn how to create, update, delete, and list data in that database using SQL commands in Java through JDBC.

Chapter Eleven — The Stocktracker Data Access Class

An application for MoneyMark Trading is being developed that expands on the program created in Chapter 10 that verified users through a log on process and then allowed them to track their stock holdings. The new program has similar functionality, but will retain user and stock information in a database. The Password class already developed will be enhanced so Password objects can be saved to a database. This application will make use of a separate class to access the database and then will present the data to the user in a GUI format.

This chapter presents some database design concepts, and then illustrates how to complete three tasks necessary to support the GUI Stock Tracker application. The majority of what is created in this chapter will have no visible result to the user, but will support the GUI application supplied on the Data Disk.

As a result of the type of DBMS being used, the first task is to create the environment for the database (Figure 11-1a). This requires using an administrative utility accessed through the Windows Control Panel. The second task is to create the internal structure for the database and insert an initial user record into the database (Figure 11-1b). A new utility program will create this structure and initialize the database. For the purpose of this program, a simple console user interface is sufficient because it is used only once. The third and final task is to create a data access class, StockTrackerDB (Figure 11-1c). This class provides access to the database for other applications. All programs, except the utility program, only access the database through calls to methods of the StockTrackerDB class.

(a) Task 1: Create ODBC Data Source Name and assign to database

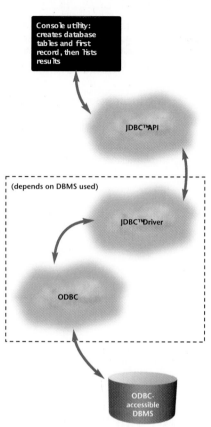

(b) Task 2: Create and execute console utility program

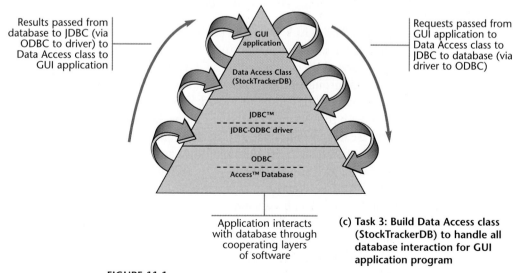

(c) Task 3: Build Data Access class (StockTrackerDB) to handle all database interaction for GUI application program

FIGURE 11-1

Program Development

The program development cycle and corresponding tasks for this project are shown in Table 11-1.

Table 11-1   StockTrackerDB Class Development Tasks

	DEVELOPMENT PHASE	TASK(S)
1	Analyze the requirements	Analyze the prototype stock-tracking application problem.
2	Design the solution	Design the logic to solve the problem.
3	Validate the design	Confirm with the user that the design solves the problem in a satisfactory manner.
4	Implement the design	Translate the design into code. Include internal documentation (comments and remarks) within the code that explains the purpose of the code statements. Design and code the applications used for creating the database structure and for accessing the database and presenting the data to the user.
5	Test the solution	Test the application for creating the database and then test the application for accessing both user and stock data. Find and correct any errors (debugging) until they are error-free.
6	Document the solution	Print copies of all source code, including the database creation program code.

Analysis and Design

Figure 11-2 shows the requirements document that initiates the development cycle for the StockTrackerDB class. This document illustrates that a request may require programs to initialize the application environment, as is done with the creation of a database.

PROBLEM ANALYSIS   The problem of providing a means of retaining information about users and their respective stocks and providing access only to authorized users is solved by a GUI, StockTracker. Access to a database is obtained through a data access class, StockTrackerDB. Access is controlled by means of a user ID and a password, both of which are contained in a database along with the associated user first name, last name, and stock information. The database maintains a relationship between a user and the stocks held by that user. Further, users with administrative access will perform user maintenance functions, such as adding new users and deleting, updating, and listing current users. A third class, MakeDB, creates the database structure and initializes the database with data for a single, known record, so the database is accessible by the GUI application. Because a Microsoft Access database is used, the Windows environment must be configured to make the database accessible to the programs that interact with it.

REQUEST FOR NEW APPLICATION

Date submitted:	December 10, 2007
Submitted by:	Mark Dunit, analyst
Purpose:	An application is needed to provide database access for a stock-tracking application under construction for client, MoneyMark Trading. The GUI application allows users to track their own customized account list of stock holdings. As the GUI will change over time, a program must be available that will provide database access independent of the GUI.
Application title:	StockTrackerDB, MakeDB (one-time utility)
Algorithms:	The password must conform to the recently developed Password class.
Notes:	1. Programs using this data access program must handle all user interfaces, accessing the database only through this program. A Microsoft Access database will be used. 2. User data consists of an ID, first name, last name, password, and an indicator for an administrative or non-administrative user. User IDs must be unique and used to access user data. Given a User object, the program can add, update, or delete the user data in the database. Given a user ID, the program can return the User object. The program can return from the database a list of all user IDs, the first and last names of each, and whether or not each is an administrator. 3. For each stock, one stock symbol and one corresponding description exists. The description is the name of the stock. The symbol is the unique access to stock data. The program can add a stock given a symbol and a description. The program can delete a stock for an existing stock symbol. The program can provide a stock description (name) given an existing stock symbol. 4. The program maintains the relationship between users and stocks. One user can have zero to many stocks, and one stock can have one to many users. Stocks held by at least one user are retained in the database. If a stock is removed from a user's holdings and no other user holds that stock, the stock and its description are removed from the database. If a user is deleted from the system, all stock holdings for the user must be deleted. Users cannot delete a stock, only their stock holdings. 5. Given a user ID, the program can provide a list of stocks held by the user. The program can add or delete a stock holding given a user ID and stock symbol. 6. A utility program should create the database structure and one administrative user entry in the database. This user entry will be used for the initial user log on so that additional users may be added by the application. Subsequent executions should restore the database to its initial state.

Approval Status:	X	Approved
		Rejected
Approved by:	Wilson Davis, Director of IT, AccessFour Software	
Date:	December 11, 2007	
Assigned to:	M. Mick, Programmer	

FIGURE 11-2

DESIGN THE SOLUTION Once you have analyzed the problem and understand the needs, the next step is to design the user interface and required classes. To develop the GUI application for this chapter requires some new classes and an interface, as well as modifications to existing classes. A few existing classes are used without changes. Because most of the GUI application uses techniques already presented, and it uses another class to access the database, the source code for all of the GUI components is provided on the Data Disk.

The application requires that only validated users have access; therefore, before the application can be used, a database must be in place and have at least one valid user. This is accomplished by a utility program, MakeDB.java, which creates the structure and initial data for the database, as indicated by the requirements document. The MakeDB.java program executes only once, when the database initially is created, adding a temporary user ID and password that can be deleted after permanent user data is entered. In order for a working database to be available for subsequent use, the MakeDB.java program is developed first.

Another new class, StockTrackerDB, provides an interface to the database independent of the application using the database. Placing the database access methods in a separate class allows for more than one application to use the database in a consistent fashion. This allows the functionality of the database to be independent of the user interface, as the requirements document indicates. The StockTrackerDB class provides the capability for the GUI program to add, delete, update, and list users, as well as maintain stocks and user stock lists. It is the second class developed in this chapter.

All other code not previously developed is provided on the Data Disk. The first source code provided is STLogon.java, which is provided to create the initial log on window, similar to the LogonFrame class from the previous chapter. The STLogon class allows users to log on to the system using a unique user ID. It also incorporates the main() method from the StockListDemo class, which, therefore, no longer is needed.

The next source code provided on the Data Disk is the stock-tracking application itself, StockTracker.java. This application associates a list of stocks with a given user and presents that list in a GUI format. It allows administrative users access to user maintenance and maintains a drop-down list of stock holdings for the current user. If the user has any existing stock holdings, the first stock symbol appears in the drop-down list box. The stocks are maintained in alphabetic order using all capital letters. If the user has no stocks, the list box is empty. Stocks that are added to the user's holdings do not affect the stock holdings of other users. When deleted from the list, the stock and its description are deleted from the database, but only if no other users hold that particular stock. Whether adding or deleting a stock holding, users can type a stock symbol in the stock text box. If deleting, users may select an existing stock holding from their drop-down list. As indicated earlier, all database interaction is performed through the data access class, StockTrackerDB.

The Data Disk also contains the source code, UserMaintFrame.java, which provides the GUI for adding new users and for updating, deleting, and listing existing user data. This GUI does not display the stocks associated with a user; however, if a user is deleted, all stock holdings for the deleted user are removed from the database, as well. This functionality is available only to administrative users. This GUI provides a series of windows appropriate for the performing function, which is communicated from the main application class, StockTracker. Again, all database interaction is performed through the data access class, StockTrackerDB.

A User class is necessary for this application; however, the User class from the previous chapter is insufficient and requires a number of changes to hold additional information. Therefore, an updated source code file, User.java, incorporating the needed changes is provided on the Data Disk.

Finally, a new interface in the source code file, STAction.java, provides a set of named constant values used by the StockTracker class when requesting behavior from the UserMaintFrame class. As you have seen, interfaces typically are small files and may consist of only constants with no method headers. The STAction interface provides for a consistent use of some constant values and also is provided on the Data Disk.

Designing a Relational Database

Before creating the Java program that initializes the database, it is necessary to design the database in terms of the tables it will contain, as well as the content of each table. As noted earlier, a relational database is comprised of data in tables, grouped in rows and columns. A column represents an individual data element, or field, such as a user ID, first name, or last name. All of the columns represent the logical contents of the table. The rows contain the actual data values for a given record, such as a particular user ID or first name.

In this application, a table is needed to hold information about a user, specifically the user ID, first name, last name, password (an object), and an indication of whether the user is an administrative user. Table 11-2 lists the tables and fields used in the StockTracker database. Because an Access database will be used, the Access data type and size, where appropriate, are listed with each field. Text fields should be large enough to accommodate the largest possible, or allowed, value to be stored. Other fields, such as fields for binary objects, do not require a specified size, because the size is based on the type of data.

Table 11-2 StockTracker Database Tables and Fields

TABLE NAME	FIELD NAME	DATA TYPE	FIELD SIZE
Users	userID	Text	20
	lastName	Text	30
	firstName	Text	30
	pswd	Long Binary	n/a
	admin	Boolean	n/a
Stocks	symbol	Text	8
	name	Text	50
UserStocks	userID	Text	20
	symbol	Text	8

When designing tables for a database, you must consider what data you want to store and how that data relates to a given record. For a given row and column, there exists only a single value, never a set of values. When the condition of having no repeating groups is satisfied, the data is said to be **normalized**. More specifically, such data is said to be in **first normal form**, because additional rules of **normalization** can be applied to database design. Data that repeats for a record typically becomes another table. For example, a user record for the stock-tracking system has one user ID, one first name, and one last name, but may have zero, one, or many stock holdings. If space is reserved for a fixed number of stock holdings per user, when the user has no holdings, that space is wasted. Further, the user could not track more stock holdings than the maximum the record accommodates. A more flexible solution is to put this data in another table and then establish a **relationship**, which is an association between fields (columns) in the two tables. The **cardinality** of a relationship is described as one-to-one, one-to-many, or many-to-many, depending on the number of records in a table that may relate to a given record in another table.

Tip

Relationship Cardinality

The cardinality of a relationship between records in a table is one-to-one only if one record in a given table relates to only one record in a second table; one-to-many if one record relates to multiple records in a second table; and many-to-many if multiple records are related to multiple records in a second table. Many-to-many relationships typically are modeled by a third table.

In order to manipulate the data efficiently and establish relationships between tables, at least one index must be established per table. An **index** is an external data structure built from a field or group of fields and is used to identify and sort records in a table. An index for a table is used as you would use an index in a book; you use a keyword (index) to look up the location of where that data exists. A **primary key** is an index with a unique, non-null value for each record. Only one primary key can exist for a given table. A primary key often is used to prevent duplicate records and to access a given record more efficiently than simple sequential retrieval. A primary key is not required unless it is specified as a foreign key in another table. A **foreign key** is one or more fields in a table that reference the primary key field(s) of another table. It is acceptable for a foreign key to have the same name as the referenced field, because they exist within different tables. Because the fields reference the same information, using the same field name makes this obvious and is a common practice, although it is not required. In the case of the Users table, the userID field is the primary key because it contains a unique value for each user record. The UserStocks table also has a field, userID, which is a foreign key to the Users table.

Tip

Naming Foreign Keys

A foreign key field does not have to be named the same as the primary key it references. It is commonplace to do so, however, not simply because the two fields contain the same data. Using the same name makes the relationship between the tables more obvious.

Each user record may be associated with zero, one, or many stock holdings. It is redundant to maintain a separate stock name for each stock holding. Each stock symbol is associated with only one stock name, regardless of the number of users holding shares of that stock. The Stocks table is created to hold each stock symbol and its associated stock name. Because the stock symbol uniquely identifies a stock, the symbol then is used as the primary key. The relationship of users to stocks is modeled by the UserStocks table, which represents the stock holdings for each user. The purpose of the table is to relate the Users table to the

Stocks table. Therefore, it consists only of foreign keys to the Users and Stocks tables, respectively. It is common to name a table such as this with a name indicative of the relationship. Figure 11-3a illustrates the three tables, their fields, primary keys (in bold), and the relationships between the tables.

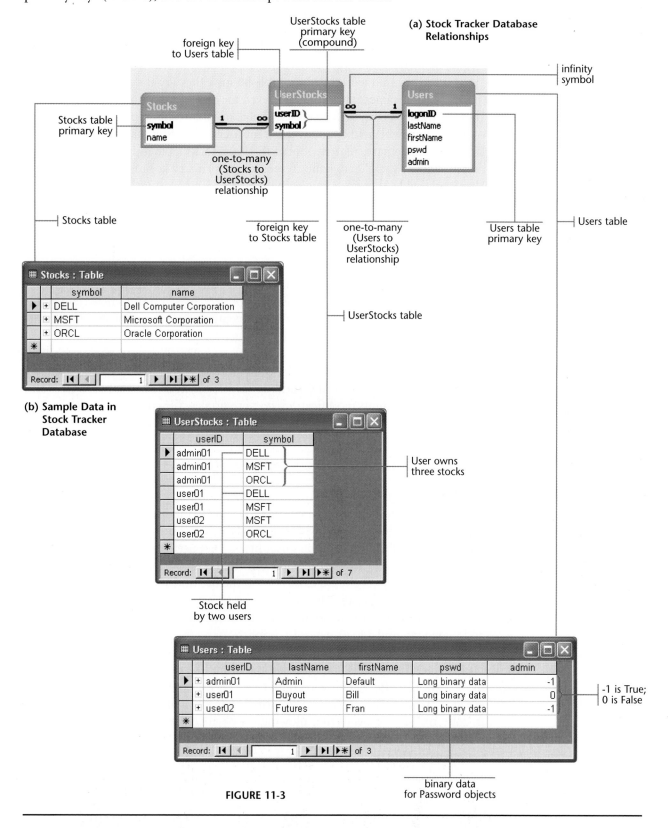

FIGURE 11-3

The lines connecting the tables indicate relationships, where the number 1 and the infinity symbol (∞) represent the cardinality of the relationships, with infinity representing many. Each User record, with a unique userID as the primary key, may have many (including zero or one) stock holdings, so the userID foreign key may appear many times in the UserStocks table; in other words, it is a one-to-many relationship. Each unique stock only has one name; however, one stock symbol may be held by many different Users. Again, this is a one-to-many relationship. A given symbol is unique in the Stocks table, and a given userID is unique in the Users table because they are the primary keys of their respective tables. They each, however, may appear multiple times in the UserStocks table, because a given user may have many different stocks, and a given stock may be held by many different users. The combination of a particular userID and a particular symbol in the UserStocks table must be unique, because these two fields together represent the primary key of this table. The UserStocks table, therefore, models a many-to-many relationship between the Users table and Stocks table.

Figure 11-3b on the previous page displays some sample data in the database. After completion of this chapter, your data should be similar.

PROGRAM IMPLEMENTATION   Once the solution is designed and validated, the next step in the development cycle is to implement the design, as shown in Table 11-1 on page 692. For this project, in addition to new classes, the Activator class and the various PasswordException classes previously created are used. Because these classes require no changes for use in this project, only the class files and not the Java source files are needed. This illustrates the reusability of these classes, which was the intent in their design. The User class needs to be modified significantly to contain additional information. The Password class also could be used without modification, because no new functionality is required; however, for objects to be stored to disk, a minor addition is necessary.

Understanding Persistent Objects

Previously, objects such as Password were used in the Java programs but were not saved to disk. Therefore, when the programs terminated, the objects were destroyed. Because the objects were not saved, the test program in the previous chapter required the addition of a user before that user could log on to use the program. Obviously, this is acceptable only in a test program. In a realistic application, data as objects should exist beyond the lifetime of the application. Achieving this requires the ability to save an object to permanent storage.

Saving an object to nonvolatile storage, such as a floppy disk or hard drive, and making it available for later use implies saving the current state of the object before the program terminates. The **state** of an object is the value of its attributes, or variables, at a given point in time. If there were no concern about saving the state of the object, then you could create a new object each time the program executes, as was done previously. **Persistence** is the ability of an object, including its state, to be saved over time, allowing the object to be restored later. Implementing persistence for an object, however, is different than simply saving some data to a disk file.

Implementing the Serializable Interface

In an earlier chapter, data was saved to a disk file using the Java Input/Output classes from the java.io package; however, this action did not include saving objects. The Input/Output classes are extended with support for encoding an object into a byte stream that subsequently can be stored to disk. They also support the complementary reconstruction of the object from the stream. The process of encoding the state of an object into a stream is called **serialization**. Serialization encodes not only the data in a class, but also other information, which includes the class name and signature. Serialization is used in the process of storing an object to a persistent state and often carries the connotation of persisting to permanent storage, although it need not do so. Restoring a serialized object for use in a program is called **deserialization**. Recall that an object also consists of methods as well as its attributes. While the methods are not saved with each object, the object is marked so programs using a modified definition of the object cannot access a previous version of the object.

Tip

Serialization and Deserialization

Serialization is simply the conversion of an object into a stream. Serializing to a byte stream allows the object to be manipulated as binary data, which can be saved to persistent storage or transmitted across a network. Here is an analogy: think of a brick house as the object. Serialization would be taking the house apart, brick by brick. Transmitting the serialized object across a network would be like sending the bricks in sequence (serially) to a new location. Deserialization would be rebuilding the house, one brick at a time.

For an object to be serialized, it must implement the Serializable interface, which has no methods or fields. An interface with no methods or fields is called a **marker interface**, because it serves to identify the object only semantically; in this case, it is identified as serializable and deserializable. Classes that inherit from a serializable parent also are serializable.

In this application, Password objects are serialized so they can be stored in a database. Consequently, the Password class from the previous chapter must be modified to implement the Serializable interface. Figure 11-4 on the next page displays the modified code for the Password class.

JAVA UPDATE Java 2 v5.0

Serializing Enums
The new class Enum implements java.io.Serializable—therefore, Enum objects may be serialized. However, Enum constants are serialized in a different manner than typical serializable or externalizable objects. While the differences may be ignored in many cases, they may affect customization of the serialization process.

When an object uses the default serialization mechanism, the class of the object, the class signature, and the values of all non-transient and non-static fields are written to the persistent storage. Also, each serializable class is uniquely identified by a serialVersionUID field, either declared in the class or computed from the class definition by the Java virtual machine. Of course, serialization only writes out fields of objects that implement the java.io.Serializable interface.

For Enum objects, only the name is serialized, not the field values of the constant. Also, the serialization process for Enum constants cannot be customized; any class-specific writeObject and writeReplace methods defined by Enum types are ignored during serialization. Finally, for Enums, any serialVersionUID field declaration is ignored as all Enum types have a fixed serialVersionUID of 0L.

```
 1   /*
 2         Chapter 11: The Password Class
 3         Programmer:  Michael Mick
 4         Date:        December 12, 2007
 5         Filename:    Password.java
 6         Purpose:     To provide a reusable Password class which uses PasswordException
 7   */
 8
 9   import java.util.*;
10   import java.io.*;
11
12   public class Password implements Serializable
13   {
14       final static int MIN_SIZE = 6;
15       final static int MAX_SIZE = 15;
16           static int maxHistory = 4;
17           static int expiresNotifyLimit = 3;
18
19       private int maxUses = 120;
20       private int remainingUses = maxUses;
21       private boolean autoExpires = true;
22       private boolean expired = false;
23
24       private ArrayList pswdHistory;
25
26
27       // Constructors for objects of class Password
28       public Password(String newPassword) throws PasswordException
29       {
30           pswdHistory = new ArrayList(maxHistory);
31           set(newPassword);
32       }
```

FIGURE 11-4

In addition to Password, other classes from the previous chapter also are needed, as mentioned earlier. The following steps obtain the needed files and then open the existing Password source code file in TextPad.

To Open an Existing Java Program in TextPad

1. Insert the Data Disk in drive A.

2. Copy the files listed in Table 11-3 from the location where you saved or compiled them in the previous chapter (the Chapter10 folder or the location specified by your instructor) to the Chapter11 folder on your Data Disk or a location specified by your instructor.

3. Start TextPad. If necessary, click Line Numbers on the View menu to display line numbers.

4. Open the file, Password.java, from the Chapter11 folder or the location specified by your instructor.

   The file, Password.java, on the Data Disk in drive A is opened in TextPad (Figure 11-5).

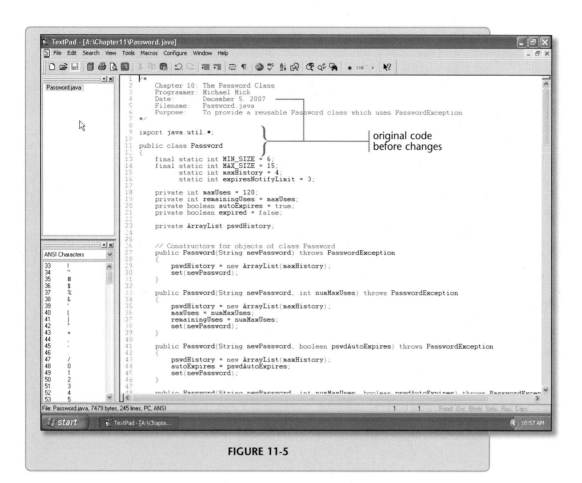

FIGURE 11-5

Table 11-3 Files Needed from Chapter 10

FILE TYPE	FILE NAME
class	Activator.class
	PasswordException.class
	PasswordExpiredException.class
	PasswordInternalException.class
	PasswordInvalidException.class
	PasswordInvalidFormatException.class
	PasswordSizeException.class
	PasswordUsedException.class
Java	Password.java

The Password class requires two changes to the source code, as shown in Figure 11-4 on page 700. Because Serializable is an interface, the class definition must be modified to implement it. In order for the compiler to locate the interface definition, however, Password.java must import the java.io package. The following steps implement the Serializable interface in the Password class.

To Implement the Serializable Interface

1. Insert line 10 as shown in Figure 11-4 on page 700. In the comments, insert your own name as programmer, if necessary, and enter the current date.

    TextPad displays the beginning lines of code for the Password class, including the initial comments and the import statements, in the coding window (Figure 11-6).

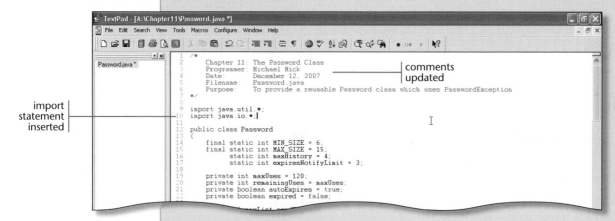

FIGURE 11-6

2. Modify the class header line as shown on line 12 in Figure 11-4. Save and compile the changes.

    TextPad displays the code for the Password class header which now implements the Serializable interface (Figure 11-7).

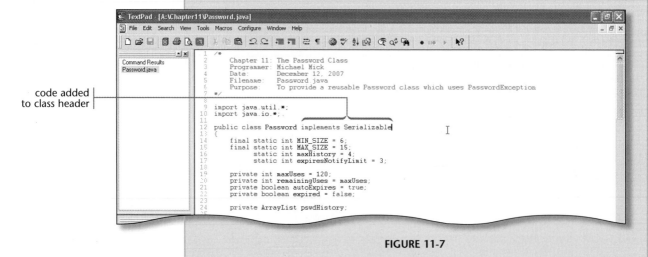

FIGURE 11-7

The changes to the Password class now are complete, and objects created from this class can be serialized and made persistent. Because this project will use a Microsoft Access database for persistence, prior to creating the database tables, the database itself must be created and identified as a data source accessible through a special software driver.

Registering an ODBC Data Source Name

Access comes with special driver software called **ODBC** (Microsoft's Open Database Connectivity) that allows programs to make method calls, similar to the JDBC API. The ODBC driver is necessary in order to interact with the DBMS software, referred to as the **database engine**, for a Microsoft Access database. At one time, this was standard for database access, and all major database vendors also had ODBC drivers for their products.

To use ODBC to interact with a database, the database must be registered as an ODBC data source name. A **data source name** is the name used instead of the actual database name when establishing a connection to the database. Once an ODBC data source name is created, it can be registered with an existing database, or a new database with no tables can be created and simultaneously registered with the data source name. Registering a database with ODBC is done through the Control Panel in Windows and is independent of Java, your Java programs, and the JDBC API.

The following steps register a new ODBC data source name.

To Register an ODBC Data Source Name

1. Click the Start button on the Windows taskbar and then point to Control Panel on the Start menu.

   Windows displays the Start menu and highlights Control Panel on the Start menu (Figure 11-8). Your menu options may differ.

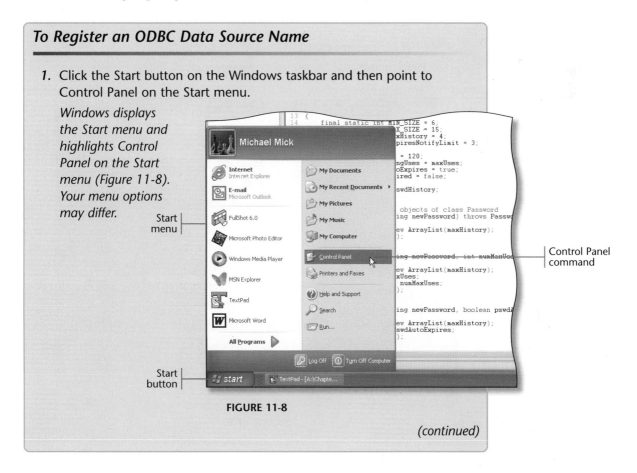

FIGURE 11-8

(continued)

2. Click Control Panel. If necessary, click Switch to Category View in the Control Panel area.

The Control Panel window opens (Figure 11-9).

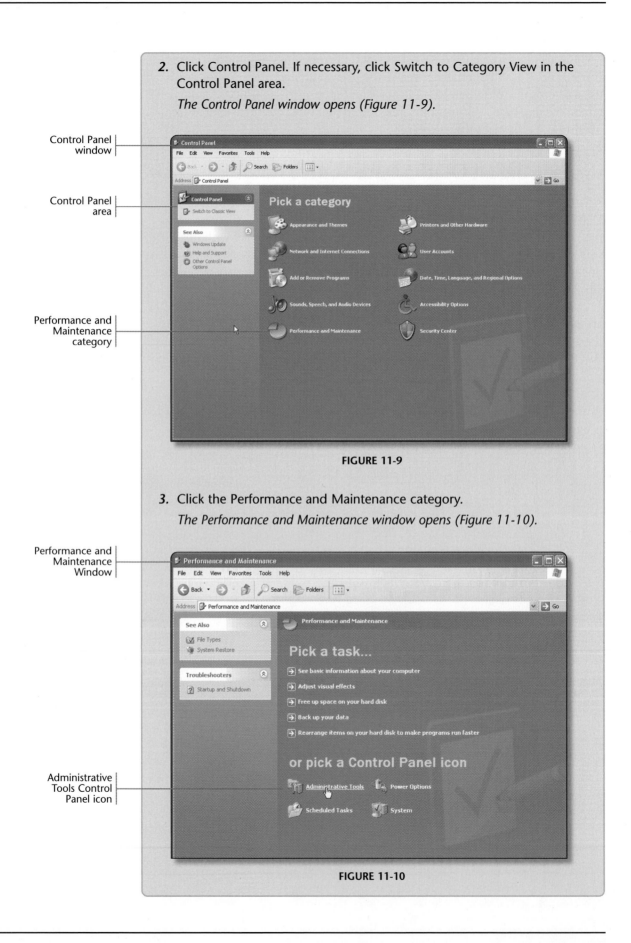

Control Panel window

Control Panel area

Performance and Maintenance category

FIGURE 11-9

3. Click the Performance and Maintenance category.

The Performance and Maintenance window opens (Figure 11-10).

Performance and Maintenance Window

Administrative Tools Control Panel icon

FIGURE 11-10

4. Click the Administrative Tools Control Panel icon.

The Administrative Tools window opens, and the Performance and Maintenance window is closed (Figure 11-11). Your window may not display all of the same icons, depending on your system configuration.

Administrative Tools window

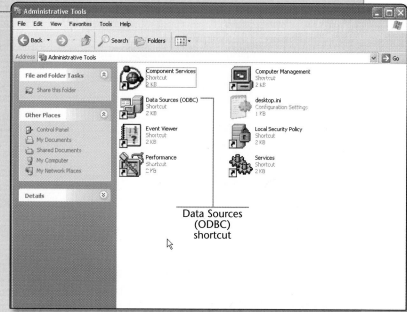

Data Sources (ODBC) shortcut

FIGURE 11-11

5. Double-click the Data Sources (ODBC) shortcut. When the ODBC Data Source Administrator dialog box is displayed, if necessary, click the System DSN tab.

The ODBC Data Source Administrator dialog box displays ODBC data sources available to all users on this machine (Figure 11-12). Your list of ODBC System data sources may vary.

System DSN tab

ODBC System data sources

ODBC Data Source Administrator dialog box

Add button

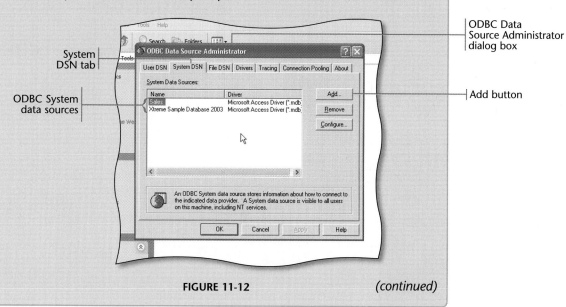

FIGURE 11-12   *(continued)*

6. Click the Add button. When the Create New Data Source dialog box is displayed, if necessary, scroll down and then click Microsoft Access Driver (*.mdb) to select it.

The Create New Data Source dialog box displays available ODBC drivers as shown in Figure 11-13.

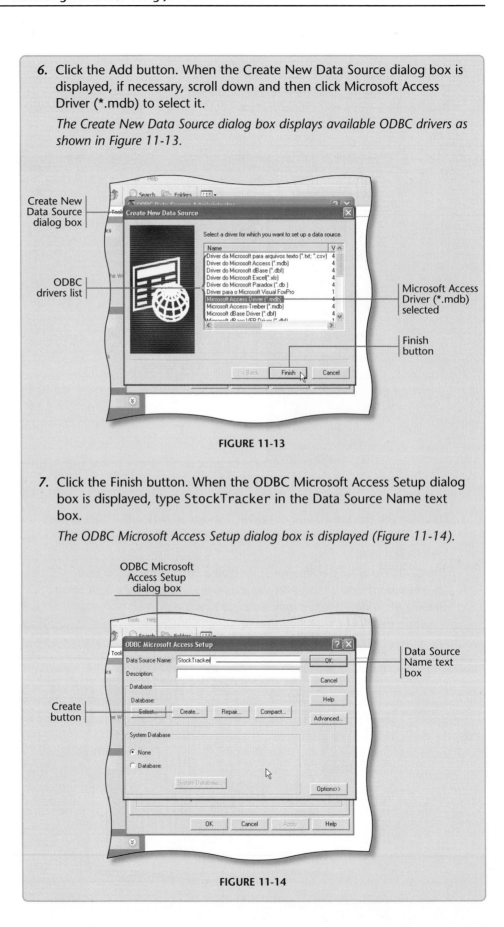

FIGURE 11-13

7. Click the Finish button. When the ODBC Microsoft Access Setup dialog box is displayed, type StockTracker in the Data Source Name text box.

The ODBC Microsoft Access Setup dialog box is displayed (Figure 11-14).

FIGURE 11-14

8. Click the Create button. When the New Database dialog box is displayed, select a: (or a location indicated by your instructor) in the Drives list. Double-click Chapter11 (or a location indicated by your instructor) in the Directories: list box. Type StockTracker.mdb in the Database Name text box.

   The New Database dialog box displays the new database name in the Database Name text box (Figure 11-15).

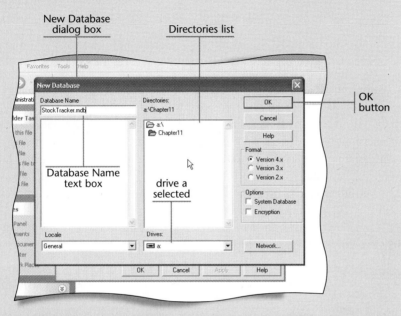

FIGURE 11-15

9. Click the OK button. When the ODBC Microsoft Access Setup message box is displayed, click OK. Click the OK button in the ODBC Microsoft Access Setup dialog box.

   The database now is accessible through the ODBC data source name, StockTracker (Figure 11-16).

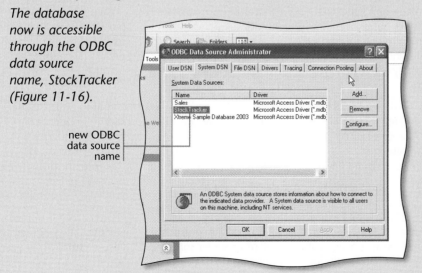

FIGURE 11-16

(continued)

> ***10.*** Click the OK button in the ODBC Data Source Administrator dialog box. Click the Close button on the Administrative Tools window title bar.
>
> *The ODBC data source name is registered and the ODBC data source is available for use.*

Once an ODBC data source exists, a connection to the database may be established. This connection is made within a Java program by using JDBC™.

Connecting to a Database Using JDBC™

A major benefit of using JDBC™ is **interoperability**, which means the underlying database used in an application can change with essentially no change to the application. Using the JDBC™ API to access a database keeps the application isolated from the peculiarities of a specific DBMS, as long as an appropriate driver is used. A **JDBC™ driver** is software for a specific DBMS and effectively translates between the functionality of the JDBC™ API and the corresponding commands of the DBMS. The application program uses the JDBC™ API, keeping the Java code consistent regardless of the DBMS used; JDBC™, in turn, communicates to the DBMS through the specific JDBC™ driver. Table 11-4 lists the four types of JDBC™ drivers.

Table 11-4   JDBC™ Driver Types

TYPE	NAME	DESCRIPTION	PROS	CONS
Type 1	JDBC-ODBC Bridge	Calls go through Bridge, then to driver, then to native database interface	Access to many databases through ODBC drivers	Performance degraded; ODBC, ODBC driver needed for specific database on local (client) machine
Type 2	Native-API/ partly Java	Variation on JDBC-ODBC bridge, but converts JDBC calls into database-specific calls and so communicates directly with database server	Better performance than Bridge	Requires binary code (vendor database library) on client machine; lower performance than Types 3 and 4
Type 3	net-protocol/ all-Java	Three-tiered; translates calls into DBMS-independent net protocol, then translated to DBMS protocol by middleware server	Can handle multiple Java clients connecting to multiple databases; supports advanced features, such as logging, auditing, caching, and load-balancing; in general, the most flexible solution	Requires database-specific coding in middle tier; traversing query result sets may take longer due to path through backend server
Type 4	Native protocol/ all Java	Similar to Type 2 but 100% Java; converts JDBC calls into native calls for database	Performance; no special client or server software needed; drivers can be downloaded dynamically	Needs different driver for each database

Loading a JDBC™ Database Driver

To use a specific database with JDBC™ requires having the appropriate driver available. The driver typically is provided by the database vendor. Before vendors began providing JDBC™ drivers for their databases, the availability of ODBC drivers was leveraged by Java with the introduction of the JDBC-ODBC Bridge. The **JDBC-ODBC Bridge** is a JDBC™ driver that makes calls to the ODBC driver for access to the database engine. This was the first type of driver available for general use and is provided with JDBC™.

As indicated earlier, a utility program needs to be created first in order to create the database structure and initial data for the database. Figure 11-17 displays the code for the utility program, MakeDB.java.

```java
1  /*
2      Chapter 11: The MakeDB Class
3      Programmer: Michael Mick
4      Date:       December 12, 2007
5      Filename:   MakeDB.java
6      Purpose:    To build an initial database for the StockTracker application
7  */
8
9  import java.sql.*;
10 import java.io.*;
11
12 public class MakeDB
13 {
14     public static void main(String[] args) throws Exception
15     {
16         Class.forName("sun.jdbc.odbc.JdbcOdbcDriver");
17
18         String url = "jdbc:odbc:StockTracker";
19
20         Connection con = DriverManager.getConnection(url);
21         Statement stmt = con.createStatement();
22
23         // The following code deletes each index and table, if they exist.
24         // If they do not exist, a message is displayed and execution continues.
25         System.out.println("Dropping indexes & tables ...");
26
27         try
28         {
29             stmt.executeUpdate("DROP INDEX PK_UserStocks ON UserStocks");
30
31         }
32         catch (Exception e)
33         {
34             System.out.println("Could not drop primary key on UserStocks table: "
35                             + e.getMessage());
36         }
37
38         try
39         {
40             stmt.executeUpdate("DROP TABLE UserStocks");
41         }
42         catch (Exception e)
43         {
44             System.out.println("Could not drop UserStocks table: "
45                             + e.getMessage());
46         }
```

FIGURE 11-17

(continued)

```
47
48          try
49          {
50              stmt.executeUpdate("DROP TABLE Users");
51          }
52          catch (Exception e)
53          {
54              System.out.println("Could not drop Users table: "
55                              + e.getMessage());
56          }
57
58          try
59          {
60              stmt.executeUpdate("DROP TABLE Stocks");
61          }
62          catch (Exception e)
63          {
64              System.out.println("Could not drop Stocks table: "
65                              + e.getMessage());
66          }
67
68          ////////// Create the database tables /////////////
69          System.out.println("\nCreating tables ............");
70
71          // Create Stocks table with primary key index
72          try
73          {
74              System.out.println("Creating Stocks table with primary key index...");
75              stmt.executeUpdate("CREATE TABLE Stocks ("
76                              +"symbol TEXT(8) NOT NULL "
77                              +"CONSTRAINT PK_Stocks PRIMARY KEY, "
78                              +"name TEXT(50)"
79                              +")");
80          }
81          catch (Exception e)
82          {
83              System.out.println("Exception creating Stocks table: "
84                              + e.getMessage());
85          }
86
87          // Create Users table with primary key index
88          try
89          {
90              System.out.println("Creating Users table with primary key index...");
91              stmt.executeUpdate("CREATE TABLE Users ("
92                              +"userID TEXT(20) NOT NULL "
93                              +"CONSTRAINT PK_Users PRIMARY KEY, "
94                              +"lastName TEXT(30) NOT NULL, "
95                              +"firstName TEXT(30) NOT NULL, "
96                              +"pswd LONGBINARY, "
97                              +"admin BIT"
98                              +")");
99          }
100         catch (Exception e)
101         {
102             System.out.println("Exception creating Users table: "
103                             + e.getMessage());
104         }
105
106         // Create UserStocks table with foreign keys to Users and Stocks tables
107         try
108         {
109             System.out.println("Creating UserStocks table ...");
110             stmt.executeUpdate("CREATE TABLE UserStocks ("
111                             +"userID TEXT(20) "
112                             +"CONSTRAINT FK1_UserStocks REFERENCES Users (userID), "
113                             +"symbol TEXT(8), "
114                             +"CONSTRAINT FK2_UserStocks FOREIGN KEY (symbol) "
115                             +"REFERENCES Stocks (symbol))");
```

FIGURE 11-17

```
116          }
117          catch (Exception e)
118          {
119              System.out.println("Exception creating UserStocks table: "
120                              + e.getMessage());
121          }
122
123          // Create UserStocks table primary key index
124          try
125          {
126              System.out.println("Creating UserStocks table primary key index...");
127              stmt.executeUpdate("CREATE UNIQUE INDEX PK_UserStocks "
128                              +"ON UserStocks (userID, symbol) "
129                              +"WITH PRIMARY DISALLOW NULL");
130          }
131          catch (Exception e)
132          {
133              System.out.println("Exception creating UserStocks index: "
134                              + e.getMessage());
135          }
136
137
138          // Create one administrative user with password as initial data
139          String userID = "admin01";
140          String firstName = "Default";
141          String lastName = "Admin";
142          String initialPswd = "admin01";
143          Password pswd = new Password(initialPswd);
144          boolean admin = true;
145
146          PreparedStatement pStmt =
147                      con.prepareStatement("INSERT INTO Users VALUES (?,?,?,?,?)");
148          try
149          {
150              pStmt.setString(1, userID);
151              pStmt.setString(2, lastName);
152              pStmt.setString(3, firstName);
153              pStmt.setBytes(4, serializeObj(pswd));
154              pStmt.setBoolean(5, admin);
155              pStmt.executeUpdate();
156          }
157          catch (Exception e)
158          {
159              System.out.println("Exception inserting user: "
160                              + e.getMessage());
161          }
162
163          pStmt.close();
164
165          // Read and display all User data in the database.
166          ResultSet rs = stmt.executeQuery("SELECT * FROM Users");
167
168          System.out.println("Database created.\n");
169          System.out.println("Displaying data from database...\n");
170          System.out.println("Users table contains:");
171
172          Password pswdFromDB;
173          byte[] buf = null;
174
175          while(rs.next())
176          {
177              System.out.println("Logon ID        = "
178                              + rs.getString("userID"));
179              System.out.println("First name      = "
180                              + rs.getString("firstName"));
181              System.out.println("Last name       = "+rs.getString("lastName"));
182              System.out.println("Administrative  = "+rs.getBoolean("admin"));
183              System.out.println("Initial password = "+initialPswd);
184
```

FIGURE 11-17

(continued)

```
185              // Do NOT use with JDK 1.2.2 using JDBC-ODBC Bridge as
186              // SQL NULL data value is not handled correctly.
187                 buf = rs.getBytes("pswd");
188                 if (buf != null)
189                 {
190                     System.out.println("Password Object   = "
191                              + (pswdFromDB=(Password)deserializeObj(buf)));
192                     System.out.println("  AutoExpires     = "+ pswdFromDB.getAutoExpires());
193                     System.out.println("  Expiring now    = "+ pswdFromDB.isExpiring());
194                     System.out.println("  Remaining uses = "
195                              + pswdFromDB.getRemainingUses()+"\n");
196                 }
197                 else
198                     System.out.println("Password Object  = NULL!");
199             }
200
201          rs = stmt.executeQuery("SELECT * FROM Stocks");
202          if(!rs.next())
203              System.out.println("Stocks table contains no records.");
204          else
205              System.out.println("Stocks table still contains records!");
206
207          rs = stmt.executeQuery("SELECT * FROM UserStocks");
208          if(!rs.next())
209              System.out.println("UserStocks table contains no records.");
210          else
211              System.out.println("UserStocks table still contains records!");
212
213          stmt.close(); // closing Statement also closes ResultSet
214
215      } // end of main()
216
217      // Method to write object to byte array and then insert into prepared statement
218      public static byte[] serializeObj(Object obj)
219                              throws IOException
220      {
221          ByteArrayOutputStream baOStream = new ByteArrayOutputStream();
222          ObjectOutputStream objOStream = new ObjectOutputStream(baOStream);
223
224          objOStream.writeObject(obj); // object must be Serializable
225          objOStream.flush();
226          objOStream.close();
227          return baOStream.toByteArray(); // returns stream as byte array
228      }
229
230      // Method to read bytes from result set into a byte array and then
231      // create an input stream and read the data into an object
232      public static Object deserializeObj(byte[] buf)
233                              throws IOException, ClassNotFoundException
234      {
235          Object obj = null;
236
237          if (buf != null)
238          {
239            ObjectInputStream objIStream =
240              new ObjectInputStream(new ByteArrayInputStream(buf));
241
242            obj = objIStream.readObject(); // throws IOException, ClassNotFoundException
243          }
244          return obj;
245      }
246  } // end of class
```

FIGURE 11-17

The utility program must be executed before using the database for the first time. It also may be executed to reinitialize the database to its beginning state. Each time the program runs, it deletes and rebuilds all tables in the database and establishes the original record as the only data contents.

The following steps open a new Java program source file.

To Open a New Java Program in TextPad

1. With the Data Disk in drive A, click the New Document button on the Standard toolbar.

2. Click File on the menu bar and then click Save As on the File menu. When the Save As dialog box is displayed, click the Save in box arrow and then click 3½ Floppy (A:) in the Save in list.

3. Double-click the Chapter11 folder or the location specified by your instructor.

4. Type MakeDB in the File name text box. Click the Save as type box arrow and then click Java (*.java) in the Save as type list. Click the Save button in the Save As dialog box.

5. Enter lines 1 through 15 as shown in Figure 11-17 on page 709. In the comments, insert your own name as programmer and enter the current date.

TextPad displays the code for the initial comments, import statements, class header, and main() method header (Figure 11-18). The import statement for the java.sql package provides the framework for installing database drivers as well as accessing and processing data in a database. The main() method uses the throws Exception clause to claim any uncaught exceptions.

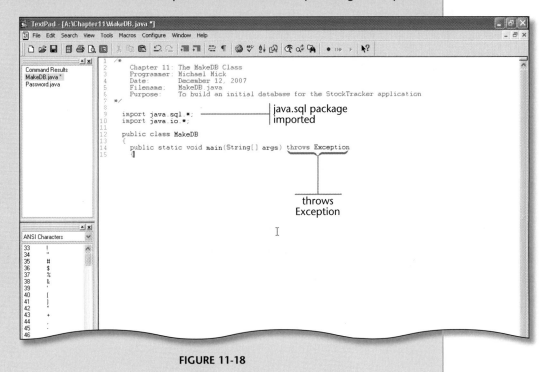

FIGURE 11-18

Before a Java program can connect to a database using the JDBC™ API, the appropriate JDBC™ driver must be loaded. While the driver must be appropriate for the type of database, and in some cases to the specific database being used, all drivers can be loaded in the same fashion. In fact, more than one driver can be loaded by a program. The **forName()** method in line 16 is used to load a JDBC™ driver. This is a static method in the class, Class, and is used to return a Class object associated with the given string name. **Class** objects represent instances of classes (and interfaces) running in a Java application. They are constructed automatically by the JVM and have no public constructor. A call to Class.forName("X") causes the class, X, to be loaded and initialized. Using this method call with a database driver loads and initializes the driver class.

Because ODBC is used to connect to a Microsoft Access database, the JDBC-ODBC Bridge driver must be loaded. The following step enters code to load the JDBC-ODBC Bridge driver.

To Load a JDBC™ Database Driver

1. Enter line 16 as shown in Figure 11-17 on page 709.

The Class.forName() method is entered (Figure 11-19). This class method loads and initializes the JDBC-ODBC driver.

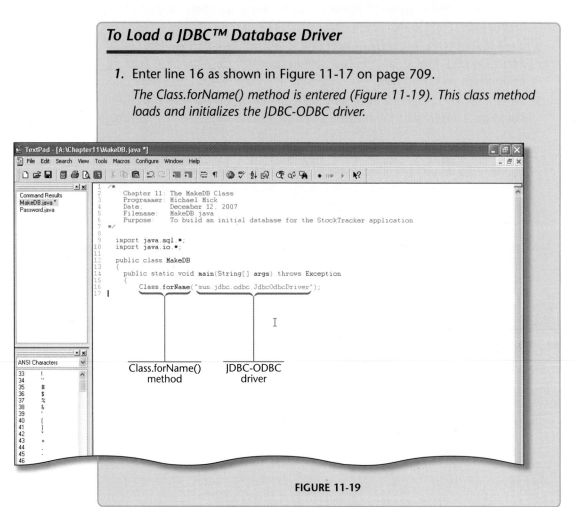

FIGURE 11-19

Only a single driver is needed to access an ODBC data source, even if multiple databases are to be accessed via ODBC.

Establishing a JDBC™ Connection

Once an appropriate driver is loaded, a connection must be established to the database. Obtaining a **connection** locates a specific database and establishes a **database session**, which is the communication pathway between the user program and the database. A connection lasts from when the user program connects to the database until the program disconnects or terminates. Obtaining a connection is the database equivalent of opening a file, and it is within the context of a connection that SQL statements are executed and results are returned. To obtain a connection, line 20 calls **getConnection()**, passing a case-sensitive parameter. The parameter is an address for the database in the form jdbc:subprotocol:subname, where the subprotocol is odbc and the subname is the data source name. Overloaded forms of this method provide additional parameters, such as a user name and password, if required by the database. The getConnection() method is a static method of the **DriverManager** class, which provides the basic services for managing a set of JDBC™ drivers. When this method is called, the DriverManager attempts to locate a suitable driver from the set of registered JDBC drivers and then establish a connection to the database. If a database access error occurs, an SQL exception is thrown. This may happen if the data source name or the database to which it refers does not exist, which is why they were established first. If successful, the method returns a Connection object. A **Connection object** models a database connection, and its **createStatement()** method is used to create a Statement object, as is done in line 21. A **Statement object** typically is used for executing static SQL statements and, once created, can be used to execute different statements until the Statement object is closed. A **static SQL statement** is a statement in which the parameters do not change as the program executes. Table 11-5 on the next page lists the SQL statements used in this chapter. By convention, the SQL statement keywords are listed in capital letters. Optional portions are enclosed within square brackets ([]) and repeating patterns are indicated by ellipses (…).

Table 11-5   SQL Statements

STATEMENT	SYNTAX	ACTION
DROP	DROP INDEX indexName ON tableName	Delete index, indexName, on table, tableName
	DROP TABLE tableName	Delete table, tableName, from database, deleting all data in table
CREATE	CREATE TABLE tableName (fieldName1 data Type Specification[, fieldName2 data Type Specification, …])	Create new table in database; constraints may be specified for each field after data type
	CREATE [UNIQUE] INDEX indexName ON tableName (field1[, field2, …])	Create new index for table; UNIQUE may be omitted if duplicate values allowed
INSERT INTO	INSERT INTO tableName VALUES (field1 value[, field2 value, …])	Insert full record into database; values or NULL must be present in order fields were created
UPDATE	UPDATE tableName SET column1 = field1 newValue[, column2 = field2 newValue, …] WHERE searchCondition	Update fields listed with new values given for records matching search condition
DELETE	DELETE FROM tableName WHERE searchCondition	Delete from table records matching search condition
SELECT	SELECT field1[, field2, …] FROM tableName WHERE searchCondition ORDER BY field1[, field2, …] [DESC]	Query database and return values for selected fields from records matching search condition sorted by field list; ascending is default, descending optional

The following step enters code to establish a JDBC™ Connection and create a Statement object.

To Establish a JDBC™ Connection

1. Enter lines 17 through 22 as shown in Figure 11-17 on page 709.

Lines 17 through 22 establish a database connection and create a Statement object for executing SQL statements (Figure 11-20).

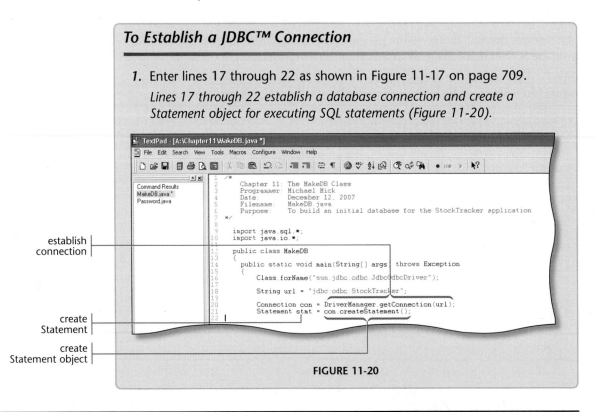

FIGURE 11-20

Once a Statement object is created, SQL statements to update or query the database may be passed through JDBC™ to the database.

Dropping Tables and Indexes in a Database

Although many DBMS products support a wide range of features, most actions are of two types: a query or an update. A **query** returns a set of data results based on the parameters of the query. An **update** is used to add, modify, or delete data from the database. A Statement object has a number of methods for executing SQL statements. The method commonly used to perform updates is **executeUpdate()**, which executes SQL statements, such as INSERT, UPDATE, DELETE, or an SQL statement which returns no value.

Executing the utility program for the first time creates the needed tables along with their respective indexes. Subsequent executions of the utility program restore the database to its initial state; however, because the tables and indexes already exist, they cannot be created again until they are deleted from the database. Deleting the indexes and tables before recreating them must happen when the indexes and tables exist. For the initial program execution, however, deleting nonexistent indexes and tables generates a series of exceptions. These exceptions are expected, and catching them allows execution to continue. The deletion of an index or a table is called a **drop** and is done with the SQL DROP statement.

An index can be dropped explicitly from its table and usually is done when the index no longer is needed for searching or sorting but the table is to remain. An index also is dropped implicitly when the table is dropped. The order in which tables are dropped is important. A table cannot be dropped if it contains any fields referenced as foreign keys in other tables. The table containing the foreign key must be dropped first. Recall that the UserStocks table represents a many-to-many relationship between the Users and Stocks tables. It contains foreign keys for each of these tables, and so it must be dropped before the Users and Stocks tables are dropped. The steps on the next page enter code to drop the StockTracker database tables and their respective indexes.

To Drop Indexes and Tables in a Database

1. Enter lines 23 through 37 as shown in Figure 11-17 on page 709.

The SQL statement, DROP INDEX, is used to drop the single index on the UserStocks table (Figure 11-21). Even though the index in this case is comprised of two fields, representing two foreign keys, it still is only one index.

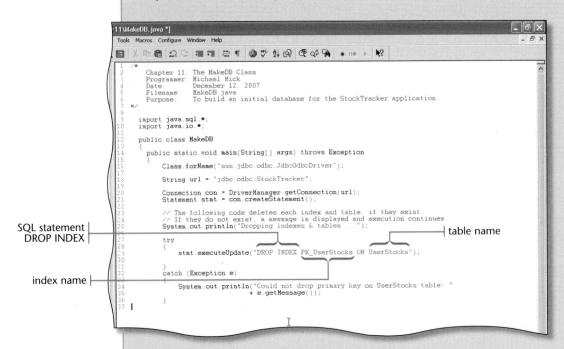

FIGURE 11-21

2. Enter lines 38 through 47 as shown in Figure 11-17.

The SQL statement, DROP TABLE, is used to drop the UserStocks table (Figure 11-22). Dropping the table would drop the index implicitly, if it had not been dropped already.

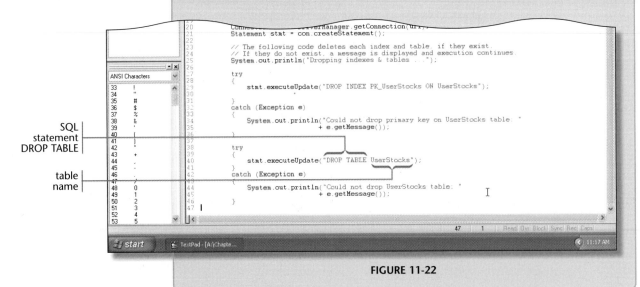

FIGURE 11-22

> **3.** Enter lines 48 through 67 as shown in Figure 11-17 on page 710.
>
> *The Users and Stocks tables are dropped, and their respective indexes are dropped implicitly (Figure 11-23). Because the UserStocks table was dropped first, there are no foreign keys referencing fields in either of these two tables.*

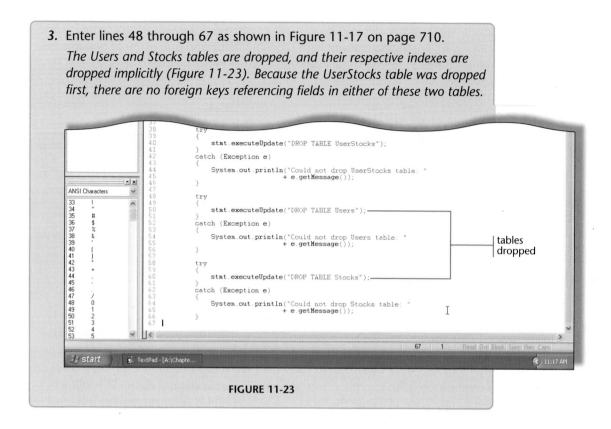

```
37
38    try
39    {
40        stmt.executeUpdate("DROP TABLE UserStocks");
41    }
42    catch (Exception e)
43    {
44        System.out.println("Could not drop UserStocks table. "
45                            + e.getMessage());
46    }
47
48    try
49    {
50        stmt.executeUpdate("DROP TABLE Users");
51    }
52    catch (Exception e)
53    {
54        System.out.println("Could not drop Users table. "
55                            + e.getMessage());
56    }
57
58    try
59    {
60        stmt.executeUpdate("DROP TABLE Stocks");
61    }
62    catch (Exception e)
63    {
64        System.out.println("Could not drop Stocks table. "
65                            + e.getMessage());
66    }
67
```

tables dropped

FIGURE 11-23

Once it is certain that the tables and indexes are dropped, it is safe to create them. You cannot create a table or an index that already exists, which is why they had to be dropped first.

Creating Tables, Indexes, and Keys

When creating tables, the order can be important; the relationships between the tables must be considered. Because the UserStocks table is comprised of fields that are foreign keys to the Users and Stocks tables, these two tables must be created before the UserStocks table.

CREATE TABLE is the SQL statement to create a new table. The table name is defined and then the fields in the table are listed along with their data types, lengths, if appropriate, and any constraints. A **constraint** is a rule that restricts the data value entered in a column. Constraints can be of two types, integrity or value. An **integrity constraint** is used to identify a primary or a foreign key. A **value constraint** is used to specify the allowable value of data in a column, such as a data range, a specific data value, or whether the data value must be unique or not null. If a field is marked as NOT NULL, then a value is required; specifically, it must contain some data. Constraints can be applied at one of two levels. A **table constraint** restricts the field value with respect to all other values in the table. For example, a primary key must have a unique value for each record, and a primary key constraint is a table constraint. A **column constraint** (also known as a field-level constraint) limits the value placed in a specific column, regardless of values in other records. A constraint can be named by using the **CONSTRAINT** keyword, and the given name must be unique within the entire database, not just the table. Typically, primary and foreign key constraints are given names. Such names typically use an identifier, such as PK for primary key and FK for foreign key, along with the table name and one or more possible field names. Table 11-6 lists some examples of constraints and their respective SQL keywords.

Table 11-6 SQL Constraints

TYPE	LEVEL	EXAMPLE SQL KEYWORDS
Integrity	Table	PRIMARY KEY
Integrity	Column	FOREIGN KEY
Value	Table	UNIQUE
Value	Column	NOT NULL

Lines 68 through 104, as shown in Figure 11-17 on page 710, create the Stocks and Users tables. Individual field names, types, sizes, and named constraints are listed within field declarations, which are separated by commas. The tables are created by calling the executeUpdate() method, each within a separate try block, allowing execution to continue even if any one table creation throws an exception. Such an exception would occur if a table already exists. The following steps enter code to create the Stocks and Users tables and primary key indexes.

To Create Tables with Primary Keys

1. Enter lines 68 through 86 as shown in Figure 11-17.

The SQL statement, CREATE TABLE, is used to create the Stocks table (Figure 11-24). Following the table name is a comma-delimited list of fields, types, sizes, and constraints within parentheses. The field, symbol, of type TEXT with a maximum length of 8, has a value constraint of NOT NULL, meaning it cannot have a null, or empty, value. It also is used as the primary key. The field, name, is of type TEXT with a maximum length of 50.

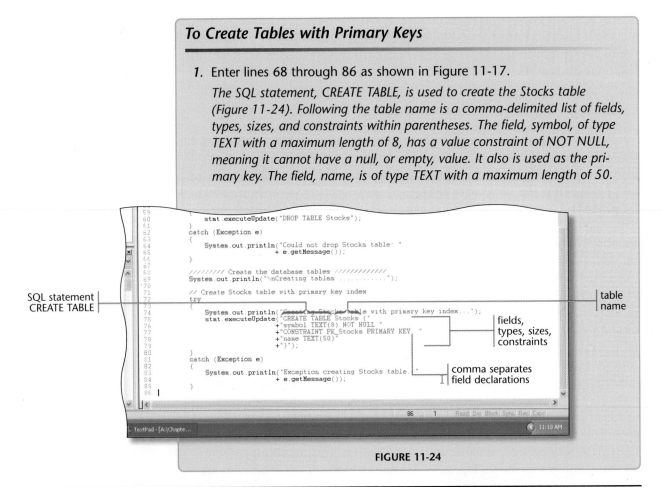

FIGURE 11-24

2. Enter lines 87 through 105 as shown in Figure 11-17 on page 710.

The Users table is created with five fields (Figure 11-25). The first three fields are of type TEXT, with the field, userID, used as the primary key. The other field types used, LONGBINARY and BIT, have implicit field lengths.

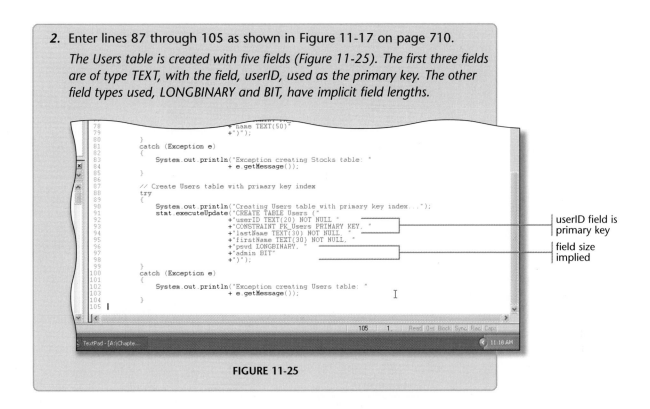

FIGURE 11-25

The data type, **LONGBINARY**, is used to store large binary objects and will be used to store Password objects in this database. The number of bytes is not specified, but with Access, it has a maximum size of 2.14 gigabytes. Microsoft Access synonyms for this data type are IMAGE, GENERAL, and OLEOBJECT. In ANSI SQL, this also is referred to as a binary large object, or BLOB. The data type, **BIT**, is a Boolean, or logical, type that results in a true or false value. A true value is equal to -1 and a false value is equal to 0. In Microsoft Access, this data type uses one byte for storage and has synonyms of YESNO, LOGICAL, and LOGICAL1.

As indicated earlier, the UserStocks table represents a many-to-many relationship between the Users table and the Stocks table. It consists of two fields: userID, which is a foreign key to the Users table, and symbol, which is a foreign key to the Stocks table. As such, the creation of this table had to be placed after the creation of the previous two tables. This table will be created without designating a primary key, as the primary key index will be created later. Creating a foreign key requires creating a reference in the current table to the table and primary key field name(s) in the related table. This is done with the **REFERENCES** keyword.

The step on the next page enters code to create the UserStocks table with foreign keys to the Users and Stocks tables.

To Create Tables with Foreign Keys

1. Enter lines 106 through 122 as shown in Figure 11-17 on pages 710 and 711.

   The UserStocks table is created containing two fields, each of which is a foreign key to another table (Figure 11-26). The field, userID, is a foreign key to the Users table field, also named userID, and the field, symbol, is a foreign key to the Stocks table field, also named symbol.

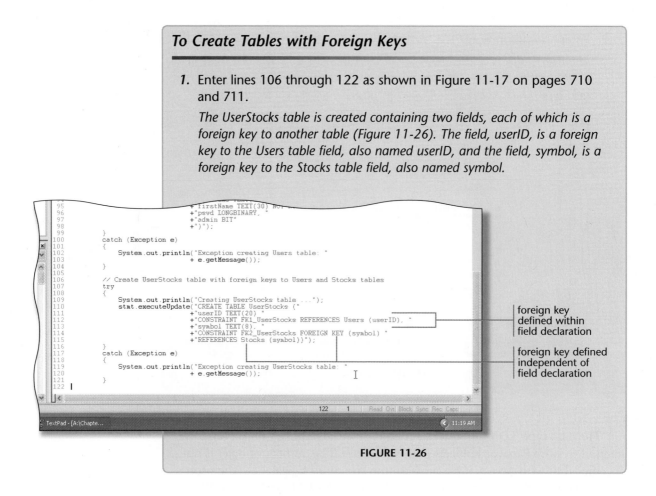

FIGURE 11-26

The UserStocks table was created containing foreign keys to other tables. Two different approaches are illustrated. Lines 111 and 112 define a constraint within the userID field declaration. Line 113 defines the field, symbol, and then lines 114 and 115 define a constraint independent of the field definition. These two approaches allow flexibility in defining individual field constraints. Additionally, the second approach allows primary and foreign key constraints consisting of multiple fields to be defined after all fields are declared.

UserStocks was not created with a primary key. Although often used, a primary key is not required for all tables. As you might expect, a new index can be created on an existing table and is accomplished by using the **CREATE INDEX** keywords. The syntax for creating an index is similar to the syntax used for creating a table. Adding the **UNIQUE** keyword means that only unique values can be used for the compound key. For the previous tables, the indexes were created at the same time as their respective tables. Because this table already exists, the **ON** keyword is used to associate the new index to the proper table name, with the field names following within parentheses. The **WITH** keyword declares additional options for the index. **PRIMARY** indicates that the new index also will be the primary key. **DISALLOW NULL** prevents null values from being allowed in the index.

The following step enters code to create a primary key index on the UserStocks table.

To Create a Primary Key Index on an Existing Table

1. Enter lines 123 through 136 as shown in Figure 11-17 on page 711.

An index for the UserStocks table is created and designated as the primary key (Figure 11-27). The WITH keyword is used to declare the index options, such as PRIMARY and DISALLOW NULL.

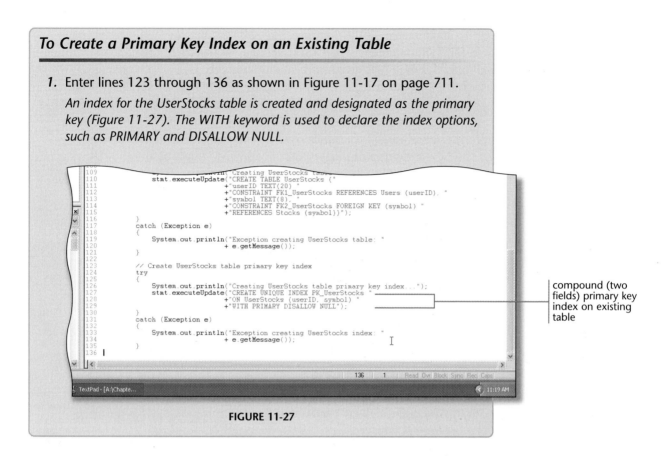

compound (two fields) primary key index on existing table

FIGURE 11-27

The tables and their relationships in the StockTracker database now are defined. Normally, the Statement object no longer would be needed and would be closed at this point. The Statement object, however, will be used later to verify the initial data added to the database, after which it will be closed. In order for the Stock Tracker application to use the database, one valid administrative user record must exist. This is a result of the application design, requiring that only an administrative user can add a new user to the database. By using the utility program to add initial data for a generic administrative user, the Stock Tracker application can be used later to either change the password for the administrative user, or add a new administrative user and delete the initial generic user, thus providing for greater data security.

Creating and Executing a Prepared Statement

Microsoft Access is a relational database, allowing the capability to define relationships between tables via fields, but it does not support manipulation of objects in a similar manner. Therefore, data in a user record is stored as individual fields in the database so those fields can be used when selecting records, defining keys, and obtaining results. Consequently, a User object, even though used in the application, is not stored as an object in the database. The user password field in the user record, however, also is an object. It can be stored in the database as an object because it is not necessary for the DBMS to be able to access the components of a Password object directly. Rather, this object will be serialized, as discussed earlier, and then written to the database. On retrieval, this data will be deserialized and the Password object reconstructed.

To add a record to the database, the executeUpdate() method is used with an SQL INSERT statement. The INSERT statement inserts into a table the comma-delimited list of values given inside a set of parentheses. To insert values for a user record into an SQL statement, including the value of a serialized Password object, a prepared statement is used. A **PreparedStatement** is a Statement object used to execute a precompiled or dynamic SQL statement. A **dynamic SQL statement** has parameter values that can change as the program executes.

All SQL statements must be compiled by the DBMS before they are executed. In many cases, a prepared statement is sent to the DBMS and compiled when it is created. When the prepared statement is executed, the DBMS simply can run the statement without compiling it again. This can make a PreparedStatement object more efficient to use than a Statement object if the same SQL statement is executed many times. Additionally, **placeholders**, represented as question mark (?) characters in the SQL statement, allow the same prepared statement to be used with different parameter values each time it is executed.

Lines 139 through 144 create the initial data for the database. These variables also are used later to set values for the PreparedStatement object. Line 143 creates a Password object from the initial string password value supplied.

The following step enters code to create a PreparedStatement object with placeholders for five dynamic parameters.

To Create a PreparedStatement Object

1. Enter lines 137 through 147 as shown in Figure 11-17 on page 711.

A PreparedStatement object is created with placeholders for five parameters to be set later (Figure 11-28). The variable values listed are the initial data recorded in the database.

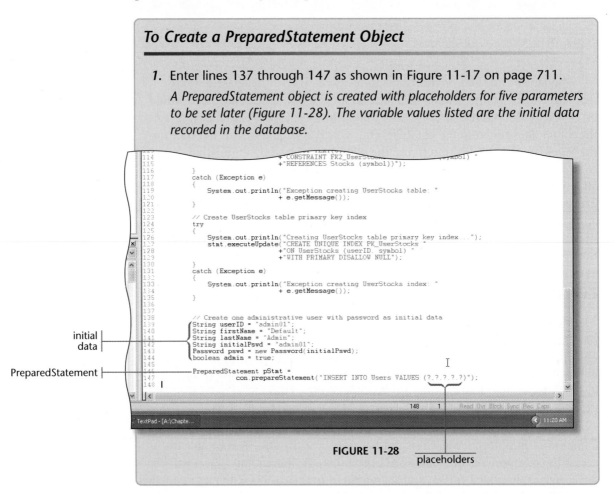

FIGURE 11-28

initial data

PreparedStatement

placeholders

PreparedStatement objects have methods that set a designated parameter to a given value for a particular data type, such as **setString()**, **setBytes()**, and **setBoolean()**, used in lines 150 through 154. The parameters are designated according to the order in which they appear in the prepared statement, with 1 representing the first parameter. Because no method is available to insert a Password object into a prepared statement, a method, serializeObj(), is created that will serialize an object into a byte array. That method is called in line 153 to serialize the Password object, pswd. The returned byte array is passed to the setBytes() method, setting the byte array in the PreparedStatement, pStmt, at the fourth placeholder. After all data values have been set, line 155 executes the PreparedStatement by calling its executeUpdate() method. Note that the same method name for a Statement object has a string containing an SQL statement as a parameter, but a PreparedStatement object does not, because the SQL statement already has been created and passed to the DBMS. Finally, line 163 calls the close() method, inherited from Statement, which immediately releases the Statement object's database and JDBC resources.

The following step enters code to set the data values for and execute a PreparedStatement.

To Execute a PreparedStatement

1. Enter lines 148 through 164 as shown in Figure 11-17 on page 711.

The String, Password, and Boolean values are set in the PreparedStatement object, and the prepared statement is executed (Figure 11-29). The PreparedStatement then is closed.

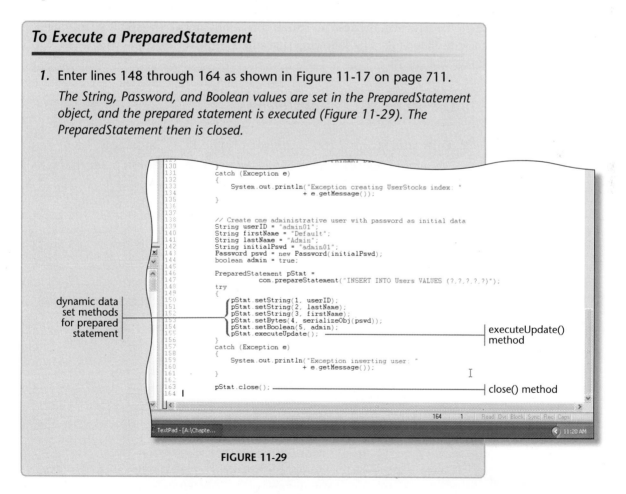

FIGURE 11-29

At this point, the database contains three tables: Users, Stocks, and UserStocks. When the completed program executes, the table, Users, contains a single record of data. This is the initial state for the database; each time this utility program executes, it sets the database to the initial state. While it is expected that this program is executed only once to establish the database initially, it is possible to perform additional executions, deleting any subsequent additions or changes made to the database within these three tables. To verify that the Users table contains only the expected data and that the other tables do not contain any records, a query is executed on each table.

Creating and Executing SQL Database Queries

The **executeQuery()** method of either a Statement or PreparedStatement object is called to perform an SQL query. Typically, an SQL **SELECT** statement is executed when performing a query. Values of the specified columns are returned for all records matching the search condition in the WHERE clause. Results of a query are returned as a **ResultSet object**, which is a table of data representing the database result set. By default, only one ResultSet object per Statement object can be opened at the same time. A ResultSet object is closed automatically when the Statement is re-executed or closed. The same is true for a PreparedStatement, because it also is a Statement object, as it inherits from Statement.

The asterisk in line 166 indicates that all columns or fields of the Users table are to be returned. Because no search conditions are set, the result set also will include all records. The following step enters code to create and execute an SQL Query Statement.

To Execute an SQL Query Statement

1. Enter lines 165 and 166 as shown in Figure 11-17 on page 711.

The executeQuery() method of the Statement object returns a ResultSet object containing the results of the query (Figure 11-30).

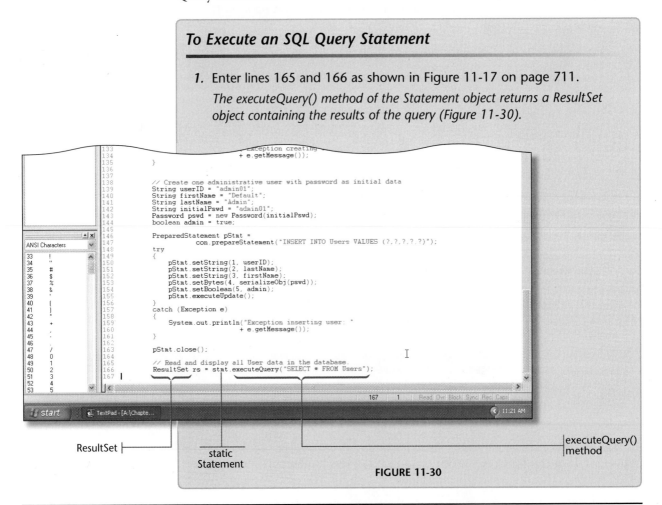

```
133             .ception creating
134                  + e.getMessage());
135     }
136
137
138     // Create one administrative user with password as initial data
139     String userID = "admin01";
140     String firstName = "Default";
141     String lastName = "Admin";
142     String initialPswd = "admin01";
143     Password pswd = new Password(initialPswd);
144     boolean admin = true;
145
146     PreparedStatement pStmt =
147                  con.prepareStatement("INSERT INTO Users VALUES (?,?,?,?,?)");
148     try
149     {
150         pStmt.setString(1, userID);
151         pStmt.setString(2, lastName);
152         pStmt.setString(3, firstName);
153         pStmt.setBytes(4, serializeObj(pswd));
154         pStmt.setBoolean(5, admin);
155         pStmt.executeUpdate();
156     }
157     catch (Exception e)
158     {
159         System.out.println("Exception inserting user: "
160                  + e.getMessage());
161     }
162
163     pStmt.close();
164
165     // Read and display all User data in the database.
166     ResultSet rs = stmt.executeQuery("SELECT * FROM Users");
167
```

ResultSet

static Statement

executeQuery() method

FIGURE 11-30

Once a query has been executed, if any data was returned, the result set data can be processed for any of the selected column values.

Processing a Result Set from an SQL Query

Results of a query are processed on a row-by-row basis. A ResultSet object maintains a type of pointer called a **cursor** to point to the current row of data. A cursor initially is positioned before the first row. The **next()** method of a ResultSet moves the cursor to the next row, returning true if the next row is valid and false if no rows remain. Because this method returns a Boolean value, it is used within an if() to test if any records were returned, as shown in lines 202 and 208, or within a loop to iterate through the result set, shown in line 175. A default ResultSet object has a cursor that moves forward only, from the first row to the last. Only a single iteration through the ResultSet is allowed.

A ResultSet object implements a number of getter, or accessor, methods for data of various data types. These methods are used to retrieve column values from the current row by passing the column name to the method appropriate for the data type of the column. The ResultSet contains only column values for those columns selected in the query. Because an asterisk was used to select all columns in the table, values for all columns are available for each row of data returned. The getString() method (in lines 178, 180, and 181) returns the String value in the given row at the named column, while getBoolean() in line 182 likewise returns a Boolean value. Line 183 displays the original password value entered, because the Password object stores only an encrypted value and will not display the password value at any rate. Because no method exists to obtain an object from the ResultSet, another method, deserializeObj(), must be created to deserialize the Password object, reversing the process of the serializeObj() method mentioned earlier.

Line 187 uses the getBytes() method of the ResultSet object, rs, to retrieve the value of the column, pswd, as a byte array. This technique should not be used with JDK 1.2.2 using the JDBC-ODBC Bridge because an SQL NULL data value is not handled correctly. If a null value is returned for the byte array, this means the database had no value for the Password object, which should not happen unless the database has been corrupted. If a byte array is returned (not null), then the byte array is deserialized into an object using the deserializeObj() method, yet to be written. This method returns an Object which then is downcast to a Password object and assigned to an appropriate reference variable. It is safe to downcast to a Password object because the deserialized object originally was serialized from a Password object. Once a Password object is obtained, it can be used to extract information about the Password — such as whether it automatically expires, whether it is expiring now, and the number of remaining uses — by calling the appropriate accessor methods of the Password class.

The steps on the next page enter code to process the results of a query returned in a ResultSet object.

To Process the ResultSet of a Query

1. Enter lines 167 through 200 as shown in Figure 11-17 on page 711 and 712.

   The results of a query are obtained from a ResultSet object and displayed (Figure 11-31). Additional steps are included to deserialize a Password object and then obtain instance values by calling Password class accessor methods.

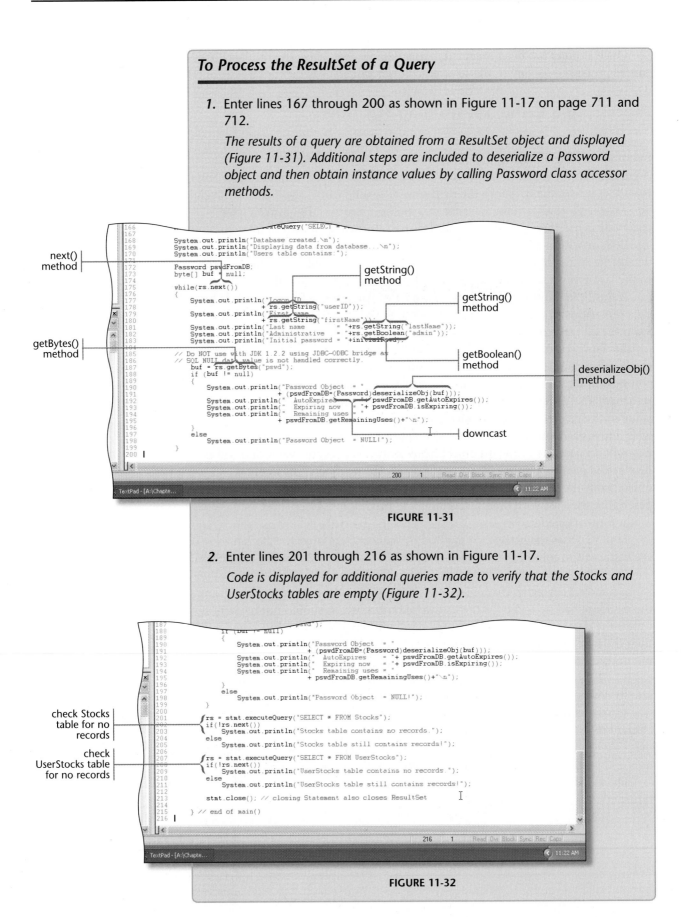

next() method

getBytes() method

getString() method

getString() method

getBoolean() method

deserializeObj() method

downcast

```
166          ...teQuery("SELECT * ...
167
168      System.out.println("Database created.\n");
169      System.out.println("Displaying data from database...\n");
170      System.out.println("Users table contains:");
171
172      Password pswdFromDB;
173      byte[] buf = null;
174
175      while(rs.next())
176      {
177          System.out.println("Logon ID        = "
178                  + rs.getString("userID"));
179          System.out.println("First name       = "
180                  + rs.getString("firstName"));
181          System.out.println("Last name        = "+rs.getString("lastName"));
182          System.out.println("Administrative   = "+rs.getBoolean("admin"));
183          System.out.println("Initial password = "+initialPswd);
184
185      // Do NOT use with JDK 1.2.2 using JDBC-ODBC bridge as
186      // SQL NULL data value is not handled correctly.
187          buf = rs.getBytes("pswd");
188          if (buf != null)
189          {
190              System.out.println("Password Object  = "
191                      + (pswdFromDB=(Password)deserializeObj(buf)));
192              System.out.println("   AutoExpires    = "+ pswdFromDB.getAutoExpires());
193              System.out.println("   Expiring now   = "+ pswdFromDB.isExpiring());
194              System.out.println("   Remaining uses = "
195                      + pswdFromDB.getRemainingUses()+"\n");
196          }
197          else
198              System.out.println("Password Object  = NULL!");
199      }
200  |
```

```
200    1    Read Ovr Block Sync Rec Caps
```
```
TextPad - [A:\Chapte...                                          11:22 AM
```

FIGURE 11-31

2. Enter lines 201 through 216 as shown in Figure 11-17.

   Code is displayed for additional queries made to verify that the Stocks and UserStocks tables are empty (Figure 11-32).

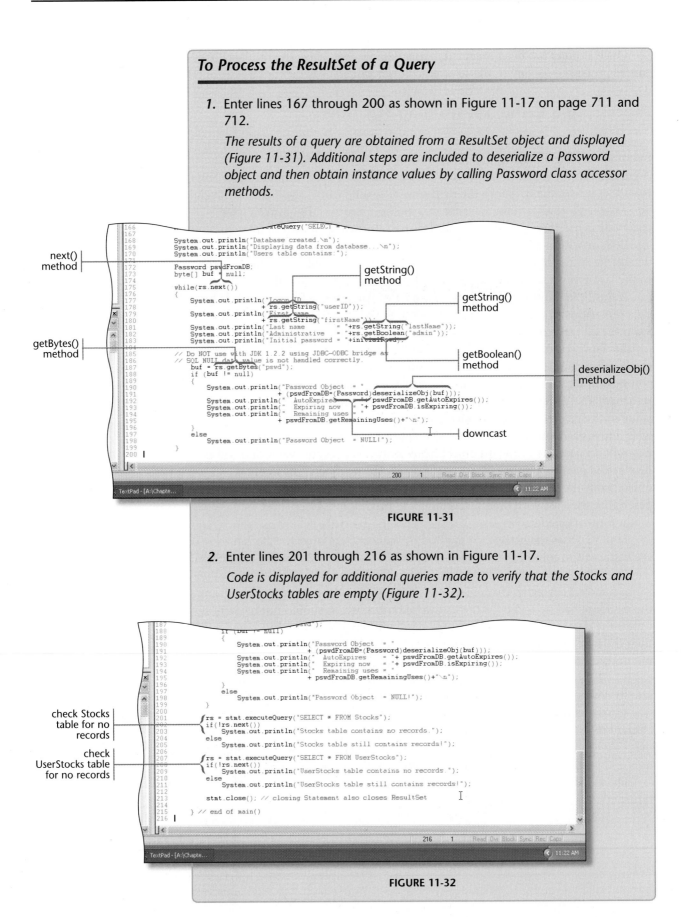

check Stocks table for no records

check UserStocks table for no records

```
187                  ...wd");
188          if (buf != null)
189          {
190              System.out.println("Password Object  = "
191                      + (pswdFromDB=(Password)deserializeObj(buf)));
192              System.out.println("   AutoExpires    = "+ pswdFromDB.getAutoExpires());
193              System.out.println("   Expiring now   = "+ pswdFromDB.isExpiring());
194              System.out.println("   Remaining uses = "
195                      + pswdFromDB.getRemainingUses()+"\n");
196          }
197          else
198              System.out.println("Password Object  = NULL!");
199      }
200
201      rs = stmt.executeQuery("SELECT * FROM Stocks");
202      if(!rs.next())
203          System.out.println("Stocks table contains no records.");
204      else
205          System.out.println("Stocks table still contains records!");
206
207      rs = stmt.executeQuery("SELECT * FROM UserStocks");
208      if(!rs.next())
209          System.out.println("UserStocks table contains no records.");
210      else
211          System.out.println("UserStocks table still contains records!");
212
213      stmt.close(); // closing Statement also closes ResultSet
214
215  } // end of main()
216  |
```

```
216    1    Read Ovr Block Sync Rec Caps
```
```
TextPad - [A:\Chapte...                                          11:22 AM
```

FIGURE 11-32

All code dealing with SQL and JDBC™ now is written. Remaining tasks for the application are the creation of methods used to serialize and deserialize a Password object.

Serializing an Object

Earlier, the Password class was modified to implement the Serializable interface. It was necessary to modify the Password class so Password objects could be serialized and deserialized; however, no methods were implemented. As explained earlier, the Serializable interface simply is a marker interface, identifying the object as a Serializable object. This allows an object to be serialized by using the **writeObject()** method in the class, ObjectOutputStream, and deserialized by using the **readObject()** method in the ObjectInputStream class. Classes requiring exceptional handling during serialization and deserialization can implement special methods with prescribed signatures to provide the needed behavior. In many cases, however, the default behavior is sufficient to serialize and deserialize an object.

The serializeObj() method serializes any Serializable object into a byte array and then returns the byte array to the caller. Line 221 creates a new ByteArrayOutputStream object. The **ByteArrayOutputStream** class implements an output stream where data is written to a byte array. The size of the array automatically increases as data is written to it. Data can be retrieved from the array as a String or as a byte array, or it can be written to another output stream. In line 222, the ByteArrayOutputStream object is used to create a new ObjectOutputStream object which provides the writeObject() method, used in line 224, to serialize the object passed as a parameter to the serializeObj() method. In line 225, the **flush()** method is called to ensure that any buffered output bytes are written through to the underlying ByteArrayOutputStream. The **close()** method in line 226, comparable to the close() method in other classes previously mentioned, closes the stream, releasing any associated resources. Finally, the toByteArray() method of the ByteArrayOutputStream object is called, creating a newly allocated byte array with the size and contents of the output stream buffer and returning the contents as a byte array, which is returned to the caller of the serializeObj() method.

The step on the next page enters code to serialize an object to a byte array.

> **Tip**
>
> ### Closing a ByteArrayOutputStream
>
> Closing an ObjectOutputStream releases resources, but closing a ByteArrayOutputStream has no effect. Interestingly enough, the methods in the ByteArrayOutputStream class can be called after the stream has been closed. This avoids the need for a byte array to temporarily hold the returned value of the toByteArray() method call.

The following step enters code to serialize an object to a byte array.

To Serialize an Object

1. Enter lines 217 through 229 as shown in Figure 11-17 on page 712.

The serializeObj() method uses a ByteArrayOutputStream and an ObjectOutputStream to serialize an object to a byte array (Figure 11-33).

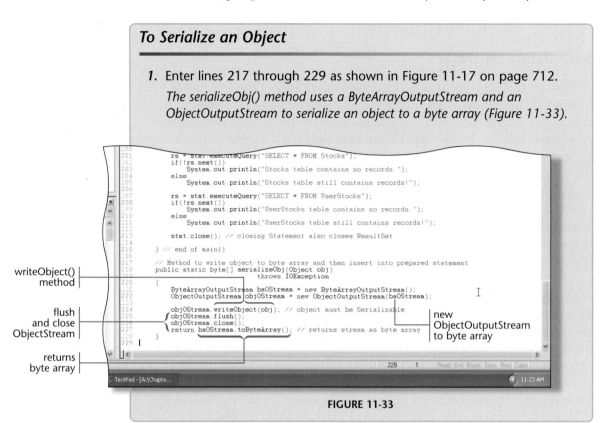

writeObject() method

flush and close ObjectStream

new ObjectOutputStream to byte array

returns byte array

```
200
201  rs = stmt.executeQuery("SELECT * FROM Stocks");
202  if(!rs.next())
203      System.out.println("Stocks table contains no records.");
204  else
205      System.out.println("Stocks table still contains records!");
206
207  rs = stmt.executeQuery("SELECT * FROM UserStocks");
208  if(!rs.next())
209      System.out.println("UserStocks table contains no records.");
210  else
211      System.out.println("UserStocks table still contains records!");
212
213  stmt.close(); // closing Statement also closes ResultSet
214
215  } // end of main()
216
217  // Method to write object to byte array and then insert into prepared statement
218  public static byte[] serializeObj(Object obj)
219                  throws IOException
220  {
221      ByteArrayOutputStream baOStream = new ByteArrayOutputStream();
222      ObjectOutputStream objOStream = new ObjectOutputStream(baOStream);
223
224      objOStream.writeObject(obj); // object must be Serializable
225      objOStream.flush();
226      objOStream.close();
227      return baOStream.toByteArray(); // returns stream as byte array
228
229  }
```

FIGURE 11-33

Deserializing an Object

Deserializing an object is the reverse process of serialization. An object that has been serialized and saved to a byte array, for example, is deserialized by converting the data in the byte array into a stream and then reading (deserializing) the stream data into an object of the original type. This process is what the deserializeObj() method follows.

Line 240 takes a non-null byte array and creates a ByteArrayInputStream object, which then is used to create a new ObjectInputStream object. Line 242 uses the readObject() method to deserialize the data to an object of type Object. Recall that the Object class is the parent, or root, class of the class hierarchy in Java. All objects have this class as a superclass and, consequently, all objects are of type Object. The deserializeObj() method returns the object, relying on the caller to properly downcast to the expected class, which was done earlier in the call to this method. If a null byte array was passed as a parameter, then a null object reference is returned by this method.

The following step enters code to deserialize a byte array to an object.

To Deserialize an Object

1. Enter lines 230 through 246 as shown in Figure 11-17 on page 712.

    The deserializeObj() method converts a byte array into an ObjectIntputStream to deserialize a byte array to an object (Figure 11-34).

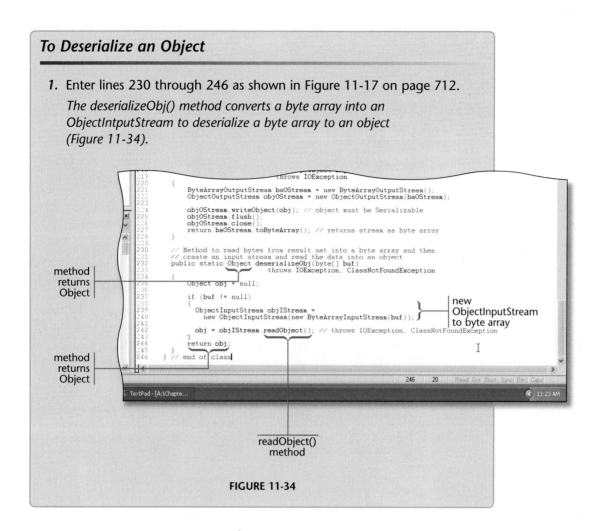

FIGURE 11-34

The utility program used to create the database tables and insert one record into the Users table is complete.

The steps on the next page save and compile the MakeDB class and then execute the MakeDB program to create new Users, Stocks, and UserStocks tables in the StockTracker database.

To Create the StockTracker Database Tables

1. With your Data Disk in drive A, click Tools on the menu bar and then click Compile Java.

2. If the MakeDB class contains errors, fix them in the coding window and then recompile the program.

   TextPad automatically saves and then compiles the source code for the MakeDB class.

3. Click Run Java Application on the Tools menu.

   The console program, MakeDB, displays the contents of the created tables (Figure 11-35). The error messages displayed are expected because the program initially tries to drop the tables before they are created.

error messages

tables created

initial data

remaining tables empty

FIGURE 11-35

OTHER WAYS

1. To save and compile, press CTRL+1
2. To run program, press CTRL+2

With the database created and an available, valid user record stored, the database now is enabled for use by an application. Because the Stock Tracker application will not access the database directly, a new class must be created to provide that access.

Tip

Verifying the Database Structure

You can examine directly the tables created by opening the database in Microsoft Access. You should see each table, and by examining in design mode, see the fields and their respective Access data types. Opening a table will allow you to see any data added to the table. Click the Relationships button and you can see the relationships between tables.

Creating a Data Access Class

The previous classes, and in particular the StockTracker class, have responsibility for the user interface and for controlling the flow of actions between what the user sees on the screen and the data that goes to or from the database, but not for accessing the database itself. Keeping that capability separate requires creating a **data access (DA) class**, which is a class given the responsibility of accessing the data from its persistent storage and providing it to the requesting application.

By separating out data access from the way the data is viewed, or presented, a level of abstraction is inserted, providing greater flexibility for storing the data. The DA class becomes a model of the database to the GUI program, allowing the GUI to request data while ignoring the type of database used, or whether a database is used at all. This technique allows the method of storing the data to change without affecting how the data is accessed by the GUI, only by the DA class. An additional function that may be abstracted, or separated, into another class is the control of how the data is used. In this case, the control class decides whether a user may add or delete other user records, or the number of unsuccessful log on attempts allowed, apart from the code for the actual user interface. This separation into a model, view, and control is a type of pattern for software design called **model-view-controller (MVC)**. Often, the control and view are combined into a **model-delegate**. Although not a strict implementation of all aspects of the MVC pattern, the StockTrackerDB class represents a model of the database, while the STLogon, StockTracker, and UserMaintFrame classes handle their respective view and control responsibilities. Figure 11-36 displays the code for the StockTrackerDB class.

```
1   /*
2        Chapter 11: The StockTrackerDB Class
3        Programmer: Michael Mick
4        Date:       December 12, 2007
5        Filename:   StockTrackerDB.java
6        Purpose:    To provide a data access class for the StockTracker database
7   */
8
9   import java.io.*;
10  import java.sql.*;
11  import java.util.*;
12
13  public class StockTrackerDB
14  {
15      private Connection con = null;
16
17      // Constructor; makes database connection
18      public StockTrackerDB() throws ClassNotFoundException,SQLException
19      {
20          if(con == null)
21          {
22              String url = "jdbc:odbc:StockTracker";
```

FIGURE 11-36

(continued)

```
23
24              try
25              {
26                  Class.forName("sun.jdbc.odbc.JdbcOdbcDriver");
27              }
28              catch(ClassNotFoundException ex)
29              {
30                  throw new ClassNotFoundException(ex.getMessage() +
31                          "\nCannot locate sun.jdbc.odbc.JdbcOdbcDriver");
32              }
33
34              try
35              {
36                  con = DriverManager.getConnection(url);
37              }
38              catch(SQLException ex)
39              {
40                  throw new SQLException(ex.getMessage()+
41                          "\nCannot open database connection for "+url);
42              }
43          }
44      }
45
46      // Close makes database connection; null reference to connection
47      public void close() throws SQLException,IOException,ClassNotFoundException
48      {
49          con.close();
50          con = null;
51      }
52
53      // Method to serialize object to byte array
54      private byte[] serializeObj(Object obj) throws IOException
55      {
56          ByteArrayOutputStream baOStream = new ByteArrayOutputStream();
57          ObjectOutputStream objOStream = new ObjectOutputStream(baOStream);
58
59          objOStream.writeObject(obj); // object must be Serializable
60          objOStream.flush();
61          objOStream.close();
62          return baOStream.toByteArray(); // returns stream as byte array
63      }
64
65      // Method to deserialize bytes from a byte array into an object
66      private Object deserializeObj(byte[] buf)
67                      throws IOException, ClassNotFoundException
68      {
69          Object obj = null;
70
71          if (buf != null)
72          {
73              ObjectInputStream objIStream =
74                  new ObjectInputStream(new ByteArrayInputStream(buf));
75
76              obj = objIStream.readObject(); //IOException, ClassNotFoundException
77          }
78          return obj;
79      }
80
81      ///////////////////////////////////////////////////////////////////////
82      // Methods for adding a record to a table
83      ///////////////////////////////////////////////////////////////////////
84      // add to the Stocks Table
85      public void addStock(String stockSymbol, String stockDesc)
86                  throws SQLException, IOException, ClassNotFoundException
87      {
88          Statement stmt = con.createStatement();
89          stmt.executeUpdate("INSERT INTO Stocks VALUES ('"
90                          +stockSymbol+"'"
91                          +",'"+stockDesc+"')");
92          stmt.close();
93      }
94
```

FIGURE 11-36

```
95      // add to the Users table
96      public boolean addUser(User user) throws SQLException,IOException,
97                                              ClassNotFoundException
98      {
99        boolean result = false;
100
101       String dbUserID;
102       String dbLastName;
103       String dbFirstName;
104       Password dbPswd;
105       boolean isAdmin;
106
107       dbUserID = user.getUserID();
108
109       if(getUser(dbUserID) == null)
110       {
111           dbLastName = user.getLastName();
112           dbFirstName = user.getFirstName();
113           Password pswd = user.getPassword();
114           isAdmin = user.isAdmin();
115
116           PreparedStatement pStmt = con.prepareStatement(
117               "INSERT INTO Users VALUES (?,?,?,?,?)");
118
119           pStmt.setString(1, dbUserID);
120           pStmt.setString(2, dbLastName);
121           pStmt.setString(3, dbFirstName);
122           pStmt.setBytes(4, serializeObj(pswd));
123           pStmt.setBoolean(5, isAdmin);
124           pStmt.executeUpdate();
125           pStmt.close();
126           result = true;
127       }
128       else
129           throw new IOException("User exists - cannot add.");
130
131       return result;
132     }
133
134     // add to the UserStocks table
135     public void addUserStocks(String userID, String stockSymbol)
136                 throws SQLException,IOException,ClassNotFoundException
137     {
138         Statement stmt = con.createStatement();
139
140         stmt.executeUpdate("INSERT INTO UserStocks VALUES ('"
141                         +userID+"'"
142                         +",'"+stockSymbol+"')");
143         stmt.close();
144     }
145
146     ////////////////////////////////////////////////////////////////////
147     // Methods for updating a record in a table
148     ////////////////////////////////////////////////////////////////////
149
150     // updating the Users table
151     public boolean updUser(User user) throws SQLException,IOException,
152                                              ClassNotFoundException
153     {
154       boolean result = false;
155
156       String dbUserID;
157       String dbLastName;
158       String dbFirstName;
159       Password dbPswd;
160       boolean isAdmin;
161
162       dbUserID = user.getUserID();
163
164       if(getUser(dbUserID) != null)
165       {
166           dbLastName = user.getLastName();
167           dbFirstName = user.getFirstName();
168           Password pswd = user.getPassword();
169           isAdmin = user.isAdmin();
170
```

FIGURE 11-36

(continued)

```
171              PreparedStatement pStmt = con.prepareStatement("UPDATE Users SET lastName = ?,"
172                               +" firstName = ?, pswd = ?, admin = ? WHERE userID = ?");
173
174          pStmt.setString(1, dbLastName);
175          pStmt.setString(2, dbFirstName);
176          pStmt.setBytes(3, serializeObj(pswd));
177          pStmt.setBoolean(4, isAdmin);
178          pStmt.setString(5, dbUserID);
179
180          pStmt.executeUpdate();
181          pStmt.close();
182          result = true;
183       }
184     else
185          throw new IOException("User does not exist - cannot update.");
186
187     return result;
188   }
189
190
191   ////////////////////////////////////////////////////////////////////////////
192   // Methods for deleting a record from a table
193   ////////////////////////////////////////////////////////////////////////////
194
195   // delete a record from the Stocks table
196   private void delStock(String stockSymbol)
197            throws SQLException,IOException,ClassNotFoundException
198   {
199       Statement stmt = con.createStatement();
200       stmt.executeUpdate("DELETE FROM Stocks WHERE "
201                   +"symbol = '"+stockSymbol+"'");
202       stmt.close();
203   }
204
205   // delete a record from the Users table
206   public void delUser(User user) throws SQLException,IOException,
207                               ClassNotFoundException
208   {
209       String dbUserID;
210       String stockSymbol;
211
212       Statement stmt = con.createStatement();
213
214       try {
215          con.setAutoCommit(false);
216
217          dbUserID = user.getUserID();
218          if(getUser(dbUserID) != null)   // verify user exists in database
219          {
220             ResultSet rs1 = stmt.executeQuery("SELECT userID, symbol "
221                         +"FROM UserStocks WHERE userID = '"+dbUserID+"'");
222             while(rs1.next())
223             {
224                try
225                {
226                   stockSymbol = rs1.getString("symbol");
227                   delUserStocks(dbUserID, stockSymbol);
228                }
229                catch(SQLException ex)
230                {
231                   throw new SQLException("Deletion of user stock holding failed: "
232                                  +ex.getMessage());
233                }
234             } // end of loop thru UserStocks
235
```

FIGURE 11-36

```
236                     try
237                     {  // holdings deleted, now delete user
238                         stmt.executeUpdate("DELETE FROM Users WHERE "
239                                             +"userID = '"+dbUserID+"'");
240                     }
241                     catch(SQLException ex)
242                     {
243                         throw new SQLException("User deletion failed: "+ex.getMessage());
244                     }
245                 }
246                 else
247                     throw new IOException("User not found in database - cannot delete.");
248
249                 try
250                 {
251                     con.commit();
252                 }
253                 catch(SQLException ex)
254                 {
255                     throw new SQLException("Transaction commit failed: "+ex.getMessage());
256                 }
257             }
258             catch (SQLException ex)
259             {
260                 try
261                 {
262                     con.rollback();
263                 }
264                 catch (SQLException sqx)
265                 {
266                     throw new SQLException("Transaction failed then rollback failed: "
267                                             +sqx.getMessage());
268                 }
269
270                 // Transaction failed, was rolled back
271                 throw new SQLException("Transaction failed; was rolled back: "
272                                         +ex.getMessage());
273             }
274
275         stmt.close();
276     }
277
278     // delete a record from the UserStocks table
279     public void delUserStocks(String userID, String stockSymbol)
280             throws SQLException,IOException,ClassNotFoundException
281     {
282         Statement stmt = con.createStatement();
283         ResultSet rs;
284
285         stmt.executeUpdate("DELETE FROM UserStocks WHERE "
286                             +"userID = '"+userID+"'"
287                             +"AND symbol = '"+stockSymbol+"'");
288
289         rs = stmt.executeQuery("SELECT symbol FROM UserStocks "
290                             +"WHERE symbol = '"+stockSymbol+"'");
291
292         if(!rs.next()) // no users have this stock
293             delStock(stockSymbol);
294
295         stmt.close();
296
297     }
298
299     ////////////////////////////////////////////////////////////////////////////
300     // Methods for listing record data from a table
301     // Ordered by:
302     //       methods that obtain individual field(s),
303     //       methods that obtain a complete record, and
304     //       methods that obtain multiple records
305     ////////////////////////////////////////////////////////////////////////////
306
307     // Methods to access one or more individual fields
308
```

FIGURE 11-36

(continued)

```
309     // get a stock description from the Stocks table
310     public String getStockDesc(String stockSymbol)
311                     throws SQLException, IOException, ClassNotFoundException
312     {
313         Statement stmt = con.createStatement();
314         String stockDesc = null;
315
316         ResultSet rs = stmt.executeQuery("SELECT symbol, name FROM Stocks "
317                             +"WHERE symbol = '"+stockSymbol+"'");
318         if(rs.next())
319             stockDesc = rs.getString("name");
320         rs.close();
321         stmt.close();
322
323         return stockDesc;
324     }
325
326
327     // Methods to access a complete record
328
329     // get User data from the Users table
330     public User getUser(String userID) throws SQLException, IOException,
331                                     ClassNotFoundException
332     {
333         Statement stmt = con.createStatement();
334
335         String dbUserID;
336         String dbLastName;
337         String dbFirstName;
338         Password dbPswd;
339         boolean isAdmin;
340
341         byte[] buf = null;
342         User user = null;
343         ResultSet rs = stmt.executeQuery("SELECT * FROM Users WHERE userID = '"
344                             +userID+"'");
345         if(rs.next())
346         {
347             dbUserID = rs.getString("userID");
348             dbLastName = rs.getString("lastName");
349             dbFirstName = rs.getString("firstName");
350
351             // Do NOT use with JDK 1.2.2 using JDBC-ODBC bridge as
352             // SQL NULL data value is not handled correctly.
353             buf = rs.getBytes("pswd");
354             dbPswd=(Password)deserializeObj(buf);
355
356             isAdmin = rs.getBoolean("admin");
357             user = new User(dbUserID,dbFirstName,dbLastName,dbPswd,isAdmin);
358         }
359         rs.close();
360         stmt.close();
361
362         return user; // User object created for userID
363     }
364
365
366     // Methods to access a list of records
367
368     // get list of selected fields for all records from the Users Table
369     public ArrayList listUsers() throws SQLException,IOException,
370                                     ClassNotFoundException
371     {
372         ArrayList aList = new ArrayList();
373         Statement stmt = con.createStatement();
374
375         ResultSet rs = stmt.executeQuery("SELECT userID, firstName, lastName, admin "
376                             +"FROM Users ORDER BY userID");
377
```

FIGURE 11-36

```
378        while(rs.next())
379        {
380            aList.add(rs.getString("userID"));
381            aList.add(rs.getString("firstName"));
382            aList.add(rs.getString("lastName"));
383            aList.add(new Boolean(rs.getBoolean("admin")));
384        }
385
386        rs.close();
387        stmt.close();
388
389        return aList;
390    }
391
392    // get all fields in all records for a given user from the Userstocks table
393    public ArrayList listUserStocks(String userID) throws SQLException,IOException,
394                                                 ClassNotFoundException
395    {
396        ArrayList aList = new ArrayList();
397        Statement stmt = con.createStatement();
398
399        ResultSet rs = stmt.executeQuery("SELECT * FROM UserStocks "
400                                   +"WHERE userID = '"+userID+"' ORDER BY symbol");
401        while(rs.next())
402            aList.add(rs.getString("symbol"));
403
404        rs.close();
405        stmt.close();
406
407        return aList;
408    }
409 }
```

FIGURE 11-36

The following steps open a new Java program named StockTrackerDB.

To Open a New Java Program in TextPad

1. Click the New Document button on the Standard toolbar.

2. Click File on the menu bar and then click Save As on the File menu. When the Save As dialog box is displayed, click the Save in box arrow and then click 3½ Floppy (A:) in the Save in list.

3. Double-click the Chapter11 folder or the location specified by your instructor.

4. Type StockTrackerDB in the File name text box. Click the Save as type box arrow and then click Java (*.java) in the Save as type list. Click the Save button in the Save As dialog box.

(continued)

5. Enter lines 1 through 16 as shown in Figure 11-36. In the comments, insert your own name as programmer and enter the current date.

TextPad displays the code for the initial comments, import statements, class header, and instance variable for the StockTrackerDB class (Figure 11-37). The instance variable, con, is accessible only by instance methods in the class.

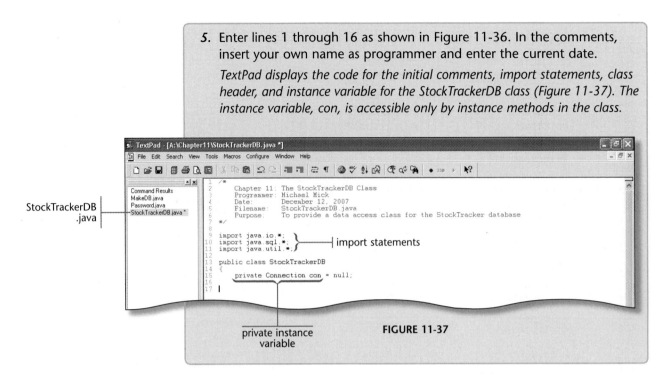

FIGURE 11-37

Because the StockTrackerDB class is a model, or representation, of the database to another program, it should connect to the database when an instance of the class is created. Therefore, the StockTrackerDB constructor loads the JDBC™ driver and makes the database connection, similar to what was done earlier. The connection, once made, is referenced by the instance variable, con, defined on line 15 and available for use until the data access class no longer is needed by the user application.

The following step enters code to create the constructor for the data access class, StockTrackerDB.

To Create a Data Access Class Constructor

1. Enter lines 17 through 45 as shown in Figure 11-36 on pages 733 and 734.

The constructor loads the JDBC-ODBC driver and obtains a Connection object for the StockTracker database (Figure 11-38).

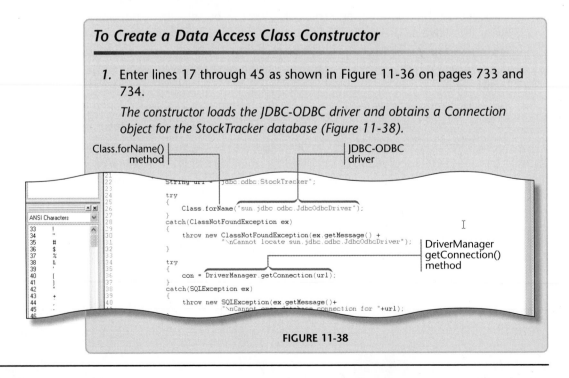

FIGURE 11-38

Because a StockTrackerDB object opens a connection to the database as soon as it is created, that connection should be closed when the StockTrackerDB object no longer is needed by the application program. The application program then calls a method to indicate when the data access class no longer is needed, and the connection is closed. Lines 47 through 51 comprise the close() method of the data access class. Line 49 closes the Connection, and line 50 sets the reference to null.

The following step enters code to create the close() method to close the connection for the data access class, StockTrackerDB.

To Close a Connection

1. Enter lines 46 through 52 as shown in Figure 11-36 on page 734.
   The connection to the StockTracker database is closed (Figure 11-39).

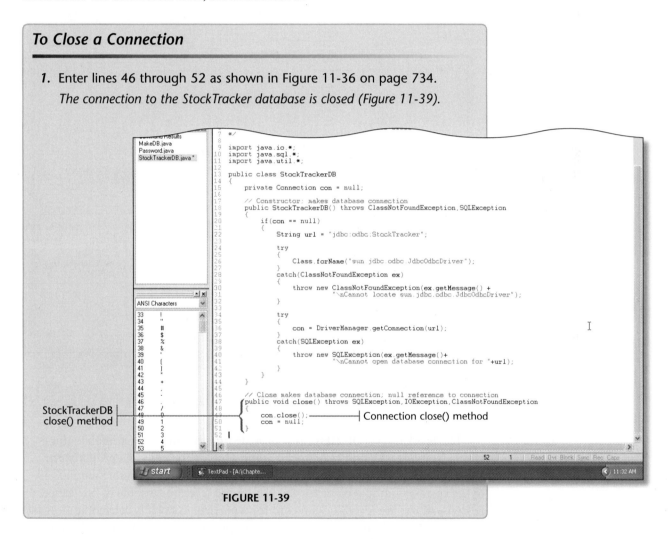

FIGURE 11-39

In the MakeDB class, methods were written to serialize and deserialize an object. These methods were necessary to be able to store a Password object in the database. The StockTrackerDB class also must be able to serialize and deserialize a Password object. The MakeDB methods were public and static, but only because that class called those methods directly from its main() method. The MakeDB is considered a one-time utility and, therefore, cannot be expected to be available whenever the StockTrackerDB class is used. Additionally, these methods are used only within the StockTrackerDB class, and so should be made private. Otherwise, the methods are exactly the same as the corresponding methods written earlier.

The following step enters code to create the serializeObj() and deserializeObj() methods for the StockTrackerDB class.

To Serialize and Deserialize Objects

1. Enter lines 53 through 80 as shown in Figure 11-36 on page 734.

   The methods, serializeObj() and deserializeObj(), display in the StockTrackerDB class (Figure 11-40). They are identical to the methods written earlier, except for being private.

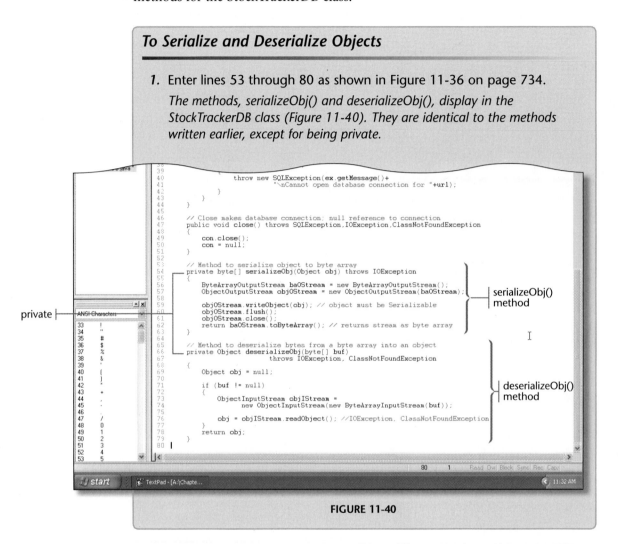

FIGURE 11-40

The StockTrackerDB class must provide functionality to manipulate three tables, Users, Stocks, and UserStocks, while keeping the contents properly synchronized. For example, deleting a user record from the Users table requires all of the corresponding records for the user in the UserStocks table to be deleted. Likewise, if the last UserStocks record for a particular stock is deleted, indicating that no users hold this stock, then the corresponding stock must be deleted from the Stocks table. Although the order in which these methods are created does not matter, they should be arranged in a logical grouping that makes later maintenance easier. This can be accomplished by locating together methods that use the same table. If a method needs access to multiple tables, however, it might be difficult to determine where in the program to place the method. Generally, four actions are typical with database programs: adding new records, updating existing records, deleting existing records, and obtaining a list of one or more selected fields for one or more records. By grouping methods according to actions, rather than tables used, the program is structured for ease of maintenance.

Adding Records with an SQL Insert

The data access class must provide the ability to add records for the Stocks table, for the Users table, and for the UserStocks table. Adding a record is done by executing an update for an SQL INSERT statement, similar to what was accomplished in the MakeDB class.

The following steps enter code to add records for the Stocks, Users, and UserStocks tables.

To Add Records to Database Tables

1. Enter lines 81 through 94 as shown in Figure 11-36 on page 734.

   TextPad displays the addStock() method (Figure 11-41). This method calls the Statement method, executeUpdate(), to execute an SQL INSERT statement, and the variables appended are enclosed within single quotes.

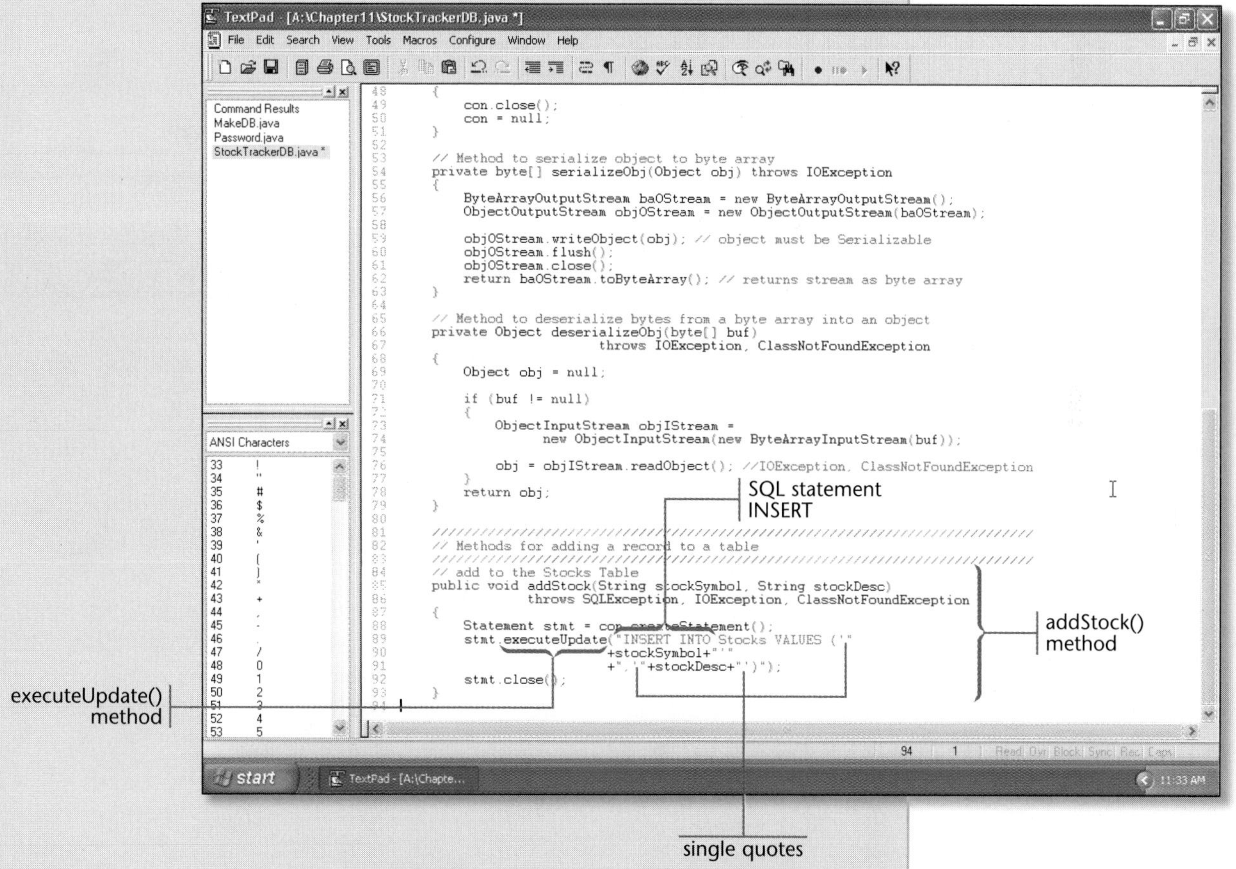

FIGURE 11-41

(continued)

2. Enter lines 95 through 133 as shown in Figure 11-36 on page 735.

TextPad displays the addUser() method (Figure 11-42). This method requires a User object as a parameter. It uses a PreparedStatement object, serializing the Password object before inserting it as a variable value.

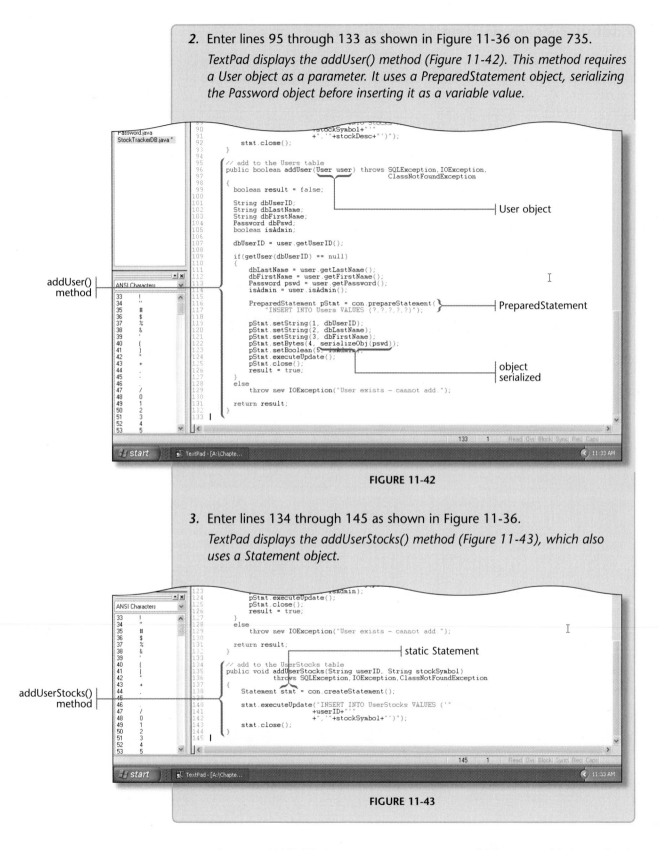

FIGURE 11-42

3. Enter lines 134 through 145 as shown in Figure 11-36.

TextPad displays the addUserStocks() method (Figure 11-43), which also uses a Statement object.

FIGURE 11-43

As demonstrated, either a Statement or a PreparedStatement object can be used to modify the database.

Modifying Records with an SQL Update

Of the three tables in this database, only the Users table can be updated. UserStocks either has a record for a given user and stock combination or it does not, so records are only added or deleted, not updated. Although the Stocks table could be updated, the only field is the stock name. The stock name field is entered when a stock initially is added to the database and is not expected to change; therefore, no provision currently exists for updating Stock table records.

The SQL **UPDATE** statement is used to update field values in a given record. The SET clause indicates a comma-delimited list of fields and their new values. This list does not have to be in the order created in the table, nor does every field have to be assigned a new value. If a field is not listed with a new value, it retains its value prior to the update. The update is applied to all records matching the search condition following the WHERE keyword.

The following step enters code to update a record in the Users table.

Using a WHERE clause in an UPDATE

Typically, the search condition specified in a WHERE clause of an SQL UPDATE statement references the primary key, which is unique for each record. If the search condition specified criteria other than a primary key, then the update is applied to all matching records, which may be more than one record.

To Update a Record in the Users Table

1. Enter lines 146 through 189 as shown in Figure 11-36.

TextPad displays the updUser() method (Figure 11-44). Much like the addUser() method, this method requires a User object as a parameter and sets a serialized Password as a dynamic parameter to a PreparedStatement.

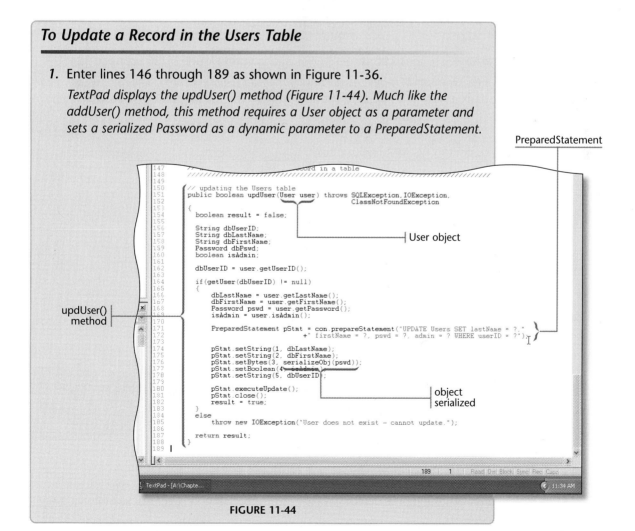

FIGURE 11-44

If a future application needs to update a different table in this database, the StockTrackerDB class easily can be modified to include the appropriate method without affecting other applications using the current code.

Performing an SQL Delete

Just as all three tables required methods to add records, consequently all three require methods to delete records. According to the requirements document, any user can delete a stock from their holdings, but not directly from the Stocks table. A public method is needed to delete a specific user stock from the UserStocks table. Because only the StockTrackerDB class can delete a stock record, and only if a stock is no longer held by any user, the method for deleting a Stocks table record is made private.

The SQL **DELETE** statement is used to delete from a given table all records that match the search condition following the WHERE keyword. Much as with the UPDATE statement, if the search condition matches multiple records, all records are deleted. If the search condition is a primary key, then only one record at most is deleted, because primary keys are unique.

The following step enters the code to delete a record from the Stocks table.

To Delete a Record in the Stocks Table

1. Enter lines 190 through 204 as shown in Figure 11-36 on page 736.

TextPad displays the delStock() method (Figure 11-45). The method is private and can be called only from within the StockTrackerDB class.

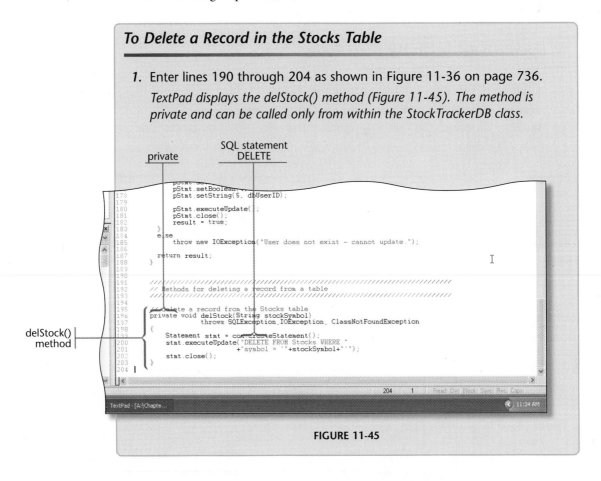

FIGURE 11-45

Deleting a Stocks record is relatively simple. Because of the relationship between the tables, deleting records from the Users or UserStocks tables is more complex.

Committing a Transaction to Delete Related Records

Deleting a record from the Users table is more involved because a user may have one or more stock holdings; therefore, any records for the user in the UserStocks table must be deleted prior to deleting the user record. Furthermore, the user may be the only user holding a given stock. The program must verify if this is the case and, if so, delete the record for that stock from the Stocks table. When tables have related records, it is likely that a change, such as deleting a record in one table, may require changes in one or more records from one or more additional tables. Such changes are considered an individual transaction. A **transaction** is a logical unit of work. If the entire transaction cannot be completed successfully, then no portion of it should be completed. For example, given a group of related records, it is possible to delete some of the records and then encounter an error condition that prevents deletion of the remaining records. Such a situation would leave the database in an inconsistent state. To avoid this, the deletions can be grouped as a transaction. In a transaction, if all changes are applied successfully, then the program can **commit** the transaction, meaning all of the changes are saved. If all the changes are not made successfully, then the program can **rollback** the changes made, undoing them and leaving the database without any of the changes applied.

By default, new connections automatically commit SQL statements as individual transactions. Setting a connection's auto-commit mode to false allows multiple SQL statements to be grouped into a single transaction. Line 215 calls the setAutoCommit() method of a Connection object, disabling the auto-commit mode. All subsequent SQL statements are treated as a single transaction until either the **commit()** method or the **rollback()** method is called to commit the statements or roll them back, respectively.

Line 217 gets the user ID from the User object passed to the method. Line 218 verifies that the user record exists in the database. Lines 220 and 221 query the UserStocks table for all records associated with a given user. The loop beginning on line 222 iterates through the ResultSet, obtaining the symbol for each stock held by the user; then in line 227, it calls the method, delUserStocks(), which deletes the entry from the UserStocks table and, if necessary, calls delStocks() to delete the stock from the Stocks table. If a stock or stock holding could not be deleted, an SQLException is thrown in line 231. An SQLException is used for database access errors and distinguishes them from other exceptions, in an analogous manner to the PasswordExceptions created earlier. Once all stock holdings for the user are deleted, lines 238 and 239 delete the user record from the Users table. Note that line 247 throws an IOException, not an SQLException, if the user record is not found. This prevents attempting to execute either a commit or a rollback. Neither is valid, because no user record was read, so no deletes were performed; therefore, no transactions exist to commit or rollback.

If all the statements complete without error, line 251 commits the statements as a single transaction. If an error occurs, line 262 rolls back the transaction, undoing all deletions. If the rollback fails, line 266 throws a new SQLException. If the rollback was successful, lines 271 and 272 throw an SQLException indicating that the transaction failed and was rolled back. If no errors occur, line 275 closes the Statement.

The following steps enter the code to delete related records within a transaction and then commit or rollback the transaction.

To Commit a Transaction to Delete Related Records

1. Enter lines 205 through 216 as shown in Figure 11-36 on page 736.

TextPad displays the beginning of the delUser() method (Figure 11-46). The setAutoCommit() method disables the auto-commit mode of the connection to allow a multiple-statement transaction.

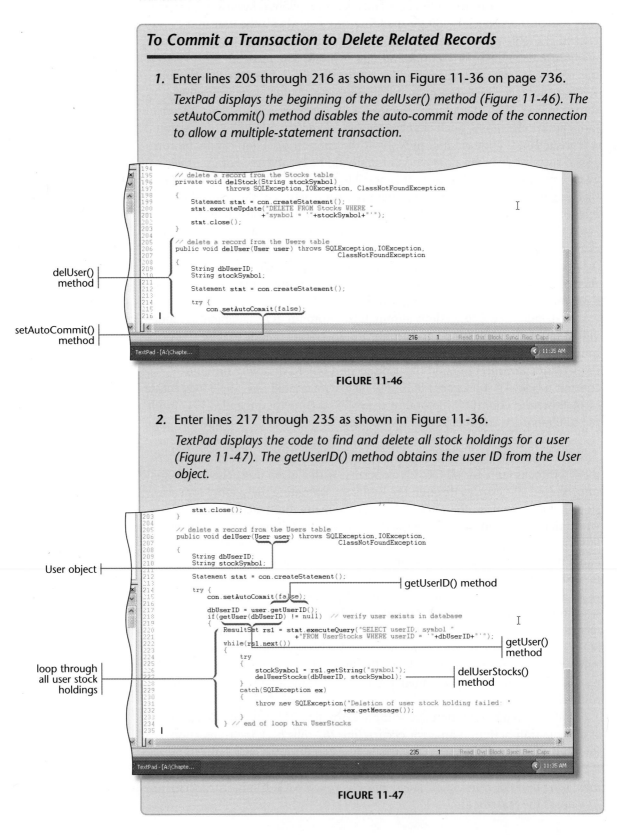

FIGURE 11-46

2. Enter lines 217 through 235 as shown in Figure 11-36.

TextPad displays the code to find and delete all stock holdings for a user (Figure 11-47). The getUserID() method obtains the user ID from the User object.

FIGURE 11-47

3. Enter lines 236 through 248 as shown in Figure 11-36 on page 737.

TextPad displays the code to delete the user record (Figure 11-48). All stock holdings for this user, and any of the same stocks no longer held by any user, are deleted.

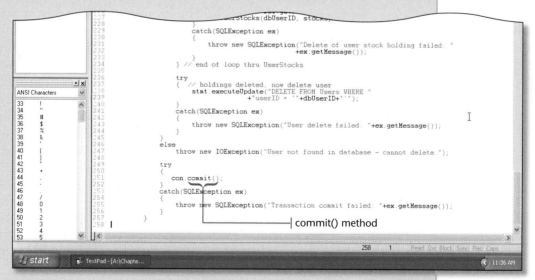

```
217            ...userID();
218        if(getUser(dbUserID) != null)  // verify user exists in database
219        {
220            ResultSet rs1 = stmt.executeQuery("SELECT userID, symbol "
221                            +"FROM UserStocks WHERE userID = '"+dbUserID+"'");
222            while(rs1.next())
223            {
224                try
225                {
226                    stockSymbol = rs1.getString("symbol");
227                    delUserStocks(dbUserID, stockSymbol);
228                }
229                catch(SQLException ex)
230                {
231                    throw new SQLException("Deletion of user stock holding failed: "
232                            +ex.getMessage());
233                }
234            } // end of loop thru UserStocks
235
236            try
237            {  // holdings deleted, now delete user
238                stmt.executeUpdate("DELETE FROM Users WHERE "
239                            +"userID = '"+dbUserID+"'");
240            }
241            catch(SQLException ex)
242            {
243                throw new SQLException("User deletion failed: "+ex.getMessage());
244            }
245        }
246        else
247            throw new IOException("User not found in database - cannot delete.");
248
```

SQL delete of user record

FIGURE 11-48

4. Enter lines 249 through 257 as shown in Figure 11-36.

TextPad displays the code to commit the transaction (Figure 11-49). If the commit fails, a new SQLException is thrown to trigger the rollback.

```
227            ...erStocks(dbUserID, stock...
228            }
229            catch(SQLException ex)
230            {
231                throw new SQLException("Delete of user stock holding failed: "
232                            +ex.getMessage());
233            }
234        } // end of loop thru UserStocks
235
236        try
237        {  // holdings deleted, now delete user
238            stmt.executeUpdate("DELETE FROM Users WHERE "
239                            +"userID = '"+dbUserID+"'");
240        }
241        catch(SQLException ex)
242        {
243            throw new SQLException("User delete failed: "+ex.getMessage());
244        }
245    }
246    else
247        throw new IOException("User not found in database - cannot delete.");
248
249    try
250    {
251        con.commit();
252    }
253    catch(SQLException ex)
254    {
255        throw new SQLException("Transaction commit failed: "+ex.getMessage());
256    }
257 }
```

commit() method

FIGURE 11-49

(continued)

> **5.** Enter lines 258 through 277 as shown in Figure 11-36 on page 737.
>
> *TextPad displays the code to rollback the transaction, close the Statement, and complete the method (Figure 11-50). If the rollback fails, a new SQLException is thrown.*

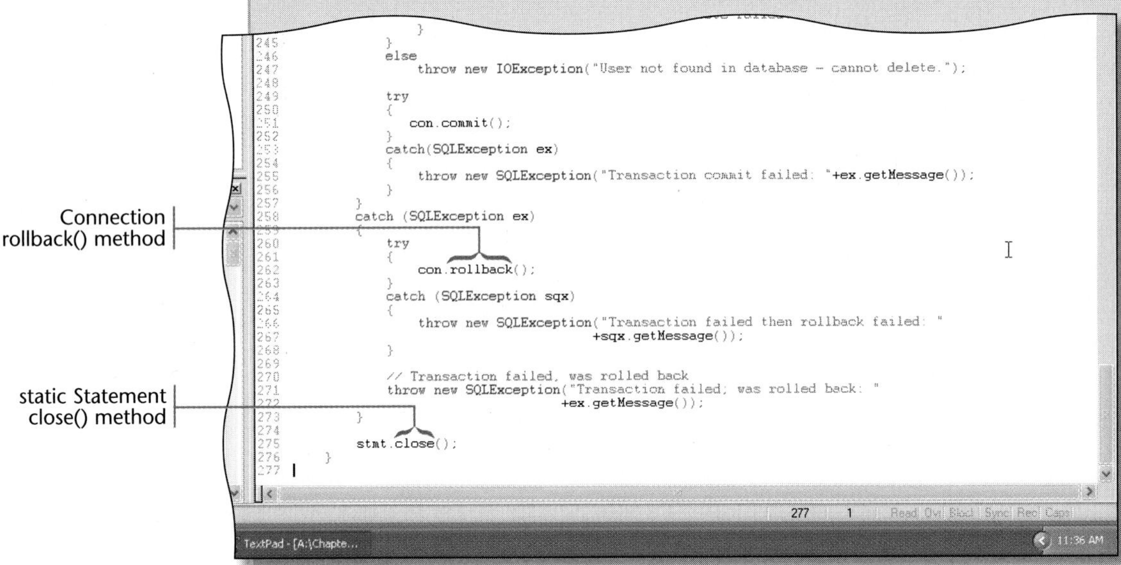

```
245         }
246         }
247         else
248             throw new IOException("User not found in database - cannot delete.");
249
250         try
251         {
252             con.commit();
253         }
254         catch(SQLException ex)
255         {
256             throw new SQLException("Transaction commit failed: "+ex.getMessage());
257         }
258     catch (SQLException ex)
259     {
260         try
261         {
262             con.rollback();
263         }
264         catch (SQLException sqx)
265         {
266             throw new SQLException("Transaction failed then rollback failed: "
267                                 +sqx.getMessage());
268         }
269
270         // Transaction failed, was rolled back
271         throw new SQLException("Transaction failed; was rolled back: "
272                             +ex.getMessage());
273     }
274
275     stmt.close();
276 }
277
```

Connection rollback() method

static Statement close() method

FIGURE 11-50

Notice how line 227 calls the method, delUserStocks(), to delete a stock holding for a user. This method will be written next. The requirements document indicates that a stock no longer held by any user should be deleted. It is possible that when this method is called, the stock holding to be deleted is the last for this stock. Lines 285 through 287 delete the current stock holding for the user. To determine if any other users hold this stock, the UserStocks table is queried in lines 289 through 290. Earlier, you learned that the next() method of a ResultSet returns true if the next row is valid and false if there are no more rows. As was done in the MakeDB class, line 292 checks if no users were found to hold this stock and if there were none, the delStock() method, coded earlier, is called in line 293. Line 295 closes the local Statement object for this method. Notice that each of the methods, delUser(), delUserStocks(), and delStock(), contain a local Statement object. Multiple statements may be opened on a single connection and, in this case, they all can use the same reference name because they are local to each method.

The following step enters the code to delete a user stock holding and, optionally, call a method to delete the stock record if the stock no longer is held by a user.

To Delete a User Stock Holding

1. Enter lines 278 through 298 as shown in Figure 11-36 on page 737.

TextPad displays the delUserStocks() method (Figure 11-51). The method checks if the stock is held by other users and, if not, calls the delStock() method to delete the stock record.

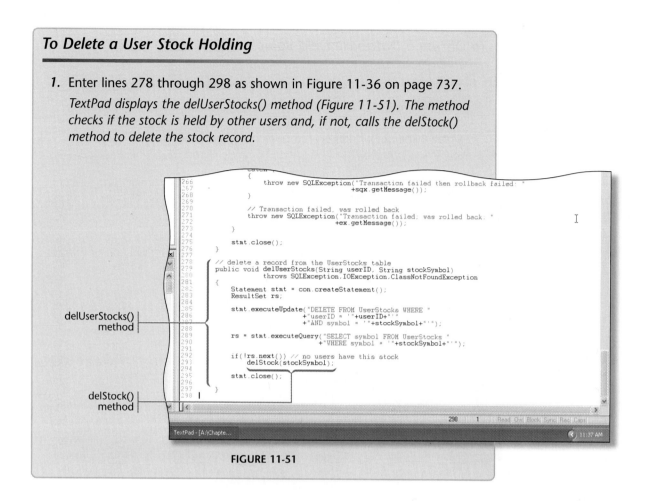

FIGURE 11-51

The final database actions needed are those that query the database and return one or more fields from one or more records.

Obtaining Database Field Values

According to the requirements document, the program must be able to return a stock description (name) for a given stock. As was illustrated earlier, this involves running a query where the search condition matches a single primary key value, which is done on lines 316 and 317. If a matching record is found, on line 319 the desired field is obtained from the result set. Line 323 returns the obtained value to the calling program. If no result was obtained, a null value, set on line 314, is returned.

The step on the next page enters the code to obtain a single value from a record in the database.

To Obtain a Database Field Value

1. Enter lines 299 through 325 as shown in Figure 11-36 on pages 737 and 738.

TextPad displays the getStockDesc() method (Figure 11-52). The returned value is the description of a stock record obtained from the ResultSet getString() method.

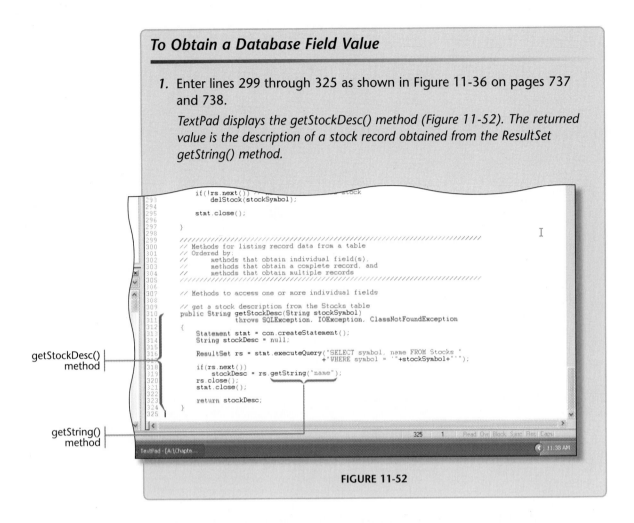

getStockDesc() method

getString() method

```
         if(!rs.next())                         ...tock
            delStock(stockSymbol);

293
294
295    stmt.close();
296
297 }
298
299 //////////////////////////////////////////////////////////////////////////////
300 // Methods for listing record data from a table
301 // Ordered by:
302 //       methods that obtain individual field(s),
303 //       methods that obtain a complete record, and
304 //       methods that obtain multiple records
305 //////////////////////////////////////////////////////////////////////////////
306
307 // Methods to access one or more individual fields
308
309 // get a stock description from the Stocks table
310 public String getStockDesc(String stockSymbol)
311             throws SQLException, IOException, ClassNotFoundException
312 {
313    Statement stmt = con.createStatement();
314    String stockDesc = null;
315
316    ResultSet rs = stmt.executeQuery("SELECT symbol, name FROM Stocks "
                   +"WHERE symbol = '"+stockSymbol+"'");
317
318    if(rs.next())
319       stockDesc = rs.getString("name");
320    rs.close();
321    stmt.close();
322
323    return stockDesc;
324 }
325
```

325   1   Read Ovr Block Sync Rec Caps

TextPad - [A:\Chapte...   11:38 AM

FIGURE 11-52

When given a user ID, the program also should return all of the user fields as a User object. As was noted earlier, using an asterisk in the SQL SELECT statement as the selected fields causes a return of all fields for the selected record. This is done in lines 343 and 344 and, again, by matching a single primary key value, a single record is obtained. Lines 347 through 357 use the result set data to create a User object. If no result was obtained, the User reference is left as null. Finally, the User object, or null, is returned to the calling program.

The following step enters the code to obtain all field values from a user record and return them as a User object.

To Obtain All Database Field Values

1. Enter lines 326 through 364 as shown in Figure 11-36.

TextPad displays the getUser() method (Figure 11-53). The method returns a User object with data from a user record.

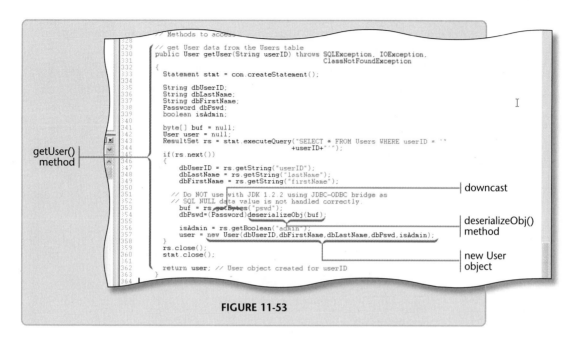

FIGURE 11-53

Finally, the requirements document indicates that the program should return two lists of values. The first case is a list of selected fields for all users that contains multiple records from a result set. The second case is a list of all stocks held for a given user. Both cases return multiple records from the result set, using the **ORDER BY** clause to sort them. Because the result sets are closed before either method returns, the data must be saved into structures the methods can return. Each method iterates through its respective result set and stores the results into an ArrayList. The ArrayList object then is returned.

The following steps enter the code to create a list of field values from multiple records and return them in an ArrayList object.

To Obtain a List of Fields from Multiple Database Records

1. Enter lines 365 through 391 as shown in Figure 11-36 on pages 738 and 739.

TextPad displays the listUsers() method (Figure 11-54). The method returns a list of selected fields sorted by userID for all records from the Users Table.

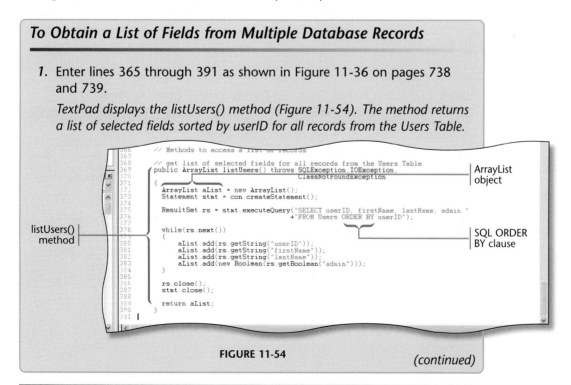

FIGURE 11-54

(continued)

2. Enter lines 392 through 409 as shown in Figure 11-36 on page 739. Save and compile the StockTrackerDB.java source code file.

TextPad displays the listUserStocks() method (Figure 11-55). The method returns all fields in all records sorted by symbol for a user from the Userstocks Table.

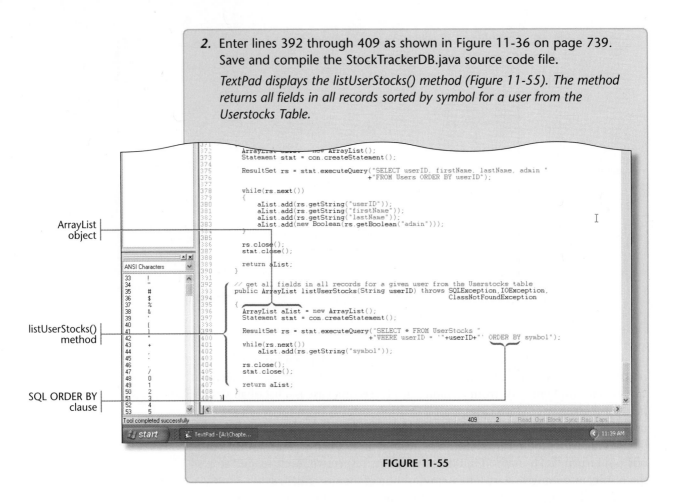

FIGURE 11-55

The StockTrackerDB class now is complete. To test the class, the code for the GUI application, StockTracker, must be compiled and executed. The remaining source files for the complete application, listed in Table 11-7, are provided on the Data Disk.

Table 11-7   GUI Source Code Files for the Stock Tracker Application

FILE NAME	PROGRAM FUNCTION
STAction.java	Interface for named constants
STLogon.java	GUI for initial log on screen
StockTracker.java	GUI for stock maintenance functions, add, delete, stock list; displays user maintenance add, delete, update, and list buttons for administrative users only
User.java	User class definition
UserMaintFrame.java	GUI for user maintenance functions, add, delete, update, and list users

All of the remaining classes can be compiled individually; however, compiling the initial log on class causes all classes used in the application to compile also.

The following steps open the initial log on class and compile the remaining related classes for the Stock Tracker application.

To Compile Related Classes

1. Click the Open button on the Standard toolbar.
2. When the Open File(s) dialog box is displayed, if necessary, click the Look in box arrow and select the Chapter11 folder (or the location specified by your instructor).
3. Click the file, STLogon.java, and then click the Open button.
4. Compile the class, STLogon.

TextPad displays the code for the STLogon class (Figure 11-56). The remaining classes for the application are compiled also.

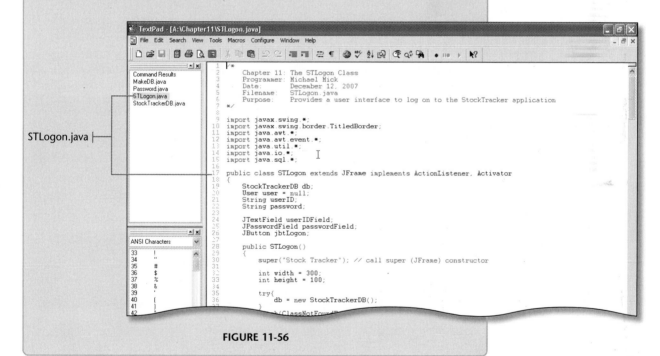

FIGURE 11-56

The remaining classes were compiled because the compiler tries to locate all classes used in the initial log on GUI and, if not found, attempts to locate and compile the source code. As each class depends on another related class, the compiles cascade until all needed classes are compiled. This cascade of compiles works only for source code files without existing matching class files. If a class file exists, its source code file must be explicitly compiled.

Testing the StockTrackerDB Data Access Class

Once all source code files are compiled, the Stock Tracker application may be tested, using the StockTrackerDB data access class to manipulate the StockTracker database. Table 11-8 lists the various stocks that are to be entered as test data for the application.

Table 11-8	*Stock Symbols and Descriptions*
STOCK SYMBOL	STOCK DESCRIPTION
msft	Microsoft Corporation
Orcl	Oracle Corporation
Dell	Dell Computer Corporation

The following steps use the Stock Tracker application to test the StockTrackerDB data access class.

To Test the StockTrackerDB Data Access Class

1. Press CTRL+2 to run the STLogon class. When the Stock Tracker Log on window opens, type admin01 in the User ID text box and then type admin01 in the Password text box.

The program opens the Log on window of the Stock Tracker application (Figure 11-57). The password text appears as asterisks. Because Password objects are used, all of the rules established in the Password class apply to passwords entered in this application.

FIGURE 11-57

2. Click the Log on button.

The Stock Tracker application window opens (Figure 11-58). Because the initial user, Default Admin, was added as an administrative user, the buttons for user maintenance are displayed.

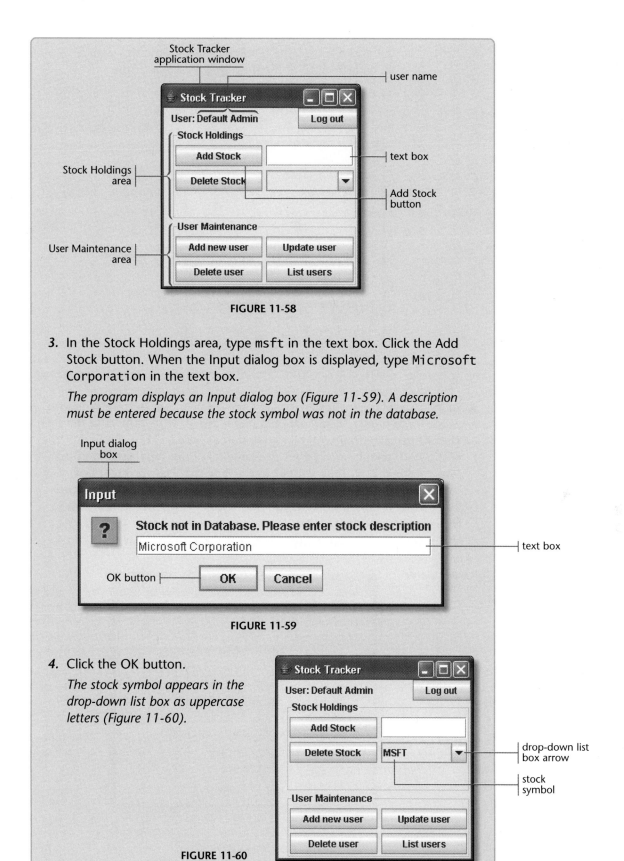

FIGURE 11-58

3. In the Stock Holdings area, type msft in the text box. Click the Add Stock button. When the Input dialog box is displayed, type Microsoft Corporation in the text box.

The program displays an Input dialog box (Figure 11-59). A description must be entered because the stock symbol was not in the database.

FIGURE 11-59

4. Click the OK button.

The stock symbol appears in the drop-down list box as uppercase letters (Figure 11-60).

FIGURE 11-60

(continued)

5. Repeat Steps 3 and 4 to add the remaining stock symbols listed in Table 11-8 on page 756. Click the drop-down list box arrow.

All of the stock symbols entered appear in the drop-down list box as upper-case letters, regardless of how they were entered (Figure 11-61).

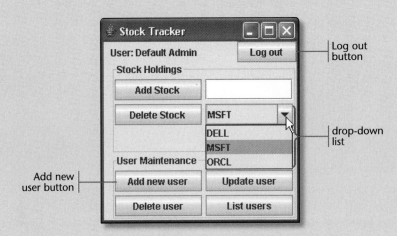

FIGURE 11-61

6. In the User Maintenance area, click the Add new user button. When the Stock Tracker: User Maintenance window opens, type user01 in the User ID text box in the Add New User area. Type Bill in the First Name text box. Type Buyout in the Last Name text box. Type user01 in the Password text box. Type user01 in the Re-enter Password text box. If necessary, click Yes as the Auto Expires option and then type 5 in the Uses Left text box. If desired, you may substitute your own test data for these and subsequent values.

The Add New User area displays the entered data (Figure 11-62).

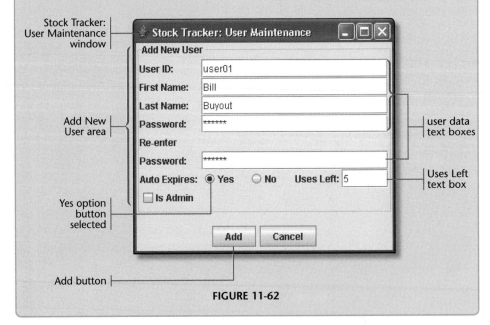

FIGURE 11-62

7. Click the Add button.

The program displays the New User Added dialog box with the user ID and first and last name of the new user that was added to the database.

New User Added
dialog box

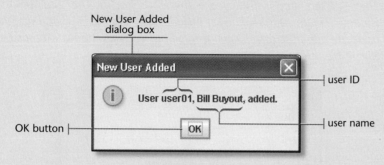

OK button

user ID

user name

FIGURE 11-63

8. Click the OK button. When the Stock Tracker window opens, click the Add new user button in the User Maintenance area. Type user02 in the User ID text box in the Add new user area. Type Fran in the First Name text box. Type Futures in the Last Name text box. Type user02 in the Password text box. Type user02 in the Re-enter Password text box. Click No for the Auto Expires option and then click the Is Admin check box to select it.

The Add New User area displays the entered data (Figure 11-64). The Uses Left text box no longer is editable.

No option button
selected for Auto
Expires option

Is Admin check
box selected

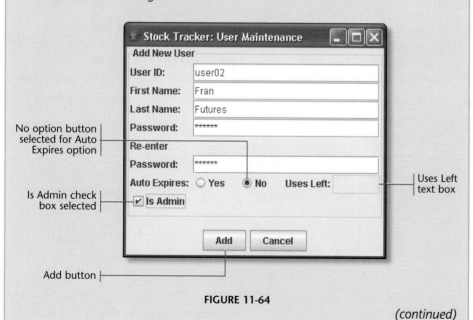

Uses Left
text box

Add button

FIGURE 11-64

(continued)

9. Click the Add button. When the New User Added dialog is displayed, click the OK button. When the StockTracker window opens, click the List users button in the User Maintenance area.

   The List Users area is displayed in the Stock Tracker: User Maintenance window (Figure 11-65). The list includes user IDs, names, and whether the users are administrative users. A scroll bar appears if data extends beyond the visible screen.

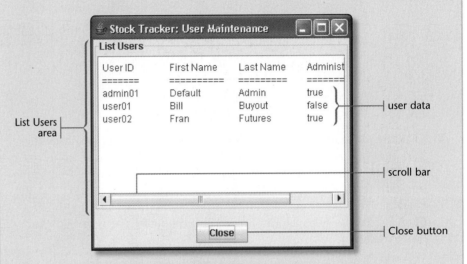

FIGURE 11-65

10. Click the Close button. When the StockTracker window opens, click the Log out button. When the Stock Tracker Log on window opens, type user01 or the first user ID you added in the User ID text box. Type user01 or the first password you added in the Password text box.

   The log on information is entered in the Stock Tracker window text boxes (Figure 11-66).

FIGURE 11-66

11. Click the Log on button. When the Change Password dialog box is displayed, type secure1 in the text box.

   The user must enter a new password when the current password expires (Figure 11-67).

Change Password
dialog box

text box

OK button

FIGURE 11-67

12. Click the OK button. When the Verify Password dialog box is displayed, type secure1 in the text box. Click the OK button.

The Stock Tracker application is displayed with the new user as the current user (Figure 11-68). The user maintenance area is not visible because this user is not an administrative user. No stocks display because this user has no stock holdings.

user name

Stock Tracker
application
window

User
Maintenance
area not
displayed

empty
drop-down
list box

FIGURE 11-68

13. Repeat Steps 3 and 4 to add the stock holdings for this user. Click the drop-down list box arrow.

The stock holdings display for this user (Figure 11-69). Stock descriptions were not added because the stocks already existed in the database.

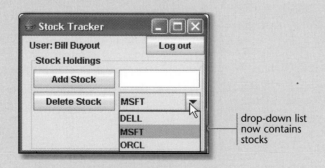

drop-down list
now contains
stocks

FIGURE 11-69

(continued)

14. Click DELL in the drop-down list to select it.

The selected stock symbol appears in the text box and in the drop-down list box (Figure 11-70).

FIGURE 11-70

15. Click the Delete Stock button. Click the drop-down list box arrow.

The stock is removed from the user's holdings (Figure 11-71). The text box is cleared.

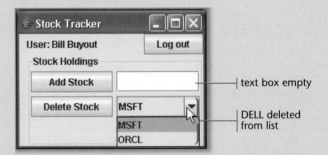

FIGURE 11-71

16. Click the Log out button. Repeat Steps 10 through 13 on the previous page to log on as another user and add stock holdings. Type `user02` in the User ID text box and then type `user02` in the Password text box. When prompted, type `secure2` as the new password. Repeat Steps 3 and 4 to add only the first two stocks as stock holdings for this user. Click the drop-down list box arrow.

The current user displays only two stock holdings (Figure 11-72). Only the first user, Default Admin, holds the stock, DELL. Because the User Maintenance area is displayed, the current user must be an administrative user.

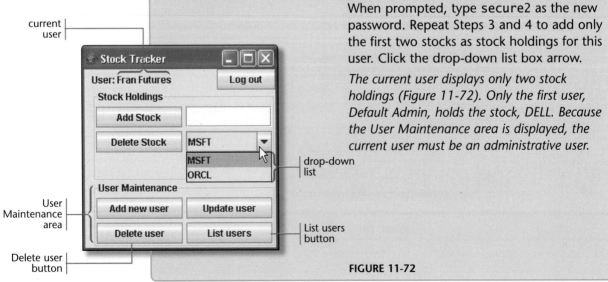

FIGURE 11-72

17. Click the Delete user button. When the Enter User ID dialog box is displayed, type user01 in the text box.

The Enter User ID dialog box displays the ID of the user to delete (Figure 11-73).

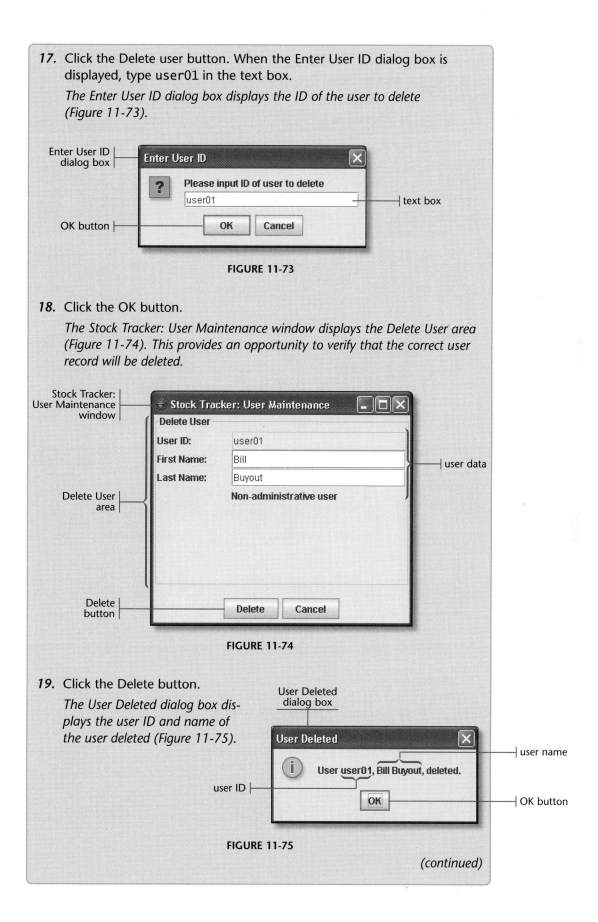

FIGURE 11-73

18. Click the OK button.

The Stock Tracker: User Maintenance window displays the Delete User area (Figure 11-74). This provides an opportunity to verify that the correct user record will be deleted.

FIGURE 11-74

19. Click the Delete button.

The User Deleted dialog box displays the user ID and name of the user deleted (Figure 11-75).

FIGURE 11-75

(continued)

20. Click the OK button. When the StockTracker window opens, click the List users button in the User Maintenance area.

The Stock Tracker: User Maintenance window displays the List Users area with user01 deleted (Figure 11-76).

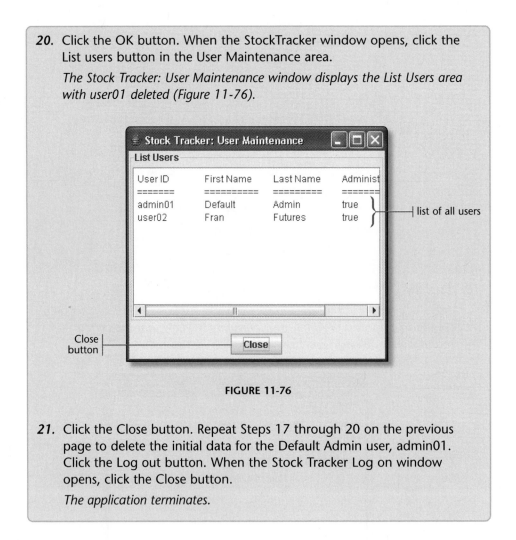

FIGURE 11-76

21. Click the Close button. Repeat Steps 17 through 20 on the previous page to delete the initial data for the Default Admin user, admin01. Click the Log out button. When the Stock Tracker Log on window opens, click the Close button.

The application terminates.

The Stock Tracker application has been successfully used in testing the StockTrackerDB data access class. If you have Microsoft Access available on your system, you can open the database and examine the tables and the records in each table directly.

Print the Source Code

After testing the application, source code for the StockTrackerDB class and the MakeDB class should be printed. The following steps print the source code for both programs.

To Print Source Code

1. In the TextPad window, click StockTrackerDB.java in the Selector Window to display the StockTrackerDB source code. Click the Print button on the Standard toolbar.

The StockTrackerDB source code is displayed in the coding window.

2. Click the Print button on the Standard toolbar.

The StockTrackerDB source code is printed.

3. Click MakeDB.java in the Selector Window to display the MakeDB source code.

The MakeDB source code is displayed in the coding window.

4. Click the Print button on the Standard toolbar.

The MakeDB source code is printed.

Quitting TextPad

After you create, save, compile, test, and print the source code for the MakeDB and StockTrackerDB classes, you can quit TextPad. The following step quits TextPad and returns control to Windows.

To Quit TextPad

1. Click the Close button on the TextPad title bar.

The TextPad window closes and the Windows desktop is displayed.

OTHER WAYS

1. Press ALT+F, X

Chapter Summary

In this chapter, you learned about designing a relational database, how to implement the Serializable interface, about persistent objects, and how to serialize and deserialize objects. You registered an ODBC data source name and learned how to load a JDBC™ driver and make a database connection in a Java program. You learned how to drop tables and indexes and then create tables, indexes, and primary and foreign keys in a database. You learned how to create and execute SQL statements to add, delete, update, and query records in a database and then how to process a result set within a Java program. You learned how to group statements into transactions and how to commit or rollback a transaction. You learned about using a data access class as a model of a database to application programs. Finally, you used a GUI application to test the interaction of a data access class with a database.

What You Should Know

Having completed this chapter, you now should be able to perform the tasks shown in Table 11-9.

Table 11-9 Chapter 11 What You Should Know

TASK NUMBER	TASK	PAGE
1	Open an Existing Java Program in TextPad	700
2	Implement the Serializable Interface	702
3	Register an ODBC Data Source Name	703
4	Open a New Java Program in TextPad	713
5	Load a JDBC™ Database Driver	714
6	Establish a JDBC™ Connection	716
7	Drop Indexes and Tables in a Database	718
8	Create Tables with Primary Keys	720
9	Create Tables with Foreign Keys	722
10	Create a Primary Key Index on an Existing Table	723
11	Create a PreparedStatement Object	724
12	Execute a PreparedStatement	725
13	Execute an SQL Query Statement	726
14	Process the ResultSet of a Query	728
15	Serialize an Object	730
16	Deserialize an Object	731
17	Create the StockTracker Database Tables	732
18	Open a New Java Program in TextPad	739
19	Create a Data Access Class Constructor	740
20	Close a Connection	741
21	Serialize and Deserialize Objects	742
22	Add Records to Database Tables	743
23	Update a Record in the Users Table	745
24	Delete a Record in the Stocks Table	746
25	Commit a Transaction to Delete Related Records	748
26	Delete a User Stock Holding	751
27	Obtain a Database Field Value	752
28	Obtain All Database Field Values	752
29	Obtain a List of Fields from Multiple Database Records	753
30	Compile Related Classes	755
31	Test the StockTrackerDB Data Access Class	756
32	Print Source Code	765
33	Quit TextPad	765

Key Terms

Homework Assignments

Identify Code

Identify the code elements shown in Figure 11-77 and describe what they do.

```
1    Class.forName("sun.jdbc.odbc.JdbcOdbcDriver");
2
3    String url = "jdbc:odbc:StockTracker";
4
5    Connection con = DriverManager.getConnection(url);
6    Statement stmt = con.createStatement();
7
8
9    stmt.executeUpdate("CREATE TABLE Stocks ("
10                       +"symbol TEXT(8) NOT NULL "
11                       +"CONSTRAINT PK_Stocks PRIMARY KEY, "
12                       +"name TEXT(50)"
13                       +")");
14
15
16   String stockDesc = null;
17
18   ResultSet rs = stmt.executeQuery("SELECT symbol, name FROM Stocks "
19                       +"WHERE symbol = '"+stockSymbol+"'");
20
21   if(rs.next())
22       stockDesc = rs.getString("name");
23
24   rs.close();
25   stmt.close();
26
```

FIGURE 11-77

1. _____   4. _____

2. _____   5. _____

3. _____

Understanding Error Messages

Figure 11-78a displays a portion of a Java program. Figure 11-78b displays the compilation error messages. Using what you know about error messages, list the coding errors that caused TextPad to display these errors.

```
1
2   public class Errors implements Serializable
3   {
4       private Connection con = null;
5
6       public Errors() throws ClassNotFoundException,SQLException
7       {
8           String url = "jdbc:odbc:StockTracker";
9           Class.forName("sun.jdbc.odbc.JdbcOdbcDriver");
10          con = DriverManager.getConnection(url);
11      }
12
13      public byte[] serializeObj(Object obj) throws IOException
14      {
15          ByteArrayOutputStream baOStream = new ByteArrayOutputStream();
16          ObjectOutputStream objOStream = new ObjectOutputStream(baOStream);
17
18          objOStream.writeObject(obj);
19          objOStream.flush();
20          objOStream.close();
21          return baOStream.toByteArray();
22      }
23
24
25
```

(a)

```
1   A:\Chapter11\Errors.java:2: cannot resolve symbol
2   symbol  : class Serializable
3   location: class Errors
4   public class Errors implements Serializable
5                                  ^
6   A:\Chapter11\Errors.java:4: cannot resolve symbol
7   symbol  : class Connection
8   location: class Errors
9       private Connection con = null;
10              ^
11  A:\Chapter11\Errors.java:6: cannot resolve symbol
12  symbol  : class SQLException
13  location: class Errors
14      public Errors() throws ClassNotFoundException,SQLException
15                                                    ^
16  A:\Chapter11\Errors.java:13: cannot resolve symbol
17  symbol  : class IOException
18  location: class Errors
19      public byte[] serializeObj(Object obj) throws IOException
20                                                    ^
21  A:\Chapter11\Errors.java:10: cannot resolve symbol
22  symbol  : variable DriverManager
23  location: class Errors
24              con = DriverManager.getConnection(url);
25                    ^
26  A:\Chapter11\Errors.java:15: cannot resolve symbol
27  symbol  : class ByteArrayOutputStream
28  location: class Errors
29              ByteArrayOutputStream baOStream = new
    ByteArrayOutputStream();
30              ^
31  A:\Chapter11\Errors.java:15: cannot resolve symbol
32  symbol  : class ByteArrayOutputStream
33  location: class Errors
34              ByteArrayOutputStream baOStream = new
    ByteArrayOutputStream();
35                                                ^
36  A:\Chapter11\Errors.java:16: cannot resolve symbol
37  symbol  : class ObjectOutputStream
38  location: class Errors
39          ObjectOutputStream objOStream = new ObjectOutputStream(baOStream);
40          ^
41  A:\Chapter11\Errors.java:16: cannot resolve symbol
42  symbol  : class ObjectOutputStream
43  location: class Errors
44          ObjectOutputStream objOStream = new ObjectOutputStream(baOStream);
45                                              ^
46  9 errors
47
48  Tool completed with exit code 1
49
```

(b)

FIGURE 11-78

Using the Java API

The Java API is a good tool to look up information about a class with which you may be unfamiliar or to check the syntax of commands and methods you wish to use in your programs. While connected to the Internet, start a browser, type http://java.sun.com/j2se/5.0/docs/api/index.html in the Address text box, and then press the ENTER key to view the Java API Specification on the Sun Web site. (Or, if you downloaded the documentation from the CD-ROM that accompanies this book, navigate to the installed version of the Java SDK documentation on your system. Open the index.html file in the docs\api folder.)

With the Java API Specification open in the browser window, perform the following steps.

1. Use the scroll bar in the lower-left frame, if necessary, to scroll to the PreparedStatement link. Click the PreparedStatement link.

2. When the Interface PreparedStatement page is displayed, read the paragraph that describes the PreparedStatement interface, as shown in Figure 11-79.

3. Scroll down to the Method Summary table. Click the link for the executeQuery() method. When the method definition is displayed, drag through the definition and the executeUpdate() method definition to select them. Click File on the browser's menu bar and then click Print on the File menu to print a copy of the definitions. When the Print dialog box is displayed, click Print selection and then click the Print button in the Print dialog box.

4. Scroll to the top of the Interface PreparedStatement page. Under the line, All Superinterfaces, click the Statement link.

5. When the Interface Statement page is displayed, read the paragraph that describes the Statement interface. As you did in Step 3 above for a PreparedStatement, display, select, and print the executeQuery() method and the executeUpdate() method definitions for a Statement.

6. Compare the PreparedStatement executeUpdate() and executeQuery() method definitions with those for a Statement and answer the following questions:

   a) How do the corresponding methods for a PreparedStatement and a Statement differ?

   b) Disregarding dynamic versus static, can both objects process the same SQL statements?

   c) The text indicated that an update or delete might affect more than a single record. Do either or both of these objects tell you the number of records updated or deleted by an SQL statement? If so, describe how you would obtain that information.

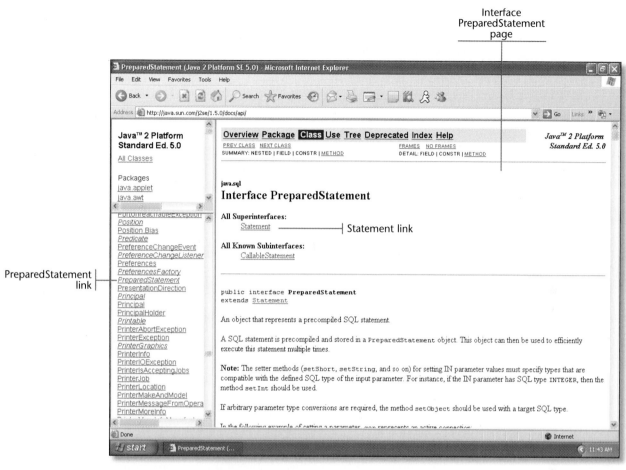

FIGURE 11-79

Short Answer

1. The number of records in one table that may relate to a given record in another table is represented by the _____ of the relationship.

2. A(n) _____ is a rule that restricts the data value that can be entered in a column.

3. A(n) _____ class accesses data from persistent storage and provides it to a requesting application.

4. A(n) _____ is software for a specific DBMS used to translate between the calls to the JDBC™ API and the corresponding commands of the DBMS.

5. Constraints may be of two types: a(n) _____ constraint or a(n) _____ constraint.

6. A(n) _____ is an index with a unique, non-null value for each record; only one is allowed for a table.

7. A(n) _____ is a type of pointer that points to the current row of data.

(continued)

Short Answer *(continued)*

8. A(n) _____ is the action of undoing changes made to a database before completing a transaction.

9. _____ is another term for the DBMS software.

10. The _____ class provides the basic services for managing a set of JDBC™ drivers.

11. Calling the _____ method for an output stream ensures that any buffered output bytes are written.

12. A database _____ is used to add, modify, or delete data from the database.

13. _____ is the process of encoding the state of an object into a stream.

14. A(n) _____ is a logical unit of work.

15. An interface with no methods or fields is called a(n) _____.

16. An association between columns in two tables is called a(n) _____.

17. A(n) _____ returns a set of data results based on a set of parameters.

18. A(n) _____ is one or more fields in a table that reference the primary key field(s) of another table.

19. _____ is a type of software design pattern that separates data access, the way the data is viewed, and control of how the data is used.

20. _____ is the capability of an object, including its state, to be saved over time.

21. The communication pathway between the user program and the database is called a(n) _____.

22. The first stage of database design in which there are no repeating groups is called _____.

23. To _____ a transaction means that all changes are saved.

24. Obtaining a(n) _____ is the database equivalent of opening a file.

25. The deletion of an index or a table is called a(n) _____.

Learn It Online

Start your browser and visit scsite.com/java3e/exs. Follow the instructions in the exercises below.

1. **Chapter Reinforcement TF, MC, and SA** Click the Chapter Reinforcement link below Chapter 11. Print and then answer the questions.

2. **Practice Test** Click the Practice Test link below Chapter 11. Answer each question, enter your first and last name at the bottom of the page, and then click the Grade Test button. When the graded practice test is displayed on your screen, click Print on the File menu to print a hard copy. Continue to take practice tests until you score 80% or better. Hand in a printout of the final practice test.

3. **Crossword Puzzle Challenge** Click the Crossword Puzzle Challenge link below Chapter 11. Read the instructions, and then enter your first and last name. Click the Play button. Complete the crossword puzzle. When you are finished, click the Submit button. When the crossword puzzle is displayed, click the Print button.

4. **Tips and Tricks** Click the Tips and Tricks link below Chapter 11. Click a topic that pertains to Chapter 11. Right-click the information and then click Print on the shortcut menu. Construct a brief example of what the information relates to in Java to confirm you understand how to use the tip or trick. Hand in the example and printed information.

5. **Newsgroups** Click the Newsgroups link below Chapter 11. Click a topic that pertains to Chapter 11. Print three comments.

6. **Expanding Your Horizons** Click the Expanding Your Horizons link below Chapter 11. Click a topic that pertains to Chapter 11. Print the information. Construct a brief example of what the information relates to in Java to confirm you understand the contents of the article. Hand in the example and printed information.

7. **Search Sleuth** Select three key terms from the Key Terms section of this chapter and then use the Google search engine at google.com (or any major search engine) to display and print two Web pages for each key term.

Debugging Assignment

Find and fix the error in each line of code. Each line contains only one error. Indented lines continue the previous statement.

```
1. forName("sun.jdbc.odbc.JdbcOdbcDriver");
2. String dbn = " AutoParts";
3. Connection con = getConnection(dbn);
4. Statement stmt = DriverManager.createStatement();
5. stmt.executeUpdate("CREATE TABLE StockItems itemID INT "
6.    +"CONSTRAINT PK_Item PRIMARY, "
7. +"CONSTRAINT FK1_Item REFERENCES PartDesc (partno) "
8. +"qtyOnHand INT, price SINGLE, cost SINGLE");
```

Programming Assignments

1 Designing a Relational Database Table

Modify the relationship diagram shown in Figure 11-3 on page 697 for the StockTracker database to include a new table for recording stock trades. The StockTrades table will capture for all users both buy and sell transactions of a given stock; the date and time of the transaction; the price per share of the stock; the number of shares bought or sold; and the total price paid or received, including any fees paid. Indicate the field(s) used as keys and the relationship(s) to any other table(s). Identify the cardinality of all relationships. Explain how your selection and order of keys used would prevent duplication of records and provide access to all transactions for a) all stocks for a given user, b) a particular stock for a given user, and c) only buy or sell transactions.

2 Creating a New Table for an Existing Database

Make a copy of the StockTracker database and name it, StockTracker2. Create an ODBC data source name, also named StockTracker2, that references this database. Write a Java utility program that will create the new table designed in Assignment 1, adding it to the StockTracker2 database. The program can be a console program and does not need a GUI interface. The new table should include all of the fields listed in assignment 1. Additionally, it should create the key(s) and relationship(s) indicated in your design. In the program, create some test data and add to the database, remembering to keep data in the tables synchronized (i.e., do not add a transaction for a nonexistent user or stock), which may require writing data to other tables in the database as well. Finally, using Access, open the database, click Tools on the menu bar and then click Relationships. Verify that the relationship diagram looks like your original design. *Hint:* Use the data type INT to create an SQL numeric field.

3 Implementing a Serialization Utility Class

Create a Java class, ObjUtil, that will provide object serialization and deserialization methods for use by any other class. This class has no constructor, as no object of the class will be created. Rather, the two methods, much like methods in the Math class, are called without an object. After creating and compiling the new class, test it by using its methods in place of the corresponding methods in the MakeDB and StockTrackerDB classes. *Hint:* Review static methods.

4 Using a Database Query Result

Write a Java program to query the StockTracker database for all users and all stocks held by each user. List the user's ID, first name, and last name followed by their stocks, including both the stock symbol and stock description (name). This can be a console application that produces output to the screen, as shown in Figure 11-80. Use the project, StockTracker, to add additional users and stocks, if necessary. For an extra challenge, use only the StockTrackerDB data access class to obtain data from the database.

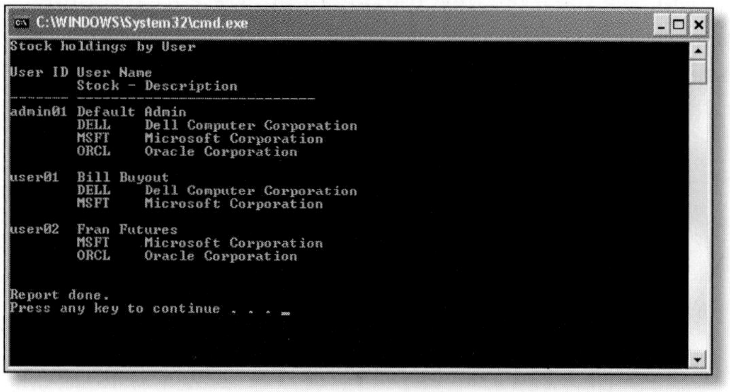

FIGURE 11-80

5 Using a Prepared Statement for Dynamic Queries

Modify the solution for Assignment 4 above to allow a single user ID to be entered at the keyboard. Use a prepared statement for all SQL commands, and do not use the StockTrackerDB data access class. Again, this can be a console application that produces output to the screen, as shown in Figure 11-81. *Hint:* Review the Stringlength() method and the use of a BufferedReader to get input at the command line.

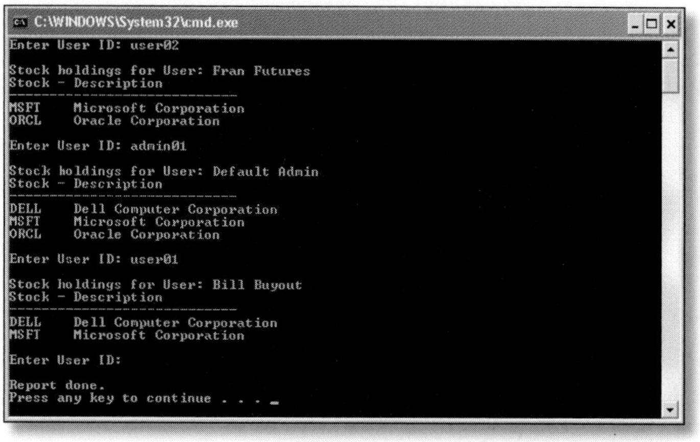

FIGURE 11-81

6 Replacing an Interface with an Enum Class

The project in this chapter utilizes an interface, STAction, to provide a list of constant values. This list is more properly provided via an enumerated list. Modify the STAction.java file to change it from an interface to an Enum class. Modify all source code that uses STAction to reflect this change. Compile the changed classes and test the modified project.

Notes

Utilizing Servlets for Web Applications

Objectives

You will have
mastered the material in
this chapter when you can:

- Understand the Model-View-Controller
  pattern
- Describe Java Web application components
- Use JavaScript in an HTML document
- Describe HTTP GET and POST methods
- Describe the servlet life cycle
- Process HTTP requests in a servlet
- Implement session tracking with HTTP
- Redirect and forward HTTP requests
- Acquire data from a Web service
- Synchronize multithreaded code on an object
- Create a JavaServer Page (JSP)
- Modify a deployment descriptor
- Enable servlet reloading with Tomcat
- Test a Web application

Introduction

In earlier chapters, the programs were designed to be used by one person at one time on one computer. Even when multiple classes were used for different purposes, such as separating interaction with a database from the user interface, you still were working with a single program running on the computer where the program was stored. Today, with the Internet playing a key role in how people use computers, applications that originally were designed for use on a single local computer now are **Web-enabled**, meaning they utilize a connection to a Web server and can be accessed from anywhere in the world.

As you learned in Chapter 1, many programmers use Java servlets to develop database-driven applications for a variety of purposes and deploy them over intranets, extranets, and the Web. For example, if a company's human resource department needs to deploy an employee benefits application that is accessible via the Web, a programmer can use Java servlets, JavaServer Pages, and JDBC™ to develop a program to meet those needs.

In this chapter, you will learn how to create a Web-enabled version of the StockTracker application as a servlet, as well as how to add functionality not available to a local, or nonnetworked, version. The Model-View-Controller (MVC) pattern discussed in Chapter 11 — which involves the separation of the user interface from the controlling logic of the program and from the interaction with the database — will be discussed further in this chapter. You will learn how to use servlets and JavaServer Pages (JSPs) to provide dynamic Web page content. The user interface takes the form of Web pages displayed in a Web browser on a client machine, while the application logic moves to a Web server capable of executing a Java servlet. The data access class, StockTrackerDB, from the previous chapter is used once again to interact with the database. You will learn how to implement session tracking with HTTP, limiting transactions to users who have successfully logged on to the system. Finally, you will use the application to access a Web service, thus providing a quote for a selected stock.

Chapter Twelve — The Webstocks Web Application

MoneyMark Trading liked the previous StockTracker application developed for tracking stock holdings; however, as many applications now are being offered over the Web, they want this application to be Web-enabled so they can make it available to clients via their Web site. In addition to providing the functionality of the previous application, the new Web-enabled version, called the WebStocks Web application, should utilize Web connectivity to obtain online stock quotes as requested by the user.

The user will interact with this application through Web pages displayed on the client machine (Figure 12-1a). The browser, therefore, is the client software responsible for displaying the user interface. Web pages, either static or dynamic, are provided by a Web server (Figure 12-1b). A **static Web page** is a Web page that exists in its entirety on the Web server before it is used. The content of a static Web page does not change with each use. A **dynamic Web page** is a Web page that is created as needed and usually is customized upon each use. A dynamic Web page often contains data extracted from a database.

When using the WebStocks Web application, the first Web page a user views is a static Web page that provides the user with a form to enter a user ID and password. After the user ID and password are verified, the user can view additional dynamic Web pages that allow the user to manage stock holdings; if the user is an administrator, access is provided to user information. These functions are the same as those provided by the StockTracker application created in Chapter 11, except in a Web-enabled format. Additionally, the WebStocks Web application has the ability to obtain a stock quote for any user with at least one stock holding (Figure 12-1c). The Web pages providing the user interface for managing stocks, displaying stock quotes, and managing user accounts are dynamic Web pages created either by a servlet or a JSP.

The WebStocks Web application also uses the data access class, StockTrackerDB, to provide access to the database on the server via JDBC™ (Figure 12-1d). Depending on the application, the database could exist on a server separate from the Web server and the client machine (a multi-tier architecture) or on the same machine as the Web server (a two-tiered architecture). In this chapter, a two-tiered client/server architecture will be used, so the database will reside on the same computer as the Web server. Further, to facilitate testing, both the client (the Web browser) and the server (the Web server software) will execute on the same physical machine.

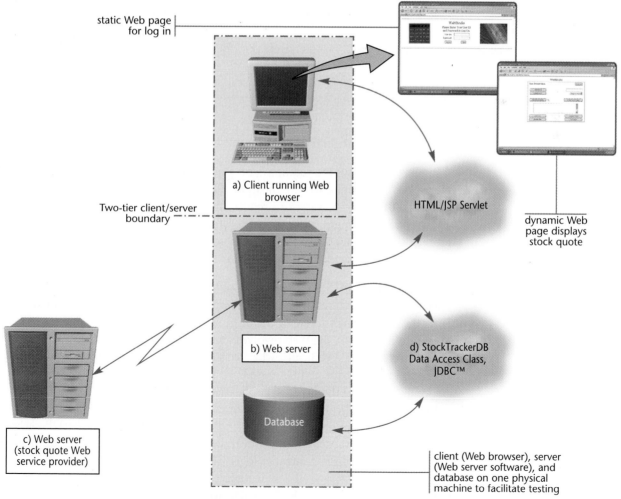

FIGURE 12-1

Program Development

The program development cycle and corresponding tasks for this project are shown in Table 12-1.

Table 12-1   WebStocks Web Application Development Tasks

	DEVELOPMENT PHASE	TASK(S)
1	Analyze the requirements	Analyze the Web-based stock-tracking application problem. Determine any new functionality added to the original application.
2	Design the solution	Design the logic to solve the problem. Determine which parts of the application will use scripting tools (HTML, JSP) versus what will be done in the servlet.
3	Validate the design	Confirm with the user that the design solves the problem in a satisfactory manner.
4	Implement the design	Translate the design into code. Include internal documentation (comments and remarks) within the code that explains the purpose of the code statements. Design and code the servlet and corresponding HTML documents and JavaServer Pages that interact with the servlet.
5	Test the solution	Test the application by publishing the servlet, HTML documents, and JavaServer Pages to the Web server and then testing the Web application by accessing both user and stock data. Find and correct any errors (debugging) until they are error free.
6	Document the solution	Print copies of all source code, including the HTML documents and JavaServer Pages.

Analysis and Design

Figure 12-2 shows the requirements document that initiates the development cycle for the WebStocks Web application. The requirements document illustrates that application development can require skills in a variety of areas, such as Java, HTML, JavaServer Pages, and databases. This implies that an application can be built by a single developer, well-versed in complementary development tools, or by a team of developers, each having a particular specialty.

PROBLEM ANALYSIS   The problem of Web-enabling an application is not focused on the core functionality of the application, as this was determined during the development cycle of the original application. Rather, adapting an application for use via the Web involves analyzing how the application is implemented on the Web; specifically, what technologies are available for use and how much existing code can be reused. Also, a programmer must consider if functionality beyond the original application must be added.

In this Web application, a number of classes developed earlier are usable without modification, including the User, Password, and StockTrackerDB classes. The original StockTracker class, however, was created for a local application and, while it incorporated the controller logic from the MVC pattern, it also handled much of the user interface (the view logic). Using the StockTracker class to build all of the user interfaces in a Web format, while possible, would increase the size

REQUEST FOR NEW APPLICATION

Date submitted:	December 17, 2007
Submitted by:	Mark Dunit, Analyst
Purpose:	An application is needed to provide the same functionality as the StockTracker application, yet be accessible via the Web. In addition to allowing users to track their own customized list of stock holdings, the application must retrieve an online stock quote for a given stock and display the result at the user's request. Again, user maintenance functions are allowed only for administrative users.
Application title:	WebStocks Web Application
Algorithms:	Online stock quotes are retrieved from the Yahoo stock ticker service, a CGI program that returns a comma-delimited list of data for a stock or stocks, with each list returned on a separate line. The service is accessed at http://quote.yahoo.com/d/quotes.csv followed by a parameter list of ?symbols=<symbolList>&format=<variables>&ext=.csv; where <symbolList> is the stock symbol or symbols sent (comma-delimited), and <variables> is the list of data requested from the service, with no embedded blanks or commas. The extension must be .csv, for "comma separated values." A list of variables that can be passed to the service include: s = Symbol 19 = Last Trade dl = Date of Last Trade cl = Change c = Percent Change tl = Time of Last Trade o = Open Trade h = High Trade x = Name of Stock Exchange g = Low Trade v = Volume 11 = Price a = Ask Price b = Bid Price n = Company Name j = 52-week low k = 52-week high p = Previous Close The program should request the following: sl1d1t1c1ohgv
Notes:	1. The application uses the same StockTracker database as the StockTracker application, accessed through the same StockTrackerDB data access class. 2. All user interfaces are accessible through a Web browser. Users are presented with an initial logon screen. If the logon attempt is successful, a main Web page displays stock and, if an administrator, user maintenance functions. 3. Users can request a stock quote that displays in a text area on the main Web page. Users also can clear a previous quote from the text area. 4. The Web server used for this application supports JSP and servlets. Browsers are expected to support JavaScript and to allow cookies. 5. A successful logon for a user is assigned a session, lasting until the user closes the browser or the session times out. An unsuccessful logon attempt beyond the maximum allowable will invalidate the session. An invalid session will require a user to close the browser before attempting to logon again.

Approval Status:	**X**	Approved
		Rejected
Approved by:		Wilson Davis, Director of IT, AccessFour Software
Date:		December 20, 2007
Assigned to:		M. Mick, Programmer

FIGURE 12-2

of the source code greatly and complicate its logic. By using HTML or JSP for the user interfaces, a Web page developer can create the user interface Web pages while a Java developer builds the servlet, thus allowing specialization of developer skills and shortening development time. Finally, by accessing a service available on the Web, significant additional functionality is provided with little development effort. Relying on a previously existing component to provide a service, rather than developing the code, is an example of another level of code reuse to improve productivity.

DESIGN THE SOLUTION Once you have analyzed the problem and understand the needs, the next step is to design the application in terms of the MVC pattern discussed earlier. Designing the solution requires you to make decisions about the types of components needed, whether servlets, HTML documents or JavaServer Pages, as well as the processing each component will do. Careful thought should be given to the responsibilities of each component of the MVC pattern when designing the application.

The Model-View-Controller (MVC) Pattern

A pattern is a standard approach to solving a particular programming problem. Recall that the Model-View-Controller (MVC) pattern has three layers:

1. the model, which defines the business rules layer;
2. the view, which defines the user presentation layer; and
3. the controller, which defines the application layer responsible for managing the application flow.

When developing an application using the MVC pattern, keep each layer as independent of the others as possible to make later modifications easier. When using a database, adding a data access layer keeps the application independent of the particular DBMS being used.

Using the MVC pattern provides more flexibility and maintainability by creating the user views separate from the controller logic. As its name implies, the controller component is used to direct, or control, the flow of the application, particularly the interaction between views of the data and the database itself (Figure 12-3). Individual user views may be static Web pages created in HTML or dynamic Web pages created using JSPs or servlets, depending on whether dynamic data is displayed on the page.

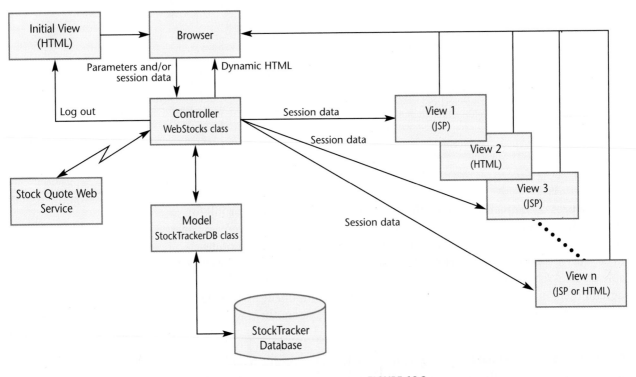

FIGURE 12-3

In this project, the controller component is a servlet. Analogous to an air traffic controller or police officer directing traffic, the controller servlet is responsible for directing requests for the next Web page view from the user, except in those few cases when a Web page invokes another Web page directly. In all cases where data must be obtained from the database, the request flows through the controller servlet. Only the controller servlet contains logic for accessing the database; database access is handled entirely through the data access class, StockTrackerDB, which models the database for the application. Additionally, the servlet obtains stock quote data from the Web service and then provides the data to the requesting view. Obviously, all requests and responses between the browser and the Web pages (whether HTML or JSP) and servlet communicate through the Web server, which is not included in Figure 12-3 for the sake of simplicity.

> **Tip**
>
> **Model-View-Controller Pattern**
>
> A pattern is a standard approach to solving a particular programming problem. The Model-View-Controller pattern has three layers: the model, which defines the business rules layer; the view, which defines the user presentation layer; and the controller, which defines the application layer responsible for managing the application flow. Keep each layer as independent of the others as possible to make later modifications easier. When using a database, adding a data access layer keeps the application independent of the particular DBMS.

Understanding Web Application Processing

Understanding the interaction between the servlet, JavaServer Pages, and HTML documents is important for deciding how to structure a Web application. It also is necessary to understand how data is incorporated into dynamic Web pages, which makes a Web application possible. Static Web pages can have some limited user interaction through client-side processing of data; however, dynamic Web pages require server-side processing.

Client-side refers to processing that uses resources available only on the client. An example of a client-side process is verification that an input field is not empty. **Server-side** refers to processing that uses resources on the server, as in verifying that the value of a user ID input field exists in a database. Server-side processing requires communication between the client (browser) and the Web server. Web applications often use a combination of client-side and server-side processing.

Static Web Pages

A Web browser interacts with a Web server using the same set of rules whether the Web page is static or dynamic. Web browsers and Web servers communicate with each other using **Hypertext Transfer Protocol**, or **HTTP**, which is a standard set of rules, or protocol, used for communication over the Internet. A request for a Web page from the browser to the Web server is known as an

HTTP request; the response from the Web server is known as an **HTTP response**. For static Web pages, the HTTP request specifies an address or URL for an HTML document on the Web server as the **target**, or requested resource.

The initial page displayed by a browser must be obtained with an absolute, or full, address. An **absolute address**, such as

```
http://www.scsite.com/catalog/books.html
```

specifies the full path needed to obtain the target Web page. An address also can be a **relative address**, such as

```
java2e.html
```

which means the location of the requested file, java2e.html, is determined relative to the location of the requesting page, which must have been obtained from the same server. For example, if the Web page at the address http://www.scsite.com/catalog/books.html includes a link that uses the relative address, java2ehtml, the link tells the browser to request the page, http://www.scsite.com/catalog/java2e.html.

If a user requests a static Web page, the Web server returns it identically for every request received, without modification in the HTTP response. When received, the browser displays the file as a static Web page (Figure 12-4).

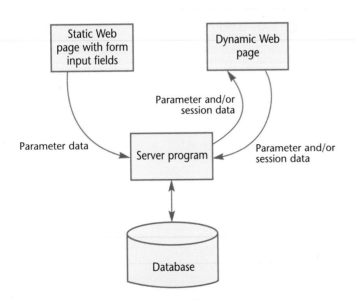

FIGURE 12-4

Dynamic Web Pages

For dynamic Web pages, the HTTP request typically contains some data that is used to tailor the HTTP response. As in the static request, the address specifies the resource requested from the Web server. If the request is for a dynamic Web page, the target of the request is not an HTML document but some type of server-side Web application, such as a servlet, or a JSP. The request is passed to the Web server, which, in turn, passes the request to the Web application. The Web application then processes the request, possibly by accessing a database, passing the request and additional data to a JSP as a part of the Web application, or even accessing a service from another remote Web application. The Web application then passes a response back to the Web server, usually as a dynamically-generated HTML document. The Web server returns the HTML document as an HTTP response to the browser. The browser displays the returned HTML document without concern as to how it was generated, either from a static HTML document or dynamically from a Web application (Figure 12-5).

FIGURE 12-5

PROGRAM IMPLEMENTATION   Once the solution is designed and validated, the next step in the development cycle is to implement the design, as shown in Table 12-1 on page 780. In this project, only one new class is created; however, 10 existing classes from Chapter 11 are reused. Because the project requires no changes to these classes, only the class files and not the Java source files are needed. Table 12-2 lists the class files from Chapter 11 that are reused for this application.

Table 12-2   Reused Class Files from Chapter 11

FILE NAME
Password.class
PasswordException.class
PasswordExpiredException.class
PasswordInternalException.class
PasswordInvalidException.class
PasswordInvalidFormatException.class
PasswordSizeException.class
PasswordUsedException.class
StockTrackerDB.class
User.class

Table 12-3 lists the HTML and JavaServer Page files used to provide views of the data in the WebStocks Web application. As indicated in the table, many of these files are provided on the Data Disk in the Chapter 12 folder.

Table 12-3   HTML and JSP Files for the WebStocks Web Application

FILE TYPE	FILE NAME	DESCRIPTION	SOURCE
JSP	mainForm.jsp	Main form displayed after successful log on	Created in chapter
	chgPswd.jsp	Supplies new password data after password expires	Data Disk
	delUser.jsp	Supplies verification to delete selected user	Data Disk
	listUsers.jsp	Supplies list of current users	Data Disk
	stockDesc.jsp	Supplies new stock description	Data Disk
	updUser.jsp	Supplies updated user information	Data Disk
HTML	index.html	Initial static Web page	Created in chapter
	addUser.html	Supplies new user information	Data Disk
	badUserID.html	Displays error message for add or delete of invalid user ID	Data Disk
	reqDelUser.html	Requests ID of user to delete	Data Disk
	reqUpdUser.html	Requests ID of user to update	Data Disk

JSP files are Web pages with one or more sections of Java code, called a **scriptlet**, embedded within the HTML. Many text editors or specialized Web page editors can be used to create these files; however, not all Web page editors will properly handle the scriptlets included in the JSP files. TextPad can edit JSP files, although color highlighting of code is not configured by default. You can customize TextPad by creating or using syntax files for a particular programming or scripting language, many of which are available for download from the TextPad Web site. Use TextPad Help as described in Appendix C to obtain instructions for installing TextPad syntax files and enabling syntax highlighting for JSP files.

Calling a Servlet from an HTML Form

A static Web page, as shown in Figure 12-6, provides the initial user interface for the WebStocks Web application. After the Web page is loaded in the user's browser, it displays an HTML form where the user can enter a user ID and password and then click a Log on button to submit that data to the Web server.

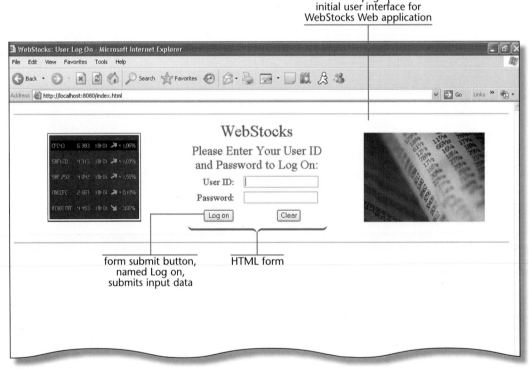

FIGURE 12-6

Creating a New HTML Document in TextPad

Recall from Chapter 1 that HTML is a set of tags that specify how the elements of a Web page display. Figure 12-7 displays the HTML code for the initial Web page for the WebStocks Web application.

```
1   <!--
2       Chapter 12: The WebStocks Web Application
3       Programmer: Michael Mick
4       Date:       December 20, 2007
5       Filename:   index.html
6       Purpose:    Provides the initial log on page for the WebStocks Web application
7   -->
8   <html>
9   <head>
10     <title>WebStocks: User Log On</title>
11     <script LANGUAGE=JAVASCRIPT>
12     <!-- hide script from older browsers
13       function validate(myForm)
14       {
15         if(myForm.userID.value=="")
16         {
17             alert("Please enter a user ID.");
18             myForm.userID.focus();
19         }
20         else if(myForm.password.value=="")
21         {
22             alert("Please enter a password.");
23             myForm.password.focus();
24         }
25         else
26             myForm.submit();
27       }
28     //-->
29     </script>
30   </head>
31   <body text="#824423" onLoad="document.logonScreen.userID.focus()">
32   <hr>
33   <table>
34     <tr>
35       <td width="33%" align="center">
36           <img border="0" src="tickerScrn.wmf" width="187" height="170">
37       </td>
38       <td width="33%">
39         <form name="logonScreen" method="POST" action="../servlet/WebStocks">
40           <table width="328" height="206">
41             <tr>
42               <td width="328" align="center" colspan="3" height="36">
43                   <font size="6">WebStocks</font></td>
44             </tr>
45             <tr>
46               <td width="328" align="center" colspan="3" height="54">
47                   <font size=5>
48                   Please Enter Your User ID <br>
49                   and Password to Log On:</font>
50               </td>
51             </tr>
52             <tr>
53               <td width="126" align="right" height="22">
54                   <font size="4">User ID:</font></td>
55               <td width="6" height="22"> </td>
56               <td width="196" height="22">
57                   <input type="text" name="userID" size="20">
58               </td>
59             </tr>
60             <tr>
61               <td width="126" align="right" height="19">
62                   <font size="4">Password:</font></td>
```

FIGURE 12-7

(continued)

```
63                    <td width="6" height="19"> </td>
64                    <td width="196" height="19">
65                        <input type="password" name="password" size="20">
66                    </td>
67                </tr>
68                <tr>
69                    <td align="right" width="126" height="37">
70                        <input type="button" value="Log on" onClick="validate(logonScreen)">
71                    </td>
72                    <td width="6" height="37">   </td>
73                    <td align="left" width="196" height="37">
74                                
75                              
76                        <input type="reset" value="Clear">
77                    </td>
78                </tr>
79            </table>
80        </form>
81    </td>
82    <td width="34%"><p align="center">
83        <img border="0" src="stockListing.jpg" width="239" height="171">
84    </td>
85    </tr>
86 </table>
87 <hr>
88 </body>
89 </html>
```

FIGURE 12-7

HTML provides tags for a variety of input elements, such as text boxes, buttons, and check boxes, which can be used to collect in an HTML form on a Web page. An **HTML form** is a section of a Web page, which is defined within HTML <form> </form> tags and is comprised of input elements for collecting data from users. These input elements are designated with an <input> tag. Most forms have two special types of button — a submit button and a reset button — although neither is required. Clicking a **form submit button** causes the information on the form to be sent to the server for processing. Clicking a **form reset button** causes all input elements to be reset to their initial values. Form submit and reset buttons often display names other than submit and reset. For example, the form submit button shown in Figure 12-6 on page 786 displays the name, Log on.

The following steps start TextPad and create an HTML file that serves as the initial Web page for the WebStocks Web application.

To Create a New HTML Document in TextPad

1. Insert the Data Disk in drive A.
2. Copy the files listed in Table 12-2 on page 785 from the location where you saved or compiled them in the previous chapter (the Chapter11 folder or the location specified by your instructor) to the Chapter12 folder or a location specified by your instructor.

3. Start TextPad. If necessary, click Line Numbers on the View menu to display line numbers.

4. Click File on the menu bar and then click Save As on the File menu. When the Save As dialog box is displayed, click the Save in box arrow and then click 3½ Floppy (A:) in the Save in list.

5. Double-click the Chapter12 folder.

6. Type `index.html` in the File name text box and then click HTML (*.htm*,*.stm*) in the Save as type list. Click the Save button in the Save As dialog box.

The file named, index.html, is saved as an HTML file in the Chapter12 folder on the Data Disk in drive A (Figure 12-8).

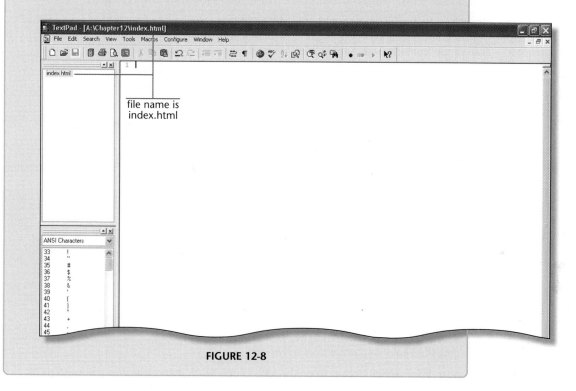

FIGURE 12-8

Table 12-4 on the next page lists HTML tags used in this chapter. Note that HTML tags are not case-sensitive. The first tag entered in most HTML files is the <html> </html> tag pair, which indicates the beginning and end of the HTML document (lines 8 and 89 in Figure 12-7). Almost all other tags are nested within this pair.

An HTML comment, however, can be placed anywhere within the document, even outside of the <html> </html> tag pair. Line 1 in Figure 12-7 displays a beginning HTML comment tag, which continues through the ending comment tag in line 7.

The <head> tag on line 9 indicates the start of the header section of an HTML document. The header section, enclosed by the <head> </head> tag pair, contains document header information such as the page title, which is contained within the <title> </title> tag pair. The Web page title for the Web page currently viewed in the browser is displayed in the browser title bar. Line 10 indicates that the Web page has a title of WebStocks: User Log On.

Table 12-4   Common HTML Tags

HTML TAG	FUNCTION
<!— comment text —>	Indicates the beginning and end of a comment.
<html> </html>	Indicates the beginning and end of a Web document.
<head> </head>	Indicates the beginning and end of the header section of a Web document (used for the title and other document header information).
<title> </title>	Indicates the beginning and end of the Web page title. The title displays in the browser title bar, not in the body of the Web page itself.
<body> </body>	Indicates the beginning and end of the main section (body) of the Web page.
<h*n*> </h*n*>	Indicates the beginning and end of a section of text called a heading, which uses a larger font than normal text. In the tag, <H*n*>, *n* indicates the size of the heading font, which can range from <H1> through <H6>.
<p> </p>	Indicates the beginning of a new paragraph; inserts a blank line above the new paragraph. The end tag of </p> is optional. It will insert a blank line below the new paragraph, unless followed by a new paragraph.
 	Indicates a new line. Following text displays on the next line with no intervening blank lines.
<table> </table>	Indicates a table, consisting of rows and columns. Tables often are used to position elements in a Web page.
<b> </b>	Indicates the beginning and end of a section of bold text.
<i> </i>	Indicates the beginning and end of a section of italic text.
<u> </u>	Indicates the beginning and end of a section of underlined text.
<ul> </ul>	Indicates the beginning and end of an unordered (bulleted) list.
<ol> </ol>	Indicates the beginning and end of an ordered (numbered) list.
<li> </li>	Indicates that the item in the tag is an item within a list.
<hr>	Inserts a horizontal rule (i.e., a horizontal line).
<a> </a>	Indicates the beginning and end of a hyperlink.
<img src="*url*">	Inserts an inline image in the page. The URL in quotation marks specifies the location of the image.
<center> </center>	Indicates that the text, graphic, or other elements between the tags should display centered on the Web page.
<script> </script >	Identifies script code. Although not required, the script statements usually are enclosed in comment tags, so browsers not supporting scripting do not render the code as text.
<right> </right>	Indicates that the text, graphic, or other elements between the tags should display right-aligned on the Web page.

Many HTML tags can contain attributes that further describe how the tag should format text, align objects, and so on. Attributes typically take the form

```
<tag attribute="value">
```

For example, as shown in line 43 of Figure 12-7 on page 787, the <font> tag includes a size attribute, which is set to a value of 6, using the code

```
<font size="6">WebStocks</font>
```

to set the font size of the word, WebStocks, to 6. A tag often can include several attributes; the <font> tag, for example, has attributes of size, color, face, and more.

Editing HTML code using a text editor, as opposed to using a GUI Web page editor, can be confusing. Code readability is improved by using good indentation as well as color syntax highlighting, if your text editor supports that feature.

Tip

Writing HTML Code

If you create HTML documents with a GUI Web page editor, the HTML tags often are created for you; however, reading the code can be difficult. If you code HTML with a text editor, such as TextPad, using syntax highlighting and indenting the tags in a consistent manner improves readability, which also improves maintainability.

Using JavaScript in an HTML Document

Some of the HTML and JSP files in this chapter also contain a small amount of JavaScript code, such as that shown in lines 12 through 28 in Figure 12-7. JavaScript is often confused with Java and sometimes with JSP. As you learned in Chapter 1, JavaScript is a scripting language used to insert functionality within an HTML document. Netscape Navigator and Microsoft Internet Explorer both support JavaScript, so that if you include JavaScript in an HTML document, you can use either of these browsers to interpret it.

JavaScript syntax is similar to Java, as well as C and C++, but is a simpler language than Java and supports less functionality. JavaScript is **object-based**; that is, it uses built-in objects. JavaScript uses an object model to reference built-in objects. Two such built-in objects are the **document object**, which is the HTML document, and the **window object**, which is the browser window. Unlike Java, however, JavaScript cannot create hierarchies of user-defined objects. JavaScript can define variables by using the keyword, **var**, as in

```
var myData;
```

however, the variable is undefined in value and has no declared data type until a value is assigned.

JavaScript is case-sensitive and has statements and operators similar to Java. Ending JavaScript statements with a semicolon is optional; however, it is recommended practice to use them, making the code easier to relate to Java.

When including JavaScript in an HTML file, the JavaScript code should be enclosed in the <script> </script> tag within the <head> </head> tag. The <script> tag has an attribute, language, which identifies the type of script language used. Line 11 in Figure 12-7 on page 787 uses JAVASCRIPT as the value of the language attribute, to indicate that the script enclosed by the <script> </script> tag conforms to the syntax for JavaScript.

The JavaScript code in the HTML file can be executed at this point in the document or it may include one or more functions defined for later use. By defining functions used by the document within the <head> tag, they are loaded and available before the user can do anything that would call them.

Lines 12 through 28 display a user-defined JavaScript function enclosed in HTML comment tags to hide the JavaScript from older, incompatible browsers. A **JavaScript function** is a callable section of code, much like a method. The function, validate(), in line 13 has a single parameter, myForm, indicating the form for which the function is called. A single HTML document commonly has only one form; however, having multiple forms in a single HTML document is valid.

Note that no data type is specified for the form parameter. Unlike Java, JavaScript is a **loosely typed** language, meaning that you do not have to declare the data type of a variable. JavaScript determines the data type from the data itself. Although this may seem advantageous when writing code, if not done with great care, it can lead to errors that are difficult to solve.

A function, such as validate(), can create local variables, have parameters, or access form fields directly. When accessing form fields directly, fully qualified names must be used, beginning with the word, document, followed by the form name, and then the field name, as in document.form.userID.

JavaScript also has many built-in functions that can be useful. Line 15 includes an if() function to check the userID field of the form to determine if its value is a null, or empty, string. Note that, because the form name, myForm, is passed as a parameter to this function, the parameter, myForm, is used as an alias for the document.form reference.

If the user ID is a null string, a built-in function, **alert()**, is called in line 17 to display a dialog box with a message telling the user to please enter a user ID and an OK button. Line 18 then calls another built-in function, **focus()**, which requests focus for the userID field. Having **focus** means that a form field can accept user input. This places the insertion point in the userID text box. Lines 20 through 24 perform the same action for the password field. If both fields contain values, then the **submit()** built-in function for the form is called in line 26, causing the form data to be submitted to the Web server.

The following steps enter the JavaScript code used in the HTML document, index.html.

To Enter JavaScript in an HTML Document

1. With the TextPad window open, enter lines 1 through 10 as shown in Figure 12-7.

   TextPad displays HTML statements in the coding window (Figure 12-9). A comment section, the beginning tags for the HTML document, head section, and title are included in lines 1 through 10.

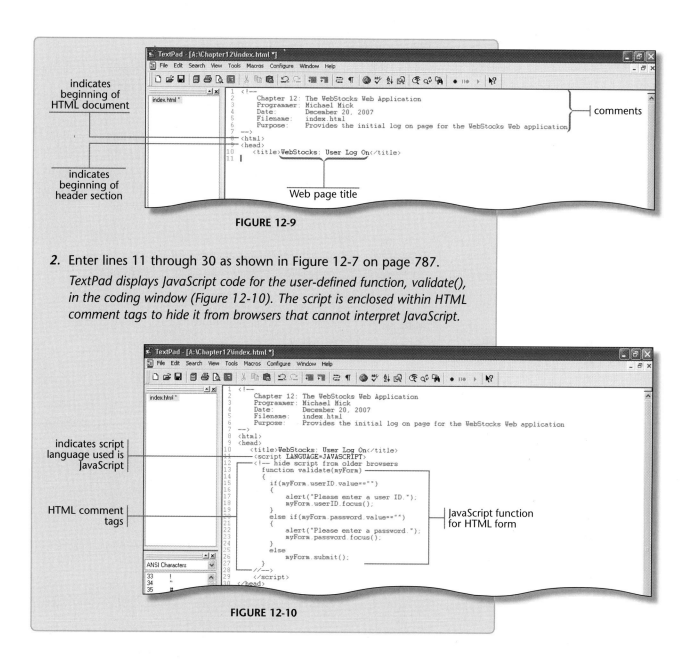

indicates beginning of HTML document

indicates beginning of header section

comments

Web page title

FIGURE 12-9

indicates script language used is JavaScript

HTML comment tags

JavaScript function for HTML form

FIGURE 12-10

2. Enter lines 11 through 30 as shown in Figure 12-7 on page 787.

TextPad displays JavaScript code for the user-defined function, validate(), in the coding window (Figure 12-10). The script is enclosed within HTML comment tags to hide it from browsers that cannot interpret JavaScript.

The head section of the HTML document is complete. Next, the body of the HTML document is coded. The body of the HTML document, which is enclosed within <body> </body> beginning and ending tags, includes code for the majority of what the user sees on the Web page.

HTML Tags and Tag Attributes

Within an HTML document, event handlers also may be included in an HTML tag, in a manner similar to the attributes mentioned previously. As you have learned, an event is an action that occurs, typically as a result of a user's action, such as placing the mouse pointer on an item on the screen and then clicking a mouse button, or requesting that the browser load a Web page. In HTML, an **event handler** associates an event with the JavaScript code that is performed when the event occurs. An event handler has the general form of

```
<tag eventHandler="JavaScript code">
```

Event handlers can be combined with attributes in a tag. The JavaScript code to execute normally is in the form of a function call, although not exclusively.

The <body> tag on line 31 in Figure 12-7 on page 787 contains both a text attribute and an event handler. The text attribute sets the text color to a value, expressed as three hexadecimal (base-16) numbers representing the red, green, and blue (RGB) values in the color. These values range from 00 to FF, for 256 different values each, to allow you to specify a color value from #000000 (black) to #FFFFFF (white). Standard colors, such as those listed in Table 12-5, also may be referenced by their name, as in white, blue, red, black, and so on.

Table 12-5   Standard Color Names and RGB Values

COLOR	NAME	RGB VALUE
	Aqua	#00FFFF
	Black	#000000
	Blue	#0000FF
	Fuchsia	#FF00FF
	Gray	#808080
	Green	#008000
	Lime	#00FF00
	Maroon	#800000
	Navy	#000080
	Olive	#808000
	Purple	#800080
	Red	#FF0000
	Silver	#C0C0C0
	Teal	#008080
	White	#FFFFFF
	Yellow	#FFFF00

The event handler, the **onLoad() method**, executes when the document is loaded by the browser. In this case, the onLoad() method calls the focus() method for the field, userID, in the form, logonScreen, of the current document. The focus() method thus places the insertion point in the userID text box.

The <hr> tag in line 32 indicates that a horizontal rule, or line, will display on the page, above a three-column table used to position elements on the Web page. The table is defined using the table tag (<table>) in line 33; each row in the table is defined using a row tag (<tr>). Within each row are column tags (<td>)

to define the number of columns. As indicated in lines 35 and 36 of Figure 12-7 on page 787, within the first row, the first column has a width that is one-third (33%) of the entire table width. Within the table cell, the image tickerScrn.wmf is center-aligned and scaled to a height and width given in screen pixels.

Creating a Form in an HTML Document

The form begins in the next column, with a table nested within the form. In line 39, the <form> tag introduces a form with a name attribute of logonScreen. This is the same form referenced earlier in the onLoad() event handler of the <body> tag. Two other attributes, method and action, are assigned values.

HTTP GET AND POST METHOD ATTRIBUTES   The **method attribute** of a form specifies which HTTP method, either Get or Post (case-insensitive), is used to send a request for service to the server. Requests usually are accompanied by form data, sent as a series of name=value parameters. The **Get method** is the default HTTP method for sending data. It transfers parameters by appending them to the URL, making them visible to the user. The Get method executes slightly faster than Post and allows the user to bookmark parameters along with the Web page; however, the amount of data that can be sent via the Get method is restricted to 4 KB of data or less. Additionally, the Get method restricts form data to ASCII characters only. The **Post method** sends parameter data without appending to the URL, so the data are not directly visible to the user, although they are not necessarily secure, either. If the parameters should not be visible, or more than 4 KB of data must be transferred, then the Post method must be used.

ACTION ATTRIBUTES   The **action attribute** of a form specifies the address of a program which will process the form data when the form is submitted, either by the Get or Post method. Typically, this specifies a program on the Web server, such as a CGI program or, as shown in line 39, a servlet. Unless a complete URL is listed in the action attribute, it defaults to a location relative to the document. The address for a servlet is specified with servlet/ before the servlet name, indicating that a servlet is requested. What appears as a servlet folder is translated on the server to the actual folder for the servlet, as discussed later.

OBTAINING FORM DATA WITH INPUT TAGS   Within a form, input tags are used to collect data from the user. An input tag can have several attributes, depending on the type of the input element. Input tags of the type, text, as shown in line 57, display a text box in a form. Input tags of the type, password, as shown in line 65, display a text box normally used to enter a password. A text box with a password type automatically displays asterisks rather than the data entered by the user, although the entered data is sent to the server as plain text. For both text and password input elements, the size attribute controls the displayed width of the text box in characters; the name attribute assigns the element a name, such as UserID or password.

An input tag with the type attribute of button displays a button that the user can click. Typically, a form includes a button when some action other than an immediate submission of the data is needed. Line 70 defines a button which, when clicked, calls the JavaScript validate() function and passes a reference to the form, logonScreen. Line 76 defines a button of type reset, which causes all input elements to be reset to their initial values, as discussed earlier. In each case, the value attribute of the button defines what appears as the button label.

The following steps enter the code to create an HTML form that calls a servlet.

To Call a Servlet from an HTML Form

1. Enter lines 31 through 39 as shown in Figure 12-7 on page 787.

TextPad displays HTML statements beginning the body and then the form in the coding window (Figure 12-11). The form is named logonScreen. When the document is loaded, the userID field in the logonScreen form will have focus. The form, logonScreen, uses the Post method to send data to the WebStocks servlet.

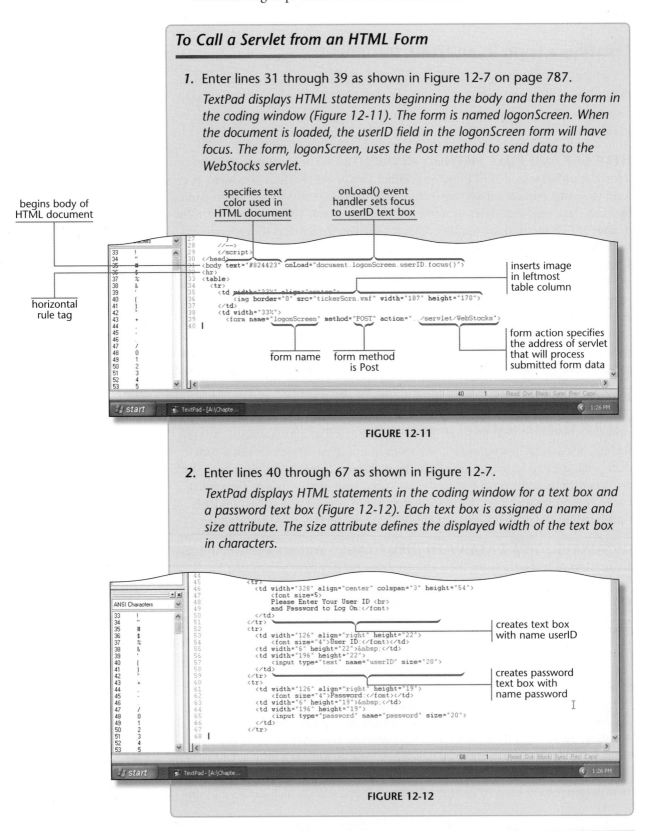

FIGURE 12-11

2. Enter lines 40 through 67 as shown in Figure 12-7.

TextPad displays HTML statements in the coding window for a text box and a password text box (Figure 12-12). Each text box is assigned a name and size attribute. The size attribute defines the displayed width of the text box in characters.

FIGURE 12-12

3. Enter lines 68 through 89 as shown in Figure 12-7 on page 788. Save the file again by clicking the Save button on the Standard toolbar.

TextPad displays HTML statements in the coding window for two buttons (Figure 12-13). The Log on button calls the JavaScript validate() function when clicked, passing a reference to the current form, logonScreen. The reset button, which will display the label Clear, resets all input data fields on the form. The code inserts an image that displays in the third table column.

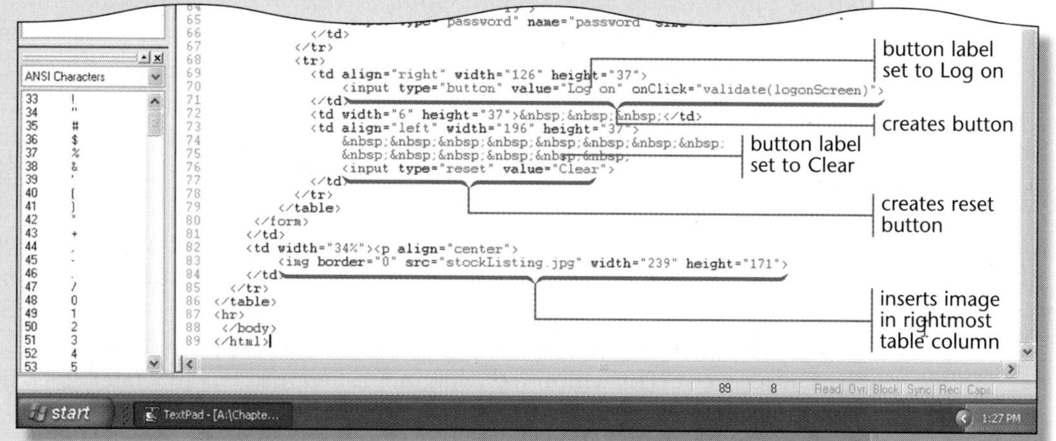

FIGURE 12-13

The code for the Web page, index.html, is complete. Because HTML source code is loaded and interpreted by a browser, you do not compile it as you would Java source program.

Creating a Servlet

The code in line 39 of the initial Web page, index.html, sends form data to a servlet named WebStocks. As previously noted, a running Java Web application depends on many components, including servlets and JavaServer Pages. Recall that a servlet is a Java class that runs on a Web server, rather than being launched from a browser. Instead, the servlet is loaded into and runs inside a servlet container running on the Web server. A **servlet and JSP container** is software that allows a Web server to work with servlets and JavaServer Pages. The container actually comprises two containers, one for processing servlets and one for JSPs, and often is referenced as a servlet container or JSP container, depending on the purpose being served. As you will learn later in this project, the Tomcat Web server is both a servlet container and a JSP container, and also can function as a Web server.

Java Servlet Processing

A servlet receives and responds to requests from clients, such as a Web browser. A servlet using HTTP extends the **HttpServlet** class, which provides access to HTTP request and HTTP response objects. These objects encapsulate HTTP requests and responses, respectively, so they can be accessed easily within the servlet.

Servlets are efficient because they run within the process of the servlet container, much as an applet runs within a browser. A **process** is a term for a program that is executing. A servlet is loaded with the first request and then remains loaded to handle subsequent requests. To handle multiple requests within a single process, servlets are multithreaded. **Multithreading** involves using the same instance of a process for multiple, concurrent uses, each known as a **thread of execution**, or **thread**. Each request causes the servlet container to create a separate thread within the single process. This is more efficient because starting a process uses more system resources than creating a thread. Using threads effectively is a more complex task for the programmer because the code must be made thread-safe. Code that is **thread-safe** avoids unwanted interaction between the threads, so the actions of one thread will not interfere with the actions of another. Because threads run the same instance of a program, each thread gets its own copy of local variables, but all threads of an instance share the same instance variables.

When a request is passed to a Web server running a servlet container (for example, the Tomcat Web server), the request is forwarded to the servlet container, which determines whether a static or dynamic resource was requested. Static resources, such as a static Web page, are opened, read, and returned to the client by a special class within the container called the DefaultServlet class. If a dynamic resource such as a servlet is requested, the servlet either is loaded directly or a class called, InvokerServlet, will load and execute the servlet.

The Servlet Life Cycle

Every servlet must implement specific methods while it executes. The methods init() and destroy() are provided to manage resources held for the life of the servlet. The init() method is called when a servlet is first loaded, similar to the init() method for an applet. The destroy() method is called when the servlet container determines that the servlet should be removed from service.

Between the init() and destroy() methods, the service() method is called each time a request is received. The HttpServlet class implements the service() method and defines helper methods, doGet() and doPost(), for Get and Post requests, respectively. The HttpServlet service() method routes each request to the appropriate method. A servlet using HTTP needs only to extend HttpServlet and override the desired methods. Typically, a servlet will override only doGet() or doPost(), depending on the type of request to which it responds, although both may be overridden. If resources, such as a database connection, must be obtained for the life of the servlet and then released, the init() and destroy() methods also are overridden to ensure that the resources are maintained for the life of the servlet.

Recall that line 39 in Figure 12-7 on page 787 of the code for the initial Web page, index.html, sends form data to a servlet named WebStocks. The WebStocks servlet is the controller in the MVC model for this application. As such, most of the Web pages in this application either submit data to this servlet or are directed by this servlet for display to the user, or both. In some cases, the servlet actually creates the Web page; however, this is done only for illustration as it violates the MVC model. Figure 12-14 displays the code used to start creating the WebStocks servlet.

```
1    /*
2          Chapter 12: The WebStocks Web Application
3          Programmer: Michael Mick
4          Date:       December 20, 2007
5          Filename:   WebStocks.java
6          Purpose:    Provides controller logic for the WebStocks Web application
7    */
8
9    import javax.servlet.*;
10   import javax.servlet.http.*;
11
12
13   import java.io.*;
14   import java.sql.*;
15   import java.util.*;
16   import java.net.*;
17
18   public class WebStocks extends HttpServlet
19   {
```

FIGURE 12-14

The following steps create a new Java servlet in TextPad.

To Create a New Java Servlet in TextPad

1. Click the New Document button on the Standard toolbar. If necessary, click Line Numbers on the View menu to display line numbers.

2. Click File on the menu bar and then click Save As on the File menu. When the Save As dialog box is displayed, click the Save in box arrow and then click 3½ Floppy (A:) in the Save in list.

3. Double-click the Chapter12 folder or the location specified by your instructor.

4. Type WebStocks in the File name text box and then click Java (*.java) in the Save as type list. Click the Save button in the Save As dialog box.

5. Enter lines 1 through 19 as shown in Figure 12-14. In the comments, insert your own name as programmer and enter the current date.

   TextPad displays the code for the initial comments, import statements, and class header for the WebStocks class (Figure 12-15).

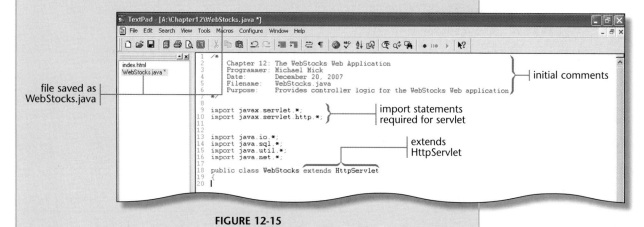

FIGURE 12-15

As shown in line 18 in Figure 12-15 on the previous page, the WebStocks class extends the HttpServlet class, which is not available in the standard SDK. The HttpServlet class instead is provided as part of a package with the servlet container, Tomcat, which is used in this project. The package is provided in a Java Archive (JAR) file, named servlet-api.jar, in the C:\Program Files\Apache Software Foundation\Tomcat 5.5\common\lib folder. Recall from Chapter 8 that a Java Archive (JAR) file is a compressed archive file, used to contain related files in a package. It is common for packages to be distributed in this format, and Java can access the classes directly from the JAR file without extracting them. To use the HttpServlet class, the import statements using the javax packages must be included.

Overriding Servlet init() and destroy() Methods

The WebStocks servlet uses the StockTrackerDB class to access the database, as did the StockTracker application. When a StockTrackerDB object is created, it establishes a connection with the database. Establishing a database connection is a relatively slow process, which you do not want to repeat with each new request. In a production environment, particularly one using a multi-tiered architecture where the database is located on a server separate from the application, connection pooling frequently is used. **Connection pooling** is a technique for creating multiple database connections and then assigning them in a round-robin fashion to servlet threads. In this chapter, connection pooling is not used; instead, only one connection is used for simplicity. Thus, you will override the init() and destroy() methods of the StockTrackerDB class to ensure the database connection is maintained for the life of the servlet.

Figure 12-16 displays lines 20 through 69 of the WebStocks servlet code. Line 20 establishes the variable, db, for the StockTrackerDB object. Recall that, because servlets are multithreaded, instance variables such as db are shared among multiple threads. Therefore, only one StockTrackerDB object needs to be created.

```
20    StockTrackerDB db;
21
22    public void init() throws ServletException
23    {
24        try
25        {
26            db = new StockTrackerDB();
27        }
28        catch (SQLException e)
29        {
30            System.out.println("WebStocks: SQLException creating new database object.");
31            e.printStackTrace();
32            System.exit(1);
33        }
34        catch (ClassNotFoundException e)
35        {
36            System.out.println("WebStocks: ClassNotFoundException "
37                            +"creating new database object.");
38            e.printStackTrace();
39            System.exit(1);
40        }
41    }
42
```

FIGURE 12-16

```
43      public void destroy()
44      {
45          try
46          {
47              db.close();
48          }
49          catch (IOException e)
50          {
51              System.out.println("WebStocks: IOException closing database.");
52              e.printStackTrace();
53              System.exit(1);
54          }
55          catch (SQLException e)
56          {
57              System.out.println("WebStocks: SQLException closing database.");
58              e.printStackTrace();
59              System.exit(1);
60          }
61          catch (ClassNotFoundException e)
62          {
63              System.out.println("WebStocks: ClassNotFoundException "
64                          +"closing database.");
65              e.printStackTrace();
66              System.exit(1);
67          }
68      }
69
```

FIGURE 12-16

Lines 22 through 41 override the init() method to create a StockTrackerDB object. The init() method is called by the servlet container exactly once to indicate to a servlet that it is being placed into service. Because the init() method is called only once when the servlet is loaded, only one StockTrackerDB object is created. The init() method throws a ServletException if an exception that interferes with the servlet's normal operation occurs.

As shown in lines 28 through 39, the constructor for a StockTrackerDB object throws two exceptions. These exceptions are caught, generating an error message and exiting the program, as this indicates an error in establishing the database connection. In each case, the printStackTrace() method for the exception is called to display a stack trace on the console. A **stack trace** is a list of methods, called leading, to the exception and typically is seen when an exception is not handled. After displaying the stack trace, the program exits by calling the System.exit() method and passing a value of 1. Passing a nonzero value indicates that the program exited abnormally.

Likewise, when the servlet no longer is needed, the connection to the database should be closed. Lines 43 through 68 override the destroy() method, calling the close() method of the StockTrackerDB object to close the connection (line 47). The close() method, like the init() method, throws three exceptions that are caught, producing a stack trace and then exiting.

The following steps enter the code to override the servlet init() and destroy() methods.

To Override the init() and destroy() Servlet Methods

1. Enter lines 20 through 42 as shown in Figure 12-16 on page 800.

   TextPad displays the init() method for the servlet (Figure 12-17). The init() method creates a new StockTrackerDB object, establishing a connection to the database.

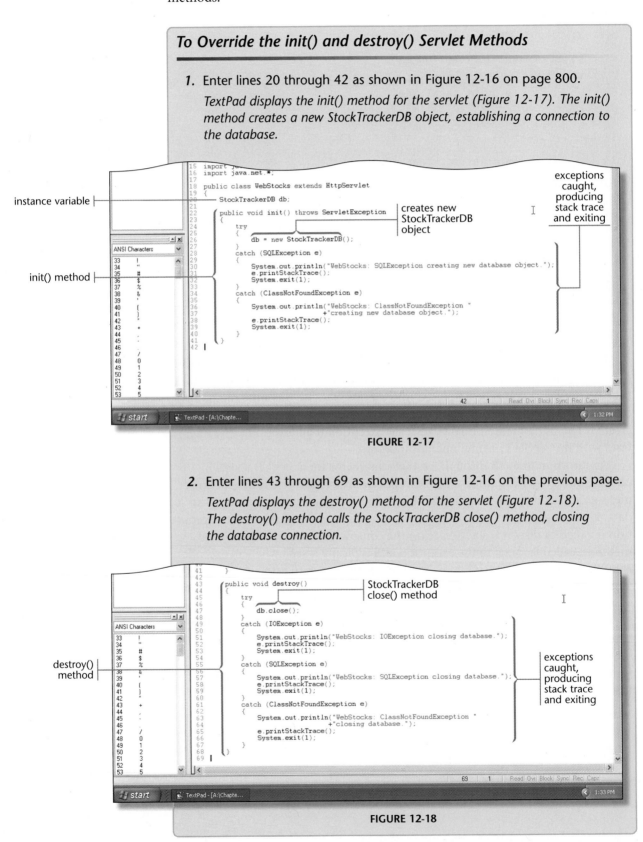

FIGURE 12-17

2. Enter lines 43 through 69 as shown in Figure 12-16 on the previous page.

   TextPad displays the destroy() method for the servlet (Figure 12-18). The destroy() method calls the StockTrackerDB close() method, closing the database connection.

FIGURE 12-18

Because the init() method is called when the servlet is loaded, and the destroy() method is called when the servlet is removed from service, these methods are called only once, regardless of the number of threads created for the servlet.

Processing HTTP Requests in a Servlet

At the heart of servlet processing is receiving a request and sending a response. As discussed above, the HttpServlet class provides the methods doGet() and doPost() that are called to process either a Get or a Post, depending on the method used to send an HTTP request. By overriding either or both of the doGet() and doPost() methods, a servlet can process Get requests, Post requests, or both. If both Get and Post requests are to be treated alike, one of the methods can call the other, rather than duplicating code.

Both the doGet() and doPost() methods have an HttpServletRequest object and an HttpServletResponse object as parameters. The **HttpServletRequest object** encapsulates the request passed from the browser through the Web server to the servlet. The request object itself is created by the servlet container. The **HttpServletResponse object**, also created by the servlet container, provides HTTP-specific functionality for sending a response.

In sending a response, a servlet can create a Web page dynamically by writing HTML code as output that the server returns to the browser on the client machine. As a preliminary step, the **setContentType() method** must be called to set the character encoding, or MIME type, of the content being returned by the server to the browser. **MIME (Multipurpose Internet Mail Extensions)** is a specification for formatting messages, particularly those using character sets other than ASCII, so that they can be sent over the Web. Many e-mail client programs support MIME, enabling them to send and receive graphics, audio, and video files. Web servers insert a MIME header at the beginning of a Web transmission, allowing receiving clients to select an appropriate application to process the type of data being sent. Browsers have a built-in ability to process certain data types — such as HTML, JPG, and GIF files — while other types may require additional helper applications, such as Adobe Acrobat Reader or RealPlayer.

Figure 12-19 on the next page, displays lines 70 through 88 of the WebStocks servlet code. Line 84 sets the setContentType() method to set the MIME type to text/html, indicating that a text- or html-encoded document will be written. Line 85 uses the HttpServletResponse response object method, called the **getWriter() method**, to return a PrintWriter object that the servlet can use to send character text to the Web browser on the client machine. Using the getWriter() method is similar to a console application using the PrintStream object, out, of the System class, as in System.out.println(); however, the output is not directed to the console, but to the requesting client through the Web server.

```
70      public void doGet(HttpServletRequest req, HttpServletResponse res)
71                      throws ServletException, IOException
72      {
73          doPost(req,res);
74      }
75
76      public void doPost(HttpServletRequest req, HttpServletResponse res)
77                      throws ServletException, IOException
78      {
79          User user = null;
80          String userID;
81          String password;
82          boolean validAction = true;
83
84          res.setContentType("text/html");
85          PrintWriter out = res.getWriter();
86
87          res.setHeader("Expires","Tues, 01 Jan 1980 00:00:00 GMT"); // no cache allowed
88
```

FIGURE 12-19

Browsers have the ability to store, or cache, pages locally so that, if a page is requested, it may be obtained from the client cache rather than requesting it be sent again from the Web server. Using caching helps to improve performance by avoiding the transmission of pages that have not changed or expired. By setting the expired date of the page to a past date, as is done on line 87, the browser is forced to load the page from the server rather than from cache. This ensures that each response processed by the browser is from the server and not a cached copy of a previous response.

The following steps enter the code to process HTTP requests in a servlet by overriding the doGet() and doPost() methods.

To Process HTTP Requests in a Servlet

1. Enter lines 70 through 75 as shown in Figure 12-19.

   TextPad displays the doGet() method for the servlet (Figure 12-20). The doGet() method calls the doPost() method, passing the request and response objects.

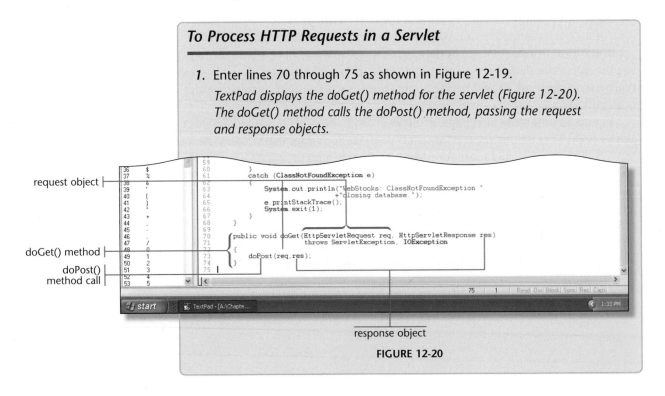

FIGURE 12-20

2. Enter lines 76 through 88 as shown in Figure 12-19.

TextPad displays the doPost() method for the servlet (Figure 12-21). Each thread has a unique copy of local variables, unlike instance variables, which are shared by threads.

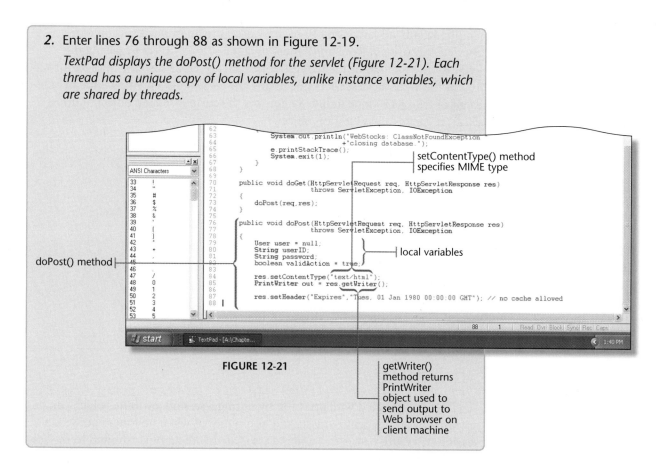

FIGURE 12-21

setContentType() method specifies MIME type

local variables

doPost() method

getWriter() method returns PrintWriter object used to send output to Web browser on client machine

Because both the doGet() and doPost() methods are to be treated alike, the doGet() method in lines 70 through 74 calls the doPost() method, which starts in line 76, rather than duplicating the same code.

Implementing Session Tracking with HTTP

Recall that Web browsers and Web servers communicate with each other using HTTP. HTTP is a **stateless protocol**, meaning that it does not maintain state; that is, it does not provide a means of maintaining information about a connection between requests. A **session** is a series of requests from the same user. The Web server cannot determine that a request from a browser belongs to the same session as a previous request.

Session tracking provides a way to identify a user across more than one request and, optionally, to store persistent information about the user between those requests. Through the servlet API, Java provides a mechanism for HTTP session tracking by creating a session object of type HttpSession, which has a unique identifier. A **session object** models the user session and is created by the servlet container when the browser makes its first request to a site. A session may time out if the time between client accesses exceeds some maximum; a session timeout means that the maximum interval between accesses was exceeded, and the server invalidated the session. Session timeouts often are set to 30 minutes between accesses, although they can vary by server or by application. A servlet also can invalidate a session explicitly, if needed.

By default, all JavaServer Pages have access to an implicit session object. Servlets that are not from a JSP must obtain a session object by calling the getSession() method of the request object. Figure 12-22 displays lines 89 through 103 of the WebStocks servlet code. Using the getSession() method with an argument of true, as is done in line 89, returns the current session object; if none exists, it creates a new session object.

```
89      HttpSession session = req.getSession(true); // get current session
90
91      if(logonValidated(req,res,session))
92      {
93          if(session.getAttribute("uses") != null) // remove temporary data
94              session.removeAttribute("uses");
95
96          if(session.getAttribute("userList") != null)
97              session.removeAttribute("userList");
98
99          if(session.getAttribute("pswdExpired") != null)
100             session.removeAttribute("pswdExpired");
101
102         userID = (String)session.getAttribute("userID");
103
```

FIGURE 12-22

Data is associated with a session by setting a session attribute, which can be retrieved by subsequent requests and also removed when no longer needed. A **session attribute** consists of a name associated with an object bound to the session. Session attributes are stored on the server and only the session identifier, or session ID, must be passed back to the browser. The browser returns the session ID with each subsequent request, allowing identification of the user session, as well as access to the session attributes. The session object provides the **setAttribute() method** to associate a name and an object with the session. The method will **bind** an object to the session, meaning it attaches the object to the session ID. The **getAttribute() method** returns the object associated with an attribute name, if it is bound to the session. The object must be downcast to the appropriate type. If the object does not exist, null is returned. The **removeAttribute() method** removes a bound attribute name and object from the session, if needed.

Session identifiers can be sent to the browser using **URL encoding**, also called **URL rewriting**; however, this requires writing significant code to add the session ID to the URL for every transaction. By default, the servlet API uses a cookie to store the session ID, and the browser passes the cookie to the server with each request. A **cookie** is a message given to a Web browser by a Web server, which the browser stores in a text file on the client machine and then returns to the server with subsequent requests. No additional coding is needed for session tracking using cookies, although custom cookies may be created for other purposes. The only drawback is that the browser must be set to accept cookies or this type of session tracking will not work. URL encoding works regardless of the browser cookie setting; however, it requires more coding effort and also displays the session ID in the URL.

Using URL Encoding versus Using Cookies

By default, the servlet API uses a cookie to store the session ID, and the browser passes the cookie to the server with each request. No additional coding is needed for session tracking using the default cookie. The only drawback is that the browser must be set to accept cookies or this type of session tracking will not work. Session identifiers instead can be sent to the browser using URL encoding, also called URL rewriting, which involves writing code to add the session ID to the URL for every transaction. URL encoding works regardless of the browser cookie setting; however, it requires more coding effort and also displays the session ID in the URL.

The following step enters the code to implement session tracking with HTTP by obtaining a session and using session attributes.

To Implement Session Tracking with HTTP

1. Click the Save button on the Standard toolbar to save the program. Enter lines 89 through 103 as shown in Figure 12-22.

   TextPad displays the code to obtain a session object and then get and remove session attributes (Figure 12-23). If a requested session attribute is null, then that attribute is not stored. Because the program is lengthy, the entered code should be saved regularly, even before the program is complete.

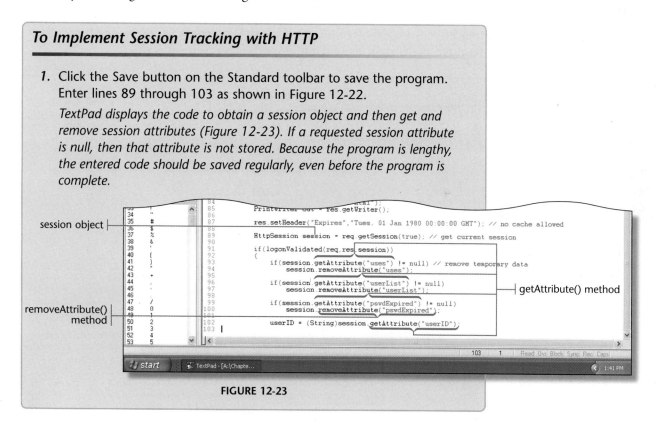

FIGURE 12-23

Redirecting an HTTP Request

Recall that user validation, as well as most subsequent requests, uses the servlet as a controller. Parameters and session attributes are used to help the servlet direct the next appropriate action for the application. In most cases, this involves performing some function in the servlet and then forwarding the request to the appropriate HTML page or JavaServer Page. To **forward** a request involves sending the current request and response objects so that the receiving resource can act upon them. To **redirect** a request is to cause the browser to send a new request to a different resource. In the case of a user who logs off of the application, the current session is explicitly invalidated so session data no longer can be used. Also, the browser is directed to request the log on page to replace the page currently displayed by the browser. This requires subsequent users to log on and be validated. When the user clicks the Log out button, a parameter is sent with a value of the text of the button.

Figure 12-24 displays lines 104 through 109 of the WebStocks servlet code. Line 104 uses the **getParameter() method** of the request object to obtain the form field parameter value associated with the name, logout. Parameter values are returned as strings. If the result is not null, meaning that a parameter value associated with the name, logout, was sent, then line 105 verifies the value of the parameter. If the user has chosen to log out, line 107 calls the **invalidate() method** for the session to invalidate the current session. Line 108 then calls the response **sendRedirect() method**, which causes the server to convert the supplied URL from a relative to an absolute URL, if necessary, and then send it to the browser. The browser then sends a request for the new URL, just as when the user initially logged on to the application. When redirecting a request to another resource, the current request and response objects are discarded.

```
104        if(req.getParameter("logout") != null &&
105            req.getParameter("logout").equals("Log out"))
106        {
107            session.invalidate();
108            res.sendRedirect("/index.html");
109        }
```

FIGURE 12-24

The following step enters the code to redirect an HTTP request.

To Redirect an HTTP Request

1. Enter lines 104 through 109 as shown in Figure 12-24.

TextPad displays the code to invalidate the session object and redirect the request to the log on Web page (Figure 12-25).

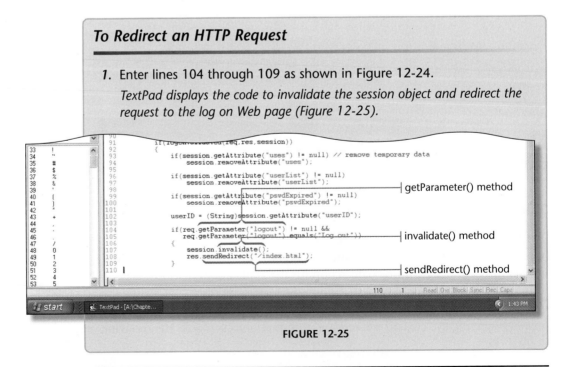

FIGURE 12-25

Forwarding an HTTP Request

For valid user actions other than logging out, the servlet must determine the appropriate resource needed and then send the current request to the appropriate resource. With the exception of logging out, which redirects the HTTP request, each user selection on a Web page requiring action by the servlet — for example, adding a stock, deleting a stock, changing a password — passes a hidden parameter to the servlet. This parameter, WSaction, determines which action the servlet takes to respond to the request. Depending on the action requested, the servlet may complete one or more tasks, including getting another parameter value, calling a method, removing an attribute, or setting an attribute to indicate the name of the next resource to use. Because the called methods throw exceptions, the calls are within a try block.

Figure 12-26 displays lines 110 through 199 of the WebStocks servlet code. For example, lines 119, 123, 127, and 131 each call a single method. The called method will set the attribute for the next resource, as appropriate. The code on lines 135 through 138 gets a parameter value, passes that value to a method call, sets an attribute representing the result of the call, and then sets the attribute for the next resource to use.

```
110                  else
111                  {
112                      try
113                      {
114                          String action = req.getParameter("WSaction");
115                          if(action != null)
116                          {
117                              if(action.equals("addStock"))
118                              {
119                                  addStock(req, session);
120                              }
121                              else if(action.equals("addStockDesc"))
122                              {
123                                  addStockDesc(req, session);
124                              }
125                              else if(action.equals("delStock"))
126                              {
127                                  delStock(req, session);
128                              }
129                              else if(action.equals("chgPswd"))
130                              {
131                                  chgPswd(req, session);
132                              }
133                              else if(action.equals("getQuote"))
134                              {
135                                  String stock = req.getParameter("stockSymbol");
136                                  String quoteRequest = getQuote(stock);
137                                  session.setAttribute("quote",quoteRequest);
138                                  session.setAttribute("forwardTo", "mainForm.jsp");
139                              }
140                              else if(action.equals("clearQuote"))
141                              {
142                                  if(session.getAttribute("quote") != null)
143                                      session.removeAttribute("quote");
144                                  session.setAttribute("forwardTo", "mainForm.jsp");
145                              }
146                              else if(action.equals("addUser"))
147                              {
148                                  addUser(req);
149                                  session.setAttribute("forwardTo", "mainForm.jsp");
150                              }
```

FIGURE 12-26   *(continued)*

```
151            else if(action.equals("reqDelUser"))
152            {
153                ArrayList userData =
154                    getUserData(req.getParameter("delUserID"));
155                if(userData.size() > 0) // the user exists
156                {
157                    session.setAttribute("userData",userData);
158                    session.setAttribute("forwardTo", "delUser.jsp");
159                }
160                else
161                    session.setAttribute("forwardTo", "badUserID.html");
162            }
163            else if(action.equals("delUser"))
164            {
165                delUser(req.getParameter("delUserID"));
166                session.setAttribute("forwardTo", "mainForm.jsp");
167            }
168            else if(action.equals("reqUpdUser"))
169            {
170                ArrayList userData =
171                    getUserData(req.getParameter("updUserID"));
172                if(userData.size() > 0) // the user exists
173                {
174                    session.setAttribute("userData", userData);
175                    session.setAttribute("forwardTo", "updUser.jsp");
176                }
177                else
178                    session.setAttribute("forwardTo", "badUserID.html");
179            }
180            else if(action.equals("updUser"))
181            {
182                updUser(req);
183                session.setAttribute("forwardTo", "mainForm.jsp");
184            }
185            else if(action.equals("listUsers"))
186            {
187                listUsers(session);
188                session.setAttribute("forwardTo", "listUsers.jsp");
189            }
190            else
191                validAction = false;
192
193            if(validAction)  // forward to resource
194            {
195                RequestDispatcher dispatcher =
196                    getServletContext().getRequestDispatcher("/"+
197                        (String)session.getAttribute("forwardTo"));
198                dispatcher.forward(req,res);
199            }
```

FIGURE 12-26

In some cases, the receiving resource differs, depending on what the user entered or the result of a database query. If a request to delete a user sends a valid user ID, then line 158 sets a session attribute, forwardTo, to the delUser.jsp Java Server Page as the receiving resource. That receiving resource allows the user to verify the data before deletion.

If an invalid user ID was entered, then line 161 sets the receiving resource as the HTML page, badUserID.html, which displays an error message. Similar action is taken on lines 175 and 178 when a request to update a user is received.

For any valid requested action, the servlet will forward the request to the resource that displays the result to the user, whether a JSP or an HTML page. To forward a request to another resource, the servlet uses a RequestDispatcher object. A **RequestDispatcher object** receives requests and sends them to a given resource on the server. The servlet container creates the RequestDispatcher object for a servlet context, using it as a wrapper around a server resource located at a particular address. The initial configuration for the Web application, provided by the server when the servlet is initialized, supplies a **servlet context**, which defines the scope of the Web application within the server. A **ServletContext object** defines the set of methods that a servlet uses to communicate with its servlet container.

As shown in lines 195 through 199, because the servlet extends HttpServlet, the servlet can get a ServletContext object by calling the HttpServlet method, **getServletContext()**, shown in line 196. The ServletContext method, **getRequestDispatcher()**, then is called to obtain a RequestDispatcher object. This method requires a path to the resource including the resource name, which must begin with a slash (/) and is relative to the current context root. The resource name is obtained from the corresponding session attribute in line 197. This value, along with the slash, provides the required path passed to the getRequestDispatcher() method.

Line 198 calls the forward() method of the RequestDispatcher object. The RequestDispatcher **forward() method** forwards a request from a servlet to another resource (servlet, JSP file, or HTML file) on the server. Because the process occurs on the server side rather than the client side, forwarding a request is more efficient than redirecting, which requires additional communication between the client and server. Forwarding also transfers the request and response objects originally received, rather than forcing the client to generate a new request.

The following steps enter the code to process the requested action and forward the HTTP request.

To Forward an HTTP Request

1. Click the Save button on the Standard toolbar. Enter lines 110 through 150 as shown in Figure 12-26 on page 809.

   TextPad displays code that gets the WSaction parameter, calls appropriate methods, and sets attributes, including one for the receiving resource name (Figure 12-27).

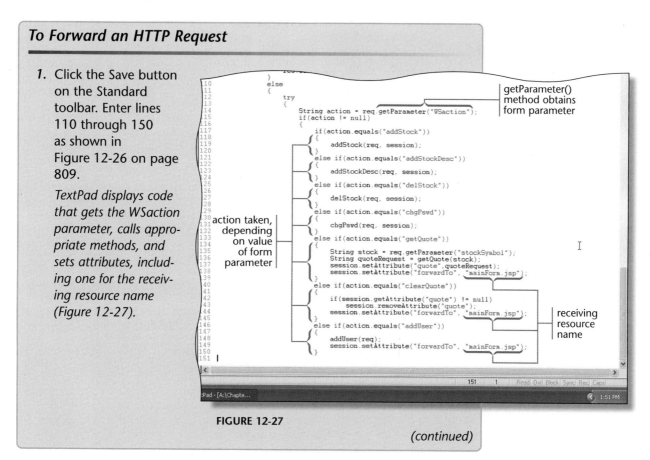

FIGURE 12-27

continued*(continued)*

2. Enter lines 151 through 192 as shown in Figure 12-26 on page 810.

TextPad displays the code for the remaining actions, including setting other JSPs or HTML pages as the receiving resource name (Figure 12-28).

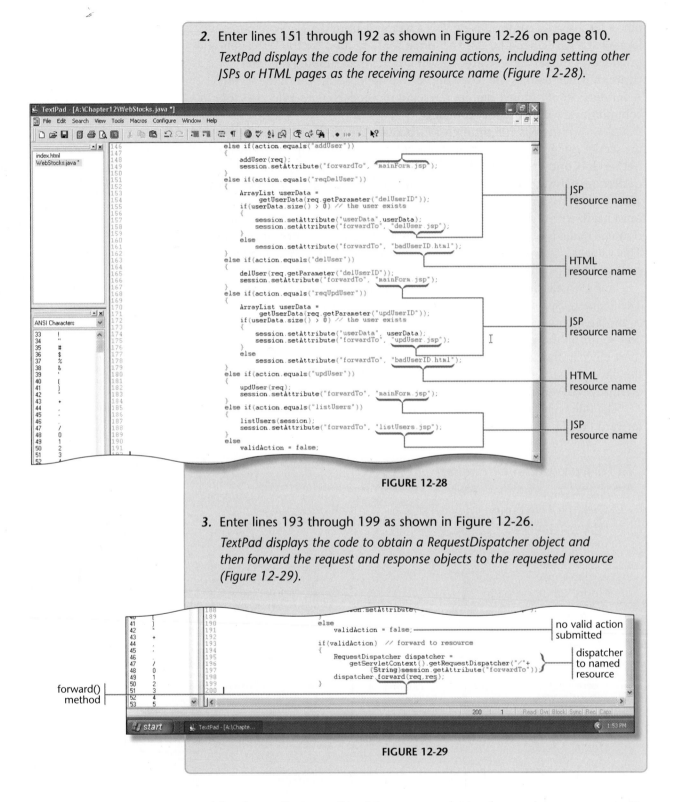

FIGURE 12-28

3. Enter lines 193 through 199 as shown in Figure 12-26.

TextPad displays the code to obtain a RequestDispatcher object and then forward the request and response objects to the requested resource (Figure 12-29).

FIGURE 12-29

After forwarding or redirecting a request, the servlet continues to execute. By arranging the logic to drop to the end of the doPost() method, the servlet thread completes.

Outputting HTML Code from a Servlet

In addition to forwarding or redirecting a request to another servlet, a JSP, or an HTML page, a servlet can write the HTML code directly back to the server, which then sends it to the client browser. This approach embeds the HTML code for a Web page in the Java servlet. As a result, the HTML code is written by a Java programmer, not a Web page designer. HTML tools cannot be used to create the Web page. Therefore, unlike a JSP, the page is not visible until the servlet executes and creates it, which makes designing the page more difficult. Finally, this approach subtracts from the goal of the MVC approach to separate the user interface from the controller code; it is presented here for illustrative purposes only.

The WebStocks servlet includes code that outputs a simple HTML Web page with an error message when an invalid action or null action is requested or when an error, such as an SQL Exception, occurs. As discussed earlier, writing HTML code to the client browser is similar to writing output to the console using the System.out object. Because a PrintWriter object was obtained and the MIME type was set in lines 84 and 85, all that remains is to use the println() method just as you would with System.out. Figure 12-30 displays lines 200 through 276 of the WebStocks servlet code.

```
200                         else
201                         {
202                             out.println("<html>");
203                             out.println("<head>");
204                             out.println("<title>WebStocks Internal Error</title>");
205                             out.println("</head>");
206                             out.println("<body text=\"#824423\" bgcolor=\"white\">");
207                             out.println("<h1>Internal Error</h1>");
208                             out.println("An invalid action was requested: "+action);
209                             out.println("</body>");
210                             out.println("</html>");
211                         }
212                     } // end of if action != null
213                     else
214                     {
215                         out.println("<html>");
216                         out.println("<head>");
217                         out.println("<title>WebStocks Internal Error</title>");
218                         out.println("</head>");
219                         out.println("<body text=\"#824423\" bgcolor=\"white\">");
220                         out.println("<h1>Internal Error</h1>");
221                         out.println("A null action was requested");
222                         out.println("</body>");
223                         out.println("</html>");
224                     }
225                 } // end of try
226                 catch(PasswordException ex)
227                 {
228                     out.println("<html>");
229                     out.println("<head>");
230                     out.println("<title>WebStocks Password Error</title>");
231                     out.println("</head>");
232                     out.println("<body text=\"#824423\" bgcolor=\"white\">");
233                     out.println("<h1>Invalid Password</h1>");
234                     out.println(ex.getMessage());
235                     out.println("</body>");
236                     out.println("</html>");
237                 }
```

FIGURE 12-30   *(continued)*

```
238                    catch(SQLException ex)
239                    {
240                        out.println("<html>");
241                        out.println("<head>");
242                        out.println("<title>WebStocks Error</title>");
243                        out.println("</head>");
244                        out.println("<body text=\"#824423\" bgcolor=\"white\">");
245                        out.println("<h1>SQL Exception</h1>");
246                        out.println(ex.getMessage());
247                        out.println("</body>");
248                        out.println("</html>");
249                    }
250                    catch(IOException ex)
251                    {
252                        out.println("<html>");
253                        out.println("<head>");
254                        out.println("<title>WebStocks Error</title>");
255                        out.println("</head>");
256                        out.println("<body text=\"#824423\" bgcolor=\"white\">");
257                        out.println("<h1>IO Exception</h1>");
258                        out.println(ex.getMessage());
259                        out.println("</body>");
260                        out.println("</html>");
261                    }
262                    catch(ClassNotFoundException ex)
263                    {
264                        out.println("<html>");
265                        out.println("<head>");
266                        out.println("<title>WebStocks Error</title>");
267                        out.println("</head>");
268                        out.println("<body text=\"#824423\" bgcolor=\"white\">");
269                        out.println("<h1>Class not found</h1>");
270                        out.println(ex.getMessage());
271                        out.println("</body>");
272                        out.println("</html>");
273                    }
274                } // end of if log out else
275            } // end of if logon validated
276        } // end of doGet()
```

FIGURE 12-30

The following steps enter the code to output HTML code from a servlet.

To Output HTML Code from a Servlet

1. Click the Save button. Enter lines 200 through 225 as shown in Figure 12-30 on the previous page.

TextPad displays the code that outputs a simple HTML Web page when an invalid action or null action is requested (Figure 12-31).

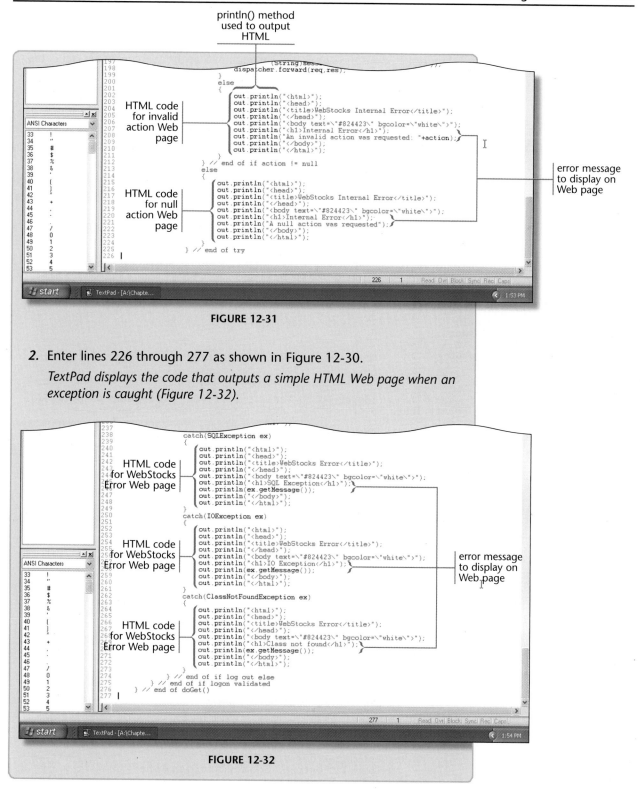

printl() method used to output HTML

HTML code for invalid action Web page

error message to display on Web page

HTML code for null action Web page

FIGURE 12-31

2. Enter lines 226 through 277 as shown in Figure 12-30.

TextPad displays the code that outputs a simple HTML Web page when an exception is caught (Figure 12-32).

HTML code for WebStocks Error Web page

HTML code for WebStocks Error Web page

HTML code for WebStocks Error Web page

error message to display on Web page

FIGURE 12-32

The first method called within the doPost() method is logonValidated(), which begins on line 278. This method determines if the user already has logged on to the Web application; if the user is not logged on, the logonValidated() method manages the log on process. Passing the request, response, and session objects allows the logonValidated() method to have access to the session attributes and to forward the request to an appropriate JSP.

Figure 12-33 displays lines 278 through 325 of the WebStocks servlet code. Line 291 checks for the existence of a session attribute, userName. If this attribute does not exist, the user has not yet successfully logged on to the application. The session object has a method which can determine if the session is a new or previously created session; however, a user trying multiple attempts to log on will use the same session each time. Using the same session is necessary to be able to count unsuccessful attempts and limit them to three for a session, as is done on lines 293 through 297. If this limit is exceeded, the user will have to establish a new session by closing the browser and reopening it. This discourages attempts by others to guess at a user ID and password.

```
278    private boolean logonValidated(HttpServletRequest req, HttpServletResponse res,
279                                   HttpSession session)
280                            throws ServletException, IOException
281    {
282        User user = null;
283        String userID;
284        String password;
285        boolean valid = false;
286        int tries = 0;
287
288        PrintWriter out = res.getWriter();
289
290        // Check if user already logged on for session; if not, attempt to do so
291        if(session.getAttribute("userName") == null) // not a validated user
292        {
293            if(session.getAttribute("attempt") == null)    // no previous attempts
294                session.setAttribute("attempt",new Integer(0)); // track attempts
295
296            tries = ((Integer)(session.getAttribute("attempt"))).intValue();
297            if(tries < 3) // 3 tries
298            {
299                userID = req.getParameter("userID");
300                password = req.getParameter("password");
301                if(userID != null && password != null)
302                {
303                    session.setAttribute("userID", userID);
304                    try
305                    {
306                        user = getUser(userID);
307                        if(validUserPswd(user, password))
308                        {
309                            session.setAttribute("userName", user.getFirstName()
310                                            +" "+user.getLastName());
311                            session.removeAttribute("attempt");
312
313                            if(user.pswdIsExpiring())
314                                session.setAttribute("uses",
315                                            new Integer(user.getPswdUses()));
316                            if(user.isAdmin())
317                                session.setAttribute("admin", new Boolean(true));
318
319                            session.setAttribute("stocks",
320                                            getStockList(userID));
321                            // call general screen
322                            RequestDispatcher dispatcher =
323                              getServletContext().getRequestDispatcher("/mainForm.jsp");
324                            dispatcher.forward(req,res);
325                        }
```

FIGURE 12-33

If a user ID and password are entered, then a method, validUserPswd(), is called to check the user password (line 307). If the user ID and password are valid, the user has successfully logged on and the attribute, userName, is created on lines 309 and 310. This attribute contains the name of the user that is displayed on the main Web page. With a successful log on, the attribute for the number of attempts is cleared (line 311) and other attributes are set to indicate whether the password is expiring (lines 313 through 315), to indicate if the user is an administrator (lines 316 and 317), and to provide a list of user stock holdings from the database (lines 319 and 320). The request then is forwarded to the main Web page for the application (lines 322 through 324).

Figure 12-34 displays lines 326 through 438 of the WebStocks servlet code. If the password entered is not valid, then a PasswordInvalidException is thrown on line 328. The method, validUserPswd(), which is called on line 307, throws a PasswordException for an invalid password, because it calls the User method, validate(), which throws a PasswordException. Therefore, the throw on line 328 is executed only when the user value is null. For this reason, it passes an error message rather than using the default message. A general Exception could have been used; however, it would not be caught on line 341. Because a password cannot be valid for a null user ID, it is acceptable to reuse this existing exception with an appropriate error message. In a larger application, an exception class hierarchy for the User class would be created and used, similar to what was done for the Password class.

If the user password has expired, lines 331 through 340 forward the request to a different JSP, allowing the user to enter a new password. Finally, if a user enters an invalid user ID or password or does so three or more times (lines 341 through 370); enters no user ID or password or an exception is caught (lines 371 through 419); or exceeds the maximum number of log on attempts (lines 420 through 438); then an appropriate HTML page is written by the servlet to the client, as discussed previously. Under such conditions, the log on attempt is not valid, and logonValidated() will return a value of false. The logonValidated() method returns a value of true only when the user has previously logged on successfully. It returns false the first time a user logs on, even if successful, so the doPost() method will take no other action and the servlet thread will complete. This is necessary because forwarding a request to another resource does not stop the servlet from continuing to execute subsequent code.

```
326                        else
327                        {
328                            throw new PasswordInvalidException("Invalid user id");
329                        }
330                    }
331                    catch(PasswordExpiredException ex)
332                    {
333                        session.setAttribute("pswdExpired", "yes");
334                        session.setAttribute("userName", user.getFirstName()
335                                            +" "+user.getLastName());
336                        session.setAttribute("pswd", password);
337                        RequestDispatcher dispatcher =
338                            getServletContext().getRequestDispatcher("/chgPswd.jsp");
339                        dispatcher.forward(req,res);
340                    }
341                    catch(PasswordInvalidException ex)
342                    {
343                        session.setAttribute("attempt",new Integer(++tries));
344                        ex.resetCount();
345
```

FIGURE 12-34

(continued)

```
346                            if(tries < 3)
347                            {
348                                out.println("<html>");
349                                out.println("<head>");
350                                out.println("<title>WebStocks Logon Error</title>");
351                                out.println("</head>");
352                                out.println("<body text=\"#824423\" bgcolor=\"white\">");
353                                out.println("<h1>Invalid User ID or Password</h1>");
354                                out.println(ex.getMessage());
355                                out.println("</body>");
356                                out.println("</html>");
357                            }
358                            else              // allows only 3 tries
359                            {
360                                out.println("<html>");
361                                out.println("<head>");
362                                out.println("<title>WebStocks Logon Error</title>");
363                                out.println("</head>");
364                                out.println("<body text=\"#824423\" bgcolor=\"white\">");
365                                out.println("<h1>Too many attempts to log on!</h1>");
366                                out.println(ex.getMessage());
367                                out.println("</body>");
368                                out.println("</html>");
369                            }
370                        }
371                        catch(PasswordException ex)
372                        {
373                            out.println("<html>");
374                            out.println("<head>");
375                            out.println("<title>WebStocks Logon Error</title>");
376                            out.println("</head>");
377                            out.println("<body text=\"#824423\" bgcolor=\"white\">");
378                            out.println("<h1>PasswordException</h1>");
379                            out.println(ex.getMessage());
380                            out.println("</body>");
381                            out.println("</html>");
382                        }
383                        catch(ClassNotFoundException ex)
384                        {
385                            out.println("<html>");
386                            out.println("<head>");
387                            out.println("<title>WebStocks Logon Error</title>");
388                            out.println("</head>");
389                            out.println("<body text=\"#824423\" bgcolor=\"white\">");
390                            out.println("<h1>ClassNotFoundException</h1>");
391                            out.println(ex.getMessage());
392                            out.println("</body>");
393                            out.println("</html>");
394                        }
395                        catch(SQLException ex)
396                        {
397                            out.println("<html>");
398                            out.println("<head>");
399                            out.println("<title>WebStocks Logon Error</title>");
400                            out.println("</head>");
401                            out.println("<body text=\"#824423\" bgcolor=\"white\">");
402                            out.println("<h1>SQLException</h1>");
403                            out.println(ex.getMessage());
404                            out.println("</body>");
405                            out.println("</html>");
406                        }
407                    }
408                    else
409                    {
410                        out.println("<html>");
411                        out.println("<head>");
412                        out.println("<title>WebStocks Logon Error</title>");
413                        out.println("</head>");
414                        out.println("<body text=\"#824423\" bgcolor=\"white\">");
415                        out.println("<h1>Missing User ID or Password</h1>");
416                        out.println("</body>");
417                        out.println("</html>");
418                    }
```

FIGURE 12-34

```
419            }
420        else
421        {
422            out.println("<html>");
423            out.println("<head>");
424            out.println("<title>WebStocks Logon Error</title>");
425            out.println("</head>");
426            out.println("<body text=\"#824423\" bgcolor=\"white\">");
427            out.println("<h1>Session invalidated.</h1><br>"
428                +"<h1>The maximum for log on attempts was exceeded!</h1>");
429            out.println("</body>");
430            out.println("</html>");
431        }
432    }
433    else
434        valid = true;
435
436    return valid;
437  }
438
```

FIGURE 12-34

The following steps enter the code to validate a Web application log on for a user.

To Validate a User Log On to a Web Application

1. Enter lines 278 through 325 as shown in Figure 12-33 on page 787.

TextPad displays the code to validate a user log on and, for a valid attempt, sets attributes and forwards the request to the main Web page, mainForm.jsp (Figure 12-35).

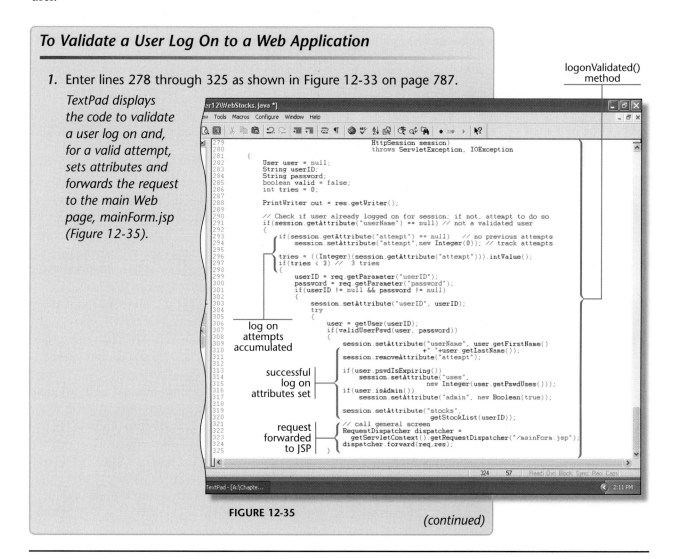

FIGURE 12-35

(continued)

> *2.* Enter lines 326 through 438 as shown in Figure 12-34 on the previous page.
>
> *TextPad displays the code that outputs simple HTML Web pages when an invalid user password or other log on error occurs (Figure 12-36). The method returns a boolean value, indicating a successful or an unsuccessful log on attempt.*

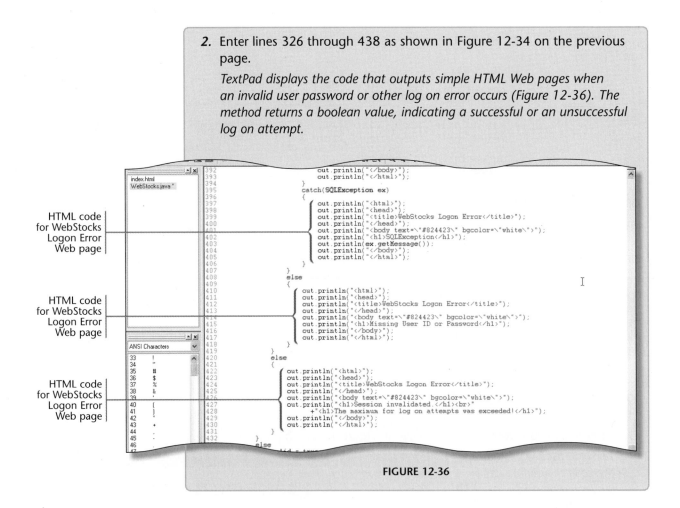

HTML code for WebStocks Logon Error Web page

HTML code for WebStocks Logon Error Web page

HTML code for WebStocks Logon Error Web page

FIGURE 12-36

Acquiring Data from a Web Service

As described in the requirements document, this application is to use a service to obtain online quotes for one or more stocks. A **Web service** is an application component service made available on a Web server for use by other Web-connected programs. Web services are not designed for human interaction. They exchange data over the Web from program to program and, thus, have no user interface.

Many Web services are standardizing on Extensible Markup Language (XML) as a means of formatting and exchanging data. **Extensible Markup Language** (**XML**) is a document markup language, similar to HTML in style, but extensible, in that you can define your own custom tags. XML increasingly is used to encode data transported over the Web. XML also is used to store server configuration data for Tomcat, as discussed later in this chapter.

The Yahoo! stock quote Web service used in this application is a CGI program that returns a list of data requested for one or more stock symbols, in a comma-delimited format rather than in XML. A format that is **comma-delimited** is textual data with the data fields delimited, or separated, by commas. Each record, or group of related fields, typically ends with a new line (\n) or return (\r) character. Using the Yahoo! stock quote Web service involves connecting to the proper URL, along with a series of URL encoded parameters, and receiving the one or more lines of data returned, one stock per line. Connecting to a URL and receiving a returned stream of data is an easy task in Java.

Figure 12-37 displays lines 439 through 467 of the WebStocks servlet code. The getQuote() method beginning in line 439 requires a stock symbol as a parameter and then, in lines 449 through 451, creates a new URL object using the address of the Yahoo! stock quote Web service and the necessary parameters to obtain a quote for the stock symbol. In general, creating a connection to a URL is a multistep process: a connection object is created for a remote object specified by a URL; setup parameters and request properties are manipulated, if necessary; the actual connection is made; and the remote object at that URL becomes available for access. Line 453 calls the **openConnection() method** of the URL to create a connection object. No additional setup parameters need manipulation, so line 454 calls the **connect() method** to make the actual connection. Lines 455 and 456 get the input stream of data from the connected URL and wrap the input stream with a buffered reader in order to read the data one line at a time. Recall that wrapping a BufferedReader around an InputStreamReader buffers the input to make reading the data more efficient. Lines 458 and 459 read each line of data and append it to a StringBuffer. A new-line character is inserted after each line because the BufferedReader readLine() method removes the end of line character from the data stream.

```
439     private String getQuote(String stockSymbol) throws IOException
440     {
441         StringBuffer buf = new StringBuffer();
442         String dataLine;
443
444         try
445         {
446             // Sends stockSymbol
447             // Retrieves s=symbol l1=price d1=date of last trade t1=time of last trade
448             // c1=change (+increase or -decrease) o=open h=high v=volume
449             URL servicePage = new URL("http://quote.yahoo.com/d/quotes.csv?symbols="
450                                 + stockSymbol
451                                 + "&format=sl1d1t1c1ohgv&ext=csv");
452
453             URLConnection conURL = servicePage.openConnection();
454             conURL.connect();
455             BufferedReader data =
456                 new BufferedReader(new InputStreamReader(conURL.getInputStream()));
457
458             while ((dataLine = data.readLine()) != null)
459                 buf.append(dataLine + "\n");
460         }
461         catch (MalformedURLException ex)
462         {
463             System.out.println("Bad URL: " + ex.getMessage());
464         }
465
466         return buf.toString();
467     }
```

FIGURE 12-37

Because the URL class constructor throws an exception if the URL is formed improperly, the exception is caught and a message is displayed on the console (lines 461 through 464). Because the URL does not change, this error never should occur; however, the exception must be either caught or thrown. If an invalid stock symbol is entered, the Web service returns a result indicating fields not applicable for the stock.

The StringBuffer contents are returned on line 466 on the previous page as a String consisting of one line of comma-delimited results per requested stock. In lines 136 and 137 (Figure 12-26 on page 809), this String is set as the session attribute, quote, which is used by the JavaServer Page, mainForm.jsp, to display the stock quote. To see the data returned by the service, you can enter the URL in the address text box of a browser, and the returned comma-delimited text is displayed in the browser window.

Viewing Stock Web Service Data

Because the Yahoo! stock quote service returns text, you can view the returned data in a Web browser. To do so, type the URL and corresponding parameters in the address box of your Web browser and then press the ENTER key. For example, type

```
http://quote.yahoo.com/d/quotes
.csv?symbols=BA&format=sl1d1t1c1ohgv&ext=csv
```

to get a quote for stock BA. You can replace this symbol with another valid stock symbol, or with multiple symbols separated by commas. Be sure they are enclosed within a single set of quotation marks. To see the results returned for an invalid stock, type

```
http://quote.yahoo.com/d/quotes
.csv?symbols=yy&format=sl1d1t1c1ohgv&ext=csv
```

The following step enters the code to acquire data from a Web service.

To Acquire Data from a Web Service

1. Click the Save button. Enter lines 439 through 468 as shown in Figure 12-37 on the previous page.

    TextPad displays the code to obtain data from the Yahoo! stock quote Web service (Figure 12-38).

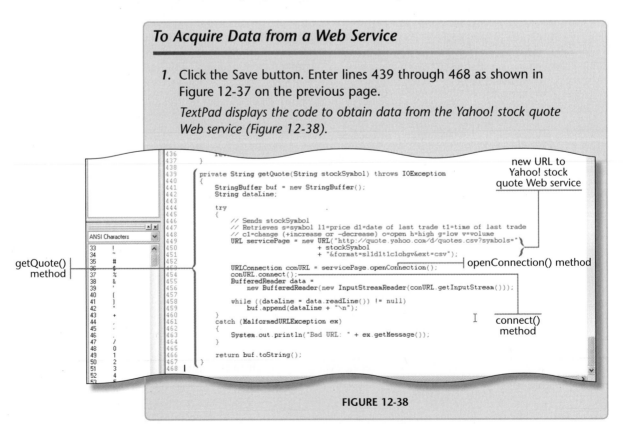

FIGURE 12-38

Using a Web service can be quite convenient; however, you must know the format of the request and of the returned data and be certain that the Web service will continue to be available. If it is unavailable for any reason, some functionality of your program will be disabled.

Synchronizing Multithreaded Code on an Object

Recall that servlets are multithreaded, meaning the same code may be executed concurrently by different threads. Each thread gets a separate copy of local variables, meaning those variables are thread-safe by definition. Code that modifies a shared resource, such as data in a database or an instance variable, however, must be given mutually exclusive access to that resource, thereby making the code thread-safe. Additionally, if the value of data can change, code accessing that data also should be made thread-safe.

The **synchronized** keyword provides thread-safe code by locking access to an object within a method or block of code. Java associates a lock, or **monitor**, with every object. Before the code in a synchronized block or method, the compiler automatically inserts the necessary code to acquire the monitor for an object and code to release the monitor before the method returns or the block ends. To declare a method as synchronized, place the synchronized keyword before the return type, as in

```
public synchronized void myLockedMethod()
```

Any method may be declared synchronized. Constructors, however, do not need to be synchronized because they only execute when creating an object, which only can happen in one thread for any given new object. A block of code is synchronized by using the synchronized statement, as in

```
synchronized (expression)
{
    statement(s);
}
```

where expression is the object to lock. Although any object can be used for the monitor, the monitor object typically is an object used within the synchronized code.

Synchronization can be difficult to understand. As an analogy, let three motorcycles represent three methods or blocks of code, three people represent three threads, and one helmet represent the object providing the lock. Only the person with the helmet can operate one of the three motorcycles, so the motorcycles are synchronized on the helmet. Without the helmet, the other two people (threads) must wait to use one of the remaining motorcycles, even though they are not in use. When the first person returns the helmet, the next person may use it with any of the synchronized motorcycles. In this analogy, waiting for a helmet makes the motorcycles thread-safe; that is, it limits the use of any of the motorcycles to one person (thread) at a time.

All of the variables used by the remaining methods, including the method parameters, are local variables and, therefore, are thread-safe. The exception is the StockTrackerDB object, db, which is an instance variable. Additionally, this object reads from and writes to the database. For these reasons, these methods, all containing code that accesses the database, need to synchronize that code on the StockTrackerDB object, db. This is true whether the methods update the database or retrieve data while another thread may be updating the database.

Figure 12-39 displays lines 469 through 505 of the WebStocks servlet code. When a user tries to add a stock, if the user already holds the stock, he or she is returned to the mainForm.jsp Web page (lines 469 to 484). Line 487 includes a monitor to synchronize access to the database. While holding the monitor, on line 489 the thread calls the method, getStockDesc(), to determine if the stock exists in the database. If the stock is not in the database, the request is forwarded to a stockDesc.jsp JavaServer Page to obtain a description for the new stock. If the stock does exist in the database, it is added to the user's stock holdings, and a new list of stock holdings is added as the session attribute, stocks. If the session attribute, stocks, already exists, it is replaced with the new list as its value. The request then is forwarded to the mainForm.jsp JavaServer Page.

```
469    private void addStock(HttpServletRequest req, HttpSession session)
470        throws ClassNotFoundException, IOException, SQLException
471    {
472        String userID = (String)session.getAttribute("userID");
473        String stockSymbol = req.getParameter("stockSymbol");
474        String stockDesc = null;
475        boolean hasStock = false;
476
477        // determine if user already holds the stock
478        ArrayList al = (ArrayList)session.getAttribute("stocks");
479        for(int i=0; i < al.size(); ++i)
480            if(stockSymbol.equals((String)al.get(i)))
481                hasStock = true;
482
483        if(hasStock) // user already holds this stock
484            session.setAttribute("forwardTo", "mainForm.jsp"); // send to main scrn
485        else
486        {      // add stock to user holdings
487            synchronized (db)
488            {
489                stockDesc = db.getStockDesc(stockSymbol);
490            }
491
492            if(stockDesc == null) // stock not in DB
493            {
494                session.setAttribute("stockSymbol", stockSymbol.toUpperCase());
495                session.setAttribute("forwardTo", "stockDesc.jsp"); // get description
496            }
497            else
498            {
499                addToUserStocks(userID,stockSymbol);
500                session.setAttribute("stocks", getStockList(userID));
501                session.setAttribute("forwardTo", "mainForm.jsp"); // to main scrn
502            }
503        }
504    }
505
```

FIGURE 12-39

A thread attempting to access any code locked on an object is blocked until the monitor is released, unless the thread is already the owner of the lock. Figure 12-40 displays lines 506 through 522 of the WebStocks servlet code. When a thread calls the method beginning on line 506, addStockDesc(), it obtains the monitor on line 514. While holding the monitor, on line 517 the thread calls the method, addToUserStocks(), which also synchronizes on the same StockTrackerDB object.

```
506    private void addStockDesc(HttpServletRequest req, HttpSession session)
507          throws ClassNotFoundException, IOException, SQLException
508    {
509        String userID = (String)session.getAttribute("userID");
510        String stockSymbol = (String)session.getAttribute("stockSymbol");
511        String stockDesc = req.getParameter("stockDesc");
512
513
514        synchronized (db)
515        {
516            db.addStock(stockSymbol,stockDesc);
517            addToUserStocks(userID,stockSymbol);
518        }
519        session.setAttribute("stocks", getStockList(userID));
520        session.setAttribute("forwardTo", "mainForm.jsp");
521    }
522
```

FIGURE 12-40

Because the same thread already owns the monitor, the code executes. If it did not, then a deadlock condition would result. **Deadlock** is a condition where two locks each are waiting on the other to release before execution can continue. The execution of synchronized code is mutually exclusive in time for separate threads, not for the same thread. Figure 12-41 displays lines 523 through 532 of the WebStocks servlet code. When two different threads call the method beginning on line 523, addToUserStocks(), the first thread gets the monitor and the second thread must wait until the monitor is released. This is because the database access on line 529 is synchronized on the StockTrackerDB object.

```
523    private void addToUserStocks(String userID, String stockSymbol)
524                    throws SQLException,IOException,ClassNotFoundException
525    {
526        stockSymbol.trim(); // remove any leading, trailing whitespace
527        synchronized (db)
528        {
529            db.addUserStocks(userID,stockSymbol.toUpperCase());
530        }
531    }
532
```

FIGURE 12-41

Understanding Synchronization

Synchronization can be difficult to understand. As an analogy, let three motorcycles represent three methods or blocks of code, three people represent three threads, and one helmet represent the object providing the lock. Only the person with the helmet can operate one of the three motorcycles, so the motorcycles are synchronized on the helmet. Without the helmet, the other two people (threads) must wait to use one of the remaining motorcycles, even though they are not in use. When the first person returns the helmet, the next person may use it with any of the synchronized motorcycles. Waiting for a helmet makes the motorcycles thread-safe!

Tip

Figure 12-42 displays lines 533 through 545 of the WebStocks servlet code. The delStock() method obtains the user ID from the session attribute, userID. The symbol for the stock to be deleted is obtained from a parameter set by a form on the requesting Web page. The StockTrackerDB object contains a method, delUserStocks(), to delete a stock for a user. The method requires that the caller supply a user ID and a stock symbol. Because this method belongs to the StockTrackerDB object and can update the database, the method call is placed within a block of code synchronized on the StockTrackerDB object. If no exception is thrown, then the call was successful and the session attributes, stocks and forwardTo, are set accordingly.

```
533     private void delStock(HttpServletRequest req, HttpSession session)
534               throws ClassNotFoundException, IOException, SQLException
535     {
536         String userID = (String)session.getAttribute("userID");
537         String stockSymbol = req.getParameter("stockSymbol");
538         synchronized (db)
539         {
540             db.delUserStocks(userID, stockSymbol);
541         }
542         session.setAttribute("stocks", getStockList(userID));
543         session.setAttribute("forwardTo", "mainForm.jsp");
544     }
545
```

FIGURE 12-42

Figure 12-43 displays lines 546 through 575 of the WebStocks servlet code. The chgPswd() method obtains the new password from a parameter value on line 550, as the user entered this value as input to a form. The current password and user ID values are obtained from session attributes rather than parameters, requiring that the user be successfully logged on to the application, at least to the point of identifying a valid user ID and password, before changing the current password. At the present time, this method is called only when the user's password has expired, and so the session attribute indicating an expired password now must be removed (lines 555 and 556). Recall that a Password object exists as part of a User object, reflecting the "has-a" relationship between the User and Password classes. Changing a user's password must be done by calling the User method, changePassword(), requiring a User object. A User object is obtained from data in the database for the current userID (line 560), the User's password value is changed to the new password value (line 561), and the database is updated with the new user data (line 562). Because these statements access and update the database in succession, they are placed within a code block synchronized on the StockTrackerDB object. A session attribute is set to forward the request and result to the proper JSP for display to the user (line 565).

Because an exception forces a user to change an expiring password when first logging on to the application, the remaining session attributes were not set and now must be set to complete the log on process (lines 567 through 573).

```
546        private void chgPswd(HttpServletRequest req, HttpSession session)
547            throws ClassNotFoundException, IOException, SQLException,
548                PasswordException
549        {
550            String pswd1 = req.getParameter("pswd1");
551            String pswd = (String)session.getAttribute("pswd");
552            String userID = (String)session.getAttribute("userID");
553            User user = null;
554
555            if(session.getAttribute("pswdExpired") != null)
556                session.removeAttribute("pswdExpired");
557
558            synchronized (db)
559            {
560                user = db.getUser(userID); // get user object from DB for this ID
561                user.changePassword(pswd, pswd1);   // change password
562                db.updUser(user);                   // update database
563            }
564
565            session.setAttribute("forwardTo", "mainForm.jsp");
566
567            if(user.pswdIsExpiring())
568                session.setAttribute("uses", new Integer(user.getPswdUses()));
569
570            if(user.isAdmin())
571                session.setAttribute("admin", new Boolean(true));
572
573            session.setAttribute("stocks",getStockList(userID));
574        }
575
```

FIGURE 12-43

Figure 12-44 displays lines 576 through 613 of the WebStocks servlet code. The addUser() method on line 576 obtains data for a new user from parameter values entered as input to a form (lines 580 through 586). Because all parameter data are returned as Strings, user fields of other data types are created and their values determined from the corresponding parameters (lines 588 through 602). A new User object is created (lines 604 and 605), and the password for the new user is set as expired, forcing the user to change the password upon the first use (line 606). Only the call to the data access class method, addUser(), actually affects the database, and so it is placed within a block of code synchronized on the StockTrackerDB object (line 610).

```
576        private void addUser(HttpServletRequest req)
577            throws ClassNotFoundException, IOException, SQLException,
578                PasswordException
579        {
580            String userID = req.getParameter("userID");
581            String userFirstName = req.getParameter("userFirstName");
582            String userLastName = req.getParameter("userLastName");
583            String newPassword = req.getParameter("pswd1");
584            String autoExpires = req.getParameter("autoExpires");
585            String numUses = req.getParameter("uses");
586            String adminChecked = req.getParameter("isAdmin");
587
588            boolean isAdmin, autoExp;
589            int uses = 0;
590
```

FIGURE 12-44

(continued)

```
591            if(adminChecked != null && adminChecked.equals("Yes"))
592                isAdmin = true;
593        else
594                isAdmin = false;
595
596            if(autoExpires.equals("Yes"))
597                autoExp = true;
598        else
599                autoExp = false;
600
601            if(autoExp && numUses != null)
602                uses = Integer.parseInt(numUses);
603
604            User user = new User(userID, userFirstName, userLastName,
605                            newPassword, autoExp, uses, isAdmin);
606            user.expirePassword(); // cause new user to have to change password
607
608            synchronized (db)
609            {
610                db.addUser(user);
611            }
612        }
613
```

FIGURE 12-44

Figure 12-45 displays lines 614 through 626 of the WebStocks servlet code. If the supplied userID is not null, then the database is accessed through the StockTrackerDB object to get the corresponding User object for the userID (line 621). This is necessary because the StockTrackerDB delUser() method, used to delete a user from the database, requires a User object as an argument (line 622). Because the User object is obtained from the database immediately before deleting the user, and both of these calls are placed within a block of code synchronized on the StockTrackerDB object, the delUser() method will be called only for a valid, existing user. If the userID does not match an existing user, an exception is thrown by the StockTrackerDB getUser() method.

```
614        private void delUser(String userID) throws ClassNotFoundException,
615                                        IOException, SQLException
616        {
617            if(userID != null)
618            {
619                synchronized (db)
620                {
621                    User user = db.getUser(userID); // throws exception if user not found
622                    db.delUser(user);
623                }
624            }
625        }
626
```

FIGURE 12-45

Figure 12-46 displays lines 627 through 660 of the WebStocks servlet code. This method obtains form data from parameters, much as does the addUser() method (lines 632 through 637). Because it is updating an existing user, a User object for the given userID is obtained from the database (line 641), and the mutator methods for the various User fields are called to set their new values (lines 644 through 655). If a new password value is supplied, however, the User method, adminChangePassword() is called (lines 642 and 643). Recall that this method does not require that the current password be supplied before changing the password value; this allows an administrator to change the password of another user. It also sets the new password as expired so the user will have to change the password during the next log on process.

```
627      private void updUser(HttpServletRequest req)
628              throws ClassNotFoundException, IOException, SQLException,
629                     PasswordException
630      {
631          // cannot change userID or uses left for password
632          String userID = req.getParameter("userID");
633          String userFirstName = req.getParameter("userFirstName");
634          String userLastName = req.getParameter("userLastName");
635          String newPassword = req.getParameter("pswd1");
636          String autoExpires = req.getParameter("autoExpires");
637          String isAdmin = req.getParameter("isAdmin");
638
639          synchronized (db)
640          {
641              User user = db.getUser(userID);
642              if(newPassword.length() > 0)
643                  user.adminChangePassword(newPassword);
644              user.setFirstName(userFirstName);
645              user.setLastName(userLastName);
646
647              if(isAdmin != null && isAdmin.equals("Yes"))
648                  user.setAdmin(true);
649              else
650                  user.setAdmin(false);
651
652              if(autoExpires.equals("Yes"))
653                  user.setAutoExpires(true);
654              else
655                  user.setAutoExpires(false);
656
657              db.updUser(user);
658          }
659      }
660
```

FIGURE 12-46

Figure 12-47 on the next page displays lines 661 through 680 of the WebStocks servlet code. Each time a user attempts to log on to the application, this method is called to validate the password for the user. The User validate() method is called to perform the validation of the password for an existing user (line 669). Recall that if a password is set to expire automatically, then the Password object within the User object will increment its use count. The count is modified in the computer memory; however, the new value will be lost if not written to the database. Therefore, if the user password is set to expire automatically, the User object containing a Password with an incremented use count is updated to the database (lines 670 and 673). As in earlier methods, the method updating the database is synchronized on the StockTrackerDB object.

```
661     private boolean validUserPswd(User user, String password)
662             throws ClassNotFoundException, IOException,
663                    SQLException, PasswordException
664     {
665         boolean valid = false;
666
667         if(user != null)
668         {
669             user.validate(password); // throws PasswordException
670             if(user.pswdAutoExpires())  // if tracking uses
671                 synchronized (db)
672                 {
673                     db.updUser(user);   // update use count in database
674                 }
675             valid = true;
676         }
677
678         return valid;
679     }
680
```

FIGURE 12-47

Figure 12-48 displays lines 681 through 691 of the WebStocks servlet code. The getStockList() method returns an ArrayList containing the stock holdings for a given userID (line 681). Because the data access class, StockTrackerDB, contains a method that also returns an ArrayList of stock holdings from the database for a given userID, it is called within a synchronized block of code. Although this method only accesses and does not update the database, by placing the call within a block of code synchronized on the StockTrackerDB object, the stock holdings of the user cannot be changed by another thread during this access, as long as the other thread also uses synchronized access to the StockTrackerDB methods.

```
681     private ArrayList getStockList(String userID)
682             throws ClassNotFoundException, IOException, SQLException
683     {
684         ArrayList al = null;
685         synchronized (db)
686         {
687             al = db.listUserStocks(userID);
688         }
689         return al;
690     }
691
```

FIGURE 12-48

Figure 12-49 displays lines 692 through 703 of the WebStocks servlet code. Like the previous method, this method also obtains an ArrayList from a StockTrackerDB method within a synchronized block of code (line 699). Instead of returning the ArrayList object, however, it is set as a session attribute (line 701).

```
692     private void listUsers(HttpSession session)
693            throws ClassNotFoundException, IOException, SQLException
694     {
695         ArrayList rs;
696
697         synchronized (db)
698         {
699             rs = db.listUsers();
700         }
701         session.setAttribute("userList", rs);
702     }
703
```

FIGURE 12-49

Figure 12-50 displays lines 704 through 715 of the WebStocks servlet code. This method returns a User object given a userID (line 704). The User object is created by the StockTrackerDB method, getUser(), called within a synchronized block of code (line 711). Recall that the StockTrackerDB method returns either a User object or, if the userID does not exist, a null reference. The object (reference) then is returned to where the method was called, as in line 306 on page 816 in the logonValidated() method.

```
704     private User getUser(String userID)
705                throws ClassNotFoundException, IOException,
706                   SQLException
707     {
708         User user = null;
709         synchronized (db)
710         {
711             user = db.getUser(userID); // get user object from DB for this ID
712         }
713         return user;
714     }
715
```

FIGURE 12-50

Figure 12-51 on the next page displays lines 716 through 747 of the WebStocks servlet code. This method also returns an ArrayList containing user data retrieved from the database. Again, method calls that access the database are in a synchronized block of code (line 724). If a valid User object is obtained, the required data is added to the ArrayList and then returned to the caller (lines 727 through 745). If a valid User object is not obtained, no user data is added to the ArrayList; therefore, the size of the ArrayList is zero. This is used by the caller to determine if any data was added to the list (line 155 on page 810 in the doPost() method).

```
716      private ArrayList getUserData(String userID)
717                  throws ClassNotFoundException, IOException, SQLException
718      {
719          ArrayList userData = new ArrayList();
720          User user = null;
721
722          synchronized (db)
723          {
724              user = db.getUser(userID); // get user object from DB for this ID
725          }
726
727          if(user != null)
728          {
729              userData.add(userID);
730              userData.add(user.getFirstName());
731              userData.add(user.getLastName());
732              if(user.isAdmin())
733                  userData.add("Administrator");
734              else
735                  userData.add("Nonadministrator");
736
737              if(user.pswdAutoExpires())
738                  userData.add("Yes");
739              else
740                  userData.add("No");
741
742              userData.add(String.valueOf(user.getPswdUses()));
743          }
744
745          return userData;
746      }
747  }
```

FIGURE 12-51

The following steps enter the code to synchronize threaded code on an object — in this case, a data access object.

To Synchronize Multithreaded Code on an Object

1. Enter lines 469 through 505 as shown in Figure 12-39 on page 824.

TextPad displays the code to add a stock (Figure 12-52). If the user already holds the stock, he or she is returned to the main Web page. If the stock already exists in the database, a method is called to add it to the user's stock holdings in the database, and a new list of stock holdings is added as the stock's attribute. If the stock's attribute previously existed, it is replaced. If the stock is not in the database, the request is forwarded to a Web page to obtain a description for the new stock. Access to the database is synchronized.

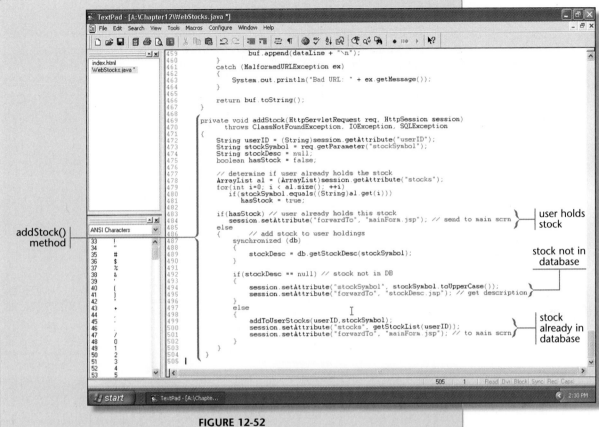

FIGURE 12-52

2. Click the Save button. Enter lines 506 through 522 as shown in Figure 12-40 on page 825.

TextPad displays the code to add a stock description (Figure 12-53). After adding a new stock and description, the stock is added to the user's stock holdings. A new list of stock holdings is added as the stock's attribute. If the stock's attribute previously existed, it is replaced.

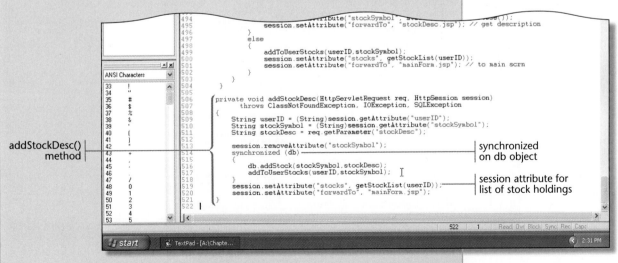

FIGURE 12-53

(continued)

3. Enter lines 523 through 532 as shown in Figure 12-41 on page 825.

TextPad displays the code to add a user's new stock holding to the database (Figure 12-54). The stock symbol is trimmed and changed to uppercase before the data access class method is called.

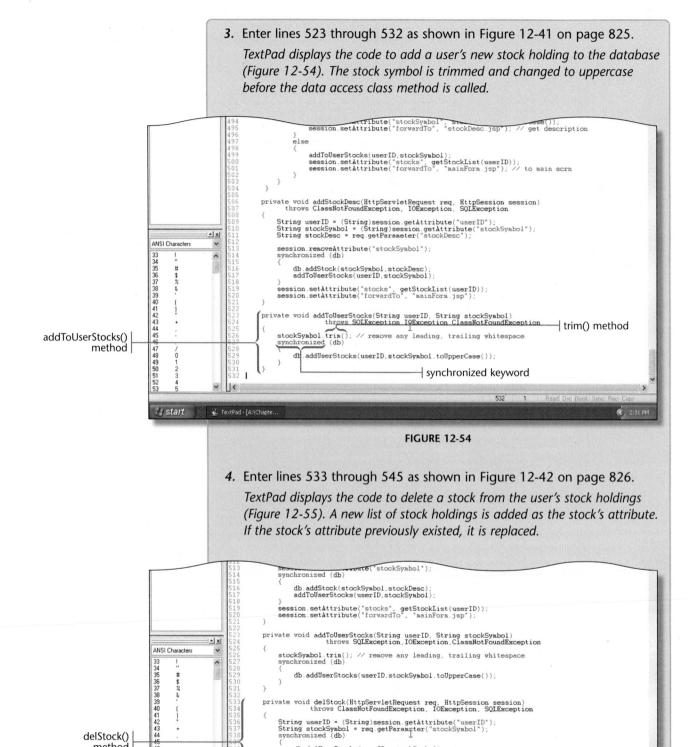

FIGURE 12-54

4. Enter lines 533 through 545 as shown in Figure 12-42 on page 826.

TextPad displays the code to delete a stock from the user's stock holdings (Figure 12-55). A new list of stock holdings is added as the stock's attribute. If the stock's attribute previously existed, it is replaced.

FIGURE 12-55

5. Enter lines 546 through 575 as shown in Figure 12-43 on page 827.

TextPad displays the code to change the user's password (Figure 12-56). Because this happens when the user initially logs on with an expired password, user attributes are set for use by the main Web page, including the number of remaining uses for an expiring password, whether the user is an administrator, and the user's stock holdings.

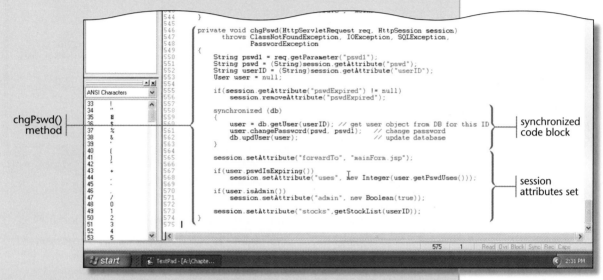

FIGURE 12-56

6. Enter lines 576 through 613 as shown in Figure 12-44 on page 827.

TextPad displays the code to add a new user (Figure 12-57). The new user's password is set as expired, forcing a change of the password at the user's next successful log on.

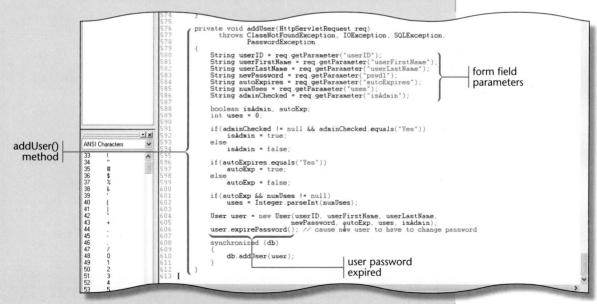

FIGURE 12-57

(continued)

7. Click the Save button. Enter lines 614 through 626 as shown in Figure 12-45 on page 828.

   TextPad displays the code to delete a valid user (Figure 12-58). If the user ID is not found, an exception is thrown by the data access class.

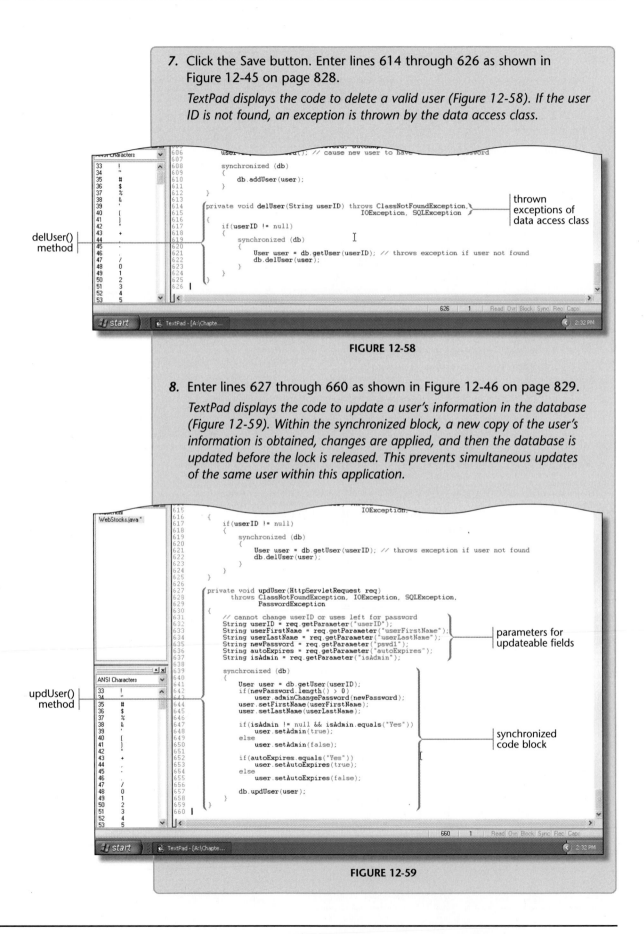

FIGURE 12-58

8. Enter lines 627 through 660 as shown in Figure 12-46 on page 829.

   TextPad displays the code to update a user's information in the database (Figure 12-59). Within the synchronized block, a new copy of the user's information is obtained, changes are applied, and then the database is updated before the lock is released. This prevents simultaneous updates of the same user within this application.

FIGURE 12-59

9. Enter lines 661 through 680 as shown in Figure 12-47 on page 830.

TextPad displays the code to validate the password for a user (Figure 12-60). If the password automatically expires, the number of remaining uses is updated in the database.

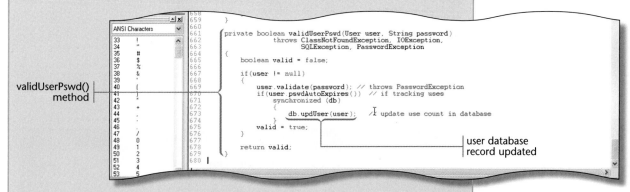

validUserPswd() method

user database record updated

FIGURE 12-60

10. Enter lines 681 through 691 as shown in Figure 12-48 on page 830.

TextPad displays the code to get the user stock holdings list as an ArrayList (Figure 12-61). This is similar to the StockTracker application.

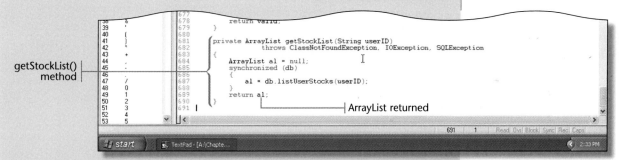

getStockList() method

ArrayList returned

FIGURE 12-61

11. Enter lines 692 through 703 as shown in Figure 12-49 on page 831.

TextPad displays the code to get the list of users as an ArrayList (Figure 12-62). This is similar to the StockTracker application, except that the list is stored as a session attribute rather than displayed. The attribute is used subsequently by a JavaServer Page to display the list.

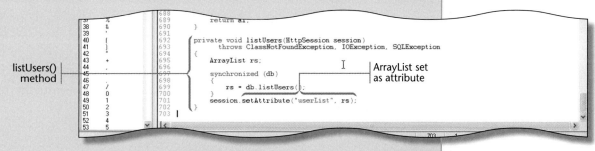

listUsers() method

ArrayList set as attribute

FIGURE 12-62

(continued)

12. Enter lines 704 through 715 as shown in Figure 12-50 on page 831.

TextPad displays the code for a utility method that obtains a User object from the database (Figure 12-63).

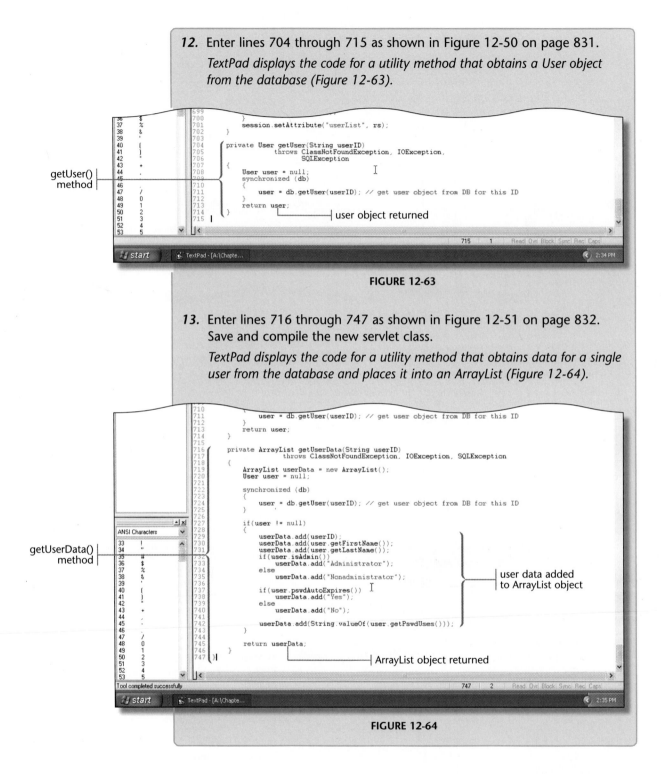

FIGURE 12-63

13. Enter lines 716 through 747 as shown in Figure 12-51 on page 832. Save and compile the new servlet class.

TextPad displays the code for a utility method that obtains data for a single user from the database and places it into an ArrayList (Figure 12-64).

FIGURE 12-64

The controller servlet is complete; however, the user interface is not. The main Web page, which is a JavaServer Page, must be created before the application can be tested.

Creating a JavaServer Page

A JavaServer Page is quite similar to an HTML page because it consists largely of HTML code. JSPs are Web pages with one or more sections of scriptlets surrounded by JSP tags and embedded within the HTML. Just as certain characters called tags indicate HTML elements, JSPs also have special tags to separate JSP scriptlets from HTML. Table 12-6 lists JSP tags. Tags typically are not case-sensitive.

Table 12-6 JSP Tags

TAG	PURPOSE
<%	Begins a scriptlet that contains one or more Java statements
%>	Ends all JSP sections, except JSP comments
<%=	Begins an expression that can be converted to a string
<%@	Begins a JSP directive for conditions that apply to the entire JSP, such as a page directive for an import attribute
<%—	Begins a JSP comment; JSP comments, just as Java comments within a scriptlet, are not compiled or executed; however, HTML comments are compiled and executed, but are not displayed by the browser
—%>	Ends a JSP comment
<%!	Begins a JSP declaration; declares instance variables or methods

Because most of a JavaServer Page is HTML code, it is easier for a Web designer to write the portion of the JSP that displays the view to the user. A JSP also is similar to a servlet, in that it contains sections of Java code as you might expect to find in a Java program. As shown in Table 12-6, tags provide the capability to insert scriptlets, string values, comments, JSP directives, methods, and Java declarations of instance variables and methods within an HTML document. Because a JSP is a hybrid of HTML and Java code, often a Web designer will create the HTML portion and then a Java programmer will write the Java portion within the HTML.

With a JSP, one or more sections of Java code, surrounded by JSP tags, are embedded within the HTML; the JSP is translated into a servlet that is compiled when it is first called to execute. The resulting servlet contains statements that output the HTML code, as would be done with any servlet that creates a Web page. It is important to note that the resulting product of a compiled JSP is a servlet that executes on the server. Although JSP is embedded in HTML source code and may appear to be somewhat like JavaScript, it is a server-side resource and does not execute on the client-side.

You may notice that a new or changed JSP initially displays more slowly than a similar Web page and more quickly thereafter. When the JSP first is requested from the Web server, the JSP container translates the JSP into a servlet, replacing the .jsp extension with _jsp.java, and then compiles it, causing the JSP to take extra time to display. Subsequent calls use the compiled code and display a result more quickly. If a compiler error is generated, it displays as a Web page and references line numbers from the generated source code. This may be difficult to relate to the original JSP source code, so it is advantageous to know how to view the generated servlet source code, which is stored in the Tomcat 5.5\work\ Catalina\localhost_\org\apache\jsp folder.

It also is important to note that the compiled JSP servlet, just as any other servlet, runs as a multithreaded instance on the server; therefore, the concerns regarding variable usage still apply. JSPs can create and access objects from other Java classes as any other Java program can; however, to use your own classes, they must be created within a package. The classes are not directly accessible if using the default package.

Tip

Viewing JSP-Generated Java Source Code

When a JSP first is requested, the JSP container translates the JSP into servlet source code and then compiles that source code. To view the generated source code, open the folder at C:\Program Files\Apache Software Foundation\Tomcat 5.5\work\ Catalina\localhost_\org\apache\jsp and look for the Java source file, xxx_jsp.java, where xxx is the name of your JSP.

Tip

JSPs are Server-Side Resources

Because a JSP looks so much like HTML, it is easy to forget that a JSP is a server-side resource, not a client-side resource. Do not think of a JSP as an HTML page that contains Java code. When creating a JSP, the code is HTML and Java, and it looks much like an HTML Web page. In terms of how it works, however, always think of a JSP as a Java servlet that outputs HTML code. That is exactly what a JSP is when compiled and executed.

According to the specification for this application, the main Web page in the WebStocks Web application, named mainForm.jsp, should look like the main user interface in the StockTracker application. This page contains an HTML form and is written using JSP, because it must collect user input as well as display dynamic data from the StockTracker database. Just like the StockTracker application, the WebStocks Web application displays the user maintenance portion of the user interface only if the user has administrator privileges. By using a JavaServer Page, the HTML portion of the page provides a form for collection of user input, while the Java portion allows dynamic data obtained from the database to be displayed. Based on this dynamic data, the portion of the interface that deals with user maintenance optionally is displayed.

The JavaServer Page, mainForm.jsp, uses JavaScript to do some client-side processing as shown in Figure 12-65. Lines 14 through 27 define a function that verifies whether a stock symbol was entered before submitting the form. This function is called when the user clicks a button that requires a stock symbol be entered, such as adding or deleting a stock, as was done in the StockTracker application. The function also is called when the user requests a stock quote. If no stock symbol was entered, line 18 calls the alert() function to issue a warning to the user. If a stock symbol was entered, lines 23 and 24 change the entry to all uppercase and then line 25 calls another method, setAction(), to set a hidden input field indicating the action requested and to submit the form field data to the server.

```
1   <!--
2   /*
3     Chapter 12: Main JSP form for the WebStocks Application
4     Programmer: Michael Mick
5     Date:       December 20, 2007
6     Filename:   mainForm.jsp
7     Purpose:    Provides the primary GUI for the WebStocks Application
8   */
9   -->
10  <head>
11  <title>WebStocks: Main Form</title>
12  <SCRIPT LANGUAGE=JAVASCRIPT>
13  <!--
14    function checkSymbol(stockAction)
15    {
16      if(document.mainForm.stockSymbol.value == "")
17      {
18        alert("Please enter a stock symbol.");
19        document.mainForm.stockSymbol.focus();
20      }
21      else
22      {
23        document.mainForm.stockSymbol.value
24          = document.mainForm.stockSymbol.value.toUpperCase();
25        setAction(stockAction);
26      }
27    }
28
29    function clearQuote()
30    {
31      mainForm.quoteList.value = "";
32      setAction("clearQuote");
33    }
34
35    function setAction(doEvent)
36    {
37      document.mainForm.WSaction.value = doEvent;
38      document.mainForm.submit();
39    }
40
41    function checkUses()
42    {
43    <%
44      int uses;
45      if(session.getAttribute("uses") != null)   // expiring password
46      {
47        uses = ((Integer)(session.getAttribute("uses"))).intValue();
48    %>
49        alert("Password is expiring after "+
50          <%= uses %>
51          +" more use(s).");
52    <%
53      }
54    %>
55    }
56  //-->
57  </SCRIPT>
58  </head>
59  <body text="#824423" onLoad="checkUses()">
```

FIGURE 12-65

The following steps create a new JavaServer Page in TextPad.

To Create a New JavaServer Page in TextPad

1. Click the New Document button on the Standard toolbar. If necessary, click Line Numbers on the View menu to display line numbers.

2. Click File on the menu bar and then click Save As on the File menu. When the Save As dialog box is displayed, click the Save in box arrow and then click 3½ Floppy (A:) in the Save in list.

3. Double-click the Chapter12 folder or the location specified by your instructor.

4. Type mainForm.jsp in the File name text box and then click JavaServer Page (*.jsp) in the Save as type list. Click the Save button in the Save As dialog box. If you did not install a JSP syntax file for TextPad, you will have to select All Files (*.*) in the Save as type list.

5. Enter lines 1 through 28 as shown in Figure 12-65 on the previous page. In the comments, insert your own name as programmer and enter the current date.

   TextPad displays the code for the initial comments, head, title, and script tags, and the JavaScript user-defined function, checkSymbol() (Figure 12-66). The color used for syntax highlighting of your code may differ, depending on your configuration for this file type (.jsp).*

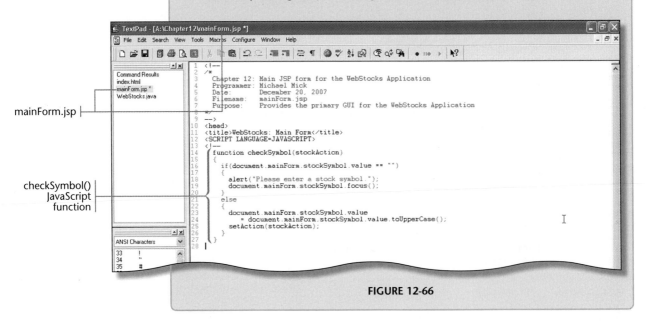

FIGURE 12-66

Not all actions on the main page of the WebStocks application require a stock symbol. Clearing a retrieved quote, for example, is done regardless of whether a stock symbol was entered. Lines 29 through 33 in Figure 12-65 define a function to clear the quote text area of the main form, named quoteList. Once cleared, the hidden input field is set to indicate the action taken and then the form field data is submitted to the servlet. Because the setAction() method exists to accomplish these last two steps, it is called after the text area is cleared.

The following step enters the code to clear the stock quote text area.

To Clear the Stock Quote Text Area

1. Enter lines 29 through 34 as shown in Figure 12-65 on page 841.

   TextPad displays the JavaScript function, clearQuote(), in the coding window (Figure 12-67). Changing the value of a text area replaces the contents displayed to the user with the new value. Setting the value to an empty string clears the text area.

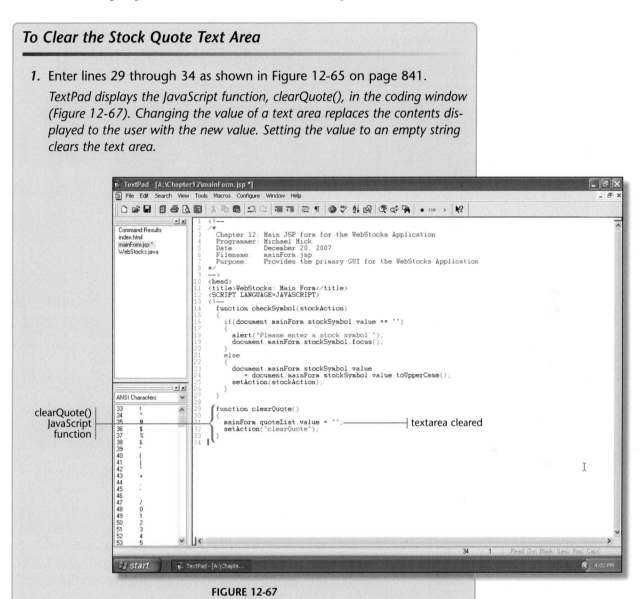

clearQuote()
JavaScript
function

textarea cleared

FIGURE 12-67

Because multiple functions performing different processes also must set the hidden form field data and submit the form, a function, setAction(), is used to execute the common code (lines 35 through 39 in Figure 12-65). The hidden form input field, WSaction, is not seen by the user; however, its value is passed to the server just like any other form field. The value for the hidden field is obtained from the function parameter. The setAction() function then calls the form submit() built-in function, which causes the form data to be submitted to the server, in the same manner as if the user clicked a submit button.

The following step enters the code for the setAction() user-defined method.

To Create the setAction() Method

1. Enter lines 35 through 40 as shown in Figure 12-65 on page 841.

TextPad displays the JavaScript function, setAction(), in the coding window (Figure 12-68). The parameter value is assigned to a hidden field in the main form and then the form is submitted to the server.

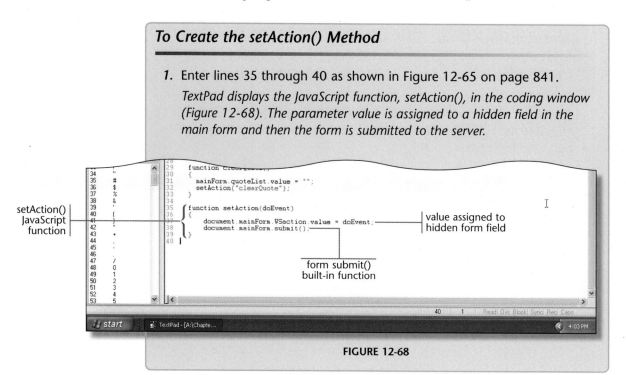

FIGURE 12-68

An additional JavaScript function is needed to alert users if their passwords are soon to expire. This alert displays when the current page initially is loaded for the user. To function properly, data from the server is needed to determine when to trigger the alert message.

Using Session Data in a JSP Scriptlet

Transmitting data from a form to the server is straightforward. As discussed earlier, when a form is submitted, the form field data is passed as name=value parameters to the form-processing program on the server. The field value can be set either programmatically or by input from the user. A program on the server, whether a servlet, CGI, or JSP, can obtain the parameter data and use it to create a Web page dynamically as a reply to the browser, as you have done already. If that dynamic Web page must again send parameter data to the server, the Web page is created with a form and form fields. When the new form is submitted, the form field data is transmitted to the Web server again.

Unfortunately, this can result in a large amount of data passing back and forth between the browser and the server and thus can degrade performance. Rather than passing data to the Web page to be processed by JavaScript code, a JSP can use data on the server to create a Web page dynamically, just as any other servlet. Recall that a JSP has access to an implicit session object stored on the server. Lines 41 through 55 in Figure 12-65 define a function, checkUses(), to display a warning if the password is expiring. The embedded JSP uses the session object to check an attribute, uses, which is set by the servlet. When servlet is called again, it will remove this attribute so the message displays only when the user first logs on and only if his or her password is expiring.

The following step enters the code to use session data in a JSP scriptlet.

To Use Session Data in a JSP Scriptlet

1. Enter lines 41 through 59 as shown in Figure 12-65 on page 841.

TextPad displays the JavaScript function, checkUses(), in the coding window (Figure 12-69). JSP tags surround the Java scriptlet code that obtains the session attribute, uses. The alert() function uses a string expression surrounded by JSP tags.

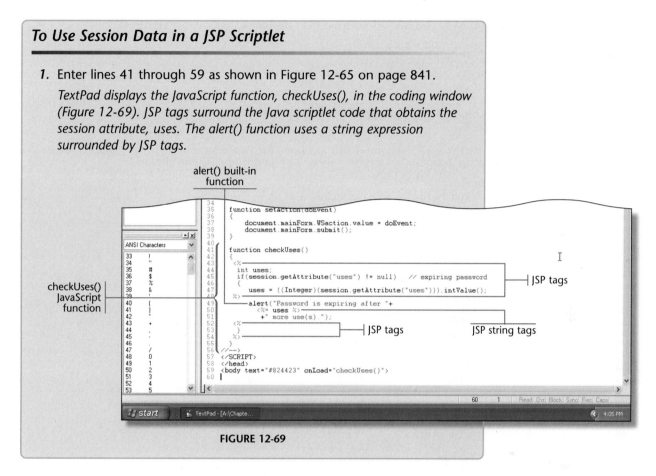

FIGURE 12-69

Recall that the onLoad() event handler executes when the page is loaded by the browser. In line 59, this event handler calls the checkUses() method when the form is loaded.

Using a JSP Page Directive

Because a JSP contains Java code, you will need to be able to import classes, either from the SDK or from other packages, for use in any of the Java code in the JSP. A **JSP page directive** sets conditions that apply to the entire JSP file, not just a single section of JSP code. Figure 12-70 on the next page displays lines 60 through 151 of the code for mainForm.jsp. A page directive is displayed on line 60, using the import attribute to import the java.util package of classes. Note that an assignment operator is used, unlike in a Java program. If multiple classes are imported, all imported classes are listed within the double quotes and separated by commas. An alternative is to use multiple JSP page directives.

```
60  <%@ page import="java.util.*" %>
61    <center>
62    <table border="0" cellspacing="0" width="55%" height="369" cellpadding="0">
63      <tr>
64        <td height="27" align="center">
65          <font size="5">WebStocks</font>
66        </td>
67      </tr>
68      <tr>
69        <td width="42%" height="341" align="center">
70          <form name="mainForm" method="POST" action="../servlet/WebStocks">
71            <table border="2">
72              <tr>
73                <td width="491" height="261" align="center">
74                  <table border="0" width="84%" cellpadding="2" height="119"
75                    cellspacing="0">
76                  <tr>
77                    <td height="26" colspan="3">
78                      <b>User:
79                      <%-- display user name from DB --%>
80                      <%= (String)session.getAttribute("userName") %>
81                      </b>
82                    </td>
83                    <td align="right">
84                      <input type="submit" name="logout" value="Log out">
85                    </td>
86                  </tr>
87                  <tr>
88                    <td width="42%" align="right" height="18"> </td>
89                    <td width="9%" height="18"> </td>
90                    <td width="176%" height="18" colspan="2"></td>
91                  </tr>
92                  <tr>
93                    <td width="42%" align="right" height="26">
94                      <input type="button" name="addStock" value="      Add Stock      "
95                        onClick="checkSymbol('addStock')">
96                    </td>
97                    <td width="9%" height="26"> </td>
98                    <td width="176%" height="26" colspan="2" align="right">
99                      <input type="text" name="stockSymbol" size="20">
100                   </td>
101                 </tr>
102                 <tr>
103                   <td width="42%" align="right" height="26">
104                     <input type="button" value="   Delete Stock   " name="delStock"
105                       onClick="checkSymbol('delStock')">
106                   </td>
107                   <td width="9%" height="26"> </td>
108                   <td width="176%" height="26" colspan="2" align="right">
109                     <Select size="1" name="StockList"
110                       onChange="mainForm.stockSymbol.value=mainForm.StockList.value">
111                     <%
112                     // build stock list from DB
113                     ArrayList al = (ArrayList)session.getAttribute("stocks");
114                     if(al.size() < 1)
115                     {
116                     %>
117                       <option selected>Add a stock</option>
118                     <%
119                     }
120                     else
121                     {
122                     %>
123                       <option selected>Select a stock</option>
124                     <%
125                       for(int i=0; i < al.size(); ++i)
126                       {
127                     %>
128                         <option value = <%= (String)al.get(i) %> >
129                           <%= (String)al.get(i) %>
130                         </option>
```

FIGURE 12-70

```
131                          <%
132                            }
133                          }
134                        %>
135                      </select>
136                    </td>
137                  </tr>
138                  <tr>
139                    <td width="42%" align="left" dir="ltr" height="24"> </td>
140                    <td width="9%" height="24"> </td>
141                    <td width="176%" height="24" colspan="2"> </td>
142                  </tr>
143                  <tr>
144                    <td width="42%" align="right" height="37">
145                      <input type="button" value="Get Stock Quote" name="getQuote"
146                        onClick="checkSymbol('getQuote')"></td>
147                    <td width="9%" height="37"> </td>
148                    <td width="176%" height="37" colspan="2" align="right">
149                      <input type="button" value="Clear Stock Quote"
150                        onClick="clearQuote()"></td>
151                  </tr>
```

FIGURE 12-70

The following step enters the code for the JSP page directive.

To Use a JSP Page Directive

1. Click the Save button. Enter line 60 as shown in Figure 12-70.

TextPad displays the JSP page directive with the import attribute (Figure 12-71). The package, java.util, is imported for use in the JSP file.

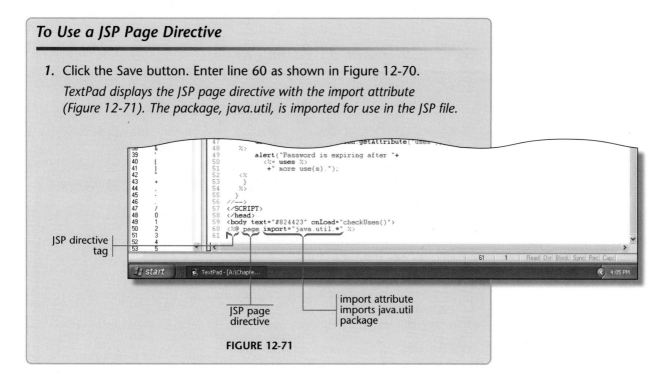

FIGURE 12-71

As discussed earlier, all JSPs have access to an implicit session object by default. If you do not want a JSP page to be able to access a session object, use the JSP page directive with the session attribute, as in

```
<%@ page session="false" %>
```

Your pages will run faster and use less memory in the JVM; however, if you try to access the session object, you will receive a fatal error from the JSP container.

Using a String with a JSP String Tag

As shown in Figure 12-70 on page 846, much of the JavaServer Page is HTML, just like the HTML page coded earlier. Sections of the page where Java code is embedded are enclosed within JSP tags.

The **JSP string tag**, <%=, must be followed by an expression that evaluates to a string. Because a session attribute is stored as an Object, it must be down-cast to the appropriate object type before its value can be used in code. In the code for mainForm.jsp, the code in line 47 in Figure 12-65 on page 841 down-casts the session attribute value, uses, to an Integer object because the session attribute originally was assigned an Integer object. It then retrieves the int value, not a String, which is used within the JSP string tag inserted in the message dis-played by the alert() method in lines 49 through 51. The expression, uses, is an int; however, when an integer is output, the String.valueOf(int) method is called implicitly, obtaining a String value just as with System.out. This leaves the int variable, uses, available for numeric manipulation, if necessary. If a String vari-able were used, its value could not be changed because a String is immutable.

Line 80 in Figure 12-70 also uses a String — retrieving the session attribute, userName, casting it to a String, and placing it within a JSP string tag for direct output on the Web page.

The following step enters the code to use a String with a JSP string tag.

To Use a String with a JSP String Tag

1. Enter lines 61 through 151 as shown in Figure 12-70.

TextPad displays scriptlet and string tags used in the JSP (Figure 12-72). Code within scriptlet tags is just like code in a servlet. Code within a JSP string tag must evaluate to a String or the JSP will not compile.

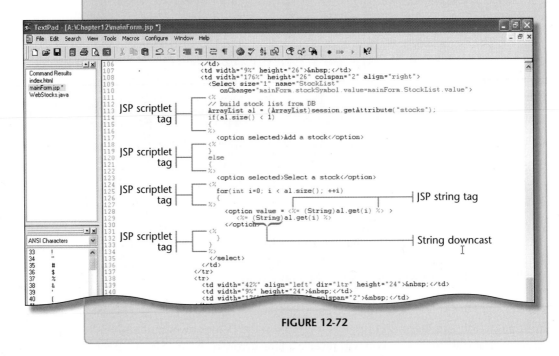

FIGURE 12-72

Using Local Variables in a JSP Script

To declare an instance method or instance variable in a JSP script, you must use a **JSP declaration tag** which begins with the tag, <%!, as shown in Table 12-6 on page 839. Recall that instance variables are shared among all threads of a servlet, including servlets generated from a JSP. Local variables declared within a script, however, are thread-safe and require no special tags in addition to being within a scriptlet. If you define a variable of a class from another package, you will need to import the package as discussed earlier.

Recall that when the WebStocks servlet retrieved a quote from the Yahoo! stock quote server, it stored the resulting String object as the session attribute, quote. This string contains comma-delimited data, with each record separated by a newline character (\n). Displaying the string as a whole would not be informative to a user, as it contains delimiters. A **delimiter** is a character, such as a comma or a newline, used to separate data fields, particularly in a stream of textual data. The data fields must be separated out, with the delimiters discarded. Separating out delimited data is called **parsing**. Each data field then can be formatted as desired and displayed in a meaningful way to the user.

Because the data is returned as a String object, a StringTokenizer object can be used to parse the string. A **StringTokenizer object** allows an application to break a string into tokens. A **token** is a set of characters separated from other tokens by one or more delimiters; that is, the data fields.

Figure 12-73 on the next page displays lines 152 through 196 of the code for mainForm.jsp. Lines 160 and 161 create a new StringTokenizer object, using the String from the quote session attribute and a set of delimiters. The set of delimiters is a string that contains the delimiter characters — in this case, a double quote ("), a comma (,), and a newline (\n). Because the double quote is itself enclosed within double quotes, it must be preceded by a backslash, similar to the newline character. The **hasMoreTokens() method** in line 167 tests if more tokens are available from the StringTokenizer's string. Each stock quote has nine requested fields, as outlined in the requirements document in Figure 12-2 on page 781. The **nextToken() method** in line 170 returns the next token from the StringTokenizer. The data for each of the nine fields is placed into a StringBuffer array for later manipulation. Once the array is loaded, each field is printed to the HTML textarea which begins on line 154. A **textarea** provides a scrollable text box that displays multiple rows of data on a Web page. Recall that with a servlet, you had to get a PrintWriter object to print data to the Web page. The JSP already has a default PrintWriter object named, out, used in lines 163 through 190 to print data to the Web page.

```
152    <tr>
153      <td width="154%" align="center" height="103" colspan="4">
154        <textarea rows="5" name="quoteList" cols="46"><%
155        if(session.getAttribute("quote") != null) // a quote exists
156        {
157          StringBuffer[] data = new StringBuffer[9];
158          StringBuffer spacer =                    // used to align report items
159                new StringBuffer("                    ");
160          StringTokenizer st = new StringTokenizer(
161                (String)session.getAttribute("quote"),"\",\n");
162
163          out.println("Symbol Price Trade Date/Time");
164          out.println("    Change    Open    High    Low    Volume");
165          out.println("==========================================");
166
167          while(st.hasMoreTokens())
168          {
169            for(int i=0; i < 9;++i)
170              data[i] = new StringBuffer(st.nextToken());
171
172            out.print(data[0]);  // stock symbol
173            out.print(spacer.substring(0, (12 -
174                (data[0].length()+data[1].length()))));
175            out.print(data[1]);  // stock price
176            out.print(" ");
177            out.print(data[2]);  // stock last trade date
178            out.print(" ");
179            out.println(data[3]);    // stock last trade time
180            out.print(spacer.substring(0, (10 - (data[4].length()))));
181            out.print(data[4]);  // stock price change
182            out.print(spacer.substring(0, (8 - (data[5].length()))));
183            out.print(data[5]);  // stock open price
184            out.print(spacer.substring(0, (8 - (data[6].length()))));
185            out.print(data[6]);  // stock high price
186            out.print(spacer.substring(0, (8 - (data[7].length()))));
187            out.print(data[7]);  // stock low price
188            out.print(spacer.substring(0, (11 - (data[8].length()))));
189            out.println(data[8]);  // stock volume
190            out.print("\n");
191          }
192        }
193        %>
194        </textarea>
195      </td>
196    </tr>
```

FIGURE 12-73

The length of the data fields can vary, depending on the details for a given stock, so aligning the output can be difficult. Recall that StringBuffer objects provide methods to obtain the length of the string data and to obtain a substring of the data, given a starting location and length. Defining a StringBuffer consisting of 20 space characters, as is done on line 158, allows substrings of spaces for various lengths to be used for aligning the report output. Subtracting the length of a data field to display from the number of spaces available yields the number of space characters needed to align the output as desired (lines 173 through 188). Displaying the first field and then calculating the length of the first and second fields together allows the first field to be left-aligned and the next to be right-aligned. Subsequent fields are right-aligned, as well. Because the data is too long to fit on a single line within the textarea, it is placed on two lines, with the second line indented under the first.

The following step enters the code to use local variables in a JSP script.

To Use Local Variables in a JSP Script

1. Click the Save button. Enter lines 152 through 196 as shown in Figure 12-73.

TextPad displays code for defining and using local variables in a JSP (Figure 12-74). Each thread gets a unique copy of the local variables, so the code is thread-safe.

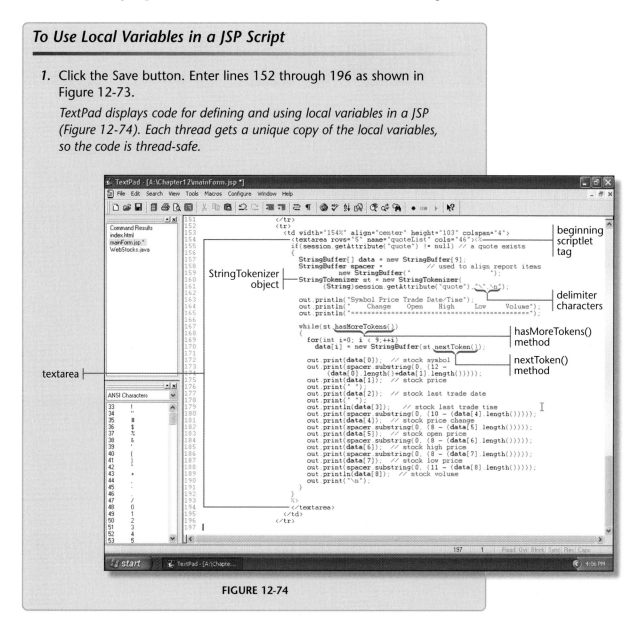

FIGURE 12-74

Optionally Creating HTML in a JSP

Recall that the main Web page displays the user maintenance section of the GUI for administrative users only. Consequently, the JSP should not create the HTML code for regular users. Figure 12-75 on the next page displays lines 197 through 239 of the code for mainForm.jsp. By using a JSP, the admin session attribute for the current user can be examined to determine if the user is an administrator (line 197) and, if so, output the necessary HTML code for the user maintenance portion (lines 200 through 225). If the user is not an administrator, this section of HTML code is not output to the resulting Web page. By creating the HTML page dynamically, this decision is made during execution of the application.

```
197                          <% if(session.getAttribute("admin") != null) // user is an admin
198                          {
199                      %>
200                        <tr>
201                          <td width="44%" align="right" height="26">
202                            <input type="submit" value="         Add User          "
203                                    name="addUser"
204                                    onClick="mainForm.action='..//addUser.html'">
205                          </td>
206                          <td width="11%" align="right" height="26"> </td>
207                          <td width="123%" align="right" height="26" colspan="2">
208                            <input type="submit" value="         Update User       "
209                                    name="updUser"
210                                    onClick="mainForm.action='..//reqUpdUser.html'">
211                          </td>
212                        </tr>
213                        <tr>
214                          <td width="44%" align="right" height="26">
215                            <input type="submit" value="     Delete User       "
216                                    name="delUser"
217                                    onClick="mainForm.action='..//reqDelUser.html'">
218                          </td>
219                          <td width="11%" align="right" height="26"> </td>
220                          <td width="123%" align="right" height="26" colspan="2">
221                            <input type="submit" value="          List Users       "
222                                    name="listUsers"
223                                    onClick="setAction('listUsers')">
224                          </td>
225                        </tr>
226                      <%
227                          }
228                      %>
229                        </table>
230                      </td>
231                    </tr>
232                  </table>
233                  <input type="hidden" name="WSaction">
234                  </form>
235              </td>
236            </tr>
237          </table>
238        </center>
239  </body>
```

FIGURE 12-75

The following step enters the JSP code to optionally create HTML based on the value of the admin session attribute.

To Optionally Create HTML in a JSP

1. Enter lines 197 through 239 as shown in Figure 12-75. Click the Save button on the Standard toolbar to save the JSP file.

   TextPad displays code for optionally creating HTML code in a JSP (Figure 12-76). If the attribute, admin, is set (not null), then the HTML code is generated; otherwise, it is not.

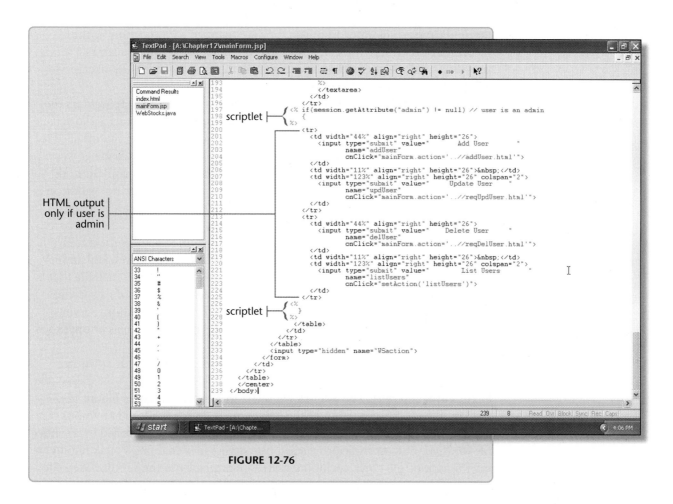

FIGURE 12-76

The JSP is complete. It is not compiled at this time. The JSP container will create the corresponding servlet code and compile it when the JSP is first loaded.

Testing Servlets and JavaServer Pages

To test a servlet, it first must be compiled and then the resulting class file must be placed in an appropriate location on the Web server. HTML files and JSP files also must be copied to their respective locations on the Web server. The Web server must be started, including the JSP and servlet containers, then a Web browser can be used to load the initial Web page for the Web application. For this project, Tomcat provides the servlet container, JSP container, and Web server.

Before using the servlet, JSPs, and HTML documents, two issues with Tomcat must be addressed: deployment descriptors and servlet reloading. The following sections address these two issues.

Modifying a Deployment Descriptor

Web applications typically are distributed within their own packages. For simplicity, this text used the default package. With Tomcat, classes in the default package are not accessible within JSPs. In a similar fashion, servlet classes placed in the default servlet folder, as opposed to files mapped to a specific package for the application, will not load unless they are mapped for execution by the InvokerServlet within Tomcat. Recall that if a dynamic resource such as a servlet is requested, the servlet either is loaded directly or a class called InvokerServlet will load and execute the servlet.

Servlets usually are loaded from WEB-INF\classes under the application's root folder. For Web applications using the default package, the root folder is the default root folder, located at webapps\ROOT within the Tomcat folder. If you installed to the default location as described in Appendix B, the full path for this folder is C:\Program Files\Apache Software Foundation\Tomcat 5.5\webapps\ROOT. All HTML documents and JSP files are placed in this folder, if they are not within an application package. Compiled servlet class files then are located in C:\Program Files\Apache Software Foundation\Tomcat 5.5\webapps\ROOT\WEB-INF\classes.

To have the InvokerServlet execute servlets from the default servlet folder, a file in the WEB-INF folder may need modification. This file is web.xml and is called a deployment descriptor. A **deployment descriptor** is an XML file that is used to configure a Web application. Servlets in packages may have a specific entry in the deployment descriptor that maps to the servlet location. Servlets without a specific entry in the deployment descriptor are known as **anonymous servlets**.

To load anonymous servlets, the deployment descriptor needs an entry indicating that all servlets called with a relative URL of servlet/* will be executed by the InvokerServlet. The asterisk (*) refers to any servlet name. Figure 12-77 displays the modified portion of the deployment descriptor for anonymous classes in the default class folder. The color highlighting is controlled by a syntax file for XML files. As indicated earlier, free syntax files enabling syntax highlighting for various file types, including XML, are available on the TextPad Web site.

```
41
42    <!-- added the following for invoker servlet -->
43        <servlet>
44            <servlet-name>invoker</servlet-name>
45            <servlet-class>
46                org.apache.catalina.servlets.InvokerServlet
47            </servlet-class>
48        </servlet>
49
50        <servlet-mapping>
51            <servlet-name>invoker</servlet-name>
52            <url-pattern>/servlet/*</url-pattern>
53        </servlet-mapping>
54
55    </web-app>
56
```

FIGURE 12-77

Loading anonymous servlets originally was enabled by default in Tomcat. The web.xml file in the conf folder (e.g., C:\Program Files\Apache Software Foundation\Tomcat 5.5\conf) has the required XML tags, but they are commented out to reduce potential security issues. Using anonymous servlets is not advisable in a production environment; however, it is acceptable for development, and it is necessary if your classes use the default package. Although the conf\web.xml file could be modified to remove the comments, it is easier, and safer if you are unfamiliar with XML, to modify the deployment descriptor (web.xml) in the root WEB-INF folder.

The following steps modify the deployment descriptor to allow Tomcat to locate anonymous servlets in the default servlet folder.

To Modify a Deployment Descriptor

1. Use TextPad to open the file, web.xml, in the folder located at C:\Program Files\Apache Software Foundation\Tomcat 5.5\ webapps\ROOT\WEB-INF.

TextPad displays the file, C:\Program Files\Apache Software Foundation\ Tomcat 5.5\webapps\ROOT\WEB-INF\web.xml, in the coding window (Figure 12-78).

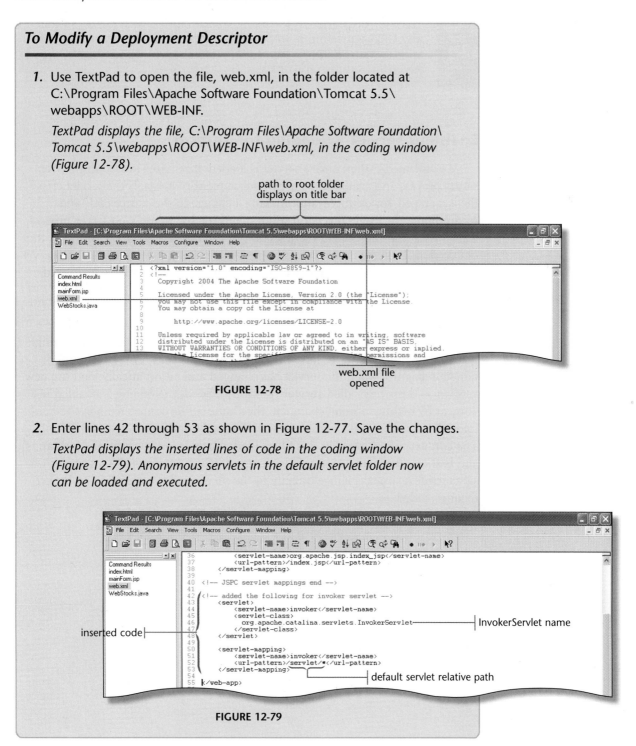

FIGURE 12-78

2. Enter lines 42 through 53 as shown in Figure 12-77. Save the changes.

TextPad displays the inserted lines of code in the coding window (Figure 12-79). Anonymous servlets in the default servlet folder now can be loaded and executed.

FIGURE 12-79

After modifying the deployment descriptor, any servlet placed in the default servlet folder can be located and executed by the Tomcat servlet container. JSPs are placed in the root directory, as are any other Web pages.

Mapping Servlets in Deployment Descriptors

Traditionally, requests for servlets are mapped to servlet/* so that any URL requesting a servlet simply precedes the servlet name with servlet/. Patterns other than servlet/* can be used; this pattern is simply customary.

Enabling Servlet Reloading for Tomcat

As indicated earlier, once a servlet is loaded, it remains loaded in the Web server process and available for use by subsequent requests. If the servlet class file is changed, for example, after making a change to the source code and recompiling, the original version still remains loaded in the Web server process. This means that subsequent requests do not use the new servlet version but the old version. To allow new requests to use the new servlet version, the Web server must be stopped and restarted, which will cause the new servlet to be loaded upon the next request for it. In a production environment, this may be acceptable.

In a development environment, however, having to stop and restart the Web server each time you update a servlet can be needlessly time-consuming. It would be much better to have the Web server (actually, the servlet container) recognize when the servlet has changed and automatically load the new version — a process called **servlet reloading**. Servlet reloading is enabled in Tomcat by making a small change to the Context file, context.xml, in the conf folder (e.g., C:\Program Files\Apache Software Foundation\Tomcat 5.5\conf). The context information in this file is loaded by all web applications (webapps) and is shown in Figure 12-80. This change is new with Tomcat 5, as earlier versions made a similar change directly to the server.xml file, which is no longer recommended.

```
1    <!-- The contents of this file will be loaded for each web application -->
2    <Context reloadable="true">             <!-- Enabled Tomcat Servlet reloading -->
3
4        <!-- Default set of monitored resources -->
5            <WatchedResource>WEB-INF/web.xml</WatchedResource>
6            <WatchedResource>META-INF/context.xml</WatchedResource>
7
8            <!-- Uncomment this to disable session persistence across Tomcat restarts -->
9            <!--
10           <Manager pathname="" />
11           -->
12
13   </Context>
```

FIGURE 12-80

The following steps enable servlet reloading for Tomcat.

To Enable Servlet Reloading

1. Use TextPad to open the file, context.xml, in the C:\Program Files\Apache Software Foundation\Tomcat 5.5\conf folder.

TextPad displays the file, context.xml, in the coding window (Figure 12-81). Your context.xml file content may be somewhat different, depending on the default options set.

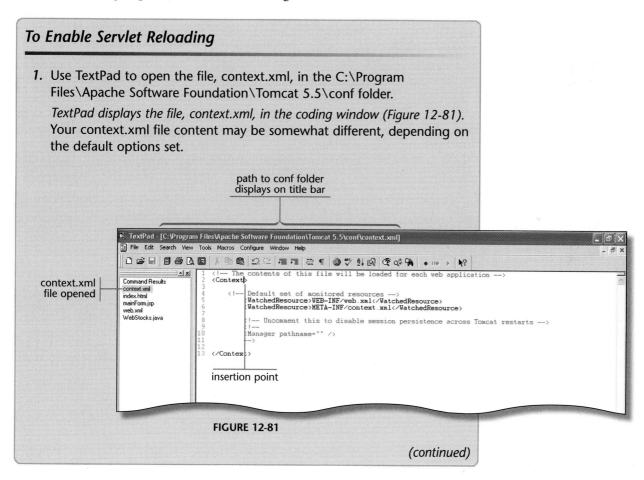

FIGURE 12-81

(continued)

2. In the TextPad window, locate the line of code containing the
<Context> XML tag. Position the insertion point at the end of the tag
and then type `reloadable="true"` as shown in Figure 12-80 on the
previous page. Save the changes.

*TextPad displays the inserted line of code in the coding window
(Figure 12-82). Modified servlets now will be reloaded automatically.
Your line numbers may be different, depending on the options set in
your context file.*

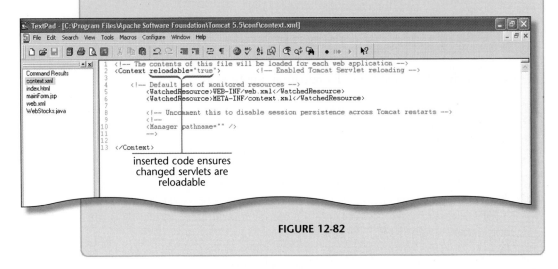

inserted code ensures
changed servlets are
reloadable

FIGURE 12-82

Due to performance considerations, servlet reloading should be enabled only
in a development environment, not in a production environment.

Testing the WebStocks Web Application

The WebStocks Web application consists of the servlet class file, HTML
file, and JSP file you created; the class files that you copied earlier; and the additional files provided on the Data Disk. All of these files must be copied to their
respective server folder locations before the Web application can be started.
Recall that the HTML and JSP files for this application are placed in the default

root folder (C:\Program Files\Apache Software Foundation\Tomcat 5.5\
webapps\ROOT) and the class files are placed in the default WEB-INF\
classes folder (C:\Program Files\Apache Software Foundation\Tomcat
5.5\webapps\ROOT\WEB-INF\classes). You may need to create the folder,
classes, in the default WEB-INF folder if it does not already exist.

To begin using the WebStocks Web application, users request the initial log
on Web page by entering the appropriate URL in the address text box of their
browser. If a specific Web page is not listed for the URL, the default Web page for
the Web site is displayed, typically index.html. The initial Web page then invokes
the servlet when its form is submitted.

Because the local machine is acting as the server, the URL entered in the
browser address text box is different than the typical address. For this application,
the complete address to the initial Web page is http://localhost:8080/index.html.
The keyword, **localhost**, specifies the local system. Because the local machine is
the server, localhost is used in place of a host address beginning with www. By
default, Tomcat accepts requests on port 8080. A **port** is a logical connection
address on the server for a particular application. This is listed after the host
address, separated by a colon. Because the initial Web page is located in the root
folder of the server, the path is /. This is followed by the Web page file name,
index.html, which also is the default page name.

The following steps start the WebStocks Web application.

To Start the Webstocks Web Application

1. Verify that the Data Disk is in drive A.

2. If necessary, create the default servlet folder, classes, in the WEB-INF
   folder, to create the folder located at C:\Program Files\
   Apache Software Foundation\Tomcat 5.5\webapps\ROOT\WEB-
   INF\classes. Copy the files as listed in Table 12-2 on page 785 and the
   WebStocks.class file you created in the Chapter12 folder on the Data
   Disk to the default servlet folder or a location specified by your
   instructor.

3. Copy the files as listed in Table 12-3 on page 785 in the Chapter12
   folder on the Data Disk, including the HTML and JSP files you created,
   to the default root folder. Also copy the two image files, tickerScrn.wmf
   and stockListing.jpg, as these are used for the initial Web page.

4. Start Tomcat using the Apache Service Manager located in the system
   tray. If you do not have the Apache Service Manager icon displayed in
   your system tray, see Appendix B to start the application, and then use it
   to start the Tomcat Service.

(continued)

5. Open your Web browser and then type http://localhost:8080/index.html in the address text box. Press the ENTER key.

The browser displays the WebStocks: User Log On Web page, index.html, for the WebStocks Web application (Figure 12-83). The Start Tomcat shortcut opens a command prompt window that stays active while Tomcat is running.

WebStocks: User Log On Web page   Web page address   User ID: text box

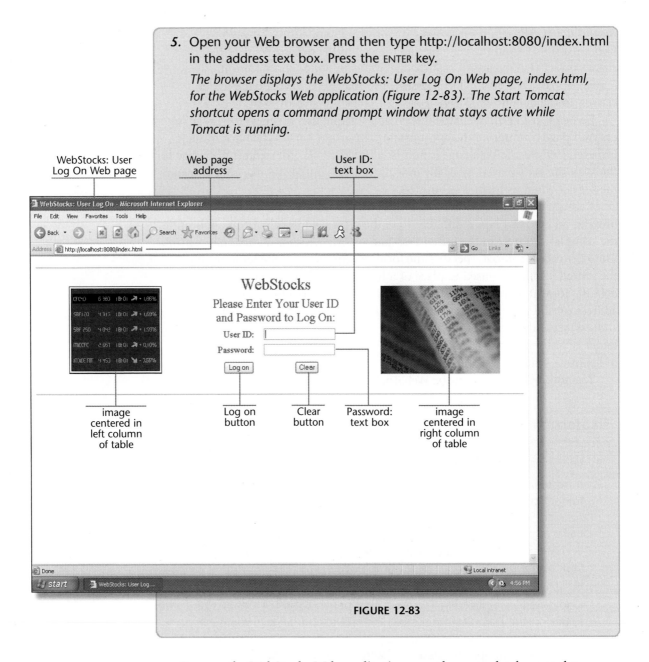

image centered in left column of table   Log on button   Clear button   Password: text box   image centered in right column of table

FIGURE 12-83

Because the WebStocks Web application uses the same database as the StockTracker application, you can log on using any user ID already entered. If the database was newly created or recreated, the default user ID, as used in the previous chapter, is available for use.

You should test the application using the same functions used to test the StockTracker application. Because these duplicate the steps taken in Chapter 11, they are not listed in detail again. However, the WebStocks application has the additional capability of obtaining online stock quotes. To test this functionality, your computer must be on a network connected to the World Wide Web.

The following steps obtain online stock quotes using the WebStocks application.

To Obtain Online Stock Quotes with the WebStocks Application

1. Type admin01 in the User ID text box and then type admin01 in the Password text box of the WebStocks: User Log On Web page. Click the Log on button.

   The WebStocks: Main Form Web page is displayed (Figure 12-84). The user name, Default Admin, is displayed on the page. Your application may display a different name if the user data was modified. Because the user is an administrative user, the buttons for user maintenance display. If you have modified the user or password with the StockTracker application, you must use the modified values to log on.

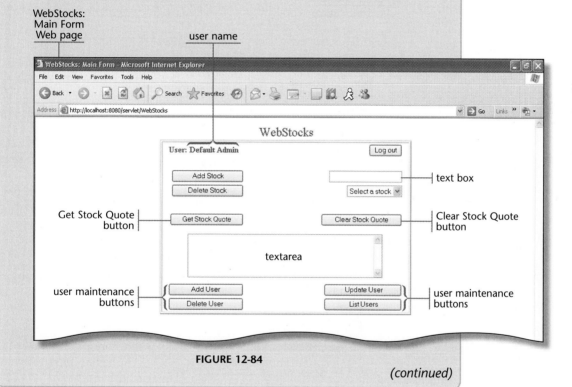

WebStocks:
Main Form
Web page

user name

text box

Get Stock Quote
button

Clear Stock Quote
button

user maintenance
buttons

user maintenance
buttons

FIGURE 12-84

(continued)

2. Type msft in the text box. Click the Get Stock Quote button.

The form is submitted to the servlet, and when the Web page redisplays, the textarea displays a formatted quote for the stock (Figure 12-85). If the stock, msft, already is in the stock holdings list for the user, it can be selected from the drop-down list box rather than typing it in the text box.

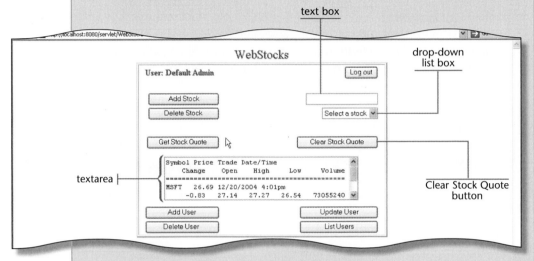

FIGURE 12-85

3. Click the Clear Stock Quote button. Type msft,orcl,sunw in the text box.

The quote is removed from the textarea (Figure 12-86). The form also is submitted to the servlet to reset the quote session attribute. The quote service can return simultaneous quotes for multiple stocks; however, the symbols must be entered manually in the text box, delimited by commas, and have no embedded spaces.

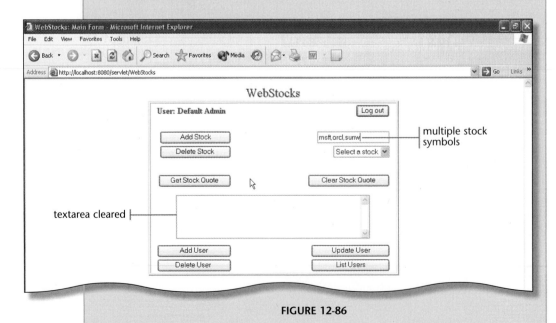

FIGURE 12-86

4. Click the Get Stock Quote button. When the Web page displays the stock quotes, use the scroll bar to view the second and third quotes.

The form is submitted to the servlet and when the Web page redisplays, the textarea displays a formatted quote for each of the three stocks (Figure 12-87). Only two stock quotes are visible at the same time.

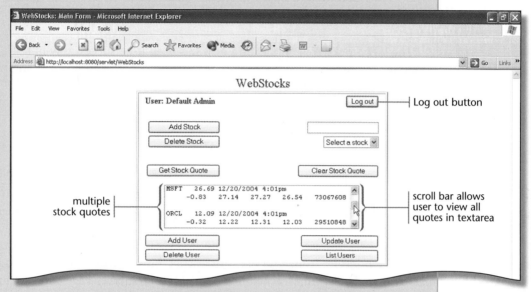

FIGURE 12-87

5. Click the Log out button.

The user is logged out and the initial Web page is displayed (Figure 12-88). The current session is invalidated, and a successful user log on is required to use the application.

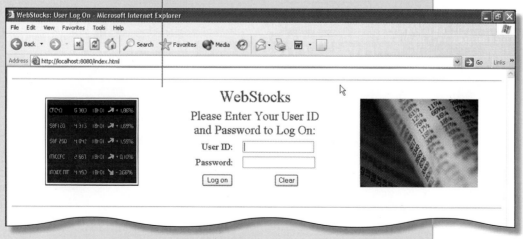

FIGURE 12-88

(continued)

> **6.** Close the browser and then right-click the Apache Service Manager icon in the system tray. Click Stop service on the shortcut menu. Close TextPad.
>
> *The browser and TextPad windows are closed, and the Tomcat server is stopped. The Apache Service Manager icon changes from a green arrow to a red square when the service stops.*

The WebStocks Web application now has been used successfully in testing the online quote functionality. As with the StockTracker application, if you have Microsoft Access available on your system, you can open the database and examine the tables and the records in each table directly.

Chapter Summary

In this chapter, you learned more about the MVC pattern and the components of a Java Web application. You created an HTML page that used JavaScript functions and that submitted form data to a servlet. You learned about the servlet life cycle, implemented session tracking, and learned how to forward and redirect HTTP requests. You learned how to output HTML pages with a servlet, and how to use a Web service from a servlet. You learned how to synchronize code to make it thread-safe. Your learned how to create a JavaServer Page and how to use session data in a JSP scriptlet. You learned how to use JSP page directives and string tags and how to declare and use local versus instance variables in a JSP. You learned to optionally create portions of a Web page in a JSP. You learned about deployment descriptors and enabling servlet reloading with Tomcat. Finally, you used a browser to test a Web application that interacts with a database and retrieves online stock quotes.

What You Should Know

Having completed this chapter, you now should be able to perform the tasks shown in Table 12-7.

Table 12-7   Chapter 12 What You Should Know

TASK NUMBER	TASK	PAGE
1	Create a New HTML Document in TextPad	788
2	Enter JavaScript in an HTML Document	792
3	Call a Servlet from an HTML Form	796
4	Create a New Java Servlet in TextPad	799
5	Override the init() and destroy() Servlet Methods	802
6	Process HTTP Requests in a Servlet	804
7	Implement Session Tracking with HTTP	807
8	Redirect an HTTP Request	808
9	Forward an HTTP Request	811
10	Output HTML Code from a Servlet	814
11	Validate a User Log On to a Web Application	819
12	Acquire Data from a Web Service	822
13	Synchronize Multithreaded Code on an Object	832
14	Create a New JavaServer Page in TextPad	842
15	Clear the Stock Quote Text Area	843
16	Create the setAction() Method	844
17	Use Session Data in a JSP Scriptlet	845
18	Use a JSP Page Directive	847
19	Use a String with a JSP String Tag	848
20	Use Local Variables in a JSP Script	851
21	Optionally Create HTML in a JSP	852
22	Modify a Deployment Descriptor	855
23	Enable Servlet Reloading	857
24	Start the WebStocks Web Application	859
25	Obtain Online Stock Quotes with the WebStocks Application	861

WHAT YOU SHOULD KNOW

Key Terms

absolute address *(784)*

action attribute *(795)*

alert() *(792)*

anonymous servlets *(854)*

bind *(806)*

client-side *(783)*

comma-delimited *(820)*

connect() method *(821)*

connection pooling *(800)*

cookie *(806)*

deadlock *(825)*

delimiter *(849)*

deployment descriptor *(854)*

document object *(791)*

dynamic Web page *(778)*

event handler *(793)*

Extensible Markup Language (XML) *(820)*

focus *(792)*

focus() *(792)*

form reset button *(788)*

form submit button *(788)*

forward *(807)*

forward() method *(811)*

getAttribute() method *(806)*

getParameter() method *(808)*

getRequestDispatcher() *(811)*

getServletContext() *(811)*

getWriter() method *(803)*

Get method *(795)*

hasMoreTokens() method *(849)*

HTML form *(788)*

Hypertext Transfer Protocol (HTTP) *(783)*

HTTP request *(784)*

HTTP response *(784)*

HttpServlet *(797)*

HttpServletRequest object *(803)*

HttpServletResponse object *(803)*

invalidate() method *(808)*

JavaScript function *(792)*

JSP declaration tag *(849)*

JSP page directive *(845)*

JSP string tag *(848)*

localhost *(859)*

loosely typed *(792)*

method attribute *(795)*

MIME (Multipurpose Internet Mail Extensions) *(803)*

monitor *(823)*

multithreading *(798)*

nextToken() method *(849)*

object-based *(791)*

onLoad() method *(794)*

openConnection() method *(821)*

parsing *(849)*

port *(859)*

Post method *(795)*

process *(798)*

redirect *(808)*

relative address *(784)*

removeAttribute() method *(806)*

RequestDispatcher object *(810)*

scriptlet *(786)*

sendRedirect() method *(808)*

server-side *(783)*

ServletContext object *(811)*

servlet and JSP container *(797)*

servlet context *(811)*

servlet reloading *(856)*

session *(805)*

session attribute *(806)*

session object *(805)*

session tracking *(805)*

setAttribute() method *(806)*

setContentType() method *(803)*

stack trace *(801)*

stateless protocol *(805)*

static Web page *(778)*

StringTokenizer object *(849)*

submit() *(792)*

synchronized *(823)*

target *(784)*

textarea *(849)*

thread *(798)*

thread-safe *(798)*

thread of execution *(798)*

token *(849)*

URL encoding *(806)*

URL rewriting *(806)*

var *(791)*

Web-enabled *(778)*

Web service *(820)*

window object *(791)*

Homework Assignments

Identify Code

Identify the code elements shown in Figure 12-89 and describe what they do.

```
506        private void addStockDesc(HttpServletRequest req, HttpSession session)
507              throws ClassNotFoundException, IOException, SQLException
508        {
509            String userID = (String)session.getAttribute("userID");
510            String stockSymbol = (String)session.getAttribute("stockSymbol");
511            String stockDesc = req.getParameter("stockDesc");
512
513            session.removeAttribute("stockSymbol");
514            synchronized (db)
515            {
516                db.addStock(stockSymbol,stockDesc);
517                addToUserStocks(userID,stockSymbol);
518            }
519            session.setAttribute("stocks", getStockList(userID));
520            session.setAttribute("forwardTo", "mainForm.jsp");
521        }
```

FIGURE 12-89

1. _____

2. _____

3. _____

4. _____

5. _____

6. _____

7. _____

Understanding Error Messages

Figure 12-90a on the next page displays a portion of a JSP program and Figure 12-90b on page 869 displays the same portion of the JSP program after it is converted to a Java servlet program. Figure 12-90c on page 870 displays the relevant portion of the error messages generated when the JSP container loads and compiles the JSP. Using what you know about error messages, list the coding errors that caused the browser to display these errors from the JSP container.

```
12  <SCRIPT LANGUAGE=JAVASCRIPT>
13  <!--
14    function checkSymbol(stockAction)
15    {
16      if(document.mainForm.stockSymbol.value == "")
17      {
18        alert("Please enter a stock symbol.");
19        document.mainForm.stockSymbol.focus();
20      }
21      else
22      {
23        document.mainForm.stockSymbol.value
24          = document.mainForm.stockSymbol.value.toUpperCase();
25        setAction(stockAction);
26      }
27    }
28
29    function clearQuote()
30    {
31      mainForm.quoteList.value = "";
32      setAction("clearQuote");
33    }
34
35    function setAction(doEvent)
36    {
37        document.mainForm.WSaction.value = doEvent;
38        document.mainForm.submit();
39    }
40
41    function checkUses()
42    {
43  <%
44      int uses;
45      if(session.getAttribute("uses") != null)    // expiring password
46      {
47        uses = ((Integer)(session.getAttribute("uses"))).intValue();
48  %>
49        alert("Password is expiring after "+
50          <%= uses %>
51          +" more use(s).");
52  <%
53      }
54  %>
55    }
56  //-->
57  </SCRIPT>
58  </head>
59  <body text="#824423" onLoad="checkUses()">
60  <% page import="java.util.*" %>
61    <center>
62    <table border="0" cellspacing="0" width="55%" height="369" cellpadding="0">
63      <tr>
64        <td height="27" align="center">
65          <font size="5">WebStocks</font>
66        </td>
67      </tr>
68      <tr>
69        <td width="42%" height="341" align="center">
70          <form name="mainForm" method="POST" action="../servlet/WebStocks">
71            <table border="2">
72              <tr>
73                <td width="491" height="261" align="center">
74                  <table border="0" width="84%" cellpadding="2" height="119"
75                      cellspacing="0">
76                    <tr>
77                      <td height="26" colspan="3">
78                        <b>User:
79                        <%-- display user name from DB --%>
80                        <%= (String)session.getAttribute("userName") %>
81                        </b>
82                      </td>
```

FIGURE 12-90a

```
45        out.write("<SCRIPT LANGUAGE=JAVASCRIPT>\r\n");
46        out.write(
          "<!--\r\n   function checkSymbol(stockAction)\r\n   {\r\n
          if(document.mainForm.stockSymbol.value == \"\")\r\n     {\r\n          alert(\"Please
          enter a stock symbol.\");\r\n          document.mainForm.stockSymbol.focus();\r\n
          }\r\n      else\r\n     {\r\n          document.mainForm.stockSymbol.value\r\n          =
          document.mainForm.stockSymbol.value.toUpperCase();\r\n
          setAction(stockAction);\r\n      }\r\n   }\r\n\r\n  function clearQuote()\r\n   {\r\n
          mainForm.quoteList.value = \"\";\r\n      setAction(\"clearQuote\");\r\n   }\r\n\r\n
          function setAction(doEvent)\r\n   {\r\n      document.mainForm.WSaction.value =
          doEvent;\r\n        document.mainForm.submit();\r\n   }\r\n\r\n   function
          checkUses()\r\n   {\r\n");
47
48    int uses;
49    if(session.getAttribute("uses") != null)   // expiring password
50    {
51        uses = ((Integer)(session.getAttribute("uses"))).intValue();
52
53        out.write("\r\n        alert(\"Password is expiring after \"+ \r\n          ");
54        out.print( uses );
55        out.write("\r\n          +\" more use(s).\");\r\n");
56
57    }
58
59        out.write("\r\n   }\r\n//-->\r\n");
60        out.write("</SCRIPT>\r\n");
61        out.write("</head>\r\n");
62        out.write("<body text=\"#824423\" onLoad=\"checkUses()\">\r\n");
63        page import="java.util.*"
64        out.write("\r\n   ");
65        out.write("<center>\r\n   ");
66        out.write(
          "<table border=\"0\" cellspacing=\"0\" width=\"55%\" height=\"369\"
          cellpadding=\"0\">\r\n       ");
67        out.write("<tr>\r\n       ");
68        out.write("<td height=\"27\" align=\"center\">\r\n          ");
69        out.write("<font size=\"5\">WebStocks");
70        out.write("</font>\r\n       ");
71        out.write("</td>\r\n       ");
72        out.write("</tr>\r\n       ");
73        out.write("<tr>\r\n       ");
74        out.write("<td width=\"42%\" height=\"341\" align=\"center\">\r\n          ");
75        out.write(
          "<form name=\"mainForm\" method=\"POST\" action=\"../servlet/WebStocks\">\r\n
          ");
76        out.write("<table border=\"2\">\r\n              ");
77        out.write("<tr>\r\n              ");
78        out.write("<td width=\"491\" height=\"261\" align=\"center\">\r\n              ");
79        out.write(
          "<table border=\"0\" width=\"84%\" cellpadding=\"2\" height=\"119\" \r\n
          cellspacing=\"0\">\r\n              ");
80        out.write("<tr>\r\n                 ");
81        out.write("<td height=\"26\" colspan=\"3\">\r\n                     ");
82        out.write("<b>User:\r\n                   ");
83        out.write("\r\n                   ");
84        out.print( (String)session.getAttribute("userName") );
85        out.write("\r\n                   ");
86        out.write("</b>\r\n                  ");
87        out.write("</td>\r\n                  ");
```

FIGURE 12-90b

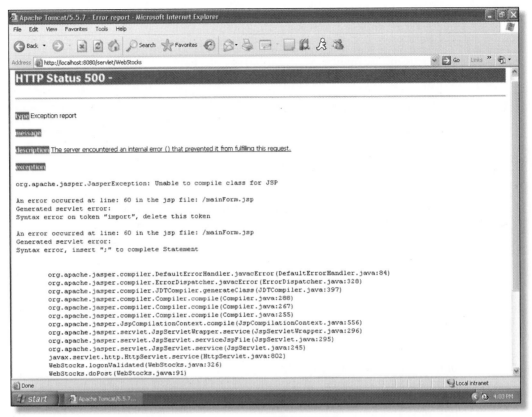

FIGURE 12-90C

Using the Servlet and JavaServer Pages API Documentation

The Servlet and JavaServer Pages API documentation is a good tool to look up information about servlet and JSP components, such as cookies and HTTP sessions. The documentation is supplied with the servlet and JSP container, Tomcat, in a folder created during installation. Start a browser and type C:\Program Files\Apache Software Foundation\Tomcat 5.5\webapps\ tomcat-docs\servletapi\index.html in the address text box and then press the ENTER key to view the documentation.

With the Servlet and JavaServer Pages API documentation open in the browser window, perform the following steps.

1. Use the scroll bar in the lower-left frame, if necessary, to scroll down to the Cookie link. Click the Cookie link.

2. When the Class Cookie page is displayed, read the first three paragraphs that describe the Cookie class, as shown in Figure 12-91.

3. Drag through the first three paragraphs describing the Cookie class to select them. Click File on the browser's menu bar and then click Print on the File menu to print a copy of the description. When the Print dialog box is displayed, click Print selection and then click the Print button in the Print dialog box.

4. Scroll to the Constructor Summary table. Click the link for the Cookie() constructor. When the constructor definition is displayed, read the definition and then drag through the definition to select it. Print a copy of the definition.

5. Scroll to the Method Summary table. Click the link for the setMaxAge() method. When the method definition is displayed, read the definition and then drag through the definition to select it. Print a copy of the definition.

6. Based on your reading, answer the following questions:

   a. What is the total number of cookies each Web browser is expected to support?

   b. Is there a limit on cookie size? If so, what is it?

   c. In what units is the maximum age of a cookie expressed?

   d. What does a positive max age mean? What does a negative max age mean?

   e. Can a cookie value be changed after the cookie is created?

   f. What reason, if any, is there to set a zero max age for a cookie?

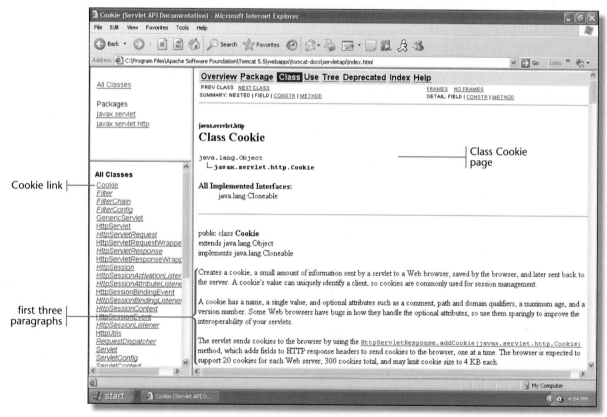

FIGURE 12-91

Short Answer

1. Applications that are written or rewritten to work using a Web server are called _____.

2. A(n) _____ is a Web page that is created as needed and often contains data content extracted from a database.

3. A(n) _____ is a Web page that exists in its entirety on the Web server before it is used.

4. _____ refers to processing that uses resources available only on the client.

5. _____ is a standard protocol used by Web browsers and Web servers to communicate with each other over the Internet.

6. A(n) _____ specifies the full path needed to obtain a Web page.

7. A(n) _____ is software that allows a Web server to work with servlets and JavaServer Pages.

8. A(n) _____ is a term for a program that is executing.

9. Using the same instance of a process for multiple, concurrent uses is known as _____.

10. Each one of multiple, concurrent uses of a process is called a(n) _____.

11. Code that avoids unwanted interaction between the threads is termed _____.

12. A section of Java code embedded within the HTML of a JSP is called a(n) _____.

13. When clicked, a(n) _____ causes the information on a form to be sent to the server for processing.

14. When clicked, a(n) _____ causes all input elements on a form to be reset to their initial values.

15. _____ is a scripting language with syntax similar to Java that is used to insert functionality within an HTML document.

16. A callable section of code in JavaScript, much like a method, is called a(n) _____.

17. The data type of a variable does not have to be declared in a(n) _____ language.

18. A built-in object in JavaScript representing the HTML document is the _____ object.

19. A built-in object in JavaScript representing the browser window is the _____ object.

20. The JavaScript function, _____, presents a dialog box with a message and an OK button.

21. A form field must have _____ to accept user input.

22. An action that occurs, typically as a result of a user's action, is called a(n) _____.

23. A(n) _____ associates an event with the JavaScript code that is performed when the event occurs.

24. The form _____ specifies the address of a program that will process the form data when the form is submitted.

25. The form _____ specifies whether GET or POST is used to send a request to the server.

26. A(n) _____ is a list of the methods called leading to an exception, typically seen when an exception is not handled.

27. The character encoding of the content being returned by the server to the browser is called the _____.

28. _____ provides a way to identify a user across more than one request.

29. A(n) _____ is stored on the server and consists of a name associated with an object bound to the session.

30. Adding the session ID to the URL for every transaction is called _____.

31. A message given to a Web browser by a Web server, which the browser stores in a text file and returns on subsequent requests, is called a(n) _____.

32. The _____ defines the scope of the Web application within the server.

33. _____ a request from a servlet to another resource discards the current request and response objects.

34. An application component service made available on a Web server for use by other Web-connected programs is a(n) _____.

35. _____ is a document markup language, similar to HTML in style, but extensible, in that you can define your own custom tags.

36. _____ data is textual data with the data fields separated by commas.

37. The _____ keyword provides thread-safe code by locking access to an object within a method or block of code.

38. A(n) _____ is a lock that Java associates with every object.

39. _____ is a condition where two locks each are waiting for the other to release before execution can continue.

40. A JSP _____ sets conditions that apply to the entire JSP file.

41. A(n) _____ is a character used to separate data fields, particularly in a stream of textual data.

42. A(n) _____ is a set of characters separated from other tokens by one or more delimiters.

43. A(n) _____ is an XML file that is used to configure a Web application.

44. Servlets without a specific entry in the deployment descriptor are known as _____.

45. With _____ enabled, the servlet container recognizes when a servlet has changed and automatically loads the new version.

Learn It Online

Start your browser and visit scsite.com/java3e/exs. Follow the instructions in the exercises below.

1. **Chapter Reinforcement TF, MC, and SA** Click the Chapter Reinforcement link below Chapter 12. Print and then answer the questions.

2. **Practice Test** Click the Practice Test link below Chapter 12. Answer each question, enter your first and last name at the bottom of the page, and then click the Grade Test button. When the graded practice test is displayed on your screen, click Print on the File menu to print a hard copy. Continue to take practice tests until you score 80% or better. Hand in a printout of the final practice test.

3. **Crossword Puzzle Challenge** Click the Crossword Puzzle Challenge link below Chapter 12. Read the instructions, and then enter your first and last name. Click the Play button. Complete the crossword puzzle. When you are finished, click the Submit button. When the crossword puzzle is displayed, click the Print button.

4. **Tips and Tricks** Click the Tips and Tricks link below Chapter 12. Click a topic that pertains to Chapter 12. Right-click the information and then click Print on the shortcut menu. Construct a brief example of what the information relates to in Java to confirm you understand how to use the tip or trick. Hand in the example and printed information.

5. **Newsgroups** Click the Newsgroups link below Chapter 12. Click a topic that pertains to Chapter 12. Print three comments.

6. **Expanding Your Horizons** Click the Expanding Your Horizons link below Chapter 12. Click a topic that pertains to Chapter 12. Print the information. Construct a brief example of what the information relates to in Java to confirm you understand the contents of the article. Hand in the example and printed information.

7. **Search Sleuth** Select three key terms from the Key Terms section of this chapter and then use the Google search engine at google.com (or any major search engine) to display and print two Web pages for each key term.

Debugging Assignment

The Debug.jsp program is a JSP that displays some simple output. The program has several syntax, semantic, or logic errors in the program code. Perform the following steps to debug the program.

1. Start TextPad and open the file, Debug.jsp, from the Chapter12 folder on the Data Disk.

2. Read through the code and fix any errors that you see. Insert today's date and your name as the programmer in the comment header.

3. Save the file. Start Tomcat.

4. Copy the JSP file to the Tomcat default root folder, or a location specified by your instructor. Open a browser and type `http://localhost:8080/Debug.jsp` in the address text box.

5. When the program compiles, the browser displays the compilation errors. Fix the first error and then repeat Step 4.

6. When you have fixed all the syntax and semantic errors so that the program will execute, look for run-time and logic errors. Fix all errors, if any, and execute the program again.

7. When the program produces the output as shown in Figure 12-92, print a copy of the source code. Close the browser. Close TextPad. Stop Tomcat.

FIGURE 12-92

Programming Assignments

1 A Web Page Greeting in JavaScript

Create a Web page that displays a greeting along with the current date, similar to Figure 12-93. Use only HTML and JavaScript to create the Web page. Obtain the current date with JavaScript by defining a variable and assigning a new Date object, as in

```
var today = new Date();
```

Save the Web page code as Greeting.html and then copy it to the Tomcat default root folder, or a location specified by your instructor. Start a browser and type `http://localhost:8080/Greeting.html` in the address text box. Print the page when it is displayed in the browser.

FIGURE 12-93

2 A Web Page Greeting in a Servlet

Create a Web page identical to the one created in Programming Assignment 1 using only a servlet to create the Web page. Import java.util.Date in order to create a Date object. Constructing a default Date object obtains the current date, as in

```
Date today = new Date();
```

Print the servlet code. Compile the servlet and copy the class file to the Tomcat default servlet folder, or a location specified by your instructor. After starting Tomcat, start a browser and type `http://localhost:8080/servlet/GreetingServlet` in the address text box. Print the page when it is displayed in the browser.

3 A Web Page Greeting in a JavaServer Page

Create a Web page identical to the one created in Programming Assignment 1 using only a JavaServer Page to create the Web page. Import java.util.Date and create a Date object as was done in Programming Assignment 2. Copy the JSP file to the Tomcat default root folder or a location specified by your instructor. After starting Tomcat, start a browser and type `http://localhost:8080/Greeting.jsp` in the address text box. Print the page when it is displayed in the browser. Programming Assignments 1 through 3 display the same date and approximate time when the local server is used as the host; however, if files from Programming Assignments 2 and 3 were placed on a Web server other than the local host, the displayed date and time could differ significantly. Write a paragraph to explain why this could happen.

4 Creating HTML Forms in Java

Write a Java servlet, HTMLBank.java, that creates the HTML form as shown in Figure 12-94. Use an instance variable for the balance. If the user enters a valid amount in the Amount text box and then clicks the Deposit button, add the amount to the balance; if the user clicks the Withdraw button, subtract the amount from the balance. If no amount was entered, or if the amount is negative or zero, output a simple HTML page that displays an appropriate error message. Compile the servlet and install it in the default servlet folder. Start Tomcat. Start your Web browser, type `http://localhost:8080/servlet/HTMLBank` in the address text box, and then press the ENTER key. To execute a second thread, start another instance of your Web browser and load the servlet in it, as well. Switching between the two instances, perform transactions with each. Recall that an instance variable is shared among multiple threads. Write a short paragraph that explains how the displayed balance verifies that the variable, balance, is shared. **Hint:** Recall the use of a DecimalFormat to format numeric output. Use the static method, Double.parseDouble(StringVariable), to convert the String from the text box parameter, amount, to a double. Be sure that an amount was entered before converting to a double.

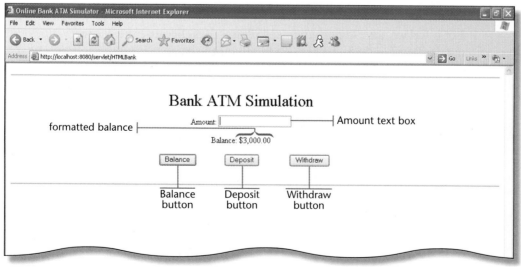

FIGURE 12-94

PROGRAMMING ASSIGNMENTS

5 Synchronizing Threads

Modify the program in Programming Assignment 4 to synchronize access to the instance variable, balance. Save the program as SyncBank.java. Because balance is a double and not an object, it cannot be used as the monitor. Use synchronized methods or synchronized blocks of code, as appropriate. Simultaneously test two threads as was done in Programming Assignment 4. Because the threads can complete too quickly to determine if they are interfering with each other, delay the adding of a deposit by inserting the following code within the synchronized block or method:

```
// Delay a deposit for a visible amount of time
try
{
  Thread.currentThread().sleep( 10000 );   // sleep for milliseconds
}
catch ( InterruptedException e ) {}
```

Write a short paragraph that explains how the displayed balance verifies that access to the variable, balance, is synchronized.

6 Implementing Session Tracking

Modify the program in Programming Assignment 4 to use session tracking to store the balance as a session attribute. Save the program as SessionBank.java. Use a local variable for the account balance, removing the instance variable. Do not use synchronization. Recall that session attributes are stored as Objects and must be downcast. Simultaneously test two threads as was done in Programming Assignment 4. Do not include a delay in the code for a deposit. Write a short paragraph that explains why the two threads do not interfere with each other. *Hint*: Because a Double object cannot be modified, use the Double method, doubleValue(), to return an intrinsic double value.

7 Forwarding a Request and Using Session Data in a JSP

Modify the program in Programming Assignment 6 to remove the code for the user interface. Save the program as JSPBank.java. Because the balance is updated and displayed, a JSP must be used to obtain the balance from the appropriate session attribute. Create a JSP, named bank.jsp, to display the form and bank balance. Recall from Assignment 4 that a negative or zero amount for a withdrawal or a deposit generates an error message. The error messages for an invalid deposit or invalid withdrawal are HTML pages, not JSPs. The servlet forwards the request to the appropriate JSP or builds an appropriate HTML page.

8 Tracing the init() and destroy() Servlet Methods

Start TextPad and open the WebStocks.java file. Insert a new line at the beginning of the init() method and then type System.out.println ("Opening a connection to the database"); on that line. Insert a new line at the beginning of the destroy() method and then type System.out.println("Closing the database connection "); on that line. Compile the servlet and then place the class file in the Tomcat default servlet folder, or a location specified by your instructor. Start Tomcat and then log on to the WebStocks Web application. Log off the WebStocks Web application. Log on and log off again. In the folder, C:\Program Files\Apache Software Foundation\Tomcat 5.5\logs, locate and open the text file, stdout_yyyymmdd, where yyyymmdd represents the current year, month, and day. Scroll to the end of the file. The window should resemble Figure 12-95. Stop Tomcat. Based on the text displayed and your knowledge of the servlet, answer the following questions:

1. When is a connection to the database opened?
2. How often is a connection made to the database?
3. Once made, when is the connection to the database closed?

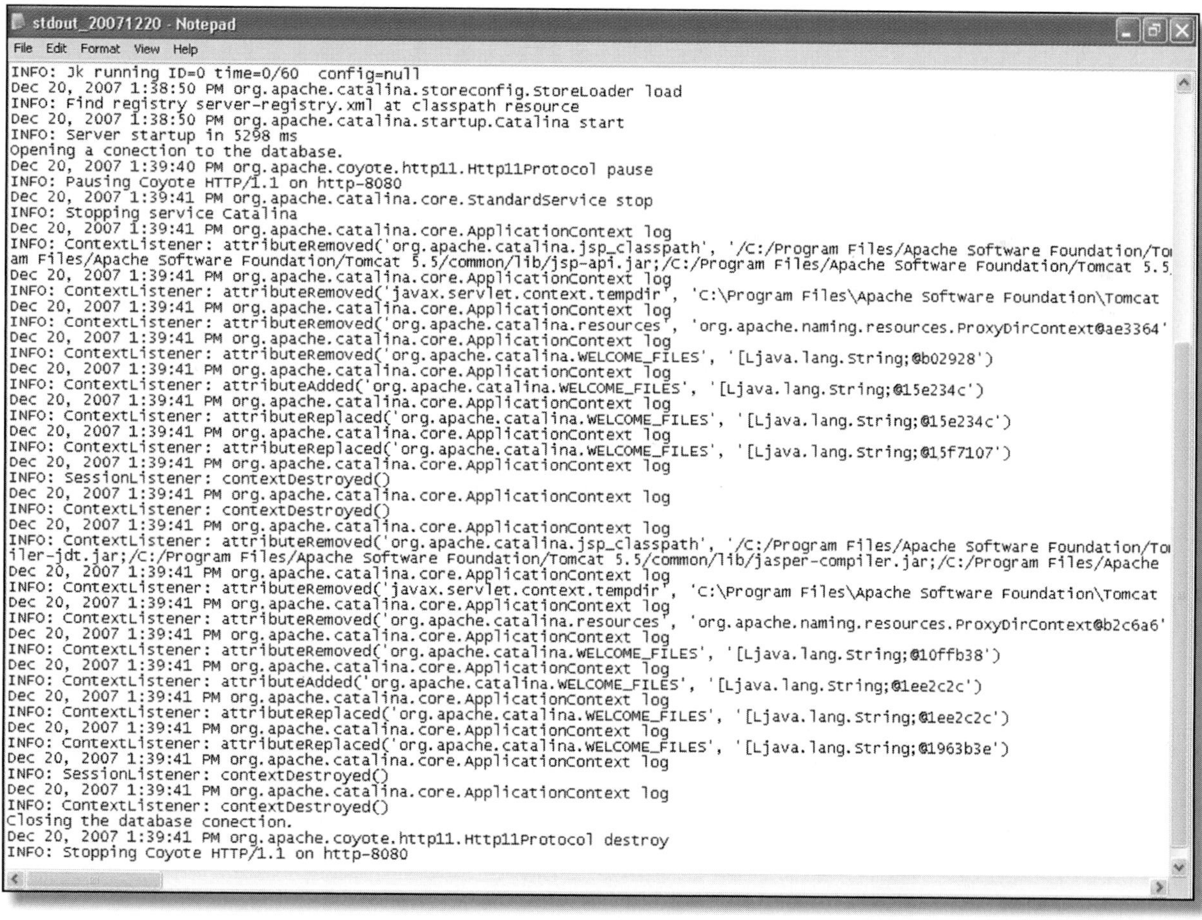

FIGURE 12-95

Notes

APPENDIX

A

Flowcharting, Pseudocode, and the Unified Modeling Language (UML)

Appendix A explains how to prepare, use, and read program flowcharts, pseudocode, and basic Unified Modeling Language (UML) diagrams. Chapter 1 includes an introduction to flowcharting and flowchart symbols beginning on page 16. Pseudocode is introduced on page 18, and the UML is discussed briefly on page 25.

Guidelines for Preparation of Flowcharts

Before the flowchart can be drawn, a thorough analysis of the problem, the input data, and the desired output results must be performed. The program logic required to solve the problem also must be determined. On the basis of this analysis, a **general flowchart** illustrating the main path of the logic can be sketched. This flowchart can be refined until the overall program logic is fully determined. This general flowchart is used to make one or more **detailed flowcharts** of the various branches of and detours from the main path of the program logic. After each detailed flowchart has been freed of logical errors and other undesirable features, such as unnecessary steps, the actual coding of the program in a computer language can be undertaken.

Straight-Line Flowcharts

Figure A-1 illustrates a general, straight-line flowchart. A **straight-line flowchart** is one in which the symbols are arranged sequentially, without any deviations or looping, until the terminal symbol that represents the end of the flowchart is reached. Once the operation indicated in any one symbol has been performed, that operation is never repeated.

FIGURE A-1

Flowcharts with Looping

A general flowchart that illustrates an iterative, or repeating, process known as **looping** is shown in Figure A-2. The logic illustrated by this flowchart is in three major parts: initialization, process, and wrap-up. A flowline exits from the bottom symbol in Figure A-2 and enters above the diamond-shaped decision symbol that determines whether the loop is to be executed again. This flowline forms part of a loop inside which some operations are executed repeatedly until specified conditions are satisfied. This flowchart shows the input, process, and output pattern; it also uses a decision symbol that shows where the decision is made to continue or stop the looping process.

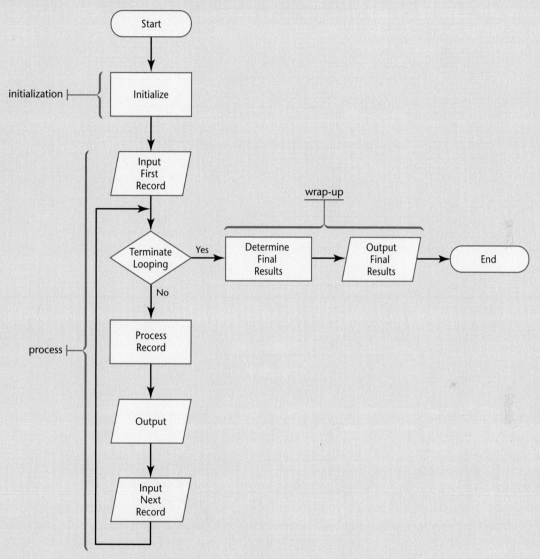

FIGURE A-2

Figure A-2 contains three braces that show the initialization, process, and wrap-up operations. For example, setting the program counters to 0 may represent an initialization operation and displaying the values of counters may represent a wrap-up operation.

Like the straight-line flowchart, a flowchart with looping may not have all the symbols shown in Figure A-2, or it may have many more symbols. For example, the process symbol within the loop in Figure A-2, when applied to a particular problem, may expand to include branching forward to bypass a process or backward to redo a process. It is also possible that, through the use of decision symbols, the process symbol in Figure A-2 could be expanded to include several loops, some of which might be independent from each other and some of which might be within other loops.

A flowchart shows a process that is carried out. Flowcharts are flexible; they can show any logical process no matter how complex it may be, and they can show it in whatever detail is needed.

The two flowcharts illustrated in Figure A-3 represent the same program, which accepts and then displays a record. The program then loops back to the accepting operation and repeats the sequence, accepting and displaying any number of records. A connector symbol, represented by a circle with a letter or number in it (in this case, A), may replace returning arrows and lines, as it also indicates the continuation of the looping process.

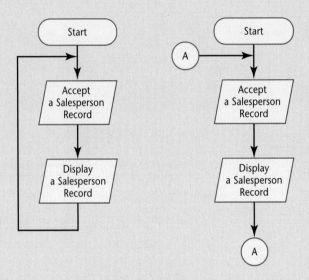

Endless Loops

FIGURE A-3

Although the flowcharts in Figure A-3 illustrate two ways a loop can be represented, the particular loop that is shown is an **endless loop**, also called an **infinite loop**. This type of loop should be avoided when constructing programs. In order to make a program finite, you must define it so that it will terminate when specified conditions are satisfied.

Figure A-4 illustrates the use of a counter that terminates the looping process. Note that the counter is first set to 0 in the initialization step. After an account is read and a message is displayed on the screen, the counter is incremented by 1 and tested to find whether it now is equal to 15. If the value of the counter is not 15, the looping process continues. If the value of the counter is 15, the looping process terminates.

For the flowchart used in Figure A-4, the exact number of accounts to be processed must be known beforehand. In practice, this will not always be the case because the number of accounts may vary from one run to the next.

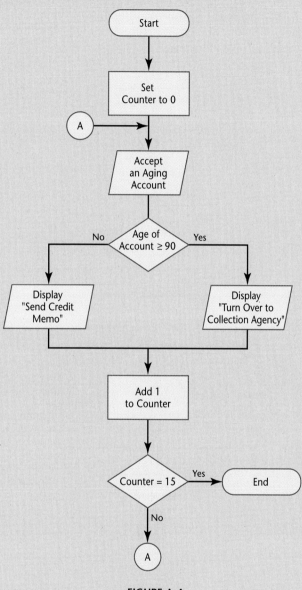

FIGURE A-4

A way to solve this type of problem is shown in Figure A-5, which illustrates the use of an end-of-file test to terminate the looping process. The value –999999 has been chosen to be the last account number. This kind of value sometimes is known as the **sentinel value** because it guards against continuing past the end-of-file. Also, the numeric item chosen for the last value cannot possibly be confused with a valid item because it is outside the range of the account numbers. Programs using an end-of-file test, such as the one shown in Figure A-5, are far more flexible and less limited than programs that do not, such as those illustrated in Figures A-3 and A-4 on pages A.04 and A.05.

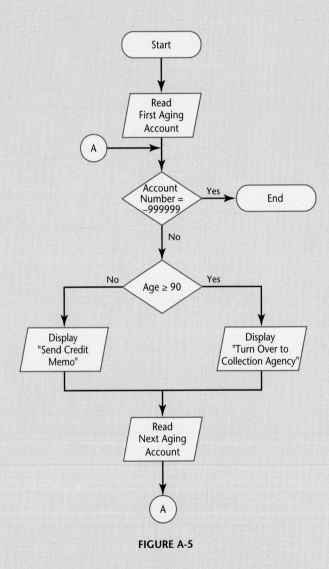

FIGURE A-5

Another flowchart with a loop is shown in Figure A-6, which illustrates the concept of counting. The flowchart incorporates the end-of-file test.

Simple computer programs do not require complex flowcharts and sometimes do not require flowcharts at all. As programs become more complex with many different paths of execution, however, a flowchart not only is useful but usually is a prerequisite for successful analysis and coding. Indeed, developing the problem solution by arranging and rearranging the flowchart symbols can lead to a more efficient solution.

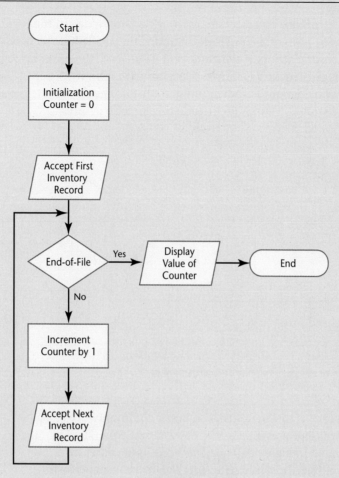

FIGURE A-6

Control Structures

The logic of almost any procedure or method can be constructed from the following three basic logic structures:

1. Sequence structure
2. If…Then…Else or Selection structure
3. Do While or Repetition structure

The following are two common extensions to these logic structures:

Do Until (an extension of the Repetition structure)

Select Case (a multiple choice extension of the Selection structure)

The **Sequence structure** is used to show one action or one action followed by another, as illustrated in Figures A-7a and A-7b. Every flowchart in this book includes this control structure.

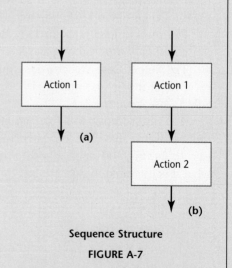

Sequence Structure

FIGURE A-7

The **If…Then…Else structure** represents a two-way decision made in the logic of the program. The decision is made on the basis of a condition that must be satisfied. If the condition is not satisfied, the program logic executes one action. If the condition is satisfied, the program logic executes a different action. This type of logic structure is shown in Figure A-8a. The If…Then…Else structure also can result in a decision to take no action, as shown in Figure A-8b. The flowcharts presented in Figures A-4 and A-5 on pages A.05 and A.06 include this logic structure.

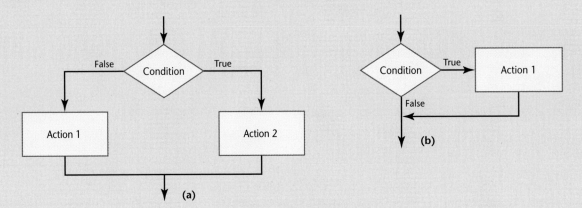

If…Then…Else Structure

FIGURE A-8

The **Do While structure** is the logic structure most commonly used to create a process that will repeat as long as the condition is true. The Do While structure is illustrated in Figure A-9 and has been used earlier in Figures A-2, A-5, and A-6. In a Do While structure, the decision to perform the action within the structure is at the top of the loop; as a result, the action will not occur if the condition is never satisfied.

The **Do Until structure** (Figure A-10) also is used for creating a process that will be repeated. The major differences between the Do Until and the Do While structures are that (1) the action within the structure of a Do Until always will be executed at least once, (2) the decision to perform the action within the structure is at the bottom of the Do Until loop, and (3) the Do Until loop exits when the condition is true.

Figure A-10 illustrates the Do Until structure, and the flowchart presented in Figure A-4 on page A.05 includes a Do Until structure.

The **Select Case structure** is similar to the If…Then…Else structure except that it provides more than two alternatives. Figure A-11 illustrates the Select Case structure.

A logical solution to a programming problem can be developed through the use of just these five logic structures. The program will be easy to read, easy to modify, and reliable; most important of all, the program will do what it is intended to do.

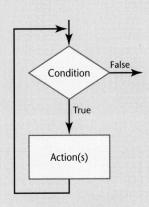

Do While Structure

FIGURE A-9

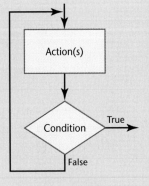

Do Until Structure

FIGURE A-10

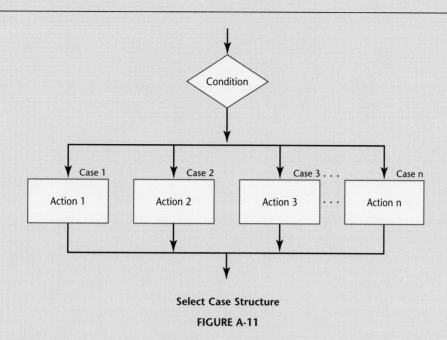

Select Case Structure

FIGURE A-11

Flowcharting Tips

The following recommendations can help make flowcharts more efficient and easier for others to understand. These suggestions assume that the input, processing, and output of the problem are defined properly in a requirements document.

1. Sketch a general flowchart and the necessary detail flowcharts before coding the problem. Repeat this step until you are satisfied with your flowcharts.

2. Use the control structures described on pages A.07 and A.08.

3. Put yourself in the position of the reader, keeping in mind that the purpose of the flowchart is to improve the reader's understanding of the solution to the problem.

4. Show the flow of processing from top to bottom and from left to right. When in doubt, use arrowheads as required to indicate the direction of flow.

5. Draw the flowchart so that it is neat and clear. Use the connector symbols to avoid excessively long flowlines.

6. Choose labels for each symbol that explain the function of the symbols in a clear and precise manner.

7. Avoid endless loops; construct loops so that they will be terminated when specific conditions are satisfied.

The reason that flowcharts are so important is simple: the difficulties in programming lie mostly in the realm of logic, not in the syntax and semantics of the computer language. In other words, most computer errors are mistakes in logic, and a flowchart aids in detecting these types of mistakes. For an additional example of a flowchart, see Figure 1-14 on page 18.

Pseudocode

Pseudocode is a program design technique that uses natural English and resembles Java code. It is an intermediate notation that allows the logic of a program to be formulated without diagrams or charts. Pseudocode resembles Java code in that specific operations can be expressed as commands that the program will execute. The following three examples illustrate pseudocode:

> Accept Employee Record
> MaleCounter = MaleCounter +1
> Display Employee Record

What makes pseudocode appealing to many programmers is that it has no formal syntax, which allows programmers to concentrate on the design of the program rather than on the peculiarities of the programming language's syntax.

Although pseudocode has no formal rules, the following guidelines are commonly accepted by most programmers:

1. Begin the pseudocode with a program, procedure, or method title statement.

> Monthly Sales Analysis Report Procedure

2. End the pseudocode with a terminal program statement.

> End

3. Begin each statement on a new line. Use simple and short imperative sentences that contain a single transitive verb and a single object.

> Accept EmployeeNumber
> Subtract 10 From Quantity

4. Express assignments as a formula or as an English-like statement.

> WithholdingTax = 0. 20 × (GrossPay − 38.46 × Dependents)

or

> Compute WithholdingTax

5. To avoid errors in the design, avoid using logic structures not available in the programming language being used.

6. For the If…Then…Else structure, use the following conventions:

    a. Indent the true and false tasks.

    b. Use End If as the structure terminator.

    c. Vertically align the If, Else, and End If statements.

The conventions for the If…Then…Else structure are illustrated in Figures A-12 and A-13. (Java implements the structure in code with the keywords, if and else.)

```
If Balance < 500 then
        Display Credit OK
Else
        Display Credit not OK
End If
```

```
If GenderCode = male then
        MaleCount = MaleCount + 1
        If Age > 21 then
                MaleAdultCount = MaleAdultCount + 1
        Else
                MaleMinorCount = MaleMinorCount + 1
        End If
Else
        FemaleCount = FemaleCount + 1
        If Age > 21 then
                FemaleAdultCount = FemaleAdultCount + 1
        Else
                FemaleMinorCount = FemaleMinorCount + 1
        End If
End If
```

FIGURE A-12   **FIGURE A-13**

7. For the Do While structure, use the following conventions:
   a. If the structure represents a counter-controlled loop, begin the structure with Do.
   b. If the structure does not represent a counter-controlled loop, begin the structure with Do While.
   c. Specify the condition on the Do While or Do line.
   d. Use End Do as the last statement of the structure.
   e. Align the Do While or Do and the End Do vertically.
   f. Indent the statements within the loop.

The conventions for the Do While structure are illustrated in Figures A-14 and A-15 on the next page. (Java implements the structure in code with the keywords, do and while.)

8. For the Do Until structure, use the following conventions:
   a. Begin the structure with Do Until.
   b. Specify the condition on the Do Until line.
   c. Use End Do as the last statement of the structure.
   d. Align the Do Until and the End Do vertically.
   e. Indent the statements within the loop.

```
SumFirst100Integers Procedure
        Sum = 0
        Do Integer = 1 to 100
                Sum = Sum + Integer
        End Do
        Display sum
End
```

FIGURE A-14

```
EmployeeFileList Procedure
        Display report and column headings
        EmployeeCount = 0
        Accept first Employee record
        Do While Not End-of-File
                Add 1 to EmployeeCount
                Display Employee record
                Accept next Employee record
        End Do
        Display EmployeeCount
End
```

FIGURE A-15

The conventions for the Do Until structure are illustrated in Figure A-16. (Java implements the structure in code with the keywords, do and until.)

```
SumFirst100Integers Procedure
        Sum = 0
        Integer = 1
        Do Until Integer >100
                Sum = Sum + Integer
                Integer = Integer + 1
        End Do
        Display Sum
End
```

FIGURE A-16

9. For the Select Case structure, use the following conventions:

   a. Begin the structure with Select Case, followed by the variable to be tested.

   b. Use End Case as the structure terminator.

   c. Align Select Case and End Case vertically.

   d. Indent each alternative.

   e. Begin each alternative with Case, followed by the value of the variable that equates to the alternative.

   f. Indent the action of each alternative.

These conventions are illustrated in Figure A-17. (Java implements the structure in code with the keyword, switch.)

```
Select Case CustomerCode
        Case 100
                HighRiskCustomerCount = HighRiskCustomerCount + 1
        Case 200
                LowRiskCustomerCount = LowRiskCustomerCount + 1
        Case 300
                RegularCustomerCount = RegularCustomerCount + 1
        Case 400
                SpecialCustomerCount = SpecialCustomerCount + 1
End Case
```

FIGURE A-17

For an additional example of pseudocode, see Figure 1-15 in Chapter 1 on page 19.

The Unified Modeling Language (UML)

Just as flowcharts describe algorithms, object-oriented design (OOD) has a standard method to depict, or diagram, concepts for design purposes. The Unified Modeling Language (UML) is a notation used to describe object behaviors and interaction. The UML is a graphical language used to represent how a system behaves or should behave. The UML is a relatively new language, having been developed in the 1990s from a number of competing object-oriented design tools.

In OOD, each class can have one or more lower levels, called **subclasses**, or one or more higher levels, called **base classes** or **superclasses**. For example, a class for Secretaries is a subclass of the Employee class. Person is a base class or superclass of Employee. The relationship among the classes, subclasses, and base classes is called the **hierarchy**. A **high-level class diagram** is a UML diagram used to show the hierarchical relationships among classes (Figure A-18).

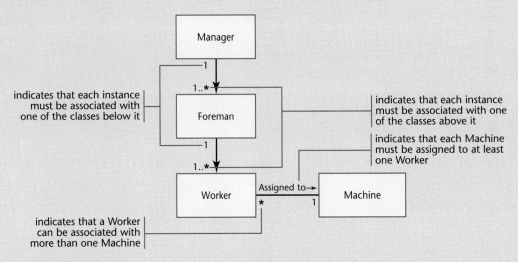

FIGURE A-18

Associations describe the manner in which instances of a class, or objects, are related. For example, two instances of a Worker class can have the association of being coworkers. This type of association is **bidirectional**, meaning each instance is associated with the other. Some associations are **unidirectional**, which means that only one class is associated with the other. For example, a Worker instance can be assigned to operate an injection molder machine, which is an instance of the class Machines. The Worker is associated with the injection molder instance because a Worker must know how to operate the injection molder, but the injection molder does not have any information about or relationship to the Worker. In this way, the association between the Worker and Machine class is unidirectional.

The high-level class diagram shown in Figure A-18 depicts a hierarchy in which an instance of the Manager class can have several instances of the Foreman class associated with it; each instance of the Foreman class can have several workers associated with it; and each instance of the Worker class can be assigned to exactly one machine. Each class is represented by a box with the class name inside the box. Relationships are designated by lines between the classes.

The 1 below the Manager class indicates that each Manager class must have at least one Foreman class associated with it; the 1 below the Foreman class indicates that each Foreman class must have at least one Worker class associated with it. The 1..* above the Foreman class indicates that each Foreman class must be associated with at least one Manager class above it; the 1..* above the Worker class indicates that each Worker class must be associated with at least one Foreman class above it. The Assigned to label indicates that each Worker class is assigned to one Machine class. The 1 next to the Machine class indicates that each Machine class must be assigned at least one Worker class. The * next to the Worker class indicates that a worker can be associated with more than one Machine class.

Object-oriented programming (OOP) and OOD use many unique terms to describe program elements. In object-oriented terminology, the data stored about an object is called an attribute or property. An **attribute** or **property** is an identifying characteristic of individual objects, such as a name, weight, or color. An **operation** is an activity that reads or manipulates the data of an object. In OOD, an operation is a type of service. In OOP, the code that may be executed to perform a service is called a **method**.

A **detailed class diagram** is used to provide a visual representation of a class, its attributes, and its methods (Figure A-19 and Figure A-20). Figure A-19 shows the general form of a detailed class diagram. Figure A-20 shows a specific example of a detailed class diagram for the Foreman class. The Foreman class contains six attributes and five methods. The rules of the UML prescribe that each attribute and method begin with lowercase letters and that each method name is followed by parentheses. The parentheses indicate that the methods are procedures in the class. A detailed class diagram also can have additional notations.

Class name
Class attributes
Class methods

FIGURE A-19

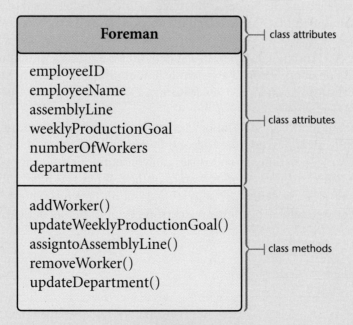

FIGURE A-20

Messages and Events

Message sending is a key component of object-oriented design because it describes how objects work together. For an object to do something, it must be sent a message. The **message** must have two parts: (1) the name of the object to which the message is being sent, and (2) the name of the operation that will be performed by the object. As you have learned, an operation is an activity that reads or manipulates the data of an object. An operation also can send additional messages while it performs its task.

Messages are sent through an interface to the object. Just as a user interface allows a program to accept data and instructions from the user, the **interface** is the way that an object receives messages.

As an example, suppose each time an assembly-line worker turns on a machine (an object), the machine tracks how many times it has been turned on by incrementing a counter. To turn on the machine, the worker presses a button on a panel to send a message to the machine. The button on the panel is the interface to the on() method of the machine, and pressing the button is the event that sends a message to execute the on() method. When the on() method executes, part of its operation is to increment the numberTimesOn counter, which is an attribute of the machine. Suppose that the shop also uses an automated system to operate its machines, so that the machines can be turned on remotely using a computer. The interface that the computer uses to turn on the machine is different from the one the worker uses. The on() method that executes on the machine, however, remains the same and the on() method still increments the numberTimesOn counter attribute when it executes.

In OOD terminology, the operation, increment counter, is a service and the message, turn machine on, is called a **request for service**. Remember that in OOP terminology, the service is called a method and the message is what is sent when an event, such as a user pressing the on button, occurs. **Sequence diagrams** are used to represent the relationships among events and objects. In a sequence diagram, messages or events are shown as lines with arrows, classes are shown across the top in rectangles, and class names are underlined and prefaced by a colon (Figure A-21). As you read the sequence diagram, time progresses from top to bottom, and the time the object is active is shown by vertical rectangles.

Figure A-21 illustrates a sequence diagram for a Foreman assigning a Worker to a Machine. The Foreman object in the first column interacts with other objects through the Foreman Interface. The Foreman sends a message through the Foreman Interface to find a Worker based on the worker's name. Next, the Foreman finds a Machine to assign the Worker based on the worker's skill. Finally, the assignment is made.

As shown in Figure A-21, nothing happens in a system unless a message is sent when an event occurs. At the conclusion of an operation, the system will do nothing until another event occurs. This relationship of events causing operations is a key feature of OOP, and programs that are constructed in this way are said to be **event driven**.

The UML is a powerful tool because it can be used to describe any item, process, or concept in the real or imagined world. Its usefulness goes well beyond the programming world. People working in different disciplines or working in different industries can communicate concepts using the UML in a standard and well-understood manner. Another feature of the UML is that many types of diagrams provide different views of the same system, or object, in addition to the ones shown here. Different views of the same system are useful depending on a person's or object's role in the system.

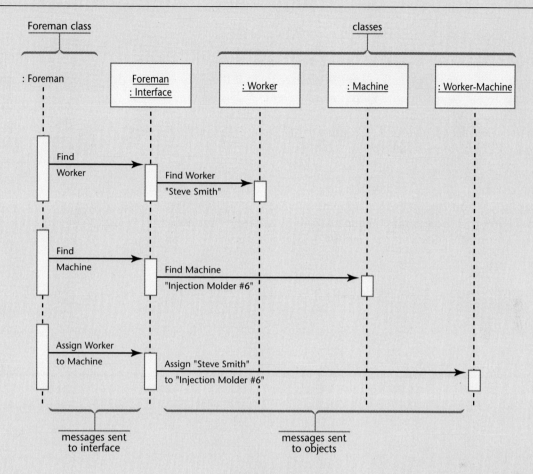

FIGURE A-21

Homework Assignments

1. In the flowchart in Figure A-22, what are the values of I and J at the instant just after the statement J = J + 1 is executed for the fifth time? What are the values of I and J after the statement I = I + 2 is executed the tenth time? (A statement such as J = J + 1 is valid and is read as *the new value of J equals the old value of J plus one* or, equivalently, *the value of J is to be replaced by the value of J plus one.*)

2. Consider the section of a flowchart shown in Figure A-23. It assumes that an absent-minded person is going to work. This individual usually has the car keys but occasionally forgets them. Does the flowchart section in Figure A-23 incorporate the most efficient method of representing the actions to be taken? If not, redraw the flowchart portion given in Figure A-23.

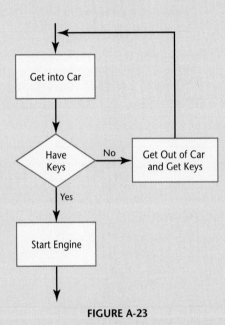

FIGURE A-23

3. In the flowchart shown in Figure A-24, what values of I and J are printed when the output symbol is executed for the fiftieth time?

4. An opaque urn contains three diamonds, four rubies, and two pearls. Construct a flowchart that describes the following events: Take a gem from the urn. If it is a diamond, lay it aside. If it is not a diamond, return it to the urn. Continue in this fashion until all the diamonds have been removed. After all the diamonds have been removed, repeat the same procedure until all the rubies have been removed. After all the rubies have been removed, continue in the same fashion until all the pearls have been removed.

5. In the flowchart represented by Figure A-25, what are the values of I and J at the instant the terminal symbol with the word End is reached?

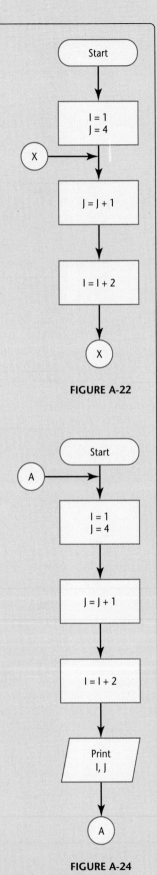

FIGURE A-22

FIGURE A-24

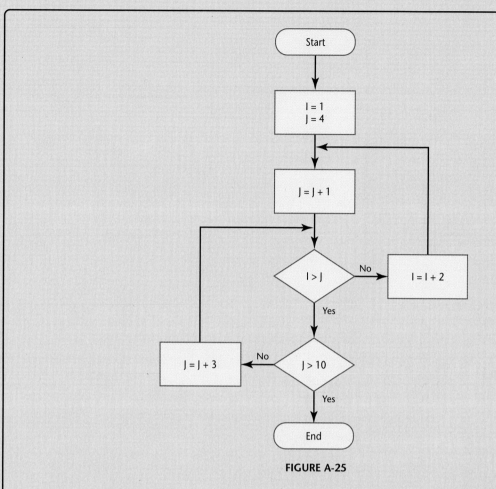

FIGURE A-25

6. Draw one flowchart, and only one, that will cause the mechanical mouse to go through any of the four mazes shown in Figure A-26. At the beginning, a user will place the mouse on the entry side of the maze, in front of the entry point, facing up toward the maze. The instruction Move to next cell will put the mouse inside the maze. Each maze has four cells. After that, the job is to move from cell to cell until the mouse emerges on the exit side. If the mouse is instructed to *Move to next cell* when a wall is in front of it, it will hit the wall and fall apart. Obviously, the mouse must be instructed to test whether it is *Facing a wall* before any *Move*. The physical movements and logical tests the mechanical mouse can complete are listed following Figure A-26.

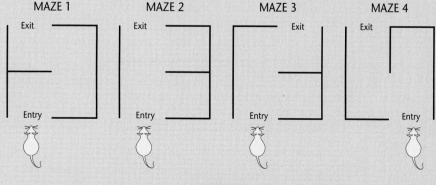

FIGURE A-26

(continued)

6. *(continued)*
   a. Physical movement:
      (1) Move to next cell. (The mouse will move in the direction it is facing.)
      (2) Turn right.
      (3) Turn left.
      (4) Turn around 180 degrees. (All turns are made in place, without moving to another cell.)
      (5) Halt.
   b. Logic:
      (1) Facing a wall? (Through this test, the mouse determines whether a wall is immediately in front of it, that is, on the border of the cell it is occupying and in the direction it is facing.)
      (2) Outside the maze?
      (3) On the entry side?
      (4) On the exit side?

7. Develop a detailed class diagram for an electric dishwasher. List at least eight attributes, including number of racks, model, and color. List at least six methods, including addDishes() and addDetergent().

8. Develop a high-level class diagram that shows the relationships among a manufacturer's inventory of finished products in its warehouses. The company has many warehouses that are managed by the inventory-control supervisor. Each warehouse contains many bins of products. Each bin contains one product type.

9. Develop a sequence diagram that shows how the inventory-control supervisor in assignment 8 assigns a product to a bin in a warehouse.

B

Installing the Java™ 2 SDK, TextPad, and Tomcat

This appendix explains how to install the three software applications used in this text: the Java™ 2 Software Development Kit (SDK), which provides the tools to compile and execute Java programs; the text editor software, TextPad, which provides an environment to create and modify programs; and Tomcat, which provides the server software needed to run servlets and JavaServer Pages™ (JSP). These resources are available free at their respective Web sites, as well as on the CD-ROM that accompanies this text. To install this software on your computer system, you must be logged in to an account or system that gives you the authority to make the necessary modifications to the environment.

Installing the Java™ 2 Software Development Kit (SDK)

The Java™ 2 SDK can be obtained by downloading the required software from Sun Microsystems at java.sun.com or from the CD-ROM that accompanies this text. The following steps show how to install the SDK from the CD-ROM to a location on your hard drive (C:). If necessary, substitute the destination location with one specified by your instructor.

To Install the Java Software Development Kit (SDK)

1. Insert the CD-ROM into your CD-ROM drive. If the CT Resources Licensing Agreement dialog box is displayed, click the Yes button. When the Course Technology dialog box is displayed, click Software. When the software files are displayed, click Sun Java™ SDK, Standard Edition 1.5.0_02.

The Course Technology dialog box is displayed with Software and Sun Java™ SDK, Standard Edition 1.5.0_02.

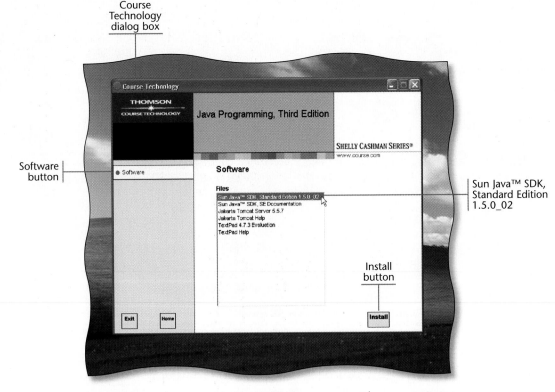

FIGURE B-1

2. Click the Install button. When the License Agreement dialog box is displayed, click I accept the terms in the license agreement.

The InstallShield Wizard dialog box is displayed briefly, followed by the License Agreement dialog box (Figure B-2).

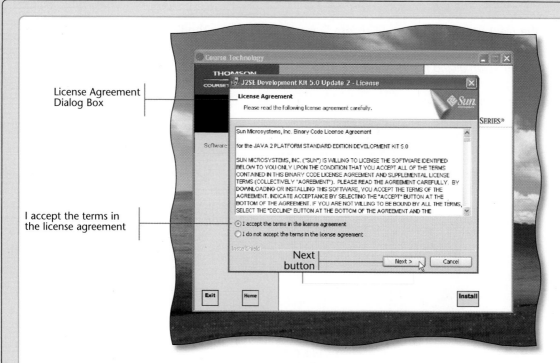

License Agreement
Dialog Box

I accept the terms in
the license agreement

Next
button

FIGURE B-2

3. Click the Next button. When the Custom Setup dialog box for the J2SE Development Kit is
displayed, verify the location to which the program features will be installed.

*The Custom Setup dialog box displays the choice of features and the default destination for the
J2SE Development Kit installation (Figure B-3). The default folder location includes the version
name. If desired, you can change the location for installing the J2SE Development Kit by clicking
the Change button. By default, all program features are installed. To save disk space, you can select
the icon of individual features, such as Demos or Source Code, to prevent their installation.*

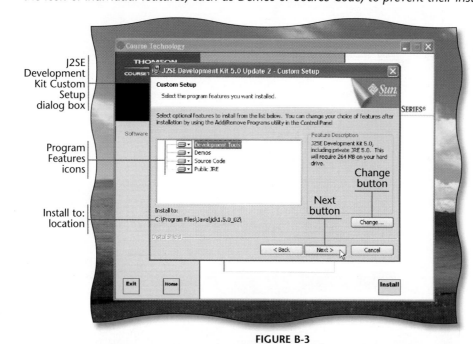

J2SE
Development
Kit Custom
Setup
dialog box

Program
Features
icons

Install to:
location

Change
button

Next
button

FIGURE B-3

(continued)

4. Click the Next button. When the Custom Setup dialog box for the J2SE Runtime Environment is displayed, verify the location to which the program features will be installed.

The Custom Setup dialog box displays the program features for the J2SE Runtime Environment (Figure B-4). If desired, you can change the location for installing the J2SE Runtime Environment by clicking the Change button.

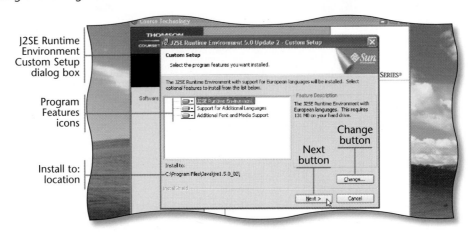

J2SE Runtime Environment Custom Setup dialog box

Program Features icons

Install to: location

Change button

Next button

FIGURE B-4

5. Click the Next button. When the Browser Registration dialog box is displayed, verify that the check box next to the browser you want to use for applets is checked.

The Browser Registration dialog box displays the browser(s) available on your system (Figure B-5). The Java™ Plug-in, which is necessary to run applets in a browser, will install for the checked browser(s).

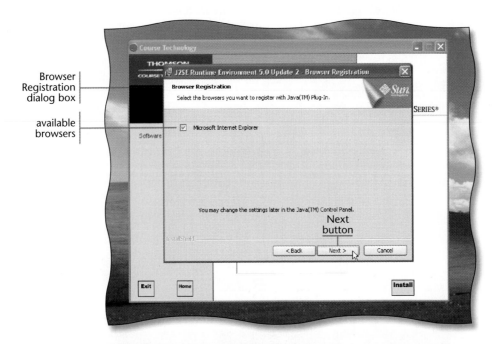

Browser Registration dialog box

available browsers

Next button

FIGURE B-5

6. Click the Next button. When the installation is complete, the Installation Completed dialog box is displayed.

The SDK installs to the previously indicated folder location (Figure B-6).

Installation
Completed
dialog box

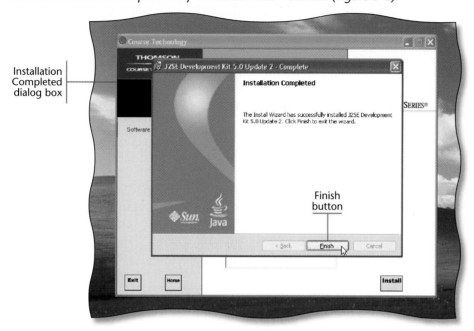

FIGURE B-6

7. Click the Finish button.

After the SDK installation is complete, you may need to restart your system for the configuration changes to take effect. If so, a dialog box displays, prompting you to restart now or later (Figure B-7). You should restart your system before installing additional software.

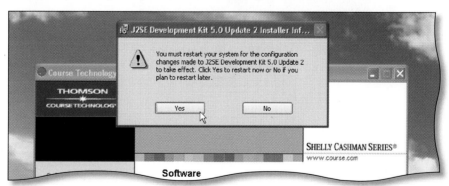

FIGURE B-7

If you need to uninstall the Java™ 2 SDK, you can use the Add or Remove Programs utility in the Control Panel.

Installing the Java™ 2 SDK Standard Edition Documentation

The Java™ 2 SDK documentation is provided in HTML format and can be viewed with a Web browser. The documentation can be obtained by downloading the required files from Sun Microsystems at java.sun.com or from the CD-ROM that accompanies this text. The following steps show how to install the SDK documentation from the CD-ROM to a location on your hard drive (C:). If necessary, substitute the destination location with one specified by your instructor.

To Install the Java™ 2 SDK Standard Edition Documentation

1. If necessary, insert the CD-ROM into your CD-ROM drive. When the Course Technology dialog box is displayed, click Software. When the software files are displayed, click Sun Java™ SDK, SE Documentation.

   The documentation is provided separately from the SDK software (Figure B-8). The documentation is available for different versions of the SDK, so you should verify that you are using the correct version of the documentation for your SDK installation.

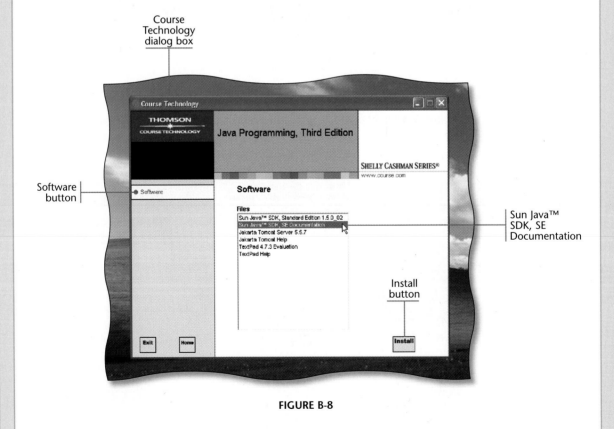

FIGURE B-8

2. Click the Install button.

The WinZip Self-Extractor dialog box is displayed with the default installation location in the Unzip to folder: text box (Figure B-9). If desired, you can modify the text in the Unzip to folder: text box to install the documentation to a location other than the default location. The documentation files are zipped, or compressed into a single archive file, to save space. The zipped file is self-extracting, so no additional software is needed to extract the files from the archive file.

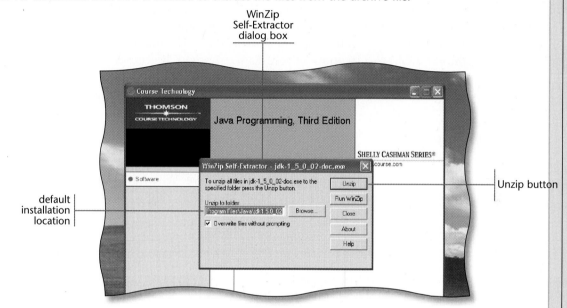

FIGURE B-9

3. Click the Unzip button.
The WinZip Self-Extractor message box is displayed, indicating that the files were successfully unzipped (Figure B-10).

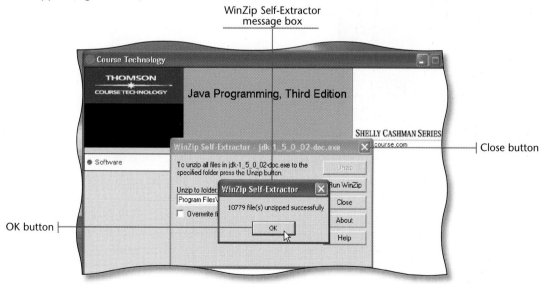

FIGURE B-10

4. Click the OK button. Click the Close button in the WinZip Self-Extractor dialog box.

Having the Java™ 2 SDK documentation installed locally may be useful; however, it is not required, as the same pages may be accessed over the Web from Sun Microsystems. The documentation is a series of hypertext documents which may require access to the Web even when accessing a local copy, as some links will refer to pages on Sun Microsystems's Web site.

Installing TextPad

TextPad can be obtained by downloading the required software from Helios Software Solutions at textpad.com or from the CD-ROM that accompanies this text. The following steps show how to install TextPad from the CD-ROM to a location on your hard drive (C:). If necessary, substitute the location with one specified by your instructor. You should install the Java™ 2 SDK before installing TextPad, as this will allow TextPad to configure itself automatically for compiling and executing Java programs.

To Install TextPad

1. If necessary, insert the CD-ROM into your CD-ROM drive. When the Course Technology dialog box is displayed, click Software. When the software files are displayed, click TextPad 4.7.3 Evaluation and then click the Install button.

   The InstallShield Wizard dialog box is displayed when the install is ready to begin (Figure B-11).

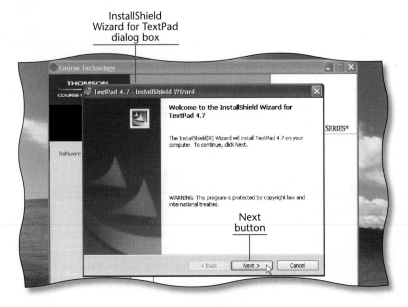

FIGURE B-11

2. Click the Next button. When the License Agreement dialog box is displayed, click the I accept the terms in the license agreement option button and then click the Next button. When the Customer Information dialog box is displayed, verify that the User Name and Organization, if any, are correct and that Anyone who uses this computer (all users) is selected.

   The Customer Information dialog box is displayed (Figure B-12). The User Name may be entered automatically. If desired, you may type a different User Name.

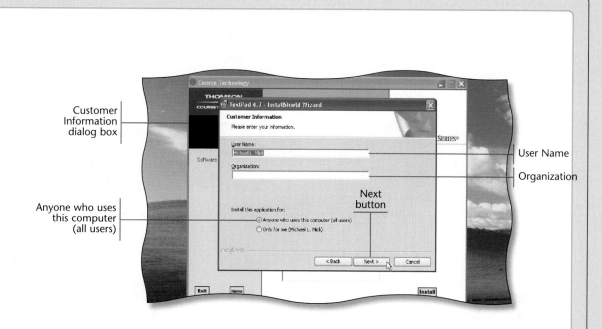

Customer
Information
dialog box

User Name

Organization

Anyone who uses
this computer
(all users)

Next
button

FIGURE B-12

3. Click the Next button. When the Destination Folder dialog box is displayed, verify that the destination folder is correct. If desired, the default destination folder can be changed by clicking the Change button.

The Destination Folder dialog box displays the folder where the software will be installed (Figure B-13). The default destination folder is indicated.

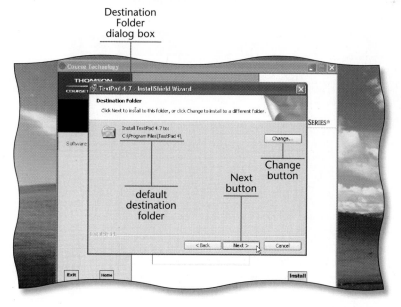

Destination
Folder
dialog box

Change
button

Next
button

default
destination
folder

FIGURE B-13

(continued)

4. Click the Next button. The Ready to Install the Program dialog box is displayed, providing a final opportunity to change any of the installation settings.

   The Ready to Install the Program dialog box is displayed prior to beginning the installation (Figure B-14).

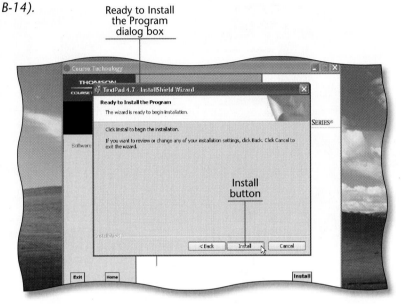

FIGURE B-14

5. Click the Install button. When the installation is complete, the InstallShield Wizard Completed dialog box is displayed. If necessary, click the Launch the program check box to deselect it.

   TextPad is installed on your computer. Because the check box is not checked, the TextPad program does not start when you click the Finish button. (Figure B-15).

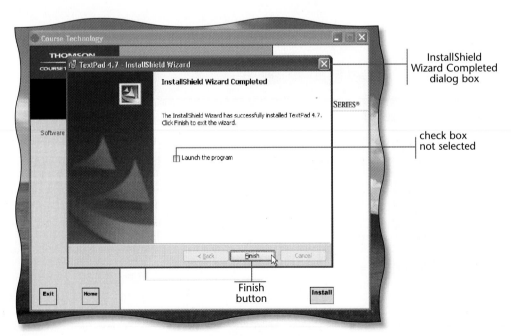

FIGURE B-15

6. Click the Finish button.

After the TextPad installation is complete, the TextPad icon is displayed on the All Programs submenu when you click the Windows Start button. TextPad documentation recommends that you have 3 MB of free disk space before attempting to install the TextPad software.

You can customize the TextPad window to display line numbers, use various colors for code elements, and provide other features to help you develop Java programs. Appendix C contains information about setting properties in TextPad to match the figures in this text.

Installing Tomcat

Tomcat is a Web server software program that supports Java servlets and Java Server Pages (JSP). The Jakarta Project from Apache Software manages the development of Tomcat and makes it freely available to users.

Tomcat is available on the Web at jakarta.apache.org/site/downloads/index.html or on the CD-ROM that accompanies this text. If you download Tomcat from the Web, be sure to download the .exe file version. The following steps show how to install Tomcat from the CD-ROM to a location on your hard drive (C:). If necessary, substitute the location specified by your instructor. Note: If you downloaded the ZIP file version, before installing you should set the JAVA-HOME environment variable first. See page APP 34.

To Install Tomcat

1. If necessary, insert the CD-ROM into your CD-ROM drive. When the Course Technology dialog box is displayed, click Software. When the software files are displayed, click Jakarta Tomcat Server 5.5.7.

   For additional information on running Jakarta Tomcat Server 5.5.7, and known issues with this version, you may open the Jakarta Tomcat help selection (Figure B-16).

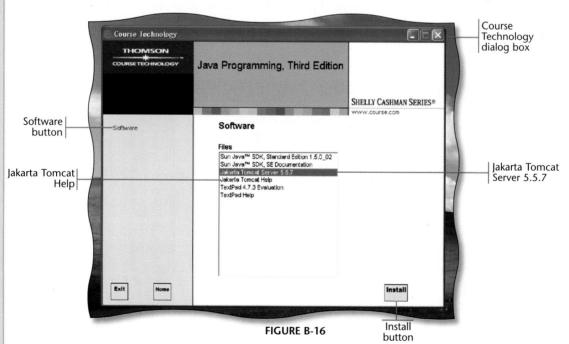

FIGURE B-16

2. Click the Install button.

   The Welcome to the Apache Tomcat Setup Wizard dialog box is displayed (Figure B-17).

Welcome to the Apache Tomcat
Setup Wizard dialog box

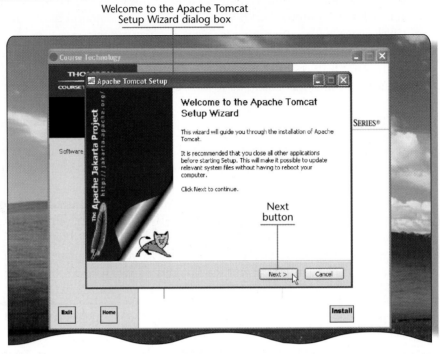

FIGURE B-17

3. Click the Next button. When the License Agreement dialog box is displayed, click the I Agree button. When the Choose Components dialog box is displayed, if necessary, click Full in the Select the type of install list (Figure B-18).

The options for a full install are displayed (Figure B-18). A full install provides documentationn as well as example programs. To save disk space, you may choose not to install optional components.

Choose
Components
dialog box

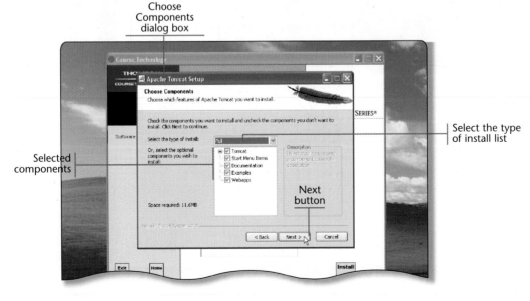

FIGURE B-18

(continued)

4. Click the Next button. When the Choose Install Location dialog box is displayed, verify the location where Tomcat should be installed.

The Choose Install Location dialog box displays the default location of \Program Files\Apache Software Foundation\Tomcat 5.5 on drive C (Figure B-19).

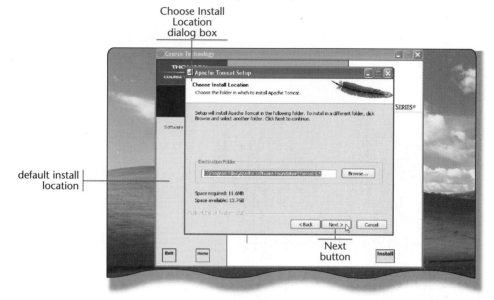

FIGURE B-19

5. Click the Next button. When the Configuration dialog box is displayed, click the Next button. When the Java Virtual Machine dialog box is displayed, verify the selected path for a Java Runtime Environment on your machine.

The Java Virtual Machine dialog box is displayed (Figure B-20). The Apache Tomcat Setup Wizard obtains the default Java Runtime Environment from the JAVA_HOME environment variable, if set, or from the system registry. You may select another path if you have multiple JRE versions installed on your machine. The JRE provides the Java Virtual Machine used to execute Java Programs.

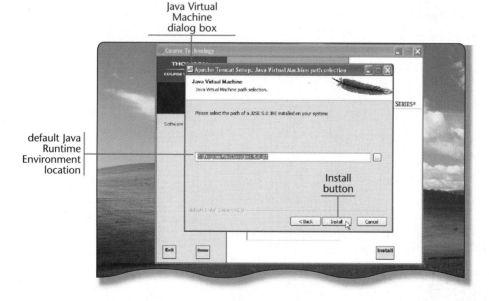

FIGURE B-20

6. Click the Install button in the Java Virtual Machine dialog box.

The Completing the Apache Tomcat Setup Wizard dialog box displays (Figure B-21).

Completing the Apache Tomcat
Setup Wizard dialog box

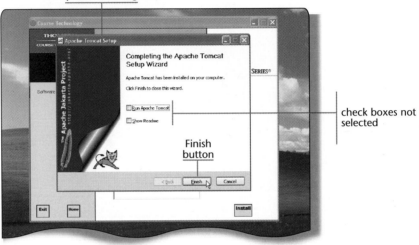

check boxes not
selected

Finish
button

FIGURE B-21

7. If necessary, click the Run Apache Tomcat check box and the Show Readme check box to deselect them. Click the Finish button.

The installation of Apache Tomcat is complete.

The Tomcat server software installs as a service under Windows XP and will start automatically. A **Windows service** is a program intended to run for an extended time, providing services to other programs. Services may be started like any other programs, or may be started automatically when the computer starts running. After installing Tomcat, you will need to add an environment variable on your system. This environment variable will be used by the Java compiler to locate certain class files when compiling servlets.

Adding a New Environment Variable

Tomcat provides a number of class files in its library which are needed when you create and use servlets. The files in this case are stored in a JAR file named servlet-api.jar. For the Java compiler to use these class files, it must know where to find them. An environment variable, named CLASSPATH, is used to identify one or more additional locations where the compiler can search for needed class files. An **environment variable** is a string that lists information about the system environment, such as a drive, path, or file name. The compiler will search for class files in the order of the locations listed in the CLASSPATH environment variable. Perform the following steps to add a new environment variable.

To Add a New Environment Variable

1. Click the Start button on the Windows taskbar and then right-click My Computer on the Start menu.

   The My Computer command is selected on the Start menu, and a shortcut menu is displayed (Figure B-22). The Start menu selections on your system may differ from those displayed.

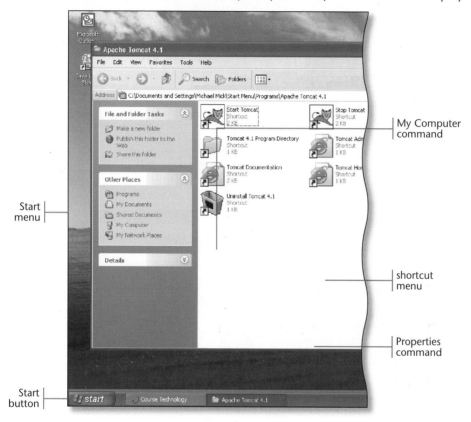

FIGURE B-22

2. Click Properties on the shortcut menu. When the System Properties dialog box is displayed, if necessary, click the Advanced tab.

The System Properties dialog box is displayed with the Advanced tab selected (Figure B-23).

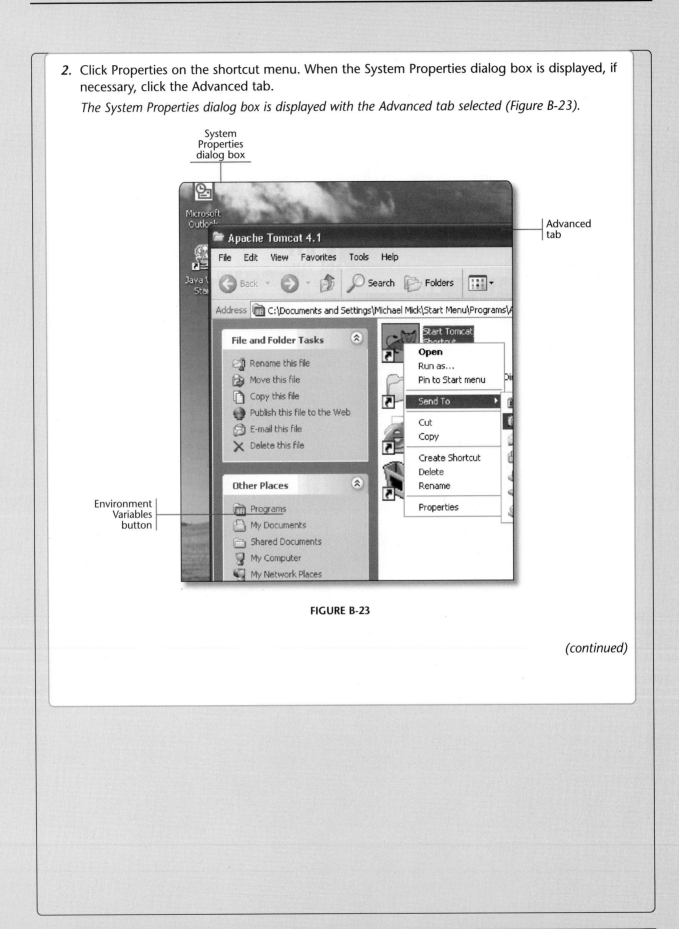

FIGURE B-23

(continued)

3. Click the Environment Variables button. When the Environment Variables dialog box is
displayed, click the New button in the System variables area. When the New System Variable
dialog box is displayed, type CLASSPATH in the Variable name text box and then type
.;C:\Program Files\Apache Group\Tomcat 5.5\common\lib\jsp-api.jar;
C:\Program Files\Apache Group\Tomcat 5.5\common\lib\servlet-api.jar
in the Variable value text box (or append \common\lib\jsp-api.jar and then also
\common\lib\servlet-api.jar to the location where you installed Tomcat).
*The New System Variable dialog box displays the environment variable name and value
(Figure B-24). Because we want the compiler to search first in the current folder and then in
the servlet-api.jar file for needed servlet classes and in the jsp-api.jar for needed jsp classes, the
CLASSPATH variable must indicate all of these locations. The current folder is indicated by a period.
Multiple locations are separated by a semicolon.*

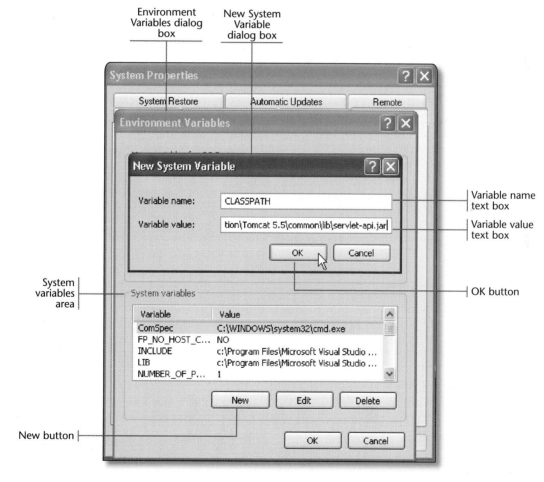

FIGURE B-24

4. Click the OK button in the New System Variable dialog box.

The Environment Variables dialog box displays the new variable name and value in the System variables area (Figure B-25).

System variables area

new variable name and value

OK button

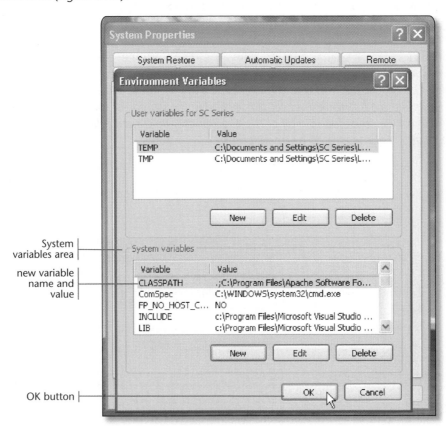

FIGURE B-25

5. Click the OK button. Click the OK button in the System Properties dialog box.

The new environment variable, CLASSPATH, is set for the system. The Java™ 2 SDK will use the CLASSPATH variable name to locate necessary files when using servlets. If needed, you may repeat the above steps to add an environment variable named JAVA_HOME, which should have a value of C:\Program Files\Java\jdk1.5.0_02\bin (or the location where you installed Java).

CONFIGURING AND TESTING THE TOMCAT SERVICE

When you use the Apache Tomcat Setup Wizard under Windows XP, Tomcat installs as a Windows service configured to run automatically. Because services do not have a user interface, it can be difficult to know when the Tomcat service is running.

The Apache Service Manager provides an easy way to determine if the Tomcat service is started or stopped. The Apache Tomcat Setup Wizard automatically installed the Apache Service Manager, which displays in the system tray when running (see Figures B-27a and B-27b). If necessary, perform the following steps to start the Apache Service Manager.

To Start the Apache Service Manager

1. Verify that all system tray icons are displayed. If the Apache Service Manager icon is not present, click the Start button on the taskbar and then point to All Programs on the Start menu. Point to Apache Tomcat 5.5 on the All Programs submenu. Point to Monitor Tomcat on the Apache Tomcat 5.5 submenu.

   The Apache Tomcat 5.5 submenu is displayed (Figure B-26). Only start the Apache Service Manager if it is not already displayed in the system tray.

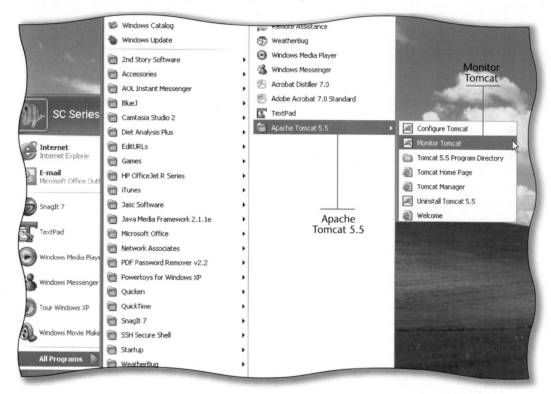

FIGURE B-26

2. Click Monitor Tomcat.

   The Apache Service Manager displays as an icon in the system tray with a green arrow on the icon indicating that the Tomcat service is running (Figure B-27a). A red square on the icon indicates that the Tomcat service is stopped (Figure B-27b). If an Application System Error dialog box is displayed, then the Apache Service Manager was already running. Only one copy of the program can run at a time.

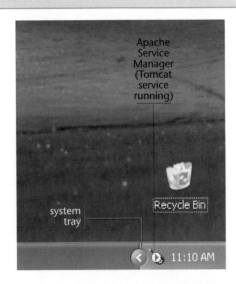

FIGURE B-27(a) and (b)

By default, the Tomcat service is set to start automatically. You may want the Tomcat service to be started manually, so it does not execute every time you boot your computer. Perform the following steps to use the Apache Service Manager to configure the Tomcat service to start manually.

To Configure the Tomcat Service

1. Right-click the Apache Service Manager icon in the system tray.

   A shortcut menu displays (Figure B-28). If the Stop service menu item is not selectable, then the service is not running. You may click About to view the license agreement. Clicking Exit will terminate the Apache Service Manager, causing it to no longer display in the system tray.

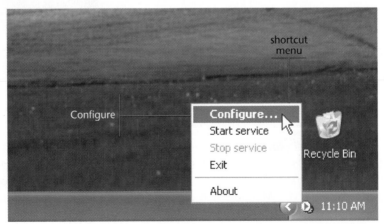

FIGURE B-28

2. Click Configure... on the shortcut menu. When the Apache Tomcat Properties dialog box is displayed, if necessary, click the General tab. In the Startup type list, click Manual.

   The Apache Tomcat Properties dialog box is displayed (Figure B-29). A startup type of Manual is selected.

Apache Tomcat
Properties
dialog box

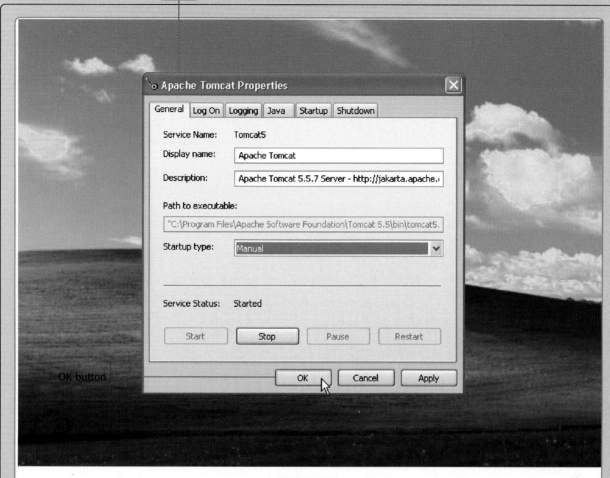

FIGURE B-29

3. Click the OK button.

The Apache Tomcat Properties dialog box closes.

Although Tomcat now is configured to start manually, the Apache Service Manager still should display as an icon in the system tray whether the Tomcat service is running or not. By the color and shape of the icon, you know quickly whether the Tomcat service is running. Perform the following steps to test the Tomcat service.

To Test the Tomcat Service

1. If necessary, right-click the Apache Service Manager icon in the system tray and then click Start service on the shortcut menu. Start your Web browser. When the Web browser window opens, type http://localhost:8080/ in the Address box and then press the Enter key.

If Tomcat is running successfully, the browser displays the Web page shown in Figure B-30. The Apache Service Manager also displays a green arrow, indicating that the service is running.

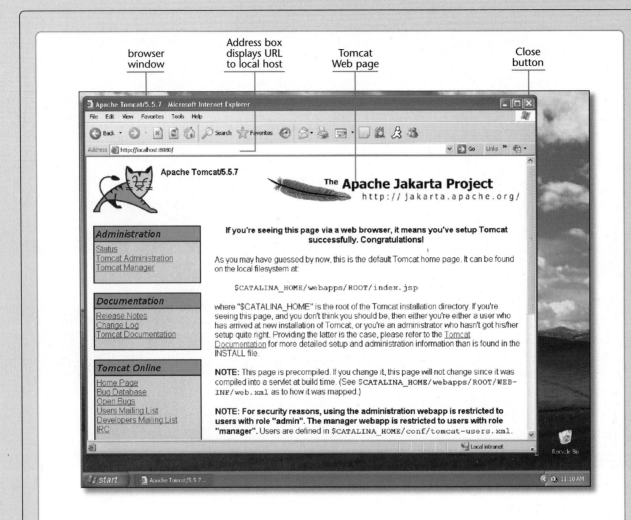

FIGURE B-30

2. Close the browser. Right-click the Apache Service Manager icon in the system tray. Click Stop service on the shortcut menu.

   The Apache Service Manager is displayed with a small red square in the center indicating that the service is stopped (see Figure B-27b).

To view the documentation for Tomcat, use your Web browser to open the file, index.html, in the folder C:\Program Files\Apache Software Foundation\Tomcat 5.5\webapps\tomcat-docs\.

C

Changing Screen Resolution and Setting TextPad Preferences

Appendix C explains how to change your screen resolution to the resolution used in this book. The appendix also explains how to set basic preferences in TextPad, so that it is better suited to your preferred work habits.

Screen Resolution

Screen resolution determines the amount of information that appears on your screen, measured in pixels. A low resolution, such as 640 by 480 pixels, makes the overall screen area small, but items on the screen, such as windows, text, and icons, appear larger on the screen. A high resolution, such as 1024 by 768 pixels, makes the overall screen area large, but items appear smaller on the screen.

Changing Screen Resolution

The following steps show how to change your screen's resolution from 800 by 600 pixels to 1024 by 768 pixels, which is the screen resolution used in this book.

To Change Screen Resolution

1. Click the Start button on the Windows taskbar and then point to Control Panel on the Start menu.

The Start menu is displayed and Control Panel is highlighted on the Start menu (Figure C-1). Your menu options may differ.

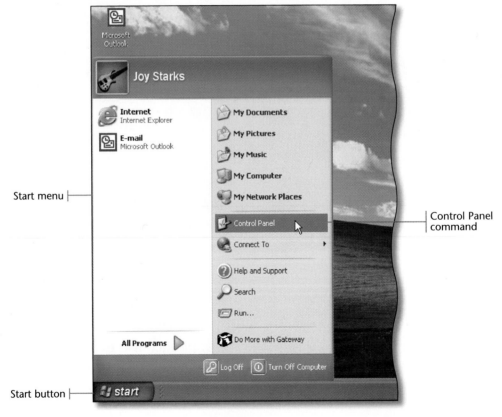

FIGURE C-1

2. Click Control Panel. If necessary, click Switch to Category View in the Control Panel area.

The Control Panel window opens (Figure C-2).

Control Panel
window

Control Panel
area

Appearance and
Themes category

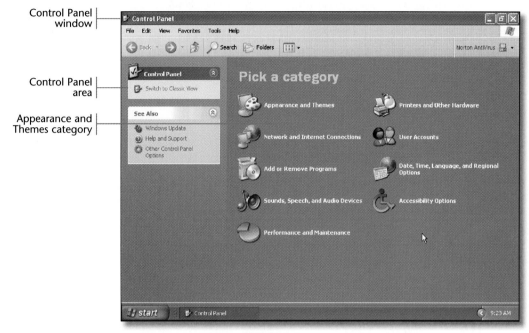

FIGURE C-2

3. Click the Appearance and Themes category.

The Appearance and Themes window opens (Figure C-3).

Appearance and
Themes window

Change the screen
resolution task

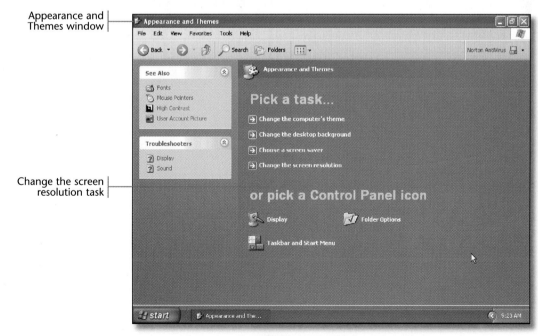

FIGURE C-3

4. Click the Change the screen resolution task.

The Display Properties dialog box is displayed, with the Settings tab selected (Figure C-4). The current screen resolution is displayed in the Screen resolution area.

Display Properties dialog box

Settings tab

Screen resolution area

Screen resolution trackbar

current screen resolution is 800 by 600 pixels

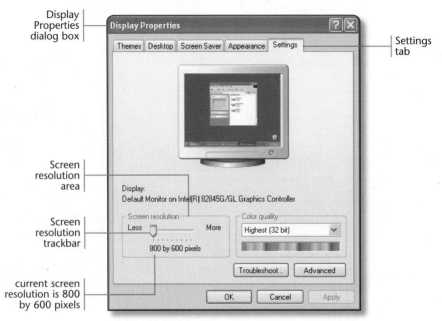

FIGURE C-4

5. Drag the Screen resolution trackbar one tick mark to the right or until the screen resolution below the trackbar reads 1024 by 768 pixels.

As the trackbar is moved one mark to the right, the screen resolution displayed below the trackbar changes to 1024 by 768 pixels (Figure C-5).

trackbar moved one tick mark to the right

screen resolution reads 1024 by 768 pixels

OK button

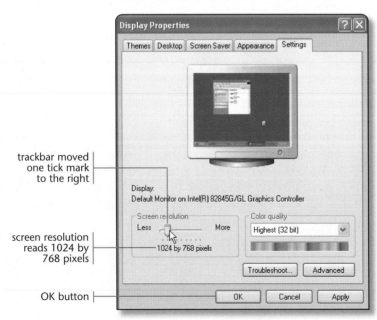

FIGURE C-5

6. Click the OK button.

The Display Properties dialog box closes. The Windows desktop is displayed at a screen resolution of 1024 by 768 pixels (Figure C-6). Your screen may flicker while the resolution change takes place.

screen resolution changed to 1024 by 768 pixels

Close button

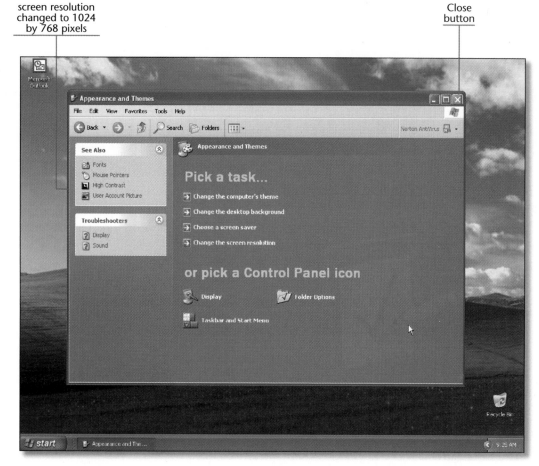

FIGURE C-6

7. Click the Close button on the Appearance and Themes window title bar.

The new screen resolution is set.

Compare Figure C-6 with Figure C-3 on page C.03 to see the difference in the display when screen resolution is set to 800 by 600 pixels or 1024 by 768 pixels. As shown in these figures, using a higher resolution allows more items, such as windows, text, and icons, to fit on the screen, but the items display at a smaller size. In Figure C-6, the Appearances and Themes window does not fill the entire screen.

You can experiment with various screen resolutions. Depending on your monitor and the video adapter installed in your computer, the screen resolutions available on your computer will vary.

When designing a user interface in Java, remember to take into consideration the screen resolutions available to the majority of users of the application. A good rule of thumb is to test your application in all of the screen resolutions in which users are likely to use the application.

Setting Preferences in TextPad

TextPad allows you to set many preferences to customize and arrange the contents and display of the coding window. This section explains how to add the available Java commands to the Tools menu; turn on line numbering so line numbers always display; and change preferences for color, font, and tabs in TextPad.

Starting TextPad and Displaying Preferences

To set preferences in TextPad, you use the Preferences command on the Configure menu to display the Preferences dialog box. Any preferences you set are saved when you quit TextPad, which means that the settings still will be in effect when you start TextPad again.

The following steps illustrate how to start TextPad and display the Preferences dialog box.

To Start TextPad and Display Preferences

1. Click the Start button on the Windows taskbar. Point to All Programs on the Start menu. When the All Programs submenu is displayed, point to TextPad.

   The All Programs submenu is displayed (Figure C-7).

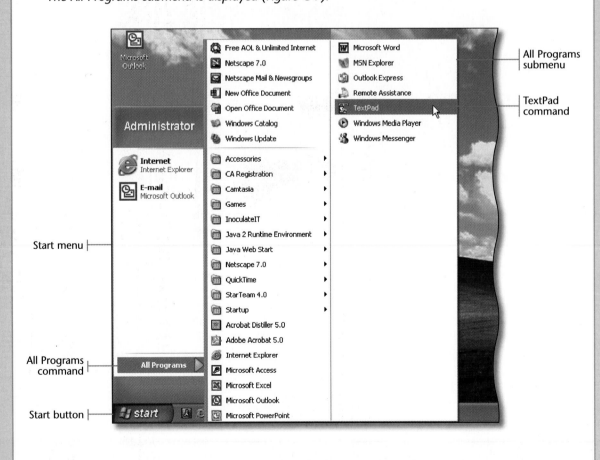

FIGURE C-7

2. Click TextPad. If a Tip of the Day dialog box is displayed, click its Close button. On the TextPad menu bar, click Configure.

TextPad displays the Configure menu (Figure C-8).

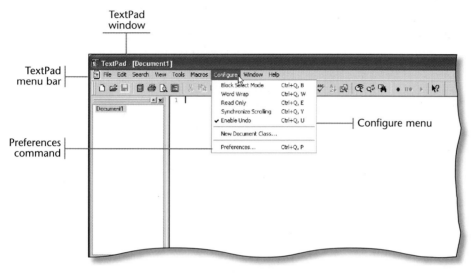

FIGURE C-8

3. Click Preferences on the Configure menu.

The Preferences dialog box is displayed (Figure C-9).

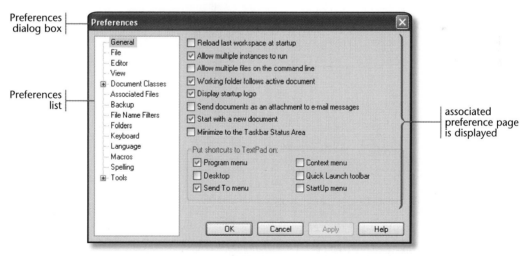

FIGURE C-9

As shown in Figure C-9, a list of preferences is displayed in a Preferences list on the left side of the Preferences dialog box. When you select a preference in the Preferences list, the associated preference page is displayed on the right.

Adding the Java Commands to TextPad

After installing the SDK and TextPad as described in Appendix B, the Compile Java, Run Java Application, and Run Java Applet commands should display on the Tools menu. You can verify this by checking the commands available on the Tools menu or checking the preferences set in the Preferences dialog box. The following steps verify that the Java commands are added and, if not, add the Java commands to TextPad.

To Add the Java Commands to TextPad

1. If necessary, click Configure in the TextPad toolbar and then click Preferences to display the Preferences dialog box. With the Preferences dialog box displaying, click Tools in the Preferences list. When the Tools page is displayed, if the form list is empty, click the Add button arrow.

   The Add button menu displays available tools (Figure C-10). If your form list already displays the Java commands, you may skip the next step.

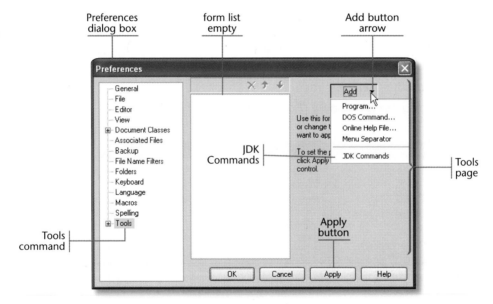

FIGURE C-10

2. Click JDK Commands on the Add button menu. Click the Apply button.

The Java commands to compile and run programs now will be listed on the Tools menu each time you start TextPad. You can assign shortcuts to any of these commands using the Keyboard page in the Preferences dialog box.

Turning on Line Numbers

Line numbers assist programmers in referencing code and fixing errors. TextPad users can set a preference to turn on line numbers so that they always display and print. The following steps show how to turn on line numbers that display on the screen as well as on printouts.

To Turn on Line Numbers

1. With the Preferences dialog box displaying, click View in the Preferences list. When the View page is displayed, click the Line numbers check box. If you want your screen to match the screens in this book exactly, click the Highlight the line containing the cursor check box so that the check mark does not display.

The Line numbers check box displays a check mark (Figure C-11). Line numbers automatically will display in the coding window each time you start TextPad.

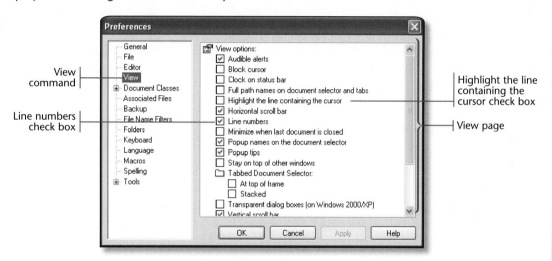

FIGURE C-11

2. In the Preferences list, click the plus sign next to Document Classes and then click the plus sign next to Java. Click Printing. When the Printing page is displayed, click Line numbers.

The Line numbers check box displays a check mark (Figure C-12). Line numbers automatically will display on all printouts printed using TextPad.

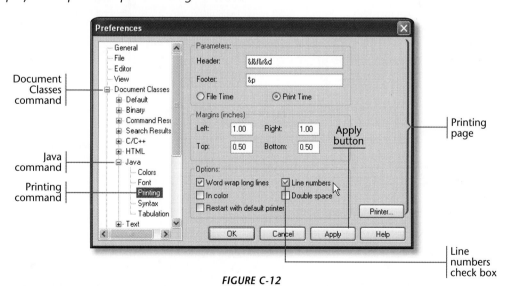

FIGURE C-12

3. Click the Apply button.

Other preferences available on the View page include turning on and off alerts, scroll bars, and tabbed document selectors or sheets. Other preferences available on the Printing page include setting print margins and setting TextPad to print in color. For example, if you want your HTML host files to print with line numbers or in color, click the plus sign next to Document Classes in the Preferences list. Click the plus sign next to HTML and then click Printing in the Preferences list. Click the In color and Line numbers check boxes and then click the OK button to set the preferences.

Setting Other Preferences

This text uses the default TextPad preferences for font, font size, color, and tabs. There may be times, however, when users need to change these settings. For example, some users may want to display code in a larger font size; others may want to set their own color coding. Sometimes, in a lab situation, users may need to reset some of these features back to the default values. The following step demonstrates how to set preferences for font, font size, color, and tabs.

To Set Other Preferences

1. With the Preferences dialog box displaying, if necessary, click the plus sign next to Document Classes and then click the plus sign next to Java. Click Colors. Click the Set Defaults button to return all color coding to its original settings. Click the Apply button.

The Colors page is displayed (Figure C-13). Clicking the Set Defaults button will restore all colors back to their default settings to match this book.

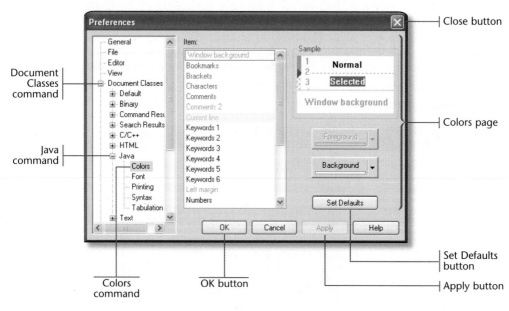

FIGURE C-13

You can change additional settings such as font, font size, and tabs using similar steps. To change font and font size, if necessary, click the plus sign next to Document Classes and then click the plus sign next to Java in the Preferences list. Click Font. When finished making changes to these preferences, click the Apply button. To change tab settings, if necessary, click the plus sign next to Document Classes and then click the plus sign next to Java in the Preferences list. Click Tabulation. When finished making changes to these preferences, click the Apply button.

For more information about changing additional settings, click Help on the TextPad menu bar and then click Help Topics. When the Help window opens, click the Contents tab and then click the plus sign next to How To to display the topic list.

The final step is to close the Preferences dialog box and quit TextPad.

To Close the Preferences Dialog Box and Quit TextPad

1. In the Preferences dialog box, click the OK button.
2. Click the Close button on the TextPad title bar.

TextPad Editing Techniques

TextPad supports many of the same editing commands as popular word processing programs. Table C-1 displays TextPad commands to navigate through the coding window. Table C-2 on the next page displays different ways to select text in TextPad.

Table C-1   Commands to Move through the Coding Window

TO MOVE THE INSERTION POINT	PRESS THIS KEY
to the beginning of the document	CTRL+HOME
to the end of the document	CTRL+END
to first non-space character on a line	HOME
to the left margin	HOME twice
to the end of a line	END
forward one word	CTRL+W or CTRL+RIGHT ARROW
back one word	CTRL+B or CTRL+LEFT ARROW
back to the end of the previous word	CTRL+D
to the start of the next paragraph	ALT+DOWN ARROW
to the start of the previous paragraph	ALT+UP ARROW
to the start of the first visible line	ALT+HOME
to the start of the last visible line	ALT+END
scroll display down one line	CTRL+DOWN ARROW
scroll display up one line	CTRL+UP ARROW
to a specified line, column, or page number	CTRL+G

Table C-2 Selecting Text in TextPad

TO SELECT	PERFORM THIS ACTION
a word	Double-click
a line	Double-click left margin or triple-click line
all code	On Edit menu, click Select All or press CTRL+CLICK in left margin
text using the mouse	Hold the left mouse button and then drag across text, click at the start of text, press SHIFT+CLICK at the end of text
text using the keyboard	Press SHIFT+ARROW, using arrow key to move in correct direction

D

Compiling and Running Java Programs Using the Command Prompt Window

Some programmers compile and run Java programs in the Command Prompt window. Unlike the TextPad software used in this book, many text editors — such as Microsoft's Notepad program — can be used to edit Java source code but have no command to compile source code or run programs. In that case, after saving the program in Notepad with the extension .java, you would enter the Java SDK compile and run commands explicitly using the Command Prompt window. In some cases, programmers must set environmental variables in order to successfully compile and run Java programs using the Command Prompt window.

Using the Command Prompt Window

This appendix describes how to open the Command Prompt window and then set properties to define how the Command Prompt window displays. It also discusses how to change to the proper drive and directory. Finally, it covers how to set the environmental variables in order to compile and run a sample program found on the Data Disk that accompanies this book.

Opening and Setting Properties of the Command Prompt Window

In Windows, the **Command Prompt window** (Figure D-1) is a way to communicate with the operating system and issue commands without using a program with a graphical user interface. Most versions of Windows contain a Command Prompt command on the Accessories submenu, which allows you to open a Command Prompt window. Opening a Command Prompt window on the desktop facilitates moving between editing programs and running them.

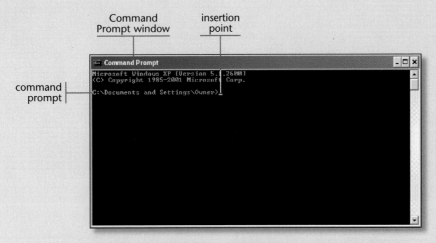

FIGURE D-1

As shown in Figure D-1, the Command Prompt window displays a **command prompt** that includes a disk drive location, followed by a subdirectory location (if any), followed by a greater-than sign (>), and finally a flashing insertion point. The insertion point designates the place where users type commands and enter responses.

The Command Prompt window normally displays light gray text on a black screen, with a default font size of 8 × 12 pixels or a similar size. In order to make the screens easier to read in this book, the Command Prompt window properties were set to use a font color of white and a font size of 12 × 16 pixels. The following steps open the Command Prompt window and set its properties to match the figures in this book.

To Open and Set Properties of the Command Prompt Window

1. Click the Start button on the taskbar and then point to All Programs on the Start menu. When the All Programs menu is displayed, point to Accessories and then point to Command Prompt on the Accessories submenu.

Windows displays the Accessories submenu (Figure D-2). Your menu options may differ.

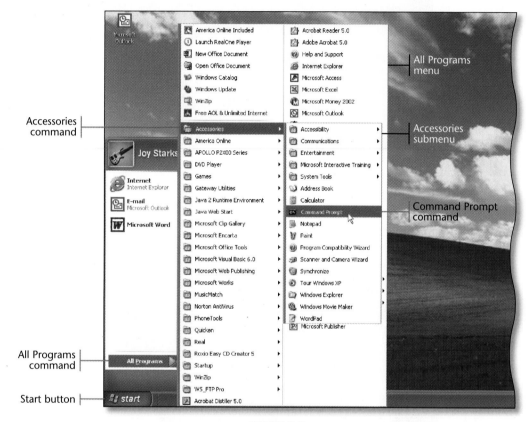

FIGURE D-2

(continued)

2. Click Command Prompt.

The Command Prompt window opens (Figure D-3). An icon and title are displayed in the title bar.

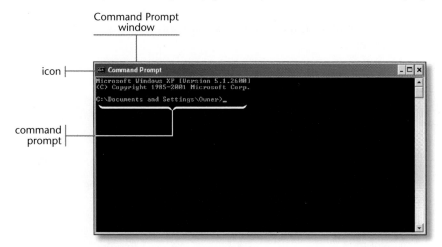

FIGURE D-3

3. Click the icon in the Command Prompt window title bar.

The Command Prompt menu is displayed (Figure D-4).

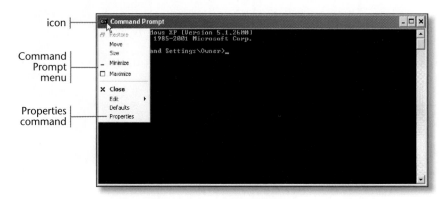

FIGURE D-4

4. Click Properties on the Command Prompt menu. When the "Command Prompt" Properties dialog box is displayed, if necessary, click the Font tab.

The "Command Prompt" Properties dialog box contains options to configure how the Command Prompt window will display (Figure D-5).

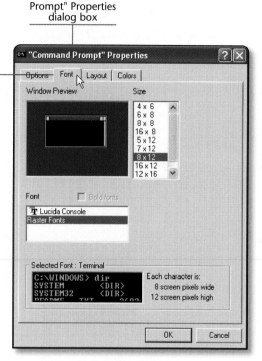

FIGURE D-5

5. In the Size box, scroll to and then click the 12 × 16 font size or a similar size font.

The 12 × 16 font size is selected (Figure D-6).

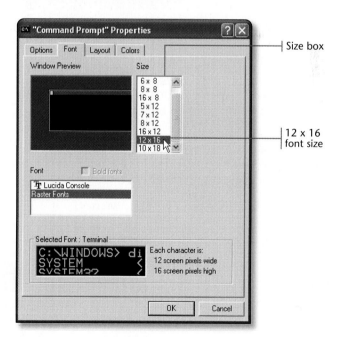

FIGURE D-6

(continued)

6. Click the Colors tab. Click the Screen Text option button to select it. In the color panel, click white. If white does not display, change each of the Selected Color Values to 255.

The screen text will be displayed in white (Figure D-7).

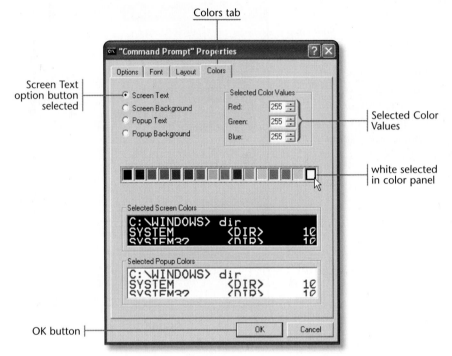

FIGURE D-7

7. Click the OK button. When the Apply Properties To Shortcut dialog box is displayed, click the Modify shortcut that started this window option button to select it.

The Command Prompt window will retain the font color and font size settings set in the previous steps (Figure D-8).

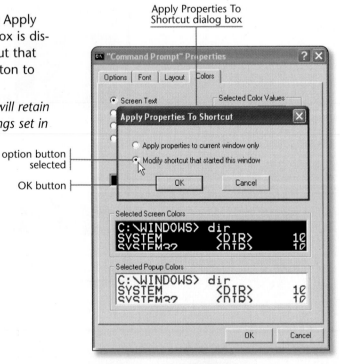

FIGURE D-8

8. Click the OK button.

The Command Prompt window displays white text with a font size of 12 × 16 pixels (Figure D-9).

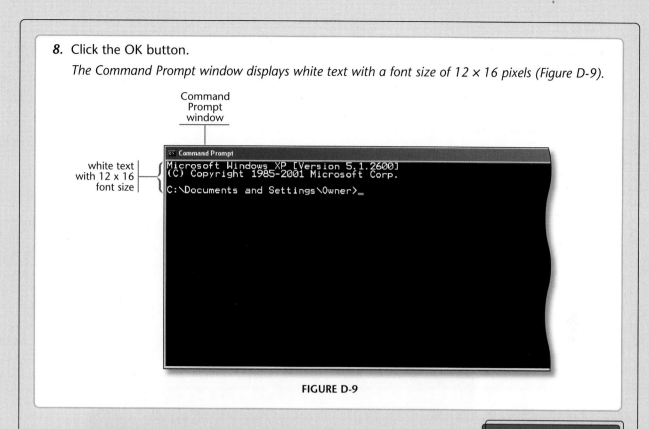

Command
Prompt
window

white text
with 12 x 16
font size

```
Command Prompt
Microsoft Windows XP [Version 5.1.2600]
(C) Copyright 1985-2001 Microsoft Corp.

C:\Documents and Settings\Owner>_
```

FIGURE D-9

Changing Drives and Directories

Operating system commands help programmers with file maintenance, peripheral control, and other system utilities. When you compile and run programs using the Command Prompt window, you need to issue some commands to the operating system, so that the Java SDK can find your files. If you save your programs on the Data Disk in drive A, for example, you will need to **log on** or instruct the operating system to access drive A. To change to a specific drive, users type the drive letter followed by a colon (:) at the command prompt. To change to a specific **directory** or folder on the drive, users type the command, cd, followed by the folder name. On most systems, the command prompt changes to reflect access to the new storage location.

The steps on the next page change the drive and directory to drive A and the Appendices folder created when you download the Data Disk. See the preface of this book for instructions for downloading the Data Disk or see your instructor for information about accessing the files required in this book.

> **OTHER WAYS**
>
> 1. Click Start button, click Run, type cmd, click OK button

To Change Drives and Directories

1. Insert the Data Disk in drive A. With the Command Prompt window still open, type a: and then press the ENTER key.

The command prompt changes to display the new drive (Figure D-10).

command to
change to
drive A

new drive A
specification

2. Type cd Appendices and then press the ENTER key.

The command prompt reflects the directory name (Figure D-11).

command to
change directory

command prompt
displays Appendices
directory on drive A

Operating system commands such as cd are helpful when compiling and running programs or performing maintenance activities using the Command Prompt window. Table D-1 displays some useful operating system commands you can use in the Command Prompt window to interact with the Windows operating system.

Table D-1 Useful Operating System Commands

COMMAND	PURPOSE
cd *directory name*	Changes directory.
cls	Clears screen of previous commands.
copy *path/filename path/filename*	Copies one or more files *from* one directory *to* another directory.
date	Displays or sets the date.
del *filename*	Deletes a file or files.
dir	Displays a list of all files and subdirectories in the current directory.
help	Displays a listing of available operating system commands.
md *directory name*	Makes a new directory.
move *path/filename path/filename*	Moves one or more files *from* one directory *to* another directory.
path *path*	Clears all search path settings and directs Windows to search only in the current directory.
rd *directory name*	Removes an existing directory.
ren *oldfilename newfilename*	Renames a file.
set classpath=*path*	Directs the Java SDK to look for classes in the specified path.
type *filename*	Displays the contents of a text file.

Pressing CTRL+C halts execution of any currently running command.

Setting the Path and Classpath Environment Variables

Recall that an environment variable is a string that lists information about the system environment, such as a drive, path, or file name. When compiling and executing from the command prompt, no IDE or VATE software has direct control over compiling and executing; only the operating system has direct control over compiling and executing. Therefore, it may be necessary to set a **path** to notify the operating system where the Java SDK is located in order to compile programs. It also may be necessary to set the **classpath** to specify the location of the Java classes in order to run the program.

The steps on the next page set the environment variables for the path and classpath at the command prompt. The steps set the path to the installed location of the Java SDK, as discussed in Appendix B. The classpath will be set to the Appendices directory on drive A.

To Set the Path and Classpath Environment Variables

1. With the Command Prompt window still open, type path = c:\Program Files\Java\ jdk1.5.0_02\bin (or enter the location of your installation of the Java SDK) and then press the ENTER key.

   The bin folder contains executable programs related to compiling and executing Java source code (Figure D-12).

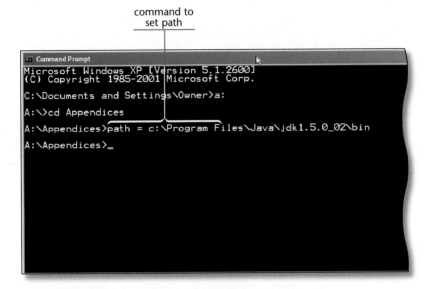

FIGURE D-12

2. With the Data Disk in drive A, type set classpath=a:\Appendices and then press the ENTER key. Do not enter spaces around the equal sign.

   The classpath is set (Figure D-13).

command to
set classpath

```
Command Prompt
Microsoft Windows XP [Version 5.1.2600]
(C) Copyright 1985-2001 Microsoft Corp.

C:\Documents and Settings\Owner>a:

A:\>cd Appendices

A:\Appendices>path = c:\Program Files\Java\jdk1.5.0_02\bin

A:\Appendices>set classpath=a:\Appendices

A:\Appendices>_
```

FIGURE D-13

The path and classpath now are set for the system. When compiling and executing in the Command Prompt window, the operating system will use these variables to obtain the value of the location where the SDK was installed on your system and to locate Java class files.

Tip

Permanently Changing the Path

If you want to permanently include the path of the Java SDK on your system, click the Start button on the Windows taskbar and then right-click My Computer. On the shortcut menu, click Properties. When the System Properties dialog box is displayed, click the Advanced tab. Click the Environment Variables button. In the System variables list, click Path and then click the Edit button. When the Edit System Variable dialog box is displayed, press the RIGHT ARROW to position the insertion point at the end of the Variable Value text box and then type ;C:\Program Files\Java\jdk1.5.0_02\bin (or the location where you installed the SDK) to append the text to the end of the existing string of characters. Click the OK button in each dialog box to accept the new settings.

Compiling Source Code and Running Programs at the Command Prompt

Programmers enter the **javac** command followed by the full name of the Java source code file in order to compile the source code into bytecode. You must enter the .java extension when compiling. Once compiled, the **java** command will run the bytecode.

The following steps compile and run the Sample Java program located in the Appendices folder using the Command Prompt window.

To Compile Source Code and Run Programs at the Command Prompt

1. With the Command Prompt window still open, type javac Sample.java and then press the ENTER key.

The program compiles (Figure D-14). You must enter the .java extension when compiling.

compile command

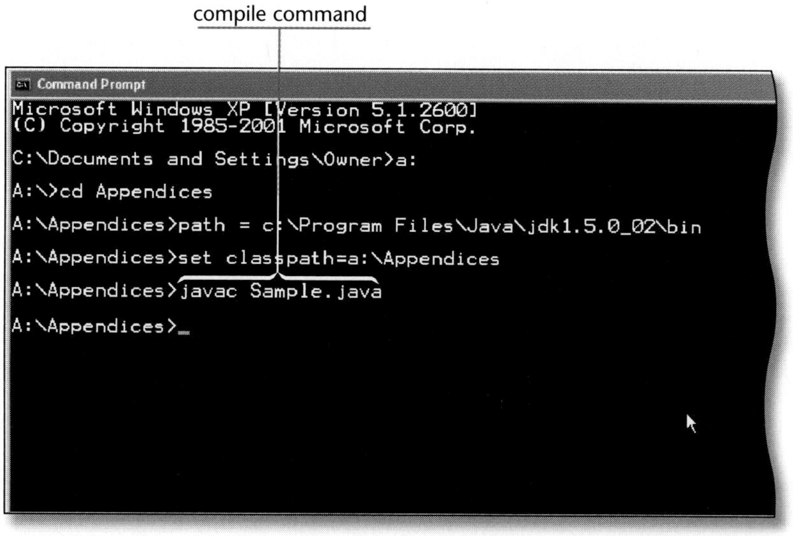

FIGURE D-14

(continued)

2. Type java Sample and then press the ENTER key.

The program runs (Figure D-15). You do not enter an extension when executing. The output from the Sample program displays.

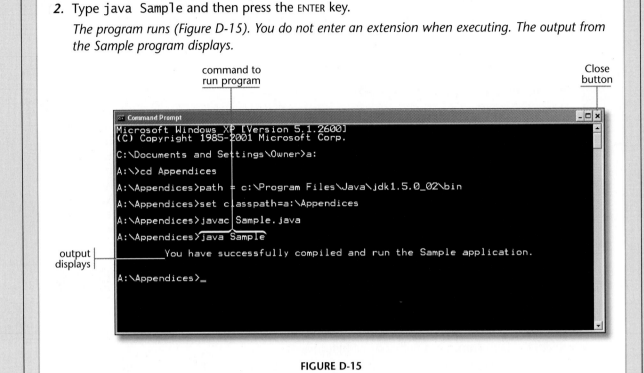

command to
run program

Close
button

output
displays

FIGURE D-15

3. Click the Close button in the Command Prompt window title bar.

The Command Prompt window closes.

When programming, compiling, and testing code, Java programmers set up their desktops in a variety of ways. Some like to have both their text editor and their Command Prompt window open at the same time, resizing each window to approximately half of the screen size. Others like to maximize the Command Prompt window in order to see more of the screen. In that case, programmers click the buttons on the taskbar to move from one window to another. Your instructor may suggest other ways to set up the desktop.

APPENDIX

E

Creating Documentation with Javadoc

Appendix E explains how to use the Javadoc utility to create HTML documentation for Java programs. The appendix also describes the various Javadoc tags used in Javadoc comments, as well as how to view and navigate the generated files.

Using the Javadoc Utility

The Java SDK contains a utility called **Javadoc**, which is used to create Java program documentation as HTML files, such as those shown in Figure E-1a and Figure E-1b. The Javadoc tool parses the special documentation comments and declarations inserted in Java source code to produce a set of HTML files that describe a package, class, interface, constructor, method, field, or any combination of those objects.

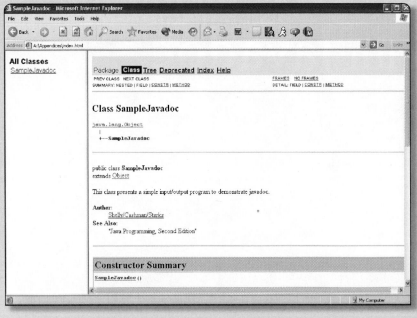

(a)

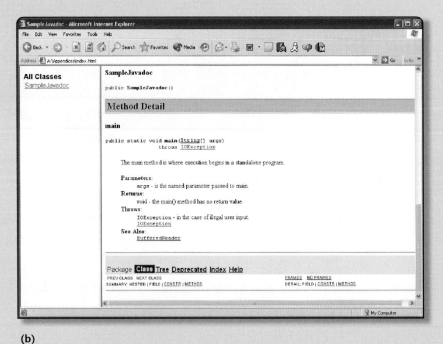

(b)

FIGURE E-1

Generating program documentation using Javadoc is a two-step process. First, you insert special comments in the source code; then, you execute the Javadoc command to create HTML-formatted program documentation.

This appendix illustrates how to use Javadoc to create HTML-formatted program documentation based on comments inserted into Java source code. This appendix uses a sample file on the Data Disk to illustrate this process; however, you can insert Javadoc comments into any existing Java source code file.

Starting TextPad and Opening an Existing File

The following steps open a program called Sample2.java, included on the Data Disk that accompanies this book. See the preface of this book for instructions for downloading the Data Disk or see your instructor for information about accessing the files required in this book.

To Start TextPad and Open an Existing File

1. Click the Start button on the taskbar, point to All Programs, and then click TextPad on the All Programs submenu.

2. When the TextPad window opens, if necessary, click the Close button in the Tip of the Day window. Click the Open button on the TextPad toolbar.

3. When the Open dialog box is displayed, click the Look in box arrow and then click 3½ Floppy (A:) in the list.

4. Double-click the Appendices folder.

5. When the list of files displays, double-click the file Sample2.java. If necessary, click View on the menu bar and then click Line Numbers to display line numbers.

TextPad displays the Java source code for the Sample2.java file in the coding window (Figure E-2).

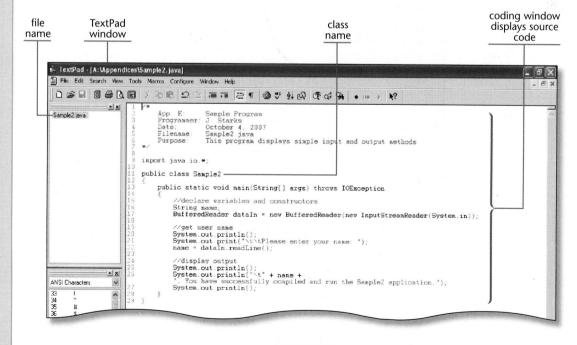

FIGURE E-2

Editing a Class Name and Saving a File with a New File Name

The program coded in the Sample2.java file asks the user for his or her name and then prints a message in the Command Prompt window. Its purpose is not to show any new coding techniques, but to illustrate how to create program documentation in HTML format.

Before editing an existing file that you may want to use again, it is a good idea to save the file with a different name. Recall that in Java, the class name must match the file name. The following steps edit the class name and then save the Sample2.java file with a new name.

To Edit a Class Name and Save a File with a New File Name

1. With the Sample2.java source code displaying in the coding window, change the file name in line 5 to SampleJavadoc.java. Change the class name in line 11 to SampleJavadoc.

2. Click File on the menu bar and then click Save As on the File menu. When the Save As dialog box is displayed, if necessary, click the Save in box arrow and then click 3½ Floppy (A:) in the Save in list. Double-click the Appendices folder or a location specified by your instructor.

3. Type SampleJavadoc in the File name text box and then, if necessary, click Java (*.java) in the Save as type list.

The Save As dialog box displays the new file name in the File name text box (Figure E-3). The comments and class name have been edited to reflect the new file name.

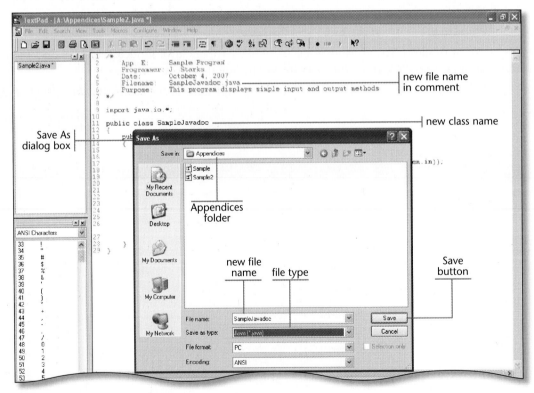

FIGURE E-3

4. Click the Save button in the Save As dialog box.

Writing Doc Comments

Recall from Chapter 2 that two types of comments are used in Java programming: line comments and block comments. Line comments are used to provide documentation for single lines of code or for short descriptions and documentation comments. A line comment, as shown in line 15 of Figure E-2 on page E.03, begins with two forward slashes (//) that cause the line to be ignored during compilation and execution. Line comments have no ending symbol.

Block comments are used as headers at the beginning of the program or when long descriptions are appropriate. As shown in lines 1 through 7 of Figure E-2 on page E.03, a block comment begins with a forward slash followed by an asterisk (/*) and ends with the symbols reversed, an asterisk followed by a forward slash (*/).

A second type of block comment — called a **doc comment,** or a documentation comment — uses special notation that allows programmers to create HTML-formatted program documentation. A doc comment is placed in the code just before the declaration of the package, class, or method it describes; the doc comment begins with a forward slash followed by two asterisks (/**) and ends with an asterisk followed by a forward slash (*/).

The doc comments then can be extracted to HTML files using the Javadoc tool. Using doc comments does not mean you are required to generate HTML files using the Javadoc tool. By using doc comments, however, you leave the option open in the event that you later decide to create program documentation in HTML using the Javadoc tool. Moreover, because doc comments follow a standard style, other programmers will have an easier time reading code with doc comments than reading code with a non-standard style of comments.

Writing Doc Comments for the SampleJavadoc Class

Figure E-4 displays the doc comments for the SampleJavadoc class. The doc comment is placed in the code just before the class declaration and begins with a forward slash followed by two asterisks (/**) on a line with no other code (line 11). The doc comment ends with the */ symbol (line 15). The doc comment can span as many lines as necessary within the beginning and ending marks. Typically, each line within a block comment begins with an asterisk and is indented for ease of reading.

```
11   /**
12    * This class presents a simple input/output program to demonstrate javadoc.
13    * @see "Java Programming, Third Edition"
14    * @author <A HREF="http://www.scsite.com/">Shelly/Cashman/Starks</A>
15    */
16   public class SampleJavadoc
17   {
```

FIGURE E-4

Placement of Doc Comments

In order for the Javadoc command to read the doc comments and convert them to program documentation, you must place doc comments directly above the package, class, or method declaration. For example, if you want to document a method named getCost(), you must place the doc comments in the code just before the getCost() method header. That way, Javadoc can associate the description and tags with the correct method. If you place other code between the doc comment and the method header, the documentation will not display the description and may generate an error.

Within the beginning and ending marks, each doc comment is made up of two parts: a description followed by block tags. A **description** is a short summary or definition of the object, as shown in line 12 of Figure E-4 on the previous page. A **tag**, or **block tag**, is an HTML notation that uses a keyword to send information to an HTML file, as shown in lines 13 and 14 of Figure E-4.

Javadoc Tags

A Javadoc tag begins with the @ sign, followed by a keyword that represents a special reference understood by Javadoc. A tag provides structure that Javadoc can parse into text, font styles, and links in the HTML files generated as program documentation.

Tags come in two types: stand-alone tags and inline tags. **Stand-alone tags** can be placed only in the tag section that follows the description in a doc comment. These tags are not set off with curly braces. **Inline tags** can be placed anywhere in the comment description or in the comments for stand-alone tags. Inline tags are set off with curly braces. Table E-1 lists commonly used Javadoc tags.

Table E-1 Commonly Used Javadoc Tags

TAG NAME	DOCUMENTATION RESULT	SYNTAX
@author	Adds an Author section with the specified name to the generated documents when the author parameter is used. A doc comment may contain multiple @author tags.	@author *name-text*
@deprecated	Adds a comment indicating that this API is deprecated and should no longer be used.	@deprecated *deprecated-text*
@exception	Is a synonym for @throws.	@exception *class-name description*
{@link}	Inserts a link that points to the specified name. This tag accepts the same syntax as the @see tag, but generates an inline link. This tag begins and ends with curly braces to separate it from the rest of the inline text.	{@link *name*}
@param	Adds a Parameter section that lists and defines method parameters.	@param *parameter-name description*
@return	Adds a Returns section with the description text. This text should describe the return type and permissible range of values.	@return *description*

Table E-1   Commonly Used Javadoc Tags *(continued)*

TAG NAME	DOCUMENTATION RESULT	SYNTAX
@see	Adds a See Also section with a link or text entry. A doc comment may contain any number of @see tags, which are all grouped under the same heading.	@see *reference*
@throws	Adds a Throws section to describe the kind of data returned to the method. It is a synonym for @exception.	@throws *class-name description*

In line 13 of Figure E-4 on page E.05, the @see tag instructs the Javadoc tool to add a See Also heading to the program documentation, with a text entry that refers the user to the textbook, Java Programming, Third Edition.

Line 14 in Figure E-4 shows a @author tag that instructs the Javadoc tool to add an Author heading, followed by the specified name, to the program documentation. The HTML tag, HREF, instructs the Javadoc tool to include a link to the Web site www.scsite.com.

Writing Doc Comments for the main() Method

Figure E-5 displays the doc comments for the main() method of the SampleJavadoc program. In line 20, the @param tag is used to define the parameters that the main() method may use. In this example, the parameter, args, is the parameter passed to the main() method. For multiple parameters, you can list multiple @param tags. When the Javadoc tool executes, the @param tag tells it to add a Parameter heading to the resulting HTML files.

```
18        /**
19         *
20         * The main method is where execution begins in a standalone program.
21         * @param args is the named parameter passed to main.
22         * @throws <code>IOException</code> in the case of illegal user input.
23         * @see BufferedReader
24         */
25        public static void main(String[] args) throws IOException
26        {
```

FIGURE E-5

The @throws tag in line 22 allows you to document what kind of exception is thrown and when that exception might occur. The @throws tag also uses a general HTML tag, <**code**>, and its closing tag, </**code**>, to create a link to the API documentation. In the case of @throws, if the exception is a Java-defined exception, you can enter the exception name between the opening and closing <code> tags; Javadoc will convert the text into a link when it generates HTML-formatted documentation.

The @see tag, as shown in line 23 of Figure E-5, is used to enter other Java keywords, methods, and data types that are related to the class or method. Again, Javadoc automatically will create a link to the API documentation for these keywords, methods, or data types when it generates HTML-formatted documentation.

Coding Doc Comments

As previously noted, doc comments should be placed directly above a definition for a class, an interface, a constructor, or a method. The following steps show how to code doc comments for the SampleJavadoc class and the main() method.

To Code Doc Comments

1. Enter lines 11 through 15 from Figure E-4 on page E.05 into the SampleJavadoc.java coding window.

   TextPad displays the doc comments for the SampleJavadoc class in the coding window (Figure E-6).

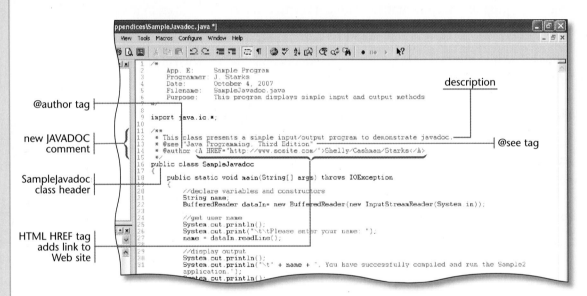

FIGURE E-6

2. Enter lines 18 through 24 from Figure E-5 on the previous page into the SampleJavadoc.java coding window.

   TextPad displays the doc comments for the main() method in the coding window (Figure E-7).

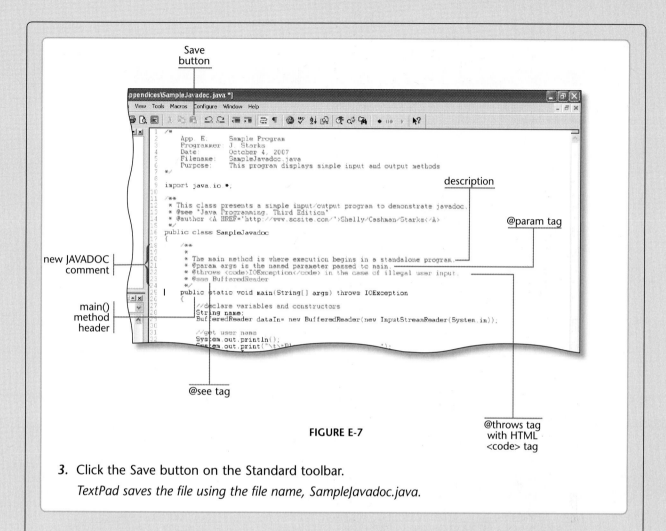

FIGURE E-7

3. Click the Save button on the Standard toolbar.

TextPad saves the file using the file name, SampleJavadoc.java.

The @see tag can take one of three different forms. The first form, as shown in line 13 in Figure E-7, tells Javadoc to display a string of text, such as a reference to a textbook; no link is created. The second form, as shown in line 22 in Figure E-7, tells Javadoc to create a link that points to the documentation for the specified keyword, method, or data type, as referenced in the Java Language Specification on the Sun Microsystems Web site. The third form tells Javadoc to create a link to a specific Web page URL, much like the @author tag in line 14.

Generating Documentation Using Javadoc

The documentation generated by the Javadoc tool consists of a number of HTML-formatted pages in the same style as the Java API Specification. These HTML-formatted pages, which include cross-reference pages, an index page, and a style sheet, use frames to display information in the Web browser window. When creating these pages, Javadoc automatically includes links to relevant Web pages in the Java API Specification based on the description and tags used in the doc comments.

Table E-2 on the next page lists some of the documentation pages created by Javadoc.

Table E-2   Documentation Pages Created by Javadoc

PAGE NAME	PURPOSE
allclasses-noframe.html	A documentation page that lists all classes using no frames.
allclasses-frame.html	A documentation page that lists all classes used in lower-left frame of index page.
classname.html	One basic file is created for each class or interface that is documented. The file is named the same as the classname with the extension .html (for example, SampleJavadoc.html).
constant-values.html	A documentation page that lists values of all static fields.
help-doc.html	A documentation page that lists user help for how these pages are organized.
index.html	An initial page that sets up HTML frames; file itself contains no text content.
index-all.html	The default alphabetical index of all classes and methods.
overview-tree.html	A cross-reference page that lists class hierarchy for all packages.
package-list.txt	A file used to link to other documentation. This is a text file, not HTML, and is not reachable through any links.
stylesheet.css	A supporting style sheet file that controls basic formatting, including color, font family, font size, font style, and positioning on the Javadoc-generated pages.

By default, Javadoc uses a standard **doclet** file provided by Sun Microsystems to specify the content and format of the HTML-formatted program documentation. You can modify the standard doclet, however, to customize the output of Javadoc as you wish, or write your own doclet to generate pages in other formats, such as XML or Rich Text Format (RTF).

Tip

Writing Doclets
You can write a new doclet from scratch using the doclet API, or you can start with the standard doclet and modify it to suit your needs. For more information on writing doclets, visit the Sun Microsystems Web site.

The Javadoc tool will generate either two or three HTML frames, based on whether you use Javadoc to document only one or multiple packages. When you pass a single package name or source file as an argument into Javadoc, it will create two frames: a main frame with an overview page and a left frame listing classes. When you pass two or more package names into Javadoc, it will create three frames: a main frame with an overview page, an upper-left frame listing all packages, and a lower-left frame listing all classes. A user viewing the documentation can remove the frames by clicking the No Frames link at the top of the overview page.

Using the Javadoc Tool

TextPad provides functionality to allow users to run Javadoc by clicking Run on the Tools menu and then entering the correct commands in the Run dialog box. When you run Javadoc, certain parameters can be used to help Javadoc link to the appropriate files. The following steps show how to run the Javadoc tool and enter required parameters to generate HTML-formatted program documentation.

To Use the Javadoc Tool

1. Click Tools on TextPad's menu bar and then click Run.

   TextPad displays the Run dialog box (Figure E-8). The Run dialog box includes text boxes for input of a command, parameters, and an initial folder.

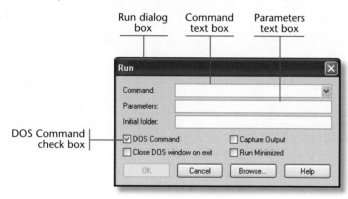

Run dialog box   Command text box   Parameters text box

DOS Command check box

FIGURE E-8

2. Type javadoc A:\Appendices\SampleJavadoc.java in the Command text box. Press the TAB key. Type -link http://java.sun.com/j2se/1.5.0/docs/api -author -d A:\Appendices\ in the Parameters text box. Press the TAB key. Type C:\Program Files\Java\jdk1.5.0_02\bin in the Initial folder text box.

   If necessary, click the DOS Command check box to select it.

   The Run dialog box displays the entered data (Figure E-9). The DOS Command check box is selected.

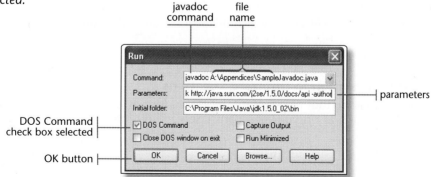

javadoc command   file name

DOS Command check box selected

OK button

parameters

FIGURE E-9

(continued)

3. Click the OK button.

The Command Prompt window displays messages about the Javadoc-generated files (Figure E-10). If your file location has changed or if your system currently is not connected to the Web, you may be prompted to connect. If you do not connect, your output may display an error or warning message, but still will generate the HTML-formatted documentation pages.

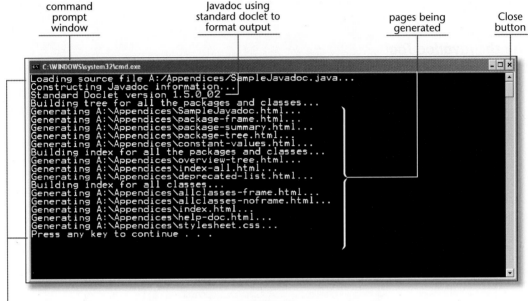

command prompt window

Javadoc using standard doclet to format output

pages being generated

Close button

Javadoc messages

FIGURE E-10

4. Click the Close button in the Command Prompt window title bar.

The Command Prompt window closes.

The –link parameter (Figure E-9 on the previous page) specifies the location of the Java API on the Sun Microsystems Web site. Using the –link parameter ensures that any links to the Java API documentation will be accessible to all users. For the documentation links to work, however, the user must be connected to the Web.

The –author parameter instructs javadoc to include the location of the author's Web page.

Creating Documentation in Different Locations

If you want the Javadoc tool to generate the HTML-formatted documentation in a different location, such as on your company's server, you may use a –d parameter, followed by the path.

Viewing Javadoc-Generated Documentation

Once Javadoc has generated the HTML-formatted documentation for your Java program, it can be viewed using a Web browser. The following steps show how to view and navigate through Javadoc-generated documentation using a Web browser.

To View Javadoc-Generated Documentation

1. Start Internet Explorer or your Web browser. When the browser window opens, type A:\Appendices\index.html in the Address text box. Press the ENTER key.

The browser displays the documentation created for the SampleJavadoc program (Figure E-11).

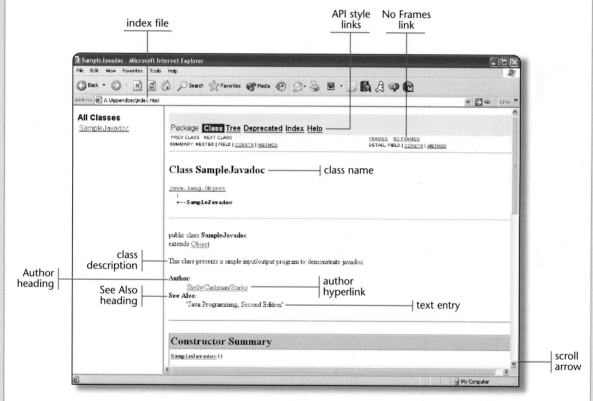

FIGURE E-11

(continued)

2. Use the down scroll arrow to display the Method Detail.

   The frame scrolls to display the Method Detail (Figure E-12).

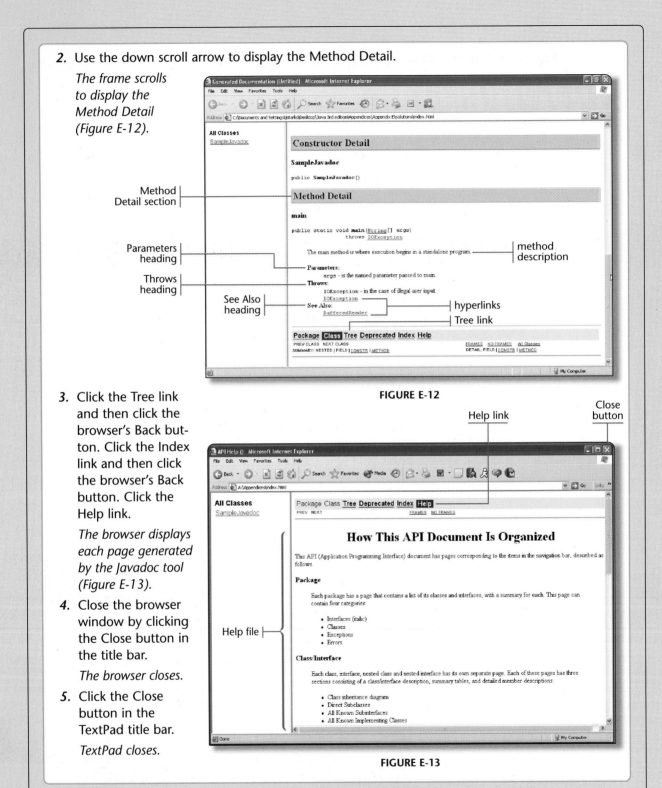

FIGURE E-12

3. Click the Tree link and then click the browser's Back button. Click the Index link and then click the browser's Back button. Click the Help link.

   The browser displays each page generated by the Javadoc tool (Figure E-13).

4. Close the browser window by clicking the Close button in the title bar.

   The browser closes.

5. Click the Close button in the TextPad title bar.

   TextPad closes.

FIGURE E-13

Businesses and programmers use Javadoc to provide documentation to users of their source code. For example, the Javadoc tool is used by Sun Microsystems to create all API documentation. For these businesses and programmers, the HTML files created by the Javadoc tool are a convenient and platform-independent way of distributing documentation online from a Web site or intranet, via CD-ROM or other media, or even as hard-copy printouts.

Index